Global Bible
Commentary

Acclaim for the *Global Bible Commentary*

If any book demonstrates the value of cultural criticism and the importance of particularity in interpretation, this is it! Scholars from diverse social locations in every continent bring their distinctive context to bear on the act of interpreting. In so doing, they shed eye-opening light on the biblical texts. The resulting critical dialogue with the Bible exposes the oppressive as well as the liberating dynamics of the texts while at the same time showing how the Bible might address the social, political, cultural, and economic dynamics of our world today. This collection can change the way you read the Bible—scholars and students, clergy and laity alike.

—David Rhoads
Lutheran School of Theology, Chicago, Ill.

In many respects—its commitments to multiplicity of readings; its abandonment of the quest for the correct reading; and its encouragement of and facilitation of culturalist and self-reflexive work—this project is the *un*-commentary. I can recommend it with enthusiasm, especially to those students who have wondered how critical, disciplined work can be engaged and even made compelling without hiding the self and its worlds.

—Vincent L. Wimbush
Professor of New Testament, Claremont Graduate University, Claremont, Calif.

Biblical scholarship, methodologically and ideologically monolingual for so long, now speaks in other tongues, as this commentary eloquently attests. As a seminary professor privileged to teach and learn from an international and multiethnic student body, I welcome the advent of this one-of-a-kind textbook.

—Stephen D. Moore
The Theological School, Drew University, Madison, N. J.

Abingdon's commentary recognizes that the Bible has historical roots but it also is alive and well in all sorts of communities around the globe. I applaud their efforts of bringing the diverse and timely voices into our professional lives, perhaps our classrooms, and to the scholarly discussions of biblical issues.

—Marla J. Selvidge
Central Missouri State University, Warrensburg, Mo.

The priority given to the contextual character of interpretation transforms the work from an academic compendium to a cultural kaleidoscope of reading. Students and scholars in Western Europe and North America will be astonished at the novelty of the interpretations that emerge from the pages of this commentary. In the *Global Bible Commentary* we have the twenty-first-century hermeneutical equivalent of Dante's community of the saints in the Rose.

—Professor Laurence L. Welborn
United Theological Seminary, Dayton, Ohio

The socio-political climate of today's globally shrinking world demands that Bible students, whether academician, pastor, evangelist, or the like, maintain a dialogue with those engaged in similar pursuits, but living in other contexts. The *GBC* facilitates this process because of its methodology. Each commentary opens with an identification of the commentator's personal social location, proceeds with an interpretation of the text, and concludes with a discussion of the text's relevance or irrelevance in the commentator's larger life setting. The result for readers of the *GBC* is the entrance into the world of others, who may not "see as we see," "think as we think," "believe as we believe," but nevertheless perceive God's word as a relevant force in their lives.

—Randall C. Bailey, PhD
Associate Professor of Bible, Faulkner University, Montgomery, Ala.

Global Bible Commentary

General Editor:
Daniel Patte

Associate Editors:
J. Severino Croatto
Nicole Wilkinson Duran
Teresa Okure
Archie Chi Chung Lee

ABINGDON PRESS
Nashville

GLOBAL BIBLE COMMENTARY

Copyright © 2004 by Abingdon Press

This book is printed on acid-free paper.

Library of Congress Cataloging-in-Publication Data

Global Bible Commentary / general editor, Daniel Patte ; associate editors,
Teresa Okure ... [et al.].
    p. cm.
Includes bibliographical references.
ISBN 0-687-06403-1 (alk. paper)
1. Bible--Commentaries. I. Patte, Daniel. II. Okure, Teresa.

BS491.3.G57 2005
220.7--dc22

2004015617

ISBN-13: 978-0-687-06403-8
ISBN-10: 0-687-06403-1

08 09 10 11 12 13 — 10 9 8 7 6 5 4 3

MANUFACTURED IN THE UNITED STATES OF AMERICA

J. Severino Croatto
(19 March 1930-26 April 2004)

This volume is dedicated

To the Memory of J. Severino Croatto

Friend, Colleague, Mentor.

Friend, ever attentive and ready to stop and take the time to be fully present to us.

Colleague, with whom we conceived this *Global Bible Commentary* and who, until the last weeks of his life, patiently chiseled at it to make it a reference work that calls its readers to hermeneutical responsibility.

Mentor, who cleared the way for this *Global Bible Commentary,* through his life-long pioneering, meticulous, and exemplary work in biblical hermeneutics and his gracious embrace of a great diversity of interpretive approaches that paved the way for the long journey following the Word through the continents, *Los caminos inexhauribles de la Palabra,* in which many could join him.

CONTENTS

ABBREVIATIONS LIST
GENERAL

abr.	abridged		HB	Hebrew Bible
approx.	approximately		Heb.	Hebrew
Aram.	Aramaic		HT	Hebrew Text
art(s).	articles(s)			
a.t.	author's translation		i.e.	*id est*, that is
aug.	augmented		ibid.	*ibidem*, in the same place
			ill.	illustrated by
b.	born		intro.	introduction
B.C.E.	Before the Common Era			
bib.	biblical		J	Jahwist or Yahwist source (of
bk(s).	book(s)			the Pentateuch)
C.E.	Common Era		Lat.	Latin
ca.	circa		lit.	literally
cent(s).	century(ies)		LT	Latin Translation
cf.	compare		LXX	Septuagint
ch./chs.	chapter(s)			
comb.	combined		MS(S)	manuscript(s)
contr.	contributor		MT	Masoretic Text
corr.	corrected			
			NT	New Testament
D	Deuteronomist source (of the			
	Pentateuch)		OG	Old Greek
d.	died		OL	Old Latin
dept.	department		OT	Old Testament
dir.	director			
diss.	dissertation		P	Priestly source (of the
Dtr	Deuteronomistic (history;			Pentateuch)
	writer)		par.	parallel
			pl.	plural
E	Elohist source (of the		posth.	posthumous
	Pentateuch)		pt(s).	part(s)
ed(s).	editor(s); edited by		pub.	published
e.g.	*exempli gratia*, for example			
Eng.	English		repr.	reprint
enl.	enlarged		repub.	republished
esp.	especially		rev. ed.	revised edition
est.	established		RGS	Religionsgeschichtliche Schule
et al.	*et alii*, and others			
etc.	*et cetera*, and the rest		sec(s).	section(s)
ET	English Translation		supp.	supplement
frg(s).	fragment(s)		trans.	translated by
Ger.	German		Vg.	Vulgate
Gr.	Greek		v(v).	verse(s)
GT	German Translation		vol(s).	volume(s)

BIBLICAL TRANSLATIONS

ASV	American Standard Version	NJB	New Jerusalem Bible
CEV	Contemporary English Version	NRSV	New Revised Standard Version
JPS	Jewish Publication Society	REB	Revised English Bible
KJV	King James Version	RSV	Revised Standard Version
NEB	New English Bible	TEV	Today's English Version (Good
NIV	New International Version		News Bible)

BOOKS OF THE BIBLE
Hebrew Bible

Gen	Genesis	Song (Cant)	Song of Songs (Song
Exod	Exodus		Solomon or Canticles)
Lev	Leviticus	Isa	Isaiah
Num	Numbers	Jer	Jeremiah
Deut	Deuteronomy	Lam	Lamentations
Josh	Joshua	Ezek	Ezekiel
Judg	Judges	Dan	Daniel
Ruth	Ruth	Hos	Hosea
1–2 Sam	1–2 Samuel	Joel	Joel
1–2 Kgdms	1–2 Kingdoms (LXX)	Amos	Amos
1–2 Kgs	1–2 Kings	Obad	Obadiah
3–4 Kgdms	3–4 Kingdoms (LXX)	Jonah	Jonah
1–2 Chr	1–2 Chronicles	Mic	Micah
Ezra	Ezra	Nah	Nahum
Neh	Nehemiah	Hab	Habakkuk
Esth	Esther	Zeph	Zephaniah
Job	Job	Hag	Haggai
Ps/Pss	Psalms	Zech	Zechariah
Prov	Proverbs	Mal	Malachi
Eccl (or Qoh)	Ecclesiastes (or Qoheleth)		

NEW TESTAMENT

Matt	Matthew	1–2 Thess	1–2 Thessalonians
Mark	Mark	1–2 Tim	1–2 Timothy
Luke	Luke	Titus	Titus
John	John	Phlm	Philemon
Acts	Acts	Heb	Hebrews
Rom	Romans	Jas	James
1–2 Cor	1–2 Corinthians	1–2 Pet	1–2 Peter
Gal	Galatians	1–2–3 John	1–2–3 John
Eph	Ephesians	Jude	Jude
Phil	Philippians	Rev	Revelation
Col	Colossians		

APOCRYPHA AND SEPTUAGINT

Bar	Baruch	Ep Jer	Epistle of Jeremiah
Add Dan	Additions to Daniel	Jdt	Judith
Pr Azar	Prayer of Azariah	1–2 Macc	1–2 Maccabees
Bel	Bel and the Dragon	3–4 Macc	3–4 Maccabees
Sg Three	Song of the Three Young Men	Pr Man	Prayer of Manasseh
		Ps 151	Psalm 151
Sus	Susanna	Sir	Sirach/Ecclesiasticus
1–2 Esd	1–2 Esdras	Tob	Tobit
Add Esth	Additions to Esther	Wis	Wisdom of Solomon

PERIODICALS, REFERENCE WORKS, AND SERIALS

AB	Anchor Bible
ABD	Anchor Bible Dictionary
ABRL	Anchor Bible Reference Library
AJBS	*African Journal of Biblical Studies*
AnBib	Analecta biblica
ANTC	Abingdon New Testament Commentaries
AsTJ	*Asbury Theological Journal*
BEATAJ	Beiträge zur Erforschung des Alten Testaments und des antiken Judentum
BETL	Bibliotheca ephemeridum theologicarum lovaniensium
BibInt	Biblical Interpretation
BJRL	*Bulletin of the John Rylands University Library of Manchester*
BJS	Brown Judaic Studies
BNTC	Black's New Testament Commentaries
BTB	*Biblical Theology Bulletin*
BZAW	Beihefte zur Zeitschrift fur die alttestamentliche Wissenschaft
CBQ	*Catholic Biblical Quarterly*
ChrCent	*Christian Century*
ChW	*Cristliche Welt*
ConBOT	Coniectanea biblica: Old Testament Series
ConNT	Coniectanea neotestamentica
CTP	Cadernos de teologia e pastoral
DB	*Dictionnaire de la Bible.* Edited by F. Vigouroux. 5 vols. 1895-1912
DBSup	*Dictionnaire de la Bible: Supplément.* Edited by L. Pirot and A. Robert. Paris, 1907-1953
EAJJ	*East Asia Journal of Theology*
Ebib	*Etudes bibliques*
EstTeo	*Estudios teológicos*
FCB	Feminist Companion to the Bible
FOTL	Forms of the Old Testament Literature

GBC	*Global Bible Commentary*
GOTR	*Greek Orthodox Theological Review*
HNTC	Harper's New Testament Commentaries
HTKNT	Herders theologischer Kommentar zum Neuen Testament
HTR	*Harvard Theological Review*
IBS	*Irish Biblical Studies*
ICC	International Critical Commentary
IDB	*The Interpreter's Dictionary of the Bible*. Edited by G. A. Buttrick., 4 vols. Nashville, 1962
IDBSup	*Interpreter's Dictionary of the Bible: Supplementary Volume*. Edited by K. Crim., Nashville, 1976
Int	Interpretation
IRM	*International Review of Mission*
ITC	International Theological Commentary
JANESCU	*Journal of the Ancient Near Eastern Society of Columbia University*
JBL	*Journal of Biblical Literature*
JFSR	*Journal of Feminist Studies in Religion*
JSNT	*Journal for the Study of the New Testament*
JSNTSup	*Journal for the Study of the New Testament: Supplement Series*
JSOT	*Journal for the Study of the Old Testament*
JSOTSup	Journal for the Study of the Old Testament: Supplement Series
JTSA	*Journal of Theology for Southern Africa*
KEK	Kritisch-exegetischer Kommentar über das Neuen Testament
NCB	New Century Bible
Neot	*Neotestamentica*
NIB	*New Interpreter's Bible*
NISB	*New Interpreter's Study Bible*
NICNT	New International Commentary on the New Testament
NICOT	New International Commentary on the Old Testament
NIGTC	New International Greek Testament Commentary
NovTSup	Supplements to Novum Testamentum
NRTh	*La nouvelle revue theologique*
NTG	New Testament Guides
NTS	*New Testament Studies*
NZM	*Neue Zeitschrift für Missionswissenschaft*
OBT	Overtures to Biblical Theology
OTG	Old Testament Guides
OTL	Old Testament Library
PROPOSITUM	*A Periodical of Third Order Regular Franciscan History and Spirituality*
Reading	Reading, a New Bible Commentary
ResQ	*Restoration Quarterly*
RIBLA	*Revista de interpretación bíblica latino-american*
RNT	Regensburger Neues Testament

SBLDS	Society of Biblical Literature Dissertation Series
SBLMS	Society of Biblical Literature Monograph Series
SBT	Studies in Biblical Theology
SemeiaSt	Semeia Studies
SJT	*Scottish Journal of Theology*
SNT	Studien zum Neuen Testament
SNTSMS	Society for Old Testament Studies Monograph Series
SP	Sacra pagina
TB	Theologisch Bücherei: Neudrucke und Berichte aus dem 20. Jahrhundert
TNTC	Tyndale New Testament Commentaries
TRE	*Die theologische Realenzyklopädie*. Edited by G. Krause and G. Müller, 27 vols. Berlin, 1977-97
VT	*Vetus Testamentum*
VTSup	Vetus Testamentum Supplements
WBC	Word Biblical Commentary
WUANT	Wissenschaftliche Monographien zum Alten und Neuen Testamen
ZAW	*Zeitschrift für die alttestamentliche Wissenschaft*
ZNW	*Zeitschrift für die neutestamentliche Wissenschaft*

CONTRIBUTORS

Abesamis, Carlos H., SJ
Socio-Pastoral Institute and
Loyola School of Theology
Quezon City, Philippines
Jesus: An Asian Perspective

Adamo, David Tuesday
Delta State University
Abraka, Delta State, Nigeria
Psalms

Almada, Samuel E.
Instituto Superior Evangélico de Estudios
Teológicos (ISEDET)
Buenos Aires, Argentina
Ezekiel 1–39

Amos, Clare
Network for Inter Faith
Concerns of the Anglican
Communion, and United Society
for the Propagation of the Gospel
London, England; and Lebanon
Genesis

Andiñach, Pablo
Instituto Superior Evangélico de Estudios
Teológicos (ISEDET)
Buenos Aires, Argentina
Joel

Arichea, Daniel C., Jr.
Union Theological Seminary, Philippines,
in Dasmarinas, Cavite, Philippines; and
Duke Divinity School, Durham, NC,
USA.
2 Timothy and Titus

Brenner, Athalya
University of Amsterdam
the Netherlands; and Haifa, Israel.
Proverbs

Beutler, Johannes, SJ
Pontifical Biblical Institute
Rome, Italy
1, 2, and 3 John

Chen, Nan-Jou
Yushan Theological College
Hualien, Taiwan
Jonah

Conti, Cristina
Seminary of the Salvation Army
Buenos Aires, Argentina
James

Cooper, Alan
Jewish Theological Seminary and
Union Theological Seminary
New York, USA
Leviticus

Croatto, J. Severino *(deceased)*
Instituto Superior Evangélico de
Estudios Teológicos (ISEDET)
Buenos Aires, Argentina
Associate Editor
Isaiah 40–55, Isaiah 56–66, and Fourth Isaiah

Da Silva, Valmor
Universidade Católica de Goiás
Goiânia, Brazil
Nahum

Demirer, Derya
Ohio State University
OH, USA; and Turkey
1 Corinthians 11 in Muslim and Christian Perspectives

Doren, Fernando
SVD, Verbo Biblical Studies Center
São Paulo, Brazil
Zephania

Duarte, Alejandro Alberto
Instituto de Theologia
Santa Beatriz de Silva
Ceuta, Spain
Matthew

Dube, Musa W.
Scripps College
Claremont, CA, USA; and
University of Botswana
Gaborone, Botswana
Mark's Healing Stories in an AIDS Context

Duran, Nicole Wilkinson
Rosemont College and Villanova
University
Villanova, PA, USA
Associate Editor
Jesus: A Western Perspective and
1 Corinthians 11 in Muslim and
Christian Perspectives

Fewell, Danna Nolan
Theological School Drew University
New Jersey, USA
Ezra and Nehemiah

Gallazzi, Alessandro
Comissão Pastoral da Terra
(Pastoral Commission of the Land);
and Theological Seminary
of the Assembly of God
Macapá, Brazil
Ezekiel 40–48

García Bachmann, Mercedes
Instituto Superior Evangélico de
Estudios Teológicos (ISEDET)
Buenos Aires, Argentina
Deuteronomy

Havea, Jione
United Theological College
North Parramatta, NSW, Australia
Numbers

Himbaza, Innocent
University of Friburg
Switzerland; and Rwanda
Habakkuk

Huang, Po Ho
Tainan Theological College and Seminary
Tainan City, Taiwan
Micah

Kalluveettil, Paul, CMI
Dharmaram College
Bangladore, India
Haggai

Kim, Jean
Moravian Theological Seminary
Bethlehem
Pennsylvania, USA and Korea
Philemon

Kinukawa, Hisako
Lutheran Theological Seminary
St. Paul Graduate School; and the
International Christian University
Tokyo, Japan
Mark

Krüger, René
Instituto Superior Evangélico de Estudios
Teológicos (ISEDET)
Buenos Aires, Argentina
Luke's God and Mammon, a Latin
American Perspective

Kwasi, Fidéle Ugira
Université Chrétienne de Kinshasa,
Kinshasa
Democratic Republic of Congo
Judges

LaCocque, Andre
Chicago Theological Seminary
Chicago, IL, USA; and Belgium
Daniel

Lee, Archie Chi Chung
Chung Chi College, Chinese University
of Hong Kong
Shatin, Hong Kong, China
Lamentations

Lee, Kyung Sook
Ewha Woman's University
Seoul, Korea
1 and 2 Kings

Liew, Tat-siong Benny
Chicago Theological Seminary, Chicago,
IL, USA; and
Hong Kong, China
Acts

Manus, Ukachukwu Chris
Obafemi Awolowo University
Ile-Ife, Nigeria
2 Corinthians

Masenya, Madipoane
University of South Africa
South Africa
Ruth

Mbuwayesango, Dora
Hood Theological Seminary, Salisbury,
NC, USA; and Zimbabwe
Joshua

Melanchthon, Monica Jyotsna
Gurukul Lutheran Theological College
Chennai, India
Song of Songs

Mendoza, Claudia
Catholic University of Argentina
(Universidad Catolica Argentina
Santa Maria de los Buenos Aires)
Malachi

Míguez, Néstor Oscar
Instituto Superior Evangélico de Estudios
Teológicos (ISEDET)
Buenos Aires, Argentina
Galations

Mihoc, Vasile
University of Sibiu
Romania
Jesus Christ: An Orthodox Perspective

Nakanose, Shigeyuki, SVD
Verbo Biblical Studies Center
São Paulo, Brazil
Zephaniah

Ngan, Lai Ling Elizabeth
George W. Truett Theological Seminary,
Baylor University
Waco, TX, USA; and China
Amos

Ntreh, Benjamin Abotchie
University of Cape Coast
Ghana
Job

Okure, Teresa, SHCJ
Catholic Institute of West Africa
Port Harcourt, Nigeria
Associate Editor
Colossians, Hebrews: Sacrifice in African
Perspective

Park, Kyung-mi
Ewha Women's University
Seoul, Korea
John

Pathrapankal, Joseph, CMI
Dharmaram Vidya Kshetrom,
Bangladore, India.
1 Corinthians

Patte, Daniel
Vanderbilt University
Nashville, TN, USA
General Editor
Introduction, Romans

Pedro, Enilda de Paula
RBP, Verbo Biblical Studies Center
São Paulo, Brazil
Zephaniah

Pixley, Jorge
Seminario Tedogico Bautista
Managua, Nicaragua
Claremont, California, USA
Exodus

Prior, John
Candraditya Centre for the Study of
Religion and Culture
Indonesia
Ecclesiastes

Richard, Pablo
National University of Costa Rica and
Latin American Biblical University
San José / Costa Rica
Jesus: A Latin American Perspective

Riches, John
University of Glasgow
Glasgow, Scotland
Ephesians

Ringe, Sharon
Wesley Theological Seminary
Washington, DC, USA
1 and 2 Peter, Jude

Rowland, Christopher
Queen's College
Oxford, United Kingdom
Revelation

Sampaio, Tânia Mara Vieira
Círculos Populares de Leitura da
Bíblia e Cursos de Formação, and
Universidade Metodista de São Paulo
Brazil
Hosea

Scholz, Susanne
Merrimack College
North Andover, MA, USA
Leviticus

Sugirtharajah, R. S.
Selly Oaks Colleges, Birmingham,
England; Serampore College, Calcutta
and Tamilnadu Theological Seminary
Madurai, South India.
Matthew 5–7: *The Sermon on the Mount
and India*

Swarup, Paul
Vidya Jyoti College of Theology
Delhi, India
Zechariah

Tamez, Elsa
Universidad Biblica Latinoamericana
Costa Rica
1 Timothy

Tofanâ, Stelian
The Faculty of Orthodox Theology of
Babes Bolyai University
Cluj-Napoca, Romania
Hebrews

Torreblanca, Jorge
Universidad Adventista del Planta
Entre Rios, Argentina
Obadiah

Upkong, Justin
University of Uyo
Uyo, Nigeria
Luke

Vassiliadis, Petros
Theological Seminary
Thessaloniki, Greece
John in an Orthodox Perspective

Wasike, Anne Nasimiyu
Kenyatta University
Nairobi, Kenya
Jesus: An African Perspective

Weems, Renita J.
Spelman College
Atlanta, GA, USA
Jeremiah

West, Gerald
University of Kwa Zulu-Natal,
Pietermaritzburg, South Africa
1 and 2 Samuel

Williams, Demetrius
Tulane University
New Orleans, LA
Philippians

Wong, Fook Kong
Baptist Theological Seminary
Hong Kong, China
1 and 2 Chronicles

Wong, Wai Ching Angela
Chinese University of Hong Kong
Shatin, Hong Kong, China
Esther

Yeo, Khiok-khng (K.K.)
Garrett-Evangelical Theological Seminary
Chicago, IL, USA; and China
1 Thessalonians and 2 Thessalonians

Zinkuratire, Victor
Catholic University of Eastern Africa
Nairobi, Kenya
Isaiah 1–39

INTRODUCTION

Daniel Patte, *General Editor*

A *Global Bible Commentary* (or *GBC*) invites its users to expand their horizons by reading the Bible with scholars from all over the world and from different religious persuasions. These scholars have approaches and concerns that often are poles apart. Yet they share two basic convictions: biblical interpretation always matters, and reading the Bible "with others" is highly rewarding.

Each of the short commentaries of the *GBC* is a readily accessible guide for reading a biblical book. Written for undergraduate and seminary students and their teachers, as well as for pastors, priests, and adult Sunday school classes, it introduces its users to the main features of the biblical book and its content.

Yet each short commentary does more. It also brings to all its users a precious gift, namely the opportunity of reading this biblical book as if for the first time. By making explicit the specific context and the concerns from which they read the Bible, the scholars show the significance of aspects of the biblical text that readers in other contexts have often taken for granted or overlooked.

How This
Global Bible Commentary
Came into Being

The contributors to the *GBC* are literally from all over the world. The associate editors, J. Severino **Croatto**, Nicole Wilkinson **Duran**, Archie Chi Chung **Lee**, Teresa **Okure**, SHCJ, and I have identified scholars on each continent—including Western Europe and North America—and from different religious persuasions. The balance of this *GBC* seeks to approximate the geographical, denominational, and gender balance of Bible readers around the world today. The *GBC* reflects the fact that almost two-thirds of the readers of the Bible are Christians in Africa, Asia, Latin America, and Oceania (ca. 1,178 billion, according to the *World Christian Encyclopedia*), as opposed to Western Europe and North America (ca. 661 million) and Orthodox Eastern Europe (ca. 158 million). Thus, approximately two-thirds of the commentators are scholars from the "two-thirds world," with a proportional and thus smaller number of contributors from the Western world (including two Jewish scholars) and the Eastern Orthodox world. In order to keep this geographical balance, we had difficulty reaching the gender balance; twenty-eight contributions are signed by women, instead of the thirty-three (half) we wanted, because the number of female biblical scholars is still relatively small, though growing, in the two-thirds world.

We, the editors of the *GBC*, asked each of these scholars to address through their commentary the question: "What is the teaching of the given biblical book for believers in your specific social, economic, cultural, and religious context?" In order to give the scholars from the two-thirds world the opportunity to address issues that colonialist attitudes had prevented them from raising, we further specified that each of the commentators should ask: "What does this given biblical book say regarding the relationship of the people of God to the world?" This question is voluntarily open. It allows each commentator to define "people of God," "world," and "relationship" in ways that are appropriate for the scholar's particular socio-economic, cultural, and religious context and for the particular biblical book.

Acknowledging
the Contextual Character
of Our Interpretations

The contextual character of this *GBC* was a challenge for many of us contributors, largely because we did not fully grasp why making explicit the contextual character of our interpretations was important. Similarly, readers of this volume, especially Western readers, will first be struck by the fascinating cross-denominational and cross-cultural insights these contextual interpretations of the biblical books bring. Yet, there is more than new insight to be gained. There are voices to be heard. First, each of the contributions involves a gentle call to stop and listen. When we listen, we hear voices that we are not used to hearing, those of biblical readers who in each context have long been silenced. These voices are soft, yet firm, and indeed most powerful and often troubling, because they articulate teachings, issues, and questions that the biblical text raises for its readers but that, on our own, we could not or would not hear.

It is when I heard such voices that my journey toward this *GBC* began. In July 1999 in Kasane, Botswana, with Musa **Dube** (see "Marks Healing Stories in an AIDS Context") as a guide, I was visiting a congregation of the Church of the Eleven Apostles. In this African Initiated Church, the priest (most often a woman) simply announced a passage (Acts 3:12-26). A woman from the congregation stood up, read it, and preached. Others followed her lead, as they felt moved by the Spirit. This preaching by the parishioners rather than by a preacher is remarkable enough. Yet I was not surprised. Dube had written about this (see *Postcolonial Feminist Interpretation* 2000, 39-42, 184-95). But I was astounded by the way this church practices communal preaching. The translation from the Setswana language whispered in my ear gave me the gist of the rich and very diverse mini-sermons, each immediately followed by prayers, with everyone on his or her knees praying aloud. After some prodding, I took my turn. Most understood my English as I elaborated on the theme "we are all children of Abraham" (Acts 3:26-27) and brought greetings from French and American churches. Seemingly the members of the congregation appreciated my words, nodding approval. I sat down. But the members of the congregation did not fall on their knees in prayer. Yet they did for the next "preachers." Embarrassingly, my mini-sermon was the only exception. After the service, I asked my translator: "What hap-

pened?" His immediate answer was: "You did not ask!" In response to my puzzled look, he explained: "As is well known" (and so, he had not translated this for me!), "one concludes a sermon with the request, 'Brothers and sisters pray for me, so that I might better understand the Scripture.'"

I knew that I have much to learn from people reading the Bible from other cultural and religious contexts. I knew that in any reading, in order to make sense of a biblical text we use our language, our culture, our religious perspectives, and our concerns. This focuses and sharpens our understanding of the text as binoculars do, but also narrows down our field of vision, becoming blinders. I also knew that only people from different contexts could show us our blind spots—the many aspects of the text that we are missing. This is why I was in this African Initiated Church! I knew all this with my head, but not with my heart. My practice was saying loud and clear that, as a European-American biblical scholar, I understood the biblical text quite well on my own, and that I did not need any help from anybody else for that. But I needed these sisters and brothers from Kasane to show me one of my blinders. Indeed, they exemplified the way to remove it. All that it takes is to ask at the end of a sermon or of a lecture: "Brothers and sisters, pray for me so that I might better understand the Scripture." When one concludes a sermon or lecture in this way, one is ready to listen to other interpretations with the expectation of learning from them.

Can Contextual Biblical Studies Be Critical?

However, who would ask "pray for me so that I might better understand the Scripture" in a church or in academic circles in Europe or North America? I have to confess that I rarely end my lectures with this formula. In academic circles it would be awkward. But thanks to the prayers of these brothers and sisters in Kasane, we Western readers can recognize that biblical scholars in other parts of the world have developed alternate strategies with the same effect: contextual biblical hermeneutics, such as a) inculturation, b) liberation, c) inter(con)textual approaches. All these critical approaches are attempts to better understand the Scripture in particular life context.

These critical approaches have been developed respectively in Africa by Teresa **Okure** and others, in Latin America by J. Severino **Croatto** and others, and in Asia by Archie Chi Chung **Lee** and others. Then, we can recognize that, in Western Scholarship, feminist approaches are themselves contextual—especially when woven together with cultural sensitivities, as in Nicole Wilkinson **Duran**'s articles on "Jesus: A Western Perspective" and (with Derya Keskin **Demirer**) on "1 Corinthians 11 in Christian and Muslim Dialogue." But for many of us trained in Western scholarship, acknowledging the contextual and cultural character of our interpretations was not an easy exercise. Articulating the context of one's interpretation is articulating that which is assumed, not articulated, while one interprets a text within it. Following a long scholarly tradition, we envision a contextual interpretation as the application of the teaching of the text to our context. And so it is, in a sense. But "application of a text to a context" is an attitude that unduly denies that the "teaching of the text" that we identified is already constructed in terms of our context. Thus, in a European-American context, an alternate strategy for becoming aware of the contextual character of our interpretations is often necessary. I found pedagogically helpful to present as equally legitimate, and plausible, several scholarly interpretations of any given text and then to invite the audience into a discussion to assess what is the "best" teaching for a specific situation. See in this volume my contextual commentary on "Romans."

All of us, contributors to this volume, struggled to make explicit the contextual character of our interpretations. We did it in different ways. But in the process, our vision of the relationship of our interpretations with other interpretations and with the biblical text began to change. As we want others to respect our (contextual) interpretations, so should we respect the interpretations of others, even when these are blatantly contextual—such as the mini-sermons of the sisters and brothers in Kasane. Consequently, the *GBC* invites its users not only to respect these "other" interpretations, but also to recognize and make explicit the contextual character of their own interpretations of the Bible. In this way, instead of belittling their own interpretations (waiting for a preacher or a scholar to give them the "correct" interpretations) the users of the *GBC* will hopefully recognize that they can respect their own interpretations and assume responsibility for them. (See the "Suggestions for Using this *Global Bible Commentary.*")

This contextual awareness applies to the reading of this volume: every reading of this *GBC* will necessarily be contextual. Therefore, my presentation of it in this "Introduction"—a reading—is also contextual. In what follows, my goal is limited to introducing this volume to a specific audience: North American undergraduate and seminary students and their teachers, as well as pastors, priests, and adult Sunday school classes. Actually, I am writing this introduction while keeping in mind the undergraduate and seminary students at Vanderbilt University—a culturally and religiously diverse group in a Western context. Readers from other contexts might be curious to eavesdrop on our conversation. But I trust that as this *GBC* is translated and/or prepared for publication in other contexts around the world, different introductions specially prepared to facilitate reading of this volume in these contexts will supplement or replace this one.

An Invitation to Read the Bible as for the First Time

Most commentaries in this *GBC* will provide us readers of the Bible in North America with the opportunity to read the biblical books as if for the first time. Why? Because each given commentary makes explicit the context and concerns from which the scholar reads the Bible. Since the scholar's contextual concerns are different from ours (often even when the commentary is written in North America), the commentary points out significant aspects of the biblical text that we have overlooked, possibly simply because we have taken them for granted.

What was for us a familiar biblical book, which no longer had anything new for us, becomes once again a surprising, disturbing, challenging, prodding, demanding, or wooing address that we cannot ignore. The muffled, subdued, tamed biblical text with which some of us might have been satisfied becomes once again alive. Then, time and again, we find ourselves having to wrestle with the text in order to extract from it a blessing, often an unexpected blessing (as happened to Jacob in Gen 32:22-32, a significant passage in Clare **Amos**' commentary on "Genesis").

Reading a biblical book as if for the first time, as a strange and alien text, is oddly enough what happens when scholars read it from a critical perspective and when believers read it as Scripture. This is understandable.

The more sensitive the scholars are about their own culture, the more aware they are of the historical and cultural gap that separates them from the biblical text. Thus, the critical outlook that we value so much in Western scholarship is sharpened when we read with scholars who make explicit the cultural and ideological perspectives from which they interpret the Bible in their part of the world— as each contributor to the *GBC* strives to do.

Similarly, the more believers read the Bible as a Word-to-live-by in all aspects of their life context, the more aware they are of the moral and religious gap that separates them from the biblical text. Thus, our ethical and scriptural sensibility is sharpened when we observe how scholars decide why choosing a particular biblical interpretation matters in their life context—which each commentator makes as explicit as possible. Accordingly, the *GBC* brings together— sometimes in side-by-side commentaries, sometimes in the same one—the critical readings of scholars and the scriptural readings of believers. As a result, the readers of this *GBC* are invited to assess scriptural

readings from a critical perspective, as conscientious preachers should do when they prepare their sermons. (The practice of scriptural criticism is further explained in Grenholm and Patte, 2000, 1-54).

Biblical Interpretation Always Matters

Biblical interpretation always matters because, for better or worse, it directly affects the lives of believers and the people around them. With this conviction, each contributor to the *GBC* begins by making explicit the specific context from which she or he writes. As a member of a community or a group, he or she asks two questions: How does reading a particular biblical book transform the common view of this life context? And, vice versa, how does approaching this biblical book with the concerns and insights arising from this particular context transform one's understanding of this book?

Biblical Interpretation Matters for Believers and Scholars

Biblical interpretation matters for believers who read the Bible as Scripture, and for preachers who do so in preparation for a sermon, because it involves choosing a Word-to-live-by. Both groups deliberately choose one of the several potential teachings of a biblical text because they think it most directly addresses concerns they have in their present life-situation. At times, this teaching simply confirms and reinforces convictions that believers already hold, although they might have some doubts about them: "I believe, help my unbelief!" (Mark 9:24—a significant verse in Hisako **Kinukawa**'s commentary on "Mark"). But in many instances, the Word-to-live-by that believers and preachers find in the biblical text deeply challenges them, changes their views of a situation, demands from them a new commitment, and transforms their way of life.

Scholars have long frowned upon this practice, because biblical interpretation also matters for them: "One should not pick and choose in a text what one likes." We biblical scholars care so much about biblical interpretation that we have devoted our entire life to preventing misuses and abuses of the Bible. Thus, it is part of our role to be suspicious of all interpretations of the Bible and to assess them. To avoid misuses of the Bible we insist that any interpretation be properly grounded in the biblical text. We, the biblical scholars involved in the *GBC* as contributors and editors, strove to play that most important role. Yet, we disagree with the traditional objection mentioned above. Picking and choosing what is particularly relevant for our life context or what is most significant for us is what *all* interpreters do.

Biblical scholars should not be surprised to hear that interpretation always involves making choices. Actually, the more rigorous we want to be in our exegesis, the more we pick and choose interpretive options. In order to ground our interpretation in the text, we scholars choose one particular critical method among many different methods and we choose a particular aspect of the text as most significant (as shown in Patte, Stubbs, Ukpong, and Velunta, 2003, pp. 54-57). Furthermore, as I have illustrated in the commentary on "Romans" in this volume, in making these methodological and textual choices, self-consciously or not, we scholars also choose a particular teaching of the text for our life context—exactly as believers do—although scholars and believers might disagree on the most appropriate choices.

In sum, nothing is wrong with picking and choosing in a text what one perceives as most significant and as most appropriate for one's particular contexts. Indeed, nothing is wrong with picking and choosing features of the texts because they are more significant from the perspective of one's religious convictions and ideologies. The most rigorous scholars do so. However, this is not to say that everything goes. The biblical scholars' role remains; we still must strive to prevent misuses and abuses of biblical texts. Two strategies are essential for this.

First, we need to assess how each given interpretation is grounded in one or another aspect of the text. But because there is a plurality of legitimate interpretations, we bibli-

cal scholars have to be more democratic and less suspicious. Rather than considering a believer's interpretation "guilty until proven otherwise," biblical scholars should consider it "legitimate until proven otherwise."

Second, we must ask the interpreters to be as aware as possible of their religious and ideological convictions. The more that interpreters make their presuppositions explicit, the less the risk that they will simply "read them into" the text. Interpretations that pretend to be objective or a mere presentation of "what the text meant" hide their presuppositions and inscribe them into the meaning of the text that should be *universally* accepted. Besides being narrow-minded, this type of interpretation is questionable because it denies any legitimacy to interpretations that presuppose religious or ideological convictions different from theirs—a problem further discussed below.

Therefore, in the *GBC*, the commentators do not hide their religious or ideological convictions. They readily disclose them in order to clarify the reasons for their interest in one or another theological feature of the biblical text. When commenting on "Hebrews: Sacrifice in African Perspective" or on Jesus' uniqueness as the only Savior of the World in "Colossians," Teresa **Okure**, SHCJ, explains why these issues are important for her as a Roman Catholic sister in Nigeria by referring to the Catholic doctrine of the Eucharist as a sacrifice, to the 2001 "Declaration of the Congregation for the Doctrine of the Faith," to the teaching of John Paul II, and to the Vatican II Council. Petros **Vassiliadis** by commenting on "John in an Orthodox Perspective" is led to emphasize what this Gospel says about "the liturgical character of the relationship of God's people and the world . . . through which this unity of humankind in God and the preliminary manifestation of the future kingdom are made present." Similar Orthodox interpretations are found in Stelian **Tofană**'s commentary on "Hebrews" and in Vasile **Mihoc**'s "Jesus Christ: an Orthodox Perspective." Paul **Swarup** on "Zechariah" and Paul **Kalluveettil,** CMI, on "Haggai" make clear the struggle of their respective Anglican and Catholic communities in India. Alan **Cooper** and Susanne **Scholz** offer their commentary on "Leviticus" as a dialogue between a Jew and a Protestant woman. As a liberal, feminist Protestant, **Lee** Kyung Sook focuses her commentary on "1 and 2 Kings" on the features of these books that reinforce the "gospel of prosperity"—a powerful movement among Protestant churches in Korea—but also on those features of these texts that undermine this movement and support the "gospel of justice" of her tradition. Similarly, though she emphasizes that her perspective is ideological and not religious, Athalya **Brenner** focuses our attention in her commentary on "Proverbs" on features of this book that are most dangerous from the perspective of her stance as "a woman scholar, Jewish, a native Hebrew speaker, a first-generation Israeli born to immigrant Ostjuden parents, a-religious, a mother to a son, divorced, living in Amsterdam and Haifa, teaching bible and Jewish studies in Amsterdam and Texas (mostly to Christians), of working-class origins, a feminist with left-oriented political opinions." Thus she highlights what Proverbs says about class distinctions and attitudes to young and old, as well as its reflected social and sexual anxieties, its shallow religiosity, and its presentation of wisdom as consumer goods.

Biblical Interpretation Matters Because of Its Powerful Effects on People

Because any interpretation results from a choice among several legitimate interpretations, biblical scholars have to join believers and preachers in asking: Is this the most appropriate interpretation for a particular life context? This question is always important when one reads a biblical text in order to identify a Word-to-live-by. A better choice of interpretation might have considerable positive consequences for the believers and those around them. But another question is even more important, although believers and preachers might forget to ask it: Whom does the chosen interpretation help and whom

might it hurt? Certain choices of interpretations have devastating effects. This is a second reason why biblical interpretation always matters.

We readily recognize unacceptable interpretations when we look at history. Think of the biblical interpretations that were used as a justification for the crusades and the massacres of "infidels," or for racism and slavery, or for the all-out attacks on indigenous peoples and their cultures in the Americas and elsewhere, or for anti-Semitism and the Shoah (or Holocaust)—as André **LaCoque** emphasizes in his commentary on "Daniel." Yes, biblical interpretation matters when millions of people are murdered or oppressed because horrible interpretations have been made.

We believers and scholars readily nod in approval. Such interpretations need to be rejected. But when we consider present-day uses of the Bible that justify other kinds of oppression, violence, and destructive attitudes, we hesitate. Part of our hesitation is due to our inability to imagine interpretations different from the one we are accustomed to. Too easily we are inclined to declare, "As everyone knows, this is what this biblical text says," even when many other readers propose different interpretations. Another part of our hesitation is due to disagreements regarding what is oppressive, violent, or destructive.

Diverse groups denounce as most harmful quite different kinds of biblical interpretations: those that justify patriarchalism and violence against women; those that justify colonialism, the violent exploitation of entire nations, and the denigration of their cultures; those that justify isolationism and the refusal to intervene to protect innocent people from dictators; those that justify homophobia and the denial of basic human rights to persons with different sexual orientation; those that justify the rejection of family values; as well as those that justify classism and the marginalization of the poor with the assumption that they are responsible for their poverty. Yes, biblical interpretation matters, when it justifies injustice and abuse of innocents, instead of calling us "to do justice, and to love kindness, and to walk humbly with your God" (Mic 6:8). But, as **Huang** Po Ho points out in his commentary on "Micah," this verse does not provide us with clear-cut criteria; we need to wrestle with it so as to receive a blessing from it! We need to debate with the text and among ourselves who should benefit from justice and kindness, who should be defended against injustice and abuse, and what is justice.

This *Global Bible Commentary* invites its users to such debates in presence of the concrete reality of economic, social, health, and cultural crises all around the world. This crisis can be summarized in numbers that are so staggering that they are beyond comprehension—"1.2 billion people live on less than a dollar per day; one billion people do not have access to clean water; more than two billion people have no access to adequate sanitation" (Serageldin, 2002, 217). But for many contributors of the *GBC* this tragedy is a very concrete part of their life context. For them, a reading of the Bible that would ignore the cruelty and starkness of poverty, hunger, devastating diseases, injustices, cultural decompositions, social and political chaos would be both meaningless and irresponsible. In an AIDS context, Botswana, Musa W. **Dube** cannot read "Mark's Healing Stories" without taking into account this situation. Similarly, one cannot ignore the spot light that each biblical text puts on one or several particular features of the economic, social, political, cultural, and religious crisis in *Argentina* when reading "Deuteronomy" with Mercedes **García Bachmann**, "Ezekiel 1–39" with Samuel Almada, "Joel" with Pablo **Andiñach**, "Obadiah" with Jorge **Torreblanca**, "Malachi" with Claudia Mendoza, "Galatians" with Néstor Oscar **Míguez**; in the *Democratic Republic of Congo* when reading "Judges" with Fidèle Ugira **Kwasi**; in *Ghana,* when reading "Job" with Benjamin Abotchie **Ntreh**; in *Indonesia,* when reading "Ecclesiastes" with John **Prior**; in *Kenya,* when reading "Isaiah 1-39" with Victor **Zinkuratire**; in *Nigeria,* when reading "2 Corinthians" with

Ukachukwu Chris **Manus;** in *Rwanda,* when reading "Habakkuk" with Innocent **Himbaza**; in *Uruguay,* when reading "James" with Cristina **Conti**. Similarly, Alejandro **Duarte** cannot ignore the political murders of eleven of his friends in *Argentina* and his situation in *Ceuta,* a small Spanish colony in North Africa, as he reads "Matthew."

It is fascinating to see how each biblical text focuses the attention on specific issues in the given concrete situation of the commentator and conversely how this concrete situation brings to light aspects of the text that otherwise do not appear to be particularly significant. This is also true of several commentaries that led several contributors to pay close attention to issues of patriarchalism and violence against women in *India,* as Monica Jyotsna **Melanchthon** did when commenting on "Song of Songs"; in the *African Amrerican* context, as Renita J. **Weems** did when commenting on "Jeremiah"; in the barrios of *Brazil,* as Tânia Mara Vieira **Sampaio** did when commenting on "Hosea," and of *Costa Rica,* as Elsa **Tamez** did when commenting on "1 Timothy." Similarly, other commentators focus their studies on the cultural plights they encounter in their context, as Madipoane **Masenya** does when commenting on "Ruth" as a *South African*; as Lai Ling Elizabeth **Ngan** does when commenting on "Amos" as an *Asian American;* as **Chen** Nan Jou does when commenting on "Jonah" as a *Taiwanese*; and as R. S. **Sugirtharajah** does when presenting the "Matthew 5–7, the Sermon on the Mount in India" as read by Raja R. Roy and Mohandas K. Gandhi.

Facing the concrete issues of their particular life contexts, other commentators lead us to raise issues concerning the responsibility (or irresponsibility!) of the churches, in *Brazil,* when reading "Ezekiel 40–48" with Sandro **Gallazzi**; in *Korea,* when read "Philemon" with Jean **Kim**; in the *Philippines,* when reading "2 Timothy and Titus" with Daniel C. **Arichea**; in the *United States,* including among *African American* churches, when reading "Philippians" with Demetrius K. **Williams**.

In the *GBC,* certain commentators find that they have to debate with the biblical text, because its taken-for-granted message was, and still is, so destructive in their contexts. It is enough here to mention four commentaries that struggle with books that were used to justify colonialism and colonialist mission: Dora **Mbuwayesango** reading "Joshua" from Zimbabwe and Southern Africa; Jione **Havea** reading "Numbers" from the South Pacific Islands; and Justin **Ukpong** reading "The Gospel of Luke" from Nigeria; and Danna Nolan Fewell reading "Ezra and Nehemiah" from the perspective of a European American mother who keeps before her the effects of colonialism on the children in the Two-Thirds World. They are struggling with the biblical text, as Jacob struggled with the angel!

Biblical Interpretations Engender Defensive Attitudes

Biblical interpretation matters so much for all of us readers of the Bible that we often become very protective of our interpretations. We are convinced that, whatever they might be, our interpretations are the "best" from the perspective of our theological or ideological views and of the life contexts that are our primary concern. Because so much is at stake, we make sure that our interpretations truly express "what the text says." We verify their legitimacy in discussion with others and by consulting appropriate resources. Then we feel that, in good conscience, we can ignore or reject all interpretations that differ from ours, and hold firm to our own interpretations.

This is a necessary attitude. Each of us needs to have a firm conviction ("naiveté," Ricoeur would say) that our choice of interpretation is the "best" Word-to-live-by before living by it in our daily lives. We have much at stake in this choice. What we do in our lives depends on it—at times our very lives depend on it. We must reach a point in our reading of the Bible when we decide to act accordingly.

Acting—praxis—cannot be indefinitely postponed, when urgent issues regarding justice for the oppressed are at stake. This is what the commentaries written from a "liberation theological" perspective directly or indirectly intimate. Here I could list most of the commentaries on the prophets. Be it enough to mention the commentaries on "Isaiah 40–55," "Isaiah 56–66," and "Fourth Isaiah" by J. Severino **Croatto** from his context in Argentina, and on "Nahum" by Valmor **da Silva** from his context in the mid-western region of Brazil. But the same urgent call for praxis in contexts involving injustice is found in commentaries on other books, such as those on "Exodus" by Jorge **Pixley**, from his context in Nicaragua; on "Luke's God and Mammon, a Latin-American Perspective" by René **Krüger**, from his context in Argentina; on "John 1, 2, and 3" John" by Johannes **Beutler**, SJ, from his context in Europe and with keen empathy for the dramatic effects of globalization as economic oppression; on "1 and 2 Peter and Jude" by Sharon **Ringe**, from her context in the United States "in solidarity with Latino/a communities in the United States, and with communities in Central America and the Caribbean"; or on "Revelation" by Christopher **Rowland.** In order to advocate and be involved in action (praxis), one must adopt a certain interpretation of the biblical book under study. This is what believers and preachers also do all the time. A quest for a Word-to-live-by must lead to living by this Word!

Yet, as liberation theologians have long underscored, one must not stop the process. Finding a Word-to-live by, and living by it is good. But we should not freeze our choice of interpretation once and for all. When we do so, we have, in effect, stopped reading the Bible. Rather we need to go back and forth between, on the one hand, living by the teaching of the biblical text with full conviction (with a first or second naiveté, Ricoeur would say) and, on the other hand, reading the text anew, with the openness to find that another choice of interpretation might be better in new circumstances or that we had overlooked an aspect of the text which turns out to be most significant. Yet, this openness is difficult to maintain by ourselves. *Reading with others* makes it much easier.

The Many Benefits of Reading the Bible "With Others"

An Invitation to Read the Bible with Others

In this *GBC*, each of the contributors offers us the opportunity to sit down and *read with* her or him a book of the Bible. What a precious gift!

These scholars take the risk of opening themselves up to us in order to expose the otherness of their views, cultures, and ideological and religious stances. They do so by making explicit how they see their life context from the perspective of a biblical book and this biblical book from the perspective of their life context. In the process, these scholars invite us to *read with them*. If we accept this invitation, we soon find ourselves reading this biblical book as if for the first time, astonished by unexpected treasures, frightened by dangerous teachings, unsettled by both the awe and the dread of an encounter with the text as a mystery.

Accepting these scholars' invitation to *read with them* is greatly facilitated by their willingness to acknowledge that their interpretations are contextual. Because we know that the interpretation of a given biblical book is concerned with a context other than ours, we do not need to be defensive. It is clear from the outset that these commentators are not reading the Bible *for us* or *to us*. They are not telling us either how we should be reading the biblical book or what interpretation of the biblical book we should adopt. On the contrary, the commentator frees us to read and re-read the biblical text on our own, both with the sharp focus provided by critical tools available in our culture and with the insights gained from the theological interests and contextual concerns that reflect our life contexts.

Some of the commentators not only invite us to *read with them*, but also exemplify in their own commentaries what *reading with others* entails. Rather than presenting their own interpretation, they present what they heard when they read with others. In a sense, this is true of most of the commentaries—our interpretations reflect our discussion of the texts with our students or with other groups. Yet, five of the commentaries were deliberately prepared by reading with a group. These commentaries include: "Numbers," which Jione **Havea** "read" in the South Pacific Islands with "a Tongan *kava*-drinking group called *Kau pakipaki folofola* ("breakers of scriptures")" in which he told and retold the story of Numbers as an island-storyteller; "1 and 2 Samuel," which Gerald **West** read with groups of southern African readers, including groups of African women; "Zephaniah," which Shigeyuki **Nakanose**, SVD, and Fernando **Doren**, SVD, Enilda **de Paula Pedro**, RBP, read with their base community in Brazil; and "Ephesians," which John **Riches** read with a contextual Bible study group in Scotland.

Reading with Others, Rather than Reading for (or to) Others

Why are the *GBC* commentators inviting others to read with them, even as they themselves read with others? To begin with, they are very aware of the disastrous effects of *reading for* others or of *reading to* others. This kind of reading has the effect of reducing others to the demeaning rank of subalterns, just as *speaking for* others and *speaking to* others do. As Spivak pointed out ("Can the Subaltern Speak?" pages 277-313), this is a typical colonialist attitude that silences the "others," stripping from them their dignity as persons, denying any value to their culture, and depriving them of their personal and communal identity. Many of the commentators from Africa, Asia, Latin America, and the Pacific Islands, as well as the commentators who are women, have suffered from this denial of their cultures and contextual concerns, when they were taught to read the Bible as Western males do. Male teachers, missionaries, pastors, and scholars from North America and Western Europe had read the Bible *to them* and *for them*.

Despite this demeaning experience, all the *GBC* scholars respect Western interpretations by male scholars, as the bibliographies and the comments make clear. Yet, as scholars in their own right they resist the temptation to do to others what others did to them. Thus, instead of reading *for us* or *to us*, they generously invite us to read *with them*, with the expectation that those who join them in reading the biblical text will have their own, distinctive interpretations for their own contexts.

Avoiding the negative effects of *reading for* (or *to*) others is one thing. Yet, *reading with* others has additional important benefits, which are reflected in the experience of the *GBC* contributors who have not personally suffered from this denial of their cultures and contextual concerns. I am referring to the European/American male contributors who are among those who represent Western Europe and North America in this *GBC* volume.

At first, several of us in this position understood our scholarly role as one of *reading for (or to) others*—teaching our students the "right" reading of the text, as we were ourselves taught. But each of us "turned" around. Through different circumstances and paths, each of us was convinced to do so because feminist, African-American, liberation, postcolonial, and other advocacy scholars generously invited us to *read with them.*

Often we European/American males had a hard time hearing this invitation—as was my case. We mistakenly thought that these advocacy scholars wanted to *read for us*—to teach us "the" right interpretation. To our mistuned ears, this is what they were telling us when they asked us to respect their interpretations and to acknowledge their legitimacy, plausibility, and validity. This was a misguided understanding of what advocacy scholars were telling us. In the same way, it would be a misunderstanding of the contributions to the *GBC* if they were to be read as *reading for us*—teaching us the right interpretation.

The contributors to the *GBC*, following in the footsteps of the pioneer feminist, liberation, and African-American scholars, do not want us to appropriate their interpretations or to mimic them. This would amount to co-opting them. Rather, they call us to recognize that our own interpretations are also framed by our own contextual and theological concerns—the first step in a long and ever ongoing journey toward abandoning our exclusivist outlook (be it imperialist, Eurocentric, androcentric, elitist, or religious) which gave us the nerve to claim that we were *reading for* everyone else whom we reduced to the status of subalterns—a strategy that European-American males unfortunately perfected.

In addition, by accepting to read with others, we begin to adopt a totally different attitude toward our own interpretations. As we learn to respect their interpretations, we find that the differences between our interpretations reflect divergent but plausible interpretive choices of three kinds: textual, contextual, and theological choices.

We have already noted that most of the commentaries of the *GBC* make explicit their contextual choices and that reading *with* the commentators helps us to perceive our own "contextual choices." It remains to mention how *reading with* the *GBC* scholars helps us to recognize the roles of culture in our textual choices and of our view of Scripture in our theological choices.

Recognizing the Role of Intertexts in Interpretations by Reading With Others

By reading *with others* we recognize that our "textual choices"—our choices of certain textual features as most significant—reflect not only the critical exegetical method we have chosen, but also a particular hermeneutical theory shaped by the intertextual dialogue in a particular culture. We always, though often subconsciously, read biblical texts in terms of familiar intertexts that lead us to pay attention to certain aspects of these texts. The parochial cultural character of our textual choices and the role of our own intertexts become most obvious when we read with interpreters from other cultures who make explicit their own intertexts. Several *GBC* commentators exemplify for us this intertextual and thus cultural character of biblical interpretations, among these: Archie Chi Chung **Lee** when he reads "Lamentations" in terms of Chinese laments; Benny Tat-siong **Liew** when he reads "The Acts of the Apostles" in terms of Chinese-American inter(con)textual stories; **Yeo** Khiok-khng when he reads "1 Thessalonians" and "2 Thessalonians" in terms of Chinese Marxist and Confucian views of hope and eschatology; Joseph **Pathrapankal,** CMI, when he reads "1 Corinthians" from the perspective of the multi-religious culture in India; as well as David Tuesday **Adamo** when he invites us to join him as he reads "Psalms" with African Initiated Churches in terms of their African religious culture. Each of these cultural perspectives highlights the significance of certain textual features that in our culture might not seem significant, exactly as our exegetical methods and hermeneutical theories lead us to highlight the significances of certain textual features. Reading with these and other GBC commentators we cannot but ask ourselves: What are the intertexts—religious or secular—in terms of which I read the biblical texts? These cultural differences are most visible when comparing the views of "Jesus: An African Perspective," by Anne Nasimiyu **Wasike**; of "Jesus: An Asian Perspective," by Carlos **Abesamis**, SJ; of "Jesus: A Latin American Perspective," by Pablo **Richard**; of "Jesus Christ: An Orthodox Perspective," by Vasile **Mihoc**; and of "Jesus: A Western Perspective," by Nicole Wilkinson **Duran**. Yet, these articles also reveal significantly different theological choices.

Recognizing the Role of Conceptions of Scripture in Biblical Interpretation by Reading with Others

By reading *with others* we also recognize that the "theological choices"—our interests in specific theological issues mentioned by the text—reflect not only our religious or a-religious interests, but also a particular conception we have of how believers relate

Scripture to their lives as a Word-to-live-by. In the process we discover that we have a choice of views of Scripture.

As readers of the *GBC*, we North American readers of the Bible are again and again surprised by the many different views of Scripture that these commentators presuppose or implement. Since the authors often do not make it explicit, I will not list specific commentaries at this point. Yet the users of the *GBC* need to be aware that different views of Scripture are presupposed by the various commentaries. Of course, quite a number of commentaries presuppose that a quest for a Word-to-live-by involves looking for a teaching that believers should implement in their lives: a moral teaching, be it a way to walk ("a lamp to my feet and light for my path," Ps 119:105), or a canon of behavior to assess who belongs or does not belong to the community, or an expression of what God wants, for instance, "to do justice, and to love kindness, and to walk humbly with [your] God" (Mic 6:8).

Yet, many other commentaries are reading biblical books for another kind of Word-to-live-by: a Word of hope, where there is no hope; a Word of love and of welcome as full members of the people of God, where there is exclusion, racism, and marginalization; a vision-giving Word, where nothing makes sense any longer and one needs to see one's life context with God's eyes; but also a troubling, disturbing Word, which is so dangerous that we have to wrestle with it and against it in darkness and with all our might to avoid being cursed by it and somehow to extract a blessing from it. This latter view of Scripture might sound sacrilegious. Does this wrestling indicate a refusal to submit to the authority of Scripture? This might be our knee-jerk reaction when we *read with* commentators who cannot but struggle with biblical texts through which they and their people have been so deeply hurt. But this knee-jerk reaction is unwarranted. Far from being sacrilegious, such wrestling readings of Scripture reflect an encounter with the Bible as "Holy." It is also a liturgical reading of Scripture, which can be a mysterious irenic

Eucharistic Presence (see Petros **Vassiliadis**) or a shattering Eucharistic Presence, a "breaking of Scriptures" comparable to the breaking of bread (see Jione **Havea**). Encountering the Sacred as Mysterious Other is encountering a reality which shakes us up, and which we cannot accept at face value without betraying it. Respecting this mystery of Scripture involves refusing to reduce it to what is obvious, recognizing that it is always more than what we understood, and wrestling with it as long as it does not allow us to acknowledge and respect the mystery of those Others who are with us.

Each of us who contributed to the *GBC* made the contextual character of our interpretations as explicit as we could so as to signal that we were not *reading for others*, but inviting others to *read with us*. Even though quite a few commentators would find it difficult to use these words, this was our way of asking from you, the users of the *GBC*: "Brothers and sisters pray for me, so that I might better understand the Scripture."

BIBLIOGRAPHY

Barrett, David B., George T. Kurian, and Todd M. Johnson. *World Christian Encyclopedia: A Comparative Survey of Churches and Religions in the Modern World.* 2nd ed. Oxford: Oxford University Press, 2001.

Croatto, J. Severino. *Biblical Hermeneutics: Toward a Theory of Reading as the Production of Meaning.* Translated by Robert R. Barr. Maryknoll, N.Y.: Orbis, 1987.

Dietrich, Walter, and Ulrich Luz, eds. *The Bible in a World Context: An Experiment in Contextual Hermeneutics.* Grand Rapids: Eerdmans, 2002. It includes essays by Justin Ukpong ("Inculturation Hermeneutics: An African Approach to Biblical Interpretation"), Elsa Tamez ("Reading the Bible under a Sky without Stars"), and by Seiichi Yagi ("Ego and Self in the New Testament and in Zen").

Dube, Musa W. *Postcolonial Feminist Interpretation of the Bible.* St. Louis, Mo.: Chalice, 2000.

England, John C., and Archie C.C. Lee, eds. *Doing Theology with Asian Resources: Ten Years in the Formation of Living Theology in Asia.* Auckland, New Zealand: Pace Publishing, 1993.

Grenholm, Cristina, and Daniel Patte. "Overture: Receptions, Critical Interpretations, and Scriptural Criticism." Pages 1-54 in *Reading Israel in Romans: Legitimacy and Plausibility of Divergent Interpretations.* Edited by C. Grenholm and D. Patte. Romans Through History and Cultures Vol. 1. Harrisburg, Pa.: Trinity Press International, 2000.

Okure, Teresa, ed. *Evaluating the Inculturation of Christianity in Africa.* AMACEA Gaba Publications Spearhead 112-114. Eldoret, Kenya: AMECEA Gaba Publications, 1990. (See especially, pages 55-88, Teresa Okure,"Inculturation: Biblical Theological Bases.")

————. *To Cast Fire upon the Earth: Bible and Mission Collaborating in Today's Multicultural Global Context.* Pietermaritzburg, South Africa: Clusters, 2000.

Patte, Daniel, Monya Stubbs, Justin Ukpong, and Revelation Velunta. *The Gospel of Matthew: A Contextual Introduction for Group Study.* Nashville, Tenn.: Abingdon, 2003.

Serageldin, Ismail. "World Poverty and Hunger—the Challenge for Science," Science 296, 2002, 54-58.

Spivak, Gayatri Chakravorty. "Can the Subaltern Speak?" Pages 277-313 in *Marxism and the Interpretation of Culture.* Edited by Cary Nelson and Lawrence Grossberg. Urbana: University of Illinois Press, 1988.

USING THE *GBC*
IN BIBLE STUDY GROUPS AND CLASSES

The *Global Bible Commentary* invites its users to:

➤ read the Bible **on their own**, going from book to book through the entire Bible.

   ♦ The *GBC* provides an excellent incentive for individuals, groups, and classes to read and study the entire Bible.

➤ read the Bible **with scholars from all over the world** and from different religious persuasions. These contributors reveal (rather than hide) the particular socio-economic, cultural, ethical, ideological, and/or religious concerns and interests that drive their reading of the biblical text in specific life contexts. Through this openness the contributors invite other readers of the Bible to dialogue with them.

   ♦ The users of the *GBC* are called upon to make explicit the contextual concerns and interests that drive their own reading of the biblical text. The *GBC* offers all a series of models for reading the Bible in terms of one's life context and for understanding one's life context in terms of a biblical text.

➤ read the Bible **with others** who, like the contributors to the *GBC,* propose interpretations of the Bible that might be quite different from ours, even though they might be part of the same group or class.

   ♦ By respecting other people's different interpretations, the users of the *GBC* who participate in group studies a) become aware of the contextual, theological, and textual choices they have made in formulating their own interpretations and b) are then in a position to better assess the choices they made and to assume responsibility for these choices: Are their interpretive choices the most helpful in their life context?

Most of this can be achieved by individual users of the *GBC,* such as preachers preparing a sermon through which they seek to address their congregations' needs by taking into account their particular situations. But the *GBC* is especially designed for Bible study groups and classes that look for a constructive and critical way of reading large portions of the Bible, if not the entire Bible, and of promoting active participation of their members.

With seventy-two contextual commentaries or articles, the *GBC* provides ample resources for two seminary or college-level classes (contrasting other interpretations, as suggested by the bibliographies, with those of the *GBC*) or for a year long Bible Study Group.

➤ For each session, one (or two) biblical book(s) and the corresponding *GBC* commentary(ies) may be assigned, asking the participants **to prepare themselves for the session by**

   ♦ reading the biblical text (with or without the help found in a study Bible such as the NISB and/or in commentaries) to write down what, in their view, this text has to say about their own life context about the "relationship between the People of God and the World" (the broad question behind the *GBC* commentaries);

♦ then, reading the *GBC* commentary on this text, taking note of

  ▪ the *differences*[1] between their own contexts and that of the *GBC* contributor, carefully identifying in both cases the particular contextual issues that are of concern for the contributor and for the member of the group/class;

  ▪ the *differences* between the ethical and theological points they underscored and those underscored by the *GBC* contributor;

  ▪ the *differences* between the features of the text they found most significant and chose to emphasize, and those chosen by the *GBC* contributor;

♦ **During the session,** following this preparation, a fruitful discussion among the members of the group can take place, which according to the goals of the group or class can be focused on one or another type of differences among the members' interpretations as compared with the one proposed in the *GBC*.

➤ After several such sessions on a series of biblical books and corresponding contextual *GBC* commentaries, a group project (or individual projects) might be to prepare a contextual commentary for their own life context, following the pattern found in the *GBC*—including, in addition, a comparison with the *GBC* commentary.

➤ A discussion of this group (or individual) project can be devoted to its refinement for eventual publication on the web-site of the *GBC*, http://www.vanderbilt.edu/AnS/religious_studies/*GBC*/, where exemplary contextual commentaries in response to those of the *GBC* will be posted following critical review. Send submissions to the General Editor: Daniel.M.Patte@vanderbilt.edu

---

[1] The focus on "differences" is essential; it is only when we recognize the differences between our interpretation and those of others that we learn from them, and thus truly respect them—rather than co-opting them, by pretending they are the same as ours, or rejecting them as meaningless.

GENESIS

Clare Amos

Network for Inter Faith Concerns of the Anglican Communion, London, England

LIFE CONTEXT OF THE INTERPRETATION

No other book of the Bible addresses the tension between universality and particularity quite as compellingly as Genesis. It begins with a vast sweep of heaven and earth and ends with a solitary human body preserved in a casket in Egypt, a body to which the destiny of a small but chosen group of people, strangers in a foreign land, is linked. And in between are surprising choices, apparently unfair exclusions, and a God who shifts shape and name and seems to have as much to learn about relating to human creation as people do about relating to their God.

Few, if any, parts of the world have felt the tension between universality and particularity as fiercely as the Middle East. Home to Abraham (perhaps the human "hero" of Genesis) and to Judaism, Christianity, and Islam, the three great world faiths that name him as father, the region struggles to this day with holy privilege and horrible pain. The pain, the privilege, and the particularity belong together. How can these three monotheistic faiths all worship the same God? How can they not? Does each one's affirmation of its own finality invalidate the truth of the others? Above all, perhaps, how can a land claimed so passionately as holy by all three faiths offer liberty and space, both sacred and secular, to each?

I spent ten formative years of my life living in the Middle East, in both Jerusalem and Beirut, Lebanon. I taught Old Testament studies there and I still relate closely to the region. I am also involved in the interfaith work of my church. These two strands belong together and provide the life context for this commentary.

It is impossible to study and teach the Hebrew Bible/Old Testament in the Middle East without being aware that its interpretations have directly affected, for good or for ill, the lives of the inhabitants of these lands. Among those whom I taught were several Christian Palestinian seminarians. For such students the question of biblical interpretation was notsimply an archaeological or intellectual exercise; it was all too relevant to present life and death. How can we expect such students to accept as canonical Old Testament books like Joshua? This book has undoubtedly been employed as a theological weapon to justify the dispossession of the Palestinian people, both Christian and Muslim. Or what about Genesis itself, with those apparently inalienable promises to Abraham and his descendants in chapters 15 and 17?

For me the problem was starkly posed by an experience of a friend of mine, a respectable, middle-class, Palestinian lady from Ramallah, a town on the West Bank. On a visit to Jerusalem my friend had a conversation with a Western tourist who, on discovering that she was a Christian living

Clare Amos is Coordinator for Network for Inter Faith Concerns of the Anglican Communion and Theological Resource Officer of the Anglican mission agency USPG. After reading for a theology degree at Cambridge University, she did post-graduate studies at the École Biblique et Archéologique Française, Jerusalem, where she specialized in the intertestamental period. She was then Course Director at St. George's College, Jerusalem, organizing short courses on the Bible and the Holy Land for clergy and theological students. Later, she taught Old Testament Studies at the Near East School of Theology in Beirut. More recently, she held positions in biblical studies at a number of theological institutions in theUnited Kingdom and is currently finishing a commentary on Genesis for the Epworth Press.

on the West Bank, informed her quite categorically that "she could not be a real Christian, because if she were a real Christian she would, of course, have been willing to leave her hometown, since she would know that God had given the land to the descendants of Abraham, Isaac, and Jacob." My friend was incredulous and I was mortified for her. As the Palestinian Anglican theologian Naim Ateek writes:

> In Israel-Palestine today, the Bible is being quoted to give the primary claim over the land to Jews. In the mind of many religious Jews and fundamentalist Christians the solution to the conflict lies in Palestinian recognition that God has given the Jews the land of Palestine forever. Palestinians are asked to accept this as a basic truth . . . Palestinian Christians must tackle the land from a biblical perspective, not because I believe that the religious argument over the land is of the *bene esse* of the conflict, but because we are driven to it as a result of the religious-political abuse of biblical interpretation. (1992, 108)

This geographical and political setting in which the scandal of particularity can feel truly scandalous is the life context from which this commentary on Genesis is offered. Genesis is a keystone of the canonical scripture of two of the Abrahamic faiths, and many of its characters are venerated in the sacred Scripture of the third. How can this book, which begins with a universal message of the goodness of God's creation, be read at last as a blessing for all? This question is not only relevant to the peoples of the Middle East, for, as we are these days only too well aware, the fate of this region seems to be fundamentally entwined with the destiny of the world.

Genesis and the Relationship Between the People of God and the World

Humanity, Earth, Land, and World

The first issue posed sharply by Genesis is the relationship between the people of God and the world itself. This subject is highly appropriate for a book that begins with a story of creation that has profoundly influenced the theologies of Judaism, Christianity, and Islam. Yet significantly, it is not precisely a *world* as a self-contained entity that is created but the "heavens and the earth" (1:1), with the focus very much on the latter. *Earth ('erets)* is a word with a range of meanings in Genesis: our entire terrestrial planet; the dry land on which humans can live and plants can grow; a particular land, territory, or political entity, such as the land of Egypt or Canaan.

These interconnections are important: they are a verbal reminder that how human beings behave on a particular spot of land will inevitably affect the earth. This point is only too obvious in Israel/Palestine today. Its political identity and the ownership of its territory is an issue that has repercussions across our planet. No land is or can be an island unto itself: developments in one country of the Middle East impinge upon the rest of the region. Pressing environmental questions like the equitable sharing of scarce water resources in the region constitute a further issue. How human beings use or abuse the land as a resource for agriculture and other aspects of human life influences history. Human sin leads to the earth being cursed and less productive (3:17). The later "violence" initiated by the human species corrupts the earth, which does not escape the ensuing cataclysmic punishment (6:13). Genesis does not allow us to compartmentalize our understanding of the earth. It tells us that ecology and politics belong together.

Furthermore, this creation in which the earth is the linchpin is "good" (1:31). The word *good* echoes repeatedly throughout the first chapter of Genesis. It is also picked up in the last (50:20) as Joseph describes God's goal through the twists and turns of his family's story as being for their "good." God wants good for human beings. He desires their very physical good, in all aspects of their lives. "The Old Testament is the great interpreter of [the] coming of God to the world which leaves no area to itself, neither nature nor history, neither love nor power, neither state nor the community of the pious" (Zimmerli 1976, 149). The same criteria apply to those within the community of faith and those outside it. God is "the Judge of all the earth" (18:25), and the inhabitants of Sodom have as much right to God's justice and concern as do Abraham and his family, even if Abraham has to remind God of this.

In the second century C.E. Marcion rejected the Old Testament as Christian Scripture precisely because it affirmed so strongly the physical and material nature of God's involvement with creation. In the Middle East today, many Arab Christians are hostile to the Old Testament/Hebrew Bible because of the way it has been used by Christian and Jewish Zionism. Yet Genesis' affirmation of God's good purposes for the whole of creation needs to be spoken and heard as a challenge by those in Israel/Palestine, whose situation is currently far from "good," and by any who have contributed to this present reality. Genesis tells us that it is not what God wants. It is not the goal of creation.

God and Humanity

When one reads Genesis as the narrative it is, one sees that God is on a voyage of discovery throughout the story. God is learning how to be God. In particular, God is learning how best to relate to God's human creation. The different sections of the book present notably different modes of interaction between God and human beings. There is the incredible intimacy of the moment of mouth-to-mouth respiration in Genesis 2:7, when God coaxes the human being into life. There is the deafening sound of the rain in the flood that silences human beings, temporarily suspending the dialogue between God and humanity. There are the many occasions when God pops up unexpectedly in dealings with Abraham, the "friend of God" (Isa 41:8), who is quite prepared to take

God to task on occasion. There are the struggles, both metaphorical and physical, that God has with Jacob.

But after that climactic moment in Jacob's life when he meets God by the Jabbok, God seems to retreat from direct intervention in the human story. In the tale of Joseph and his brothers. God appears largely as a providential force working behind the scenes and in the speech of the human characters. For better or for worse, this is Genesis' final statement about God's interaction with humanity, and it reflects most closely the situation we are in today. If human beings have been created to be in the "image of God" (1:27), then like governors of far-flung imperial provinces, they need to be sufficiently self-confident in their own natures to live without the constant intervention of their overlord and to coexist as people able to perceive the image of God in others. Genesis has guided us through humanity's childhood and adolescence to this state of comparative maturity.

Read against this background, some of the theologies that underpin the passions alive today in Israel/Palestine seem to be in a state of arrested development. It is notable how many of the flashpoints for trouble are linked to the story of Abraham. There is Hebron, whose Arabic name *El Khalil* ("the Friend") actually recalls Abraham and where, according to the tradition, he is buried. There is Jerusalem, whose temple's foundation legend is linked to the near-sacrifice of Isaac, Abraham's son. There is the area near Nablus/Shechem where a Jewish settlement has been named Alon Moreh after an altar built by Abraham. But Abraham, fascinating character though he is, is not God's final word, not even in Genesis. Humanity cannot, and is not meant to, sustain the ongoing and direct involvement of God in its affairs in the way that Abraham experienced. The history of the Middle East has been skewed by viewing God as a figure who is allowed to operate through apparently unfair divine dictates, rather than by respecting the maturity and ability of his human creation to work out for themselves the full implication of being made in the image of God. Elias Chacour, a Greek Catholic Palestinian priest from Galilee, summed up the vision of Genesis 1:26-27, which is yet far from realized:

> The true icon is your neighbour, the human being who has been created in the image and with the likeness of God. How beautiful it is when our eyes are transfigured and we see that our neighbour is the icon of God, and that you, and you, and I—we are all the icons of God. How serious it is when we hate the image of God, whoever that may be, whether a Jew or a Palestinian. How serious it is when we cannot go and say, 'I am sorry about the icon of God who was hurt by my behaviour.' We all need to be transfigured so we can recognise the glory of God in one another. (2001, 46–47)

Two by Two

Numbers are important in Genesis and they often help to structure the narrative. Particularly significant are the numbers ten, seven, and two, all of which are introduced during Genesis 1. The number two dominates much of the story of Genesis; wrestling with the benefits and difficulties of duality is a constant theme. It is not only in the flood that life is organized by "two and two" (7:9). Creation itself happens through the separation of an original unity into a series of pairs: light/dark, day/night, heaven/earth, land/sea. The human being ('adam) of Genesis 2 is first paired with the ground ('adamah). Then, after the creation of woman ('ishah), the paired relationship between the woman and the man ('ish) is the focus of Genesis 2 and 3.

But with the story of Cain and Abel in Genesis 4, the issue of *brotherhood* is introduced, a topic that will dominate the rest of the book. How should brothers (or "close kin," for the Hebrew word 'Ah often refers to a wider relationship than that of strictly siblings) relate to each other, particularly if one of the two appears to be unfairly favored by God or a parent? Should they interact with hostility or hospitality? The theme is revisited throughout the stories of Shem/Ham/Japheth, Abraham/Lot, Isaac/Ishmael, Jacob/Esau, Rachel/Leah, Joseph/his brothers, and Manasseh/Ephraim. It is not a simple question of inclusion and exclusion, for Genesis consistently makes it clear that even the less-favored brother has an important role in the schema. The interplay can be intricate, but it is evident that the ultimate well-being of the one brother/sister is linked to the fate of the other.

Genesis also draws significant connections between many of the figures in its story and national or tribal entities in the ancient Middle East (e.g., Lot is the ancestor of Moab and Ammon, Esau of the Edomites, Ishmael of the Ishmaelites, and Jacob of the Israelites). Fraternal relations—or lack of them—are a mirror through which the destinies of peoples and nations are being viewed. But it also becomes apparent that defining precisely who the people of God are is not as obvious as it might seem, not the least because the right to claim that title depends on the goodwill and cooperation of the "other." The implication of this for a reading of Genesis from the context of the Middle East today is unmistakable (see particularly the poem by Shin Shalom on p. 12).

Time and Place: In a Strange Land

The scholarly consensus regarding the date and sources of Genesis, which existed for a century after the development of the Graf-Wellhausen hypothesis, has broken down during the last twenty years. We no longer speak assuredly of J, E, D, and P sources, nor of a tenth-century Yahwist writing during the reign of David or Solomon. Detailed presentation of alternative hypotheses lies beyond the scope of this commentary, but broadly speaking, the exilic and postexilic periods have been highlighted as significant. It was during the sixth through fourth centuries B.C.E. that Genesis took its basic written shape. It therefore reflects the political and social contexts of that particular era. At that time, groups located in Mesopotamia/Persia and Egypt—perhaps even more than Palestine—were important for the ongoing life of the Jewish community. The nature of the community itself was evolving: was it a religious, a racial, or a national community? And the question of the relationship between this community and the other inhabitants of Israel/Palestine was the focus of sharp debate, with contrasting voices found on the one hand in Ezra/Nehemiah and on the other in books like Jonah or Ruth.

Genesis needs to be read with an awareness of this historical context. It is a book in which both Mesopotamia and Egypt loom large in the narrative. It is also a book that speaks of possession of the land of Canaan as a future aspiration rather than a present reality. The very last word in Genesis, for example, is *Bemitsrayim* ("in Egypt"). It is a book to be read in the Diaspora, as much as in Canaan itself. And it is also a book that consistently challenges a narrow nationalism that seeks to exclude non-Jews from sharing in the blessings being offered. "How do you live as strangers in a strange land?" is a question it poses, but the book's ironic ambiguity leaves it not entirely clear who the strangers are and which is the land that is strange. Perhaps those who live in the Middle East today—Jews, Christians, or Muslims—need to ask themselves a similar question.

CONTEXTUAL COMMENT

Structural Overview of Genesis

Genesis is a book that is appropriately named, for it is shaped by its genealogies. The Hebrew formula *'eleh toledoth*, which is variously translated as "genealogy," "generations," "history," and "story," appears a number of times in the narrative, positioned at key points to divide up the narrative:

Gen 2:4
Gen 5:1*
(the exact words of the formula vary slightly here)

Gen 6:9
Gen 10:1*

Gen 11:10*
Gen 11:27

Gen 25:12*
Gen 25:19

Gen 36:1,
(repeated in 36:9)*
Gen 37:2

These ten examples of the toledoth formula can be divided into five pairs (as above). Within each pair, one example (indicated by an asterisk) introduces a *pure* genealogy, the other a more extensive narrative connected with the family mentioned. The five pairs effectively separate the book into five sections:

1. The creation of the world and of Adam and his descendants
2. The flood and its aftermath (the story of Noah and his sons)
3. The family of Shem and Terah (the story of Abraham)
4. The family of Ishmael and Isaac (the story of Jacob)
5. The family of Esau and Jacob (the story of Jacob's sons)

Remarkably, several of the pure genealogies relate to a wider or different group than the leading characters featured in the narrative material. Genesis 25:12 lists the descendants of Ishmael, Genesis 36:1 lists those of Esau, and Genesis 10:1 includes the descendants of Shem, Ham, and Japheth. Genesis is interested in their destinies as well as the fate of the offspring of Abraham, Isaac, and Jacob. The very structure of Genesis, therefore, challenges any narrow focus on a chosen family or race. It is particularly striking that this point is made specifically through the use of genealogies, for during the postexilic period pure genealogical status seems to have become a key marker for membership in the Jewish community. To employ a genealogical device to structure the overall book in this way is itself a piece of ironic subversion. It is also a reminder in the current political context that all peoples are entitled to their roots and that any solution that seeks to deracinate Palestinians from their families, hometowns, and culture does not honor the promise Genesis offers.

The passages selected for the detailed commentary that follows include material from each of the five sections of the book. In the reflections offered we also note how the positioning and content of the toledoth references affect the wider understanding of the story.

Significant Passages
for a Contextual Reading

Genesis 1:1–2:4a:
In the Beginning . . .

There is no end to the beginning of Genesis. Modern translations like the NRSV rightly reflect the fact that the text speaks literally of "in beginning" rather than "in the beginning" (in Hebrew, *Bereshith* rather than *Bareshith*). The reference is to a process rather than a point in time. We are standing outside our world, looking at it from a distance. It was appropriate that Genesis 1 was read by the Apollo 8 astronauts on December 25, 1968, as they made the first human circumnavigation of the moon. But the telescope we are peering through in this chapter collapses time as well as space. We are being offered a perspective on the ultimate goal of creation as well as its development.

In the New Testament, John 5:17 draws on this passage to reflect that creation is not yet complete, for "the Father is still working." One way to understand Genesis 1 is as a prologue to the rest of the book. Perhaps within the book the human beings of the story will be able to become God's partners in this work of creation—for such, the Tal-

mud says, is the privilege of those who seek peace. Perhaps, perhaps not.

Genesis 1 sets the stories to come, small and large, of struggling humanity within a cosmic and transcendent framework, and it introduces a God whose ultimate sovereignty seems assured. It presents an ideal that the other forty-nine chapters (and the rest of the Bible!) struggle to realize, an ideal still to be realized today. What does it mean for human beings to be created, male and female, in the image and likeness of God? How can we really live up to the majestic monotheistic vision of this passage when so often our conception of God still seems unashamedly tribal? Is the plurality in unity of the divine, which is hinted at in Genesis 1:2 and 1:26, a reminder that we cannot easily grasp this God (*'Elohim*), either intellectually or as a convenient, divine talisman?

Yet the focus on the unity of the *one* is also interwoven with an awareness of the importance of *two*. Constantly the rhythmic cadences of the passage emphasize a sequence of pairs, which either contrast with or complement each other. Duality seems to be written into the fabric of our world's creation. A Jewish midrashic tradition suggests that Genesis begins with the word bereshith because its first letter is *b,* the second letter of the Hebrew alphabet—and so the link between our world and two is fundamental. But if duality is essential, what does this mean for our world today in which the *other* is too often perceived as alien and the alien is most definitely the other?

Genesis 2:4b–4:26:
From the Dust of the Ground

Whatever the precise literary relationship between the story of heaven and earth in Genesis 1:1–2:4a and Genesis 2:4b–3:24, as it now stands, this second passage offers a very different perspective on human beings and their place in creation. No longer are they the height of creation, in the image of God; rather, they are dust of the ground. The contrast is deliberate and realistic. The dual viewpoint itself expresses the reality of the human condition. It is the glory and tragedy of humanity that we are held in this tension which we long to resolve.

Earth and its soil, literally, form the foundation on which these chapters are based. The prefatory comment in Genesis 2:4a, which includes the toledoth formula, may even suggest that "the heavens and the earth" are in some way viewed as the progenitors of who and what is then made. Certainly the link that is made between the ground or land (*'adamah*) and the human being (*'adam*) reinforces the connection. Note that it is the human being who derives his name from the ground, not vice versa. And the role of the human being is literally to serve the ground or land. When the human beings are punished for eating the forbidden fruit, the ground suffers as much as they (3:17). The destinies of humanity and the ground are intertwined.

The geography of the scene is redolent of the Middle East, where water is precious. One possible understanding of Genesis 2:5-6 is that throughout these early chapters of Genesis it does not rain. Rain, therefore, is a new phenomenon, which arrives with a vengeance only when the great flood begins (7:6). Until then, the fertility of the ground depends completely on underground springs (2:6) that are the source of a river that "flows out of Eden" (2:10). The four branches of this great river are named (Pishon, Gihon, Tigris, and Euphrates), and in three cases they are even linked to specific geopolitical units (Havilah, Cush, and Assur). The availability of water and the continued prosperity of Eden, however, belong together. Just as human beings depend on the soil, so the soil itself depends on the continuation of the water supply.

In many ways the images touch upon the reality of life in Israel/Palestine and the wider Middle East today. Springs, rivers, and underground water resources are essential for settled life in a region that for half of each year does not normally experience rainfall. They are precious commodities and not unlimited. Currently, the population of Israel/Palestine is exploiting its available water resources close to their maximum potential or even beyond it. But the sharing of these water resources is far from equitable and it reflects the realities and asymmetries of power. Israel uses more than 80% of the Palestinian water resources and thus induces a water shortage that affects the economic, environmental, and social fabric of Palestinian society. On the West Bank, many wells that for centuries have provided water to Palestinian villages have been rendered unusable due to deep, modern wells dug to supply water to nearby Israeli settlements. Furthermore, desire to continue to control water resources is clearly a major factor in any political negotiations about the extent of a possible Palestinian state or the amount of Israeli influence in South Lebanon. As in Genesis, geopolitical entities are still linked and defined by water sources.

There is also the question of their overuse. Because of the amount of water being taken out of the Sea of Galilee, Israel's major reservoir, the water levels in the Jordan River and Dead Sea are dropping and both are becoming increasingly saline. Human beings seem to be reversing the biblical order in which they are servants of a ground nourished by water. One result of eating the fruit of the tree of knowledge has clearly been humanity's determination to control the ground rather than to serve it. In the damage done to the region's ecology, it seems that the curse pronounced on the ground (3:17) is being amply fulfilled.

While the current contextual realities reflect our expulsion from Eden, this passage in Genesis also provides a vision for a very different future. The name given to the second river, the Gihon, is fascinating. Although the text, as it stands, links the river to the land of Cush, the writer also probably intended a connection with the spring on which Jerusalem depends, also called the Gihon. What a compliment to such a small spring—to be compared to the mighty Tigris and Euphrates! Yet this exaggeration is a reminder that this water was the lifeblood on which Jerusalem, the biblical Holy City, depended. Biblical writers like Ezekiel (47:1), Zechariah (14:8), and John, the author of Revelation (22:1), recall these images in Genesis to look forward to the days when this spring will gush forth so copiously from the heart of Jerusalem that it will make even the Dead Sea fresh. By its banks will be planted the tree of life, finally accessible to human beings, with its variety of leaves and fruits "for the healing of the nations." At long last, water—the source of so much conflict in the Middle East since history began (e.g., Gen 26:16-22)—becomes the focus for peace and begins to earn the ascription *living* with which it is often credited in the Bible.

The story of Cain and Abel continues the interplay between human beings and the ground. Once again the geography of Israel/Palestine and the region underpins the narrative. One of the striking features of the terrain near Jerusalem is the amazing diversity of climate in such a small area. The difference in rainfall between Jerusalem and terrain just five miles away is striking: Jerusalem averages six hundred millimeters (19.7 inches) of rain a year, while five miles to the east of the city the rainfall has dropped to an annual three hundred millimeters (11.8 inches). Five miles further east still, the annual total is only one hundred millimeters. Inevitably, this great disparity impacts human life. Settled agricultural life is only possible with a rainfall of at least three hundred millimeters (3.9 inches) a year. With less than three hundred millimeters of rainfall a year, the only possible way of living, at least in biblical times, is as a semi-nomadic keeper of sheep and goats. This means that substantially different lifestyles exist in close proximity. It is all too easy for distrust, misunderstanding, and envy to develop, whether between individuals or larger groups seeking space in a limited amount of fertile land. This has colored the area's history in both biblical and more recent times. It also affects contemporary political dynamics. Echoes of this hostility between two brothers with such different lifestyles loom large in the misunderstand-

ings between Israelis and Palestinians, even though it would be a gross distortion to view Palestinians as semi-nomadic Abels and Israelis as settled Cains.

It is notable that it is Cain's sacrifice that is rejected, the brother who is a tiller of the ground (*'adamah*) and who offers its fruits. Is this an effect of the curse pronounced on the earth in the previous chapter? Certainly the imbalances in creation that have resulted from the action of the man and the woman in Genesis 3 seem to be having their effects on the next generation. Is the triumphal cry of Eve at Cain's birth—which seems almost designed to exclude her husband, a symptom of the lack of harmony that has developed between the couple (3:16)? And what impact will it have on the life of a child so greeted? The question YHWH poses to Cain after Abel is murdered echoes the query previously addressed to their parents. So the theme of hostile brothers, which dominates much of Genesis, has been introduced with a reminder that our actions are influenced both by previous history and by our environment. But Cain is neither released from guilt nor from his inability to look YHWH in the face (4:14). Even the ground itself becomes still more difficult to cultivate (4:12). The rest of this commentary chapter offers a pessimistic but realistic assessment of how the violence initiated by Cain multiplies geometrically as assisted by the development of human technologies. The ghosts of Cain have floated around the corridors of the Middle East ever since.

Genesis 9:1–12:3: A New Creation

Is the new creation that is promised after the flood to be an inclusive or an exclusive one? Is it to be marked by diversity or uniformity? One striking feature distinguishes God's words of blessing to Noah. A connection is made between humanity's status *in the image of God* and respect for the sanctity of human life (9:6). Cain, by his actions against his brother Abel, had thus defaced the image of God in himself. The statement in Genesis 9:6 offers a remarkably wide-ranging vision of what it means to be human. Indeed, the formulaic way in which it is set out implies that all human beings have equal rights to equal protection. It is owed to all descendants of Noah, which means everyone.

Whatever the concept of chosenness may mean later in Genesis, there is no place for preferential treatment or discrimination over this fundamental human right. Any who wage war today, justifying their actions on the basis of the Judeo-Christian tradition, would do well to remember this. Western lives are not more valuable than those of the peoples of Africa or Asia. Yet the inclusive vision does not stop there, for the covenant that God then grants is made not only with human beings but with "every living creature" (9:10, 15). Once again humanity cannot separate itself from the rest of creation of which it is a part.

Over the next two chapters, two contrasting genealogies are introduced by the toledoth formula and the story of the building of the Tower of Babel, which they envelope. These genealogies tease out some of the ambiguities of this inclusiveness. The first genealogy (10:1-32) is marked by its expansive diversity in setting out the entire *family of the nations*. It is not neat and tidy. Some names appear twice (e.g., Havilah in 10:7 and 10:28). The genealogy includes the offspring of all three of Noah's sons. Note that Ham, whose family is cursed as a result of his actions in Genesis 9:20-25, is still included in the list. However, Ham's descendants do not have a particular ethnic profile.

Genesis here has no truck with an ethnic apartheid. Rather, the connecting link in Ham's genealogy seems to be the symbolism of Ham's descendants as nations the biblical writer feared either for their empires or for their aggressive expansionism, just as Ham's misguided actions had earlier seemed to give him inappropriate control over his father. In the eyes of the writer of Genesis, the curse of slavery is thus an appropriate reversal. The repeated mention that each group had its own languages and nations accentuates the list's diversity. This makes the genealogy's position immediately before the story of the tower of Babel more intriguing and creates a discrepancy. For according to Genesis 11:1, all people spoke a single language.

It is difficult to read the account of the building of the tower without recalling modern skyscrapers and, at this time, particularly the Twin Towers of New York City. Since September 11, 2001, the analogy has often been made. In Genesis we have already had a hint that cities may not be the healthiest of locations. It was Cain or his son Enoch who built the first one (4:17). Other clues that something is amiss are found in the location Shinar (where Nimrod's kingdom also was) and "from the east" (11:2, the direction in which Adam, Eve, and later Cain settled). There are also verbal indicators that link this story with earlier episodes (chs. 3 and 6) in which humanity had overreached itself and transgressed the boundaries between humanity and divinity. Indeed, it is remarkable that the builders set about their task with an exhortation (11:4) that recalls God's own when God created humanity (1:26). Equally telling is God's reaction a few verses later (11:7), which echoes the builders' own but also reminds us of God's majestic plurality used at that moment of creation.

These people may think that they can "make" something, including "a name" for themselves (11:4), but they completely fail to realize the awesome gap between themselves and the Lord of all creation, however high their tower might be. Indeed, to understand this story we need to remember God's first instruction to humanity after their creation: to "fill the earth" (1:28). This is precisely what these builders have forgotten. In their quest for unity and homogeneity focused on one small space of earth, they have tried to no avail to obliterate God's creative vision of duality and diversity. God's purposes will not be defeated. The ironic result of God's intervention is that they do receive a name, Babel/babble, though presumably not the name they had sought. And their scattering across the earth

(11:9) is not only a punishment but also the fulfillment of God's will in creation.

Reflecting on the relationship between the people of God and the world today, there are several aspects of modern culture that this story calls into question. It challenges the way globalization is currently eroding a diversity of cultures and languages and, accentuated by the development of the Internet, is facilitating an anglophone homogeneity. The story prompts discussion about one particular nation's global hegemony, a nation whose sense of self-confidence and certainty about its own values sometimes seems to outsiders to be on a par with the arrogance of the builders of Babel. Perhaps it suggests that we should not be too quick to identify our own national or cultural perspective with a global one. It is tellingly and tragically ironic that the Twin Towers housed an institution known as the World Trade Center. Who chose that name? And whose "World" was it anyway? Is, therefore, the key challenge to God's people to respect the multifaceted nature of God's world and to acknowledge that all parts of our globe have an equal right to be part of it?

From the tower of Babel narrative we move to the second, more orderly linear genealogy (11:10-32), with one name for each of the ten generations. The clue that foreshadows a significant turning point is the breakdown of this unified, linear structure when Terah's several sons are mentioned. Once again the word *toledoth* appears (11:27), introducing this time not a genealogy but the story of Abraham that continues through Genesis 25:11.

The call of Abraham is the antithesis of what transpired at Babel. Instead of seeking security through his own autonomous efforts in his native locale, he is summoned to journey into the unknown, to find a future by renouncing his past. Instead of seeking his own name (cf. 11:4) he is offered one by God (12:2). In Islam he is given the epithet *El Khalil,* "the Friend" (of God). We have now entered a new stage of the relationship between God and humanity.

Does this new focus on a "chosen" individual and his family suggest that God is no longer interested in other human beings and peoples? Hardly. However, we understand the third of the blessings offered to Abraham ("in you all the families of the earth shall be blessed, 12:3c; Bible translations vary considerably), it is clear that Abraham's role is linked to the blessing of others beyond himself. And yet this is the figure whose tomb in Hebron has become such a focus of conflict and bloodshed. Surely Abraham, by definition, cannot be the exclusive possession of any one of the Abrahamic faiths! The portrayal of Abraham in both Christianity and Islam emphasizes that he was a "god-fearer" (in Arabic, *hanif*), someone who instinctively worshipped the One God before the establishment of a specific religious creed or system. The Qur'an's comment is remarkable: "Ye People of the Book! Why dispute ye about Abraham, when the Law and the Gospel were not revealed until after him? Have ye no understanding? . . . Abraham was not a Jew nor yet a Christian; but he was truth in Faith and bowed his will to God's . . . and joined not gods with God" (Surah 3.65, 67).

Genesis 15–16: The Challenge of Hagar

Recent studies of Genesis have suggested that the story of Abraham (and Jacob) is structured chiastically, with a series of parallels that progressively work in toward the center of this section. Viewed in this way, the unexpected center of the narrative is the account of the pregnancy of Hagar the Egyptian (ch. 16), the substitute wife of Abraham, leading into the birth of her son Ishmael, which is enveloped by two accounts of the covenant between God and Abraham (chs. 15 and 17). At first sight, the story of Hagar appears to be a diversion, a false trail, which irritatingly delays the arrival of Isaac, the favored heir. Yet look more closely and it becomes clear that this is no narrative dead end but a pathway to a vision of God whose justice refuses to be confined by national or tribal boundaries.

The first clue is Hagar's name. In Genesis names and their meanings matter and too little attention has been paid to Hagar's name. Hagar reminds us of *hager,* a Hebrew word that means something like "sojourner," "stranger," or "resident alien." In the law codes of the Old Testament, just treatment for such people is a touchstone for people's relationship with God: "You shall not wrong or oppress a resident alien, for you were aliens in the land of Egypt" (Exod 22:21).

Significantly, the first time the noun *ger* occurs in the Old Testament is in the previous chapter, Genesis 15, where it appears during the establishment of a covenant between YHWH and Abraham. During this episode these ominous words appear: "Know this for certain, that your offspring shall be aliens [ger] in a land that is not theirs, and shall be slaves there, and they shall be oppressed for four hundred years" (15:13). It is interesting that this reference to the Egyptian experience of Abraham's descendants should come so shortly before Hagar herself is introduced to us and immediately referred to as an Egyptian. The links are reinforced by the verb *'anah,* which in its intensive form means to "oppress" or "afflict." This word also makes its first appearance in Genesis in these chapters, initially describing the "oppression" of Abraham's descendants in Egypt (15:13) but then used to express the ill treatment Hagar receives at the hand of Sarah.

These verbal ties are strengthened by the fact that the same verbal stem, *'nh,* appears twice more in Genesis 16: when Hagar is instructed by an angel to return to Sarah and "submit" to her (16:9) and when Hagar is promised that YHWH has heard her "affliction" (16:11). The text offers the hint that the reason for the later slavery of Abraham's descendants in Egypt is the mistreatment that was once meted out to an Egyptian woman at the hands of Israel's founding father and mother. A demand for justice and compassion for all resident aliens, with Hagar as an archetype, is being written into the very fabric of the covenant. The seeming implication is that this covenant relationship's healthy continuance depends at least in part on the willingness of Abraham and his family to offer justice to others. A reading of Genesis committed to justice in such terms would have major consequences for Israel/Palestine today.

Genesis 20–22: Faith Put to the Test

Hagar and her son Ishmael continue to play a significant part in Abraham's story. The next narrative in which they appear is sandwiched between two episodes in which the meaning of Abraham's own status as *ger* is explored (20:1; 21:23; 21:34). Note how Abimelech, king of Gerar (surely the verbal link between this name and the word ger is deliberate?), is a man of good faith (20:6, 21:23) and treats Abraham accordingly, though demanding that Abraham should behave in a reciprocal manner.

By contrast, the expulsion of Ishmael and Hagar is one of the darkest points in the entire book, and the roles both Abraham and Sarah play in it are far from admirable. Sarah's hostility and Abraham's apparent weakness combine in a scenario that, unconsciously or not, has probably provided many with an apparent justification for ethnic cleansing. The story may even have been written as a challenge to the treatment of "foreign women [wives]" in the time of Ezra/Nehemiah when many were sent away (Ezra 9:12; Neh 13:23-27).

The writer hints at the episode's moral ambiguity. As well as framing it with the story of Abimelech, a man with "integrity" and "innocence" (20:5) who provides a contrasting foil for Abraham, the narrator offers clear parallels to Isaac's experiences (ch. 22), which are themselves introduced by the link phrase "after these things" (22:1). The parallels between the fates of the two brothers include the use of similar phrases (e.g., "bush/thicket" and "early in the morning"), the role of the angel in resolving both incidents, and the importance of the theme of seeing. Linking the two incidents in this way provides a rationale for the seemingly monstrous demand made on Abraham to sacrifice his son Isaac. Apparently the command is given as a test to discover whether Abraham "fear[s] God" (22:12), a test he has once already been subjected to when he followed God's instructions and sent Ishmael and his mother away. But was not Abraham simply using God as an excuse in the earlier incident, a convenient way of sorting out a family quarrel? We can all hear God speaking to us when it is opportune to do so, and Abraham's loyalty to God goes through many twists and turns. With the demand for Isaac, however, the purity of Abraham's faith is discovered as God requires of him the one thing that under no human circumstance would he ever have wished to relinquish. In effect, Abraham's treatment of Hagar and Ishmael provokes the fate that is apparently going to befall Isaac.

So a story of two brothers lies in these chapters at the very heart of Genesis. And Genesis 22—a chapter described as "central to the nervous system of Judaism and Christianity" (Goldin 1993, xxi) and one that resonates with Jewish theologies of the Holocaust and Christian theologies of the sacrifice of Christ—cannot be properly read without an awareness of Genesis 21, which tells the story of Ishmael, who is regarded as the ancestor of the Arabs and a hero of faith in Islam. Indeed, the linking of the these two stories takes on a further twist because Muslim tradition has come to believe that it was Ishmael rather than Isaac who was so nearly sacrificed by his father.

Even within Genesis itself, Ishmael's role reinforces the view that, in this biblical book, particularity is never allowed to totally displace universality and that the eventual destiny of Isaac's descendants will be affected by how Ishmael and his mother are treated. Ishmael will stand alongside Isaac in Genesis 25:9 for the burial of their common father in Hebron, and his descendants are given a genealogy in Genesis 25:12-18. In Genesis 16:12 a mysterious birth oracle is uttered over Ishmael. Most modern biblical translations read it as sug-

gesting that Ishmael would live at odds, in hostility, with his kin. But, in fact, the Hebrew here is ambiguous, and another possible translation is that in the future Ishmael would live "alongside his brothers." Is it too fanciful to suggest that the destiny of the Holy Land is somehow held in the tension between these two possibilities?

For these stories that Erich Auerback liked to describe as "fraught with background" (1953, 12) are also fraught with foreground in the context of contemporary Israel/Palestine. The author of Genesis repeatedly suggests that the destinies of Isaac and Ishmael are intertwined, that the descendants of both still need each other. It is ironically painful to read of the reuniting of Isaac and Ishmael in Hebron for the burial of their father and to recall that this act of brotherly unity would be unthinkable to many of their present-day spiritual descendants. An exquisite poem titled "Forms of Prayer for Jewish Worship," by the Israeli poet Shin Shalom is used during the New Year Festival in the Reform synagogues of the United Kingdom. Presented as coming from the lips of Isaac, the writer speaks to his brother Ishmael about a future that will include them both. Translated from the original Hebrew, it reads in part:

> Ishmael, my brother,
> How long shall we fight each other?
>
> My brother from times bygone,
> My brother, Hagar's son,
> My brother, the wandering one.
> One angel was sent to us both,
> One angel watched over our
>   growth—
> There in the wilderness, death threatening through thirst,
> I a sacrifice on the altar, Sarah's first.
>
> Ishmael, my brother, hear my plea:
> It was the angel who tied thee to me.
> Time is running out, put hatred to
>   sleep.
> Shoulder to shoulder, let's water our
>   sheep. (1952, 891)

Genesis 25:22-26; 27; 32–33:
The Risk of Meeting

As twins, Jacob and Esau's fraternal relationship is as intimate as is biologically possible. Conversely, their hostility is magnified, beginning in their mother's womb (25:22-23) and dominating the entire Jacob section of Genesis. Even when Jacob is in Haran (Gen 29–31) and Esau is not a protagonist in the narrative, the rivalry between the two sisters, Rachel and Leah, is recounted in such a way as to provide a contrapuntal variation on that of their husband and his brother. This theme of fraternal rivalry attains its zenith in Genesis 32 and 33 in the interplay between Jacob's encounter with a divine antagonist and his meeting the next morning with Esau, the brother he expects to meet as an antagonist but whose graciousness surprises him.

One can meet God in a variety of ways, but the two different means by which Jacob meets God approach the profoundest insights of biblical spirituality. These chapters have the quality, and the mystery, of some of the resurrection stories of Jesus. Indeed, we are about to read a story of death and resurrection in which symbolically Jacob dies and Israel is reborn. These are not comfortable chapters, and that is precisely their power. We, like Jacob, need to wrestle through them. But as Jacob himself ultimately discovered, it is only by struggle that the blessing comes and the people of God are brought to birth.

Intriguingly, these chapters fall about as far from the end of the book of Genesis as some mysterious encounters of Abraham with God in Genesis 18 fell from the book's beginning. There, too, the interweaving of the vertical and horizontal dimensions of faith was prominent; there, too, the ambiguities of the relationship between God and humanity were explored. It may be more comfortable to meet God at a noonday lunch party as Abraham did, than in the dark of night by a lonely river, but many of us can identify with Jacob's experience and make it our own.

Jacob's first meeting with God is found in the compelling account of his nighttime struggle with a divine figure (32:22-32), a story in which layer is imperceptibly built on layer. Gerhard von Rad's comment cannot be stated better.

> The content of the narrative . . . contains experiences of faith that extend from the most ancient period to the time of the narrator; there is charged to it something of the result of the entire divine history into which Israel was drawn . . . Israel has here presented its entire history with God almost prophetically as such a struggle until the breaking of the day. The narrative itself makes this extended interpretation probable by equating the names Jacob and Israel. (1972, 325)

Rembrandt painted a picture of the scene. In it Jacob is held by the wrestler in such a way that his head is gradually being forced around so that he is compelled to look his opponent in the face. Jacob will not be allowed to avoid confronting his past, his present, and his future. After a long and painful struggle in which Jacob is wounded—the angel's "touch" being perhaps an apt reprisal for the way in which Jacob had earlier deceived his father and deprived his brother of his birthright through an act of touch (27:21-23)—the key question is asked, "What is your name?" with the answer, "Jacob" (32:27).

The whole of Jacob's past life has been leading up to this question. Once before, years ago, he had been asked a very similar one by his father Isaac and had given a fraudulent response, claiming to be his brother Esau (27:18-19). The last twenty years of his life have been shadowed by that lie. This time the truth is dragged out of him. As Jan Fokkelman points out, in acknowledging that he is called Jacob, he is confessing guilt, for he has effectively named himself as "Fraud," the intrinsic meaning of his name (27:36) (1987, 51). Only when this has been publicly stated can his healing and blessing begin.

The angel responds by offering him a new name, Israel (32:28). Jacob's name is changed as a sign of his new relationship with God. This new name—and the circumstances in which it came about—will describe not only an individual but also a whole people and the history of their struggling relationship with God. However, in the later pages of Genesis and in the history of the people for whom he will be the eponymous ancestor, this name Jacob will continue to be used alongside that of Israel. Jacob cannot leave his old self entirely behind.

Is this renaming the blessing that Jacob has sought throughout his life (27:10, 27-29) and in this wrestling bout (32:26)? Probably this is what we are supposed to assume. For the content of the bald statement "and there he blessed him" (32:29) is not otherwise spelled out. To become Israel rather than Jacob is a blessing, albeit a hazardous one. Now Jacob's very name expresses God's promise to him once at Bethel, "Know that I am with you and will keep you wherever you go" (28:15). But, as he has just discovered, that, too, can be a dangerous assurance. The moment of his life when he can say, "I have seen God face to face" (32:30) and when God is most truly with him is during this wounding and lengthy struggle.

But this struggle leads to the second meeting with God in the following chapter. After the long night has ended and morning breaks again, Jacob/Israel finally meets his brother Esau and greets him with the words, "To see your face is like seeing the face of God" (33:10). The wordplay on *face* makes the connection to the events of the night before plainly obvious. We now glimpse another meaning of that dangerous divine encounter. There was indeed a connection between that strange wrestler and Esau. There are rabbinic legends that suggest the wrestler was the guardian angel of Esau, or Edom, the nation of which Esau was the ancestor (36:1), and those legends contain an important truth. Jacob's experience has changed the way he looks at Esau, and perhaps he has begun to understand that it is only by loving our brothers and sisters that we can begin to see and love

God (see also 1 John 4:12). In overcoming, for a brief moment, the duality between God and humanity, the division between human beings themselves is overcome. And in becoming one with his brother, perhaps at last Jacob has become whole. The previously quoted words of Elias Chacour (see p. 4) are relevant and remind us of what it might mean to read this story in Israel/Palestine today.

Does not the story suggest that just as any who choose to claim the name Israel only have the right to it if they are prepared to wrestle with God, so also Israel's vocation must include a willingness to wrestle with the world of national and political realities in which God's people find themselves? Daringly, this would also mean that the blessing offered to Jacob at the end of the struggle is contingent upon the goodwill of those like Esau's descendants. And if Israel turns its back on either a relationship with God or a fraternal relationship with the foreign nations (symbolized by Esau/Edom), then it becomes less than Israel. It is, and will be, a struggle. But only in the struggle will there be the blessing. Such is the mystery of being Israel. Equally, Christians, who have in their history also regarded themselves as the heir of Jacob and relegated Judaism to the position of Esau (Rom 9:13), need also to realize that their claim to be "Israel" (e.g., Gal 6:16) rests on their willingness to see God in the face of the other.

The Old Testament will never again wrestle quite so powerfully with this topic of brotherhood; perhaps it is too painful to do so. Human beings cannot bear so much reality. It is easier for Jacob to travel to Canaan and Esau to Edom than to live together face to face. But once on a dark night and a sunlit morning we were given a glimpse we cannot ignore. This blessing will not be taken from us.

Genesis 37–39; 44:18–45:3: The Perils of Recognition

Is the story of Joseph and his brothers—a story in which YHWH does not clearly intervene directly in the action—intended to illustrate what it might now mean to see God through seeing the face of one's brother?

A series of intricate verbal and thematic connections link Genesis 37, 38, and 39, the three chapters that begin this section of Genesis. They have been introduced by the final example of the toledoth formula that describes the section as "the story of the family of Jacob" (37:2), rather than simply as the tale of Joseph. The story being told here is as much Judah's as that of Joseph, and Genesis 38—rather than being the intrusion it is often treated as—provides a key link in the narrative. One of the thematic links between all three chapters is that of clothing that is used to deceive: Joseph's long-sleeved robe, smeared with goat's blood by his brothers to offer "proof" of his death to their father; the prostitute's garb worn by Tamar to mislead Judah and gain her rights; Joseph's own clothes left in the hand of Potiphar's wife in Egypt and used to falsely accuse him of rape. This is not, of course, the first time in Genesis that clothing has been used to deceive. Jacob's deception by his sons echoes the earlier time when Jacob deceived his own father, Isaac, by wearing the skin of goats in order to gain the blessing intended for his brother Esau. These thematic connections remind us that the past insists on invading the present. We are required to live with the consequences of our own past actions or those of a previous generation. That is certainly true in the Middle East.

Yet we can learn, move on, and change. And our teachers may come from some surprising places, which is the inference of the encounter between Judah and Tamar. Tamar is apparently a Canaanite, an outsider. Her marital history is hardly auspicious. Indeed, Judah's refusal to allow his youngest son, Shelah, to marry this unlucky woman seems eminently sensible, even though it left Tamar in social limbo. Tamar's sexual initiative was aimed at securing her rights and, as Judah eventually acknowledges, she is "in the right" to do so (38:26). The use here of the Hebrew root *tsadik* ("right") is striking, linking a Canaanite woman's legitimate quest for human dignity to a word so often associated with God and God's standard for humanity.

Tamar has been an unlikely instructor for Judah but an appropriate one for a man who had played a leading role in his brother Joseph's enslavement. The rabbis noted the connections: "You said to your father 'Recognize.' By your life Tamar will say to you, 'Recognize'" (*Midr. Gen. Rab.* 37.32-33). Only after this encounter with Tamar does it become possible for Judah to play the leading role in healing his family's deep hurts (44:18-34) by offering himself as a slave and a substitute for the beloved Benjamin. In Judah's speech in Genesis 44 he observes "his [Jacob's] life is bound up in the boy's life" (44:30). It is this that enables reconciliation and the mutual recognition of Joseph and the brothers. In this biblical book, in which duality has been such a prominent theme, the awareness that our lives are bound up one with another, perhaps even in a way that sometimes feels unfair, stands as a challenge whenever Genesis is read against the backdrop of today's Middle East.

CONCLUSION

Perhaps Genesis needs to come with a reader's health warning: Do not treat it as history; do not use it as a prophetic blueprint or as an unconditional charter for a specific modern political arrangement in the Middle East. Above all, read this book, which explores the development of an adult relationship between God and humanity, with the reflective heart of an adult.

In some ways it is unhelpful that so many of the stories of Genesis—including those of Noah and his flood and Joseph and his brothers—are the ones we first come to know and love as children, for Genesis is quite a dangerous book to use with young people. We risk going wrong if we try (as is often done in Christian education) to use the patriarchs simplistically as moral exemplars. To read Genesis properly requires us to stand at a slight distance from the text and explore it quizzically. The text provides us with difficult questions rather than offering easy answers.

Throughout its fifty chapters, Genesis has teased out the relationship between two and one. It is notable that Genesis 50:20 reminds us that God uses human beings to work his purposes. It is not good for human beings, or even for God, to be one and alone. Yet being two is only life-giving if both partners are prepared to engage with each other in a way that risks mutual change. Are we ever likely to be brave enough to treat the Bible itself as such a dialogue partner? And is it a message that protagonists in the Middle Eastern maelstrom will ever be ready to hear?

BIBLIOGRAPHY

Alter, Robert. *Genesis: Translation and Commentary*. New York: W. W. Norton, 1996.

Ateek, Naim S. "Biblical Perspectives on the Land." Pages 108–16 in *Faith and the Intifada: Palestinian Christian Voices*. Edited by Naim Ateek, Marc H. Ellis, and Rosemary Radford Ruether. Maryknoll, N.Y.: Orbis Books, 1992.

Auerbach, Eric. *Mimesis*. Princeton: Princeton University Press, 1953.

Brett, Mark G. *Genesis: Procreation and the Politics of Identity*. Old Testament Readings. London: Routledge, 2000.

Chacour, Elias. *We Belong to the Land: The Story of a Palestinian Israeli Who Lives for Peace and Reconciliation*. With Mary E. Jensen. Erma Konya Kess Lives of the Just and Virtuous Series. South Bend, Ind.: University of Notre Dame Press, 2001.

Dennis, Trevor. *Looking God in the Eye*. London: S.P.C.K., 1998.

Fokkelman, J. P. "Genesis." Pages 36–55 in *The Living Guide to the Bible*, edited by Robert Alter and Frank Kermode. Cambridge, Mass.: Belknap Press of Harvard University, 1987.

Goldin, Judah. Introduction to *The Last Trial: On the Legends and Lore of the Command to Abraham to Offer Isaac as a Sacrifice: The Akedah*, by Shalom Spiegel. Woodstock, Vt.: Jewish Lights, 1993.

Humphreys, W. Lee. *The Character of God in the Book of Genesis: A Narrative Appraisal*. Louisville: Westminster John Knox Press, 2001.

Rad, Gerhard von. *Genesis: A Commentary*. Translated by John H. Marks. Rev. ed. OTL. Philadelphia: Westminster Press, 1972.

Shalom, Shin. "Ishmael, My Brother." Page 891 in *Forms of Prayer for Jewish Worship*. Vol. 3, *Prayers for the High Holy Days*. Edited by The Assembly of Rabbis for the Reformed Synagogues of Great Britain. London: The Reformed Synagogues of Great Britain, 1952. Used with permission by the publisher.

Turner, Laurence A. *Genesis*. Readings, A New Biblical Commentary. Sheffield: Sheffield Academic Press, 2000.

Wolde, Ellen van. *Stories of the Beginning: Genesis 1–11 and Other Creation Stories*. London: SCM Press, 1996.

Zimmerli, Walther. *The Old Testament and the World*. Translated by John J. Scullion. London: S.P.C.K., 1976.

EXODUS

Jorge Pixley
Seminario Teologico Bautista, Managua, Nicaragua

LIFE CONTEXT OF THE INTERPRETATION

I have spent almost all of my professional life teaching in theological schools in Mesoamérica, or Middle America, which, as I understand it, includes Mexico, Central America, and the Caribbean. It is out of this context that I share with the readers of this commentary the way Exodus reads to us in Mesoamérica. Let me add a further word about this us. The context for Bible reading over the forty years of my ministry has been the people's groups, both Catholic and evangelical, that are devoted to what we call the lectura popular de la Biblia, a people's reading of the Bible.

The empirical fact of our situation is countries with formal democracies and dramatically declining lifestyles for the majority of the people. It is a situation dominated by a global market in an era when capitalism is no longer a growing productive force. The achievement of profits is now mainly a matter of financial transactions, which means there is very little increase in the production of goods, and the principal source of capital accumulation is the redistribution of wealth through banks and stock exchanges. It does not take much reflection to see that this kind of accumulation must take away from many in order for some to enrich themselves. This is possible in large measure by a merciless extraction of wealth from impoverished countries, an extraction that is only possible through a policing network of financial organizations controlled by U.S. financial interests: principally, the International Monetary Fund (IMF), the World Trade Organization (WTO), and the World Bank (WB). In our Bible study groups and church reflections, these mechanisms are understood by ordinary people.

Let me add a word about formal democracy as well. There was a period from about 1959 to 1989 when we lived in a condition of more or less open warfare between the dominant sectors of society and the poor. The means of control were military, and no holds were barred. Whole villages in countries like Guatemala experienced massacres, and countries like Mexico and El Salvador witnessed extensive torture and repressive actions. The U.S. government supported war in Nicaragua, a war whose illegal character was confirmed by the World Court in The Hague but not recognized by the U.S. government. Today, thank God, the military repression has decreased in our area. There is the possibility of electing officials. But there is also tight control from the U.S. empire, a control exercised by allowing very limited options for elected governments, so that it makes little difference which party is elected. This control is carried out by diplomatic means, but also and primarily through the U.S. control of the international financial organizations. Should any country defy the structural adjustment programs (SAPs) imposed by the IMF, it will be excluded from all benefits and most trade, as has been the case with Cuba.

This is the general context within which we in Mesoamérica read the Bible.

Jorge (George) Pixley, now retired in Claremont, Calif., taught biblical studies in Puerto Rico for twelve years, Argentina for one year, Mexico for ten years, and Nicaragua for sixteen years. His best-known books are *The Bible, the Church and the Poor* (with Clodovis Boff, 1989) and *Biblical Israel: A People's History* (1992), both translated into several languages.

Issues Raised by Exodus about the Relationship of the People of God with the World

The big issue has to do with the people of God. Who exactly constitute *the people of God?* In terms of the book of Exodus one could answer that on the surface it is the "sons of Israel" (1:1). But shortly we discover that those whom the pharaoh is oppressing are the Hebrews, which is, as we shall see, not the same thing. Further on, in Exodus 12:38, we discover that the people who departed from Egypt under Moses' leadership were "a mixed crowd." And a little further on still (12:48-49) we learn that the resident "aliens," or strangers *(gerim)*, may participate in the celebration of God's liberation of God's people if their males undergo circumcision. This ambiguity is important. The counterpart of this ambiguity in Christian Scriptures is the double character of the beneficiaries of salvation, the church (1 Cor 1:2), or the poor (Luke 6:20).

A second and major hermeneutical issue raised by this book is, who is God? The book's answer is given in no uncertain terms in Exodus 20:2: "I am YHWH your God who brought you up out of the land of Egypt, from the house of slavery" (a.t.). It is not that there are no other gods. Pharaoh was a god to the Egyptians and to obedient sons of Israel in Egypt. And the gods of Canaan are surely envisioned by the next verse which says, "You shall have no other gods before me" (20:3). The rejection and not the denial of other gods shows that the identification of YHWH, the liberating God, as Israel's God was a live and most important issue. We must read Exodus with a full consciousness of this fact.

A third hermeneutical issue of importance is the structural analysis of the societies involved. We live in a capitalistic world at the globalized stage of capitalist development. We can only know what this means by a global, structural analysis of our societies. In an analogous fashion we must analyze Egyptian society. Only when we understand the structural contrast can we understand the polemical nature of the foundation of the Israelite nation as a nation in Canaan that refused to be Canaanite. (Canaanite and Egyptian social structures were similar; at times, polemic against Egypt is really directed at Canaan.)

CONTEXTUAL COMMENT

Shiphra and Puah Disobey Pharaoh Because They Fear God (Exod 1:8-22)

The book of Exodus begins with a listing of the sons of Jacob who entered Egypt with him, eleven sons with their families. To this list it adds Joseph, the twelfth son, who was already in Egypt. This defines from the beginning the protagonist of the book: the children of Israel, or Jacob. The order of the list does not correspond exactly with any of the lists in Genesis 46, Numbers 1, and Numbers 26. In contents, it corresponds with Genesis 46 against the two lists in Numbers by including Levi and joining Ephraim and Manasseh to Joseph. The leadership of the exodus narrated in this book comes from two Levites, Moses and his brother, Aaron. What historical reality these lists represent, if any, is much debated among historians but not important for our purposes.

The second part of this chapter (1:8-14) deals with the oppression of the children of Israel by the pharaoh and his men. With verse 15 there is a shift to the story of two Hebrew midwives, Shiphrah and Puah, who bravely defy the pharaoh's order to kill the sons of the Hebrew women. Within the overall story of the book, this shift is hardly perceptible and the reader assumes that *children of Israel* and *Hebrew* refer to the same people. We shall return to this point shortly.

The pharaoh fears that the children of Israel will "join our enemies and make war on us in order to go up from the land" (1:10, a.t.), an anticipation of the exodus from the land of Egypt to seek the land of promise. The pharaoh's fear is the fear of every oppressor, ancient or modern. The oppressed are necessary to do the dirty work no citizen wants to do, but they are feared and controlled as a potential enemy.

Shiphrah and Puah fear God (1:17), and with this expression and its context we begin to know the real God and not Pharaoh, the false god. The fear of God makes these women resist the deadly orders of the king and save the lives of the male children of the Hebrew women. So it is that the first mention of God in this book introduces him as one who provokes resistance to oppression in the name of life. (We say *him* because the God of the children of Israel is, in fact, presented as male; however, we may, in our theological wisdom, question this idea about God's gender.)

We must turn to the strange shift in names (from *children of Israel* to *Hebrews*) for the midwives and the people in the midst of the story. This requires some historical research that is not strictly textual interpretation. It is necessary, nonetheless, if the text is to reveal its origins and speak to our contemporary situation. The word *Hebrew* occurs thirty-five times in the Hebrew Bible, and thirteen of those times (over a third) are in the first chapters of the book of Exodus, the story of the resistance of this people to oppression. Related forms occur in several languages of the ancient Near East, including the Amarna letters from fourteenth-century Egypt. In all of these extra-biblical references the word refers to people who are not part of the citizens of the city or land. Sometimes it refers to caravaneers who do not belong in the land but trade there. Other times it refers to immigrants who are not part of the native peoples. But most interestingly, in some cases it refers to rebels who reject the dominant order. In no case outside the Bible, and few in the Bible, does it refer to an ethnic group. The concentration in Exodus 1 and 2, stories of resistance in which the term occurs seven times, suggests that the latter meaning applies. My

suggestion, and that of some other scholars, is that the Israelites emerged as a people as a result of the rebellion of the exodus and that the protagonists of the historical event behind the story were a mixture of peasant peoples who were ripe for rebellion.

A Champion Arises
(Exod 2:1-25)

This is the legend that tells how Moses, a leader of the Hebrews and of royal extraction, was really a Levite saved by the courageous actions of his anonymous mother and sister. (Later, in a genealogy in Exodus 6:20, we will learn the mother's name, Jochebed, and later still, we will learn the name of a sister, Miriam.)

But this is a story about Moses, whose name is typically Egyptian (a part of the royal name *Tutmosis*) but is given an artificial Hebrew interpretation in Exodus 2:10. (I use *Hebrew* here in the modern sense, as the name of the language of Israel; it is never so used in the Bible.) In a surprising twist, this Moses emerges from the palace with a passion for justice, a passion whose origins are not explained, not even by reference to God. After accidentally seeing the mistreatment of a Hebrew, a matter that must have been a common sight in Egypt, Moses, in a fit of indignation, slays the oppressing Egyptian (2:11-12). Later in Midian, his land of refuge, he drives away some offensive shepherds and gives water to the animals of some young Midianite women beside a well (2:15-17). The text does not reveal or care about how this gentleman attained his passion for justice, only that his love of justice qualifies him as the man YHWH will single out to lead his people out of Egyptian oppression. For, by the end of the second chapter, God "heard" their cries, "remembered" his vows to the patriarchs, "looked" on the children of Israel, and "took notice of them" (2:23-25).

This is a good place to pause the running commentary on the text and look at the structure of Egyptian slavery. In Genesis 47:13-25, the Bible gives a good anecdotal description of the situation. The basis of the generalized slavery in Egypt was royal control over all the land. The Egyptian population was massively a peasant population that lived in small villages. Agriculture was almost totally dependent on the waters of the Nile for the irrigation of lands that received practically no rainfall. These waters were useless unless channeled and the villages protected by dikes against floods. And these works far surpassed the capacity of any given village. A very successful political system had already been devised in the fourth millennium B.C.E. whereby the king was owner of all the land of all the villages. From them he collected tribute in grain and animals, and he organized a bureaucracy of laborers who were responsible for building both the waterworks that were so vital to survival and the magnificent temples that assured the divine king would be properly worshiped by a population grateful for the blessings of the king's lands. It is apparent from the mention of the authority of the elders in Exodus 3:16 that the villages had a measure of local government. This is the social structure that Karl Marx, who studied it in its Indian form, called the Asiatic mode of production and that later Marxist thinkers more appropriately call the tributary mode of production.

The tributary mode of production is known, with variations, in Mesopotamia, India, Aztec Mexico, and other lands. What this means for Exodus is that the slaves were not just Asiatic immigrants in Egypt, they were the whole of the Egyptian population. We can speculate with some probability that local government was a matter of a council of elders in each village who could at least decide on the distribution of the productive lands among families and the selection of persons to fulfill the village's quota of forced labor. A good king knows that his authority rests on a wise use of his power over the bodies of his subjects. Exodus 1 suggests a king with a love of glory whose construction efforts pushed the system beyond the limits of tolerance and produced that uprising and emigration of slaves we know as the exodus. This simplified explanation is, I hope, suffi-cient to support the interpretation offered in this commentary.

God Reveals to Moses God's Secret Name and Strategy for Liberation (Exod 3:1-22)

This chapter has several parts, all of them important. First, God reveals himself to Moses at the "mountain of God" (3:1) and demands of him solidarity with the Hebrew people, who according to our hypothesis are those among the oppressed who are prepared to rebel (3:1-10). Next, God reveals the name by which he wills to be invoked by his people (3:11-15). Finally, God reveals to his prophet and champion the strategy to be used for liberation (3:16-22).

Nothing has been said prior to Exodus 3:1-10 about Moses' relationship, if any, with God. Presumably, he has worshiped the Egyptian gods and Pharaoh, who is one of them. Now God reveals himself to Moses as "the God of Abraham, the God of Isaac, and the God of Jacob" (3:15); that is, God is a God who is partial to the oppressed Hebrews in Egypt. God reveals further his intention to free the Hebrews from their oppression in Egypt by giving them a land of their own, the land of a list of peoples headed by the Canaanites. God also makes known his plan for Moses to go to Pharaoh as the representative of God, the God of the oppressed peasants and of the children of Israel (3:18). In one great manifestation Moses learns that God, the true God, is the God of the oppressed Hebrews, that God intends to free the Hebrews, and that he, Moses, must end his ambivalent life and opt for solidarity with the Hebrews.

Moses quite reasonably objects, saying the peasants have no reason to trust him and accept him as their leader and champion (3:13). But God has an answer: Moses will reveal to the people his knowledge of their legendary ancestors. If they ask who this God is, Moses is to reveal the secret name YHWH (3:14), though it is not clear whether the people will recognize this code name or whether they are to be stricken by the presence of a new God who wills their liberation. The book of Genesis assumes a prior revelation to the patriarchs of this private name, though nothing has been said to this respect in Exodus.

Next comes the striking presumed etymology of this name (3:14). It is a matter of debate among interpreters how this should be taken. In traditional philosophical theology it is an affirmation of God's existence as essential and necessary, as in Anselm's famous *Proslogium.* The phrase, with two identical verbal forms, is literally translated, "I will be who I will be." As such, it sounds like a refusal to answer: "I will be who I will be," or perhaps, "I will be (for you) the one who is (for you)." In rabbinical fashion I believe we should leave all of these options open as we read this significant text.

Then things get more specific about Moses' commission. He is to go to the elders of Israel and present himself as the messenger of the God of their fathers who intends to free them and give them a different land (3:16-17). They are to present themselves to Pharaoh with the reasonable demand for time off to go on a "three days' journey" to this mountain of God in order to worship there (3:18). When the king refuses, the stage will be set for measures of force that God will execute (3:19-20). Eventually, the king will let them go and they will leave with the gifts of neighbors who sympathize with their cause but are not ready for the risks of the enterprise (3:21-22). It is a simple strategy that will prove to be effective.

God Provides a Lieutenant for Moses, Gives Him Words for the King, and Initiates Him (Exod 4:1-26)

Not surprisingly, Moses feels overwhelmed by the task God has given him, which he feels surpasses his capabilities. God responds in two ways: he gives Moses the power to perform three magical tricks to impress both the children of Israel and the Egyptian king (4:1-9), and he offers Moses an assistant in the form of his brother, Aaron (4:10-16). In Exodus 7:7 we will learn that Aaron was eighty-three years old and Moses eighty! We are to assume that Aaron was born before the edict ordering the death of Hebrew male children and hence that he was raised in the village. He is not, then, like Moses, who is suspected of being one of "them." Aaron is truly a valuable addition to the very risky enterprise Moses is about to begin.

Next Moses gets words to pronounce to the king (4:21-23). These words are from God to god, from YHWH, the God of the Hebrews, to Pharaoh, the god of the Egyptians. Israel is YHWH's firstborn, and Pharaoh also has a firstborn, who is also a god or who will become one upon his adoption by the gods of heaven at this king's death. The God of the Hebrew's threat to the god of the Egyptians is: If you do not let my firstborn Israel leave to serve me (and no longer serve you) I shall kill your firstborn (4:23).

This proposed threat invites reflection. In the land of Egypt, as in other lands with tributary modes of production, the king stands far above everyone else. He owns all the land, all the cattle, and all the persons in his land. With the majority being peasants, he may dispose of their produce and labor as he sees fit. With the bureaucrats, his military and civilian personnel, he has the power to appoint and to remove. With his family, potentially dangerous rivals, he always reserves the possibility of murder. This means that in the experience of Egyptians, from the highest minister of state to the humblest peasant woman, the king is experienced as a god. And he is celebrated as such in the fastidious rituals held in the temples of the land. What we are seeing in these words is a threat to the king's hegemony from a distinct God of the peasants, or of some of them—an unheard-of event!

In modern terms we would speak of class struggle. All tributary modes of production have a built-in class struggle due to the unequal nature of the two sides: the king on the one hand and everybody else on the other. In normal times the class struggle would be entirely one-sided, from the top to the oppressed peoples. A rupture in the religious system, however, meant a loss of hegemony, and the king's control would become a matter of naked power, an unsustainable situation. What we are seeing here is that the class struggle has, in fact, invaded the religious field, something we know about in Third-World countries, where the deepest religious divisions are not between churches but within churches, crossing denominational lines. In antiquity this is a unique experience so far as I know. In the contemporary Third World, the dominant mode of production is capitalism; in it, religion has a much less central role and so the rupture of religious hegemony is not as frightening to the capitalists, whose ideological control rests only partially on religion.

Class Struggle Emerges in Plain Sight: Cracks in Solidarity (Exod 4:27–6:13)

The text rapidly discloses the dynamics of any process of liberation, what happens when an oppressed people undertake the difficult struggle for their liberation. First, Aaron, the lieutenant, meets Moses, the leader, at "the mountain of God" and they get their act together (4:27-28). They then return to Egypt, gather the elders of the villages (literally, the children of Israel), and demonstrate their signs, and "the people believed and heard how YHWH had visited the children of Israel and seen their affliction; they bowed down and worshiped" (4:31, a.t.). As I mentioned before, in a peasant society there can be no significant action without the belief that heaven is on their side, without a religious legitimization.

According to the plan, Moses and Aaron next present their request to Pharaoh in a peaceful manner: YHWH says, "Let my people go to celebrate a feast in the desert" (5:1, a.t.). Pharaoh's response is the mocking one of a tyrant who feels confident in his control: "Who is YHWH that I should obey him?" (5:2, a.t.). But then, like the U.S. authorities whose control was mocked in September of

2001 or the Russians who suffered the same fate in October of 2002, Pharaoh determines to be tough with these potential terrorists. The class struggle from above takes on a harsher appearance than before. For the men who are laboring on the pharaoh's constructions, the quota of bricks will remain the same, but now the men must gather their own straw for the bricks (5:7-9). This is the response of management that feels confident of its position and wishes to weaken the position of the labor leaders with their own base, the workers.

Those who implement Pharaoh's new get-tough policy are the overseers *(nogeshim)*, presumably servants of Pharaoh. But these, in order to establish their control, have appointed bosses *(shoterim)* from among the villagers themselves. The overseers address the workers with the new work orders only through these bosses. The response of the Israelite bosses is to go around the overseers and appeal directly to the king, the same strategy, we may note, that was used by the defenders of Indians (e.g., Bartolomé de Las Casas and Felipe Guaman Poma de Ayala) in the New World of the sixteenth and seventeenth centuries. In this manner the bosses avoid undercutting the whole system and hence their own positions. Their strategy assumes their assimilation to the system as they interpret the new harsh measures as being the willfulness of bad overseers who can be reined in by the good king, exactly as did Bartolomé and Guaman.

But unlike the Catholic kings, who had an interest in reining in their Spanish conquerors, the pharaoh is completely unsympathetic. He feels that the request for a leave is the work of Moses and Aaron promoting the laziness of the workers (5:4). And the pharaoh's strategy for this new phase of the class struggle succeeds. The Israelite bosses blame Moses and Aaron, not the king, for the new, harsher labor conditions (5:19-21).

In the face of this setback in their class struggle from under, Moses and Aaron must return to the God who commissioned them and voice their complaint (5:22). God's response is a reaffirmation of the strategy, a reminder that it had already been announced that the struggle would have to become violent before Pharaoh yielded, and a reaffirmation of divine commitment to this struggle as a fulfillment of God's promises to Abraham, Isaac, and Jacob (6:2-8).

When Moses and Aaron speak anew to the people, nobody wants to listen (6:9). Here is a weakening of solidarity, which is the nemesis of all struggles for liberation and with which only true leaders can cope. Moses and Aaron are going to prove themselves to be such. But for the moment they must return to Pharaoh with their weakened position (6:10-13). We will now have a brief parenthesis (6:14–7:7) before we pick up the story again.

Excursus: The Credentials of Moses and Aaron (Exod 6:14–7:7)

This parenthesis in the story places Moses and Aaron in their appropriate line among the children of Israel, the presumed father of all Israelites. Moses and Aaron are grandsons of Levi. The genealogy is interested in them specifically, so it only includes the first three sons of Israel (Reuben, Simeon, and Levi) in the order of the list found in Exodus 1:1-4.

YHWH the Terrorist Softens Pharaoh to Release the Children of Israel (Exod 7:8–11:10)

In Exodus 7:3 YHWH announced to Moses his intention of performing his signs and wonders (ōtōti wete-mōfti) before Pharaoh and in the land of Egypt. And the long passage we are now commenting on is, in fact, the performance of these signs and wonders, which have the triple purpose of 1) showing that YHWH, the God of the Hebrews, is a powerful God; 2) softening the heart of Pharaoh; and 3) terrorizing the population to demand the Hebrews' expulsion from the land of Egypt. After the private show of wonders before the king (7:10-13) comes a series of nine wonders plus the announcement of a tenth yet to come. Some of these are public nuisances, like the frogs (8:1-15), the lice (or gnats, vermin, kinnim,

8:16-19), and the swarms of diverse insects (`arōv, 8:20-32). Other wonders are real plagues—diseases in livestock and humans—like the great plague (deber kabēd meōd), or "deadly pestilence," on all cattle small and large (9:1-7) and the ulcers (lishchin), or "festering boils," on humans and cattle (9:8-12). We would call these plagues biological warfare today.

The next category of wonders are attacks on the sustenance of the general population—the conversion of the river water to blood (7:14-25), the great hailstorm (9:13-35), and the locusts that destroy those crops left standing by the hail (10:1-20). As one would expect, these are the wonders that have the strongest effect on the people of Egypt and even on the ministers of the king (see 9:20-21 and 10:7). These sorts of actions would create desperation in any population. We would call them sabotage today. The ministers even recognize that the land has been destroyed and the king has not yet taken note (10:7).

The next to the last wonder, the three days of darkness, coming as it does after the nuisances, the plagues, and the sabotage of the vital supplies of Egypt, has a terrifying effect even on the king, who makes the greatest concessions so far and, for the first time, threatens to kill Moses (10:28). It is surprising the king has not tried to kill him before. The last and decisive wonder, the death of all the firstborn of Egypt, is only announced in Exodus 11:1-9 and its execution is left until later (12:29-36), after the instructions for the celebration of Passover and the feast of unleavened bread (12:1-28).

Looked at as a whole, this is a series of terrorist actions. They first cause pressure on the population and finally on the king himself, who, like all rulers, is insulated from the calamities that affect ordinary people. Was it Moses and his followers or was it God who carried out these terrorist actions? Our text supposes that YHWH, the God of the Israelites, is the terrorist. This terror is used with a purpose, but then the creation of terror among any population usually is. The Brazilian, the Uruguayan, the Guatemalan, and the Argentine military dictatorships used terror against their people in the hope of wiping out subversive movements that had considerable popular support. The Israelis used terror first to clear the way for the settlements in the Near East for immigrant Jews and then to extend their domains into the occupied territories of Palestine. In this last case, it is official state policy. In the case of the Latin American military governments, it was never quite official policy and was carried out in underhanded ways by the armies of those countries, as it is today in Colombia. The interesting thing in the case of our text is that it is YHWH, the God of the Israelites, who becomes a terrorist in order to achieve his goal of freeing the people from their oppression so that they can move to a new land and set up a new nation there.

YHWH Orders Celebrations as the People Achieve Liberation (Exod 12:1–13:16)

This text combines the instructions for celebrations of ritual observances with the account of the death of the firstborn sons of humans and cattle in Egypt. It is clear that the account, hidden as it is between instructions for festivals, is secondary to the orders to hold the festivals. This in itself is interesting. One does not tell the story of YHWH's deeds of liberation to provoke new versions of these deeds but in order to interpret the festivals the people of Israel celebrate.

The Beginning of the Desert Passage, with a Victory over the Egyptian Army (Exod 12:17–15:21)

Exodus 13:17-22 explains the manner in which the people march through the wilderness guided by a cloud that gives shade by day and light by night. In the following chapters the cloud is going to constantly represent the presence of YHWH with his people. They are out of Egypt, the house of slavery! But strangely, the cloud leads them into a space between Egypt and the sea. The

wilderness wanderings are picked up again in 15:22-27, where the theme of murmuring *(lōn)* is introduced. It refers to the complaints and even, in some cases, rebellions against Moses and the liberation project. In this first case it is thirst that provokes it.

Put into the story of wandering is the magnificent story of the defeat of the army of Egypt at the Yam Suf, which probably means the Sea of the Limits; that is, the limit before entering Egypt. Exodus 14:1-31 tells of the victory at the sea when, thanks to YHWH, the Israelites cross through a dry lane and the Egyptian army is drowned under the waters. The outcome is that "the people feared YHWH and trusted YHWH and his servant Moses" (14:31, a.t.). Exodus 15:1-21 is a hymn celebrating this victory of YHWH, who is declared to be king (15:18).

The Economic Principles of the New Nation That Is Taking Shape in the Wilderness (Exod 16:1-36)

One of the key problems in the wilderness for the six hundred thousand mixed people who are becoming the people Israel is food. This problem is faced at the wilderness of Sin, midway between Elim and Sinai. The people murmur *(yil-lōnu, niphal* or passive of *lōn)* against Moses and Aaron (16:2). These protests are a serious matter, for in their trials the people dream of Egypt, the land of their bondage which they left behind. At least in Egypt they had had plenty to eat (16:3)! The revolutionary will is slipping. Moses feels his very life is threatened during the griping at Rephidim (17:4). His leadership will be challenged many times. There will even be a plan to name another leader to guide them back to Egypt (Num 14:4).

Although the complaining threatens the revolutionary project, its basis is real enough. If this great people cannot find food, the project will fail. So, even before Moses presents the problem to YHWH, God takes the initiative and promises a solution (16:4-5). This sixth chapter is centered on the provision of manna, the bread God sends from heaven. Manna becomes the survival food for the people in the wilderness. The question of meat will be dealt with in Numbers 11.

With production of the basic foodstuff resolved in the first eleven verses, the issue that takes up the rest of this chapter is the fair distribution of the manna, so that everyone's needs are satisfied. The strictly egalitarian manner in which this happens is, of course, an idealized picture. But like Luke's picture in Acts 2:41-47 and 4:32-37, it is intended as the goal toward which the community's efforts are directed. *Economy* in its root meaning derives from *oikos*, house, and *nomeuo* (= *nemo*), feeding (someone) or grazing (cattle). An economics true to its vocation must be judged by its ability to provide for the needs of all. Neither Exodus 16 nor Acts 2 and 4 give proposals for production in the long run, but in a well-run household one undertakes production to satisfy the needs of its members. This is the first intention of our text.

Another intention is to inculcate obedience to YHWH. If YHWH orders each person to gather a gomer per member of the household, then that must be all the gathering of a day. If YHWH orders that two gomers be gathered on Friday to supply the needs for two days and thus avoid working on the Sabbath, then this is what must be done. Thus, the incident of the manna is also a lesson in obedience.

Some Incidents on the Way from Sin to Sinai (Exod 17:1–18:27)

This text picks up a few of the sites mentioned in the bare itinerary of Numbers 33 and mentions incidents at the locations between Sin and Sinai (Num 33:11-15). At Rephidim there are two noteworthy incidents. The first has to do with protests, in this case formal accusations with the strong legal language of the riv motif. The occasion for the protests is the lack of water for humans and animals, obviously a most seri-

ous matter. The problem is the threat of a lynch action against Moses (17:3-4). God quickly resolves the issue by showing Moses how he can draw water out of a rock cliff at Rephidim. It is not unusual that a revolutionary experience such as this, with the scarcities that go along with revolution, provoke violent actions against the leadership, nor that the leaders take offense at the failure of their people to recognize their heroism and sacrifices.

While at Rephidim, the children of Israel are also attacked by a local group. There is a battle during which Moses and Hur stand on a hill and watch while the armed host of Israel fights with the Amalekites (17:8-16). In a new situation with the emergence of a new people it is also natural that the neighboring nations should feel threatened by the unknown element in their environment and should take preventive actions. But, as in the previous crises, YHWH saves the people from this threat.

The next two incidents involve Jethro, the priest of Midian, who had received Moses when he fled Egypt and given him one of his daughters, Zipporah, as a wife (2:21). Jethro comes to meet Moses at an unnamed "mountain of God" (18:5). We learn here that Moses had sent Zipporah and their two sons, Gershom and Eliezer, to safety in Midian with Jethro at some time during the strife in Egypt. Jethro brings them back to Moses in the wilderness. But this return of Moses' family is not what interests the text. Moses and Jethro meet each other solemnly as two great chiefs of which Jethro is the greater (18:5-7). Moses recounts to Jethro the works of and the salvation that he attributes to YHWH (18:8), and Jethro responds by officiating at a sacrifice and banquet in YHWH's honor for Moses and his leading lieutenants (18:12).

The final incident in this series, Exodus 18:13-27, attributes the bureaucratizing of the new nation to a recommendation of the Midianite priest, Jethro. Any revolution, if it is to do more than just make waves, must create the institutions that are needed for civil life in society. What Moses does at

Jethro's recommendation seems very top-down. It may be the most efficient way of handling administration, but it hardly inspires ordinary people who wish to have a role in selecting their officials.

But why are these two incidents that lift up a Midianite priest placed right in the middle of the story of the shaping of Israel after their uprising and exodus from Egypt? Let me propose that at least one factor is that Jethro is used to introduce a fundamental matter for the theology of this revolutionary people—that YHWH is greatest among the gods (see 18:11). The actions against Pharaoh are justified several times: "By this you shall know that I am YHWH" (7:17, 6:12, 29:46). Jethro gives what will be the party line: "Now I know that YHWH is the greatest of the Gods" (18:11, a.t.).

YHWH Offers a Pact for a New, Different Nation (Exod 19:1–24:14)

In a sense, this proposal by YHWH and acceptance by the "children of Israel, the Israelites" (19:6) of a constitutional basis for a new nation is the climax of the book of Exodus. Exodus is not just the story of a successful uprising against a powerful king. It is the story of the formation of the people of God as a new kind of nation based on the kingship of YHWH, the God of the poor and oppressed. This section is framed by the solemn treatment of this pact. The offer comes in Exodus 19:3-8, which is quoted in part here (a.t.):

> Moses went up to God, and YHWH spoke out to him, "Thus you shall say to the sons of Jacob and report to the children of Israel. You [pl] have seen what I did to Egypt. I put you on the wings of an eagle and brought you to me. Now you must listen and obey my voice and keep my covenant [pact]. [You are] a special property for all the earth is mine. Now you shall become a kingdom of priests and a holy nation" . . . And all the people answered as one and said, "All that YHWH has spoken we will do." And Moses took the words of the people to YHWH.

This remarkable offer by YHWH is based on the marvel of YHWH's bringing the people out of Egypt. Now they must obey YHWH and be his priests, holy among all the nations, who are also YHWH's.

Now let us look at the closure of this text in Exodus 24:3-8 (author's translation):

> And Moses entered and reported to the people all the words of YHWH and his decrees [*mishpatim*]. All the people responded with one voice and said, "All the words which YHWH has spoken we will obey." And Moses wrote out all the words of YHWH and rose early in the morning to build an altar at the foot of the mountain and twelve pillars for the twelve tribes of Israel. And he sent young men of the children of Israel to raise burnt offerings and to sacrifice bulls as communal offerings [*zevachim shelammim*] to YHWH. Moses took half the blood and put it in bowls and half he poured on the altar. He took the book of the covenant and spoke out in the ears of the people. They said, "All the words YHWH has spoken we will do and obey." And Moses took the blood and sprinkled it on the people while saying, "This is the blood of the covenant which YHWH has made with you based on all these words" [that is, decrees, laws].

The pact offered by YHWH in a set of laws spoken to Moses and communicated by Moses to the people is solemnly formalized in a ritual banquet. The holocaust (`olah) is cut up and the good meat offered to YHWH on the altar. The communal offerings (*zevah shelammim*) are divided: the fatty parts are burned on the altar and the meat distributed to be eaten by the people. In this way, a cattle-raising people formalized their agreements. The whole pact is based on the redemption from Egypt ("I bore you on eagles' wings," 19:4) by YHWH and the acceptance and obedience to the decrees of YHWH by the people who thus become the children of Israel. They are no longer Hebrews or rebels. They have all become heirs of the promises to Israel, or Jacob, even that mixed multitude of the six hundred thousand. It is solemnly celebrated with a big meal of meat and, surely also, wine and vegetables. This resembles the U.S. custom of Thanksgiving Day, when by eating a meal of turkey, all people in the United States—whether they be Polish or Mexican or Japanese in origin—declare themselves Plymouth pilgrims whom God has rescued.

Space does not permit elaboration of the words (decrees) set forth by YHWH and accepted by the people at Sinai (20:1–23:33). So let us focus on the opener: "And God spoke all these words and said, 'I am YHWH your God who brought you up from the land of Egypt, from the house of slavery. You shall not have other Gods beside me'" (20:1-3, a.t.). YHWH, the liberating God, makes this remarkable statement to the male Israelites who will soon seal with a solemn banquet their obedience to this God. They are to have no other gods alongside YHWH. This is a polemical, negative statement, an unusual way to begin a national constitution. But Israel was born in a conflict with the pharaoh, the god/king of Egypt. The Israelites begin to be one by renouncing any other gods, whether Pharaoh or Baal and the gods of the land of Canaan. This is not a monotheistic statement. The freed Israelites know from experience that the gods of Egypt are powerful, but their God is henceforth to be only YHWH. This is a reminder of the ideological class struggle in Egypt and a foretaste of the ones to come in Canaan. The Israelites will live in solidarity with the oppressed.

Now we should go back to two previous statements that prepare for this one: the confession in Exodus 15:18 that "YHWH will reign forever and ever" (a.t.) and the confession by Jethro in Exodus 18:11, "Now I know that YHWH is greater than all the Gods" (a.t.). YHWH now will reign (over Israel), a kingship that the people will celebrate in their psalms (Pss 47, 93, 95–100). There are, of course, other kings. But Israel has loyalty to YHWH and not them. This also has implications for the constitution of Israel worked out in the laws of Exodus 20 through 23, on which we cannot comment here. They do not contemplate a king, except, that is, YHWH, whose lordship was accepted from the start. Therefore, there are no jails and no sentences requiring confinement. Damages are to be repaired in kind: for a stolen cow, five cows and for a stolen sheep, four sheep (22:1-4); for bodily wounds, bodily wounds (21:23-24). If a slave owner wounds a slave, that slave shall be freed (21:26-27). The more serious offenses—murder, adultery, and blasphemy—require the death sentence. Domestic slavery is accepted for debts but limited to seven years (21:1-10). There is no generalized slavery. The lack of jails administered by a king leaves fewer alternatives to work out guilt, but it also bears witness to a new society that is a sort of popular democracy with only God as king. In this way we confirm that the exodus is not just about getting out of slavery but also about building a new society of a different sort.

YHWH's Presence in Israel Is Formalized by Cultic Institutions (Exod 24:15–31:17)

Having received the outline of the laws for life in the new Israel, Moses must now return to the mountain and receive the model of the *Mishkan,* which will be YHWH's dwelling in the midst of the Israelite camp. It must be constructed of the best materials, provided with light by a six-branch lampstand (25:31-40), perfumed by a specially designed fragrance to be kept up in an altar of incense (30:23-33), and provided with a table where fresh bread will be placed every day (25:30). There must be an altar for meat outside of the dwelling (27:1-8). Its priesthood must dress in special robes to serve at YHWH's house. To round it all out, the people must set apart one day out of each week to rest in honor of God (31:12-17). Space does not allow for further elaboration.

Israel Explores a Mistaken Answer to Revolutionary Leadership (Exod 31:18–34:35)

These chapters as a whole deal with the

Israelites' failure to understand the nature of the revolutionary leadership YHWH has provided in the person of his messenger, Moses. After many days of Moses' absence on the mountain of God, the people cry out to Aaron, "Come, make us a God who can go before us for what has happened to Moses the man who brought us out of Egypt we do not know" (32:1, a.t.). The people ascribe their exodus from Egypt to Moses, not to YHWH or their own revolutionary acts. More remarkable still is that God makes the same ascription in Exodus 32:7: "Your people whom you brought up out of the land of Egypt" (32:7, a.t.). The people, in their religious fervor, would prefer to be led directly by YHWH rather than by YHWH's agent. And Aaron is to make an image that will give them that assurance.

YHWH's reaction upon the top of the mountain is anger at this "stiff-necked" people (32:9). He offers to provide Moses with another people (32:10). But Moses will have nothing to do with this escape from the situation, and he argues with YHWH, appealing to God's self-esteem (32:11-13). Astoundingly, YHWH repents of the evil he had planned to do to the people (32:14).

A long section follows in which Moses deals severely with the people's lack of faith in him and their breach of the commandment to not make images, even images of YHWH, which was clearly the case here (see the feast to YHWH prepared by Aaron before the image of the calf, 32:5-6). Even Moses expresses his unwillingness to proceed without YHWH's presence in the camp. God's response is that in this case he would destroy the people in his anger (33:3).

God will send his angel before them (32:2), a repetition of what YHWH said in Exodus 23:20-24. What is never made clear is whether Moses himself is this angel. Angel (*malaak*) only means messenger, and Moses is certainly YHWH's messenger. The incident of the golden calf is not only a violation of the prohibition of images but also a rejection of the messenger Moses whom YHWH had appointed to lead the people. (It is, of course, also a violation of the prohibition on images of YHWH in 20:4-5 and 34:17). In some interpretive traditions this is part of the prohibition against the worship of other gods, but this does not seem possible in the Exodus 34:17 version. In any case, the real issue is not what was made but the rejection of YHWH's chosen messenger. As a symbol of this rejection, Moses takes the dwelling and moves it outside the camp, thus removing YHWH's residence from the Israelite camp. And he renames it "the tent of meeting" (*ohel 'mo`ed*); that is, the place where he, YHWH's messenger, will meet with YHWH (33:7). The cloud of YHWH's glory will rest over the tent when this happens so the people will know that Moses is meeting with YHWH. YHWH is delegating the leadership to Moses and the people know it.

Building the Tent of Meeting (Exod 35–40)

YHWH filled Bezalel of Judah and Oholiab of Dan with the spirit of wisdom, enabling them to build the tent with all its furnishings (31:1-10, 35:30-35). Chapters 35 through 39 describe the work they did, and Exodus 40 describes the inauguration of the new residence for YHWH, or place of meeting with Moses. Actually, Exodus 40 seems to reflect no knowledge of the change we have just seen in Exodus 33, from *mishkan* to *ohel mo`ed*. When all is finished, the cloud of the glory of YHWH fills the tent and Moses can no longer enter, only Aaron and his sons (Exod 40:34-38). It is again the cloud that leads the people on their long march.

CONCLUSION

What can we say? We have seen how Exodus can be read and is being read as the story of the revolutionary struggle of an oppressed people who search for their liberation, and as the story of the formation of a new society based on other principles, other, that is, than the generalized slavery of Egypt and Canaan. Because it has been and is still so read by oppressed people, it has served the African slaves in the New World and serves the oppressed peoples of the Third World in their struggle to regain their freedom and dignity. It will surely continue to do so, with or without the help of scholars!

BIBLIOGRAPHY

Buber, Martin. *Moses: The Revelation and the Covenant.* Harper Torchbooks, TB27. New York: Harper, 1958.

Childs, Brevard S. *The Book of Exodus: A Critical, Theological Commentary.* OTL. Philadelphia: Westminster, 1974.

Croatto, J. Severino. *Liberación y libertad: Pautas hermenéuticas.* 2ᵈ ed. Lima: Centro de Estudios y Publications, 1980.

————.."Yavé, el Dios de la 'presencia' salífica: Ex 3,14 en su contexto literario y querigmático." *Revista Bíblica* 43 (1981): 153–63.

Gottwald, Norman K. *The Tribes of Yahweh: A Sociology of the Religion of Liberated Israel, 1250–1050 B.C.E.* Maryknoll, N.Y.: Orbis Books, 1979.

LEVITICUS

Alan Cooper

Jewish Theological Seminary and Union Theological Seminary, New York, USA

and

Susanne Scholz

Merrimack College, North Andover, Mass., USA

LIFE CONTEXT OF THE INTERPRETATION

Alan

My reading of Leviticus emerges from two locations: from my memories of a traditional Jewish education, and from the standpoint of a Jewish biblical scholar teaching in a Jewish seminary. I have a few distinct childhood recollections of Leviticus, an odd mixture of confusion and curiosity. I remember learning that in the days of the temple, boys (probably of the priestly caste) began their study of Torah with Leviticus. My own initiation into biblical study, however, was through the more approachable books of Genesis and Joshua. We got to Leviticus in sixth grade, and I have not-so-fond memories of preparing charts of all the sacrifices, lists of who offered what animals for what purpose, which parts of the offerings were reserved for the priests, and so forth. When anyone asked why we had to know all those details, we were reminded that every day in our prayers, we petitioned God for the rebuilding of the temple and the restoration of its sacrifices. And what if the temple were to be rebuilt in our generation, and there was no one around who knew how to perform the rituals? At such moments, I was happy not to be a descendant of the ancient kohanim. I thanked God (sotto voce) that my undistinguished lineage rendered me ineligible for temple service.

When the more arcane portions of Leviticus came up in the weekly synagogue lections, my tutor (who was studying to become a rabbi) admonished me to pay careful attention, but my mind invariably wandered. Still, a couple of passages always captured my interest. Leviticus 11, which lists the clean and unclean animals, was an endless source of fascination, not least because it provides the basis of the way observant Jews restrict their diets to the present day. Why should I be able to eat a bald locust (11:22), but not a ham sandwich (11:7)? That made no sense at all. And why would the Torah be concerned about whether I might eat a bat (11:19) or a lizard (11:30)—perish the thought. And then there was Leviticus 18, the list of illicit sexual relations. What a source of mirth that was for us youngsters, especially when it was read on Yom Kippur afternoon. Picture a gaggle of boys, sitting in the back of the synagogue, refusing to admit to one another how famished we were, and giggling over whose nakedness was being uncovered. For the most part, the annual reading of Leviticus went by in a blur, the nadir being the laws concerning skin diseases and bodily emissions (Lev 13–15).

Alan Cooper, professor of Bible at both a Jewish seminary and a Christian seminary, is the director of Jewish Theological Seminary Press. His recent publications in the areas of biblical criticism and history of interpretation, include "Biblical Studies and Jewish Studies" in *The Oxford Handbook of Jewish Studies* (2002) and "The Message of Lamentations" in *JANTS* (2002). With a Lilly Endowment Faculty Fellowship he works on the history of the interpretation of Leviticus 12 (the laws of parturition).

Susanne Scholz is an associate professor of religious studies. Among her publications are *Rape Plots: A Feminist Cultural Study of Genesis 34* (2002) and *Biblical Studies Alternatively: An Introductory Reader* (2003). She is also co-editor of *Zwischen-Räume: Deutsche feministische Theologinnen im Ausland* (2000).

Fast-forward a little more than a decade to my years as a doctoral student in Bible, well versed in the text but a neophyte in terms of critical study. The object of study was referred to as "Old Testament," since the politically correct "Hebrew Bible" had not yet come into fashion. All of my teachers and fellow students were Protestants. (The Jewish professors taught Semitic languages or post-biblical Jewish literature—not Bible—and the Jewish students generally studied with them.) There was never a course on Leviticus, and as I immersed myself in critical scholarship, I learned why. My teachers were the heirs of a scholarly tradition that was antipathetic to the book and its teachings. According to the dominant critical view, its cultic prescriptions reflected a late, decadent phase of Israelite religion, far removed from the noble teachings of the prophets and all but devoid of theological interest. In this view, Leviticus adumbrated the oppressive legalism of Pharisaic Judaism, from which the Christian dispensation provided relief.

This was my first encounter with the anti-Judaism of traditional biblical criticism. It was a firsthand encounter with what Ernest Frerichs has described as the "least acceptable element in the Wellhausen program for Jewish biblical scholars," namely "the denigration of Jewish history, the elevation of the pre-exilic period to a prime status and the corresponding reading of the postexilic period as one of darkness and decline" (Frerichs 1987, 1-6). No wonder, then, that a traditionally educated Jewish scholar would find it hard to take this sort of criticism seriously.

Fortunately, alternatives were at hand, thanks to the sympathy and catholicity of my teachers. Both literary-critical and social-scientific approaches to biblical study, then in their infancy, offered promising alternatives to historical criticism. And new historical-critical paradigms were emerging that eschewed the discomfiting aspects of the Wellhausenian model. The new approaches offered ways of confronting Leviticus both critically and sympathetically, in effect turn-ing the older method on its head. Far from being a mass of incoherent and oppressive legislation, the laws of Leviticus could be seen to reflect a coherent worldview and system of thought. And since the final authors of Leviticus were almost certainly the final redactors of the Torah in its entirety, it made sense to view Leviticus not as a late and decadent appendage, but as the very center of the Torah itself.

Susanne

It is not by accident that I took the initiative to co-write with Alan an article on the book of Leviticus. As a German, in fact a "diasporic" German Christian theologian living in the United States, I am part of the post-Holocaust generation, aware of the Christian history of anti-Judaism. Christian prejudices toward Judaism continue to be very prevalent everywhere although people are not always conscious of their anti-Jewish views. In fact, Christians in the United States, including Christian fundamentalists, are usually eager to emphasize that they have nothing against Jews. They want to "like" everybody and know that anti-Judaism is "bad." Yet anti-Jewish sentiments emerge quickly when one digs deeper. In contrast, many German Christians and certainly Christian theologians in today's Germany are very aware of Christian anti-Judaism. The younger generation of theologians has been especially encouraged to develop sensitivity toward this prejudice, which has resulted in numerous education programs on the Holocaust and study programs in Israel, such as *Studium in Israel: Ein Studienjahr an der Hebräischen Universität Jerusalem. Some of us studied at the Hebrew University of Jerusalem.* Others came to places like New York and the Jewish Theological Seminary for firsthand knowledge about Jewish life in America. We are committed to creating alternative Christian positions to the anti-Jewish ones that have dominated Western history, politics, and religion for centuries.

Read in this context, the book of Leviticus is particularly intriguing. Even today, this biblical book does not command much respect or attention from Christians anywhere. I therefore consider this commentary a healing exercise for Christians in Germany, in the United States, and around the world. It will illustrate that a Christian perspective can stand next to a Jewish one without rejecting the latter. Perhaps Western Christians especially need to learn to appreciate our theological insights in the context of diverse religious traditions and practices. For too long, Western Christians have not accepted the limitations of our views, but have ignored, converted, or even killed people of other religions, Jews prominently among them. Western Christians, and perhaps Christians anywhere, have to define and be ourselves without being afraid of different positions. My comments intend to contribute toward this goal.

The exercise of co-writing this commentary reaches toward another important goal for Christians in the West and around the world. It shows that the Bible can be a valuable resource for bringing people together, even after many centuries of oppression and discrimination. Perhaps western Christians should read the Bible more often with people of different beliefs. Such reading practice might convince secularized people in the West that the Bible is not only a symbol of quaint, religiously conservative, or unsophisticated discourse, but a resource for understanding past and present culture, politics, and religion.

CONTEXTUAL COMMENT

An Overview of Leviticus

The twenty-seven chapters of Leviticus are usually divided into the following six sections: (1) Sacrificial Regulations (Lev 1–7); (2) The Beginnings of Worship (Lev 8–10); (3) Purity and Purification (Lev 11–15); (4) Yom Kippur or Atonement Festival (Lev 16); (5) Holiness Code (Lev 17–26); (6) Appendix (Lev 27).

The People of God and the Jewish-American and German-Protestant Contexts

Susanne

Christians worldwide, and German Protestants in particular (due to the historical developments of Western modernity), have a long history of ignoring the book of Leviticus as a resource for faith and religious development. Leviticus represents to them the epitome of legalistic and ritualistic religion that Jesus Christ superseded. In biblical studies, this pervasive attitude among Christians in the West and, because of the history of the western missionary movement, also around the world finds an influential expression in the work of Wellhausen, mentioned above. Wellhausen had a deep-seated aversion for "the Law" that led him to date legal materials into the late period of Israelite history. Because of his attitude, he characterized legal texts, as found in the book of Leviticus, as "pedantic," "legalistic," "ritualistic," and "repetitive" in his monumental and influential *Prolegomena to the History of Israel* in which he admits his preference for the prophetic over the legal tradition (Wellhausen 1885, 350). Following his comprehensive description of the literary-historical composition of the Pentateuch, generations of theologians came to think of biblical law as a phenomenon of the declined theological phase of post-exilic Israelite history (after 535 B.C.E.).

Wellhausen's belief reflects a long tradition of Christian/Protestant contempt for biblical law and, consequently, for Judaism. For centuries, Christians taught and learned that "Mosaic law" had ended with the coming of Christ. For instance, the famous Protestant reformer, Martin Luther, expressed openly and most aggressively the Christian supersessionist view in a pamphlet entitled "On the Jews and Their Lies," published in 1543:

Since priesthood, worship, government—with which the greater part, indeed, almost all, of those laws of Moses deal—have been at an end for over fourteen hundred years already, it is certain that Moses' law also came to an end and lost its authority (Luther, 272).

Considering the influence of Martin Luther on generations of Protestant theologians, the power of this statement is not to be underestimated. Protestant theologians especially stressed the belief that the gospel replaces the law; faith alone offers divine grace and not works (i.e., the law). According to this position, biblical law is a relic of the past that, in fact, belongs to a different religion, namely Judaism.

The rejecting attitude toward biblical law and Judaism is not limited to German theologians or to a past long gone. For instance, Mackintosh, an American contemporary of Wellhausen, declared that Christians have "taken Israel's place." In characteristic Christian manner, he contended: "Jewish worship was connected with inefficient sacrifices, a burdensome ritual, and an unpurged conscience, which gendered in the worshiper a spirit of bondage and fear" (Mackintosh 1880, vii). Nowadays, the dismissal of Leviticus is still visible in mainstream Christian lectionaries that include only one passage in the recommended preaching cycle, namely Leviticus 19:1-2, 9-18 (*Revised Common Lectionary,* 113). Similarly, the title "Oh, No! Not Leviticus!" of an online sermon expresses past and present Christian sentiments that reduce Leviticus to "a sacrificial system which is no longer relevant," "a priesthood which is no longer in existence," and "laws which are no longer binding" (online sermon by Coty Pinckney of Williamston, Mass. at http://tcpiii.tripod.com/levit1.htm). Even today, many theologians and preachers feel little need to consider the book of Leviticus as a necessary component of Christian education, life, and spirituality.

Historical-critical interpretations developed by Christian scholars in the West have done little to dismantle this prejudicial stance toward biblical law and the book of Leviticus. In fact, one could argue that Christian biblical scholarship has contributed to this mind-set. Renowned twentieth-century scholar Martin Noth, who wrote quite favorably about biblical law, defended the Christian refusal to engage Leviticus: "For it deals predominantly with cultic matters in a way which seems very monotonous" (Noth 1965/1977, 7 [original 1940]; see also Noth 1966). A generation later, Gunneweg still felt the need to debate "the theological problem of Old Testament legalism." And while he did not fully support the idea of the Old Testament as part of an "alien religion," he found it lacking due to its "pre-Christian" nature. To Gunneweg, the Old Testament was "without Christ" and "un-Christian," so that "the old language of the Old Testament" had to be translated "into the proclamation of the one act of God in Jesus Christ" (Gunneweg 1978, 220, 236). The Christian difficulty with legal materials in the Hebrew Bible surfaces most prominently in the idea that the book of Leviticus is not a literary unit, but only a fragment of the much larger Priestly source or "P" (only a few scholars have begun to question this norm; see Rendtorff 1996). Accordingly, the standard and German publication, *Die theologische Realenzyklopädie* (TRE), does not contain an individual entry on Leviticus but refers to this biblical book only in an article addressing the Priestly source (Zenger 1997).

Since the 1960s, some Christian theologians, among them German scholars of the Hebrew Bible, have become sensitive to this bias and have begun to explore the connection between biblical interpretation and Christian anti-Judaism (Eckard 1965; Osten-Sacken 1977; Boadt, Croner, and Klenicke 1980; Rendtorff 1983, 1990, 1999; Fisher 1983; Thoma and Wyschogrod 1987). Their work confirms that the Christian bias toward biblical law is indeed part of the larger problem of Christian anti-Judaism. Interestingly, not many studies discuss Leviticus in light of the Christian prejudice. However, two German and Protestant Old Testament scholars, Gerstenberger and Rendtorff, published commentaries on Leviticus as a result of their commitment to Jewish-Christian dialog. Only Gerstenberger, refers to the Christian history of reading Leviticus. Although he examines primarily the historical origins of Leviticus and is thus quite technical, he comments briefly on the negative reception of biblical law in Christian theologies. He writes:

> Christian tradition has often arrogantly distanced itself from the sacrificial practices of the Old Testament, and has strictly rejected the ceremonial legislation of the Jews. It has rendered suspicious and disparaged the Jews' entire practice of worship as well as their devotion, and through such religious slander has prepared the ground for discrimination and persecution. Perhaps the annihilation camps of the Nazi period would not have been so easily possible without this sort of centuries-long poisoning of the religious climate and the destruction of the religious soul of the Jewish people. (Gerstenberger 1996, 15)

The commentary by Rendtorff does not make such connections explicit. Meticulously dissecting every verse and half-verse, the volume reinforces the notion of Leviticus as an incoherent and arbitrary collection of rules and regulations. Thus neither study forcefully seeks to transform the negative image of Leviticus or biblical law.

Our bi-religious interpretation does not continue this trend. It aims to make meaningful the book of Leviticus for present-day readers, Jewish and Christian. We also take seriously the dominantly secular context of contemporary Western societies. For today's people, whether they are of Christian or Jewish background, Leviticus is full of strange regulations that are far removed from the technological, economic, and political structures of our world. Accordingly, Christian or Jewish commentators face the challenge to present Leviticus as a historically, culturally, and spiritually meaningful text for people who have little knowledge of the Bible and who live secular lives mostly unrelated to religious institutions. In other words, any interpretation of Leviticus must enhance our understanding of the world and our place in it. Otherwise, Leviticus and, for that matter, the Bible as a whole will slowly but surely become artifacts of the past that relate little to the realities of our time. Considering these challenges and opportunities, I look forward to offering fresh perspectives on Leviticus in our joint endeavor that bridges differences of religion, national origin, and gender.

Alan

I am a Conservative Jew, which places me in the middle of the three most prominent streams of Judaism, to the right of Reform (so to speak) and to the left of Orthodoxy. Conservative liturgy has transformed the petitionary prayers seeking the restoration of the temple and its cult into retrospective descriptions of what took place there. Few if any Conservative Jews wish to see the Jerusalem Temple rebuilt, and, for most, the idea of a restored Jewish sacrificial cult is abhorrent. The cultic prescriptions in Leviticus that are temple-bound, therefore, are solely of academic or historical interest, or they may be sources for homiletic reinterpretation and application.

On the other hand, the laws in Leviticus that govern personal behavior remain intensely important to the Jewish community. As interpreted by the authoritative post-biblical legal traditions, they constitute a regimen for life that defines Jewish identity and distinctiveness. For example, the cliché "you are what you eat" certainly applies to Jews. The extent to which Jews do or do not observe the strictures of Leviticus 11 and related texts places them along the Jewish spectrum, and often distinguishes Jews from non-Jews as well. The same applies for the laws governing menstruation and bodily emissions (Lev 15). The more rigorously one observes the laws of "family purity," the more one is associated with the Orthodox stream.

For liberal Jews, the essence of Leviticus is contained in the particular observances, but also in the sweeping admonition of 19:2, where God commands Moses to say to the Israelite, "You shall be holy, for I, YHWH your God, am holy" (authors' translation [a.t.]). Still the question is: how is that statement to be understood? Is it descriptive or prescriptive, and what, exactly, does holiness denote? No single, normative answer to those questions exists, but a rich history of interpretation offers an array of possibilities.

Three topics are, in our view, particularly pertinent to American Jews and German Christians. The first topic centers on sacrifice and retribution of guilt as described in Leviticus 1–7. Placed in the context of German guilt for the Shoah and the murder of millions of Jews during Nazi-time, the question is how to read the meticulous instructions on the atonement of one's wrongdoing in our post-Holocaust world. The second topic focuses on the issue of sexuality since in Western countries Leviticus is frequently mentioned in debates over homosexuality (Lev 18:22; 20:13). The book also addresses incest (Lev 12; 18; 20) and women's sexuality (Lev 12; 15) from an androcentric perspective that is offensive to contemporary Western views, and so merits discussion. The third topic emerging from our reading relates to the concept of holiness, which is, in our view, the most important theme in Leviticus. Marginalized from much of western religious theory and practice, holiness is an alien concept for many people today. Whether Jewish, Christian, or secular, western people have lost access to this notion. Perhaps too many people were killed during the twentieth century for holiness to make sense for westerners at the dawn of the twenty-first century. Nevertheless, we maintain that western people need to reclaim this concept; our discussion addresses the how-to.

Sacrifice and the Retribution of Guilt (Lev 1–7)

After the murder of millions of Jews during the Shoah and the relentless killings of millions of people in post-1945 wars in Korea, Vietnam, El Salvador, Somalia, East Timor, Croatia, Iraq, and the many other places of our world, the descriptions of Leviticus 1–7 on how to atone for one's individual or collective wrongdoing seem utterly outdated and passé. The seven chapters assume that people, whether lay or priest, whether an individual or a collective, commit acts of wrongdoings all the time. Hence, they require means of retribution before God. According to Leviticus, various forms of retribution are available to them: burnt offerings, cereal offerings, or peace offerings, at various costs depending on the economic status of those seeking retribution. The point of the sacrifice is to reconnect with the divinity and to reestablish the covenant broken by the individual or collective group. This notion of atonement or, to use a more contemporary term, reparation feels simply too easy and thus too corruptible. It assumes that the sacrifice of a bull, a sheep, a goat, or even cereal actually suffices for the atoning act. Are our collective sins not too great for such affordable reparation? And where is the atonement to the offended parties here on earth? Moreover, in our meat-eating societies the slaughtering of animals happens on such a regular basis and with such quantitative thoughtlessness that the very idea of sacrificing an animal as a retributive act seems too benign and innocuous in view of the massive violations perpetuated daily upon people, animals, and nature. Our world seems so much more complicated. More than a priest's efforts are necessary to pay retribution for injuries, harm, and murder inflicted.

Perhaps this distrust toward animal and cereal sacrifice is not altogether so new. Hundreds of years ago, Jews replaced the recurrent sacrifices of the first and second temple periods with prayer services. The change occurred because of the destruction of the temple in Jerusalem in 70 C.E. Could it have happened even without the destruction? Some scholars argue that the point of the sacrificial system was to give an elite group control over people and commodities. Yet it takes two to tango. People must have gotten something out of the rituals, too. Jacob Milgrom recognized in his discussions on the Levitical system that people require a means of alleviating the burdens of sin and guilt that weigh them down. We go to therapy; an

Israelite made a guilt offering. Yet the problem remains the same: how to atone adequately and effectively for one's wrongdoings? (1991, 339-345) Leviticus 1–7 reminds us of the importance of taking serious and systematic care of individual and collective sins. Spiritual and religious integrity is at stake, requiring retributive work. Such work, however, is not reduced to beautiful words or a quiet mea culpa. The descriptions of Leviticus 1–7 emphasize the physicality and rawness of the retributive action. Luckily, today's priests, ministers, and rabbis no longer smash animal blood on the four corners of an altar. Yet the repetitive and drastic rituals of Leviticus 1–7 make us wonder how to recover the concreteness of seeking retribution in our religious life. According to Leviticus, it is not enough to say, "I am sorry." It is too bland and verbal. Concrete action is required, such as building a house, sewing a dress, planting trees, or sowing corn. *Aktion Sühnezeichen,* a German post-Holocaust organization that has been sending young Germans abroad to volunteer in the effort of seeking retribution from Nazi crimes, has understood the need for retributive concreteness. Retributive action requires a level of physicality, and if it is done, Leviticus 1–7 promises retribution before God in one's individual and collective lifetime, a comforting and encouraging notion for the German post-Holocaust theologian of this commentary. Concrete action repays for the guilt by the generation that committed it. Guilt is not imagined as transmittable from generation to generation, even though the quest for understanding past sins may persist among generations to come.

Sexuality
(Lev 12; 15:18-33; 18, 20)

The issue of sexuality is central to our reading because the topic illustrates clearly the androcentric character of Leviticus. A discussion on sexuality is also necessitated by the fact that this biblical book is probably most often quoted in contemporary disputes on homosexuality (Lev 18:22; 20:13).

Though little known, Leviticus also addresses the issue of incest (Lev 18; 20) and women's sexuality (Lev 12; 15:18-33) in ways that are offensive to contemporary Western perceptions on sexuality. By focusing on this topic, we ask ourselves how to read Leviticus in our contexts that pronounce equality between women and men and, increasingly, oppose heterosexual privileges.

The notoriety of Leviticus in disputes on homosexuality has made many people believe that the Bible as a whole rejects homosexuality. Leviticus 18:22 states: "You shall not lie with a man as with a woman: that is an abomination (*tôēbâ*)" (a.t.). Leviticus 20:13 includes the death penalty: "If a man has intercourse with a man as with a woman, they both commit an abomination (*tôēbâ*). They shall be put to death; their blood shall be on their own heads" (a.t.). Many different interpretations have been proposed in opposition to and in support of homosexuality. Opponents insist that the verses also reject female homosexuality, even though the texts mention only male homosexuality. Sometimes interpreters connect the verses with other biblical passages, such as Gen 19:1-26 or Romans 1:26-27, and discuss Leviticus as one example of the biblical prohibition regarding homosexuality. Interpreters of this persuasion stress the literal meaning of the text and, thus unsurprisingly, many of them affiliate with Christian fundamentalist churches in the West.

Supporters of homosexuality are commonly on the defensive in this debate although they propose refreshing alternatives to the literal approach. They maintain that it is problematic to disconnect Leviticus 18:22 and 20:13 from the larger literary context, the Holiness Code. This code deals exclusively with cultic purity, as indicated by the cultic term *tôēbâ*. This noun, which means "abomination," signifies the transgression of a divinely sanctioned boundary in the cultic realm, and thus, according to some scholars, the verses prohibit homosexual acts as part of the religious cult. In other words, Leviticus 18:22 and 20:13 do not refer to homosexuality in the contemporary meaning of the word.

Supporters also criticize the inconsistency of the position that claims continued authority for Leviticus 18:22 and 20:13 but does not carry out the great majority of Levitical laws. For instance, Leviticus 20:10 advises that adulterers receive the death penalty, and Leviticus 19:19 prohibits the sowing of two kinds of grain or the wearing of clothing made from two different kinds of fabric. These and many other laws of Leviticus are unacceptable to most people in the West, and are also ignored by opponents of homosexuality. Their literal approach blinds them, and so they rarely recognize the inconsistency of their position. Yet discussions about the epistemological standards for reading biblical texts, including Leviticus 18:22 and 20:13, which are so desperately needed in this sometimes violent conflict over sexual practices, rarely reach audiences beyond the scholarly field.

Meanwhile, some progressive Jewish and Christian organizations ordain female and male leadership regardless of sexual orientation. To them, Leviticus 18:22 and 20:13 do not represent a standard to be followed. In such circles, the verses remain important only to understand the historical, political, and religious dimensions of homophobia in Western societies. As such, these texts offer rich and distressing evidence about the lasting influence of Leviticus even today.

The book of Leviticus also tackles the issue of incest, alas from a thoroughly androcentric stance. In Leviticus 18 and 20 the directives are always addressed to men, as if to suggest that incest is the exclusive concern of males. Women's perspectives do not exist in these texts. Accordingly, men are prohibited from having sexual intercourse with the various female relatives of their families (esp. Lev 18). Women are not imagined as subjects of incest, but are always the objects.

Scholars have long puzzled over the fact that Leviticus 18 does not mention one of the most incest-ridden relationships, that of father and daughter. Early interpretations, such as the rabbinic literature *(m. Sanh. 9:1),* noted the omission and ardently prohibited incest between father and daughter. Contemporary interpreters often explain the omission by referring to the societal structures to which this text once spoke. The argument is that in ancient Israel the sexual and reproductive functions of women always belonged to a particular man. Women were legally owned first by their father and then by their husband. In such a system incest between father and daughter was not condemned because it did not threaten male ownership. The writers of Leviticus did not include father-daughter incest because the father's ownership over his daughter's sexual and reproductive function remained undisputed, even in case of incest.

Still, this explanation is historically amorphous because we are not certain that Leviticus reflects actual or practiced law. Perhaps it represented only priestly wishful thinking. In fact, it is probable that women in ancient Israel had more rights and access to political, economic, and religious power than much of modern androcentric scholarship assumes. Due to the limited historical evidence available, much of biblical historiography has to be taken with more than a grain of salt. An alternative approach to the omission of father-daughter incest must therefore be considered.

Feminist scholars have published a plethora of studies on the problem of incest, since it has haunted women throughout the androcentric ages. The question is whether to read the laws in Leviticus as permission to fathers to sexually violate their daughters or as an important reminder about the statistical frequency with which father-daughter incest has occurred in the past and present. One's answer will depend on how one chooses to deal with biblical androcentrism. If one prefers to reject biblical literature because it has contributed so extensively to the oppression of women, one will select the first option. If one wishes to stick with the Bible, one will choose the second option. Still, both choices recognize that father-daughter incest is tremendously harmful to the daughter. That Leviticus does not prohibit this form of sexual violence with the severest penalty available to the priestly imagination remains a disturbing fact. It is high time to emphasize the omission and to read Leviticus 18 and 20 as religious documents that have contributed to the prevalence of father-daughter incest by not condemning fathers unambiguously.

Finally, Leviticus 12 and 15:18-33 deal with women's sexuality, particularly the effects of giving birth and menstruation. The brief chapter of Leviticus 12 describes the required purifications and sacrifices needed after childbirth (12:4). A woman who gives birth to a son is considered impure for thirty-three days whereas a woman who gives birth to a daughter is impure for double the amount of time, namely sixty-six days (12:5). The discrepancy exposes the implicit androcentrism according to which a girl extends the time of impurity for her mother. Yet, whether she bore a daughter or a son, the mother is required to make the same sacrifice of a one-year-old lamb and a young pigeon.

The regulations in Leviticus 15:18-33 discuss the sexual situations that make a woman impure. They relate to sexual intercourse in general and menstrual and other forms of discharge. The religiously and culturally discriminatory effects of Leviticus 15 cannot be underlined enough. According to *Wholly Woman, Holy Blood* (De Troyer, *et al*), the priestly denigration of female sexuality and biological function has contributed to the extensive woman-hatred under the conditions of patriarchal society. The priestly tradition of Leviticus associates female blood with impurity and consequently disqualifies female sexuality, a position with far-reaching negative consequences about menstruation and women's participation in religious life in general. For instance, Western Roman Catholic women had to undergo "the rite of blessing," a humiliating process of regaining religious acceptance after childbirth, until the middle of the twentieth century. In addition, throughout Christian and Jewish history female blood was usually not regarded as a connection to divine life and thus holy, but as dirty and repulsive. Leviticus 12 and 15 contributed significantly to these and many other discriminatory theories and practices about women's sexuality in Judaism and Christianity. We thus need to recognize these chapters as particularly harmful to women's well-being and equal status in Western societies.

In conclusion, there is no doubt about the androcentric-priestly attempt to assert control of women's bodily and especially reproductive functions. The struggle with sexuality certainly relates to the priestly problem of embodiment in general. The whole complex of purity and impurity is based on the notion of a disembodied God. For the priestly writers and many people even today the question is: What does it mean for humans to be created in the "image of God"— an idea also accepted by the priestly literature—while encumbered by physical bodies? God neither requires nourishment (surely we reject the notion that sacrifice is to feed God) nor needs to reproduce. Humans, of course, do both. The deviation from the divine ideal compromises the human condition and also confirms physical corruptibility and death. For the priestly imagination, things that contact, enter into, or come out of the body, therefore, were sources of impurity. The view of a body-less divinity has led to the androcentric struggle with sexuality and simultaneous God-likeness.

Since the twentieth century, the feminist movement has sharply criticized this position that denigrates human and especially female physicality. So how shall we read Leviticus when the topic is sexuality? Perhaps the biblical book can serve as a reminder that human physicality and especially human sexuality should not be taken for granted. We need to balance our created nature with the idea of being "like God" in ways that help people enjoy their sexuality responsibly and freely without harming themselves or others. Perhaps such an approach will, in turn, create a future in which sexualities, homosexual or not and female or not, will no longer be perceived as a threat to divine contact, but be welcomed and celebrated in religion and society.

Holiness
(Throughout the Book of Leviticus)

The book of Leviticus assumed its present shape as the result of a process of editing and rewriting that may have spanned several centuries. Two distinctive, even contradictory, strands of priestly ideology may be discerned within it. The earlier is contained within Leviticus 1–16, which essentially comprise a manual for priests. These chapters codify various priestly responsibilities and prerogatives and contain information that priests require in order to exercise their main sacerdotal/pedagogical function, namely to "distinguish between the sacred and the profane, and between the unclean and the clean" (10:10, a.t.). The sacrificial laws are descriptive ritual texts thinly overlaid with a prescriptive veneer that places them in the narrative context of the Sinaitic revelation (see 1:2, 4:1-2, 5:14, 5:20, etc.). The laws pertaining to such matters as clean and unclean animals, skin diseases, and bodily discharges (Lev 11; 13-15) are known as "priestly *torah*," that is, divine instruction for priests.

The priests serve as a buffer between the presence of God in the tabernacle and the outside world. Their goal is to maintain the tabernacle in a state of ritual purity, allowing only objects and persons that are ritually pure to enter into proximity to God. The concept of ritual purity is part of a bipolar scheme that divides everything into the categories of clean/pure (*tahor*) and unclean/impure (*tame'*). The typical English glosses of the underlying Hebrew words are somewhat misleading, because the operative concepts have more to do with normalcy and deviance, respectively. For humans, deviance is defined by conditions that compromise the integrity of the body (deformities, afflictions, emissions). While these notions of normal and deviant are often at odds with modern sensibilities, they do constitute a coherent system. Should the *tame'* come into contact with the holiness of God, the result would be "profanation" of God, with dire consequences.

Since the human body is created "in the image of God," according to the priestly author(s) of Genesis 1:27, it too must be protected from profanation (11:44-45). The living must avoid contact with the dead, and the flesh of "unclean" animals must not be ingested. The criteria that distinguish "clean" from "unclean" animals may not make much sense to modern readers, but once again, they appear to operate according to certain standards of normalcy and deviance. For example, edible fish are defined a priori as having fins and scales (11:9). Fish-like animals that do not possess those two characteristics are deviant, and may not be consumed. Likewise, animals that live in the water but move about on legs (like crabs and lobsters) are clearly deviant and may not be eaten.

In the later stratum of Leviticus (basically Lev 17–26), the sphere of holiness that must be protected is extended beyond the precincts of the tabernacle to encompass the entire world. Leviticus 19:2 sounds a clarion call when God commands Moses, "Speak to the whole community of Israel and say to them: You shall be holy, for I, YHWH your God, am holy" (a.t.). The emphasis on "the whole community" marks a departure from the priestly *torah* of the earlier chapters, and the idea that the entire community is in some sense holy moves away from the notion that the tabernacle is the principal venue of holiness.

In ancient times, the term *holy* (*qadosh*) was glossed as "separate, distinct." As applied to God, the term was understood to denote God's utter uniqueness; as applied to Israel, it was taken to mean that Israel was distinguished from other nations because of its special relationship with God ("a priestly kingdom and a holy nation," according to Exod 19:6; see also Lev 20:26). This notion of holiness as separateness often persists in later times, although different commentators have varying notions of what it means. There are those who discern some qualitative difference between Israel and the rest of the world; others say that what is distinctive about Israel is that God chose Israel as the vehicle for conveying God's word to all of humanity. Some suggest that, since God is incorporeal, all people should strive to purge themselves of worldliness and corporeality insofar as it is possible to do so. Others oppose this idea and say, rather, that holiness is maintained by steering a middle course between the extremes of abstemiousness and hedonism.

All of these interpreters assume that Leviticus 19:2 draws an analogy between God and the community, which suggests that people should attain to holiness by imitating God in some manner. More likely, though, the verse uses the word "holy" in two different senses. In the first sense, holiness denotes the essential characteristic of deity. It is an abstract term, in contrast to the "glory" (*kabod*) of God, which is the tangible presence of God in the world. In the second sense, holiness signifies a relationship of nearness to God, which is an equivocal matter. On the one hand, God's presence may bring great blessing to the community; on the other hand, nearness to the presence makes it incumbent upon the community to maintain itself in a state of purity or risk destruction. And that onus is no longer placed only, or even primarily, on the priests, but on every single Israelite.

The sphere of holiness, in this latter view, extends well beyond cultic matters pertaining to the tabernacle. A glance at the laws in Leviticus 19–21 shows that holiness encompasses every aspect of human behavior, including cultic matters, civil law, ethical behavior, agricultural practices, and so forth. The sequence of laws in Leviticus 19 is revealing in its randomness: honoring parents, keeping Sabbath, not making idols, not consuming the meat of a sacrifice for more than two days, leaving the edges of a harvested field for the poor, refraining from theft, deceit, false oaths, coercion, or withholding wages, etc.

Almost every one of those laws concludes with the statement, "I am YHWH," or "I am YHWH your God," which denotes the fact that God is omnipresent, and not merely resident in the tabernacle. Perhaps most characteristic is Leviticus 19:14: "You must not insult the deaf, or place a stumbling block before the blind. You shall fear your God: I am YHWH. Lest anyone think that it would be a simple matter to get away with tripping a blind person, the law serves as a stern reminder that there is always at least one witness to every human action—God. Failure in such ethical matters, no less than failure to maintain oneself in a state of ritual purity, profanes the holiness of God, and the consequence is that "the land to which I bring you to settle in will spew you out" (20:22, a.t.).

While these ideas may seem archaic at first, it is not hard to discern their continuing impact on modern culture in the West. Although the ancient purity laws are mostly dysfunctional today, they survive, for example, in modern attitudes towards sexuality, and especially in the obsession with health and hygiene. A recent article in the *New York Times* described a "purification" treatment for women at a fancy spa in New York City. Both the language and the concept are redolent of a latter-day Leviticus. It is a thoroughly secularized Leviticus, in which the ultimate goal is self-fulfillment rather than the attainment of God's blessing. In fact, one could argue that in our culture the notion of holiness as separation does not capture the imagination anymore. Whether in spa treatments, in yoga exercises, or in traditional religious settings, many Western people seek—sometimes desperately—to experience not separation but "union" with the divine. Feeling utterly alone in a money-driven world, they look for "community," and when they find it, they consider it "holy," i.e., unifying. Consequently, the priestly concern for holiness continues under changed circumstances even though the particularities of Leviticus no longer hold.

CONCLUSION

The Idea of Holiness for Jewish and Christian People in Europe and North America

According to our interpretation from Jewish-American and German Protestant contexts, the book of Leviticus provides insights into Western Jewish and Christian theological discourse, history, and culture. Leviticus also encourages people to reflect on the problem of integrating holiness into our life and the world. Although contemporary Western people will most likely wonder about the particularities of Leviticus, this biblical book provides ideas on how Jews and Christians of the twenty-first century may develop religious practice, a major concern for many people in industrial and post-industrial societies. They want to know how to cultivate religious-spiritual identities in a society in which religious-spiritual emptiness, insecure economic working conditions, and feelings of socio-political isolation and powerlessness prevail. According to our interpretation, Leviticus invites people of Jewish and Christian traditions to reflect on our "roles in the divine drama of preserving and enhancing cosmic harmony" (Wegner 1992, 42) in societies that are dominated by sociopolitical, economic, cultural, and religious forces of exploitation, oppression, and alienation. Leviticus encourages us to find religious and spiritual meaning in our everyday activities, to watch ourselves perform them, and to connect our actions with the eternal realm.

BIBLIOGRAPHY

Boadt, Laurence, Helga Croner, and Leon Klenicke, eds. *Biblical Studies: Meeting Ground of Jews and Christians*. New York: Paulist, 1980.

De Troyer, Kristin, Judith A. Herbert, Judith Ann Johnson, and Anne-Marie Korte, eds. *Wholly Woman, Holy Blood: A Feminist Critique of Purity and Impurity*. Harrisburg, Pa.: Trinity, 2003.

Eckard, A. Roy. "Jewish-Christian *Gegenüber*: Some Recent Christian Efforts in Europe." *JBR* 33 (1965): 149-155.

Falk, Gerhard. *The Jews in Christian Theology*. Jefferson, N.C.: McFarland, 1992.

Fisher, Eugene J. "The Impact of the Christian-Jewish Dialogue on Biblical Studies." Pages 117-138 in *Christianity and Judaism*. Edited by Richard W. Rousseau. Scranton, Pa.: Ridge Row, 1983.

Frerichs, Ernest S. "Introduction: The Jewish School of Biblical Studies." Pages 1-6 in *Judaic Perspectives on Ancient Israel*. Edited by Jacob Neusner, et al. Philadelphia: Fortress, 1987.

Gerstenberger, Erhard S. *Leviticus: A Commentary*. Translated by Douglas W. Stott. Louisville: Westminster John Knox, 1996.

Gunneweg, A. H. J. *Understanding the Old Testament*. Translated by John Bowden. Philadelphia: Westminster, 1978.

Luther, Martin. "On the Jews and Their Lies." Pages 121–306 in *The Christian in Society IV*. Vol. 47 of *Luther's Works*. Edited by Franklin Sherman. Philadelphia: Fortress, 1971.

Mackintosh, C. H. *Notes on the Book of Leviticus*. New York: Loizeaux, 1880.

Milgrom, Jacob. *Leviticus: A New Translation with Introduction and Commentary*. New York: Doubleday, 1991-2001.

Noth, Martin. "Die Gesetze im Pentateuch." *Gesammelte Studien zum Alten Testament*. München: Kaiser, 1957.

Noth, Martin. *Leviticus: A Commentary*. Rev. ed. Philadelphia: Westminster, 1965/1977.

"The Laws in the Pentateuch: Their Assumptions and Meaning." Pages 1-107 in *The Laws in the Pentateuch and Other Studies*. Translated by D. R. Ap-Thomas. Edinburgh/London: Oliver & Boyd, 1965.

Osten-Sacken, Peter von der, ed. *Treue zur Thora: Beiträge zur Mitte des christlich-jüdischen Gesprächs: Festschrift für Günther Harder zum 75. Geburtstag*. Berlin: Institut Kirche und Judentum, Selbstverlag, 1977.

Rendtorff, Rolf. "The Jewish Bible and Its Anti-Jewish Interpretation." *Christian Jewish Relations* 16 (1983): 3-20.

————. "Toward a Common Jewish-Christian Reading of the Hebrew Bible." Pages 89-108 in *Hebrew Bible or Old Testament? Studying the Bible in Judaism and Christianity*. Edited by Roger Brooks and John J. Collins. Notre Dame, Ind.: University of Notre Dame, 1990.

————. "Is It Possible to Read Leviticus as a Separate Book?." Pages 22-35 in *Reading Leviticus: A Conversation with Mary Douglas*. Edited by John F.A. Sawyer. JSOTSup 227. Sheffield: Sheffield Academic Press, 1996.

————."The Old Testament: Jewish and Christian Bible." *AsTJ* 54: 13-22, 1999.

Sawyer, John F. A., ed. *Reading Leviticus: A Conversation with Mary Douglas*. JSOTSup 227. Sheffield: Sheffield Academic Press, 1996.

The Revised Common Lectionary: Consultation on Common Texts. Nashville: Abingdon, 1992.

Thoma, Clemens, and Michael Wyschogrod, eds. *Understanding Scripture: Explorations of Jewish and Christian Traditions of Interpretation*. New York: Paulist, 1987.

Wellhausen, Julius. *Prolegomena to the History of Israel*. Edinburgh: Adam & Charles Black, 1885.

Wegner, Judith Romney. "Leviticus." Pages 36-44 in *Women's Bible Commentary*. Edited by Carol A. Newsom and Sharon H. Ringe. Louisville: Westminster John Knox, 1992.

Winter, Miriam Therese. *Woman Wisdom: A Feminist Lectionary and Psalter, Part One: Women of the Hebrew Scriptures*. New York: Crossroad, 1991.

Zenger, Erich."Priesterschrift." Pages 435-446 in *Theologische Realenzyklopädie*, vol. 27. Berlin/New York: de Gruyter, 1997.

NUMBERS

Jione Havea

United Theological College, North Parramatta, NSW, Australia

LIFE CONTEXT OF THE INTERPRETATION

The context of the South Pacific Islands is made up of more water than solid ground. Island-space is oceanic, fluid, and volatile, often described as a "liquid continent" and a "sea of islands." South Pacific natives identify with the ocean because it shapes us: we are oceanic.

The majority of the natives are poor, but we have a wealth of cultures (Fitzpatrick 2001; Linnekin and Poyer 1990). Our cultural wealth is not limited to the differences between the Polynesian, Melanesian, and Micronesian groups (note that Fiji is both Melanesian and Polynesian!), because there are differences within each major group. The different attitudes to tattooing, from the *pe'a* [body tattoos] marking a Samoan *Matai* [chief] and the *moko* [facial tattoos] signifying valor and beauty for Maoris, to the Tongans' disapproval of tattooing (after the missionaries outlawed the practice in 1838) testify to the diversities among, and forced upon, contemporary Polynesians. Moreover, there are differences within island groups. The many delineations of *lölenga fakamotu* [Tongan "island habits"], *Fa'a Samoa* ["Samoan way"] and *vaka-i-taukei* [Fijian "way of landowner"] testify to diversities within each group.

Nonetheless, one of the habits we share is storytelling. Like our oceanic context, island-storytelling ebbs and flows, surges and fades, with the story becoming more or less dynamic, alive, in each telling. As with other oral cultures, participants in story-telling events redirect the story. Storytelling is conversational and deconstructive.

Numbers and the Relationship of God's People to the World in the South Pacific Islands

Overview of Numbers

Numbers constructs Israel's movements from the wilderness of Sinai to the steppes of Moab, two years after the exodus from Egypt (1:1) and prior to crossing the Jordan (Num 36:13; Josh 3:1-2). It is the story of a migrating people, in between places, which prefigures the joys, pains, and anxieties of oceanic migrant communities. When read with a migrant outlook, Numbers suggests that *in-between places* (wilderness) *are places* (land of foreigners).

One concern of Numbers is to organize a new generation that had not experienced persecution in Egypt (Olson 1985), in anticipation of invading Canaan (Num 13–15, 27, 33–36). Organizing this generation involved grouping and ranking the people (as in the censuses in Num 1–2, 3–4 and 26; cf. 18), and setting them apart from outsiders (Num 22–25). The narrative favors Israelite interests, and it is hostile against what is foreign and strange. Purity (of body, practice, and race) is defined and (as if possible) protected,

Jione Havea, a native of Tonga, is a lecturer in theology at Charles Sturt University and United Theological College, NSW, Australia, and an amateur in cross-cultural studies. His recent works include *Elusions of Control: Biblical Law on the Words Of Women* (2003); "To Love Cain More Than God" in *Levinas and Biblical Studies* (ed. Tamara Cohn Eskenazi, et al., 2003); and "[Y]our Book, [Y]our Reading: Writing Tasilisili Readings" in *Methodist and Radical: Rejuvenating a Tradition* (ed. Joerg Rieger and John Vincent, 2003).

while defilement and rebellion are punished and removed (Num 5–6, 11–14, 16–17; Douglas 1993).

In such a narrative, there are many chances for people to be excluded and left behind, ousted. Among the excluded are foreigners, who are powerless against Israel as the story of Balak (Num 22–24) suggests. Despite paying divination fees, building altars, and offering repeated sacrifices, God would not consider the Moabite king's fear reasonable (Israel may "lick up" [22:4] his land as it did to the Amorites). God listens selectively, and Balak had the wrong kind of face. As "the horns of a wild ox" (23:22) for Israel, God allows, even encourages, Israel to invade and dispossess the land of "foreigners," when in fact, Israel is the foreign invader and the Moabites are the natives!

Women, too, are excluded and ostracized in Numbers. Miriam and Aaron speak against Moses but only Miriam is punished (Num 12). They speak as "big brother" and "big sister" (assuming that Miriam is the sister in Exod 2:1-10), directly and candidly, against Moses' [other] wife and privileges, and question whether he is the only one through whom YHWH speaks (cf. 16:1-35). Why does not Aaron too get a skin-change or suffer leprosy? Is Miriam punished because she is a little sister? And why keep Miriam out of the camp for seven days? Is it to show that Israel would not move without her? One of the ironies in this story is that YHWH *says to Aaron and Miriam* that he speaks "face to face, clearly, not in riddles" only with Moses (12:8)!

Zelophehad's daughters are also restricted in Numbers. They complain that their father's name may vanish from his clan because he has no son, and YHWH allows them to possess their father's inheritance (27:3-7). But after the elders complain that the daughters may squander *their* ancestral property by marrying outside their tribe, YHWH restricts them to marrying whomever "they think best" as long as they marry within their tribe (36:1-12).

They are free as long as they protect their tribe's property; in other words, they are not really free.

The dark underside of the drive for organization, for order, is the rejection of the foreign and strange, the different and abnormal. There are opportunities for their normalization and readmission (Num 19), but the received form of Numbers does not let their foreignness and strangeness become unnoticeable. The following contextual readings will allow the "ugly faces" of the foreign and the other to keep reappearing, will favor in-between places and people without advocating displacement, and thereby rebel against the Israelite biases of Numbers. Such a reading involves resisting the gender, ethnic, and spatial (land, wilderness) repressions in Numbers, with emphasis on *crossing* (migration, transgressing) rather than *arrival* (settlement, invasion).

Crossing Numbers

In form and content, Numbers deconstructs itself. It tells of Israel *crossing* the wilderness, the land of foreign people, but it does not honor the positive consequences of contacting other, foreign, cultures: no culture is immune to cultural coercion. Cultures are continually constructed; they are fluid, flexible, and dynamic rather then fixed, and humans participate in their construction. Cross-culturalism is therefore unavoidable, and so is the *crossing* of cultures.

Undermining Numbers' concern for order is the admixture of narrative and legal texts. Its content pushes for exclusion but its form manifests the intermixing and crossing of literary forms. The story of Zelophehad's daughters is an interesting example of the crossing of narrative and law, with a law issued to counter the narrative (27:8-11) and a second law issued to counter the earlier law (36:6-9). The second supplements the first, but Numbers does not erase the first law. Nor does it erase the daughters' narrative. They coexist, as if to invite readers to cross them. In light of islanders' preference for stories, the legal revisions do not control the daughters' story.

Strangers at Home

When explorers and missionaries crossed the South Pacific Ocean, they viewed the natives as "strangers." This perception was partially accurate, for our ancestors were voyagers who came to our islands—depending on which anthropologist one consults—from different places of origin. Polynesians, for example, who are approximately scattered between Aotearoa, Hawaii, and Easter Island, are said to have voyaged from the "East Indies" based on linguistic evidence and archaeological artifacts originating with the Lapita (the presumed ancestors of the Polynesians, Melanesians, and Micronesians); from Melanesia on linguistic grounds; and from the Americas based on the presence of South American *kava* and tattoo cultures. It is as if we are the descendants of three parents, and rightly so, for the nature of *being Poly-nesian* (from the Gr. "many islands") is being of multiple roots, as if one were *more or less rooted*.

We natives are not native to the South Pacific Islands! But our ancestors walked the islands before the palefaces arrived. How then did we become the only "strangers" in the islands?

Our ancestors' experiences with palefaces "materialize" or "historicize" the plight of the natives of the wilderness, such as the Amalekites, Midianites, Moabites, Edomites, Kenites, Amorites, and others, whose land Israel crossed in Numbers. The following contextual comments will privilege the faces of the foreign and strange as if, to recall Freud, to welcome the return of the repressed and oppressed.

Dipping Numbers in Island Space

The bible is not a South Pacific Island text!

How should islanders read this foreign text brought by non-natives for *their* interests? Should we advocate Hone Heke, the first Maori to sign the Treaty of Waitangi (the treaty that established New Zealand and ceded Maori control to the British): "To Jesus Christ and the book, I will turn my back and empty my bowels on them?" Do the "Balaks" of the South Pacific Islands stand a chance against the "horns of Israel" and this book, even though native-Balaks of the past failed?

A popular recent response calls for contextualization (the theme of an issue, *The Pacific Journal of Theology* 27 [2002]). Notwithstanding, whose faces are contextualized? Is not contextualization another mask, a normalized face, for globalization?

It is strange that I raise this doubt, this *rebellion,* in this contextual commentary, but rebellion is the stuff of Numbers. I will heed the guideline for my contribution by considering not only my life contexts from the perspective of Numbers but also Numbers from the perspective of my life contexts. As a consequence, I will not read Numbers "as corrective lenses," because it is difficult to find something corrective in a story that endorses the proscription of peoples like mine. Accordingly, the following "contextual comments" will not contextualize (in the sense of appropriate) Israel's crossing of the wilderness, so that native South Pacific Islanders may accept it; I will contextualize it in order to allow the foreign and strange to be different. In so doing I offer comments that are both contextual and oceanic.

CONTEXTUAL COMMENT

How these Storytelling Events Evolved

A Tongan kava-drinking group called Kau pakipaki folofola ("breakers of scriptures," appealing to "breaking bread" practices) gave me a chance to be an island-storyteller. Our custom is to open with a song and prayer and then read the selected passage several times until we have an intuitive awareness of the story. Then, while sharing kava, I begin to retell the story with the group spontaneously calling out their comments and diversions, now and then bursting into song (normally when my storytelling is not making sense, thus setting the story in new paths). Before the closing prayer (usually about three hours later) I announce the passage for our next sitting, knowing full well that most will not read it because not all are literate, or own a bible.

On the last evening that we *broke* Numbers, when I finally revealed my intention to write this commentary, the group agreed that I should *write events in island-story-telling* based on our conversations. I will begin with Numbers 25 (which we *broke* at our eighth sitting).

For events in island-storytelling to happen, I ask you, our readers, two things: reread the passages until you have an intuitive awareness of the stories, and be free to redirect the stories where and when you can. Our purpose is not to recover these stories but to let them loose, by leisurely telling them in conversation.

Numbers 25:1-18:
What's Wrong with Foreign Women?

Foreign stuff is valuable. Foreign cars, food, beer, clothes . . . they are all good. They are also expensive; maybe that's why they are valuable.

Why then was YHWH so furious when the Israelites wandered into the domains of the Baal of Peor? Wasn't their foreign food tasty enough? Is it not proper manners when you come to a foreign land to pay your respects to that land and its deities? Would not YHWH expect the same when foreigners come to his land! That they would eat his people's food, and show him respect? That his people would be hospitable to strangers who come within their gates? What is YHWH *doing*?

There are several sides to YHWH's temper. It indicates an insecure god who will not stand being seconded, a jealous god who will not share YHWH's people with another Baal, a capricious god whose vengeance transcends its cause, and a fickle god who gives ambiguous commands.

Strange events take place in this story. Because the people (*ha'am*) whored (*znh*) the daughters of Moab and yoked themselves to the Baal of Peor (25:1-2)—which means a lighter load for YHWH and Moses—YHWH demands that all the "heads of the people" (*rao'she ha'am*) be impaled in the face of the sun, i.e., in public (25:4). Whether YHWH had "ringleaders" (as in the JPS translation) in mind or, as it is written, "all of the heads of the people " involved, is not clear. Moses heard the latter (25:5), but the number of *heads* YHWH required is ambiguous. YHWH could have wanted to impale only the ringleaders (as *heads*) but Moses had a different agenda, to get rid of "all the people who yoked themselves to the Baal of Peor." Possibly Moses heard YHWH correctly, but decided that all the offenders should be impaled. What is Moses *doing*?

The command did not stop Zimri, son of Salu, from bringing home, in front of Moses and the congregation, a Midianite woman, Cozbi daughter of Zur (25:6). Both Zimri and Cozbi came from chiefly families (25:14-15), but that did not stop the son of another leader, Phinehas son of Eleazar son of Aaron, from entering the tent to spear both of them (25:7-8). Phinehas' zeal (25:11), for which he was granted a "covenant of peace" (protection from revenge from Zimri's family?) and the priesthood for himself and his descendants (25:12-13), turned back YHWH's extreme anger from Israel, but only after twenty-four thousand people were killed. YHWH's wrath was redirected to the Midianites, who were to be harassed because their hospitality was seen as trickery and deceit (25:16-18).

It is strange that YHWH was so angry, because he had earlier defended Moses when Miriam exposed his Cushite woman (Num 12:1), his other foreign woman. In other words, not all foreign women are bad. What then is wrong with Moabite and Midianite women? What is wrong with the daughters of Lot (Gen 19:30-38) and Jethro (Exod 1:1)?

What's wrong with foreign women? What about the fact that *we* are foreigners, and so are our sisters? Should our sisters be treated like whores (Gen 34:31)? Do we even have twenty-four thousand sisters? What is this storyteller *doing*?

Num 13:1–14:45: Steal Boldly!

YHWH is not sure of the state of the land YHWH is giving to Israel. Why else would YHWH tell Moses to send men to spy out the land? Sending spies also suggests that the land does not belong to Israel.

The twelve spies are leaders picked from Israel's ancestral tribes, sent to see whether the land is rich or poor, whether the people are strong or weak, few or many, and whether the towns are fortified or not. Moreover, they are charged to be bold and bring back some of the fruits of the land (13:17-20). While it is unacceptable to eat the food of the land in Numbers 25:2, this spy story permits twelve Israelites to reap what they did not sow. Trespassing and raiding are legitimized, with invasion and dispossession anticipated.

Forty days later, the spies return carrying a single cluster of grapes so huge that two men have to carry it between them on a pole. The spies also bring back pomegranates and figs (13:21-24). Surely this land is rich, flowing with milk and honey. But the land is also rich with people and cultures. This land is not empty—*terra nullius* is an illusion—because it is occupied by Nephilim, Amalekites, Hittites, Jebusites, Amorites, and Canaanites.

Upon returning, the spies disagree over what Israel should do. Some of them dread the size and power of the aboriginal custodians of the land, against whom the Israelites are like grasshoppers (13:31). Their report is contradictory: the land they spied devours its inhabitants (13:32), and they lived to inform Israel that its inhabitants are giants! Who would want to enter a devouring land, or follow someone who leads toward such a land (14:1-5)? That would be suicidal.

Caleb, on the other hand, later joined by Joshua (13:30; 14:5-10), bringing to mind the two men who carried the huge cluster of grapes, brings YHWH back into the story. There is no reason to cry or rebel, for if YHWH is pleased with Israel, then the giants would be no more than bread for them (14:5-10a). Such is the report YHWH wants to hear. To say otherwise, as did the other spies, is to rebel against YHWH, who does not usually listen to what YHWH does not want to hear.

YHWH wavers when some of the people do not want to claim the land. YHWH is at first angry, vowing to disinherit them (14:10b-12). But after Moses reminds YHWH that YHWH's honor is at stake (14:13-19), YHWH decides not to kill the people right away but to leave them wandering in the wilderness until that generation (apart from Caleb and Joshua, who said the words YHWH wanted to hear) dies (14:20-35).

Israel is caught between a devouring land and forty years in a withering land. Some of the people attempted to transgress YHWH's decision to have them die in the wilderness (14:32-33), but they failed (14:44). They failed to take the land YHWH promised earlier because they sinned, and also because the indigenous custodians of the land defended them. Yes, the custodians of Canaan, like custodians of all lands, can sometimes defeat the advances of God's people.

Numbers 5:11-31: Where Are the Stories?

Laws read as if they have universal applicability, but readers are anchored in realities from which these laws become refigured and transformed through story. In the case of Numbers 5:11-31, several stories are possible.

A man suspects that his wife has been unfaithful to him by sleeping with another man. Instead of consulting his wife or confronting the other man to see if his suspicion is legitimate, the husband must bring his wife to a priest. He then asks the priest to administer the grain offering designed to recall the iniquity (5:11-15). The suspicious husband is earnest before YHWH, the jealous God of Israel, anticipating that YHWH will sympathize with his jealousy.

This husband is not required to substantiate his jealousy (not even one witness is required, 35:30), which masks his own deficits. In other words, he is jealous because he could not satisfy his wife by giving her what she (may have) found in another man. He is jealous because he is not as capable as that other (imaginary) man.

A second man wishes to divorce his wife, so he concocts a story claiming that she has gone astray by sleeping with another man, thereby defiling herself (5:14b). The liar takes his tale to a priest (yet another man), who is eager to display his authority. This second husband is not required to produce an eyewitness either. All that is required of him is his jealousy and the appropriate ritual, a grain offering of jealousy (5:11-15).

But jealousy is a lame excuse. It proves that the husband is insecure. His jealousy exposes his lack of control (5:19, 29) because he thinks he has authority over his wife, but does not know how to deal with her.

A woman is brought to the tabernacle by her husband, who carries an offering that is supposed to recall iniquity (5:15). She is led away from the eyes of the community into the space of men, before YHWH. She watches in disgust as the priest scoops up dirt from the floor and dumps it into a clay jar filled with holy water. The priest then approaches her, dishevels her hair, making her look like a vagabond, and then makes her say "Amen! Amen!" to an oath that may make her womb discharge and her uterus drop. (Her "guilt" may cause a spontaneous abortion, a prolapsed uterus, or sterility; the Hebrew is unclear). In YHWH's presence, she is rejected (5:16-22).

As if the contents of the clay jar were not already revolting enough, the priest writes out the oath and then washes the parchment in the holy water. He then makes the accused woman drink the mixture, as if to silence her (5:23-26). Her mouth is needed to drink the repulsive water but not to say anything in her defense. She drinks the water of bitterness in her husband's interest. If she suffers the physical effects of the curse, she legitimizes his jealousy, whether true or not. She frees her husband from iniquity but becomes an execration among her people. If she passes the test, she will conceive her jealous husband's children (5:27-31). She is both there and not there—accused and rejected in the presence of YHWH, ignored and reclaimed as her husband's property.

Let us imagine that in the tabernacle's vicinity there is a third man who has slept with his neighbor's wife. He is not there, in the tabernacle, but he is there, for men like him cause wives to drink the water of bitterness. However, there is no offering, no ritual designed to recall his iniquity.

Let us imagine a fourth man who is disturbed that his sister is brought to the priest, bringing shame to her family. He cannot do anything about it, for he is not allowed to accompany her. He is helpless, but he is not required to be silent.

And there are other persons, men and women, who wonder what is being covered up in the law of jealousy. Whose interests are muddied in administering the bitter water?

Numbers 20:1-13: We Are Thirsty!

At Kadesh, the place where Miriam died and was buried, Israel could not find water to drink. And as one would expect, the people came to their leaders, Moses and Aaron, to complain.

Israel's complaints for water are a continually recurring irritant: They complained at Marah because the water was bitter, and YHWH showed Moses a piece of wood that purified the water (Exod 15:22-25a). Bitter water can be sweetened—except for the wife of a jealous husband! They again complained at Rephidim, where there was no water, and YHWH instructed Moses to strike the rock at Horeb, on which YHWH will stand, and water will come forth (Exod

17:1-7). Drinkable water is available under the feet of YHWH—except for the wife of a jealous husband!

At Kadesh, the people's complaint separates Moses from YHWH. If they were under YHWH's leadership they would have already seen death (Num 20:3). But since they are traveling with Moses and Aaron, they are dying of thirst in the wilderness, an unsuitable place for gardening (20:4-5). They wish they had died with their kindred rather than being brought into the wretched wilderness (14:32-33), the home of non-Israelites!

YHWH gives a different response this time. Moses is to take his rod and speak to the rock, in the eyes of the people, to release water (20:8). He takes the rod, but instead of speaking to the rock Moses speaks to the people, "Listen, bitter ones, should we make water come forth from this rock for you?" (20:10). He did not say a word when he struck the rock at Horeb but he speaks out at Kadesh, as if to prove himself, as if he has the courage to do differently than instructed. He speaks, and then strikes the rock twice before it releases abundant water for the people and their livestock to drink (20:11). It would have been interesting to see Moses' face after he gave the rock the first strike!

Moses should have known that YHWH does not usually accept defiance and contradiction. YHWH is not happy about losing the opportunity to show his holiness before the people (20:12a), as if YHWH too has something to prove.

Moses has cast his lot. He will not escort the people of Israel into the land God has given them. They are freed from witnessing the violence and bloodshed promised for Canaan's aboriginal custodians—brutality from which latter storytellers are not detached.

Numbers 32:1-42: Ka mate!

Reading Numbers 32 is painful for natives who have witnessed and suffered the kind of violence described in this story. They do not respond with dancing and singing, but with anguish. "Ka mate!" is the cry of despair that resounds in them as they hear the stories of the natives of Transjordan, a people whose land was conquered and whose cities, towns, and villages were totally destroyed (32:33-42).

On his deathbed, Henare Teowai of Ngati Porou, New Zealand, explained the art of the Maori *haka* (dance): *Kia korero te katoa o te tinana* (The whole body should speak). This applies to both the *peruperu* (a war dance, involving weapons, which ends with a characteristic high jump with the legs folded underneath) and *ngeri* (a short, free form of *haka*) styles. The *ngeri* style is not uniformly enacted but involves a good deal of spontaneity and creativity as performers submit to the power of the *haka*.

South Pacific Island dances have stories to tell, and performances to enact, as the well-known Maori *Ka mate* (a *ngeri* style *haka*) demonstrates:

Ka mate! Ka mate! Ka ora! Ka ora!	I die! I die! I live! I live!
Ka mate! Ka mate! Ka ora! Ka ora!	This is the hairy man
Tenei te tangata puhuruhuru	Who fetched here
Nana nei i tiki mai	And caused the sun to shine
Whakawhiti te ra	One step, another step
A upane, ka upane	One step, another step ... the sun
A upane ka upane . . . whiti te ra	shines!
Hi! I die! I die! I live! I live!	

Ka mate was first performed by Te Rauparaha, son of chief Werawera of Ngati Toa [Toarangatira], a branch of the Tainui tribe. After his father was killed and eaten, Te Rauparaha grew up to be one of the most respected warriors in Maori history, having control over the coastline from Porirua up to the Kapiti Coast by the late 1820s. But he also had moments of vulnerability, one of which gave birth to *Ka mate*.

Pursued by warriors from Ngati Maniapoto and Waikato, Te Rauparaha fled to Taupo and asked chief Tuwharetoa for help, but was refused. He moved on to Motuopuhi and sought protection from Te Wharerangi, who was reluctant at first but later permitted Te Rauparaha to hide in his kumara pit while his wife, Te Rangikoaea, sat over the mouth of the pit. There are two explanations for why she was seated over the entrance. First, since according to custom no man would put himself beneath a woman's genitals, the pursuers would discount the pit as a hiding place. In this regard, Te Rauparaha transgresses local custom in order to survive. Second, female genitals are believed to have a shielding effect, so Te Rauparaha shielded himself with Te Rangikoaea.

When the pursuers arrived, Te Rauparaha muttered *Ka mate! ka mate!* (I die! I die!), but when Te Wharerangi told them that the man they were pursuing had fled to Rangipo, Te Rauparaha muttered *Ka ora! ka ora!* (I live! I live!).

The pursuers doubted Te Wharerangi and Te Rauparaha again muttered, *Ka mate! ka mate!* And when Te Wharerangi eventually deceived them, Te Rauparaha exclaimed *Ka ora, ka ora! Tenei te tangata puhuruhuru nana nei i tiki mai whakawhiti te ra!* (I live! I live! For this is the hairy man who fetched the sun and caused it to shine again!).

Tangata puhuruhuru (hairy man) possibly refers to Te Wharerangi, a man of many *hairy* habits. But hairiness is also associated with bravery, while hairlessness (in contrast to baldness) signifies lack of courage.

Coming out of the pit Te Rauparaha performed his *haka* before Te Rangikoaea and the assembled people, adding *A upane ka upane whiti te ra, Hi!* (One step, another step, the sun shines!). *Upane* (terrace) refers to the steps cut into the side of the pit for access, and each *upane* in the *haka* represents the steps Te Rauparaha made as he emerged from the pit to see if the coast was clear. One can imagine his joy at eluding death and coming out of the dark pit into the light of day—*Whiti te ra! Hi!* It is a joyous cry after persecution and being saved by a woman's genitals. But, tragically, the indigenous peoples of the earth all too rarely shout a joyous cry. No joyous cry for the inhabitants of the kingdom of King Sihon of the Amorites, of the kingdom of King Og of Bashan, or of Gilead (32:33-42), who had the bad fortune of having a land that the Reubenites and the Gadites deemed "good for cattle" (32:1).

CONCLUSION

Island storytelling is not so much about forming conclusions as about responding, redirecting, transgressing, engaging, disagreeing, teasing, angering, crossing, challenging, and letting go. Every storytelling event begs for spontaneity and creativity, and for the storyteller not to finalize the story! However, now and then, as I do here, the storyteller gives the closing words to the story. In closing, therefore, I revisit Numbers 35:6-34.

In Israel's midst, six cities of refuge are set aside for those who have inadvertently killed someone, i.e., without intent (35:22-28). In these cities they are to be safe from the family members who would avenge the death (35:9-15). Murderers, on the other hand, shall be put to death (35:16-21), if there is more than one witness, and no ransom is to be accepted (35:30-32).

In Israel's midst were natives of the land who would hope that Israel, and their God, would take their laws seriously. Consider Numbers 35:33: "You shall not pollute the land in which you live; for blood pollutes the land, and the land can have no expiation for blood that is shed on it, except by the blood of him who shed it" (JPS).

BIBLIOGRAPHY

Bible quotations either from *Tanakh* (Philadelphia: Jewish Publication Society, 1999) or my own.

Crocombe, Ron. *The South Pacific*. Suva, Fiji: University of the South Pacific, 2001.

Douglas, Mary. *In the Wilderness: The Doctrine of Defilement in the Book of Numbers*. JSOTSup 158. Sheffield: Sheffield Academic Press, 1993.

Fitzpatrick, Judith M., ed. *Endangered Peoples of Oceania: Struggles to Survive and Thrive*. Greenwood Press "Endangered Peoples of the World" Series, 1525-1233. Westport, Conn.: Greenwood, 2001.

Havea, Sione 'Amanaki, et al. *South Pacific Theology: Papers from the Consultation on Pacific Theology, Papua, New Guinea, January 1986*. Oxford: Regnum, 1987.

Levine, Baruch A. *Numbers 1-20: A New Translation with Introduction and Commentary*. AB 4A. New York: Doubleday, 1993.

_____. Numbers 21-36: *A New Translation with Introduction and Commentary*. AB 4B. New York: Doubleday, 2000.

Linnekin, Jocelyn, and Lin Poyer, eds. *Cultural Identity and Ethnicity in the Pacific*. Honolulu: University of Hawaii Press, 1990.

Oliver, Douglas L. *Native Cultures of the Pacific Islands*. Ill. Lois Johnson. Honolulu: University of Hawaii Press, 1989.

Olson, Dennis T. *The Death of the Old and the Birth of the New: The Framework of the Book of Numbers and the Pentateuch*. BJS 71. Chico, Calif.: Scholars Press, 1985.

Sakenfeld, Katharine Doob. *Journeying with God: A Commentary on the Book of Numbers*. ITC. Grand Rapids: Eerdmans, 1995.

DEUTERONOMY

Mercedes García Bachmann

Instituto Universitario (ISEDET), Buenos Aires, Argentina

LIFE CONTEXT OF THE INTERPRETATION

Two immediate life contexts inform my reading. First, I am part of Argentina's impoverished urban middle class. Formerly we had access to education, health services, cultural events, leisure, and could pay our mortgages and travel. Currently we are losing many of these privileges, because of unemployment, reduced work hours and/or reduced salaries, bank failures, inflation, devaluation of our national currency, loans, and mortgage obligations. The country is rapidly accelerating toward almost total pauperization, with half of its population already under the poverty line.

People in large cities are also increasingly affected by assaults, robbery, and kidnapping, with policemen themselves committing many of these crimes. Because all this is new to our country, there is a general feeling of disorientation, defeat, and fear. Many migrate to richer, supposedly more secure countries (United States, Canada, Europe, Israel).

Very poor and mostly rural Pentecostal Native American peoples, among whom I teach Bible, form a second immediate life context for my reading. For me this is a difficult challenge, because I come from the culture of their conquerors. My dominant and domineering culture disdains them, ignores them, and oppresses them socially and economically, leaving them the less productive and devaluated lands. Usually the church fares no better in encouraging Native Americans to uphold their traditional values; on the contrary, the church often pushes them to abandon these values.

A wider context for this reading of Deuteronomy is formed by the Argentinean society at large. Argentina is one of the richest countries in the world in natural resources, land, water, and food production. Its population is a mixture of Europeans who came at the time of the Spanish colonization and during later migrations, indigenous population, a small number of descendants of African slaves, immigrants from Muslim countries (e.g., Syria and Lebanon), and all possible mixtures between these peoples. Despite this ethnic, cultural, and religious variety, for centuries the country viewed itself as white, European, and "civilized." Thus, it turned its back to the rest of the Latin American continent and looked toward Europe, only to discover, in the midst of crisis, that European countries do not consider Argentina as one of their peers!

My reading context also includes my vocation as clergy of a mainline Protestant denomination. In this country this means being in between a massive but formalist Roman Catholicism and so-called "new" movements (including Pentecostalism, as well as spiritism, Buddhism, and other religions). Argentina also has large Jewish and Muslim communities.

Mercedes L. García Bachmann, dean of Instituto Universitario ISEDET (Instituto Superior Evangélico de Estudios Teológicos), is a pastor of the United Evangelical Lutheran Church in Argentina and Uruguay. She holds a Ph.D in Hebrew Bible from the Lutheran School of Theology in Chicago (USA) with a dissertation on "Little Women: Social Location of Female Labor in the Deuteronomistic History" (1999). She is co-editor of *Búsquedas y señales. Estudios en Biblia, Teología, Historia y Ecumenismo* (2003), she publishes regularly in RIBLA, *Cuadernos de Teología, IRM,* and *Semeia.* Her articles are on feminist and liberation issues in the prophets, the Pentateuch, the historical books, and Ecclesiastes.

Deuteronomy and the Relationship of God's People to the World in my Life Context

Both of the life contexts in which I move are marked by old and recent wounds and perplexities, which color our thinking and feeling, and challenge our faith and the perspective of our mission as Christians. We move between the anguish that most of our people are deprived of the most basic human rights (food, shelter, health, education, job, safety) and the hope grounded in the knowledge that we have resources both in our faith and in our communities. A crisis so drastic and anthropogenic (people are starving to death) is also an opportunity for re-orienting our values: both those we personally hold and proclaim or teach, and those of our society. Deuteronomy will help in this reorientation of our values, provided that we recognize the distance between Deuteronomy's world and ours.

Deuteronomy's World and Ours

We, as well as our contemporaries around the world, have a worldview that is very different from that of Deuteronomy. For instance, in Deuteronomy laws are God-given through Moses, while in our society laws are the product of legislation and lobbying, not divine inspiration.

Nevertheless, today there is a general belief that God can act in present times as God has acted in the past, in particular during the time of the exodus. But this belief wavers, because nobody dares to ascertain how God acts: Is it through legislators or in spite of them? Through bureaucrats in the international financial system or in spite of them? Through a country's legal system or in spite of it? Or does God act in all these ways?

This uncertainty is directly related to the plight of the poor and oppressed. Imagine this scenario. Countries are obliged to pass laws that benefit transnational organizations but are detrimental to the countries themselves and to their people. Like the proverbial carrot tied in front of the donkey, promises of financial help are tied to the condition of passing these laws. Can we say that those are God-given laws? That God is acting through those deeds? Put differently: What kind of God are we speaking about? The one who inspires the market? Or the one who opts for the liberation of slaves and nobodies?

The market and economy at the time of Deuteronomy were very different from today. Consequently, this book cannot directly address these issues in our society. This alone should be enough to show that God's promises of blessings to Israel cannot be automatically applied to present-day political and socioeconomic dynamics. It would be too simplistic to conclude that God blesses certain nations with wealth and punishes others through war, starvation, and misery. While this is what the biblical text states, we also need to consider other issues raised by this text.

Where Are the Boundaries between the People of God and the World Today?

Modern business and financial transactions are led by nations that are inheritors of the Christian worldview and culture and that at times identify themselves with Christianity. Indeed, in several cases, these nations support a state or official Christian denomination, use the word "God" in their currency, or have heads of states who are also heads of churches or are related to the church in some manner. In such situations, where are the boundaries between the people of God and the world?

Boundaries are set by behavior and by deeds. This is not a new teaching: "Not everyone who says to me, 'Lord, Lord,' will enter the kingdom of heaven, but only the one who does the will of my Father in heaven" (Matt 7:21). In Deuteronomy, this concern to avoid any split between lip-service and life-service is expressed by very forceful statements and assumptions, such as the command to annihilate all "pagan" nations from the land. Yet, because the book was produced at a time when Canaanites and the other original nations no longer existed as nations (most scholars date the book's final redaction somewhere between the fifth and the fourth centuries B.C.E., during either the Persian or Hellenistic periods), its injunctions are a call to keep their faith in YHWH uncontaminated by the faith in other gods or goddesses.

Deuteronomy is not naïve in its assumptions. Danger comes not only from without (from the Canaanites) but also from within: "If anyone secretly entices you—even if it is your brother . . . or your own son or daughter" (Deut 13:6, see the whole chapter). Deeds, not credentials, are what counts. In times like ours, when most institutions—including churches—have lost their credibility, this principle of deeds rather than words is all the more important. Yet, this principle is rarely applied, even within the churches. The church/people of God should address this problem for the sake of the world; otherwise, our witness is false.

God's Concern for the Oppressed as the Basis for a More Just Society

Deuteronomy deals with at least two social contexts. The oldest parts of the book retain traces of the people's experiences before or during the earliest stages of the monarchy, when village solidarity and institutions were still strong and had a say about community life. This is particularly evident in some of the laws contained in chs. 12–26, such as those regarding community feasts (offerings, seasons, acceptable participants).

Later parts of the book, written during the monarchy, subsumed these laws into another framework. These laws increase the distance between the decision-making bodies at the village (i.e., the elders, the fathers, the Levites) and the decision-making at the capital (i.e., the court, the temple, the king). At the very least, the law adding the Levites to the list of those for whom society must care (e.g., Deut 14:28-29) belongs to the times of the monarchy, when the cult was centralized and the Levites lost their position at rural sanctuaries and had to be protected or provided for by laws such as this.

This concern for society's most vulnerable is typical of Deuteronomy. The message

"if you protect the poor you will have this land I promised you" (Deut 14:28-29) and all the passages about the poor (10:18; 14:29; 16:11,14; 24:19-21; 26:12-13; 27:19) can be understood as: "if you do not protect the poor, you will end up in a living hell." Today we are already in a living hell, whether we realize it or not. There is no safe place any longer. Many countries are poor or extremely poor, while a handful are rich and very wasteful. Beware if the rich nations do not protect the widow, the orphan, and the stranger within their gates! This warning is for wealthy societies; they have vulnerable people within their gates; they have many knocking at their gates, climbing their walls, passing over fences, or rowing boats to get in. This warning is also for the countries that are not as rich; lack of faithfulness is manifest in the smallness of their gestures to help the poor. Vulnerable people give each society an opportunity for solidarity, and thus an opportunity to bear witness to its values by turning toward those in need and by living the gospel. International organizations and governments are responsible for the plight of the poor, but so are local policies and conditions. One of Deuteronomy's messages concerns every person's responsibility toward God and toward other members of "the community of saints."

Who Belongs to the Community?

The ability to belong to the assembly of Israel is directly related to the people's behavior. Those who worship other gods or goddesses, who make images, or who entice members of Israel to do so shall never belong to the assembly of Israel. And if they did—if they were Israelites— they would be put to death. For the neighboring nations (the Egyptians) the Moabites, the Ammonites and others, there is another answer. Depending on their past deeds, either they will be ultimately accepted into Israel, or they will never belong (Deut 23:3-8).

One unanswered question remains: Do women belong to the community or not? On the one hand, Israelite women belonged to the people and had many of the same rights as male Israelites; they participated in the Sabbath and other feasts and were bound by the commandments as men were (except for coveting a neighbor's wife!). On the other hand, there were restrictions: the term "people" was also used to refer exclusively to males in the military camp (Deut 23:9-13; also 23:1), and the initiatory rite for belonging to Israel, namely, circumcision, was for males. These examples show the ambiguity of the categories. Besides an intended inclusiveness of every person belonging to an Israelite family and tribe, and a use of language to refer to the entire population, the same language was used to refer exclusively to males.

The inclusion of women and marginalized groups so that they might have the same rights and responsibilities as adult males is one of the issues of justice in our world, in many institutions, and especially in the church. The body of Christ without women is half a body, and thus it is not true to its very nature. Yes, there are plenty of women sitting in the pews, cleaning institutional facilities, and taking care of the institutions' male authorities. But this is not the same as including them (and other groups) as equals with the right to fully be who they are and to fully exercise their gifts and talents for the sake of the people of God and the world, as is God's will.

CONTEXTUAL COMMENTARY

Overview of Deuteronomy

Deuteronomy is presented as Moses' last testament on the plains of Moab, just before entering the promised land. Moses recounts for the people the great deeds of their God and the way they are to set their hearts and to behave once they are in their new home, lest they prove unworthy of God's gift and lose it. Then Moses commissions Joshua to be the people's leader, after which Moses dies and is buried somewhere on the mountain.

There are only two main characters in the whole book, YHWH and Moses. Everyone else, including Israel, does not have a direct voice and has to speak through Moses or the book's narrator.

Stylistically, Deuteronomy may be classified as a prophetic law-book with a hortatory introduction, because its hortatory or paraenetic style and its body of legal material are interrelated with the concerns of the "classical" prophets. Among these concerns are: obedience to the spirit of the law and not merely to its letter, as seen in the text's emphasis on instruction (rather than law) and on YHWH's wonders for Israel (e.g., 4:32-40; 5:23-27); remembering God's great deeds in Egypt and later in the wilderness (e.g., 1:19, 29; 2:25); the call to

Israel to repentance and conversion, as expressed in exhortations to remain faithful to YHWH (4:21-31; 5:14-15); and a concern for orphans, widows, foreigners, and other oppressed groups (10:18; 14:29; 16:11,14; 24:19-21; 26:12-13; 27:19).

The book resembles the ancient Near Eastern treaties between a suzerain and its vassal state, with stipulations governing the relationship, and blessings and curses for following them or not. Despite this clear resemblance, scholars have not been able to achieve a consensus regarding the nature of the relationship between God and Israel. While some see Deuteronomy as the book found in the temple during Josiah's time and upon which this king initiated reforms in Judah (seventh century B.C.E.), most see it as a theological elaboration from much later (fifth or fourth century B.C.E.), with no pretense of literal applicability. Deuteronomy is a sermon, rather than a law-book.

Regarding its composition, positions again differ widely. Some see it as the product of one hand (in Moses' times). With other scholars, I see it as the product of several hands, from the time of the Northern Kingdom (eighth and seventh centuries B.C.E.) to Persian and Hellenistic times (fifth to fourth centuries B.C.E.)

Theologically, Deuteronomy has a clear concern for cult centralization; the danger of idolatry, including both going after other gods/goddesses and making YHWH into a false god; and the relationship between God's actions and the community's response. Their concerns can be seen in the numerous statements (such as 1:21; 4:37-38) in which the land is presented as God's gracious gift rather than as a reward for the people's merits. At the same time these statements require Israel to live according to the covenant, lest the land expel Israel.

Deuteronomy 1:9-18, Setting up Worthy Leaders

In this pericope Moses recounts an earlier event from (Deut 1:9; also Exod 18). By comparing these two texts, we can more clearly visualize what Deuteronomy emphasizes.

In Exod 18, Jethro suggests that Moses be relieved from parts of his workload by setting up God-fearing, respected, and morally straight leaders from the community to direct and judge their own subgroups of people, leaving only major cases for Moses to adjudicate. In Deuteronomy, Moses himself proposes the same idea.

While the Exodus account emphasizes that judges are to be morally upright persons who would not accept bribes or be partial in judging, Deuteronomy also underscores their wisdom or intellectual abilities. Judges must be "wise, discerning [or able to understand] and reputable [well known]" (1:13; see 1:15). Although many commentaries propose to change this latter passive participle into an active one, ("they know well") this is not necessary, as "being known" implies having a reputation built on actions, a desirable condition for a leader.

Who would be chosen for this task is left for the people to decide, as the text makes clear (Deut 1:13). Since the people themselves choose their leaders, Deuteronomy seems to leave more room for the people's participation than its literary source does

(i.e., Exodus). Yet, Deuteronomy presents this appointment of judges as initiated by Moses, while Exodus says that a foreigner, Moses' father-in-law, initiates it.

The charge to avoid partiality in favor of the powerful ("the great") against the weak ("the small") and to resist intimidation (1:16-18) is a sign that such manipulations of justice were known and lamented. Although obviously not new, manipulation of justice by the rich and the powerful is one of the most serious difficulties of our world today, at both ends of the injustice (e.g., those who accept bribes are as immoral as those who give bribes!) These range from small gifts or privileges at the community level up to political appointments, federal funds deposited into personal accounts in Swiss banks, and fixed federal political campaigns. The examples are too many and too embarrassing to mention in detail. Money and power seem to be the new gods that use whatever is needed to control their slaves and to increase their number—some of them voluntary slaves, but the vast majority are victims of the system.

Moses' words to the leaders demonstrate the problem: "you shall not be intimidated by anyone, for the judgment is God's" (Deut 1:17). In other words, they should be "God-fearing" (as Exod 18:21 describes them). Many people, at least on the decision-making level, do not know or remember that "the judgment is God's." They have no good reason to fear human justice, as they buy people who then protect them. But why do they have so little fear of God's judgment? Does this come from secularism? From a lack of evidence of God's power in the everyday world? From a lack of faith? From the churches' lukewarm message about political responsibility? From the churches' own corruption? I do not have the answer, but I suspect that several of these factors play a role in the attitudes of leaders who ignore their responsibility toward God as they manipulate justice.

Another question can be asked: Were there women among these leaders? In Deut 1:9-18, the masculine is used, but it never states whether "men" means males only or people (as is often the case in Hebrew). Thus, it is not clear whether there were also women among those leaders. Since it makes a difference to be led in worship, in church, in school, at work, or in politics by a woman rather than by a man, we must ask this important question, even if the text does not give us the answer.

Deuteronomy 4:1-8, Only YHWH you Shall Adore

Despite its frequent shifts from singular to plural forms when addressing Israel, 4:1-40 is a literary unit added to Deuteronomy at a late stage (vv. 41-49 are an even later editorial addition to vv. 1-40). Here again, the text recounts an experience already narrated: the annihilation of those who had chosen to follow the Baal of Peor (or Baal-peor) and the preservation of those who had clung to YHWH. Why cling to YHWH? The answer is most directly expressed in 4:7-8: "For what other great nation has a god so near to it as the Lord our God is whenever we call to him? And what other great nation has statutes and ordinances as just as this entire law that I am setting before you today?" This rhetorical question put by Moses to the people (the obvious answer is "none") marvelously summarizes their experience of YHWH's works of salvation for the people. Implied in this rhetorical question are profound teachings about God's nature: God is near and powerful. God has the power to deliver God's people from enemies; to provide for all their needs in the desert; to give the land allotted to them; and to give them the commandments, statutes, and judgments necessary to make of them a holy and unique people, as God is holy and unique. This is the God that the people should follow rather than the "god" of the free-market economy. Through Christ we have been given the opportunity of sharing in that closeness with this holy, unique God, and thus we can understand the depth hidden in so simple a question. Yet, this understanding must lead to acting!

Deuteronomy 4:15-20, The Nations' Allotments and the Relationship of Israel with Other People

Starting with Deuteronomy 4:15, the text develops the prohibition of image making (the second commandment). Here it is not worship of other gods or goddesses that is forbidden, but the worship of YHWH through any kind of image. Lest Israel, influenced by its neighbors, starts to think, "maybe this or that figure is acceptable," the text makes a long list of those images that are not to be worshipped: images of males or females, beasts of the field, birds, creeping things on the earth or fish. Further, Israel is not to worship the sun, the moon, or the stars, as other peoples do. Israel is to worship YHWH and none other. This commandment addresses the danger of turning an image or object into YHWH and using it to try to manipulate YHWH, and the danger of copying other nations in their worship of gods or goddesses represented by animals or natural phenomena.

This passage contains the curious expression "the sun, the moon, the stars, and all the heavenly host . . . that YHWH your God has allotted to all the peoples under heaven" (v. 19, a.t.). As I work with people who are first-generation Christians coming from ancestral worship religions, the question often arises as to whether their ancestors knew God or not, whether there were manifestations of God or whether they died as "pagans"—pagans, that is, according to the Christian theology preached to them. These verses in Deuteronomy clearly state that Israel considered other peoples as also having some relationship with God, even if those people did not recognize the relationship. Perhaps to speak of a knowledge of God would be far-fetched, but no nation is left without some hint that there is a special, unique divinity. Israel, on the other hand, has a firsthand knowledge of the Creator and thus has no reason to worship creatures.

This seems to be a wonderful way of

dealing with the mystery of God's revelation and especially with those nations or peoples who have not received it. Even they have received created elements (which they worship) from YHWH! God is never too distant, even for peoples who do not know God! Yet God is also distant enough not to be our toy.

Deuteronomy 7:1-26, The Land, Gift of God for Life, and Israel's Relations with Other Peoples

What will Israel find when it enters the land? Will the land be ready for the taking? Not quite. It will be occupied by several nations, all of them stronger and more numerous than Israel. However, this will not be a problem, as YHWH—not Israel— will drive them out. Since the number of nations is the symbolic number seven, it should not be taken literally, but should be interpreted as referring to any possible enemy, present and future (7:22-24). Israel's responsibility is not to drive other nations out of the land; this is YHWH's work. Israel is to keep free from any influence from those other peoples by "utterly destroying them," especially their religious symbols, by avoiding any covenant with them, and by declaring banned any property of theirs, especially gold or silver set aside for sacred use.

From our perspective in Argentina, we intensely dislike the passage's militaristic tone. Most of our world has suffered or suffers military conquest, explicitly or implicitly connected to Christianity or to another religion. In past centuries, the American continent was conquered and devastated in the name of Christianity and Christian empires. Recently, one Muslim country, with extremely poor people but with rich oil resources, has been devastated by a North-Atlantic coalition for alleged "reasons of national security." The dictator of another country has been denounced as *the* enemy and thus demonized. The economic and political interests that motivate wars should be unmasked, especially when a holy war is

proclaimed against a demonic enemy. No true religion can allow itself to be used as a justification for the murder of other peoples, when the murders are actually perpetrated for political and economic reasons. As I write, I hear on the radio a world leader stating that a short war against a country would be beneficial for business!

A second reading is nevertheless also possible. When one takes into consideration that Deuteronomy was written much later than the events it narrates, and that its final redaction dates at least from postexilic times (fifth century B.C.E. and after), then this militaristic language can be viewed symbolically. Israel is about to make a new start in the land that is ruled by a Persian emperor. Thus, no nation is to be driven out from the land by military force; only the militaristic image remains. Yet, Israel must overcome the temptations of idolatry, of ritualism instead of obedience, and of social structures that oppress their own people. Israel and every other people, ours included, must overcome these temptations.

This second reading is the central teaching of this passage for us today. There are features of our lives that are harmful for our faith or our lives; we must not allow them to tempt us. Today, however, many of us would reason that "utterly destroying them" is no solution, as these harmful elements would probably still be accessible to us. Learning to "live with the enemy" is another, more realistic, way of looking at dangers that, in the end, remain present in our lives because we welcome them.

Deuteronomy 8:1-10, Learning to Live in the Wilderness

Chapter 8 continues Moses' address to the people. As before, the remembrance of God and God's works is central in this chapter. The first ten verses concentrate on remembering God's presence with the people in the wilderness, until they reached the promised land. The last ten verses emphasize that Israel should take care not to forget God. Freely adapting several scholars' statements, we note that memory is the best remedy for fear, for temptation, and for lack of solidarity among the people. Remembrance implies positioning oneself in matters important for oneself and for the community. It means having God in the past as a beacon, in the present as a companion, and in the future as the goal of humanity for completion and fulfillment. When we have a sense of history, we can see that events are not just random occurrences but symptoms of circumstances that affected us individually and corporately in the past and will continue to affect our lives in the present and future.

The very example put by the text illuminates our experience today. In the desert, people had manna, a daily miracle provided by God. Today, millions of people do not enjoy the miracle of a daily meal. They live in another kind of wilderness, from which there seems to be no way out. Otherwise, how can anyone explain that our country (to take but one example), which is among the five major producers of food in the world, has half of the population living in poverty and malnourished?

Manna is a miracle, not only in what it means as food supply, but in what it means as a divinely delivered object lesson. In the wilderness, Israel had to learn to trust God and not their own initiatives, a lesson especially hard for those who believed themselves to be God. In the wilderness, they had to be disciplined and trust in Someone they could not see, carry with them, or manipulate.

Manna is also a miracle in that it became a test case for solidarity and trust through food distribution. In the wilderness, no one was hungry, for God provided enough for the day. Any manna not used that day was spoiled by the next day (except, as we know, on the Sabbath). What would happen if we applied the same principle today? Imagine a situation of complete trust in God and full solidarity with human beings (if you are in solidarity with your own family and friends, what is special about it?), in which food is not stockpiled to the detriment of another person's life. Concrete images for this

vision are many; what is most important is that these images inspire our churches and our societies to action. For today the miracle of manna is not working.

Some Deuteronomic Laws Concerning the Poor

Perhaps there is no more realistic witness to our sinful condition than the Bible itself. A people is called out of bondage to be free and to receive from God, who liberated them. Yet, against all advice Israel requests a king like the other nations, enslaves its own members, and does not hold to its historical memory that requires a way of life that would exhibit the special relationship it has with YHWH.

There is always a thin line between prophetic criticism and ethnocentrism when we look at a society other than our own, as is the one reflected in the Bible. On the one hand, we do not want to compromise certain rights for us or for other people, even if we recognize that it would be anachronistic to expect current formulations in the text. For example, we do not expect the Bible to state every person's right to be free and not to be sold or treated as an object. On the other hand, there is always the danger of unfairly imposing our own criteria without considering other relevant facts, for example, data not contained in the text, such as slave laws from other societies. Furthermore, religion and its manifestations are never pure because they are always subject to the surrounding culture, both now and in the ancient world.

Standing in the tension between vision and reality, the kingdom of God and sin, love for the biblical witness and critique of that same witness for what is not redemptive in it, we now turn to some of the legal material in Deuteronomy to see what it says about the love for God and people that surpasses much of human society and culture.

Several laws are concerned with the poor of their time. The typical Deuteronomic formula unites the resident alien or stranger, the fatherless, and the widow (e.g., Deut 10:18, 14:29, 24:19-21, 27:19, and others). These are the three categories of people deprived of land (this is unclear in the case of the child, but otherwise the child would probably not be mentioned as poor) and deprived of a "father," and, therefore, they need laws to protect them. Other members of the poor included the slave and the Levite. While the latter belong to the institutional religious apparatus, the former was part of a household. Thus, even if maltreated, they had a father, the head of the household, to care for them. Slaves represented a major investment by their owner, so usually it would have been unprofitable to have them starve to death.

Israelite society tried to find ways of dealing with its slaves justly and fairly, and adopted laws that prevented their masters from total control over their slaves. This is certain (at least in theory) for Israelites in debt slavery; it is less sure with regard to foreign slaves, who had nobody to look after them and their—very basic! —human rights.

That one can speak of people purely in terms of monetary investment and profit/loss shows how off the mark both ancient and modern societies are when they skew and prioritize their values solely towards the economic. At least slaves had a visible master to turn to for food. Today, the slaves of the globalized international economy do not know who owns them, and those who foster such international economic slavery through business practices solely advantageous to themselves, often do not see themselves for what they are— slave masters! When entities as nebulous as the market or neo-liberalism literally determine life and death for millions over the whole globe, when investments, money, and profit are set far higher than people, there is something very wrong, very sinful, in our global practices.

"Open your Hand to the Poor . . . ." (Deut 15:1-11)

These verses discuss release of debts (or in modern economic parlance, debt relief), an extremely important and sensitive issue in both biblical times and today. Although these verses are included among the laws,

they appear to be more like a midrash or commentary on the law on release in v. 1, "Every seventh year you shall grant a remission of debts," than as laws themselves. The style is vague and hortatory, it shows inconsistencies, and it would be difficult to know in what situations or to whose benefit they would apply. For instance, does the phrase "your needy neighbor" (15:7, 9, 11) also refer to needy foreigners? No, since Israelites are allowed to exact claim from foreigners (v. 3). On the other hand, if these poor or needy are fellow Israelites, a situation that will undoubtedly continue ("there will never cease to be some in need on the earth," 15:11), how does one reconcile this and similar assessments with v. 4, which states, "There will be, however, no one in need among you (a.t.)"? Scholars assume that a variety of sources underlie this text, the latest portion being the commentary on the law in vv. 4-6, which contradicts the assertion that there will always be poor.

One thing is clear from the text: lending and pressing for repayment are not private issues between creditor and debtor. They are social issues, and, insofar as God is involved, we could say religious issues as well. Because Israel has experienced God's blessings, not even one member of the community is to suffer the humiliation of having to take a loan. God's promise to Israel is that it will always have enough to lend to other nations and never have to borrow from them, provided Israel remains faithful to this commandment (15:1-6).

Every seventh year there will be a release of debts. The term used is *shemittah,* "dropping," a noun that appears only in Deuteronomy. Its verb form is used to prescribe the land's rest or Sabbath in Exodus 23:10. In the law concerning the land, it means that its owner shall let it rest for the year, while the poor of the country can eat from its produce. Thus, many modern commentaries think Deuteronomy 15 describes a suspension of the claims on anything loaned during that year. Yet most ancient commentaries and some modern ones think that 15:1 refers to the cancellation of the remainder of the debt, rather than merely to its suspension for one year. A suspension of the debt for one year is more reasonable and practical. Yet, this is one of those texts that raise the possibility that Deuteronomy was not a law-code meant to be practiced, but a vision that the community of holy people who follow a holy God should aspire to, something analogous to the Gospels' presentation of the church.

Although the term *Sabbath* is not mentioned in this pericope, its use here seems justified by the use of the seven year cycle for debt release, and because of the importance of the Sabbath commandment elsewhere in the book (Deut 5:12-15). Sabbath is related in the Bible and in Judaism to rest, completion, and feast. We could ask: Whose rest, whose completion, whose feast is to be celebrated in this Sabbath? All of Israel! Especially its weakest members, at least insofar as they benefit from the weekly Sabbath. According to the text, it is also a Sabbath for the lender, because his (her?) Sabbath is related to God's. It is the feast of trust for those who do not let money and possessions come between them and God or between them and their brothers and sisters of God's community!

Seen in this light, Christians in rich countries that lend money to poorer countries, need to seriously ask themselves: How are we doing as a people of God, when our churches fail to exercise any real influence on our own governments and societies regarding debts with usurious interest rates and whose price is paid with people's blood? How are we doing when a Jubilee year becomes a tourist event to some capital of Europe? In countries like mine, we need to ask: How are we doing as churches, when the highest authorities present themselves as Christians and hardly use the borrowed money for the country's advancement, but rather send it to private overseas bank accounts, —and thus steal from the people. Once again, this is not a private, individual issue—despite what banks and countries view as "privacy policy"! It is not a private issue, because, as Deuteronomy affirms, God personally intervened to make it a theological and ethical issue. Wherever we are, we Christians should recognize the debts of poor nations as a theological and ethical issue, and we must act accordingly.

More on Loans
(Deut 24:6-22)

Noteworthy among the laws concerning the poorest in society are the ones that preserve the debtor's dignity. For instance, Deut 24:10-13 prohibits a creditor from forcibly entering a debtor's home to take a pledge or collateral on the loan. Debtors have the right to control their homes and property; thus, the debtors are to bring the collateral to the creditor. If the pledge was the only cloak or blanket on which one slept, then this would be daily taken and daily returned to the debtor for the night. Forbidding the pledge of the millstone (a necessary implement for bread-making) or any of its parts preserves the debtors' dignity by allowing them to at least provide their own bread (24:6). Likewise, Deuteronomy makes provisions for the daily laborer to be paid daily at sunset; otherwise, the worker would not be able to buy food for dinner (24:14-15). When one notes that this commandment uses the verb "to oppress" in reference to the worker, one realizes how easy it is to forget that all these issues are matters of justice and of the dignity due every human being. These are not charitable measures!

Today, in many countries around the globe most human rights are violated, especially those concerning labor and the body (such as rape and torture). Rich countries violate labor rights by establishing and profiting from miserable wages. Both rich and poor nations are, at least indirectly, involved in child labor, child prostitution, and other practices that are shameful, perverse, and sinful.

The people of God have the important responsibility of confronting these and other manifestations of neo-liberal capitalism by underscoring time and time again the value of life. In this case, "people of God" is any person, church-related or not, who communes with God and his or her brothers and sisters throughout life—that is any person who obeys the spirit of the laws in Deuteronomy.

Deuteronomy 23:17-25, Exclusion in the Name of Religion

Chapter 23 contains laws concerning several issues, such as interest on loans, temple offerings, vows, purity in the military camp, and others. The majority of commentators can discern no coherence in their order. The laws, however, do have a common theme:maintaining the Israelite community's boundaries. This chapter is divided into two major clusters, 23:1-15 and 23:16-25. The first responds to the question: Who belongs to the community and who does not? The second answers the questions:What are some of the financial responsibilities of the people of God toward these insiders and outsiders?

I am especially concerned with the laws in 23:17-18 (23:18-19, HT) prohibiting certain people, notably prostitutes and consecrated men and women (Heb. *qadesh* and *qedeshah*) to make offerings at the temple. The other term, *kelev*, or "dog," appears in extra-biblical sources (e.g., Canaanite inscriptions and Hittite texts) as a self-reference by people who are servants of their divinity. The difficulty in defining whether *keleb* is literally a dog (substituting for other sacrificial animals) or represents a person, lies in the use of the noun *mehir*. *Mehir* is the price of a commodity (perhaps the price of a hired commodity?) and not the wages for a service. The terms *qadesh* and *qedeshah* come from the same root as sanctify, holiness, holy. How they became "sacred prostitute" (male and female) in the vast majority of commentaries and Bibles is a long story that is—fortunately!—starting to be reversed. So the best translation of 23:17-18 is:

There will be no woman consecrated (to other cults) among the daughters of Israel, and there will be no man consecrated (to other cults) among the sons of Israel. You shall not bring the fee of a prostitute nor the price of a 'dog' to the house of YHWH your God for any vow. For also these two are an abomination to YHWH your God (a.t.).

These texts connote views most important for the Yahwist redactor, who despised and perhaps even feared anything not clearly and exclusively devoted to YHWH. Thus, these verses are not objective descriptions, but instead are stereotyped rejections of the religious "other."

What do we say in today's world about a text like this? Its message is clear and pertinent to the confusing current religious situation—the religious shopping-mall—where individuals seek only their own self-gratification and self-fulfillment. Most Christians (to speak of our own faith) do not know the basics of their own confession and either demonize or divinize the church as they have experienced it. Most people cannot imagine another reality, one governed by God's purposes, at least not in this life. Christianity is to be faulted on this issue. A clear stance like that of Deut 23:17-18 is to be commended.

What are my misgivings about this text? The authors harshly disparage other religious practices, practices with which many Israelites saw no problem and participated: kings, prophets, common people, women, children, and perhaps even priests. Rather than explaining the dangers they see in these practices, the authors condemn them by using insults.

Those who have converted into Christianity from another faith are hurt and shamed when their former religion is degraded, insultingly described, and condemned without adequate explanation or insight. Such converted Christians constantly question the ultimate fate of their own families and friends who have not converted and who continue in their old ways. Are they condemned? What will

God do to them? Why cannot they understand? What can I do to have them saved?

We, members of the people of God, need to learn to affirm who we are and what we believe, both culturally and religiously as in Deut 23:17-18. Yet we also must avoid following this text in despising and demonizing others. Then God's work will surely be done through us.

CONCLUSION

Much of Deuteronomy cannot be directly applied to our situation today. Our situation in Argentina is characterized by: secularization; a democratic system of government with election by the people and not by God; a Roman-derived legal system rather than one derived from the Assyrians or Babylonians; a continent colonized by European countries (in our case Spain) with the sword and the cross as weapons; Christendom; a more tolerant approach to other faiths; a different awareness of human rights; and another language. These and other reasons makeit impossible to try to directly apply Deuteronomy to our context.

Nevertheless, as we have seen, we can identify with many of Deuteronomy's concerns. Seen as a postexilic product (in its final canonical version, the one we read and we take as God's word!), it is an appeal to the past in order to strengthen the faith of a people supposedly holy in the eyes of God. It is "supposedly" holy people," because, if they were faithful and holy, there would be no need to appeal to laws to bring them closer to God.

Deuteronomy is a call to regain a sense of unity and belonging as one people with a common identity. Deuteronomy's authors/ redactors addressed this call to a people weakened by internal strife and a lack of purpose. Within this people, individuals are responsible to God and to the community for their own personal and social behavior; they will not be put to death for their child's behavior or their parent's behavior (Deut 24:16). Thus, the people of God—past, present and future—must once again confess with their whole being *YHWH 'elohenu YHWH 'ekhad* "The LORD is our God, the LORD alone" (Deut 6:4).

BIBLIOGRAPHY

Christensen, Duane L., ed. *A Song of Power and the Power of Song: Essays on the Book of Deuteronomy.* Winona Lake, Ind.: Eisenbrauns, 1993.

Craigie, Peter C. *The Book of Deuteronomy.* NICOT. Grand Rapids: Eerdmans, 1976.

Driver, S. R. *Deuteronomy.* ICC. New York: Scribners' Sons, 1895.

Engelmann, Angelika. "Deuteronomium. Recht und Gerechtigkeit für Frauen im Gesetz." Pages 67-79 in *Kompendium feministische Bibelauslegung.* Edited by Luise Schottroff and Marie-Theres Wacker. 2d ed. Gütersloh: Chr. Kaiser/Gütersloher Verlagshaus, 1998.

Frymer-Kensky, Tikva. "Deuteronomy." Pages 52-62 in *The Women's Bible Commentary.* Edited by Carol A. Newsome and Sharon H. Ringe. Louisville: Westminster John Knox, 1992.

García Martínez, F., A. Hilhorst, J. T. A. G. M. van Ruiten, and A. S. van der Woude, eds. *Studies in Deuteronomy in Honor of C. J. Labuschagne on the Occasion of His 65th Birthday.* VTSup 53. Leiden/New York/Cologne: 1994.

Mayes, A. D. H. *Deuteronomy.* The NCB Commentary. Grand Rapids/London: Eerdmans/ Marshall, Morgan & Scott, 1979.

Nakanose, Shigeyuki. "Para entender el libro del Deuteronomio. ¿Una ley a favor de la vida?" *RIBLA* 23 (1996): 168-184.

Tigay, Jeffrey. *Deuteronomy.* The Jewish Publication Society Commentary on the Torah. Philadelphia/Jerusalem: The Jewish Publication Society, 1996.

JOSHUA

Dora Mbuwayesango

Hood Theological Seminary, Salisbury, North Carolina, USA and Zimbabwe

LIFE CONTEXT OF THE INTERPRETATION

The book of Joshua appears to be a blueprint for the colonization of southern Africa. During the colonial period, the indigenous peoples of southern Africa experienced cruel dispossession of their lands by the British and Boer settlers who migrated to the region to make a better life for themselves. To get ownership of the arable lands, the settlers killed and displaced the indigenous peoples from their ancestral lands. They justified their barbaric acts on the pretext of civilizing the indigenous peoples, and the missionaries who came with them saw this settlement as an occasion to convert the "natives" to Christianity. Hence the settlers and missionaries worked together in an unholy alliance. While the settlers took the lands from the indigenous peoples, the missionaries gave those peoples the Bible, which, in the missionaries' view, gave divine sanction for the peoples' displacement and dispossession. (This sentiment is well expressed in the southern African popular saying: "When the whites came they said, 'Let us pray'; when we opened our eyes we had the Bible and they had our land.") What can the book of Joshua say to the Canaanites, the dispossessed, and the exterminated? Can the God of the dispossessor be the God of the dispossessed? How can the church be a moral voice against present injustices in southern Africawithout a critical analysis of the injustices depicted in the Bible, which mirror our own?

The people of southern Africa are characterized by tribal diversity that is tied to land and identity. Tribal identities play a major role in the distribution of national resources, especially land. The church can use Joshua's narratives of the distribution of the land in its critique of the politics of land redistribution. The problem of Israel's exclusivity—both within its borders and toward those outside of its borders—can be used as a warning against discrimination against others who are now part of the southern African population.

CONTEXTUAL COMMENT

An Overview of Joshua

The book of Joshua is the last stage in the sequence of the construction of Israelite identity. Israel, above all, is identified with the land of Canaan. The first stage is depicted in the book of Genesis in which the land is promised to Israel's ancestors, to Abraham, Isaac, and Jacob. Genesis concludes with Israel not yet in this land but in Egypt. In Exodus through Deuteronomy, Moses leads Israel from Egypt through Sinai and leaves them on the verge of the promised land in the plains of Moab. The book of Joshua, the climax of the narratives of the land, takes Israel into the land of Canaan. The book of Joshua presents the ideology

Dora Rudo Mbuwayesango, a native of Zimbabwe, is associate professor of Hebrew Bible. Her publications include "Can Daughters be Sons? The Daughters of Zelophehad in Patriarchal and Imperial Society" in *Relating to the Text: Form Critical and Interdisciplinary Insights on the Bible* (2004) and "How Local Divine Powers Were Suppressed: A Case of Mwari of the Shona" in *Other Ways of Reading: African Women and the Bible* (2001).

that defines Israel's identity in terms of its relation to the indigenous peoples of Canaan as much as of its internal relations Both the external and internal aspects of Israel's identity are tied to the land of Canaan. What distinguishes Israel from the Canaanite nations is that Israel has a special relationship with its God, YHWH. The status of Israel as a chosen people and holy nation determines how Israel relates to the other nations. For Israel to be the holy nation, YHWH's own, they have to be distinct from all other peoples. For this they need to rid the land of other peoples, i.e., the Canaanites, who might be a bad influence on them. A few groups of peoples are not exterminated, such as the family of Rahab (Josh 2) and the Gibeonites who make a treaty with Israel (Josh 9). Yet, according to Joshua's presentation, not wiping out the Canaanites completely is a failure on Israel's part.

The book of Joshua can be divided into two major parts: the extermination and dispossession of the Canaanites (1–12), and the distribution of the land of Canaan among the Israelites (13–24).

Part I: Josh 1–12

The introduction establishes Joshua as the new leader who is to fulfill the task that Moses began with the exodus of the Israelites from Egypt (1:1-2). This is followed by the sending of spies (2), the crossing of the Jordan and the camp at Gilgal (3–5), the fall of Jericho (6), Achan's sin and the conquest of Ai (7:1–8:29), a covenant on Mount Ebal (8:30-35), the treaty with the Gibeonites (9), the conflict with the Amorite kings and the southern campaign (10), the northern campaign (11:1-15), and the summary of the occupation (11:16–12:24).

Joshua 6:1–12:24 presents the role of God in the conquest and the annihilation of the indigenous peoples to make room for God's chosen people. The text emphasizes the fulfillment of the command to annihilate all. The narratives do not explain why the indigenous peoples deserve such treatment from God. The narratives simply emphasize that God is giving the land to the Israelites. Thus, for Israel, receiving the land involves attempting to wipe out the Canaanites.

Part II: Josh 13–24

The second major part can be divided into two sections. The first (13:1–21:45) is about the establishment of tribal boundaries and cities. It begins with an account of the unconquered lands and a summary of the occupation of the Transjordan territory (13). The distribution of the land takes place in two phases: the allotments to the three tribes (Judah, Ephraim and Manasseh 14–17); and the allotments to the seven other tribes (18–19). The section concludes with the designation of cities of refuge and Levitical cities (20–21).

The purpose of the land distribution narratives is to show that the land was divided according to God's command. It underscores that, though divided into tribal allotments, Israel is united under the God who gave it the land. Even when that unity is threatened by some divergences, disaster is averted through compromise.

The second section (22–24) emphasizes the covenantal unity of Israel. The Jordan divides the people of Israel into two major divisions, but a strong connection remains. Thus the epilogue (22:1–24:33) highlights the idea that the fulfillment of God's promise initiates the renewal of the covenant. In covenant making, Israel comes before YHWH as one entity. Tribal and territorial land allocations do not destroy the fundamental unity of Israel as the people of YHWH. The last words of Joshua exhort the Israelites to obey YHWH in the promised land (23). The renewal of the covenant at Shechem is presented as Israel's response to Joshua's last words (24:1-28). The section concludes with notice of the burials of Joshua, Eleazar, and the bones of Joseph (24:29-33). The basic element that unites the diversified Israel is the covenant with YHWH.

The conquest and settlement of Israel in Canaan is presented as sanctioned and indeed as achieved by God. The way a group constructs its identity reflects how it relates to others. The story of Joshua 1–12 reflects the exclusivism that can lead to genocides and holocausts. The Joshua narratives ought to be shown for what they are in order to avoid the construction of identities that lead to extermination of those who are different. Joshua 13–21 raises the issue of unity in diversity. Differences within the people can lead to disorder if the common ground is not upheld. In the last section (22–24), Joshua brings unity to a diversified Israel.

Joshua's narratives are often problematic because of the ways they depict the relations between the people of God and others. God is very partial to the so-called chosen and is ruthless to the rest of the world. Israel's exclusion of other peoples leads to their extermination. The relationships among the people of God are healthier, although one can detect some intolerance for nonconformists such as Achan and the tribes settled east of the Jordan. Every effort is made to forge and maintain unity among God's people, as the second half of the book expresses.

Exclusive Identity:
The Extermination of the Other
(Josh 1–12)

Israel's identity—political, religious, and economic—is tied to the land of Canaan. How Israel came into possession of the land is the primary topic of the first section of Joshua. When the land was promised to Israel's ancestors, the Canaanites lived in it. The land had to be transferred from the Canaanites to the Israelites. The text shows how YHWH achieved this. The running theme is that YHWH had already handed over the land to the Israelites; Israel only had to follow YHWH's directions as set into law by Moses. The Israelites engaged in a Holy War, which is characterized in Joshua by the principle of *herem*—a term with connotations ranging from "thing devoted to Yahweh," to "ban," to "utter destruction." *Herem* as God's command is morally problematic (Niditch 1993, 28-77) because it

requires that the enemy be utterly destroyed; it sanctions slaughter in the name of God.

The extermination of the Canaanites begins at Jericho (Josh 6). The description of events is dramatic. The battle is won even before it has begun. It is YHWH who fights the battle, so the spoils belong to YHWH— they are *herem* (6:16-17). YHWH has already put Jericho, its king, and its mighty warriors in Joshua's hand (6:2). The Israelites simply follow YHWH's instructions: the Israelite warriors march around Jericho once each day for six days (6:3). Seven priests carrying trumpets before the ark lead the march (6:4). On the seventh day, the Israelite warriors march around the city seven times with the priests blowing the trumpets. Then all the people make a great shout, at which time the city falls flat (6:5) and the people proceed to apply the *herem* requirement—devoting things to Yahweh, applying the ban through utter destruction (6:16-19). All breathing things, "men and women, young and old, oxen, sheep, and donkeys" (6:21), are killed except for Rahab and her household who had earlier assisted the spies. The people are cautioned not to take anything that is "devoted to YHWH"— *herem*—because it would result in their destruction. Silver, gold, and vessels of bronze and iron are to be considered holy, set apart for YHWH. The city is burned down with everything in it except for Rahab (traitor to her own people), her family, and the silver, gold, and vessels of bronze and silver (6:24). Human beings are considered dispensable.

The seriousness of the *herem* ban requirement is demonstrated in the case of Achan, who took for himself some of the treasures at Jericho (7:1). The first attempt at conquering Ai was a dismal failure (7:2-5). All Israel suffered a major setback because the *herem* ban was not completely carried out at Jericho; an individual, Achan, deemed it unreasonable to destroy precious booty and saved some of the treasures for himself. Just as in the case of Jericho, Joshua had first sent spies. But the strategy they recommended resulted in a complete defeat of the Israelites. It is striking that YHWH is not depicted as playing any role in the first attack of Ai. When the battle ended in total disaster for Israel, Joshua consulted YHWH and emphasized that YHWH could not afford to allow Israel to be defeated by the Canaanites: "The Canaanites and all the inhabitants of the land will hear of it, and surround us, and cut off our name from the earth. Then what will you do for your great name?" (7:9). The greatness of YHWH's name was tied to the survival of Israel in the land of Canaan. Despite Joshua's attempt to manipulate YHWH, YHWH wanted Israel to adhere strictly to the *herem* ban principle; thus a witch-hunt was put into effect (7:13). Achan confessed that he had taken treasures from Jericho and, together with his family, was stoned and burned by all Israel (7:18-26). Then YHWH's anger died down, and ironically, the *herem* ban principle was soon modified to allow Israel to keep some of the spoils and livestock.

The second attempt at Ai met with success (8:1-29), because Israel followed YHWH's instruction (8:1-2). What happened to Jericho was to happen to Ai, but with a different strategy. The people of Ai were to be drawn out of the city in pursuit of the fleeing Israelites, and then ambushed and their city burned. The king was captured and all the people slaughtered. Joshua played an important role in the slaughter, until he had utterly destroyed all the people of Ai and hanged Ai's king. There were to be no human survivors at Ai. But, in contrast to the scene of destruction at Jericho, Israel was allowed to take for itself Ai's spoil and livestock.

Another type of relationship with inhabitants of the land is presented in the story of the Gibeonites (9:1-27). When the news of Israel's conquest of Jericho and Ai reached the other inhabitants of the land—the Hittites, the Amorites, the Canaanites, the Perizzites, the Hivites, and the Jebusites—they formed a coalition against Israel. However, one group of the indigenous inhabitants, the Gibeonites, did not join the coalition but deceived Israel into making a treaty with them. They pretended that they were not from within the land of Canaan, the land Israel had been given by its God. It is noteworthy that the Gibeonites are depicted as accepting Israel's claim on the land (9:24). It is also interesting to note that the role of the Canaanite gods is not mentioned. This omission is quite interesting considering that the rest of the book views the Canaanite religions as the greatest threat for Israel. Actually, the Israelites made a covenant with the Gibeonites in the name of YHWH (9:15). When Israel realized the deception they could not break this covenant guaranteeing the lives of the Gibeonites. Instead, Israel made the Gibeonites "cursed" slaves of Israel and servants dedicated to service in the house of YHWH as "hewers of wood and drawers of water" (9:19-27). The Gibeonites were thus kept inferior to the Israelites. In keeping with the covenant between Israel and the Gibeonites, Israel came to the rescue of the Gibeonites when they are attacked as allies of Israel by a league of five kings: Adoni-zedek of Jerusalem, Hoham of Hebron, Piram of Jarmuth, Japhia of Lachish, and Debir of Eglon. Again YHWH assured Joshua of victory (10:8) and was an active participant in the war: YHWH threw huge stones from heaven that killed lots of people in the opposite camp (10:10-11). The five kings, who were found hiding in a cave, were then tortured, killed, and hung on trees (10:16-27).

The story continues with the capture and utter destruction of several cities. The ongoing picture is that of massacres, and complete annihilation of the indigenous inhabitants "as the Lord God of Israel commanded" (10:40). Joshua's success is directly attributed to YHWH—"because the LORD God of Israel fought for Israel" (10:42). A less developed account of Israel's exploits on the northern side follows the same pattern; the Israelites slaughter all the peoples, following what YHWH had commanded through Moses (11:1-15).

Joshua 11 concludes with a summary of the Israelite military campaign in the land of Canaan, assessing what had been accomplished. First, it declares the military campaign to be complete: "So Joshua took all that land" (11:16). Joshua had to fight for the land in a protracted war because "[t]here was not a town that made peace with the Israelites, except the Hivites, the inhabitants of Gibeon; all were taken in battle" (11:19) This statement seems to claim that Israel won the land in a fair fight. But it also attempts to explain the discrepancy between the claim that Israel received the land from God and that Israel had to kill to displace other people. The explanation is given simply as YHWH's doing: "For it was the LORD's doing to harden their hearts so that they would come against Israel in battle, in order that they might be utterly destroyed, and might receive no mercy, but be exterminated, just as the Lord had commanded Moses" (11:20). This statement shifts at least part of the blame to the victims.

Another summary in 11:21-23 refers to the indigenous inhabitants as *Anakim*. The significant point is that the land is now referred to as the land of the Israelites. Although some indigenous peoples still remain in such places as Gaza, Gath, and Ashdod, a time of rest from war is ushered in and the land is ready for internal distribution. Before the distribution of the land, however, there is an additional long summary (12:1-24) that gives a select list of the conquered kings and exploits in the Transjordan and west of the Jordan.

In Josh 2:1–12:24, the conquest of the land is represented in epic style, in narratives focused on the capture of a few key cities and the practice of the *herem* ban. Because the ban required that the enemy be utterly destroyed, Israel's occupation of the land of Canaan involved systematic pillaging and killing of the current inhabitants. This extermination of the indigenous peoples did not only have divine approval; it was mandated by God. The Israelites killed in conformity with the directives of God. This presentation of God poses problems for the dispossessed. Is this an appropriate representation of God? Does God truly sanction and destroy other peoples for the sake of one nation?

To begin, we must ask if this is an accurate representation of what happened. Actually it is difficult to harmonize the narrative of Josh 1–12 with the archaeological evidence. In other words, Joshua's account is not an accurate record of what happened. There is virtual unanimity among scholars that the model of conquest narrated in Josh 1–12 is untenable (e.g., Thompson 1987, 11-40). Joshua, together with the entire corpus of narratives of early Israel, comes from authors writing many centuries later than the events described (during the exilic or postexilic period) who had no reliable information about the distant past.

Without minimizing the problematic character of this religious teaching, one can better understand it by keeping in mind the historical context of the book of Joshua. Its accounts of conquest were written either during the exilic or the postexilic period. Because it was intended to propogate an exclusive ideology among the (would-be) returnees, the book of Joshua emphasizes the question of Israel's identity and who deserves to be in the land. These narratives are constructed to give a sense of mission to the returnees; they need to fulfill what Joshua had begun but had not quite completed. Each generation is responsible for furthering the original intent of YHWH. If the Canaanites did not deserve to be in the land during the times of Moses and Joshua, then they do not deserve to be in the land now—whoever are the "Canaanites" who occupy the promised land as the people comes back from exile.

Furthermore, the narratives are characterized by storytelling techniques (Miller and Hayes 1986, 56-60). Thus, the book of Joshua, as part of a larger narrative beginning with Genesis and ending in 2 Kings (from creation to exile), portrays the self-understanding of a people as envisioned and represented by its writer. In other words, the book of Joshua is a literary creation that reflects the religious perspectives of the writer who seeks to connect Israel's identity as YHWH's people to the Land of Canaan. The story aims to show that Israel deserved the land of Canaan and that the Canaanites were not supposed to occupy the land. Thus, this story postulates a unique religious origin for the people. As the Pentateuch has shown, Israel has been chosen by YHWH and invited into a covenantal relationship, with the promise that they will receive the land. In the book of Joshua, the Israelites receive possession of the land promised by YHWH their God.

The purpose of the book of Joshua, like the other narratives in the corpus (Genesis –through 2 Kings), was to inculcate in the people of Israel an identity that was based on the land.

Two important criteria defined Israel's understanding of itself as a people: religion and land. It was basically through religion that they had obtained their land. Their God, YHWH, had given it to them. Their continual possession of the land depended on their religious faithfulness and purity. Thus, in the belief that they had to remove all temptations in order to be faithful to YHWH, they developed the ideology of the total destruction of the indigenous inhabitants of the land. The *herem* ban required that the enemy be utterly destroyed as a sacrifice to the deity who had made the victory possible. The writer of Joshua appealed to the *herem* ban tradition to relate the identity of the chosen people to the doctrine of the separation of the holy from the unholy. Israelites should separate themselves from the impurity of others.

This being said, it remains that the conquest narratives in Josh 1–12 are very problematic in the context of southern Africa. The depiction of the God of Israel as an exclusivistic God can only be most troubling for us. Is not God a universal God, rather than a very partial God who engages in the extermination of other peoples in favor of one nation? Should the people of God be a people that cannot tolerate others? Should the ideal world be exclusively occupied by God's people? The book of Joshua seems to demonstrate that people of different ethnicities and religions cannot live side by side in an environment characterized by mutual respect. Is this really the case, and even if so, is this the lesson that we need to hear? In order to have a moral voice and to speak against present-day injustice, the church needs to voice its objections to the Christian use of the Bible to justify or ignore injustices. Does not the book of Joshua fuel such misuses of the Bible?

How a people constructs its identity reflects how they relate to those who live among them and to those who are different. The ideology of divine entitlement is a dangerous one. Yet, the book of Joshua can help the people of God to construct its identity in a sound way, namely by acknowledging and making explicit the revulsion we have for its narratives. Precisely because these stories of relentless massacres shock us, they warn us that the construction of identities that are exclusive and religiously sanctioned—however overt or covert this religious exclusivism might be—leads to genocide and extermination of entire ethnic groups.

Internal and External Relations: Land Distribution (Josh 13–19)

Joshua 13–19 deals with the distribution of the land that had been cleared of Canaanites. This section is introduced by a disclaimer: there are still Canaanites that Israel has not yet conquered and driven out (13:1-7). Yet Joshua is now old and has to distribute or allocate tribal possessions before he dies. YHWH promises to drive out the remaining Canaanites: "I will myself drive them out from before the Israelites" (13:6). The section emphasizes that the dispossession of the Canaanites will be completed at a later time. The remaining Canaanites are depicted as people who are where they are not supposed to be. They should not be among the Israelites, so that YHWH's people might remain pure.

Moses had already allotted land east of the Jordan to two and a half tribes: the tribe of Reuben (13:15-23), the tribe of Gad (13:24-28), and the half-tribe of Manasseh (13:29-31). Although they are east of the Jordan, these tribes are an integral part of YHWH's people. The distribution of land west of the Jordan is introduced by noting the people who oversee it (14:1-5), namely,

Joshua, but also Eleazar the priest, and tribal representatives. The function of tribal representatives was to avoid future disputes concerning land distribution and to ensure fairness. The land was to be allotted through lot, as a demonstration that it was YHWH who was actually controlling the distribution. The text also emphasizes that the Levites did not get a land allotment and thus no inheritable land, only cities to live in and pastures for their flocks and herds (14:3-4)—as had been determined in the time of Moses. Joshua did not introduce new policies.

The distribution of the land begins with allotment of land to a non-Israelite, Caleb the Kenizzite (14:6-15). The Kenizzite are not portrayed as peoples to be driven out of Canaan to make room for Israel. When the people of Judah come forward to receive their allotment, Caleb comes with them and makes his demand. In fact, Caleb, having joined the invaders, is now part of the tribe of Judah. Caleb receives special treatment because he was one of the spies who had come back with a positive report and encouraged the Israelites to trust YHWH and move forward to Canaan (Num 13–14). Caleb asks specifically for Hebron, which is still occupied by the *Anakim* of whom Israel was afraid in the spy episode (Josh 14:12-15). Caleb believes that he can drive them out.

This passage directly contradicts 11:21-23 where Joshua is reported to have wiped out all the *Anakim* from Hebron. This contradiction shows that the primary concern of the narrative is to explain the prominent presence of the Kenizzites among the Israelites. Because of Caleb's deeds for Israel's sake, the Kenizzites deserve to live in the promised land as equals to the Israelites. This is in contrast with the Gibeonites who are inferior—slaves and servants—and with the rest of the Canaanites who are to be driven out.

The tribal boundaries were established to avoid future boundary disputes. The tribes of Judah (15:1-63) and Joseph, made up of Manasseh and Ephraim (16:1–17:18), receive an extensive explanation of how the land was allocated to them. A somewhat abbreviated narrative follows regarding the allotment of territory to the other seven tribes (18:1–19:48).

The picture of the complete conquest is clouded by repeated notations that Israel was not able to drive out several Canaanite peoples: the Geshurites and Maacathites (13:13), the Jebusites (15:63), the Canaanites (16:10; 17:12-13). Actually, the picture of Israel in Canaan is a picture of a people intermixed with other peoples. But Israel did not live among the Canaanites in an atmosphere of mutual respect. Because of the Israelite ideology and their identity constructed on the basis of a religious exclusivism, the other inhabitants of the land had to be seen as undesirables.

The land distribution concludes with Joshua receiving his land from the Israelites. It is only after all the other tribes have been allocated their lands that Joshua asked for his share. Like Caleb, Joshua received a specific town, Timnath-serah in the hill country of Ephraim (19:49-51). What is significant in Joshua's case is that there was nothing special about the land he was given. He even took the responsibility to rebuild the city for himself. He did not really ask for special treatment and did not take a part of the best land. Joshua's humility is striking.

The church could use the example of Joshua to critique the way land is distributed in southern Africa (and especially in Zimbabwe) where the political leaders get most of the land.

In the book of Joshua the tribes were allotted land in an orderly fashion. The function of the lot was to bring about order and a semblance of equity. Although the tribes could question the amount of land, this did not lead to civil or intertribal wars.

The narratives about land distribution conclude with a section on the establishment of the cities of refuge (20:1-9) and Levitical cities (21:1-42). The Levitical cities were scattered all over the tribal territories. The Levites served as a unifying factor for the scattered Israelites. The allotments of cities of refuge and Levitical cities concluded with a general evaluation of

YHWH's role in the whole process of conquest and settlement. According to the author:

> Thus the LORD gave to Israel *all* the land that he swore to their ancestors that he would give them; and having taken possession of it, they settled there. And the LORD gave them rest on every side just as he had sworn to their ancestors; *not one of their enemies* had withstood them, for the LORD had given all their enemies into their hands. *Not one of all* the good promises that the LORD had made to the house of Israel had failed; *all* came to pass. (21:43-45)

The passage emphasizes the completeness of the conquest and settlement of Israel in Canaan. This contrasts sharply with the repeated mention that some (indeed, many) of the Canaanites were not driven out of the land. These verses serve the important purpose of emphasizing YHWH's faithfulness in fulfilling the promise of land made to the ancestors. This fulfillment is a marker of Israel's identity as a people who, unlike other nations, is YHWH's chosen people with a specific entitlement. Furthermore, Josh 21:43-45 conveys to future Israelites that the removal of Canaanites is also their responsibility. As do the rest of the narratives, these verses posit how Israel was to view and relate to the non-Israelites who lived among them. They were to be perpetual enemies.

Internal Diversity and Unity (Josh 22–24)

The conclusion of the book of Joshua focuses on the internal identity of Israel. The land distribution has been completed and now the Trans-Jordanian tribes (the Reubenites, the Gadites, and the half-tribe of Manasseh) must return east of the Jordan. The question was: Since these tribes were not properly speaking in Canaan, were they still part of YHWH's people? The question was first addressed when Joshua dismissed them with a blessing after commending them for having been committed to the military campaign west of the Jordan. Joshua emphasized the basic elements that would keep them united with the other Israelites settled in Canaan proper: observing what Moses commanded them, namely, to love YHWH faithfully (22:1-6).

When the Transjordanian tribes were about to leave Canaan proper, they also recognized the problem of their religious identity. They resolved it by building an altar near the Jordan on the western side of the river (22:10). Yet, this action was viewed as a threat by those settled in Canaan proper (designated as "the Israelites") who prepared for war against the trans-Jordanian tribes (always designated by their tribal names) (22:12). The Israelites first sent Phinehas the priest and some tribal representatives to confront the two and a half tribes. The two and a half tribes responded that they had not built an altar to offer sacrifices or to compete with the other tribes west of the Jordan. They claimed to have built it as a memorial out of fear of religious rejection by the tribes west of the Jordan, those in Canaan proper. They were afraid that the Jordan river would be taken as the boundary of the territory of YHWH's people. However, their identity was tied to the worship of YHWH, and their altar (a copy of the altar of YHWH) was to serve as evidence that they had a portion in YHWH. Their response satisfied the tribes west of the Jordan and a civil war was avoided (22:13-34)

Like Moses, Joshua gave final speeches to the Israelites that culminated with the making of a covenant—a renewal of Israel's commitment to YHWH (23:1–24:28). The first speech (23:1-16) focused on the exclusive identity of Israel. Joshua began with a brief historical narrative that went back to the call of Abraham and culminated with Israel in the land of Canaan, emphasizing YHWH's acts on behalf of Israel. These actions were evidence of Israel's special status before YHWH: "and you have seen all that the Lord your God has done to all these nations for your sake, for it is the Lord your God who has fought for you" (23:3). Joshua acknowledged that Canaanites remained in the land, but as usual he coupled this statement with the promise that YHWH would drive them out and Israel would possess all the land. God would give complete possession of the land of Canaan to Israel, but there was a condition regarding the way they should relate to the remaining Canaanites. Israelites should not mix with these Canaanites, because Canaanite religion was such a strong temptation for them (23:7-8). The Israelites were thus prohibited from having anything to do with Canaanite gods. They should neither mention the names of these gods, nor swear by them, nor serve them, nor bow to them. The Israelites should hold fast to YHWH, because "the LORD has driven out before you great and strong nations; and as for you, no one has been able to withstand you to this day" (23:9). This exaggerated presentation of the success of the Israelites in Canaan (compare with chs. 13–21) is meant to emphasize why Israel must be totally and univocally committed to YHWH, without whom no possession of the land would have been possible.

Thus, the Israelites were prohibited from intermarrying with the Canaanites by the threat that YHWH would not continue to rid them of the remaining Canaanites. Interaction with the Canaanites would lead to certain extinction for Israel: "until you perish from this good land that the Lord your God has given you" (23:13). The Canaanites were seen as a threat to the continual existence of Israel.

The final chapter in the book of Joshua (24), through its presentation of the renewal of the covenant, focuses on the identity of Israel. Once again Joshua began with a recapitulation of Israel's history, from Abraham to its present position in the land of Canaan (24:2-13), in order to demonstrate Israel's special status as compared with other nations. He emphasized that YHWH had made Israel what Israel was today: the Israelites were successful in their wars against the Canaanites because YHWH had handed the enemies over to them. Israel was indebted to YHWH because they occupied a land for which they had not labored, lived in and towns they had not built, and ate fruits from vineyards and olives they had not planted (24:13).

What YHWH had done on behalf of Israel called for a response, namely, reverence toward YHWH and service in sincerity and faithfulness. Just as Moses had invited the Israelites at Sinai to make a decision concerning exclusive service of YHWH, so Joshua asked the people to devote themselves exclusively to YHWH and reject other gods (24:14-15). Aware of what YHWH had done for them (24:17-18), the people expressed their eagerness to serve YHWH: "Far be it from us that we should forsake the LORD to serve other gods" (24:16). Joshua was not sure that they truly understood what commitment to YHWH entailed (24:19-20), but the people once again expressed their commitment to serve YHWH (24:21). Joshua then mades a covenant with them (24:22-27), and dismissed the people to their respective lands, separated by tribal geographical boundaries but united in the covenant with YHWH who had given the land to Israel.

CONCLUSION

The book of Joshua is one of the most troubling books in the Bible. It is concerned with the external and internal identity of Israel. The external identity of Israel is depicted in Josh 1–12 through the presentation of Israel's invasion of Canaan and the extermination of the original inhabitants of the land. The relationship of the people of God to the world is most disturb-

ing. With divine sanction, the Israelites exterminate the indigenous peoples of Canaan just to get their land. And when the *herem* ban is partially lifted, material goods such as gold, silver, bronze, and iron are deemed more precious than human life. Human beings are dispensable.

The picture of God in the book of Joshua is also disturbing. God is depicted as a partisan God who favors one nation, who takes what belongs to certain nations to give to another, and who demands the extermination of other peoples. This portrayal of God reflects the negative attitude of the people of God toward non-adherents to their particular religion.

The second half of the book, chs. 13–24, is more concerned with the internal identity of God's people. The narratives of the distribution of the land emphasize the unity of the covenant people and the lengths to which Israel is prepared to go to maintain internal unity. The narratives emphasize the essential elements for keeping Israel as one entity despite tribal and geographical boundaries. The purity of the Israelite religion requires not only separation from the external other but also rejection of internal corrupting elements. Commitment to YHWH and national unity despite the diversity within the people of God is a positive element, because it does not negate diversity within God's people. Yet this internal unity may still be a dangerous construction, because it is sealed by YHWH's gift to the people of God of a land taken away from other people.

The book of Joshua serves mainly as a warning against constructing a religious identity that is exclusive. To say the least, such an identity that has no room for tolerance may lead to discrimination and/or genocide.

BIBLIOGRAPHY

Boorer, Suzanne. *The Promise of Land as Oath: A Key to the Formation of the Pentateuch.* BZAW 205. Berlin: de Gruyter, 1992.

Chidester, David. *Savage Systems: Colonialism and Comparative Religion in Southern Africa.* Studies in Religion and Culture. Charlottesville Va.: University Press of Virginia, 1996.

Comaroff, Jean, and John Comaroff. *Christianity, Colonialism, and Consciousness in South Africa.* Vol. 1 of Of Revelation and Revolution. Chicago: University of Chicago Press, 1991.

Dube, Musa W. *Postcolonial Feminist Interpretation of the Bible.* St. Louis, Mo.: Chalice, 2000.

Kwok Pui-lan. *Discovering the Bible in the Non-Biblical World.* Bible and Liberation Series. Maryknoll, N.Y.: Orbis, 1995.

Lemche, Niels Peter. *The Canaanites and their Land: The Tradition of the Canaanites.* JSOT-Sup 110. Sheffield: JSOT Press, 1991.

Lind, Millard C. *Yahweh is a Warrior: The Theology of Warfare in Ancient Israel.* Foreword by David Noel Freedman. Introduction by John H. Yoder. A Christian Peace Shelf Selection. Scottdale, Pa.: Herald, 1980.

Miller, James Maxwell, and John H. Hayes. *A History of Ancient Israel and Judah.* Philadelphia: Westminster, 1986.

Niditch, Susan. *War in the Hebrew Bible: A Study in the Ethics of Violence.* New York: Oxford University Press, 1993.

Prior, Michael. *The Bible and Colonialism: A Moral Critique.* Biblical Seminar 48. Sheffield: Sheffield Academic, 1997.

Thompson, Thomas L. *The Origin Tradition of Ancient Israel. 1. The Literary Formation of Genesis and Exodus 1-23.* JSOTSup 55. Sheffield: JSOT Press, 1987.

JUDGES

Fidèle Ugira Kwasi

Université Chrétienne de Kinshasa, Democratic Republic of the Congo
Translated from French by Aline Patte

LIFE CONTEXT OF THE INTERPRETATION

At the beginning of the twenty-first century, Africans, especially Congolese, face an unprecedented crisis that affects their economy, their culture, and their identity. Since gaining independence in 1960, forty years of political and economic mismanagement has led to the neglect of basic individual and social needs. Thus, a crucial question for us is: Can we find a dependable model of management and leadership to help us recognize the actual needs of our people and to meet these needs?

Democracy and the free market economy are promoted as the panacea for the sound development of any nation. But are they appropriate for the Democratic Republic of the Congo (République Démocratique du Congo, RDC) and other African nations? If so, should democracy and the free market in RDC simply duplicate the form they have in other countries? Or should they take particular African characteristics so that Africans might be true participants in the global exchange promoted by the globalization of the free market economy? In order to be true participants, we Africans must convey to others our particular African perspectives on democracy and on exchange as the basis for community life and economy. But how can we convey our perspectives when we do not have the necessary means of mass communication? Finally, what is the place of religion in all this? Is there a particularly African expression of religion, which, if it were taken into account, would allow us Africans to rediscover our identity and to develop an ethic for our individual and community life?

This commentary seeks to address these questions from the perspective of protestant churches in RDC. As an expression of God's will, as Scripture, the book of Judges can be a basis for developing the ethic that we need to envision our lives as individuals and as a community. When looking through the lens of the book of Judges, we soon see that life in our society today is distorted beyond recognition by sin, and that efforts to find solutions to our social, economic, and cultural problems are characterized by self-serving attitudes rather than by a true quest for justice in line with the justice of Yahweh. The description of the frame of mind of people in the time of the judges readily applies to our present situation in the RDC: "In those days there was no king in Israel; all the people did what was right in their own eyes" (17:6; 18:1; 19:1; 21:25).

I first propose an overview of the book of Judges and of the meaning of the substantive, šapat, "judge," then I focus my comments on four features that are repeated with variations throughout the book. My comments will pay more attention to the contextual reading of these

Fidèle Ugira Kwasi, born in Democratic Republic of the Congo (RDC), received his doctorate in theology and Old Testament from the Faculté Universitaire de Théologie Protestante de Bruxelles. A professor of Old Testament and Christian Ethics, he has published several articles in the field of Christian ethics, is the co-author of *Prédication comme acte de libération* (Preaching as a Liberating Act, 1995), and is completing a book on *Les perspectives d'une pastorale d'éveil pour la Nation* (Prospects for a Pastoral Theology of Awakening for the Nation).

features, because the proclamation of God's Word always takes place in a specific context. I will suggest ways in which this text can be related to our present context in the RDC. Therefore, discussions of specific historical critical scholarship (Yee 1995) will not be taken up.

CONTEXTUAL COMMENT

An Overview of the Book of Judges

The book of Judges can be outlined as follows:

1:1–2:5: The first introduction is focused on the vicissitudes of the installation in Canaan. It seeks to answer the question: Why did God not drive out all the Canaanites from the land? Judges 2:1-5 answers: because Israel has not obeyed God's commands (2:2).

2:-6–3:6: The second introduction is more doctrinal. It is framed by a reminder of the faithfulness of the people of Israel in Joshua's time (2:6-9) and by an explanation for the fact that Philistines, Canaanites, and other peoples remained in the promised land (3:1-6). Its central part summarizes the theological lesson of the period of the judges: "Whenever the LORD raised up judges for them, the LORD was with the judge, and he delivered them from the hand of their enemies . . . But whenever the judge died, they would relapse and behave worse than their ancestors, following other gods . . . So the anger of the LORD was kindled against Israel" (2:18-20). The purpose of God's preservation of the people of the land is "to test Israel, whether or not they would take care to walk in the way of the LORD as their ancestors did." (2:22).

3:7–16:31: The central part of the book presents the stories of the twelve judges of Israel following the above pattern—a four "R's" cycle proposed by Arnold: rebellion, ruin, repentance, rest (1995, 77). This cycle is particularly clear in the cases of the six major judges: Othniel, Ehud, Deborah, Gideon, Jephthah, and Samson). Yet this cycle progressively disintegrates. The repeated religious and moral relapses throughout the book of Judges convey to the readers a sense of ongoing moral deterioration throughout this period.

Two conclusions correspond to the two introductions:

17:1–18:31: The first conclusion tells of the establishment of a shrine for an idol and the worship of this idol under the leadership of a Levite, first in the hill country of Ephraim then at Dan (see the corresponding condemnation of worship of idols in the second introduction, 2:6–3:6).

19:1–21:25: The second conclusion tells the story of the crime of the people of Gibeah (the rape of the concubine of a Levite), and the war against the Benjaminites who had refused to punish the guilty.

My comments are limited to the second introduction and to the main body of the book of Judges, because they are most directly linked to our context in the RDC.

Who Are the "Judges"?

The verbal root, *šapat,* ordinarily means to judge, to decide, to dispense justice, to do what is right, to condemn, to punish. Yet its basic meaning is "to put right a problematic situation," because to exercise justice means to remedy violated rights, for instance, to give freedom to the oppressed (Cazelles 1973, 266; Vernard 1970, 4-5).

With this general observation in mind, we can recognize how the book as a narrative defines the character "judges." First, we can note that the book title, "Judges," refers to the men and women called by YHWH to save Israel from a situation of distress during the period from Joshua's death (2:16-19) until the time of Samuel, the last judge (1 Samuel). This particular title emphasizes that Israel's salvation is initiated by God: "Then the LORD raised up judges, who delivered them out of the power of those who plundered them" (Judg 2:16). Israel, as the beneficiary of God's grace, was called first to give thanks to God and then to participate in the realization of the mission God entrusted to her.

Šapat also means to judge in the sense of exercising a judiciary power and of governing (4:4; 10:2, 3; 11:27; 12:7-14; 15:20; 16:31). This connotation has important implications for sub-Sahara Africa in general and for the RDC in particular. The main question is whether or not Africa is really "governed." One can doubt it when one considers how far behind our countries are in economic and technological development, how large is the indebtedness of our countries even though there are very few signs of the envisioned development for which money was borrowed, and how extensive and cruel is the poverty among the working classes both in rural and urban areas. There are, of course, leaders who busily speak and act in the name of the people. But in many cases it is difficult to say whether they govern and serve the people or are primarily concerned to amass colossal fortunes for themselves. Are not European, North and South American, and Asiatic bankers surprised by the extravagant deposits that these "leaders of the people" make in their foreign bank accounts?

If "to govern" also means "to manage," it follows that there are laws that apply to all. But what is happening? The very persons who elaborate and promulgate these laws do not abide by them. Accordingly, they are above the laws, and thus "outlaws." For them, "to govern" means to have power and to hold on to this power. But when governing means holding on to power at all costs, development and change cannot be contemplated, let alone implemented. Then it is inconceivable to govern in the sense of "judging" that is, of "putting right a problematic situation," and of exercising justice by remedying violated rights, and bringing freedom to the oppressed. Are we not in a situation where the Lord should raise up judges, who will deliver the impoverished people of the RDC from those who plunder them (see 2:16)?

The designation, "judges," raises also the problem of titles that people attribute to themselves. Bypassing the usual principles of promotion in the army, a corporal who becomes a leader in one specific situation attributes to himself the rank of general. Similarly, both in African Initiated Churches and missionary-originated churches, leaders proclaim themselves Bishop, Archbishop, Monsignor, Patriarch, etc., without taking into account either the ecclesiastical traditions or the responsibilities that these titles entail.

By contrast, according to Vincent (1958, 10), the designations "judges," "saviors" or "judges-deliverers" are not honorary titles. Rather these terms describe the service to which they were called by God. Judges are people chosen by God who receive a special charisma: "the spirit of the LORD took possession of" them (6:34, about Gideon; see also 3:10, about Othniel; 11:29, about Jephthah; 13:25; 14:6, 19; and 15:14, about Samson). Their role is to reestablish the rights of YHWH in a situation compromised by unfaithful people. Through their charismatic authority, they lead their tribe into battle and to victory—sometimes only their clan and rarely a group of tribes, except in the cases of Gideon and of Deborah and Barak. Thus, the judges are "deliverers" called forth by YHWH in a difficult period of Israel's history. Following this success, they do not "hold on to power" and rule over all Israel. Their mission is simply to reestablish and maintain Israel's faithfulness to YHWH, to build up the nation of Israel, and to bring about the victory of YHWH over Baal. In sum, the judges are people who have been chosen by God for a mission of salvation, not to grasp and abuse power.

Throughout the book of Judges one finds the repetition of a cycle going from moral and religious degradation, to divine punishment, to repentance (crying out to God), and to God sending a judge to deliver the Israelites from their oppressors. My contextual comments are therefore focused on statements that represent each step of the cycle:

1) "The Israelites did what was evil in the sight of the LORD . . . " (2:11; 3:7, 12; 4:1; 6:1; 10:6; 13:1);
2) "They abandoned the LORD, and worshiped Baal and the Astartes" (2:13; also 2:11, 19; 3:6-7; 10:6, 10, 13);
3) "So the anger of the LORD was kindled against Israel, and he gave them over to plunderers who plundered them, and he sold them into the power of their enemies all around" (2:14 and 15; also 3:8; 4:2, 9; 6:1; 10:7; 13:1);
4) "But when the Israelites cried out to the LORD, the LORD raised up a deliverer [or judge] for the Israelites" (3:9, 15; 6:6, 7; 10:10, 12); and the enemy "was subdued that day under the hand of Israel" (3:30; 4:23; 8:28; 11:33).

"The Israelites Did What Was Evil in the Sight of the Lord . . . "

"The Israelites did what was evil in the sight of the LORD": such a statement (2:11; 3:7, 12; 4:1; 6:1; 10:6; 13:1) refers to the moral and religious deterioration that characterizes the first step of the narrative cycles that reoccur in the book of Judges. From the outset, it signals that any quest for justice and peace in economic and social development is doomed to failure as long as the nation does not conform to God's will, which is the indispensable basis for individual and community morality. The description of the moral crisis and its consequences for a developing nation, Israel, in the time of the judges is quite instructive for African nations that are presently going through similar crisis. The people of Israel repeatedly failed to trust in God, to whom they owed their life as individuals and as a people, and rebelled against the One who sustained their life through a comforting presence and an eternal law. The vicissitudes of Abimelech's short-lived monarchy (9:1-57) and Samson's marriage with a Philistine woman (14:1-20) illustrate well the ethical decline of this period.

Abimelech did not have any charismatic or other qualities that could prompt people to follow him and to support his quest for power. What did he do? Underhandedly, he exploited kinship and tribal relationships to assert himself (9:2-3). He used the money "out of the temple of Baal-berith," money tainted by idolatry, to hire "worthless and reckless fellows" (9:4). With them, he committed a heinous crime: he killed seventy of his brothers (9:5). He had forgotten the implacable law (a part of the covenant with Noah) stating that "Whoever sheds the blood of a human, by a human shall that person's blood be shed" (Gen 9:6). Not only did Abimelech die in terrible conditions, but also in a shameful way: from a woman's hands (Judg 9:52-53). Therefore, he begged his armor-bearer, "Draw your sword and kill me, so people will not say about me, 'A woman killed him'" (9:54).

Samson's case is another example (14:1-20). In marrying a woman from the uncircumcised Philistines he transgressed his parents' teaching, failing to honor his father and mother (Exod 20:12). When "his father and mother" reminded him of their teaching, "Is there not a woman among your kin, or among all our people, that you must go to take a wife from the uncircumcised Philistines?" (Judg 14:3a-b), he rudely demanded of his father: "Get her for me, because she pleases me" (14:3c). When the noble ideal to obey God's word is absent, people driven by self-centered motivations enter a cycle of moral deterioration with far-reaching consequences. Nevertheless, unlike Abimelech, Samson did not deny his faith; he continued to pray to YHWH until the last trial of his life (16:28-31).

The last part of the book of Judges is punctuated by a refrain that summarizes what the author sees as the generalized moral deterioration of that period: "In those days there was no king in Israel; all the people did what was right in their own eyes" (or, as the French translations underscore, "each person acted as he or she pleased" i.e., according to what felt good to them; 17:6, 18:1; 19:1; 21:25). Each time it is repeated, this refrain introduces an outrageous set of events showing religious and moral degradation; then, even as people seek to redress some problematic situations, they engender worse situations that are presented as punishments from God.

In present-day Africa, "all the people act as they please" in their search for "justice" and "peace." Without any sense of direction and any grounding for understanding what justice and peace are, this quest readily brings about catastrophic situations, discouragement because no solution to these crises can be envisioned, and then desperate reactions that make these situations even worse. The book of Judges provides a sense of history in which God plays a role and provides stability and a sense of direction that is most needed in our context.

The book of Judges shows that the misfortunes and successes of Israel are correlated to periods characterized, respectively, by Israel's unfaithfulness and by God's gracious interventions. More specifically, periods of prosperity, as in the time of Joshua (2:7), are correlated to faithfulness to God and the covenant. By contrast, periods of misfortune (when Israel is confronted or oppressed by other peoples) are interpreted as resulting from not obeying God's covenantal commandments (2:2). In this way, the book of Judges calls us to reintegrate in today's theology a quest for the meaning of history, seeking to discern the significance of each event from the perspective of the covenant with God. This lesson is illustrated by the way the book of Judges interprets the significance of the presence of other peoples in the promised land: "They were for the testing of Israel, to know whether Israel would obey the commandments of the LORD, which he commanded their ancestors by Moses" (3:4). In this time of transition between Joshua (2:7) and the monarchy ("in those days there was no king in Israel"), Israel is on a quest for a sense of identity and a correlated sense of morality.

These features of the book of Judges are helpful for our contextual and hermeneutical reflections in this commentary, because Sub-Sahara African nations are in a similar kind of transition. The religious fervor of Africans, especially of Congolese, is well-known. They massively participate in the religious services of the Roman Catholic, Protestant, Kimbanguist, and Orthodox churches, as well as in the very popular gatherings of the powerful charismatic movement. Nevertheless, they have a deep feeling of hopelessness. They are distraught by the breakdown of all political, economic, and social infrastructures that deprives them of any opportunity to obtain the bare minimum they need to survive: food, clothing, housing, security, and the most rudimentary form of health care. In other words, they are in the first stage (concern for physiological needs) of the five-stage pyramid of human needs proposed by Abraham Maslow (Kanawaty 1996, 3-25). Deeply dissatisfied, they wonder if there is any hope of moving beyond this obsession with satisfying their own physiological needs and those of their dependents. Consequently, individuals, groups, and communities rationalize all kinds of evil or dubious deeds by claiming that they are justified because they must survive.

Since March 30, 1970, for instance, several churches established by the Protestant missions in the Belgian Congo since 1878 have gathered together to form the Church of Christ of Congo (Église du Christ au Congo, ECC). Yet, despite the massive and increasing poverty among the population, the ECC leaders have chosen not to publicly display their identity and their "protestant" ethics by intervening in public affairs, because of the constant threat of political balkanization. The church cannot take the risk of identifying with one or the other faction, can she? If this faction were to be defeated the church would be endangered. But by hiding her identity and her ethical commitments, is not the church compromising her prophetic mission? The ECC collaborates with the state to manage essential services: public schools, public health care, and many social and economic development projects. Remaining involved in all these important social services without speaking up against dubious practices in the name of the ethical teaching of the church is, in my opinion, quite problematic. The ECC cultivates an ominous ambiguity in the midst of the immense crisis that affects our nation. Instead of hiding our identity, it is crucial that the "Christian" option be made explicit in such a situation. We Africans seem to have lost all sense of direction and of identity, precisely because we have excluded God from any part of the decision-making in our society. We cannot possibly serve others and help our nation, whose sovereignty is constantly undermined by people who "act as they please," by exclusively thinking about our own selfish interests rather than the needs of the community and of those around us.

"They Abandoned the LORD, and Worshiped Baal and the Astartes"

"They abandoned the LORD, and worshiped Baal and the Astartes": this statement in 2:13 is repeated in different forms in 2:11, 19; 3:6-7; 10:6, 10, 13, and in numerous passages about following or worshiping other gods. It first appears in the second introduction of Judges, 2:6–3:6, and at the beginning of its central part, 3:7–16:31, as an expression of the main reason for Israel's decline: the rejection of God as the supreme authority. For Israel in the time of Joshua, true worship is not the worship of a generic "God"—it is not the worship of "Elohim"—but the worship and service of YHWH, that is, of the One who powerfully intervened in their lives (2:7). The worship and service of YHWH is a response to his interventions. If one does not know YHWH's works, one does not know YHWH; then one cannot worship YHWH and ends up worshiping other gods (2:10-11). The great work of YHWH for Israel is, here as well as throughout the Hebrew Bible, that YHWH "had brought them out of the land of Egypt" (2:12).

Regarding the issue of faith or faithfulness toward God, it is important to remember with Oyen (1974, 17), that reflections on God, on God's nature, and on the existential problems of life with God are not central issues in the Hebrew Bible. There is no enigma or mystery to be accepted by or through faith. Rather the people's relationship to God is pri-marily a matter of concrete interaction between God and God's people, which is for Israel a call to obedience and sanctification. It is a matter of remembering the works of YHWH for Israel. As Oyen emphasizes:

The substance of faith is its "ethical" aspect. The very concept of election conveys that Israel has been called to obedience: Israel must sanctify the God who is holy, by doing God's will on earth, by making God's glory shine, by walking in the light of life while remaining in God's light and being faithful to God. Worship is living with God, and as such it is above all *abhoda,* service. This means . . . becoming aware of the Presence of a God who is with us. As a tree is recognized by its fruits, so the level of a people's faithfulness is recognized by its politics. Participating in political coalitions or alliances with the dominant powers of the time was a sign that Israel's awareness of the recent past, marked by YHWH's powerful interventions, was fading away and therefore did not provide the ethical framework that governed Israel's life. This fading awareness of God's role in their life by a "generatio . . . who did not know the LORD or the work that he had done for Israel" (2:10) was the basic reason for the moral deterioration pictured in 2:11–3:6.

The deep immorality that Israel exhibits is directly linked to their rejection of YHWH demonstrated by their worship of other gods (2:11). The phrase "doing what was evil in the sight of the LORD" is found at least sixteen times in the book of Judges: 2:11, 15; 3:7, 12; 4:1; 6:1; 9:23, 56, 57; 10:6; 11:27; 13:1; 15:3; 20:3, 12, 13, 34, 41. This evil is directly or indirectly related to worshiping "the Baals." While Baal is a designation of the Canaanite storm god, more generally it simply means Lord. Worshiping Baal is being confused about who is LORD.

We now understand that there are different sociological models in constructing the origins of the Israelites. The main trend in scholarship is to see the people of Israel as emerging from the indigenous Canaanites. The culture and religion of the Baals and Astartes are part of the makeup and milieu of Israel. (Gottwald 1999 and Gottwald and Horsley 1993). Since harvest is not possible without rain, a drought engenders the tragedy of famine. How to have the assurance that rain will fall? As Briend says,

They [the Canaanites] turn towards the gods and in particular towards Baal, the great storm god, who is also the fertility god. In order for rain to fall in due course, Baal must show favor to human beings; therefore, they must gain his goodwill in the hope that he will be victorious in his fights against the forces of death; the coming of fertilizing rain is a sign of this victory. (1970, 7)

For the people, rain is a life and death matter: "To whom should Israel turn in order to benefit from this rain? To Yahweh or to Baal? It was a difficult choice. Was not Yahweh the God of the desert? Is Yahweh really the master of the rain and seasons?" (Briend 1970, 6). The book of Judges shows that the Israelites answered this question by opting to remain with their worship of Baal while pledging allegiance toYahweh (2:11; 3:7; 10:6). Besides Baal, Judges also mentions "the Astartes" (2:13; 10:6), the goddess of fecundity and love. Astarte was broadly worshiped in the Ancient Near East: women were to pay homage to her in order to be assured of giving birth to many children.

Abandoning YHWH, "the God of their ancestors, who had brought them out of the land of Egypt" and following "other gods, from among the gods of the peoples who were all around them" (2:12) certainly was, from the point of view of the Israelites, a matter of survival. But following these other gods and being at their service in the hope of gaining their favor as a matter of survival is quite different from serving YHWH, who has given life and a national identity to Israel by bringing them out of the land of Egypt.

The contextual question for us in African countries is: In our desperate situation, should we follow those who blindly and haphazardly search for any means of survival by going in all kinds of direction at once—following all kinds of "Baals" and "Astartes"? Or should we avoid this panic-driven attitude? Should we not remember "the Lord, the God of [our] ancestors, who had brought [us] out of the land of Egypt"— when we think of the colonial bondage as our land of Egypt? The Israelites of the period of the judges failed this test. Will we?

Our situation is similar to that of Israel during the period of the judges. The mismanagement of the four first decades of independence have resulted in a chaotic situation that could accredit the colonialist thesis that Africans are totally incapable of governing themselves because, accordingly, they have neither a past nor a civilization that could ground their nations. Without an anchor in our history and civilization, we seem to be engaged in a frantic race for development (are we not a developing country?) without any sense of direction, because we do not remember where we come from. Indeed, what is development without a culture? Without reference points, such as "the God of our ancestors"? Without landmarks, such as being brought out of the land of Egypt? Struggling for survival through economic, social, and political development is necessary. But doing so without direction is counterproductive, preventing any possibility of providing the basic necessities of life for most, as we can plainly see today.

M. Frederico Mayor, former general director of UNESCO (United Nations Educational, Scientific, and Cultural Organization), has shown that there will be no real and lasting progress without an ethic of development for framing international relations, the establishment of peace and security, and the protection of the environment. The formulation of such an ethic is necessary, he notes, to govern "international relations so that freedom, including the freedom of exchange of goods and capitals, that has demonstrated its efficiency, will not be synonymous with a cynical 'free for all' or 'every one for oneself.'" He continues:

It should not be shaped by the law of the mighty, but should weave together concerns for justice, human rights, equal opportunities, and, do we dare say it, a sense of kinship among all. If, and only if, these conditions are met, the road towards democracy will not stumble upon stagnation, indeed upon a worsening of the economic situation that would pave the way of a resurgence of totalitarism." (Mayor 1991, 8)

Therefore, for Mayor, it is essential to give priority to the development of education, science, and culture, because they have a key role in the realization of a promising future.

Similarly, Max Cerrans emphasizes the close relationship between development and culture. Actually, he notes the primacy of culture over the economy. Without culture, in the broad sense of the term, there is no development. But a culture cannot be pulled out of thin air:

> Soul of a nation, it [the culture] cannot be separated from the life of individuals and peoples. But it is as vulnerable as a baby bird; it is at the mercy of voracious predators such as alienation, fashion, will to power, economic ambitions. Thus, in order to give to culture the space it needs to flourish, people must carefully nurture it and protect it from a multitude of enemies. (Cerrans 1991, 7)

Following the dreadful and deadly slave trade between the fifteenth and nineteenth centuries, and following centuries of colonization that has destroyed most life-structures, Africans are today deprived of resources. They did not benefit from their significant contributions in the struggle against totalitarianism during the two World Wars and then against communism between 1945 and 1989. Gaining political independence did not result in much progress. Indeed, it engendered much unnecessary violence, as was the case in the conflicts with Great Britain in South Africa, with France in Algeria, and with Portugal in Angola, without speaking of the civil wars in our countries. We can anticipate similarly disappointing and even tragic results for our current willy-nilly participation in the ongoing process of globalization. All these struggles were and still are driven by an idealized quest for freedom, for serving others, and

for peace. Yet these efforts were to no avail, because they were framed neither by our cultures, nor by an affirmation of "the God of [our] ancestors," nor by an acknowledgment of God's role in our history. What would the value of a world order be if it is not warranted by YHWH?

This suggestion is apparently anachronistic. Yet it also seemed so to the people of Israel in the generations after Joshua. Indeed, what people can claim to have gained independence without some kind of support from YHWH, even if this independence is quite precarious, as was the case for Israel? As Israel learned from the judges, not being grateful to YHWH for one's existence as a people is nothing less than a sin and can lead only to further moral, economic, and social deterioration.

"Following other gods" (2:12, 19) is also a violation of the covenant on Sinai (Exod 20:3), as the verb "hâlak" suggests. As a consequence of their "bowing down" to these other gods (Judg 2:12, 17, 19; see Exod 3:12), the Israelites "provoked the LORD to anger" (Judg 2:12), or "kindled the anger of the LORD" (2:14, 20; 3:8; 10:7).

Even though this theme is found only in two of the six cycles concerning major judges—the cycles of Othniel, 3:7-11, and Jephthah, 10:6–12:7—the fact that the author of Judges uses these verbs several times in a few verses to describe Israel's unfaithfulness demonstrates how seriously the author viewed this sin of abandoning the worship of YHWH to worship other gods. Through differences in wording and through the sheer weight they acquire, these repeated statements change in meaning (Arnold 1995, 81). Thus, in 2:11-13, we first find a reference to moving away from God (2:11a), then to following idols (2:11b); then we come back to the theme of abandoning God, now in a more developed way (2:12a); followed by a new reference to following idols (2:12b). Finally in 2:13 both themes are summarized once again: "They abandoned the LORD, and worshiped Baal and the Astartes" (2:13).

Yet, even more significant for the author is the condemnation of the Israelites because they "did what was evil in the sight of God," whatever this evil might be (3:7, 12; 4:1; 6:1; 10:6; 13:6), and as a consequence "the LORD gave them (or sold them) into the hand of" their enemies (3:8, 12-13; 4:2; 6:1; 10:8-9; 13:6). These features are found in each of the cycles.

"He Gave them / Sold them over/ to Plunderers"

This third feature is first summarized in the doctrinal introduction: "So the anger of the Lord was kindled against Israel, and he gave them over to plunderers who plundered them, and he sold them into the power of their enemies all around, so that they could no longer withstand their enemies" (2:14).

This verse spells out the harsh punishment that YHWH inflicted upon Israel for their rejection, whether by worshiping other gods or more generally by doing "what was evil in the sight of God." The intensity of YHWH's anger against the people that YHWH had brought out of Egypt to Canaan is expressed by the verb *harah,* translated "to kindle" (2:14, 20; 3:8; 6:39; 10:7). Yet, as the cycles (rejection of YHWH, punishment, crying to YHWH, and YHWH sending judges) show, YHWH does not cease to love Israel. This punishment is designed to bring Israel back to YHWH, who was the God of their ancestors and also their own God. The consequence of rejecting YHWH is that Israel becomes unable to resist their enemies: "the LORD sold them into the hand of" their enemies (3:8, 12-13; 4:2; 6:1; 10:8-9; 13:6) who are presented as "plunderers" in 2:14. They have abandoned YHWH; now it is Israel's turn to be "abandoned." Then they cannot resist their enemies.

In the RDC and other African nations, abandoning God by excluding God from decision-making is a common practice. People dream of a new Eldorado, be it located in Europe, America, or Asia; individual and national decisions are made from this perspective. For instance, each year many Africans mortgage their lives in trying to migrate illegally to Europe through the Strait of Gibraltar or to America by boarding

ships moored on their shores. From the perspective of Judges read as normative Scripture, certain Christian Congolese conclude that these illegal emigrants abandon God and that in turn God abandons them into the hands of plunderers. Who knows the number of those who die in these illegal migrations? Of stowaways who have been thrown overboard by sailors? And who knows the number of those who have arrived on other shores to be entrapped by exploitation in these new countries, and have turned to the illusory refuge of alcohol or drugs? Here in Africa, because people allow the vision of this new Eldorado to govern their decision-making instead of God, the result is disastrous: rampant injustice, war, social disintegration, political, economic, and cultural violence, and insecurity. "The LORD gave them over to plunderers" (2:14). Thus, the "kadogo"—children soldiers of the RDC, of Angola, of Mozambique, of Liberia, of Sierra Leone, of Somalia—are vagabonds in the streets of our cities who disturb, aggress, or assault many unfortunate passersby. Political promises are not kept. Social systems are nearly or completely collapsed. Rebellions are launched, and who knows when they will end. God has been excluded from decision-making, and now people cannot resist their enemies. Judges raises for us a question that needs to be pondered: What does it mean to include God in one's decision-making? The different books of the Bible propose several models, in addition to the one suggested by Judges. So the question remains open.

The Israelites Cried Out To the Lord; the Lord Raised Up a Deliverer; Their Enemies Were Subdued; the Land Had Rest

The two-stage statement, "when the Israelites cried out to the LORD, the LORD raised up a deliverer for the Israelites" (3:9) concerning Othniel, is repeated with little variation in 3:15 concerning Ehud. Yet, the pattern progressively falls apart in the following cycles. The first part of the statement occurs in 4:3 and is simply followed by the mention that "at that time Deborah, a prophetess, wife of Lappidoth, was judging Israel" (4:4), then by the story of Deborah and Barak defeating Sisera, the Canaanite general who ultimately died at the hand of another woman, Jael (4:5-24). This victory is celebrated by the song of Deborah (5:1-31). In 6:6-7, we twice find the first part of the statement, "the Israelites cried out to the LORD," but YHWH's initial response is to send a prophet who calls the people to repentance (6:8-10). Nevertheless, God appoints Gideon as deliverer without waiting for Israel's repentance. In 10:10-16, when the Israelites cry out, they also confess their sins, then put away the idols and "worshiped the LORD, and he could no longer bear to see Israel suffer" (10:16); then in a tortuous way, Jephthah, the son of a prostitute, delivers Israel (10:17–12:7). Finally, in the case of Samson (13:1–16:31), the pattern unravels completely: there is no mention of the Israelites crying to YHWH, and Samson, who was a judge for twenty years (15:20; 16:31), is himself morally depraved—breaking his Nazirite vows and having intercourse with non-Israelite women.

Those who passively read the Bible expecting to find in it ready-made models to imitate will be disappointed. The colorful characters presented in this book have in several cases dubious moral lives. Yet they are "judges" who right the wrongs suffered by oppressed people, sometimes resembling figures such as Zorro or Robin Hood, heroes of the oppressed poor (see Venard 1970, 4–5). But there are also among them more subdued characters who bring about justice in a more peaceful manner. Are we not told that Deborah "used to sit under the palm . . . and the Israelites came up to her for judgment" (4:5), in this case settling their litigations? Yet, this courtroom-like activity must be understood in the broader sense of "judging" in the sense of "delivering" Israel from those who oppressed or plundered them, as is repeatedly emphasized in 2:16, 18; 6:9; 8:34; 9:17.

The individual stories of the judges are very different from each other. But in each case, the Spirit of YHWH empowers them or YHWH raises someone known for some kind of weakness. Othniel was "Caleb's younger brother" (3:9-10). Ehud is ironically described as a "left-handed Benjaminite" (Benjamin means "son of the right hand"!) (3:15). Deborah was a woman, who at first believed she needed the help of a man, Barak, and who is presented as "a prophetess" (4:4) who sends the Israelite army into battle by her prophetic proclamation (4:14). Gideon, from the weakest clan and the least in his family (6:15), is presented as a very reluctant judge who again and again requires signs that YHWH will intervene (6:1–8:31). Jephthah was the son of a prostitute, ostracized by his family and associated with outlaws (11:1-3). And, as mentioned above, Samson (13:1–16:31) is presented as a most unlikely judge because of his very dubious morality. Yet each is somehow "raised up" and empowered by YHWH as a deliverer. This empowerment is often expressed as a possession by the Spirit, making clear that the deliverance is a gracious gift from God, a manifestation of God's presence in the life of Israel (3:10; 4:10; 6:34; 13:25; 14:6, 19; 15:14, 16) (see Kwasi Ugira (1999, 134-35). The gift of the Spirit or a word from the LORD (e.g., 6:11-16, 25-26) is each time a call to a specific vocation to accomplish a precise task, in time and space.

Phrases referring to the way the enemy "was subdued [or humiliated] that day under the hand of Israel" (3:30; 4:23; 8:28; 11:33) underscore how the grace of YHWH is manifested toward the (repentant) people. The Israelites, who were totally unable to resist the enemies used by YHWH for their punishment, are now empowered to subdue them. Then peace reigns in the country as a divine blessing: "So the land had rest forty years" (3:11, 30 [here eighty years]; 5:31; 8:28), although in the case of Jephthah (12:7) and Samson (16:31), the author cannot say that there was peace for Israel.

CONCLUSION

The book of Judges has much to teach to us in sub-Sahara Africa regarding how to emerge from four decades of chaotic political and economic transition, and this without paying further the high price Israel paid for having rejected YHWH. Indeed, YHWH is the only and true signpost pointing to a new social, economic, political, and cultural community order. As the *Traduction Oecuménique de la Bible (TOB)* points out in its notes (1975, 455-56), we should not forget that the book of Judges is first of all a work that originates and reflects Israel's faith. In the Song of Deborah (Judg 5, one of the oldest texts of the Hebrew Bible), Israel's faith is already characterized by the conviction that "the God of Israel is the one who sustains God's people during the most difficult times" (TOB 455). Strikingly and most realistically, the book of Judges does not hide Israel's or the judges' weaknesses. On the contrary, it emphasizes them, so as to make even clearer the patience of God, who untiringly sends leaders to deliver the tribes from oppression. The *TOB* continues:

> Of course, the heroes of the book of Judges belong to a time marked by harsh ways of life and views of morality that are quite different from ours. The subterfuge of Ehud, the murder of Sisera by Jael, the sacrifice of Jephthah's daughter, the love affairs of Samson might shock us, but, through these narratives that do not seek to cover up the actual reality of life, one should learn to discover how God intervenes to guide a people by giving them leaders empowered by the Spirit (3:10; 6:34; 11:29; 13:25; 14:6, 19; 15:14). (*TOB* 455-56)

Thus, this book invites us, in Africa, to look again at the long period of transition that we are in. We can recognize that, in our desperate struggle for survival we have adopted attitudes in which YHWH is not the ultimate reference point; therefore divine punishment is to be expected. It becomes apparent from what precedes that a nation is not primarily founded on a will to power, although power is a valuable tool for the service and well-being of others. Rather, different clans, tribes, and peoples are gathered together into a nation in three ways: (1) by referring to the same God, as the Israelite tribes did through their shared faith in the God of Abraham, Isaac, and Jacob; (2) by remembering their shared experience, a remembrance that constitutes a national culture, as the Israelites remembered that they came out of Egypt; and (3) by recognizing that they need to help each other in order to survive.

Africans must transform their current denial of their identity and of their religious experience into a constructive use of these as the foundation of their emerging nations. Yet a basic question remains: What does it mean for us, in our concrete situations, to remain faithful to YHWH? What does it mean not to bow down in the presence of the gods of neighboring peoples? Is it not what happens through political and diplomatic efforts in interior and international affairs?

Indeed, often people assume political positions, but they fail to serve the nation and its population, even as they enrich themselves. Thus, for most people, the word "politics" has become synonymous with "lie," a sign of cynicism and of alarming ethical emptiness. Thus, Africans have progressively lost any sense of community identity and its ideals of service and responsibility toward others. In this way, four decades of mismanagement reflect and engender this double emptiness that results in the tragic pauperization of the large majority of the population, including farmers in the villages and workers in the cities.

In a country such as the Democratic Republic of Congo (RDC) where, according to governmental statistics, at least 80 percent of the population identify themselves as Christians (Roman Catholic 50 percent, Protestant 20 percent, and Kimbanguist 10 percent), and in a culture where the resonance between the African traditional cultures and the Hebrew Bible are numerous (see also in this volume the commentary on 1 and 2 Samuel by Gerald West), it is appropriate to emphasize that faith in YHWH is the only way to overcome our loss of community identity and of ethical grounding. By rediscovering their fundamental relationship with YHWH, Congolese people could rediscover their deep relationship with each other in a community and a nation. It is therefore urgent to support current efforts in that direction, even if they are modest, and maybe to discover in these efforts "how God intervenes to guide a people by giving them leaders empowered by the Spirit" (*TOB*, 455-56),

From this perspective, it is also urgent to reformulate theological education in Africa so that theology and biblical studies be fully contextualized, taking into account the given social contexts and the economic needs of the people in this context. It is a matter of integrating in our daily experience both theological reflection and the study of the Bible in order to glorify YHWH, the living God who is manifested in our experience.

In the present struggle of our society to survive, Congolese people need to anchor their lives in a "law." But rather than adopting the law of the globalization process, they should turn to Scripture and to the book of Judges. Yet, in this book, they should not expect to find ready-made models that they can passively adopt and emulate in their lives. This point is true also of the other books of Scripture, and in the case of the model judge, Jesus Christ. Rather this book and the rest of Scripture accompany us through our lives, constantly calling us to repent and to rediscover the presence of God at work among us in deliverers whom God sends to us and the empowerment we receive from God to walk together toward a time of justice and peace "so the land [might have] rest [many] years" in Africa (3:11, 30; 5:31; 8:28).

BIBLIOGRAPHY

Concordance de la Traduction Œcuménique de la Bible TOB. Paris: Cerf; Villiers-le-Bel: Société biblique française, 1993.

Arnold, D. *Ces mystérieux héros de la foi. Une approche globale des Juges.* Saint-Légier, France: Emmaüs, 1995.

Briend, Jacques. «La fascination des Baals. » *Journal de la vie. La Bible aujourd'hui. Commentaire biblique* 45 (1970): 3-15.

Cazelles, Henri. *Introduction à la Bible. Edition nouvelle. T.II. Introduction critique à l'Ancien Testament.* Paris: Desclée et Cie, 1973.

Cerrans, Max. «Développement: et la culture dans tout ça?» *Sources UNESCO* 25 (1991).

Gottwald, Norman K *The Tribes of Yahweh: A Sociology of the Religion of Liberated Israel, 1250-1050 B.C.E.*. Sheffield: Sheffield, 1999.

Gottwald, Norman K and Richard A. Horsley, ed.. *The Bible and Liberation: Political and Social Hermeneutics,* Maryknoll, N.Y.: Orbis Books, 1993.

Kanawaty, George, ed. *Introduction à l'étude du travail.* 3rd ed. Geneva: International Labour Office, 1996.

Kwasi Ugira, F. «Esprit et mission dans la perspective sapientiale.» *Revue Congolaise de Théologie Protestante* 13 (1999): 124-142.

Mayor, M. Frederico. «Vivre libre, vivre mieux. » *Sources UNESCO* 30 (1991).

Oyen, Hendrik Van. *Ethique de l'Ancien Testament.* Trans. Etienne de Peyer. Nouvelle série théologique 29. Geneva: Labor et Fides, 1974.

Rad, Gerhard von. *Théologie de l'Ancien Testament. T.I. Théologie des traditions historiques d'Israël,* 3rd ed. Trans. Etienne de Peyer. Geneva: Labor et Fides, 1971.

Traduction Œcuménique de la Bible. Ancien Testament. Paris: Cerf, 1975.

Venard, J. «Juges ou sauveurs.» *Journal de la vie. La Bible aujourd'hui. Commentaire biblique* 44 (1970): 2-11.

Vincent, Albert, trans. *Le livre des Juges; Le livre de Ruth.* 2nd ed. Paris: Cerf, 1958.

Yee, Gale A., *Judges and Method: New Approaches in Biblical Studies.* Minneapolis : Fortress, 1995.

RUTH

Madipoane Masenya (ngwana' Mphahlele)

School of Theology and Biblical Religions, University of South Africa-UNISA

Pretoria, South Africa

LIFE CONTEXT OF THE INTERPRETATION

The book of Ruth is interpreted in the present commentary in an African-South African Christian context. The adjective "African" in the phrase "African-South African" refers to the indigenous peoples of South Africa. Though its meaning is contested by some in South Africa today, with many now claiming Africanness, we use this term to identify the context of those South African peoples who have always been known as Africans, such as Sothos, Ndebeless, and Xhosas.

In this context, the Christian Bible, despite its unfortunate colonial and missionary history (see West on 1 and 2 Samuel and Dora Mbuwayesango on Joshua in this volume), still plays an important role as a spiritual resource in people's lives. As a Northern Sotho Christian, I cannot claim to speak for all Christians in South Africa. I will therefore read the book of Ruth informed by my Northern Sotho social location. However, due to many similarities between African-South Africans, my commentary will make sense to many Bible readers in this context.

My location as a woman in this context will also influence my reading of the book of Ruth. I will employ the *bosadi* (womanhood) approach, which is cognizant of the unique context with its various oppressions that shape female African-South African Bible readers (Masenya, 2004). The context is Christian because I presuppose an audience of those African Christians who are motivated by their faith to regard the Bible as an important spiritual resource.

Life Context and Hermeneutical Issues

Challenges in the African-South African Christian Life Context

One of the challenges facing African peoples in post-apartheid South Africa is an identity crisis. A history that defined non-white peoples in terms of the hen "superior" race damaged Africans' self-identity. The hierarchical construction of people on the basis of race—white, colored, black, Indian—affected how the Bible was received by Africans. African women continue to experience these hierarchies daily as they grapple with a patriarchal culture. In this culture, the married adult male or female defines normative humanity; neither a woman nor a man can be regarded as fully human without a marriage partner. Marriage then becomes idolized and the received interpretations of the Bible reinforce this process. For women in my context, both African patriarchy and androcentric Bible interpretations remain serious challenges to their identity.

In addition, the South African masses face the challenge of survival amid adverse conditions of hunger, unemployment, and the AIDS epidemic, to name but three.

Madipoane Masenya (ngwana' Mphahlele) [child of Mphahlele] earned her PhD from the University of South Africa (UNISA). An associate professor of Old Testament, she is the author of *How Worthy is the Woman of Worth? Rereading Proverbs 31:10-31 in African-South Africa* (2004). She has also published articles on the Bosadi (Womanhood) reading of texts from the Hebrew Bible. She is an ordained minister in the International Assemblies of God Church (IAG) in South Africa.

Hermeneutical Issues Raised by this Life Context

This life-context raises for us the following hermeneutical questions:

1. If the church affirms that God is not partial and does not exclude any person, and that all humanity bears God's image, how can those with damaged identities be empowered to take their rightful place in God's divine scheme?

2. Given the patriarchal systems entrapping many Christian women and always connecting their identity with their marital status, which hermeneutics can affirm women who voluntarily choose to live outside the expected norms?

3. Can the people of God in present-day Africa, confronted with the desolation of poverty, disease, and too many premature deaths, confess a God who intervenes in human affairs? Can Christians still view themselves as agents of God's *hesed* (botho, loving-kindness, faithfulness) in this death-dealing context?

The Book of Ruth and Its Challenges

a) *Challenging an identity crisis:* The book of Ruth presents the story of a foreign widow who refused to succumb to the societal definitions of womanhood in her time. In our life-context, Ruth could serve as a model of a person who emerges as a winner, despite the many strikes against her.

b) *Challenging the idolization of marriage:* Though the book of Ruth gives readers the impression that a better life for women only takes place within marriage, by reading this book against the grain we will show that, although marriage is positive when it is not abusive, single people can still experience life in its fullness.

c) *Challenging our doubts about God's intervention in life:* Through the lives of Naomi and Ruth, readers see God intervening in a situation of lack (of food, life, etc.) to bring about plenty.

CONTEXTUAL COMMENT

An Overview of Ruth

This story is unique in the Hebrew Bible and in my own context because it portrays a strong bond between a widowed mother-in-law and her daughter-in-law. The commitment of a young woman to an old woman in a male-centered world continues to amaze modern readers of this story.

The narrator of the story situates its events during the time when the judges ruled in Israel, and there was a famine in the land (1:1). It should however be noted that, historically, no famines are associated with this period. Similarly, the virtues of kindness and care exemplified by the characters in this story are in a sharp contrast with the evil that typified the period of the judges in Israel (eg., the rapes of women, the hostility and the wars in Judges). However, the book of Ruth's present canonical position in the Christian Bible, following the Greek and Latin manuscripts, makes sense. It marks the transition between the time when the Israelites were ruled by the judges (the book of Judges) and the introduction of the monarchy (the books of 1 and 2 Samuel and 1 and 2 Kings)—hence the book of Ruth's happy ending with the birth of a son who becomes the great-grandfather of David.

This canonical location also makes sense to scholars for whom the story's purpose is the legitimation of the Davidic dynasty. From such a perspective this story is dated sometime in the preexilic period. Yet, on the basis of its archaic style, including Aramaisms, some commentators have dated the book of Ruth in postexilic times. Some have argued that, in this context, the foregrounding of a successful foreign woman in Israel was a protest against the policies of Ezra-Nehemiah regarding marriages with foreigners (Ezra 9–10; Neh 10:28-30; 13:3, 23-30). After presenting the different positions of scholars regarding the dating of the book of Ruth, Sasson argues: "It is clear that none of the approaches summarized above, taken either singly or in combination, could be expected to yield a convincing date in which *Ruth* was set in writing. For neither 'internal' (i.e., onomastic, anthropological, theological, linguistic) nor 'external' (i.e., historical, contextual, folklorist, genealogical) evidence is compelling enough to establish a credible period in which our scroll was either authored or committed to writing" (1989, 251). Nevertheless, the trend among recent scholars is to date the book in the pre-exilic period. Though they are not agreed on the date, there is a widespread understanding that its author comes from the royal court (Nielson 1997, 29). Arguments in favor of the conclusion that the book's purpose was the legitimation of the Davidic dynasty make sense. What would not make sense—and would have also hindered the scroll's acceptance in the canon—is a view of this book as a story exclusively concerning the commitment of a foreign Moabite widow to an old Israelite widow.

As it now stands, the story was basically meant to show the divine legitimation of the Davidic dynasty by revealing that YHWH, the God of Israel, can "make a way out of nowhere." However, while the Hebrew Bible's male narrators affirm women by using them to achieve males' ends, they do not care whether the means used to achieve those ends are conventional or not (consider Esther, Tamar, Rachael). Yet, we must hasten to say that due to the ambiguity of the language used by the narrator, it is difficult to argue with certainty whether what Ruth does with Boaz at the threshing floor (3:1-14) is problematic or not.

Irrespective of the difficulties related to the dating and purpose of this tale, in my view the narrator has succeeded in relating a story of courage and hope in the midst of desolation.

As a response to the situation of famine in Bethlehem, Elimelech, his wife Naomi, and their two sons set out for Moab (1:1-2), a country that historically did not fare well with Israel. After the death of Elimelech, the two sons marry Moabite women. They also die, leaving no sons (1:3-5).

Naomi learns that YHWH has provided food for the people back home and therefore decides to return (1:6). Knowing that wives' security lies with their husbands, Naomi is kind enough to allow her daughters-in-law to return to their mothers' houses, because their future with her would be insecure (1:8-14). Orpah heeds Naomi's advice, but Ruth does the unusual: she clings (davaq) to an old woman (1:14b).

In the traditional Northern Sotho context, Ruth's decision would make sense. In this culture, one's husband's death is not supposed to "release" the widow from the deceased family, because *lebitla ga le hlalwe* (the grave may not be divorced) or *lebitla la mosadi ke bogadi* (the grave of a married woman is at the husband's place). In fact, in this culture Naomi would not have advised her two daughters-in-law to return to their families. Orpah's action would therefore have been viewed with distaste.

Ruth silences her mother-in-law's objection by making an amazing commitment, which is often used in Christian circles for matrimonial ceremonies: "Where you go, I will go; where you lodge, I will lodge; your people shall be my people, and your God my God. Where you die, I will die—there will I be buried. May the LORD do thus and so to me, and more as well, if even death parts me from you!" (1:16-17)

On arrival in Bethlehem, Ruth takes the responsibility to support the family. She "happened" to glean in the field of Boaz (2:3), Naomi's next of kin. Through cooperation, the two widows defeat the temptation of low self-esteem and acquire for themselves two people important for their survival in that world: a husband and a son!

Overcoming an Identity Crisis

Most modern readers' descriptions of the biblical characters' actions are at odds with those that the original hearers or the characters would have proposed. By deciding to describe Ruth in this commentary as someone who challenged negative societal stereotypes, I do not claim that this was necessarily how Ruth viewed herself. As modern readers we bring our own concerns and perspectives to the story in an attempt to make sense out of it. Thus, my starting point is that—like many women in my context—Ruth had an identity crisis.

As a Moabite married to an Israelite man (1:4), Ruth was in a precarious situation due to the historical rivalry between the Israelites and the Moabites (as expressed by the story of the Moabites originating from an incestuous relationship between Lot and his daughters, Gen 19:37). Some commentators have attributed the calamity that befell Abimelech's family to God's punishment for his choice of Moab. Fewell and Gunn explain Naomi's hesitancy to return with Ruth on the basis of Naomi's embarrassment by the *Moabite* daughter-in-law (2000, 233-239).

As a woman in a world in which female security rested with men (fathers or husbands), Ruth was at a disadvantage. As a young widow whose husband had left no sons, her identity was challenged even more (1:5).

However, Ruth's boldness leads us to doubt that she simply accepted as her lot the several strikes put on her by society. Despite her precarious position, she does the extraordinary.

First, she dares to challenge the patriarchal status quo by clinging not to a man but to an old woman, who is a symbol of desolation and insecurity (Ruth1:16-17). By so doing, Ruth challenges daughters-in-law who always perceive their relationship with their mothers-in-law in a negative way to think otherwise. She challenges young widows who become totally helpless and hopeless after the death of their husbands to accept that after a period of mourning, life can and must continue. Ruth reminds women who believe that they can only achieve success in life if they are supported by men that even disempowered women can make things happen.

Furthermore, Ruth is bold enough to initiate a marriage with Boaz (3:9) by asking him to "spread his cloak over" her.

Her story reminds all of us, particularly the powerful, that God is not partial to any person. God uses whoever is available to achieve God's purposes. Therefore, what is important to God is not how we are defined on the basis of race or gender, but our availability as agents of God's transforming *hesed* in the lives of our neighbors. The Hebrew word *hesed*, variously translated as kindness, lovingkindness, faithfulness, or loyalty (1:8, 2:20, 3:10), used both about God and persons, is one of the key concepts in the book of Ruth. In it, God uses a non-Israelite woman from Moab to achieve God's plan for the world (4:13-22).

Overcoming the Idolization of Marriage

Naomi's exhortation to her daughters-in-law (1:11-13) reveals that marriage was a very important institution for (wo)men's lives in that world. Thus in 3:1-3, the women plan to get a marriage partner for the younger widow.

Based on her life experiences as a woman in Israel, Naomi knew that women, particularly younger ones, could not find security outside marriage. She therefore knew the importance attributed to males in that context. Her words of exhortation therefore revolve around husbands or sons.

Many modern women readers have found this tale unappealing, precisely because of the significant role played by men as providers of better lives for women. Readers are left with the impression that the importance of men in the story denies Naomi and Ruth their independence. Though certain commentators laud Ruth for her boldness and courage in a volatile situation, others regard her as an example of a woman who succeeds because she plays according to patriarchal rules. According to this latter interpretation, Ruth dares to visit a male sphere in the night searching for marriage. She ultimately wins a husband and fulfills tthe main expectation of a patriarchal marriage, bearing a son. In sum, the lesson is that Ruth the Moabite could only become acceptable by allowing herself to be assimilated according to the rules of Judahite patriarchy.

Such an interpretation raises a caution flag above the story of Ruth, which is understandable in particular contexts. It helps some modern women readers to make sense of this tale, particularly those who can afford to refuse any compromise with patriarchal rules because of their class and social status. Unfortunately, this interpretation forgets that, given the circumstances of the time, these two women probably did the best they could do to survive as poor widows. I, therefore, agree with Katherine Sakenfeld when she says:

> Although the story of Ruth is one of women making decisions and taking action on their own, their action takes place in the context of this traditional assumption about women's place in socio-economic structure. Indeed in Israel's society, such an assumption was probably realistic and prudent, as there appears to have been minimal structural provision for the well being of unmarried adult women in that culture. (1999, 25)

In other contexts—indeed, in many settings today—women simply cannot afford to step out of the social situations structured by patriarchal rules. In such circumstances, women will still find the story of Ruth and Naomi affirming and hope-giving.

Conversely, in many African contexts, we also need to resist readings of this story that simply find in it a confirmation of the common opinion that marriage offers the only possible meaningful life for women. Since the idolization of marriage is still rife in many African contexts, we need to raise a caution flag above this type of interpretation. We need to remind young women that God's purposes for individual women and men can still happen apart from marriage; life, and the fullness thereof as designed for them by God, can still flourish without marriage. Women and men who choose to lead celibate lives should not be marginalized by those who have come to regard marriage as a norm. It must, however, be emphasized that our achieving this aim as people of God may not happen soon, as there are few examples of voluntary celibacy either in our African cultures or in the Bible. However, if as readers of the Bible we acknowledge the gap between the time of the biblical events and our time, we might be enabled to liberate the word of God from the cultural bonds with which we have chained it. This does not mean denying any value to the book of Ruth, but rather focusing on what it says about God's intervention in human life.

God's Intervention in Human Life

The events in the story of Ruth remind us of those that occur in the book of Esther. God's actions are basically veiled in both books. In the book of Ruth, however, mention is made occasionally of YHWH and the characters' understanding of God's intervention in their lives.

If we keep in mind that this story is in the Hebrew Bible, we can appreciate that the events unfolding in it might not have been accidental. Did all the men in Naomi's family die so as to show that YHWH could bring hope in a situation of despondency and that humans should acknowledge God's intervention in this situation? Did Ruth decide to leave her homeland and to cling to an old widow so as to make clear that she was clinging to God? Was it an accident that she ended up gleaning in the right field, or was she led by God's hand to that field? From this perspective, we can recognize that God uses ordinary human beings to direct the course of events and thus to bring food to the hungry, security to the insecure, and lineage and a future to the desperate. In the lives of Naomi and Ruth, we therefore witness the work of God's transforming hand to end death-dealing situations in people's lives.

The tale therefore reminds the church that we can trust this same God even as we are overwhelmed by different challenges in our own contexts. God's business is with people and it is in God's nature to work through willing human agents for the welfare of all humanity.

CONCLUSION

Two widows allowed themselves to be used by God to transform their undesirable situation into a better one. They refused to be victims of circumstances. The Northern Sotho proverb says, *Kgomo go tsoswa yeo e itsosago*— literally, only a cow that tries to get up (from its fall) will be lifted up. This means that only those people who make the effort to get out of their helpless situations will be helped. If we as individuals and participants in structures of power become willing agents and take upon ourselves the responsibility to transform our hopeless situations, we, like Ruth and Naomi, can trust God to make us rise above those circumstances.

BIBLIOGRAPHY

Dube, Musa W., ed. *Other Ways of Reading: African Women and the Bible,* Atlanta: SBL, 2001.

Fewell, Danna N., and David M. Gunn, "A Son has been born to Naomi! Literary Allusions and Interpretation in the Book of Ruth." Pages 233-239 in *Women in the Hebrew Bible: A Reader.* Edited by Alice Bach. New York: Routledge, 1999.

Masenya (ngwana' Mphahlele), Madipoane J. *How Worthy is the Woman of Worth? Rereading Proverbs 31:10-31 in African-South Africa.* New York: Peter Lang, 2004.

Masenya, Madipoane J. "Ngwetši (Bride): The Naomi-Ruth Story from an African-South African Women." JFSR 2 (1996) Pages 81-90.

Nielson, Kirsten. *Ruth: A Commentary.* Translated by Edward Broadbridge. OTL. Louisville: Westminster John Knox, 1997.

Sakenfeld, Katharine D. *Ruth. Int.* Louisville: Westminster John Knox, 1999.

Sasson, Jack M., *Ruth: A New Translation with a Philological Commentary and a Formalist-Folklorist Interpretation.* 2d ed. Biblical Seminar. Sheffield: JSOT, 1989.

1 AND 2 SAMUEL

Gerald West

School of Theology, University of KwaZulu-Natal, Pietermaritzburg, South Africa

LIFE CONTEXT OF THE INTERPRETATION

The Bible is an ambiguous book in South Africa. It was brought to the southern areas of the continent by European explorers, missionaries, and other more obvious colonial agents. The Bible was a part of the colonial package, and although it has become an African book, the legacy of its arrival lives on. For southern Africans, then, the Bible is both a problem and a solution (Mofokeng 1988). The problem is twofold. First, the Bible has been used by a white minority—whether they be the various colonial-settler communities that have occupied southern Africa since the 1600s or their progeny who have become, in some sense, white Africans—to wrest control of the land from indigenous peoples. As the popular African anecdote proclaims, "When the white man came among us, he had the Bible and we blacks had the land; he then said to us, 'Let us pray.' After the prayer, when we had opened our eyes again, we had his Bible and he had our land." This is the problem of a Bible that has played a significant role in colonization and apartheid.

Second, the Bible is problematic in Africa because this single book speaks with divergent voices. Even for those who find the Bible a liberating book, it sometimes bites the very hand that embraces it for liberation. There are parts of the Bible, to put it bluntly, that are not appropriate for southern Africa (e.g., Col 3:22). So the problem is not only the use to which the Bible has been put; the Bible itself is also intrinsically problematic in that some texts are ideologically loaded

against those who would struggle for survival, liberation, and life (Mosala 1989).

But the Bible is not only a dilemma and a problem in Africa, it is also a solution. The Bible is an African book that has power, whether opened or closed. As a closed (iconic) book, the Bible is used in southern Africa to protect and heal those who hold it. As an open book, the Bible contains many elements that resonate with southern Africans. Without much difficulty, they hear God speaking to them from the pages of their Bibles.

An Overview of 1–2 Samuel, and the People of God, within Southern Africa

1 Samuel and its Relationship to Judges as Empowering for African Readers

One of the immediate problems that any reader encounters when reading the book of 1 Samuel on its own is that the story seems to assume knowledge readers do not have unless they have read the book of Judges. There are a number of missing narrative connections for the readers of 1 Samuel. For example, what is the ceremony of national repentance in which Samuel leads the people in 1 Samuel 7 all about? Why are the people repenting? There is no obvious answer in 1 Samuel, though it might be argued that the fault lies with Hophni and Phinehas (and perhaps Eli). But if we, as readers, remember Judges 2:11, we immediately know what is going on. In Judges 2:11, one of a set of theological summary

Gerald West is the author of *Biblical Hermeneutics of Liberation: Modes of Reading the Bible in the South African Context* and *The Academy of the Poor: Towards a Dialogical Reading of the Bible* (1999); he is the co-editor with Musa Duba of *The Bible in Africa: Transactions, Trajectories, and Trends* (1999).

passages (the others are 1 Samuel 12 and 2 Samuel 7), the problem is clear: Israel repeatedly falls into apostasy against God. Whenever this happens, God allows a foreign oppressor to dominate Israel for a time, which, in turn, makes Israel cry out to God, who responds by sending a judge to deliver them. This is why the people are repenting in 1 Samuel 7. It also comes as no surprise to the reader of Judges and 1 Samuel when Samuel, that the greatest of the judges, defeats the Philistines, the greatest of Israel's enemies (7:13). In fact, the early chapters of 1 Samuel sound very similar to certain chapters in Judges. Samuel is a judge, and his story shares many similarities with the stories of other such figures in the book of Judges.

These similarities between Judges and 1 Samuel have led some scholars to suggest that there may have been an earlier version of the book of Judges, perhaps a Deuteronomic version in which 1 Samuel 1–12 formed a part of the Deuteronomic book of Judges (Jobling 1998, ch. 2). According to this view, Samuel is the apex of the Deuteronomic book of Judges. He is the most complete judge—the best example of what this form of leadership has to offer. Samuel's story is, then, the climax of the Deuteronomic book of Judges.

However, Jobling argues (1998, 33–35) that later editors, who did not share this high opinion of the charismatic form of leadership typified by the judges and who wished to promote kingship, modified the Deuteronomic book of Judges and concluded it at its present canonical ending with a negative assessment of the period of the judges. "In those days there was no king in Israel; all the people did what was right in their own eyes" (Judg 21:25). To emphasize their ideological position, these pro-monarchy editors inserted the book of Ruth after Judges because Ruth begins with a potentially negative interpretation of the time of the judges. "In the days when the judges ruled, there was a famine in the land" (Ruth 1:1).

The high point of the period of the judges, the judgeship of Samuel, was then inserted as a prologue to what might have

been another Deuteronomic book dealing with kingship (1 Samuel 13–2 Kings 25). Samuel, instead of representing the climax of a tribal and charismatic form of local leadership, now appears as a transitional leader to the pinnacle of leadership forms, the monarchy.

Southern Africans who have this account of ideological contestation in the Bible explained to them have little problem with making sense of this suggestion. They are only too familiar with the way in which the "winners" rewrite texts. Interestingly, in Africa some communities believe that "Europeans have kept secret those parts of the Bible that provide the key to their wealth and technology. . . . This belief seemed confirmed," writes Elizabeth Isichei, "by the discovery that the Apocrypha are omitted in Protestant Bibles, and by gnostic texts with titles such as the *Gospel of Thomas*" (1995, 295). A further twist is evident in a story from Avaira, in the western Niger Delta, where local people tell of a lost Bible that is far fuller and richer than the usual version in use. This lost Bible was originally and miraculously given to the Isoko Christians, but it was then taken away and either lost or destroyed by the missionaries (Isichei 1995). As this example from West Africa indicates, Africans can easily understand how those with power will use it to manipulate texts to suit their own purposes. This is, after all, their own experience with the Bible. Not only was the Bible used to denigrate their indigenous culture and religion, but, even when they had embraced the Bible as their book, it was turned against them by the forces of apartheid in South Africa.

A reading of 1 Samuel that recognizes that the final form may not be the last word and that a careful literary reading of the text can detect other suppressed emphases and voices is potentially empowering, explaining as it does that the Bible is a site of struggle. What you read and how you read it does make a difference. While ordinary African Christians do not read the Bible with careful attention to character, plot, structure, and narrative point of view, these literary features clearly indicate that 1 Samuel has been a site of struggle in the past as it may be in the present. Most southern Africans have no difficulty recognizing this.

Besides offering an empowering methodological move for identifying different ideological layers within the text, a close reading of 1 Samuel has other potential benefits for southern African readers.

African Resonances with 1 Samuel

The tribal context of Judges, with its clear echoes in 1 Samuel, even in the early cases of the monarchy, resonates with southern African readers:

♦ the polygamous family into which Samuel is born (1:2)
♦ the eating of meat that has been sacrificed (1:4)
♦ the rivalries of polygamous family life (1:5-6)
♦ the acute problem of barrenness and the yearning for a male child (1:10-11)
♦ the dedication of a child to a particular office in life (1:22)
♦ the disappointment when the children of leaders abuse their privilege (2:12-17)
♦ the recognition by other tribes of a new young leader beginning to emerge (2:20)
♦ the word of warning from a prophet-like figure to the leadership (2:27-36)
♦ endemic conflict with neighboring tribes (4:1–7:14)
♦ the presence of local deities (5:1-2)
♦ the dependency on and centrality of cattle in community life (6:7)
♦ agricultural life (6:13)
♦ the slaughtering of an animal as a way of communicating with the deity or ancestors (7:9)
♦ the leader's role of judge among the people (7:15)
♦ tensions between more local and charismatic forms of leadership and more central and dynastic forms of leadership (8:1-22)
♦ the importance of stature in a leader (9:2)
♦ the need to visit a seer on occasions (9:6-10)
♦ the presence of shrines in the community (9:13-14)
♦ the importance of hospitality to visitors and strangers from neighboring tribes (9:19, 22-26)
♦ possession by spirits (10:10)
♦ the importance of remembering the ancestors and their deeds and the recitation of the origins and traditions of the tribe (12:6-18)
♦ the younger boys looking after the herds in the field (16:11)
♦ women dancing and singing in recognition of the exploits of their men (18:6-7)
♦ the plotting of a king or chief against his rivals (18:12–24:22)
♦ the exile of rivals and their alliances with the chief of a neighboring tribe (27:1-12)
♦ the importance of mediums and dreams and the consultation of the ancestors (28:6-25), and much more resonates with the African reader of 1 Samuel.

This is a profound point. Missionaries and colonial agents used the Bible to denigrate and demonize the religious and cultural practices of the Africans, insisting that their forms of Christianity were far superior. And yet, once African Christians became familiar with the Bible, they were amazed to find that their religion and culture were mirrored in texts like 1 Samuel. These similarities between the Bible and their life contexts became a resource to recover aspects of their African religion and culture that the missionaries had damaged (Sanneh 1989). Much of African biblical scholarship to date has focused on showing the similarities between precolonial African culture and religion, and the Bible, particularly the Old Testament, as most Africans would refer to the Hebrew Bible (West and Dube 2000).

For example, the missionaries insisted that veneration of the ancestors—those "living dead" who inhabited the spirit realm and continued to watch over and guide their people through dreams and portents—was demonic. And yet here, in 1 Samuel 28, we find Saul consulting a diviner (v. 8) who, in turn, enables Saul to consult with his ancestor, Samuel (v. 11), whom the text describes as "a god, coming up out of the ground" (v.

13, a.t.); (see Mafico 2000). Here we have the living dead warning Saul. And here, God as in many African traditional religions, is present but remote. It is the ancestors who are available for consultation.

According to some African biblical scholars, each of the "fathers" of Israel—including Abraham (Gen 15:1), Isaac (Gen 31:42), and Jacob (Gen 49:24)—worshiped his own god with its own name. Thus, it could be argued, the term *Elohim* appears to have been a generic noun, meaning "gods" or "ancestral spirits" (the form is plural), although later it became the designation of the supreme deity, YHWH. In support of this suggestion, Temba Mafico (2000) discusses 1 Samuel 28. Here, as indicated, Saul asks a medium to summon Samuel. When the medium sees the spirit of Samuel, she tells Saul (literally), "I see *Elohim* [gods or spirits] coming up from the earth" (28:13). The medium (or *sangoma,* as she would be called in Zulu) called Samuel; but what she sees are "*Elohim* [gods] coming up," among whom is Samuel, one of the ancestors. The Israelites, like most Africans, trusted these gods because they were the gods whom their ancestors had trusted and venerated. When the living departed, they joined the living dead who watched over their people. Samuel lived on after his death, guiding those who came after him.

Texts like this, therefore, are profoundly empowering because they recover and rehabilitate damaged aspects of indigenous culture and religion. However, the recovery of some aspects of traditional culture is not welcomed with the same degree of enthusiasm by all sectors of African society. African women often find themselves doubly disadvantaged. Not only do most forms of colonial Christianity discriminate against them as women, but revitalizing indigenous culture often causes further subjugation. It is not easy for an African woman to condemn aspects of her traditional culture when this culture is being rehabilitated from its denigration and destruction by missionary and colonial forces. Women are called to affirm their indigenous culture, not condemn it; yet increasingly, African women are breaking their silence on this matter, putting their interests as women before the interests of their patriarchal culture.

Silenced Women Speak in 2 Samuel

The stories of abused women in 2 Samuel have proved to be a particularly valuable resource for African Christian women. The story of David and Bathsheba is readily understood as a narrative about a king or leader using his power to control women. Although there is considerable scholarly debate about whether Bathsheba was raped by David, with some scholars arguing that there are indications in the text that she was a willing participant, most African women readers are adamant—Bathsheba was raped. David is the subject of the verbs in 11:1-4; David "saw," "sent," "sent" again, and "lay with her." Bathsheba is the object here. And though she is the grammatical subject of a number of phrases ("she came to him," "she returned to her house," and "she conceived"), she remains the object of David's authority and agency. It is only in 11:5b that she takes initiative and "sent and told David, 'I am pregnant.'" Most African women can understand exactly why she now sends a message to David. As a married woman whose husband has been away for some time and who has purified herself from her menstruation (11:4), she knows that David is responsible for her pregnancy. In a patriarchal society she is vulnerable and has limited choices. Will her husband believe that the king raped her? Will her husband, a foreigner (11:6), have any recourse against the king? Will the king allow her to bear his child and remain with her husband? Where do her greatest chances for survival, and the survival of her child, lie?

That Bathsheba was raped is supported by Nathan's condemnation of David; David has "taken" Uriah's wife to be his wife (12:9), and what David did in secret, "I [God] will do this thing before all Israel, and before the sun" (12:11-12)—a clear foreshadowing of Absalom's rape of David's "concubines" in 16:22. If this is not clear enough, Nathan's prophecy that God "will raise up trouble against you [David] from within your own house" (12:11) includes the incident in the next chapter when David's son, Amnon, unambiguously rapes David's daughter, Tamar. Before we come to this text, it is worth noting that it is Ahithophel, David's former counsellor (15:12) and Bathsheba's grandfather (cf. 11:3 and 23:34), who counsels Absalom to "go in to your father's concubines, the ones he has left to look after the house; and all Israel will hear that you have made yourself odious to your father, and the hands of all who are with you will be strengthened" (16:21). It is not implausible that Ahithophel

is driven to betray David and align himself with the rebellious Absalom to avenge what David did to his granddaughter.

There is, of course, no excuse for Ahithophel's proposal of sexual assault; there can be no mitigation for the way men use women in their contestations for power or in their plots for revenge. As readers, we hope that the narrator rejects such acts as clearly as we do; and perhaps he does, for the terrible tale of Tamar's rape is told with remarkable sensitivity to the woman's perspective, and she, more than any woman in the Bible, is not silent.

CONTEXTUAL COMMENT

How This Contextual Commentary Was Developed

The following commentary was created through the community development and research organization, the Institute for the Study of the Bible & Worker Ministry Project (ISB&WM) of the School of Theology at the University of Natal. We began working with the text of Tamar's story several years ago, when local communities of Christians invited us to assist them with finding empowering ways to read the Bible, particularly those parts that concern the issue of violence against women (West 2000). Ordinary readers of the Bible are a constituent part of African biblical scholarship and cannot be ignored in any discussion of biblical texts and their interpretation in Africa (Okure 1993; West 2002). Increasingly, women's groups have invited the ISB&WM to participate in workshops on the theme of violence against women. Our contribution to these workshops has been varied. We have offered some resources for facilitator training, encouraged groups of women to network with each other both ecumenically and regionally, and put the group in contact with relevant nongovernmental organizations and government departments; but our major contribution has been to facilitate a contextual Bible study.

Tamar's Story: 2 Samuel 13:1-22

In workshops on the theme of violence against women, we in the ISB&WM usually work with 2 Samuel 13:1-22, a neglected and marginalized text which is found in few lectionaries and seldom publicly read (and certainly never on a Sunday). Having made sure that counselors are available, we use the following framework.

2 Samuel 13:1-22 is read aloud to the group as a whole. After the text has been read, a series of questions follow.

1. Read 2 Samuel 13:1-22 together again in small groups. Share with each other what you think the text is about.

Each small group is then asked to report back to the larger group. Each and every response is summarized on newsprint. After the report, the participants return to their small groups to discuss the following questions.

2. Who are the main characters in this story and what do we know about them?
3. What is the role of each of the male characters in the rape of Tamar?
4. How does Tamar respond throughout the story?

When the small groups have finished their discussion, each group is invited to present a summary of their discussion. This is done in a variety of ways. If there is time, each group is asked to report on each question, but if time is a constraint then each group is asked to report on only one question. The full report, which the group's scribe records, is then displayed for everyone to read at some other time. The reports can also be presented more creatively by way of drama, poetry, or song. After this report, the small groups reconvene to discuss the following questions.

5. Are there women like Tamar in your church and/or community? Tell their stories.
6. What is the theology of women who have been raped?
7. What resources are there in your area for survivors of rape?

Once again, the small groups present their report back to the plenary group. Creativity is particularly vital here, as women often find it difficult to articulate their responses. A drama or a drawing may be the only way in which some groups can report. Finally, each small group comes together to formulate a plan of action.

8. What will you now do in response to this Bible study?

The plan is either reported to the plenary or presented for other participants to examine after the Bible study.

In our experience, the effects of this Bible study are substantial. Women are amazed that such a text exists, angry that they have never heard it read or preached, relieved to discover that they are not alone, and empowered because the silence has been broken and their stories have been told. As one women said, "If such a text exists in the Bible, how can we be silent about these things in the church?"

The initial opening question generates a host of responses as readers share their early impressions of this seldom-read text. Ordinary readers readily engage with questions 2, 3, and 4, returning to the text again and again to find out as much as they can about each of the characters, missing nothing. They note how Jonadab, a relative of Amnon's, attempts to draw himself nearer to the potential heir to the throne of David by identifying his restrained lust. Reminding Amnon that he is indeed "son of the king" (13:4) and thereby implying that he should have whatever he wants, Jonadab provides a plan for the rape of Tamar. The readers also observe the slow pace of the story, with the graphic description of the plan and its execution, as they delve into 13:5-11. David, it seems to them, is somewhat irresponsible and unable to detect that Amnon's request is a ruse (13:6), and so he sends Tamar to be raped (13:7). (Some readers remember the earlier stories in 2 Samuel and comment on how often damage is done when David "sends.") Whatever restraint Amnon may have had now collapses as he premeditates the rape of his sister (13:9-14).

Women readers, in particular, applaud the clear and careful way in which Tamar approaches her task and her defense. She trusts her brother and willingly serves him while he is sick, and even when she finds herself trapped, she argues articulately with him. First, she says a clear no (13:12), which should be enough. Second, she reminds him that he is her "brother" (13:12). Third, she makes it clear that she is not a willing participant and so names what he is doing, "forcing" her (13:12). Fourth, she reminds him of their cultural heritage and communal values, "for such a thing is not done in Israel" (13:12). Fifth, she declares his intentions to be "vile" and evil (13:12). Sixth, she appeals to what she hopes is some recognition of her situation, reminding him of the consequences of his actions for her (13:13). Seventh, she then turns the question on him, asking what the consequences of such an act would be for him (13:13). Eighth, she offers him a way out, at considerable cost to herself, suggesting that he speak to the king about marrying her (13:13). Alas, even this most articulate of all biblical women is not listened to, "and being stronger than she, he forced her and lay with her" (13:14).

Even after the rape she does not remain silent. She argues with Amnon again, this time urging him not to abandon her to the consequences of rape (13:16). But the male ego again refuses to hear, and she is forcefully (again) removed (13:16-17).

Tamar's public acknowledgment of the rape (13:19) is met with mixed reactions by women readers as they both applaud her decision "to go public" and worry about the cost of such a public statement in a patriarchal society. They find some comfort in Absalom's offer of sanctuary but reject his silencing of her (13:20). Finally, they are appalled by David's empty anger and his impulse to protect his son (13:21).

Clearly, each of the male characters—whether it be David, Amnon, Jonadab, the servants, or Absalom—plays a role in the rape of Tamar, though their roles are different. This is how many men it takes to rape a woman!

The narrator's point of view is interesting; most readers comment that this male character (presuming the narrator to be a male) is surprisingly sympathetic to the concerns of women. They are grateful that he names rape for what it is: a violent assault on a woman (13:14). They are amazed by how articulate Tamar is and find many of her arguments convincing. They especially like the fact that she finds aspects of her cultural and religious heritage potentially liberating, even if they are often used to oppress and dominate. Most of all they are astounded that such a text exists in the Bible, for they find it a remarkable resource with which to raise and discuss rape in their own contexts.

Questions 5, 6, and 7 provide plenty of opportunity for precisely such discussions, with many women finding "sacred space" in which to share the unshareable. They quickly discover that they are not alone, and soon they name the Davids, Amnons, Jonadabs, servants, and Absaloms in their own experiences. Clearly, professional counseling is required in many such situations, and it is irresponsible to proceed without it.

Question 8 provides an opportunity "to do something about it," and groups come up with wonderfully creative action plans, including composing a liturgy for their local church and challenging the local police station to provide resources for the survivors of rape.

Implicit in the Bible study as outlined above are all the elements of the contextual Bible study process. The study begins and ends with community consciousness questions. Questions 1, 5, 6, 7, and 8 draw on the readings and resources of the local community group. The contributions of all participants are affirmed by using small groups and writing up all responses. Responses to question 1 elicit the public transcript; participants offer interpretations they have received and feel are safe to proclaim publicly. They know what they are expected to believe about the Bible. However, there are usually some responses that are more ambiguous and potentially provide space for more authentic interpretations, interpretations that articulate something of their own experiential and working theologies. If the group becomes a safe place, if there are resources to articulate what is often incipient and inchoate, and if there is an understanding with the others in the group, elements of a lived faith may gradually be more overtly and vigorously voiced.

Clustered between the community consciousness questions are a series of critical consciousness questions (questions 2, 3, and 4). These questions—the contributions of the socially engaged biblical scholars—provide resources for careful and close readings of the text. In this example, the critical consciousness questions draw on literary modes of interpretation, posing questions about characters, plot, setting, and so on. Such structured and systematic questions are not usually in the repertoire of ordinary readers, though once asked, the questions are readily grasped and appropriated. The advantage of using questions that draw on literary modes of interpretation is that they do not require any input from the socially engaged biblical scholar ("the expert"). The questions are contribution enough, and ordinary readers make of them what they will. However, in many instances ordinary readers want access to resources that are only available to the "trained" reader. For example, participants may want to know the significance of Tamar tearing her clothing. In such cases, the socially engaged biblical scholar may offer sociohistorical resources in response to this question, preferably by drawing on parallels in the participants' own socio-historical context.

In our experience, literary-type questions almost always lead into socio-historical-type questions; this is important because it indicates the need ordinary readers have to locate faith in real, concrete contexts. But beginning with literary-type questions and allowing sociohistorical-type questions to emerge from the participants, keeps the powerful presence of the biblical scholar firmly in check. Equally important, by waiting for the questions to arise from the participants, we can be sure that we are answering questions of interest to them rather than questions of interest to biblical scholars.

Critical consciousness questions facilitate a more careful and close reading of the text than is usually the case among ordinary readers. They give the text a voice and, in so doing, open up potential lines of connection with faith trajectories in the biblical tradition that have been neglected or suppressed. Women discover that they are not alone; their terror can be found in the Bible. While this "text of terror" (Trible 1984) perhaps offers little comfort, it does at least acknowledge the reality of their experience.

The concluding community consciousness questions (5, 6, 7, and 8) ground the Bible study firmly in the lives of the participants. In responding to these questions, community consciousness and critical consciousness fuse and fashion faith interpretations (Patte 1995) that make sense and are an expression of the lived, working theologies of ordinary believers. Whether these incipient and unclear faith interpretations are articulated depends on how safe the contextual Bible study process is. In safe places, women who have been touched by Tamar tell their stories, help and hold the pain of their sisters, and plan for the transformation of their churches and communities. Unfortunately, not all Bible study groups are safe, and some women may remain silent. But the potential is there, implicit within the contextual Bible study process and this text, for the articulation, owning, and acting out of those interpretations and theologies by which ordinary readers of the Bible live.

Rizpah's Story: 2 Samuel 21:1-14

The end of the Tamar story reminds readers that what has happened to Tamar, just as what happened to Bathsheba, has repercussions. Because of what Amnon did to Tamar, Absalom "hated Amnon" (13:22). Nathan said to David, "Now therefore the sword shall never depart from your house" (12:10), and it truly does not. The rest of David's reign is littered with dead bodies: Absalom kills his brother Amnon (13:23-36) and is thereby forced to flee from his father's presence (13:37-39), Absalom mounts a rebellion against his father and is eventually killed (15:1–18:33), and the narrative ends with the death of Sheba (20:1-22).

True, there are moments of remarkable insight and faith amidst all the maneuvering, scheming, and death. David's ongoing struggle between his public responsibilities and his personal life—beginning, of course, with David's remaining at home while his army goes out to war in 11:1—is typified in his instruction to the army that they should "deal gently" (18:5) with his rebellious son Absalom, as well as in his profound mourning for Absalom when the more politically astute Joab disregards David's instructions and kills him (18:14-15). David can be wonderfully human! David can also be full of faith, as when he abandons Jerusalem to Absalom's army (15:14), trusting that, if he finds favor "in the eyes of the Lord," God will restore his throne to him (15:25), but knowing that if God takes "no pleasure" in him, he will lose his kingdom (15:26).

Overall, however, the narrative of 2 Samuel comes to an end with little wholeness or hope in the life of David, Samuel's heir. There are attempts at the end of 2 Samuel to bring together a series of short, unrelated texts (chs. 21–24) that the editors were apparently unable to integrate into the narrative framework that forms the bulk of 1 and 2 Samuel. Each of these textual units provides glimpses of the complexity of the materials available to those who composed the story of David's reign, particularly as they have not been constructed into a coherent narrative. One of these fragments (21:1-14) has been especially useful in the South African context.

I came across this text for the first time while teaching a course called the "Succession Narrative" (2 Samuel 9–1 Kings 2). While most commentators see Rizpah as a prop in someone else's plot, I recognized her as someone with a story of her own. She reminded me of others I had seen sitting silently, so it was with excitement and expectation that I entered my class on the day we were to discuss this text. We had been reading 2 Samuel together regularly and the class was familiar with our literary approach. I allowed the class to guide our reading, but I watched closely, waiting for Rizpah to speak. It was with growing disappointment that I realized she would not speak. David, the Gibeonites, and even the almost absent Saul were given voice, but not Rizpah.

The class consisted almost entirely of black South Africans, mostly from poor and marginalized communities. Less than a quarter of the class were women, and they did not speak at all. The male discussion concentrated on the characters of David and the Gibeonites, and their stories and theologies were closely examined. Even when I intervened and said, "We have heard the stories and theologies of the fathers, but what about the stories and theologies of the mothers?" the women remained silent still, quietly shaking their heads. I know now that they were sitting silently in solidarity with Rizpah.

I have used this text often in various contexts, some of them safe, sequestered sites in which women and some men read with Rizpah. The commentary presented here is a communal reading of 2 Samuel 21:1-14, based on a series of contextual Bible studies

in various communities in South Africa. All of these Bible studies were facilitated by me and shaped by my interpretive and social interests. However, the contextual Bible study process is an enabling process in which trained scholars read the Bible with ordinary, untrained readers from poor and marginalized communities. Therefore, the concerns, questions, needs, and experiences of these other readers have substantially shaped the interpretation.

As facilitator of the reading process, I offered and enabled a variety of questions from literary, postmodern/poststructuralist, and liberationist perspectives. So, for example, questions on the limits of the text enabled readers to recognize 2 Samuel 21:1-14 as a literary unit, and questions about the characters in the text encouraged a close and careful reading that focsed on the text itself rather than on their remembered reconstructions of the larger story of David. I also offered questions that probed the gaps, juxtapositions, presences, absences, and ambiguities within the text, and in so doing provided resources for a postmodern/poststructuralist reading. Ordinary readers, of course, brought their many resources for reading and "re-membering." They also brought their experiences as the marginalized poor to the reading process.

The reading of this text offered here is a communal product that draws deeply on the readings of those who know Rizpah better than I do. Rizpah has come to live with us and we have become her people. With her we have begun to recognize, recover, and revive the subjugated discourses and hidden transcripts of the biblical tradition and make them our own. We have also come to articulate and own the incipient and inchoate readings and theologies by which we live. I have seen Rizpah often before, although I did not know her name, but I have only begun to hear her story by reading with others who know her.

In each of the various groups in which this text was read, a similar reading framework was used. This framework expresses the commitments of the contextual Bible study process, a process that has been developed by African biblical scholarship and includes commitments to read the Bible from the perspective of the organized poor and marginalized, to read the Bible communally, to read the Bible critically, and to read the Bible for social and individual transformation. The ISB&WM prefers to work with organized groups because they already have a sense of identity and cohesion that enables them to "talk back" to those of us who work with them and to act for social transformation in their context.

In reading 2 Samuel 21:1-14 we used the following questions.

1. Read this passage together and tell the story to each other.
2. What is this passage about? Share your responses in the group.
3. Who are the major characters in the story and what do we know about them?
4. What is David's theology in this text? What is the Gibeonites' theology? What is Rizpah's theology? What is the narrator's theology?
5. Which theology do you identify with and why?
6. What challenges does this text pose for the church in South Africa today?

Questions 1, 2, 5, and 6 focus on community consciousness and concentrate on forms of engagement with the text and each other. Questions 3 and 4 focus on critical consciousness, concentrating on forms of critical distance generated by a close and careful reading of the text.

Not everybody read with Rizpah, so our reading was a marginal reading located among other contended readings. Most readers initially read with David, a godly character whom they knew and trusted from their readings of other texts. This story seemed to confirm their confidence in David; his response to the famine is to "seek the face of God" (v. 1a, a.t.). But then some readers pointed out that the famine was already in its third year (v. 1a). Why had it taken David so long to "seek the face of God"? Was David was not as close to God as he should have

been? Unease with David grew when he did not immediately choose the first option offered by the Gibeonites: restitution through "silver or gold" (v. 4a). How could he agree to restitution through blood? Was David was not as close to his people as he should have been? Or, as some argued, was David being particularly sensitive to the power dynamics implicit in the situation, namely, that because the Gibeonites were a marginalized community, their initial response was one of deference (v. 4a)? Being aware of relations of power, David gave them the space to articulate their real request by making it clear to them that he was giving them the right to decide: "What do you say that I should do for you?" (v. 4b).

Perhaps, some said, David was even using this opportunity to rid himself of potential opposition from Saul's house. David might have been using the Gibeonites to execute his own political interests. This line of reasoning appeared to be supported, some readers argued, by the repeated presence of Saul and his house in the story. Participants pointed to the reference to Saul's "house of blood" (v. 1b, a.t.) and the Gibeonites' reminder that Saul was "the chosen of God" (v. 6a; in the Hebrew text and some translations), and they drew on what they knew about the tensions between David and Saul from other texts. This would explain, they suggested, why David did not take up the opportunity to offer financial compensation (v. 4a). Some went further and argued that David's refusal to take this option and the repetition of the question allowed or even prompted the Gibeonites to make the decision they did. They understood the unspoken intent of David's repeated question: David wanted Saul's family to be eliminated as a potential threat to his throne. Realizing this, the Gibeonites obliged David, either for reasons of their own or because they had little option given their position. In their initial request, the option of "silver or gold" is grammatically linked to "Saul and his house" and the option of "putting to death" is linked to "anyone in Israel" (v. 4a, a.t.). But when David asks the second time, the object of the killing is clear, though Saul is not mentioned by name (vv. 5-6a).

None of the readers liked the idea of David using the Gibeonites for his own ends; in fact, those reading with David became more and more uncomfortable with his actions in this story. But the majority reading with the Gibeonites applauded David for doing the appropriate thing. Some form of restitution was clearly implied by God's statement (vv. 1b and 2b), and, rather than imposing his form of restitution, David asked the Gibeonites for theirs. When they behaved deferentially, David rightly recognized this as the behavior of a vulnerable and marginalized group, and he persisted until they felt free to state their preference. David was being remarkably sensitive to the power dynamics in that situation.

These readers went further, arguing that the perspective of the Gibeonites was appropriate and right. Many of these black South African readers were adamant that the Gibeonites were right to demand blood restitution; they too knew what it was to be systematically slaughtered. Blood restitution was an appropriate response to a "house of blood" (v. 1b, a.t.) that "consumed" and "planned to destroy" (v. 5), particularly when the house in question was that of a ruler who had used his power to oppress and decimate the vulnerable and marginalized.

This reading led to a heated discussion of capital punishment, which was at that time being debated by the new Constitu-tional Court in South Africa. Those reading with the Gibeonites insisted that the death penalty must remain and be reactivated (there being a moratorium at that time), so that those guilty of blood crimes could be appropriately punished. Those reading with the Gibeonites and those reading with David, sharing as they did a similar theology, felt that David was right when he gave seven relations of Saul into the hands of the Gibeonites (v. 9a), and that the Gibeonites were justified in "exposing/hanging/impaling them" (v. 9a, a.t.). Further, they insisted that their opinions were substantiated by the final sentence of the story: "And God answered prayer for the land after that" (v. 14b, a.t.). The

phrase "after that" clearly refers to the handing over and exposing/hanging/impaling of the family of Saul.

But it was not clear to everyone that this phrase should be interpreted in this way. What about Rizpah, some asked? Does she not have a part in this story? All the small groups, in working through the questions previously outlined, had agreed that Rizpah was one of the major characters; yet she had played no role in the discussion thus far. The question was pertinent and provoked a deep disquiet in all the readers. Rizpah, it slowly began to emerge, had also done the right thing: she had shown honor to the dead.

Reading from a largely African culture, most readers were very uncomfortable with the exposing/hanging/impaling (v. 9) of the bodies. Even those who were deeply committed to the perspective of the Gibeonites found this practice difficult to understand. Relatives of the dead must be allowed to bury the dead properly. In their culture, disrespect toward the dead was, and is, wrong. Cracks began to appear in the dominant reading.

Those who read with David found fresh resources for their interpretation. While Saul had broken the oath of Israel to the Amorites (v. 2b), David had kept his oath to Jonathan by sparing Mephibosheth (v. 7). This showed that David honored his relationships, even with those who had a claim to the throne. Moreover, David honored the dead by gathering the bones of Saul, Jonathan, and their relatives who had been hanged/exposed/impaled and giving them a proper burial (vv. 12-14a). In this respect, then, David had a different theology than the Gibeonites. So, some suggested, the phrase "after that" (v. 14b) included not only right restitution but also right burial. But this reading in turn opened additional fissures and gaps in the text. Those who read with Rizpah (mainly women) located their interpretations in these places. By providing a proper burial for the dead of Israel, they argued, David had been responding to Rizpah's actions. It was only "when David was told what Rizpah . . . had done" (v. 11) that he responded appropriately. She had shamed and challenged him by her solidarity with the dead. How were Rizpah's actions to be interpreted? What was Rizpah saying in her silence?

Among those who read with Rizpah were those who emphasized her silent solidarity with the dead. She was doing what women all over the world do: caring for the dead. And because she was in a marginalized position as a woman and a concubine (v. 11), to care for and bury the dead (including her children) properly, she stayed in solidarity with them, doing what she could to honor them. Others who read with Rizpah emphasized the deafening silence of her protest. Although silent, by publicly associating herself with the victims of the king's policy, she was engaging in a political act of protest. She was caring for the dead because men with power do not care for the living. This was one of those rare moments when the hidden transcript of women's resistance to dominant ideologies and theologies ruptured the public transcript of deference and disguise. What was usually acted and spoken offstage by women behind the backs of the dominant, now found a public forum at center stage. The "after that" in the final sentence (v. 14b), these readers argued, referred to Rizpah's actions, not David's. God's response was associated with Rizpah's resistance. This was clear from the narrative because the rains, which were God's response, were directly related to Rizpah's actions (v. 10a). The narrator tells us that Rizpah stayed in solidarity with the dead "from the beginning of harvest until rain fell on them from the heavens" (v. 10a). The silent cries of Rizpah and her dead were heard by God.

While the narrator seems to suggest, these readers continued, that David might have heard God speak when "he sought the face of God" (v. 1a, a.t.), God did not speak again. And Rizpah never spoke. But Rizpah's act of solidarity with the victims of the theology of David and the Gibeonites demanded a response from David and God. God responded first, when the rain fell on Rizpah and the dead (v. 10a). David then also responded, recognizing, we hope,

another more accountable, responsible, and compassionate theology.

Finally, it was pointed out, Rizpah was not alone in her solidarity with the dead and her protest. While she was the only one to risk death by defying the male leadership, she could not have survived day and night, month after month (v. 10) without the support of her sisters. Perhaps even Saul's daughter, Michal (or Merab), was among those who sustained and strengthened Rizpah. However, Michal, like the leaders of the Gibeonites, may have actively embraced the dominant theology of retribution and death. Perhaps the class position that came with being a daughter of a king made it difficult for her to identify with her sisters. Certainly these African readers knew that the class position of white women in South Africa often has this consequence. And their experience of black male leaders, in both civic and church structures, who have lost their community consciousness and have abandoned *ubuntu* (a person is a person because of other people), made the theology of the Gibeonite leaders uncomfortably familiar. This was the saddest aspect of this story for those who read with Rizpah: that marginalized communities of people could embrace a theology of domination and death.

It would be nice to report that this is where our readings rested. But this reading too was deconstructed. Those who read with David continued to claim textual clues for their interpretation, contending that the juxtaposition of the final two sentences ("they did all that the king commanded" and "God answered prayer for the land after that" [v. 14]) was clear textual attestation that it was David's actions that elicited God's response. Those reading with the Gibeonites responded to Rizpah by reminding those who read with her that theologies of compassion and life had been easily co-opted by apartheid and that such theologies were inadequate if apartheid and its architects were to be completely destroyed.

Thus, this text remains contested. Perhaps the narrator's primary point is that contending theologies of life and death coexist in our communities. The Bible, like the church, is a site of struggle. But those of us who came to know Rizpah cannot forget her. She is our sister and we are her people (West 1999, 121–22, 165). The narrative of who we are has been rewritten by her story; the prophetic force of her life has become a factor in our lives. By sharing in her story we have also been strengthened in our struggle for survival, liberation, and life.

CONCLUSION

In this contextual commentary I have attempted to offer both a sense of how southern Africans go about engaging with the Bible and what they find in their encounters with the Bible. For most southern Africans, the Bible is their book even though they recognize the ambiguity of its arrival among them and question the readings of the Bible that have been used to oppress them. The text and world of 1 and 2 Samuel resonate with their world and are familiar to them, and parts of 1 and 2 Samuel do speak to their lives in empowering ways.

BIBLIOGRAPHY

Isichei, Elizabeth. A History of Christianity in Africa: From Antiquity to the Present. Grand Rapids: Eerdmans, 1995.

Jobling, David. 1 Samuel. Berit Olam Studies in Hebrew Narrative and Poetry. Collegeville, Minn.: Liturgical Press, 1998.

Mafico, Temba L. J. "The Biblical God of the Fathers and the African Ancestors." Pages 481–89 in The Bible in Africa: Transactions, Trajectories, and Trends. Edited by Gerald O. West and Musa W. Dube. Leiden: Brill, 2000.

Mofokeng, T. "Black Christians, the Bible and Liberation." Journal of Black Theology 2 (1988): 34–42.

Mosala, Itumeleng J. Biblical Hermeneutics and Black Theology in South Africa. Grand Rapids: Eerdmans, 1989.

Okure, Teresa. "Feminist Interpretation in Africa." Pages 76–85 in Searching the Scriptures: A Feminist Introduction. Edited by Elisabeth Schüssler Fiorenza with Shelly Matthews. 7 vols. New York: Crossroads, 1993.

Patte, Daniel. Ethics of Biblical Interpretation: A Reevaluation. Louisville: Westminster John Knox, 1995.

Sanneh, Lamin. Translating the Message: The Missionary Impact on Culture. American Society of Missiology Series 13. Maryknoll, N.Y.: Orbis, 1989.

Trible, Phyllis. Texts of Terror: Literary-Feminist Readings of Biblical Narratives. OBT 13. Philadelphia: Fortress, 1984.

West, Gerald O. The Academy of the Poor: Towards a Dialogical Reading of the Bible. Sheffield: Sheffield Academic Press, 1999.

West, Gerald O. "Contextual Bible Study in South Africa: A Resource for Reclaiming and Regaining Land, Dignity and Identity." Pages 595–610 in The Bible in Africa: Transactions, Trajectories, and Trends. Edited by Gerald O. West and Musa W. Dube. Leiden: Brill, 2000.

West, Gerald O. "Indigenous Exegesis: Exploring the Interface Between Missionary Methods and the Rhetorical Rhythms of Africa: Locating Local Reading Resources in the Academy." Neot 36 (2002): 147–62.

West, Gerald O., and Musa W. Dube, eds. The Bible in Africa: Transactions, Trajectories, and Trends. Leiden: Brill, 2000.

1 AND 2 KINGS

Kyung Sook Lee

Ewha Womans University, Seoul, Korea

LIFE CONTEXT OF THE INTERPRETATION

The significant changes that Christianity in Korea underwent during the last fifty years seem to be very similar to the changes in theological perspective that the sources of 1–2 Kings underwent when the Deuteronomistic Historians "redacted" them as they wrote these books. The big difference is that in Korea, the Deuteron-omist theological perspective is used to oppress other cultures and traditions, while in 1–2 Kings it was developed to help the people survive in a national crisis.

Unlike many other Asian countries, which were colonized by western countries (e. g. Great Britain, France, and the U.S.A.), Korea was colonized by the Japanese. Christianity was brought to Korea not by colonizers, but by missionaries associated with progressive nationalists. As a result, in the late 19*th* century, Christianity contributed much to the reform of a feudalistic Korean society, then to national independence from Japan, equality between men and women, and the abolition of classicism. Thus, until 1945 in Korea, Christianity was a tiny minority associated with the weak in our society and proclaimed a message of justice, liberation, and empowerment for women and marginalized people.

Following the establishment of the independent government (1948) and the Korean War (1950–53), a very different kind of Christianity became prevalent. Koreans were strongly influenced by the U.S.A., and Christianity gradually became very popular as the religion of the powerful Americans. Since 1970, economic boom and rapid growth of the church (now about 30 percent of the population) have coincided. In the process, the Korean churches underwent significant changes. They have become more and more authoritative and seem to have readily accepted the patriarchal and dualistic theology of western churches. At times, the Bible and the churches became tools of (imperialist) oppression; pastors and church leaders were endowed with an absolute authority to which lay people should simply submit by remaining quietly obedient. As a result, Christianity exacerbates the conflicts between classes, sexes, and religions. Christians become more and more exclusive and aggressive in their relations with other Asian religions and cultures.

It is no wonder, then, that Christians in Korea, and in other parts of Asia, experience an identity crisis. How can we keep both our Asian identity and our Christian identity? How can we go back to the early Christian spirit to achieve equality, freedom and social justice?

To answer these questions, we should be clear on the following points. First, Christianity is the way to follow Jesus Christ, who was always on the side of the righteous, oppressed, and marginalized people: the poor, the weak, women and children. Christianity has no right to oppress the other religious people and their cultures.

Kyung Sook Lee (D. Th. Göttingen), Professor of Old Testament and Director of the Ewha Institute for Women's Theological Studies, is a frequent participant in meetings of the World Church Council and Faith and Order. Her many publications include, *Women in the Old Testament* (1994), *God, History and Women in the Old Testament* (2000), "Die Koenigsbuecher," in *Kompendium Feministische Bibelauslegung* (1999); "The Biblical Hermeneutics of Liberation from the Perspective of Asian Christian Women," in *Feminist Interpretation of the Bible and the Hermeneutics of Liberation* (2003).

Second, the Bible is indeed the word of God, but expressed in human language. It was written in a concrete situation, by a certain group of theologians to address specific needs in this situation. What we read in the Bible is "contextual theology." In 1–2 Kings we hear what various human voices have to say about God and in the name of God during the period of exile. Understanding these voices and the tensions between their theological perspectives might help us clarify the present day tensions in Korea between a) the powerful Christian movement and its gospel of prosperity and b) the Christianity associated with the weak and the poor and its gospel of justice for the oppressed and the marginalized, with which many Korean feminist theologians are most concerned.

CONTEXTUAL COMMENT

Deuteronomistic Historians as Redactors

It is widely accepted that the so-called Deuteronomistic Historians were a group of theologians who wrote the history of Israel in the books going from Joshua to 1–2 Kgs. The Deuteronomistic Historians were not "authors," but rather redactors who brought together diverse scribal Israelite traditions. Yet they did so creatively by organizing these into a coherent literary work from the perspective of their theological outlook and in terms of their particular interests concerning history, prophecy and laws.

The Deuteronomistic Historians wrote 1–2 Kgs in the exilic period around 550 B.C.E. in search of answers to their questions regarding the reason for Israel's exile and for ways to make possible Israel's future survival as a nation. Why the exile? They answered: Israel had sinned against God/Yahweh who punished her. Will Israel survive? They responded: Yahweh is righteous and strong, and he will save Israel again, when the people turn away from their transgression.

In their effort to address their contextual questions from the perspective of this "high theology," the Deuteronomistic Historians pronounced judgments against many kings and queens, especially those of the northern kingdom. Yet we can sense that these judgments are often in tension with the ways that these sources of the historians portrayed those kings and queens. The Deuteronomistic Historians' judgments, therefore, often seem anachronistic and unfair.

From the perspective of their high theology, the Deuteronomistic Historians severely criticized the worship of foreign Baals in both kingdoms (1 Kgs 16:31-32, 18:18, 22:53; 2 Kgs 8:18.27 etc). Furthermore, they criticized sacrifices at any place other than Jerusalem as transgressions against God. Consequently, every king of the northern kingdom was condemned because each of these kings offered his sacrifice at Bethel and Dan, where Jeroboam erected altars and where the people worshiped instead of going to Jerusalem. The stereotypical description of this worship as pagan (worshipping golden calves) seems to be an unfair criticism of a sanctuary dedicated to Yahweh, although it was not built around the ark, as it was in Jerusalem. Thus, the concept of the "sin of Jeroboam" (repeatedly denounced from 1 Kgs 13 to 2 Kgs 23) directly reflects the Jerusalem- and Judah-oriented theological perspective of the authors. Each king was exclusively judged in terms of these narrow religious criteria, without taking into account his political, economic, social, and military achievements.

This high theology was formulated after King Josiah's reform in 622 B.C.E. and can be summarized by the slogan: "One nation, one God, one temple" or Judah, Yahweh, the Jerusalem temple. Subsequently, during the exile, the Deuteronomistic Historians wrote 1–2 Kings from this perspective, in order to give hope to the nation. For instance, 2 Kings ends with a ray of hope for Israel, namely the story of King Jehoiachin's release from prison and eating at the table of the King of Babylon. But, in their quest for a way to help

Israel survive as a nation, the Deuteronomistic Historians adopted a more and more narrow religious outlook to the point of exclusivism and intolerance of other peoples and religions—a theological outlook in tension with the sources that the redactors used.

For the Korean churches, this type of teaching needs to be carefully assessed, because it can easily serve as a justification for the authoritative, exclusivist, and dualistic attitudes which have become prevalent in our churches and are so problematic in our Asian context. Thus we will examine most attentively the structures of authority and the theological perspective of 1–2 Kgs, and pay close attention to the textual ambivalences that suggest that 1–2 Kgs are in tension with the views of its sources. Recognizing this two-fold contextual theology inscribed in the text will be most helpful in helping us to recognize the contextual character of our own theological stances today.

Structure of 1–2 Kings and its Sources

1–2 Kings synchronizes the annals of the two separate kingdoms to bring together their two histories into the single history of a single people. The history of each king begins with a formula that follows a clear pattern, identifying: a) the king's first year of reign as related to the reign of the monarch of the other kingdom; b) the number of years he reigned; c) in the case of the kings of Judah, how old he was when he became a king and the name of his mother; and d) an overall judgment of the king. All the kings of the northern kingdom, without exception, were judged negatively. Three kings of Judah—David, Hezekiah and Josiah—were highly praised, while other kings of Judah received only limited approval. The closing formula for the history of each king has a similarly stereotypical pattern, including: a) the mention of the annals in which the king's acts were written; b) the king's death; c) in the case of the Judean kings, the king's burial; and d) the name of the successor.

The presentations of the many prophets, among whom Ahijah, Elijah, Elisha, Isaiah, and Hulda, follow a stereotypical pattern, emphasizing prophetic promises and their fulfillments. The prophets are described as messengers of Yahweh, who proclaimed the divine will and judgment, and who uttered prophecies subsequently fulfilled. This stereotypical pattern shows that the stories of the prophets should be read as folktales, rather than as reliable historical documents. This observation is especially the case with the stories of Elijah and Elisha that were divided into many parts as they were paired with stories about the kings; it is very difficult to reconstruct the chronological order of the events.

Many scholars think that the Deuteronomistic Historians used a collection of miracle stories about Elijah and Elisha, in addition to the royal sources that these historians explicitly mention: "The Book of the Acts of Solomon" (1 Kgs 11:41), the "Annals of the kings of Israel," and the "Annals of the kings of Judah." These last two sources included the stories of each king's wars, building projects, and conspiracies.

In summary, 1–2 Kgs, as we have it, not only reflects the theological views of the redactors, i.e., the Deuteronomistic Historians, but also the different theological perspectives of at least three sources. Consequently, 1–2 Kgs necessarily involve a diversity of voices. It is most helpful for the Korean context to bring to light the tensions between these different voices. We will do so by paying close attention to the role of women and of prophets in key stories:

1) Solomon, Abishag, and Bathsheba (1 Kgs 1–2);
2) Solomon, the temple, the Queen of Sheba, and foreign wives (1 Kgs 8, 10–13);
3) Division of the Kingdom, Ahijah the Prophet, and Jeroboam (1 Kgs 11–12);
4) Ahab and Jezebel (1 Kgs 16:29–22:53): The Story of a Wicked Foreign Woman? Or of Royal Tyranny?
5) Elijah, Elisha, the Israelite Servant and Naaman, and the Shunammite Woman (1 Kgs 17–2 Kgs 9)

6) Rampage in the Name of Yahweh and the Making of a Wicked Woman (2 Kgs 9—11)

Solomon's Accession to the Throne, Abishag, and Bathsheba (1 Kings 1–2)

1 Kings begins with the ambivalent story of Solomon's accession to the throne (1 Kgs 1). Was Solomon the legitimate successor of David, or not? Adonijah, the eldest surviving son of David, should have been the king. Why did Solomon become king? Because his mother, Bathsheba, and Nathan "reminded" David of his promise to make Solomon his successor. But did David ever make such a promise, or was this simply a court intrigue around an old king as 1 Kgs 1:11-14 suggests? Was it because Adonijah too hastily proclaimed himself king without consultation with David? Is this story told in order to contest the legitimacy of Solomon's kingship by revealing the intrigue behind it? Or, on the contrary, to give legitimacy to it? Or even to justify the blood revenge that, after David's death, Solomon enacted against his potential opponents (1 Kgs 2:13-46)?

The ambivalence of this opening story frees us to read it from the perspective of a hermeneutic of suspicion and to observe the role of two women in it: Abishag and Bathseba.

Abishag

Abishag was a young and beautiful Shunammite woman brought to David in order to be his attendant and to "revitalize" the old David. Despite much debate, it is not clear what her function was to be (Schroer: 118-119). Although she did not have a sexual relationship with David (1 Kgs 1:4)—she was neither David's wife nor his concubines—she remained David's property. Thus, from the perspective of the story, after David's death, Solomon, and no one else, had the right to possess her. The story of Abishag, including that Adonijah wanted to have her (1 Kgs 2:13-25), was told simply to justify Solomon's blood revenge; Adonijah

had to die. Thus, the Deuteronomistic Historians treated Abishag as an object, not a person. Who was she? How did she feel? How did she live after David's death? Nothing is reported. She was not viewed as a human being. She was an object, not a subject. Her story was exclusively told from the perspective of his story.

Bathsheba

Like Abishag, Bathsheba was brought to David as a sexual object (2 Sam 11:4). Her former husband, Uriah, had to die, because she had become pregnant by David (2 Sam 11:5-27). Many male scholars and even feminist scholars have considered her a cunning woman who intentionally seduced David and made her son Solomon a king (Klein:41-64). However, this logic is not plausible. What else could she do when King David sent for her? (In agreement with Gerald West and women from Zululand, *1 and 2 Samuel*, in this volume). Here in 1 Kgs 1–2 she takes an active role as heroine in a life and death struggle over the kingship of her son. Even though the text might be read as telling the story of intrigue by a cunning woman, it can also be read as referring to an actual promise made by David. Then her reaction, as a mother whose son's future and life are in danger, is natural. From this perspective, she acted as a person who had actually heard David's proclamation that Solomon should become a king. By lying about such a matter, she would have endangered not only herself, but also her son, and all his friends. What she did for Solomon's succession was a brave and intelligent way of negotiating the logic of politics with deadly consequences for her son. It is not fair to judge her with any other moral principles.

As a queen mother, Bathsheba was highly respected by King Solomon and others. Adonijah came to ask a favor of her (to have Abishag as his wife, 1 Kgs 2:13-18), treating her as a respected adviser of the royal court. When she visited Solomon to talk about Adonijah's request, Solomon greeted her very politely, bowed down to her, and led her to sit at his right side. It is not clear whether she knew the meaning and implication of Adonijah's request for Abishag. Even if she recognized that Adonijah was trying to reclaim the kingship for himself, and thus contributed to the killing of her son's opponent, this was once again part of the life and death struggle for the kingship.

It is very interesting to note that we hear Bathsheba's voice only as the mother of Solomon. We do not hear her voice as the wife of Uriah or of David, except for her announcement, "I am pregnant" (2 Sam 11:5). In sum, for the Deuteron-omistic Historians, a woman was a human being only through motherhood; she had an identity primarily as the mother of a son.

For our context in Korean churches today, the view of women presented in the stories of Abishag and of Bathsheba in 1 Kgs 1—2 is disquieting. Yet, we can see a more positive role of women emerging: that of *gebirah*. Even though this term is usually translated "queen mother," it becomes apparent in 15:12-13 that it designates a function that can be given to a woman or taken away from her. These verses are quite puzzling (who is the mother of whom in this story?), if one takes *gebirah* to be exclusively a designation for the mother of the king. Yet it makes quite a lot of sense if *gebirah* is a title, which can be given to, and taken away from, a woman who was a counsellor and mediator for the king. This title and function were not automatically that of the mother of the king, although it was the normal case. A gebirah must have been a woman with a powerful position and with an influence comparable to that of other counsellors at the royal court.

Solomon, the Temple, the Queen of Sheba, and Foreign Wives (1 Kings 8, 10–13)

The following chapters, (1 Kgs 3—4), underscore Solomon's wide-ranging wisdom (e.g., 4:33), and include the famous story about Solomon's wise decision regarding each of two women claiming the same child as hers (3:16-28). It is a traditional story adopted and adapted by the Deuteronomistic Historians (see Gressmann) that also demonstrates that motherhood and life bear witness to each other. 1 Kgs 5–7 describes Solomon's growing power, the consolidation of the kingdom, international relationship, and the construction of the temple.

1 Kings 8, the dedication of the temple, shows that Solomon adopted both the Near Eastern theology of God as the supreme resident, whom the king represents and serves, and the concept of a temple as the place of divine residence (De Vries: xxvi). Yet ambivalence is maintained. God's presence in the temple was indeed implied by the presence of the ark (1 Kgs 8:1-11). But the whole idea that God resides in the temple was alien for the Israelites (see 2 Sam 7:5-7; Isa 66:1-2), so the Deuteronomistic Historians simply said that it was God's name that dwelled in the temple, "the place of which you said, 'My name shall be there,'" (1 Kgs 8:29); God's dwelling is heaven. The Jerusalem temple became the place chosen by God toward which the Israelites should address their supplications to God (1 Kgs 8:29-40). Yet, in another ambivalence, this temple is not limited to Israel: the foreigner's prayer would also be heard by God in the temple (1 Kgs 8:41-43).

Scholars agree that 1 Kgs 8, in its entirety, is the product of the Deuteronomistic Historians. Solomon was just the mouthpiece for their theology—a contextual theology for exiled Israelites. Thus, the main concern of 1 Kgs 8 is not the temple itself, but the people who were carried away captive; if they repent, Yahweh will bring them back to the land (1 Kgs 8:33.46-53). The people can live secure in this hope, because of Yahweh's promise to the Davidic dynasty; David's successor will sit on the throne of Israel forever, "if only your children look to their way, to walk before me as you have walked before me." (8:25).

The Queen of Sheba's Visit

If the visit of the Queen of Sheba (today, possibly Yemen) to check Solomon's wisdom and glory (1 Kgs 10) is historical, we meet a ruling queen of the Orient around 930 B.C.E.; but it is probably a legend.

The Queen of Sheba came to Jerusalem with a great retinue, and with camels bearing spices, gold, and precious stones as presents for King Solomon. Convinced by the prosperity she sees and by Solomon's wise answers to all her questions, she said, "your wisdom and prosperity far surpass the report that I have heard. Happy are your wives! Happy are your servants . . . " (1 Kgs 10:7-8). It sounds erotic. Indeed, many love stories about the Queen of Sheba and Solomon have been spun in Jewish, Arabic, and African literatures. Yet by introducing this legend in 1 Kgs, the Deuteronomistic Historians use the Queen of Sheba to highlight Solomon's wisdom, wealth, and luxury.

Solomon's Luxury and His Foreign Wives

The high praise of Solomon's glory and wealth is followed directly by criticism and judgment. The Deuteronomistic Historians also knew that Solomon was a tyrant and that all of his luxury cost people's agony and sacrifice. Deuteronomy 17:16-18 was explicit: a king should not possess many horses and wives and much silver and gold. But Solomon had many horses (twelve thousands, 10:26), and the opulence of his life style described in 4:22-28 was such that it was calculated that his food provision for one day was enough to feed 14,000-32,000 people and involved enough meat for 3,000-4,500 people.

Solomon had seven hundred wives and three hundred concubines (1 Kgs 11:3); even if this number was exaggerated, the royal court needed thousands of attendants. In addition, to accomplish all his constructions—including that of the temple, of his house and those of his wives, and military bases—Solomon "conscripted forced labor out of all Israel . . . thirty thousand men" (5:13). The people had to suffer under the yoke of that kingdom's glory. Unfortunately, the Deuteronomistic Historians did not criticize Solomon from the social justice perspectives of Deut 17, but from their own religious views.

The Deuteronomistic Historians who praised Solomon so highly in 1 Kgs 3–10, needed to explain the kingdom's division. For this he put the blame on Solomon's foreign wives who, in his old age, "turned away his heart after other gods" (11:4). As punishment, the kingdom would be torn apart (11:9-13.34-35). So, indirectly the Deuteronomistic Historians blamed the foreign wives and concubines for the division of the kingdom, not the social injustices.

But are these women even to be blamed for Solomon's apostasy? Or are they simply turned into scapegoats for the king's wrongdoing? The tensions in the text point to another, more historical reality. We are told that Solomon had many wives—including foreign wives—from his young age; but never before was he designated as a sinner for this, and his kingdom enjoyed prosperity. Solomon had erected the high places for the foreign gods of his foreign wives so that they could offer incense and sacrifices to them (11:7-8). This action was probably a diplomatic gesture at the time of these marriages, aimed at sealing political alliances. Throughout Solomon's reign, it was not forbidden for foreigners to worship their own gods in Jerusalem. Some scholars suggest that Solomon might have intended to erect images of foreign gods in Yahweh's temple in order to symbolize the nations waiting in humble attendance upon God of Israel (De Vries: xxvii, Schroer:130-131). Thus, against the the Deuteronomistic Historians' claims (11:7-8), the presence of these altars for foreign gods might not have been an actual sign of idolatry. Rather, as Lang (55) suggests, they demonstrated that Yahweh was the national and supreme God, and the other foreign gods were humble guest gods that could be worshipped with their altars in Jerusalem.

Thus, the very tensions in the text show that it is the Deuteronomist historian who turned Solomon's foreign wives into scapegoats for his apostasy. Unfortunately, the Deuteronomistic Historians' interpretation of that part of history has conveyed and continue to convey the message that women, in general, are dangerous and seductive.

Division of the Kingdom, Ahijah the Prophet, and Jeroboam (1 Kings 11–12)

For our context in Korea, three issues stand out in the retelling of the division of the Kingdom: the cause of this division, the role of the prophet, and the Deuteronomistic Historians' condemnation of Jeroboam.

1 Kings makes it clear that there were political tensions during the last years of Solomon's reign and that these were due to Solomon's political failures and his disregard for the people. 1 Kgs 12 says that the dissatisfaction of the people was the crucial issue: the people's yoke was too heavy to carry. Therefore, Jeroboam rebelled against Solomon (11:26). Why? The text first explains it by describing him as one who was put in charge of "forced labor of the house of Joseph" (11:27-28).

Indeed, after Solomon's death, returning from Egypt where he had fled (11:40), Jeroboam went with the people to the new king, Rehoboam, to ask him to lighten their service and yoke: "Your father made our yoke heavy. Now, therefore, lighten the hard service of your father and his heavy yoke that he placed on us, and we will serve you" (12:4). But Rehoboam fiercely rejected this plea (12:11). Thus, historically a) Solomon's heavy yoke and Rehoboam's arrogance against the people were the real cause of the kingdom's division; and b) Jeroboam was the leader of triumphant popular movement to free the people from the oppressive rule of Solomon and Rehoboam that resulted in the independence of the north.

This movement for social justice, consistent with the message of the classical prophetic books prophets, is still visible in 1–2 Kgs, although it is now covered up by the Deuteronomistic Historians' theological perspective. Thus, the successful champion of social justice, Jeroboam, is presented by the prophet Ahijah as fulfilling a prophecy

regarding the punishment for the sins (apostasy) of Solomon and his successor, Rehoboam (11:29-39). In the process, both the prophetic role and the justice issues that Jeroboam advocated are radically transformed.

The role of the prophet Ahijah is strictly limited by the Deuteronomistic Historians' reduction of the prophetic role to the pattern of "prediction and fulfillment." Here, prophets are the servants of Yahweh who announced the divine will and judgment, an announcement which is soon to be fulfilled. The primary concern for social justice and ethical teaching that we find in the classical prophetic books is absent. For Korean readers, this truncated view of the role and message of prophets can be dangerously misleading.

Similarly, the Deuteronomistic Historians radically transformed the figure of Jeroboam: the champion of social justice becomes a sinful figure. Throughout the rest of 1—2 Kgs we will find reference to the "sin of Jeroboam" (e.g., 1 Kgs 15:26.34, 16:19.26). Following the division of the kingdom, Jeroboam became king of Israel, (the northern kingdom), and Rehoboam king of Judah (12:20). The Deuteronomistic Historians tells us that Jeroboam built Shechem on the hill of Ephraim and resided there (12:25). He made two golden calves and set one in Bethel and other in Dan (1 Kgs 12:26-29). Objectively, it was quite natural for Jeroboam to set up altars in Israel, so that the people of the northern kingdom would not go and worship in Jerusalem. But in the eyes of the Deuteronomistic Historians this became the "sin of Jeroboam," a heinous sin: worshipping elsewhere than in Jerusalem.

Was it a condemnation of idolatry? It is what the Deuteronomistic Historians propose by speaking about the two golden calves—implicitly referring to Exodus 32:4. But many scholars debate this issue. For Jeroboam, it would not have made any sense to set up altars to worship Baal in the form of golden calves. Historically speaking, Jeroboam most probably set them as pedestals or thrones for Yahweh, as the ark did in

Jerusalem, in order to establish the cult of Yahweh at Bethel and Dan.

At any rate, the condemnation of Jeroboam on the basis of this Jerusalem-oriented theology is clearly anachronistic. It interprets Jeroboam's actions (922-901 B.C.E.) and those of his successors (e.g., 1 Kgs 15:26.34, 16:19.26) from the perspective of the cultic reform of Josiah after 622 B.C.E.

Ahab and Jezebel (1 Kings 16:29–22:53): The Story of a Wicked Foreign Woman? Or of Royal Tyranny?

Omri, and his son, Ahab, kings of the northern kingdom with Samaria as its capital, were economically and politically successful. But Ahab was most strongly criticized by the Deuteronomistic Historians because he married Jezebel, "daughter of King Ethbaal of the Sidonians." It was a political marriage to consolidate economic and diplomatic relations between Israel and Sidon of Phoenicia. In 1 Kgs 16:31-33, we read that "he erected an altar for Baal in the house of Baal, which he built in Samaria," and that he went and served Baal and worshipped him. The reader thus might have the impression that Ahab did not worship Yahweh, but Baal. But this is once again an anachronistic judgment of Ahab from the perspective of the cultic reform of Josiah. From a historical perspective we have to say that as the King of Israel, Ahab necessarily worshipped Yahweh, because Yahweh was the national God of Israel and Judah. Certainly, Ahab tolerated Baal's worship and erected the altar, probably for his wife and her attendants, who wanted to worship their gods in Samaria—as Solomon built altars for the gods and goddesses of his foreign wives in Jerusalem.

But for the Deuteronomistic Historians this activity was the occasion to paint Jezebel as the most wicked woman in the history of Israel, probably because she was a very powerful queen. Two very negative stories about Jezebel—the story of her persecution of Yahweh's prophets and that of Naboth's vineyard—show that the depiction of Jezebel as a wicked woman was superimposed by these redactors.

The "flashback" mention in 18:4 and 13 of Jezebel's persecution of Yahweh's prophets interrupts so much of the flow of the story that the NRSV sets 18:4 between parentheses. This mention was clearly added to the pre-existing story regarding Elijah, Ahab, and the conflicts between the prophets of Yahweh and those of Baal (18:1-46) in order to blame Jezebel for this conflict. Was not this foreign princess responsible for the presence of the cult of Baal in Israel? Should she not be blamed for this conflict?

The same anachronistic condemnation of Jezebel is found in the story of Naboth's vineyard (1 Kgs 21:1-19; 2 Kgs 9:30-37). In 1 Kgs 21 we read an artistically interesting story with a nice plot concerning a wicked foreign queen, an innocent Israelite king who is manipulated by the wicked queen, a prophetic condemnation, and God's promised intervention. But as soon as one looks more closely at the text, it becomes clear that the Deuteronomistic Historians have once again painted a foreign woman as cunning and wicked. As many scholars have pointed out, contradictions in the story show that it was retold with a new antagonist—Jezebel. Where was the vineyard? In Samaria (21:18, 22:38)? Or in Jezreel (21:1-16)? Who was the instigator of the crime? Jezebel (21:1-16) or Ahab (21:17 -22 and 27-29)? Scholars, Oeming, Miller, and Rofe, appropriately conclude that the wicked role of Jezebel was inserted by the Deuteron-omistic Historians in an older Naboth's vineyard story. That story originally concerned a political conflict between the royal court and a rich landlord—a conflict won by the royal court through a power game and the use of intrigue.

If this analysis is correct, 1 Kgs 21 presents not so much Jezebel's wickedness, but rather an other instance of the Deuteronomistic Historians' hatred for foreign women, here in the person of Jezebel. The royal tyranny upon landlords in Israel, which was exposed and prophetically denounced by the earlier form of the story, is now almost hidden.

Elijah, Elisha, the Israelite Servant and Naaman, and the Shunammite Woman (1 Kings 17–2 Kings 9)

Elijah and Elisha

The narratives about the prophets Elijah and Elisha are interwoven with stories about kings in 1 Kgs 17–2 Kgs 9 that tell about their role in conflicts between Baal and Yahweh worshippers. As precursors of the classical prophets, Elijah and Elisha spoke in the name of Yahweh and proclaimed God's will. These main differences are that as "men of God" they performed many miracles and took part in the political movement against the house of Omri and Ahab.

The stories of Elijah's miracles resemble those popular legends of the never failing jar of meal and oil (1 Kgs 17:10-16) and of revived sons (17:17-23). Such stories about Elijah and Elisha, similar to the miracles ascribed to Moses (and Jesus), establish the legitimacy of Elijah or Elisha as a "man of God," who is a true prophet and an agent of God's power: "Now I know that you are a man of God, and that the word of the LORD in your mouth is truth" (1:24).

The narrative in 1 Kgs 18, the events on Mount Carmel, evokes in the readers loyalty to Yahweh as the only God, through its mocking polemic against other gods. This is true of the entire story of Elijah that rejects all forms of syncretism. One cannot believe both in Yahweh and in Baal; one must choose between them. According to Lang and Albertz, this strict monotheistic theology originated with Elijah.

For us in Korea, as people who live in a multi-religious society, this theology of Elijah raises the very serious question: Did the Israelites worship other gods such as Asherah, Astarte or Baal during the period of the monarchy? Was Moses the father of monotheism as many scholars assumed? Or was it Elijah, as Lang and Albertz propose?

And did the Deuteronomistic Historians emphasize during the exilic period Elijah's monotheism in order to better address the needs of the exiled community in Babylon which was tempted by syncretism or apostasy? Therefore, is this strict rejection of syncretism a particular "contextual theology"?

As we already noted, the Deuteronomistic Historians do not say that Omri, Ahab, and Jezebel, abandoned the cult of Yahweh. The problem was that they did not eliminate the cult of Baal, and in fact tolerated it—indeed, Jezebel promoted it. How common was this simulta- neous worship of Yahweh, Asherah, and Astarte in Israel? It is much discussed (Schorer:130-132). Yet we can say that it is in such a tolerant context that Elijah stood up to start the religion exclusively devoted to "Yahweh."

As we compare the stories about Elisha in 2 Kgs 2–8 with those concerning Elijah, we find many similarities between the two prophets. After Elijah's ascension (2 Kgs 2:1-15), Elisha exhibits the same kind of power as Elijah did. Despite corrupted texts (esp. 2 Kgs 7) and grotesque stories (2 Kgs 2:23-25; 6:25-30), the narrative shows that Elisha demonstrated his ability as a man of God by performing miracles, as Elijah did. Yet a distinctive trait is that, in many instances, Elisha did not talk with the people directly, but only through Gehazi. While Elisha enjoyed authority as a man of God and had inherited Elijah's mantle, he did not inherit his spirit. Another distinctive trait is that Elisha's main interest seems to lie more in political than in religious affairs. Thus, he tells the Shunammite woman, who had helped him, that he could speak on her behalf to the king or to the commander of the army (2 Kgs 4:13), showing his political connections. Similarly, Elisha and his prophets were behind Jehu's conspiracy in Israel (2 Kgs 9:1-13) and Hazael's small uprising against Ben-Hadad of Aram (2 Kgs 8:7-15).

The Israelite Servant and Naaman

The story of Naaman, commander of the army of the king of Aram (2 Kgs 5) is very interesting from our multi-religious perspective. Naaman was a man of Aram, and he suffered from leprosy. A "young girl captive from the land of Israel" (5:2) advised him to visit Elisha, and Naaman followed her advice. His leprosy was cured through Elisha, and Naaman said: "There is no God in the all earth except in Israel" (2 Kgs 5:15). Naaman wanted to become a worshipper of Yahweh. But because of his nationality as an Aramean and his position in the King's court, he would have to bow down in the house of Rimmon. When Naaman asked Elisha if Yahweh would pardon him for that, Elisha said to him, "Go in peace" (2 Kgs 5:19), meaning that Yahweh will pardon him.

In this story, Yahweh is very generous. Elisha, in the name of Yahweh, has understood the situation of the foreign army commander and permitted him to worship Yahweh in his own way. Here Elisha is not exclusive and judgmental but inclusive and open to the foreigners. This is a most important passage for people who live in a multi-religious society such as ours. Another significant feature of this text is that a young girl from Israel gave such kind and worthwhile advice to the commander of the Aramean army. Despite her precarious situation as a young girl, taken captive during a raid in Israel by the Arameans and made a servant of Naaman's wife, she represents the wisdom of Israel.

The Shunammite Woman

In the miracle stories of Elijah and Elisha, the wonder workers are males, and most of the recipients are women. Each of these women is very poor and in desperate situations. Either she has nothing to eat (e.g., 1 Kgs 17:8-16), she has no son, her only son is dead, or she is a poor widow in debt (2 Kgs 4:1-7). It is a pity that these stories give us the general impression that women are always in need, and that males, like priests or prophets, should protect them. Happily, the story of the Shunammite woman breaks this pattern.

The Shunammite woman is a wealthy woman who was childless, and who supported Elisha by providing housing and food. She had a son as predicted by Elisha, but her son died, and through Elisha, her son was brought back to life (2 Kgs 4:8-37). However, if we read the story carefully, it becomes clear that the Shunammite woman was more than the beneficiary of the miracle, she also was its initiator. Like most women in these narratives, she has no name, but she has a voice, speaks for herself, makes decisions, and acts independently as a fully human subject. When she heard that Elisha was passing through Shunem, she takes the initiative to invite him to stop there for a meal and to build a room where he could stay whenever he would come to Shunem. When Elisha wanted to show his gratitude for her hospitality, she refuses his suggestion that she could receive some favor of the king or the commander of the army: "I live among my own people." (2 Kgs 4:13).

She is the true initiator of her son's resuscitation. When the boy is sick, her husband simply asks a servant to bring him to his mother. Following his death, she acts very quickly. She lays her son on Elisha's bed, saddles the donkey, and directs the servant to ride speedily to Elisha. She insists that Elisha revive her son and the prophet does as she says. Several feminist scholars (Shield, Van Dijk-Hemmes, and Siebert-Hommes) also emphasize that in the story of resuscitation in 2 Kgs 4:18-37, the real miracle worker is the Shunammite woman, and the real power rests with the woman.

Rampage in the Name of Yahweh and the Making of a Wicked Woman (2 Kings 9–11)

Jehu, the Revolutionist

Through the intermediary of a young prophet, Elisha anointed Jehu as the king of Israel (2 Kgs 9:1-6), with the following mandate from Yahweh:

> "Thus says the LORD the God of Israel . . .
> You shall strike down the house of your
> master Ahab, so that I may avenge on
> Jezebel the blood of my servants the

prophets, and the blood of all the servants of the Lord. For the whole house of Ahab shall perish; I will cut off from Ahab every male, bond or free, in Israel. . . . The dogs shall eat Jezebel in the territory of Jezreel, and no one shall bury her." (9:6-10).

It was a conspiracy in the name of Yahweh. And dutifully Jehu killed the following: Joram, son of Ahab, king of Israel, as well as Ahaziah, king of Judah who was visiting him (9:17-28), Jezebel (9:30-37), seventy sons of Ahab (10:1-11), and forty-two brothers of Ahaziah, king of Judah (10:12-14), loyalists of Joram in Samaria (10:15-17). In alliance with Rechab (10:10-16), Jehu enforced a strict and exclusivist cult of Yahweh, killing all the worshippers of Baal and destroying Baal's temples (10:18-28). All were killed in the name of Yahweh, in very brutal massacres. The stories certainly include exaggerations; for instance, the numbers of "forty-two" or "seventy" (used in the narrative) are favorite numbers in folk tales. In the end, Jehu was criticized because he did not turn away "from the sins of Jeroboam" (10:29)—an explanation of the political defeats and the shrinking territory of Israel (10:32-33). Yet, throughout the main body of the narrative, the very cruel and zealous Jehu was evaluated quite positively by the Deuteronomistic Historians because he suppressed Baal's worship.

Athaliah

In another very cruel story, Athaliah is depicted as the most wicked woman in the Bible (2 Kgs 11). To keep her power in the kingdom of Judah, she has even tried to kill her grandson. Athaliah, a princess of the northern kingdom, was married to King Jehoram of Judah to strengthen the relationship between Israel and Judah. Her husband, Jehoram, reigned eight years in Judah, and her son, Ahaziah, became king of Judah (8:16-24). Thus, she was the queen mother, the *gebirah*. But as a result of Jehu's revolution, she lost not only her brother, King Joram of Israel, but also her son, King Ahaziah of Judah, and many other members of the royal families (see above). According

to 2 Kgs 11:1, "when Athaliah, Ahaziah's mother, saw that her son was dead, she set about to destroy all the royal family," including her grandson, Joash (11:2, spelled Jehoash in 11:21), who was rescued by Jehosheba. This is a strange and unrealistic story. Why did Athaliah proceed with this massacre? It is not explained and difficult to understand. As the *gebirah,* she had and would continue to have vast political power, especially if her grandson was on the throne. So the Deuteronomistic Historians' report that Athaliah wanted to kill Joash is not plausible. Of course she might have had many enemies in the court and tried to eliminate them to secure her position in the royal court of Judah. But it is a real exaggeration to say that this activity involved trying to kill all the royal family, including her grandson. Once again, the Deuterono-mistic Historians' picture does not match the reality of history. The Deuteronomistic Historians took the side of the Jerusalem group led by the priest Jehoiada, depicting him as a hero and Athaliah as a sinner, a wicked woman. Here again, a power hungry conniving man is affirmed and positively described, while a powerful woman is vilified.

What is most likely is that after Jehu's coup, there were political conflicts in Judah between the people of Jerusalem and the "people of the land" (mentioned often in 2 Kgs 11:14-20). Perhaps the people of Jerusalem, who agreed with Athaliah's marriage to Jehoram and understood the benefits of the alliance between the north and south, were on her side, while the "people of the land" did not want to have Athaliah in their court, because she was not from David's house but from the family of Ahab and Jezebel. Because of Jehu, Athaliah was totally cut off from Israel, and had an enemy inside her family, Jehosheba. Jehosheba, a sister of King Ahaziah, probably not a daughter of Athalia (11:2-3), stole Joash and supported Jehoiada, the priest (she became his wife, according to 2 Chr 22:11). Then, apparently, the priests of Jerusalem and the "people of the land" joined force in a conspiracy against Athaliah. Jehoash (Joash) took his seat on the throne of the kings (2 Kgs 11:19) and all the "people of the land" rejoiced, while the city (Jerusalem) was quiet. But to justify this take-over by the party of the priest and of the "people of the land" and the killing of Queen Athaliah, did she need to be vilified? Of course, this is part of the Deuteronomistic Historians's customary literary way of presenting all women power in a negative light.

Josiah's Reform and Prophetess Huldah

The Deuteronomistic Historians wrote about the fall of Israel in a stereotypical way: Throughout its history, Israel has sinned all the time; they went after false idols, like the golden calves and sacred poles; they worshipped all the hosts of heaven and Baal; and of course committed "the sins of Jeroboam" (2 Kgs 17:7-18. 21–23) The fall of the northern kingdom, Israel, in 722 B.C.E., is the just judgment for all these sins.

The situation of Judah was different. It involved paying tributes to the Assyrian king, oscillating between cultic reforms under King Hezekiah, (2 Kgs 18–20), and "abominations," under king Manasseh and Amon (2 Kgs 21). King Amon's servants assassinated him in the palace. But once again, "the people of the land" intervened. They killed all the conspirators and made Amon's son, Josiah, king of Judah (21:23-24). Again we have to ask: Who were these "the people of the land?"

Josiah's reform is the climax of 1 and 2 Kings. Josiah is one of the three kings (together with David, and Hezekiah) who are highly praised in the Deuteronomistic Historians' work because they contributed to establishing or reforming the cult of Yahweh. The catalyst for Josiah's reform was the discovery of a "book of the law" (2 Kgs 22:3-11), which most likely was similar to the Book of Deuteronomy. The high priest Hilkiah made this discovery during repair work in the temple and was ordered by the king to "Go, inquire of the LORD. . . . concerning the words of this book" (22:13). And together with other priests, Hilkiah went to the prophetess, Huldah (22:14).

Who was Huldah? In the Hebrew Bible there are not many prophetesses. Miriam (Exod 15, Num 12) and Deborah (Judg 4—5) were the female figures in the pre-monarchical period. Isaiah's wife was also called a prophetess (Isa 8:3), but we do not know if her title as a prophetess means that she functioned as a prophetess, or whether she was simply given the title because she was the wife of a prophet. So it appears that Huldah is the first prophetess mentioned in the biblical texts.

The mention of Huldah in 2 Kgs 22 gives us the information that in the monarchical time women prophets existed, even in relationship with the royal court, and had a prophetic role in important events. The priests did not hesitate to visit Huldah, the prophetess. This procedure was simply the appropriate thing to do when sent by the king to "inquire of the LORD." The fact that it was a woman, a prophetess, who was consulted, did not require any explanation or justification.

"The prophetess Huldah [was] the wife of Shallum son of Tikvah, son of Harhas, keeper of the wardrobe; she resided in Jerusalem in the Second Quarter, where they consulted her" (2 Kgs 22:14). She declared to the delegation sent by the king that God would bring disaster on Jerusalem and its inhabitants, but after Josiah's death, because he had repented (22:15-20). We do not know if she was a prophetess of the temple an independent prophetess. But one thing is clear: what she told the delegation in 22:16-20 is a summary of the Deuteronomistic Historians' theology. It is not a trivial matter, that the Deuterono-mistic Historians put their own theology in the mouth of a woman. And the fact that they do it in such a matter of fact way shows that there probably were many other prophetesses besides Huldah.

Following Huldah's oracle, King Josiah started the cult reform: he eliminated all "high places," where sacrifice outside Jerusalem had been practiced (23:8-9); he demolished the altar in Bethel "erected by Jeroboam son of Nebat, who caused Israel to sin" (23:15). The Deuteronomistic Historians did not write about the political or economic effects of this cult reform. Actually, we do not know how successful it was. Nor is it clear whether the people of Judah were happy with this reform or not. But its influence was most significant, because many books of the Hebrew Bible were written or edited by Deuteronomistic historians echoing this reform, including Deuteronomy.

Following King Josiah's death, the "people of the land" once again intervened, making Jehoahaz, son of Josiah, king in the palace of his father. As usual they lent enthusiastic support to the restoration or continuation of the Davidic dynasty. Whether they were a rich and privileged group or some

kind of democratic movement with high aspirations cannot be ascertained.

In spite of Yahweh's promise to David and Jerusalem, and according to Huldah's oracle, Judah fell (in 598 B.C.E., with complete exile in 587 B.C.E.). Judah met the wrath of Yahweh. 1 and 2 Kgs tried to explain these events theologically in various ways, but these books did not fully succeed. 2 Kings ends with the story of Jehoiachin, finally released from prison and able to dine regularly in the king's presence. This ambiguous report about King Jehoiachin as an honored captive in the royal circle would likely give some hope to the people of Judah. Judah's future was open. This was the contextual theology of hope and survival that the Deuteronomistic Historians proclaimed at that time.

CONCLUSION

What we read in 1-2 Kings is a theological interpretation of history by the Deuteronomistic Historians, not an objective history. Deuteronomistic Historians wrote these books in the concrete situation of the crisis of their national defeat. They tried to answer the questions: Why? and How? Why the exile? How could we survive in exile? The answer—By adopting an exclusive theology: "One God, one nation, one temple." Yahweh, Judah, and the Jerusalem temple. This was a contextual theology that addressed these problems. This exclusive theology provided a way to repent and to survive by allowing the exiled people to remain in a community clearly distinct from the other nations and religions that their faith required them to exclude. This contextual theology was, therefore, a matter of repentance and survival for the exiled people of God.

Such an exclusive theology became problematic in our context, because this contextual theology of survival was misinterpreted in an imperialistic way in Korea. Yet, all along, we noted other voices in this text: the memory of other traditions and theologies much more open to other

people and ways. Behind what was the almost systematic vilification of women, and especially of foreign women, as part of the theological pattern of the Deuteronomistic Historians, we noted in 1-2 Kgs that women in Israel have played very important roles in society. But these stories were seldom told in a positive way, because the Deuteronomistic Historians had no interest in "her-story." So we should use our imagination very freely to figure out how they contributed to the society. In 1–2 Kgs, Yahweh is jealous of his covenant, but he is also depicted as holy, righteous, mighty, and attentive to the people, including non-Israelites, such as Naaman. In short, Yahweh acts according to the law of causation—sins call for punishments, but Yahweh's actions are also shown to be above this law. God is gracious and generous and gives us hope even in times of crisis. By developing their contextual theology to give that hope to the people of their time, the Deuteronomistic Historians invite us to develop our own Korean contextual theology for our time that will bring real hope for the poor, the weak, women, and children.

BIBLIOGRAPHY

Ahlstroem, G. W. *Aspects of Syncretism in Israelite Religion* (Lund: Gleeup, 1963).

Brenner, Athalya, ed., *Samuel and Kings*. A Feminist Companion to the Bible 7, Second Series (Sheffield: Sheffield Academic Press, 2000). See especially: Lillian R. Klein, "Bathsheba Revealed," pages 47–64; Mary E. Shields, "Subverting a Man of God, Elevating a Woman: Role and Power Reversals in 2 Kings 4," pages 115–124; and Jopie Siebert-Hommes, "The Widow of Zarephath and the Great Woman of Sunem: A Comparative Analysis of two Stories," pages 98–114.

De Vries, Simon J. *1 Kings*. WBC 12 (Waco. Texas: Word Books 1985).

Lang, Bernhard "Die Jahwe-allein-Bewegung, Die Geburt des biblischen Monotheismus," pages 47-83, in Bernhard Lang, ed. *Der einzige Gott* (Muenchen: Koesel Verlag, 1981).

Lee, Kyung Sook "Die Koenigsbuecher," pages 130–145 in *Kompendium Feministische Bibelauslegung,* ed. Luise Schottroff and Marie-Theres Wacker (Guetersloh: Chr. Kaiser/Guetersloher, 1999).

Schroer, Silvia "Toward a Feminist Reconstruction of the History of Israel," pages 85–176, in Luise Schottroff, Silvia Schroer, Marie-Theres Wacker, eds. *Feminist Interpretation, The Bible in Women's perspective,* translated by Martin and Barbara Rumscheidt (Minneapolis: Fortress, 1998).

Van Dijk-Hemmes, Fokkelien, "The Great Woman of Shunem and the Man of God: A Dual Interpretation of 2 Kings 4:8-37," pages 218-30, in Athalya Brenner, ed. *Exodus-Deuteronomy* Feminist Companion to the Bible 5 (Sheffield: Sheffield Academic Press, 1994).

1 AND 2 CHRONICLES

Fook-Kong Wong

Hong Kong Baptist Theological Seminary, Hong Kong, China

THE LIFE CONTEXT OF THE INTERPRETATION

This commentary is written from the perspective of a Chinese Christian teaching in a Baptist seminary in Hong Kong. Since the majority of people in Hong Kong are of Chinese origins, Chinese cultures dominate in this Special Administrative Region (SAR) of China. Western cultures also exert a strong influence because of the SAR's colonial roots as well as its roles as an international port and financial center. Other important groups include new immigrants from the mainland as well as Filipino maids from the Philippines. Despite its relative homogeneity in terms of racial mix, it is religiously heterogeneous. Buddhism and Taoism predominate, but other religions like Islam, Sikhism, Hinduism, Mormonism, Jehovah's Witness, and Judaism are also represented. The Christian community in Hong Kong has a significant voice in society despite being a numerical minority. Hong Kong has enjoyed tremendous economic growth in the last three decades. Many people's standard of living is on par with that of the developed world. Politically Hong Kong was a British colony until 1997, at which point it returned under the sovereignty of China. It is currently governed under a "one country, two systems" arrangement that allows Hong Kong a measure of political freedom while being part of China.

1 and 2 Chronicles: The Relationship of God's People to the World in this Life Context

My perspective on 1 and 2 Chronicles is that they were written for the descendants of the Jews who had returned from exile, whose priorities and sense of identity were not necessarily the same as their parents. Furthermore, the initial excitement of returning and rebuilding the temple had worn off. The hope for the emergence of a new king (perhaps Zerubbabel) had also fizzled out. What remained was the grim reality of daily life in Palestine. In these circumstances the Chronicler (that is, the author-redactor of 1 and 2 Chronicles) rewrote Israel's history to encourage his people. The following are some issues about the relationship of God's people to the world that are raised by a reading of Chronicles.

First, there is the issue of cultural iden-tity. A notable feature of 1 Chronicles is that it begins with nine chapters of genealogies. One function of the genealogies was to connect the Jewish community in the Chronicler's time to its roots. These extensive genealogies were one of the Chronicler's ways of explaining to these later generations why their forefathers had returned to Jerusalem. They also reflect his attempt to rekindle in his readers the same passion that had driven their ancestors to return to the land of Israel. The Pentateuch and the Deuteronomistic History addressed the same concern in their own way.

Historically Hong Kong was a city of immigrants. The population grew mainly through the influx of new immigrants until the 1960s, when the Communist Chinese government and the colonial government in to the colony. Nevertheless, new immigrants

Fook-Kong Wong is a professor of Old Testament whose publications include *A Commentary on First and Second Chronicles* (2003); "Echoes of Zechariah 4:6 in Chronicles," *Interpretations of Scripture and Literature* (in Chinese, 2003); and "A Response to Professor Jack Sasson's 'The Origin of the Hebrew Religion,'" in *Hebrew Origins* (Jack Sasson, 2002).

have continued to arrive on the shores of Hong Kong up till the present. With more than 95 percent of the population being Chinese, Hong Kong people have retained many of the Chinese customs that they inherited from their ancestors on the mainland. Many people still believe in *feng shui* (relating to life conditions in particular contexts). Chinese love opera, follow Chinese customs in matters of marriage and burial, and celebrate Chinese festivals that have been passed down for centuries.

On the other hand, due to its years under colonial rule and its development as a global city, Hong Kong people have also developed an international sense of identity. For example, they cherish values like human rights, equality before the law, democracy, freedom of expression, transparency, and competitiveness. This fusion of east and west makes them distinct from both their former British rulers as well as from their present Chinese government. Like the Jewish Diaspora who returned to Jerusalem, they find that their values are not quite the same as those who never left their homeland. One result of the handover is that Hong Kong people now have a chance to rethink and redefine their cultural identities.

Second, an important aspect of Jewish identity advocated by the Chronicler was a deep commitment to and worship of YHWH. On this issue, the situation in Hong Kong differs from that of the Chronicler. Less than 10 percent of the population are Christian. Many people would look to Confucianism, Buddhism, Taoism, or forms of syncretistic popular belief as their religious roots. Although religious pluralism has always existed, the church enjoyed a special status from their former Christian government. For example, they were provided with land for schools, social services, and hospitals, and they were given leadership in certain ceremonies like marriage ceremonies and national functions. These privileges can no longer be taken for granted and the church is treated like any other non-profit organization. This change of status is not necessarily bad but it requires adjustment on

the part of the church to meet the new challenges. In this post-handover situation, a deep commitment to God is even more vital for the survival and growth of the church.

A third problem highlighted by reading Chronicles in light of the context of Hong Kong is the sense of crisis facing Hong Kong people. Property values and the stock market are down, the economy is in bad shape, and so many endure the shame of not being able to provide for their families. Furthermore, China's entry into the World Trade Organization would spell the end of Hong Kong's role as China's window to the world. We do not know whether the Chronicler's intended readers enjoyed strong leadership or if they were facing a specific crisis. What we do know is that the Chronicler felt the need to appeal to Israel's former heroes and God's powerful intervention in the past to encourage them. These exhortations are as valuable today as they were in the time of the Chronicler.

The last problem addressed by the Chronicler is that of materialism and spiritual apathy. It is evident from the biblical accounts that many of the returnees were more oriented toward materialism than toward spirituality. In the other biblical texts of the period, each with its own agenda (see the commentaries in this volume), we find suggestions that the rebuilding of the temple stopped for almost eighteen years while the greater portion of the returnees looked after their own self-interest (Hag 1). The Sabbath was not diligently kept (Neh 13:15-22) and offerings to the temple were not properly observed (Mal 1). The situation does not seem to have changed much in the time of the Chronicler. Against the prevalent materialism and spiritual apathy, the Chronicler emphasized a God-centered, worship-centered lifestyle. From the perspective of our Baptist tradition, the same problem of materialism and spiritual apathy affects the greater society and even the church today. The churches in Hong Kong should reevaluate their priorities and not let material possessions replace God as the center of their lives.

CONTEXTUAL COMMENT

An Overview of the Books

The name of the two books in Hebrew is *dibrê hayyāmîm* ("the words/matters of the days"). The books were mainly a chronicle of the kings of Judah. Kings of the northern kingdom were only mentioned when their stories intersected with their Judean counterparts. Scholars used to think that Chronicles and Ezra-Nehemiah had the same author and, in fact, that the latter was the continuation of Chronicles. This view has been challenged vigorously in the last few decades. Many scholars today think that Chronicles and Ezra-Nehemiah were by different authors. A related issue concerns the unity of the book. Many theories have been forwarded regarding the composition of the book (Japhet 1993, 5-7; Williamson 1982, 12-15, 41). A major trend today is to see substantial unity in the book, and this is the view followed here.

Chronicles was written in the later part of the Persian period (at the earliest toward the middle of the fourth century B.C.E.). The Pentateuch and the Deuteronomistic History were already in circulation and the Chronicler used them as his sources. Consequently, there is a lively discussion regarding the purpose of his work (e.g., to refute the Samaritans, to substantiate the claim of the Davidic house to rule over Israel, or to establish the exclusive legitimacy of the Jerusalem cultic institution). Although the purpose of the book is still under discussion, it is clear that the Chronicler emphasized certain themes, which included the importance of the temple in Jerusalem, and the worship of YHWH centering on the temple; the divine choice of the Davidic dynasty; all of Israel as the people of God; immediate retribution, guilt and atonement; and God's miraculous help in times of crises.

Genealogies
(1 Chronicles 1-9)

Extensive genealogies occupy the first nine chapters of 1 Chronicles. The genealogies begin with Adam and end with the appearance of David. These genealogies can be analyzed as follows (Dorsey 1999, 146):

A Israel's past (1:1-54)
   B Royal tribe: Judah (2:1–4:23)
      C Peripheral tribes (4:24–5:26)
         D Center: Tribe of Levi (6:1–81)
      C' Peripheral tribes (7:1–40)
   B' Royal tribe: Benjamin (8:1–40)
A' Israel's present (9:1–34)

This analysis reveals that most of the materials pertain to the tribes of Israel. The list in chapter 1 was a summary of the genealogical lists in Genesis; the details given in Genesis were omitted, leaving only a chain of names that linked Adam to Israel (Jacob). The focus on the tribes was therefore a deliberate choice rather than the result of a limitation of the Chronicler's sources. It is apparent that the Chronicler wanted to get to the tribes of Israel as soon as possible, but he did not want to omit the ancestors who preceded Israel. He did not just want to anchor his readers' identity in their Jewish roots but also in the greater human family. The ideology of the genealogies in chapter 1 urged Israel to realize the ideal that God had intended for the whole world (Johnstone 1997, Vol.1, 30).

These genealogies are similar to Chinese genealogical records kept by the head of families or at local temples. Some Chinese families can trace their genealogy back a few centuries using these records. In Hong Kong economic status and educational affiliations have taken over the role once held by one's pedigree. This change is understandable, but one's roots still serve or should serve important functions. Genealogical roots connect people to their cultural roots, imbuing their lives with a meaning greater than that of the individual, and keep them moored in times of great change. Furthermore, regardless of the differences that exist between mainland and Hong Kong Chinese, these two groups do share a common past in history. Until the merging of their horizons in the future, this shared past serves as a bridge between them.

From our Baptist theological perspective, the genealogical lists in Chronicles bear witness to God's intimate knowledge and remembrance of his people. Lists of names make for boring reading until one realizes that each name represents a person who once lived, loved, and had a story. Take, for example, the name Tiras (1 Chr 1:5). Who was this man? What did he look like? How many wives and children did he have? Did he lead a happy life? Was he a good man? We do not know and will probably never know on this side of eternity. This man represents the majority of people in this world. We are only a name on many lists kept by governments, companies, and schools. People outside of our circle of friends and family will never know our stories. By contrast, God saw fit to include Tiras' name in the Bible. God remembers his life as vividly as when he was living in this world. Similarly God loves each of us and remembers us even when our memories have faded from this life. Revelation 2:17 tells us that God will give each of us a new name that only God and the receiver of the name knows. This level of intimacy contrasts powerfully with the alienation and impersonality that exist in the world today.

An ugly side effect of the economic problem facing Hong Kong is that people feel alienated even from their family and friends. The shame of not being able to provide for one's family or to keep up with one's peers imprisons many people in their own private cell, figuratively and, sometimes, literally. As a result, suicide rates have gone up alarmingly. If only people knew that they were not alone and would never be alone even if their relatives and friends were to forsake them. God knows, loves, and remembers all our lives. We are not just a name (or a number) but a valuable person before God.

David
(1 Chronicles 10–29)

David and Solomon were the most important kings in Chronicles, and they were the models used to measure the reigns of the other kings. The narratives of David (1 Chr 10–29) and Solomon (2 Chr 1–9) respectively comprise about 39 percent and 15 percent of the total narratives devoted to the kings. Together they occupy more than half of the materials on the kings. Although the Chronicler followed the Deuteronomistic Historian in emphasizing David and Solomon's importance, he differed in his choice and arrangement of sources.

A major difference in the Chronicler's portrayals of David is that he concentrated on David's role in preparing for the building of the temple and its liturgy. More than half of the Davidic narratives is devoted to the story of bringing the ark into Jerusalem (13:1-14; 15:1-43) and to the preparation to build the temple and the paraphernalia related to its worship (17:1-26; 21:18–26:32; 28:1–29:25).

The Chronicler's account of David's life could be divided into two sections. The first section (1 Chr 10–21) narrates David's rise to power and culminates in his bringing of the ark into Jerusalem. It ends with the purchase of the future site of the temple. The second section (1 Chr 22–29) evolves around his preparation for the building of the temple and centering worship in the temple. If 1 Chronicles were the only book that we possessed about David, we would imagine that David spent the first part of his life establishing his kingdom and the second part preparing for worship in the temple. First Chronicles 21 is thus the hinge or center of the Davidic narrative.

In this pivotal passage, the Chronicler presents David as sinning by taking a census. The parallel version in 2 Samuel 24 is similar on many points, but it also contains significant differences; it actually contains one of the major differences between the narratives about David in Chronicles and in Samuel. In 1 Chronicles, chapter 21 functions as a bridge that connects the younger David's military and political successes to the spiritual achievements of his later years (1 Chr 22–29). The main literary device used by the Chronicler to achieve this effect is the addition of 1 Chr 21:28–22:1. These verses and their content are unique to Chronicles. In 2 Sam 24 the Deutero-nomistic Historian does not associate the incident of the census with the choice of the site of the temple, nor does he state that the temple was built on Ornan's threshing floor. By ending his story of the census with David's declaration that Ornan's threshing floor was the divinely chosen site of the future temple (1 Chr 22:1), the Chronicler changes the emphasis of the story from God's punishment to God's choice of the site of the temple. He immediately continues to describe David's preparation for the building of the temple (1 Chr 22), the division and duties of the temple personnel (1 Chr 23–26), and, finally, the handing of the throne and the work of building the temple to Solomon (1 Chr 28–29). The Chronicler repeats his interpretation of the census story in 2 Chronicles 3:1 by stating that the site of the temple is the threshing floor of Ornan the Jebusite.

The same incident is reported in 2 Samuel 24, but its function is very different. Second Samuel begins with the coronation of David (2 Sam 2) and goes on to describe one victory after another. Here, the turning point of David's life is his adultery with Bathsheba and the murder of Uriah, her husband (2 Sam 11). From this point onward, there is a series of incest, murder, and rebellions in David's court. The census is the last of this series of calamities in 2 Samuel. When we meet David again in 1 Kings 1, he is a feeble old man who requires a young woman's body heat to keep him warm. Therefore, the census in 2 Samuel 24 functions as the culmination of God's wrath against David for his sins of adultery and murder.

The incident that marks the downfall of David's life in 2 Samuel becomes in Chronicles the bridge to greater spiritual achievements in his later years. The bloodshed that led to the coronation of David over all the tribes (2 Sam 2–5), his adultery with Bathsheba (2 Sam 11), and the troubles in his court (2 Sam 12–24) are all left out of Chronicles. David's life is reinterpreted as a role model of spiritual zeal.

It has been noted, quite correctly, that biblical writers generally eschewed mythology. The Priestly writer (who gave us a good portion of the Pentateuch) and the Deuteronomistic Historian (who gave us a major portion of our materials on the kings of Israel and Judah) suppressed mythological materials in their books. This could be said of the Chronicler as well. Nevertheless archetypical figures found in myths are not absent from Chronicles. David and Solomon are presented as two prominent archetypical figures. Indeed, the other kings in Chronicles can also be viewed as archetypical figures of good or bad leaders. The fact that they are presented as historical figures rather than mythic heroes makes no difference to their paradigmatic function in the book as figures of good or bad leadership.

Hong Kong also faces a grim present and an uncertain future. However, the period of the fifties and sixties in Hong Kong was worse than the present. Through the intelligence, entrepreneur spirit, and sheer hard work of many unsung heroes, Hong Kong has made tremendous economic and social improvements during these past decades. These unsung heroes can serve as role models for this generation. With better infrastructures and the same work ethic, there is great cause for hope for the future. On a different note, from the context of our Baptist tradition, we can also emphasize that individual Christians can also remember their past to give them hope for the future. There are heroes of the faith in Christianity just as there are heroes in Israel's history. The author of the book of Hebrews expressed it well when he exhorted his readers to take courage from past heroes of the faith and, ultimately, from Jesus himself to run the race of their lives (Heb 12:1-2).

Solomon
(2 Chronicles 1–9)

The story of Solomon is even more significant in showing the Chronicler's interest in temple building and worship activities.

Actually, 67 percent of these narratives are devoted to the temple and worship (2 Chr 2:1–7:22). The story of Solomon can thus be divided into two interrelated parts. Following the introductory chapter, in the first part, 2 Chr 2:1–7:22, Solomon accomplishes the task that his father gave him by building the temple. In the second part, 2 Chr 8–9, God blesses him with great wealth and fame as a reward for building the temple. The introduction to this second part presents the completion of the temple as a prelude to the other deeds that Solomon accomplished: "At the end of twenty years, during which Solomon had built the house of the Lord and his own house, Solomon rebuilt the cities that Huram had given to him, and settled the people of Israel in them (8:1-2).

It is easy for Christians in the Baptist tradition to miss the message of the Chronicler because it is presented in a form that is not immediately relevant to them. Christians do not worship in a temple. Even when Christians use expressions like "temple of God" to describe their place of worship, such expressions do not come close to conveying the significance of the temple for the Chronicler. As we noted, for the Chronicler the temple was the only place that YHWH had chosen for his people to worship him. Therefore, a God-centered, worship-centered life should have the temple as its focal point. The Chronicler used the story of the wealthiest king in Israel's history to emphasize his message that God gives material blessings to those who prioritize their spiritual life, that is, worship in the temple and "wisdom and knowledge." This message,

conveyed by the retelling of Solomon's story in two interrelated parts, is concisely expressed in 2 Chronicles 1:11-12:

> God answered Solomon, "Because this was in your heart, and you have not asked for possessions, wealth, honor, or the life of those who hate you, and have not even asked for long life, but have asked for wisdom and knowledge for yourself that you may rule my people over whom I have made you king, wisdom and knowledge are granted to you. I will also give you riches, possessions, and honor . . ."

Materialism and spiritual apathy are as rampant today as they were in the time of the Chronicler. They are as great a problem in the church as in the broader society. The drive to accumulate possessions is acute in the Christian community, which offers weekly scheduled opportunities for believers to show off their possessions and to compare their wealth status with each other. Thus this teaching of Chronicles can easily translate for Christians into a "gospel of prosperity." Yet, such an interpretation would miss the point of the Chronicler's message, which calls for a God-centered, worship-centered life. God should replace material possessions as the center of our lives.

Other Judean Kings
(2 Chronicles 10–36)

When we compare the Chronicler's handling of the Judean kings' materials with that of the Deuteronomistic Historian, we observe that he gives quite a bit more attention to some kings than the Deuteronomistic Historian. The following table illustrates this point.

Kings of Judah	Number of verses in 2 Chronicles	Number of verses in 1 and 2 Kings
Rehoboam	58	34
Abijah	23	8
Asa	47	16
Jehoshaphat	101	51
Hezekiah	117	95

When compared to the narratives in Kings, it becomes apparent that the materials unique to Chronicles inevitably include narratives about God's interventions in dire situations. For example, both Kings and Chronicles mention the invasion of Shishak (1 Kgs 14; 2 Chr 12) but they differ in emphases. In Kings the invasion of Shishak is a punishment on Judah for their unfaithfulness to YHWH. The Chronicler, on the other hand, includes a section about Rehoboam and his people humbling themselves before YHWH (2 Chr 12:5-8). As a result, God tells them through the prophet Shemaiah that they will be spared destruction although they will have to serve Shishak. By including this material, the Chronicler emphasizes God's intervention to save the people from total destruction rather than emphasizing their punishment.

The part of Abijah's narrative unique to Chronicles describes a battle between Abijah and Jeroboam on Mount Zemaraim (2 Chr 13:3-20). Jeroboam sets an ambush behind the army of Judah so that they are attacked from both directions. At the critical moment, when all seems lost, they cry out to YHWH. As a result God routs Jeroboam and the Israelite army before Abijah and Judah.

Similarly, a part of Asa's narrative that is not found in Kings pertains to the invasion of Zerah, the Cushite (2 Chr 14:8-14). Zerah's army is almost twice the size of Asa's army. Realizing their disadvantaged position, Asa cries out to God for help. God answers his prayer and strikes the Cushite before Asa and Judah. Chronicles also contains a unique narrative about Jehoshaphat and an invasion of a coalition of Moabites, Ammonites, and Edomites (2 Chr 20:1-30). Jehoshaphat gathers his people before God in fear and trembling. God tells him that he will not even need to fight the battle. On the morning of the battle, Jehoshaphat appoints singers to sing praises to YHWH before their enemies. At that moment YHWH causes the invaders to turn on one another.

Finally, Hezekiah's narrative also has a section about an enemies' invasion (2 Chr 32). As above, when Hezekiah prays to God for help, God sends an angel to annihilate the leaders of the Assyrian army. Hezekiah's account differs from the preceding ones in that this section is also found in Kings. The sections not found in Kings include materials about his religious reforms (2 Chr 29-31). Hezekiah's narrative also differs from the above in that the agent of God's intervention (i.e., an angel) is specified. None of the above narratives tell us how God saves God's people.

In summary, the narratives unique to Chronicles illustrate God's miraculous intervention to save God's people from certain destruction. These kings do not win because they are stronger than their enemies. In fact, in each case they are presented as weaker than their enemies. They win only because God intervenes directly to rescue them. It is on account of this trust in God's power that the Chronicler encourages his readers to "be strong and courageous" (1 Chr 19:13; 22:13; 28:20; 2 Chr 15:7; 32:7) in the face of hardship and danger.

There is a great deal of insecurity and pessimism in Hong Kong these days. The once roaring economy is down and the unemployment rate is up. Christians are not impervious to the gloom. In Baptist churches (and certainly other churches), offerings are dwindling and more people are seeking counseling for various reasons. Many Christians who thought they had faith in God have awakened to the realization that their confidence was really placed in themselves or in the economy. In the face of overwhelming odds, self-confidence may not be sufficient. In times like this we can learn from the Chronicler's admonition to his readers. We, too, can be strong and courageous if, in addition to possessing a healthy sense of self-worth, we can trust in God's love and power. To put it differently, we may need a higher power to pull us through in certain circumstances. Perhaps God will intervene directly to save us from our distress just as God did in the narratives of Chronicles. Or God may give us the fortitude to overcome the challenge facing us.

CONCLUSION

The last three decades have seen an increasing appreciation of 1 and 2 Chronicles as historiography and literature. Likewise, we might note an increasing appreciation of the books' theological messages, which are as applicable to Christians today as they were to the original Jewish readers. First, the Chronicler encouraged his readers to appreciate their cultural roots while keeping an international outlook. Obviously the issue is not as simple as telling people who their ancestors are. I doubt the Chronicler thought that the problems and discouragements facing his readers would disappear just because he reminded them of their cultural roots. They did not have a choice about the circumstance in which they found themselves, but they could choose to face it with a positive attitude. The Chronicler hoped to rekindle in them the same zeal that drew their ancestors back to Jerusalem. Hong Kong people did not have a choice either. Nobody consulted them about the handover. Yet they do have a choice about how to react to this situation. Hopefully a rediscovery of their historical and cultural roots will help ease some of the frustrations and adjustments that come with the change of government.

Second, the Chronicler challenged his readers to worship God and to place God at the center of their lives. The fact that he emphasizes this message again and again shows that he perceived this to be a problem for his readers. Materialism and spiritual apathy are deceptive vices. Believers today, as in the Chronicler's days, have legitimate reasons for seeking material well-being for themselves and their families. The difficulty lies in discerning what is enough. When does a legitimate need replace God as the center of our lives? Chronicles does not define what constitutes contentment; rather the Chronicler focused his readers on the need to put God first and then he let them decide on their other priorities.

Third, the Chronicler admonished his readers to trust in God's love and power to pull them through difficulties that were too much for them to handle. Since we do not have much information about the situation of the Chronicler's intended audience, we do not know exactly what the Chronicler had in mind. What we know is that he highlighted God's ability to help them defeat their enemies despite being the smaller and weaker party in the conflict. While we might be in quite different situations today, God still loves us and has the power to lead us through tough times.

BIBLIOGRAPHY

De Vries, Simon John. *1 and 2 Chronicles*. FOTL 11. Grand Rapids: Eerdmans, 1989.

Dillard, Raymond B. *2 Chronicles*. WBC 15. Waco, Tex.: Word, 1987.

Dorsey, David A. *The Literary Structure of the Old Testament: A Commentary* on *Genesis–Malachi*. Grand Rapids: Baker, 1999.

Japhet, Sara. *I & II Chronicles: A Commentary*. OTL. Louisville: Westminster John Knox, 1993.

Johnstone, William. *1 and 2 Chronicles*. 2 Vols. JSOTSup 253-254. Sheffield: Sheffield Academic Press, 1997.

McConville, J. Gordon. *I and II Chronicles*. Daily Study Bible. Philadelphia: Westminster, 1984.

Noth, Martin. *The Chronicler's History*. Trans. H.G. M. Williamson. JSOTSup 50. Sheffield: JSOT, 1987.

Williamson, H. G. M. *1 and 2 Chronicles*. NCBC. Grand Rapids: Eerdmans, 1982.

EZRA AND NEHEMIAH

Danna Nolan Fewell

Theological School, Drew University, New Jersey, USA

LIFE CONTEXT OF THE INTERPRETATION

One needs only to peruse the reports from UNICEF databases and the World Health Organization to realize something of the appalling conditions in which most of the children of the world live. As an upper middle-class Caucasian female biblical scholar from North America who also happens to be a parent, not only do I live with an awareness of the disparity between my own experiences and those of women and children around the globe, but I also stand implicated in a national politic that continues to ignore the rights and needs of children as it presses forward a questionable, only thinly disguised, religiously-driven agenda. During the last decade 53 million people—one out of every 115 people on earth—were uprooted from their homes and became displaced within their countries or refugees across borders. An estimated 80 percent of the refugees and displaced persons were women and children. Up to 5 percent of these refugee populations—often more in emergency evacuations—were children separated from their families (UNICEF, 2001). I am a citizen of a country that has contributed mightily, both through its aggression and its indifference, to this global dilemma.

As a person who trains leaders for various kinds of religious communities, I am compelled to ask: In a world where so many children are sick, hungry, dying, abandoned, displaced, and violated, in a world where politics take precedence over matters of life and death, what difference does reading the Bible make? If reading the Bible is to make a difference, we may be forced to read between the lines, looking for the ways in which children are repressed, exploited, violated, and ignored by the religious and political agendas of the biblical world and of the Bible's readers today.

This is why, in the following pages, I chose to read Ezra between the lines, retelling the story by paying close attention to the minor characters in it, so that we may hear the other side of this story.

Danna Nolan Fewell, professor of Hebrew Bible, general editor of Semeia Studies (SBL) and of Biblical Limits (an interdisciplinary series devoted to the Bible and postmodern culture), Routledge Press, has published many articles. She is the author of *Circle of Sovereignty: Plotting Politics in the Book of Daniel* (1988/1991) and *The Children of Israel: Reading the Bible for the Sake of Our Children* (2003); the coauthor of *Compromising Redemption: Relating Characters in the Book of Ruth* (1990), *Gender, Power, and Promise: The Subject of the Bible's First Story* (1993), and *Narrative in the Hebrew Bible* (1993) and the editor of *Reading Between Texts: Intertextuality and the Hebrew Bible* (1992) and the co-editor of *Bible and Ethics of Reading*, Semeia 77 (1997).

Material in this *GBC* chapter is adapted from Danna Nolan Fewell, "The Genesis of Israelite Identity: A Narrative Speculation on Postexilic Interpretation," in *Reading Communities, Reading Scripture: Essays in Honor of Daniel Patte* (ed. Gary A. Phillips and Nicole Wilkinson Duran, Harrisburg, Pa.: Trinity, 2002), 111–118 and *The Children of Israel: Reading the Bible for the Sake of Our Children* (Nashville: Abingdon, 2003), 55-63 and used with permission from the publishers.

CONTEXTUAL COMMENT

An Overview of Ezra and Nehemiah

The books of Ezra and Nehemiah were originally a single book called Ezra (separated in the Christian Bibles beginning in the third century C.E.). The overall work is dated either ca 400 B.C.E. or ca 300 B.C.E., according to the scholars' assessment of how quickly it was written after the events it narrates. Scholars think that Ezra-Nehemiah incorporates material from several sources, including many of the passages in the first person that come from memoirs of Ezra (perhaps Ezra 7:27–8:34; 9:1-15 and Neh 7:73–8:18) and of Nehemiah (Neh 1:1–7:73, and parts of 12:27-43 and 13:4-31), and quite a number of lists (of returnees, Ezra 2:1-70; 8:1-14; and Neh 7; of those who put away "foreign" wives and children, Ezra 10:18-44; of those who worked on the walls, Neh 3; of residents of Jerusalem, of priests and Levites, Neh 11:3–12:16).

Ezra (1:1-3) begins where Chronicles (2 Chr 36:22-23) ends—the proclamation by the Persian king, Cyrus, of the liberty to the exiles. Then, the author of Ezra-Nehemiah redacts the many sources along a theological perspective according to which the returned exiles were a godly remnant with a commitment to the covenant that distinguished them from other people and ensured they would avoid repeating the errors that caused the exile.

Ezra-Nehemiah can be outlined as follows (Klein 1992, 738-739):

I. Ezra 1:1–6:22. The Return from Exile
  A. Decree of Cyrus, 1:1-11
  B. List of Returnees, 2:1-70
  C. Rebuilding of the Altar and of the Temple's Foundation, 3:1-13
  D. Opposition from Various Groups, 4:1-24
  E. Continuation of the rebuilding of the Temple, 5:1–6:22
II. Ezra 7:1–10:44. Ezra's Return and Initial Work

  A. Ezra's return with a Group of Exiles, 7:1–8:36
  B. Crisis over intermarriage with women of the land, 9:1-15
  C. Ezra's reform "to Restore Ritual Purity" by putting away "foreign" wives and children, 10:1-44
III. Nehemiah 1:1–7:73a. Return of Nehemiah and Rebuilding of Walls of Jerusalem
IV. Nehemiah 7:73b–10:39. Ezra's Reading of the Law and Liturgical Responses
V. Nehemiah 11:1–13:31. Nehemiah's Further Acts and Reforms—concluding with another condemnation of mixed marriages (13:23-31)

Interpretive Choices and My Focus on Ezra 9–10 and Neh 13:23-31

Choice # 1

From the perspective of my life context, I choose to focus my attention on Ezra's initial reform, with its requirement that Israelite men divorce and send away their "foreign" wives and children (Ezra 7-10).

Choice # 2

I read Ezra 9–10 from the perspective of Jonathan, son of Asahel, who, with a few others, opposed Ezra's proposed removal of foreign wives and their children (1:1-44): "Only Jonathan the son of Asahel, and Jahaziah the son of Tikvah made a stand against this . . . " (10:15, a.t). I take into account that the gesture reported in Ezra 10:15 is ambiguous. It is possible to render it with the JPS translation: "Only Jonathan son of Asahel and Jahzeiah son of Tikvah remained for this purpose . . ." Yet, with most translations and commentators, I understand it as a gesture of opposition.

Choice # 3

My rereading of Ezra 7–10, in "The Scene" below, takes into account that many of the books of the Hebrew Bible were written in the first part of the Persian period (ca 538-332 B.C.E.), that is, the time of Ezra (who launched his reform against mixed marriage ca 457/458 B.C.E.) and Nehemiah (governor of Judah ca 445-433 B.C.E.). In my view, Genesis was also probably written during this period: see Fewell (1997); Davies (1995); Carroll (1991); and Mullen (1997). For an overview and assessment of these arguments, see Heard (2001).

Choice # 4

This rereading is based on scholarly reconstruction of the situation upon the return of the exiles. Eskenazi and Judd (1994) suggest that an imbalance in the ratio of women to men may have been part of the initial problem for the returnees. Returnees married women who stayed in the land of Israel during the exile. This dialogue suggests that, at some point, the number of returning women increased to an adequate proportion.

Choice # 5

"The Scene" below is a proposed dialogue between Jonathan the son of Asahel (10:15) and Shechaniah the son of Jehiel (10:2-3). Jonathan's tentativeness regarding the "land of our fathers" reflects current theories that Jewish identity and the corresponding land claim were political constructions of the post-exilic period. In addition to the work of Davies (1995) cited above, see also Hamilton (1995).

Choice # 6

The issue of marriages with "women of the land" which Ezra presents as a religious issue, an issue of purity, also had a social and economic dimension that recent studies have investigated. In "The Scene" below, I seek to take into account the main results of such studies. Particularly important is the work of Daniel Smith-Christopher (1991: 263-64). Using the sociological theory of hypergamy, he argues that the men involved were attempting to "marry up" on the social ladder. He supposes that the "foreign women" were not ethnically foreign at all, but were

Jewish women who had not been in exile. He follows Williamson (1985) who argues that "the peoples of the land" (i.e., the surrounding community that had remained in the land) controlled much of the territory and enjoyed economic and social advantages that the returned exiles did not share. Willa Mathis Johnson (1999), exploring how Persian marriage practices play into Persian politics of land control, pushes the hypergamy theory further and argues that the "foreign women" were women from Persian noble families who were given, along with access to Persian controlled land in Palestine, to some of the men of Judah who were in positions of leadership. This would have kept Judahite allegiance to Persian authority strong. See also Heard (2001: 179-82), who sees in the telling of the Laban stories a reflection of the hypergamy argued by Smith-Christopher. "Mesopotamian" wives would have been perceived as more geographically and politically connected to the Persian government and consequently not the same kind of threat to ethnic identity as the "people of the land."

Choice # 7

There is also a political dimension to Ezra's reform, related to his person and position. To what extent was Ezra acting as an official of the Persian government and following an agenda that was politically acceptable by the Persians? See Kenneth Hoglund's explanation of the Ezra-Nehemiah reform in which he argues that ethnic exclusivity conformed to Persian political policy (particularly 1992, 237-44). Hoglund suggests that "[b]oth reformers [Ezra and Nehemiah] were sent to the Restoration community in the mid-fifth century precisely because of the need to insure continued control over the community in the face of the challenges resulting from the Egyptian Revolt" (1992, 244). This might explain why Egyptians are explicitly named in the list of peoples with "abhorrent practices" in Ezra 9:1, where all the other peoples named would have been associated with territories in immediate proximity to Judah.

Choice # 8

As for the issue regarding whether or not early Israelites originally separated from the "people of the land," despite rewritings of earlier history in the Persian period (see choice # 3), these texts could not leave out foundational traditions which show the ancestors of Israel closely interacting with the people of the land. For instance, regarding Genesis 12, one might assume, as many have in the past, that Hagar was part of the property Abraham received from the king of Egypt in exchange for Sarah (Gen 12:16). Later interpreters speculated that Hagar was Pharaoh's own daughter. But then the story of Abraham sending away Hagar and her son can be viewed as a justification to dismiss the foreign wives and their children. The question of the ethnic origin of Sarah remains open. On this point, see Miscall, (1983, 23-45). Finally, according to the Genesis narrative (25:1-6), Abraham also sent away the children of his third wife, Keturah. This text, too, would have supported the Ezra-Nehemiah reform.

Choice # 9

Bracketing out the social, economic, and political dimensions of the context in the time of Ezra and Nehemiah and the many traditions regarding the close interactions of Israel with people of the land, Ezra posits that it is because of a lack of purity that Israel was punished and lost the promised land. Ezra's prayer indicates this assumption:

> From the days of our fathers to this very day, we have been in great guilt. And because of our iniquities, we, our kings, and our priests have been handed over to foreign kings, to the sword, to captivity, to plunder and to disgrace to this day (Ezra 9:7 a.t.).

Literary Context

> At the end of these things, the leaders came near to me [Ezra], saying, The people of Israel and the priests, and the Levites, have not separated themselves from the people of the lands, the like of their corruptions of/to the Canaanite, the Hittite, the Perizzite, the Ammonite, the Moabite, the Egyptian, and the Amorite. For they have taken from their daughters for themselves and for their sons and they have intermixed the holy seed with the people of the lands . . . (Ezra 9:1-2, a.t.)

> And Shechaniah, the son of Jehiel, of the sons of Elam answered and said to Ezra, We have been unfaithful in relation to our God and have taken foreign women from the peoples of the land. Yet there is hope for Israel concerning this thing. Now, let us cut a covenant with our God to expel all the women and those born from them according to the counsel of Adonai and those who tremble at the command of our God and by the law, let it be done according to the law (Ezra 10:2-3, a.t.).

Only Jonathan, the son of Asahel, and Jahaziah, the son of Tikvah, made a stand against this action (Ezra 10:15, a.t.).

The Scene

Despite the rain, the assembly was large. Under the threat of having their property confiscated and their families ostracized from the congregation, all the returning Israelites had come to Jerusalem to hear what Ezra had to say. His message was brief and to the point:

> You have been unfaithful: You have brought home foreign women to compound the offense of Israel. Now confess to YHWH, God of your fathers, and do his desire: Separate yourselves from the people of the land and from the foreign women (Ezra 10-11 a.t.).

The drenched crowd, eager to escape the rain, agreed to Ezra's demand and then dissipated to institute the new policy of ethnic purification. A few lingered behind. Jonathan son of Asahel grabbed the arm of Shechaniah son of Jehiel.

"What do you want?" asked Shechaniah.

"I want to know just what in Sheol is going on," demanded Jonathan. "You wouldn't let me speak in the assembly. You wouldn't take my questions or hear my objections. I demand to know what you think will come of all this."

"Oh, did you wish to contest this action?" asked Shechaniah. "I thought you were gesturing to show your support."

Jonathan glared at him.

"What will come of all this," continued Shechaniah, ignoring the glare, "is the purification of God's people. We cannot have the holy seed of the sons of the exile contaminated by being mixed with the people of the land."

"This hasn't been considered a problem before. Why all this sudden concern for purity?"

"Well, I wouldn't call it 'sudden,'" replied Shechaniah. "Foreign women have been a problem all along according to some versions of our history."

"Are you referring to a version that you may have had a hand in writing yourself?" Jonathan asked sarcastically. *[See Choice # 3 above.]*

"I tell the truth as I see it—and as Ezra the priest sees it, I might add. The prophets have long warned us about the uncleanness of the peoples of the land."

"Says who?" Jonathan demanded.

"Says Ezra [see Ezra 9:10-12]. He *is* a priest. Do you doubt that he speaks the truth?"

"Do you think priests have cornered the market on truth?" retorted Jonathan. "The *truth* is that you are disrupting—no, worse—destroying lives with this new edict. You are tearing families apart. You are leaving women and children homeless with no place to go and no way to take care of themselves."

"Hard decisions sometimes have to be made," replied Shechaniah calmly. "We must now take care of our own women, the women of Judah, who have come back with us from captivity. They deserve homes and families as well. Their rights must be protected and our communal identity must be kept intact and preserved from polluting influences." *[See Choice # 4 above.]*

"Your concern for the returning women is touching. You surely count your own sister and daughter among that number." Shechaniah's jaw tightened, but Jonathan continued. "But let me ask you this: If we were all to marry among ourselves, how, in the long run would this be of any help to us as a community? If we all do this, we could very well remain landless. You know as well as I do that the so-called 'foreign' women of whom you speak come from families that are now in control of the land. If God has really promised us this land, if it is indeed the land of our fathers, then we have a responsibility to reclaim it. *[See Choice # 5 above.]* If the only way we can regain possession of it peaceably is to marry back into it, so be it. There is nothing wrong with living in peace with the others who inhabit this place." *[See Choice # 6 above.]*

Shechaniah looked disapproving. "We must have faith. If God wants to give the land back to us, then God will do it in his own good time. But it will only be done as long as the lines of inheritance are clear. He will only give it to the holy seed. Thus, we must make sure that that seed remains separate from all the peoples of the lands and uncorrupted by them and their practices. Remember our father Abraham once refused to accept property from the king of Sodom lest anyone should say that the king of Sodom made Abraham rich [see Gen 14]. So, we, too, cannot be accepting property from the likes of the people who are now squatting here, lest we come to believe ourselves obligated to people who are different from ourselves. We must remember that the land is a gift from God."

"A gift from the Persian government is more to the point!"

"What do you mean by that?"

"Think about it. Ezra is an official of the Persian government, the government that permitted us to return to this place and that wants to keep a tight rein on what we do here. Those of us who have returned will always be indebted to the Persian government. Unless, of course, our identities as released captives somehow get confused with those who have been living here all this time. They, of course, owe no debt to the Persians, do they? In fact, one might imagine that they could come to resent the Persian government for bringing us here and complicating their lives." *[See Choice # 7 above.]*

"That's rubbish. This is not about politics. It's about what YHWH demands of us as his people. He does not want us associating with or accepting property from the people of the land! The story of Abraham teaches us this quite clearly."

Jonathan shook his head. "Yes, well, I seem to remember Abraham associating with plenty of the 'people of the land.' He was not above compromising with them about grazing or water rights. He even purchased real estate from them [Gen 21:22-33; 23:1-20]. And he certainly had no problem accepting property—or women either for that matter—from the Pharaoh of Egypt. *[See Choice # 8 above.]* Are you really sure God cares so much about how we reacquire the land or whether or not our seed is 'pure'? When in our history have we ever been 'pure'?"

"That's precisely the point," trumped Shechaniah smugly. "That's why we lost the land to begin with." *[See Choice # 9 above.]*

"That's absurd," countered Jonathan. "I can't believe that God wants to put women and children at risk just for the sake of some narrow-minded view of who can or cannot be one of God's people."

"Well, you had better recall your history, brother. As you yourself just noted, our father Abraham had a foreign wife. An Egyptian. And like these women who need to be expelled, she bore him a mixed son."

"So?"

"So, don't you see?" said Shechaniah, trying to hold his impatience in check. "In the beginning, Abraham wasn't satisfied with the woman he had brought with him from the land of the Chaldeans either. He didn't think that Sarah could provide much of a future for him. And so he took an Egyptian woman, who came with much wealth, to provide him a son. A strong, healthy first-born son who would, he thought, secure the promise of land and blessing that God had made to him. But his efforts to make God's promise come to pass were clearly misguided. God had a surprise for Abraham. His wife Sarah, the woman from his very own

family, who had traveled with him to this land, was able to bear him a child after all."

"Well," Jonathan looked skeptical, "whether Sarah was really from Abraham's very own family has always been debatable, hasn't it? Just because he said so on occasion to save his skin doesn't mean it was necessarily true. But, that aside, what's your point?"

"The point is that we must marry our own kind. Even if it means sending back to the land of captivity for brides from our families left behind there. Just as Rebekah was secured for Isaac and Rachel and Leah were secured for Jacob, the sons of the exile must find appropriate brides, no matter what the cost. And if they can bring back from Chaldea property and large families to add to our diminished economy and population here, all the better."

"And all the better, too, if these women share the interests and values of the Persian government, eh, Shechaniah? We certainly wouldn't want to become involved with people who might be likely to show resistance to the Persians. Isn't that what's at the heart of this?" *[See Choice # 6 above.]*

"The main thing," responded Shechaniah, pointedly disregarding that last remark, "is that our sons come back here to settle the land. Only those who marry women from their own kind will be allowed to possess it. That's how Esau lost his right to the land, remember? He married women of the land, and they made everyone's lives bitter. That's why Jacob inherited the family birthright and blessing."

"I seem to have heard the story differently," says Jonathan. "As I recall, didn't Jacob trick Esau out of the birthright and blessing? In fact, isn't it just possible that you're doing a similar thing now?"

"Don't be ridiculous. Isaac and Rebekah knew what was best for the family. That's why Jacob was admonished not to take a wife from among the women of the land. Remember, it was Isaac who was the son of the covenant. He was the holy seed, born of those coming from Chaldea to claim this land. Rebekah was from his very own family. He was heir to the land and the heir after him was the son born of this perfect union who emulated his values.

"Yes, that's all very well, but the land wasn't even theirs yet. The possession of the land was still generations away."

"Yes, and perhaps that is the case for us as well. But that doesn't mean we shouldn't be attending to the purity of the holy seed who will receive it. Sarah knew that the inheritance could not be shared. That is why she insisted that the Egyptian woman and her son had to go. God saw the wisdom of this. He supported her and encouraged Abraham to do the same. That's why I say, sometimes we must make difficult decisions. God insisted that that foreign woman and her child be sent away long ago; God insists that these foreign women and their children be sent away today. It's just as simple as that. God has a greater plan for us." [See Choice # 8 above.]

"Your acquiescence to this 'greater plan' wouldn't have anything to do with the fact of your own father's second marriage, would it?" Jonathan looked at Shechaniah with renewed scrutiny. "Hasn't your father taken a woman from 'the people of the land' as you call them? And don't you have brothers who have come from that union? [As expressed in Ezra 10:26, since Shecaniah is a descendant of Elam; 10:2.] Is that why you're so enamored with these stories of divinely sanctioned disinheritance? Shechaniah, I would have expected better of you."

Shechaniah became indignant. "Don't try to shame me, Jonathan! I'm simply trying to follow God's will. God told Abraham to put away that Egyptian woman and her son. Abraham was obedient. It's clear from the story that we must do the same."

"But what if, unlike you, we love our families?" contended Jonathan. "We love our children. We don't want to be parted from them. We don't want to abandon them."

"No. I'm sure Abraham didn't want to be parted from Ishmael either," Shechaniah replied with an air of cold superiority. "But he did as he was told. Abraham was willing to give up not only this mixed child, but even the child of promise when God asked him to. If our father Abraham was willing to sacrifice his children, then so must we be. Sometimes God seemingly asks us to give up our futures. We don't know why. We must simply have faith and do as he has commanded us and trust that he will provide what he has promised."

"Yes, well, with *your* brothers out of the way, that will certainly provide for you, won't it?" said Jonathan sarcastically. "What about for those you're sending away? Where will these women go? How will they take care of themselves and their children? How will they live? You are insisting that we cut them out of our lives, out of our families, out of our community, and yet you offer no provision for them."

"Well, my brother, you might certainly give them something to tide them over." Shechaniah smiled indulgently. "When Abraham sent the Egyptian and her son away, he didn't send them empty-handed. He made provision."

"You call a loaf of bread and a skin of water *provision?* Wasn't Abraham supposed to have been a fairly wealthy man? Did you really believe that he did the right thing by his wife and his child?" [see Waters, 1991: 187-205].

"Well, granted, one might call this compassionate conservatism," conceded Shechaniah. "But the point is, that the woman and her child survived just fine. *God took care of them.* Abraham didn't have to. So you should not worry about these foreign women and their children whom we now must cast out of our own families. God will take care of them. We must take care of our own kind."

"And just *who* determines who 'our own kind' are?" asked Jonathan.

"Why, Ezra is putting officials in place to check the genealogies. You needn't worry. This will all be handled properly," Shechaniah said.

"No doubt," said Jonathan, shaking his head and slowly walking away. "And soon we'll believe that this has always been God's will."

CONCLUSION

The question is indeed: Is it God's will that women and children be uprooted from their homes, be forced to live in unsafe conditions, be victims of economic disparity? Can we simply continue thanking God for all the blessings our children receive and ignore the appalling fact that so many children are sick, hungry, dying, abandoned? As Shecaniah, son of Jehiel, did when supporting Ezra's reform, can I, an upper-middle-class Caucasian biblical scholar from North America, continue to stand implicated in a national politic that continues to ignore the rights and needs of children as it presses forward policies that favor the imperial interests of multi-national corporations? As it makes autocratic pronouncements identifying entire groups of people as "evil" and "other?" As it puts at risk the lives of our children and the children of others in combat and through neglect as it pursues courses of aggression under the guise of self-protection? In some ways the biblical world and the (post)modern world are not so very far apart. Children suffer in both as result of the theology and politics of adults. Should we not find our lives interrupted, disrupted, and unsettled by this? Should we not read between the lines of both the Bible and our culture? Should we not speak out and act on behalf of the children?

BIBLIOGRAPHY

Carroll, Robert P. "Textual Strategies and Ideology in the Second Temple Period." Pages 108–124 in *The Persian Period*. Vol. 1 of *Second Temple Studies*. Edited by Philip R. Davies. JSOTSup 117. Sheffield: JSOT Press, 1991.

Davies, Philip R. *In Search of "Ancient Israel."* JSOTSup 148. Sheffield: Sheffield Academic, 1995.

Eskenazi, Tamara C. and Eleanore P. Judd. "Marriage to a Stranger in Ezra 9–10." Pages 266–85 in *Temple Community in the Persian Period*. Vol. 2 of *Second Temple Studies,* Edited by Tamara C. Eskenazi and Kent H. Richards. JSOTSup 175. Sheffield: JSOT Press, 1994.

Fewell, Danna Nolan. "Imagination, Method, and Murder: Un/Framing the Face of Postexilic Israel." Pages 132–52 in *Reading Bibles, Writing Bodies: Identity and the Book*. Edited by Timothy K. Beal and David M. Gunn. Biblical Limits. London: Routledge, 1997.

Hamilton, Mark W. "Who Was a Jew? Jewish Ethnicity during the Achaemenid Period." *ResQ* 37 (1995).

Heard, R. Christopher. *Dynamics of Diselection: Ambiguity in Genesis* 12-36 *and Ethnic Boundaries in Post-Exilic Judah*. Semeia Studies. Atlanta: SBL, 2001.

Hoglund, Kenneth G. *Achaemenid Imperial Administration in Syria-Palestine and the Missions of Ezra and Nehemiah*. SBLDS 125. Atlanta: Scholars Press, 1992.

Johnson, Willa Mathis. "Interethnic Marriage in Persian Yehud." PhD diss. Vanderbilt University, 1999.

Klein, Ralph W. "Ezra-Nehemiah, Books of." Pages 731-742 in *The Anchor Bible Dictionary. Volume 2*. Edited by David N. Freedman. New York: Doubleday, 1992.

Miscall, Peter. *The Workings of Old Testament Narrative*. Semeia Studies. Philadelphia: Fortress, 1983.

Mullen, E. Theodore, Jr. *Ethnic Myths and Pentateuchal Foundations: A New Approach to the Formation of the Pentateuch*. Semeia Studies. Atlanta: Scholars Press, 1997.

Patte, Daniel. *Ethics of Biblical Interpretation: A Reevaluation*. Louisville: Westminster John Knox, 1995.

Smith-Christopher, Daniel." The Mixed Marriage Crisis in Ezra." Pages 243–65 in *Temple Community in the Persian Period*. Vol 2 of *Second Temple Studies*. Edited by Tamara Eskenazi and Kent Richards. JSOTSup 175. Sheffield: JSOT, 1991.

UNICEF End Decade Databases. New York: UNICEF, 2001.

Waters, John. "Who was Hagar?" Pages 187–205 in *Stony the Road We Trod: African American Biblical Interpretation*. Edited by Cain Hope Felder. Mineapolis: Fortress, 1991.

ESTHER

Wong Wai Ching Angela

The Chinese University of Hong Kong, Shatin, Hong Kong, China

LIFE CONTEXT OF THE INTERPRETATION

The book of Esther is highly interesting in a postcolonial context like Hong Kong. In such a context, the story of Esther, a Jewish woman sent to a Persian court, reminds Hong Kong people of the supreme power of both the British Empire over local Chinese before 1997 (when Hong Kong was "returned" to China) and also of the distant and yet strong majestic presence of the Beijing government in Hong Kong. People in Hong Kong struggle to live between two competing sets of values: those of the prevalent Western law and those of a reasserted Chinese national and cultural identity. So people in Hong Kong are like the body of Queen Esther. Both are the site of multiple contests between colonialism (the Persian court/the British) and nationalism (Jews in Persia/Hong Kong Chinese); between the sovereign (the king/the British parliament/ the Beijing government) and the people (Jews/Persians/people of Hong Kong); as well as between men (the king/Haman/ Mordecai/men in Hong Kong) and women (Vashti/Esther/other courtesans/women in Hong Kong). Most of all, given the current resurgence of wars, of terrorism, and of wars on terrorism around the world, the story of Esther invites us to struggle with the complex and yet vital issues concerning the relationships among rival peoples of different ethnicities, cultures, and religions.

In the Hebrew Bible, the book of Esther is classified as one of the Writings. It is tradi-

tionally associated with the Jewish festival of Purim, which celebrates the victory of the Jews over their enemies through the actions of two courageous Jewish national figures— a hero, Mordecai, and a heroine, Esther. Sandra Berg suggests that the book of Esther should be understood as a novella telling the story of the survival of Diaspora Jews, which was told and retold during years of Jewish Diaspora (1979, 167–187). It champions a sense of identity not only for the original audience—a people struggling for survival—but also, in other times and places through history, for Jewish communities threatened by foreign powers. Consequently, despite the fact that this story originated among people living in a foreign land among neighbors of other ethnicities, it is highly nationalistic, openly calling for ethnic loyalty and for a heroic victory over "others." This is a story about two figures who live with other people in a society and work together with them as colleagues in the court. Despite these implied bonds between Jews and Persians, from the start the story sharply contrasts the identities of the Jews and of the Persians. Exaggerated literary portrayals set Jews and Persians in dramatic opposition; they are ridiculed for being locked in antagonistic relations, battling each other throughout the story. By the end of the story, the book of Esther celebrates the survival of a colonized community, the Jews, from destruction by the imperial

Wong Wai Ching Angela is associate professor in the Department of Modern Languages and Intercultural studies and in the Department of Religion, and she serves on the Committee on Gender Studies. Active in Asian ecumenical circles, she is a member of the Presidium of the Christian Conference of Asia (2000–2005) and of the Board of Trustees of the United Board for Christian Higher Education in Asia (2003–2006). Her publications include many articles and most recently *The Poor Woman: A Critical Analysis of Asian Theology and Contemporary Chinese Fiction by Women* (2002) and *Gender and Change in Hong Kong: Globalization, Postcolonialism, and Chinese Patriarchy* (2004).

community. At first, the court politics of Persia seems to posit a situation characterized by ongoing and constructive multicultural coexistence, which has disintegrated by the end of the book. Therefore, this story is alarming, because it suggests that such coexistence is extremely fragile, and can readily disintegrate as a result of misguided governmental decisions and political intrigues.

CONTEXTUAL COMMENTARY

Colonialism and Violence

It is believed that the book of Esther was composed in the eastern Jewish Diaspora of the Persian Empire because of its setting in Susa, its knowledge of the Persian court and its surroundings, and its total lack of interest in Judah and the temple. The book seems to address a Jewish audience who lived under foreign rule and were trying to deal with their ethnic identity in a society in which they were a minority. The book of Esther portrays a world in which Esther and her people lived in constant danger of persecution and oppression, a situation at odds with the scholarly opinion that Jews lived in harmony with their Gentile neighbors and rulers for most of the Persian period (538–332 B.C.E.). However, Esther reflects an attitude that is relatively sympathetic toward the Persian king and toward Gentiles—an attitude that would be unthinkable during the harsh treatment of the Jews by the Seleucid rulers (1–2 Macc) in the later part of the Hellenistic period (198–143 B.C.E.). Therefore, the story of Esther certainly predates the Seleucid period, and even the Hellenistic period, and was written in the postexilic period.

As a novella about Diaspora Jews, the book of Esther is a story told from the perspective of a Diasporic community struggling for survival in a land that was not their own. It concerns the tension and hostility they encounter. The story takes the literary form of a historical fiction framed around banquets and feasts, described in the beginning (Esth 1), the middle (Esth 5), and the end (Esth 8–9). The first banquet flaunts the imperial power, glory, riches, and lavishness of the Persian court, evoking by contrast, in the mind of the readers, the modest means of the Jewish community. The Purim feast at the end of the narrative (Esth 8–9) signifies the harsh reality and cruelty of ethnic conflicts and power politics between two peoples living under the same imperial rule and how these conflicts affect the fate of these two peoples. The feast of Purim (the word *Purim* means "lots") commemorates the reversal of fate for the Jewish people from imminent destruction to momentary salvation. But the joy and laughter of this celebration are quite disturbing because they take place in the midst of death, loss, and destruction inflicted on another community. Just before the celebration, casualties are numbered at seventy-five thousand (9:16).

During the height of the colonial era from the seventeenth to the nineteenth century, the peoples who lived in the lands that were to become Asian countries suffered extensive political and cultural destruction through the violent establishment of artificial borders without regard for existing communities, ethnicities, and families. By throwing together peoples from different languages, ethnicities, and religions, the establishment of these borders generated suspicions and tensions among them and brought about conflicts that are still unresolved. An outstanding example is India: its creation during the colonial period; its breaking up into four nations—India, Sri Lanka, Bangladesh, and Pakistan; the ongoing conflicts and tensions between (the new) India and its neighbors; and the ongoing ethnic rivalries within the present national boundaries of each of the countries. The scale of the destruction that result from the colonial period is tragically attested to in Sri Lanka, where the ethnic rivalries between the Tamils and Singhalese communities have claimed the lives of tens of thousands of civilians. Mass killings of people of particular tribes, clans, languages, ethnicities, and religions were not only an integral part of the history of modern nation-building but are still daily occurrences in Indonesia, Pakistan, India, Philippines, Cambodia, Myanmar, and China.

Read from this Asian context, the Hebrew Bible does not offer us a paradise where we might escape this world of conflicts and hostilities. In many ways the Hebrew Bible in general, and the book of Esther in particular, are representative of the long tradition of human brutality and violence since the beginning of history. Esther reminds modern readers of the ties between colonialism and violence and of how tension and hostility, when built up among different peoples brought together by imperialist powers, result in cycles of reciprocal revenge and persecution.

Strategies for Resisting Structures of Authority

Among other literary features, the book of Esther uses a folktale motif as its most effective textual strategy (Niditch 1985, 451). A similar strategy was used in other court novellas in the Hebrew Bible, including the stories of Daniel (Babylonia) and Joseph (Egypt). In these stories, powerful people are negatively portrayed and their laws, policies, and style of rule are ridiculed. In the book of Esther, the Persian court and its king are subtly mocked by a series of ironic subplots: the presentation of the king's extravagance (1:4-8); the demeaning, offhanded dismissal of the original queen, Queen Vashti (2:17); the treatment of young women in the cities as prostitutes (2:3-4, 8-9); the investiture as queen of a Jewish woman of low status and origin (2:15-18); the hanging of the chief official of the kingdom, Haman (7:8-10); and the king's permission to the Jews to carry out massive killings of his own people (8:11–9:16). Throughout the story, the king is portrayed as stupid, passive, and incompetent; he is never in control of the situation and is manipulated by people around him (the seven legal advisers and administrators, 1:14-22; courtiers, 2:2-4; Haman, 3:8-11; 7:3; 8:3; 9:13; and Esther). In effect, the Persian king is a laughingstock.

From this literary perspective, the disturbing depiction of the massacres that serve as a backdrop to the joyous celebration of the Jews at Purim appears as the culmination of the sarcasm and irony that we find throughout the book. It is a literary device for crying out the anguish that has accumulated for a people living in a foreign land and being subjected to unrelenting threat, danger, antagonism, and suspicions because of their different culture and religion. This cry also testifies to the violence that arises from people's anxiety, from their fear of others. It also testifies to the difficulties that peoples of different origins encounter as they seek to coexist.

The tragedy is that the book of Esther and similar literary expressions of anxiety and fear are rarely used as venues for cultivating mutual understanding and acceptance among communities in conflict. Rather, they are used to glorifying a nationalism that promotes the establishment of an exclusive community by a victory over ethnic rivals gained through revenge and destruction. The history and location of Hong Kong exemplify such a situation. Today Hong Kong is a city situated between a huge country, China with its various ethnic minorities, and the rest of Asia with its thousands of different races and languages. Hong Kong is the heir to one of the world's richest and oldest cultures and traditions, and at the same time it is one of the world's most successful colonial territories. It is a part of the world's largest communist country and one of the greatest "free" capitalist economic centers of the world. For a long time, this hybridity has made of Hong Kong a testing ground where people from various different backgrounds and cultures could learn to live together. Chinese intellectuals have described people of Hong Kong as a people finding their identity in the city rather than in the nation.

Nevertheless, like all communities confronted with imminent economic and political hardships, the people of Hong Kong have become defensive. In response to a shrinking economy, the people of Hong Kong, following their local government, have begun to define more narrowly who belongs to the community by drawing strict lines of demarcation between old and new immigrants, between Chinese and other Asians, and between rich people, be they expatriates or foreign investors, and poor migrant workers. As a result, the earlier Chinese settlers of Hong Kong are adopting an increasingly negative attitude toward the poor, the new immigrants, and the migrant workers, who contribute as much to the city as they themselves do. The book of Esther could serve as a reminder of the causes of this negative attitude and its disastrous consequences, and thus as an appeal to the diverse people of Hong Kong to return to the mutual understanding they exemplified so well for the rest of the world. This book also suggests a strategy for challenging political, colonial, and cultural authority structures: irony, the use of folktale motifs to mock these authorities and to create a space that is free from oppression.

Political Authority, Nationalism, and Women

One also needs to recognize how political authority structures and nationalism affect individuals, especially women. The female protagonist, Esther, has not always fared well in commentaries. This is an appropriate assessment; her role is quite ambivalent.

The story of Esther begins with the banishment of Queen Vashti, who refuses to display her beauty before the king's guests and become an object of the men's gaze (1:11-12). Together with many young women from all the provinces of the Persian Empire, with no choice and no capacity to resist, Esther is not only put in the harem (2:5-8) but also actively seeks to beat out all the other women (2:9-15). She succeeds and becomes the new queen of King Ahasuerus (2:16-18). In so doing, Esther makes it pos-

sible for Mordecai, her uncle, to have the political means to neutralize Haman's plot to exterminate all the Jews in Persia and to turn it around into the destruction of the enemies of the Jews (9:1-17).

For feminist interpreters, Esther poses difficulties. Esther is a lower-class woman who is subordinated to the power of the king and the imperial orders, a classical concern for feminist scholars. But Esther is also a woman who gains access to power and becomes queen by using her body, namely her beauty and sex. Nevertheless, she is commonly praised for her role as a national heroine who demonstrates wit and courage as an active and daring participant in the struggle for the survival of her people.

The book of Esther is a book of gender politics about women living under imperial orders as much as a national tale about a people surviving the threat of ethnic destruction. In effect, any female in the book is limited to the role ascribed to her in the men's world with its nationalistic agenda. Even as the queen, Esther is not given any other alternative than that of working for the national interest of her people (4:1-17). In this sense, Esther, Vashti, and the other courtesans, chosen from among the most beautiful women in the country, are sacrificed for the country as a whole. Keeping the political status quo, the imperial order—or reversing it in the name of nationalistic survival—involves maintaining a patriarchal order in which women are reduced to objects.

However, the two queens, Vashti and Esther, reject their fate. Both of them disobey the king: Vashti refuses to be reduced to an object of man's gaze (1:12), and Esther, against the proper, imperial practice, takes the initiative of approaching the king in the inner court without being summoned (4:11; 5:1). Thus, both Vashti and Esther violate the authority of the imperial power and threaten the status quo of the patriarchal structure represented by the king. But both ultimately fail. In Vashti's case, the threat is so great that an edict has to be proclaimed to rescue male authority: "all women should bow to the authority of their husbands, both high and low alike" (1:20, author's translation). Esther is less threatening; she acts as she was urged to do by a man, a patriarchal figure, her adoptive father Mordecai (2:7; 4:1-17), although he acknowledges her authority and acts "as Esther had ordered him" (4:17) and the sway of her beauty and sexuality on the king hides

her breach of the imperial order (5:1–7:10). Thus Esther secures the survival of her people; the Jews' annihilation by an evil faction in the imperial structure, Haman's faction, is avoided. But, as we previously noted, the imperial structure remains; the oppression and destruction of one group by another is still the rule (9:1-16).

CONCLUSION

The book's perceived lack of religiosity has made difficult its broad reception over the years. Believers find most disturbing the complete absence of any mention of God, covenant, and prayer. The heroine of the book, Esther, is married to a non-Jew, lives in a completely Gentile environment, and there is no suggestion that she upholds the dietary laws. Except for Esther's fasting before entering the inner court without being summoned by the king (4:16), and Mordecai's reminding her of a certain control of events from another place ("another quarter," 4:14), the book is totally secular; indeed, it has been seen as one of the most secular in the Hebrew Bible.

The retreat of God into the background allows the human characters to take the front stage. The name *Esther* in Hebrew, *Hadassah* ("I am hiding" or "I will hide") seems to communicate this aspect of God's role (Beal 1997, 2; also Berg 1979, 178). Human beings take control of their fate and are responsible for their actions. The God of history found in Exodus now hides behind human plans and acts in Esther. There will be no "exodus" from the present oppression in Diaspora, where the Jews must stay and transform destruction into redemption. Esther even opens a slight possibility for collaboration among ethnic and religious communities. Yet the concluding event of the story, the establishment of the Purim festival, turns out to be brutal and bloody. One ethnic group triumphs over another, and the spirit of revenge is too strong to be contained. The story ends in tragedy not only for the Persian enemies of the Jews but also for the victorious Jews, who have

become like their enemies. In the end, both groups are losers.

Since the tragedies of September 11, 2001, and of the subsequent unilateral declaration of war on terrorism that the U.S. government wages all around the world from Afghanistan to Pakistan, to the Philippines, to Iraq and the Middle East, the mass destruction of peoples and lands assaults our hearts and minds. Despite years of constructive efforts toward peace and reconciliation, rival communities are once again divided; they are pushed to see themselves as "us" versus "them"; an unprecedented level of hatred rises and engenders desperation and thirst for revenge. People are overwhelmed by feelings of vulnerability and helplessness. With the world's strongest military power determined to eradicate all those who are against it, and the unilateral affirmation of the legitimacy of preemptive wars, any effort to bring people of different origins and creeds together seems ever more futile.

Can we still envision the possibility of building communities where feelings of fear, threat, and betrayal are deeply entrenched? Or should we abandon this struggle as pointless? In the midst of conflict, trust between communities is very fragile. Believing that peace processes are worthwhile becomes more and more difficult. The violence on September 11 was massive because of the latest technological advancement. But what really aggravates this calamity is the subsequent spirit of revenge, taking the form of a sweeping resolve from all sides to use violence for violence. In this situation we need an even more fervent determination to rebuild communities across divisions and boundaries. We must devote ourselves to exploring and reflecting on the possibilities for building a multicultural community that includes many ethnicities, languages, religions, and cultures. Our reading of Esther does not provide us with models or solutions. But, as we have seen, it invites us to struggle and pursue this task, especially today in a postcolonial Hong Kong set in a multicultural Asia.

BIBLIOGRAPHY

Aichele, George, and Tina Pippin, eds. *Violence, Utopia, and the Kingdom of God: Fantasy and Ideology in the Bible*. London: Routledge, 1998.

Beal, Timothy K. *The Book of Hiding: Gender, Ethnicity, Annihilation, and Esther*. Biblical Limits. London: Routledge, 1997.

Bechtel, Carol M. *Esther. Int.* Louisville: Westminster John Knox, 2002.

Berg, Sandra Beth. *The Book of Esther: Motifs, Themes, and Structure*. SBLDS 44. Missoula, Mont.: Scholars Press, 1979.

Brenner, Athalya, ed. *A Feminist Companion to Esther, Judith and Susanna*. FCB 7. Sheffield, U.K.: Sheffield Academic Press, 1995.

Bush, Frederic W. *Ruth, Esther*. WBC 9. Waco: Word Books, 1996.

Clines, David J. *Ezra, Nehemiah, Esther: Based on the Revised Standard Version*. New Century Bible Commentary. London: Marshall, Morgan, and Scott, 1984.

Craig, Kenneth M., Jr. *Reading Esther: A Case for the Literary Carnivalesque*. Literary Currents in Biblical Interpretation. Louisville: Westminster John Knox, 1997.

Crawford, Sidnie Ann White. "Esther." Pages 131–37 in *The Women's Bible Commentary*. Edited by Carol A. Newsom and Sharon H. Ringe. Exp. ed. Louisville: Westminster John Knox, 1998.

Levenson, Jon D. *Esther: A Commentary*. OTL. Louisville: Westminster John Knox, 1997.

Niditch, Susan. "Legends of Wise Heroes and Heroines." Pages 445–63 in *The Hebrew Bible and Its Modern Interpreters*. Edited by Douglas A. Knight and Gene M. Tucker. Philadelphia: Fortress, 1985.

JOB

Benjamin Abotchie Ntreh

Department of Religious Studies, University of Cape Coast, Cape Coast, Ghana

LIFE CONTEXT OF THE INTERPRETATION

I am writing this commentary from the West African context. In this context, we have the problems of poverty and HIV/AIDS pandemic that confront both the church and the general population. The West African subregion has everything that any part of the world could wish for to make it rich. However, West Africa is one of the poorest regions of the world. Similarly, West Africa used to have strict sexual taboos. Its people were, to a large extent, very healthy. However, with the advent of modernization and urbanization, sexual taboos are no longer observed and the respect for traditional medicine practitioners have also eroded. Thus, poverty and HIV/AIDS stare us in the face. HIV/AIDS infection and its effects are reaching crisis proportions. Moreover, there are some myths concerning how HIV/AIDS is acquired. There are also claims by some herbal specialists and religious leaders that they can cure the infection.

I propose to address these issues using the book of Job. It deals with the lack of knowledge on the part of Job and his friends regarding the way to address the issues concerning Job's suffering. Thus, the book can address the issues of lack of knowledge regarding poverty and the spread of HIV/AIDS in this subregion of Africa. Similarly, the book of Job is relevant in addressing economic exploitation that is also rife due to the same ignorance. To achieve this, I will use sections from the following chapters that represent the gist of the book and shed light on the problems identified above: Job 1; 3; 4; 8; 11; 29; 32; 38 and 42.

Analysis of the Life Context

The economies of West African nations (except Liberia) have been based on the legacy of their colonial past. West Africans did not get the opportunity to create economies for themselves. In their interaction with powerful nations of Europe and America, the African nations were disadvantaged. The relationship that developed between Africa and the former colonial powers has made African people permanently dependent on the West. Thus, the poverty that we shall talk about here is human-made and vicious. It is important to analyze the factors that have created the present situation for West African people.

Before Europeans came to West Africa, most African peoples considered the land (the earth) on which they lived as God-given. Thus, Africans associate the land with their past, present, and future. In most West African societies there is the belief that the earth, as an independent deity, gave birth to the first human beings. Through the land, Africans are associated with their ancestors, the living, and the yet unborn. Again, Africans see the Again, Africans see the land not merely as the source of their livelihood, but also as the mother who receives them after this life (Dickson 1984, 58-59, 161;

Benjamin Abotchie Ntreh, professor of biblical Hebrew and Old Testament studies and head of the Department of Religious Studies at the University of Cape Coast in Cape Coast, Ghana, is secretary of the Ghana Association of Biblical Exegetes. Dr. Ntreh is a specialist in African biblical hermeneutics who has published articles on African interpretations of the Bible, including "Towards an African Biblical Hermeneutics" (1990), "Methodological Challenges of Old Testament Scholarship in the African Context" (1998), "The Survival of Earth: An African Reading of Psalm 104" (2001). Dr. Ntreh is an ordained minister of the Presbyterian Church of Ghana.

Zahan 1979, 23; Mbiti 1990, 26-27, 100). Land is, therefore, never sold or bought. It is for the entire people, and the king or chief holds it in trust for the people. Its possession runs in families and clans that constitute the community. Thus, the worse thing that can happen to an African is to be forcibly removed from his/her native land. Separation of the Africans from their ancestral home (land) is believed to bring disaster to the family and the community at large, and it is the most humiliating thing to dispossess someone from his/her land (Mbiti 1990: 156, 214). Therefore, Africans will fight with all their beings to hold on to their ancestral land.

West African people also know that the land is a sacred trust and therefore they care for it, because their survival depends on mother earth. So when West Africans are about to cultivate the land they seek permission from God for its use (Boulaga 1984, 182; Dickson 1984, 58-59). When the Africans were living this simple life, they were able to produce enough food to feed their people. However, West African people are always willing to share with others part of their land with the expressed understanding that they are not giving it away.

When European colonizers came to Africa, West Africans thought of them as people who needed land to live on and, therefore, gave them part of the land for that reason. However, through manipulations, the Europeans were able to assert themselves against the West Africans and take as much land as possible for themselves. Colonial powers further changed the land tenure system, acquiring large portions of the land and selling these to large timber and mining companies, as well as to other Europeans for use as commercial farms. As a result of this process, the West African people were dispossessed from their native land. West Africans were subsequently employed to work in these farms, mines, and timber companies. They were underpaid and the greater portion of the proceeds from these mines and timber firms were repatriated to Europe, to the disadvantage of the Africans. Thus, although one may see that mining or logging

of timber is taking place, it does not mean that the West African people benefit from the products that are taken out of the land. Very often, West African nations have been told (and they seem to agree) that clearing forests is an easy means of earning some foreign currency for their development projects. Therefore they exploit their own forests for the timber. There are records of the fast disappearing forest in West Africa.

> Liberia, for example, obtained about $84 million from wood exports in 1980, just over 11% of its total export earnings. About 80,000 hectares [approx. 2.47 acres] of forest were being logged per year out of its remaining 900,000 hectares of primary forest—a rate that would completely remove the nation's forest in 11 years. . . . The Ivory Coast (la Côte d'Ivoire) is the biggest timber exporter in Africa, and its foreign exchange earnings amounted to over $300 million in 1980. Ivory Coast's area of closed forest declined by two-thirds in 20 years, from 12 million hectares in 1956 to four million in 1977. However, agriculture destroyed 4.5 times as much forest as logging, a ratio that may be similar in other parts of Africa. Ivory Coast's timber exports are expected to begin to fall within the present decade. In Nigeria, most of the exploitable forests have already been logged. Once a major timber exporter, Nigeria has banned timber exports and may have to import wood for its own needs. In Ghana, too, the country's forest resources, outside the relatively small area of reserved forests, are rapidly reaching a state where they can only provide a minimal output of commercial timber (Timberlake 1986, 106-107).

Similarly, ordinary West Africans, having been put in this vicious cycle of poverty, are unable to purchase the fuel from their oil fields. They, therefore, cut wood and use it as fuel for cooking. This hastens the deforestation that has already taken place through the cutting of timber from the forests of West Africa. Almost all the minerals mined are sent to Europe and America, and the mines cause irreparable damage to the land.

West African farmers are urged to grow cash crops in order to enter Western markets.

Africans need to produce that which West-erners would consume, such as cocoa, coffee, tea, and other products that Africans them-selves do not consume. In a very subtle way the church in Africa is involved in pushing West Africans towards this sort of farming. Some of the missionary churches, under European leadership, started experimental farms to train young Africans to produce for European markets. West Africans have been told over and over again that their economic prosperity lies in producing more such agri-cultural products. Conversely, the prices of these cash crops continue to fall day by the day, losing about one third of their value in less than a decade between the mid-1970s and mid-1980s (see Timberlake 1986, 33–34). In any case, these cash crops need more fertilizer and farm machinery that need to be imported with the scarce foreign exchange earnings of these West African countries. Again, in the words of Timberlake,

> Over the past decade [1975–1985], real income from cash crops has declined; production of cash crops has declined; African shares in world markets of most commodities have declined; govern-ments' balance of trade has worsened, and most African countries are sinking deeper into debt. Yet, between 1974-76 and 1982, the area devoted to major export crops such as coffee, cocoa, tea, sugar, cotton, tobacco and hard fibers grew by 11.4%, according to FAO figures quoted by the Economist Intelligence Unit (UK) (Timberlake 1986, 70).

In spite of these facts, Africans are labeled as lazy people. Is this justified?

Traditionally, there were only a handful of cities in Africa. Since most West Africans lived close to their communities and their land, they observed most taboos, especially sexual taboos. However, with the advent of modernization and its accompa-nying urbanization, most young West Africans have moved from their original rural communities to the new urban centers. In the urban centers, traditional societal forces that helped them to live according to the tenets of the society, including sexual norms, do not exist. Now, in the face of new values and the absence of traditional forces to regulate behavior, young West Africans exercise their newly found free-dom. Young West Africans in the urban centers are more likely to be more promis-cuous than those in the village. Thus, the spread of HIV/AIDS is prevalent in urban centers. However, when young West Africans who have contracted HIV go back to their villages they introduce it in the vil-lage when they have unprotected sex. This sort of trend is so familiar that there does not seem to be an end in the near future. Closely related to this issue is the role of the traditional medicine practitioner. In tra-ditional West African settings, the role of traditional medicine practitioners was very much respected. However, in their encoun-ters with Europeans, West Africans have come to realize that, as far as curative med-icine is concerned, the systematic (scien-tific) European medicine has better efficacy than traditional African medicine that is closely associated with superstition and fear of the gods.

CONTEXTUAL COMMENT

An Overview of Job

The book of Job is a debate on the issue of the generally accepted notion that goodness is rewarded and evil is punished. To give a context for the debate, the writer presents a man called Job who was "blame-less and upright, one who feared God, and turned away from evil" (Job 1:1). However, the book tells us that misfortune of the great-est magnitude came upon Job. The rest of the book is a debate on the reasons why Job might have been suffering. The reader of the book is made aware that Job's suffering has nothing to do with any sin on his part. Rather, it is a test as to whether he had been worshipping God for nothing (Job 1:9-10).

Initially, the suffering of a person with such qualifications was viewed with shock. Neither Job nor his three friends could speak. Everyone could see that Job was suffering, but no one could relate this suffering to any known sin of the man. The ice was broken when Job finally tried to declare himself innocent and accused God of misjudgment (3:1-26). The declaration infuriated Job's friends who accused him of trying to cover up his hidden sins (4:5-27; 8:1-22; 11:1-20; 15:1-35; 18:1-21; 20:1-29; 22:1-30; 25:1-26:14; 27:13-23). Job insisted that he had not committed any sin. (6:1-7:21; 9:1-10:23; 12:1-14:22; 16:1-17:16; 19:1-29; 21:1-34; 23:1-24:25; 26:1-27). In the end, God appeared and rebuked Job and his friends for saying what they did not understand (38:1-41:34). Howevers, God asked Job to offer sacrifices on behalf of his friends for forgiveness (42:7-9), and Job's fortunes were restored (42:10-17).

Original State of Job and His Demise

In the context of the debate is set. Job has ordered his life in such a way as to avoid the evil that came upon him (Job 1:1-5). Job's status corresponds to the expected description of him. He is very much endowed with all sorts of goodness. He has a perfect number of children—three daughters and seven sons (Job 1:2; 1 Sam 2:5; Ruth 4:15; Habel 1985, 87). In terms of property, Job is unmatched in his time. He owns "seven thousand sheep, three thousand camels, five hundred yoke of oxen, and five hundred donkeys and very many servants" (Job 1:2-4; cf., Gen 12:13; 24:35). Furthermore, in religious matters, Job is not complacent. He offers sacrifices for the known and unknown sins of his entire family. All expect, therefore, that such a person will enjoy the favor of God (Prov 3:7; 14:16; 16:6). Thus, for the sages of the time, there is no way that Job should meet any mishap, because goodness is rewarded and evil is punished.

In spite of all this, evil of a very great magnitude comes upon Job and his family. Job, "a blameless and upright man who fears God and turns away from evil" (1:8; see 1:1), is plagued with untold suffering. He loses all his children, property, and servants in a single day. His own body is covered with sores. The setting for the predicament is put in the realm of the spirit world—a debate between God and the tester (Satan) about why Job worships God for nothing. While God holds the view that Job worships him for free, Satan holds the view that Job's devotion to God is based on God's protection of Job and his family and the property he has received from God (1:6-12). The ground for this contest is something that is beyond the comprehension of both Job and the people of his time. The pathetic thing is that Job is not even aware of what is happening to him. Yet, initially, he accepts his loss, as one would expect of a devout worshipper of God. He said, "the LORD gave and the LORD has taken away; blessed be the name of the LORD" (Job 1:21b).

Nations of West Africa are all endowed with natural resources—gold, bauxite, manganese, diamonds, and oil. There are forest areas that help to make West Africa most convenient for wholesome living. There are vast spans of land that are rich in nutrients to sustain food production for the populace. West Africa, until about the mid-1960s, had sufficient food for its peoples. There are lots of countries that do not have these natural resources and yet are rich. However, since the 1970s, the West African sub region has become one of the most deprived regions of the world. Its inhabitants go hungry and poverty stares the nations in the face. West Africans are poor even though they have more than any country needs to be rich. Children die from malnutrition every day; approximately "20 percent of all babies born in Burkina Faso and Sierra Leone die before their first birthday" (Timberlake 1986, 6). However, the nations of West Africa have not complained about why and how they became so poor. They seem to have accepted this state of affairs. However, this was not to last forever.

Three friends of Job come to visit and mourn with him concerning his loss (2:11-

12). For seven days, neither Job nor his friends, utter a word (2:13). Then Job breaks the silence by indirectly cursing the day he was born and calling the forces of darkness to reverse the order that God has created (3:1-26). The outcry here makes Job's attitude different from his earlier response. Job's physical pain seems to have affected his mental state. Job's outcry is understood as an indirect curse on God and the created world order (Habel 1985, 106-107). Job complains bitterly that he does not deserve to receive that sort of punishment. His state does not correspond to what is expected of a person with his lifestyle—"a blameless and upright man who fears God and turns away from evil" (Job 1:1, 8). Job's reaction infuriates his friends who, one by one, accuse him of being pompous and arrogant (4:1ff).

Like Job, nations of West Africa complain about the unfair world economic order that has been the bane of their demise. Yet, the more West Africans complain, the more they are told that they are lazy and that it is due to their laziness that they are poor. The traditional teaching of the church is that poverty is the consequence of evil—laziness. Africans have responded that they have been forced into this situation by powers greater than they are, and that they are not made to take any decision on the prices of their goods. The West African people wonder why their efforts have not yielded the desired riches.

The churches in the region made it part of their task to raise the people of West Africa from their poor state through education. Initially, most of the mission-initiated churches established experimental farms to train young West Africans in the production of cash crops. However, Africans do not consume most of these cash crops. Rather, they are meant for European and American markets. Thus, Africans ask why their efforts do not yield the desired riches that they were promised would come with this sort of farming. They blame their European colonizers for their predicament. In their view, the failure of Europeans to promote the interests of West Africa was due to their insatiable colonial exploitation. West Africans go further and say that however nice, enlightened, and good-hearted certain individual colonial officers might have been, their functions and authority fit into a pattern of colonial administration which was itself conditioned by the central and overall need to extract the riches of the colonies and transfer them overseas. Thus, it is most apparent to West Africans that any benefits that they might have received in the process—through the building of roads, the construction of a harbor, or some welfare program—were merely accidental. Benefits for West Africans are not the underlying purpose of these projects by their colonizers and of the colonial rule (Nkrumah 1963: 31). Africans are very aware that if the development of these resources were not going to benefit the Europeans themselves they would not have invested in such projects. This is what business is all about. A person or nation shows interest in that which he/she knows can yield profit for him/her. This was recently described as the unfavorable economic order.

The churches in West Africa often condoned this state of affairs simply by envisioning their role as preparing their members for life in heaven rather than on earth. Thus, the church in West Africa has, to a large extent, made itself to be of no or little earthly value. In addition, West Africans wonder why HIV/AIDS seems to discriminate and affect only the urban and rural poor. People of West Africa, as well as of other parts of Africa, believe that HIV/AIDS was created to eradicate them. They see HIV/AIDS as an infection of strangers. They see this as a creation of Europeans to eradicate the African population. On the other hand, the churches most often see the HIV/AIDS pandemic as God's punishment for the promiscuity of West Africans. Consequently and unfortunately, West Africans do not acknowledge their own complicity in the spread of HIV/AIDS, because they do not see how they can fight against what God has willed.

Job's Friends Attack Him

In chapter 4, Eliphaz is the first of Job's friends to respond to Job's outcry. On the one hand, Eliphaz agrees with Job's assertion that good people need not be punished (Job 4:7). He goes on to say that no human being can be good before God (Job 15:14; 22:2-3). On the other hand, he also holds the view that it is the wicked that is punished (Job 4:8). In effect then, Eliphaz is asserting that Job's apparent righteousness might be an outward show. He goes on to say that God is not affected by the goodness of humans or the angels. This is to say that even if Job were good, that goodness did not affect God in any way.

In chapter 8, Bildad, like Eliphaz before him, also thinks that God does not wrongly punish the righteous. He sees punishment as a means by which God corrects the erring ones. Thus, he urges Job to make supplications for any hidden sins that might be in his life (Job 8:1-7). In the end, Bildad seems to suggest that the end will definitely be good for Job because God will restore him to his rightful position (8:20-22; Habel 1985, 178; Terrien 1954, 975). It seems that Bildad's words suggest that Job should repent for God to restore him to his rightful place. What this means then is that Bildad doubts that Job truly is "a blameless and upright man who fears God and turns away from evil" (Job 1:1, 8). Later, Bildad expresses the view that human beings can never be reckoned as righteous before God since God does not reckon the heavenly bodies and beings as justified before him (25:4-6).

In chapter 11, Zophar, like the two other friends of Job, believes that there is something that God knows that might have escaped Job (Job 11:5-6). He holds that the wicked prosper only temporarily (Job 20:5-8; 13-14). For Zophar, therefore, Job's possessions at the beginning of the book may not, after all, be a sign of his supposed goodness and blessing from God (Job 27:13-21). He, therefore, believes that Job should learn from what is happening to him, repent and be spared the ultimate punishment— death.

It seems unthinkable that Africa, with so many natural resources, should be as poor as it is now. While West Africans blame colonialism as the cause of their present predicament, the former colonial powers claim that they did much to help West Africa to get out of the doldrums. The former European colonizers have told West Africans that their natural resources were useless to them until the Europeans developed these resources with their own capital investments (Kwame Nkrumah 1963, 21). Yet, the question remains: Will it be possible that at some time in the near future the rich resources of West Africa will be of some benefits to its inhabitants? Unfortunately, for West African nations, their leaders who freed them from colonizers thought that they were making transactions with their former colonial overlords, who may represent Job's friends, for their mutual benefit. Rather, those transactions have contributed to the underdevelopment of the subregion and the further development of Europe and America.

Again, it is wrong for West Africans to be accused of being lazy or to be told that they lack human resources for their own development. West African nations use their scarce foreign earnings to train the human resources that they need. However, they are not able to retain such trained experts. Many of these experts from West Africa, trained in Europe and America, refuse to return to their countries because it is in Europe and America that they can get remuneration commensurate with their qualifications. Those who do return get frustrated by the lack of equipment. It is, therefore, not a sign of laziness when West African nations continue to be underdeveloped.

Furthermore, European and American countries, corporations, and functionaries have been involved in a lot of projects in Africa to reverse the trend of deprivation that exists on the continent. The International Monetary Fund (IMF), the World Bank, and other development partners of Africa have pumped millions of dollars into West Africa. These development partners—Europe, America, and their allies who manage the IMF and its subsidiaries—cite this as evidence that they are interested in the growth and development of West Africa. They, therefore, blame West Africans themselves as their own enemies. They cite the corruption and inefficiency of governments in West Africa to support this stance. This is similar to Job's friends who accuse him of being the cause of his own predicament. While these people play God, they take no responsibility for the programs that they prescribe as the antidote for the underdevelopment of West Africa, although these programs never seem to work in West Africa even with inspectors from these financial institutions present.

The church in West Africa has also not been able to help Africans answer why their efforts have not yielded the desired results. In the area of HIV/AIDS, the church has largely taught "abstinence." For adults, the Christian church advocates, "being faithful" to one's own partner. The church does not want to get involved in the issue of condoms. Thus, the church only talks about the AB (Abstinence from sex, Being faithful to one's partner) of the ABC (Abstinence from sex, Being faithful to one's partner, and using Condoms) strategy for combating HIV/AIDS. However, the church has not been able to stop premarital sex among its members. Thus, the church does not effectively address the increasing rate of infection. To complicate the issue, practitioners of African traditional medicine persons have made claims that they are able to cure HIV/AIDS. This has brought false hopes to some who continue to live dangerous sexual lifestyles. No one accuses the West African in any complicity in the spread of the virus. Yet, the views of the West Africans makes this issue relevant for discussion here. Traditionally, West Africans, like most African peoples, think that God or enemies inflict disease. In this vein, the majority of West Africans do not accept the spread of HIV/AIDS merely as infection. They do not seem to understand how sex that is created by God could turn out to be the cause of so much devastation.

Thus, like Job whose worldview makes him think that God unfairly treats him, the mind of the West African complicates the issues involved in the spread of HIV/AIDS. In that same vein, the role of the majority of the Christian church has not helped. Although there are a good number of unwed parents in the church, it has tended to be oblivious to the effects of its belief that advocating the use of condoms in the HIV/AIDS campaign will encourage promiscuity. However, this stance has made many believe that HIV/AIDS inflects only promiscuous persons. In the process, church members who would otherwise be saved from infections with the use of condoms, are infected due to this stance of the church.

Job's Responses

In chapters 6; 9; 12; 16; 19; 21; 23; 26; 27 and 29-31, Job denies that he had some secret sins. In chapters 29-31, after three rounds of attacks by his friends, Job gives his final response. He yearns for the days of old when God was readily available to him when he called upon him. He remembers the time when he lived in good health, prosperity, and wealth. Job also cites the former state of affairs when he had the respect of his fellows; princes and nobles regarded him with esteem. He had the final word in courts. He was also providing comfort to those in distress. Job's situation has changed due to no known sins that he could put his finger on and this causes him pain. At this time Job had—shalom—total well-being. The situation is particularly painful for Job because, now, younger men have the audacity to question the validity of the basis of his earlier prosperity.

Africa is in the same precarious situation. As has been said already, West African nations are deprived of their trained experts. This is a cry of all West African nations. Like Job, who finds that his righteousness has not benefited him at all, the more people the West African nations train the more they lose to the developed nations.

Elihu's Intervention

Chapter 32 introduces Elihu, a young man, who has been standing by listening to Job and his friends. Elihu introduces himself as one who is not qualified to be part of the debate between Job and his friends. However, after eavesdropping for some time, Elihu concludes that the elderly have not done justice to the issues at stake. Elihu is annoyed with Job and his friends because they are all wrong. He accuses Job of justifying himself and he accuses Job's friends of accusing Job without evidence. Elihu speaks forcefully but without sympathy for the suffering. Elihu advises that Job and his friends should rather seek God's judgment concerning Job's situation (32:12; 36:22). He also advises Job to listen to the thunder as God's speaking in with all God's majesty. However, Job would have none of this (37:3-7). He would rather have God himself come to make things plain to him, as he has persistently said (Job 31:35-37).

The International Monetary Fund (IMF) enters the arena of the discourses between West African nations and developed nations as an independent arbiter. The IMF reproves the developed nations of stifling the West African nations. However, the IMF also interprets the present state of West Africa as due to bad economic practices. Thus, according to the IMF, West African nations are to be blamed for their own predicaments. The IMF has suggested reforms that are expected to get West Africa out of the depressed economic situation. However, none of their recommendations have worked. The IMF has suggested that developed countries should try to help developing countries. However, no developed country adheres to this suggestion, just as no one pays attention to Elihu in the book. The IMF interventions give West African nations a breathing space from the constant criticism of the developed countries. And although West African nations suspect that the IMF is a front-organization for the developed nations, the IMF tries, as much as possible, to assert itself in a way that makes it possible for it to indict both the developed nations and the developing nations. However, since the IMF indicts West African nations for their shortfalls, they feel the IMF is not fair; thus, like Job, they seek a much fairer advocate.

God Vindicates Job

God (Yahweh) then appears out of the blue and answers Job and his three friends (Job 38). Yahweh's words to Job are intimidating. Job is overwhelmed by what he hears. Yahweh asks him questions—about creation and the created order—to which Job obviously has no answer. Yahweh goes on to state what he does in sustaining the creation (Job 38:39-41). Then Yahweh tells Job to state whether he had any ways of sustaining any part of creation. Job had asked for a lawsuit against God. Now after God appears, Job is made to see that he acted in ignorance. So Job confesses that he has spoken of things of which he had no understanding (Job 40:3-5). Job confesses that he had earlier heard of God, but now he has seen God. This is the answer that Job got. He did not get a solution to the problem at hand. Rather, he got an experience that was as satisfying as getting an answer for his quest (Job 42:1-6). This concluding section makes clear that Job's friends had been wrong all along. They had made claims about things that they knew nothing about. They had accused Job for nothing, when they thought that what was happening to him was due to some hidden sin. God then askes Job to pray for them. Job is to forgive them as God has forgiven them. Job is then restored to his former status. He has the same number of children as he had before, although this time the daughters were more beautiful than they were before. Furthermore, Job got double the property he had lost. This restoration did not seem to be the real answer that Job was looking for. It seems that Job was more satisfied that God had come to vindicate him.

West African countries need to recognize that the solutions suggested by the International Monetary Fund and developed countries cannot get them out of their present state of economic dependence on the West, since neither Europe nor America would help them to come to par with them on the economic ladder. Thus, African nations need to seek their own solutions to their problems, whether they be HIV/AIDS or economic. Here, there is no real equivalent to the role of God in the context of West Africa. However, West African nations seem to take solace in Strategic Investors (SIs) or Foreign Direct Investors (FDIs) as the way forward. These SIs and FDIs seem to stand on a higher moral ground in that they do not seem to be directly associated with the activities of either the developed nations or the IMF. It is important to note that Job's satisfaction came when God appeared and exonerated him (42:1-6). In like manner, West African nations are satisfied when they are solely responsible for their predicaments. The restoration of Job's property and children came after he had expressed satisfaction at the appearance and explanation of God (42:10-17). West African nations cannot hope for such an appearance. Yet, West African nations can hope that with new African initiatives their situation can be changed for the better.

CONCLUSION

At the beginning of the book, Job is described as "a blameless and upright man who fears God and turns away from evil" (Job 1:1, 8). According to the wisdom and understanding of the time, no evil should have come unto Job. In spite of this qualification, Job is plagued by a series of unimaginable problems. When Job complained that it was a mistake and that he was being punished wrongly, his friends who had come to sympathize with him accused him of hidden sins. West Africa finds itself in a similar situation in that West African nations have been endowed with all the natural resources that any country would wish to have. However, West Africa finds itself as one of the poorest regions in the world. Like Job's friends, European and American colonizers accuse Western Africans of being the cause of their poverty and for the HIV/AIDS pandemic. As Job blamed God, West African nations blame their former colonial powers for their present precarious state of existence. These former colonial powers have replied that if they had not spent their own resources to develop the natural resources, the resources would not have been of any use to West Africans, who then would have been worse off. However, just as Job goes through a series of arguments with his friends to prove his innocence, West Africa rebuffs the arguments of its former colonial powers by pointing out the unfavorable economic order engineered by developed nations. Again, West African nations see the same unfavorable world economic order as that which has deprived West Africa of its human resource base. For West Africans then the HIV/AIDS pandemic is also directly related to this economic situation. Finally, Job seems to have been satisfied when God directly exonerated him of any wrongdoing. As Job was exonerated from the accusations of his "friends," so the book of Job calls for an exoneration of West Africans from the accusations of their European and American "friends." However, unlike in the book of Job where Job's vindication is coupled with the restoration of his property, there does not seem to be any hope for West Africa that their situation will change in the near future. It seems then that West African nations must satisfy themselves with understanding more clearly the circumstances that have created their present situation, in particular the role of neo-colonial economic exploitation. On this basis, West African nations have to work out their own strategies to get out of this predicament, since it is humanly impossible for developed countries to abandon their position toward West Africa, or for other regions of the world to be on par with developed countries on the economic or any other sphere of life.

BIBLIOGRAPHY

Alter, Robert. *The Art of Biblical Narrative.* New York: Basic Books, 1981.

_____. *The Art of Biblical Poetry.* New York: Basic Books, 1985.

Boulaga, F. Ebouassi. *Christianity without Fetishes.* Translated by Robert Barr. Maryknoll, N. Y.: Orbis Books, 1984.

Dickson, Kwesi A. *Theology in Africa.* Maryknoll, N.Y.: Orbis Books, 1984.

Habel, Norman C. *The Book of Job.* OTL. Philadelphia: Westminster, 1985.

Mbiti, Jon S. *African Religions and Philosophy.* 2d Rev. and enl. ed. Oxford: Heinemann, 1990.

Newsome, Carol A. Pages 239–253 in "Job and his Friends." *Interpretation* 53 (1990).

Pope, Marvin H. *Job.* The Anchor Bible 15. 3d ed.. Garden City, N.Y.: Doubleday, 1982.

Rodney, Walter. *How Europe Underdeveloped Africa.* Washington, D.C.: Howard University Press, 1981.

Rowley, Harold Henry. *The Book of Job.* NCB. 2d ed. Grand Rapids: Eerdmans, 1978.

Scoot, R. B. Y. *The Way of Wisdom in the Old Testament.* New York: The Macmillan Co./Collier-Macmillan, 1971.

Terrien, Samuel. "The Book of Job." Pages 875–1198 in vol. 3 of *The Interpreter's Bible.* Edited by G. A. Buttrick. 12 vols. Nashville: Abingdon, 1954.

Timberlake, Lloyd. *Africa in Crisis: the Causes, the Cures of Environmental Bankruptcy.* Philadelphia: New Society Publishers, 1986.

Zahan, Dominique. *The Religion, Spirituality and Thought of Traditional Africa.* Translated by Kate Ezra and Lawrence M. Martin. Chicago: University of Chicago Press, 1979.

PSALMS

David Tuesday Adamo

Department of Religious Studies, Delta State University, Abraka, Delta State, Nigeria

LIFE CONTEXT OF THE INTERPRETATION

In Africa the existence of evil ones and enemies is painfully real. Evil spirits, witches and wizards, sorcerers and ill-wishers are a constant source of fear and anxiety (Adamo 2000). The early missionaries who introduced Western Christianity to Africans mainly taught them to discard their traditional ways of dealing with enemies and evil spirits. They did not teach African converts how to use the Bible to solve their everyday problems. The Eurocentric ways of reading and interpreting the Bible have not met the real needs of African converts: how to confront food scarcity, the power of enemies, diseases, and even death. For Africans, Western Christianity brought by the missionaries not only failed to reveal the secrets of the Western power and knowledge used to conquer and oppress them, but actually contributed to the prejudice and oppression of colonialism.

We African Christians searched the Bible time and again with our own eyes to see whether it could help us to solve our particular problems. In the process we discovered in the Bible a worldview and culture that has great affinities with our own. We discovered in both the Old and New Testaments realities similar to those we find in Africa: miracles, satanic powers, hunger, and the deliverance of the oppressed. In the biblical miracle stories, we found many healing techniques we are accustomed to, such as potent words, touching, prayers, and ordinary water. Then we had to ask: how can we read the Bible to meet our daily needs as African Christians?

African Indigenous Churches, particularly those in Nigeria, began to interpret the Bible in an African way for the African context. This "African cultural hermeneutics" (Adamo 2001, 43-46, and Adamo 1999, 66-90) makes the African sociocultural context the subject of interpretation and thus analyzes the biblical text from the perspective of the African worldview (Ukpong 1995, 3-14; Adamo 2000, 336). From this African outlook, Western biblical interpretation appears as an intellectualist quest for an objective universal truth. By contrast, African interpretations are *existential and pragmatic* in nature, and *contextual* in approach" (Ukpong 2002, 17).

This contextual commentary discusses how the book of Psalms is read and interpreted in a particular African context, the African Indigenous Churches in Nigeria with sizable memberships (1985 statistics from Barrett, Kurian, Johnson 2001, 553-554)—especially Christ Apostolic Church (1.3 million), Cherubim and Seraphim (500,000), Church of the Lord (Aladura) (1.4 million), and Celestial Church of Christ (3.1 million). Without rejecting Western interpretations, I want to show how a great many ordinary people interpret the Psalms using an African conceptual frame of reference. As strange as it may seem at first to non-Africans, this method of interpretation is widespread not only in Nigeria (see the above statistics), but also more broadly in West Africa, most other parts of Africa, and the African Diaspora. My report is based

David Tuesday Adamo, professor of Old Testament in Nigeria, has also taught at Southern Methodist University and Texas Christian University in the USA. He is the author of many articles and of four books: *Black American Heritage* (1985, reprinted in 2001); *Africa and Africans in the Old Testament* (1998); *Reading and Interpreting the Bible in African Indigenous Churches* (2001); and *Exploration in African Biblical Studies* (2001).

upon visits to these churches, detailed discussions withinformants, and publications used by these churches, including Ade-boyejo (1988), Adewole (1991), Ogunfuye (no date), and Olatunji, Abe, and Jolugba (no date).

CONTEXTUAL COMMENT

The Importance of the Book of Psalms

The book of Psalms has an important place among the Old Testament books. It is one of the most frequently quoted books in the New Testament. It is the book of the Bible that the Christian community turns to in times of joy, sorrow, pain, confusion and danger (Weiser 1962, 19). Anderson is emphatic on the unique place given to the book of Psalms by the Christian church:

Today in Roman Catholic and Eastern Orthodox churches—especially where the ancient monastic usage is still preserved—the entire Psalter is recited once each week. In the Anglican church the Psalms are repeated once a month. And in other churches in the Protestant tradition the profound influence of the Psalter is evident in responsive reading of selected psalms or in the singing of hymns influenced by psalms such as "All People That on Earth Do Dwell" ("Old Hundred"—Ps. 100) or "A Mighty Fortress is Our God" (the great Reformation Hymn—Ps. 46). (1974, 3-4)

Anderson continues by emphasizing, in the words of Christoph Barth, that the renewal of the church cannot be envisioned "without the powerful assistance of the Psalms" (quoted in Anderson 1974, 4). Apart from public worship, individuals have found edification and comfort in sorrow and afflictions in the Psalms, because of their unique way of speaking about God and to God. This is why the Psalter is the favorite book of the saints (Weiser 1962, 19). Throughout the centuries, the Psalms have received special attention among Christian lay people, clergy, and scholars all over the world, because the Psalms have often brought some kind of transformation to the believers' life and faith.

Because of the importance of the Psalms, Western biblical scholars continuously work to discover the correct approaches for understanding them. These approaches include determining the authors and dates of the psalms according to the superscription, determining their literary types and forms, and determining their basic theological thought. Yet these multiple Western scholarly approaches have not really helped believers to read the Psalms as potent prayers that can transform one's life and faith—what African believers long for.

The reconstruction of the community worship settings of the psalms and their corresponding classification—as "Hymns or Songs of Praise," "Acts of Thanksgiving," "Psalms of Trust and Confidence in God," "Petitions and Laments," "Wisdom Poems," and Processional Liturgies and Blessings" (introduction and notes to the Psalms in the *New Interpreter's Study Bible*, NISB)—is a step toward the "existential and pragmatic" interpretations that Africans seek. However, it is not yet the "*contextual* approach" Africans are looking for (see Ukpong 2002, 17). To many Africans who were converted to Christianity, even this latter approach by Western scholars appears too mechanical and distant. It does not meet their daily needs in their context. For Africans who were given the Bible and faith in God as substitutes for their traditional medicine, charms or amulets, and potent words, the question is: How do we use this Bible and faith as concrete and effective means to gain protection from enemies and evil spirits, to gain healing from sicknesses, and to gain successes in work, school, and business? The answer to this multifold question has been found by Africans, especially the African Indigenous Churches who have used an African cultural hermeneutic. They have discovered distinctive ways of classifying the psalms into curative (or therapeutic), protective, and success psalms, and they use them for these purposes in conjunction with rituals involving natural artifacts.

Reading Psalms Therapeutically

Before the arrival of Christianity in Africa, Africans had developed effective indigenous therapeutic systems. Dealing with peculiar problems, such as diseases, sorcerers, witches, enemies, and lack of success in life, involved such practices as the use of mysterious or potent words, herbs, animal parts, living and non-living things, and water; fasting; prayers; laying on of hands; sacrifices; and divination. Although Western missionaries convinced African Christian converts to discard such means of addressing their problems, they did not offer any concrete alternatives. They did not provide other charms, incantations, divination, sacrifices, medicines, or other cultural ways of protecting, healing, and liberating people from the evil powers in African forests. African believers therefore searched the Bible to find the power that they thought the missionaries refused to show them. The members of the African Indigenous Churches found this power and these potent words especially in the book of Psalms. Some psalms are therefore classified as "therapeutic psalms." The reading of the Bible is combined with the African indigenous method of healing. Herbs, prayer, fasting, and the use of God's name are employed in the healing process in addition to the use of psalms. It is believed that virtually all types of illnesses are curable with the combination of reading the Bible and the use of African indigenous materials.

The psalms classified as therapeutic include Psalms 1, 2, 3, 4, 6, 7, 8, 18, 19, 20, 21, 24, 25, 27, 28, 29, 40, 49, 51, 53, 62, 100, 102, 109, 115, 119, 121, 126, 127. Because of limited space I will demonstrate how only a few of the above psalms are read and interpreted in African Indigenous Churches, especially in Nigeria.

For the above therapeutic psalms to be effective, absolute faith in God and the Bible (God's Word) is a prerequisite; the use of herbs, prayer, fasting, and the recitation of the potent names of God is also required.

Psalms 1, 2, and 3 as Therapeutic Psalms

STOMACH TROUBLE

In an African context, Psalms 1, 2, and 3 belong to the classification of therapeutic psalms. Instead of seeking to establish the authorship, date, and literary forms so as to classify these psalms as Western scholars do, we African readers classify them according to their use for stomach pain. Although there is no mention of stomach pain in these texts, the African indigenous interpreters believe these texts to be potent for stomachache because this has been revealed to the interpreter (the priest or prophet, leader of one or another of the African Indigenous Churches) in a vision by God—as my informant told me and as can be read in the publications of these churches (see Adeboyejo 1988). These psalms are also considered as potent words, like the African so-called incantations, because the Bible itself said that its words are sharper than a two-edged sword (Heb 4:12). For these psalms to be effective one should read them in the context of a ritual. In this case the prophet prescribed: take a bowl of water and then read Psalms 1, 2, and 3 above the bowl of water; pronounce the holy name of God, *Walola Asabata Jah* forty-eight times; mix together fried oil, potash, salt, and fresh egg and put these in the water; sip it little by little. There is a perfect assurance that the stomach pain will disappear (Adeboyejo 1988).

The above ritual action and the repetition of God's name make this text become performative. A closer look at the three psalms shows that the name of God, YHWH, is mentioned twelve times. The recitation of these passages also repeats the name YHWH twelve times. This practice is based on the African belief that names of God are potent when recited in rituals.

GYNECOLOGICAL PROBLEMS

Barrenness and infant mortality are major problems in Africa and are largely responsible for divorce and polygamy. In most indigenous societies in Africa, priests and diviners are contacted before any marriage contract to make sure that the spouse will not be barren or experience infant mortality. Psalm 1 can be used therapeutically to cure gynecological problems such as miscarriages in women (Ogunfuye 78). As soon as a woman is aware that she is pregnant, she should read Psalm 1 daily in the morning and evening. Prayer in the name of "Eli-Ishaddi, Jehovah shallom," should accompany the process. Then this Psalm becomes performative and one can count on God's protection from harm.

Barrenness and Psalm 51

Psalm 51 is a prayer for God's cleansing and forgiveness: "Wash me thoroughly from my iniquity, and cleanse me from my sin" (51:2). Adewole, a prophet of one of the African Indigenous Churches, prescribes the use of this psalm for women who have taken much medication for barrenness. It is prescribed for this purpose because of the belief in Africa that most barrenness results from sin and from God's anger. When God forgives and cleanses the barren woman, God, who is the author of children, will have mercy and give a child to the barren woman after she reads Psalm 51. This psalm is also to be read in conjunction with Gen 15:1-5, 21:1-8 and 1 Sam 1:9-20. In Gen 15:1-5 and 21:1-8, God promised Sarah, who was barren, that she would conceive and bear a son. In 1 Samuel 1:9-20 Hannah was also barren; she prayed to the Lord and God blessed her with a son. In an African interpretative context, when the above passages are read a certain number of times and specific ritual acts are performed as instructed, the words become potent. Thus, very early in the morning while naked and after she might have had

sexual intercourse with her husband, a barren woman who desires a child should read these passages (Ps 51, Gen 15:1-5, 21:1-8, 1 Sam 1:9-20) with faith three times above coconut water or raw native egg. This reading is accompanied by a prayer for (blessing of) drink, and by pronouncing, for effectiveness, "Jehovah Shiklo-hirami" twenty-one times and "Holy Mary" twelve times (Adewole 1991, 22).

Alternatively, and in other places, a barren woman reads Psalm 51 in conjunction with a ritual that includes getting ocean water, honey, and original perfume, and taking them to the "mercy land" (a sacred place nearby) for three days. The detailed instructions for this ritual include: start at midnight on Tuesday; be happy always; face your husband alone and eat many fruits, bananas, oranges, and coconuts; burn heavy incense in your house every night and sprinkle perfume; put three crosses in the water; sing three songs for forgiveness of sins with your husband; sing three songs for mercy and three for praises; and call the following holy names: Jehovah, Jesus Christ, Holy Michael, *El Shadai, Jehova-Jireh,* and *El-braka-bred-El* twenty-one times. The wife and husband should pray naked while facing the four corners of the house, starting from the east; thank God for hearing their prayers and roll to the right and left; remind God in prayer of his promises in Genesis 15:4 for human beings to multiply, of God's promises to Sarah, Elizabeth, and Hannah and that all were fulfilled (Gen 21:1-3, Luke 1:13, 1 Sam 2:21); give thanks to God with the confidence that the prayer is answered. Repeat this ritual every month (Adewole 1991, 44-45).

Safe Delivery

For safe delivery, the prophet Adewole recommends the reading of Psalms 34, 59, and 60 in the context of a ritual including drinking and bathing in spring water from a rock (on Monday, Wednesday, and Friday) and calling the name of Holy Mother Mary (Adewole, 1991 25). These passages are good for safe delivery according to the prophet Adewole. Psalms 34, 59, and 60 talk about deliverance from afflictions and from one's enemies: "I sought the Lord, and he answered me, and delivered me from all my fears" (34:4); "Deliver me from those who work evil; from the bloodthirsty save me" (59:2); "O grant us help against the foe, for human help is worthless" (60:11). These psalms are chosen by the prophets of African indigenous churches for child delivery, perhaps as a result of a fervent African belief (particularly by the Yoruba people of Nigeria) that every person has an enemy, known or unknown, who brings afflictions to that person. The time of childbearing, when a woman is especially vulnerable to afflictions and pain, warrants the ritual reading of powerful passages such as Psalms 34, 59, and 60, which are regarded as the main prayers for God's deliverance from affliction by enemies who are prepared to torture to death a woman in travail. The potency of these psalms is guaranteed when they are recited many times with prayer, fasting, and faith in God.

Infant Mortality

Psalm 126, a psalm of praise ("When the LORD restored the fortunes of Zion," 126:1), is also a prayer to God for the restoration of the Israelites' fortunes: "Restore our fortunes, O LORD" (126:4). Prophet Ogunfuye recommends it as a prayer to prevent infant mortality (Ogunfuye, 78) because it deals with how God freed the children of Israel from captivity. By restoring them when they had lost hope, God filled their mouth with laughter (Ps 126:1-2). The reason for reading this psalm to prevent infant mortality is the belief that infant mortality is a particularly serious risk for a woman who has already lost and buried several children. Like the children of Israel in captivity, she has wept over and over again for the loss of her children. Like Israel, which, all of a sudden, was delivered from captivity, the woman prays that she will be delivered from her own "captivity." As Psalm 126:6 says, "Those who go out

weeping, bearing the seed for sowing, shall come home with shouts of joy, carrying their sheaves." The reading of this psalm, following precise instructions for the accompanying ritual, definitely changes the travail of a woman with a long history of stillbirth and infant mortality into the joy of a mother of healthy children. The prophet says that a woman with a history of infant mortality should start reading this psalm as soon as she is aware of her pregnancy. She should read this psalm daily over the water for bathing, for washing, and for drinking throughout the period of her pregnancy. She should continue the process immediately after delivery and as she washes the baby with the water until it is fully-grown. With the reading of this psalm as instructed, the early death of such child is unthinkable, says the prophet. In addition, Psalm 126 could be written on four pure parchments with the holy names Sinni, Sinsuni and Semanflaf, and set in the four corners of the house of a pregnant woman with a history of "born-to-die" children (*abiku* in Yoruba and *ogbanje* in Ibo of Nigeria).

Cough

For cough, the prophet Adewole prescribes the reading of Psalms 24, 84, and 91 three times after taking a mixture of honey and palm oil. The prophet also says to call the holy names *Jah-Kurajah Jah Kulah* three times at every reading of the psalms and every taking of the mixed drink. Throughout this ritual, the prophet says to "pray and wait for the power of God" (Adewole, 42). The reading of Psalms 24, 84, and 91 after taking the mixed honey is said to be very effective. While honey and palm oil have some nutrients that suppress cough, the reading of the above passages and the pronouncement of the holy names of God sanctifies the honey and the oil for potency. When asked for the reason for choosing these particular psalms as effective for cough, the prophets answer, as in the other cases, that these have been revealed to them in a dream or a vision. Yet we can note that the effectiveness of these psalms is related to absolute trust in God who is the creator of all things and can use any material substance to heal and to reveal God's glory. "Pray and wait for the power of God," the prophet instructs. These psalms say: "The earth is the LORD's and all that is in it" (24:1); "The LORD of hosts, he is the King of glory" (24:10); "O LORD of hosts, happy is everyone who trusts in you" (84:12); "say to the LORD, 'My refuge and my fortress; my God, in whom I trust'" (91:2); "Those who love me, I will deliver; I will protect those who know my name" (91:14).

Reading and Interpreting the Psalms for Protection

Protection in African Traditional Religions

All over the world people are concerned with protection, including protection from destruction of people, crops, houses, land, trees, water, clothes, and all other properties. Protection from loss of life is most seriously sought. The process for seeking protection and the nature of the protection sought by African indigenous people differs remarkably from that of Western people. Africans living in Africa have to face some peculiar problems due to their perception of the world around them.

To indigenous Africans, the presence of witches, sorcerers, evil spirits, and various other enemies are painfully real. They believe that these witches, sorcerers, evil spirits, and enemies are responsible for all the evil events that happen in their lives and all over the world. In African traditional religions, many kinds of artifacts are used to protect children and adults. These include animate and inanimate objects, such as stones, sand, trees, leaves, human parts, animals, water, and urine. The use of such artifacts reflects how serious the issue of protection is in African Traditional Religions. There are three major methods of protection in African indigenous tradition: traditional medicine for the body; the use of a charm, or amulet (tira in Yoruba language), or some materials wrapped by the

medicine man (babalawo or onisegun or oologun) with parchment to be put into the pocket or worn on the body; and the use of potent words ogede in Yoruba language. This use of imprecatory potent words or incantations is one of the major ways of protecting oneself against enemies. Traditionally when Africans identify an enemy but do not possess the potent words or charm to deal with such an enemy, they consult a medicine man (babalawo) who gives them some potent words or a charm, either for protecting themselves or for attacking their enemy. The words must be recited at a certain place, time, and number of times to be effective. This is the background in which the African Indigenous Churches read and interpret the book of Psalms as a means of protection against enemies or other forces.

Psalms as Potent Words for Protection

The following psalms are identified for protection according to African readings: 1, 2, 4, 5, 8, 9, 10, 11, 12, 13, 14, 23, 27, 30, 40, 36, 46, 51, 53, 55, 64, 68, 70, 72, 74, 88, 90, 91, 104, 109, 114, 116, 119, 121, 124, 125, 126, 127, 130, and 147. According to the prophets of African Indigenous Churches, these psalms have been identified as protection psalms partly because of their content but primarily because they have been prescribed by the spirit of God in dreams or trances. The choice of these psalms is also based upon the African belief that the words of God must be more powerful than the African potent words (incantations) because the Bible is the sword of the Spirit (Eph 6:17) and sharper than a two-edged sword (Heb 4:12).

Prophet Adeboyejo was emphatic concerning the use of Bible as an "incantation and shield for Christians":

I implore everybody to endeavor to read Holy Bible after this special arrangement especially every time because BIBLE is the word of Son of Mary, particularly it was *incantation* and shield for Christians. I beg you in the name of Merciful God to refrain from retaliation for yourself, because enemies will be footstool for the children of God to reach the position of honor and glory. (Adeboyejo, 1)

Many of the psalms used for therapeutic purposes are also appropriate for protection from nearby enemies. This is the case of Psalms 1 and 2, but Psalms 5 and 10 are also appropriate. These psalms are believed to be potent words, like *ogede* in African traditional religions. Apart from the revelation in a vision to the prophets, these psalms derive potency from words that refer to God's protection of the righteous against enemies. Psalm 1:6 says, "for the Lord watches over the way of the righteous, but the way of the wicked will perish." The wicked are the enemies who pursue the righteous. Reading these psalms is a way of seeking refuge in God not only in one's heart but also more openly in words, as Psalm 2:11 says, "Happy are all who take refuge in him." (see also 5:11). Reading the psalm invokes God's help against one's enemies: "Give ear to my words, O LORD; give heed to my sighing. Listen to the sound of my cry, my King and my God, for to you I pray. . . . For you are not a God who delights in wickedness; evil will not sojourn with you" (5:1-2, 4). With Psalm 10:12 the believers pray: "Rise up, O LORD; O God, lift up your hand; do not forget the oppressed." Thus, they pray for God's intervention against their enemies, about which the psalmist says: "Their mouths are filled with cursing and deceit and oppression; under their tongues are mischief and iniquity" (10:7). In other words, thanks to God's intervention brought about by the potent words of the psalm, the curse of the enemies shall not be effective.

In the case of more distant enemies running after the believer and declaring war, Psalm 10 must be recited also as a potent word of protection. But this needs to take place in the context of rituals: for instance, the prophet teaches that one should fast until twelve noon and pray three times, that is, in the morning, afternoon, and evening, and should pronounce the holy name *Jara ta ajaja momin* seven times (Adeboyejo, 16).

Other psalms are to be used as potent words for protection for one day: Psalms 13, 46, 91, 116, 121, 125, and Job 5:18-27. These passages are to be read repeatedly, partly because their contents concern the protection of God's children. For example, "God is our refuge and strength, a very present help in trouble. . . . 'Be still, and know that I am God! I am exalted among the nations, I am exalted in the earth'" (Ps 46:1, 10). "A thousand may fall at your side, ten thousand at your right hand, but it will not come near you. . . . no evil shall befall you, no scourge come near your tent" (Ps 91:7, 10). These potent words are regarded as capable of bringing God's intervention as Christians read and claim the words and their potent effects. While reading these passages, the prophet instructs the believers to pronounce the following holy names: *Esiel, Angla, Jehovah Emmanuel*. One must also say the following words:

> See and know that I am He no God after me, I am He that can kill you and make you alive. I am He that can heal; nobody can escape from my power or shadow. I spread my hand toward the heaven. I said I am He who is living forever *animo animon, alimon, taftian*. The Lord saves and keeps me (Amen) (Adeboyejo 1988, 16).

After pronouncing these holy names, some special prayers must be said,

> . . . Thou are my power and shield, sword in presence of my enemies, my enemies will run back. They shall fall because God will be in His holy place. Everlasting God, command Thy angels who [are] stationed at four corners of the world, Holy Michael, Gabriel, Raphael and Uriel to protect me and to fight my cause in all ways from today (Amen). (Adeboyejo 1988, 12)

Protection for Travelers

The prophets of African Indigenous Churches also teach that if one is planning to travel, the recitation of Psalm 102:4-18 will protect one from a motor accident, shipwreck, airplane crash, or any other travel-related accident. Apart from the fact that this psalm is prescribed in a vision from God to the prophets, its content refers to someone who is almost dead and who prays to the Lord for life. In Psalms verses 11 and 24, say, "My days are like an evening shadow; I wither away like grass. . . . 'O my God,' I say, 'do not take me away at the mid-point of my life, you whose years endure throughout all generations.'" This prayer contains potent words of God, as do the so-called African incantations. It is capable of preventing death for travelers when repeated because the word of God is powerful. This power is immediately and mysteriously activated as one reads the passage or writes it on a parchment to be worn or put in one's pocket.

Similarly, Evangelist Luke Jolugba, the founder and pastor of Cherubim and Seraphim Church (in Isanlu, Kogi State, Nigeria), teaches that reciting Psalm 54 as potent words protects travelers (Olatunji, et al., 39). Evangelist Luke Jolugba assigned the power of delivering travelers to Psalm 54 not only because this was revealed to him in a vision, but also because it includes a prayer of deliverance and the claim that the Lord has performed that deliverance: "For he has delivered me from every trouble, and my eye has looked in triumph on my enemies" (54:7). Reading this psalm will bring deliverance from expected trouble and the threat of death, because it is a potent word from God.

Prophet Ogunfuye claims that other psalms, namely Psalms 17 and 119:105-112, when read with special prayers, bring protection for travelers. According to him Ps 17 should be recited when enemies are trying to make your journey a failure and you have no defense. God's words in Psalm 17 become one's prayer and defense. The psalm specifically affirms "my steps have held fast to your paths; my feet have not slipped" (17:5) and asks God to: "Guard me as the apple of the eye; hide me in the shadow of your wings, from the wicked who despoil me, my deadly enemies who

surround me" (17:8-9). Psalm 119 also reflects the power of God's word in averting one from the path of death, which is the path of darkness. It says, "Your word is a lamp to my feet and a light to my path" (119:105). The prophet Ogunfuye instructs that this psalm must be read together with the holy name *Jerora* and with the following prayer:

> O God my Savior, I beseech Thee in Thy power to come down from Thy heavenly abode and deliver me from all my adversaries who now compass round about me to do me evil. . . . Let Thy holy angels guard me throughout my journey. Give me Thy holy spirit to overcome all obstacles. . . for the sake of Thy adorable holy name, *Jehovah Jerora*. [Amen.] (Ogunfuye , 17)

This prayer is an essential part of the recitation of the biblical text that becomes effective in the life of the petitioner, protecting him or her from seen and unseen enemies.

Protection for Military and Paramilitary People and Hunters

According to Prophet Ogunfuye, the words of Psalm 60 are potent words for soldiers, police, others going to war, and hunters going to hunt at night, when read with appropriate prayers. The author of the booklet *The Uses of Psalms* sees the same psalm as potent words for protection for hunters and as a bulletproof shield when used with the holy name *JAH* (Ogunfuye, 24, 29, 40). Although it is claimed, as in every other case, that this psalm was chosen for this situation because of a vision, it is apparent to me that this vision took into account the content of the psalm, which reflects the situation of war, as mentioned in its introductory words (60:1, referring to battle with the Arameans and with the Edomites) and as expressed in its body. Thus, the soldiers, police, and hunters can identify with first the lament and then with the prayer of the psalm: "Have you not rejected us, O God? You do not go out, O God, with our armies. O grant us help against the foe, for human help is worthless. With God we shall do valiantly; it is he who will tread down our foes" (60:10-12). According to the African Indigenous Churches the words of this psalm will act as a powerful shield or protection for people going to war—as the African potent words, *ogede,* do, but more powerfully so—by chanting the words and mentioning the holy name of God. The name of God in African theology is significant and potent to achieve the desired purpose.

Protection Against Slanderers

Prophet Ogunfuye prescribes Psalms 14, 36, and 137 as potent words for protection from someone trying to lie about a person. These psalms should be read three times with the holy name "*Mupateka Jehovah Afeni*" and "*Eli Sumete,*" with the following prayer:

EL-YAH, Agla, Adonai, Jod, He, For, He: God of Abraham, God of Isaac and God of Jacob, God of Shadrach, Meshach and Abednego, God the Father, God the son and God the Holy Ghost, grant to us according to our hearts desire. [Amen] (Ogunfuye, 31).

Once again the content of these psalms certainly influenced their choice for the protection of those who are being slandered. Psalm 14 is about someone who lies and deceives him or herself by saying in his or her heart that there is no God. Psalm 36 has the same content. It is about wicked people: "The words of their mouths are mischief and deceit . . . They plot mischief while on their beds" (36:3-4). According to 36:12, these workers of deceit and iniquity will fall: "There the evildoers lie prostrate; they are thrust down, unable to rise." And this will happen when these potent words are recited again and again.

The Bible as an Amulet or Charm for Protection

I have stated above that the use of charms or amulets is one of the indigenous ways of seeking protection in Africa. The African Indigenous Churches make use of these methods in their approach to interpretation of the Bible. Based on their belief in the power of words, the Bible is written on parchment, worn around the neck, hung on the doorpost of a house, or kept under a pillow overnight. Prayers are offered for the effectiveness of the charms.

The use of psalms as protection from enemies, witches, and wizards is a common phenomenon in African Indigenous Churches in Nigeria. Prophet Ogunfuye seems to specialize in the use of the Bible, especially the book of Psalms, for protection, cure, and success. For protection against "secret enemies, evil doers and trouble mongers" (Ogunfuye, 7, 35, 51-52), Ps 7 should be written on a pure parchment and put in a special consecrated bag and kept under one's pillow. It should be written on the parchment with the following special prayer:

O merciful Father, Almighty and everlasting King, I beseech Thee in the holy name of *Eel Elijon* to deliver me from all secret enemies and evil spirits that plan my destruction always . . . let thy holy angels disperse them so that they may not come nigh unto my dwelling place. Hear my prayer now for the sake of holy *Eel Elijon.* [Amen] (Ogunfuye, 7)

Psalm 7, prescribed in a vision to the prophet for children of God who are persecuted by secret enemies, can be understood to refer to such enemies. Psalm 7:1, "O LORD my God, in you I take refuge; save me from all my pursuers, and deliver me," is a prayer for deliverance from all of one's enemies, seen and unseen, known and unknown, that persecute the believers. The last verse in this prayer affirms the power of this prayer and the righteousness of God by praising the LORD for the answered prayer: "I will give to the LORD the thanks due to his righteousness, and sing praise to the name of the Lord, the Most High" (7:17). The writer believes that it is impossible that his or her prayer remains unanswered. So also, all Christians who pray this prayer, and who carry these words written on parchment to show their belief that God is faithful and has answered their prayer, will see their enemies mysteriously destroyed.

Reading and Interpreting Psalms for Success

For us to understand Afrocentric methods of interpreting the Psalms for success in life, it is important to discuss what success means in African tradition. Success pertains to the totality of life. For men, it concerns getting a job, obtaining job promotions, getting rich, having many wives and children, traveling without accidents, and more. Success in romantic relationships is also important and is cherished; therefore, marital disharmony or divorce indicate a lack of success in marriage and in life. Similarly, one's inability to find a suitable and loving spouse is a lack of success. Winning court cases is success in life. Finding favor in the sight of God and people is success. African traditional religions do not dispute that God is the author of all kinds of success, or that no one can really achieve success without God. In addition to hard work, Africans employ prayers, rituals, potent words, and faith in God to enhance their opportunities for success.

Means of Enhancing Success in African Traditional Religions

The same methods that were used for protection are also applied in order to be successful. One important way by which African indigenous people attempt to enhance success is the use of "medicine" called *awure* in the Yoruba language of Nigeria. *Awure* literally means something that activates success or that uncovers it. This type of medicine that brings good luck may be in the form of potent words, indigenous soap, or a concoction of herbs and other ingredients. Whenever an important venture is being embarked upon, there is a strong awareness that enemies, human or spiritual, seen or unseen, are struggling to undermine the venture. This thought is indisputable in a typical African traditional society. Hence, when one embarks upon an

important venture like starting a business, building a house, taking a spouse, looking for a new job or attending an interview, a medicine-man is often consulted to increase the chances of success.

Reading and Interpreting Psalms for Success

Some psalms were identified by the Christian converts in Africa and used with some indigenous materials as potent words to bring success. African Christians believe that the success psalms have the power to bring success if used with faith and rituals, such as prayer, fasting, and the performance of specific symbolic actions involving a combination of animate or inanimate materials. Christians in Africa who were not comfortable with using pure indigenous ways of obtaining success—mostly because of condemnation by the Western Christians and missionaries—had to find alternative methods for achieving success. They turned to the Christian Bible and found similar potent words, especially in the Psalms. As in previous cases, the prophets of African Indigenous Churches identified specific psalms for each given situation. A few examples will suffice.

Success in Examinations

For success in studies and/or examinations, Psalms 4; 8:1-9; 9; 23; 24; 27; 46; 51; 119:9-16; 134 are identified. For students who want to improve their memory and be sure of success in all their examinations, Prophet Adeboyejo instructs them to use Ps 4 with the following ritual.

> Cut four candles each into three parts; light them around him or her; put some salt under each candle and then read Psalm 4 eight times, calling the holy name *Alatula Ja Ajaralhliah* seventy-two times (Adeboyejo, 5). "Answer me when I call, O God of my right! You gave me room when I was in distress. Be gracious to me, and hear my prayer. . . . know that the LORD has set apart the faithful for himself; the LORD hears when I call to him. . . . I will both lie down and sleep in

peace; for you alone, O LORD, make me lie down in safety." (Ps 4:1, 3, 8).

The prophet recommends Psalm 4 (and a few other psalms, e.g., 8, 9, 23, 24) for success in studies and examination not because its content has anything to do with examination or the sharpening of memory, but simply because this psalm has been prescribed in the spirit during visions. Yet this psalm also contains powerful words of the spirit that can change one's life if repeated in the context of recommended rituals. As Psalm 119 underscores, putting the word of God in one's heart has powerful effects in the life of the believer. It can prevent sin: "I treasure your word in my heart, so that I may not sin against you" (119:11). It can sharpen one's mind for understanding: "Give me understanding, that I may keep your law and observe it with my whole heart" (119:34). Treasuring in one's heart the words of Psalm 4, and "know[ing] that the LORD has set apart the faithful for himself; the LORD hears when [one] call[s] to him" (Ps 4:3) is a powerful word that gives understanding and confidence to the students. This might be why Ps 4 was chosen for this particular situation.

Securing the Love of a Woman or Man

Psalm 133 is classified by the prophets as the psalm that will aid one to secure the love of a woman or a man. This may be so because of the first verse, "How very good and pleasant it is when [brothers] live together in unity!" (133:1). This praise for harmonious living with brothers can be understood to refer to any loving relationship, including that between a man and a woman. This passage is believed to be capable of bringing about the desired blessing as promised in Psalm 133:3: "For there the LORD ordained his blessing." When God gives this blessing that looks and feels like precious oil or dew (133:2, 3), the praise of God will be possible. For example, if any man is looking for a girlfriend or a lovely wife and has a history of failure in such endeavors; if a wife is losing the love of her husband; or if a husband is looking for the love of his wife who is probably at the verge of divorcing him, these individuals should read this psalm while performing the following ritual prescribed by Prophet Adeboyejo:

> Draw some water with your mouth into a bottle. . . . Then call the name of the woman/man and the name Eve/Adam 21 times. Read Psalms 133, Ruth 1:16-17 and Song of Solomon and John 1:1-4 into the water at midnight and if the person is known give the water to her/him to drink (Adeboyejo, 27).

CONCLUSION

The fact is that the "Bible is God's word in human language which implies human culture with its ideology, worldview, orientation, perspective, values, and disvalues" (Ukpong 1995, 17-32). I have taken all these aspects of human culture into consideration in an African context.

At first glance, non-African readers may be tempted to dismiss Afrocentric methods of interpretation. They may want to ask: should we not make a distinction between "uses" of the Bible and "interpretations?" But if one takes a closer look at the African interpretive methods and at the interpretive methods of the Old Testament prophets and Jesus, one cannot but rethink this initial reaction. Some Old Testament prophets and Jesus used potent words, prayers, touching, water, and material means to promote healing, protection, and success in life. The African methods of interpreting the Psalms for healing, for protection, and for success are widespread among different denominations in Africa, despite slight variations. One important fact is that the efficacy of the psalm as potent word is never doubted. The most essential ingredient of this is faith in God's words and the power of God's name.

Because Western methods of interpretation are not the only legitimate and universal methods, and since all interpretations are contextual (including Western interpretations), African biblical scholars should acknowledge the legitimacy of this type of African interpretation and encourage this interpretation with some possible modification. Admittedly, care must be taken since not all aspects of African culture are acceptable. We must be able to sieve and discard aspects of our culture that are not compatible with African Christianity. But the first step is to become aware of this mode of interpretation, and to take the time to appreciate its cultural character and its important role in the life and faith of many African believers.

BIBLIOGRAPHY

Adamo, David Tuesday. "The Use of Psalms in African Indigenous Churches in Nigeria." Pages 337-349 in *The Bible in Africa: Transactions, Trajectories, and Trends*. Edited by Gerald West and Musa Dube. Boston: Brill, 2000.

——. *Reading and Interpreting the Bible in African Indigenous Churches*. Eugene, Ore.: Wipf and Stock Publishers, 2001.

——. "African Cultural Hermeneutics." Pages 66-90 in *Vernacular Hermeneutics*. Edited by R. S. Sugirtharajah. Bible and Postcolonialism 2. Sheffied: Sheffield Academic Press, 1999.

Adeboyejo, T.N. *St Michael Prayer Book*. Lagos, Nigeria: Neye Ade & Sons, 1988.

Adewole, Sam Akin. *The Revelations of God for 1992 and the Years Ahead Plus some Effective special Psalms to solve various Problems*. Lagos, Nigeria: Celestial Church of Christ, 1991.

Anderson, Bernhard W. *Out of the Depths: The Psalms Speak for Us Today*. Philadelphia: Westminster Press, 1974.

Barrett, David B., George T. Kurian, and Todd M. Johnson, eds. *World Christian Encyclopedia: A Comparative Study of Churches and Religions in theModern World*. 3 vol. Oxford: Oxford University Press, 2001.

Crenshaw, James L. *The Psalms: An Introduction*. Grand Rapids: Eerdmans, 2001.

McCann, J. Clinton, Jr. A *Theological Introduction to the Book of Psalms: The Psalms as Torah*. Nashville: Abingdon, 1993.

Ogunfuye, Chief J. O. *The Secrets of the Uses of Psalms*. 3d ed. Ibadan, Nigeria: Ogunfuye Publication, no date.

Olatunji, Joel, Israel O. Abe, and Samuel Jolugba. *Itan Igbesi Aye Ajihinrere Oni Luke Jolugba Ati aofin Ijo Pelu Awon Eto Isin Kerubu & Serafu*. Isanlu, Nigeria: Kerubu ati Seraful, no date.

Ukpong, Justin. "Rereading the Bible with African Eyes." *Journal of Theology for Southern Africa* 91 (1995): 3-14.

————. "Inculturation Hermeneutics: An African Approach to Biblical Interpretation." *The Bible in a World Context: An Experiment in Contextual Hermeneutics*. Edited by Walter Dietrich and Ulrich Luz. Grand Rapids: Eerdmans, 2002.

Weiser, Artur. *The Psalms, A Commentary*. Trans. Herbert Hartwell. OTL. Philadelphia: Westminster Press, 1962.

PROVERBS

Athalya Brenner

University of Amsterdam, The Netherlands, and Haifa, Israel

LIFE CONTEXT OF THE INTERPRETATION

This mini meta-commentary will proceed from the contextual, idiosyncratic, and personal to the accepted, the "classical," in four stages or rounds that relate to each other dialogically. The linear arrangement does not mean that, while reading Proverbs or any other biblical text, this reader necessarily indulges in a highly structured and conscious readerly exercise. Rather, in my own reading the various elements become hopelessly mixed. I have attempted to separate the various strands in order to make my own intellectual and emotional kitbag available to readers operating from other backgrounds.

With covert and also overt judgment springing from my context (described in the "First Round" of my reading), I will note the following in the book of Proverbs: class distinctions, attitudes toward young and old, a conservative respect for age, a shallow religiosity, the perpetuation of attitudes toward the Other within and without society, the presentation of Wisdom as a consumer good, the implied gender relations, and the social and sexual anxieties that feature, perhaps despite the authors' and editors' intentions.. In so doing, I will ponder my ambivalence regarding the question, What is there in Proverbs for contemporary readers? Some self-deconstructive tensions that I find in the book will be exemplified by briefly discussing two of my favorite passages: Prov 30:18-20 and 26:23. (The translation of these verses and all other translations from the Hebrew are my own, and the biblical references follow the order and numbering of the Hebrew text.) In so doing, I invite you to contemplate, ponder, or muse over the double-edged teachings of many verses in Proverbs and to become aware of how much of such teaching these verses contain.

First Round: Issues Raised By Proverbs About My Context and By My Context About Proverbs

This reader is a woman scholar, Jewish, a native Hebrew speaker, a first-generation Israeli born to immigrant Ostjuden parents, a-religious, a mother to a son, divorced, living in Amsterdam and Haifa, teaching bible and Jewish studies in Amsterdam and Texas (mostly to Christians), of working-class origins, a feminist with left-oriented political opinions. This brief statement of identity and of context reflects my deep awareness that its components have influenced my reading of Proverbs as well as other texts. The world in which I live and with which I identify myself cannot be defined, simply and straightforwardly, as "western." Rather, I see myself as both orientalized and westernized. First, I see myself as orientalized, because Israel is decidedly and increasingly Levantinized. I am a native of Israel, with Hebrew as a native language, and I have a working knowledge of Arabic; I prefer the foods, smells, music, etc., of the Levant. On the other hand, Israel is

Athalya Brenner is an Israeli and nonreligious Jew. In addition to being professor of Hebrew Bible/Old Testament in the Netherlands, she is the Roslyn and Manny Rosenthal Distinguished-Professor-in-Residence at Brite Divinity School (Fort Worth, Texas), and she has an honorary PhD from the University of Bonn (the Catholic Theological Faculty, 2002). She is the author of *The Israelite Woman* (1985) and *The Intercourse of Knowledge* (1997), co-author of *On Gendering Texts* (1993), and compiler/general editor of the Feminist Companion to the Bible series from Sheffield Academic Press (19 volumes). She lives in Amsterdam and Haifa, Israel.

westernized and orientalizing (in Edward Said's sense), and so am I, whether I like it or not. My westernization has increased since I accepted the Amsterdam professorship. And, importantly, the world I feel I belong to is a secular world, even though my business is to study and teach texts that are, by western and non-western cultural consent, religious texts.

Thus, unlike most interpreters in this volume, I suspect, my attention to matters of faith—explicit and implicit—lags far behind my interests in literary structure, forms and content; issues of gender and class; episte-mological questions; and the biblical text's influence on early twenty-first century life, mine (in the various locations I move between) and that of others. In my secular world, I am neither finely attuned to, nor desperate to find, an underlining religiosity in this religious collection that we call "bible," "*tenakh,*" or "scripture." I do not feel a compulsion to subordinate the norms and values of Proverbs to higher, underlying religious sentiments that are greatly in evidence in other parts of the Hebrew Bible. And it is no hardship or sorrow for me to concede that, in Proverbs, "religion," the monotheistic impulse, or "Yahwism," functions much like "religion" does in Imperial Rome at the start of the first millennium C.E.—that is, as a general background for sustaining societal stability and the politico-economic status quo. Religious devotion, inasmuch as it is present in Proverbs, seems to me a matter of a certain, pale, background *praxis*: mostly confessional lip service rather than *faith* or even, to a large degree, rather than *ritual*. On this point the comparison with Rome breaks down: there ritual did function as background *praxis*, and in a big way. Would it be an anachronism, then, to label the gleaned, generalized culture of Proverbs—following the example of Rome—as largely secular, old-fashioned, conventional, and conformist (promoting continuation rather than change)? I do not think so. Add to that Proverbs' decidedly urban, male, autochthonic, and elite-class concerns (as would seem from screening its contents), and the implications are many.

From this perspective, the acclaimed "universality'" of this "wisdom" collection is seriously impaired when located in its implied context, and its traditional "wisdom" character is undermined by the questions: Whose wisdom? By whom? For what purpose? Of what kind? Is the wisdom of the well-fed, advocated as guidelines for life, beneficial for the hungry or even for the less well-fed? These are questions that I cannot help but raise about Proverbs from our present day context. A hermeneutic of suspicion is in order.

Everything in Proverbs points to an urban, fairly affluent, royally governed setting; nothing points specifically to a certain place or a named city. Most commentators hasten to posit Jerusalem as the likely place of composition. However, I submit that the tenuous Solomon and Hezekiah links are not sufficient for so doing. Since I do not feel compelled to bracket together Proverbs and orthodox Yahwism, or to find a clearly defined connection to Judahite (and later Jewish) culture, or to lend the book's alleged universal character the additional halo of the holy city, I do not do it. I regret the non-specificity of locale, as I do the inability to date the book, at least in its final form. But this is no reason to assume too much; in such cases, assuming too little would appear preferable.

The lack of specificity has been construed as contributing to the book's universal appeal, or usefulness. However, in my cultural context, orientalized/westernized, secular, and concerned for the oppressed, I have to be very suspicious of the teachings of Proverbs. My chief reasons against accepting Proverbs' counsel as universally applicable "wise sayings" is its emerging social contexts, as outlined. Although kindness to inferiors is recommended, even commanded, class distinctions are not only accepted but also perpetuated. The Other within and without is not integrated. Religiosity and life philosophy are not nuanced. "Wisdom" is consumer goods, to be transferred and acquired and utilized for practical purposes. Obedience and authority are valued above independence and original initiative. Agism (in the sense of age superiority, diametrically opposed to what we call agism nowadays) is the order of the day. For me the implications of such a power structure are distasteful. This is a culture that lets fathers sacrifice their sons (Abraham and Isaac, Gen 22) or their daughters (Jephthah and his nameless daughter, Judg 11) to their supreme divine father for the collective good. This is a culture that condones sending young persons to war by elder politicians, for the collective good, every single day in the Middle East; and this is the aculture that eventually allowed the divine father to sacrifice his divine son for the same purpose. You may not agree with such an evaluation of Proverbs' counsel and its implications. But, from where I am, reflections about superior fathers and their control over their sons or son are more than disturbing.

You may object further and say, traditional honest values have a lot to recommend them. A good point: who can argue with the value of hard work, the impulse to improve and achieve, to advance up the social ladder? The problem is that when we need spiritual food, or food for the mind, we may not find it in Proverbs. For spiritual sustenance we need to turn to books that are troubling and deeply thoughtful and provocative, books with, from our perspective, a deeper understanding of the divine, such as Qoheleth and Job. Those texts, no doubt products of elite circles as well, go beyond the class-specific into the universal realm.

Turning to gender and other social issues raised by Proverbs, I am conscious of the irritating presence of what we call a glass ceiling, Sylvia Plath's bell jar if you wish.

In Proverbs opportunities for advancement and self-betterment are open to certain males only: otherwise, or so it seems, stability and social order will be adversely affected. Gender issues are a good example for this claim, as will be elaborated upon in the Commentary section, where Proverbs' two extremities, its beginning and end, will be discussed as a case study.

But before we continue, a word of advice: biblical scholars are quick to equate the gender of Proverbs 1–9 and 30–31 addressees (almost always ignorant males) with that of the speakers-in-the-text. In Hebrew, the first person singular (and plural) pronouns and verb forms are free of grammatical gender markings, and hence are identical for both grammatical genders (feminine and masculine). Consequently, when the speaker is 'anî or 'anokî (first person,"I"), unless there are additional grammatical markers, one cannot assume (as generations of readers have done, in quite a facile manner) that the speakers as well as the addressees are both male. On the contrary, in societies that promote female inferiority, women often protect internalized male values with zeal, following along the "slave and master" paradigm. This commentary, then, will not assume that the address "my son" implies a father's voice, unless the text contains good evidence to support such an assumption. This simple critical strategy opens up the possibility of understanding Proverbs differently. As discussed in the contextual comments below, Proverbs' mixed attitudes, which are at least dual-layered, about women and femaleness/femininity suggest ambivalence and ambiguity concerning other issues as well.

CONTEXTUAL COMMENT

Second [Traditional] Round: An Overview of Proverbs

Parts and structure

Apart from the book's general title (superscription), "The sayings [*mishle* traditionally translated as "proverbs," hence

the whole book's accepted title] of Solomon, son of David, king of Israel" (1:1), six more titles (10:1a, 22:17a, 24:23a, 25:1, 30:1a, 31:1) indicate the ends and beginnings of discrete units. When using a combination of the titles as well as contents as our guide,

Proverbs appears as a collection of seven-plus-one units, unequal in length and scope. Please note that my own division is slightly different from that of other scholars (Crenshaw and Fontaine, for example).

1. 1:1–9:18 *The Proverbs of Solomon, son of David, king of Israel.* This section features a preface and blueprint for the first part as well as the whole collection (1:1-7), and advice, with the literary trope or topoi of transmitting "wisdom" from parents to sons often present. An amazing personification of "wisdom" as a woman—lover, bride, friend, wife, teacher—is complemented by warnings against the "other" woman (*ishah zarah*) and a personified woman of "folly."

2. 10:1–22:16 *The Proverbs of Solomon.* This section contains short, associatively linked—or not linked at all—sayings about life, required social behaviour, personal fortune, achievements, rewards and punishments, and so forth.

3. 22:17–24:22 *Words of the Wise.* This instruction shows structural and content affinity with the Egyptian instruction of Amenemope, and also similarities to the Aramaic *Ahiqar.*

24:23-34 *These also [are Words] of [from] the Wise.* Justice, priorities, and industry (see also 6:6-11) are recommended in an appendix to this section, which shows no great similarity to the Amenemope instruction but, as indicated by its title, is an addition introduced by a subtitle.

4. 25:1–29:27 *Also these are the Proverbs of Solomon that the men of Hezekiah, king of Judah, wrote down.* This section discusses: the world, social life and conduct, and the royal court (mainly Prov 25–27); the king, poverty, and reward/punishment (mainly Prov 28–29), mostly in the form of a parable or comparison.

5. 30:1-10 (or 14, as divided by many scholars) *The Words of Agur, son of Jakeh, of Massa.* These verses offer a skeptical evaluation of life, god, and the world. As such they are extraordinary in Proverbs and closer in tone to Qoheleth.

6. 30:11-33 *Seven numerical sayings,* graded or otherwise, mainly about human relations and foregrounding (as do the next sections) gender relations. No general title or subtitle precedes this section.

7. 31:1-9 *The Words of Lempel, king of Massa, with which his mother instructed him.* These verses consist of warnings to a royal son, mainly about dangers that women and drink present to the business of ruling.

This seven-part structure (we may remember that the number seven has stereotypical, formulaic significance in the Hebrew bible and beyond it) finally climaxes in a seven-plus-one = eighth constituent structure, with an acrostic (alphabetically ordered units, in this case verses, from *aleph* to *taw*) poem, once again with no [sub]title:

8. 31:10-21 In praise of a virtuous wife (*Eshet hayil*).

Composition, authorship, dating

Although the main title relates the book to Solomon, thus pointing to ancient Jewish tradition that linked Solomon's fabled "wisdom" and knowledge of human nature and world nature (1 Kgs 3 par. 2 Chr 1:7-13; 5:8-14, 19a; 10 par. 2 Chr 9), most contemporary commentators agree that accepting Solomon as author of even the book's first collection is not only unwarranted by the content but also impossible because of the early (tenth century B.C.E.) dating this would imply.

There are no chronological indications of events, personalities, places, or nationalities in the book itself. In fact, it is wondrously non-specific in its discourse regarding "history." Whether this is a hallmark of "wisdom" literature as a whole, as some commentators will have it, is a moot point. The individual collections themselves are not always unified (excepting perhaps the first collection, Prov 1–9, and see commentary below) and their linkage to each other is artificially effected by the [sub] titles. The language is mixed, with early biblical Hebrew features as well as late ones in the same collection; thus, it is difficult to characterize any collection by its language. The Egyptian connection in the third collection indicates cultural dependence or affinity, rather than chronological specificity. The double attribution to Solomon and Hezekiah (25:1) is not convincing either, although it has value for understanding the gradual emergence of the book as we have it. Consequently, dating and authorship remain obscure. Scholars can and do imagine and re-imagine the relative chronological order of each collection vis-à-vis the others according to its relative simplicity, complexity, or title (which may have been added later, of course, by the editors!). No informed decision is possible for the parts or for the whole.

Proverbs is situated in the Writings section of the *Tanakh*, hence even according to Jewish tradition is later than the Torah and Prophets. Its attribution to the Wisdom genre presumably assured the book of its unproblematic place in the Jewish canon.

Third Round: Issues Raised in Proverbs About Life

Education

An important trope of Proverbs is advice-giving; when an advice-giving situation is conjured, it is from a parent to a "son," or from an "elder" or "elders" who are "wise," while the target audience is imaged implicitly or explicitly as male, young, "foolish," "ignorant," "insensitive," and in need of instruction and teaching. Whether this implies an actual family teaching praxis, or rather a teaching situation at schools where elder persons prepared younger males for the privileged life of public office, scribal activity, or economic viability remains uncertain despite heated discussions among scholars. What can be deduced, though, is that the literal trope points to the class situation in which such counsel could be formulated and transmitted: urban elite classes (Merchants?

Royals? Court officials? Landowners? Scribes? Priests?) that had the leisure, money, and inclination to invest in the continuance of their ways through the training of whoever needed prompting in the right direction. That the producers as well as the consumers of this seemingly oral—but for us readers literary—training were males seems to be borne out by the texts themselves, as well as by the preoccupation with female figures, personifications, and metaphors. That these texts hold incidental value for women readers (Fontaine 2002), and that women could and must have educated their male and female children alike in the home, seeps occasionally into the largely male-dominated (Newsom 1997) discourses.

The "Good Life"

The "good life" is a life of economic solvency and societal stability, in a family circle, as a socially adjusted citizen who is successful and at peace with fellow citizens and the authorities, including religious authority. A middle way is advocated, without taking financial or other risks, with a conservative attitude toward excesses or impulses. Respect for superiors is a must. Industry and eloquence are highly regarded, as are social justice and legalism.

Materialism and Rewards

Happiness and material possessions seem to be equated, at least to a large extent. The rewards of obedience, listening, acting decorously, seem in this optimistic worldview naturally to be expected.

Interpretations of misfortune

Inter-pretations of fortune and misfortune are clearly simplistic. Justice exists in this world. If you behave well, you are rewarded in kind. If you behave badly, the same applies. Conversely, if you are poor and miserable, it means you have committed social or other sins; and if you're wealthy and happy, this means you have done your duty. In a sense, the beginning of Job's story (Job 1–2) links exactly to this view, only to depart from it in Job 3.

Weaker community members

The weaker members of the community must be helped inasmuch as the condition of poverty results from misconduct and folly. Poverty is the reward of the foolish, i.e., those who do not heed the words of the wise. So help is advocated, but without recommendations to radically rethink or change the poors' situation. In other words, poverty and misfortune are accepted as the way of the world.

Norms and values

Norms and values are delineated by conventional social axioms. The family is the basic unit, to be preserved in its age hierarchy. Its authority, like other authorities, is just, correct, and benevolent. The ways of the wise, (i.e., the father and the ancestors) are to be recommended and followed with obedience. Since the chief addressees are inferior or younger males, instruction in gender relations is necessary. Sexual temptation of "strange," Other, or loose women is acknowledged but long-lasting monogamous endogamy is preferred: dallying with non-family women may lead to death. Attitudes to the young should be firm. Respect for wives and mothers is required but less so than for superior male relatives.

Views of time

Views of time are non-specific. Time should not be wasted in languid fashion; the past and past generations are favored. No national historic past, or group past, as linked to Yahwism and its special sacred places or its covenant with its god, are mentioned. The future seems to be manipulated by present action (see above).

Finally, a culture may be characterized by its anxieties as much as by the values and aspirations that it promotes. Along this line, it seems that the mini-cosmos teased (perhaps unfairly) as a summary out of the Proverbs text may be generalized by its four great fears: (1) fear of being, or appearing, non-conventional; (2) fear of being, or appearing, unsuccessful; (3) fears

of females and femininity, which seem to permeate Proverbs, even though the book starts and ends with expanded female figures. Moreover, these fears must have been internalized into female consciousness, as is apparent from the few texts that are perhaps delivered by a female speaker-in-the-text (see commentary of Prov 1–9 below); and (4) fear of death, as coupled with fear of *she'ol*, "the underworld," is overall present and used liberally, again and again, as the overkill (literally!) reward for disobedience to instruction, especially in Prov 1–9 and regarding sexual matters. Indeed, untimely death is construed as the ultimate punishment for not heeding counsel.

Fourth Round:
Contextual Commentary
Proverbs 1–9, 30:11–31:22

These chapters present the theme of the female/feminine as an uncontained container.

Proverbs 1:1–9:18 can be divided into seventeen segments, although scholars differ as to the precise demarcation lines. If we once again follow formal features (as we have done by following [sub]titles earlier), we find that direct addresses, such as "[my] son[s]" and appeals to the addressee to heed the instruction, suggest the following divisions, here listed with a précis of their contents.

(1) 1:1-7 These verses provide the title and general (editorial?) introduction to the whole collection, culminating in the declaration: "Fear of Yhwh is the beginning of knowledge" (7a). It is immediately apparent that the addressees are young, ignorant, foolish males in need of an education in the ways of the world.

(2) 1:8-19 These verses present an instruction from "father" and "mother" to son (in that order; 1:8). The subject is: do not consort with criminals looking for easy, illegal gain.

(3) 1:20-33 These verses present an instruction from a metaphorized or personified

female wisdom figure to "fools," promising reward and/or punishment for obedience or rebellion in erotic terms that will, presumably, attract attention and produce ethical behaviour.

(4) 2:1-22 An unidentified speaker addresses a "son" to extol the virtues of "Wisdom," which is here a protective agent against, and contrasted with, a "strange" or "Other" woman who commits adultery and leaves her husband. The divine punishment for falling for such a woman is death. Interestingly, both "Wisdom" and the "Other" woman are characterized by eloquence and eroticism, but not good looks.

(5) 3:1-10 "My son" is exhorted to remember the speaker's teaching in order to have a good and long life and please god and man. The details are: fear god, shun evil, pay your first fruits to Yhwh.

(6) 3:12-20 "My son" is to accept god's treatment, even if rough, for god is like a father who loves his son and therefore beats him up. The main thing is to find Wisdom and her rewards, for she is a tree of life and source of happiness. Yhwh himself used her for the creation process (see 8:22-36).

(7) 3:21-35 "My son" is given general instructions about interpersonal relations (anger, jealousy, fairness, and evil) in order to attain respect.

(8) 4:1-9 "Sons" (plural!) are invited to listen to the "father's" instruction. He appears to resort to the instruction of his own father and mother, as embedded in his own speech, in praise of Wisdom in terms of erotic promise, success, and long life.

(9) 4:10-19 "My son" is warned against wicked persons and wicked company.

(10) 4:20-27 "My son" is warned against the sins of gossip and unfairness.

(11) 5:1-23 "My son" is warned against the "strange" or Other eloquent woman.

The advice is extended to "sons" (plural): do not come near her or her house; she's a threat. Rather, stick to the indigenous, insider wife of your youth. And Yhwh sees all.

(12) 6:1-19 "My son" is warned against providing collateral for someone else's loan, against being idle, and against lying and provoking fights, etc.: all behaviors that Yhwh hates.

(13) 6:20-35 "My son" is asked to heed the instruction of his father and mother (in this order), and refrain from any contact with the "strange," Other, "foreign" woman. A diatribe against adultery, which is compared to damaging fire, follows. The main concern here is the horned husband's jealousy and its consequences.

(14) 7:1-27 "My son" is exhorted to stick to Wisdom and refrain, once more, from dallying with the "strange" and rhetorically eloquent, attractive woman. The speaker-in-the-text assumes an observant position in a house, in front of a window, and tells the "son" a story about such a woman walking the streets, calling to young "sons," catching a victim and taking him home to her bed. The boy succumbs to temptation and thus will bring a bitter end upon himself. To summarize, the speaker warns the "sons" (plural) to avoid such deadly temptation.

(15) 8:1-21 Woman Wisdom stands in the street and verbally attracts young, male passersby to her house (much like the Other woman does). Her self-advertising is articulate and persuasive, and her promises for wealth and happiness are convincing. However, her method does not vary much from the Other woman's.

(16) 8:22-36 Another portrait of personified Wisdom obtains here: Yhwh's companion from or before creation, his daughter who witnessed the creation of

the world and perhaps even helped, who plays with the cosmos and humans. As such, this is an extraordinary portrait of Wisdom and of Yhwh as father to a [metaphorical?] daughter.

(17) 9:1-18 Once again Wisdom attempts to attract ignorant male customers: this time the imagery is of a temple (her house has seven pillars!) and food (she cooks and prepares drinks), rather than sex. Her direct opposite, Woman Folly, also goes out in the street to attract customers but, like the Other woman, her attempts to promote hidden pleasures are inexplicably deadly, although her powers of persuasion are considerable.

The last three units of Proverbs, once again, display a deep concern with women and femaleness/femininity. Their limits and contents are listed below.

Proverbs 30:11-33. In this section there are seven numerical sayings (30:11-14, 15-17, 18-20, 21-23, 24-28, 29-32, 33), structured on a "3 or 3+1 formula": "there are/I know three or four things," etc. Several of these are graded, that is, the higher number constitutes a climax. All but one (30:21-23) have a comment appended to them; to define these comments as "glosses," marginal additions by ancient readers that disturb the flow, as some scholars have done, seems to me unwarranted. The subjects vary. At any rate, at least sayings 2, 3, and 4 have women in their epicentre (others deal with respect for elders and the weak in society, animal community life as against human organization, heroism, and anger). Saying 4, which stands at the center of this mini-collection, is wellknown and worth quoting here (30:18-20, translation and italics mine):

(18) Three things are [too] perplexing for me, and four I do not know

(19) The way of an eagle *in* the sky

(19) The way of a snake *on* a rock

(19) The way of a ship *in* the middle of a sea

(19) And the way of a man *in* a [young] woman

(20) So is the way of an adulterous woman: she eats and wipes her mouth, and says, "I committed no sin."

A quick comparison with other translations will show that the main differences between them and my translation are minimal: they concern the textual speaker's "wonderment" or "amazement" in 30:18, and, the prepositions used to translate the Hebrew, especially of the last (and fourth) climactic utterance. To translate the line of 30:19 as "the way of a man with a *girl*" (NRSV), or similar other translations, takes away the physical force and gender viewpoint inherent in this text, and converts perplexity into admiration. If the original Hebrew's intent and prepositions are retained, so is the anxiety and confusion of a male speaker over male sexuality meeting its female containment. To translate this perplexity into a dual-gender, universal sentiment is perhaps socially acceptable but misses the Proverbs anxiety, as repeatedly attested in this biblical text. If we take 30:20 seriously as a comment, then its placement after this consummate and minimalistic poem strengthens this interpretation further: the imagined response of an adulterous woman, light and incorporating double entendres about food and lips may be tantalizing indeed.

Proverbs 31:1-9. These verses are addressed to Lemuel, a king, "my son, the son of my womb," expressly by his mother. The warnings against women recall those of the parent in Prov 1–9. Warnings against drinking alcohol culminate in a demand to do justice and judge wisely. It seems, therefore, that the textual mother is concerned with her son's governing powers through the correct attention span, with no deviations, more than with morality or social convention. In any event, this is an explicit instance of a mother's instruction, whereas in Prov 1–9 the mother's voice was or may have been implied while never foregrounded.

Proverbs 31:10-31. This acrostic poem draws a portrait of a virtuous wife who works round the clock, keeps her family, and is commercially active, in addition to doing all traditional female crafts and tasks. She carries out economic transactions, is Yhwh-fearing, charitable, learned, and a source of praise and comfort for her sons and husband (see embedded speech of praise in 31:27-31).

This short summary of Proverbs' opening and closing units foregrounds some points that are endemic to the collection as a whole and meaningful for understanding it. To start with, these units serve as the book's frame and its framework: all the other units are enveloped by or embedded in the frame. The frame contains much discourse that is concerned with femaleness and femininity—more specifically, it elaborates the roles of a legitimate wife/lover and mother as against illicit sexual ties of a man with Other women. This is in keeping with Proverbs' general interest in safeguarding the family as an ongoing, [re]productive social institution. This impulse makes sense for social continuation and self-perpetuation. At the same time, it betrays anxiety about the social project it promotes.

This anxiety seems to be male anxiety, since most of the "instruction," if not all, is addressed to males. It would be an error, though, to presuppose—as is commonly done—that the gender identities of the instruction's producers and addressees are identical (for details see above). The only place where the textual speaker identifies himself as a "father" quoting his father's instruction is in 4:1-9; two more texts refer to the father and mother's instruction (1:8-19, 6:20-35). Other "speeches" identify the recipients as son or sons, but they do not identify the speakers. Furthermore, in Prov 7, the speaker may actually be a woman figure: Proverbs 7:6 depicts the speaker as observing through a window, from the inside of a house. Such a position typically belongs to a woman, as suggested by the biblical examples of Sisera's mother (Judg 5:28), Jezebel (2 Kgs 9:30-33), and Michal (2 Sam 6:16 par. 1 Chr 15:29), and by archaeological evidence. It is as conceivable to image a warning mother's words here as it is to imagine a father's words; perhaps a mother's admonition makes more sense, in view of Lemuel's mother's cautionary counsel against women in 31:1-9. Women are quick to internalize society's norms, out of self-defence, choice, or necessity. Hence, the gender bias of Proverbs should be redefined and nuanced further. Its business is indeed the education of [young] males; but the educators are both age-superior males and females.

Moreover, the curious persona or metaphor of wisdom as Wisdom, an erotically portrayed wife/lover and female teacher of commonsense is deeply meaningful for identifying the textual "voices" in Proverbs as well as its underlying wishes and anxieties about the promoted social order. It would make no sense to advance and sustain a female Wisdom figure, variously depicted in no less than seven units within Proverbs' first collection (Prov 1–9), and to attribute a teaching function to Lemuel's mother and the virtuous wife at the book's ending, if such a function was unimaginable as attributed to regular wives and mothers. Be the origins of Wisdom's portraits as they may—a goddess figure, a metaphor, an abstract quality metaphorized as female because its grammatical gender is the feminine (as indeed it is in Hebrew)—its prominence plausibly suggests an appreciation of womanhood—more specifically endogamous wifehood and motherhood—that is overtly absent from the androcentric world order advocated. Thus, a mixed and at least dual-layered message to and about women is implicit in the present form of the book of Proverbs, as available when studied with its extremities taken seriously as reading guides for the whole.

The virtuous wife who closes Proverbs is a paragon of virtue: no wonder that Jewish husbands still recite the poem to their wives today, either at their wedding or on Shabbath evening, according to their community's customs. Incidentally, as I have learned recently, in some Orthodox Jewish communities the poem is recited also at the graveside during a deceased woman's funeral service (in Haifa); I have no idea whether an unmarried woman receives the same ritual treatment. At any rate, during her lifetime, such a wife is convenient to have, since she has everything, apart from beauty (31:30). Like Wisdom, she is "far more precious than rubies" (31:10). In fact, she is the personification of the metaphorical/metaphorized or personified Wisdom. The essence of feminine/female achievement is a woman who has totally adapted to her required role. This is the ultimate male victory: a useful woman, the complete antithesis to the woman Other. Indeed, if we could show that this exaggerated blueprint for wifely behaviour was taught by mother to daughter—after all, the virtuous woman does have the capacity of wisdom

and Torah in her mouth, just like Wisdom the teacher (31:26)—the male victory will be complete.

Or will it? When all is said and done, this poem, this personification of wifely virtue, seems to be a male fantasy, no doubt for the benefit of the sons and their fathers, and most likely internalized by their womenfolk. Yet, the preoccupation with the female/feminine at the beginning and the end of Proverbs, the mutation of Wisdom/bride/lover/teacher into the wife, testifies to how slippery and uncertain the victory is. The dialectics remain (see Camp 1985); woman continues to exert a fatal attraction and, ultimately, retains a subject position as a central patriarchal myth (Newsom 1997, 129-131). The victory undermines itself. It is socially triumphant but, psychologically, the Woman continues to be elusive, as does Wisdom, for the males inhabiting the landscape of Proverbs.

CONCLUSION

What Is in Proverbs for Contemporary Readers?

My reading of Proverbs is perhaps disappointing to you. With covert and also overt judgment, I have made notes about class distinctions, attitudes toward young and old, a conservative respect for age, a shallow religiosity, the perpetuation of attitudes toward the Other within and without society, the presentation of wisdom and Wisdom as consumer goods, and social and sexual anxieties. I have outlined Proverbs' discourse and context—by way of generalization, and this is always unjust—as elite, urban, self-consciously conventional and aimed at conserving its way of life. All this limits Proverbs' scope and may appear to take it off the shelf of the books containing universally applicable advice for a good life.

This is indeed so, to a degree. Proverbs, like other biblical books, is universally applicable as a result of readerly consensus concerning the bible, not because it is intrinsically and fundamentally so. How-

ever, having critiqued the book's counsel as a whole, there is no denying that many of its "sayings" and aphorisms, especially in its inner parts (beyond the frame), are beautiful as well as useful. It does contain many worthy details of genuine wisdom.

Let me therefore conclude on an appreciative note. I have already indicated one of my favorites, 30:18-20, translated above. Read (and translated) with care, it rings no less than true. Another one is the difficult verse of 26:23, which mixes metallurgy and pottery images. My translation will be something like, "[Like] silver dross on [fired] clay, so are hot lips with an evil heart." This verse may therefore be another warning against the danger that women present for men (as in 31:1-9 and 23:26-33), not simply a warning against non-gendered hypocritical attitudes.

But to return to the actual image, since when can clay be silver-plated? So, taking my clue from Ugaritic and a slight emendation following the Septuagint and instances of later biblical Hebrew usage (Jer 23:31,

Pss 5:10, 12:3, 36:3, 55:22; Prov 28:23; Dan 11:32), I can also translate: "like glaze on pottery, so are smooth lips but an evil heart." If the latter translation is adopted, the reference to metallurgy disappears (as does the vague sexual undertone). But does this impoverish the imagery? Perhaps, since we are now exclusively in the metaphorical realm of pottery in the first part of the verse. On the other hand, beyond the pottery metaphor and in the second and referential part, we gain a link to a well-known image: by metonymy (from lips to the words uttered by those lips), eloquence—"smooth words," to borrow the phrase from Carole Fontaine's recent title—is implied. And eloquence, rhetorical ability, is a value to be taught in/by Proverbs. However, not all eloquence, not all smoothness, is acceptable. The Other woman's smooth words are not. Smooth words that are not backed by the right thoughts are not. Hypocrisy is not appreciated. Should we say then that that the text warns about itself, underscoring that smooth words of Wisdom have to be carefully examined?

You may prefer the "hot lips" to the "smooth lips" (i.e., "words"), in spite of the difficulty presented by silver-plated pottery. You may contemplate the double-edged idea of "smooth words" in Proverbs. You may ponder, or muse over, how one difficult verse may imply so much of Proverbs' torah: speech, orality, opacity or transparency of human response and thoughts, ethics of convenience, conveyance through imagery. And you may wish to check my opinions and translations, so as to produce your own.

BIBLIOGRAPHY

Brenner, Athalya, and Fokkelien van Dijk-Hemmes. *On Gendering Texts: Female and Male Voices in the Hebrew Bible*. Biblical Interpretation Series 1. Leiden: Brill, 1993.

Brenner, Athalya, ed. *A Feminist Companion to Wisdom Literature*. FCB 9. Sheffield: Sheffield Academic Press, 1995: see esp. Fontaine (24-49), Schroer (67-84), Valler (85-97), Yee (110-130), Camp (131-156).

Brenner, Athalya, and Carole Fontaine, eds. *A Feminist Companion to Wisdom Literature and the Psalms*. FCB 2d series 2. Sheffield: Sheffield Academic Press, 1998.

Camp, Claudia V., *Wisdom and the Feminine in the Book of Proverbs*. Bible and Literature Series 11). Decatur, Ga.: Almond Press, 1985.

————. "Woman Wisdom and the Strange Woman: Where is Power to be Found." Pages 85-112 in *Reading Bibles, Writing Bodies: Identity and the Book*. Edited by Timothy K. Beal and David M. Gunn. Biblical Limits 27. London and New York: Routledge, 1997.

————. *Wise, Strange and Holy: The Strange Woman and the Making of the Bible*. JSOTSup 320. Sheffield: Sheffield Academic Press, 2000.

————. "Woman Wisdom." Pages 548-552 in *Women in Scripture: A Dictionary of Named and Unnamed Women in the Hebrew Bible, the Apoc-ryphal/Deuterocanonical Books, and the New Testament*. Edited by Carol Meyers, Toni Craven, and Ross S. Kraemer. Boston: Houghton Mifflin, 2000.

Clifford, Richard J. *The Wisdom Literature*. Nashville: Abingdon, 1998.

Crenshaw, James L. "Proverbs, Book of." *ABD CD-Rom*. New York: Doubleday, 1992.

Crenshaw, James L. *Old Testament Wisdom: An Introduction*. Rev. ed. Louisville, Ky.: Westminster John Knox, 1998.

Fontaine, Carol R. "Proverbs." Pages 145-155 in *The Women's Bible Commentary*. Edited by Carol A. Newsom and Sharon H. Ringe. Louisville, Ky.: Westminster John Knox, 1992.

Fontaine, Carole R. *Smooth Words: Women, Proverbs, and Performance in Biblical Wisdom*. JSOTSup 356. London: Sheffield Academic Press, 2002.

Fox, Michael V. *Proverbs 1–9* AB 18A. Garden City, N.Y.: Doubleday, 2000.

Lang, Bernhard. "Lady Wisdom: A Polytheistic and Psychological Interpretation of a Biblical Goddess." Pages 400-423 in *A Feminist Companion to Reading the Bible: Approaches, Methods and Strategies*. Edited by Athalya Brenner and Carole R. Fontaine. Sheffield: Sheffield Academic Press, 1997.

McKane, William. *Proverbs*. OTL. London: SCM Press, 1995.

McKinlay, Judith E. *Gendering Wisdom the Host: Biblical Invitations to Eat & Drink*. JSOTSup 216 Sheffield: Sheffield Academic Press, 1999.

Murphy, Roland E. *Wisdom Literature: Job, Proverbs, Ruth, Canticles, Ecclesiastes, Esther*. FOTL 13. Grand Rapids: Eerdmans, 1981.

Newsom, Carol. "Woman and the Discourse of Patriarchal Wisdom." Pages 116-131 in *Reading Bibles, Writing Bodies: Identity and the Book*. Edited by Timothy K. Beal and David M. Gunn. Biblical Limits 27. New York: Routledge, 1997.

Scheid, John. An *Introduction to Roman Religion*. Translated by Janet Lloyd. Bloomington, Ind: University of Indiana Press, 2003.

Westermann, Claus. *Roots of Wisdom: The Oldest Proverbs of Israel and Other Peoples*. Trans. J. Daryl Charles. Louisville, Ky.: Westminster John Knox, 1995.

Whybray, Norman R. *Wealth and Poverty in the Book of Proverbs*. JSOTSup 99. Sheffield: JSOT Press, 1990.

'Proverbs, Book of.' Pages 320-323 in *Dictionary of Biblical Interpretation*. Vol. 2. Edited by John H. Hayes. Nashville: Abingdon, 1999.

ECCLESIASTES

John Mansford Prior

Candraditya Research Centre for the Study of Religion and Culture, Indonesia

LIFE CONTEXT OF THE INTERPRETATION

After thirty-two years of the Soeharto military regime (1967-1999), Indonesia has been left without a functioning civil society. The bureaucracy and the judiciary, the executive and the legislature, and the armed forces and their conglomerates were systematically corrupted. National and private debt became untenable while democracy and human rights were denied. Readily manipulated, the powerless are now reasserting narrow ethnic identities and strident religious allegiances. With a civil war in the Moluccas, struggles for independence in Aceh and West Papua, and civil wars or conflicts on other islands, both the discarded poor and the vulnerable middle class are sinking into a culture of resignation.

Issues Faced by Ecclesiastes and by Indonesians

A solid consensus holds that Ecclesiastes was compiled in the Judean Province of the Hellenistic Empire ruled from Egypt during the third century B.C.E. The text clearly reflects this centralized colonial power. Under the repressive Ptolemaic regime the average Israelite felt unable to change circumstances for the better. Everything was *hebel,* "breath, whiff, puff, vapor, steam," that is, "superficial, ephemeral, insubstantial, fleeting, empty, absurd, vain, incomprehensible, futile, useless, senseless, enigmatic, inconsistent, contradictory, indeed completely frustrating." Life was simply experienced as futile in a world out of control.

Ecclesiastes was written about, and for, merchants, small land holders, homesteaders, fellow bureaucrats, rulers, elders, prophets, priests, and legislators. These Jerusalem scribes who wrote the book, often at the mercy of the whims of autocratic rulers (10:20), developed and lived out a survival ethic for personal security to enable them to maneuver successfully within the establishment. Their work ethic was understandably strongly conformist, pragmatic, indeed opportunist. Their elevated yet precarious position would be threatened by any major change.

The economic milieu of Ecclesiastes was as volatile as it was arbitrary, a world full of economic opportunities and equally great risks. Money had only recently acquired a prominent role in the postexilic economy. Monetary terms appear in virtually every verse, with references to taxes, wages, rents, loans, fines, and inheritances as well as to the price of goods and services. Sounding like a pragmatic entrepreneur, Ecclesiastes uses the vocabulary of his day to subvert the preoccupations of his contemporaries.

Jerusalem had become a thriving cosmopolitan marketplace where the Sabbath rest

John Mansford Prior, PhD, has worked in Indonesia since 1973 in biblically-based awareness programs among the marginalized. He is coeditor (with John England, et al.) of *Asian Christian Theologies: A Research Guide to Authors, Movements, Sources* (three volumes, 2002-2003). Other recent publications include "Dialogue and Culture (Reflections by a Temporary Sojourner)" in *Sound the Gong: Conference on Interfaith Dialogue* (2002); "Dignity and Identity: The Struggle of Indigenous Peoples of Asia to Preserve, Purify, and Promote their Cultures," in *Proclaiming Christ to Asian Cultures: Promise and Fulfilment* (2003); and "Clashing Cultures, Contrasting Visions: Indonesian Perspective," in *Church in the Service of Asia's Peoples* (2003). He is also a contributor to Focus (Pakistan); *Ishvani Documentation and Mission Digest* (India); *East Asian Pastoral Review* (Philippines); and *Verbum* SVD (Germany).

had long since been routinely flouted (Neh 13:15-16). With royal grants, sublets, loans, bribes, and pawns, everyone with a little initiative and a connection or two was into the financial game. A socio-economic pyramid was in the making, no longer mirroring the pre-exilic agrarian hierarchy united under a royal superstructure. Even some of the poor were succeeding, provoking spiteful barbs from their "betters" (Eccl 7:21). Ecclesiastes presumes such a lively and competitive economic environment full of risk, a somewhat arbitrary, rapidly changing world, where the new-rich of today could easily become the new-poor of tomorrow.

The situation in Jerusalem presupposed by Ecclesiastes is strikingly similar to many aspects of the situation in Indonesia today, where a culture of resignation prevails both for the discarded poor and the vulnerable middle class.

The quietly accommodating, passionless sage lived in awe of a silent, distant, perplexing, unpredictable, and thus totally free deity. He recognizes his impotence and hands his fate over to *Elohim* who decides the times and limits for everything. While he does not flatly negate conventional behavior, he radically qualifies and relativizes conventional values and the revelation in which they are embedded. Ecclesiastes is critically skeptical of traditional wisdom without seeing Torah as the revelatory answer to the human quest for meaning. The ethos of Ecclesiastes strikes one as being signally "secular." With no apparent alternative to an increasingly hopeless present (3:14-15), with an elusive and unpredictable future (6:12), and with memories of a glorious past of no practical import (7:24), the sage tries to keep the flame of faith flickering and create a breathing space in which to renew confidence in life.

CONTEXTUAL COMMENT

Overview of the Book

Section one (1:1–6:9) describes our unpredictable world: human toil is futile (1:2–2:26) and the whole world elusive (3:1-8), so we should enjoy the portion God has given (3:9-22). Even virtue is unreliable (4:1-16); thus we are urged not to do anything to excess (5:1–6:9).

Section two (6:10–11:6) outlines the author's theological and ethical stance: we are not in control, but God is (6:10–7:14); therefore wisdom and justice are elusive (7:15-29). Given that the world is arbitrarily dominated by the powerful, the powerless should nurture God's gift of joy (8:1-17). The one certainty is death (9:1-10). Success is never guaranteed (9:11-16), so we should cope as best we can in a "risk society" out of control (9:17–11:6).

An end-piece (11:7–12:8) urges us to enjoy life while we are able, for old age is approaching.

Each of the three descriptive passages below is studied together with a prescriptive text urging Ecclesiastes' ethic.

Ecclesiastes 1:2-2:26 with 5:1-6:9—Face the Futility of Human Toil with Quiet Realism

Half poem, half prose, Ecclesiastes 1:2–2:26 describes a world outside human control. Key terms appear for the first time: *hebel* (futility, with thirty-eight occurrences in the book), *'amal* (human toil, with thirty-five occurrences), *yitrōn* (gain, with ten occurrences) and *tahat haššemeš* (under the sun, with twenty-nine occurrences). Despite human ingenuity, we achieve no truly new creation and we receive no clear gain. Therefore, Ecclesiastes rejects the hegemony of the new, the belief that a person's value is determined by his or her toil, a dominant worldview buttressed by a religious apparatus. Nobody can buy his or her future.

Powerless to change the course of events, the author outlines a quiet realism (5:1–6:9). As life is *hebel* we should not become obsessed with dreams, goods, or causes. We are advised to accept simple enjoyment and be happy with our lot *(sameah be-helqō)*. Life, a gift of God, is for living (5:18-20;

also 2:24-26 and 3:12-13). We should enjoy what God has given and not crave, or try to achieve, pleasure by our own efforts. We are not to strive after wealth and status but to be open to God-given enjoyment, albeit in an arbitrary portion and at unpredictable times decided by an inscrutable deity.

Thus Ecclesiastes aims for a practical ethic adequate for repressive and uncertain times. The sage aims to be supremely adequate rather than prophetically ideal, for striving after ideals is futile. While he sympathizes with the oppressed (4:1-3), the sage only obliquely condemns crimes against them.

The meaning of life has to be tested, determined, and integrated into other knowledge. The sage's allegiance is not to a divine revelation so much as to truth established through human reflection on experience. This tone is very much in tune with modernity.

Ecclesiastes 3:1-8 with 6:10–7:14—The Discovery of Meaning in an Elusive World

The famous poem "For everything there is a season . . . " is cosmic in scope ("under the heavens" 3:1, a.t.) and involves the fate of the whole world and of all humanity ("every matter", or "everything, everyone" v.1, a.t.). The world is in God's hands, and God's wisdom is overwhelming; God decides, although God's decisions are inscrutable. A sovereign God determines events; the only realistic response is to enjoy the present moment.

Ecclesiastes presupposes the absolute power of both God and the state. In the world of the sage both God and the government are distanced from the people. Both *'Elōhim* (the deity) and empire work in unfathomable ways that cannot be contested; they are not approachable or swayable. *'Elōhim*, like the emperor, is remote. God is silent throughout the text, and possibly indifferent (3:11, 18; 5:1-2; 6:1-2; 7:14; 8:17).

How should we behave when toil is useless and gain futile? In a parody of wisdom, Ecclesiastes declares that it is not even clear what is good *(tōb)*. This is the sage at his most skeptical (7:1-12). Apparently contra-

dictory proverbs underline human impotence; the juxtaposition of contrary statements is "a rhetoric of subversion" (Seow 1997, 244). The past—both revelatory history and wisdom tradition—is no firm anchor (7:10). Such skepticism fits a chaotic age where a globalizing market and communications have undermined certainty.

We should enjoy life as a gift when feasible, while facing harsh realities when necessary (7:14). We are urged to live a balanced life, being active yet not pursuing anything to excess (7:16-18), finding satisfaction *(simḥah)* in living itself (8:15, etc.) but not in power or possessions (2:1-11).

However, the text is also gender-biased, and on occasion blatantly misogynist (7:26-29). Women provide sustenance, entertainment, and sexual services as required so that men can enjoy life (9:9) and "seize the day" while still young (11:9).

Ecclesiastes 4:1-16 with 7:15-29—Open to many Narratives in a Spirituality of Dialogue

Ecclesiastes 4 opens with the first of a series of "better than" sayings (see 7:1-12 above). Whatever is "better" is outside human effort and therefore should not be sought but enjoyed when it occurs. Success driven by competition is unreliable, for the world is generally both oppressive and tragic. Therefore we should find security in quiet acceptance free of worry (4:6).

We cannot control the storm but can navigate a passage through it by being good but not excessively so, virtuous but not overzealous, diligent but within limits, wise but not too clever (7:15-18). Whatever we do should be spontaneous rather than calculated. Profit *(yitron)* from human labor *('amal)* is ephemeral *(hebel)*, for work does not exclusively define what is worthwhile in life. The portion *(heleq)* that *'Elohim* presents to each one of us gives what meaning there is to life.

Thus, in a world of contradictions the sage chooses to negotiate between opposing viewpoints. Through an ongoing dialogue Ecclesiastes bridges the gap between revelation and experience, faith and reason, salvation and indifference. The goal of the sage's dialogue is not conversion of the other but an ethic of sharing and sympathetic coexistence. For Ecclesiastes, dialogue is an all-pervasive attitude to life.

In Indonesia, Christian communities form small congregations scattered across the archipelago among minority ethnic groups. Their urge to keep to themselves in a threatening environment is overwhelming. Only half the Christian community consists of wealthy entrepreneurs, traders, and administrators, while the other half consists of marginalized indigenous groups, both those left behind in the village and those now overflowing the cities. They are finding in Ecclesiastes both the skepticism required to face the all-enveloping global market and the rooted values they need as their precarious cultures are buffeted by rapid change.

There is an all-pervading sense of powerlessness and fragmentation in Indonesia today. One reaction is to totalize experience. This reaction is seen in both the enervating individualism and the encapsulating devotion of the middle classes, as well as in the extremist politics and fanatical ethnic and religious movements of the marginalized. The encounter between the survival ethic of Ecclesiastes with the everyday resistance of the edged-out poor of today is triggering a transformation of powerlessness into creative activity. The word of Ecclesiastes is one element in the weaponry of the poor as they heighten personal and community worth through symbolic action, and enhance self-esteem and maintain relationships of mutuality in ceremony and celebration, without resigning themselves to life's current oppressive conditions.

CONCLUSION

Enigmatic resignation was the sage's way of responding to a precarious, bewildering world. He spurns evasion and declines leaps of faith. Without a trace of self-delusion, the sage persistently and doggedly clings to both the limitations and the integrity of human experience.

Ecclesiastes' conclusions remain tentative. The radical questioning of the sage invites us to take up the text itself in a nonauthoritarian manner. The sage invites us to view the unmanageable postmodern world released from any overarching narrative; he bids us work with many narratives in concert. In the end the epithet "futile" must also be applied to the book itself, for the text needs to be matched with other wisdom, experience, and value systems. The sage's accommodating survival ethic needs to be complemented with a prophetic demarcation of boundaries.

Meanwhile Ecclesiastes is a balm against the viruses of both fanaticism and indifference. It can nurture a rooted calmness, a vital condition for those wishing to break out of traditional stances that are no longer viable and witness convincingly amidst the whirlpool of conflicting values churned up by a globalizing world. When times are unpredictable, when humans are losing confidence in their own ability and God is elusive, Ecclesiastes is a necessary, though modest, guide to mission.

BIBLIOGRAPHY

Bergant, Dianne. *Israel's Wisdom Literature: A Liberation-Critical Reading.* Minneapolis: Fortress, 1997.

Ceresko, Anthony R. "Wisdom in Israel." Pages 273-82 in *Introduction to the Old Testament: A Liberation Perspective.* Maryknoll, N.Y.: Orbis, 1992.

Gottwald, Norman K. *The Hebrew Bible: A Socio-Literary Introduction.* Philadelphia: Fortress, 1985.

Mbiti, John S. *Bible and Theology in African Christianity.* Nairobi: Oxford University Press, 1986.

Prior, John Mansford. "'When all the Singing has Stopped.' Ecclesiastes: A Modest Mission in Unpredictable Times." *International Review of Mission* 91 (2002):7-23.

Seow, Choon Leong. *Ecclesiastes: A New Translation with Introduction and Commentary.* AB 18C. New York: Doubleday, 1997.

Singgih, Gerrit. *Di Bawah Bayang-bayang Maut (Under the Shadows of Death).* Jakarta: BPK Gunung Mulia, 2001. (An Indonesian contextual commentary on Ecclesiastes.)

Tamez, Elsa. *When the Horizons Close: Rereading Ecclesiastes.* Translated by Margaret Wilde. Maryknoll, N.Y.: Orbis, 2000.

———. "Ecclesiastes 3:1-8." Pages 75-94 in *Return to Babel: Global Perspectives on the Bible.* Edited by John R. Levison and Priscilla Pope-Levison. Louisville: Westminster John Knox, 1999.

Verstraelen, Frans J., Isabel Mukonyora, and James L. Cox, eds. *Rewriting the Bible: The Real Issues: Perspectives from within Biblical and Religious Studies in Zimbabwe.* Religious and Theological Studies 1. Gweru, Zimbabwe: Mambo, 1993.

SONG OF SONGS

Monica Jyotsna Melanchthon
Gurukul Lutheran Theological College, Chennai, India

LIFE CONTEXT OF THE INTERPRETATION

The well-known *Kamasutra* is often viewed as symbolic of India's open and liberal attitude to human sexuality. Yet the process of acquiring this visibility has been obscured, as the social context of the book will show, because India's treatment of human sexuality is closely bound to the structures and concerns of the normative tradition, which is oppressive to women.

The reality is that the expression of female desire and sexuality has been dictated by the Indian patriarchal culture, according to that culture's fears and constructions of desire. The manner in which women are treated—their bodies used and abused, their bodies and lives controlled by cultural and religious injunctions—is far from liberal. The culture stresses marriage for women and considers married women whose husbands are alive as *sumangalis* (as auspicious). Motherhood is held sacrosanct. In most parts of India, women do not have any say regarding their own marriage. Cultural precepts exalt parents who give away their daughters while they are still children, often with dire consequences for their lives as women. Such practices as early marriage result in sexual trauma, early pregnancy, and associated reproductive health problems. For women, the family is both the most intimate domain and also the space wherein it is most difficult to exercise their autonomy. The family is the primary source of affirmation for women, though it rarely extends beyond the limited universe of the household. Motherhood is not merely a personal aspiration but often a means to social recognition. Such expectations alienate and oppress single women, widows, and barren women and encourage prejudice, reinforced by culture and religion. Because rejection by the family means isolation, women are unable and unwilling to assert themselves over or against the family.

The patriarchal control of female sexuality in marriage is amplified by concerns for caste purity, caste status, power, and hierarchy. Kinship relations established through marriage give status and leverage in society to the immediate family, the clan, and the entire caste group. Concerns for any breach of proper caste relations remain a most potent incentive behind the enforcement of strict caste and sexual codes. Inter-caste and intra-caste marriages that infringe on cultural norms and customary practices invariably lead to direct violence perpetrated by male family members upon the couple, and especially upon the woman.

Within the institution of marriage, according to caste norms, the most disturbing aspect of gender subordination is women's lack of control over their own bodies. Heterosexuality is the norm and the satisfaction of male sexual needs is the summum bonum of sexual relations. Cultural norms demand the performance of wifely duties, the fundamental of them being the duty to participate in sexual relations with the husband—actually, the duty to never refuse sexual relations with the husband. Indian patriarchal ideology does not permit women to be sexual entities in their own right. Similarly, practices of dedicating

Monica Jyotsna Melanchthon, who teaches Old Testament and heads the Department of Women's Studies, is the author of *Rejection by God: The History and Significance of the Rejection Motif in the Hebrew Bible* (2001). She has published many articles on contextual interpretations of biblical texts and theological topics, and she is a member of the editorial board of *Dialog* (Blackwell). Melanchthon is also an active participant in programs of the Lutheran World Federation, the World Council of Churches, and the Asian Women's Resource Centre for Culture and Theology.

girls to deities, and thus to a life of prostitution, cause many of these women to experience a complete violation of their bodily integrity. The question of any true choice is totally meaningless for these poor and very young women.

Furthermore, women are disempowered by their internalization of patriarchal standards of sexuality which includes complete ignorance of their bodies and the suppression of female sexual desire. Many myths linked with fertility and sexuality—such as the myth that menstrual blood is polluting and dirty, or that women's sexuality is dangerous to society—reinforce women's negative self-image and apathy toward their own bodies and sexuality in general. These attitudes have disastrous consequences for women's health, causing women to neglect their bodies, ignore early signals of illness, and hesitate to talk about their illness. For Indian women co-opted by these patriarchal and cultural standards, the free will to decide for themselves and their bodies is, in fact, a mirage.

For Christians, the Indian social construction of women's sexuality as a site of control is reinforced by the use of the Bible. Traditional beliefs and definitions of sexuality are believed to be God-given, and discussing them is tantamount to blasphemy. These narrow definitions of sexuality are constructed on the basis of the laws pertaining to women in the Old Testament, of misinterpretations of texts like Genesis 1 and 2. Yet the primary problem for an Indian woman comes from the culture's genitalization of sexuality, which hinders her from recognizing the sacredness of her body and understanding sexuality as involving the totality of a truly mutual relation unaffected by power. Under the influence of Christianity and its self-denying philosophy, mutual, equal pleasure and respect are unwarranted, and consequently, the validation of a woman's identity becomes a difficult goal. This denial of true mutual relationship and the related genitalization of sexuality lead to the notions that women are unclean, polluting, temptresses, sources and symbols of illicit desire, moral danger, and lust. Consequently, the active participation of women in the ritual life of the church is drastically limited, the use of feminine language or symbolism for God or any other theological category is unthinkable, and marginalized women are deprived from meaningful and fulfilling relationships with God, the church, and the society.

CONTEXTUAL COMMENT

Song of Songs and Sexuality

Sexuality is a largely uncharted field and clearly in need of our involvement. Thus, in women's studies at Gurukul Lutheran Theological College and at the Asian Women's Resource Centre for Culture and Theology, we attempt to develop an alternate understanding of sexuality, and more particularly of female sexuality, freedom, and beauty. We seek to help women to find freedom by transforming themselves from objects to subjects of sexuality, by breaking out of their submissive roles and becoming active, assertive sexual agents.

Song of Songs, which is rarely read or used in the Indian churches, has become a resource for us, Christian women in India, as we attempt to explore the field of sexuality. For many the strong sexual imagery and erotic language is at first a cause for embarrassment. Yet the fact that this book is held as Scripture, and therefore as normative or prescriptive, calls for and justifies its exploration and encourages women to appropriate the truths contained in it.

Song of Songs seems to reflect the sociopolitical context of postexilic Israel. The disintegration of the Israelite nation brought about the intensification of ethnic politics, social stratification, and a struggle for identity and for maintaining the purity and distinctiveness of Jewish ancestry. The literature from this period (i.e., the Levitical laws, the social injunctions of Ezra and Nehemiah) suggests that this struggle for survival generated pressures for regulating social relations. This development was by no means an uncontested or homogenous process. Codification of social relations raised almost as many problems as it attempted to resolve. To start with, the right to create codes was implicitly or explicitly claimed by men, more often than not by priests, and justified by appeals to divine sanction. Effectively then, participation in the process of codification was denied to all women and to most men. But some of those who had been excluded from this process produced texts espousing alternate ideologies and opinions. Song of Songs is one such text. It counterbalances other statements on sexuality found in the Old Testament by describing a woman who is in control of her own sexuality and finds joy in it.

Two striking features of Song of Songs are that, although it is a book of Scripture, it does not mention the name of God and its central character is female. While it does not include injunctions of any kind, it offers an ideology that frees women from inhibitions, celebrates desire and love between a man and a woman irrespective of their social locations, and affirms a relationship free of any hierarchy. One cannot help feeling seduced by these sexually egalitarian images.

But the book has its share of problems. Scholars debate its authorship, whether it is a unified composition or a collection of poems put together by a compiler, the reasons for its canonization, and its relation to other love poetry from ancient West Asia. Scholars also ask: Is the woman character a real woman or the product of male literary artistry? Is the woman speaking for herself or is she speaking on behalf of the narrator? Does the text really portray the ideal of gender equality, since we hear so little of the male voice? To what extent was the woman truly able to exercise such sexual freedom in the social context of the time? Is the freedom expressed an idealized notion or is it real? In a traditional society like Israel, what would have been the repercussions for such an outgoing, sexually active woman? Such questions and a detailed analysis of the text dilute the excitement and the romantic fervor of the book. Nevertheless, for women, Song of Songs stands out as different in the Old Testament. It invites them to imagine and to appropriate, if possible, this alternate rendering of female desire and sexuality. What is most important for women in India is that the woman protagonist finds ways to celebrate her body and sexuality, despite the cultural constraints of her time. The strong, assertive, and confident woman of Song of Songs helps us to recognize that other female characters in the Old Testament also crossed boundaries and exercised power and agency despite the limitations of the cultural and social world in which they lived. This is what women in India need to embrace.

The Woman Protagonist: An Embodiment of Resilience

When a writer features a female as the protagonist, that writer consciously or unconsciously intervenes in a longstanding debate concerning Israelite identity and its intimate yet uneasy relationship with Israelite womanhood. The Israelite woman is a figure whose very life is marked by subordination and subservience to the male members in the society. Without an identity of her own, she needs public protection but also control through regulation. When we frame Song of Songs and its main character in this way, most significant dimensions of the text become apparent. We can recognize that Song of Songs was a subtle historical engagement with questions of social order and Israelite identity.

We can imagine the woman of Song of Songs as one of those whom the fifth-century social reform of Ezra and Nehemiah sought to control. But unlike her counterparts, she does not allow herself to become the victim of societal or religious control. That she was aware of and probably experienced the censure of the community is hinted at in 5:7, where she refers to being beaten by the sentinels who found her wandering the streets looking for her lover. Song 8:1 suggests that she was afraid of expressing her love for him in public, although the reason is not given. The lovers seem to spend stolen and quick moments together. The fact that they were always in haste and never entirely satisfied suggests that their meetings were clandestine (5:6, 8; 8:14) and that for some reason the society sought to keep them apart. The frequent assertions by the woman that her beloved was hers and hers alone and that they belonged together (2:16; 6:3; 7:10) indicate that she was convincing herself that this was the case but also trying to convince someone else (perhaps the daughters of Jerusalem) who did not think so.

Yet she is in a joyous relationship to her body. This is the secret of her health, self-sufficiency, confidence, and delight in life. She accepts and exults in her lover's appreciation of her body and she finds pleasure in the body of her lover and gives expression to it (1:9–16; 2:9). Her resilient embodiment is the basis of her primitive, enduring personhood and her irrepressible force as a subject-agent. With it, she survives her times, both literally and politically. Hers is a body personhood that seems to exceed discipline. This body personhood seems to pay little attention to social injunctions. Religious, racial, and gender taboos as well as the social norms of Israelite propriety are seemingly pushed aside or ignored for the sake of the demand of a desire expressed in the context of love. She is subversive in the face of authorities that would control her.

The body of the woman in Song of Songs is solid, reliable, and resilient. Nothing seems to have the power to corrode it—neither the violence of a tradition that decrees chastity and denial, nor that of a time period that would discipline it in other multilayered yet no less chaste terms. The canonical authority of this body, the stigmata that proclaims its value, lies in its ability to survive and resurface. It also has the power to effect reiteration across generations and across a social map that includes the author/s, and us, the readers—a social map that is also a map of India today.

Female Sexual Desire: Natural and Legitimate

Desire flows throughout the Old Testament. Biblical human beings desired the everyday goods necessary for a comfortable life: a good harvest, wine, God, women, land, security, peace, and power. Even God is portrayed as desiring certain qualities (Pss 40:6; 51:6; 68:16; 149:4; Hos 6:6). Desire is therefore never prohibited but controlled and codified (Exod 20:17; Lev 18). But the male's voice, his needs, his desires, and his constructions of reality are dominant in the Bible. In Song of Songs, the dominant voice is that of a woman, who gives expression to her wants and her needs, undeterred by the sanctions and expectations of society. She gives direct and sustained testimony to the pleasures of love. The desire she expresses is overt and its predominance in Song of Songs is unmistakable. The main program in Song of Songs is an exploration of desire, more accurately, female sexual desire.

In a canon where the perspectives of women receive scant attention, where female desire and pleasure are denied, controlled, or legislated, Song of Songs uplifts female sexual desire as something to be granted legitimacy. In a culture where the only kind of desire that women were allowed to express is the desire to please husband and family, where there was no room for the expression of personal desire, female desire is here celebrated. It is posited as natural and universal and, therefore, as not requiring any codification. This book contradicts both (a) the notion that women and union between the sexes need to be regulated and (b) the traditional understanding that female sexuality is socially constructed rather than rooted in the natural order.

The setting for the consummation of this desire and yearning for love is not confined to the four walls of a house or home (1:4; 2:4; 3:1; 8:2); it is also the outdoors, the pasture (1:7-8), the garden (4:16; 5:1; 6:2;), and the vineyard (8:12). The frequent references to nature, the seasonal changes (2:10-13; 6:11), the vegetation, the flora and fauna, and the plethora of metaphors taken from nature are striking features of Song of Songs. These images, surrounded by references to eating and drinking, are symbolic of consummated sexual love. This very prominent emphasis given to nature as the setting for the expression of desire is probably intentional, meant to accentuate the inherent connections between desire and the natural, to stress the fact that female sexual desire is instinctive, innate, and beyond legislation. Just as one has no control over nature and its times and changes, so also desire should not be curtailed or controlled.

Female Desire, Equality, and Justice

The realm of desire is commonly constructed around two locations: it is either desiring or desired, either capable of experiencing desire or of being an object of desire, either a man or a woman, either powerful or powerless. In the Indian construction of sexuality, the man is not only the focus of sociosexual relations but also in control of them. Consequently, women are constructed as the objects of such relations. They are objectified and relegated to a position of powerlessness. Then, ideal women are defined in terms of physical and mental attributes fitting this objectified position; those who do not meet this ideal are subordinated.

In Song of Songs, the characters are not placed within any particular religious, socia,l or national contexts. They are just a man and a woman. The woman does not seek permission from either a father or brother; she dreams of bringing her lover to her mother's house (8:2); she does not wait for the lover but goes in search of him (3:1-3) and brings him home (3:3-4). She manifests autonomy, sexual and otherwise, beyond all social constraints. Song of Songs is an affirmation and a triumph of the sovereignty of female sexuality as well as a celebration of the personal power and delight of the woman in her surroundings who is released from all restrictions and fears. In so doing, and most significantly, Song of Songs legitimates a particular form of desire. The desire of women upon which the book is

centered is embedded in a context where differences are denied. In this way, Song of Songs posits a definition of desire that contradicts all relations constructed as power relations, which today accompany class, caste, racial, ethnic, and religious identities.

We live in a world today where constructions of beauty are leading many women to hone their skills and their bodies in the hope of achieving a standard of beauty that will make them desirable and accepted. Embodying popular notions of beauty confers economic and social power on the individual, resulting in asymmetrical competitive relations among women and abuse by men. Those who do not meet these standards of beauty suffer lack of confidence, exclusion, and sometimes ridicule. Song of Songs at times contradicts existing notions of beauty (1:5 contra 7:1) that emphasize fairness. Here the couple expresses their desire and love for one another without any hindrance from either conventional standards of beauty or from social identities (4:1-7; 5:10-16; 6:4-10; 7:1-9).

Song of Songs is a protest against our tendency to compartmentalize "the rational and affective, the public and private, the sexual and chaste, and today's favorite, the appropriate and the inappropriate," observed Carey Allen Walsh.

> These serve pragmatic functions in life, helping to ensure our competencies as citizens, but they also hinder and stall our desire. They function too, to police desires. We are bombarded with suggestions of what we should desire and how much, and at the same time we are instructed to keep these desires to ourselves. (2000, 8)

In the Indian culture, women can pursue the gratification of desire only within the context of conjugal love. Marriage is an institution that gives the utmost power to men to own, name, mark, and control the bodies of women and rewrite abuse and aggression as love and pleasure. The relationship between the couple in Song of Songs transcends borders of convention and propriety. It emphasizes neither marriage nor procreation, which is normally considered to be the aim of union between the sexes. Neither of these is the concern. The focus instead is on mutual love, respect, and appreciation. Love and wanting to be with the lover is the central theme, something that is often neglected in social and even religious definitions of marriage.

CONCLUSION

Desire is usually born out of the experience of needing or lacking something. Song of Songs, even when allegorized as the yearning of the devotee for God, is suggestive of the complexities involved in worshipping and relating to a God who is unseen but is needed and desired. Song of Songs as a whole expresses the yearning of a woman for her lover and her inability to see him and be with him all the time, which fuels her desire and determination. She dreams (3:1-4; 5:2-7), she adjures (2:7; 3:5; 5:8), she cajoles (1:7), and she acts (3:1-4). The desire she feels is tangible and palpable; her body experiences the pain of separation, the longing to be with him. One can imagine what she is feeling and suffering when she is not with her lover. The Song is devoted to female desire and it contains a lesson for women and men. It contains a valuable message about all kinds of desire, sexual and others. The sexual desire highlighted in Song of Songs serves as a metaphor and a vehicle for all women who individually and corporately desire to usher in a new world, a world of equality, peace, and justice. The resilience of the woman, her courage, boldness, and determination, at the risk of being censured, beaten, isolated, and ridiculed are exemplary in their modernity.

They are necessary characteristics in the making of a new moment in the genealogy of the Indian woman as citizen, as agent-self, and as humanist in church and society—in sum, as an individual with a commitment to all of life, to oppressed communities, to oppressed women and men, and to nature.

The Indian woman has for centuries been at the receiving end of patriarchal abuse and misuse of power. We are witnessing today, amidst the violence that enforces the maintenance and control of women, the weakening of the absolute power that did not permit the space for the articulation or even the awareness of grievance. Today women are aware of a wrong, which the absolute power of patriarchal control does not permit us to correct. The aspiration for the wholeness of humanity has been ignited by the recognition and acknowledgement that as children of God, created in the image of God, women have a right to live as persons with identity, dignity, and worth. This has given birth to a women's movement that is working toward the establishment of an alternate society and a church that is free from asymmetrical relations, violence, and injustice. The desire for such a church and society is natural, legitimate, and just.

BIBLIOGRAPHY

Brenner, Athalya, and Carole R. Fontaine, eds. *The Song of Songs: A Feminist Companion to the Bible*. FCB Second Series 6. Sheffield: Sheffield Academic Press, 2000.

Hwang, Andrew, and Samuel Goh. *Song of Songs*. Asia Bible Commentary Series. Bangalore, India: Theological Book Trust, 2001.

Isherwood, Lisa, and Elizabeth Stuart. *Introducing Body Theology*. Introductions in Feminist Theology 2. Sheffield: Sheffield Academic Press, 1998.

John, Mary E., and Janaki Nair, eds. *A Question of Silence? The Sexual Economies of Modern India*. New Delhi: Kali for Women, 1998.

Kannabiran, Vasanth, and Kalpana Kannabiran. "Caste and Gender: Understanding Dynamics of Power and Violence." *Economic and Political Weekly* (September 14, 1991): 2130–33.

Keel, Othmar. *The Song of Songs: A Continental Commentary*. Translated by Frederick J. Gaiser. Minneapolis: Fortress, 1994.

Walsh, Carey Allen. *Exquisite Desire: Religion, the Erotic, and the Song of Songs*. Minneapolis: Fortress, 2000.

Weems, Renita J. *Song of Songs*. Pages 156–60 in The Women's Bible Commentary. Edited by Carol A. Newsom and Sharon H. Ringe. Louisville: Westminster John Knox, 1992.

ISAIAH 1–39

Victor Zinkuratire

Catholic University of Eastern Africa, Nairobi, Kenya

LIFE CONTEXT OF THE INTERPRETATION

The great hopes and aspirations that African nations had at the time of independence have largely remained unfulfilled, four decades on. The original beautiful dreams of a promised land of political freedom, social stability and economic prosperity have for many countries occasionally turned into nightmares of political chaos and economic collapse. The promised land is still a mirage. This is the situation not only in my region of Eastern Africa but practically in all sub-Saharan countries. Poor governance is responsible for economic mismanagement, social injustices, corruption, military and ethnic conflicts—all of which have contributed to the extreme poverty afflicting the majority of our people today. External factors, such as globalization with its predominantly negative impact on the young and still fragile democracies and economies of African countries, have only aggravated the situation. In addition to all these, and partly because of their influence, many positive African traditional values and cultural practices that had sustained society for centuries are fast disappearing and being replaced by foreign ones that are not fulfilling the same stabilizing role.

But it is not all doom and gloom. There are also signs that people are beginning to learn lessons from past mistakes and bitter experiences of suffering and pain. This is reason for hope. It is in the context of these concrete African realities that we want to reread and reinterpret Isaiah's harsh words of judgment and his reassuring promises of renewal.

Issues Raised by Isaiah 1–39 in Relation to the African Situation

The Israelite society that Isaiah was addressing in the eighth century had undergone great socioeconomic and political changes since the introduction of the monarchy. In the pre-monarchical times of the tribal confederation, the majority of the population were peasants living off their land in egalitarian communities under the leadership of elders. These tried to guarantee the welfare of everyone, especially the weaker members of society such as widows and orphans. Yahwism, Judah's traditional religion, permeated, inspired and directed every aspect of people's lives.

This was also the way most African societies were organized in precolonial days before the rise of the modern state. In the extended family and clan system the needs of every members were taken care of by the whole community, and there were no cases of extreme poverty or excessive wealth in the hands of a few. The central role that Yahwism played in Israel was played by traditional religions, which also guided every aspect of people's lives as individuals and as community.

In Israel during the time of Isaiah under

Victor Zinkuratire, SSS, is a Ugandan Catholic priest who teaches in Kenya. His main interest is the interpretation of the Bible in African contexts. He is general editor (with Angelo Colacrai) of the *African Bible* (Nairobi: Pauline Publications Africa, 1999), a study edition of the New American Bible annotated for African readers. He also coedited (with Knut Holter and Mary Getui) *Interpreting the Old Testament in Africa* (New York: Peter Lang, 2001). He is editor of *African Christian Studies,* a quarterly journal of the Catholic University of Eastern Africa's Faculty of Theology, and serves on the editorial board of the *Bulletin for Old Testament Studies in Africa.*

the monarchy the situation had changed. The economy had become centralized and was controlled by the ruling classes and their wealthy associates. The result was accumulation of wealth by the elite at the expense of the majority of ordinary citizens who became impoverished through the unjust and exploitative practices of the powerful. The system was based on the Canaanite model of the city state where Baalism favored a social system in which the ruling classes controlled the economy and oppressed the rest of the population (Ceresko, 2001, 160-161, 209-222). We get a clear idea of this system from Samuel's description of how kings would rule (1 Sam 8:11-18).

The society that Isaiah was addressing is somehow the kind of society that Africa has become since the introduction of the modern state. There is a pattern of similarities. In Israel the transition from the tribal confederation to the monarchy weakened the old communitarian ideals of Yahwism and tended to strengthen the influence of Baalism. Similarly, in Africa the transition from the old egalitarian way of life to the modern state system has weakened the positive values found in African traditional religions and cultural practices—a kind of African Yahwism—and strengthened the present process

of secularization, analogous to the influence of Baalism in Israel (Shorter, 1997, 11-27).

In both cases it is basically an implicit rejection of God's absolute sovereignty over human affairs in favor of a reliance on human resources, such as the political, economic and military structures of the state, including foreign alliances. This is the sin of pride that was at the root of all the disorders in Israelite society that Isaiah condemned in his prophecies of judgment: social inequalities, injustice and militarism.

If Isaiah had a message of hope it was based on the possibility that the people would return to the ideals and virtues of Yahwism adapted to the monarchical system. A creative blend of our African heritage with what is positive in modernity can also be a basis for us to appropriate Isaiah's same message of hope.

Isaiah's mission to his eighth century world of Judah and Jerusalem must serve as the model for the Church's prophetic mission to the world of Eastern Africa today. The similarity between the prophet's theological concerns and our own regarding these issues provides us with the hermeneutical key for rereading and re-appropriating his message in the context of our present socio-economic, political and religious situation.

CONTEXTUAL COMMENT

An Overview of Isaiah 1-39

Isaiah 1-39 is the first part of a large and complex collection of prophetic proclamations that originated with the preaching of Isaiah in Jerusalem between 742 and 701 B.C.E. The second part of the collection (40–55) and the third part (56–66) contain prophecies that reflect the events of the exilic and post-exilic periods respectively (see the *GBC* commentaries by Severino Croatto that follow).

The material in 1–39 is not chronologically arranged and does not all come from the time of Isaiah. It must have originated as small independent collections which can now be identified as follows: chaps 1-12 are prophecies concerning Judah and Jerusalem;

chaps 13-23 are oracles against foreign nations; chaps 24-27 are about God's judgement over the whole cosmos; chaps 28-35 contain further oracles of judgement and liberation. Chaps 36-39 are historical narratives taken from 2 Kings 18-20. Whatever can be identified as coming from Isaiah himself is limited to some utterances mostly in chaps 1-12, 13-23, and 28-33. But even these chapters contain some late oracles , such as 14:1-2; 14:32; 16:4b-5; 17:7-8; 19:16-25; 23:17-18. The rest of the prophecies come from later centuries and are re-readings of the prophet's original message by later generations to actualise it for the concerns of their own times. To be properly understood, therefore, Isaiah 1-39 must be read from the historical perspective of postexilic times. It is for this reason that our texts for contextual reading are selected both from Isaiah's original prophecies about judgement and from the later re-readings that contain messages of restoration. Our task then is to continue this same process of reinterpreting the words of Isaiah but in our own context of Africa.

Isaiah as a Prophet of Judgment

Isaiah's prophecies in the context of the eighth century were predominantly about God's judgment of Judah and Jerusalem (6:9-13). Later on, however, these prophecies were reread and re-interpreted in the new circumstances of the immediate postexilic period, and even much later, when Jerusalem and the country had been partly restored. They can therefore be fully understood only in the context of the whole book of Isaiah.

Isaiah 6:1-13: The Call and Mission of the Prophet

This is a foundational text for understanding Isaiah's concept of God, the nature of his mission as a prophet and the message of the book of Isaiah in general. The title of YHWH as the "Holy One of Israel" or Jacob is typically Isaian because it occurs twenty-six times in his book and only six times in the rest of the Hebrew Bible (Oswalt 1986, 15). For Isaiah holiness is what best defines the nature of God as the transcendent one, who is wholly other (Rudolph Otto) and exalted above humanity and the rest of creation. But this transcendent God is at the same time immanent in the world through his *kabôd*, the glorious splendour that actively fills the earth both in judgment and salvation (Croatto 1989, 58; Jensen 1987, 87). God's holiness defines not only his being but also his relationship with the world and humanity, and this is why he can say "You shall be holy, for I the LORD your God am holy." (Lev 19:2). The holiness demanded here is ethical and not just ritual. This is clear from the commands found in the Holiness Code of Lev 19. It therefore follows that God's laws are themselves an

expression of his being and that is why any sin is considered an attack on God (Ps 51:6).

This was the revelation that Isaiah received from his vision and its immediate effect was to make him profoundly aware of his own and his society's sinfulness and unworthiness (6:5). But God took the initiative to cleanse him (6:7) and sent him on a mission to preach what he has experienced: God's holiness, human sin that merits God's judgement, and the possibility of being pardoned through repentance (6:8-13).

Prominent among the moral attributes of God in African traditional religions are God's holiness, justice, righteousness, anger, pity, love and kindness (Mbiti, 1970, 31-42). When these are combined with transcendence, another attribute of God in Africa (Mbiti, 1970, 12-16) close to the biblical one, we get what can be safely considered the equivalent of Isaiah's understanding of God's holiness (Gehman, 1989, 191). One of the commonest names for God in Africa is "Creator" (*Ruhanga* in my native language, from the verb *kuhanga*, to create), and this is an indication that a fundamental concept of God in Africa is that of Life-giver, because he is the originator of life. Now life in all its manifestations is the most fundamental human value in Africa, so much so that the morality of any action is judged on whether it promotes life or diminishes it.

"For African Religion, all principles of morality and ethics are to be sought within the context of preserving human life and its 'power' or 'force'" (Magesa 1998, 38). Anything that is anti-life is therefore sin against God the Life-giver and always merits God's anger and punishment.

These are the terms and the conceptual frame of reference with which Africans can read and understand Isa 6:1-13 and the whole message of the prophet in Isaiah 1—39. The sins of Judah and Jerusalem that Isaiah condemned were all anti-life in one way or another. His prophecies of judgement as well as his message of hope can therefore be appreciated by Africans in the light of their own religious traditions regarding the nature of God.

Isaiah 1:1-31: Introducing the Major Themes of the Book of Isaiah

This opening chapter acts as an overture to the whole book of Isaiah (Brueggemann 1998, 10, Croatto, 1989, 37). It contains a selection of oracles that represent the teachings of Isaiah on the themes of judgment and salvation. As such the oracles come from different periods of the prophet's preaching and are not presented in any chronological or literary order. The purpose of the editor, who likely wrote after the fall of Jerusalem, was to convey the message that the destruction and all the suffering experienced by the nation were a punishment for disobedience and that only repentance would bring them hope for better things.

The people of Eastern Africa and the continent in general can see reflected in this chapter the vicissitudes of their own history from the simple life of pre-colonial days to the complexities of their contemporary society. Isaiah's oracle accusing Israel of ignoring their God who has cared for them like a father (1:2-4) can equally be leveled against many Africans today who have abandoned their faith in a provident God whom their forefathers recognized instinctively.

The oracle in 1:5-9 is a description of Judah and its cities that have been invaded and looted by foreigners. This is perhaps a reference to the Assyrian invasion of 701 B.C.E. under Sennacherib, when Judah was devastated and left like a badly wounded person. Many African countries have experienced similar devastation through foreign invasions, civil wars, ethnic conflicts, deforestation of land by greedy entrepreneurs, and generally by bad politics. Africa today is a badly wounded continent.

The message of the oracle in 1:10-17 is that there can be no true worship acceptable to God without the practice of justice toward the weak members of society, such as widows and orphans. The temptation to separate worship from life is a perennial one and the oracle serves as a salutary reminder to modern churchgoers. The majority of the people in Eastern Africa, including many political leaders, are Christians who regularly participate in the Sunday worship of their churches and prayer meetings and contribute generously for the upkeep of church buildings and furnishings. In spite of all this apparent piety there is a lot of oppression, social injustice and exploitation of the weak by the same people. Isaiah reminds us that there must be something wrong with our worship if it can coexist with all these social ills.

The next oracle in 1:18-20 is the high point of the chapter. The people are offered a choice, just as in Deut 30:15-20: to choose life or to choose death. If they renounce their unjust and oppressive practices "they will eat ('akal) the good things of the land" but if they refuse "they will be eaten ('akal) by the sword" (Isa 1:19-20, a.t.). The consequences of either choice are expressed by the same Hebrew verb, for emphasis. Had the people been obedient the land of Judah would have been spared the Assyrian invasion and devastation and would have continued its normal agricultural productivity for its inhabitants. Many countries in Africa, even those with favorable climate, experience severe famines because of similar military invasions, internal conflicts and economic exploitation of land and resources by greedy people in positions of power. Africans will begin to eat the good things of their lands only when these social evils are eliminated through responsible leadership, otherwise the sword of famine and disease will continue to devour them.

According to the literary structure of Isaiah 1, as identified and explained by Croatto (1989, 37-38), the remaining verses of this chapter, 1:21-31, are like an echo that repeats and reinforces the message of the previous verses by means of symmetrical correspondences based on parallelism or opposition. Hence the initial accusation that Israel does not know YHWH (1:2-4) corresponds to 1:29-31, according to which these same people have turned to the worship of other gods only to meet with frustration and even destruction. It is not difficult to see the truth of this message even today in Africa. Often those people who abandon their Christian faith to go in search of other gods in the form of wealth, power and self-indulgence. These things do not always bring them happiness and may in fact destroy them in the end.

The debilitating invasion of Judah and Jerusalem in 1:5-9 is complemented by the destruction of sinners in 1:28. Then, in 1:10-18a, the dishonest and unacceptable worship contaminated by crime and injustice is reversed by the purification of Jerusalem, once an oppressive city, which turns into a city of justice, a faithful city in 1:21-27. It is in 1:18b-20 that the two symmetrical parts converge to highlight the message of the chapter intended by the redactor, namely that in spite of sin and the inevitable judgment the possibility of being pardoned and living securely was still there. This however would depend principally on the conversion (1:16-17) of the leaders: "princes of Sodom" and "people of Gomorrah" (1:10) and those in positions of power, such as the wealthy and the corrupt judges (1:23), who were in the first place responsible for most of the political and social evils. It is this possibility of transformation, ultimately based on God's power and initiative (1:26), that gives hope to the suffering people of Africa.

Isaiah 5:1-24: The Moral and Social Crimes of Israel

The long and peaceful reign of Uzziah (783-742 B.C.E.) had brought relative wealth and prosperity to Judah but most of this wealth was in the hands of the ruling class and the merchants who controlled the economy by exploiting the majority poor. The song of the vineyard (5:1-7) is directed against these ruthless exploiters. The punch line of the song is:

He looked for justice but saw bloodshed
For righteousness (*zedaqa*) but heard cries of distress (5:7, a.t.)

In 5:8-24, six different groups of people are listed with their respective crimes, each introduced by a woe. The first group is the rich and powerful citizens who dispossessed poor peasants of their patrimonial land and houses. These large landowners would buy out small farmers to increase their property, plant more vineyards, and make huge profits to support their luxurious lifestyles. The corrupt judicial system facilitated this exploitation. Even criminal means were sometimes used, as when King Ahab grabbed Naboth's vineyard in 1 Kings 21. All this was a violation of the covenantal demands of Yahwism. According to Levitical law (Lev 25:23-34), patrimonial land was inalienable and in former times it is this law that had protected the poor from being robbed of their property permanently. In most Africa societies family land was also strictly inalienable but in today's changed social and economic systems people are sometimes forced by circumstances to sell their land, piece by piece. They then have to live as tenants providing cheap labor for their landlords in order to survive.

The next five groups of people are accused of sins that are more easily associated with the rich but poor people can also commit them. They are: the drunkards (5:11-12), the arrogant who defy God (5:18-19), those who try to justify their misdeeds through self-deception (5:20), the conceited who think they are all wise (5:21) and those who pervert justice by accepting bribes (5:23). Poor people are also capable of committing these sins. They may become heavy drinkers in order to forget their misery, or justify their stealing because they are needy, or pervert justice by accepting a bribe to give false testimony in court. The message of Isaiah was primarily addressed to the rulers but it has relevance even for the poor people of Africa.

Isaiah 5:25-30; 14:4b-23; 37:22b-29: Devastation Caused by Wars

The moral and social crimes that Isaiah condemns in 5:8-24 had serious political, military and economic consequences, which are further described in 5:25-30. The prophet interprets the military invasions from Assyria, and later from Babylonia, as YHWH's punishment of Judah for these crimes. The invading armies will scatter the population into exile and people will be starving to death (5:13-14), leaving houses desolate and land unproductive and uncultivated (5:9-10). In Africa the ambition and greed of some political leaders have brought about military invasions, oppressive military governments, civil wars and ethnic conflicts. The result is always desolate villages, homeless refugees, and loss of human life and property, interrupted cultivation of fields, hunger, disease and social unrest. For more than a decade my own country Uganda experienced all these things. This is a timely warning for leaders of nations. They carry a heavy responsibility for which they will have to account.

In 14:4b-23 we have a taunting song against the king of Babylon who has finally fallen, to the great relief of the oppressed people who have suffered for so long under his tyranny (14:4b-7). Even nature itself—the cypress and cedar forests of Lebanon—can finally rest from unrestrained destruction by the greedy tyrant seeking to increase his wealth. We know from the sad experience of many African countries that bad leaders, particularly in military regimes, who have no respect for human life have no respect for the environment either. All that matters to them is economic gain that in turn increases their ability to dominate (see Croatto 1998, 44).

In this song the fallen king of Babylon is further humiliated even in death, because, unlike the kings of the other nations who lie in tombs, his body is just thrown away (14:18-20a). In the theology of Isaiah YHWH, the sovereign ruler of all the nations of the world uses pagan nations to punish the unfaithfulness of his people (10:5). But he also punishes these nations in turn for their pride, as the poem of 14:4b-23 so dramatically demonstrates. This theological truth is also historically vindicated by the many examples of tyrants who eventually came to a bad end. The recent history of Africa provides several such examples. Even those who escape punishment to live and die in exile are considered cursed because, in many African cultures being buried away from one's ancestral home is like not being buried at all, like the king of Babylon. We cannot rejoice in the miserable end of these dictators but we can celebrate the end of an oppressive regime.

We have in 37:22b-29 a further example of YHWH reacting to the pride and arrogance of a foreign nation, this time Assyria under Sennacherib. The poem is YHWH's comforting response to king Hezekiah's prayer in 37:15-20, concerning the threats of Sennacherib and his arrogant defiance of YHWH (37:10-13). Here again we see the destructive power of war, whether from a foreign invader or from internal conflicts. The natural resources of a country get plundered (37:24) and cities and towns are reduced to ruins (37:27), a common occurrence in Africa. But in the end, the prophet assures us, it is always God's plan that succeeds. In this case Sennacherib's plan to capture Jerusalem failed (37:29) and he himself was later on assassinated by his own sons (37:38).

In addition to military invasions another form of foreign invasion has come in the form of globalization, which affects every aspect of a nation and its people's life: political, social, economic, cultural and even religious. The phenomenon of globilization itself has great potential for good but, in African countries, its benefits have so far been outweighed by its disadvantages. For example, the conditions imposed on African countries by the world is financial institutions, such as the International Monetary Fund and the World Bank, have not improved the economies of these countries. On the contrary we see the problem of poverty getting even worse.

There are also cultural invasions from the West through mass media affecting the African ways of life and at times even supplanting them and thus causing social and moral destabilization. Religious invasions too have taken place and in a few cases they have been literally devastating, as when the leaders of a religious sect in my country Uganda set fire to hundreds of their followers in a locked building. This was not a home-grown sect. The Church has also to deal with these more subtle kinds of invasions.

Isaiah as a Prophet of Hope

Redactors of Isaiah 1-39 skillfully inserted new material into Isaiah's original proclamation of judgment in order to add the message of hope. These new interpretations had a larger theological vision than Isaiah's original message. They embraced God's salvific plan not only for Israel but also for all the nations and the entire cosmos (Seitz 1992, 487-488). Their purpose was to show that the ultimate goal of God's judgment was not to destroy but to purify and impart new life. It is primarily these later reinterpretations that make Isaiah's prophecies a message of hope. Faced with so many problems that have no obvious solutions, Africans need to hear this message as an antidote to fatalism and as a prod to action.

Isaiah 2:2-5: Future Jerusalem and the Nations

As if to tone down the harsh message of the opening chapter, the redactors of the book of Isaiah inserted this magnificent poem at this strategic point to introduce the message of hope. The poem must have been well known because it is also found in Micah 4:2-3, with only minor variations. It is an expression of a natural human longing for peace, justice and prosperity in a world often characterized by military conflicts, injustices, exploitation, poverty and hunger. The poem announces a new world order from which all these evils will be banished forever. This will come about because from Mount Zion God will be in charge as ruler and arbitrator between nations so that everything will be conducted according to his wise instructions and just laws. There will be no more reason for wars and the military hardware will be converted into agricultural implements. The result will be international peace and economic prosperity.

Reading this poem in the context of contemporary Africa, with its seemingly insurmountable problems, one may be tempted to shun the challenge by trying to convince oneself that the opening phrase "In days to come" refers to the world beyond time rather than our present one. Certainly the Hebrew phrase can refer to the end time, as in Jer 49:39; Ezek 38:16; Dan 10:14; Hos 3:5), but it can also refer to events within time, as in Gen 49:1; Jer 23:20 (Oswalt, 116). It is in this latter sense that we in Africa should understand the phrase if we want this word of God to be a source of hope for us in our present hopelessness.

In a Christian context we can look to the church, sacrament of Christ's presence in the world, as the intermediate Jerusalem where all believers will agree to be guided by the law of Christ, our teacher and judge, rather than by individual or even national interests. Many African governments could easily "beat their swords into plowshares and their spears into pruning hooks" (2:4) by radically reducing their military spending in favor of reducing the widespread poverty and hunger. A reduction of arms would also reduce the temptation to use them at the slightest excuse and this would contribute to international peace. The last verse of this poem exhorts the house of Jacob to "walk in the light of YHWH" (2:5; cf. Ps 119:1, 105) as an example of obedience for the gentile nations or perhaps for the Judeans living in Diaspora. We can reread this exhortation as an invitation to us as the church, the new Israel and light of the world (Matt 5:14), to set the same example for the rest of the world to follow in promoting justice and peace.

Isaiah 35: A Happy Homecoming

Chapters 34–35 sum up and bring to a conclusion the prophet's teachings about God's sovereignty over the world in chs 13—33, and the final destinies of the arrogant nations who receive severe punishment (ch. 34) while YHWH's oppressed people are finally rehabilitated (ch. 35). Scholars see the salvation theme of ch. 35 as a link and introduction to Second Isaiah before chapters 36-39 were inserted (see Croatto, "Isaiah 40-55: Second Isaiah," in this volume). In this way ch. 34 could also be seen as the grand finale of First Isaiah, whose original theme was predominantly judgment.

The final restoration of Israel is described in terms of a desert being turned into luxuriant and productive land. It is perhaps unnecessary to ask whether the desert in 35:1 refers to the land of Judah or to the Syrian desert through which the Judeans returning from the Diaspora would pass. This is poetic language and the desert might as well be a theological description of all the damage physico-ecological, social and spiritual that arrogant and greedy human beings cause (see Oswalt, 1986, 620). This is the kind of desert that many African countries are in today. The words of the prophet reread in our context are therefore a powerful source of hope, because YHWH, the sovereign Lord of those ancient kingdoms, is also the sovereign Lord of our contemporary world and is still active in judgment as in salvation.

Christians can see the ministry of Jesus as the beginning of the fulfillment of this prophecy, as Luke 7:22 (Isa 35:5-6) shows, and we should not consider the physical healings in the New Testament merely as symbols of spiritual healing. The mission of the church is certainly to bring about spiritual liberation and transformation, but for these to be genuine they must in turn translate into social, political and economic liberation and transformation, as Liberation theology rightly stresses. Spiritual transformation must translate into good governance, environmental protection, hospitals, schools, clean drinking water, and all the other basic necessities of life that are still lacking in Africa. Working towards the fulfillment of the prophecy in Isaiah 35 is therefore a challenge to the church in its relationship to the world of Eastern Africa and the continent in general.

CONCLUSION

Isaiah's prophecies of judgment and of hope have a powerful message for the people of Eastern Africa in their present problems and aspirations. In the first place, YHWH's severe judgments against the people of Judah and Jerusalem, particularly the leaders, should guide the church on how to respond to Africa's political instability, regional armed conflicts, social and economic oppression and the resultant problem of poverty.

Moreover, a great number of people, especially the young, have allowed themselves to be seduced by the new secular culture of individualism, materialism and self-indulgence (Shorter 1997). This has led to the abandonment of many positive traditional African values and brought about a general breakdown in morals. There can be little doubt, for example, that the spread of HIV/AIDS, which is devastating many African countries, has been facilitated by the disappearance of the many social controls and taboos that regulated sexual behavior in Africans traditional society. How would Isaiah interpret the devastation being caused by this pandemic?

But Isaiah also had messages of hope for his people. Today we can already see the possibilities of rereading them as good news for Africa in the context of the many positive initiatives that the church and civil society are taking to remove the present oppressive conditions. There is now some political and economic cooperation between African states and regions to promote good governance and economic development. There are also many peace initiatives to end the widespread military conflicts in Africa. In all this, the Church is actively involved in its prophetic role of proclaiming the word of God, condemning abuses, giving moral and spiritual guidance, and supporting the poor and underprivileged members of society.

African theology of inculturation is also trying to rediscover forgotten values in the African religio-cultural, moral and spiritual traditions and to integrate them with biblical and Christian traditions in order to develop a vigorous and truly African Christianity capable of confronting and transforming today's African reality. The family institution in Africa is a primary resource and for this reason Church leaders and theologians have taken it up as the best model for the African Church. This is to teach African Christians to see themselves as the extended family of God that reaches out beyond one's clan to embrace every tribe and every nation (2:2-5). A church modeled on the traditional African family, which cared for the needs of every member and valued harmonious relations among them, would ideally promote justice and peace in all their dimensions. This is of course beautiful theology, but it is only when it becomes incarnate in the concrete life of society that the prophet's message of hope in Isaiah 1-39 will also become a liberating message for Africa.

BIBLIOGRAPHY

Bahemuka, M. Judith and Joseph L. Brockington, eds. *East Africa in Transition: Communities, Cultures and Change*. Nairobi: Acton, 2001.

Brueggemann, Walter. *Isaiah 1-39*. Interpretation. Louisville: Westminster John Knox, 1998.

Bujo, Benezet. *African Theology in Its Social Context*. Marryknoll: Orbis Books, 1992

Ceresko, Anthony. *Introduction to the Old Testament: A Liberation Perspective*. Maryknoll: Orbis Books, 2001

Clements E. Ronald. *Isaiah 1-39*. Grand Rapids: Eerdmans, 1980

Croatto, J. Severino. *Isaias 1-39*. Buenos Aires: Ediciones la Aurora, 1989

Croatto, J. Severino "Economia y poder en Isaias 1-39 (La palabra de Isais y sus relecturas)." *RIBLA* 30 (1989):43-54

Gehman, Richard J. *African Traditional Religion in Biblical Perspective*. Kijabe, Kenya: Kesho Publications, 1989.

Jensen, Joseph. *Isaiah 1-39*. Wilmington, Del.: Michael Glazier, 1984.

Magesa, Laurenti. *African Religion: The Moral Traditions of Abundant Life*. Nairobi: Paulines Publications Africa, 1998.

Mbiti, John S. *Concepts of God in Africa*. London: S.P.C.K., 1970

Oswalt, John. *The Book of Isaiah*. New International Commentary. Grand Rapids: Eerdmans, 1986.

Seitz, Christopher R. "Isaiah, Book of (First Isaiah)," pp. 472-488, *The Anchor Bible Dictionary* Vol. 3. New York: Doubleday, 1992.

Shorter, Aylward and Edwin Onyancha. *Secularism in Africa. A Case Study: Nairobi City*. Nairobi: Paulines Publications Africa, 1997.

ISAIAH 40–55

J. Severino Croatto

Instituto Superior Evangélico de Estudios Teológicos, Buenos Aires, Argentina

LIFE CONTEXT OF THE INTERPRETATION

My country, Argentina, has sunk into a deep economic, financial, moral, and spiritual depression in the last several years. The economy, especially, is mired in the worst slump in Argentine history. External financial problems ($141 billion commercial debt) strangle every attempt to develop the country's people and to satisfy their basic needs. The global market, the monopolist interests of national and international corporations, and political corruption have spoiled the country's inexhaustible resources. A traditional food-producing country—with crop yields at an all-time high in 2002—is sinking into poverty and food is increasingly unattainable for a significant percentage of the population. The wealth generated by millions of farmers and workers is unequally distributed: inequity and iniquity go hand in hand!

On the one hand, socioeconomics is deeply connected to social structures and systems; on the other hand, it is also rooted in the individual behavior of both Argentines and non-Argentines. The corruption of power and justice, the unscrupulous plunder of the country's wealth, fiscal evasion by the powerful and privileged, the drain of capital, the lack of national consciousness taking place in multinational companies and their national partners, and so on, generate numerous dire consequences: poverty for an increasing majority, deficient childhood and adolescent development, illness and disease, lack of educational opportunity, hunger, despair, and loss of hope. A future without opportunities is for all too many people the only future.

Our perception of the Argentine context is not a sense of "dependence" (using the vocabulary of sociology and classical liberation theology); rather, it is a situation of exclusion from the dominant system. The poor, the disinherited, and the unemployed are all excluded. They are leftovers. They not only lack basic needs, but also are left out of the prevalent eco-nomic system by the system itself. The system does not want their inclusion.

Analysis of the Context

In these conditions there is seemingly no hope. The only positive way out of our dilemma is creativity and solidarity. Two creative possibilities for hope exist. First, we can unite and clamor for justice and recognition, by taking the initiative to overcome the obstacles to our inclusion and our freedom.

Second, hope for Christian people is in the word of God, which does not substitute for human initiative but supports and strengthens it. The prophet we call "Second Isaiah" addressed a gloomy and distressed community. What did he proclaim to captives?

J. Severino Croatto (recently deceased) was Professor of Exegesis, Hebrew, and Religious Studies. A contributor to *Revista de Interpretación Bíblica Latinoamericana (=RIBLA)* and the *Movement of Popular Reading of the Bible,* he published 22 books, including three volumes on hermeneutics: *Exodus, A Hermeneutics of Freedom* (1981); *Biblical Hermeneutics. Toward a Theory of Reading as the Production of Meaning* (1987); *Hermenéutica Práctica. Los principios de la hermenéutica bíblica en ejemplos* (2002); three volumes on Génesis 1-11 (1974; 1986; 1997), the last one, *Exilio y sobrevivencia: Tradiciones contraculturales en el Pentateuco*; three volumes on the book of Isaiah (1988; 1994; 2001), the last one, *Imaginar el futuro. Estructura retórica y querigma del Tercer Isaías* [Isaías 56-66]; two volumes on Religious Studies (1994; 2002), the final one. *Experiencia de lo sagrado y tradiciones religiosas. Estudio de fenomenología de la religión* [2002]).

CONTEXTUAL COMMENT

Second Isaiah has an appropriate word to speak to the exiles. The Judahite's country was dismantled, and their plundered wealth forcibly brought to the center of the Babylonian empire. The country was devastated by war: its economy ruined, its agricultural production spoiled, and its cities destroyed. The kingdom of Judah became part of the (Assyrian) province of Samaria (Samerina in Assyrian records).

In this situation, to the exiles in Babylon and to the remnant in Judah YHWH seemed to be a "defeated God." The symbol of God's presence, the sacred vessels, had been captured by the conquerors (2 Kgs 25:14-15). Hope was gone.

The prophet could not give the disenchanted people any vision of salvation in the name of *that* God, could he? How could the prophet provide the hope of deliverance?

First, he needed to reconstruct the character of the "defeated God" into the character of a "sovereign, capable God."

Second, he needed to speak in the name of this *new* God by proclaiming a word of hope announcing that "liberation was possible."

Third, the prophet did not concern himself with the salvation of other nations (an alien subject!) but was concerned with his people's security and salvation. It is out of the question to speak of "nationalism vs. universalism" in this text. YHWH's universal dominion contrasts with the imperial pretensions of the Babylonian rulers and their gods. YHWH's salvific plan concerned Jacob/Israel (first part, 40:12–49:13) and Zion/Jerusalem (second part, 9:14–55:13). The prophet was urged to offer a word of hope to the people who were losing their cultural and religious identity amidst the nations and who had already lost their political independence.

Isaiah 40–55: Identifying the Most Significant Passages for a Contextual Reading

The book is divided into two symmetrical sections: the first is concerned mainly with Jacob/Israel (40:12–49:13) and the second with Zion/Jerusalem (49:14–55:13). Both topics are prefigured in the initial words of 40:1-2 and 40:9-11. Israel is dismantled, Jerusalem is in ruins, without inhabitants, and Judah is reduced to a miniscule province in the new provincial administration. This is the context of Israel's claim in 40:27: "My way is hidden from the LORD, and my right (*mishpat,* a favorable divine intervention) is disregarded by my God."

How can the people maintain their hope and ideals in so painful a situation?

It might seem better to take refuge in the great gods of the empire than to trust in YHWH: "Save me, for you are my god!"(44:17b) refers to the worship of other gods. Oppressed people may be tempted to trust in the very power that is despoiling them; however, could those gods save them? Would they save Israel? ("There is no one to save you," 47:15b). For this reason Second Isaiah is at times harshly critical of his audience's disenchantment with YHWH's ability to save them (46:5, 8, 12; 48:4, 5b, 7b, 8b, 18).

If the prophet is committed to reconfiguring the portrait of YHWH as a savior God, then he must firmly state the power of YHWH's word. The text highlights the efficacy of YHWH by using 40:6-8 and 55:10-11 as an inclusio with 46:10-11 as its central axis). This central passage especially stresses the strength and efficacy of God's word: "My plan ('asatî) shall stand, and I will fulfill all my will (hefsî)" (v. 10b, a.t.).

Several texts confirm this theme of optimism and trust in the power of YHWH's word. In different ways the prophet appeals to a *metanoia* or change of mind by the exiles. Without hope it would be impossible to escape the oppressive situation. Second Isaiah uses the people's historical memory to convince them. He expresses confidence in the LORD YHWH in many "Do not fear" oracles, stressing that other gods are impotent, mute and without existence (43:1-3a; 45:14; 46:6-7). He reiterates that YHWH creates and shapes (43:1, 15; 44:2; 45:11), that he saves and redeems (46:3-4), and that he will fulfill his plans (46:10b, 11b). A new exodus is being enacted (48:21; 49:9b-11, "I have spoken, and I will bring it to pass; I have planned, and I will do it," .46:11b). A strong message of salvation is stressed (52:10). Jerusalem (i.e., the country) is humiliated (47:6; 51:19-20, 23) and disoriented (51:18), but will be liberated (51:22). This is clearly and emphatically stated in the three "Awake, awake" oracles of 51:9, 17 and 52:1.

The community of exiles is given the title "Suffering Servant" in 52:13–53:12 and the mission of announcing salvation to the Diaspora communities (explicitly stated in 48:20b and earlier mentioned in the first two "Servant" poems of 42:1-7 and 49:1-9a). The gods of the empire have fallen down (46:1); they cannot save.

If we view chapters 40–55 as a coherent literary construction, we notice the following structure:

A   *40:1-11:* Jerusalem / YHWH's *Word* / Good news about the *way* / *Glory*

  B   *40:12-31:* YHWH argues about YHWH's power, wisdom and strength

    C   *41:1–49:12:* Rhetoric of persuasion *to Jacob / Israel* about YHWH's power and salvific will / Diasporas' return

      X   *49:13:*   Cosmic celebration for YHWH's consolation and compassion

    C'   *49:14–54:17:*   Rhetoric of persuasion *to Jerusalem* / Diasporas' return

  B'   *55:1-9:* Invitations and promises / YHWH's plan

A'   *55:10-13:* Diasporas / *Word of* YHWH / Rejoicing on the *way* of return / *Name*

The last words of Second Isaiah (55:12-13) represent a double final celebration of the Diasporas' return—the horizon of Fourth Isaiah—and of YHWH's Name, the very symbol of God's action in history.

We propose to study the following: (1) the "awake, awake" oracles of 51:9, 17; 52:1; (2) the polemical rhetoric of the fascinating oracle in 46:3-7—the text that is in the structural center of Second Isaiah and is related to the global kerygma of 40–55; (3) the overall message of the "Servant poems" (not "songs"!) in the context of a hermeneutical Latin-American *rereading*.

The "Awake, Awake" Oracles of 51:9, 51:17, and 52:1

After the first Suffering Servant poem (50:4-9a, 10-11), chapter 51 opens with a magnificent oracle of liberation (vv. 1-8). A fivefold "for . . . " (ki) in verses 2b, 3a, 4b, 6b and 8a rereads the promises to Sarah and Abraham in Genesis 12 and 17 (51:1-2a):

> For he was but one when I called him
> For the Lord will comfort Zion
> For a teaching will go out from me
> For the heavens will vanish like smoke
> For the moth will eat them up like a
>   garment

and has a promissory conclusion:

> My deliverance (*sidqati*) will be forever,
> and my salvation (*yeshu'ati*) to all generations (v. 8b).

Verse 2b should not be corrected to refer to the past (NRSV, "he *was* but one when I called him, but I *blessed* him and made him many"). It concerns the present situation of exile and Diaspora: "*For* he was but one when I called him, but I *will* bless him and make him many." The blessing concerns *the Judean Diasporas*, as in Gen 12:1-3, not the Gentile nations.

The second "for..." oracle (Isa 51:3) recalls 40:1 (in both places a twofold "comfort, comfort" / "[YHWH] has comforted / has comforted") and 49:13b, the end of the first part of Second Isaiah ("*for the Lord has comforted his people and will have compassion on his suffering ones*"). The material conditions have changed and the text lays stress on the psychological consequences of the Diaspora condition.

A programmatic salvific vocabulary of "*torah* (prophetic instruction) / *mishpat* (divine intervention) / *sedeq-sedaqah* (liberation) / and salvation" dominates the third and fourth argumentative oracles (vv. 5 and 6-7). Fourth Isaiah appears to have reworked this set of oracles by alluding to the Diaspora situation in vv. 4b ("a light to the peoples") and 5b ("the coastlands wait for me . . .").

Three "awake, awake" oracles follow this hopeful message of salvation. The first (vv. 9-11) addresses YHWH's arm as a symbol of strength and creativity. Using the mythological language of the primordial victory over the waters, the speaker points to the first exodus (v. 10b) as a paradigm for the second, future exodus of captives (v. 11, "so the ransomed of the LORD shall return").

The second oracle (vv. 17-23) is spoken to the *woman* Jerusalem, who has already been identified as the people of YHWH (v. 16b: "saying to Zion: You are *my people*"). She is invited to stand up, in opposition to Babylon, which is requested to sit on the ground and in the dust (47:1). The fortunes of the two women (i.e. cities) are changed. Babylon the oppressor will be humiliated and forced to sit on the ground, whereas the prostrated, humiliated Jerusalem will rouse herself, giving up the "bowl of staggering" into the hand of her tormentors, those who have said to her: "Bow down, that we may walk on you," treating her back like the ground (v. 23b).

Whenever I read this text, I feel YHWH is speaking directly to our context of national and individual humiliation and prostration, regardless of our personal denominational heritage.

In the third and last "awake, awake" oracle (52:1-2), we hear voices of encouragement and strength. Zion is exhorted to rise up and loosen the bond binding her neck. A prose fragment (vv. 3-6) recalls the Egyptian and Assyrian enslavements, as a historical framework for the "awake, awake" oracles.

The messenger's poem of good news (52:7-12) closes this long section and announces the coming of YHWH and his redemption: ". . . for the Lord will go before you, and the God of Israel will be your rear guard."

Isaiah 52:13–53:12: The Community of Exiles as the "Suffering Servant" Contextual Rereading

The four poems of the Servant of YHWH (42:1-7; 49:1-9a; 50:4-9a.10-11; 52:13–53:12) are redactional (Fourth Isaiah's?) compositions that supplement a basic message of salvation. The first two songs concern the proclamation of good news of salvation to the Diaspora communities all over the world, whereas the last two of them expose the suffering of the Servant of YHWH because of his obedience (50:5) and for "the many" (53:11).

Now, who is the Servant, and who are the "many"? At the textual level, the Servant can only be Israel—yet not the whole people of Israel but the community of exiles, whose sufferings and liberation (Second Isaiah) is proposed as a paradigm for the redemption of the Diasporas (Fourth Isaiah). This is clearly stated in 48:20:

> Go out from Babylon, flee from Chaldea, declare this with a shout of joy, proclaim it, *send it forth to the end of the earth,* say, "The LORD has redeemed his servant Jacob!"

This passage is a clue to understanding the character of YHWH's Servant in Isaiah. The suffering Servant of Isa 53 is no other than the suffering community of exiles, whose distress is meaningful for the rest of the people (53:5, "But he was wounded for our transgressions . . . upon him was the punishment that made us whole, and by his bruises we are healed"). The historical horizon is no longer the aftermath of Jerusalem's fall in 586 but the situation of exile some generations later. YHWH's former anger has passed away (43:28; 47:6; 54:7); now, YHWH wants Israel/Zion to be delivered from captivity, slavery, and oppression.

The Servant is the symbol of a community, not an individual. The "we-speech" of 53:1-6 confirms this statement. This distinction is relevant for my own contextual reading of the prophetic text. We can reread this Isaianic text as a paradigm of our sufferings as a nation despoiled by internal and external oppressors who have imprisoned us in the jail of poverty, unemployment, low salaries, money devaluation, and unimaginable inflation.

Nevertheless, the Suffering Servant is also the *glorified* Servant of YHWH. Two statements anticipating glorification and exaltation (52:13-15 and 53:10-12) structurally frame the Servant's passion account. This is worth noting, because their kerygmatic function is to anticipate the glorious denouement (52:13-15), and make sense of the Servant's sufferings (53:10-12). When the text was written, this ending was not yet fulfilled but seen through the eyes of hope.

This paradigm may perhaps be better actualized in my historical, economic, and political context than it was in the New Testament itself for two reasons: First, the communal character of YHWH's Servant corresponds to the character of the whole people of a country. Second, the end of the story looks forward only in hope, whereas the New Testament reading looked backward after the fact. In the midst of our distress and anguish, the character of the Servant of YHWH may be adopted as a paradigm of hope in the wilderness of our critical situation and used to make sense of our suffering. Our critical distress, but also our capacity for hope, may be an example for other communities or nations.

Isaiah 46:3-13: The Salvific Kerygma to Oppressed People

While he addresses Lady Babylon in chapter 47, the prophet (or YHWH) first refers to her gods Marduk (Bel = Ba'al) and Nabu, symbols of *imperial power* (46:1). They are already fallen (note the past tenses in 46:1). Transported on the backs of beasts of burden during the processions, they look like they are being carried out into captivity. This image suggests a reversal of fortunes for the Judahite captives. If the people were fascinated by the power of these gods and made images of them to worship (vv. 5-7), they would experience the powerlessness of these gods to answer or save. Twice in this oracle people are accused of not believing in YHWH (vv. 8, 12).

Who then is YHWH?

Speaking ironically, YHWH reminds the house of Jacob/Israel that *they* have been *borne* from their birth and will be *carried* even to their old age (v. 3). The Babylonian gods cannot save them, but YHWH has made them, will *bear*, *carry* and save them (v. 4).

YHWH alone (v. 9) is the one who *carries*, the one who fulfills his plan (v. 10b, 11b) and changes "former things" (v. 9a), the one whose deliverance is near (v. 13a). The Hebrew text stresses the LORD's action through a fivefold repetition of "I" (*'ani*) referring to YHWH speaking to his addressees (v. 4): "*I* am he, *I* will carry you, *I* have made, *I* will bear, *I* will carry and will save."

The oracle's conclusion, "I will put salvation in Zion, for Israel my glory" (13b), recalls in chiasmic form ("Zion/Israel")—the continuous series of promises to Israel (40:1–49:13) and Zion (49:14–55:13).

Confronted by economic and financial superpowers in our contemporary historical situation, we can profitably reread this chapter of the Isaianic tradition and plumb its reservoir of energy and hope in the midst of our distress.

CONCLUSION

We started our commentary by describing the horrific political and economic conditions of our people and the devastating psychological and spiritual effects of those conditions. Second Isaiah's message is a quite fitting and appropriate word of hope in the midst of Argentina's terrible present tribulation. Its message is not one of resigned conformity but an exhortation to struggle for better living conditions. The catchword of the Second Isaiah passages we have examined is: liberation is possible. In other words, change is possible. Regaining hope is the way to regain life.

BIBLIOGRAPHY

Croatto, J. Severino. *Exegesis of Second Isaiah from the Perspective of the Oppressed: Paths for Reflection.* Pages 219–36 in *Reading from this Place II.* Ed. F. Segovia and M. Tolbert. Minneapolis: Fortress, 1995.

———. *Isaías. La palabra profética y su relectura hermenéutica. II: La liberación es posible.* Buenos Aires: Lumen, 1994.

Miscall, Peter D. "Isaiah: New Heavens, New Earth, New Book." Pages 41–56 in *Reading Between Texts.* Edited by Danna Nolan Fewell.

Literary Currents in Biblical Interpretation. Louisville: Westminster John Knox, 1992.

Darr, Katheryn Pfisterer. *Isaiah's Vision and the Family of God.* Literary Currents in Biblical Interpretation. Louisville: Westminster John Knox, 1994.

Willey, Patricia Tull. *Remember the Former Things: The Recollection of Previous Texts in Second Isaiah.* SBLDS 161. Atlanta: Scholars Press, 1997.

ISAIAH 56–66

J. Severino Croatto

Instituto Superior Evangélico de Estudios Teológicos, Buenos Aires, Argentina

LIFE CONTEXT OF THE INTERPRETATION

Argentina has recently collapsed into a national crisis because of market speculation, the dismantling of all nationalized utilities and corporations, the corruption of power, the financial institutions' voracity, the perversion of the economic system, the ineffectiveness of politicians, the venality of judges, the unjust labor relations, and television programs that model theft and crime. This crisis has generated among people, especially among the lower classes and the poor, a lack of confidence in politicians and the judiciary.

Fortunately, the society has expressed its anger *(bronca)* and denounced the wicked guides, the false shepherds now exposed as wolves. In other words, the people of Argentina are spiritually sound enough to react against lies and injustice, having demonstrated the strength and ability to defend themselves.

At the same time, base communities have imaginatively developed initiatives of solidarity and survival throughout the country. Even the most marginalized not only claim their right to live but also propose new ways of escaping oppression and oblivion.

Amidst the pervasive, extreme national economic and political collapse, wretched people are urging us to rise again and to imagine a future for Argentine society and for every individual Argentine.

Third Isaiah and the Relationship of God's People to the World in My Life Context

Crisis situations, usually socio-economic in origin, produce an extreme *perturbation* in individuals and communities. What are the spiritual and religious effects upon these perturbed individuals and their communities? Perhaps a sense of *disenchantment* and *insecurity*. Perhaps, even worse, an attitude of indifference to things religious: "God doesn't protect me," so I abandon him (Isa 40:27).

Yet the effect may be completely different: generating the *confidence* to *complain* to God. Such a complaint expresses the feeling of being abandoned and unprotected by God, and concludes with a *request for* God's new manifestation in the present. The appeal to God's "historical memory" is decisive. It is still possible to envision an intervention of this God who seems to be absent and remote. The long prayer of criticism in Isa 63:7–64:11 comes to mind in this context.

What are the causes of our spiritual disruption? What are our leaders doing for the benefit of poor and hungry people? Why have we fallen into this situation of economic and moral collapse? The pericope on fasting in Isa 58:1-14 may be appropriate for reflecting on this issue.

J. Severino Croatto (recently deceased) was Professor of Exegesis, Hebrew, and Religious Studies, at Instituto Superior Evangélico de Estudios Teológicos (ISEDET). A contributor to *Revista de Interpretación Bíblica Latinoamericana (=RIBLA)* and the Movement of Popular Reading of the Bible, he published twenty-two books, including three volumes on hermeneutics: *Exodus, A Hermeneutics of Freedom* (1981); *Biblical Hermeneutics. Toward a Theory of Reading as the Production of Meaning* (1987); *Hermenéutica Práctica. Los principios de la hermenéutica bíblica en ejemplos* (2002); three volumes on Génesis 1-11 (1974; 1986; 1997), the last one, *Exilio y sobrevivencia: Tradiciones contraculturales en el Pentateuco*; three volumes on the book of Isaiah (1988; 1994; 2001), the last one, *Imaginar el futuro. Estructura retórica y querigma del Tercer Isaías* [Isaías 56-66]; two volumes on Religious Studies (1994; 2002), the final one, *Experiencia de lo sagrado y tradiciones religiosas. Estudio de fenomenología de la religión* [2002]). This *GBC* volume is dedicated to his memory. His warm collegiality and great contributions to both the academy and the church will be missed.

At the same time, we cannot remain prostrate on the ground in our misery and distress. As Second Isaiah has taught us earlier, we should wake up and stand up in hope. A word of liberation is addressed to the sufferers, but it must also be heard by those who have power to undo the national disaster we are enduring in Argentina. Studying Isa 61:1-3 from a fresh perspective may yield insights appropriate to my context.

CONTEXTUAL COMMENT

Isaiah 56–66: Most Significant Passages for my Contextual Reading

Third Isaiah is a multifaceted work. A conflicted community is splintered into the just and the wicked. This situation is depicted mainly in chs. 56:9–59:8 and 65–66 in which there is a harsh prophetic denunciation of those "devotees" who have misinterpreted God's favor for the oppressed, an oracle about true and false or appropriate and inappropriate fasting (58:1-14).

Isaiah 60–62 describes Jerusalem's reconstruction with ch. 61, the structural center, presenting a message of liberation and everlasting joy. We can appropriate this prophetic message for ourselves in our context of distress and oppression (see below).

Chapters 59:9-21 and 63–64 separate this central section from the beginning and closing units (56:9–59:8 and 65–66). Both sections consist of a community prayer (59:9-15a + 63:7–64:11) and a decisive intervention by YHWH (59:15b-20 [21] + 63:1-6), bracketing the central promises of liberation and restoration (60–62).

I find it very exciting to analyze both the psalm of 59:9-15a and the complaint of 63:7–64:11 because they are almost completely ignored by Bible readers in spite of their limitless reservoir of meaning.

The following structural and compositional arrangement of Isa 56–66 helps one to visualize the rhetorical development of the passage:

A-A': First *inclusio* (essential message). Return of the Diaspora (56:1-8 + 66:18-24).

B-B': Main *inclusio*. Criticism of violence and injustice, negligence toward oppressed and wanting people, various kinds of worship of other Gods (mainly in 56:9–58:14 + 59:1-8, and in 65–66, at the beginning and the end of the section 56–66; cf. 65:1-7, 11-12; 66:1-2a, 3-4, 5b, 6, 14b-17). There are *two* groups in these accusations: the corrupt, violent, and iniquitous individuals; and the just (or righteous) (57:1, 13b), all called "my servants" (65:8, 9, 13, 14, 15; 66:14).

Inside this main section of judgment oracles, we see salvific promises addressed to, or about, the "contrite and humble in spirit" (57:13b, 14-19, and 65:8-10, 15b-25). In this same section we also see four antithetical parallels between beatitudes and woes (65:13-15a), the same that motivated, I think, Luke's presentation of blessings and maledictions in two parallel sets (6:20-26).

C-C': Confession of sins (59:9-15a [1-15a] + 63:7–64:11).

D-D': YHWH's vindication, extended from Israel to the nations (59:15b-20 [21] + 63:1-6).

E-E': The New Jerusalem vs. the "nations" (60 + 62). Promises to Zion extend into the final oracles (B') of 65:18b-19a and especially 66:7-14a.

X: Central proclamation: 61:1-11: *To loose/to comfort* . . . Promises of redemption to Israel.

Arranging this structure as a pyramid (reading from below left upwards, and then down on the right side) we have:

X
61   Liberation message

E   60   **E'** 62 Jerusalem glorified/ Nations at its service

D   59:15b-20[21]   **D'** 63:1-6 YHWH's actuation

C   59:1-15a   **C'** 63:7–64:11 Poems / confession of sins

B   56:9–58:14   **B** 65:1–66:17 Criticism (+ promises)

A   56:1-8   **A'** 66:18-24 Return and inclusion of diasporas

This structure reflects an additional redaction of the Isaiah tradition known as Third Isaiah. I think this redactional layer on top of Third Isaiah belongs to the hand of a final redactor tentatively designated as "Fourth Isaiah," who organized and structured the whole canonical book called "Isaiah" (see the next commentary). For this part of my study I selected passages that more surely belong to Third Isaiah, who probably wrote during the Persian period, fifth to fourth centuries B.C.E.

Isa 58:1-14: The Fast Agreeable to God

This chapter is one of the foundational prophetic texts for Latin American exegesis and theology. Its main purposes are to distinguish true religiosity from false praxis and to propose a coherent model of behavior for those searching for God. The theme of regular fasting, especially after the temple's destruction in 586 B.C.E., symbolizes that which appears pleasing to God, but is in reality what God *does not* want (v.5). The verb "choose" *(bakhar)* is decisive in YHWH's discourse, "Is such the fast that *I choose* ('ebkhar), a day to humble oneself?" (v. 5).

Fasting is not wrong; it belongs to the traditional set of cultic obligations; the ritual helps the people to remember the nation's catastrophe and moves them to repentance and confession of sins. Nevertheless, God, who judged the nation, had called the nation through the prophets to practice social justice, to promote the cause of orphans and widows (Isa 1:17), to act justly one with another, and to not oppress the alien (Jer 7:5-7). Between the practice of fasting and the practice of social justice, YHWH *chooses* the second one (Isa 58:6-7, 9b-10a).

This fundamental *choice* (to practice justice, to undo the yokes of oppression, to be in solidarity with the poor and the hungry) is the opposite of *delight* in fasting and nearness to God without an accompanying concern for the oppressed and hungry (Verses 2-3, and further, v. 13).

If we look closely at the set of behaviors of which YHWH approves, we may be surprised that we do not find here any word about cultic obligations, not even on a "yahwistic" confession of faith. All the concepts belong to the socio-economic realm:

> to loose the bond of injustice,
> to undo the thongs of the yoke,
> to let the oppressed go free,
> And to break every yoke,
>
> . . . to share your bread with the hungry,
> and bring the homeless poor into your house,
> when you see the naked, to cover them , and not to hide yourself from your own kin (vv.6-7).
>
> If you remove the yoke from among you,
> the pointing of the finger, the speaking of evil,
> if you offer your food to the hungry and satisfy the needs of the afflicted (vv.9b-10).

The first set (vv.6-7) is made up of *seven* claims, four about social conditions (prison/enslavement [because of debts?]) and three about economic conditions. The second set (vv.9b-10) is a shortened form of the previous one, with a reference to two misbehaviors concerning the realm of speech-communication (false accusation and evil speaking against others) in the second colon.

This message is pertinent for us as Christians in our present distressed context as we experience a gradual, steady increase in both poverty rates and lack of essential resources. Do we please God by multiplying our cultic services? Or by freeing people from economic and social dire needs and by providing the necessary means for survival? God's own choice is clear in the prophetic word. Do we make the same choice? Do we align ourselves with God?

Further, Isaiah's message is not directed to the people in need but to those in society capable of freeing and nourishing the needy precisely because they *have the power* to free others or the resources to aid the needy. The prophet's criticism is not directed against the common people but against the upper socioeconomic classes. The fourfold claim in v. 6 implies that the responsibility for this situation of hunger and need lies with the addressees, as verse 3b makes clear ("Look, you serve your own interest on your fast day, and oppress all your workers"). This claim is not just exhortation; rather, it expresses a demand for *justice*.

This is a sound message for our "Christian" society, which sometimes delights to "seek God" in religious rituals and practices but exploits employees, domestic help, or even those who are severely indebted. The political and ruling segments of society all too frequently promote their own interests or try to maintain their privileges without doing anything for and at the expense of those in society who suffer and are disenfranchised. Sometimes people in the church are busier with worship services and other church activities than with concrete economic and social issues. The acid criticism of Third Isaiah's teaching is very pertinent to both cases.

Even the Sabbath may merely be an opportunity for some to pursue their own pleasures and to talk about business (v. 13). The last expression suggests that the Israelites had distorted the relationship between the sacred day and economic and social justice. In both cultic practices and Sabbath keeping a *religious* practice is neither preceded nor followed by the true worship that is concerned with justice. If YHWH's worshipers practice justice, liberation, solidarity with and care for the needy, "Then you shall call, and the LORD will answer; you shall cry for help, and he will say, *Here I am*" (verse 9a, the thematic center of ch. 58). God is encountered and worshipped *primarily* in practicing justice and identifying with the poor (Matt 25:31-46).

Isa 61:1-3: How Can We Hear a Prophetic Word in a Situation of Distress?

The meaning of this short prophetic oracle is simultaneously both simple and inexhaustible. It is neither a prophetic "call narrative" (at the redactional level of the whole canonical book of "Isaiah" there is only one calling, Isa 6) nor a "Messianic" consecration, as I have argued elsewhere in my full commentary on Third Isaiah (Croatto 2001, 248-249). Throughout the entire book, the prophet proclaims (structurally and thematically) a central message of liberation from "chains": economic, financial, political, and so on. *Seven* verbs of action express this global liberation:

> to *bring* good news to the oppressed,
> to *bind* up the brokenhearted,
> to *proclaim* liberty to the captives,
> and *release* to the prisoners;
> to *proclaim* the year of the Lord's favor,
> and the day of vengeance of our
>   God;
> to *comfort* all who mourn;
> To provide for those who mourn in
>   Zion—to give them a garland
>   instead of ashes . . . (verses.1-3a).

The reader can easily distinguish three types of socio-economic chains (oppressed, captives, prisoners) and two types of subjective chains (brokenhearted, mourners). Sadness and heartbreak are not a purely spiritual dimension but the direct consequence of socio-economic distress. Thus the text addresses both human corporeality and interiority. Our proclamation of the word of God must also address both aspects of the human condition.

The divine intervention proclaimed in this text presupposes that overwhelming, dominant *powers* directly cause the oppression. The known lexicon of vengeance expresses this reversal of fortunes (see also Isa 34:8, 63:4). For the prophets, debts and other obligations that cause imprisonment, enslavement, and suffering have their source in the iniquitous behavior of society's powerful and dominant. This idea is absent from the Jubilee legislation; the "year of favor" (v.2a) has nothing to do with the Jubilee Year or similar concepts. Second, the prophets cannot support the idea of fixed dates in the future for any release; they urge liberty and release *now*. Therefore absolutely no correlation exists between the prophetic claims of Isa 61:1-3 (and even less so for Luke 4:19) and the Jubilee Year.

As we passed over the year 2000 (the chronological date!) and the proclamation of a (mainly) spiritual Jubilee by the Catholic Church, so many words and good intentions on foreign and internal debt in our world remained void of real-ization. Everyone has forgotten the claims of the prophets.

If we recapture the prophetic demand of proclaiming release at *any time,* including the present, perhaps we can retain the appeal of God's word and hear it afresh. This is what we desire, what we require, in my country in our present hour of distress. Isaiah 61:4—a verse clearly distinguished from the surrounding context, as is widely recognized—is fantastically appropriate in my life context. Even though the economy and the human spirit lie in ruins, we still hope to "build up the ancient ruins," to "raise up the former devastations," and to "repair the ruined cities, the devastations of many generations [of wrong politics]."

The poem's last verse encourages us to rebuild hope and reality, in order that "the LORD God will cause righteousness and praise to spring up before all the nations" (v.11b).

The Confession of 59:9-15a and the Complaint of 63:7–64:11

The first of these two units speaks about the absence of *mishpat, sedaqah* and *[yeshu'ah]*. All these terms point to the historical experience of YHWH's salvific presence. In the present conditions of the praying community, this soteriological presence is absent. What are people to do? Will they despair and sink into pessimism, as many in my context now do? The text points to an alternative, but what is it?

After describing the situation of confusion and disorientation (59:9-11), the text records a profound "confession of sins" (59:12-15a). This kind of prayer implies that we recognize our misdeeds and sins, and prepares us to hear the promises of salvation (59:15b-20).

The second unit (63:7–64:11) is a long prayer in the style of a complaint or lament to YHWH because of the present situation of misery, despair, and hopelessness. Two significant motifs in the complaint are: (1) YHWH's past great deeds, now strangely absent; and (2) the invocation to the Lord as "our father" (three times!) and "the one who redeems us." As we shall read in the final address, both titles open the heart to hope, to expectance of divine favor.

The long prayer begins by recording the past benefits (*hasde-*) of YHWH as they are registered in Israel's memory (63:7). The abundance of his benefits expresses the historical acknowledgment of YHWH's gracious deeds. "He became their savior in all their distress" (63:8b). Moreover, "in his love (*be'ahabato*) and in his pity he redeemed them; he lifted them up and carried them all the days of old" (63:9b).

Two main reflections follow from this historical salvific background: (1) The actual situation of distress produces a brief but profound confession of sins by the community (63:10; 64:6-7); (2) Instead of an extensive confession of sins (as in 59:12-15a), a long lament about YHWH's *absence* in the present situation is the main subject of the prayer. This lament has two sections. In the first section, 63:11-14, the author reports the community's remembrance of God's decisive intervention in the marvelous events of the exodus. But God is now absent. Where is the one who brought them up out of the sea? Where is the one who put God's holy spirit within him (i.e. Moses) (63:11b; a tradition also seen in 2 Kgs 2:9-10, 15; Mark 1:10).

In the prayer's second section (63:15–64:11) the community directly addresses God and questions YHWH's behavior: "Where are your zeal and your might?" (63:15b); "Why, O LORD, do you make us stray from your ways . . . ?" (63:17a). At the same time, they blame YHWH for not reenacting the glorious deeds of the past in the present (64:1-4). They also remind God: "You are our father" (three times, 63:16a, b; 64:8), "our Redeemer from of old is your name" (v. 16b). This expression of confidence gives way to the last claim:

> After all this, will you restrain yourself, O Lord?
> Will you keep silent, and punish us so severely? (64:12 [11])

In my country's present distress, this community prayer inspires us to question God, to renew our hope, and to look to the future for a transformation of our current dire situation.

Indeed, in the midst of our distress, people and institutions at every level are demonstrating a tremendous solidarity and sense of community. New projects and new ideas that promote solidarity, justice, development, and community are following the numerous protests against politicians, banks, judges, corporations, and violence and corruption.

CONCLUSION

The main teaching of the texts we have considered concerns our response to the actual social situation. We are not to despair but to hope in YHWH's salvific intervention. This hope, however, requires us to recognize our misbehaviors and our sins, both personally and socially, and to imagine a new future, a "new heavens and a new earth" (65:17; 66:22).

Hope and do not despair: this is the last word in the prophetic message.

BIBLIOGRAPHY

Brueggemann, Walter. "The Hope of Heaven . . . on Earth." *BTB* 29 (1999): 99-111.

Croatto, J. Severino. *Imaginar el futuro. Estructura retórica y querigma del Tercer Isaías (Isaías 56–66)*. Buenos Aires: Lumen, 2001.

———. "El profeta de la liberación recibe el espíritu de Yavé (Comentario hermenéutico de Isaías 61:1-3)". *Ihr Völker alle, klatscht in die Hände*. Fests. Erhard S. Gerstenberger. Ed. Rainer Kessler et al. Münster: LIT Verlag, 1997.

———. *"Vom levitischen Jubeljahr zur prophetischen Befreiungszeit (Exegetische Erwägungen zu Jesaja 61 und 58 in Zusammenhang mit dem Jubeljahr)."* Pages 97-121 in Weltdorf Babel. Globalisierung als theologische Herausforderung. Ed. Giancarlo Collet. Münster: LIT Verlag, 2001.

Gray, Mark. "The Quest for Justice with Reconciliation: The Rhetoric of Isaiah 58:6-10." *Breaking Bread, Building Justice: The Mission of the Church in a World of Hungers.*

FOURTH ISAIAH

J. Severino Croatto
Instituto Superior Evangélico de Estudios Teológicos, Buenos Aires, Argentina

LIFE CONTEXT OF THE INTERPRETATION

Argentina's difficult situation is the result of recent unusually bad social and economic policies and an increasing financial dependence on international agencies. Our external debt has grown as never before, we have a severe trade deficit, and economic productivity has almost ground to a halt. Many Argentines have become a new diaspora by fleeing to other countries in search of a new life for themselves and their families. Those that have emigrated, and even those that remain behind, are losing their sense of *community* and *identity*. For many Argentines, there is no future and no hope, but only dispersion, emigration, and loss of identity. The final redactor of Isaiah addressed an ancient audience that faced such a reality. Perhaps the words of Fourth Isaiah address the hopelessness of today's Argentina.

Issues Raised by Fourth Isaiah

Masses of people from Argentina are migrating to Europe, the United States, Australia, and other countries, searching for a better life. As a consequence, their families are disrupted or at least divided. They are compelled to start a new life in a different culture. At the same time, they begin to *lose their roots*, being in a liminal state of not belonging to either their host culture or their original Argentine culture. If they get a good position, they tend to forget their country of origin.

For the ancient Judeans, the Diaspora was not, at least as represented in some texts, at all pleasant. The traditional faith was forgotten and the "ways of YHWH" were no longer practiced.

First Isaiah (1–39) describes the social injustice, corruption, and foreign invasions that caused the nation's poverty, hunger, and devastation. Second Isaiah (40–55) addresses the captives in Babylon and affirms YHWH's capacity and determination to redeem and restore.Third Isaiah (56–66) speaks to a community drawn into internal conflicts (discrimination; worship of other Gods; neglect of oppressed, poor, and hungry people; lack of justice, and superficial religiosity).

Despite these distinctions, the entire book of Isaiah presupposes a situation of devastation, dispersion, exile, alienation, oppression, and despair, which closely resembles our experience in Argentina today. It is in the midst of such distress that signs of hope and reconstruction are proclaimed, which constitute the final and overarching message of the book called "Isaiah."

J. Severino Croatto (recently deceased) was Professor of Exegesis, Hebrew, and Religious Studies. A contributor to *Revista de Interpretación Bíblica Latinoamericana (=RIBLA)* and the *Movement of Popular Reading of the Bible,* he published 22 books, including three volumes on hermeneutics: *Exodus, A Hermeneutics of Freedom* (1981); *Biblical Hermeneutics. Toward a Theory of Reading as the Production of Meaning* (1987); *Hermenéutica Práctica. Los principios de la hermenéutica bíblica en ejemplos* (2002); three volumes on Génesis 1-11 (1974; 1986; 1997), the last one, *Exilio y sobrevivencia: Tradiciones contraculturales en el Pentateuco*; three volumes on the book of Isaiah (1988; 1994; 2001), the last one, *Imaginar el futuro. Estructura retórica y querigma del Tercer Isaías* [Isaías 56-66]; two volumes on Religious Studies (1994; 2002), the final one. *Experiencia de lo sagrado y tradiciones religiosas. Estudio de fenomenología de la religión* [2002]).

CONTEXTUAL COMMENT

Fourth Isaiah: Most Significant Passages for a Contextual Reading

In each of the three "Isaiahs" we find themes that do not correspond to any of the prophets or redactions we call First-, Second-, or Third Isaiah. All of these texts use similar language, describe the prophet in similar terms, and address situations of a later date, later even than Third Isaiah. This data leads me to conclude that there was a final redactor, a Fourth Isaiah, who produced the canonical Isaiah.

The theological reflection in these texts also echoes later conditions: the dominant political power is no longer Babylon or even Persia, but "the nations." This indicates that there is a new situation of dispersion and oppression throughout the known world. I think that the texts about the "islands" (11:11; 24:15; 41:1; 42:10, 12; 49:1; 59:18; 66:19) also correspond to the horizon of a Fourth Isaiah rather than to the Second Isaiah or even the Third Isaiah.

Some exegetes speak of a "redaction level." This is correct, but only if we admit that the redactor, Fourth Isaiah, is a full author, who establishes a framework for an enormous literary and theological work and writes with a *special* and *distinct* program that concerns the various Diasporas and the province of Yehud. This Fourth Isaiah is the person behind the magnum opus we simply call "Isaiah."

The main themes and their figurative representations displayed in the whole book are as follows:

a) The return of the Diasporas	b) The nations	c) The New Jerusalem
+	-	+
"Sons and daughters"	Inversion of situations	Reconstruction
"Numerous"	At the service of…	Repopulation
"Ends of the earth"	Wealth taken from…	New economy
YHWH's splendor	"They will know"	"You will know"
		Joy and exultation
11:9-16; 27:12-13; 35:9-10;	(13-23); 14:1-2, 26-27; 34;	1:27; 4:3-6; 14:32b; 16:5;
43:5-7; 49:12, 22; 55:12;	43:3b-4; 51:21–52:2; 49:23; 45:14;	49:14-26; 54:1-17;
56:8; 60:4, 9b; 62:10; 66:18-21	59:18b; 60:12, 14; 63:1-6	59:20a; 60 + 62; 66:7-14

Each theme, consisting of promises to the Diasporas and the future of Jerusalem, as well as the fortune of the nations, is found in each of the three sections of the book of Isaiah.

The descriptions of the situation of Jerusalem in Persian times and that of the different Diasporas throughout the Empire, explain the critical moment Judeans are living in their human lives and in relation to YHWH. Is there still time to hope and expect salvation? Fourth Isaiah imagines a new future, in which a symbolic Jerusalem will gather together the whole people, whether living in the Diasporas or in Yehud.

The Symbols of the Invitation to the World Diasporas

Isa 11:9-16

This text most clearly states the calling of Judean Diasporas. Beginning with the transition oracle of 11:10, the non-Davidic shoot—which points to a *new* dynasty!—is exhibited as a signal or flag (*nes*) to the nations. In order to understand several passages that involve the "nations" (*goyim*) or "peoples" (*'ammim*), it is necessary to interpret these terms as referring, not to foreign nations as such, or to the Gentiles, but *to the realm* where the Judean communities live all over the world (for this ecumenical horizon, see v.11b).

With this context in mind, we can now understand the phrase, "the *nations* shall inquire of him" (v.10b), a most strange idea if "nations" refers to "Gentiles." When the motif "flag *to* the nations" (not "for," NRSV) appears in v.12, it is explicitly stated that the aim is to assemble the outcasts *of Israel*, and gather the dispersed *of Judah*, and this will happen "from the four corners of the earth." There is no question of calling the Gentiles; rather, the newcomers will expand their territory and plunder the neighboring peoples (v.14). Verses 15-16 imagine the returning "remnant that is left of his [YHWH's] people" crossing the sea (now the River Euphrates) for a second time and introduce the conclusive thanksgiving of ch. 12.

It is worth noting that the promises referring to the Diasporas are preferably inserted at the end of the main sections of the present book of Isaiah. The best examples are:

11:11-16 (end of 2–11);
35:10 (end of 1–35);
49:12[-13] (end of the first part of 40–55);
55:12-13 (end of the second part of 40–55);
66:18-21, at the end of 56–66, as well as of the whole book of Isaiah.

This compositional device clearly signals the reader that the recovering of the dispersed people is one of the main redactional (i.e., Fourth Isaiah) themes of the whole book.

Isa 66:18-21

This pericope speaks about the return of the western Diasporas (though a return from other directions is not excluded). The symbolic names of different peoples derive from Ezekiel 27 (an oracle against Tyre and its commerce throughout the Mediterranean).

YHWH is described as coming "to gather all nations and tongues" (v.18b). He "will set a sign among them" (v.19a). The "nations" are where the Judean Diasporas live. The next phrase should be translated as follows (not as NRSV does): "and I will call from them [i.e. from the nations] the-survivors-unto-the-nations (Tarsis . . .) and they shall declare my glory among the nations" (v.19b). The formula "the survivors unto the nations" refers to the different Diasporas in earlier times. It does not refer to a future international going and coming of a group of survivors.

That the promises concern the Judean communities abroad is most clearly stated in v.20, which says, "They [the nations] shall bring all your kindred from all the nations . . . . . ." The *nations* themselves will transport the returning Judeans home. The call for liberation, gathering, and return is for the Diasporas, not for the Gentiles.

Such a benediction appears to be nationalistic or even chauvinistic to modern readers. I think that universal salvation was not a vision of the different authors/redactors of canonical Isaiah. For them, the critical situation was the ruined nation of Judah—in reality, the very small province of Yehud—and the dispersed people of Israel, in a tragic state of destruction and annihilation. How does a person or a people escape this mire of hopelessness?

Universalistic interpretations of such texts as these are part of a Christian missionary hermeneutic based upon the insights of New Testament writers (see Acts 13:46-47 with Luke 2:29-32 [Simeon's praise] and 24:44-48).

The New Exodus Motif

Both Isa 48:20-21 and Isa 49:9b-13 give us an exegetical clue for understanding the double redaction and double context of Second Isaiah's literary composition.

Indeed, Isaiah 40–55 is not a unitary composition; rather, it is a proclamation in exile *reread* much later when the nation was rapidly disintegrating. Chronologically, we can think of an exilic phase of the text, reworked later sometimes during the Persian-Hellenistic period. So, we read Isa 40–55 not from the perspective of the Babylonian captivity but largely from perspective of the canonical book, i.e. Fourth Isaiah.

Isa 48:20-21

In this passage, the first level of redaction is the work of the exilic prophet, known as "Second Isaiah." If 48:20a echoes the voice of this messenger of YHWH to the captives in Babylon; v.20b, on the other hand, represents the kerygma of this same liberated group (the Israel-Servant) to the diasporas dispersed all over the earth ("the end of the earth"). This mission is accredited to the Servant in 49:1-9a, who will "restore the survivors of Israel" and be "a light to the nations" (the Judean communities amidst the nations, v.6), so that God's "salvation may reach to the end of the earth," as is restated in v.6b.

Isa 49:9b-13

When we bypass the Servant's poem of 49:1-9a, we reach the climactic promise for the gathering of the dispersed people of Israel: "Lo, these shall come from far away, and lo, these from the north and from the west, and these from the land of Sinim (i.e. Syene?)." This last toponym symbolizes the far south (south of Egypt). The east is not mentioned because the release or gathering from the region of Babylon supposedly is (symbolically) a past event already programmatically recorded in 48:20a.

Whereas the crossing of the desert was narrated in perfect tenses (*qatal*) in 48:21— "They *did* not thirst when he led them through the deserts; he *made* water flow for them from the rock . . . "—it is depicted in imperfect or future tenses (*yiqtol*) in 49:9b:

"They *shall* feed along the ways. . . they *shall* not hunger or thirst . . . ". This new desert crossing reenacts the ancient, paradigmatic, first exodus.

The New Jerusalem

Promises of a renewed Jerusalem appear throughout Isaiah:

1) The New Jerusalem shall be redeemed (*padah*) by justice and righteousness (1:27). These two words (*mišpat* and *sedāqah*) do not concern human values, as they do in chs. 1–39, but rather YHWH's ability to act and to save (also found in different layers of chs. 40–55, prominently, and 56–66).
2) YHWH's spirit will cleanse Jerusalem (4:2-5). This very late passage takes theological motives from the exodus and wilderness traditions.
3) Again, the city shall be protected and fecund (49:14-26; 51:17–52:2), full of sons and daughters (54:1-17), wealthy and blessed (60 and 62), full of joy and giving birth to a *new nation* (66:7-14).
4) 14:32b summarizes in a few short lines the message of the entire canonical book (Fourth Isaiah): "The LORD has founded Zion; and the needy among his people will find refuge in her."

I am not saying that all of these New Jerusalem oracles belong to Fourth Isaiah. Rather, I am emphasizing this final redactor's profound interest in Jerusalem's re-foundation (14:32b) as a symbol for the new Judah, presently in ruins. Jerusalem herself is imagined as a herald of good tidings ("Here is your God!") to the cities of Judah in 40:9. Jerusalem's restoration prefigures the renewal of the country of old. And the condition for this event is the return, the re-gathering of the worldwide diasporas.

The promises of Jerusalem's restoration and the Diaspora's return, inserted in chs. 1–39, may be a mark of Fourth Isaiah's literary hand.

CONCLUSION

How can these hopeful promises be read in the political, social, cultural, and even religious context in which Argentine believers have to experience God's presence in the midst of distress, increasing poverty, disenchantment, desperation, and pessimism?

Similar questions faced the final "constructor" of the book of Isaiah. Since the ancient Israelites were in a situation similar to the current crisis in Argentina, the prophet *did* think it worthwhile to plant the seeds of hope in their heartbroken spirits. Can we hear the prophet once again? Can we hear his word of hope today?

Every individual and every community tries to survive, no matter what the circumstances. In the midst of social dissolution and the loss of cultural and social identity it is possible to imagine a different future, a New Jerusalem, a new people with new visions and possibilities. These imaginative, prophetic promises call us to raise our spirits and to renew our hope in order to reconstruct the economic, social, and cultural conditions we enjoyed.

At the level of final redaction, all the prophetic books end with a hopeful word, as with Isa 66:18-24. This redactional technique itself is a message. We want to re-appropriate Fourth Isaiah's message of hope and future reconstruction of society and culture.

In Argentina today, we want to reestablish hope; we want to create for our own diasporas a country with new economic possibilities, with an honest and just ruling class; we want to reconfigure the political system in order to make life fulfilling and productive for all people.

Fourth Isaiah, the author of the present canonical form of the book "Isaiah," is a guide in our search for a new nation.

BIBLIOGRAPHY

Berquist, Jon L. *Judaism in Persia's Shadow: A Social and Historical Approach.* Minneapolis: Fortress, 1995.

Clements, Ronald E. "Isaiah: A Book without an Ending." *JSOT* 97 (2002): 109-126. (I remain unconvinced about Clements' characterization of 5-25 as an "apocalyptic book" and its suggested identification with Duhm's missing "Fourth Isaiah.")

Croatto, J. Severino. "Composición y querigma del libro de Isaías." *RIBLA* (2000): 35-36, 39-70.

JEREMIAH

Renita J. Weems

Spelman College, Atlanta, Georgia, USA

LIFE CONTEXT OF THE INTERPRETATION

The context from which I write is that of a North American woman whose ancestors were brought to this country hundreds of years ago as slaves to what was thought to be a New World. Having been stripped of language, culture, religion, kin, and prevented from fully assimilating into their new environs has influenced the way the slaves, and their descendants after them, would view reality. Their image of themselves as wanderers, exiles, and outsiders would be affixed permanently to the cultural imagination of African Americans. Four hundred years of degradation, segregation, discrimination, and pseudo-attempts at integration leave me, and other slaves' descendants, feeling that we are neither fully American nor genuinely African.

Not insignificantly, the Bible played an instrumental role in domesticating slaves and making black people in America feel predestined to their second class status. But the Bible has also played a part in helping slaves (and their descendants) find the will to struggle for a new world order. The same goes for the role the Bible has played in the lives of North American Christian women. It has been a force both for rationalizing women's subordination and for inciting women to agitate for their rights. The vision blacks and women in this country have struggled for, utopic though it may be, is deeply rooted in biblical prophets' vision of justice and freedom. My writing about Jeremiah is, therefore, to traverse in both familiar and unfamiliar territory. As a child of the American south, where slavery and Jim Crow laws were the norm, and where the church, the Bible, and Protestant Christianity were permanent fixtures of the soul, and having come to consciousness during the height of the Civil Rights, Anti-Vietnam and Women's Movements, I understand, firsthand, what the Jewish feminist poet, Adrienne Rich means when she, born and raised in post World War II America by secular Jewish parents, describes herself as "split at the root." I am North American; I am of African descent; and I am a woman. I am both the product of a dominant culture and a victim of that culture. I am a First World woman with Third World commitments. I am a Western woman raised in a patriarchal culture, but also who has profited from my country's exploitation of the labors of women living in less developed countries. Multiple identifies and shifting loyalties inform my reading of Jeremiah. As a descendant of African slaves, a woman, a daughter of the American south, an ordained Protestant minister, a mother and wife, and a professor at a black women's college, mine is a context which has taught that texts are simultaneously to be submitted to and struggled against.

Renita J. Weems is Camille and William Cosby Professor of Humanities (2003-2005) at Spelman College. Besides the several books for lay church women that she has written on women's spirituality and the Bible—including *What Matters Most: Ten Lessons in Living Passionately from the Song of Solomon* (2004) and *Listening for God: A Minister's Journey Through Silence and Doubt* (2000)—her scholarly writings have focused on the prophets, womanist and feminist biblical criticism, and cultural studies, including two books, *Battered Love: Marriage, Sex, and Violence in the Hebrew Prophets* (1995) *Just a Sister Away: A Womanist Vision of Women's Relationships in the Bible* (1988). She was the first African American woman to earn a PhD in Old Testament studies (which she received from Princeton Theological Seminary).

Analysis of Life Context as Viewed from Jeremiah

Ministers, theologians, and students of Christian scriptures are accustomed to focusing on the book of Jeremiah exclusively as religious literature, viewing the oracles attached to the prophet as the word of God and his legacy as that of a prophet of hope. But much can be gained by viewing the book as "survival" or "protest" literature. Edited in its final form during fifth century Persian domination, the book of Jeremiah certainly qualifies as belonging to diaspora writings. This is literature written to explain how an individual or a people found themselves as part of a catastrophic or traumatic event, and how they managed to survive whole. Amy Tan's *Joy Luck Club*, Elie Wiesel's *Night*, and W.E.B. DuBois' *Souls of Black Folks* are contemporary books that fall in this category. Rather than trivializing their suffering or interpreting it away, the writers face their community's suffering with courage and in protest.

The book of Jeremiah purports to stem from an audacious prophet living sometime during the seventh and sixth centuries B.C.E in the tiny kingdom of Judah. He sought to give guidance to his country in the face of the tumultuous political events of his day. While there's little doubt that many of the oracles contained in the book date back to the prophet, there's also little doubt that the book is the product of editors and theologians of a later generation who sought to interpret their political context in light of the prophet's preaching.

Jeremiah is a prophet at odds with the royal class—kings, priests, scribes, and other prophets of his day—and continues to be a role model for speaking truth to the powerful, for giving voice to suffering, and for resisting the dominant values of the empire. The nation's fate seemed always to be on the verge of a national crisis, domination, or in danger of instituting political or religious policies that threatened its special covenant relationship with God. But that seems never to have dampened the tiny kingdom's belief in itself as unique, nor its appetite to be self-defining.

Jeremiah is an ideal text in uncertain times. War, terrorism, insurgency, weapons of mass destruction, occupation, and globalization are topics that currently dominate the news. When American planes, commandeered by Middle East terrorists, crashed into the World Trade Center in New York, Americans were dumbfounded. Everyone wanted to know, "How could this happen to us?" and "Where was God?" Pundits and prophets were invited before television audiences to answer. It was shock and horror reminiscent of the sort the inhabitants of Judah felt when a foe from the north succeeded in breaking through the walls and terraces of Jerusalem and laying waste the city's precious national symbols. "Is the Lord not in Zion?" the traumatized fanatics of the day wanted to know. For a few months after September 11, 2001, the shock and grief shook American citizens out of their self-complacency. For a while there we were less interested in television celebrities and were more likely to engage strangers in conversation, show compassion toward the homeless and poor, and talk openly about God, faith, and our shared humanity. But at the time of this writing, things are back to normal, sort of. We have been encouraged by our leaders to go back to the way we were living before 9/11 and not let threats of increased terrorism keep us from spending, traveling, enjoying life, and showing our resolve to remain a dominant power around the world. Back to sloganeering: "national security," "axis of power," "weapons of mass destruction," and "Let's roll." Back to hearing the false promises of court prophets: "Peace! Peace!" when there is no peace. America is a superpower, after all. "If prophecy is essentially a ministry of disclosure, a stripping bare," as Hans Wolff once said, then Jeremiah serves as an example of what it means to speak truth to power. His example is precisely the work of suspicion and recovery that we need from modern prophets. Jeremiah is a book for crisis times, and America's insistence upon securing its position as a global power will attract as much disaster and grief inside its borders as it imposes upon others.

The book of Jeremiah gives us, citizens who are 'split at the root,' torn by our love for this country and our disgust over its abuse of power, hope. It teaches us how to grieve and how to help our country find new language and a new heart after ruin, so that we can construct a new basis for our existence as a nation.

CONTEXTUAL COMMENT

Overview of Jeremiah

Jeremiah's ministry spanned the administration of five kings: Josiah (640-609 B.C.E.), Jehoahaz (609), Jehoiakim (609-597), Johoiachin (597), Zedekiah (597-587). In the course of his forty-year career, the prophet's attitudes toward his nation and its fate changed, probably numerous times. He likely endorsed King Josiah's campaign to restore autonomy to Judah, especially the measures he undertook to purge the land of foreign religious practices and to call the nation back to worship of Yahweh exclusively. "Repentance" and surrendering one's whole heart to God were constant themes of his message. He later grew critical when Judah's inhabitants had grown comfortably numb to abuses and threats. He was quick to denounce Judah and Jerusalem and to condemn the land to disaster in his early years, when he spoke with divine dissatisfaction with all forms of injustice. But he was also quick to preach newness and restoration when disaster struck.

The prophet is identified as Jeremiah ben Hilkiah, a descendant of the priests of Anatoth in Benjaminite territory (Jer. 1:1-3). His career spanned a period of great turmoil and transition in the ancient Near East: the tiny southern kingdom of Judea was caught in the middle of the Egyptian, Assyrian, and growing Babylonian military conflict. Two historical events in particular were at the centerpiece of the prophet's ministry① the religious reforms of Josiah (621 B.C.E.), and the demise of Judah, along with the exile of its high-born citizenry (597 and 587). Narratives in 2 Kings 21–25, 2 Chronicles 33–36 and books associated with other prophets living and preaching around the same time, such as Zephaniah, Nahum, Habakkuk, and Ezekiel, broaden our perspective on the period. The book of Jeremiah offers historians a wealth of insight into the conspiracies, intrigue, and drama that marked the final years of Judah.

Not all oracles and narratives found in the book can be traced back to the prophet himself. Most scholars agree that the book is a construction of the person and message of Jeremiah by exiles looking back on the demise of Judah and the profound theological crisis that followed. As exiles forced to live out their existence in captivity, battling to resist the cultural and ideological trappings of their captors, and desperate to keep their own traditions energized and their hope in home and Yahweh alive, the gôlah (exile) community would have been acutely interested in the oracles of a prophet like Jeremiah. The exiles saw in his oracles an example of what it meant to preach under the pressure to conform to the dominant ideology. Seeing through the false prophecies, flawed ideologies, and fake claims to power of his day to discover the truth of Yahweh's word and will for Yahweh's people, made his ministry a role model for subsequent generations of prophets and the basis for comprehending where Judah went wrong as a nation.

Jeremiah's career involved two impossible tasks: Leading his people as they mourned the loss of everything they knew and loved and helping them imagine the better future God had for them. His oracles focus on three major themes:

1. Judah and Jerusalem have sinned and will be punished.

2. The Hope of Zion Rests with the Exiles

3. From Grief will Come Newness

To be a prophet during the reigns of Josiah, Jehoiakim, and Zedekiah was to be swept up into the high stakes game of imperial politics, geopolitical contests, and international intrigue. To be a prophet was to be a mouthpiece for God before audiences that wanted to hear anything but what the moral, just, and righteous thing was to do. To acquiesce to God's call to stand in the halls of the royal palace and Temple and speak Truth to power was to court rejection, assault, vilification, imprisonment, and likely death. To say yes to God was to declare no to the status quo.

Prophets were anything but naive. They understood well the dangers that faced them and were not eager to accept the chance to be vilified by their countrymen. In times of insecurity and fear, the calls to repentance and conscience that Jeremiah issued were not always well received. Officials and court prophets shouted "treason" and threatened imprisonment (Jer 28). Close friends urged reason and caution. But how can the prophet look the other way when his enemy is dead set on silencing him? There is no shame in wishing to avoid persecution. It is what sane and sensible people do. And being sensible, Jeremiah tried getting out of the job by complaining to God that he was too young and much too inexperienced for such a responsibility. But God would not take "no" for an answer.

The last we hear of Jeremiah is after Jerusalem has been sacked and King Jehoichin languishes in prison. Jeremiah writes that the "good figs" (Jer 24:10), those taken into Babylonian captivity, are to settle down in Babylonian exile. "Build homes and plant gardens" he urges the traumatized band of captives, to the dismay of some. He does not urge the people to acquiesce to slavery, but he urges them to trust that God will bring something new and beautiful out of their misery and trauma. After all, restoration was always the plan.

At the end of his career, Jeremiah himself was carted off to Egypt, kicking and screaming to the end, (along with Baruch his secretary) by friends who feared reprisals from Babylon for the murder of the governor Nebuchadnezzar had appointed (Jer 43). Thus, at least one of the reasons his audience could trust his message was that he personally had nothing to gain and everything to lose if what he preached proved true. Jeremiah most likely did not even live to see his message vindicated.

The Composition of Jeremiah

A major shift has occurred in studies of the book of Jeremiah. Most commentators now agree that the "final form of the book" is addressed to the generations of exiles who lived sometime after the period of Jeremiah. Previous scholarship focused on trying to delineate the "authentic" oracles of Jeremiah from the work by later editors: the narratives and stories that developed about him, and the editorial insertions that brought his work in line with Deuteronomic thinking. It is quite likely that Deuteronomists in the sixth century used Jeremiah's oracles as a basis for responding to the questions and concerns of later generations who continued to wrestle with the aftermath of the exile. But distinguishing original material from later scribal expansion and prophetic person from interpreting community cannot be done with any certainty.

Buoyed by the promises of higher criticism, modern interpreters are desperate to (re)assemble the original words of the "real" Jeremiah, believing that to do so is to know the true words (and perhaps mind?) of God. Needless to say, such notions are borne out of an almost fanatical attachment to texts, documents, and the printed word. For ancient audiences the life and message of "Jeremiah" as paradigm says something about the working of God in history. The editors carefully brought together these traditions—poetry and prose, authentic oracles and secondary material about the prophet and the tradition he represented—for readers who are prepared to go beyond a one-dimensional theology of God. God does not speak one time. God speaks, and has spoken, says Jeremiah and the Deuteronomists, again and again to each succeeding generation, in words that borrow from the past (though not confined to the past), and with fresh new meanings for each generation, in light of their own particular historical circumstance. Our job is then to trust the judgment of the final editors who saw the convergence between Jeremiah's distant words and God's perennially new efforts to persuade creation to trust God whole-heartedly.

The book of Jeremiah does not conform to that which moderns understand as "book." Its contents lack a unified structure, because it is not a book so much as a collection of prophetic materials which have passed through a long and complex history of transmission—as is suggested by the fact that the Greek translation of the book is shorter than the Hebrew text. What is significant is how this sixth century prophet preaching in a time of crisis came to embody what it means to remain faithful to God while eking out a living in the belly of an empire which worships power, ridicules pathos, and battles against alternative thinking.

A Call to be a Prophet to the Nations (1:4-19)

Superscriptions are appended to prophetic books to make abundantly clear how important historical context is for understanding the message of the prophet. Whatever timeless truth later readers might think they perceive in the message must be accounted for in the life context of the messenger. Jeremiah prophesied during the reigns of kings whose policies set the tiny kingdom on an inescapable destiny.

A prophet "knows what times it is," used to say Abraham Heschel (2001, 10) the Jewish theologian. Jeremiah warned from the beginning that soon Judah's world would take a radical turn. Life as the citizens of the tiny nation knew it would never be the same again. In a few years descendants of Israel would measure time in terms of *Before* and *After* the sixth century B.C.E. and mourn the loss of *before*.

An alert reader is expected to notice the similarities between Moses' and Jeremiah's call stories. Deuteronomic editors traced the prophet's authority back to Moses. Both Moses and Jeremiah complained of being

much too ineloquent for the task. Yahweh met Moses's objection (he was a stammerer) by providing Aaron as his mouthpiece and Jeremiah's objections by placing the words directly on his lips (Jer 1:9).

Little did Jeremiah know that humility, feelings of insecurity and unworthiness were his best qualifications for the job of prophet at the close of the seventh century and beginning of the sixth. Everything the people of God cherished and believed about God, themselves, and their traditions was about to be turned on its head. A spokesman who eschewed emotion and took great pride in his image as a cool headed rational speaker would be totally ineffective in conveying God's heartache and Judah's horror at the disaster that awaited the tiny kingdom. Crying out and wrangling with God have their place in the stages of grief. One of the reasons the ministry of Jeremiah continues to capture the hearts of readers is because the prophet did not shy away from pain. He endured this pain rather than offering smug interpretations of it.

Many see Jeremiah's commission to be "a prophet to the nations" as an indication of God's sovereignty over not just Israel, but the whole world. Others see it as a nod to the collection of oracles against foreign nations that is part of the book (25:15-38; 46-51). But neither goes far enough. Distinguishing Jeremiah as a prophet to the nations makes clear that his preaching could not be confined to Judah alone, but was for the world as a whole. The moral decay and religious idolatry that other prophets saw at the local level, Jeremiah would see as pan-endemic of the disintegration of the moral universe as a whole. Prophets who see more than the royal mythmakers are particularly dangerous.

In the black North American context we can point to modern prophets like Martin Luther King, Jr. and Malcolm X, whose movements became of interest to government officials when they refused to confine their remarks to black people's struggle in North America. When they began to make connections between American racism and the Vietnam War, the struggle for human dignity and the struggle against poverty, the struggle of black people in his country and the wave of colonial revolutions in Asia, Africa and Latin America, they became dangerous. Like Jeremiah, prophets who preach locally but who comprehend the global implications of their work, must be silenced.

Recall King's now famous "I Have A Dream" speech in which King called upon America to deliver on the "promissory note" of the Declaration of Independence–that all of its citizens be guaranteed their rights of life, liberty, and the pursuit of happiness. "Injustice anywhere is a threat to justice everywhere," King wrote from a Birmingham jail.

If God had permitted Jeremiah to confine his remarks to Judah, his burden might have been bearable. After all, he had centuries of human experience to back his predictions that the current political course would lead to disaster. But the call to be a prophet to the nations raised the bar. His predictions would reach the unthinkable. Jerusalem, the holy city, was doomed. To confirm his calling, God gave Jeremiah two signs (1:11-14): an almond tree (Hebrew: *shaqed*) which represented God's assurance that "I am watching–*shoqed*—over my word to see that it happen"; and a boiling cauldron tipping away from the north toward the south to symbolize the political problems stirring up in the direction of Mesopotamia that would soon spill over into the southern kingdom.

Divine Judgment Against Judah and Jerusalem: You Are the Problem (2:1–25:38)

Promises of reconciliation do not follow immediately on the heels of the threats of destruction and punishment. The first twenty-four chapters are filled largely with oracles of judgment, wherein one finds only scattered hints of the possibility of Israel's renewal (e.g., Jer 3:11-18; 16:14-18; 18:1-16). Not until chapters 30–31 is there a sustained attempt to paint in broad strokes a picture of hope and restoration.

In the meantime, some of the most blistering language shows up here in the earliest chapters of the book, leaving no doubt in any-

one's mind what a commission to "uproot and tear down, destroy and overthrow" entails. Judah and Jerusalem are the object of the prophet's harshest gaze. He compares the city to a loose wife, a lusty, neighing horse, willful children, a wild vine, a partridge who steals the hatchlings other mother birds lay, and a band of traitors. Images are piled on imageries as Jeremiah hopes to pierce the numbness and complacency gripping the rebellious nation. Apostasy, idolatry, deceit, injustice, and feigned innocence are the nation's sins against God. Genuine repentance and a return to radical loyalty to the God of their ancestors were their only hope. "Hope for what?" you and I ask more than 2,500 years later. Grace? Judah was doomed. Prophets wrestle with this question all the time. How do you talk about grace without letting folks feel that they have gotten off the hook for their sins? Isn't punishment an intrinsic consequence of sin? Shouldn't it be? Never mind prophets: parents struggle every day with the murky side of *lex talionis*. Is it possible to reinforce to a child the rules that govern a family without always having to resort to punishment?

One can imagine the shock and discomfort of Judah's citizens at hearing this lunatic prophet go on and on about the sky falling (2:29; 5:7-9). The inhabitants had a royal Zionist ideology which spoke of God's unconditional assurances to Judah in the form of the Temple, the Davidic monarchy, and the law book which had been discovered a few years earlier during some Temple repairs. "Why all the *Sturm* and *Drang* about disaster falling the city?" some must have asked. "Does it take all that?" still others surely wondered.

This is not language and imagery spoken in the hopes of wooing listeners back to their first love. It intends to electrocute its audience into action by shocking and shaming them, and by pummeling them with the inescapability of his claims. Jeremiah punctuates his message with rhetorical questions and sexual imagery either because he thought his audience especially obdurate or because he felt the historical crisis facing them warranted hyperbole to cut through their moral fog. The more obstinate the audience the better a poet the prophet must be.

Destruction Comes!

What kind of language does Jeremiah use throughout this first section, (Jer 2:1–25:38) to convey his message? Whatever language that works is one response. Language that works is language that pierces the comfortable numbness that grips one's audience. For a listener to stomp away muttering "How dare you!" is not necessarily a bad thing. Plucking up and uprooting is wrenching, both to audience and speaker By forcing the inhabitants to imagine themselves as a promiscuous wife, Jeremiah enhances the highly emotional tone of this block of material—a tone of urgency, agitation, desperation, and frustration. No interest is shown in these opening chapters for developing a coherent train of thought or a carefully reasoned argument to impress listeners. Attention is on evoking emotions and overwhelming the senses so as to shake Judah out of its complacency. Have they gone so far as to cut ties with their entire past, their God, and their ancient landmarks? Jeremiah asks (Jer 6:16). Being autonomous is fine, but it has its limits, he argues. "We need to recognize that such a sense of call in our time is profoundly counter cultural," writes Walter Brueggemann, "because the primary ideological voices of our time are the voices of autonomy—to do one's own thing, self-actualization, self-assertion, and self-fulfillment" (1986, 19). Nations whose policies communicate that they are autonomous, self-sufficient, and able to exist in isolation from other nations, unaccountable to anyone for their crimes within its borders and without, are nations that have some waking up to do.

The image of Judah the loose wife certainly comes to the point. "What do you mean that you dress in crimson, that you deck yourself with ornaments of gold, that you enlarge your eyes with paint?" (Jer 4:30) the poets asks. Just as a woman finds her identity in relationship ("Can a girl forget her ornaments, or a bride her attire?" Jer 2:32), so do God's elect find the reason for their existence in the God who created them. "I remember the devotion of your youth, your love as a bride, how you followed me in the wilderness in a land not sown" (2:1). The covenant at Sinai is depicted in terms of a marriage where the bride accepts her husband and follows him into a new life. Continuing to draw on women's experiences to make his point, Jeremiah compares Judah's coming travails to that of a woman in labor (Jer 4: 31; cf. 31:15) and to a mother humiliated at her sexual undoing by her abusers (Jer 13:26).

Acutely familiar with the culture's assumptions about female sexuality and a husband's rights over his wife, the prophet sought rhetoric that would draw a direct parallel between a wife's shameless, loose conduct (Judah's sin of rebellion and idolatry) and the "justifiable" measures a dishonored husband takes to punish his wife and bring her back into line (the disaster God was preparing to unleash upon Judah and Jerusalem). Here is an instance where poetry can go awry. Sometimes a metaphor raises more questions than it answers, creates more problems than it solves, oppresses as much as it empowers. Like a woman raped and ravaged by an intimate assailant, Judah will come to know shame and humiliation from the hand of the one she betrayed. Men are expected to be shocked at hearing themselves compared to a ravaged woman, but they get the inference about power and subjugation. Beyond the account about wives leading their husbands into idolatry, there is little talk about Jeremiah's interactions directly with women. He claimed that his decision to not take a wife was God's choice (Jer 16:2).

But women hearing God's wrath compared to rape and assault will probably respond with disgust or curiosity (or a combination of the two). Disgust makes women throw up their hands and walk away at this poem's hopelessly androcentric worldview. That's one option. But that response doesn't change things. It leaves the status quo unexamined and unchanged. Women readers can choose to hold their disgust at bay long enough to stay with the poetry and press certain questions: What is in the image of a naked, mangled female body that grips the religious imagination? What does God's love for God's people and claim upon them have to do with the power husbands in patriarchal cultures have over their wives? What does a loving God have in common with a jealous, violent husband who stalks his wife and attacks her? These are the kinds of questions that touch on the ethics of interpretation. We see here that patriarchy makes connections between women's bodies and men's fantasies where there are none intrinsically. (The one image from male sexuality the prophet draws from, "Remove the foreskins of your heart" [4:4], makes no connection with power and violence, but with remorse and contrition instead.) Choosing to face the language of female sexuality in Jeremiah and to face the consequences of a faith that has come down to us through the lens of patriarchy, can be empowering. Facing reality forces readers to speak up about the ways in which religious texts distort reality, re-inscribe sexual abuse, force connections where there are none, and hide behind language about authority to maintain the status quo.

Finally, exactly who does Jeremiah lay the blame upon for Judah's crimes against God? Who is guilty? Every citizen? Are the poor as much to blame as the rich? Are women and children to be punished alongside men? Eventually, every theologian has to answer the question "What kind of God metes out punishment by the slaughter of innocents?" If it were left up to Jeremiah, the poor (e.g., translate the marginalized, the forgotten, the voiceless, and the invisible citizens) would be excused (Jer 5:4). But Jeremiah is forced to conclude that everyone, from the least to the greatest, is guilty (Jer 6:6) and will be forced to suffer. This sounds curiously like the reasoning of the ruling class who deprive the poor when it is time to divide up the riches but conscripts them in when time comes to distribute the burden.

Much of the prophet's preaching was directed at the public sphere of policy making—the policies and preachments of kings, priests, scribes, the ruling elite, merchants, and other prophets. Jeremiah's audience was male, those who had a certain relationship to power and decision making could appreciate some of the assumptions about rights, duty, power, violence, shame and honor embedded in such imagery. The bulk of his preaching was directed at those whose social, economic, political, and religious rankling placed Judah at risk abroad. But in the end, his belief in corporate responsibility would force him to conclude that everyone is guilty, from the least to the greatest. Does that mean that no citizen is innocent,—that everyone is accountable, when her country is guilty of crimes against another? Jeremiah certainly thought so. And sometimes so do I. Like shareholders who share in their companies' profits (however ill-gotten), like trust fund heirs who share in the wealth accumulated (however unjustly) by their benefactors, and like lottery winners who break the bank at the luck of a draw (however much was squandered in the process of getting the lucky ticket), we sue for our right to share in the riches. We must also be willing to suffer being sued (or made to pay) for our share of responsibility in the evil, wickedness, and wrongdoing that it may have taken to amass such wealth.

Temple Sermon: "Remember Shiloh"—Jer 7 and 26

The oracles associated with Jeremiah's famous "Temple Sermon" are found in chapter 7, with a narrative version of the infamous event located in chapter 26. We are told in the latter chapter that the dating for this event was the beginning of Jehoiakim's reign (609 B.C.E.). As a result of that sermon, Jeremiah was put on trial for his life. Every nation has its share of national symbols that (are supposed to) have the effect of stirring up pride, patriotism, and collective consciousness. The fact that every Judean monarch could trace his lineage directly back to David was one such cherished symbol for Judah. The notion that Zion (another name for Jerusalem) was the very city of God conjured up feelings of safety in the hearts of its citizens. The glorious sight of Solomon's Temple in the center of the city, along with its cult designed to fortify its grandeur, was breathtaking enough to reinforce notions of Jerusalem as the dwelling place of God.

But Jeremiah positioned himself outside the gates of the Temple to break the public calm as worshipers streamed in and out the Temple for worship. He insisted that having the Temple was no substitute for keeping the Torah, eschewing idolatry, showing justice to the widow and orphan, and worshiping God with one's whole heart. "Remember Shiloh!" he shouted as they hurried along with their pious expressions.

Shiloh too was a center of worship, and it was not spared. Worshippers were incensed as worshipers are wont to be when they have to put up with prophets standing up in their pulpits breathing threats and damnation. No one comes to church to hear sermons titled, "You're the Problem." People want to hear about pleasant things from their pulpit, like grace, love, mercy, peace, joy, forgiveness, kindness, and heaven. If the preacher must talk about sin, certainly let it be someone else's sin. But when it is their sin under the microscope this week, their favorite president that is being criticized in the sermon, their beloved country under indictment, their sense of security (*shalôm*) that is under threat, a prophet must be prepared for retaliation. Small wonder that priests and other prophets were the first to bring charges against Jeremiah (26:10-11). It reminds one of the criticism of white clergymen in Birmingham that led Martin Luther King, Jr. to write his "Letter from a Birmingham Jail." Calling everyone a whore and a sinner is one thing but threats against the Temple (read: "church," "ministry" "other ministers") were threats against their livelihood and positions. The warnings threatetned Jeremiah's own livelihood as well. You know you are likely to be in the presence of a true prophet when, if what he or she is preaching is true, he or she has as much (if not more) to lose as everyone else.

A circle of women, wives in particular, are singled out both here in the Temple Sermon in Jeremiah 7 and again in Jeremiah 44 for their willful refusal to cease and desist from certain idolatrous practices. Jeremiah accuses the women of engaging in rituals that make clear their devotion to the Queen of Heaven (44:15-25; cf. 7:18). Some believe the "Queen of Heaven" is a reference to the Mesopotamian astral goddess Ishtar who was probably introduced into the culture during Assyrian rule. Others believe it is a reference to Ashtoreth/Astarte, an equivalent Canaanite goddess recognized for her powers over fertility and war. Judean women are guilty of idolatry, Jeremiah insists, and their husbands of failing to control their wives (44:20-23, 26-30). The women saw things differently and do not mind saying so. Reality does not add up, they say in essence. Disaster did not follow disobedience and lack of covenant loyalty to the God of Israel. Disaster followed upon the heels of the reforms Josiah instituted which criminalized performing rituals to any God other than Yahweh. Disaster may have been averted had their rituals not been criminalized. This is one of those stories that shows that women were as much on the margins of the cult and worship in Israel as they generally were on the margins of power in the society (Patrick Miller, 2001, 638). What remains unclear is whether the women saw what they were doing as exchanging worship of Yahweh with worship of the Queen of Heaven, or proposing a balance in the religious realm similar to the one found throughout nature that complemented worship of Yahweh (a male god) with worship of the Queen of Heaven (a female goddess). Whichever was the case, Jeremiah would never be able to see things from the women's point of view. Not (just) because he was sexist. He was wholeheartedly devoted to Yahweh, the one God, and could not think of placing any other God before or beside Yahweh: "Has a nation changed its gods even though they are no gods? But my people have changed their glory for something that does not profit" (Jer 2:11).

Lamentations: "My Head, A Fountain of Tears" Jer 11:18-12:6; 15:10-21; 17:14-18; 18:18-23; 20:7-13

Grief, anguish and weeping permeate Jeremiah's prophecy. Women are called upon to lead the people in weeping over the nation's disaster (9:17-19). Bereft of her offspring, Rachel weeps inconsolably (31:15). Even the earth and its creatures shed tears at sight of the heap of ruins that is now Jerusalem (9:10). How can the prophet be expected to contain his own emotions in the face of all this trauma? Poems referred to alternately by scholars as "Jeremiah's confessions" or "Jeremiah's laments" portray him as a prophet besieged by anguishand loneliness are scattered throughout the book. It is this material that lends weight to his image as "The Weeping Prophet." It is quite possible, as some have supposed, that the reason this material was included among his oracles was to enhance his reputation as a true prophet who stood in the tradition of the prophet *sans pareil* Moses. Neither sought the prophetic office, and both suffered greatly for their obedience. But there is another way to make use of this material thousands of years later when the matter of Jeremiah's calling is taken for granted. When we encounter the oracles of weeping and gnashing of the teeth in the book we are reminded of the anguish God feels watching the rebellious actions Judah exhibits (5:9, 29) leading up to her destruction in 587 B.C.E. and the grief God feels in the face of her destruction and its aftermath (8:18). Many times it's not quite clear who is weeping: the prophet or the inhabitants or God. In two poems the figures of God and Jeremiah converge and remain indistinguishable (8:18-21; 9:1-3). Elsewhere the image of God alone lamenting is unforgettable (12:7-13). The anthropomorphic imagery of a grieving God, an anguishing God, a God at her wits' end reminds us that God is not immune to human suffering and human need. The prophet's pain is God's pain. After all, from the beginning God promised "I am with you . . . " (1:8, 19; 7:7). The undignified spectacle of God weeping must have further complicated Jeremiah's reputation as a prophet worth hearing. Sympathy is not simply what you want when you are being ravaged by pain. You want relief, vindication, healing, deliverance. "Is the Lord not in Zion?" (8:19) they wanted to know when the Babylonians breached the city

walls. The God they sought was the God of war, battle, retribution, and vindication. In other words, "Where is God?" This is a question African Americans have lots of experience asking in their long and torturous history as exiles on these North American shores. Prophet after prophet has risen up and tried to answer the question for each new generation of black people born in this country who have had to face racism in its mutations over the centuries. Those prophets are to be commended for their efforts. But what they had to say has all but been forgotten. It is the music of African Americans that has had the most lasting impression: the slave songs, the blues, the spirituals, the jazz, the rhythm and blues tunes, the protest songs, the rap music, the gospel music that have endured as generation after generation has sought solace in the face of such unanswerable questions as "Where is God?" "How Are We To Make It?" "Now what?" "How long?" "What's Going on?" "Where is the Love?" or "Does God Care?" In the dominant culture, no tears, no groaning, no public wailing is allowed. Real men do not cry. I have always been fascinated with the composure fathers and husbands have been known to exhibit in television interviews within hours of a son's murder, a daughter's kidnap, a wife's plane going down in flames, the loss of a long held job that is being outsourced to some place in India. Since when did numbness get equated with strength? Jeremiah cries on behalf of every man unable to cry.

A few weeks after the September 11 tragedy a late night CNN talk show celebrity hosted a panel of religious experts from a wide range of religious traditions around the question, "September 11: Where Was God?" Six prominent religious leaders from a wide range of religious perspectives (Christian, Muslim, Jew, New Age, Buddhist) were invited to come discuss the topics of God, suffering and evil. Six religious leaders, each of them men. Where were the women panelists? Even Jeremiah knew the importance of enlisting women's help when the task is to help audiences connect with the pathos of our loss and comprehend the depth of our own culpability. After all, women are most familiar with weeping and grief. Women banding together in circles professionally or spontaneously keening and mourning over their dead is a familiar sight in almost all parts of the world. A television panel being watched by millions of people may not be the place to begin keening over the dead if you are a woman who has been invited on the panel, but it is as good a place as any to say that some things are about the heart and not just the mind. After all, it is usually the empire's inability to feel, care, or empathize with the pain of their subjects—the outcries of those they have colonized, the hunger of those they have profited from—that makes them vulnerable to desperate acts of opposing it. Ours is a world where grief is treason, a failure of nerve, a flaw in leadership, says Walter Brueggemann (1986, 18). When God weeps, the awful distance and difference between God and people is bridged. Simone Weil wrote, "The love of our neighbor in all its fullness means being able to say to him (or her) 'What are you going through?'" (1951, 126). When we are able to empathize with the fears, tears, and pain of those we have kept at arm's length—the shopkeeper with eight mouths to feed weeping over his business that has been blown to smithereens, the little girl keening over her grandfather's body as it lay in a heap on the Gaza banks, the young mother in the Philippines with fingers gnarled from sewing buttons on jeans that will be sold in the US at a price twice her monthly wage—the awful distance between us will be shortened. Tears are a bridge, sometimes providing the shortest distance between you and the stranger.

Conflict and Controversy (26:1–29:32): Whom to Believe?

Whereas the laments and judgment speeches of chapters 2–25 let us in on the internal world of the prophet, his ire and his anguish, this next block of material lets us in with greater detail on some of the external events that prompted his ire and precipitated his anguish.

Conflict

Evidently Jeremiah was not the only prophet preaching in Jerusalem. The oracles found in the book of Habakkuk suggest that the ministries of the minor prophet and major prophet overlapped, though neither gives any indication in the contents of the books that either was aware of the other. But one prophet in particular is remembered, probably because his preaching stood in direct opposition to that of Jeremiah. His name is Hannaniah ben Azzur (Jer 28:1-17).

In the fourth year of Zedekiah, ambassadors from the surrounding nations convened in Jerusalem to deliberate with the King of Judah concerning a common uprising against the Babylonian king. Hannaniah the prophet was convinced that within two years there would be a speedy return of Jehoiachin and his fellow exiles as well as the return of the Temple vessels which had been carried off by Nebuchadnezzar. This was a time of terrible uncertainty. People were torn thinking, "What shall I believe?" Even Zedekiah himself vacillated from one policy to another. The supreme need of the hour was that someone might know the facts and declare them, and thus give the people an indication of the line of action to take. Jeremiah upbraided prophets, priests, and kings for their obstinacy, their double mindedness, their simply not knowing God as they should and thus leaving themselves vulnerable to the myth-making of partisan fanatics. Sound bites, spins, stomp speeches, classified memos, speeches spoken from the Rose Garden (the official White House backdrop for many important speeches by the President of the United States) are the contrivances of the royal machinery intended to say a lot, but tell as little (truth) as possible. Prophets who benefit from the royal payroll can not afford to speak truth (6:14; 8:11; ch. 28). Pashur the priest imprisons Jeremiah in the Temple for his frightful pronouncements (20:1-6). King Jehoiakim builds a grand palace in the hopes of communicating to all around that despite appearances security and prosperity prevail, while ignoring the cause of the poor and needy (22: 13-17). Jeremiah writes a letter to those in exile warning them against trusting the promises of false prophets who stir their hearts into believing that a speedy return to Jerusalem, was in view. He urges them to settle in for the long haul; and a respondent writes a disgruntled letters to the officials back in Jerusalem accusing Jeremiah of misleading people with his doomsday messages (ch. 29). Things get so bad that when Jeremiah shows up at the Temple with a yoke of wood around his neck urging the ambassadors, king, and people to submit voluntarily to the Babylonian power, Hannaniah stepped up and tore the yoke from Jeremiah's shoulders and repeated his own prophecy of speedy deliverance. Well, what did Jeremiah do? "But Jeremiah the prophet went his way" (Jer 28:11). What else can any of us do when we are outgunned by the official mythmakers? It was not his problem; it was God's problem. It was up to God to defend God's prophet and God's prophecy. It always is, which is a good thing to remember when it is you against them. If God does not vindicate your interpretation of things —well, then you have lost the battle anyway.

Despite appearances, when it comes to prophets and their preaching, it is never easy to tell true ones from false ones—not back then and not now. The truth is not revealed from a prophet's behavior, from his mannerisms, from his smooth talk, nor the grandeur of the hall from which she preaches; the truth is not even revealed from the very words of the prophet. The test of truth—if any at all— is history. History winnows out the truth from deceit. In the meantime, we live in the uncertainty and gamble on what our hearts tell us is the word of God, and pray that if we are wrong then may God have mercy on us all. Jeremiah earned his place in the canon because history proved him right—not because anyone believed him at the time. In the meantime, he preached God's word as he understood it. And he died without the benefit of seeing his suffering vindicated. This is what makes his book important to people living in colonized circumstances who know first hand that there are no easy answers. That's reality.

Book of Consolations
(30:1–33:26)

These four chapters pick up the theme of the possibility of reconciling with God scattered throughout the book and carries them through with a consistency of purpose. The centerpiece of this collection is Jeremiah 31:31-34.

A prophet can go insane trying to keep straight her twin impossible tasks, to destroy and overthrow on the one hand, and to build and plant on the other hand. We have seen already that there are more than enough oracles in the book to warrant seeing in the prophecy the rationale for God's wrath and judgment and the model for weeping and grieving in the face of hopelessness. But what to make of the oracles that fall within 30:1–33:26 which have come to be known alternately as *the book of consolations* and *the little book of hope*? Either these oracles are clear evidence of the hand of an exilic editor tampering with the prophet's legacy and trying to make the prophet out to be more hopeful than history and circumstances allowed him to be; or the legacy of Jeremiah refused to be pigeonholed.

Survival Literature is what such books have come to be referred to. They are written to explain how and why people find themselves in these situations and, once in the environment, how they manage to survive whole. Rather than trivializing pain or interpreting it away they face it squarely. That was Jeremiah's legacy to the gôla (exiled) community living decades after him. There is no need, as some interpreters have done, to debate whether these oracles date back to the prophet. Survivors of catastrophic events, unspeakable horror, prolonged suffering will tell you that you hope, or you die—first your will, and then your flesh.

How does a Christian (or any person of faith) live in an empire? Especially when that empire claims the blessing of God to govern? How does one continue to believe in God when deceit, injustice, avarice, abuse of power, gluttony, war, and a lack of moral conscious are inherent to life in the empire?

One must, like Jeremiah, be able to see beyond destruction to newness, and beyond despair to gloriously fresh possibilities. The despair among the poor (which those in power thrive on), says: "The future looks like the present. God's purposes will not get accomplished, so why bother?" The cynicism that keeps capitalism going says: "God's will will come through, but not for a long, long time . . . so I'd better cut a deal and get by the best I can." What does hope say? Hope says, "Pain is not forever. Wounds heal. Death does not have the final word." Hope is possible because for Jeremiah judgment was never an end in itself. It was the means for bringing God's people into a new and more lasting relationship with the divine. The old order passes away, making way for a new order to rise up from out of the ashes. This is possible because our pain is God's pain and God's pain is our pain. And despite what was uttered when you were in the throes of pain "My hurt is incurable, my wound is grievous. Nothing will heal this pain" (30: 12, 13), it is possible to begin anew with God, as though it was the first time being introduced to God.

One does not have to use religion to escape colonized reality and to spiritualize the new life God promises God's people. The promise to the *gôla* scattered throughout the diaspora that there will be of festive, exuberant, indulgent homecoming celebration (31: 10-14) is rooted into the very real and material world of human existence in time and space. The exiles clung to the dream of one day returning to their homeland, just as the Jews cling to the belief that they have a right to occupy a homeland that was theirs for centuries, and the Palestinians cling to the hope of reclaiming what was taken from them by superpowers around a table decades ago. Not surprisingly—home—whether it's going home or coming home, is a recurring theme in African American religious music and preaching. Because centuries have passed since we were brought to these shores, and we are quite possibly far more American now than we are African, we have no homeland to call our own. Home is wherever God is, if not over here (on this side of human history) then over there (on the other side of human history).

CONCLUSION

It's certainly the case that the book of Jeremiah expects too much of its readers. Readers of the book are expected to be able to look beyond one-dimensional theology to a God who is set upon avenging wrong when a nation sins and restoring the health of that nation when it has been duly punished. Curses and praise, judgment speeches and salvation oracles, weeping and singing stand side by side without apology. Similarly, deciding whom in Jeremiah to identify with and where one's context fits best is demanding work. It is not easy; it is certainly not a comfortable task. Is my context that of Babylon, the megalomaniacal empire, or Judah, the tiny kingdom desperately grabbing for power out of its own driving insecurity and fear? Am I Jeremiah the activist, fighting and complaining at the same time? Or am I like the citizens of Judah: clueless as to what the fuss is all about? Where do I stand in the prophet's

preaching? Am I more Babylonian than I am a Judean, more elitist and obstinate in my thinking than compassionate and caring? Do I see the poor and marginalized, or am I too committed to putting distance between anything or anyone that reminds me that for the things I have accumulated someone was made to suffer? Is there anything Jeremiah-like in my commitments? These are the questions each reader must ask for herself at every turn of the book's pages.

Jeremiah puts us on edge with ourselves. We read his oracles and cannot always be sure when God is speaking or when the prophet is speaking. We do not know for sure if we are like the headstrong and lascivious wife in his poems or the basket of bad figs hopelessly condemned to death. And perhaps all of this is as it should be. We are to remain on edge and trust God. There are no happy endings in the book, because history remains open. There is still a chance that the land might repent. The prophet dies in exile in Egypt without seeing his words vindicated. He leaves us a legacy of what it means to speak into the silence and say what must be said. "We must re-vision Christian faith as a combative, argumentative, and emancipatory" practice that seeks "the well-being of all," argues Elisabeth Schüssler Fiorenza (1992, 163).

Jeremiah insists that we all have a stake in what happens to our country. We do not have to have degrees from the illustrious Kennedy School of Government or the Wharton School of Business to have an opinion about the moral future of our country. For too long we have left it up to the so-called experts. We have a duty to speak, to dissent, and to demand a better case for compromising our most fundamental principles as Christians and citizens than has thus far been made. As citizens we must demand a better excuse than fear and greed. We must love this world too much to see countries complicit in their own worst stereotypes. Right after September 11 2001, Americans asked in much anguish,

"Why do they hate us?" If we persist in making war the first rather than the last option, we will soon find out. The answer will be clear.

The book of Jeremiah says much about the working of God in human history. When in Jeremiah 30–33 he envisions a new beginning and a new covenant initiated by God, he did not imagine God as just touching up the canvas. He imagined God painting a different picture of life with a completely new canvas. Hope was the brightest color applied to the canvas (Jer 31:31-34). The goal of the covenant was the formation of a new completely different world order, one that starts with a new humanity where "I will be their God, and they will be my people." God is one who so empathizes with the world as to identify with broken societies, exiled communities, tortured victims and lands laid waste. We must return again and again to the book of Jeremiah because he reminds us of what is so unimaginable at times—that out of ruin can come resurrection and out of an evil heart can come compassion and empathy for the Other.

BIBLIOGRAPHY

Bauer, Angela. *Gender in the Book of Jeremiah:* New York: Peter Lang, 1999. *A Feminist-Literary Reading.* Studies in Biblical Literature 5.

Brueggemann, Walter. *Hopeful Imagination: Prophetic Voices in Exile.* Philadelphia: Fortress, 1986.

Dubbik, Joep. "Jeremiah: Hero of Faith or Defeatist? Concerning the Place and Function of Jeremiah 20:14-18" *JSOT* 86 (1999): 67-84.

Heschel, Abraham J. *The Prophets.* Perennial Classics. New York: Perennial, 2001.

King, Martin Luther, Jr. "I Have A Dream" Speech (1963). Online: http://usinfo.state.gov/usa/infousa/facts/democrac/38.htm. Distribution statement: Accepted as part of the Douglass Archives of American Public Address (http://douglass.speech.nwu.edu) May 26, 1999. Prepared by D. Oetting http://nonce.com/oetting).

"Letter from Birmingham Jail" April 16, 1963. Quoted from http://almaz.com/nobel/peace/MLK-jail.html.

Miller, Patrick D. "The Book of Jeremiah" in *The New Interpreter's Dictionary of the Bible* (Nashville: Abingdon, 2001) pages 553-936.

O'Connor, Kathleen. "Jeremiah." Pages 169-177 in *The Women's Bible Commentary.* Edited by Sharon Ringe and Carol Newsom. Louisville: Westminster John Knox, 1992.

Schüssler Fiorenza, Elisabeth. *But She Said.* Boston: Beacon, 1992.

Sharp, Carolyn. "The Call of Jeremiah and Diaspora Politics," *JBL* 119/3 (2000): 421-438.

Weems, Renita. J. *Battered Love: Marriage, Sex, and Violence in the Hebrew Prophets.* (Minneapolis: Fortress, 1995).

"Huldah, the Prophet: Reading a (Deuteronomistic) Woman's Identity." Pages 321-340 in *A God So Near: Essays in Honor of Patrick D. Miller.* Edited by Brent A. Strawn and Nancy R. Bowen. Winona Like, Ind.: Eisenbrauns, 2003.

"Reading Her Way Through the Struggle: African American Women and the Bible." Pages 57-77 in *Stony the Road We Trod.* Edited by Cain Hope Felder. Minneapolis: Fortress, 1991.

Weil, Simone, *Waiting for God.* Translated by Emma Gruafurd. New York: Putnam, 1951.

LAMENTATIONS

Archie Chi Chung Lee

Chung Chi College, The Chinese University Of Hong Kong, China

LIFE CONTEXT OF THE INTERPRETATION

My Life Context

It is generally held that Asian people have been cursed with suffering and poverty that sharply contrasts with the blessed and rich traditions of religiosity and spirituality. Yet, most of the world's great living religions have their roots in Asia. There is also no denying the painful history of the common people in South, Southeast, and East Asia. The oppressed and marginalized poor in these regions bear witness to this terrible human plight. Their voices echo in both written and oral folk literature. Living memories of many family catastrophes, social tragedies, or national calamities are still fresh and hurting for our wounded generation. These experiences have been inscribed on the theological agendas of Dalit theology (India), Homeland Theology (Taiwan), Theology of Struggle (The Philippines), and Minjung Theology (Korea), to cite just a few examples. The aboriginals and minority nationals in various Asian countries (Indonesia, East Malaysia, Myanmar, Northern Thailand, Taiwan, Mainland China, etc.) who are victims of oppression and injustice are still struggling to have their voices heard.

Humiliating defeats in war, loss of geographical integrity, deprivation of human dignity, and the forced surrender of independence in the face of Western imperialism constitute my context. With the exception of Thailand and Japan, colonization is a shared experience among the Asian countries. Furthermore, the invasive and destructive forces of cultural imperialistic ideology and economic exploitation are pervasive and ongoing in much of Asia.

The recent tragedy of the 1989 Tiananmen Square Massacre in China exemplifies the socio-political complexities of national calamities in Asia. For the Chinese people, this event is part of an unresolved entanglement of fate and destiny that affects the coming decades. Young lives were sacrificed in the crackdown on the pro-democracy, anti-corruption student movement. The ruling power condemned the demonstration as "counter-revolutionary turmoil." More than 160 families that had loved ones killed in the massacre publicly petitioned on behalf of their lost children for justice and vindication.

The mothers from these families who lost their children have established the Tiananmen Mothers' Campaign under the leadership of Ding Zilin, whose seventeen-year-old son was one of the first and youngest killed in Tiananmen. After fourteen bitter years the authorities still deny these legitimate mourners and justified lamenters the possibility of public mourning and remembrance of the dead. The mothers demand the publication of a detailed list of the names of the dead and injured. The mourners' rightful and valid quests for a listening ear are articulated in songs, poems, testimonies, and declarations collected in publications and on the Internet.

Archie Chi Chung Lee is a professor of Hebrew Bible and a specialist of cross-textual hermeneutics, especially Chinese text and the post-exilic biblical tradition. He is the author of several books including *A Commentary on the Book of Koheleth* (in Chinese, 1990); *Doing Theology with Asian Resources: Ten Years in the Formation of Living Theology in Asia (1993, ed.); and Interpretation of the Megilloth* (in Chinese, 2003); as well as numerous articles in academic journals.

Cross-Textual Reading in Asian Biblical Hermeneutics

The dynamics of texts and their contexts have gained currency as an interpretative paradigm in recent theology and biblical studies. Most scholars are familiar with this paradigm and assume that texts not only have their own contexts but also must be interpreted in terms of this original context. In addition, the reader's context also contributes to the reading process. The recognition of the impact of language, history, cultural background, and socio-political settings on textual interpretation is beyond dispute.

Asian biblical hermeneutics have never ignored the importance of context. But Asia should not be regarded as merely a context in which the Bible is to be understood and applied, as if the Asian texts and the undeniably rich, multi-textual traditions of Asian countries have nothing to offer. The contextual approach often, though not necessarily intentionally, relegates Asia, its texts, and traditions to a subordinate role. They are considered mostly in order to facilitate the communication of the gospel, and therefore denied any real substance and content. In such cases, one presupposes a dual concept of revelation, giving theological currency to the so-called specific and final revelation over and against an ongoing general revelation.

The cross-textual approach used here intends to rectify this problem in contextual hermeneutics (Lee 1993). While the Bible and its subsequent readings grow out of various contexts, we cannot overlook the fact that other texts contributed and continue to contribute to the formation of the canon and to enrich its interpretation. First, the Bible and its traditions of interpretation cannot be imagined without the ancient Near Eastern (West Asian) cuneiform tablets, Greco-Roman classics, Rabbinic traditions, Latin literature, and even Muslim writings. Furthermore, from the perspective of cross-textual interpretation, the reader's socio-political situation is regarded as a social text that participates in the process of interpretation. It is with this crossing between texts that I read Lamentations. Both lament literature from Chinese classical literature and the lived experiences of Chinese in mainland China and Hong Kong constitute the texts to be read along with Lamentations. Being nurtured by Chinese cultural texts, I am framed by the ethos and pathos of Chinese culture, which provides the framework for the comprehension and articulation of my life experiences. My cross-textual reading of Lamentations tries to make sense of both contemporary human suffering and the responses to tragedy captured in Chinese cultural texts. In brief, cross-textual interpretation takes seriously the worlds of the two literary texts: the world of the Chinese cultural texts and the world of the biblical text, Lamentations. The readers' role is crucial. By actively engaging the world of the text, readers take a strategic position to gaze at life with a much wider horizon, merging these two cultural worlds. This fused horizon will enhance the understanding of the familiar native text (the cultural texts) and of the Bible, an acquired text from West Asia, which is itself embedded in diverse interpretations and entangled with the long and rich history of Christianity.

CONTEXTUAL COMMENT

Reading Lamentations and Chinese Laments Cross-Textually

The feelings of hurt and pain and, above all, the desire to pursue life despite constant threats of death are inscribed in the various classical and contemporary writings of Asian people. These are the texts that I read with the biblical book of Lamentations. More specifically, in this commentary, I refer to both Chinese cultural and social texts. My chosen cultural texts are the Chinese laments in the *Book of Poetry* (*Shijing,* eleventh to seventh centuries B.C.E.), the *Book of the South* (*Chu Ci,* fourth century B.C.E.), and *The Lament for the South (Ai Jiangnan Fu)* by Yu Xin (513-81 C.E.). My chosen social text is the Tiananmen Square Student Movement of 1989 and the laments of the Tiananmen mothers after the massacre.

Jerusalem's destruction in 586 B.C.E. is no doubt a watershed in the religion of Israel. It exerts a tremendous impact not only on the subsequent development of faith in YHWH, but also on the appropriation of Israelite faith traditions by later generations. The exilic experience of suffering constitutes the essential core of the theology of humanity in biblical faith.

The five poems in Lamentations are not arranged in historical or logical sequence. In terms of literary form, the first four chapters are acrostic compositions, with a stanza for each of the twenty-two letters of the Hebrew alphabet. Though not strictly acrostic, chapter 5 has twenty-two verses, which formally resembles an acrostic poem.

Lamentations 1–2

Lamentations 1 and 2 must be seen together as related, twin chapters. The two poems are similar in acrostic form, but also in emotional intensity and dramatic characteristics. The different voices represent speakers who express their lament in turn, and their voices weave together very artistically. The differences in the two chapters are nevertheless striking. The ruined capital city of Jerusalem, the city of God, is personified as a devastated, widowed mother in chapter 1. Her body is violently battered (1:15). Her present condition is contrasted with her former status as a graceful princess. She has been rendered lowly and lonely (1:1-2). Here femininity is nationalized and motherhood politicized, just as in the student demonstrations at Tiananmen Square, where Mother China was nationalized and politicized. The students adopted this metaphor to rebuke the predominantly male leadership, which failed (and continues to fail) to care for the people's suffering and falls short of showing mercy to the children of China. Mother China becomes weak and suffers humiliation herself. Her children are starving. And a request for Mother China's help only ends in violent execution.

I Want Mother

Why do you shed tears?
Because Mother is critically ill.
Why are you so happy?
Because people of the whole nation
    are helping.
Mother is saved; your esteemed body
    is safe.
Mother in good health, loves her
    children.
I want our Mother
Because she gives love to us,
Brings warmth to humankind.
I love my Mother
Because Mother raised us into
    adulthood,
Brought us to the path of brightness.
Bless our Mother Country:
Good health, live long to millions
    of years.
Long live Mother Country! Long live
    democracy and freedom!
*(Wu and Yang 1999, 104. A poem copied
from a poster at Tiananmen Square on
May 25, 1989, signed "A Student of the
Capital." All poems cited from Tiananmen below are rendered into English by
the author.)*

As an abandoned widow, Zion laments the death of her people at the hands of the invading enemy. God is conceived as the divine power that is responsible for causing the present suffering. That God inflicts pain and authorizes destruction on God's own people is a prominent theme (1:1-10). But the poet does not ignore or condone the sins of the people. Lamentations 1:5 illustrates the poet's ambiguity regarding the agency of and motivation for destruction. The cruel enemy, the sins of the people, and God are all to some degree responsible.

The mother's plight in chapter 2 is that of a natural human mother who laments the tragic loss of her children. But the poet also describes God as the absolute agent of destruction bringing every single act of destruction to the city, the temple, its altar, the palace, and the city's residents. Violence is everywhere and is total (2:1-10). God has become a merciless enemy: "Zion's role as the object (even victim) of God's attack stands out in the Hebrew as it is marked by a special (untranslatable) Hebrew particle that identifies definite direct objects" (Dobbs-Allsopp 2002, 79). God is unmistakably the subject of twenty-nine out of the first thirty-one verbal forms (Dobbs-Allsopp 82). The consequence of the fierce and outrageous divine rampage against the city is best under-scored by the images of the starving infants and babies (2:11-12). The shift from the third person singular description of God's attack in 2:1-10 to the first person singular emotional outbreak in 2:11-22 indicates the change in point of view from the narrator/poet to the real physical mother's grief (vv. 11, 12, 20, 22). "Those whom I bore and reared my enemy has destroyed" (v. 22) indicates a mother's deep despair at the death of her children. Poems from the Tiananmen Square student demonstrations in 1989 take up this metaphor in laments. The Tiananmen Square poets develop this metaphor in personifica-tion and mother-child imagery.

Crying Over Child: To the Child Killed by Nine Gun Shots

1. Child, all that you love to eat
   I have lain,
   Here they come:
   Cakes with fillings,
   Shredded meat with bean sprouts.
   Mum was thrift, what you wanted
       to eat
   Would not always be provided.
   Child, you'd better take
   A few bites.
   Having eaten these, you'd then
   Remember your Mama.

2. Child, all through the night Mum
       has sewn
   For you a white cloth.
   Though the breeze of spring has
       just gone,
   Summer's just come;
   But
   You have to go afar,
   You will never return

to see your Mama.
Child, anyhow,
Put it on.
Put it on, you'd think about Mama.

3. Last night
   Mum heard gunshots. In the blaze
   Unarmed civilians,
   Fallen one after the other.
   Then they brought you
   Back in a stretcher.
   At that time
   You could no longer take a glance
   At your Mum.
   Just then you were still vivacious!
   Toward Mum, you could still make
       funny faces.
   How come you've nine gun wounds in
       your body?
   Blood gushing out
   All the way along the High Street
   To the courtyard!

4. They said you were a rioter,
   They said
   You'd sabotage the 20-million-lives-
       built great palace.
Nevertheless
Mum knows
You were just a naïve child
Pulling Mum's hand yesterday
Urged Mum to take you to the park.
(*Dagong Bao*, a Hong Kong newspaper, June 18, 1989)

Another poem describes the rising of the souls of those who were crushed to death. The souls address their mother in lament and bid them not to go to Tiananmen to look for them as the Square is deserted (one poem laments the vanishing of "the world's largest square," Wu and Yang, 52) and white terror reigns instead:

We can hear
Your cries
Mother, please don't
Go to the Square again to find us.
Here is white all over
Tents, banners,
Commander's outpost, boardcast station

All have been demolished
Teachers, classmates and friends
All gone. Gun smoke disperses
Thousands of lives
Have turned into ashes with a blink of the
    eyes.
*(Hong Kong Singtao Evening Post, June
11, 1989)*

One better understands Lamentations 2:12
after reading it in light of the Chinese political lament. The Chinese text presents an
event closer to our experience and it helps to
expand our imagination on the biblical text:

They cry to their mothers,
"Where is bread and wine?"
as they faint like the wounded
in the streets of the city,
as their life is poured out
on their mothers' bosom. (Lam 2:12)

The realities of hunger, grief, and death
dominate the Tiananmen poetry. The feelings evoked by such realities are expressed
through the portrayal of a mother-child relationship:

Mama
I am hungry, but I cannot eat.
Mama, I am not afraid
If I die, I am afraid the blood of China
    turns cold.
Mama, we are not rioters
We cry out with our lives. (Wu and Yang,
    90)

These poems commonly convey the
agony of being wrongly accused of anti-rev-
olutionary activity and instigating riots.
"Mama! We Have Not Done Anything
Wrong" is a title of a poem in which a
lamenter begs his or her mother to believe in
him or her: "Even the wide and deep valleys
will express their prudence in echoing our
cry" (Wu and Yang, 38).

Finally, Lamentations 1 and 2 embody a
prayer of lament to God and a petition for
divine response: "Look, O LORD, and see"
(1:11; 2:20), "O LORD, look at my affliction"
(1:9), and "See, O LORD, how distressed I

am" (1:20). This very petition is significant
because the lamenters pour out their sorrow,
anger, and protest in order to force God to
respond.

A careful reader will note that the divine
is suppressed in these Chinese laments. The
poets only raise a cry for mercy to the
metaphorical Mother China, begging her to
look at their pain and suffering and to be
compassionate toward their agony (Wu and
Yang, 26-33).

Lamentations 3

"I *['ani]* am one who has seen affliction"
is how the speaker introduces himself and
reveals his identity in chapter 3. The man
uses an individual lament form to speak of
his personal plight at the hands of God (3:1-
18). This same narrator continues speaking
in the next two sections, asserting his hope
in God (3:19-24) and describing his basis for
such a hope (3:25-39). The poem then shifts
to a communal lament using the first personal plural "we," *nakhnu* (3:40-47). The
final supplications naturally draw the whole
lament to an appropriate end (3:48-66).

Many scholars defend the male-gendered
arrangement of Lamentations (Dobbs-Allsopp, 106-107). The common scholarly
assumption is that chapter 3 is a lament of
"the everyman" who not only counterbalances Zion's female voice but also transcends
his plight with trust and hope in God. Here
lies the exact problem of reading Lamentations through the perspective of our traditional gendered theological discourse. This
so-called center of Lamentations has attracted
much attention, questing for hope in the midst
of human distress and misery. While Widow
Zion in chapter 1 and the crying mother in
chapter 2 find no hope in lament, the "everyman" in chapter 3 is portrayed as a humble
confessor and a faithful man upon whom
God's salvation will be bestowed. To balance,
decenter, and de-emphasize chapter 3, my
commentary is brief.

Lamentations 4

This poem is also an acrostic but has only
two lines to each stanza (chs. 1–2 have three

stanzas per verse, and ch. 3 uses each of the 22 alphabets three times, but each verse has only one stanza). The poet presents the people's distress at Zion's destruction differently; he presents a survivor's third-person eyewitness report (vv.1-20) instead of a metaphorical personification and dramatic dialogue. This form reduces the intensity of the emotional outpouring. The last two verses contain a curse on Edom and a word of comfort for Zion. Edom's punishment will come while Israel's is complete and will never recur.

The community, represented in the first person plural "we," is heard in the recounting of the horrible experience of Jerusalem's invasion (Dobbs-Allsopp, 133-34). The poem begins by recounting the disaster experienced by the people, beginning with the plight of children and the suffering of innocent babies denied their mothers' milk (4:2-4). The famine causes untold suffering for the children. Even, the rich, used to plenty, experience the doom of hunger and poverty, as Zion's sin is greater than Sodom's (4:5-9). A ghastly horrific scene of cannibalism, the otherwise compassionate mothers eating their own children (4:10), captures the attention of most readers, ancient and contemporary. It dramatically encapsulates the sheer horror of Jerusalem's siege and subsequent fall. This passage highlights the desperate agony of a compassionate, loving mother driven, by starvation, to eat her own children.

The second section (4:11-16) begins and ends by portraying YHWH's fierce anger as the agent of the city's destruction. This literary frame underscores the role and importance of YHWH's anger.

As this commentary is being written, the new and deadly disease, SARS, threatens to be an international epidemic. Because it is so highly contagious, the disease severs physical contact between human beings. Both SARS patients and those suspected of having the disease are denied the right to be with loved ones when they so badly need support. Since not even family members are not allowed in the intensive care units, no one can visit and encourage the patients who desperately struggle with this painful, deadly disease. Many SARS victims die in total silence and isolation.

Emotionally upset, physically exhausted, and deeply terrified medical professionals have risked their lives to care for SARS patients. In order to protect their families and the public from catching SARS, they have been isolated as well: many have not been home for many weeks.

Despite the promotion of public solidarity and a concerted societal effort to fight against the disease, as witnessed in China, Taiwan, and Hong Kong, SARS has also led to caution and discrimination among human beings. Lamentations 4:15 echoes in our modern setting. In this very difficult verse the enemies directly address the people of Israel:

"Get away! Unclean" they call to them
"Get away! Don't touch"
"For they have gone away and must wander," they say.
"They shall no longer abide among nations." (Hillers 1992, 143)

Lamentations 5

Instead of closing with a positive theological affirmation or praise anticipating the reversal of Jerusalem's misfortune, Lamentations 5 presents an unresolved puzzle in Israel's faith. The long-awaited divine intervention and redemptive act do not appear; the hoped-for reversal does not occur; and the book closes without a hymn of thankful jubilation.

The open-endedness of the prayer in chapter 5 embodies a profound recognition of divine freedom and mystery that does not offer any guarantee but, at best, leaves readers on a hopeful note. This unimposing posture invites all persons to an ongoing participation and partnership in the unceasing quest for life in the midst of death. This uncertainty empowers those who are already deeply hurt by human existence; instead of threatening them, this ambiguity saves them from the deep abyss in which they could so readily plunge. The uneasy, perturbed mutter, "unless you have utterly rejected us, /

and are angry with us beyond measure" (5:22), highlights this ambiguity.

This final chapter facilitates intercultural dialogue and cross-textual enrichment. It truthfully portrays a human quest for meaning beyond the boundaries of the Judeo-Christian world of faith. No doubt, it is most significant that in the last part of Lamentations one has the privilege to address God: "Remember, O Lord, what has befallen us; look, and see our disgrace!" (5:1). The poet appeals to God's everlasting reign (5:19) and contrasts it with God's present abandonment of the people (5:20). It is hard to envision God's eternal rule alongside a view of God as one who abandons and totally rejects forever God's very own humanity (5:22). Yet, such a prayer of restoration and renewal is an invaluable human language that all sufferers have at their disposal.

Since time immemorial, lamentation has been an integral part of Chinese life. As the Chinese have struggled against atrocities throughout the centuries, and their lament literature has been a resource for the survivors. From the time of the Shang dynasty (1766–1027 B.C.E.), the Chinese have expressed their cries of agony and pain in poetry similar to laments in other cultures.

The Chinese politician and prominent poet Yu Xin (513–81 C.E.) was an ambassador to Western Wei in the north. Western Wei invaded his country, Liang, in the south, and destroyed the capital city, Jiangling, in 554. He was taken captive and remained in the foreign court for twenty-eight years until he died. His unfulfilled longing for his homeland fills all his writings. The most representative is *The Lament for the South,* which follows the model and continues the tradition of the ancient southern Chinese literary creation *The Songs of the South* (Chuci), attributed to Qu Yuan (343–277 B.C.E.), who was also exiled in a foreign land away from the same ruined capital city, Jiangling. Their shared reality of exile in a foreign land and empathy for the sufferings of the common people connects the two poets across some eight hundred years. They also recollected the glorious past and contrasted it with the cruel present of homelessness and deep sorrow. Both Qu Yuan and Yu Xin's laments speak from a survivor's perspective—the same perspective found in each poem in Lamentations (Dobbs–Allopp 46).

Though the confession of sin and the complaint against God, two characteristics of Lamentations and other biblical laments, do not appear in Yu Xin's lament, Xin assumes and acknowledges the will of Heaven. In Xin's *The Lament for the South,* the exclamation "How could Heaven have been so drunk?" attempts to show that the human situation has gone terribly wrong, beyond our normal comprehension. Yet Yu Xin rejects any basis for questioning Heaven, an intelligent rational being in the mystery of divine-human collaboration. The poet connects the will of Heaven to the complexities of human sociopolitics *(ren shi).*

Captured Lament and Its Release

Voices of lament are captured and inscribed in literary form in the biblical canon. The process of canonization, however, instead of releasing the power and impact of human laments, has fossilized the deep human sentiments expressed in the historical moment, turning them into domesticated theological resources. The fierce and intractable character of human cries from the depth of existence in Lamentations has been subdued. Berlin views this interpretation of Lamentations positively: "it eternalizes the catastrophic moment and its aftermath, freezing it in time, probing it from various perspectives, and preserving it forever" (2002, 1). However, the voice of theological professionals too often overshadows the cry of the suffering multitudes.

Traditional theological concerns have prevailed in the history of the book's interpretation. Tracing its theological roots has been the major objective of reading Lamentations in Christian communities and academic circles (Gottwald). The framework of sin and punishment, the concern for and defense of theodicy, and the demand for repentance—viewed as the only hope by those in the midst of seemingly unending desperate human situations—together constructed a workable theological agenda. Yet, one has to realize that such a theological scheme imposed on Lamentations only serves an ecclesiastical interest. For the sake of those suffering tremendous pain in Asia and other parts of the world, we must explore alternative readings. The voice of the exiled and desperate community must be released in this current time of sorrow and loss so that grief-stricken and wretched people can make their own voices heard with all their power. Famines, wars, and violence have relegated too many human souls to an appalling existence. For them, the book of Lamentations has survived and, in its role as literature of survival, will continue to provide the means of survival for suffering humanity (Linafelt, 2000).

For Christian communities, the loss of lament has been costly. Some interpreters have noted this loss and have called for a recovery of the lament tradition to enrich Christian life (Brueggemann 1986). Glossing quickly over life's tragic moments so as to enter quickly into superficial joy and insubstantial hope has deprived us of the value of lament. A renewed interest in Lamentations helps us to recover the church's precious lament tradition, which we cannot afford to lose.

In reading Lamentations one observes that defeat by the enemy, the city's grave sin, and YHWH's punishment are three causes for the miserable, tragic plight of Jerusalem and its people. But ultimately YHWH is "the architect of the consequence of sin" (Hunter 1996, 115). Though the presence of a transcendental personal God is absent from Yu Xin's *Lament,* he nevertheless articulates the mystery of the workings of the natural order. The four-character Chinese phrase: "Heaven's will, human affair" *(tian yi ren shi)* in Yu Xin's *Lament* (Line 65) neither exhibits an either/or choice nor a both/and mentality. The tension between the divine and the human factors is properly maintained, and the ambiguity helps humans to resist the temptation to view human suffering one-dimensionally. Both Lamentations and the Chinese Lament give mourners a voice in times of pain and grief. Cries of lament do not necessarily address God directly, but they are human emotional outpourings that enable people to weep over atrocity and to be released from its slavery. The profundity of lament in poetry must be further explored cross-culturally and treasured as an indispensable human heritage that enriches human existence and enables every wounded community to survive with human dignity.

BIBLIOGRAPHY

Berlin, Adele. *Lamentations: A Commentary.* OTL. Louisville: Westminster John Knox, 2002.

Brueggemann, Walter. "The Costly Loss of Lament." *JSOT* 36 (1986): 57–71.

Dagong Bao, a Hong Kong newsapaper, June 18, 1989.

Dobbs-Allsopp, F. W. *Lamentations.* Int. Louisville: Westminster John Knox, 2002.

Gottwald, Norman K. *Studies in the Book of Lamentations.* SBT 14. Chicago: A. R. Allenson, 1954.

Lee, Archie. "Biblical Interpretation in Asian Perspective." *AJT* 7 (1993): 35-39.

Linafelt, Tod. *Surviving Lamentations: Catastrophe, Lament, and Protest in the Afterlife of a Biblical Book.* Chicago: University of Chicago Press, 2000.

Hillers, Delbert. *Lamentations: A New Translation with Introduction and Commentary.* 2ᵈ rev. ed. AB 7A. New York: Doubleday, 1992.

Hong Kong Singtao Evening Post, June 11, 1989.

Hunter, Jannie. *Faces of a Lamenting City: The Development and Coherence of the Book of Lamentations.* BEATAJ 39. Frankfurt am Main: Peter Lang, 1996.

Wu, Xuanren, and Yang Qing, eds. *Lament Songs and Flaming Blood: Anthology of Original Poems from the Democracy Movement, 1989.* (In Chinese: *Zhuang Ge Zhu Xue: Ba Jiu Min Yun Yuan Shi Sou Ji.*) Hong Kong: Shi fang / Zhongguo Deng Huo Xing Dong, 1999.

Yu Xin. *The Lament for the South.* Translated by William T. Graham, Jr. Cambridge Studies in Chinese History, Literature, and Institutions. Cam-bridge: Cambridge University Press, 1980.

EZEKIEL 1–39

Samuel E. Almada

Instituto Universitario ISEDET, Buenos Aires

LIFE CONTEXT OF THE INTERPRETATION

The context from which I wish to interpret the book of Ezekiel is South America, with a particular focus on the crisis facing the Argentine Patagonia—my place of origin. The Patagonia is a vast region that enjoys great natural wealth, with vital oil reserves, drinking water and numerous forests. The climate is favorable for raising sheep, whose meat and wool represent one of the chief supports of the local economy. This territory is not densely populated and it offers many attractions for tourism.

The neo-liberal policies of the past several years, coupled with the obscure conditions of enforced privatization on the part of the principal industries of the Argentine State (petroleum, electric, airline, telephone, etc.), the long-standing exploitation associated with privately owned farming land, in addition to soaring rates of unemployment, have all contributed to the deprivation of the people who, as a result, feel as though they are foreigners in their own land.

This has brought about devastating consequences to Argentina, which is currently experiencing the greatest political and social crisis in its history. Great wealth still exists, production increases each year and large profits are generated—but these profits do not translate into improved living conditions for the local residents; they remain in the hands of a few. Among these are the insatiable multinational businesses and monopo-

lies that invest their profits back into their headquarters, as well as politicians and corrupt, ambitious local business people.

Presently (in 2002), while in the midst of the great crisis—and perhaps as a result of it—some conflicts have worsened with regard to key aspects that affect the future development of the Patagonian region. One of these aspects relates to macroeconomics, and is reflected by the tensions between integration projects that are both regional (Mercosur: Brazil, Argentina, Uruguay, Paraguay) and continental (Free Trade Agreement of the Americas, driven primarily by the United States). Agreements are important in all areas, but what matters is that the timing and local interests be respected—not that the strongest impose their will. Some even talk about exchanging debt for land or for installation of military bases.

In short, the situation of profound iniquity and injustice is at the root of all national and international problems, especially for those of us who find ourselves on the side of the most unfortunate, for this has led and continues to lead many countries and nations to a political, economic, and social situation that is unsustainable and unfeasible. There is transference of wealth from the poorest countries toward the wealthiest countries, and the disparities among the wealthiest minorities and the poorest majorities has reached scandalous proportions. What is our responsibility

Samuel E. Almada, a native of Patagonia (Argentina), is a member of the Baptist Evangelical Church of Argentina. After studying at the Baptist Seminary in Buenos Aires, in Jerusalem, and Strasbourg, he received his doctorate from Institutio Universitario ISEDET, where he now teaches and coordinates the theological program for native people. He has published articles (in Spanish) in *RIBLA* and *Cuadernos deTeologia* (CuT): on biblical studies and hermenentics: reading Isaiah 52:13-53:12 in light of popular readings (CuT, 1995), the Jubilee (RIBLA, 1999), Ezekiel and hope for exiles (CuT, 2000), interreligious and intercultural hermeneutics (CuT 2001), and Obadiah, injustice and punishment (RIBLA 2001).

as Christians? Is it possible to change this situation? Can the prophetic message of the Bible help us find these answers?

Analysis of the Context

Hermeneutic perspective

Our hermeneutic (interpretive) perspective falls along the lines of *hermeneutics of liberation*, inscribed in a theological movement that originated in Latin America over thirty years ago, and whose relevance and legitimacy are justified because of the situation already described that, far from improving, has worsened in an alarming way in the past several years.

In this sense, we approach the text primarily keeping in mind the present *socio-political* and *socio-economical* aspects that interact with analogous situations that are reflected in the biblical texts that are being studied. We must take into account the situation of *poverty* and *exclusion*, given that more than half of the Argentine population falls below the poverty line. We add to this the fact that, historically, a high percentage of this country's population belonged to the middle class. Consequently, the people have suffered great degradation that is reflected in a *spiritual crisis* no less important: discouragement, lack of confidence and difficulty in facing the future with hope, which has led many Argentines to leave the country. The crisis has also reached the level of *political representation*, where unresolved historical issues emerge, generalized corruption takes place and the nation is on the verge of dissolution.

But the crisis also presents the opportunity for change, for becoming more mindful and creating new endeavors—all of which represents a great challenge for churches, the peoples of God, faith communities. From the faith perspective, we see in the Bible that Yahweh (the God of Israel) is the Lord of the world and of history, and rejects all types of oppression and injustice. Therefore, in order to be faithful to God, believers must make a commitment to fight against injustice and oppression. What is essential here is the *liberating praxis* (action), since that is where

the God of the Bible and of history is revealed, and from there we have a better perspective to reread and to actualize the message of the Bible. This liberating perspective can also guide us as we read the Bible, beginning with the account of the Exodus, and has a notable expression in ideology and the message of the prophets of Israel. The book of Ezekiel, a true representation of a biblical prophesy, takes the major traditions of God's people (the Exodus, the covenant, the establishment in the land of their fathers) and revises them in light of the historical circumstances of Ezekiel's time.

The search for new horizons

How can a person rebuild hope and be restored to faith while experiencing *desolation, dispersion* and *disappointment*? This is a question that arises from our own reality, and is probably similar to the questions asked by the dispersed communities of Israel during the times of the exile. Ezekiel's prophesies are testimonies of a community of believers who faced difficult living conditions, and they offer valuable clues as we attempt to understand the crisis and look toward the future.

So in order to better understand the context of the exile and "diaspora" (scattering) we must also take into account the events that prompted this situation and their consequences in the new setting. The destruction of Jerusalem and the Temple brought about a profound crisis of faith. The captivity, the exile and the constant threat of assimilation on the part of the dominant culture resulted in an identity crisis and a lack of perspective.

The impact of the disaster in Judah and the exile represents a true point of inflection in the memory of the Israelites, and will require a significant effort of theological elaboration that would lay a foundation for a new historical beginning and new perspectives. The crisis situation turned out to be a decisive moment for remembering, and this way, the *liberation of the captives*, the *return of the exiled to their land,* and the *restoration to the community*, were recreated as a new paradigm of the saving action of Yahweh for his people.

CONTEXTUAL COMMENT

The Book of Ezekiel in Its Context

The book of Ezekiel's historic setting is the exile and the diaspora of the nation of Israel after the destruction of Jerusalem and the Temple in the year 586 B.C.; the prophet and his message are set in Babylon (1:1-3), where there were several exiled communities.

Ezekiel's prophecies were written as theological interpretations of the political and religious tragedies of the nation of Israel, and at the same time, they attempt to restore this community as it faces the future.

The end of the monarchy, the loss of land, the destruction of Jerusalem and the Temple—all resulted in the obvious destruction of the theological platform that held the institutional life of the nation and forced profound changes in thought, beliefs and practices of the people.

The people exiled in Babylon, besides being relatively few in number and being exposed to a different dominant culture, lived with other deported groups of diverse origins. Some of these groups, however, learned to use their circumstances to create new horizons. For example, they formed groups to recreate some kind of community life while being able to maintain their language, rituals, and customs.

Faith in Yahweh was one of the binding ties, although now it was not related to the Temple and sacrifices in Jerusalem, but to earlier traditions dating back to the constitution of the nation. In the exile, communities began to congregate in a traditional teaching setting, which came to have a preponderant role in its practices and religiosity. Prophetic traditions that were once discredited in the era of the monarchy were now recovered; poetic material for liturgical use was now being collected and composed; some rituals and precepts, particularly the Sabbath, Passover, circumcision on the eighth day, and various dietary customs, fulfilled a function of protection and transmission of values and principles of their own.

All of this allowed some communities of the exile to maintain their identity and recreate their faith, as they are considered to be a paradigm, the forerunners of the *utopian* return and reunion of *all* the dispersed people in the world to the lands of their fathers.

Ezekiel, from the Priesthood to Prophetic Ideology

[handwritten marginal note: But do they conflict?]

The prophet Ezekiel—which was the name attached to the collection of oracles—was the son of a priest, had been a priest himself, and was strongly tied to the activities of the Temple. He soon found himself exiled with his fellow citizens. His Jewish name has pertinent programmatic connotations and its meaning can be translated as "God will strengthen" (*y^{e}hezqe'l*).

A notable characteristic of Ezekiel is the rare transformation from priest to prophet, and the combination of literary material that represents these two different profiles, which are oftentimes antagonistic in biblical tradition.

As a priest, Ezekiel participated in the institutionalized worship practices at the Temple in Jerusalem, and he inherited its traditions. But later, forced by external circumstances and a personal experience with Yahweh, he was transformed into a *messenger of the new*, a true prophet, impassioned, combative, and unpredictable.

The priestly profile remains behind the prophet; the priestly prestige and language are still present, although they are now implemented in new perspectives. Nevertheless the prophetic tradition of Ezekiel retains the basic characteristics of the classic prophetic message: he denounces sin, announces judgment, and calls to conversion.

On the one hand, the priestly and Levitical influence can be recognized in the frequent use of juridical terms linked to the priesthood, and the recurring reference to the Holiness Code (Lev. 17–29). On the other hand, one can find a certain affinity with major prophetic traditions such as Isaiah, Jeremiah, Hosea, Amos, and often resorting to common traditions.

Collection of Oracles and Cycles of Superimposed Rereadings (1st, 2nd and 3rd Ezekiel)

In its present rendering, the book of Ezekiel—the same applies to other prophetic books (e.g., Isaiah, Jeremiah, Zechariah) and many other books of the Bible—reflects a relatively complex process of formation through which different traditions originating from various periods and locations were interwoven. This process usually included the collection, the organization, and revision of materials, from different perspectives and with purposes that relate to each stage.

In this way the prophet Ezekiel can be thought of as the initiator of a community and/or of a school in Babylonia; the oral and written traditions of this community or school were progressively developed until taking on a definite form at a later date (probably in the Greek period). This gives us a first clue that enables us to talk about First, Second, and Third Ezekiel as "cycles of superimposed rereading" (see further down).

Among the literary particularities of the book, one finds a wide variety of literary styles and genres, with an abundance of symbolic material and sometimes unusual content: surprising visions (Ezek 1–3; 8–1; 37:1-14; 40–48); clever symbolic actions (4:1-5; 12:1-7; 21:23-32; 37:15-28); diverse allegories and metaphors—many of them influenced by popular mythology from that context (16; 17; 23; 27; 31; 32:1-16; 32:17-32); and oracles with traces of what would later be developed into an apocalyptic and eschatological representation (Ezek. 38–39).

In the overall structure of the book of Ezekiel we can identify an introduction (1:1—3:15) and two lengthy parts: A (3:16—33:33) and B (34:1—48:35). Part A includes primarily the denunciation of sin including its judgment and condemnation; Part B consists of oracles of deliverance and promises of restoration. We shall see later on how these positive and negative oracles turn out to be an ingenious means of reversing the order of past situations and of articulating a message of hope.

Each of the *cycles of rereading* (1st, 2nd and 3rd Ezekiel) reflects a particular literary point of view. Each originates in a particular school and/or community and thus each cycle is recognizable in a specific collection of texts and literary units.

First Ezekiel is the name suggested for Part A, 3:16–33:33, the first set of oracles of judgment and condemnation, which corresponds to a literary point of view and prophetic tradition prior to the destruction of Jerusalem (see 33:21). The material is presented in a prophetic style that rebukes sin and announces judgment. In this sense, the duplicated narrative describing the prophet as a watchman (3:16-21 and 33:1-9) who warns the people of the threatening dangers and is responsible for them, has two functions. In addition to playing an important role in the prophetic ministry, the watchman narrative supports and intensifies, by way of inclusion, the critical perspective and the tone of judgment within the entire section. In Part A, we can also differentiate the sections containing prophesies of judgment upon Israel and Judah A-I (3:16–23:49), and A-II (24:1–33:33), other nations (chapters 25–32).

Part B, 34:1–48:35, corresponds to a perspective of writing after the catastrophe and portrays a less critical content expressing a frank and optimist tone. But here we also find material that corresponds to different literary points of view. On one hand, we have subunit B-I (34:1–39:29) that includes the oracles of deliverance, restoration and return to the land; and on the other hand, we have B-II (40:1–48:35) that paints a picture of restoration and reestablishment in the land.

Second Ezekiel is the name given to the material associated with the announcements of deliverance and restoration that are found primarily in B-I (34:1–39:29). This second cycle adopts the literary point of view of the exiled communities during a period long after the destruction of Jerusalem and the exiles (probably during the Persian period).

Second Ezekiel rereads the oracular material in First Ezekiel and, as a result, has left many imprints in Part A. In Part A-I (3:16–23:49), for example, we find several oracles of deliverance (see 11:14-21; 16:59-63; 20:33-44) that complement oracles of judgment, therefore inverting situations in the past. In this way, the focal point changes. What were originally oracles of judgment and punishment become in this new light an explanation and interpretation of the disaster. In Part A-II (24:1–33:33) something similar happens. Different oracles against other nations were brought together when they were reread. In the process they were organized in a concentric structure that has its nucleus in a brief announcement of deliverance of Israel (28:24-26). Once again the announcement of punishment and retribution turns into a message of comfort for victims and is a foretaste of their vindication and restoration.

Third Ezekiel basically constitutes what is known as the torah, or constitution of Ezekiel (B-II: 40–48), and at the same time is presented as one of the three "visions of God." This also involves a late postexilic literary point of view, and offers an alternative vision of the future that includes restoration and reestablishment in the land of the fathers (this section will be discussed further in a separate study by Sandro Gallazzi).

The question remains whether the third literary point of view of Ezekiel also corresponds to the final author, or perhaps there was a fourth writer. The final editor (3rd or 4th Ezekiel) is a true author and not merely a gatherer of materials, and would have been the person responsible for assembling the three "visions of God" (mar'ot 'elohim,1:1-3; 8:1–11:25 and 40:1–48:35), and for offering in this way an important structural outline for the book of Ezekiel as a whole (see further down the analysis of the visions). This phase is set toward the end of the Persian period.

The only material that is difficult to fit into the proposed classification (1st, 2nd, 3rd Ezekiel) is the oracle against Gog and Magog (38:1–39:20), because it is quite different from the rest. There are many indications that relate it to the Greek period and

seem to condemn the occupation of Palestine by the Seleucids. If it were the case, these oracles would correspond to a different literary point of view with considerably less significance in the shaping of the book, because of its late introduction into it.

From Judgment to Deliverance: the Oracles of Ezekiel 3–39

The first part, A-I (3:16–23:49), is primarily the denunciation of the misdeeds of the people of Israel and the corresponding condemnation of these sins. The material that is covered varies in form and content: symbolic actions that announce the destruction of Jerusalem and the exile (4 and 5); denunciation and condemnation of the mountains of Israel and its people (6 and 7); visions of the abominations in the temple (8-11); message directed against Israel's false prophets and prophetesses (13), and against idolatry (14:1-11); allegories and elegies against kings and princes of Israel (17; 19; 21); and a survey of the history of Jerusalem and Israel, oftentimes presented in symbolic language (16; 20; 23).

The language is often repetitive and heavy. Recurring themes include unfaithfulness, breaking of the covenant, and sociopolitical sins. Israel's rebellious past is brought to the forefront, as a negative sign, which sets the tone for an initial interpretation of the catastrophe. This theological way of reading the events leads us to interpret misfortune (here the exile) as Yahweh's judgment or punishment toward his unfaithful people (cf. 5:5-17 and 9:1-11). Nevertheless, this first tentative assessment starts the process of remembrance that will help work through and overcome the crisis. Recognizing the negative aspects of the past, analyzing mistakes and confessing one's fears is not easy—but it is a first and necessary step to move ahead.

Forgetting the past is precisely one of the wrong attitudes emphasized. In the message of Ezekiel, regaining one's memory, is closely linked to knowing Yahweh and his character. The concept of knowing Yahweh is the recurring and emphatic common thread that appears throughout chapters 1–39, and is commonly recognized in the formula recurring frequently in the discourses—"You shall know that I am Jehovah." This formula seems to be associated with both the oracles of *judgment/condemnation* (6:10) and the auspicious promises of *deliverance/restoration* (37:14); it ties together these two extremes that form the basic structure and style of the book of Ezekiel, and especially in chapters 3—39.

These two extremes (judgment and restoration) are also juxtaposed in different passages and literary subunits as a way of reversing the negative meaning of the first one. This phenomenon results from the rereadings used as literary and theological means to modify the original message. A typical example of this is where prophesies of restoration are juxtaposed to those of condemnation. This juxtaposition is expressed in a variety of combinations and structures. One of the most common structure combines a long prophesy of judgment [negative (-)] followed by a brief prophesy of deliverance [positive (+)], as in Ez. 16:1-58 (-) and 59–63 (+); 17:1-21 (-) and 22–24 (+); 20:1-38 (-) and 39–44 (+).

Prophesies of Judgment on the Nations and the Restoration of Israel (Ezek 24–33)

In Part A (3:16–33:33), we also find a collection of prophesies of judgment on other nations (25–32); against neighboring nations (Ammon, Moab, Edom, Philistia, 25), and other "super-powers" represented by their kings and/or cities (Tyre, 26:1–28:19 and Egypt, 29:1–32:32).

The pronouncements of judgment on neighboring nations (25) accuse these nations of behaving like malicious neighbors, of rejoicing over Israel's misfortune, and hoping to profit territorially from Judah's destruction.

We find greater pronouncements of condemnation on the super-powers of the time of Israel: Tyre and its rulers, Egypt and its Pharoah. Tyre was a major seaport that

enjoyed prosperity due to her international commerce, but her wealth and glory led to her arrogance and destruction (28). This glorious city is depicted allegorically as a mighty overloaded ship that wrecks and sinks into the abyss of the sea due to the excessive weight of its wares and riches (27:25-36).

Egypt was a super-power that had attempted, time and again, to take control of Palestine in order to secure its raids toward the North. This nation is also charged for its lack of moderation, for encouraging the rebellion against Babylon, and particularly for halfheartedly supporting the house of Israel (29:1-7). Therefore, Egypt's fall is also connected to her wealth, majesty, and pride (cf. Pharaoh's descent to hell with his people, 32:17-32).

The oppression that Israel suffered at that time justifies these negative pronouncements aimed at other nations; furthermore, the very reality of the *dispersions* makes the subject of *nations* relevant at all times. If Yahweh punishes his people through other nations, Yahweh's redemptive will may allow a confrontation with other powers in the world.

Although in the narrative of the book of Ezekiel the message was addressed to other nations and their rulers, we should not overlook the fact that the true addressees and recipients of these oracles were none other than the *people of Israel*. From this perspective, one can recognize that there is an indirect yet very clear sign: every accusation, pronouncement of punishment, and curse against the enemy brings about comfort, encouragement, and hope to the victim-nations. Furthermore, we should not forget that all the judgments against other nations are associated with situations that involve Yahweh's people, to whom in the following verses many glorious promises are made. For example, in 35:1–36:15, the proclamation of destruction of the mountains of Edom is followed by promises of the restoration of the mountains of Israel; and in chapters 38–39 the oracles against Gog and Magog forecast the victory of Israel.

The judgments on other nations are found in chapters 25 through 32, which are framed by chapters 24 and 33. The correlation between these two chapters is evident. In 24, we read prophesies concerning the destruction of Jerusalem (24:1-14) and the coming of a fugitive messenger (24:25-27); in 33 these prophesies are fulfilled, and the messenger comes with the news of the nation's destruction (33:21-29). Inside this frame, we find judgments upon the nations in the east and north (25:1–28:23) that correlate to the judgments on the people of Africa (29–32). Sandwiched in between these oracles is a brief prophesy about the *restoration of the house of Israel* (28:24-26) in direct opposition to the oracles against her neighbors (see 28:26b).

This is yet another example of the juxtaposition of oracles of judgment and oracles of deliverance that will reverse past situations. Here we have two lengthy collections of oracles of judgment on nations (25:1–28:23 and 29:1–32:32) that have as their nucleus the prophesy of the *restoration of the house of Israel* (28:24-26).

God's Visions and the Structure of the Book of Ezekiel

(1.6.1) IMAGES AND SYMBOLS

Apart from 37:1-14 Ezekiel describes three great visions (1:1-3–3:13; 8:1–11:25; 40:1–48:35), all of which are interrelated. Only these three visions are presented as "visions of God" (*mar'ot élohim*) (1:1; 8:3 and 40:2), and together they provide a common thread throughout the chapters.

The first vision (Ezek 1:1–3:15) describes a moving object likened to a glowing metallic chariot on which four living beings (*hayyot*) emerge. The thunder and other phenomena that accompany this vision remind us of the theophanies from the days back in the desert (cf. Exod. 19:16-20; Deut. 4:10-12; 5:2-5) and symbolize the presence or special manifestation of Yahweh in the midst of his people. The glowing metal reminds us of Yahweh's *pillar of fire and the cloud* that guided and protected his people through the

wilderness (cf. Ex.od 13:21-22; 40:34-38; Num. 9:15-23). The *vision of the metallic chariot* (Ezek 1:4-28) combined with the *vision of the scroll* that the prophet was commanded to eat (2:1–3:11) form one great vision. The vision of the scroll can be classified under the narrative literary form of prophetic *call*.

The *second vision* (Ezek 8–11) recaptures the image of the glowing metal (10), that is associated with the "glory/splendor (presence)" (*kabôd*) of Yahweh. But now this is viewed in a new context of judgment and condemnation. Here the "glory (presence)" of Yahweh has departed from the Temple and Jerusalem (10:18-22 and 11:22-24), as a sign of punishment for the shameful sins of his people (see Ezek 8; 9; 11:1-13).

The *third vision* (Ezek 40–48) introduces a new setting and delineates the distinctive characteristics of a new order to be assumed by the people of Israel as well as their restoration. The literary examples of both the exodus and the establishment of the people in their land are supported by the suggestion that they are connected to the renewal of worship to Yahweh, whose presence among the people assures life and blessing. The *road back to the temple through visions* in Ezek. 8–11 recurs in 43–46, but in light of a *return.*

VISIONS AND STRUCTURE OF THE BOOK

The three visions accompany and represent three pivotal moments in the book: introduction (1:1–3:15), judgment and condemnation (3:16–33:33), deliverance and promises of restoration (34:1–48:35); and they constitute one of the central threads. Images and symbols are introduced in the first vision that are later used and amplified in the second and third visions.

The *departure* of Yahweh's "glory/presence" from the Temple and from Jerusalem, in the context of the second vision (Chs. 8–11), can be interpreted as a punishment for the people's sins. But considering the experience of the exile and the dispersion, such an incident might suggest that Yahweh did not abandon his people, but rather moved East (see 10:19; 11:23) and was with the exiles (11:16). This implies making a concerted effort to reread the passage with new theological perspectives that help us understand and accept the situation; and at the same time, it allows us to overcome the theological paradigms of the past.

In a similar way, the *return* of Yahweh's "glory" through the vision of the new sanctuary (see Ezek 43), also implies the return of the exiles to their land, the restoration of the nation and the renewal of worship of Yahweh, in addition to righteous actions (11:17-20).

The Nation's Deliverance and its Restoration: A Key Text (Ezek 34–39)

Chapters 34–39 incorporate the major oracles of deliverance and promises of restoration; and they represent a particular literary point of view that we have related to Second Ezekiel. The text can be subdivided into seven parts (34; 35:1–36:15; 36:16-38; 37:1-14; 37:15-28; 38:1–39:20; 39:21-29) on the basis of a literary feature. All of the subunits begin with the same introductory formula: *The word of the Lord came to me saying* (see 34:1; 35:1; 36:16; 37:15; 38:1), with the exception of the oracle that concludes the section (39:21-29), and 37:1 that presents a particular variant. The content of this section can be summarized as follows:

34:1-31 Prophesy against malicious shepherds: restoration of Yahweh's flock and the establishment of a covenant of peace

35:1–36:15 Prophesy against Mount Seir: Blessing on the mountains of Israel

36:16-38 The impurity of the Israelites, the holiness of Yahweh and the restoration of the house of Israel in a renewed land

37:1-14 The revival of the dry bones and the restoration of the house of Israel

37:15-28 The reuniting of the nation and the everlasting covenant of peace

38:1–39:20 The attack by Gog, king of Magog: Victory in the house of Israel

39:21-29 Conclusion: Prophesy of deliverance

Reversal of Past Circumstances

The series of contrasts made between the oracles of judgment and the oracles of deliverance in the literary subunits of Ezekiel 34–39 are apparent, and have two aims: On one hand, *to remove the old order*, and on the other, *to affirm Yahweh's new vision of future salvation.*

Accordingly, the judgment on malicious shepherds and oppressors (34:1-10) is contrasted with the promise to rescue, bring back, and reunite the flock that has gone astray (34:11-16). The harsh judgment on the mountains of Edom (35:1-15) is contrasted with the prophesy of blessed restoration of the mountains of Israel (36:1-15). The profane conduct (impurity) of the Israelites that resulted in a defiled land and their scattering (36:16-20), will be corrected (cleansed) and will lead to the restoration of the community to their land, with abundance and safety (36:21-38). Starting from dried and dispersed bones, a nation is called together, reconstituted and encouraged (37:1-14); the old divisions in the nation are done away with and replaced with national unity (37:15-28). The powerful invading nation from the North will not be able to stand up against the modest nation of Israel, and will unexpectedly find its grave in a foreign land (38-39).

Second Ezekiel's Kerygma

The message of the book of Ezekiel, as a whole, has an optimistic tone, and it makes use of ideological and theological devices that guide the scattered communities to rediscover their own identity and history, while affirming the commitment made with the vision of deliverance and restoration proposed here. This vision singles out what is *special and unique about the God of Israel*, and *God's prodigious actions in favor of his people.*

The prospect of deliverance is the central message of the whole work, that we have particularly connected to Second Ezekiel. This literary perspective represents the point of inflection between the past in need of transformation (1ˢᵗ Ezekiel) and the vision of future reconstruction (3rd Ezekiel). Three aspects of this perspective are highlighted:

Knowing Yahweh and his Power

Knowing Yahweh will most likely strengthen a person's faith in God's vision of the future and in a God that is able to perform the prodigious actions of the past. Such a faith implies experiential *knowledge* of the basic precepts that bring about justice in the community. This is not merely head knowledge, but a profound experience of purification and transformation—unquestionably a "new heart and a new spirit" (cf. 11:19; 18:31; 36:26).

Heschel on knowledge (Hosea)

To know or recognize Yahweh implies actions more than words; it means specifically to become involved in Yahweh's vision for the future and for life. *Yahweh's honor* and *reputation* are at play in the power for liberation and salvation at work in the history of his people. The importance given to this issue is revealed in the numerous expressions of *recognition* ("you will know that I am Yahweh") found throughout Ezekiel. 3–39.

A New and Everlasting Covenant

The establishment of this new covenant not only implies a new knowledge and a new relationship with Yahweh, but a series of promises, as well. These promises concern the return of the scattered people and the restoration of the community to their land, with a multitude of blessings as described in 34:25-31 and 37:20-28.

The Return and Reuniting of the Dispersed

In the end, the vision of the future that is being proposed has as its objective the return, the reuniting of the dispersed and the restoration of the community. Although it may sound utopian, it is entirely possible.

CONCLUSION

The Revival of the Dried Bones (Ezek 37:1-14)

The symbolic language utilized in the vision in Ezekiel 37 makes it easy to formulate a synthesis of the oracles of deliverance and salvation and to summarize the kerygma of the book as a whole. The narrative captures the major preoccupations of a people torn apart and dispersed; with all hope lost, they run the risk of being assimilated by a dominant culture. This vision can serve as a backdrop for our reflections on our life-context in Argentina alluded to in the beginning, and for our interpretation of the situation in light of Ezekiel as Word of God for us.

The End of a System

The image of the dried bones may very well represent the situation of desolation and uncertainty that we Argentines find ourselves living in during this present crisis. The motif of death involves a perspective of radical judgment on history and reflects the end of a socio-economic and political paradigm or system. Ezekiel's prophecy suggests a sharp breakup with the past, and a radically new vision of the future that would put an end to the spiral of oppression, injustice, and corruption that led to the present situation. In the context of Ezekiel, the oppressive structure was the Temple and the sacrifices in Jerusalem; in our context, it is the neo-liberal structure that places human life at the service of money in its worst form, and many people in power and "Christians" support it because it protects their own interests over and above the common good.

The rulers of Argentina learned the pure and hard neo-liberal theory, as a way of becoming integrated into the global economy. This process had its origins during the military dictatorships of the 1970's, and continued with the subsequent democratic governments with varying characteristics, having had their glory days in the 1990's. The present result of this process shows the resounding failure of a system created to resolve problems of wealth distribution and to organize social life in a just and humane way for the people. Moreover, it should be noted that Argentina is not the exception, and that this crisis is not simply a product of internal corruption, since the majority of the countries in the Third World experience similar situations of financial collapse or near collapse.

In this context, it is striking that the promoters of the neo-liberal model continue to state that this is the only model that works and that there are no alternatives—that if not this model, then chaos. This may be true for those who act as the only hegemonistic power on earth. But the book of Ezekiel beckons us to search for new ways and alternatives. Although the details of the new vision for the future are unknown, and while this vision and its potential results still remains to be assessed, the only certainty we have is that a more just and humane system is possible.

Identity crisis

The country is experiencing an identity crisis in a climate of dissolution and general insecurity. Although it is painful, the crisis forces us to look at ourselves in a more honest way, to examine our lives in relation to others, and finally, it offers us an *opportunity for change*.

A nation's *identity* is an elemental component when it comes to participation at the local, regional, or global level, or involvement in socioeconomic, cultural and religious issues. From a position of power, it is difficult to respect and appreciate those who are different, and what is at stake here is our identity as citizens and as Christians.

Argentina, as well as many other countries in this South American continent, was settled during the times of the conquests, and nothing stopped these powerful groups of "civilized people" and "Christians" from despising, overpowering, and killing entire populations in certain regions. There was no place for people who were different.

The official history of the country reflects a concerted effort in hiding and denying others. But because of the current crisis a deeper truth comes to light: our mestizo faces and our ethnic, cultural, and language diversity. Our challenge at the present time, as believers, is to receive people who are different as truly sent from God.

Confession and Point of Inflection

Ezekiel's prophetic message underscores the *potentiality of a dissolved nation*, that is actualized through the *confession* in which the nation *understands and assumes* its own decomposition: "Our bones are dried up, and our hope is lost; we are cut off completely" (37:11b). From this rock-bottom place, a *new conscience* begins to take root where the *impossible is possible*; dry bones revive, dispersion changes into community, weakness into strength and widespread pessimism into hope.

Towards a Community of Life and Hope

New Faith in the God of Life

Knowing the God of life gives new faith and new assurance, and implies a serious examination of our commitment as believers in past and present history. This also implies a spirituality and a theology that is expressed in our commitment to life, justice, and freedom. It is imperative that we rid ourselves of insipid religiosity and of our service to personal salvation; it is not enough to be "children of Abraham." Mahatma Gandhi said: "What horrifies me more than those who do evil is the indifference of the righteous people."

The restoration of our identity and dignity as Christians and citizens depends on our identity with and commitment to the poor, those at the margins of society, and the unloved. In Argentina these segments have increased considerably, and the time has come for our awareness and solidarity with the needy.

This new conscience also has implications for our global vision. Globalization cannot be sustained if the power and interests of a few minorities are globalized, and their economic and cultural models are imposed on everyone else. It is time to recognize that the injustices and inequalities are not fortuitous results, nor are they consequences of an involuntary accident that cannot be conclusively understood and explained. They are not even a product of the incompetence of technicians. Rather they result from a premeditated program implemented with tenacious determination by certain minorities that aim at astutely appropriating what does not belong to them. This is why we must pay closer attention to actions rather than allowing ourselves to be mesmerized by diplomatic speeches uttered at international conferences and forums.

New faith in the God of hope promotes globalization of solidarity and integration among people of different ethnicity, culture, and languages. This is why the new Christian faith should be ecumenical, inter-religious, and intercultural.

The Possibility of a New Vision of the Future

The prophet Ezekiel remembered and evoked the past in order to imagine the future. For example, he alluded to the *deliverance from the country of Egypt* (20:33-35), to the *Promised Land* (20:42; 47:1–48:29), to the *covenant* (34:25; 37:26) and to *Torah* (40–48). This critical contemplation through which Ezekiel reanalyzed the past was the underlying principle that made possible a new vision of the future.

Similarly, our assurance as a faith community is based on the Word of God that declares that a new and just order is possible. This new order includes liberation from all types of oppressive forces—primarily financial ones—and a return to placing greater value on life. This implies getting rid of corrupt and selfish behaviors of the past, promoting a unified ethic in favor of the common good. This life plan affirms the unity of the nation, the return of those who have dispersed because of the crisis, and the restoration of the community to her land.

All this can be summarized in the establishment of a *covenant of peace, of well-being and of security* (*berit shalom*), according to Ezekiel 34:25-30 and 37:21-26. This covenant involves observing God's commandments for life and collaborating with our neighbors in the building of a just and unified society. Only this will guarantee prosperity to the nation, fertility to the earth, and God's presence with his people. Only this will assure reactivation in the economy, fair distribution of wealth, and will prevent us from becoming slaves again to the interests of others.

Well-Being and Security in a Renewed Land

Ezekiel's message portrays a close relationship between the people and their land and between the conduct of the nation and the situation of the country. Given this portrayal, one can initially interpret the disaster, the dispersion of the nation, and the infertility of the land as the consequences of the sin of the people that inhabited the land (see 36:17-19). Then, the process of *reunion and restoration of the nation* has its correlation in the process of *renewal of the land and nature* in general (see 36:8-13 and 47:9-12). Few books of the Bible show such an important life-relationship between the people and the land, and place this life-relationship within the framework of a new covenant with the God of life (see 34:25-30 and 37:21-26). The hope for a state of well-being and of security for the nation is brought to fruition in a renewed and generous land.

In this sense, the word of God invites us to a deeper communion, not only with human beings, but also with the land and nature in general; and this partnership highlights an important aspect of our commitment as Christians and the mission of the churches. It not only involves a greater knowledge of the macro- (universe, astronomy) and micro- (atoms, genetics) cosmos, but above all, an understanding of the interdependence and permanent interaction among different forms of life, matter, and energy. Therefore, our faith communities are held responsible for ecological projects and the care for the environment. Similarly, the economic, social, and political processes should also be compatible and maintain affinity with the ability to sustain life in its diversity.

BIBLIOGRAPHY

Albertz, Rainer. *A History of Israelite Religion in the Old Testament Period*. Louisville: Westminster John Knox Press, 1994.

Almada, Samuel E. "La profecía de Ezequiel: Señales de esperanza para exiliados. Oráculos, visiones y estructuras". *Revista de Interpretación Bíblica Latinoamericana* 35/36 (2000):103-121.

Croatto, J. Severino. *Biblical Hermeneutics. Toward a Theory of Reading as the Production of Meaning*. Maryknoll, NY: Orbis, 1987.

LaCocque, André. "De la mort à la vie (Ézéchiel 37)." Pages 191-222 in *Penser la Bible*. Edited by Paul Ricoeur - André LaCocque. Paris: de Seuil, 1998.

Parunak, H. van Dyke. 1978 *Structural Studies in Ezekiel*. Massachusetts: Harvard University. 1980 "The Literary Architecture of Ezekiel's *mar'ot elohim*." *JBL* 99 (178):61-74.

Ricoeur, Paul. "Sentinelle de l'imminence." Pages 223-245 en *Penser la Bible*. Edited by Paul Ricoeur and André LaCocque. Paris: de Seuil, 1998. [sobre Ez 37]

Schwantes, Milton. *Sufrimiento y esperanza en el exilio*. Santiago: Rehue, 1991.

Zimmerli, Walter. *Ezechiel*. BKAT 13/1-2; Neukirchen-Vluyn: Neukirchener, 1969.

——Ezekiel 1: A Commentary on the Book of the Prophet Ezekiel. Hermeneia. Philadelphia: Fortress, 1979.

——Ezekiel 2: A Commentary on the Book of the Prophet Ezekiel. Hermeneia. Philadelphia: Fortress, 1983.

EZEKIEL 40–48

Alessandro Gallazzi

Comissão Pastoral da Terra, Amapá, Brazil

Translated from Portuguese by Cristina Conti

LIFE CONTEXT OF THE INTERPRETATION

The Pastoral Land Commission (Comissão Pastoral da Terra) participates in the struggle for life and justice of the peasants, the river people, and the landless of Amazonia. The Commission is trying to be a sign of life and resistance against the violence of the multinational corporations, the devastating timber industries, the profiteering of the mining companies, and the deceitful projects of a government that is often corrupt and exclusively committed to the interests of the powerful.

In this wonderful land, native, black, mestizo, and white people form the multiethnic richness of the Amazonian population. Yet this population suffers from oppression by the wealthiest and most powerful countries, which are always trying to impose their will and their cultural and economic projects as the best, the most civilized, and even the most "Christian." Such a permanent attack on the fullness of nature and on the lives of peoples demands an explanation and motivates us to proclaim, once more, a word that can be good news for the Amazonian poor.

Analysis of the Context

An Annoying Reality

The present-day context is marked by ongoing conflicts and is made even worse by a history of evangelization in which, all too often, the word of God was used to justify oppression and to legitimate the privileges of the powerful and their allies, the churches.

The Christian religion that was imposed by the conquistadores was the mighty mechanism of ethnic, cultural, and social domination that subjugated our peoples. Their ancestral religions were labeled primitive superstitions, their cultures and ways of life were considered savage, and popular religion—a fruit of the encounter between Christianity and ancestral religions, too hastily classified as syncretism—was manipulated in order to generate servitude and conformity.

Christian monotheism was supposed to proclaim a Father who in his love welcomes everyone, brings life to all, and wants all of us to be brothers and sisters. Instead, the proclamation of Christian monotheism often became the mirror image and the legitimization of the European monarchies and the carbon copy of a theocratic, imperialist church. This church was more anxious to expand its frontiers and power than to announce the gospel of life, grace, and liberty.

The religious experiences of the Latin American peoples were rarely respected as legitimate and creative life experiences. In many cases, these religious traditions were reduced to simple folklore and used as a tourist attraction.

Alessandro Gallazzi, born in Italy, has lived in Brazil since 1973, working with the Pastoral Land Commission, an ecumenical grassroots organization fighting for the rights of the poor and the preservation of the environment. A member of the Latin-American biblical movement, he teaches at the Theological Seminary of the Assembly of God at Macapá and is on the editorial board of RIBLA (*Revista de Interpretación Bíblica Latinoamericana*). His many publications include a book on Esther (*Ester: a mulher que enfrentou o palácio*, 1987), 1 Maccabees (*1º Macabeus: autocrítica de um guerri-lheiro*. 1993), Judith (*Judite: a mão da mulher na história do povo*, 2001), the Sadducee's theocracy (*A Teocracia Sadocita: sua história e ideologia*, 2002), and two volumes of essays on post-exilic biblical studies (2003).

Theoretical Perspective and Methodology

It is in this context that I read Ezekiel 40–48. These chapters narrate the theoretical project that Israelite intellectuals developed in Babylon for the Jews who remained in Judea. The purpose of this project concerned the priestly and monarchical elites, who had lost their leadership positions because of the exile; it was a matter of restoring them to power.

We will use "conflict" as the interpretive key to the text and read these pages "from the margin," from the perspective of oppressed peoples, in order to see how the text takes sides. This twofold approach is not easily implemented, because Ezekiel 40–48 does not make explicit the conflicts it seeks to resolve; actually it often conceals its position in these conflicts. Ezekiel 40–48, like all the priestly writings, aims at speaking the word of God authoritatively. In order to secure their sacred power, the priestly writers usually "forget" or suppress the conflicts behind the text, sacralize and universalize history, and transform what they view as transgression of the covenant into heresy and set aside every prophecy that threatens the sacred order they seek to maintain.

Using conflict as an interpretive key, I will show that these priestly teachings were never neutral, eternal, or universal. They had an origin, a history, a community basis, and were partisan. Rather than being content with the "literal sense" of this text—that is with the sense that individual believers seek for their religious lives by reading it exclusively for its universal a-historical teaching—I will study its historical development to see when, how, and why these teachings were formulated.

Why does Ezekiel begin to use words such as *Zadokites and Levites*; *prince*; *people of the land*; *foreigners*; *pure and impure*; *sacred and profane*; *sacrifice for the sin*; *oblation* as stereotypes? By freeing these words from their sacral dimension, we will be able to discern how even a biblical text can be used to defend a project of oppression.

The Horizons of the Study of Ezekiel 40–48

Our analysis of Ezekiel 40–48 will reveal the mechanism of domination behind the *Gott mit uns* ("God with us") engraved on the belts of Hitler's soldiers; the *In God we trust* printed on the dollar bill that reigns supreme from Wall Street; or the old and modern anti-Islamic crusades, fought in the name of a so-called Judeo-Christian civilization.

This analysis will open our eyes to recognize when and how power inside our churches follows the logic of oppression and exclusion. Our eyes will open to discover the reason for intolerance toward other religions, and even toward other Christian churches.

Finally, this analysis will make us aware of why the androcentric image of God as a patriarchal merciless and punishing judge is still so prevalent and powerful at all levels of society in Amazonia and also in the outside world that so forcefully impinges upon the lives of Amazonians. This study will show how this image of God is instilled in our hearts by a veneration of the temple and how it conceals the experience of a God—Father/Mother, friend, full of tenderness and compassion—who wants us to be brothers and sisters in communion with everyone and everything.

CONTEXTUAL COMMENT

Although Ezek 40–48 has often been dated as from 572 B.C.E. (Ezek 40:1), it was probably written a century later, around 460 B.C.E. The name, the memory, and the authority of the priest Ezekiel, prophet of the exiled, were used to give credibility to the text.

The Pre-Text: The Conflict that Produced the Text

Somewhat later, in 445 B.C.E., Hanani, talking to Nehemiah, summarized the situation of Jerusalem and the survivors of the exile who were living in Judea:

The survivors from captivity, who are down there in the province, live in great misery and humiliation; the walls of Jerusalem are in ruins and her gates are burnt. (Neh 1:3, a.t.)

They returned from Babylon, knowing they were the remnant of the faithful people, purified by the trial of the exile. They returned, full of projects, to restart everything once more. They enthusiastically began the reconstruction of the Lord's temple, trusting the promises of restoration that, after Cyrus' victory, the prophet, often designated as Second Ezekiel (34–37), had announced to the communities of the deportees.

My servant David shall be king over them and they shall have only one shepherd for all. . . . They shall dwell in the land where their parents dwelled. . . . I shall establish with them an everlasting covenant, a covenant of peace. . . . My dwelling shall be in their midst: I shall be their God, and they shall be my people. (Ezek 37:24-27, a.t.)

Nothing of that kind happened: the Babylonian captivity had ended almost a century before and the dreams of reconstruction of the Second Ezekiel and the Second Isaiah were still unfulfilled.

The restoration of the Davidic monarchy failed after the mysterious disappearance of Zerubbabel. The sanctuary, even after it was rebuilt, did not get the support of the people and could no longer be maintained. Above all, the repatriates did not succeed in recovering their lands or rebuilding the city. The dream of the everlasting alliance of peace had turned into a reality of misery and humiliation. There were several reasons for this situation:

- The Judean peasants, who had received their lands from the Babylonians after the fall of Jerusalem (2 Kgs 25:12; Jer 39:10), did not recognize any entitlement to the heirs of the exiled, and resisted the restoration efforts.
- Afraid of losing their power, the governors of the neighboring provinces acted in their own economic and polit-

ical self-interest, and obstructed the repatriates' projects (Ezra 4; Neh 3:33–6:19, HB).

- Most of the deportees, probably the best educated, had stayed in Babylon, and did quite well in both business and as members of the imperial administration's bureaucracy.

The resulting unrest in Judea created problems for the Persian court, which was already worried about Egypt's attempts to gain autonomy from Persian rule. The emperor wanted a stable Judea, submissive to his interests, that had an effective capital city, a solid internal organization, and a peaceful population.

The Context: The Group that Produced the Text

The situation also worried the Israelites in the Diaspora. The lack of peace and tranquility in Judea cast suspicion on the rest of the Israelites.

The Judahite circles, connected to the scribes of the Persian court, developed a project for Judea that could simultaneously satisfy both the imperial court and the Israelite Diaspora. The temple was to be the center of Judea's socioeconomic and political life and the cultic and symbolic center for all the Israelites, both those in Judah and those in the Diaspora. This is the context from which Ezekiel 40–48 arose.

I think this was the book "of the law of God, which is also the law of the king" (Ezra 7:12-26, a.t.) that was in Ezra's hands when he came, sent by the emperor, to Jerusalem. No other text of the time had envisioned an endeavor with such political and economic connotations and visualized such well-defined social relations, so that Judea would be the pacifying agency that Artaxerxes wanted in the region.

The Text: The Proposal to Solve the Conflict

The vision of the new temple covers the first three chapters (Ezek 40–42) of the text.

A man of God (40:3) describes the concrete, minute details and measurements of the temple's sanctuary: gates, atriums, courtyards, halls, and holy places. A massive wall surrounds the temple to "separate the sacred from the profane" (42:20, a.t.).

The glory of the LORD—in exile in Babylon with his people—now returns to this temple, making it the place where God will dwell in the midst of God's people forever (43:1-9). The sanctuary becomes a sacred space of supreme holiness, a "holy of holies" that must never be profaned (43:7-9; 44:6-9). The law of the temple demands: "The whole area on top of the mountain is a holiest place" (43:12, a.t.).

The remaining chapters (43:13–48:35) describe the new regulations and territorial boundaries of the theocracy installed, both in Judea and Jerusalem, by the triumphant presence of the Lord's glory. Jerusalem a city whose name will be: "YHWH-is-there" (48:35, a.t.).

The Prince = the High Priest

The *prince* has, in these pages, a central and indispensable place. He has important privileges in the cult: he sits by the eastern gate, which is locked for everyone else, because it is the gate through which God had entered (Ezek 44:1-3). There, he will "eat bread in front of YHWH" (v. 3, a.t.), an exclusive prerogative of the priests (Lev 24:8-9). Also, he will attend the Sabbath and the new moon holocausts and peace sacrifices (Ezek 46:2).

Ezekiel 45:17 says that the holocausts, the oblations, and the libations belong to the prince. He himself will perform the distinctively priestly sacrifice for the sin, oblation, holocaust, and peace sacrifices, in order to do expiation for the house of Israel (Ezek 45:22 and 46:12).

Should the prince be viewed as someone who was performing the temple functions of pre-exilic kings or as a priest? Considering what the text itself said about the Zadokite priests, making them a special group, privileged and separated from all the others (Ezek 44:15-31), I do not think it is correct to read in these texts that the prince performs the functions of the preexilic kings. Furthermore, the fact that the prince has the right to the greater part of the holy share of land, offered to YHWH (Ezek 45:7) shows that he belongs to the priestly group. In sum, everything implies that the prince is the high priest himself, in his function as "chief of the temple." This is the new figure that will replace the figure of the Davidic king. The Israelites in the Diaspora could much more easily identify themselves with a people faithful to the covenant and centered around the temple and with a high priest than with a body politic centered around a king.

The Land of God = The Land of the Temple

This political vision needed economic support. It was essential that the Zadokite priests, the dominant political group, control the land.

The texts of Ezek 45:1-8 and 47:13–48:-35 solve the issue by giving the new land economy a truly theological basis. The text imagines that, on returning from the exile, the whole land of Israel will be distributed to each of Israel's tribes in individual strips of land (each 12.5 km. = 7.8 mi. wide) running from the Mediterranean up to the Jordan. One strip, though, will be a "holy share" reserved for the priests, the Levites, and the prince/high priest.

The priests—theoretically without an inheritance in Israel, as their inheritance is God himself (Ezek 44:28)—will, in actual fact, manage in God's name the greater and best part of the land between Bethlehem and Gibeon, almost all of the land of the small post-exilic Judea! The land acquires a new theological aura. Because the land belongs to God (Lev 25:23), the right to manage it belongs to God's representatives: the prince/high priest, the Zadokites, and the Levites.

Those who work on God's land will have to pay tribute to God's representatives (Ezek 45:13-16). Thus the temple will be, at the same time, God's sanctuary, the high priest's palace, and the storehouse of the Zadokites and the Levites!

In order to avoid the conflicts that had marked the preceding eighty years, though, it was necessary to recognize the rights of the "people of the land." These were the farmers of Judea who had received land after Jerusalem's destruction and depopulation and who continued to own or, at least farm, the land. The authors of this text knew that it was impossible to build a peaceful Judea without recognizing the land ownership rights of the local Judahites. Ezekiel 47:22-23 legislates that the "children of the aliens" also have the right to own the land.

The Altar as Economic Center

At the center of the holy share is the temple; a temple that, as Artaxerxes desired, would be a state-owned "tax center." At the center of the temple is the sacred and publicly visible altar. The public altar would be the theocracy's tax-center where people pay tax in post-exilic Judea.

This gigantic (36 ft. or 10.9 m. tall) square altar (43:13-17) has a base measuring 900 sq. ft. (83.6 sq. m.), on which there were three concentric platforms before reaching the altar stone, which measured 6 x 6 yards. Never did the altar have such enormous proportions. As conceived in Ezekiel 40–48, the altar is a powerful theological and economic symbol. It is through this altar that God and the people of Israel are connected.

A fountain of life-giving and fecund water, coming out of the holy of holies, will run by the altar and descend to the Dead Sea, which will be restored to life. The fish proliferate, the trees bear fruit every month, and the leaves heal wounds, because its water comes from the sanctuary (Ezek 47:1-12). For God to offer such blessings, the altar must always be in operation, with a complex process of sacrifices and offerings occurring on and around it. This process will guarantee a continuous supply for the priests' table and the central storehouse.

The Holy of Holies and the Holiest Meals

Ezekiel 40–48 introduces new sacrificial rites: the oblation, the sacrifice of atonement

for sin, the sacrifice of compensation. Completely absent from Deuteronomy, these rites insure that the Zadokites and their families will have a continual supply of consecrated food obtained from the rest of the people.

Originally, the oblation was the offering of a present to God, mostly in combination with a holocaust and, like the latter, completely burnt (Num 16:15; Judg 6:18; 13:19, 23; 1 Sam 26:19; Jer 14:12). Our text, however, reserves the oblation as food for the priests (Ezek 44:29). God will be satisfied with a handful of flour, burnt as a memorial. The remainder will be exclusively for the priests (Lev 2:1-3).Even more importantly, apart from its ritual significance, the oblation will be a compulsory complement to most of the other sacrifices and is spelled out in detail (Ezek 46:5,7,11,14-15).

The sacrifice of atonement for sin, or sin offering, is practically absent from pre-exilic texts (mentioned only in 2 Kgs 12:17 outside of priestly texts) and never referred to in Ezek 1–39. Sin offering occupies a central space in the liturgy of the second temple: it will be performed during the great festivals (Ezek 45:17b-25), during the consecration rites (Ezek 43:18-23), and to recover purity that was lost by involuntarily transgressing one or another of the many legal and cultural regulations. Through this sacrifice, the transgressor will have the guarantee of having this sin forgotten. The sin offering makes up for the sin (the same word, *hkt' h,* is used for both sin and sin offering).

The whole society of the second temple will be organized around this system of purity, impurity, and the rituals necessary to maintain or restore purity. The Zadokites' main function was "to teach the people to distinguish between the sacred and the profane, and make them know the difference between pure and impure" (Ezek 44:23, a.t.).

The work of Ezra and Nehemiah regulated and adapted social, political, and religious program of Ezek 40–48 to the diverse life situations that developed in the postexilic era. The book of Chronicles would be the ultimate expression of the ideology behind Ezek 40–48 at the beginning of the fourth century B.C.E.—found still later in Qumran's Temple Scroll (11Q19-20).

It was not easy to enforce these liturgical, social, and economic regulations among the people of Judea. The people's reaction, especially the women's, are seen in such significant texts as the Song of Songs, Qohelet, and the books of Ruth, Job, and Jonah.

CONCLUSION

Our base communities read Ezekiel 40–48 critically because its teachings are totally unacceptable in our context. A critical study that shows that the teaching of these chapters reflect the interests of the privileged group that produced it helps us recognize that it is precisely the kind of teaching that contributes to the plight of the peoples in the Amazonian regions. This teaching is tragically implemented in our lives through the powerful and oppressive role of the transnational corporations. But for our base communities, Ezekiel 40–48 remains most important, because it helps us recognize where the same kinds of organizations, enterprises, and ideologies are at work in our context today. This critical reading of Ezekiel 40–48 and its hierarchical ideology also helps us recognize that there are alternative hierarchical ideologies, such as those of earlier prophets, of Jesus of Nazareth and the early church. In light of our Christian base communities' reading of Ezekiel 40–48, we better understand the conflicts within the Jewish "family" between the priestly party (in line with Ezekiel 40–48) and Jesus and the early church (in line with the other prophetic tradition):

- why the "chief priests and rulers" and the main authorities delivered Jesus up "to be condemned to death and crucified" (Luke 24:20, a.t.);
- why immediately after Jesus' death, "the curtain of the temple was torn in two, from top to bottom" (Mark 15:38);
- why Stephen was killed (Acts 7:54-60) because he denied the temple (vv.:48-50);
- why Paul proposed to the communities a model of church without priests with a unique access to the divine (1 Cor 12:4-31);

- the importance of worshiping God in spirit and truth (John 4:23) and the significance of a new Jerusalem without a temple (Rev 21:22).

The absence of the temple and of the priesthood, especially in their sacrificial roles as necessary mediators between God and human beings, is one of the most distinctive characteristics of the New Covenant's ecclesial project.

This critical study of Ezekiel 40–48 helps us to clarify the liberating force of Jesus' proposal, based on forgiveness and the right of the poorest, the smallest, the women, and the impure. According to the gospel, the only offering that will do is that of forgiveness:

> Forgive us our debts, as we also have forgiven our debtors. . . . Judge not, that you be not judged. . . . and the measure you give will be the measure you get. (Matt 6:12; 7:1-2, RSV)

This reflection may contribute to overcoming the notion of God as judge and master and replacing it with the experience of the true God, Father and Mother, full of tenderness and mercy.

From the socioeconomic and cultural perspective of our base communities there is also another reason for this critical reading of Ezekiel 40–48. In Latin America there is a conflict between the church of the temple—official, despotic, structured, static, and eternal—and the church of the house, the base communities—spontaneous, helpful, provisional, and on its way forward. To know the temple's instruments of oppression will help us to better recognize the instruments used today to control, oppress, and even condemn everything that is new, different, other, or secular. Such knowledge will help us to be truly critical, i.e., to resist using religion to dominate peoples and consciences. It is going to empower us to confront and resist the economic programs and projects that outsiders (through trans-national corporations and globalization) seek to implement in our land and devastate our people.

BIBLIOGRAPHY

Anderson, Gary, A.. "The Interpretation of the Purification Offering (*hata't*) in the Temple Scroll (11Q temple)." *JBL* 111 (1992): 17-35.

Dijkstra, Meindert. "The Altar of Ezequiel: Fact or Fiction?" *VT* 42 (1992): 22-36.

Gallazzi, Sandro. *A teocracia sadocita. Sua história e ideologia.* Macapá, Brazil: 2002.

———. "Nunca descuidaremos da casa de nosso Deus (Ne 10,40)—Aspectos da economia do segundo templo." *RIBLA* 30 (1998): 59-77.

———. "Jubileo: aquí y ahora." *Alternativas* 13 (1999), also *RIBLA* 33 (1999): 64-80.

Garmus, Ludovico. "Ezequiel e a terra: um projeto exílico de reforma agrária." *EstBíb* 13 (1987): 21-36.

Kilpp, Nelson."Neemias - perfil de um político." *EstTeo* 29:2 (1989): 175-183.

Marx, Alfred. "Sacrifice pour les péchés ou rite de passage? Quelques reflexions sur la fonction du *hata't.*" *RB* 96 (1989): 27-48.

Maier, Johann, *Il giudaismo del secondo tempio.* Brescia, Italy: Paideia, 1991.

Monari, Luciano. *Ezequiel, um sacerdote profeta.* São Paulo: Paulinas, 1992.

Sacchi, Paolo. *Storia del secondo tempio.*Turin: SEI, 1994.

———. "Il puro e l'impuro nella Bibbia. Antropologia e storia." *Hen* 1 (1984): 65-80.

Schaper, J. "The Jerusalem Temple as an Instrument of the Achemenid Fiscal Administration." *VT* 45 (1995): 528-539.

Spadafora, Francesco, ed. "Ezequiele." *La Sacra Bibbia.* Turin: Marietti, 1960.

Zimmerli, Walther. *Ezekiel* (2vols.) Philadelphia: Fortress, 1983.

DANIEL

André LaCocque

The Chicago Theological Seminary, Chicago, Illinois, USA

LIFE CONTEXT OF THE INTERPRETATION

Few biblical books are more directly relevant for the present time than the book of Daniel. Its lucidity in engaging the powers and the variegated manifestations of historical evil is striking. My own fascination with this Hebrew Bible apocalypse dates from the time when, as a young teenager, I was confronted, like the whole of Europe, with pure evil. It was pure evil because it was unencumbered by any ethical restraint. The Nazi brainwashing of its followers (though many of the SS murderers had PhD's) inaugurated an unprecedented occurrence in history and set a point of no return. For the first time, a horde of "beasts" (Dan 7:1-8) was unleashed with the exclusive purpose of Jewish genocide and with a total absence of guilt. Killing defenseless people of all ages became a "sacred duty," a meritorious act, because it contributed to the "eradication of vermin." Massacre, rape, humiliation, and radical dehumanization became the ultimate virtues of fanatics transformed into killing machines.

It is then that I encountered God, a God that I readily intuited was inseparable from his martyred people and, through them, from all the downtrodden of the world. I also fell in love with the Hebrew Scriptures, testimony of this nation-witness who had "recognized" God, as the prophet Ezekiel insists. The inseparability of Scripture from "the people of the Book" is the ultimate rule guiding its readers.

Daniel and the Relationship of God's People with the World

When reading a biblical text, one should never forget that Israel is steadily speaking about Israel and to Israel. No principle, perhaps, is more urgent when one opens the book of Daniel because the book's composition was motivated in the first place by what constituted an unprecedented upsurge of evil at that time: the first historical pogrom of the Jews organized by a state with all its resources. In 168/167 B.C.E. Antiochus IV Epiphanes, a successor to Alexander the Great in the Middle East, decided that the Judeans had exhausted the grace period before adopting the state's doctrine called Hellenism, an enlightenment imported by Alexander's colonists and aimed at superseding all philosophical and religious traditions in the conquered territories. The Jews were being coerced into abandoning their "backward" religion. The persecution lasted three years, from 167 to 164, and the subversive book of Daniel was written during that period, shortly before Antiochus's death and the end of the pogrom. Internal evidence attests to this: there is a noticeable shift from prophecy *post eventum* (after the fact), with a basically correct overview of historical events in Daniel 11:42, to the inaccurate prediction of the tyrant's death by "fall[ing] upon the mountains of Israel" (Ezek 39:4; cf. Isa 10:5-11 and Joel 3:2).

Within this first all-out religious persecution, the least one can say of the book of

André LaCocque is Emeritus Professor of Hebrew Scriptures and Emeritus Director of the "Center for Jewish-Christian Studies" at the Chicago Theological Seminary. He has written many books, including *Daniel in His Time* (1988), *Romance She Wrote, A Hermeneutical Essay on Song of Songs* (1998) and *Thinking Biblically* (with Paul Ricoeur) (1998), a commentary on *Ruth* (2004). Honored by a Festschrift: *The Honeycomb of the Word, Interpreting the Primary Testament with André LaCocque* (2001).

Daniel is that it is an engaged document. In fact, it could not be more so, for the author was convinced that Antiochus was the last and ultimate incarnation of historic evil and that the contemporary events of the second century B.C.E. were the last before the end of the world. Hence, Daniel's visions are neither abstract developments nor speculations about happenings to come some twenty-two cen-turies later. They do not allude to Hitler, Stalin, Saddam Hussein, or other recent and contemporary tyrants. Rather, they specifi-cally speak of the prohibition of all Jewish religious practices by a "beastly" regime, of a time when circumcising a boy was marking him for slaughter and when people of all ages were dying as martyrs for their faith and were honoring God rather than Caesar.

CONTEXTUAL COMMENT

An Overview of Daniel as Narrative and Apocalypse

Daniel's conception of history is, to a large extent, consistent with that of the rest of the Bible. History has a beginning and an end. It is linear, not cyclical. The events are not repetitive. Daniel, however, introduces an uncommon dimension. The history it envis-ages is universal; it is no longer the *Heils-geschichte* (salvation history) of the Prophets, focusing on internal and external events as they exclusively affect Israel. Daniel's synop-sis divides human time into four successive periods of decline. Humanity as a whole (not just Israel) is regressing toward a historical point very much in the image of the initial chaos, before God created the cosmos. Thus, Daniel's horizon encompasses more than the Judeans/Jews, and the expected eschatologi-cal event is itself cosmic. This different emphasis, in comparison with prophetic eschatology, is decisive.

With Daniel, we can say that history knows no duplication of itself; it does not endlessly cycle. But, on the other hand, there is some justification in saying with the sage, "There is nothing new under the sun." This is particularly true with regard to evil, as it is singularly devoid of invention. Circumcision marked infants for destruction not only in 168/167 B.C.E. but again in medieval Europe and twentieth-century Germany. The Hebrew Scriptures were not only forbidden reading in the Antiochan period, when scrolls were seized and burned, but they were also forbid-den in the medieval *auto da fe*'s (act of faith) and modern Nazi Germany (as were the books of Daniel and Revelation in the territo-ries occupied by the Japanese during World War II). The Jew is the image of human suf-fering, and so what was originally an internal literature of lament and praise (such as the book of Psalms) becomes a subversive docu-ment authentically reflecting the universal cry for justice and faith in Providence.

The book of Daniel belongs in the cate-gory of "dangerous" literature. It is a political manifesto, a denunciation of evil and human callousness. At times, such protests have become powerful enough to stir revolutions. In the first decades C.E., the ancient rabbis decided against preserving the apocalyptic literature (with the exception of Daniel) when they witnessed the repeated bloody insurrections against Rome by Jewish parties cultivating apocalyptic books. The rebels were finding some kind of assurance in those texts that the enormous military superiority of the Roman legions would be no match for the angelic armies sent by God in the escha-ton (end time). This had the direst of conse-quences: Jerusalem was razed to the ground by the Romans and rebuilt under a different name, after which no Jew was allowed to enter. For centuries Palestine ceased to be the Jewish homeland, until certain modern developments. Within this old/new perspec-tive, the book of resistance bearing the name of Daniel cannot be ignored.

The Nature and Composition of Daniel

The nature of the book is mixed. There are stories about Daniel and his three compan-ions at the court of Nebuchad-nezzar of Babylon and there are Daniel's own visions about the end time. We may call the former *Daniel A* and the latter *Daniel B*. The ostensible time for the entire manuscript is the sixth century B.C.E., right after the destruction of Jerusalem by the Babylonians. Daniel A, which occupies the first half of the book, is undoubtedly much older than Daniel B, which shifts to a sort of autobiographical report by Daniel of his eschatological visions. Thus, the book is bigeneric, both narrative and apocalyptic. It is also bilingual, being written in both Aramaic (Dan 2:4–7:28) and Hebrew (Dan 1:1–2:4; 8:1–12:13) without a clear indication as to why it was done so. Furthermore, Daniel is also bitemporal, as the time of the narrative is set in the sixth century while, as we have seen, events of the second century prompted the final composition.

Much can be inferred from these dualities. One could suggest that the stories in Daniel A have been reused and reshaped by the author of Daniel B according to his own purposes. In both parts, the hero is Daniel (whether this is the name of the actual author or not). Daniel is a wise courtier on the model of other comparable stories (Ahikar from Egyptian literature, as well as Joseph and Esther in the Hebrew Bible); he is able to interpret the signs of the time and the divine "secrets" embedded in dreams, strange scripts, visions, and biblical prophecies. In short, Daniel is able to unveil (*apocalyptō*) what is hidden.

Fitting such an extraordinary mantic capacity of the seer, the style and diction for reporting this operation of unknotting (*pesher,* decoding) the mysteries are often forbidding. Many misled readers of the apocalypses have taken advantage of these difficulties for promoting fantastic solutions to historical "riddles" (Ezek 17:2), without regard for the *Sitz im Leben*—the date, the authorship, and the intent of the documents. On this score as well, Daniel is dangerous literature!

In a commentary as condensed as the present one, a considerable amount of information on Daniel must remain unmentioned. I have attempted in other works to show the astounding novelty of the book's theology. Both the book and its theology provide an indispensable background for readers of intertestamental and New Testament literature. Here I have selected three representative passages: Daniel 7, Daniel 3, and Daniel 12.

Daniel 7

Earlier, I sounded a cautionary note about abstracting the book and discrete texts thereof from their moorings for the sake of identifications with modern villains. True, the apocalyptic periodization of history, where four empires in succession jealously vie to be first in terms of monstrosity, provides a much used pattern that is open to repeated *aggiornamentos* (updating, modernization). In the time of Daniel's composition, the vile man was Antiochus, someone representing the "Greek empire" and number four on the list of beasts (Dan 7:7, 19). Although this empire was seen as the last avatar of the universal evil by the *khasidim* (pious ones) of the time, it was, however, succeeded in the first century B.C.E. by Rome. The fourfold pattern was simply revised (by *2 Baruch* or *4 Ezra*), with the fourth position now occupied by the Romans. This way, the apocalypse never dies: the fourth beast is always a new incarnation in the "evil empire" of the moment. (Such a contemporizing process has been deemed acceptable as long as it is consciously a second reading, based on a first reading that is respectful of the historical context of the document.) This guaranteed that Israel would not be absent from any interpretation and the Scripture would not be snatched away from the people of the Book, the very people who first produced the Scripture—a caution not always heeded by modern "interpreters" of apocalypses.

Evil always remains the same; only the victims are different. To all of the victims, in all the periods of history, Daniel is powerfully effective as good news to the oppressed. It is powerful, although—or perhaps because—it does not speculate on any potential improvement in the situation of the poor but announces the end of all oppressive regimes and the end of history and the world as we know them. The change is as radical as can be. The end is a return to the point zero from which God inaugurated and will inaugurate God's reign, the divine kingdom whose nature cannot be associated with the historical parodies portrayed in Daniel 7:1-8.

The kingdom of God wipes out all historical political regimes. Even a political messiah plays no role here. The kingdom to come has at its head the ultimate human being, the *bar enosh* (Son of Man), in stark contrast to beasts like Nebuchadnezzar or Antiochus IV. The human and humane One comes from heaven, while the four monsters pretending to lead the people are coming from the primordial ocean, the waters of chaos. They are wallowing in debauchery and brutality, but God will set up a tribunal and delegate judgment to the One who does not compete with the beasts for power, fame, and honors, but receives "dominion, glory and kingship" from God over all nations forever (Dan 7:14).

Daniel 7:1-8

From the primordial chaos emerge four beasts representing the four successive empires, which allegedly span the historical duration of the world (Dan 2:31-45). The first beast is Babylon; the second is Media; the third is Persia; and the fourth, the fiercest beast of all, defies description. This fourth beast symbolizes the Macedonia of Alexander the Great. The Western power grows an awesome horn that represents Antiochus the Fourth. The latter's arrogant attitude is mentioned here and also in Daniel 8:23, while his obscene mouth (Dan 7:25) is again featured in Daniel 11:36 (see also Ps 12:3; Rev 13:5). With this last offspring of the world empires, history comes tragically to an end, as no grosser evil could conceivably erupt.

The date is 168/167 B.C.E., when Antiochus has defiled the Jerusalem temple and inaugurated the religious persecution previously mentioned. The high priest of the time, a holy man by the name of Onias III, is offhandedly dismissed and replaced by a toady of Antiochus named Jason. For an account of these events, we turn to Daniel 9, where the author presents the all-important Jeremaian motif of the "seventy (weeks of) years" (Dan 9:24, author's translation [a.t.]) expected to elapse between the first wave of exiles to Babylon until the final restoration (Jer 25 and 29). Daniel receives the revelation that these prophetic texts must be understood in terms of "weeks of years," thus bringing the time of the promised breakthrough 490 years after 587 (or 605, the date of Jeremiah's oracle), which is roughly the epoch when the book of Daniel was actually written. These seventy (weeks of) years are divided in Daniel 9:24-26 into three parts, each of which is marked by an event concerning an "anointed one," or messiah (a.t. throughout):

- ♦ Verse 25: "Until an anointed, there will be seven weeks."
- ♦ Verse 26: "After sixty-two weeks, an anointed will be cut off."
- ♦ Verse 24 (which is really the conclusion of this pericope): "He has fixed seventy weeks until a Holy of Holies is anointed [anew]."

The author is convinced that he is witnessing the last gasps of a dying history. Consequently, he states that seven weeks have passed from 605/587 to the anointment of the high priest Joshua. Then an era of sixty-two weeks have ended with the removal ("cut off") of the high priest Onias—unless we must understand his being cut off in more radical way, since Onias was assassinated in 171 by the usurper high priest Menelaus (see Dan 11:22; 2 Macc 4:7-11). The last week will culminate with the anointment of the renewed temple—a true prophecy that Judas Maccabee will bring to fulfillment in the winter of 164 B.C.E. and which will coincide, in Daniel 7, with the advent of the kingdom of God.

Indeed, the Son of Man is enthroned as the last and true High Priest (Dan 7:14) in the transcendent temple, the abode of the "Ancient of Days" (Dan 7:9-10, a.t.), which is also the ultimate court of judgment. As such, the "Human One" (Dan 7:13, a.t.) is given the dominion, glory, and kingship that has been usurped for a fleeting moment by the beasts and their cronies. For he is the lieutenant of God, who is Creator, Judge, Savior, and King. These divine powers are delegated to the Son of Man, whose judgment over all nations is a re-creation of the universe.

Remarkably, the nature of God's substitute is both angelic and human, on the model provided by Ezekiel 8–11 and 43. Ulrich B. Müller notes that "one should describe him as a celestial hypostasis of the people . . . rather than of God," (1972, 35), for he must first be introduced into God's presence since he comes from elsewhere (Dan 7:13). As to the human dimension of the figure, the old messianic expectation of Israel comes to mind. The Davidic, or royal, aspect however, is replaced here (due to political and economical circumstances) by an Adamic, or populist, evocation. And, as to the angelic aspect, the book of Daniel makes it clear that the celestial patron of Israel is the archangel Michael (Dan 10:21). Thus, the Son of Man enthroned at the right side of God, is indeed an hypostasis of sorts of the elect people.

Daniel 7:15-28

The collective dimension of the figure called Son of Man is underscored in the third part of the chapter. Here, the attributes of the Human One are shared by the people of the "saints," a qualifier generally reserved for angels but which is used here (Dan 7:25, 27) to designate the complex nature of God's people. They share with the Son of Man the visibility of God, as shown in Daniel 7:13 and manifest in Ezekiel 1:26. This daring development of Daniel 7 on the basis of Ezekiel is of the utmost importance for students of the New Testament with regard to its confession of Jesus of Nazareth as Christ and Lord and the collective dimension of its identification.

Daniel 7 is prophetic, visionary, and paraenetic. It proclaims the end of suffering for the persecuted of the second century and the marginalized of all times, as well as the vindication of their demand for justice and the glory of the reign they will soon share with their angelic patron forever. Such a happy ending has nothing in common with a Hollywood scenario, for its transcendence does not translate the poor into another world. As the text of Ephesians 6:12 reads, "For our struggle is not against enemies of blood and flesh, but against the rulers, against the authorities, against the cosmic powers of this present darkness, against the spiritual forces of evil in the heavenly places." (See also Dan 10:20–11:1.) Thus, the struggle is not exhausted in facing contingent foes but has cosmic dimensions, which also characterize the ultimate victory of the downtrodden. This struggle, in which the empirical is both hiding and revealing the transcendent, is brilliantly described in our second text.

Daniel 3

As already stated, Daniel A, which features the story of Nebuchadnezzar's colossus, has been reworked to accommodate an agenda that is specific to the second century—for instance, the king's self-deification (Dan 6:6-10) or the death of the martyrs (Dan 3 and 6:17-23).

Daniel 3:1-18

Nebuchadnezzar sets up a golden statue (probably of himself). The story is clearly imaginary; its ending in Daniel 3:28–4:3 makes this unquestionably evident. But the Greek translation of the LXX "historicizes" the tale by dating the event to the eighteenth year of the king, 587 B.C.E., the very year the Babylonians ruined Jerusalem.

Remarkably, the statue erected by the potentate is not specifically called an idol, which perhaps restricts the story's scope to a question of religious preference: iconic or aniconic? The issue here is not only deeply religious—the statue demands to be worshiped (a liturgical term appears in the Aramaic text)—but it is also political. The colossus makes a statement of ultimate power that will soon be shown for what it actually is: a crematorium, an urn for ashes.

The dictatorial regime demands limitless dedication from all. The display of its totalitarianism is to be celebrated with fanfare and hymns. The popular enthusiasm suffers no shade of doubt. Any opposition is met with the dismemberment of the foolhardy. At the sound of the trumpet, everyone must make merry! (Dictatorships throughout history, including the present, possess haunting echoes of Daniel 3.)

The cult of the emperor is anachronistic any time before the era of Antiochus's religious and cultural madness (see also 1 Macc 1:41-53), but it has since been replicated ad nauseam. The throngs are raptured by the state's orchestration of its power and they hail the superman at the helm of the state machine. At his death, for no Stalin or Mao is immortal, they lament the demise of their god.

All this would be utterly comic were it not for the fact that the clown does not laugh. The symbol of the Babylonian state is significantly and ominously empty and hollow, but it can be heated to incandescence. The colossus, in which the throngs recognize the representation of their king and the symbol of the state's power, is also a Moloch-like furnace to swallow up the dissidents. Everybody must sing the same tune. The strength of the regime is in uniformity and conformism; its dynamism is in the endless repetition of the same liturgical prostration before the statue, a manifestation of a grotesque hubris. *Ave Caesar! Kaisar kyrios!*

At this juncture, Daniel 3 is a call to martyrdom (see 1 Macc 1:57-63; 2 Macc 6–7). In the vast Babylonian empire, three young people do not conform. Only three! This is a minority if ever there was one. They have already shunned the royal diet in Daniel 1; now they refuse to be a party to the tyrant's insanity. Fitting the pacifism of the book (see Dan 11:34 as an allusion to the Maccabean insurrection being "a little help"), the three adopt an attitude of passive resistance (3:1-12). But even that is judged intolerable by the totalitarian ideology.

Some two centuries later, the Roman historian Tacitus said that the Jews are the enemies of humanity. Their very presence in Babylonia or in Nazi Germany is enough to clog the mechanism of the dictatorial state.

That nation, Israel, always a "minority," even on its own land, possesses the uncanny vocation of alterity, of total otherness.

Daniel 3:13-18

These verses constitute one of the highest peaks in the biblical landscape. The Jews' refusal stirs the tyrant's fury (Dan 3:13), who now erupts with terrible threats and with affirmations that no one can be saved from his absolute power, not even a god (Dan 3:15). The three respond with a flashing and staggering statement. Their stance of fidelity to God will not change, whether God is able (or willing) to save them or not. Their faith does not belong to the realm of the magical. Their love is unconditional; it does not expect any kind of reward. There is one tradition of interpreting Job 13:15? which, incidentally, was recited by one of the Jews hiding in my home in 1941? "Though G-d may slay me; G-d will I trust."

Thus, the king of Babylon is utterly defeated.

Daniel 3:19-30

This is a story of martyrdom. If, as is extremely probable, the story is originally much older than the apocalyptic part of the book, it surely became particularly relevant at a time when thousands of people lost their lives for refusing to worship the Antiochan state and its idols (see the next section on Daniel 12). The statue-furnace is overheated and the three men— Shadrach, Meshach, and Abednego (as they are known by their Babylonian names)—are thrown alive into the oven. Before the second half of the twentieth century, such a motif may have been regarded as a narrative overstatement. However, since then it has become tragically descriptive of actual occurrences in Auschwitz and elsewhere. No one then escaped. No fourth personage visibly came to cool off the flames and rescue the Jewish children. This, indeed, was the possibility contemplated by the three when Nebuchadnezzar was threatening them: "whether God does or not." But the narrative in Daniel 3 speaks of a highly unusual occurrence: Nebuchadnezzar witnesses the presence of a fourth person in the furnace with the potential martyrs. It is a complex figure, a divine-human epiphany, strikingly resembling the one we met in Daniel 7. Here, the person "has the appearance of a god" (Dan 3:25; or, of the gods, a.t.). The Greek version of Theodotion's commentary on this verse calls him, "the vigilant angel watcher Daniel"! Daniel is not as absent from this chapter as it first seems.

Of utmost importance is that salvation is occurring within the furnace (Dan 3:24-27). This motif is most compelling. It avoids all magical hocus-pocus and shows God (or God's hypostasis) participating in the suffering of God's children. God goes to hell with them and becomes a co-victim. As Elie Wiesel tells us in his book *Night*, God is there, "He is hanging here on this gallows" with the young lad tortured by the SS (1982, p. 62).

Such is the response to the maniac king. To murder someone does not require the slightest skill. Evil, as we have seen here, is always similar to itself, the antipode of creativity and invention. That is why Israel's God is the living God rather than the God of death; this principle needs to be remembered when we turn to Daniel 12. In contrast, Nebuchadnezzar or other potentates in Daniel A, are only capable of bringing death to their people. Power creates a feeling of being granted a license that is inaccessible to any other, even the license to kill.

Shadrach, Meshach, and Abednego were saved by the presence of a fourth being. Daniel A thus anticipates another enormously important breakthrough, namely that of the doctrine of the resurrection of the just. This will retain our attention in the third text selected for commentary. But before we turn to Daniel 12, it is to be noted that Daniel 3 ends with a highly surprising royal confession praising the Jewish God, a motif that is also present elsewhere in the book. An example of this is found in the "outrageous" text of Daniel 2:46-49, which depicts Nebuchadnezzar

falling on his face and worshiping Daniel!

The difference with another comparable text—Acts 14:11-13 in which Barnabas and Paul are mistaken as Jupiter and Mercury? is that Daniel does not protest. Why is he not repelled by this nonsense of the Babylonian? Because, according to prophetic texts, the nations must fall before Israel and lick the dust of their feet (Isa 45:14, author's interpretation). The amusing paradox is that the king who thought of himself as a god is now worshiping a man, Daniel. He tried to cloak the truth about himself under the pretense of self-divinity, but the truth was revealed to him (Dan 2:47) and, hard as it may be to hear, it is a liberation brought about by Daniel-Israel to the nations.

In most of the stories reported by Daniel A, the foreign potentate is credited with premonitory dreams, like those of the pharaoh in Genesis 41. Such visions of the night are deemed God-sent and testify to God's concern with the nations. But, as in Genesis 41, the dream remains a puzzle to the king. Its meaning escapes him and the dream would have remained a cipher without Joseph or Daniel. In short, the divine self-revelation is universal, but its decoding is particular to Israel. It is not that Israel is better than others (see Deut 9, esp. v. 6), but Daniel-Israel dialogues with God and receives the key to the code (Dan 2:18-19, 27-29, 47; 4:6). This notion is at the heart of apocalyptic literature.

The decoding (*apocalyptō*) of the divine secrets—embedded in history, in nature, in life—brings the greatest powers to their knees (see Dan 3:28-30). True, Daniel B does not share the optimism of Daniel A with regard to the empire's ability to convert to Israel's God. This "impossible possibility" (Barth 1957, *Church Dogmatics,* III. 3, 351) is predicated by the acknowledgment that God is the King of all kings and that God "gives [the kingship] to whom he will" (Dan 4:25, a.t.; see also Dan 4:34). Such a gift is for the sake of "practicing justice and showing mercy" (4:24, a.t.), and these are the criteria by which the sovereign is tested. In fact, justice is the divine justice and mercy is the divine mercy as God practices them with God's people. On the part of the potentate, they thus amount to an *imitatio Dei* (imitation of God), which the text dubs praising the Lord (Dan 4:34).

Is Nebuchadnezzar really capable of *metanoia* (change of mind)? Hardly (Dan 5:21). History seldom confirmed Israel's expectation in this regard. No historical Nebuchadnezzar ever fell on his knees before God; no Darius ever adopted Judaism; no Antiochus IV repented in extremis (barring 2 Macc 9:11-12). Israel knows that. But the possibility of the empire hosting justice and mercy is affirmed in spite of all objective evidence and must be maintained for sanity's sake. Relenting is a true potential because no individual and no collectivity, no king and no kingdom, is shut off in a secret chamber of evil—in which case no one would be guilty. Nebuchadnezzar's empire is evil because it may be the home of justice and mercy. When the powers that be refuse to open up the secret chamber, the king goes mad (Dan 4:28-32). The warrants of the ever-potential metanoia of the state are precisely the Jew at the foreign court, the "Hebrew" in Nineveh (Jonah 1:9), the Christian in Asia Minor (1 Pet 4:16). These are the carriers of sanity in the midst of insanity.

Sanity is the knowledge that history is aiming toward an ultimate event that telescopes, condenses, synchronizes, and judges history (Dan 7). It is the event from the beginning, the absolute *kairos*. In Daniel 12, it coincides with the resurrection of the martyrs.

Daniel 12

Daniel 12 is the first time (with Isa 26:19, which was written around the time of Dan 12) that Scripture clearly proclaims an individual resurrection. There are reasons why Israel had been reluctant to speculate about an afterlife. I have explored some of them elsewhere (LaCocque 1979, 235–40). It is important here to realize that the author of Daniel 12 is much less preoccupied with his own fate after death than with God's sovereignty and justice. The martyrs of the second century B.C.E. do not deserve to be revived, but God's equity does not tolerate the termination of innocent, faithful lives at the whim of a demonic tyrant, who could then delude himself and others by claiming to be the master of life and death. To defeat the despot, God receives the martyrs' deaths as a holy oblation instead of "the wages of sin."

Resurrection in Daniel 12 is not general; it is reserved for the *maskilim* and *matsdikim* (the sages and those who justify [others], Dan 12:3, a.t.). The same restriction is again present in 2 Maccabees 7 and *1 Enoch* 90:33. But *Psalms of Solomon* 3:11b-12 extends the privilege to the righteous in general. Finally, *1 Enoch* 51:1 speaks of a general resurrection; a conception picked up by mainstream Judaism and Christianity.

Already in the sixth century B.C.E., Deutero-Isaiah had assimilated redemption and (re)creation. Ezekiel (especially chapter 37) emphasized the same connection. With the contribution of Daniel 12, a correspondence is established of creation, redemption, and resurrection. The apocalyptic text even goes further and pinpoints resurrection as the major event of and beyond history. The end is like the beginning, a victory over chaos and death. The end-time is Eden retrieved.

CONCLUSION

So the book of Daniel comes to its end as befits its eschatological message. The vision is not of a "pie in the sky" but expresses the firm assurance that the *maskilim* and *matsdikim* (the sages and "righteous") are the powerful ferment of this world's salvation. Daniel ends on a realistically sober note:

"The wicked shall [continue to] act wickedly and not understand . . . Happy is the one who perseveres [until] the end of days" (Dan 12:10-13; a.t.). The end of days are always the days of our life! As one of the Jews hiding in my home in 1941 recited, "Though God may slay me; God will I trust."

BIBLIOGRAPHY

Barth, Karl. *Church Dogmatics,* 14 volumes, Edinburgh: T & T Clark, 1956–1975.

Collins, John J. *Daniel: A Commentary on the Book of Daniel.* Hermeneia. Minneapolis: Fortress, 1993.

Collins, John J., and Peter W. Flint, eds. *The Book of Daniel: Composition and Reception.* 2 vols. VTSup 83. Leiden: Brill, 2001.

Fewell, Danna Nolan. *Circle of Sovereignty: Plotting Politics in the Book of Daniel.* 2nd ed. Nashville: Abingdon, 1991.

Hartman, Louis F., and Alexander A. Di Lella. *The Book of Daniel.* AB 23. Garden City, N.Y.: Doubleday, 1978.

LaCocque, André. "Allusions to Creation in Daniel 7." Pages 114–31 in *The Book of Daniel: Composition and Reception.* Edited by John J. Collins and Peter W. Flint. VTSup 83. Leiden: Brill, 2001.

-------- . *The Book of Daniel.* Translated by David Pellauer. Atlanta: John Knox Press, 1979.

-------- . *Daniel in His Time.* Studies on Personalities of the Old Testament. Columbia: University of South Carolina, 1988.

Müller, Ulrich B. *Messias und Menschensohn in jüdischen Apokalypsen und in der Offenbarung des Johannes.* SNT 6. Gütersloh: Gütersloher Verlagshaus Mohn, 1972.

Rowland, Christopher. *The Open Heaven: A Study of Apocalyptic in Judaism and Early Christianity.* New York: Crossroad, 1982.

Wiesel, Elie. *Night.* New York: Bantam, 1982.

HOSEA

Tânia Mara Vieira Sampaio

Methodist University of Piracicaba, Brazil

LIFE CONTEXT OF THE INTERPRETATION

The city of São Paulo, well-known as the powerful engine that leads Brazil, is a densely populated industrial metropolis where almost eighteen million people live. Its daily life is full of contradictions that affect every human being regardless of social class, ethnic group, age, or gender.

A few years ago in a peripheral neighborhood (a barrios) of São Paulo, a group of marginalized women, with bodies marked by the practice of prostitution from a tender age, deeply moved us, the facilitators of a grassroots Bible study goup ("Círculos Populares de Leitura da Bíblia"), by their baffling questions. Could we celebrate the sacrament of the Eucharist with them? What does the Bible say about women like them? Is it true that God does not like them? Would God bless them only if they abandon prostitution?

Their questions reflect the message they have heard again and again from priests and pastors who have closed the doors of their churches to them, denying them access to their "sacred spaces" and to God as long as they do not radically change lifestyle. But for these women, giving their bodies to prostitution is not a choice, still less a pleasure. For the great majority of them, it is an inescapable part of the endless cycle of poverty in which they are caught and of the relentless abuse they suffer from a patriarchal society that both condemns prostitution and condones it for the pleasure of men, even as it totally deprives women of their dignity.

Remembering Jesus' freeing God from the temple, where the sacerdotal class imprisoned God behind ritualistic sacrifices, has led me to read the Bible with grassroots Bible study groups that have included among their readers people with graduate degrees as well as people with more limited education. Hearing the questions of these women who are marked by the stigma of marginalization, we addressed their questions by reading the Bible in dialogue with them. We paid attention to certain texts that the mainline churches had stopped reading both in community worship and in theological reflection. Thus we noted that in the texts about Rahab (Josh 2:1-3, 6:17-25, Matt 1:5, Heb 11:31, and Jas 2:25) she is always designated as "a prostitute" (except for Matt 1:5). Yet these references to her social status are never used to condemn her or to say that she is unworthy. On the contrary, the prostitute Rahab has a place among the most famous names of the history of salvation, joining Abraham, Moses, and others. Actually Rahab is introduced as one of the pillars of our faith.

As I read Hosea, my dialogue with these women led me to raise new questions. I began to realize that, in the logic of patriarchal oppression, they have been expelled from home, and that prostitution is for them a means of survival and a practice of resistance against many forms of violence against them. Looking at their situation from

Tânia Mara Vieira Sampaio, PhD in Religion (Old Testament), is a leader of "Círculos Populares de Leitura da Bíblia" (Grassroots Bible Study Groups). She trains facilitators for this movement, which since the 1970s has been most fruitful in promoting the development of popular biblical hermeneutics among marginalized people in Brazil and in other parts of Latin America. She is the author of Movimentos do corpo prostituído da mulher - aproximações da profecia atribuída a Oséias (1999).

Hosea's perspective, I believe we should not merely see these women as victims, although their victimization must be denounced. Rather, we should recognize, support, and encourage the ways they resist violence, struggle for dignity, and fight for survival, their own and that of their dependents.

My desire to read Hosea with these women was motivated by hearing their stories of the violence that they have endured since childhood or adolescence. As little girls, many of them were sexually abused by their fathers, stepfathers, uncles, friends of the family, or neighbors. Others were sold by their families for money to feed the rest of the family. Some, lured by the promise of money that they wanted to buy fashionable clothes or trinkets, gave themselves without being aware of the real consequences. Many were raped by men in homes where they worked as housekeepers, or were forced into sexual relations by bosses promising them a better salary, which they desperately needed to support sick relatives. For people with limited education, that is, for the great majority of Brazilians, selling one's body is more profitable than any available job.

The many forms of violence in our country and in the world cannot go unmentioned; otherwise we lose the will and ability to confront them. Violence is related to racial, class, gender, religious, and cultural differences. Violence, whether physical, emotional, economic, or social, affects a person's very integrity. Thus, violence should not be viewed as a peripheral social issue, concerning marginalized people alone; it is an issue that concerns the condition of human relations in society.

Our personal and pastoral responsibility demands of us that we proceed to a critical reevaluation of religious discourse in all our denominations. We need especially to assess those religious discourses that legitimate and reinforce cultural and social patterns that label women as guilty while absolving men of any guilt and responsibility.

Prostitution had contradictory connotations in Hosea's society. While it carried preconceived stigmas, it was an accepted social role. This observation already raises the possibility that Hosea was not so much concerned with prostitution as a social institution, but with the purpose for which it was used.

If this be the case, we need to carefully evaluate the complex implications of Hosea's view of prostitution for both women and men, and especially for their respective places in society. Hosea implies (and makes explicit in ch. 4) that women were neither viewed as guilty nor punished for practicing prostitution. The crux of the problem is elsewhere. Prostitution is presented as a social function performed by women as a means of subsistence (Hos 2:4-17). It was condoned by priests, in order to extort money and swindle the people (Hosea 4:4-19), and used by the prophet as a metaphor to reveal a twisted social reality. The prophetic critique was not aimed at the different levels of people's unfaithfulness. It was a broader critique of the social order, including a critique of a use of power comparable to prostitution by certain segments of the population, and in particular by the priests.

CONTEXTUAL COMMENT

Hosea's Different Prophecy in Its Time and Space

The prophecy of Hosea has a beauty and scope different from the theological traditions of its time. This brief commentary presents a sampling of these innovations, but also a deconstruction of the stereotypes that centuries of interpretations have created out of Hosea's metaphors by reducing the prophecy to a religious critique mirrored in the prophet's marriage. These stereotypical images will be deconstructed through a close examination of the text, aimed at providing evidence of the misogynist hermeneutics of traditional interpretations developed in a patriarchal perspective. Their reductionism is already visible in the subtitles that the translators added to the text, which have influenced our understanding of the textual units. Keeping in mind the women from the barrios of São Paulo, we seek to renew the reading of Hosea by reconsidering its central theme, prostitution. Rather than making the a priori assumption that the reference to prostitution is a universal metaphor that we can understand in terms of our own views of prostitution, whatever they might be, we must recognize that this metaphor referred to prostitution as a social reality in the kingdom of Israel of the eighth century b.c.e., intertwined with other social realities, such as agricultural work, palace intrigues, military activities, religious rituals in daily life and in the sanctuaries, and internal and external political alliances.

The prophetic text attributed to Hosea is one of the most poorly conserved books of the Hebrew Bible. While this textual fact creates difficulties for the exegetical-hermeneutic process, it also opens new possibilities and justifies a quest for its mysteries through new hermeneutic venues. The first question raised by this book concerns its authorship. Many agree that the greater part of the text comes from the prophet Hosea. Yet, this prophetic book has long pericopes instead of the brief and punctual public discourses characterizing other prophetic books of the time (e.g., Amos 3:3-15; Mic 3). These longer pericopes indicate the presence and role of a prophetic circle that redacted the prophecies. With this awareness, one can recognize a plurality of voices in the text that reveal the interactions of people in their daily lives.

This prophetic text refers to the final period of the northern kingdom, from the last years of the reign of Jeroboam II (786-746 B.C.E.) to the reign of Hoshea son of Elah (732-724 B.C.E.)—kings of the dynasty of Jehu (1:1-4). Hosea 1 makes explicit that the focus of the critique is the dynasty of Jehu. Hosea 2–3 reflect the economic prosperity and political tranquility that marked the reign of Jeroboam II. Hosea 5 and subsequent chapters describe signs of the growing crisis in Israel due to external pressures from Assyria. Indeed, following the subjugation by Tiglath-Pileser III (king of Assyria) of part of the territory of Israel around 733 B.C.E., a climate of violence and insecurity prevailed in Israel (4:1-3). The final chapters (13–14) refer to events close to the years 724-722 B.C.E., dates of the fall of Samaria and the end of the northern kingdom (13:10-11).

Most scholars agree that the final composition of the book took place in the southern kingdom after 722 B.C.E., as is indicated by several allusions to Judah as parts of posterior additions pointing to the salvation of Judah, by contrast with Israel.

An Overview of Hosea

On the basis of different language styles, scholars commonly divide the book of Hosea into two large units: Hosea 1–3 and Hosea 4–14, with several subdivisions for the second unit. However, following Sherwood (1996, 117-149), I propose to break down the book in terms of its shifts from micro- to macro-social relationships among men and women. This perspective divides the books into two large blocks, Hosea 1–4 and 5–14. Chapter 4 belongs to the first section, along with 1–3, because it refers to the primary relationships in Israelite life. These are micro-power relationships among men and women, including marriage, procreation, collective work in the field, production and distribution of goods, as well as particular occasions, such as harvest in Hosea 4, when collective activity leads to festivities and religious rituals.

Hosea 4 is thus a hinge between the two large sections, because like 1–3 it deals with daily life in harvest time, and because it combines a strong critique of the priests—as a group who represent the State—with a description of actual prostitution and adultery as common occurrences in Israel that affected the relationships between women and men. In Hosea 4, the critique of the priest, and behind him of the monarchic state, unmasks what happened in the daily lives of families. When this is recognized, the previous chapters (1–3) acquire a historical and concrete social force that demands a revision in the interpretation of the metaphors and symbols, traditionally understood as the primary theological teaching of a prophecy safely removed from social realities.

Methodologically, we must keep in mind that structures and content are closely interrelated and frame the meaning of the prophetic book. Therefore, the concrete details found in the text concerning daily life in the eighth century B.C.E. convey the historicity of the experience of Hosea and Gomer with prostitution and of its relationship with the events of the last twenty years in the kingdom of Israel. While the first section, Hosea 1–3, focuses on the domestic domain and its peculiar social relationships of power, the second, Hosea 5–14, widens the scope to include the macro-power social relationships of the monarchic state, the king's court, his army, priests, etc. By this observation I do not intend to disconnect the domestic sphere from the public sphere, but to indicate how each is intertwined with the other. The book of Hosea establishes a direct correspondence between public and private spaces. By suspending the interpretation of the metaphors long enough to consider the actual social relationships reflected by the book of Hosea, we can recognize how traditional interpretations, which have read this book in terms of very different cultural situations, have distorted the book's views of prostitution and its overall message.

In this contextual commentary, I consider different features of the micro-social domain presented in Hosea 1–4, and put them in dialogue with similar features of the macrosocial domain presented in Hosea 5–14. I go from the space of the house to that of the palace, from the workspace in the harvest to the fertility rites, from the space of pregnancy and childbirth to that of militarization, from the tribute paid by workers to the sanctuary and the erection of idols.

Prostituted Bodies on the Move (Hosea 1:2)

Prostituted bodies on the move open the prophecy. Resisting bodies move through the prophecy. Transgressing bodies on the move challenge the reading of the prophecy and call for reinterpretation! Yahweh said to Hosea, "Go, take for yourself a wife of prostitutions and children of prostitutions; for the land prostituted itself, forsaking Yahweh." (1:2 a.t.)

After a brief reference to the historical period (1:1), the prophetic discourse immediately deals with marriage and the situation of prostitution in Israel. Hosea goes to Gomer's father to take her in marriage (1:3), in line with the custom of the time. The union follows in part usual customs. Yet it is also presented as out of the ordinary. According to the text, the condition of the woman and her children as being "of prostitutions" is connectd to the disobedience of the land. In the text, prostitution stands out as a social condition that infiltrated the household, breaking into it as a practice present throughout the country.

We cannot ignore the clear mention of the two houses that were united through the marriage of the children: The word of Yahweh that came to Hosea *the son of Beeri* . . . 'Go, take for yourself a wife of prostitutions . . . ' So he went and took Gomer the *daughter of Diblaim* (1:1-3, a.t.)

The mention of the names of Beeri and Deblaim is significant. Pronouncing the father's names within daily relationships upheld the houses and the families; at a marriage it established ties of solidarity between the houses.

The force of prophetic originality is in details that may not seem important. In 1:2 Gomer is presented as a "woman of prostitutions"—note the plural, "prostitutions"—and, at the same time, as the daughter of Deblaim. The fact that "prostitutions" is in the "abstract plural" (Wolff 1974, 13) indicates that it does not refer to an individual characteristic of Gomer, but rather to the circumstance in which Gomer was. She was involved in prostitutions without being excluded from the patriarchal family structure. She was taken in marriage from within her father's house.

The text does not use the verb *zanah* (to prostitute self) with the name of Gomer. The text does not say that she prostituted herself; rather, it affirms that the "land prostituted itself." Therefore, interestingly, the weight falls on the land, and not exclusively on the woman who marries the prophet. She was a young woman who belonged to her father's house, from whence she was taken in marriage. The prostitution(s) marking her body seems strange. From whence would such a condition come? In general, a prostitute is not found in her father's house, but rather in places where she practices prostitution.

The prophetic text continues to surprise us when we consider a statement often ignored by commentators. Hosea 4:14 mentions, in the plural, that "the daughters prostituted themselves and the brides practiced adultery" during the times of the harvest (4:14). This indicates that women other than Gomer were in a similar situation, and, consequently, that other women and men were in the same situation as Gomer and Hosea. In this text, <u>prostitution is not a general metaphor; the prophet sought to confront an</u> actual aspect of Israel's way of life.

Fertile Prostituted Bodies and Children of Prostitutions

Gomer's body of prostitutions is the same body that gives life. She is pregnant, but her pregnancy is marked by a previous reality; prostitution affects her children: "they are children of prostitutions" (1:2). Therefore, from the start they bear pejorative names (1:4-9). What would bring a parent to receive a son or a daughter by giving him or her a name that proclaims a curse rather than a blessing? The text makes it explicit: these names are sharp critiques of the monarchy:

> Name him Jezreel . . . and I will avenge the blood of Jezreel on the house of Jehu, and will cause the kingdom of the house of Israel to cease.
> Name her Lo-Ruhamah; for I will no longer have mercy on the house of Israel.
> . . .
> Name him Lo-Ammi; for you are not my people, and I will not be yours.
> (1:4, 5, 6, 9, a.t.)

Each child's name announces punishment on the king's dynasty, the destruction of the state of Israel and its army, a suspension of YHWH's deep love and the rupture of the covenant that YHWH had made with his people during the exodus out of Egypt. All the critiques are directed against the state of Israel, and not against the woman and her children. Rather the woman's body is the prophetic word proclaiming the destruction of the political structures that feed on the life of her children.

The power that the state strives to acquire is in the procreating body of the woman. Children are important in the tribal structures of Israel. They are needed both as laborers in the field and as soldiers on military fronts, the two basic structures of the tribal economic system. Either the children's bodies, marked by prostitution, are sacrificed for the sake of the national power structure, or this tribal system is destroyed, and the children have the possibility to live.

Similar critiques of the monarchic power structures of Israel are found throughout the book of Hosea, especially in passages regarding political issues concerning the kings, economic issues related to the harvest, and the use of religion for political and economic manipulation in the turmoil in the last twenty years of the northern kingdom.

Kings, Prostitution, and Women's Power: Transforming Conditions of Subordination into Spaces of Power

> They have set up kings, but not by me.
> They have made princes, and I didn't approve.
> Of their silver and their gold they have made themselves idols,
> that they may be cut off. (8:4, a.t.)

> I have given you a king in my anger,
> and have taken him away in my wrath (13: 11, a.t.)

A power that constituted itself against YHWH's will is responsible for the husband-wife dispute about the support of the children, and about the origin of the goods needed to sustain the household.

> Contend with your mother! Contend, for she is not my wife,
> neither am I her man; and let her put away her prostitution from her face, and her adulteries from between her breasts; Lest I strip her naked. . . .
> Indeed, on her children I will have no mercy; for *they are children of prostitutions.* (2:2-4, a.t.)

In the husband-wife dialogue, the children are first summoned to clarify the situation. The children are urged to ask what they need from their mother. The rest of the dialogue demonstrates the complexity of the situation. Yet the critique of the woman's prostitution allows the hard facts to emerge. Her prostitution was not for luxury items and pleasures; she brought home the basic necessities of life:

> "For their mother has prostituted herself. She who conceived them has done shamefully; for she said, 'I will go after my lovers, who give me my *bread* and my *water,* my *wool* and my *flax,* my oil and my *drink*'" (2:5, a.t.).

To a certain extent, prostitution was a space for women's power. By bringing home the basic necessities of life they threatened their husbands' authority and claims of ownership. Contesting Gomer's prostitution also requires one to question the food that she brought home to her children and husband. Despite the long tradition of theological interpretation, merely blaming the woman's body is not enough. Men are also implicated in the situation of prostitution that is found throughout the nation.

When analyzing the power relationships between Gomer and Hosea from this perspective, Hosea 2:6-23 becomes understandable. The renewal of their relationship is due neither to the woman's condemnation nor to her repentance. On the contrary, the text emphasizes that the new relationship between the woman and the husband occurs when he is no longer called "my Baal," my owner (2:16), but rather "my man" i.e., the

man with whom I freely associate myself, a conception that is considerably stronger than the translation "my husband." The new matrimonial bond is no longer established through the customary exchange of gifts between two families, as in the first chapter, but through a covenantal agreement between the woman and the man. This new relationship is between the woman who, in her condition of prostitution, has been empowered to be a full partner in this covenant and the man who is also free to enter this covenant by resisting the existing social structures.

> I will betroth you to me forever. Yes, I will betroth you to me in righteousness, in justice, in loving kindness, and in solidarity. I will even betroth you to me in faithfulness; and you shall know Yahweh. (2:19, 20, a.t.)

Life is renewed insofar as the demands of the existing social and political structures are denied. Indeed, the renewal of the couple's relationship also signals the reversal of the names of the children. As we noted above, these names are sharp critiques of the monarchy and of the political, military, and social structures. The renaming of the children announces the end of this political order and of its militaristic projects. The covenant with YHWH announced in Hosea 2 reflects the renewed power relationship between women and men in daily life and leads toward the transformation of conditions of subordination into spaces of power, even if they are merely spaces where survival or resistance becomes possible:

> "In that day *I will make a covenant for them* with the animals of the field, and with the birds of the sky, and with the creeping things of the ground . . .
> It will happen in that day, I will respond," says Yahweh,
> "I will respond to the heavens, and they will respond to the earth;
> and the earth will respond to the grain, and the new wine, and the oil; and *they will respond to Jezreel [God sows].* I will sow her to me in the earth; *and I will have mercy on the Lo-Ruhamah [No-Mercy]* and I will tell *Lo-Ammi [Not-My-People]*

'You are my people; and they will say, 'My God!'" (2:18-23, a.t.)

In the same line, the brief third chapter presents a synthesis of the new relationship between the woman and the man, and between Israel and YHWH. Not only will the woman stay home without prostituting herself, but the man will do the same. Simultaneously, the kingdom of Israel will remain a long time without a king, without a prince, and without religious ceremonies. Without these political and religious factors, prostitution ceases in the nation; when these political and religious factors are present, prostitution proliferates:

I said to her, "You shall stay with me many days. *You shall not prostitute yourself,* and you shall not be with any other man. *I will also be so toward you.*" For the children of Israel shall abide many days without king, and without prince, and without sacrifice, and without sacred stone, and without ephod or idols (3:3, 4, a.t.).

As long as Israel has a king, princes, sacrifices, sacred stones, ephods, or idols, the life-context is quite problematic. This observation rescues Gomer from her isolation as a particular prostitute whom a prophet married. Her prostitution is part of a much broader social and political situation. The suspension of prostitution on the part of the woman and the man is tied to the destruction of the state of Israel. Or, more positively, the restructuring of the household as a covenantal relationship requires the destruction or the reinvention of the exercise of power by the monarchy. Prostitution, in the book of Hosea, is the condition that marks the life of all people in the nation. Prostitution is not simply a symbol or a metaphor used to make a theological point against the priests and other political leaders. Prostitution marks the life of priests and political leaders because they expropriate the life of men, women, and children and interfere with the household rules of solidarity *(hesed)*.

Kings and princes are denounced in Hosea as senseless, deceitful, and consumed by internal (7:1-7) and foreign political intrigues (5:1-15; 7:8-16; 8:8-14; 10:6-15).

They make the king glad with their wickedness, and the princes with their lies (7:3). They are all hot as an oven, and devour their judges. All their kings have fallen (7:7). Israel is swallowed up. Now they are among the nations like a worthless thing. (8:8)

The religious space is also under critique. One can no longer find mercy or solidarity *(hesed)* there (6:6), because the priests have identified themselves with the political and social structures that sustain the state. Thus, again and again the book of Hosea disqualifies the priests from religious leadership.

They feed on the sin of my people, and set their heart on their iniquity. (4:8) As gangs of robbers wait to ambush a man, so the company of priests murder in the way toward Shechem, committing shameful crimes. (6:9)

State-Sponsored and Priest-Supported Prostitution

Hosea 4 includes severe condemnations of the priests' actions. In 4:1-4, they are made responsible for the people's sin and their lack of knowledge of YHWH; in 4:9-19, they are accused of confusing worship of YHWH with foreign religious practices and thus of making it impossible to pronounce the name of YHWH (4:15).

A central point of this chapter clarifies the target of the prophetic critique when it alludes in 4:10-13 to the harvest time, as 9:1-2 also does. The wheat threshing floors (9:1) are spaces for work and simultaneously for the religious rituals of thanksgiving. It is harvest time; the work yields its fruit. It is the moment to stomp on the harvested grapes and to savor the new wine (4:11). In the short and intense harvest time, men, women, children, and the elderly have to work together. The enormous amount of work leads to fatigue. The shade of the trees (4:13) welcomes tired bodies and gives them the deserved pleasure of rest.

The prophet is impervious to the idyllic beauty of communal human labor and of the harvest festival with its popular and religious celebration. The gifts from the earth in return for labor are acknowledged in religious rites of thanksgiving for the earth's fertility. Yet the priests are strongly criticized for mixing thanksgiving toward YHWH with fertility rites, which strip bodies of their dignity and violate the rules that preserve life and household solidarity.

> Indeed the spirit of prostitution has led them astray, and they have been prostituted to their God. They sacrifice on the tops of the mountains, and burn incense on the hills, under oaks and poplars and terebinths, because its shade is good. Therefore your daughters prostituted themselves, and your brides commit adultery. I will not punish your daughters when they play the prostitute, nor your brides when they commit adultery (4:12-14, a.t.).

Daughters, young women of marrying age that are still in their father's house, daughters-in-law, and brides are involved in prostitution and adultery. In the time and space of the harvest, the women of the households are drawn into Canaanite fertility rites, promoted by priests (4:14, 15).

The force of this chapter demands a revision of the common misogynist readings. The text explicitly states, "I will not punish your daughters . . . nor your brides" (4:14), and there is no word of condemnation against the other women, be they prostitutes or sacred prostitutes. But the priests' attitudes are very explicitly condemned. When considering Gomer's prostitution and adultery in light of the harvest celebrations, it becomes evident that she participated in the harvest and its festivities in her role as Deblaim's daughter and then as Hosea's wife. Was the nation and the household equally affected by this practice? Was it appropriate for people to object to the participation in fertility rites by women of their households? Why would the priests promote such activity as part of popular religiosity?

The power struggles in the historical context of the northern kingdom indicate that it was urgent for the kingdom to increase procreation; young hands were needed to work the land that provided the resources needed by the state and to pay the tributes required for foreign alliances, and young males were needed in the army. Thus, it appears that the priests concealed within religious practices the economic and political use of the bodies of women, men, and newborn children. The priests equated the procreative women's cycle to that of nature, so that the harvest festivities would become the encounter between bodies, which, in the pleasure of the shade trees, while resting with good wine, generated a crop of new children.

One can now understand why, even before their birth, the children carry the mark of prostitution in their bodies. They are children conceived on the wheat threshing floors at harvest time, rather than in the household, where an average span of three years was maintained between pregnancies for the welfare of the woman and of the child.

The kingdom of Israel urgently wanted to defend its sovereignty against Assyria. With religion as a means of peaceful coercion and the fetish of pleasure as a concealment, the political and religious powers exploited bodies, as we saw in Hosea 2–3. This conclusion is supported by paying attention to the conversations between husband, wife, and children about the marks of prostitution and adultery that are in their bodies, about the origin of the goods that sustain the household, and finally about the covenantal marriage envisioned on a radically different basis. When these power structures are exposed, the last chapters of the book of Hosea become more meaningful.

> Ephraim's glory will fly away like a bird. There will be no birth, no pregnancy, and no conception. Though they bring up their children, I will bereave them, so that not a man shall be left. (9:11-12, a.t.)

This text, and a similar passage in 13:13, which curiously are often interpreted as punishments, make sense as an expression of resistance rather than victimization. The bodies that circulate in the texts transgress the orders of the state. A woman's body that is not ready for procreation—that refuses conception, pregnancy, or childbirth—and a newborn child who refuses to grow (13:13) constitute threats to the state rather than punishment of women's bodies or of the people.

This prophetic proclamation comes from the guts of one who does not see any sense in engendering sons and daughters, or in feeding them, since conditions are such as to make life impossible for them. The desire that no child be born is an expression of hope and of protest. It fits with other proclamations of the book of Hosea that liturgically reject the powers sustaining the state, as in the following example:

Assyria can't save us. We won't ride on horses; neither will we say any more to the

work of our hands, 'Our gods!' *for in you the fatherless finds mercy.* (14:3, a.t.)

These words that open the conclusion of the prophetic text criticize the way of religious space was used to support the state in the last years of the kingdom of Israel. If in the religious harvest spaces (4:4-19) and in the sanctuaries (8:4-7) there are forces of trickery that expropriate the life of the people, it is in the liturgical proclamation that the prophet denies the state and reaffirms the children's lives. The text approves neither foreign alliances, nor silver and gold transformed into idols, nor the army, nor robbed lives, but mercy toward the small ones and toward the orphans.

CONCLUSION

In this reading of Hosea, I considered Gomer and Hosea as subjects with choices, desires, misconceptions, struggles, and points of view at different times in their lives, like the women in the barrios of São Paulo. In the process I have focused our comments on passages that describe the relationships between women and men in micro-social spheres and their correspondence to relationships in the macro-social spheres.

This focus helped to show prostitution as a social practice that was widely experienced by the people of Israel in the eighth century b.c.e. The recognition that prostitution occurred throughout the nation and affected many women besides Gomer should not hide the role of men (see 4:14). Without the presence and the participation of men, the practice of prostitution would not be viable. This observation is a first step toward overcoming the stigma that disqualifies prostituted bodies, especially the woman's body in androcentric cultures like ours. In such cultures, msen are not associated with the social image of prostitution.

On the basis of this reading of prostitution in Hosea, it becomes possible to envision ways to avoid reducing the teaching of Hosea to the analogy that says the prophet is

to the woman as YHWH and fidelity are to infidelity. In addition to stigmatizing the woman's body, such analogies conceal significant aspects of the text concerning people's lives and their experiences before God, turning certain aspects of the text upside down. When it becomes clear that the priests, the kings, and the princes constitute the social groups Hosea criticized, it is no longer possible to view the analogy of the marriage as the key to Hosea's prophecy.

Since, according to our interpretation, the misogyny assigning culpability to the woman's body cannot be grounded in the text of Hosea, the question is: From whence does it come? What is the conception of the world that calls for such interpretations? Who benefits from such misogyny?

While I cannot begin to answer these questions here, I can at least affirm that it is possible to develop a study of Hosea that is led in our space and time by the bodies of these women. Furthermore, I can answer one related question: Who is hurt by interpretations of Hosea that posit analogy between Gomer and Hosea, woman and man, unfaithful people and YHWH? In our grassroots Bible study groups, we have heard the answer in the bewildering question of women with bodies marked by prostitution: Is it true that God does not love us?

Despite the difficulties of breaking away from "fossilized interpretations," Latin American exegetes and hermeneutes dare to practice hermeneutics of suspicion and to question the privileged space of these interpretations by reading the Bible in other spaces, such as grassroots Bible study groups where all are welcome.

BIBLIOGRAPHY

Alonso Schökel, L., and José L. Sicre Diaz. *Ezequiel – Doze profetas menores – Daniel – Baruc – Carta de Jeremias*. Vol. 2 of *Profetas* São Paulo: Edições Paulinas, 1991.

Gebara, Ivone. *Teologia ecofeminista: ensaio para repensar o conhecimento e a religião*. São Paulo: Olho d'Água, 1997.

Jarschel, Haidi. "Corpo de Mulher, corpo culpabilizado." Pages 49-56. in Revista *Mandrágora* nº 1, *Direitos Reprodutivos e Aborto*. Pós-Graduação em Ciências da Religião, Instituto Metodista de Ensino Superior, São Bernardo do Campo, 1994.

Sampaio, Tânia Mara Vieira. *Movimentos do corpo prostituído da mulher - aproximações da profecia atribuída a Oséias*. São Paulo: Ed. Loyola, 1999.

Sherwood, Yvonne. *The Prostitute and the Prophet: Hosea's Marriage in Literary-Theoretical Perspective*. JSOTSup 212. Sheffield: Sheffield Academic Press, 1996.

Weems, Renita J. *Battered Love: Marriage, Sex, and Violence in the Hebrew Prophets*. Minneapolis: Fortress, 1995.

Wolff, Hans Walter. *Hosea: A Commentary on the Book of the Prophet Hosea*. Translated by Gray Stansell. Edited by Paul D. Hansen. Hermeneia. Philadelphia: Fortress, 1974.

Yee, Gale A. *Composition and Tradition in the Book of Hosea: A Redaction Critical Investigation*. SBLDS 102. Atlanta: Scholars Press, 1987.

JOEL

Pablo R. Andiñach

Instituto Universitario ISEDET, Buenos Aires, Argentina

Translated from Spanish by Rubén Muñoz-Larrondo

LIFE CONTEXT OF THE INTERPRETATION

There are several connections between Joel's message and the Latin-American realities of poverty and marginalization. Years of grassroots struggle for justice and equality have only resulted in social repression and a reinforced system of exploitation of the natural resources of the poorer nations for the benefit of the rich and powerful nations. Living conditions have deteriorated during the last twenty years. The level of

extreme poverty of twenty and thirty years ago had somewhat declined, but it has again reached unthinkable levels. In Argentina, for example, the neoliberal economic policies of the governments have brought back levels of hunger, illiteracy, and appalling unhygienic conditions not seen for a generation. Joel refers to a similar social reality in Judah. However, many in the world are still totally unaware of such dreadful reality.

CONTEXTUAL COMMENT

An Overview of the Book

The book of Joel is composed of two different but carefully balanced parts. The first and oldest part, 1:1–2:17, presents the devastation of the country by foreign military invasion. Joel uses the image of a locust invasion, evoking vivid natural images in the minds of the readers. The people suffering from such devastation are in tears and cry out in lamentation. The second and more recent part, 2:18–4:21, contains words of comfort for the oppressed and of judgment against their enemies. Some vivid images of this section became a staple of later apocalyptic literature, for instance, "the sun shall be turned to darkness and the moon to blood" (2:31 [HB 3:4]), and "the sun and the moon are darkened" (3:15 [HB 4:15]).

These two parts include material from different origins and times and were the product of complex redactional work. Thus, dating these parts and identifying their

respective social contexts is quite difficult. It is enough to say here that the process of final redaction took place during the later part of the postexilic period (400-350 B.C.E.) or perhaps at the beginning of the Hellenistic period. It was a time when foreign powers oppressed and abused the people of God who, though unable to hope for a quick liberation, remained convinced that God would have the last word and would not forget the downtrodden. The concluding verses (3:18-21 [HB 4:18-21]) proclaim the coming of God's final judgment against the oppressors.

The connection between the two parts is logical, as a question is related to an answer. The first part describes the military invasion using the image of a locust invasion (explicitly mentioned in 1:4, suggested through out). The second part (2:20; 3:2-3; [HB 4:2-3]) clarifies the fact that it is an actual military invasion. The surprising "thing" of 1:2 ("Has such a thing happened in your

Pablo R. Andiñach, former dean of the Instituto Universitario ISEDET (Instituto Superior Evangélico de Estudios Teológicos) and professor of Old Testament, is the author of *El fuego y la ternura. Comentario al Cantar de los Cantares* (1997), *Iglesias Evangélicas y Derechos Humanos en la Argentina 1976-1998*, (2001), with Daniel Bruno, "Zechariah" in *International Bible Commentary* (1999) and "Genesis" and "Tobias" in *Comentario Bíblico Latinoamericano* (forthcoming).

days?") is shown to be God's liberation in 3:16-17 [HB 4:16-17)]. The invitation to repent (2:12-17) corresponds to the out-pouring of the Spirit (2:28-29 [HB 3:1-2]). In this way, the second part rereads the first part to discern in it a new historic reality. The final text goes beyond the first experience of the invasion as a locust plague and of repentance; it becomes a denunciation of oppression and a proclamation that God wants to restore a forgotten justice.

Remembering Oppression (Joel 1:2-4)

The book begins with an exhortation to remember some past events. Because justice has not been reestablished, one must remember these dreadful events; otherwise evil and suffering would triumph by being forgotten. The formula, "tell your children of it, and let your children tell their children, and their children another generation" (1:3), evokes what is expressed in a legal context in Deuteronomy 6:7.

Joel 1:4 describes a locust invasion, a regular and well known occurrence in the ancient world. All vegetation was destroyed, with devastating and long-term consequences for both people and animals, deprived of food. It even affected religious services, because of the lack of oil and other products necessary for the rituals.

This mention of the locusts in 1:4 is used to keep alive the memory of the destruction brought about by a foreign army. Like an invasion of locusts, this military invasion affects all of life, including its political, cultural, and religious realms. People had to adapt their daily lives to the demands of the occupying troops. Joel 2:17 expresses Israel's grief and pain of being occupied by a foreign nation, and of being exposed to mockery for not having a God who protects her.

Countries that are economically dependent upon foreign nations today have experiences similar to that of Israel in Joel's time. In order to disguise the subjugation they impose upon others, colonialist nations and people in power promote forgetfulness in the

name of reconciliation. The powerful are said to have "lovingly" brought peace, despite the horrendous acts that they have perpetrated with impunity. In the name of a twisted concept of love, the oppressors insist that the victims should forgive them without asking for any compensation for their loss and without expecting any expression of repentance for the aggressions. In Argentina, politicians and even religious leaders have insisted that the mothers of the hundreds of "disappeared persons" (the "*desaparecidos*" whose corpses have not yet been found since their disappearance in the time of the military dictatorships) should forgive and forget for the sake of national reconciliation. Meanwhile, the same politicians and religious leaders pardon the murderers without requiring them to acknowledge the illegality of their actions. Joel recognized this mode of behavior in his time, and objected that, without remembrance, there is no possibility of justice. Children must be told what has produced the oppression they are experiencing. Keeping alive the memory of history and clear-minded analyses of the causes of injustice, social repression, and economic exploitation are necessary to maintain the hope for justice among those who suffer from oppression.

The Day of YHWH

Joel proclaims the coming of "the day of YHWH" in 1:15; 2:1-2, 10-11, 28-32; and 3:14-17. Through repetition, this important theme becomes more and more concrete as the book unfolds.

In 1:15 and 2:1-2, the prophet simply proclaims that the day of YHWH "is near." Yet this simple phrase assures the people that the current military invasion and occupation "before our eyes" (1:16) is not the day of YHWH. They have to wait a little longer. The key question is: Is the foreign invasion they are suffering a model for the day of YHWH? Or is the proclamation of the day of YHWH a warning directed against the invaders and oppressors? In the first case, the future event could be understood as a judgment upon Israel, and its proclamation would involve a call to repentance to avoid YHWH's punishment of the chosen people, a punishment that would resemble the invasion by foreign troops (2:12-17). In the second case, the current destructive and oppressive prefigures the day in which YHWH will obliterate the enemy and avenge injustice. Which is it? The first part, 1:1–2:17, does not provide a clear answer, but the second part resolves this ambivalence when YHWH *speaks*: "In response to his people the LORD said" (2:19), and promises both restitution to Israel of what is lost and punishment of the oppressors (2:19-20). Similarly, 2:28-32 and 3:14-17 describe the salvation of Israel and the final judgment of the enemies. In sum, the proclamation of the day of YHWH is not an announcement of an eschatological invasion that would destroy the economic and religious life of Israel. On the contrary, it announces that there will be justice for those who have been deprived of justice, salvation from oppression for those who have been marginalized by history, and freedom for those who are now captive and enslaved, even as the oppressors are in turn sold into slavery (3:7).

The text also announces that "the day" will come as "destruction from the Almighty" (1:15). The Hebrew root for "destruction," *shod,* meaning to "devastate," or to "ruin," has a clear human connotation, similar to the verbs to "exploit" or to "oppress" (cf. Isa 16:4). And the same root is used as a designation for YHWH, Shaddai ("Almighty" in NRSV), forming a word pun: "The day of YHWH comes as devastation from the Devastator." This language suggests that YHWH's intervention will resemble that of the foreign armies that have devastated Judah. Thus, in a quick reading one might confuse the description of the devastation of the day of YHWH with that of the devastation suffered by Judah. Yet, in light of the second part of the book, the destruction of YHWH refers to the future punishment of those who have oppressed Israel.

This reversal of destinies is illustrated in the proclamation of the destruction of the neighboring nations in the valley of Jehoshaphat (3:1-8). The fact that the nations are exploiting others and enjoying their wealth gives the impression that God is on their side. Joel's message comforts those who work for justice knowing that ultimately God will vindicate them.

The Spirit Given to the Marginalized People (Joel 2:28-32, [HB 3:1-5])

Joel 2:28-32 [HB 3:1-5] is generally understood in terms of its citation in Acts 2. However, it has an important message in and of itself as a part of the book of Joel. To begin with, these verses contain a powerful critique against the Israelite religious authorities' monopolization of YHWH, viewed as the God of the priests and of the temple. In addition, these verses indirectly introduce a distinction between the God of Israel and the gods of the other nations. The God of Israel is not a God who guarantees military successes or wealth. Rather, YHWH communicates with everyone: the poor, the young, the old, women and men, and male and female slaves. Surprisingly and significantly, this list does not include priests.

Joel 2:28-32 builds upon the proclamation that Israel will be repaid for economic losses ("I am sending you grain, wine, and oil," 2:19; "I will repay you for the years that the swarming locust has eaten," 2:25) and God's assurance, "I am in the midst of Israel" (2:27). YHWH's presence with them promises the dawning of a new situation radically different from their present experience, and especially different from the experiences of the young, the elderly, and the slaves.

In the context of a foreign military occupation, in which the land is destroyed, young people are deported or enslaved, and all feel totally powerless to confront the arrogance of the powerful—the proclamation of the possibility of a different society is a marvelous act of liberation. This liberation includes the liberation from internal oppression for those marginalized by society. In that day, marginalized people (including women, slaves, the young, and the elderly) will proclaim God's word and thus delineate and bring about a new world, according to God's will.

From a sociological perspective, this democratization of the gift of prophecy is a critique of the distribution of power, including political power as it relates to the temple. It is probable that the background for this text is a power struggle in Jerusalem. Be that as it may, Joel evidently refuses to classify the inhabitants of Judah into well-defined categories, to which he alludes elsewhere: elders (presupposed in 1:2), priests (1:8, 14; 2:17); and small landowners (1:11), by contrast with the marginalized, male and female young people, the elderly, and female and male slaves. These marginalized people, including the female and male slaves, receive not only freedom, but also a privileged status: they will speak for God, a privilege that not even their masters had possessed.

This passage clarifies the kind of justice that will be brought about "in that day." It is a justice for the oppressed, for the marginalized, and for female and male slaves in Judah who, by definition, were viewed as excluded from those chosen by YHWH. This statement of liberation and recognition of the slaves' dignity emerges because of Israel's experience of being oppressed and exploited as an entire nation. Slaves and other marginalized people in Israel should be liberated from the marginalization they suffer within Israel.

The Triumph of the Weak
(Joel 3:9-14 [HB 4:9-14])

The call to war addressed to all nations, urging them to come to Mount Zion, is full of irony. Instead of being a call to nationalistic war, it is a call to God's judgment upon the oppressive nations. The oppressors believe that they are coming once again to destroy this weak people and their ineffective God. Instead, they will be destroyed and judged by the God of this people. A deep sense of powerlessness is common among oppressed peoples. And oppressors reinforce this self-perception to ensure that the oppressed remain convinced that they cannot change the present reality. In many cases, this sense of powerlessness is religiously sanctioned, through affirmation that the state of affairs is according to God's will. The author of Joel develops this ironic call to war to expose this fallacy of God's support for oppression and to show the weakness of the powerful.

Thus, Joel 3:10 (HB 4:10) ironically turns the images of Isaiah 2:4 and Micah 4:3 upside down. The irony includes persuading the enemies to melt their plowshares into swords and to transform their pruning hooks into spears. The passage ends with another allusion to the day of YHWH and its nearness (3:14). In contrast to earlier passages, the hearers do not fear its coming, because the day of YHWH will reveal justice and salvation for the oppressed. Justice is commensurate to the suffering and injustice to which people have earlier been subjected.

The Proclamation of Liberation
(Joel 3:16-21 [HB 4:16-21])

The book of Joel ends with words of hope. This active hope is based on the conviction that changes must take place so that this postponed justice might become a reality.

Joel 3:17b announces that "Jerusalem shall be holy, and strangers shall never again pass through it." That is, foreign invaders shall never again rule over Jerusalem and Israel. This verse proclaims God's presence and protection for God's people, while showing explicitly that those who have committed crimes against Israel and have been mentioned throughout the book are indeed foreigners.

This promised new situation, wherein Israel will never again be subjugated by a foreign nation is not presented in the text in terms of a new age or an eschatological reality. The emphasis in 3:17 is geographical rather than chronological. Once again, Joel balances eschatological and historical realities. This balance is necessary to avoid spiritualizing YHWH's justice by isolating it from historical injustice. The mention of Egypt and Edom in 3:19 does not refer to historical revenge, but functions as a signal of the historicity of judgment; real nations will be judged.

The people who hear these words can thus have a great expectation and a profound hope; true justice may become a reality in history and in their daily lives.

CONCLUSION

Joel's message to Latin America, as well as to all those who experience oppression and injustice, is that God is neither absent nor indifferent to the world's problems. God's liberating action is revealed even in situations that are difficult to comprehend and in which God's presence is difficult to recognize. Joel demonstrates that seeking God's will leads people far away from arrogant and powerful leaders. Joel leads believers who long for liberation to struggle and pray for a world in which everyone will have the opportunity to enjoy justice and peace.

Today, powerful nations continue to exploit and to raid the treasures of the "weak ones" with the conviction that they will never have to give an account of their oppression of others. Joel's voice reveals that the nature of true human justice can clearly be recognized as the mirror image of human injustice and that we have not yet heard God's last word. People are running in all directions to scrounge for their daily bread and with the hope of concrete and real justice, even as the social, economic, and political systems deny them access to necessary resources and rob them of their right to live with dignity. Joel inspires us to believe in a divine and eschatological justice that will reinforce rather than cancel the hope for a healthy human justice that is effective for everyone.

BIBLIOGRAPHY

Alonso Schoekel, Luís. "Joel." Pages 923-950 in *Profetas II*. Madrid: Cristiandad, 1980.

Andiñach, Pablo R. "The Locust in the Message of Joel." Pages 433-441 in *VT42*, 1992.

Prinsloo, Willem. *The Theology of the Book of Joel*. BZAW 163. Berlin: de Gruyter, 1985.

Sweeney, Marvin A., and David W. Cotter, eds. *The Twelve Prophets*. Berit Olam. Collegeville, Minn.: Liturgical, 2000.

Wolff, Hans Walter. *Joel and Amos: A Commentary on the Books of the Prophets Joel and Amos*. Edited by S. Dean McBride, Jr. Translated by Waldemar Janzen, S. Dean McBride, Jr., and Charles A. Muenchow. Hermeneia. Philadelphia: Fortress, 1977.

AMOS

Lai Ling Elizabeth Ngan

George W. Truett Theological Seminary, Baylor University, Waco, Texas, U.S.A.

LIFE CONTEXT OF THE INTERPRETATION

The United States of America is a nation of immigrants. Except for Native Americans, everyone can trace his or her ancestry to other countries. Chinese Americans are no different. We started arriving in the United States as early as the 1840s. Our experience in the past century and a half has not been an easy one.

Like many immigrants, Chinese immigrants came from desperate social and economic conditions in our home country in hopes of grasping new opportunities and making a better life for our families. The earliest immigrants were attracted to America by the prospect of gold mining and jobs on the transcontinental railroad. They faced a myriad of problems, however, as they struggled to survive and to assimilate despite discrimination in both the private and public arena (see Lennon, 2003).

The Chinese Exclusion Act of 1882 was the first law enacted in the United States to bar the entrance of would-be immigrants based on race. This law was enforced until after WW II, when the new immigration acts of 1952 and 1965 removed any reference to "race" as a deciding factor for quota and for entrance into this country. Subsequently, immigration in the second half of the twentieth century has changed the face of America. As for Chinese immigrants, entrance to the United States is no longer limited to merchants, diplomats, and students; now laborers and families can begin new lives in the "Golden Mountain," the land of opportunity. Chinese immigrants now can have access to education, jobs, citizenship, and the protection of law.

The new wave of immigrants since the 1970s, including Chinese and other Asians, found new opportunities for entering American life. The rapid development of technology and communication, the advances in science and medicine, and the embracing of a diverse, multicultural society have fostered an accepting atmosphere where personal achievements and personal choices can flourish. Asian immigrants can choose to assimilate nearly unobtrusively into mainstream American society. Those who can master the English language, acquire educational degrees, and land decent jobs can move into the middle and upper-middle classes. Asian Americans who have assimilated into American society are quite privileged, because few immigrants from Asia and other parts of the world successfully attain this level of the American dream.

We Asian American Christians, are often torn between two worlds, constantly trying to negotiate several sets of cultural, social, and religious values. For many, the ability to assimilate and be successful in American society is considered a sign of blessing. The question of one's Asian-ness or American-ness is softened by one's willing contribution and dutiful participation in church programs and activities. If one is doing well at work, in life and in church, then one must be doing well with God. Material and spiritual blessings readily go hand in hand. A question that needs to be raised is: is this position theologically sound?

Lai Ling Elizabeth Ngan, a native of Hong Kong, China, teaches Hebrew Bible and biblical Hebrew in a Baptist seminary in the United States. A member of the Ethnic Chinese Biblical Colloquium and the Society of Biblical Literature's Committee on Underrepresented Racial and Ethnic Minorities in the Profession, she contributed "Amos: Introduction and Commentary" to *The IVP Women's Bible Commentary* (2002).

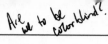
Are we to be colorblind?

Another question that needs to be raised concerns the cost of assimilation. What are the implicit and explicit costs to self and to others for participating in the values and norms of the dominant culture? How "white" does an Asian need to be in order to be an American? How much of our cultural heritage do we have to reject or deny? How far are we willing to go to perpetuate the myth of the "model minority"? At what price are we willing to sell ourselves and our souls?

Like many Americans, Asian Amer-icans are guilty of exploiting those who are in a less advantaged position. How much do we, knowingly and unknowingly, contribute to the oppression of others, including new immigrants and overseas Asians who are vulnerable to economic and political exploitation? How much do we willingly participate in oppressive social structures because they provide the key to personal gain? Do we give a second thought to the plight of garment workers locked in cramped work spaces behind barred doors, or of restaurant workers who work fifteen-hour days seven days a week at slave wages, or of children forced to work in family industries to supplement family income despite the existence of child labor laws? These disturbing conditions exist not only overseas but presently in the United States. What about the high-tech companies that expect their Asian workers to work extra hours and on weekends without extra pay or complaints? What about tax cuts that put a few more dollars in our pockets but close off services and assistance that new immigrants need? How does one balance upward mobility and personal integrity? How far can we go and still claim to be the church, the people of God? When is enough enough?

Asian Americans who have blended into mainstream American society enjoy many social and economic powers that other Asians around them do not have. We wield a certain amount of political clout and influence. Asian American lobbyists, activist groups, and social and legal services are readily available in major cities throughout the United States. American society, however, has not yet become totally color-blind. Although Asian Americans have made great strides in recent decades, their skin color will always mark them as "other" in a white-dominated society. The power and privileges that Asian Americans enjoy are not, therefore, inalienable in the eyes of many; continued vigilance and negotiation are necessary. What we have is borrowed power.

Most immigrant groups that have achieved a high level of acceptance and assimilation into America face a similar situation. From a social and cultural perspective, we have borrowed power from the dominant culture. But from a theological perspective, our power is on loan from above, and therefore it should not be used for personal gain but for the common good. The question is: what will we do with this borrowed power? Will we use it for good or for evil? If it is to be used for good, then what prophetic and social responsibility does a privileged minority have to confront and convert unjust social structures and praxis? If communal good is the goal, the responsible life must extend beyond ourselves; it must permeate our communities and the world.

We live in a complex, pluralistic world that includes very diverse cultures, values, beliefs, religious traditions, and sacred texts. This cultural and religious pluralism is present here in the United States, although we find here only a small sample of the pluralism that exists in Asia. There is no single dominant religious tradition in Asia. Asians are practitioners of all major religions. Thus, for Asian American Christians living in a postmodern world with an awareness of cultural and religious diversity, the question is: How should we proclaim the truth claims of the Christian tradition? How should we speak of God and for God? What does the Christian God have to do with the rest of the world?

The book of Amos addresses a number of social contextual issues that Asian American Christians face in the twenty-first century. As is the case with privileged and well-established Asian Americans, the upper crust of ancient Israelite society became rich on the backs of the poor and disenfranchised in their society. To maintain an opulent lifestyle, they participated in social structures with legalized oppression of the weak and vulnerable. Those who were abused were not foreign enemies, but their own people. Such a practice directly contradicted their claims that they knew the God of the covenant and belonged to God's people. Their attitude is so unlike that of God, who cared for them when they were weak and vulnerable (Amos 2:9-11)! As Asian American Christians, we need to become more aware that we participate in exploiting the poor, the weak, and the vulnerable as we eagerly seek upward mobility, financial stability, and social status. This exploitation takes place both inside and outside the church: in the way we treat new immigrants or the needy who come to church to seek assistance; in the way ministers are treated as hired hands; and in the way landlords and CEOs treat their tenants and workers. The real cost is shouldered not only by the exploited, but also by the exploiters. When we forget that others are human beings created in the image of God, we also run the risk of forgetting that we ourselves are, likewise, made in God's image.

The upper class in ancient Israel rose in status and wealth by obeying and gaining the favor of the monarchy. In this sense, their privilege and power were not inherent or inalienable, but borrowed. In a hierarchical, patriarchal society, one's standing on the ladder of social structures was clear enough: the king had power over other males in his kingdom, males had power over females who were in their household, and women had power over the poor. Thus, though the rich women of Samaria had less power and privilege than their male counterparts, Amos still indicted them for their participation in the oppression of the poor. Although Asian Americans, including Asian American women, have limited and mainly borrowed power, the prophet would not have dismissed our responsibility to the vulnerable and needy in our community. Lest we become complacent and self-congratulatory in our current social status and accomplishments, we need to be more intentional about taking up the prophetic mantle to speak up and correct the wrongs in our world (5:24).

The book of Amos does not indict foreign nations for not knowing YHWH and not obeying the torah, but it indicts them for their crimes against humanity. Their inhumane treatment of neighbors was considered rebellion against YHWH. Only Judah and Israel, who should have known YHWH, were indicted for rejecting God and the torah (2:4). In Amos, however, YHWH is portrayed as the sovereign Lord of all nations who moves peoples at will and punishes the nations for their rebellion. Whether or not the nations have recognized YHWH as their God, YHWH will, nevertheless, judge all nations with equity.

CONTEXUAL COMMENT

An Overview
of the Book of Amos

Amos has the distinction of being the first prophet to have his oracles and visions collected into a book included in the Christian canon. The book provides only scanty information about the prophet, but he was apparently a "missionary" who lived in the southern kingdom of Judah and was sent by God to preach to the northern kingdom of Israel. Not only was he an outsider from a less developed country, he did not even have the proper professional credentials to be a prophet. His ministry probably lasted only a short time and is dated to around 750 B.C.E., two years before the earthquake in the time when Uzziah was king of Judah and Jeroboam II was king of Israel (Amos).

The book of Amos begins with a series of oracles against the nations for their indecent and outrageous treatment of neighboring peoples. Their acts of violence are considered not mere transgressions, but rebellion against YHWH, who will hold them accountable and punish them with destruction by war. Even Judah was rebellious "because they had rejected the *torah*, or instructions, of YHWH" (2:4, a.t.). However, the leaders of Israel, who were indicted for social injustice perpetrated against their own people, were the primary target of Amos' preaching. YHWH's judgment would surely come, but the goal of Amos' preaching was to turn the people from wrong to right before it was too late.

How Unlike God!
(Amos 2:6-12)

The early years of the reign of Uzziah (783-742 B.C.E.) and Jeroboam II (786-746 B.C.E.) were marked by peace, prosperity, and piety. Together, these two kings had reclaimed the territory that was once held by David, subdued neighboring powers, secured peace, and promoted economic growth and international trade. The religious scene could not have been better. The people were religiously active, filling temples and shrines with worshippers and filling altars with endless sacrifices. Underneath the pleasant façade, however, something rotten was festering.

The prophet proclaimed a series of five indictments against the Israelites for their treatment of the poor and vulnerable in their society (2:6-7). They were selling the righteous for money and the poor for the price of a pair of shoes. These charges perhaps referred to debt slavery or bribery in court; nevertheless, human life was devalued and human dignity was ignored. The Israelites were so land-hungry that even the bit of dust clinging to the head of the poor was a target of possession. The needy were treated with contempt and violence, and the powerless were pushed out of the way in the rush to acquire more.

A rather curious charge against the Israelites was that "father and son go in to the same girl" (2:7). What were father and son doing with this girl? "Go in" is not used as a euphemism for sexual relations elsewhere in the Hebrew Bible. Yet Shalom Paul (1991, 81-83) convincingly argues for such a usage based on Akkadian parallels and similar vocabulary to the charges against the Judahites in Amos 2:4b, where sons were walking after their fathers and were led astray by idolatrous worship. Who was this young woman? Was she a street prostitute or a cult prostitute, or was she another defenseless member of society? The last suggestion seems most likely since Hebrew has specific words for the first two categories, and the word Amos used indicates a young woman of high birth at marriageable age or a high-ranking maidservant (Exod 2:5; 1 Sam 25:42; Esth 2:9; 4:4, 16), though not a slave. Apparently, she did not belong to any other male, so the law did not prohibit the offense that was committed against this girl by father and son. According to the prophet, however, it was an affront to God that profaned God's holy name.

The abuses of the weak and vulnerable in society were in stark contrast to what YHWH did for the Israelites during their periods of weakness. The five charges in Amos 2:6-7 are countered by the reminder of five undeserved acts of compassion from YHWH (2:9-11). God sided with them when they were powerless. Throughout their historical experience, YHWH destroyed their enemies, delivered them from slavery, cared for them in the wilderness, gave them a land as their possession, and provided religious leaders to guide them. Repeatedly, the emphasis is on the contrast between what YHWH did when they were weak and vulnerable and what they are doing to the poor and needy in their midst. How unlike God they are!

Guilty as Sin
(Amos 4:1-3, 6:1-7)

After a summary of the charges "against the whole family that [YHWH] brought up out of the land of Egypt" (3:1, see 3:1-15), the prophet launches a series of attacks against specific power groups in the nation. He targets the ruling class because they are responsible for the plight of the poor and they have the power to do something about it.

The primary audience of the oracles was the male leaders in Israel, but women were neither immune from these charges of oppression nor were they shielded from their responsibility: "Hear this word, you cows of Bashan" (4:1). The rich women of Samaria were charged with "*oppressing* the poor, *crushing* the needy and *saying* to their lords, "Bring, that we may drink" (4:1, a.t.). The series of participles indicate that these were continuing offenses and demands. Their unquenchable desire for more was responsible for the injustice and oppression in society. The association of wine and feasting with the rich upper class, a frequent occurrence in Amos, suggests that these women demanded from their husbands not the mere necessities of life, but luxuries and an extravagant lifestyle.

The wealthy women of Samaria, like other women in patriarchal societies, were restricted to the domestic realm. The public and political arena belonged to males. These women, however, lacked neither power nor influence in their families, and in society, though they asserted this ower indirectly through the males. For sure, these women did not have the same power as the males, but in comparison to other women and males from a lower socio-economic status, they were in a privileged position. The power and privileges that they had were borrowed power, granted when their desires meshed with the desires of the males who had charge over them and withdrawn when they dared to step out of line. Yet, for Amos, the insecure possession of power could not be used as an excuse for not assuming responsibility for their actions. These women of Samaria were held responsible for their participation in and promotion of a lifestyle that perpetuated oppression. For Amos, the ethical

implications of the covenant applied to both men and women.

In 6:1-7, the prophet proclaims a series of "woe" oracles against the leaders of Israel, who think they are "the first of the nations" (6:1) and who receive homage and accolades from others (6:1d). Amos taunts them for living with a false sense of security and superiority (6:1b). They thought they could not be touched by evil and that they were immune from harm (6:3a), though their actions wreaked havoc in the lives of many (6:3b). They could afford luxurious idleness, feasting on choice cuts of meat, improvising songs for entertainment, drinking wine excessively, and lavishly pampering their bodies with the finest oils, but they were totally oblivious to the stench of death around them.

The charges in Amos 2:6-8 and 8:4-6 are that the rich upper crust of society enjoyed an indulgent, luxurious life at the expense of the poor whom they cheated and abused. And "YHWH swore by the pride of Jacob: Surely I will never forget any of their deeds" (8:7, a.t.).

Seek Good and Live
(Amos 5:4-24)

As with all prophetic preaching, the goal of Amos' proclamation is not merely to condemn what is wrong, but primarily to turn the hearts and minds of the hearers back to God. What is sought is nothing less than true repentance. The tone of anguish is clear in 5:4-24. Amos pleads with the Israelites to seek what is good (5:14), that is, to seek God (5:4, 6), so that they might live. Amos's deepest wish is that they will turn and live.

Amos seeks to turn the Israelites' worldview upside down with his preaching. He counters the popular beliefs and praxis of the day by offering the people of God an alternative view of what God desires for them. Contrary to the popular belief that active participation in religious services will bring blessings and security, Amos calls upon the people to seek God and not "Bethel," the "house of God" (5:4-6).

Bethel, Gilgal, and Beer-sheba were sacred places because they were memorials connected to the ancestors and to the history of the conquest of the land (5:4-6). But, Amos claims, these sanctuaries cannot save, any more than cultural heritage, past accomplishments, or ethnic pride can. Their many festivals and rituals will not elicit the desired response from God (5:21-23). Their only hope is to be found in God who is above all (6:8) and who says to the house of Israel and to us, "Seek me and live" (5:4).

The people wrongly assumed and claimed that "the God of hosts" (5:14-16) was with them. Perhaps this assumption came from the claim that they were the covenant people of YHWH. Perhaps their special status suggested immutability and entitlement to God's blessings and protection. The prophet, however, claims that the God of hosts will be with them only if their social praxis is in line with an ethical and moral life. "Seek good and not evil . . . Hate evil and love good" (5:14-15).

In the Hebrew Bible, "evil" is not an abstract concept; it takes on concrete manifestations. Good and evil are exhibited by one's actions. To seek and to love good is to "establish justice in the gate" (5:15). Amos accuses the people to "turn justice into wormwood and cast righteousness down to the ground" (5:7, a.t.). The pairing of "justice" and "righteousness" is of central importance in Amos. This word pair, which is also found in 5:24 and 6:12, is completely unknown in the law codes of the Torah but is more commonly found in the wisdom literature of the Hebrew Bible (Paul 1991, 245). Justice and righteousness are not abstract attributes; they are concretely expressed in individual and communal life. Justice refers to the behavior and praxis that result from an ethical, moral way of living, and righteousness refers to the right relationships with other people that flow from a right relationship with God. The horizontal relationship to neighbors is inseparably bound to the vertical relationship to God.

"But let justice roll down like waters, and righteousness like an ever-flowing stream." This famous verse of Amos 5:24, which is etched on the Civil Rights Memorial in Montgomery, Alabama, will forever be linked with Martin Luther King, Jr.'s speech, "I Have a Dream." The cry for a just and righteous society in the recent civil rights movement is the same cry expressed by Amos as the reality that God desires, namely, a community where every aspect of life is permeated with just praxis and right relationships. As flowing water covers every surface of every object and fills every crevice, and mighty streams cleanse away rock and debris, so just and righteous living must touch and cover every fiber of the interwoven relationships in society. Justice and righteousness have the power to change the course of life and sweep away obstacles to wholeness.

The people of ancient Israel apparently thought that they were righteous and that God was on their side. They were eagerly looking forward to "the day of YHWH," believing that it would be a day of brightness and light, a day when God's wrath would fall on their enemies and they themselves would be exalted (5:18-20). The prophet, however, counters their expectations with talk of darkness and gloom. Amos was the first prophet to use the phrase "the day of YHWH" in his oracles, but the way he uses it suggests that it was a popular, if misguided, concept in his time. The day will come and it will be inescapable. But, as illustrated by the simile of a person who narrowly escapes from a lion and a bear only to arrive home and be bitten by a snake (5:19), the day of YHWH will not be a day of rejoicing but a day of woe. It is unimaginable to long for such a doomed encounter.

The Lion Has Roared, Who Can but Prophesy?
(Amos 1:1-2; 3:3-8; 7:10-15)

Amos 7:1–9:6 contains a series of visions concerning the certainty and severity of

God's judgment on Israel. All the standard commentaries note the structure of this section and its parallelisms. Sandwiched between the third (7:7-9) and the fourth vision (8:1-3), is a narrative describing the confrontation between Amos and Amaziah, the priest of Bethel (7:10-17). Amaziah challenged Amos' right to preach in Israel, because of the threat that his preaching posed to the monarchy and to social stability. Amos, however, countered the charge with the irresistible nature of God's call (7:15), an echo of the earlier declaration, "The lion has roared; who will not fear? The Lord GOD has spoken; who can but prophesy?" (3:8)

Amos readily acknowledged that he did not have the professional credentials to be a prophet (7:14-15). He was neither a prophet nor had he received training to be a prophet. He was a herdsman and a dresser of sycamore trees. But contrary to the romantic notion that Amos was an uneducated backwoodsman who was given supernatural insight into Israel's corruption, Amos may have been a well-to-do businessman who became aware of the abuses in Israelite society through his business dealings with the northern kingdom. God probably used this awareness to stir in him a prophetic voice.

A number of hints support this portrait of Amos. Amos 1:1 describes Amos as being at Tekoa among the "shepherds," a term that designates a "sheep breeder" or a "sheep dealer" and that is also used in 2 Kings 3:4 to describe King Mesha of Moab. This term suggests that Amos was more likely an owner of herds than merely a hired hand. His knowledge of international affairs and domestic conditions further suggests that he was well aware of his world. The book of Amos is also replete with numerical sayings, rhetorical questions, similes, and wisdom themes. This wisdom literary genre is expressed in some of the best Hebrew in the Bible. These hints suggest that Amos may have been an educated businessman who found himself awkwardly out of place in the north as a prophet. As a privileged outsider, he preached the message that inspired him and sought to right what was wrong. He risked rejection and condemnation for his unpopular message, but when YHWH calls, can one afford to remain popular?

Asian Americans who have assimilated well into American society are privileged outsiders too, at least a privileged minority in the United States. If God has also privileged us with new eyes to see, will we, like Amos, go where we are sent and share our new vision? Will we be willing to risk rejection and unpopularity? Will we seek to make right what is wrong?

God is God of All

The passages in Amos concerning God's dealings with foreign nations (1:2–2:3, and 9:7-11) and the three doxologies (4:13, 5:8-9, 9:5-6) emphasize the sovereignty of "YHWH of hosts." Whether or not the nations recognize YHWH as their God, Amos says that they are accountable to YHWH and face YHWH's judgment. The prophet does not fault the nations for not knowing God, but their violence toward neighboring peoples is seen as rebellion against God. For this violence, they will be judged and punished.

Amos emphasizes that YHWH watched over all the nations, not merely Israel. Without their knowledge or consent, God moved peoples at will (the Israelites from Egypt, the Philistines from Caphor and the Arameans from Kir) and can also move each back to its place of origin. The special relationship that Israel has with YHWH calls Israel to be particularly responsive to God. It does not mean that they are greater than the peoples of Calneh, Hamath, Gath, or Ethiopia (6:2; 9:7) or that they can act with impunity. The covenant relationship brings with it greater responsibility, for the Israelites are supposed to know God.

YHWH is also the God of creation (4:13, 5:8-9, 9:5-6). YHWH is the one who created and watches over nature. YHWH turns morning into darkness and deep darkness into day. YHWH made the stars and formed the constellations, molded the mountains, and commanded the seas; nature responds to YHWH's voice. At YHWH's roar, "the pastures of the shepherds wither, and the top of Carmel dries up" (1:2); at YHWH's touch, mountains melt, rivers buckle, and destruction flashes out (5:9). YHWH's awesome power and the yielding response of nature struck a sense of wonderment in all who witnessed such displays of might. The only appropriate response of the creatures is to fall down and worship the God of all.

Asian American Christians face the difficulty of reconciling their ethnic and religious identity as Asian American and Christian with the claims of competing Asian religious traditions and multiple sacred texts, yet the book of Amos proclaims uncompromisingly that the sovereign God we worship is the God of all.

CONCLUSION

What does the book of Amos say to Asian Americans who have entered mainstream American society and have successfully achieved a comfortable share of financial and political security?

We must acknowledge our place as privileged minorities who owe a debt of gratitude to those who have struggled before us and those who continue to struggle in the world. Yet, we must also carefully consider our role in social and economic systems that exploit and oppress other human beings. An American ideal that we can embrace is the freedom to choose. We have the freedom and power to make lifestyle choices. As suggested above, like Amos we are privileged outsiders and minorities who, in this position, are often given by God new eyes to see. The question is then: will we, like Amos, take the risk of being rejected by choosing to make right what is wrong? In the face of death-dealing social and economic options, will we choose to live humanely and compassionately? Will we choose to be more like God in our dealings with others? Will we choose solidarity with the exploited and minimize our participation in social and economic systems that promote the rise of a few at the expense of the many?

Though Asian Americans may only have borrowed power, it is power, nonetheless. This power is a double-edged sword that can be used for good or for evil, for communal welfare or personal gain. Again, our choices carry life-altering consequences. To choose what is good is to choose God. To choose what is good is to choose life. Our personal choices have a rippling effect in our larger communities by funneling our energies, resources, and power in one direction or the other. Our goal should be nothing less than the permeation of justice and righteousness in every facet of life. As the people of God, a people living in covenant relationship with God and with neighbors, Asian American Christians have a responsibility to bring about a just and equitable society by letting justice and righteousness "roll down like waters" (5:24). As a privileged people, we Asian Americans need to recognize that we can contribute significantly to the transformation of the world and to the ushering in of the kingdom of God. It is time to take up the prophetic mantle and to shoulder our responsibilities to neighbors and God.

BIBLIOGRAPHY

Andersen, Francis I., and David Noel Freedman. *Amos: A New Translation with Introduction and Commentary*. AB 24A Garden City, N.Y.: Doubleday, 1989.

Lennon, Thomas, series producer. *Becoming American: The Chinese Experience*. A Bill Moyer Special. A three-part film series, aired on PBS on March 25-27, 2003.

De La Torre, Miguel A. *Reading the Bible from the Margins*. Maryknoll, N.Y.: Orbis, 2002.

Hayes, John H. *Amos: The Eighth-Century Prophets: His Times and His Preaching*. Nashville: Abingdon, 1988.

Ngan, Lai Ling Elizabeth. "Amos: Introduction and Commentary." Pages 446-456 in *The IVP Women's Bible Commentary*. Edited by Catherine C. Kroeger and Mary J. Evans. Downers Grove, Ill.: InterVarsity Press, 2002.

Paul, Shalom M. *Amos: A Commentary on the Book of Amos*. Hermeneia. Minneapolis: Fortress, 1991.

Sanderson, Judith E. "Amos." Pages 205-209 in *The Women's Bible Commentary*. Edited by Carol A. Newsom and Sharon H. Ringe. Louisville: Westminster John Knox Press, 1992.

OBADIAH

Jorge Torreblanca
Universidad Adventista del Plata, Entre Rios, Argentina

LIFE CONTEXT OF THE INTERPRETATION

Obadiah's message gains relevance if we just take into account the current international situation and the economic globalization of recent decades. This process has been characterized by repeated promises of worldwide neo-liberal economic solutions, according to which the free market economy would resolve all individual and societal ills. Globalization introduces new marketing techniques, while commerce and technology affect and transform the production and distribution of goods and services. The results of this globalization process for our cultures in Latin America as well as for the social and political life of our countries, in my case, Argentina, are totally unpredictable.

Our Life Context
in Light of Obadiah

The problem with globalization is that it does not globalize the benefits. In light of Obadiah, people ignore the kinship that unites them with other people around the world. While there have been moments when some have benefited from technological breakthroughs and the ability to travel to developed countries, most people in Latin America have been deprived of peace, food, housing, employment, educational opportunities, and healthcare. Structural differences and inequality between the haves and the have-nots increase daily. Rich nations do frequently meet to discuss how to help the poorest nations. But mistrust by the have-not nations and peoples is appropriate. These initiatives, no matter how good and well-intentioned they might be, are belied by the worsening situation of the very Latin American people these international programs are supposed to help.

We find Argentina within this general context of economic globalization and increasing disparity between the rich and the poor. Real and pressing problems are visible in the political system (e.g., the notorious case of having five presidents within a month; the lack of trustworthy candidates), in the judicial system (incompetence, corruption) as well as in the economy (external and internal debts, default). Because of the enormous external debt, the living conditions in Latin America steadily deteriorate (see the issue of RIBLA, 1990, devoted to external debt and biblical studies). More and more people are reduced to a state of poverty; decent housing is out of reach; schools, when they are open, are overcrowded; prenatal care for mothers and healthcare for children is less and less available; more and more children die.

The many people who are devastated and deeply humiliated by poverty and misery emphatically and publicly repudiate the "professional" leaders of the political bodies by calling for their resignation. But theirs is also a cry of resignation; they have no hope for any kind of change. They dream of emigration, because the country "cannot go on." Is there any sign of hope in the depth of such despair? Of safety in the turmoil of such insecurity? Of peace in the midst of such anguish?

Jorge Torreblanca (ThD, Instituto Universitario ISEDET, Buenos Aires) teaches at the River Plate Adventist University (Libertador San Martín, Entre Ríos, Argentina). He has served as Dean of Theology and Vice President for Academic Affairs at the Bolivian Adventist University (Cochabamba). The recipient of a scholarship from the World Council of Churches (Geneva, Switzerland) he has published several articles on the prophets (especially Jeremiah) including in RIBLA, and co-edited a book, *Entender la Palabra. Hermenéutica Adventista para el Nuevo Siglo* (2000).

CONTEXTUAL COMMENT

An Overview of Obadiah

In content and structure, the Hebrew Bible's shortest book has not attracted the attention of many scholars; there are no novelties in Obadiah's message. The title reads "Vision of Obadiah"; the phrase is commonly used in other prophetic books to announce the prophetic word. The rest of this short oracle against Edom is written in literary rhythmic prose, and the genre is the usual "oracle against other nations" found throughout the prophetic corpus.

These twenty-one verses have an interesting literary structure. According to both David A. Dorsey and Samuel E. Almada (who has the clearer proposal), Obadiah is organized according to a beautiful concentric symmetric structure (a chiasm).

a (1) summon of the nations / war against Edom / oracle of YHWH;

  b (2-4) destitution and humiliation of the arrogant by YHWH;

    c (5-7) Esau's ruin / betrayal and defeat by his allies;

      d (8-11) that day / utter and eternal destruction of Edom by YHWH;

      xx (11-14) cases and charges against Edom/ the day of the disgrace of Judah;

      d' (15-16) the day of YHWH / revenge / all nations against Edom;

    c' (17-18) survival on Mount Zion / Jacob-Joseph will completely devour Esau;

  b' (19-20) restitution of possessions to the sacked and deported;

a' (21) triumphant return of the deported / trial to Esau / royalty of YHWH.

Commentators stress that the book's main topic is the manifestation of God's justice to the people that God has chosen and with whom God is in a covenantal relationship (17-21). The prophet seeks to promote trust in God despite the tragic events of the fall of Jerusalem. Without emphasizing the negative aspects of the situation, he speaks with an almost jingoist and disturbingly vengeful tone in order to stress another central topic: the proclamation of judgment against all nations (11-16), because God is the Lord of history, a Sovereign who knows the destiny of all nations.

As with any prophet, Obadiah proclaims his oracle in a concrete historical situation, triggered by the events of 587 B.C.E., and with the clear intention of facing up to the stark reality of his time. The destruction of Jerusalem and the sacking of its symbols by the current hegemonic power, Babylon, with the support of its unexpected allies, Edom among them, was a severe crisis for Judah and its people. Tradition has it that Edom is the neighboring country populated by the descendants of Esau, Jacob's brother. The people of Edom have not respected the reconciliation between the brothers (Esau-Jacob) and have constantly opposed Israel/Judah. From the time of the patriarchs, through the time of Moses in the wilderness, to the time of the judges and the kings, the biblical account shows a strained relationship between Israel and its neighboring brother. But in aiding Babylon during the destruction and deportation of Jerusalem, Edom went beyond all acceptable limits.

For Obadiah, this enmity has arisen out of Edom's cruelty, wickedness, and longing for power. Edom went as far as signing an alliance with the powerful and considered itself protected and invulnerable. But Edom was not the only evil or enemy nation. Edom represents all the nations that rebel against God, as become clear in 15-16, where all the nations are together with Edom subjected to divine judgment. Edom becomes a symbol for all antagonism against God, God's sovereignty, and God's person. Pride, arrogance, and self-confidence are sins that challenge YHWH, and will not stand.

One of the keys for reading Obadiah is to remember that the oracle, despite being ostensibly addressed to Edom, is addressed to the people of Israel. Obadiah pronounced it so that his people, Israel, would listen, and so that a proper relationship might be restored between God and God's people. Obadiah's message is in response to the needs of the remnant of God's people, particularly those left in Judah. Since the prophet does not recount the Edom's vile misdeeds in detail, he merely presupposes them in his oracle, thus showing that his intention lies elsewhere. His goal is not to review Edom's betrayal but to generate hope for Judah out of desperation, safety out of insecurity, and peace out of anguish. But how does he do it?

Obadiah's Contextual Teaching: "You too Were like One of them"

The reason for YHWH's disparagement of Edom's attitude and deeds is explained in vv. 11–14, the center of the chiasm. The charges against Edom are vividly expressed in apodictic statements that point out what the accused should not have done. The final phrase of v. 11, "you too were like one of them," summarizes Obadiah's message: You, my kindred, are like me, but on that occasion, you were like one of them, those who are not our kindred. Regarding Edom's response to the destruction of Israel, the accusation moves in crescendo toward the most serious misdeeds:

12a You should not have looked (with pleasure) at Jerusalem's destruction;

12b You should not have rejoiced about it;

12c You should not have boasted ("enlarged your mouth");

13a You should not have entered the gate of the destroyed city;

13c You should not have stolen (put your hand in its wealth);

14a You should not have posted yourself in the crossroads (to ambush fugitives);

14b You should not have handed over the survivors as prisoners.

One action led to another. Not content with looking with pleasure at the disaster which engulfed their neighbors, the Edomites went on to enjoy this sight, then they stole from the ruins, as anonymous snipers they assassinated the survivors, and finally they openly handed over as prisoners

those who could have escaped the massacre. The condemnation targets moral issues: betrayal, pride, callous insensitivity, robbery, and assassination. Yet to limit the teaching of this text to an entirely personal moral message, such as "God does not like people who engage in such behavior," and "we should strive for God's ways of humility and service, and shun arrogance and pride," would be to miss Obadiah's main message.

The prophet's message is not about individual morality. Notice that the text always speaks about a nation; one should not be misled by Obadiah's personification of the nation. This socio-political dimension must not be overlooked. Obadiah seeks to address the heavy oppression that the "new order" of Babylonian imperialism and its structure of centralized power imposed upon the subjugated people: exiled Israel and those remaining in Judah. The country was impoverished because the main cities were destroyed. The settlement of foreign peoples in Judah (the Edomites among them), altered the nation's ethnic composition and brought about social tensions. The deportation of skilled workers and the governing class impoverished Judah. Because of looting by the invading Babylonians, their control of commerce, and the taxes they imposed, Judah's possessions and resources were transferred from the poorest people to the Babylonian court and the attendant centers of power. Economic, social, and political instability and tension made the rural areas suffer the worst, as they were powerless to escape exploitation by rich and powerful people—the very ones targeted by the prophets' ongoing accusations.

The most important result of Judah's defeat was that kinship ties within the community were broken. There was no mutual help. Blood relations and kinship were forgotten. The haves did not share with the have-nots, the totally destitute. People did not fear God, and thus ignored the Levitical laws that forbade selfish interest, usury, exploitation of kindred, and that also required generosity and sharing with the less fortunate. According to Obadiah, YHWH rejects these attitudes, common in Israel.

How does Obadiah intervene in the name of God ("says YHWH") in this very disastrous concrete historical situation? His prophecy celebrates Zion's (or Israel's) future recovery, and proclaims that evil Edom and Babylon's good fortune will come to naught; they will be repaid for their evil. But, "says YHWH," God's people (Israel) will be returned to their former glory when God restores their nation and makes them rulers over their former oppressors.

This proclamation reveals the underlying intent of the rest of the book. But more importantly, it shows that the entire book's goal is to reassure the defeated and oppressed Israelites. Furthermore, it shows that Obadiah's oracle seeks to change the lives of the people. It holds before them as a permanent motivation that God is the supreme sovereign who is still in control of life and history. Furthermore it emphasizes the certainty that God will exercise justice: "For the day of the Lord is near against all the nations. As you have done, it shall be done to you; your deeds shall return on your own head" (15). The prophet knows that hope transforms the attitude that people have toward their present situation, and thereby changes a people's way of life. Indeed, as a people they will continue to struggle. But now they will do so with hope, because they are no longer on an inexorable path to destruction. Step by step they see themselves as moving forward in a new era when the use of power will be used in a positive and constructive way, rather than in an oppressive and destructive one.

CONCLUSION

The prophet speaks in the name of YHWH to expose the self-deceit of oppressive powers and their allies, in his time as well as today in Argentina. The oppressive and exploitative powers view people as nothing more than tools to be disposed of as soon as they have used them and reached their treacherous objectives. People who ally with and serve exploitative powers only deceive themselves. They are not in control. They think they reinforce their control through their corrupt, arrogant nationalism, and their violent use of the power they have been given by the oppressive powers. This thought is merely a temporary illusion; they are fooling themselves. This applies to the kindred people (Edom, other Argentineans), and among them especially to the political, financial, and economic elites who ally themselves with the exploiting foreign power. After their indoctrination, they rule mercilessly in the name of the exploiting powers. They manage with pride and without regard for the majority of people hurt by economic adjustments imposed by the exploiting power.

This is the reality we face in Argentina today. So God's people wonder: How can we analyze the present national disaster, which devastates us both morally and materially? What can we do as the people of God in this situation? Where can we look for hope? Is there a way out of this current deprivation, powerlessness, and suffering? Does God care for us? Will God continue to allow those arrogant people who are responsible for the situation to be successful? What does God want from us?

Obadiah addresses these questions to us. Obadiah's message generates hope for security and restoration. The present situation will not be permanent. Those who are powerful live in an illusionary conceit. There are deeds that must not be done between kindred, and a high price will have to be paid for such misdeeds.

The country will recover when the kingdom is managed according to YHWH's will. For this, the remnant of God's people must understand and incorporate in their life God's holiness: "it shall be holy" (v. 17). This holiness is beyond narrow nationalism, and involves a different lifestyle; a cooperative, communal lifestyle, which of necessity entails drastic changes in society's power structures. The biblical diagnosis of the crises and their solutions in Obadiah's time remains true and highly relevant in our era.

BIBLIOGRAPHY

Almada, Samuel E. "Abdías: la injusticia no quedará impune." *RevistB* 63 (2001): 150-168.

Dorsey, David A. *The Literary Structure of the Old Testament.* Grand Rapids: Baker, 1999.

RIBLA, Deuda externa. Vol. 5-6, 1990. (A special issue of RIBLA devoted to "Biblical Studies and the External Debt").

JONAH

CHEN Nan Jou

Yu-Shan Theological College and Seminary, Hualien, Taiwan

LIFE CONTEXT OF THE INTERPRETATION

A story told by the famous Taiwanese Buddhist nun Dharma Master Cheng Yen:

> One day my mother told me on the phone the very sad news that my youngest brother in military service was killed by one of his friends by accident. Mother asked me: "What should we do." I composed myself as much as I could and said to her: "Mother, your child is gone. No matter what we do, we cannot bring him back to life. The Buddha teaches that there is a law of cause and effect at work in our lives. Perhaps nothing could have averted this tragedy. What you must do is to change your attitude and try not to cling to the thought that your son was a victim. Instead, you can turn your thoughts to the mother whose son killed your son by accident. She must be feeling more painful than you are. She must be extremely sorry for what happened, and she must also be very afraid of what is going to happen to her son at military court. His life is in your hand. If you in compassion can speak for him, he can still live. Your child is dead. Now you must have compassion for all people. Other people's children are also your children. You must speak up for the young man who killed your son by accident." . . . At the military court my mother did speak for the young man, saying it was an unintentional homicide, that she did not hate him, and asked the court to give him an opportunity to begin a new life. What a story of mercy and love it is. (*Cheng Yen, Chu Chai e Hsin Lin (The Mind Free from Delusion)* 1991, 18-19. Translation from Mandarin Chinese by C. S. Song used with permission.)

A local church minister in Taiwan told his congregation the story of this merciful and loving mother during a Sunday morning sermon without mentioning the part of the teaching of Buddha. After the service, a member of his congregation came to him to express appreciation and said: "Dear pastor, the story you told this morning is very moving. Where did you read it?" The minister replied frankly: "I am glad to know that it is helpful to you. It is taken from a Buddhist book." On hearing the reply, this man became angry and turned away from the pastor. Was it right for him to be angry?

Christianity came to Taiwan in 1865. At present, including both Protestants and Roman Catholics, only about 4 percent of Taiwan's twenty-three million people are Christian. However, influenced by old missionary fundamentalist evangelical thoughts, many Taiwanese Christians tend to think that there is nothing of value in non-Christian religions. Such thinking, reflected in the reaction to the sermon mentioned above, not only makes the Christian mission in Taiwan difficult, but also creates considerable tension between Christians and the followers of other religions.

If God is the God who created the heaven and the earth, the God who rules the world, and the God who is the Lord of history, God must have been with us in Taiwan from the

Chen Nan Jou, Vice-President of Yu-Shan Theological College and Seminary, is Professor of Christian Ethics, teaching and doing research in theology of mission and theology and culture. He is Director of the Center of the Programs of Indigenous Theology and Mission. His many publications include the following books (in Chinese): *The Socio-Political Ethics of the Presbyterian Church in Taiwan* (1991), *Mission and Ethics* (1995) *and Theology of Identifying* (2003).

beginning, before the arrival of the Christian missionaries. The God of Israel who brought Israel out of the land of Egypt, the Philistines from Caphtor, and the Arameans from Kir (Amos 9:7), must also have done something in the history of the Taiwanese people. The history and the cultures of Taiwan must possess traces of God. They must possess theological significance and relevance.

Nevertheless, this is very difficult for many Christians to accept. They think that if our cultures and non-Christian religions have theological relevance and significance, then the preaching of the gospel to non-Christians would become ridiculous and meaningless. They are angry about endeavors to explore the theological significance of other cultures and religions. Is it right for them to be angry? If there is theological significance in other religions, then how do we conceive of Christian mission? What is Christian mission in a religiously and culturally pluralistic society? How do we do mission in such a context?

It is very important for us as Christians in a society of religious and cultural diversity to study the Bible to learn who God is and what is the right Christian attitude toward non-Christian religions. How does a Christian evaluate the so-called "non-Christian cultures?" How do we as Christians discern the theological meanings of Taiwanese history and cultures? We may get some insights from the book of Jonah, which tells us the story of God, the nature of God, and how God deals with those who follow other religions. Through the dialogue between God and Jonah, we may discern God's character and action, get to know more about God, and more appropriately respond to God's mercy and love.

CONTEXTUAL COMMENT

In the postexilic period, the books of Ezra and Nehemiah reflect a xenophobic attitude toward Gentiles, but the book of Jonah provides a contrasting view of the relationship of Jews with non-Jews. Therefore, Jonah is a most useful book for Christians hoping to learn the nature of God and how to interact with the followers of non-Christian religions.

Jonah is written in the form of a didactic story. The storyteller asks people who are not pleased about God's compassion and concern for the followers of other religions, "Is it right for you to be angry?" (4:4, 9)

"But this was very displeasing to Jonah, and he became angry" (4:1). Why was Jonah displeased and angry? He was not pleased about God's decision to spare Nineveh (3:10). Why was Jonah concerned with God's decisions? Why did Jonah become angry when God forgave the people of Nineveh? Jonah was sent to denounce their wickedness (1:2; 3:2) and told them that Nineveh would be overthrown after forty days (3:4). Perhaps Jonah became angry because he thought that God's merciful decision made him a false prophet. Perhaps Jonah was dissatisfied because his people's enemy, the wicked Ninevites, did not receive the punishment from God that he expected. Fundamentally, the issue behind Jonah's anger was that God acted differently from how he thought God should act.

In fact, Jonah's understanding of God was right on many points. He knew that God is a just God (1:2). This may have been the reason that Jonah ran away from God and did not go to Nineveh at the book's beginning. He wanted the people of Nineveh to be punished for their wickedness. He knew God is the God of creation (1:9), redemption (2:6, 9), and the Lord of the world and its history (1:12; 4:3). He knew that God is the God who hears prayers (2:7). He knew and experienced God's mercy and love (2; 4:2).

But Jonah was not aware that God's mercy and love toward the followers of other religions were beyond his imagination. He was not aware that he knew God only in part. If we view Jonah's understanding of God's mercy and love in light of Psalm 103 instead of Exodus 34:6-7, we may conclude that the storyteller wants to remind the hearers/readers that (God) "does not deal with us according to our sins, nor repay us according to our iniquities. For as the heavens are high above the earth, so great is his steadfast love toward those who fear him; as far as the east is from the west, so far he removes our transgressions from us" (Ps 103:10-12). There is a chasm between Jonah's understanding of God and God's real character and mind. Therefore, the storyteller reports that God said to Jonah, "Is it right for you to be angry?" (Jonah 4:4).

This question applies not only to Jonah and Jews of that period, but also to us today. Many modern Christians still think that all other religions are evil and that their believers are incapable of good. These Christians are angry about theological works that try to discern the theological relevance and significance of the non-Christian cultures and religions. They are angry with theologians who argue that other religions also reflect the truth, and angry at the theology that argues that God's salvation extends to believers of other religions. "Is it right for you to be angry?" is a question for those who have the same attitude as the person who was infuriated at the use of a Buddhist story in a Christian sermon.

In fact, in the book of Jonah, non-Jews are depicted as devout, religious people. When Jonah's ship threatened to break up, every sailor cried out to his own god for help (1:5). They selflessly did everything they could to save Jonah's life although they knew that he was the cause of the fierce storm (1:13). The people in Nineveh were also very religious. After learning that they were going to perish for their wicked ways and injustice, they humbled themselves and repented. Both the sailors and the people of Nineveh were willing to turn to God.

This is not to claim that people with religious piety are necessarily righteous before God. Yet, acknowledging people's piety and the merits of other religions is a necessary attitude for relating to followers of other religions. If we envision other cultures and religions from the perspective of creation, we might recognize that they also manifest God's mercy and love in familiar ways.

Jonah did not answer God's question (4:4). The storyteller seems to say to the hearers/readers that Jonah was not aware of his real situation. Jonah did not realize that God's ways are better than our ways, and God's thoughts are higher than our thoughts. Therefore, God made a bush grow tall enough overnight to give shade to the angry Jonah. Jonah, very pleased with the bush's growth that shaded him from the hot sun, was infuriated when it died. Then, God said to Jonah, "Is it right for you to be angry about the bush?" (4:9). The storyteller calls the hearers/readers to be involved in the dialogue between Jonah and God. Jonah said that he was right to be angry enough to die for the death of a bush that he had neither planted nor tended. God replied that if Jonah cared for a bush, why was it wrong for God to be concerned about the people of Nineveh and extend mercy and love to them? (4:10-11). The comparison is not between a bush and human life, but between Jonah's thoughts and God's thoughts, between Jonah's selfish concern for the death of a shade tree and God's gracious concern for the salvation of a great city. Beyond Jonah and his people, God was concerned about all of humankind. Jonah does not comprehend the actual nature of God's mercy and love.

God asked Jonah, "Is it right for you to be angry?" What was the message that the storyteller wanted to deliver to the Jewish people in his time? That they should renounce or "turn from" (shuv, 3:8) any kind of intolerance toward people with other beliefs. The storyteller wants all hearers/readers to know that God's mercy and love transcend the boundary of ethnicity and religion, and to respond to this merciful and loving God.

For Christians, this book also asks: Is this vision of God's mercy not what Jesus showed to the world when he preached the gospel of the kingdom of God? When he broke the boundaries of culture and religion? We have no right to be angry if God wants to show mercy and love to the people of other religions. We have no right to be angry if God would like to accept the believers of other religions into God's kingdom. We have to be open-minded to the believers of other religions, for we can never know how the Spirit of God works among them (see John 3:8).

We live in a world in which many misunderstandings, misinterpretations, and misapprehensions exist between different cultures and religions. There are tensions between Western Christians and the Muslims in the Arabic world, and between Christians, Hindus, and Buddhists in South Asia. We *must* be aware that God's mercy and love extend to all. One of the obstacles to Christian mission today is that Christians have Jonah's attitude toward other religions. As long as this Christian bigotry remains, it will be hard for the Christian communities to participate in God's mission by witnessing to God's mercy and love, denouncing evil, and being peacemakers.

CONCLUSION

The book of Jonah does not present Jonah's story, but rather the story of God as merciful and loving. The storyteller conveys that God's mercy and love are beyond our comprehension. God is love. Where there is love, there is God. Far from defending God, Christian bigotry and denominationalism harm the proclamation of this good news.

Following the teaching of the book of Jonah, Christians should participate in God's mission not because they think that they hold all the truth and that all other religions are evil, but because they have experienced God's compassion and salvation for all. Bringing this good news to other people does not involve denying their culture and religion, and thus their identity. Rather it involves appreciating the merits of other religions and acknowledging what God has done among their followers before they ever heard about the gospel. Then people from different religions can work together in building a society of justice, peace, and love. Then the daily prayer for the coming of the reign of God will not be in vain.

BIBLIOGRAPHY

Limburg, James. *Jonah: A Commentary.* OTL. Louisville: Westminster John Knox, 1993.

Salters, R. S. *Jonah and Lamentation.* OTG. Sheffield: JSOT Press, 1994.

Sasson, Jack M. *Jonah.* AB 24B. N.Y.: Doubleday, 1990.

Song, C. S. *Christian Mission in Reconstruction: An Asian Analysis.* Maryknoll, N.Y.: Orbis, 1977.

Trible, Phyllis. "The Book of Jonah," in *NIB* 7, Pages 463–529. Nashville: Abingdon, 1996.

Yen, Cheng. *Chu Chai e Hsin Lin (The Mind Free from Delusion).* Translated by C. S. Song. Taipei Hsi Tai Publishing Company, 1991.

MICAH

Huang Po Ho

Tainan Theological College and Seminary, Tainan, Taiwan

LIFE CONTEXT OF THE INTERPRETATION

The message of Micah, derived from the sociopolitical and economic situation in the context of the international political dynamics of the eighth century B.C.E., has become more pertinent in the Third World with the development of economic globalization. Micah has a special appeal for Third World people who struggle to free themselves from the shackles of internal and external oppression. These personal experiences give them new insights as they approach this text as the Word of God. The sense of being dependent on powerful others for one's political, social, and economic future was very real for the Israelites during the period of Micah. Their national fortune was totally at the mercy of the imperialistic aspirations of Assyria, Egypt, and Babylon, which was emerging as a world power. The superpowers striving to control the world and the great empires engaged in "world wars" were becoming a reality (Alfaro 1989, 1-2).

The book of Micah offers no personal data of the prophet, nor does it narrate the call of the prophet. However, as the heading of the book (1:1) states, Micah lived in the days of kings Jotham (742–735), Ahaz (735–715), and Hezekiah (715–687), with a prophetic ministry during the last two reigns. He was, therefore, a contemporary of Isaiah and Amos.

The background of the prophetic pronouncement of Micah appears to be similar to the life context of the people in Taiwan, to which the writer of this commentary belongs. Intercontextual dialogue between the two contexts promises a better perception of the meaning of the book of Micah and a deeper appreciation for the struggles of the Taiwanese people to liberate themselves from internal and international conflicts.

Taiwan is historically a colonized land. The Dutch, Spanish, Chinese Ming dynasty, Manchurian, Japanese, and Chinese Nationalists have ruled this land at one time or another. Its population is quite diverse. In addition to ten aboriginal tribes, there are three ethnic Han groups that have migrated from southern China and, most recently, a significant number of workers who have migrated from Southeast Asia.

Christian churches have existed here for more than a century, but unfortunately they have kept their foreign identity and remained detached from the plural cultures and religions of the Taiwanese people. The Presbyterian Church in Taiwan has tried to play a prophetic role by advocating human rights and self-determination for the Taiwanese people, when it was under martial law and internationally isolated by the diplomacy of China, and by attempting to calm down conflicts among ethnic groups. The church paid a very high price for the role it played; many of its pastors and church workers, including its former general secretary, were imprisoned.

Huang Po Ho, president of Tainan Theological College and Seminary, Taiwan, is an ordained minister of the Presbyterian Church in Taiwan, an officer of the Programme of Theology and Cultures in Asia, and was the Moderator of the Council for World Mission from 2001 to 2003. He is the author of one book in English, *A Theology of Self-Determination* (1996), and more than twenty books in Chinese, including *A Theology from the Womb of Cultures* (1987) and *The Shaping of Christian Identity* (1997).

Post-Colonial Taiwan and Micah

Taiwan formally ended its colonial history with the first direct presidential election of 1996. Yet remnants of colonial influences remain strong in domestic and international relations.

The "divide and rule" policy implemented by the colonial authorities has created ethnic strife among the different groups in Taiwan. There are ongoing questions and tensions regarding both personal identity (is it Taiwanese or Chinese?) and political options for either independence from or unification with China. Internationally, though the formal colonial rulers are no longer present, the geopolitical importance of the island has sandwiched the country between China and the United States. China sees Taiwan as its window to breathe the air of the Pacific Ocean, which eventually may enable it to become a member of the international superpower's club. The United States considers Taiwan as its flag carrier to protect it from direct confrontation with China. In effect, neither China nor the United States allows the people of Taiwan to exercise their right of self-determination and to decide their own destiny.

Christians in Taiwan, though they are a small minority (less than 5 percent, including Catholics and Protestants), have maintained a negative attitude toward the cultures and religions of the native people. Generally speaking, most Christians adopt a "superiority mindset" and view the Taiwanese people and their cultures and religions as pagan and unworthy. Because of this attitude, Christians and their churches are perceived by the Taiwanese as alien. Furthermore, Christian mission is mostly manifested as a preoccupation with the number of converts, instead of a commitment to actualize the reign of God.

The efforts of the Presbyterian Church in Taiwan (the only Protestant church that existed before World War II) to identify itself with the people led it to emphasize political concerns. Since 1971 three major public statements issued by the church consistently insisted that the fate of the Tai-wanese people should not be dictated by the political superpowers and that the people's right to self-determination needed to be respected. These statements called for political reforms in the nation and sought international recognition of the Taiwanese people's effort to establish a society truly characterized by justice, peace, and freedom. They also appealed to the superpowers not to deny the rights of the Taiwanese people and not to isolate them from the international community when they mend their relationship with China. In these critical times, the statements urged both the churches and the people in Taiwan to speak the truth with love and to respect each other in order to create a sense of solidarity regardless of differences in political views, ethnicities, religions, denominations, and ideologies. The statements also expressed deep concerns for human corruption as evidenced by declining morality, the erosion of social security, and ecological destruction for the sake of rapid economic development. Finally, the statements appealed to the global community and especially the churches around the world to reiterate the principles of basic human rights and the right to self-determination, while supporting the people in Taiwan in their effort to establish a new and independent country, where "steadfast love and faithfulness will meet; righteousness and peace will kiss each other. Faithfulness will spring up from the ground, and righteousness will look down from the sky" (Ps 85:10-11).

Thirty years have passed since the first statement was issued by the Presbyterian Church of Taiwan, and thankfully the political and economic situation of Taiwan has significantly progressed toward the open, democratic, and economically developed society envisioned by these statements. However, the societal way of life in Taiwan remains far from satisfactory, if not worse than before. Moral corruptions, distortions of human spirituality, and ethnic conflicts have made contemporary Taiwan a society without consensus with regard to communal values, concepts, and ethos. In addition, the globalization process implemented in the economic order of society has deeply affected the weakest sections of our society, including the aborigines, traditional farmers, fishermen, women, and children. Furthermore, international isolation and missile threats exercised by China over the island remain a persistent challenge to the existence of the country and a weight on the life of its people.

While reading the book of Micah, the people in Taiwan hear the proclamation of hope for a new creation out of a situation of suffering and pain. The apparent similarity between the threats to the people of Judah

thousands of years ago and to the Taiwanese people today—in both cases, there is an imminent danger of national destruction—calls Taiwanese Christians to interact critically with the message of the prophet.

Yet we also note that Micah's forceful prophecies unfortunately did not prevent the southern kingdom from being conquered. Neither has the message proclaimed by the Presbyterian Church in Taiwan brought peace and reconciliation to the people of different ethnic groups in Taiwan. Do these situations warrant a critical review of the messages being proclaimed?

CONTEXTUAL COMMENT

The book of Micah arises out of the tributary mode of production represented by the Israelite monarchy. The structural elements of this mode of production are inscribed in its text (Mosala 1989, 118). The material condition out of which the text of Micah was produced was similar to that of some other prophetic texts, including an earlier text and later interpolations, prolonging the message of the prophet for another situation. Thus, many biblical scholars recognize a literary disjunction between Micah 1–3 and Micah 4–7. The first three chapters are genuinely from the prophet Micah, while the following three chapters are later interpolations.

Micah 1–3: Helping Us to Recognize the Root of the Socioeconomic Problems in Taiwan

Micah 1–3 arose in the context of the eighth century B.C.E. The prophet attributes God's wrath to the socioeconomic condition during the time of Ahaz and Hezekiah. Earlier in its history, under Uzziah (767–739), Judah had followed the established tradition of engaging in war to strengthen the political and economic powers of the monarchic kingdom. However, the gross injustice and the unequal control of resources, along with massive corruption by the ruling oligarchy and its officials, weakened the power of Judah. In this weakened situation, King

Ahaz (735–715) perceived an impending danger from Judah's powerful neighbors, Israel and Aram. To escape the threat of the neighbors, Judah entered into a military treaty with Assyria, including an agreement to pay a huge tribute to the Assyrian ruler. While Israel and Samaria were conquered by the Assyrians, Judah became a vassal state of the imperialist Assyria. The alliance with Assyria forced Judah to reorganize its socioeconomic structures and its cultic practices. Judah as a nation had lost its autonomy, including its ability to determine its own future and to worship the God who liberated Judah from oppression.

The juxtaposed poems of Micah 1–3 can be briefly reviewed against this background.

1:2-7. The prophet depicts the coming of the Lord to punish Samaria for its idolatry.

1:8-16. Micah laments the destruction of the cities of Judah.

2:1-13. In these two poems of doom against the powerful in Judah (2:3-5, 6-7, and 10-11), Micah warns Judah against its reorganization of its socioeconomic structures according to which those who have power (2:1) devise ways of appropriating the fields and houses of the people (2:2) and act as "an enemy" of the people, oppressing "the peaceful," women, and children (2:8-9). Yet these two poems of doom are followed by a promise to the remnant for Israel (2:12-13).

3:1-12. In another series of poems of doom, Micah condemns the corrupt rulers of Judah (Jacob) and Israel who do "not know justice" and "who eat the flesh of my people" (3:1-4), and "who abhor justice," "build Zion with blood," and "give judgment for a bribe" (3:9-11). This passage also speaks against the false prophets who are at the service of the rich and "who cry 'Peace' when they have something to eat [i.e., given to them], but declare war against those who put nothing in their mouths" [i.e., against those who do not give them food or money] (3:5, cf. 3:11). This section concludes with a verse that Jeremiah quotes a century later: "Zion shall be plowed as a field; Jerusalem shall become a heap of ruins, and the mountain of the house a wooded height" (Mic 3:12 and Jer 26:18)

Is this not the situation of Taiwan? Do not the Taiwanese people experience this kind of uncertainty because Taiwan opted to side with the imperialistic United States in order to gain protection from the missile threats of China? Is it not the case that this political option has brought about an economic situation imposed by the imperialist powers that, through its globalization process, has forced the aborigines into unemployment and marginalization? As the church in Taiwan has read and reread Micah 1–3, its message has contributed to a critical self-understanding of our situation and helped the church to recognize the root of the socioeconomic problems of its people.

Micah 4–7
and Its Ambivalent Message

Micah 4–7, as Mosala argues, reflects the royal Zionist ideology that began to evolve during the time of David and, after refinements, became the dominant self-consciousness of the nation in the later reigns, culminating after 587 in the ideological activity of the priestly class during the Babylonian exile (1989, 119). Mosala points out that the central themes of the monarchical ideology were stability, grace, restoration, creation, universal peace, compassion, and salvation.

This monarchical ideology contrasts radically with the ideology of premonarchical Israel, characterized by such themes as justice, solidarity, struggle, and vigilance. The latter part of the book of Micah is eloquent in its silence on the ideological struggle waged by the oppressed and exploited class of monarchical Judah. Apart from making available a body of information about the material situation of oppression that it could not suppress, Micah 4–7 simply luxuriates in an elaborate ideological statement of self-comfort by dwelling on issues like the Lord's universal reign of peace (4:1-4), God's promise of return from exile (4:6-13), the promise of a ruler from Bethlehem (5:2-5), the Lord's salvation (7:8-20), and so forth (Mosala 1989, 120). These chapters clearly reflect the character of a ruling class document, which serves the interest of the dominant and established sections of society.

4:1-5. This new section begins with the well-known poem about universal peace (also found in Isa 2:2-4) "they shall beat their swords into plowshares, and their spears into pruning hooks; nation shall not lift up sword against nation, neither shall they learn war any more" (4:3). Yet, as we shall discuss below, this message is not as "universal" as it first looks.

4:6–5:5. This promise of restoration after the exile is in effect the promise of a new age in Zion, which will be ushered by the coming of a righteous ruler from Bethlehem (5:2, as quoted in Matt 2:6): "And they shall live secure, for now he shall be great to the ends of the earth; and he shall be the one of peace" (5:4b-5).

5:6-15. In this new age, the present order will be reversed (but the structure of power will remain the same): Judah (Jacob) will be a mighty nation "like a lion among the animals of the forest, like a young lion among the flocks of sheep" (5:8) and all foreign elements—chariots, fortified cities, idolatry of all kinds—will be removed from "the remnant of Jacob."

6:1-8. Following this vision of a new age, Micah returns to the present reality, an

[handwritten margin note: Troubles lie in relations w/ strong imperialists (US)]

unfaithful Israel, by presenting a lawsuit in which the Lord challenges the people for breach of its covenantal commitments. This poem concludes with a statement of God's requirements: "To do justice, and to love kindness, and to walk humbly with your God" (6:8), that we further discuss later.

6:9-16. The doom sayings continue with curses against the dishonest economic practices of the wealthy (6:10-12).

7:1-7. The exploitation of the powerless by the powerful ("the official and the judge ask for a bribe, and the powerful dictate what they desire; thus they pervert justice," 7:3) leads to the disintegration of all true human relationships: "Put no trust in a friend, have no confidence in a loved one . . . for the son treats the father with contempt, the daughter rises up against her mother, the daughter-in-law against her mother-in-law; your enemies are members of your own household" (7:5-6).

7:8-20. This concluding passage is often called (since H. Gunkel) a liturgy of hope, in which Jerusalem and God are in dialogue, beginning with the suffering people's expression of confidence in God and concluding with a hymn to the faithful and compassionate God (7:18-20).

The churches in Taiwan frequently mention two passages from this second part of the book of Micah, 6:6-8 and 4:1-4.

Micah 6:6-8:
Justice, Love—For Whom?

Despite its brevity, Micah presents a complex variety of ways in which God relates to human beings. God's wrath, a mode of God-human relation that causes disaster and suffering, is viewed as a punishment for human sin. The calamities that the people will endure are the consequences of human behavior. This assumption has led Micah to inquire: "What does the LORD require of [us]?" (6:8) and "With what shall I come before the Lord?" (6:6), and to formulate his faith statement: "He has told you, O mortal, what is good; and what does the Lord require of you but to do justice, and to love kindness, and to walk humbly with your God?" (6:8). This passage has been commonly interpreted as a message denouncing formal liturgical practices and demanding deeds that are morally correct and commendable. However, it is important to point out that the prophet was rejecting particular religious practices to which his people were deeply committed.

Reading this passage from our pluralistic religious context first reveals that the God of Israel pragmatically desires human obedience in the form of particular social behavior rather than mere liturgical practices, even if they are most cherished. From our contextual perspective, it also appears that this passage resembles other prophetic traditions that posit a dualism opposing the people of Israel and so-called pagans. Accordingly, the prophet's demand to satisfy God's will by doing justice, acting with lovingkindness, and walking humbly in the path of God exclusively concerns the people of God.

Unfortunately, nothing in this passage suggests that the prophet has any concern for justice and love beyond Judah and Israel; this justice and this love do not extend to people other than the people of the Lord. The prophet's blind spot, sacrificing other people's security in the zealous attempt to secure national security, is also evident in the prophetic role of churches in our part of the world. The recent escalation of military tension between Taiwan and China, which threatens the security of twenty-three million people in Taiwan, has driven the Presbyterian Church of Taiwan to advocate Taiwan's independence and the people's right to self-determination. During that time, the China Christian Council has followed the policy of its government to support the unification agenda. These different attitudes have caused tensions not only between the two churches but also among the people in the two countries. Of course, one could argue that the prophetic message of Micah is constrained by the identity of the prophet; his prophecy was at the service of his people. But such constraint would contradict his own message of universal peace proclaimed in 4:1-4. In the same way, the fact that the Presbyterian Church in Taiwan is at the service of its people does not mean that its primary objective should not be the proclamation of universal peace.

Micah 4:1-4: A Message of Universal Peace?

Another oft-repeated passage of Micah is the promise of universal peace in the kingdom of God (4:1-4). Part of this passage is inscribed on the wall of the United Nations building. However, conflicts among member nations of the United Nations never cease, even though they have committed themselves to upholding this motto.

If we read the passage carefully enough, we will agree that the so-called universal peace proclaimed by the prophet, in fact, is once again a version of peace limited to the people of God or centered upon it.

In days to come the mountain of the Lord's house shall be established as the highest of the mountains, and shall be raised up above the hills. Peoples shall stream to it, and many nations shall come and say: "Come, let us go up to the mountain of the Lord, to the house of the God of Jacob; that he may teach us his ways and that we may walk in his paths." For out of Zion shall go forth instruction, and the word of the Lord from Jerusalem. (4:1-2)

The peace proclaimed here is perceived from the specificity of the Israelites' exclusive claim to be the people of God. Unfortunately, the universal concept of peace conveyed in the following verses (4:3-4, "they shall beat their swords into plowshares . . .") is clothed in an imperialist structure driven by imperialist interests, although this time the empire is that of the people of God, as 5:8 expresses most directly: "And among the nations the remnant of Jacob, surrounded by many peoples, shall be like a lion among the animals of the forest, like a young lion among the flocks of sheep, which, when it goes through, treads down and tears in pieces, with no one to deliver." Since the message of "universal peace" that the United Nations follows is cast in this imperialist mode, the United Nations has unsurprisingly failed to bring real world peace and has been unable to resist attempts for hegemonic manipulation.

CONCLUSION

Three distinguishing characteristics can be attributed to the society of Taiwan: religio-cultural plurality, economic globalization, and sociopolitical neocolonization. To read the book of Micah in this threefold context by using a postcolonial perspective reveals the limitations of its message. People of different cultures and religions seem to be excluded from his message. Also the concern for justice and peace advocated by the prophet is constrained by his nationalist ideology. Both in Micah's time and today for the churches and people of Taiwan, such a message fuels conflicts more than it provides tangible solutions to these conflicts.

BIBLIOGRAPHY

Alfaro, Juan I., OSB. *Justice and Loyalty: A Commentary on the Book of Micah.* ITC. Grand Rapids: Eerdmans, 1989.

Hillers, Delbert R. *Micah: A Commentary on the Book of the Prophet Micah.* Edited by Paul D. Hanson with Loren Fisher. Hermeneia. Philadelphia: Fortress, 1984.

———. "Micah, Book of." Pages 807–10 in *ABD.* Vol. 4. Edited by David Noel Freedman. New York: Doubleday, 1992.

Mosala, Itumeleng J. *Biblical Hermeneutics and Black Theology in South Africa.* Grand Rapids: Eerdmans, 1989.

NAHUM

Valmor da Silva,
Catholic University of Goiás, Goiânia, Brazil
Translated from Portuguese by Rubén Muñoz

LIFE CONTEXT OF THE INTERPRETATION

This interpretation of Nahum has come out of the midwestern region of Brazil, a region marked by the traditions of its indigenous peoples and by its recent assimilation into the national scene. The author of this interpretation comes from a humble, poor family from a rural region in the south of Brazil. He participates in Christian base communities and ecumenical movements and practices contextual interpretation of the Bible that defends their human rights, and supports people who struggle for justice, based on the experience of the oppressed. The downfall of oppressive powers resonates with the author, as it did with Nahum.

In this context, the prophecy of Nahum represents a cry of freedom by people who suffer from injustice, as they witness the destruction of their oppressors. This cry expresses, on the one hand, a strong faith in a God who brings about justice, and, on the other, the irony of the oppressor's downfall. In the time of Nahum, this was the situation of people subjugated as a result of war, as they witnessed the destruction of the armies who had conquered them. This is the current reality of colonized nations, as they proclaim their freedom from those who have exploited them. This is the case of starving people as they witness the defeat of the economic groups who have exploited their labor.

Imagine how unjustly-condemned people feel when they see the restoration of their rights. Consider the reactions of victims of torture, when they witness the end of their executioners. Think about the feelings of groups who have been enslaved, when they see the destruction of those who enslaved them.

Now is the time to hear the cries of children performing degrading work, of little girls forced into prostitution, and the soft complaint of the elderly whose salaries and pensions are not enough to buy the medications they need. Now is the time to hear the weeping of women who suffer discrimination, of exploited Brazilian natives (Indians), of marginalized blacks and countless others. Nahum's voice makes us listen to the disturbing cry of each of these peoples. The expected fall of Nineveh is a symbol of radical changes in the global situation. Nahum's voice carries the cry of resistance of all oppressed people when he cries out in the face of the fall of Nineveh, a symbol of radical change.

Issues Raised by Nahum about the Relationship of the People of God with the World

Nahum's prophecy is a forceful appeal to people and communities who live in situations of oppression. It presents its readers

Valmor da Silva studied theology and biblical studies in Rome. He received his PhD from the Methodist University of São Paulo. Convener of the Master Program in Religious Studies, he teaches courses in history, society, and biblical literature, including comparative studies of wisdom traditions in the Bible, the Ancient Near East, and Brazil. His publications include books focusing on apocalyptic themes in the New Testament (on 2 Thessalonians, *Segunda epístola aos Tessalonicenses: Não é o fim do mundo*, 1992, and *Jesus, milagreiro e exorcista*, 2000; and a translation of García Martínez's *Textos de Qumran*, 1995), a book on the history of the people of God (*Caminhos da Bíblia: Uma história do povo de Deus*, 2003), and many articles, including one on Nahum (2000).

with a challenge: remain a silent accomplice of injustice, or cry out and tear down the tyrannical powers. Nahum invites its readers to denounce injustice, to restore the usurped rights, and to proclaim the just judgments of God.

CONTEXTUAL COMMENT

Overview of Nahum

The name Nahum means "comforted by God," but his language is hard and shocking. He speaks from the point of view of oppressed people, to whom he directs his consolation. Because of this, he uses irony to describe Nineveh's brutal power, and shows great emotion when describing the downfall of this cruelty. Historically, this prophecy should be dated between 663 and 612 B.C.E. Thebes or No-Amon, in Egypt, fell in 663 (Nah 3:8) and Nineveh, the Assyrian capital, fell in 612. The whole book ironically commemorates the destruction of the Assyrian empire.

Juda was ruled by Manasseh (687–642), followed by Amon (642–640). Manasseh left a legacy of cruelty, religious decadence, and collaboration with Assyria. Soon after Amon's reign, Josias (640–609) undertook an internal reform, perhaps supported by Nahum.

Faithfulness to a prophetic mission is transformed into a vision of hope at the downfall of the cruelty represented by Nineveh (1:1). Nahum challenges the people of God to see that God is not passive before injustice (1:2-8). God discerns between those who struggle for peace and those who promote wars (1:9-2:1). The downfall of oppressive power is cause for celebration among the oppressed (2:2-11), and those who stockpile weapons of destruction die from their own violence (2:12-14). Sad is the end of this bloody city, because no one will have compassion on it (3:1-7). History itself confirms this sequence of defeat (3:8-11), showing that human arrogance is worthless (3:12-17). Finally, Nahum challenges his readers by using violent and ironic language   used to describe the destruction of this unjust power (3:18-19). It is Nahum's tone of voice we need to hear to perceive his irony. Thus, rather than focusing on several passages of this book, we need to hear Nahum's entire speech, from beginning to end, carefully listening for its tone.

"YHWH is a Jealous and Vengeful God" (Nah 1:1-8)

The title of the oracle (1:1) is followed by a hymn to the sovereignty of God over the world and its history (1:2-8). The acrostic poem, that follows the first half of the Hebrew alphabet, exalts divine justice. Far from being neutral, God reveals fury against the oppressors and divine goodness toward those who seek God's refuge. It is this conviction that the psalm sings.

The God of Nahum is a jealous, vengeful, angry, furious, powerful God of justice (1:2-3). Although these characteristics are shocking for us, they are a protest against Assyria, which considered itself the ruler of the world. In the presence of threatened human life, God rises up in fury. God is jealous, passionate, and vengeful invindicating those whose rights have been usurped (1:2). But the end of the poem affirms that God is good—a shelter in tribulation—and welcomes those who take refuge in God (1:7). In the presence of those groups of people whose rights have been taken away for far too long, we might need to hear both sides of this message.

"Oppression Will not Rise up a Second Time" (Nah 1:9–2:1)

This section consists of three oracles directed to Judah, and two against Assyria. God manifests his choice one more time. Judah can be reassured that evil will be reduced to nothing, like dry straw and thorns, and oppression will not rise up a second time (1:9-10). The yoke of oppression will be broken (1:12-13), and the people will be able to have their celebrations in peace (1:15; cf. Is 52:7). This is a clear positive announcement of joy and liberation.

From Assyria, comes the wicked advisor Belial (1:11), whose name will have no more descendants (1:14). A nation that is skilled in cruelty will now drown in its own violence. Assyria produced this mysterious advisor Belial, who plots to do evil. The name Belial is composed of the words "no" and "useless," meaning uselessness, nullity, or emptiness. It came to designate evil and, later, what is impious, immoral, and diabolical. Here it already appears as a person's name in order to refer to the evil, diabo-lical power of the Assyrian empire. Historically, Belial could be Sennacherib, who, in 701 B.C.E., took possession of Judah as we see in 2 Kings 18:13-16. The oracles express the triumph of justice over oppression, the victory of peace over war, and the dominion of love over hate—a message of hope many need to hear today.

"A Destroyer Is Rising up against You" (Nah 2:2-11)

With eloquent poetic expression, the text describes the destruction of Nineveh, capital of Assyria. Its words convey excitement and approval before the destruction of this powerful city. The text abounds with irony in describing the terror of the enemy warriors. It provocatively mocks their efforts to ward off the assault of the city. With vivid realism it pictures the heat of battle, mixing together various references to the color "red"—the red of the enemy shields, the red of their uniforms and of their chariots, and certainly the red of the heads that will roll and the blood that will be spilled. It ridicules the soldiers, tripping over their own feet, the water undermining the palace, the queen with her servants screaming in flight, the widespread looting and sacking. The text concludes: "Hearts melt with fear; knees tremble, strength is gone, faces grow pale" (2:11, a.t.).

Nineveh's fall signified Judah's liberation, and represented the possibility of the restoration of the kingdom of Israel, and the reunification of both kingdoms. It is for this reason that Nahum's description of this event is so forceful and emotional. Historically, the fall of the Assyrian empire was due to the combined forces of the Medes and of the Babylonians, who united to attack the capital city. According to some sources, an unusual overflow of the Tigris River contributed to the fall of Nineveh. Other sources mention that a canal of water was diverted to enter the city. In both cases, the foundations of the city walls could have been weakened by water, as seems to be suggested by the following verses from Nahum: "The gates by the river burst open; the palace is filled with terror" (2:6, a.t.) and, "Like water from a broken dam the people rush from Nineveh!" (2:8, a.t.).

"Where Is the Lion's Den?" (Nah 2:12-14)

The lion was used as a symbol of Assyrian power. Figures of lions were present in Assyrian art, in the palaces, on weapons, and in inscriptions. The lion—a bloody and indomitable beast, ready to attack and devour its prey—perfectly symbolized the ferocity of the Assyrian army. Nahum utilizes the same symbol but with heavy irony: "Where is the den of lions, the cave of the lion cubs? When the lion left, the lioness remained, together with their cubs" (2:11, a.t.). Nahum continues: "The lion killed his prey and tore it to pieces for his mate and their cubs; he filled his den with the torn flesh of his prey" (2:12, a.t.). A divine oracle proclaims the final just condemnation: "The sword will devour your cubs. It will disappear your preys and no more will be heard the voice of your messengers" (2:13, a.t.). The ferocity is emphasized by words relating to lions ("lions, lioness, cubs, prey"). the repetition of the words "den" and "cave," and by the use of the verbs "tear to pieces" and "fill with prey." Assyria, the ferocious lion, is destroyed by its own violence.

In the midst of this description of how the

Medes and Babylonians defeated the Assyrians and put an end to their cruelty, Nahum has God declare, "I am against you" (2:13, repeated in 3:5). In the prophet's conception of things, God cannot allow injustice. Because God has divine power, God cannot but intervene when goodness and justice are violated. God cannot remain inactive when seeing oppression. God's hand of justice is ready to intervene against those who dare to challenge justice. This gives hope to many in the world today.

"Woe to You, City of Blood" (Nah 3:1-7)

Having satisfied his desire for justice, Nahum sings a funeral hymn for Nineveh, the devastated prostitute (3:1-7). She is described as a city of blood, lies, loot, and plunder, as befits the city's tradition of cruelty. But the prophetic elegy concentrates on the mountain of dead bodies in this city of ruins. Oppression was defeated; it has become but a heap of corpses. The capital city is presented as a prostitute and a witch because of her power of seduction. Both images, prostitution and witchcraft, have been used by various prophets and have political connotations well beyond any sexual allusions. To prostitute oneself, in this case, was to betray the people for political or economic interests, as an "attractive whore full of deadly charms, who enchanted nations and seduced them" (3:4, a.t.). However, once again, the empire stumbles and falls, and becomes a public spectacle of destruction. To end this ironic elegy, Nahum plays with the meaning of his own name, "consoled," and poses the question: "Who has any sympathy for her? Who will want to console her?" (3:7, a.t.).

"And You, Nineveh, Are You any better than Thebes, the Capital of Egypt?" (Nah 3:8-11)

To complete the sense of happiness upon the fall of powerful Assyria, Nahum reminds his readers that No-Amon, the Egyptian city of Thebes, had the same fate (3:8-11). Just as Thebes was attacked by Assyria in 667 B.C.E. and sacked in 663, so Nineveh is now destroyed by the Medes and Babylonians. Its city walls and fortresses are useless to protect it. Useless also is the support of Ethiopia, Egypt, Put, and Libya (3:9). Violence will be defeated. The descriptions of children beaten to death and enemy warriors, in chains like trophies of war are shocking but realistic in the light of Assyrian cruelty (3:10). Unfortunately, this is often also today's reality.

"All Your Fortresses Will Be like Fig Trees with Ripe Figs" (Nah 3:12-17)

This new scene stresses the fragility of Assyrian strength. A variety of ironic images are scattered throughout the text. Nineveh is a fig tree with figs in season, so ripe that they are falling off the trees (3:12); the city's secure gates will be thrown open, and fire will destroy the bars across its gates (3:13); the edge of the great river is without water; Assyria's soldiers, accustomed to dominating others, now tread on clay like slaves making bricks (3:14); Assyria, which once had an army as numerous as locusts, is now devoured by this same fury, as crops wiped out by invading locusts (3:15); its merchants, guards, and scribes now have flown away, like a swarm of insects that disappears suddenly (3:16). Once more, destructive power is defeated by its own weapons.

"Woe to You, Emperor of Assyria" (Nah 3:18-19)

Nahum ends with an ironic funeral lament upon Assyria, particularly directed at its emperor (Nah 3:18-19). The sleeping emperor and his noblemen are taken by surprise. The valiant lion, always vigilant, is now asleep. While the empire's commanders sleep, its army scatters . The empire is terminally ill, incurably diseased. Nineveh is dead and now the people it has oppressed clap their hands in joy. It is the applause of victory for the destruction of evil.

CONCLUSION

Nahum confronts violence and combats it by using the same language of violence. By using irony, he ridicules the Assyrians' violent power and thus disarms the brutality.

With the same touch of irony, he declares, without circumlocution, that God does not tolerate oppression. In the end, God is justice, and when there is opposition to God's justice and God's essence, God protests. In the presence of abusive power, as in the case of Nineveh, Nahum invites us to pity the powerful rather than envy them.

Then we can hear the cries of the oppressed. It becomes clear that remaining silent is to become accomplice to injustice. Our role as people of God is to denounce injustice, as Nahum did.

The God of Nahum challenges our churches today. This is a God who is strong and just, resists evil, and takes the side of oppressed people. God is not passive, does not tolerate evil, and is not at all neutral. May the promoters of war be defeated by their own weapons. May evil drown in its own cruelty.

BIBLIOGRAPHY

Bonora, Antonio. *Naum, Sofonias, Habacuc, Lamentações—Sofrimento, protesto e esperança.* São Paulo: Paulinas, 1993.

Rossi, Luiz Alexandre Solano. *Como ler o livro de Naum: A história pertence a Javé.* São Paulo: Paulus, 1998.

Schökel, Alonso L. and J. L. Sicre Díaz. *Profetas* 2. São Paulo: Paulinas, 1991.

Silva, Valmor da. "Naum, a boca justiceira de Javé." *RIBLA* 35/36 (2000): 212–19.

HABAKKUK

Innocent Himbaza

Rwanda and University of Fribourg, Switzerland

Translated from French by Aline Patte

LIFE CONTEXT OF THE INTERPRETATION

In this commentary, I read Habakkuk in the context of Rwanda and the African great lakes region. Rwanda is a small country surrounded by Uganda, Tanzania, Burundi, and the Democratic Republic of Congo. It is well known for its mountain gorillas, but also sadly for the genocide in 1994. Rwanda's christianization started in 1900 with the arrival of the Missionaries of Africa (Pères Blancs). Most of the population is Christian. It is a country with a long history that, like the surrounding countries, has known both quiet and troubled times, bloody changes of governments, and confrontation with the AIDS epidemic. Immersed in these socio-political problems, some believers are questioning God, while others are committed to following God.

Analysis of the Context

The context reflected in Habakkuk, Rwanda's present socio-political context, and the context of the African great lakes region are almost identical. The philosophical and religious predispositions of this region's inhabitants influence their Christian life and their answer to the question: Should Christians believe that the events in their lives include divinely ordained punishments? Divinely ordained rewards? Many Christians have questions of theodicy: Why is God allowing believers to suffer and die unjustly? Why is injustice not punished?

The prophet Habakkuk asked the same questions (1:2-5, 12-13). The prophet appealed to God, asking that violence and oppression stop and that justice be restored. Could Christians from this part of Africa, who appeal to God in this way, be helped by God's answer to Habakkuk? Will Rwandan Christians have the courage to promote social, economic, and political justice, when for many of them the word "politics" is synonymous with corruption?

One more aspect of the Rwandan context is that today many churches are experiencing a revival, a return to God, in which an ever-growing number of Christians become once again (or for the first time) active in their churches. More and more Christians are putting their trust in God, as did Habakkuk, no matter what the crisis, no matter what their personal circumstance. The prophet's main message is that trusting God in all circumstances is a path to life (2:4; 3:17-19). For Habakkuk, such trust is placed in a faithful God who promised to intervene in the believer's life and in the world. Is Habakkuk a model of encouragement for Christians? Do those who fill the churches have the same conviction that Habakkuk did?

God tells the prophet that the wicked think that they are beyond God's reach, but will not survive. Even though at that moment the prophet might not think it possible, the righteous will eventually win. In the

Innocent Himbaza, after studying in his native Rwanda, then in Jerusalem, received his PhD from the University of Fribourg, Switzerland, where he teaches Old Testament exegesis and also serves as pastor of a Reformed church parish. He is the editor of "Leviticus" in the forthcoming new edition of the Hebrew Bible: *Biblia Hebraica Quinta* (BhQ). His publications include several books, including a detailed analytical study of translations of the Hebrew Bible in Rwandese languages, *Transmettre la Bible. Etude exégétique de la traduction de l'Ancien Testament: le cas du Rwanda* (2001), and an inculturated study of Esther, "Entre culture et théologie, une lecture d'Esther 1" *ETR* (2000).

meantime, Habakkuk must trust God and follow God's commandments. Is it possible for the Christians in the African great lakes region—confronted by the AIDS epidemic, poverty, and political instability—to follow Habakkuk's example?

By taking note of God's interventions in history, Habakkuk is convinced that one must trust in God no matter what. He acknowledges that there are serious problems, yet he also knows that the believer can surmount these problems with God's help. Can reading and appropriating Habakkuk's words help believers in Rwanda and the great lakes region who, for decades, have had to deal with continual turmoil and frequent war?

CONTEXTUAL COMMENT

Overview of the Book of Habakkuk

The prophet Habakkuk is not well known. The most substantial historical reference we have is the mention of the Chaldeans, i.e., the neo-Babylonians (1:6). This sets the date of Habakkuk's preaching at the end of the seventh century B.C.E.

The prophet denounces the injustice suffered by the people (1:2-4). This injustice remains unpunished. Then God announces the judgment coming from a foreign nation (1:5-11). Habakkuk laments again, for God is using a nation that brings even more injustice and arrogance (1:12-17). God answers again (2:1-4) by emphasizing that the righteous need to be confident (or faithful). Even though injustice seems to win, it does not have the last word. Chapter two concludes with five curses against the oppressors and their deceptions (2:5-20).

Chapter three contains a psalmodic prayer in which the prophet reviews history and notes that God has intervened for the salvation of God's people in powerful ways since the exodus (3:8-15). Habakkuk reassures himself with this retrospective glance. He cannot but be confident in God, in spite of the present situation (3:16-19).

Habakkuk 1:1-13

In this passage, the prophet expresses his concern for the suffering that the righteous endure. When God responds by announcing the punishment of the wicked by means of another nation, Habakkuk cannot accept it. He believes that this will only increase the injustice. The Chaldeans are indifferent to other nations except as lands to conquer; they destroy them brutally. They worship their own strength as their god.

For Habakkuk, a God who is the benevolent sovereign of the universe cannot act in this way. He could accept that God uses a nation to punish another one, but does not understand why God does not intervene when this nation exceeds its divinely mandated mission and brutalizes others.

I have often heard reactions similar to Hab 1:2, "O Lord, how long shall I cry for help, and you will not listen?" among the nations at war in the African great lakes region.

The great temptation for many Christians in Rwanda is "to hope for heaven" and forego "the world." They think they need not concern themselves with social and political injustice, and that they should focus all their attention on their personal relationship with God. How very different from Habakkuk's attitude! The prophet denounces human injustice and wants "the world" to be changed. He asks God: Why do you accept oppression (Hab 1:3)? Why are you silent when the wicked swallow up the righteous (Hab 1:13)? However, there are other Christians in Uganda who are aware that their mission as Christians involves participating in the country's social and political life. A major intercessory movement promoting Christian values is reaching more and more people in Uganda and even developing beyond its borders. The participation of Christians in every aspect of life can change the world for the better, without condoning the misdeeds of those in power.

Habakkuk 2:1-4

The prophet waits for God's answer. God asks the prophet to write down the answer on tablets and to wait for the realization of the vision at the "appointed time" (2:3). God's answer (2:4) is that the righteous live by their confidence (in God) and that the wicked will perish. Ralph Smith thinks that God asks the prophet to only write "the righteous live by their confidence/faith" on the tablets (107). The book of Habakkuk speaks of *confidence* or *trust* (faith) in a God who is faithful to the promise of salvation made to God's people who are suffering violence and injustice. When confronted by a social, political, or economic crisis, believers can call on God and ask God to intervene. They can trust in God, who helps them to live in the world and who can improve its destiny.

This passage is viewed as the book's central message. Jewish tradition says that it summarizes all God's commandments. Indeed, according to *b. Mak. 23b-24a*, Moses received 613 laws. David came and reduced them to eleven (Ps 15). Isaiah came and reduced them to six (Isa 33:15-16). Micah reduced them to three (Mic 6:8). Isaiah came again and reduced them to two (Isa 56:1). Amos came and reduced them to one (Amos 5:4). But Rabbi Nahman b. Isaac said: "It is Habakkuk who came and reduced them to one, as it is said: the righteous will live by their faith" (Hab 2:4 [faith in the sense of confidence in God and faithfulness]).

Although Jesus has summarized the law another way, Paul gave this passage great importance by putting it at the center of his definition of the gospel in Romans 1:16-17 and Galatians 3:11, where "faith" might be understood as "confidence" as the reformer Martin Luther understood it. Hab 2:3-4 is quoted a little differently in Hebrews 10:37-38 (10:37 speaks of a person who is to come; giving to the verse a stronger messianic connotation; 10:38 insists that the believers must not regress or not abandon their faith). All these interpretations appear to isolate faith from the believers' daily life. One must not forget that for Habakkuk, faith and commitment in the world are closely bound together and must not be separated.

Waiting without ceasing, as the prophet does, is also the challenge given to Christians. Habakkuk insists that believers must persevere in their faith and in their expectation that God fulfills promises. Together with their commitment in the world, Christians must stand firm in this faith in a God who is faithful to the promise that God's people will be saved from the violence and injustice described in Hab 1:2-4 and 2:5-20.

Habakkuk 3:10-15, 17-19

A review of history shows the prophet that God has intervened for the people's salvation. Habakkuk talks of God's presence among the people in a picturesque way, mentioning some well known historical facts, such as the exodus. In these verses, God is shown to be stronger than the stars and the forces of nature. God is depicted as a warrior that nothing can resist. The almost mythical way God is depicted in these verses makes God unique. Nothing or no one accomplished what God did. This is also an assurance of security for the future. If God has accomplished such great wonders in the past, why would God not do the same today? In this way, Habakkuk is a comforting witness for those who seek guidance in order to believe. God is faithful and can be trusted.

Habakkuk 3:17-19 is one of the passages in the Bible that best expresses the believer's faith in God. Problems remain: trees that bear no fruit, empty stalls, drought-withered crops. However, the prophet knows that, in spite of everything that can happen, he can have confidence in God. No one else can save him, and his salvation is in God's hands.

The prophet's fear is changed to confidence. He now can go through difficulties; he can wait for God's intervention with joy and exultation. Beyond these present difficulties is life for the one who believes in God.

Here Habakkuk gives a good answer to believers who lose courage and think that God has forgotten them. Even though God is beyond all understanding, God is worthy of our confidence.

CONCLUSION

The prophet Habakkuk tells us that God rejects human injustice and idolatry. Although believers may think that God is not acting, they should still be faithful.

Habakkuk's attitude challenges believers who are not involved in the world. Habakkuk appears to say that the church/people of God and the world should not be envisioned as two different "geographical worlds." Believers and non believers live together. The mission of the church involves working to make the world go in the right direction. Believers should promote social justice and civic peace for everyone. Indeed, if Christians emphasize Christian values, and if these values are increasingly accepted, the world will become better and better. Much human suffering will be avoided.

Reading Habakkuk, we are learning that God has been, is, and will be the Almighty. God has not changed. Christians, particularly those who are frequently confronted by sociopolitical difficulties, are urged to trust in God. Let us hope that many of those who fill today's African churches already have this understanding.

BIBLIOGRAPHY

Baumgartner, Antoine J. *Le prophète Habakuk: Introduction critique et exégèse, avec examen spécial des commentaires rabbiniques du Talmud et de la tradition.* Leipzig: W. Druglin, 1885.

Haak, Robert D. *Habakkuk*, VTSup 44. Leiden, New York, Copenhagen, Cologne: Brill, 1992.

Linden, Ian, Jane Linden, and Paulette Gêraud. *Christianisme et pouvoirs au Rwanda* (1900-1990). Paris: Editions Karthala, 1999.

Robertson, O. Palmer. *The Book of Nahum, Habakkuk, and Zephaniah.* NICOT. Grand Rapids: Eerdmans, 1991.

Scott, James M. "A New Approach to Habakkuk ii 4-5a." *VT* 35 (1985): 330-340.

Sibomana, André. *Gardons espoir pour le Rwanda. Entretiens avec Laure Guilbert et Hervé Deguine.* Paris: Desclée de Brouwer, 1997.

Smith, Ralph L. *Micah—Malachi.* WBC 32. Waco, Texas: Word, 1984.

Sweeney, Marvin A. "Structure, Genre and Intent in the Book of Habakkuk." *VT* 41 (1991): 63-83.

Vuilleumier, René., and Carl A. Keller. *Michée Nahom Habacuc Sophonie.* CAT XIb. Genève: Labor et Fides, 1990.

ZEPHANIAH

Shigeyuki Nakanose, SVD
Fernando Doren, SVD
and
Enilda de Paula Pedro, RBP
São Paulo, Brazil

LIFE CONTEXT OF THE INTERPRETATION

Using the method of *leitura comunitária* (communitarian reading) of the Bible, we begin our study of this text with a concrete situation from our context.

Mateus Barbosa de Sousa, three-and-a-half years old, has the weight of an eight month-old baby and the height of a nineteen month-old child. Mateus lives with his father, mother, and three brothers in the poorest *barrio* of a town called Itinga, in the Vale do Jequitinhonha, in the north of Minas Gerais, Brazil. On December 11, 2001, the family's hut was visited by a doctor who diagnosed Mateus as a victim of Kwashiorkor, the worst form of malnutrition, which is very common in Africa. This type of malnutrition results from a lack of protein contained in mother's milk and in meat.

The first symptoms of the disease are fatigue, irritability, and lethargy. A child begins to suffer diarrhea, anemia, and slow motor control. If the illness is not treated, the child loses immunity and the body begins to swell. Mateus, for example, cannot walk and has a bloated appearance. The evolution of the disease can lead to mental retardation and death. Every child who has Kwashiorkor will suffer severe consequences for the rest of his or her life, even if the disease is treated. Little Mateus is a living portrait of the tragedy that strikes millions of Brazilians: the harsh reality of hunger, misery, and poverty. In Brazil, thirty million people live in extreme poverty, with a monthly income of less than R$80.00 (approx. US $25.00). This fact is a scandal, given that the Brazilian economy ranks among the ten largest in the world. In one percent of the population alone is concentrated the wealth equivalent to that of fifty percent of the poorest. Fifty-three million people live below the poverty line and twenty three million persons like Mateus live in extreme poverty (Mendonça 2002, 82-93)

It is in solidarity with the suffering of these people that we read the book of Zephaniah and its prophetic outcry for the systemic change of those social, economic, political, and religious structures that are not life-giving.

Shigeyuki Nakanose, ThD, serves as a Divine Word Missionary. He received his doctorate in biblical theology from New York Theological Seminary. For ten years he has been director of the Centro Bíblico Verbo in São Paulo, Brazil (see http://www.cbiblicoverbo.com.br/). His many publications include *Josiah's Passover* (English 1993, Portuguese 2000).

Fernando Doren, an Indonesian Divine Word Missionary, is a graduate (M.Div. and M.A. in missiology) from the Catholic Theological Union in Chicago. He works with the Landless, Workers Movement in São Paulo and as a coordinator of the Pastoral Land Commission. As an integrating member of Centro Bíblico Verbo, he has participated in several commentaries (in Portuguese), including *On the Acts of the Apostles,* vol. 1 (2001), and vol. 2 (2002); *Commentaries on First and Second Peter* (2002); and *Commentaries on Second and Third Isaiah (Isaiah,* 40-66) (2004).

Enilda de Paula Pedro is a religious Sister of the Good Shepherd and a member of the Centro Bíblico Verbo in São Paulo. She earned her master's degree in biblical theology from the Universidade de Nossa Senhora da Assunção, São Paulo, Brazil. Her many publications include *Como Ler o Livro de Oséias* (1995), which she co-authored with Shigeyuki Nakanose.

CONTEXTUAL COMMENT

An Overview: Zephaniah, an Outcry of the Poor of the Land

The book of Zephaniah is a prophetic outcry on behalf of the exploited and miserable "poor of the land" (2:3, author's translation [a.t.]), including peasants and shepherds (2:6), against court officials (1:8-9), merchants (1:10-11), rich people (1:12-13), foreign oppressors (1:4-6; 2:4-15), and Jerusalem, which is called a "soiled, defiled, oppressing city" (3:1).

The prophetic ministry of Zephaniah (whose name means "God protects or hides") may be dated early in the reign of Josiah, while Josiah was still a child (between 640-630 B.C.E), and before his religious reform (621-609 B.C.E.; see 2 Kgs 22:1–23:30). At this time the worship of foreign gods, such as Baal and Milcom, and astrology, common in the time of Manasseh, were still practiced (1:4-5).

Zephaniah begins with a genealogy (1:1) that shows that, although he was a Cushite (of black descent, and thus not from David's dynasty—as discussed below), his great-grandfather was King Hezekiah, who, during his reign (716-687 B.C.E.) took advantage of a crisis in the Assyrian Empire to promote political and religious reforms (2 Kgs 18:7). He sought to centralize the nation's economic, political, and religious life in Jerusalem and the temple, calling for a renewal of the covenant with YHWH, and for a rejection of the worship of other deities (2 Kgs 18:4; 2 Chr 31). But these reforms were interrupted by the invasion by the Assyrian king, Sennacherib (701 B.C.E.), and Hezekiah's successor, Manasseh (687-642 B.C.E.), restored the worship of the Assyrian gods and other deities in the temple in Jerusalem (2 Kgs 21:1-18; 2 Chr 33). After the assassination of Manasseh's successor, Amon, the "people of the land" enthroned his son, Josiah (640-609 B.C.E.), who was only eight years old (2 Kgs 21:24; 22:1).

Who were the "people of the land" who to some extent controlled the nation of Judah while Josiah was a child, in the time of Zephanaiah? They were great landowners living in the cities; although they were neither princes nor priests, they belonged to the influential elite (1 Sam 8:22; 2 Kgs 25:19; Jer 52:6). The "people of the land" should not be confused with the "poor of the land" (2:3, a.t.; 3:12); the people of the land included those who oppressed and exploited the poor. The peasants and other poor of the land had to supply food and other goods for trade with the Assyrians, for the royal court, and also for the elite people of the land with their luxurious lives: "I will punish the officials and the king's [children] and all who dress themselves in foreign attire" (1:8). In this context, Zephaniah became the spokesperson for the poor of the land.

A. 1:1 Introduction (post-exilic addition)

B. 1:2-18 Judgment and condemnation—the day of the Lord
a) Universal punishment, especially upon Judah (1:2-6); b) "The day of the LORD is at hand" (1:7); c) Oracles against violence and fraud, business obsession, and accumulation of wealth; anticipation of the day of the Lord (1:8-18).

C. 2:1-3 The transformation comes from the poor of the land: the prophetic proposal

B'. 2:4-3:8 Judgment and condemnation of:
a) the Philistines (2:4-7); b) the Moabites and Ammonites (2:8-11); c) Ethiopia (2:12); d) Assyria (2:13-15); e) Jerusalem, the rebellious, "soiled," and "oppressing" city (3:1-5); and f) all the earth (3:6-8).

A'. 3:9-20 Conclusion (post-exilic addition): Rereading Zephaniah's prophecy—Promises

The prophecy attributed to Zephaniah was read and reread during the exilic and post-exilic periods, when the book of Zephaniah received its final literary form, with a chiastic organization, ABCB´A´ that emphasizes its center.

The book of Zephaniah is like a window through which we can simultaneously see, on the one hand, the harsh life of the poor of the land in the time of Judah, and the opulent life of the economic, political, and religious elite of Jerusalem, and on the other hand, the plight of present-day poor of the land in Brazil and the opulence of the present-day wealthy.

Judgment and Condemnation of Judah and the Nations (1:2-18 and 2:4–3:8)

Opening the book of Zephaniah as a window on his time, one discovers wealth (1:13), such as houses of cedar (2:14), wine-producing vineyards (1:13), herds of cattle, and especially sheep (2:6). However, what was done with what the peasants and shepherds produced? The greater part went to Jerusalem to supply the palace and the wealthy houses, and the rest was commercialized by merchants and moneychangers (1:10-11). Gold and silver circulated in the hands of a privileged few (1:18), and was used to buy foreign goods (1:8) and to pay tribute to Assyria.

Civil construction was in full development. The cities were protected by fortified walls and high towers (1:16). Wealthy families in luxurious houses in Jerusalem lived off the work of the peasants. For these reasons the prophet denounced Jerusalem as "rebellious, blood-stained, and oppressing" (3:1, a.t.).

The prophecy pronounces this harsh judgment and condemnation against all those mentioned above, who participated in the oppression of the people by devouring all that the poor of the land were producing. Indeed, the princes, the judges, and other authorities were like lions that devoured the people, or like ferocious wolves (3:3). The religious leaders were no better; the prophets were reckless and traitorous; the priests profaned the worship of God, doing violence to the law (3:4). All were corrupt, so much so that they knew "no shame" (3:5).

This total corruption was rooted in the political situation and the efforts of all these leaders to maintain themselves in power even as they lived in submission to Assyria. The Assyrian imperialism, which was still strong during the beginning of King Josiah's reign, had a religious dimension, involving the adoption of the Assyrian gods, the heavenly army (1:5). The conflict that occurs on earth between the armies of Judah and Assyria reflects the struggle between the YHWH of "the poor of the land" (2:3) and the deities of Assyria and of the neighboring countries, with whom is associated a "YHWH of the official religion" in Jerusalem (1:4-6).

Indeed, in the official religion these other deities are worshiped side by side with this official YHWH. But this God does does not intervene in human affairs, either to reward or punish (1:12). Thus, people perceive their behavior to be irrelevant. They believe they are totally free to act as they wish. They believe that they can practice injustice, oppressing the poor and weak, and that nothing will happen.

However, history shows the opposite. The God of life is at work—the Lord of history, who judges and condemns. The Lord judges the neighboring nations, located at the four cardinal points (2:4-15): Philistia (west), Moab and Amon (east), Ethiopia and Egypt (south), and Assyria (north). God also intervenes in history to teach a lesson to the leaders of Jerusalem, but they are not converted (3:1-4).

Prophetic proposal of Zephaniah (2:1-3)

In this situation Zephaniah and the group that he represents proclaim the imminence of the day of YHWH—the God of the poor—as the day of punishment (1:7). But what is the day of the YHWH? Originally, the day of the Lord was understood as the day of the Lord's intervention to save the people of Israel from the hands of their enemies (i.e., Josh 10:12-14). This hope for salvation remained in the hearts of the people. Yet, Amos reinterpreted the meaning of this day of intervention; it would be a day of darkness and judgment (see Amos 5:18-20 and the commentary on Amos in this volume). Zephaniah interpreted it similarly, as is clear from 1:14-18.

Zephaniah warned the people about the road to self-destruction that they were taking (1:2-3), as Amos, Micah, and Hosea also did (Hos 4:1-3; also Paula Pedro and Nakanose 1995, 36-41). The leaders of Judah were bringing the day of YHWH upon themselves through their decisions and actions (Zeph 1:14-18).

Zephaniah and the group that he represented went even further. In addition to their warnings and criticisms of the present situation, they presented a concrete proposal:

> Seek YHWH all you poor of the land, who obey God's commands. Seek uprightness, seek poverty: you may perhaps find shelter on the Day of YHWH's anger. (2:3, a.t.)

The suffering and oppressed people were called upon to assume their own destiny, to become the protagonists of their own history, and to reconstruct society on the basis of the interests of the poor of the land, of those women and men who fulfilled the will of YHWH by practicing justice and solidarity (seeking poverty in solidarity with the poor of the land, 2:3). This reconstruction meant reorganizing the society to make it more humane. The day of YHWH, the central point of Zephaniah, would be inaugurated with a communion sacrifice, a banquet prepared for the guests who were sanctified in the struggle for justice and for life (1:7). The impious and the unjust would not participate in this banquet.

Other proposals for reform also responded to the harsh reality of the people, in particular the reform undertaken by King Josiah around 621 B.C.E.

Josiah's reform was in fact quite similar to the economic, political, and religious reform initiated by Hezekiah (Nakanose 1993, 14-92; 2000, 65-228). Josiah turned Jerusalem into Judah's economic, political, and reli-

gious center. He undertook the purification of the temple, getting rid of the Assyrian gods and the statues of popular religions. Yet, in the process, the temple became the only place for worship, so that the rural peasants and farmers were obliged to go to the temple for worship and to present their offerings. Furthermore, Josiah's troops persecuted and murdered many poor of the land, because their popular religion, away from Jerusalem, was suspect (2 Kgs 23:4-25).

In sum, Josiah's reform project was very different from the proposal made by Zephaniah. Zephaniah was from Cush, a region in Ethiopia and was probably a black man. He was not related to the Davidic dynasty and its projects (Gamelera 1989, 21-25). He represented the impoverished of the country and the city, victims of the violence of the governing elite. It was in the interests of these oppressed persons that he formulated his proposal for social reform, which had at its heart, justice and solidarity with the poor of the land.

The Rereading of the prophecy of Zephaniah: Promises (3:9-20)

Zephaniah's reform proposal was kept alive in the hearts and practices of the poor who faithfully preserved the dream of the poor of the land of his era. This proposal was read and reread during the exilic and post-exilic periods, by the poor and humble of the land (3:12), the lame, and the outcasts (3:19; cf. Ps 146), probably persons linked to the communities of Second and Third Isaiah (see Croatto on Isa 40–55 and 56–66 in this volume). Among these people in exile or after the exile, in a situation quite similar to that at the time of Zephaniah, emerged Zephaniah 3:9-20.

To the exiled and the impoverished, the remnant from the catastrophic Babylonian exile, who were subjected to the iniquity of their leaders who dominated holy Mount Zion (3:11b), the following promise was made: the people would be rescued and gathered (3:19-20; cf. Isa 56:8).

The remnant of Israel, the poor and the humble (3:12) who did not practice wickedness like their leaders, would inhabit Zion, Jerusalem, Israel (3:14-16; cf. Isa 54:14). They would look after their own people, because their leaders had not fulfilled their responsibility (3:15; cf. Isa 14:30; Ezek 34). The guarantee they were given was that God was in their midst (3:15, 17; cf. Isa 66:1-2) as their true king (3:15), the God who does not tolerate wickedness (3:18-19).

This conviction gave strength to the oppressed people to clamor for a just society (3:11-13). It was their motivation for rejoicing and gladness (3:17b), and it enabled the small remnant of Israel to organize itself in a spirit of solidarity and justice as the leaven of society (3:18b-20). Furthermore, the group of the poor and humble of the land called for the conversion of all peoples and for new international relations (3:9-10).

CONCLUSION

B earing in mind the present living conditions of Brazilians, as the church—the people of God—it is necessary to encourage the various initiatives that spring up from the grassroots. In the Brazilian context, the *Comunidades Eclesiais de Base* (the base Christian communities) are certainly a privileged space where the oppressed, the poor, and the excluded find their place. These communities are fertile ground where the poor become the protagonists of history and of the transformation of society. Here are the grounds where today's poor of the land make their silent cries heard.

As Brazil increasingly becomes the living place of many church traditions, ecumenism and ecumenical work may offer another way to deal with the injustice that is at the root of the people's suffering. The *Movimento dos Trabalhadores Sem Terra* (Landless Workers' Movement, known as MST), has

become a way for many faith traditions to come together to tackle the problem of injustice. By promoting justice for rural and urban workers, *the Comissão Pastoral da Terra* (the Pastoral Land Commission) has been an important meeting place for religious leaders. The same support needs to be offered to other movements in society at large, even if they are not church related.

In this globalized era, it is imperative for Christians to globalize their dreams, sharing their experiences and ideals with other social movements that also work to create a just, egalitarian, and peaceful world. The World Social Forum, which has met three times in Porto Alegre, Brazil, may be a real sign of this hope. Participating in the non-governmental organizations may be an alternative way—outside the unjust globalized structures—to respond to the cries of the impoverished and excluded ones, such as Mateus.

BIBLIOGRAPHY

Gamelera, Sebastião S. *Sofonias, Filho de Negro, Profeta dos Pobres da Terra. RIBLA* 3. Rio de Janeiro: Vozes, 1989.

Mendonça, Ricardo. "O paradoxo da Miséria." *Veja.* Special issue: *Miséria: O grando desafio do Brasil* (January 23, 2002), 82-93.

Nakanose, Shigeyuki. *Josiah's Pass-over: Sociology and the Liberating Bible.* The Bible and Liberation Series. Maryknoll, N.Y.: Orbis, 1993.

———. *Uma História para Contar: A Páscoa de Josias.* São Paulo: Paulinas, 2000.

Paula Pedro, Enilda de., and Shigeyuki Nakanose, *Como ler Oséias: Reconstruir a Casa.* São Paulo: Paulus, 1995.

HAGGAI

Paul Kalluveettil, CMI

Dharmaram College, Bangalore, and Marymatha Seminary, Thrissur, India

LIFE CONTEXT OF THE INTERPRETATION

Abject poverty, inborn superstitions, fundamentalist religious attitudes, and illiteracy condemn the majority of the people of Asia to a life of misery. To them the book of Haggai (the prophet's name means "celebration," "festival," Meyers 1987, 8) proclaims a way to make their life a celebration and a festival.

A temple issue divides the Hindu and Muslim people in India, generating hatred and bloodshed fueled by religious fanaticism. Politicians are keen to exploit the issue for their own advantage. The primary theme of Haggai concerns the reconstruction of the temple. For Christians in the Indian context this theme is not to be interpreted in its literal sense. The temple has to be understood as a metaphor, which refers to human beings as living temples (1 Cor 6:19).

Another aspect of the life context from which I write this commentary is the church in India, with such a complex history that it might be best to speak of it as a multifaceted reality, the churches in India (see *1 Corinthians* in this volume by Joseph Pathrapankal). In this Indian Christian perspective, the book of Haggai challenges the church and the people of God to "conscientize" themselves and the citizens of their country so that they may recognize their call to become living temples of God. The church's task is to help the nations construct living temples in the hearts of the people, and to make their lives in the company of God's celebration. Like Haggai, the church must teach others how to remain optimistic in the midst of difficulties, and to learn to live in the hope of God's future.

CONTEXTUAL COMMENT

An Overview of Haggai

Haggai addressed the people who had returned from Babylon. His ministry lasted from August 29 to December 18 in 520 B.C.E. (Achtemeier 1986, 94). The people were shocked to see their beloved temple in utter ruin (1:4, 9), and they were discouraged, thinking that they could never restore it to its former glory. The economic situation was wretched. Since the majority of people had to struggle for their daily existence (1:5-6; 2:16-17), they had no time or interest in rebuilding the temple. Therefore, the prophet addressed the people with words of encouragement and inspiration.

Temple as a Medium of Prosperity (Hag 1:8; 2:9, 18-19)

Haggai 1:8 presents an important message with several theological dimensions:

> "Go up to the hills and bring wood and build the house, so that I may take pleasure in it and be honored, says the LORD."

Paul Kalluveettil, a native of Kerala, India and a member of the Carmelites of the Mary Immaculate (CMI), holds a master's degree and a doctorate from the Biblical Institute, Rome. He is a professor of Old Testament and Semitic languages, and was director of the Centre for Biblical Studies at Bangalore. He has served as the vice president of the Society of Biblical Studies, India, and the secretary of the Catholic Biblical Association, India. His numerous publications in English and Malayalam (the language of South India) include three volumes of *Vachana Bhashyam* (*A Theological Introduction to the Old Testament,* 1995–2002) and *Declaration and Covenant* (*Analecta Biblica,* 1982).

The loving God of the Bible dreams of living with human beings. For this purpose God called Abraham and elected Israel and gave them the land, saying, "I will be your God and you will be my people." This covenant promise was realized when YHWH lived among them, "the people of the land," in the temple of Jerusalem (Hag 2:2-5). Thereby the land became the symbol of divine presence and blessing. The people of Israel experienced oneness as members of a family in the presence of YHWH. For them, life became a celebration with the Lord and their fellow human beings. In the temple, in a self-giving way, YHWH became present to the people, and the people gave themselves to YHWH. Thus the temple became the place of God-realization and self-realization.

With the destruction of the temple (1:2)—the medium of blessings—the people felt that YHWH had abandoned them. They attributed their wretched existence to YHWH's absence. At this time Haggai announced the good news: "I am with you, says the LORD" (1:13). YHWH desired to become one with them, to live among them in the temple, and fill them with the choicest blessings (2:9, 18-19) so that they might once again be festive. God would be pleased with them and wipe out every source of misery from their midst. The divine glory would be revealed in the Lord's new house, as in the times of their ancestors (2:3-8). It would bring them prosperity, satiation, comfort, joy, and peace (2:18-19).

Haggai instructs the people first to build a "house" for YHWH. This is what YHWH asks of them (1:8). Then YHWH will bless them and build a life for them (2:18-19). Their present selfishness will produce only counter results (1:2-4, 6, 9-11). The people wholeheartedly listen to Haggai and enthusiastically begin to rebuild the temple.

Like Haggai, the church, especially in Asia, has to stir up the people (who are tempted to lead inert, discouraged lives) to become active and dynamic in the service of others. In lives of active service, Christians are "rebuilding the temple"; we are rebuilding temples of the Holy Spirit (1 Cor 6:19).

A Stirred-up Community
(Hag 1:13, 14; 2:4)

"And the LORD stirred up the spirit of Zerubbabel . . . and the spirit of Joshua . . . and the spirit of all the remnant of the people" (1:14). In Haggai's time, the purpose of being stirred up was to build the temple. This community was to be inspired and led by the Spirit of God. The word 'spirit' (Hebrew *ru'ah*) is used thrice in the text. The Hebrew word to 'stir up' (*'wr*) means to wake up the sleeping ones (cf. Isa 50:4; Zech 4:1); to activate the inert and to spur on the indolent (cf. Isa 41:2, 25; 45:13) (Wolff 1988, 52-53).

Haggai promises YHWH's abiding presence in the midst of the people (1:13; 2:4). God will guide their activities and give them strength, so that they can "stand firm" (used thrice in 2:4) and "work." The covenant community is a dynamic fellowship. Its work is to build God's temple, which is the symbol of the divine presence.

In the context of India a literal reading of the text is out of the question. It is better to understand 1:14 as a paradigm of the new covenant community, which is called to be God's stirred-up people, a community that lives, moves, and has its being in God (cf. Acts 17:28).

Every endeavor to evoke God's presence may be understood as building up the temple. Every human being is a living temple of God. Hence every effort made for the betterment of humanity amounts to reconstructing the house of God. The covenant community is destined to engage fully in such an endeavor. Since its trust is in God, it can stand firm in vicissitudes and oppositions (cf. Pss 46:2; 144:2).

To be a faithful servant of humanity, the church as a people of God has to become a community that moves according to the whisperings of the Spirit, who stirs them up, leads them, counsels them, and strengthens them. Thus the text addresses the people in the developing countries who are inclined to lead an apathetic and dormant life, because of despair, pessimism, and absence of hope for the future. YHWH wants to arouse such people and inject into them the dynamism of the Spirit.

The World of Signs
(Hag 2:3, 6-7, 23)

The book of Haggai speaks in signs, which are intended to lead us to the signified. The first sign is the temple that the people are constructing. To the people who are discouraged about their modest construction in comparison with the magnificent temple of Solomon (2:3), YHWH requests them not to look to *yesterday* but to *tomorrow*, when "Once again, in a little while, I will shake the heavens and the earth and the sea and the dry land; and I will shake all the nations, so that the treasure of all nations shall come, and I will fill this house with splendor" (or "glory," 2:6-7). This solemn declaration refers to future events that will occur in the world. The Lord will soon interfere in the world's history, and God will defeat the existing evil social structures. God's purpose is to bring salvation and a new structure into the universe. Then all the nations will spontaneously come to Jerusalem with their silver and gold as offerings to the Lord of cosmos. The glory of the rebuilt temple will be greater than the glory of Solomon's edifice (2:9). But its greatest glory will be the presence of YHWH.

Human beings will not bring about such a radical change in the world. YHWH will bring about this transformation. The people must believe in God's power, and evaluate and live the present time in the light of God's future for them. They must lead a life fully absorbed in the glorious vision and celebrate this vision now. To the Hindu mind, this vision is surprisingly positive. For Hindus who believe in fate *(karma),* a belief that leads people to a resigned, melancholy life, celebrating the vision of God's future for them is an astonishing prospect.

The second sign is the person Zerubbabel, the governor of Judah. The prophet reports that YHWH will "make you like a signet ring; for I [YHWH] have chosen you" (2:23). What this passage signifies is the coming of the Messiah who belongs to the Davidic dynasty. For us Christians, this promise is fulfilled in Jesus Christ, the son of David who served as the signet ring of God. And the call to lead a life fully absorbed in the glorious vision of God transforming the world is a positive message that we need to live out so as to share it with Hindu people, transforming their vision of a life marked by resignation to fate *(karma).*

CONCLUSION

Haggai speaks to Christians in India. In a context of abject poverty where the majority of people are condemned to a life of misery, Christians are to be fully engaged in constructing living temples in society. The book invites the Indian church to stir up the indigenous community and transform it into a celebratory congregation, full of dynamism and optimism in the service of others. If the church listens to the word of God, "I am with you" (1:13), then the Lord will stir up her spirit (1:14) and make her a signet ring (2:23) so that she can become a catalyst in the Indian society.

BIBLIOGRAPHY

Achtemeier, Elizabeth. *Nahum–Malachi. Int.* Atlanta: John Knox Press, 1986.

Meyers, Carol L, and Eric M. Meyers. *Haggai, Zechariah 1–8: A New Translation with Introduction and Commentary.* AB 25B. Garden City, N.Y.: Doubleday, 1987.

Smith, Ralph L. *Micah–Malachi.* Dallas, Tex.: Word, 1984.

Wolff, Hans Walter. *Haggai: A Commentary.* Translated by Margaret Kohl. Minneapolis: Augsburg, 1988.

ZECHARIAH

Paul Swarup

Diocese of Delhi, Church of North India, Vidya Jyoti College of Theology, Delhi

LIFE CONTEXT OF THE INTERPRETATION

Iinterpret Zechariah in India, a pluralistic country, with a population of over one billion people. Hindus account for about seventy five to eighty percent of India's population, and Muslims follow with about twelve percent. Christians comprise a tiny fraction of the population (about three percent, or perhaps six percent when the independent churches are counted). Our society is multicultural, multireligious, and multilingual. Politic-ally, however, the Hindu fundamentalist party is very powerful; its ideology revolves around *Hindutva,* according to which everyone must accept being under the Hindu umbrella or be regarded as anti-India and anti-national. Christian mission is viewed with suspicion, partly because Christianity is identified with Western culture and colonialism.

Conversion is the main bone of contention between Christians and Hindus. A few years ago, an Australian doctor named Graham Staines, who had spent over thirty years in India working with lepers, was burnt alive along with his two sons, accordingly, because he was involved in converting tribal people. Although the killers were jailed, many states have passed anti-conversion laws to prevent the propagation of the gospel. For the majority of Hindus, no exclusive claims should be made about Jesus or by him; at most, Jesus may be considered as one among the many Gods.

The first theological issue that this situation raises involves the exclusive claims made about Jesus Christ as the only way to salvation. The second concerns the church's mission to serve the poor and the *dalits* ("untouchables") of society. The Hindu fundamentalist groups expect us to make compromises on our theology and to stop our service-mission to the poor and the dalits.

Another major question for us concerns the delimitation of the people of God in India. In addition to the mainline churches, as many as three hundred and seventy independent denominations exist, with no sense of unity. Although their congregations multiply and grow at an impressive rate despite persecution, they also constantly divide into splinter groups as soon as there is dissent. Furthermore, there has been a tremendous amount of unfaithfulness within both independent and mainline churches in India; many of the leaders, bishops, priests, and pastors—the "shepherds"—abuse their power. Selfishness, nepotism, corruption, sexual perversion, immorality, greed, and sloth have infiltrated the church. The people of God need to repent and be filled with God's spirit to walk in God's ways.

The book of Zechariah addresses the preceding issues quite directly. Zechariah 1:2-6 issues a direct call to the people of God to return to YHWH so that YHWH can also return to them. The people of God in India need to hear Zechariah's message about repentance as a change of direction affecting all of daily life (rather than a mere change of minds and hearts). The repentance we need

Paul Swarup, an Anglican priest at St. James Church, Delhi, holds a doctorate from Cambridge University, where he wrote a dissertation titled *An Eternal Planting, A House of Holiness: The Self-Understanding of the Dead Sea Scrolls Community* (2003). His publications include *God Brings His Justice to Light in His Time* (2003), articles in *Apologia* (2003) and *Transformation* (2004), and a co-authored book titled *Understanding Jesus* (India SPCK, 2004).

concerns theft, change of minds and hearts). The repentance we need concerns theft, lying, and corruption in business (which are punished by a curse in 5:1-11), and oppressive, unfaithful shepherds (10:3; 11:4-5). Indeed, we need to be cleansed from sin, impurity, and idolatry (13:1-3).

Despite the threats and actual persecution, we need to find ways of administering true justice, of showing mercy and compassion (especially toward the powerless, as Zechariah calls his readers to do toward the widow, the fatherless, the alien, and the poor), and of speaking with integrity (7:8-10; 8:16-17). Then we will not need to make compromise about our theology when speaking about God and Christ; people will know that God is among us and will come to us to seek God (8:1-23).

As far as the issue of conversion is concerned (should we refrain from trying to convert people because of the political pressure?), Zechariah underscores that when people take God seriously, their lives are radically transformed. They are changed from the inside out, and are sustained and nurtured by God's Spirit, just as Zerubbabel was empowered for the task of completing the temple (4:6). In other words, Zechariah reminds us that converting people is not a human accomplishment, but God's accomplishment. Despite our many shortcomings of which we need to repent, God is really at work in India, in and through the many fragmented denominations as well as the mainline churches. Zechariah, through his vision and oracles, helps us to see God's involvement in our lives.

CONTEXTUAL COMMENT

An Overview of the Book of Zechariah

The name Zechariah could mean "YHWH remembers" or "YHWH pays attention." This name is appropriate for a book that emphasizes that, indeed, YHWH remembers the people when they cry out or when they repent and turn to YHWH.

The title, which appears in 1:1 and subsequent remarks in 1:7 and 7:1, dates the book during the reign of Darius, the Persian king, that is, about 518–520 B.C.E.

The book gives very little biographical information about Zechariah himself. But mentions of Zechariah in Ezra 5:1, 6:14, and Nehemiah 12:16 suggest that he was born in Babylon and was among those who returned in 538 B.C.E. under the leadership of Zerubbabel (see Zech 4:8-10) and Joshua (also spelled Jeshua), the high priest (see Zech 3:1-9; 6:11). He was both prophet and priest, having succeeded Iddo as head of a priestly family (Neh 12:16). Zechariah was a contemporary of Haggai and they both encouraged the people of Judah to complete the rebuilding of the temple (Zech 4:8-10). However, Zechariah was

more interested in the spiritual renewal of the people than in the building of the temple.

The book of Zechariah can be subdivided into two parts (following most scholars; Webb 2004 includes 7-8 in Part II):

Part I: Chapters 1–6
  Call to repentance (1:1-6)
  Visions with Oracles (1:7–6: 15)
  Address to Bethel (7:1–8:23)
Part II: Chapters 8–14
  Two oracles (9–11 and 12–14)

A Call to Return to the Lord (1:1-6)

The key message of the first part of the book is summarized in 1:2-6: "Return to me, says the LORD of hosts, and I will return to you" (1:3). Their ancestors, despite repeated warnings from YHWH through the prophets, did not repent and turn from their evil ways. This refusal to repent resulted in the destruction of the temple and of Jerusalem, and in the exile to Babylon. But the word of the Lord stands firm (1:6) and the same call of repentance is now addressed to Zechariah's generation through the prophet. Unlike previous generations, those who have returned from exile have repented of their sinful ways, acknowledging that they have been rightly punished for them (1:6b), and paving the way for YHWH's return to them. The book of Zechariah therefore invites the people of God to reclaim their identity as the sons and daughters of God and to return to God, who gives meaning to life and is the source of strength for the present and hope for the future (Ollenburger 1996, 748). As noted above, the churches in India need to hear this message of repentance.

Immediately after this opening message, Zechariah presents a sequence of eight visions: the man on the red horse (1:8-17); four horns and four blacksmiths (1:18-21); the man with a measuring line (2:1-13); priestly vestments for the high priest (3:1-10); the lampstand and the two olive trees (4:1-14); the flying scroll (5:1-4); the woman in a basket (5:5-11); and the four chariots (6:1-8), concluded by the crowning of Joshua (6:9-15).

Vision 1:
The Man on the Red Horse
(1:8-17)

Zechariah sees a man riding a red horse, as well as three other horses that patrol the earth and report to the angel of the Lord on the red horse that the whole world is at rest and in peace. Then the angel of the Lord pleads with YHWH, "how long will you withhold mercy from Jerusalem and the cities of Judah, with which you have been angry these seventy years?" (1:12). YHWH asks the angel to proclaim that peace and prosperity will be restored again to Jerusalem (1:13-17).

Zechariah's prophetic vision enables him to engage past tradition with the present crisis. The key theological message that stands out in this vision is that there is life if one returns to YHWH. This message is much needed for the churches in India in view of our own crisis, which is due to corruption of all kinds and failure to serve as the people of God in our society. We, laity and clergy, are in tremendous need of repentance. The proclamation that there is life if we return to YHWH is an invitation to repent.

Vision 2:
Four Horns and Four Blacksmiths
(1:18-21)

In the second vision Zechariah is shown four horns and four blacksmiths. The horns symbolize the nations that have scattered Israel and Judah, and the four blacksmiths are other nations that YHWH has used to bring about judgment. The message of these verses is that YHWH's sovereignty is not restricted to the people of God alone; YHWH is Lord of the nations and other communities, which are also accountable for what they do. Thus, it might be most appropriate for churches in India to team up with non-governmental organizations unrelated to the churches for the sake of affirming justice and peace and for the transformation of a marginalized group of children (Swarup 2004).

Vision 3:
The Man With a Measuring Line
(2:1-13)

Zechariah sees a surveyor who is going to measure the boundaries of Jerusalem but who is then interrupted and told that Jerusalem will be a city without walls. YHWH himself will be a wall of fire around the city and God's glory will dwell within it (2:4-5). The meaning of the vision is further developed by the vivid affirmation that whoever plunders or touches God's people actually pokes "the apple of my [YHWH's] eye" (2:8; cf. Deut 32:9-10). YHWH will, therefore, be the one who brings about retribution on the nations that have exploited God's people.

Vision 4:
Priestly Vestments for the
High Priest
(3:1-10);
The Crowning of Joshua
(6:9-15)

Zechariah now sees Joshua, the high priest, standing before the angel of the Lord, and Satan accusing him. YHWH rebukes Satan, because Joshua is like a burning stick that has been snatched out of the fire (a reference to his surviving the Babylonian exile, 3:2). Satan's accusations are explained by Joshua's filthy clothes, which represent his sins. His filthy garments are removed and he is clothed with fine garments, symbolic of his cleansing (3:3-5), which makes him ready to walk in God's ways. Joshua will now assume charge of YHWH's house and his courts, and have direct access to the divine council (3:6).

The vision continues with YHWH's proclamation, "I am going to bring my servant the Branch" (3:8). This reference to a messianic Davidic figure is also used in 6:12 (and in Jer 23:5, 33:15; cf. with a different vocabulary in Isa 11:1). In 6:9-15, which describes the crowning of the high priest Joshua, YHWH further states that Joshua is the man who is the "Branch." This designation means that that the office of the "Branch"—Joshua, and also the coming anointed, the Messiah—would be both a priestly and a royal office and that he would be the one who would build the temple of YHWH.

In 3:9 YHWH places in front of Joshua a stone with seven facets and an inscription, through which God will remove the sins of Jerusalem in a single day. This stone could be a priestly symbol if we interpret it in terms of 6:9-15 (where Joshua, the crowned Branch, will build the temple) or a reference to the stone associated with Zerubbabel (if we interpret in terms of 4:6-10).

Vision 5:
The Lampstand and the
Two Olive Trees
(4:1-14)

In the fifth vision, the lampstand (in the temple?) has an abundant supply of oil (God's power) for the bowls of its seven lights from the two olive trees that represent "the two anointed ones" (4:14), the priestly and the royal offices that are the conduit for God's power. More immediately, the two olive trees seem to evoke the figures of Joshua (3:1-10) and Zerubbabel, who,

YHWH promises (4:9), will complete the building of the temple. Zerubbabel is to carry out God's work with the power of YHWH's Spirit: "Not by might, nor by power, but by my spirit, says the Lord of hosts" (4:6). This teaching regarding the rebuilding of the temple applies to all the tasks of the churches in India, including the cleansing (3:1-10) and the building of the people of God. A quietist attitude grounded in confidence in God's Spirit, rather than wielding power in confrontation with others, is in order: "Not by might, nor by power, but by [God's] spirit."

Vision 6:
The Flying Scroll
(5:1-4)

Zechariah is now shown a huge flying scroll upon which is written a curse for everyone involved in robbery and false witness; they will be destroyed (see also Lev 19:11-15). For the churches in India, the brief description in 5:1-4 is enough to evoke the situation of our churches, whose members continue to behave in their daily lives like everybody else in society. The text describes a situation in which the exiles had returned to Jerusalem and were free from political oppression, yet they maintained a corrupt judicial system, with perversion of justice, bribes, false witnesses, and thieves.

Vision 7:
The Woman in a Basket
(5:5-11)

Here Zechariah is shown a measuring basket containing the iniquity of the people, symbolized by a woman ("Wickedness," 5:8), who is taken to Babylon where a temple will be built for her. The removal of the basket and the woman symbolizes that YHWH will eliminate corrupt economic practices (such as stealing, 5:1-4) within Judah. This vision also expresses that economic corruption is closely associated with idolatry. The economic sphere and the religious are closely linked; from our context in India, we can readily perceive the text's implication that if one is corrupt, then the other is bound to be corrupt also. [Editors' Note: Regarding the gender bias in this text, see the commentaries on Jeremiah and on Hosea in this volume.)

Vision 8:
The Four Chariots
(6:1-8)

The four chariots symbolize the agents of judgment, who cover all four directions of the earth. The vision shows the sovereignty of YHWH over all the nations.

Address to Bethel
(7:1-8:23)

The title of this section, 7:1, shows that the address to Bethel takes place two years after the visions of the preceding chapters. The people of Bethel send a delegation asking whether they should continue with the ritual practice of fasting and mourning for the destruction of the temple. Through the prophet, YHWH questions their motives, reminding them that before the exile the message of the prophets called them to administer true justice and to show mercy and compassion rather than to oppress the weak and the vulnerable, the widow, the alien, and the orphan and to devise evil against each other (7:9-10; cf. 8:16-17)). But the people of Judah would not listen and were sent into exile (7:11-14). This past reversal from prosperity to adversity because of persistent disobedience prefigures for Zechariah another reversal from adversity to prosperity when YHWH will come back to the people with compassion (8:1-23). Indeed YHWH will reestablish the covenant, repeating the covenant formula: "They shall be my people and I will be their God, in faithfulness and in righteousness" (8:8). Thus their days of fasting will become days of celebration (8:19). In sum, if they practice justice and peace rather than evil (8:16-17), then the nations around them will know that YHWH dwells among them and they "shall come to seek the LORD of hosts in Jerusalem"(8:22).

This latter message is most significant for the churches in India in answer to our ques-

tion: How does one communicate the gospel in a context where we cannot initiate theological proclamations? As we practice justice, show mercy and compassion, especially toward the powerless, and speak with integrity, people will know that God is among us and will come to us to seek God (8:1-23).

Two Oracles: The Messianic Future and the Consummation of the Kingdom of God
(Zech 9–14)

Zechariah 9–14 consists of two oracles. The phrase "An Oracle," occurs in 9:1 and 12:1. The theme of this section, somewhat apocalyptic, is the rule of God, manifested first in the coming of his Messiah, the human king (Zech 9), and revealed finally in the coming of God himself, the divine king of the whole world (Zech 14). We will review the many features of this oracle that are interpreted as prophecies fulfilled in the New Testament texts, even though this is not the place to discuss the latter texts.

First Oracle: The Advent and the Rejection of the Messiah
(Chs. 9–11)

The oracle opens with a description of YHWH stripping Zion's enemies of their power, in a systematic sweep going from northern Syria to the Philistines in the south, and finally settling down in the temple to secure Zion from the threat of invasion or oppression (9:1-8).

Then Zion is called to rejoice: "Lo, your king comes to you; triumphant and victorious is he, humble and riding on a donkey, on a colt, the foal of a donkey" (9:9). Zion is called to celebrate because God is coming to dwell in Zion, bringing peace—not riding a war horse but a donkey, that is, the foal of a donkey—as is properly understood in John 12:14-15 and misunderstood in Matthew 21:5-7 (which envisions two animals) when this prophecy is applied to Jesus' entrance in Jerusalem. While the "king" can be identified with YHWH (as I suggested above), it has been traditionally and appropriately understood as referring to a future Davidic king who is humble and peaceful (as in Zech 3:8; 4:6; 6:12). YHWH has already prepared the way for the coming of this king so that he will have no need to engage in war. This king will come in peace, offering that peace to all the nations, and exert universal dominion (9:10). "On that day" this king will therefore bring deliverance to Israel according to YHWH's covenant of blood with them (9:11-17; cf. Exod 24:3-8).

In the rest of the oracle (Zech 10–11) concerning the challenge of restoring all of Israel to Zion, the central issue is that of leadership; the people wander like sheep who "suffer for lack of a shepherd (10:2). The crisis of leadership is such that the shepherds are misleading the people rather than assisting them to walk in the ways of YHWH. Therefore, YHWH promises to take care of his people, and to bring them back to the land (10:3-12).

In chapter 11, Zechariah is asked to take on the role of shepherd (11:4), because their own shepherds are not interested in the welfare of the sheep but rather in making money (11:5). YHWH removes three shepherds who had failed to fulfill their role (11:8). However, the response of the flock is most disappointing. They detest YHWH who in turn grows weary of them. YHWH's response to them is quite drastic: "Let the dying die, and the perishing perish. Let those who are left eat one another's flesh" (11:9, NIV). The breaking of the staff named "Favor" symbolizes the covenant that is broken between YHWH and the people (11:10). The shepherd then seeks his pay, indicating the severance of the relationship. The people pay him thirty pieces of silver, the price of a slave (see Exod 21:32). Zechariah then takes the money to the temple and flings it into the temple's "treasury" (or "to the potter," 11:12-13). Zechariah is also made to break his second staff, "Unity, annulling the family ties between Judah and Israel" (11:14). Then God sends the people a worthless shepherd (11:15-17).

The key theological message is that rejecting God and the good shepherd (here either God or the prophet, earlier the messiah) and detesting his loving care and his discipline results in the coming of other leaders who are tyrants. The people of God need to be continuously fed and nourished by faithful shepherds who feed their flock.

Second, detesting the good shepherd leads not just to the breakup of the covenant community, but to a breakdown in the covenant relationship with God (11:10-11). The result of rebellion against God is disaster. Therefore, Zechariah preaches repentance, an essential part of proclaiming the reign of God.

But the key issue is again of the response of the people. Will the flock again "detest" and reject its true shepherd, or will it rejoice at the shepherd's coming and be willing to be ruled by him? This is the crux of the matter for the future of God's people. For the churches in India and elsewhere, with the fulfillment of these prophecies in the coming of Jesus the Messiah (i.e., Matt 26:14-16; 27:3-10), the stage is set for the final showdown in God's relationship with the people, and ultimately with the world at large.

Second Oracle: God as King Over All the Earth (Zech 12–14)

The final oracle concludes with YHWH becoming king of the world: "And the LORD will become king over all the earth; on that day the LORD will be one and his name one"(14:9). The phrase, "on that day," repeated again and again, indicates a future time when YHWH will fulfill promises:

a) to empower Jerusalem to destroy the nations that attack her (12:2-9);

b) to give the house of David and the inhabitants of Judah a spirit of compassion and supplication (12:10-14) (so much so that they will mourn for one they have pierced, identified in John 19:37);

c) to cleanse them from sin and impurity, so that there is no room for idolatry and false prophets (13:1-6).

Nevertheless, God will allow the good shepherd to be struck and the sheep to be scattered, although a remnant will be spared and purified (13:7-9).

The oracle concludes with the coming "day of the Lord," which involves a battle with all the nations attacking Jerusalem. Many will flee from the city before YHWH intervenes (14:1-5). Then YHWH will be "king over all the earth" (14:9). Those who reject God will be punished with various plagues (14:12-15). However, the survivors of the neighboring nations will also participate in the celebration of the Feast of Booths (Tabernacles, *Succoth*) to worship "the King, the LORD of hosts" (14:16). YHWH reigns forever and ever and dwells in their midst; therefore Jerusalem will be holy, with no room for any idolaters (14:17-21).

CONCLUSION

We have noted two major issues for the churches in India, one internal and one external. Within the churches in India there is a tremendous need for repentance both from the laity and the clergy. For the churches to be purged, there needs to be a turning toward God, particularly on the part of the shepherds—the clergy, bishops, and other leaders. A problem exists when those who claim to be the people of God behave no differently than those who do not. As we noted earlier, the shepherds have become greedy to the extent that we are not concerned for the flock of God. It is in this context that the message of Zechariah is a clarion call to repent and to return to the Lord so that the Lord will also return to us. "Render true judgments, show kindness and mercy to one another; do not oppress the widow, the orphan, the alien, or the poor" (7:9-10).

The external challenge is the pressure on us Christians, a tiny minority in a sometimes hostile Hindu world, to make compromises on our theology and our service-mission. Part of the issue is our concern to convert others. Yet, as we have noted, Zechariah's message is that transformation or conversion can never be accomplished by force, and that it is partly a response to the people of God's practice of justice, compassion, and integrity. Ultimately, Zechariah's strong message is that God is in control and is working in the midst of the people and the world—they are God's people and God's world. Beyond Zechariah, as Christians we make a similar claim when we affirm that the rule of God as king—that is, the kingdom—has been inaugurated with the coming of Jesus and will be consummated with his second coming.

BIBLIOGRAPHY

Conrad, Edgar W. *Zechariah*. Readings. Sheffield: Sheffield Academic Press, 1999.

Ollenburger, Ben C. *The Book of Zechariah. NIB* 7. Abingdon: Nashville, 1996.

Swarup, Paul. " 'Conversion' and the Gospel in a Pluralistic Society." *Anglican Life in Mission: Second International Consultation, Limuru, Kenya,* July 2003. Special issue of *Transformation* 21:1 (2004): 54-60.

Tuckett, Christopher M, ed. *The Book of Zechariah and Its Influence*. Aldershot, Hampshire, U.K. and Burlington, Vt.: Ashgate, 2003.

Webb, Barry G. *The Message of Zechariah: Your Kingdom Come*. The Bible Speaks Today Series 50. Downers Grove, Ill.: Intervarsity Press, 2004.

MALACHI

Claudia Mendoza

School of Theology, Catholic University of Argentina, Buenos Aires

LIFE CONTEXT OF THE INTERPRETATION

I am from Argentina and am forty years of age. I hold a degree in biblical theology, and am a member of the Catholic Church. I have taught Bible studies for more than ten years in the city of Buenos Aires at several institutions that have prepared catechists, professors of religious studies, theologians, and priests.

My country is presently experiencing a terrible and lingering crisis. This crisis is not only socio-economic, but judicial and political as well. More than half of the population (53 percent) falls below the poverty line. Our unemployment rate is alarming (more than 20 percent), and every day we witness, with dismay, the vast impoverishment of the middle class and the heartbreaking misery of the many excluded who suffer from hunger and malnutrition in a country that produces enough food to satisfy more than three times the needs of the entire population. Meanwhile, a large number of the leading class—most of whom are negligent, incompetent, and possibly corrupt—diligently strive to hold on to their privileges. An external debt, which realistically is not repayable, robs many generations of a future. Many Argentines, at least those who are able, have emigrated from this country in search of jobs and many more wander through the streets, dragging their families along, rummaging through garbage in search of food or something to sell. These are the so-called *cartoneros* [those who live in cardboard boxes]—the new icons of misery who out-line the night's urban landscape, trekking through the city streets with their pushcarts. Packing the late-night trains, they return to their lives in the outlying neighborhoods. They think of the future with more anguish and uncertainty than hope.

Malachi and the Relationship of God's People With the World in Argentina

As God's people, what should we do in this context of misery and hunger, where respect is lacking and dignity is violated, and where horizons are obstructed and threatened? As an educator, I ask myself, how I should teach the book of Malachi. What does the prophet have to say to seminarians, catechists, and committed Christians in my city and in my country? What would God, through the words of Malachi, say to the *cartoneros* of my city?

The book of Malachi urges us to respond to its message. With its dialectical or disputational style and its simple, straightforward technique, Malachi does not hesitate to call things the way they are. Its piercing gaze can cleverly unveil behaviors that seem innocent but hide a profound irreligiosity and a blatant disregard for God's will. Such behaviors inevitably lead to a deteriorated relationship with the living God.

Malachi was probably rebuking a nation of people who, like the Argentines, suffered from hunger and misery, humiliation, hopelessness, and anguish. (According to my

Claudia Mendoza, while doing research on Malachi toward her doctorate, teaches introductory courses in Biblical studies at Facultad de Teología. Universidad Católica (UCA), Buenos Aires, Argentina. She also teaches Holy Scriptures in the context of the Instituto Salesiano de Estudios Teológicos, as well as of the Instituto Teologico Franciscano "Fray Luis Bolaños," and several Diocesans biblical study groups in the Noreste Region of Argentina.

estimation, the backdrop of the book was the impoverished Jerusalem, which fell victim to the Persian economic imperialism and her collaborators, a few years before the activities of Nehemiah.) How can we not be enlightened and find comfort in these pages while we heed the admonition that demands the kind of action that would help defeat misery and exclusion!

CONTEXTUAL COMMENT

An Overview of Malachi

The reader of Malachi soon discovers, perhaps with surprise, that rather than denouncing the perverse system that has left the majority of the nation in misery, the prophet seems to concentrate on other realities, which are apparently less urgent and dramatic, and maybe even insignificant when compared to the realities of hunger and marginalization.

In the beginning of the book, the prophet offers this hurting nation a sign of God's love: the definite destruction of her hated neighbor Edom (Mal 1:2-5). Then, in the lengthiest portion of the book he rebukes the priests harshly (2:1-9), accusing them of dishonoring God's name and defiling the Lord's table by not controlling the quality of the offerings (1:6-14). By neglecting their duty to teach the requirements of the *torah* ("instruction" or "law" in most translations; cf. 2:6-8), the priests lead the people to defile the altar of the Lord (1:14; 2:8) and to become unfaithful to the covenant by marrying foreign women (2:10-16). Then, when the people "weary" God by asking, "Where is the God of justice?" (2:17) when those who do evil are not punished, the prophet promises, in a spectacular eschatological description, the coming of the God of justice to the temple (3:1-2). God will first purify the Levites (3:3) so that the offerings brought by Judah and Jerusalem will be acceptable (3:1-4). Then the prophet rebukes those who oppress the weak—after he "bear(s) witness against" the sorcerers, adulterers, and liars (3:5). He then accuses the nation of defrauding God by not paying their tithes and offerings (3:6-12). He ends, in another eschatological description, with a God who listens patiently to the complaints of the righteous who become discouraged because they feel that serving God is in vain when they gain no benefits from obeying his commands (3:13-15).

When evildoers trample on the weak with impunity (3:5), when it seems as though God no longer loves the righteous (1:2; 3:13-15) and does not intervene on their behalf (3:15); when anguish and hopelessness crush even those who fear God (3:14); when there is hardly a distinction between the righteous and the wicked (3:18) because we do not see God doing justice (2:17); it seems almost cynical to consider tithes and offerings (1:6–2:9; 3:6-12) and fidelity in marriage (2:10-16) as distinctive of God's people. How do we demand tithes and pure offerings of the *cartoneros* in my city? How do we call the poor who rummage through the garbage "abominable traitors" because they do not live in a faithful marriage relationship? (2:10-16). How do we refer to seminarians preparing themselves for the priesthood as "wicked" when they do not teach the standards of purity to people who are dying of hunger? (2:1-9). And how do we find the signs of God's powerful love in the destruction of our neighbor? (1:2-5). How do we give hope to a hurting nation that longs for justice, promising them, in God's name, that some day, their offerings will be pleasing and acceptable! (3:2-4)?

Apparently, Malachi intends to lead us incisively toward a discussion of this kind, challenging us, provoking us, and bothering us. The temptation is to close the book and accuse the author of engaging in empty ritualism, of being an antiquated conservative, and of being more interested in filling the coffers of the temple than the stomachs of the people. But let us open our hearts to hear what he has to say. Don't we believe that

God is speaking to us directly through him? With his provocative style he urges us to sharpen our gaze so we can get a closer look at the essence of God's people, which could seem out of place and unimportant in a context such as this. But in the eyes of the prophet, it inexorably reveals the quality of our faith. This is not an invitation to examine our solidarity or charity toward those who suffer, or our commitment to liberation or political action; rather it is an invitation to focus on how we honor—or dishonor—God in celebration and in faithfulness to our covenant commitments.

After an initial moment of perplexity, let these questions resonate and let us be receptive to the implicit questions the prophet is asking us: Aren't we aware of the attitudes that are actually hidden behind worship practices? Have we not thought about what it means to have worship no matter how it is done? As people of God, what are we telling the world about God when they see us honoring God any which way? Are we, by our actions, proclaiming to the world that we worship the great King and Lord (1:14)?

If we think of ourselves as the church—as God's people in relationship with our world—we need to understand that we are not part of a charitable organization. For this reason we must take notice of what the *mal' ?kî* (messengers of God) are telling us. So who are these "messengers of God?" As Malachi indicates, they are God's ministers (2:7). In other words, those who, by occupation, fulfill the roll of teaching competently and legitimately about God's will. But the appeal is extended to everyone, because each member of the holy nation has a duty to hear and to make known what God has to say.

Malachi 2:1-9: A Longing for a Joyful and Faithful Service

Malachi 2:1-9 does not seem to be the most appropriate passage in terms of a contextual reading. It talks about God's covenant with Levi, and it is not immediately clear what significance it might have for present-day humanity. If we take a closer look, the prophet seems to challenge us to communicate God's will competently and faithfully. First of all, he addresses those who ought to know and teach God's will but appear to neglect it in their own lives. The will of God is life and peace for God's people (2:5), a people invited to a festive celebration of the Lord. Therefore, the prophet insists on rebuking those who allow the people to approach the "great king" without taking into account his honor and dignity, without realizing what it means to sit at the table of such a noble Lord.

Malachi explicitly gives a "miswâ" (commandment)—and a firm warning—that clearly shows the seriousness of the obligation of those who watch over the honor and respect of the Lord and the torah, but have not determined in their hearts to reverence the Lord as they ought to (2:1-2). He threatens to break their arms—rendering them incapable of worshipping—and to spread waste matter on their faces (2:3 LXX). He then remembers nostalgically the "covenant with Levi," made in favor of the people in order to give them life and *shalôm* (fullness, complete fulfillment, 2:4-5). The people found his teaching to be true—never unrighteous—because Levi walked with God, living a good and righteous life. He turned many toward God (2:6). Because of the true wisdom (*da'at*) coming from his lips, the people sought his instruction (*tôrâ*), knowing that he was a legitimate "messenger of the LORD of hosts" (2:7) and a bearer of blessing.

On the other hand, if the Levites stumble, they "cause many to stumble" and thus violate the covenant (2:8), weakening the people's authentic relationship with God. This relationship is founded in love and respect for God's sovereign will because God is offered intimately in the divine word (cf. Exod 33:11; Bar 4:1; John 14–15). If they turn into halfhearted and negligent officials (Mal 1:13), the Levites interfere with the flow of life and blessing that the Lord wants to shower on the people (cf. Hos 4:6).

CONCLUSION

Malachi prompts us to ask ourselves, How do we see God as our Lord and Father? How do we get close to God? How do we come into God's presence? The prophet suggests that dignity comes from God; in God we find justice. God is the source of all blessing. For God's people, the source of our identity is in our relationship with God. If this relationship becomes corrupt, the meaning of our existence as a people becomes threatened. From there, with respect for our Father and Lord, we must permanently rediscover our own mission and openly examine the task before us each day.

For Malachi, the quality of our faithfulness is manifested in the way we worship and serve God as Father and Lord—the way we celebrate the joy of living in God's presence, not focusing on the outward details of rituals, but rather on the complete and communal expression of a life centered in God. The function of the Levites was to ensure that the people worshipped God appropriately.

Today we also need "Levites" who would ensure that God is honored and would hand out invitations to the distinguished guests of the great Host—guests who have spent the day rummaging through the garbage but who now must get ready for the party because, as sons and daughters, they are allowed to partake of the banquet and celebrate. We need Levites to look after the party even in the midst of misery and poverty—even when it seems that there are more pressing issues at God's table—because that is where each person, each *cartonero*, regains honor and dignity. That is where, after searching all day, one finds the "better part," which shall not be taken away (Luke 10:42).

BIBLIOGRAPHY

Berquist, J. "The Social Setting of Malachi." *BTB* 19 (1989): 121–126.

Childs Brevard S. *Introduction to the Old Testament as Scripture*. Philadelphia: Fortress, 1979.

Dentan, Robert C. "The Book of Malachi." Pages 1115–1144 in vol. 6 of *The Interpreter's Bible*. Edited by G. A. Buttrick. 12 vols. Nashville: Abingdon, 1956.

Fischer, J. A. "Notes on the Literary Form and Message of Malachi." *CBQ* 34 (1972): 313-320.

Kaiser Walter C., Jr. *Malachi: God's Unchanging Love*. Grand Rapids: Baker, 1984.

Ogden, Graham S., and Richard R. Deutsch. *A Promise of Hope—A Call to Obedience: A Commentary on the Books of Joel and Malachi*, ITC. Grand Rapids: Eerdmans, 1987.

JESUS:
AN AFRICAN PERSPECTIVE

Anne Nasimiyu Wasike
Kenyatta University, Nairobi, Kenya

LIFE CONTEXT OF THE INTERPRETATION

After the Second Vatican Council, African people have been and are continuing to formulate Christologies that are meaningful and relevant to the varying contexts on the continent. These contextual Christologies differ from one another through denominational, political, social, cultural, ethnic, and linguistic influences (whether Anglophone, Lusophone, or Francophone). Africa had received the Western understanding of Christ, inherited from the early Christians who linked the Hellenistic understanding of Logos to Christ the Messiah in order to bridge the gap between creation and redemption and counteract the early gnostic beliefs (Nasimiyu-Wasike 1989, 129). A number of African theologians use inculturational models while others use liberational models to answer the question of who Jesus is for the African people.

Nevertheless, there are unifying elements in African Christologies, including strong reliance on the Bible and church tradition, the importance of African traditional teachings, the use of indigenous African symbolism and imagery, the significance of the sociocultural context, and the real contextual situations in which African people live.

Widely accepted images of Jesus in Africa include Christ as the Greatest Ancestor (John S. Pobee: Ghana), Christ the Proto-Ancestor (Benezet Bujo: Congo/Zaire), Christ the Brother-Ancestor or Elder Brother (Charles Nyamiti: Tanzania), Jesus as Healer, Liberator, Savior, and Mother (Theresia Hinga and Nasimiyu-Wasike: Kenya; Jean-Marc Éla: Cameroon; Mercy Amba Uduyoye and Elizabeth Amoah: Ghana). The use of these images depends on the historical, cultural, or social context of the interpreter. On the one hand, the African people view religion as a means to free people from hunger, suffering, injustice, and oppression; on the other hand religion is seen as a source which renews, revitalizes, enhances people's prosperity, fertility, and good health, and provides them with total protection from evil. Thus, Jesus is believed to effect positive changes in people's lives.

When one asks the question: "Who is Jesus Christ for the African person?" several images and models of Jesus Christ come to the forefront including the cosmological, anthropological, eschatological, and liberationist models. This essay will focus on the most prominent images of Jesus that speak to the African people, especially women.

Jesus the Nurturer of Life

Strong resilient elements within the African cultural heritage influence the formulation of Christological statements. ncestor veneration, the Master of Initiation Rites, and the medicine men and medicine women are important in the life of any community. In African Christology, we find Jesus assum-

Anne Nasimiyu Wasike, PhD Duquesne University, Professor in Systematic Theology is a lecturer in conferences all around the world ranging from missiology, EATWOT (Ecumenical Association of Third World Theologians), Franciscan Conferences, to the United Nations Commission on the Status of Women. Among her many articles and chapters in books, the most directly related to this article are: "Christology and an African Woman's Experience," in *Jesus in African Christianity: Experimentation and Diversity in African Christology* (1989) and in *African Faces of Jesus* (1991), "Mary, the Pilgrim of Faith for African Women" in *The Bible in African Christianity* (1997), "Witnesses to Jesus Christ in African Context at the Dawn of A New Millennium" (1997).

ing various roles in the human situation. He was always concerned about the people and their welfare. He reached out to the poor and vulnerable with compassion, care, and love. Traditionally, African mothers were seen as the embodiment of all virtues of the community, providing these exact same values of compassion, care, and love. They were like a quietly burning candle that gives both life and light to others. In John 6:1-12, when Jesus sees the crowd of people he asks his disciple Philip, "Where are we to buy bread for these people to eat?" (6:5). With five loaves and two fishes he is able to feed five thousand men plus uncounted women and children. Here Jesus puts others first and, as a nurturer of life, is very much concerned with their welfare. He demonstrates the qualities of a mother to both male and female disciples. Jesus is a nurturer of life, especially the life of the weak. Jesus's motherhood is characterized by nourishment, protection, and care for the poor, the vulnerable, the oppressed, and the marginalized (Mark 10:13-16). The way Jesus relates to the people, especially the disciples, shows a warm tenderness, affection, receptivity, and a readiness to restore life to an integrated wholeness (Wasike 1998, 7). In John 13:4-14, when Jesus washes his disciples' feet, he demonstrates what he means by service. When the disciples had been fishing all night and had caught nothing, Jesus acts out the roles played by mothers by lighting a charcoal fire and preparing breakfast for the tired disciples (John 21:9-13). All Christians are challenged to nurture one another. This nurturing is not to be left to women alone, but it is a responsibility for all women and men called to follow the example of Jesus.

Jesus the Liberator

When Jesus embarks on his ministry, he clearly declares that his mission is to proclaim freedom for the prisoners and release for the oppressed (Luke 4:14-21). He asks all persons, women and men, not to accept hardships and pain fatalistically but to find ways to eliminate inhumane conditions and create a better place for all (Nasimiyu-Wasike 1989,

131). He helps people to cope with concrete life situations of hunger, unemployment, fear of evil spirits, and diseases (today, especially HIV/AIDS and related diseases), barrenness, broken relationships, and death (Jer 8:21-9:1). Jesus is the liberator, the Savior and the Redeemer of all, especially of women who find themselves doubly oppressed by poverty and patriarchy (John 8:3-11). He sets women free from ostracism, from blood-taboos, and other distorted views that are a response to women's natural physiological processes (Luke 8:43-48 and Gal 5:1). In their spontaneous response to Jesus' summoning, African women are aware of his presence and his sharing in their daily struggles of birthing, nurturing, maintaining, and protecting life. African women talk about Jesus, believe in Jesus, and relate closely to Jesus who is truly a friend and companion (John 4:7-26).

Childbearing is central to African women's self-image. Mercy Amba Oduyoye brings out this element when she analyzes the visit of Mary to Elizabeth (Luke 1:39-57). The narrative of Mary and Elizabeth exchanging pregnancy announcements is a very important one for African women. Mary, a younger woman, visits Elizabeth, an older woman, to share her unfamiliar experience, to support her, and to journey with her in this strange phenomenon. Both Mary and Elizabeth share the experience of extraordinary conceptions due to special divine intervention. This biblical scene speaks to the situation of childless African women who pray for God's intervention in the face of the dreaded reproaches of the clan's people. Mary and Elizabeth are overjoyed at God's saving power, which comes through women (Luke 1:42). As the unborn communicates to the unborn, God's future plan of setting humanity free is discerned by women and is made ready by women to be communicated among and by women to the whole of humanity (Oduyoye 2001, 51).

In the events of his life Jesus championed what is life-giving, and was in solidarity with the poor and the marginalized of his time. He was obedient and dependent on God the Father who alone has life (Phil 2:6-

8). In obedience to the mission he was given by God the Father, he became a victim of repressive violence together with the oppressed. Jesus' death was the result of his option for the poor, the marginalized, and the oppressed. As Jean-Marc Éla has strongly emphasized, to follow Jesus is to live out his subversive plan and stance for the poor against situations of misery and oppression (1988, 109). The presence of misery and oppression is a basic form of the world's sin that contradicts the reign of justice and the freedom inaugurated by Jesus Christ (Rom 6:16-23). The poor and the marginalized are living out Jesus' passion in their lives. They are the presence of the Crucified God who has to be rediscovered in the world today. In Matt 5:3-12 and Luke 6:20-26 Jesus clearly affirms that all people are citizens of the kingdom; he counsels them in various walks of life and shows that his concern is not only the spiritual, but all aspects of human life. In these texts Jesus' concern is for building bridges of friendship that would enable people to live together in mutual harmony as sisters and brothers. He teaches his disciples to live out their lives in justice and respect for others (Luke 3:10-14).

Jesus suffered, died, and was resurrected so that humanity could have the fullness of life (1 Cor 15:22). His own suffering sets humanity free, because in his resurrection Jesus is the victorious one, the conqueror, and thus the one who annuls the powers of Satan, all the witches, the evil spirits and satanic agents and emissaries. As such, Jesus calls women and men to work at eliminating the sufferings which are brought about by discrimination and inequalities and to create a better human social order for all (Gal 3:26-28). Jesus continues to suffer with the downtrodden of society. These people's struggle becomes God's struggle (Wasike 1989, 131). Jesus suffers with those who suffer and works in them to give birth to new human relationships based on mutual respect and shared responsibilities with one another (Matt 20:25-28; 25:31-46). The HIV/AIDS pandemic has added new burdens to the African woman and the girl-child. Life is

being threatened as thousands continue to die on a daily basis. In African traditional societies, women and girls were never killed during war because they carried within themselves the future generations; killing women and girls leads to self-extinction. Currently the highest casualties of HIV/AIDS in Africa are female. There are approximately forty million people in the world living with the HIV virus. Of these about thirty-three million people live in Africa and twenty-two million of these are women and girls (USAIDS Report 2001). This is a very gloomy picture for the African continent. But despite all this, Jesus is suffering with those who suffer, and there is hope within the people's collective spirit that God will not abandon them but will restore life in God's own time (Rom 5:12-21). Paul gives hope in assuring us that humanity and the whole creation are in need of liberation (Rom 8:20-23). Christ as the cosmological liberator reconciles all things to God. God liberates creation because it too participates in humankind's sin and redemption. Humanity's exploitation and use of creation has united the world's destiny to its own.

Jesus the Healer

Jesus as healer restores harmony and wholeness to the broken, wounded, and sick world. In his own lifetime Jesus went about curing people suffering from diseases both natural and spiritual: epilepsy, paralysis, leprosy, hemorrhage, blindness, and possession by evil spirits. When Jesus healed individuals, he did it both spiritually and physically. The sick person's faith initiated the healing. In Mark 2:5-11 Jesus cured the paralytic by saying to him, "Son, your sins are forgiven ... stand up, take your mat and go to your home." In this way he demonstrated that spiritual wellness and physical healing are closely linked; one leads to the other or they occur simultaneously. His approach to healing was integral and holistic. Jesus restored the vision of two blind persons after they affirmed that they believed in his healing power. Jesus touched their eyes and said, "According to your faith let it be done to you" (Matt 9:27-30). Again in Luke 8:40-48 Jesus insisted that someone had touched him. The woman who had hemorrhaged for twelve years stepped forward in fear and trembling, and explained why she had touched him. Jesus replied, "Daughter, your faith has made you well; go in peace." Therefore, the link between healing and faith is intrinsic and allows the two elements to function as two sides of the same coin. Jesus' healing ministry is continued in the church through the sacraments. The African Instituted Churches have attempted to maximize this model of Christ the healer, the Victorious One, and the Conqueror in order to tap this fundamental faith element that is deeply rooted in the African psyche.

In his life Jesus endeavored to restore individuals and societies to wholeness (Wasike 1989, 133). At the same time he invited his disciples both then and now to participate in this process of restoration and reestablishment. As Christians who have experienced the liberating power of Jesus Christ we are summoned to witness to God's love and care for the universe and at the same time to demonstrate the sustained human responsibility of creating a harmonious new world.

BIBLIOGRAPHY

Amoah, Elizabeth. "Christology and Popular Religions: An African Constructive Statement." Pages 88-98 in Voices From The Third World Vol. 18, no. 2. Ecumenical Association of Third World Theologians. Colombo, Sri Lanka: Asian Theology Center, 1995.

Ela, Jean-Marc. My Faith as an African. Tr. John Pairman Brown and Susan Perry. Maryknoll, N.Y.: Orbis, 1988.

Oduyoye, Mercy Amba. Introducing African Women's Theology. Introductions in Feminist Theology 6. Cleveland, Ohio: Pilgrim, 2001.

Okure, Teresa. "An African Historical Perspective on EATWOT Christologies and Popular Religions." Pages 138-142 in Voices From the Third World Vol 18, no. 2. Ecumenical Association of Third World Theologians. Colombo, Sri Lanka: Asian Theology Center, 1995.

———. "Witnesses to Jesus Christ in African Context at the Dawn of a New Millennium." PROPOSITUM: A Periodical of Third Order Regular Franciscan History and Spirituality 2:1 (2000): 4-12.

Nyamiti Charles. Christ as Our Ancestor: Christology from an African Perspective. Gweru, Zimbabwe: Mambo, 1984.

Schreiter, Robert J, ed. Faces of Jesus in Africa. Faith and Cultures Series. Maryknoll, N.Y.: Orbis, 1991.

Stinton, Diana. "Jesus of Africa: Voices of Contemporary African Christology." Pages 287-313 in The Myriad Christ: Plurality and the Quest for Unity in Contemporary Christology. Edited by T. Merrigan and J. Haers. BETL 152. Leuven: Uitgeverij Peeters and Leuven University Press, 2000.

Waliggo, John Mary. "African Christology in a Situation of Suffering." Pages 93-111 in Jesus in African Christianity: Experimentation and Diversity in African Christology. Nairobi, Kenya: Initiatives, 1989.

Wasike, Anne Nasimiyu, "Christology and an African Woman's Experience." Pages 123-135 in Jesus in African Christianity: Experimen-tation and Diversity in African Christology. Edited by J.N.K. Mugambi and Laurenti Magesa. Nairobi, Kenya: Initiatives, 1989.

JESUS: AN ASIAN PERSPECTIVE

Carlos H. Abesamis, S.J.

Socio-Pastoral Institute and Loyola School of Theology, Quezon City, Philippines

LIFE CONTEXT OF THE INTERPRETATION

Using the valid exegetical methods of historical criticism and sociological analysis, I am attempting, in this essay, to offer a biblical reading of Jesus based on how the text presents him. In this way, I attempt to avoid imposing any private, eisegetical reading upon the text. Additionally, I read the text through the eyes or "eyeglasses" of the poor. Does this not muddle the text and distort the image of Jesus? On the contrary, by using the eyes of the poor, one sees the biblical Jesus as if for the first time and challenges the traditional views of Jesus and his mission that are held by many in the Philippines and elsewhere. Although the poor are often taught to aspire to the salvation of their souls in heaven, and thus to distrust their own perspective and to subordinate their concerns for food, shelter, and justice, they resonate with the core of Jesus story as found in the gospels. Jesus' worldview and that of the poor are similar; they both see life in the same way. This realization is the result of working with the biblical text while being in touch with the poor in the Philippines. Another result of reading in an Asian context, where silent contemplation is at home, is a renewed appreciation for the contemplative aspect of Jesus.

The biblical reading we offer would resonate with a Philippines that is in Asia and where 80 percent of the people are poor, the victims of four hundred years of Spanish colonization and an ongoing neo-coloniza-tion by the United States and the transnational corporations.

The core of the Jesus story revolves around two "essentials" of Jesus. Jesus was a person (1) connected with the Source, his Abba, and (2) totally poured out in mission —a mission for total salvation, both human and cosmic.

The First Essential: Jesus' Connection with the Source

In the context of the Philippines, the religious or spiritual life of Jesus becomes most visible. Jesus was intimately connected to the Source, and that Source was his Father.

> He was like a mountain stream directly in touch with the Original Spring.
> Like an artesian well, he was connected with the Water Source.
> He was like a tree whose roots drink from the Water Veins beneath the earth.
> He was like a battery connected with the Power Source.

Being connected with the Source, Jesus' inner being is fully charged with the Divine, and his outer aura, luminous with the Divine. To use other metaphors:

> He was like a sponge, drenched and soaking wet.
> He was like a cloud fully seeded, pregnant, heavy with rain.
> He was like a piece of paper, wet with the signature of God.
> He was a torch ablaze, ablaze with the Divine Flame.

Carlos H. Abesamis, S. J., is a professor of Scripture in the Philippines. He is co-founder of the Socio-Pastoral Institute (SPI), and a founding member of the Ecumenical Association of Third World Theologians (EATWOT) and the Conference of Asia Theologians (CATS). His publications include, "Some Paradigms in Rereading the Bible in the Third World" in *Mission Studies* (1990), *What Is Inside the Wooden Bowl? Or How (not) to Move Toward a Contextual Theology* (1997), *What Is in It for Mr. and Mrs. Pobre? The Jubilee Year and the Sabbatical Year of the Bible* (1999), and *A Third Look at Jesus: A Guidebook Along a Road Least Traveled* (2000).

Jesus was bursting with *divine Energy* because he was *in touch with the Abba,* and we add, *through silent communion.* This is implicitly or explicitly supported by the biblical data.

Now during those days he went out to the mountain to pray; and he *spent the night* in *prayer* to God. (Luke 6:12, author's italics; also Mark 1:35; 6:45-46)

With unerring intuition, John the evangelist portrays a Jesus who says:

The Father and I are one. (John 10:30)

Do you not believe that *I am in the Father and the Father is in me?* The words that I say to you I do *not speak on my own;* but the *Father who dwells in me does his works.* Believe me that *I am in the Father and the Father in me;* but if you do not, then believe me because of the works themselves. (John 14:10-11; also Matt 12:28; Mark 5:25-31; Luke 4:18; 5:17)

The Second Essential: Jesus' Outpouring in Mission for Total Human and Cosmic Liberation

The second "essential" about Jesus is this: he was totally poured out in mission. And, we hasten to add, his mission was for total salvation, human and cosmic.

I start with my childhood catechism. I was taught that Jesus' mission was to die to save my soul from sin, and to give me sanctifying grace in this life, so that when I die I might go to heaven where I will see God face to face. This view of Jesus' mission is very common in the Philippines.

Now that I am an adult, however, I find that formulation to be *correct but too narrow.* The biblical text challenges this narrowness.

New World and a New History for Humankind and Creation

The overall lifework and mission of Jesus was, as is commonly viewed, the proclamation of salvation. But what was the salvation Jesus proclaimed? He proclaimed the "kingdom of God" (Mark 1:14-15), also desig-

nated "new heavens and a new earth" (2 Pet 3:13) or the "age to come" (Mark 10:29-30). The kingdom of God is a new world on earth, to be consummated at the end of history. In fact, it is a new universe, as the biblical testimonies will show. At any rate, it is not a specific designation for heaven. We are not saying that there is no heaven. There is indeed a heaven: YHWH's abode in the firmament "above." To avoid the use of the name of God, Matthew spoke of the "kingdom of heaven." But he did not use the kingdom of God as a synonym for heaven.

Inspired by the book of Isaiah (Isa 26:19; 29:18-19; 35: 5-6; 40:9; 42:1-4; 52:7; 58:6; 61:1-2), Jesus proclaimed the kingdom of God as: the good news of liberation for the poor, liberty to the captives, sight to the blind, freedom to the oppressed, the jubilee year release of slaves, rest for the land, recall of the debts of the poor, and the restoration of the land, property, and houses of dispossessed ancestors (Luke 4:16-20). It is a new world replete with various blessings for individuals and all humanity, especially the poor and oppressed.

During his lifetime Jesus summarized his work of salvation thus: "the blind receive their sight, the lame walk, the lepers are cleansed, the deaf hear, the dead are raised, and the poor have good news [of liberation and justice] brought to them" (Matt 11:2-5; also Luke 7:18-23). Jesus' message in the Gospels contains no word about forgiving sins or saving souls for heaven. His message is about health, life, justice, and liberation.

A rich source of information about the kingdom of God can be found in the beatitudes (Matt 5:3-11; Luke 6:20-22). The kingdom of God is a new earth for humankind, promised specifically to the meek (Gk. *praus*) or considerate. In that new earth, there will be justice and liberation for the poor (Luke 6:20), a blessing for the poor in spirit, food for those who had suffered from hunger, righteousness for those who desired it, joy and comfort for the sorrowful, mercy for the merciful, a vision of God for the pure in heart, and divine sonship and daughtership for the peacemakers (Matt 5:3-10; Luke

6:20-21). Again, the kingdom of God is a new earth where human beings, individually and collectively, will experience a new and different history.

Matthew 19:28 pictures biblical salvation as *palingenesia* (Luke 22:29-30 uses basileia, "kingdom"). Various translations attempt to render this breathtaking reality in Matthew: "when all things are reborn," "at the renewal of all things," "the renewal of the earth," "regeneration," "new world," "when everything is made new again," "when the world experiences a rebirth," "a reborn universe."

The kingdom of God then means a new world experiencing total salvation—a new universe experiencing total well-being.

Good News to the Poor: Justice and Liberation

In sum, salvation for Jesus refers to the liberation of the whole person and the universe and the many blessings of well-being in this life. There is a whole range of life-blessings: from food and healing to divine filiation. Which of these is of the greatest concern for Jesus? This is an important question. The biblical data bid us to throw all hesitation to the winds. Jesus' greatest concern is justice and liberation for the poor. How can we say this? Because "good news to the poor" was so often on his lips. We take careful note then of the following:

(1) The obvious and unalloyed meaning of "good news to the poor" is nothing more and nothing less than justice and liberation for the poor;

(2) This good news is always mentioned in key mission statements (Matt 11:2-6 par. Luke 7:18-23; Luke 4:16-21; Luke 6:20 par. Matt 5:3);

(3) It is the only detail always mentioned in these mission statements; the other details (health for the sick, life for the dead, and the vision of God for the pure in heart) are not always mentioned;

(4) This good news occupies a special spot in the lists of blessings, either the prominent first or the climactic last.

Risky Business

But proclaiming good news to the poor is risky business. For Jesus, not only the proclaiming of good news to the poor, but the whole mission for total salvation turned out to be a risky affair. His mission meant that he:

- put primacy on the human being and human life over and against the accepted tradition and law (e.g., Mark 2:15-17; 2:23-28; 3:1-6; Luke 16:20-22);
- was a non-conformist and a rebel against tradition (Mark 2:21-22; Mark 7);
- was an uncompromising critic of the value-system or ideology of the establishment (Matt 9:13; 23:23; Mark 2:7; Mark 8:15);
- staged a double assault—in word and deed—against the most massive institution, the temple (Mark 11:15-19; 13:1-2).

Is it any wonder that Jesus made enemies? Conflict was an integral part of his story.

The Death and Resurrection of Jesus

Is it any wonder that some people would want to get rid of him?

> The Pharisees went out and immediately conspired with the Herodians against him, how to destroy him. (Mark 3:6)

And they did. The Romans, the imperialist power of the time, and their collaborators, threatened by his proclamation of the kingdom of God, killed Jesus through an officially sanctioned state execution. This is the *historical aspect* of Jesus' death.

In itself, Jesus' execution would already have had a weighty significance. It was the death of a rebel for the sake of the kingdom, of a martyr for justice and the oppressed. But another meaning was also given to his death, a death in atonement for sin (John 1:29; Rom 3:21-25; Eph 5:2). This is the *meaning through the eyes of faith* or the *theological aspect* of Jesus' death.

This Jesus did not remain death's captive. He was raised from the dead. As Paul succinctly states: Jesus was "handed over to death for our trespasses and was raised for our justification" (Rom 4:25).

Jesus' Return and the Kingdom's Realization

All stories have closure. Jesus' story has his Parousia ("return," or more, popularly, "second coming") at the end of time. The kingdom inaugurated at his first coming will be realized at his second coming (Luke 21:25-28; 1 Thess 2:19; 3:13). With Jesus' Parousia, the final and definitive kingdom of God will have come. Our world of unresolved pain, hunger, and thirst will be restored to wholeness.

This final and definitive salvation is *apokatastasis pantôn* (Acts 3:21), a thrilling reality, variously translated "universal restoration," "when all things will be made whole again," "restoring all things to perfection." This text denotes a world where there is justice (also Rom 8:19-23, 1 Cor 15:24-28, Eph 1:9-10, 2 Pet 3:13, Rev 21:1-5). Can one find a more concise expression of the dream of the poor?

The Parousia or Jesus' return is therefore a salvific event. It is the Victory-Day, *the day of the coming of the kingdom!* Our complete redemption is at hand (Luke 21:27-28). Whether or not we take Jesus' Parousia literally, its basic message is that our present history of mourning, pain, suffering, and death will give way to a new creation where all things will be made new!

Though indeed we can hope for a heaven after each one of us dies, heaven is not our final goal. Our final goal is a new earth, in fact, a new universe, where all reality will experience total well-being.

Final Thoughts

It is clear that the Jesus of my childhood catechism was a pale shadow of the biblical Jesus as seen through the eyes of the poor. The main salvific events cannot be limited to Jesus' death and resurrection. Rather, the main events are in Jesus' life and work, foreshadowing his Parousia.

Salvation is not just freedom from sin but liberation from all evils: personal evil (Jesus restored sick individuals to health), social evil (he blessed the hungry at large), historical evil (he promised "liberty to the oppressed," recognizing the oppression found in human history), and cosmic evil (he will come again to vanquish all evil cosmic powers).

Salvation is not for disembodied souls but for human individuals (the sick, the poor, the sinner, the resurrected person), for humankind (the poor, the hungry, the peacemakers) and for nature, creation, and the universe (the regenerated universe, all things united in Christ, God being all in all.).

The blessings of salvation in the here and now are not limited to sanctifying grace but extend to all life-giving blessings, such as food, land, health, forgiveness of sins, and life with God. The blessings of final salvation are not limited to seeing God face to face but extend to all life-promoting blessings: personal, social, historical, and cosmic (food, justice, divine filiation, and resurrection). "Total human and cosmic well-being" is a pale, fallible human way of describing this tremendous, sublime reality. "For now we see in a mirror dimly, but then we will see face to face" (1 Cor 13:12).

The final goal of salvation is not just heaven after a person's death, but the kingdom of God at the end of history. It is a new world and universe with a new history.

BIBLIOGRAPHY

Abesamis, Carlos H. *A Third Look at Jesus: A Guidebook Along a Road Least Traveled.* 3rd ed. Quezon City, Philippines: Claretian Publications, 2000.

JESUS: A LATIN AMERICAN PERSPECTIVE

Pablo Richard

National University of Costa Rica, Heredia, Costa Rica

Translated from the Spanish by Rubén A. Muñoz

LIFE CONTEXT OF THE INTERPRETATION

Jesus has many faces in Latin America. The most traditional and popular are the child Jesus, the merciful Jesus (image of the Sacred Heart), and the suffering Jesus. New faces are appearing: the Indian Jesus, the black Jesus, the Campesino Jesus, the young Jesus (almost a hippie), the revolutionary Jesus (with Che Guevara's face), Jesus interacting with women, the itinerant or charismatic Jesus, Jesus the liberator of the poor, and Jesus confronting the authorities. Similarly, base community Bible studies (el movimiento bíblico popular) among the people in Latin America have brought to light many faces of the historical Jesus implicit in the gospels.

Biblical exegesis has made great strides during the last thirty years. However, a large chasm still exists between the praxis of exegesis and the church. In the Latin American base community Bible studies, exegesis has truly served the people of God whenever those with pastoral responsibilities have also engaged in exegetical reflection. The quest for the historical Jesus is a joint venture between exegetes with pastoral orientation and community workers with biblical training.

The Quest for the Historical Jesus in Mainline Exegesis

Our starting point is the birth of critical biblical studies that made a distinction between the historical Jesus and the Christ of the church. This distinction has liberated the Christian faith from ecclesiastical dogmatism. A harsh critique of the church motivated this quest for the historical Jesus. With Albert Schweitzer (1875–1965) and Rudolf Bultmann (1884–1976) came the collapse of the first quest. Schweitzer conclusively demonstrated that nineteenth-century reconstructions of the historical Jesus were more reflections of the individual exegete's personal interest and culture than historical reconstructions. For Bultmann, proceeding from Schweitzer's insight and interpreting through the lenses of existentialism, it was enough to know that Jesus existed; what he taught or did is not relevant for Christian theology. Christianity was born at Easter. Bultmann's students Käsemann, Bornkamm, Fuchs, and Ebeling later initiated a second quest and rekindled the hope that critical research might find at least a minimal core of authentic tradition.

Finally, a third quest came from English-speaking scholars (e.g., E. P. Sanders, G. Theissen, J. D. Crossan, J. P. Meier, B. Mack, M. Borg, G. Vermes). Against Bultmann, they believe in the possibility of reconstructing the historical Jesus. Their optimism is based on their view that there is a social continuity between Jesus of Galilee and early Christianity, and (for some) a the

Pablo Richard, a Chilean priest and professor of exegesis, studied in Santiago, as well as in Vienna, Rome, Jerusalem (École Biblique), and Paris (Sorbonne). He is Doctor Honoris Causa from the Faculté Libre the Théologie Protestante, Paris and the Director of the Ecumenical Research at the National University of Costa Rica. He also teaches at Universidad Bíblica Latinoamericana. His publications include *Death of Christendoms, Birth of the Church: Historical Analysis and Theological Interpretation of the Church in Latin America* (English, 1987); *Apocalypse: A People's Commentary on the Book of Revelation* (English, 1995); and *El Movimiento de Jesús antes de la Iglesia: Una interpretación liberadora de los Hechos de los Apóstoles* (1998).

ological continuity between the historical Jesus and the Christ of faith. In this quest, scholars use the social sciences to discern what in the text reflects the historical Jesus and the post-Easter Christian community. This quest has had a great impact in Latin America. Yet we need to struggle with its political implications, as Elisabeth Schüssler Fiorenza has recently done from her feminist perspective in *Jesus and the Politics of Interpretation* (2001).

The Quest for the Historical Jesus from a Latin American Perspective

A series of exegetical studies by Albert Nolan (1978), Rafael Aguirre (1998), Pablo Richard (1995), Jon Sobrino (1978), and Julio Lois (1996, who presents the christological work of Gustavo Gutierrez, José Comblin, Juan Luis Segundo, Leonardo Boff, Hugo Echegaray, and Carlos Bravo) point in a distinctive direction.

While there is in the First World a third quest for the historical Jesus, we in Latin America engage in what I propose to call a fourth quest. It does not presumptuously claim to supersede the insights of the former quests, as if its goal were to invalidate their results. The fourth quest is rather a constructive effort to use and adapt the best of this First-World research to a different context.

The characteristics of this fourth quest are:

The Historical Jesus from the Perspective of the Poor and Marginalized in the Third World

The concept of a "Third World" is vague. Yet, it becomes concrete when one thinks about the peoples, cultures, and religions of Latin America, Africa, Asia, and Oceania where 70 percent of the population live in poverty and are marginalized. Since the sixteenth century, Christianity came to these regions through European colonial expansion. For this reason, in its theology and its culture, our Latin American form of Christianity has a deeply marked Eurocentric character. The question is: How can we envision a historical Jesus and a reading of the

Gospels from the margins, that is, from the perspective of marginalized peoples and cultures, rather than from the perspective of the dominant former colonial center powers? Since, statistically speaking, the main religions of the world (including Christianity) are Third-World religions, we cannot simply follow the exegetical practices of Europe and the United States. Such practices ignore the social, cultural, and religious reality of the Third World.

Thus, in Latin America, the quest for the historical Jesus is performed from the perspective of the poor, the oppressed, and the marginalized by considering the economic, social, political, cultural, and religious contexts and the related issues of gender and generation gap. Behind the scholars of the First World, there is a library. Behind the scholars of the Third World there are continents of poor and marginalized peoples.

Many First-World exegetical works, especially about miracles, exorcism, myths, and visions, address questions arising from a modern and secular mentality. In Latin America, we study the same topics but from the perspective of the poor and of the Third-World cultures. Here, our problem is not secularization, but the fact of oppression and the need for liberation. Especially since the fourth and fifth centuries C.E. early Christianity institutionalized itself by assuming the Greco-Roman social structure, culture, and philosophy. Imperial Christianity was born. Today, in Latin America, we try to reconstruct the history of Christianity in the opposite way, not from a triumphant position of power but from the margins in solidarity with poor. Instead of critical biblical studies as the exclusive property of Western scholars, we argue for radically reorienting the quest for the historical Jesus from the perspective of the peoples, cultures, and religions of the so-called Third World.

The Historical Jesus in the Context of the Origins of Christianity

In Latin America, the quest for the historical Jesus is less Jesus-centered, because it is envisioned in the broad context of the *Jesus*

Movement and from the perspective of a concern for the *origins of Christianity as a global reality.*

It might be useful to start with two general points. First, the "historical Jesus" is the Jesus before his death. Second, the Jesus Movement, before his death, as well as after his resurrection, was without doubt a historical reality. Jesus and his disciples, both male and female, formed a movement that was religious, messianic, and charismatic, but it also had a clearly marked social structure.

From a Latin American perspective, it is important to reconstruct the historical reality of the Jesus movement in the time *after* his resurrection and *before* the church. The continuity between the dead Jesus and the resurrected Jesus is the foundation for the post-resurrection Jesus movement. His body— although transfigured, glorified, and exalted —remains the same (the texts insist that he is not a ghost; that he can be touched; that he eats with his disciples; that the marks of his crucifixion can be touched; and hence that the tomb is empty). Therefore, this movement, empowered through the Holy Spirit and the Word, breaks free from institutional, religious, and cultural constraints, and organizes itself in houses.

The Acts of the Apostles shows the historical character of the Jesus movement after his resurrection (30 C.E.) and before the full organization of the churches (after the year 70 C.E.). If one wants to reconstruct the Jesus movement before the organization of the church, one needs to consider the seven authentic letters of Paul (1 Thessalonians, 1-2 Corinthians, Galatians, Philippians, Philemon, and Romans); the "Galilean Gospel" (the Q Source); the pre-synoptic traditions; and perhaps the Gospel of Mark. It is easily demonstrable that during these years this group truly was a "movement," and not yet a "church." Jesus himself founded this movement, and its historical nature can be reconstructed as accurately as one can reconstruct the historical Jesus.

In the same quest for historicity, one should reconstruct the historical apostolic churches after the year 70 C.E. and before the

era of Christianity. The *Judeo-Christian trend* gave birth to the models of the church reflected in Matthew's Gospel and the Epistle of James. By contrast, the *Hellenistic trend* emerges in the models of the church presented in the post-Pauline letters (Colossians, Ephesians, the Pastoral Epistles, the Epistle to the Hebrews, and 2 Thessalonians), Luke-Acts, the two Epistles of Peter, and the Epistle of Jude. The *tradition of the Beloved Disciple* introduces another model, found in the Fourth Gospel and the three Epistles of John. Finally, the *apocalyptic trend* engendered the model of the church in the Book of Revelation. The variety increases if one adds the writings of the Apostolic Fathers (*Letters of Clement,* Ignatius of Antioch, Polycarp, Diognetus and the *Shepherd of Hermas*) and the New Testament Apocrypha.

In sum, the quest for the historical apostolic church shows that, after the year 70 C.E., there was a plurality of church models. Unfortunately, this original diversity was soon lost in the process of institutional unification and in the establishment of the hegemony of the Constantinian Christianity that led to Western Roman Catholicism.

The First-World exegetes of the third quest, especially J. P. Meier, insist that the gospels must be read from the perspective of the historical Jesus, rather than from a theological or dogmatic standpoint—a fundamental and pertinent decision. However, from a Latin American perspective, I argue for a broadening of this principle so as to incorporate the quest for the historical Jesus into a quest for the Jesus movement and for the historical apostolic churches, so as not to impose on the New Testament the same ecclesiastical problems that arose through the establishment of hierarchical power structures in later Western Christianity, whether in Roman Catholic or Anglo-Saxon Christianity.

The Historical Jesus Understood as a Function in the Church's Re-formation

In our global quest of historicity, we make a distinction between:

—the historical Jesus prior to Christianity,

—the Jesus movement prior to the church, and

—the emergence of the apostolic churches *prior to* Christendom.

In the quest for this "before" we do not look behind but ahead. This is not a disengaged historical quest, but a quest performed in order to find a new foundation for the churches in our world today. *Behind* the biblical texts there is *memory;* however, by looking *ahead* of these texts we are looking for a way to live out the Christian faith in our ecclesial communities.

The problems with which contemporary churches struggle are therefore important in our quest for the historical Jesus. The scientific quest for this "prior to" is motivated by the needs that Jesus' disciples have today as they strive to live their faith, that is, by the needs of the Jesus movement in the present world. This quest is particularly motivated by the urgent need for the church's re-formation and for once again basing our churches on the model of the ancient apostolic church.

Today, our communities and ecclesial movements look for a historical basis by which to live in the same way as the earliest Christian communities. Today, in view of the great diversity of religious opinions, one needs a special gift of discernment or a canon (measuring stick) to define with some assurance what it means to be a Christian and a church. The reading of the New Testament from the historical perspective described above gives us this reference, this discernment, and this canon.

The contemporary Latin American base community Bible studies strive to give the Bible to the people of God, so that, with the Bible in their hands, in their hearts, and in

their minds the people of God may discover for themselves the Jesus of history, the Jesus movement, and the apostolic churches. The re-formation of the present-day church will begin from this process of biblical study. The people of God cannot do this on their own; they need the guidance of critical biblical scholars and critical biblical studies, the guidance of the clergy, and of the Magisterium (for us Roman Catholics). At the same time, the people of God need to be organized in communities and movements with the authority, legitimacy, freedom, assurance, creativity, and autonomy that come from the direct knowledge of the word of God. Throughout the church's history, biblically based movements structured in this manner always ended up as a reformation.

In the contemporary church, the historical Jesus is absent. The Apostles' Creed (most likely, from the third-century C.E.) confesses: "I believe in Jesus Christ... who was ... born of the Virgin Mary, suffered under Pontius Pilate. . . . " It says nothing about the events in between Jesus' birth and crucifixion; it mentions nothing of the life of the historical Jesus, of his proclamation of the kingdom of God, of his miracles, of his exorcisms, or his parables. The Nicene Creed (fourth century) similarly omits mention of Jesus' life. In the subsequent catechisms, including the current catechism of the Roman Catholic Church, this pattern persists; there is no detailed presentation of the story of the historical Jesus. The theological and dogmatic view of Jesus is dominant. The Latin American base community Bible studies strive to rescue this historical Jesus and the historical Jesus movement in order to re-form the contemporary church by reestablishing it on its historical, apostolic foundation.

CONCLUSION

In the quest for the historical Jesus, three themes are particularly relevant in Latin America: Jesus' humanity, sociological perspectives, and Jesus' project. Emphasis on the *complete humanity of Jesus* opposes the present-day, docetic, dominant heresy

that denies the humanity of Jesus. Our quest for a historicalJesus emphasizes his fully human consciousness and avoids portraying later dogmatic Christologies as features of the historical Jejus.

Sociological exegesis from the perspective of the poor and the marginalized can join European and Anglo-Saxon exegetical studies that incorporate geographical, economic, social, and political analyses in the quest for the historical Jesus and the origins of Christianity. In general, this is a welcome and insightful approach. Yet, in Latin America, we believe that it is essential to conduct these analyses from the engaged perspective of the struggle of the poor for their liberation, rather than doing so from a disengaged, so-called objective perspective.

Jesus' historical project, the kingdom of God as manifested in his liberating actions is, for us, more important than the historical Jesus in himself. The study of the miracles, the exorcisms, and the parables are conducted not in terms of their tension with modern thought, but in terms of the vision that they present for the liberation of the poor. Jesus did not define the kingdom of God, except in the stories he told and the story of his deeds, told by the evangelists in their texts. It is noteworthy that Jesus identified the kingdom of God not with the Davidic monarchy, not with the sanctity of the temple, and not with the fulfillment of the law, but with the lives of the poor.

BIBLIOGRAPHY

Aguirre, Rafael. *Del movimiento de Jesús a la Iglesia cristiana: Ensayo de exégesis sociológica del cristianismo primitivo.* Estella, España: Editorial Verbo Divino: 1998.

Ellacuría, Ignacio, and Jon Sobrino, eds. *Mysterium liberationis: conceptos fundamentales de la teologia de la liberacion.* Madrid: Editorial Trotta, 1990.

Lois, Julio. "Christology in Liberation Theology." Pages 223–251 in *Systematic Theology: Perspectives from Liberation Theology: Readings from Mysterium Liberationis.* Edited by Ignacio Ellacuría and Jon Sobrino. Maryknoll, N.Y.: Orbis, 1996.

Nolan, Albert. *Jesus before Christianity.* Maryknoll, N.Y.: Orbis, 1978.

Richard, Pablo. *Apocalypse: A People's Commentary on the Book of Revelation.* Bible and Liberation Series. Maryknoll, N.Y.: Orbis, 1995.

———. *El movimiento de Jesús antes de la Iglesia: Una interpretación liberadora de los Hechos de los Apóstoles.* Costa Rica: Dei, 1998.

Sobrino, Jon. *Christology at the Crossroads: A Latin American Approach.* Translated by John Drury. Maryknoll, N.Y.: Orbis, 1978.

———. *Jesus the Liberator: A Historical-Theological Reading of Jesus of Nazareth.* Translated by Paul Burns and Francis McDonagh. Maryknoll, N.Y.: Orbis, 1993.

JESUS CHRIST:
AN ORTHODOX PERSPECTIVE

Fr. Vasile Mihoc

Orthodox School of Theology, Sibiu University, Sibiu, Romania

LIFE CONTEXT OF THE INTERPRETATION

Orthodoxy, as defined in the Orthodox Church, is less a doctrinal system than the experience of communion with God in Christ. This definition explains the unique place of christological thinking in the Orthodox Church. Understanding the identity of Jesus Christ correctly is an existential necessity for an Orthodox, because believing in the person of Jesus Christ also means living an intimate life of communion with him. Being in Christ and being in the church, the body of Christ, is one and the same. We know who we really are as Christians by correctly formulating who Jesus Christ is and what his work of salvation means for us. For an Orthodox Christian the rejection of christological heresies is also an existential necessity, and not simply a theoretical debate. Erroneous christological formulations are directly related to concrete, existential distortions of Christians' self-understanding and way of life.

Following the holy tradition of the church fathers and of the ecumenical councils, Eastern Orthodoxy confesses Christ as true God and true human, as the divine Savior and the Lord of the world. Orthodox Christians read all of Holy Scripture through the light of this faith in the *theanthropic* Christ.

Jesus Christ: True God and True Human (*Theanthropos*)

The Orthodox understanding of Jesus Christ, firmly grounded in the biblical revelation, was deepened and received a clear expression during the patristic era in the context of controversial christological heresies. The Nicene Creed and the christological definition of the Fourth Ecumenical Council (Chalcedon, 451 C.E.) are fundamental to the Orthodox understanding of Jesus Christ. The Nicene Creed confesses, against Arian heresy, faith in Christ as "true God from true God" who has become human, who died, rose from the dead, ascended to heaven, and is seated at the right hand of the Father. As for the definition of Chalcedon, it reacts against some erroneous understandings of how the two natures, divine and human, are united in Christ. According to the confession of faith in Chalcedon, Jesus Christ is both divine and human, or to use the corresponding Greek expression, he is the *theanthropos,* the God-Man. (*Theanthropos* is coined from two Greek words: *theos* "God" and *anthropos* "human being.") From an Orthodox perspective, a major shortfall of modern views of Jesus Christ is that his humanity is affirmed in such a way as to detach it from the *theanthropic* (or *theandric*) person.

As the *Son of God,* Christ, is the second person of the Holy Trinity. He is of the same divine nature as the Father and the Holy Spirit. He eternally pre-existed his coming into the world. Saying that "God sent his Son" (Gal 4:4), Paul presupposes the pre-existence of the Son, because only one who

Vasile Mihoc, an Orthodox priest and a professor of New Testament studies, is interested in the Orthodox interpretations of the Bible through the centuries, especially as practiced by the Greek Fathers. He has published numerous works in Romanian, including his most recent books: *All Year Sundays Exegetical Sermons* (2001) and *Introduction to the Study of the New Testament,* vol. 1 (2001). He is coeditor of *Bibel in Orthodoxer und Westlicher Perspektive* (2000). He is a very active member of the *Studiorum Novi Testamenti Societas* and of the World Council of Churches.

already exists could be sent. According to John, the Logos was God and was with God in the beginning and all things were made through him (John 1:1-3). The Logos and eternal Son of God became man when he was conceived through the Holy Spirit and born on earth by the Virgin Mary. Because Jesus was conceived through the Holy Spirit, and because he is not only human but also true and fully God, the Most Holy Virgin is rightly venerated as the Mother of God (Gr. *theotokos*). As a man, the incarnate Logos received the Jewish name *Jesus*, because he was born and lived as a Jew among Jews. The incarnate Son of God presented himself and was witnessed by his followers as the *Christ* (Messiah), the Anointed of YHWH announced by the Old Testament prophets while they were as yet expecting his advent upon earth. According to the New Testament, Jesus the Christ is not simply the Son of David, but also the Son of God, born of the Father from all eternity. To Jesus' question, "Who do you say that I am?" Peter—and with him the church of all times— answers with this confession of faith: "You are the Christ, the Son of the living God" (Matt 16:15-16, RSV).

Nature (*physis*), person (*hypostasis*), and *theanthropos* are terms used by the church fathers and the ecumenical councils in their struggle to formulate an adequate Christology in contrast with the heresies of the time (Arianism, Nestorianism, or Monophysitism). The mystery of Christ is the mystery of the two natures and of their *theandric* union. There is an aesthetically beautiful simplicity in the ordering of the church fathers' Christology, which examines in sequence three questions: the deity of Christ, his humanity, and the union of the divine and human natures in one person.

Christ Is Fully God

When a child in the manger or when agonizing on the cross, he does not cease to fully participate either in the life of the Most Holy Trinity, or in the divine Providence of the universe by his all-present power. In the Nicene Creed we confess that Christ is "of one substance" (Gr. *homoousion*) with the Father.

When we call Christ our Savior, we confess that he is not only human, but also God. Christ the Savior is God because God alone can save. Salvation consists in the fact that God the Logos was present in all the stages of the human life of Jesus. For Cyril of Alexandria, for example, salvation came precisely from the fact that "one of the Holy Trinity suffered in the flesh." In each of his works two energies are present: the divine energy and the human energy. It will, therefore, be childish to try to determine a "psychology" of Christ, to reconstruct "his spiritual life" or even to write a "life of Christ." Discussion about the man Jesus from Nazareth does not lead to a correct understanding of who Christ is. Jesus' fellow citizens from Nazareth knew better than any of us about the civil status of Jesus, "the carpenter's son" (Matt 13:55). Yet, it was impossible for them, "because of their unbelief" (Matt 13:58), to adequately answer the question: "Where then did this man get all this?" (Matt 13:56), that is, "Where did [he] get this wisdom and these deeds of power?" (13:54).

Christ Is Fully Human

The Church condemned as a dangerous heresy the docetism that denied the real humanity of Christ, presenting this humanity as only "apparent." In becoming human, the Son of God becomes a human individual, Jesus of Nazareth, who was born as a child, "grew in wisdom and stature" (Luke 2:52), lived to maturity in human life, was crucified, and died on the cross. Yet, Christ is not a human person in the sense that we are. His humanity does not have a hypostasis of its own among the innumerable hypostases of humankind. The person of Christ, divine in nature, "en-hypostasizes" the human nature, as Leonce of Byzance says (*Contra Nestorianos et Eutychianos* 1, Migne, PG 86, col. 1277): the personality of Christ is the personality of the pre-existent Logos that assumes our human nature.

The Mystery of the Incarnation

If it is clear from the Scripture that Jesus Christ is truly God and truly human, one fundamental question remains: how are these two natures united in the unique person of Jesus Christ? The Council of Chalcedon (451) described this union by using four negative adverbs: "unconfusedly, immutably, indivisibly, and distinctly." The first two qualifications are opposed to Monophysitism, and the other two to Nestorianism. The four negative definitions express the mystery of incarnation. We cannot make presuppositions (and this is the meaning of the four negations of the formula of Chalcedon) regarding the way in which the divine and the human coexist in one and the same person *(hypostasis)*. What we can say is that, without being confused, the two natures of Christ are united. The divine energies irradiate Christ's divinity and penetrate his humanity, making it divine from the moment of the incarnation. The transfiguration reveals in part to the apostles the fire of the divine energies that irradiates the human nature of their Lord. This interpenetration of the two natures is called in Greek *perichoresis* (Maximus the Confessor), or, in Latin, *communicatio idiomatum.*

The Mystery of Christ

By the incarnation, the Son of God assumed our human nature. The Greek Fathers teach that the incarnate Son of God has saved that which he has assumed. He is the Suffering Servant of God who heals through his wounds and is victorious through his sufferings. Christian believers understand themselves to be saved from sin and death by Jesus' sacrificial death, the meaning of which was validated and confirmed in his resurrection. This understanding of salvation by faith in the crucified and risen Lord is repeatedly attested in the apostolic witness and commonly believed in Christian communities. From the very beginning they worshipped him as "Lord and Christ" (Acts 2:36, RSV). "Jesus is Lord" (Rom 10:9) is the heart of Christian confession of faith. This confession implies the Lord's permanent presence with his followers (Matt 28:20), in his church, through the Holy Spirit. The mystery of Christ includes the revelation of the Holy Spirit, who manifests his presence in the earthly Jesus and who makes him continually

present in the church. This living communion that we have with Christ through the Holy Spirit makes us Christians.

At the same time, we confess the Lord Jesus as the Christ of the *Parousia*, as the one who comes in the glory of God. The incarnation of the Son of God, his earthly work of proclaiming the gospel, his death on the cross, his resurrection and ascension to the right-hand of the Father, and his second coming are all stages of God's work for the salvation of the world.

The Theanthropic Understanding of the Holy Scripture

The concept of *theanthropos* is the key for an Orthodox understanding of Christ, as it is the fundament and the norm of the Orthodox approach to the Holy Scripture. The Gospels depict Christ acting distinctively by his two natures. Each nature works according to its properties. Thinking in the theanthropic perspective, the church fathers sought to valorize the christological texts of the Scripture by reference to one or the other of the two natures or to their union in the unique person of Christ.

Thus, for instance, Athanasius of Alexandria says that the skilled exegete, like an honest moneychanger, should consider attentively any biblical text referring to Christ, in order to discern if it refers to his humanity, to his divinity, or to the relation between the two natures:

> Expressions used about His Godhead and His becoming man, are to be interpreted with discrimination and suitably to the particular context. . . . He who expounds concerning His Godhead is not ignorant of what belongs to his coming in the flesh: but discerning each as a skilled and 'approved moneychanger', he will walk in the straight way of piety; when therefore he speaks of His weeping, he knows that the Lord, having become man, while he exhibits his human character in weeping, as God raises Lazarus" (Athanasius, *On the Opinion of Dionysius,* chap. 9, Nicene and Post-Nicene Fathers, vol. 4, Schaff, 1980: 179).

Gregory the Theologian is such a skilled

"moneychanger" when he explains the apparent contradictions of the biblical affirmations about Christ by the interpretation of the two natures:

> "He hungered–but he fed thousands . . ."
> He was wearied, but he is the Rest of them that are weary . . .
> He was heavy with sleep, but he walked lightly over the sea . . .
> He prays, but he hears prayer.
> He weeps, but he causes tears to cease.
> He asks where Lazarus was laid, for he was man; but he raises Lazarus, for he was God.
> He is sold, and very cheap, for it is only thirty pieces of silver; but he redeems the world . . .
> As a sheep he is led to the slaughter, but he is the Shepherd of Israel, and now of the whole world also.

> As a Lamb he is silent, yet he is the Word . . .
> "He is . . . wounded, but he heals every disease . . .
> He dies, but he gives life . . ."
> (Gregory Nazianzen, *Orat.* XXIX, 20, *Nicene and Post-Nicene Fathers,* vol. 7, Schaff, 1980: 309)

In his treaty *On the Orthodox Faith* (or *Dogmatics*), John of Damascus, the most systematic of the Oriental Fathers, offers a summary of the manner in which the patristic writers distinguished between the biblical ways of speaking about Christ. He said that the Scriptures contain four types of references regarding Christ, depending on how he is considered: 1) *before* the incarnate theandric union; 2) *during* the time of incarnate union; 3) *after* the union; and 4) after the resurrection.

CONCLUSION

To conclude, Orthodox theology regards as fundamental and indispensable elements of Christology:

1) The identification of the person of Christ with the Son of God, the second person *(hypostasis)* of the Holy Trinity. In all he was and did, Jesus of Nazareth was not only a human being, but also God. He suffered death as a man, but by his resurrection from the dead the real hypostasis of Christ was proved to be not the biological one, but the eschatological or the Trinitarian hypostasis. 2) The *hypostatic* union of the two natures—divine and human—in Christ. For the Orthodox the starting point of christology is the *hypostasis,* the person. This fact is of greatest significance, for it stresses that the basis of ontology is the person, both with regard to God and also, in Christ, with regard to the human being. Christ is who he is only as a person, that is, in freedom and love. And thanks to Christ, humans can exist and affirm their existence as personal.

BIBLIOGRAPHY

Grillmeier, Alois. Christ in Christian Tradition. Translated by John S. Bowden. New York: Sheed and Ward, 1965.

Lossky, Leonce of Byzance (*Contra Nestorianos et Eutychianos* 1, Migne, PG 86, col. 1277

Meyendorff, John. *Christ in Eastern Christian Thought.* Crestwood, N.Y.: St. Vladimir's Seminary Press, 1975.

The Nicene and Post-Nicene Fathers. Series 2. Edited by Philip Schaff and Henry Wace. 1890-1900. 14 vols. Repr. Peabody, Mass.: Hendrickson, 1994.

Oden, Thomas C. *The Word of Life.* Systematic Theology 2. San Francisco: Harper SanFrancisco, 1992.

Patrologia Graeca. Edited by J. P. Migne. 162 vols. Paris, 1857–1886. See Patrologia Graeca (Electronic PG) http://rosetta.reltech.org/reltech/PG/info.html.

Patrologia Latina. Edited by J. P. Migne. 217 vols. Paris 1844–1864. See Patrologia Latina Database Home Page. Online:http://pld.chadwyck.co.uk/.

Vladimir. *The Mystical Theology of the Eastern Church.* Translated by the Fellowship of St. Alban and St. Sergius. Crestwood, N.Y.: St. Vladimir's Seminary Press, 1976.

Zizioulas, John D. *Being as Communion: Studies in Personhood and the Church.* Foreword by John Meyendorff. Contemporary Greek Theologians 4. Crestwood, N.Y.: St. Vladimir's Seminary Press, 1985.

JESUS: A WESTERN PERSPECTIVE

Nicole Wilkinson Duran
Villanova University, Villanova, Pa., USA

LIFE CONTEXT OF THE INTERPRETATION

Like other parts of the world, the West has its own Jesus, who looks like us, speaks to and for us, and loves us best. Unlike other parts of the world, we have unfortunately exported our Jesus to all parts of the world, where by virtue of his superior purchasing power and firepower, he has dominated and done his best to crucify his local counterparts. As a product of western Presbyterian Sunday schools and graduate school classrooms, and a woman, in some ways resistant, but in most ways native to western and particularly American culture, I am looking most of all in this essay for the Jesus of my own people—the educated, Euro-American, Christian elite.

Probably the most popular western Jesus has been our reading of John's Jesus. The Jesus my students know and love is sweetly mystical, self-proclaiming, forever delineating his own position in relationship to God and humanity. Kind, patient, spiritual, perfect, distant, ephemeral, *nice, he* shows up in church pictures and stained glass with titles like, "The Good Shepherd," and "Suffer the little children to come unto me." His kingdom is not of this world, thank God. He does not tell us what to do with our money or who our neighbor is, but murmuring mysticism goes quietly, with dignity, to his painless cross, and we let him go gratefully, with satisfaction—it is finished.

Chasing the Historical Jesus as a Western Project

It is partly in opposition to this gentle, ghostly Christ that the western project of chasing the historical Jesus has developed. The Jesus of western scholarship is not nearly as nice as that of the western church; continually reinvented and redefined, he remains forever desperate to overturn the tables of any church he enters. The effort to define who Jesus was historically has been in part an effort to free Jesus and his teachings from an over-spiritualized interpretation.

But the historical Jesus is a western phenomenon. In fact, as Elisabeth Schüssler Fiorenza has pointed out, the scholars engaged in that effort are almost exclusively western men. With the exception of a few white women, the scholars who gather to define and describe the historical Jesus are white men. Why are western male scholars and virtually no others drawn to this project? What are they looking to define, in defining the historical Jesus over and over again, each in his own way? Kwok Pui-lan suggests that for the West, Jesus is the ideal native, the perfect Other, against whom we define and critique ourselves. Thus our Jesus is "foreign . . . yet tamable, because Jesus, though a 'savage,' is a noble one" (83). So the same segment of the population that dominates and obliterates all difference

Nicole Wilkinson Duran, after teaching the New Testament in the United States, South Africa (Zululand), and Turkey, is currently teaching part-time at Rosemont College and Villanova University. With her husband, she is raising twin sons in the suburbs of Philadelphia, Pa. She has published articles on topics ranging from gender and race in Esther, to body symbolism in the story of John the Baptist's execution, and edited (with G. Phillips) *Reading Communities, Reading Scripture* (2002). She is an ordained Presbyterian minister and does occasional preaching and adult Christian education.

insists on a different Jesus to demonstrate its tolerance—some of our best friends are Other. Constructing Jesus as the Other means that although he is not like us, we understand him best, and it means that there is an Other that our touch has not destroyed.

The West continues, despite the protests of postmodernism, to seek ultimate truth in facts (that hard, pure, western word), historical and scientific. The Quest for the Historical Jesus has sought to use western historical and social scientific thinking to uncover, discover, (unclothe, disrobe) the true Jesus, over against the Jesus of subjective impressions, the various Jesuses that the rest of the world experiences. For to the extent that Jesus is historical, he is inaccessible to present experience in all its variety.

The Quest for the Historical Jesus as Theological and Ideological

Perhaps in this sense the Quest is not so far from religious pursuits as it may seem. The iconoclastic, secularist discipline of historical Jesus research can itself be seen as a religious phenomenon. After all, what can we westerners do? We have no ancestors, no ongoing life of those who have died, no cyclical sense of life's ongoing power. The dead are dead, for us; the past is past and cannot be touched, despite our longing. In a strictly and fully western place, the rules of epistemology form walls that no past experience, not even the resurrected Christ himself, can transgress. From within that structure, our only possible experience of Jesus is looking through certain, prescribed lenses into the past we can know only in this one prescribed way. Our only hope of contacting Jesus is in the actual process of defining and redefining him—perhaps what scholars seek is less the perfectly historical end product than the process of searching for it, and the chance that it provides to talk to Jesus without embarrassment.

Though in some ways diverse, the historical Jesuses of the West currently divide into two camps: the eschatological prophets and the teachers of wisdom. The eschatological Jesus may be apolitical, otherworldly, rebellious in a strictly religious sense (see particu-larly Ehrman), while the teacher of wisdom is a social critic and a bit of an intellectual. Indeed the argument over this issue seems to be about whether or not Jesus was relevant socio-politically. The currently predominating opinion that Jesus was a non-eschatological teacher of wisdom presents Jesus as someone with his feet on the ground, not advising his followers to sit and wait for the end-time, but suggesting that they search for and indeed create the kingdom of God among themselves (e.g, Crossan, Mack). Given the western separation of religious and secular, it makes sense that eschatology, and the intensely religious worldview from which it emerges, comes to be seen (despite historical evidence to the contrary) as a kind of anesthetic, clouding an accurate perception of and weakening real resistance to political oppression. The more political our Jesus is, the less his teaching requires the religious belief that underlies eschatology.

American Scholars' Rejection of Jesus as a Revolutionary

American scholars are at least more or less unanimous in maintaining that although in some ways a rebel, a lightening rod, and a catalyst, the historical Jesus was not a revolutionary. That is to say, he neither led an armed movement against the Roman Empire nor advocated the Empire's overthrow. However, in Mark's gospel there is no indication that Jesus disapproves of his followers' violent attempts to prevent his arrest; instead, he rebukes the arresters themselves (Mark 14:47-49). Only in the later gospels—all of them friendlier with the Romans than is Mark—do we hear Jesus rebuke his followers, even healing the arrester's slashed ear (Luke 22:50-51; cf. Matt 26:51-54; John18:10-11).

The conclusion that violence is entirely anathema to Jesus, then, is surely not the only possible historical reading. But it seems to me that we persist in reading the text this way for two reasons: first, if Jesus had been a revolutionary, then scholars and believers would be in the uncomfortable position of seeing him as a failed revolutionary, since Rome was to remain in power in Palestine for centuries into the common era. Being on the winning side of history ourselves, we cannot accept as our own a Jesus who was a loser. Second, and more importantly, like the Roman Empire of Jesus' own time, we Americans see ourselves as on the side of peace. No matter what manner of evil we may wreak upon the globe, no matter what tortures we fund, fuel, or perform around the world, no matter how much murder and destruction must come to rest on our doorstep, that door is closed. We are innocent, by definition. We love peace and promulgate peace around the world. Even our missiles are peacemakers. We have our methods, as did the Romans, but deluded or blind, we remain innocent of those as well. Like the Roman Empire of Jesus' time, then, any motion of impatience, any gesture of anger or pain, any reaction making its way back to us from our far-flung deeds seems unprovoked, a sucker punch, a slap in the face to an innocently playing child.

With such a concept of ourselves, how could we admit into our number a Jesus who is not as innocent as we are, as peace-loving, as enamored of harmony, as terrified of disorder? Our Jesus cannot accept the sword as an alternative. The sword is a choice of desperation, and the American Jesus must remain as far from despair as is the nation. Thus on the popular level we embrace the crucified Jesus of the Gospel of John, who dies without a hint of despair, with a decorum beyond obedience. It's not hard to die a human death when one is God to begin with.

The rules of historical criticism have precluded much conversation between the historical Jesus and any other conception of Jesus—the Jesuses of other cultures, imagined by other methods. But the fact that historical scholars were not discussing with others how their own cultures shaped their images of Jesus has not meant that those factors had no influence, but rather that the influence was unexamined and often unconscious. For when we portray Jesus it has been less who we are that shapes our portrayal than who we imagine ourselves to be, and so the Jesus we project is one who resembles not the westerner himself so much as the westerner's ideal. Aspects of western experience that do not fit that ideal western self are excluded from conversation with the Jesus tradition.

So the sword is excluded from the western Jesus' teaching and ministry, although the West has the sword in its left hand as it holds onto this Jesus with its right. And thus, as Mark Lewis Taylor has pointed out, Jesus the arrested, executed criminal is not the western Jesus, although the United States imprisons more of its population than any other nation on earth, and clings to capital punishment as though for its social salvation (2001, xi).

What if We Imagine a Less Privileged Western Jesus

What if we imagine a western Jesus who is less privileged, less innocent? What if we imagine him from the perspective of my own nation, in which two million people are imprisoned in conditions ranging from grim to horrifying (Taylor xiv, 19) and in which over three thousand prisoners currently await execution? (36). Jesus was, however briefly, a prisoner. Like the twenty-three men executed in Texas in the year 2003, he was disposed of by the state as harmful to society. Stripped of his agency and his clothes, costumed, blindfolded, and beaten, might he, like incalculable numbers of American prisoners, have been raped? It is clear in the Synoptic Gospels that Jesus' body becomes entirely an object to his captors, whose actions appear pointless except to display their power over that body. They undress him, dress him, and mock him, rather like children with a doll. But they are not children, but men exerting unlimited power over another man—this dynamic in American prisons breed violence, and amid the violence, rape.

But why bring rape into the story of Jesus? There is no mention of rape in the text of the passion in the Gospels, and so no solid ground on which to build this case. But the biblical narratives never mention a man's rape of a man, although certainly such things happened in the biblical world. If the Gospels' authors had heard such rumors, would they have repeated them? Yet the burden of proof must be on those of us who speculate—not to prove that it happened, but to prove the usefulness of imagining that it might have. What difference would it make to understand Jesus as the victim of rape as well as arrest, torture, and execution? For me it means a different

understanding of his powerlessness and his identification with the powerless, an identification with the often invisible, largely African-American prisoners of my country, and a new level of identification with women, who, whether or not they have experienced rape, have lived with its threat as part of their defining daily experience.

CONCLUSION

Jesus is not western by origin. Middle Eastern, African, Asian perhaps, but he comes from nowhere that has ever been culturally contiguous with Western Europe. But to say that Jesus is not western by origin is to disguise the degree to which Jesus is western historically. He was not born here, but grew up and spent so long here, an exile or a captive, that his return to the parts of the world closer to his birthplace has most often been by means of western ships and planes, western languages, and the pursuit of western interests.

He is, in many ways, one of us, so how can he free us from our own sins, which he shares? But the question is less about Jesus

than about myself. How can I find a western Jesus who is truly the Other who opens me to Others? How can I find a western Jesus who is neither the western man's pet Other nor the western man himself, a Jesus who is not here to confirm my own position of privilege? How, Jesus asks, can Satan cast out Satan (Mark 3:23-27)? How can I read this text against my own white, elite interests? To paraphrase further, if western interests are divided, then those interests cannot stand, and their end has come. So from the western camp of Satan, perhaps it is our duty to provide that division, to speed the inevitable end of the dominance of our Jesus.

BIBLIOGRAPHY

Arnal, William E., and Michel Desjardins, eds. *Whose Historical Jesus?* Studies in Christianity and Judaism 7. Waterloo, Ont., Canada: Wilfrid Laurier University Press, 1997.

Borg, Marcus J. *Meeting Jesus Again for the First Time: The Historical Jesus and the Heart of Contemporary Faith.* San Francisco: HarperSanFrancisco, 1994.

Crossan, John Dominic. *The Historical Jesus: The Life of a Mediterranean Jewish Peasant.* San Francisco: HarperSanFrancisco, 1991.

Crossan, John Dominic, Luke Timothy Johnson, and Werner H. Kelber. *The Jesus Controversy: Perspectives in Conflict.* The Rockwell Lecture Series. Harrisburg, Pa.: Trinity, 1999.

Ehrman, Bart D. *Jesus: Apocalyptic Prophet of the New Millennium.* New York: Oxford University Press, 1999.

Kwok Pui-lan. "Jesus/the Native: Biblical Studies from a Postcolonial Perspective." Pages 69-85 in *Teaching the Bible: The Discourses and Politics of Biblical Pedagogy.* Ed. Fernando F. Segovia and Mary Ann Tolbert. Maryknoll, N.Y.: Orbis, 1998.

Prothero, Steven. *American Jesus: How the Son of God Became a National Icon.* New York: Farrar, Strauss and Giroux, 2003.

Mack, Burton L. *A Myth of Innocence: Mark and Christian Origins.* Philadelphia: Fortress, 1988.

Meier, John P. *A Marginal Jew: Rethinking the Historical Jesus.* ABRL. New York: Doubleday, 1991.

Schüssler Fiorenza, Elisabeth. *Jesus and the Politics of Interpretation.* New York: Continuum, 2000.

Taylor, Mark Lewis. *Executed God: Way of the Cross in Lockdown America.* Minneapolis: Augsburg Fortress, 2001.

MATTHEW

Alejandro Duarte

Instituto de Teología Santa Beatriz de Silva, Ceuta, Spain

Translated from Spanish by Daniel Patte

A Severino Croatto, que supo vivir aquello que enseñó

Two life contexts focus my interpretation of Matthew. I was in Argentina during the period of the military dictatorship (1976–1983). During this very difficult time eleven of my close friends and companions were killed. I wept and still weep for my companions, as Rachel was "weeping for her children, refusing to be consoled because they are no more" (Matt 2:18). In both the cases of the killings in Bethlehem and in Argentina, there is deep grief and a cry against these injustices. Most importantly these tragedies constantly remain with me as I reflect on the ways the "little ones" (10:42; 18:1-14) are exploited, marginalized, and excluded. Violence against the little ones can take the form of the direct violence that killed my eleven friends, but it can also take the form of the no less terrible structural violence of a neoliberalism that is totally unable to sustain any program of solidarity with the poor and the weak in our society. Survival of the strongest and of richest—social Darwinism—is the order of the day, while the large majority of the population remains socially invisible. The "little ones" and the "innocents" (as the murdered children in 2:16 are often called) are today the majority of the world's population. They are denied any social role, any prospect for the future, and who are silenced by ideologies that mark their words as incorrect, inappropriate, and pointless, because they do not conform to the hegemonic designs of the rich and powerful.

All those who oppose injustice must speak about the complicity of many in this injustice. Buenos Aires, which has the social means to protect its inhabitants, has become like Jerusalem in Matthew 2; it rejects those who come from "outside" (like the magi) because they stand outside of its power structure and do not share its visions. While excluding these outsiders, they also exclude many others within our society such as malnourished children, neglected sick, underprivileged women, and elderly people without access to healthcare and other forms of aid. For me, Matthew 2 and the killing of the children is a mirror in which one can see present-day Buenos Aires.

Severino Croatto always taught us that biblical hermeneutics is a reflection on the text within our own context and with those with whom we share our reflections. Consequently, in biblical studies we need as clear a picture as possible of both our view of our social location and of the different views we take with us after reflecting on the text.

For me the theme of the little ones is articulated by Matthew in chap 2, the beginning of his story about Jesus–the passage I shall particularly emphasize; as well as in chapter

Alejandro Duarte, a lay-Catholic theologian, studied at the Catholic Faculty of Theology of Buenos Aires and with J. Severino Croatto at the Instituto Universitario ISEDET, and at École Biblique of Jerusalem. He had a pastoral ministry in the suburbs of Buenos Aires, leading grassroots Bible study groups. In Ceuta (a small Spanish enclave in North Africa) he is the director of the of the grassroots biblical program of the Dioceses of Ceuta, in addition to being professor of Biblical Studies at the Theological Institute.

[Translator's note: In Spanish, as in Greek, a single word is used to express what English calls justice and righteousness—an important concept in Matthew. Throughout, I translate this concept with "justice" and its cognates with "just," because this is the major connotation in Duarte's contextual commentary.]

18, Matthew's presentation of the organization of the community; and finally in chap 28, where, through the resurrection, Jesus is at the service of the little ones with whom he will be "to the end of the age" (28:20) and calls his followers to a service through which they will also share in his resurrection.

The other experience that colors my reading of Matthew includes the seven years I spent in Jerusalem and my present situation as an immigrant in Spain, because of teaching opportunities. My successive moves from Catholic Argentina to Jerusalem, with its small Christian minority, and to increasingly multicultural Catholic Spain, has motivated me to use an analytical tool that elucidates the complexity of multicultural and multireligious situations. What self-perception does one have when one is religiously, culturally, and socially up-rooted from one's world? These concerns led me to return to the biblical text. Yet, it is not so much to discover the relevant lessons Matthew has for my context(s). My primary goal as I read Matthew is to discover how to formulate the critical questions we need to address to biblical texts in such multicultural, social, economic, political, and religious situations.

These contextual issues led me to focus my comments on Matthew 2, a Matthean passage with multiple resonances, and to situate my analysis on Matthew's life context. Biblical scholarship has shifted focus, first with redaction criticism (see Strecker [1971], Davies and Allison [1988–1991], and Luz [1985–2002]), then toward sociocultural historical critical studies, epitomized in Warren Carter's work. As necessary and as fruitful as this shift of focus was, I believe it does not yet suffice to address my concerns. There is more to this passage. This passage offers us analytical tools by inviting us to emulate the ways Matthew uses authoritative traditions to confront those who have opted for the imperial project and have forgotten the most defenseless. This will be clarified by paying close attention to the traditions to which Matthew alludes. Then, we will be in a position to see that the Gospel of Matthew is a relentless condemnation of Jerusalem and of those who collaborate with the Empire.

As such, this text becomes a useful tool for every diaspora or marginalized community, because it shows us the destructive or oppressive role of verbal manipulation and teaches us how to make a clear distinction between liberating and oppressive discourses. Through its Christology and ecclesiology, Matthew presents a way of constructing spaces and communities that are actual alternatives to the global and totalizing reality of our present world.

CONTEXTUAL COMMENT

An Overview of Matthew

The Gospel of Matthew was probably written in Antioch and reflects Christian communities in Syria and Galilee in the generation after the fall of Jerusalem (ca. 80s C.E.). It is probable that this Gospel originated and was read in a series of communities, rather than in a single community that could be precisely located. Among other things, Matthew addresses diaspora Jews about the implications of Jesus' coming and about God's promises for God's people, city, and temple.

Matthew as Narrative and Salvation History

Matthew's theology is a salvation history, primarily presented in a narrative form. Thus, I first read Matthew as a narrative. As is any narrative, this gospel is a complete whole—each of its parts is to be studied within the context of the rest of the story. Here, I will address the sacred world presented by this gospel as an alternate to all other belief systems. We, the readers, have the option to locate ourselves either inside or outside the symbolic sacred world proposed by the text.

Matthew constructs this symbolic world by the use of literary oppositions and chiastic arrangements (Patte 1987; Davies and Allison 1988-91). Of special importance for me is the chiastic correspondence among many features of Matthew chapters 1–2 and 26 –28 (Patte, 1987, 16-42, 353-405).

This Gospel is for a church (neither a people nor a religion) in transition and in the process of defining itself. Thus, it forcefully emphasizes the quest for Christian identity by little ones and marginalized people. This theme is already expressed by the theological concepts of faithfulness to the law (as interpreted by Jesus) and of the destiny of God's people, which should be read in terms of the separation and tension caused by Jesus the Messiah, the authoritative teacher and redeemer sent by God. For Matthew, the key of history is christological: past, present, and future should be viewed in light of Christ.

Matthew simultaneously presents a narrative plot about Jesus and theological sub-themes. Consequently, the interactions among several possible meanings, traditions, and typologies shape each passage. Furthermore, Matthew is constructed for hearers (rather than readers) and their different ways of relating to the text. For them, chiastic structures, speeches, and the high points of the story are most significant. Matthew's history is a sacred history in which God intervenes. But it is neither a history of Israel, nor a history that ends with Jesus, nor again a history of the Church, as we conceive of it today. It is a history in which the Old Testament is neither forgotten nor abandoned, but fulfills the great promise of God, clarified in Jesus who emphasizes this promise in the history of Israel in the canon of Scripture. Matthew opens up the sacred history of Abraham to include Jesus, as well as events of his own days and of the future. Thus, we should pay attention to the periodization of sacred history posited by Matthew, for whom the central event is Jesus, and for whom the continuing presence of Jesus is a promise for the future. For Matthew, sacred history is a history of

salvation given to those who respond to Jesus' teachings and deeds with complete ethical commitment.

Ethical Commitment and Moral Life as a Response to God's Presence with Us

The ethics of this gospel is not an ethics of principles to be implemented, but an ethics of response to the presence of God and Christ in my/our history. It is the promise "God with us" that is fulfilled not only in the birth narrative, but also in all of chapter 2— including the death of the innocents—in the middle of the Gospel (chapter 18), and in victorious and permanent form in the last speech (chapter 28). The death of Jesus means victory for the little ones, to whom the Lord, God and Jesus, gives full hope, by being present in the midst of the community.

In Matthew, justice is fulfilled when the law, as interpreted by Jesus, is fulfilled. In this way the law remains valid through the authority of the resurrected one, who gives a dynamism to the law that permits a *halakah* which is itself dynamic, rather than rigid (5:17-48). The total fulfillment of the law is the fulfillment of the prophets. Thus, Matthew invites us to pass from the code of holiness to the code of mercy (9:10-13), which he defines in terms of human needs and of the values of justice and love.

Matthew's Christological Titles and Jesus' Praxis

Matthew's Christology is the concrete expression of Jesus' convictions, identity, and significance that articulates all of Matthew's theological views: history, the Old Testament, and the Law. The primary title that Matthew gives to Jesus is "Son of God," a title closely connected with Emmanuel (1:23) and Savior (1:21). This title is given to Jesus as a revelation of the Father (3:17; 17:5), is the primary issue of the temptation (4:1-11), and is presupposed at Gethsemane by Jesus' prayer to "My Father" (26:39, 42; see also 11:27; 24:36). The title is used in the High Priest' accusation (26:63; 27:43), in the on-lookers' mockery at the cross (27:40), and in the centurion's confession (27:54). "Son of God" is the title used to confess one's faith (see also 14:33; 16:16).

"Son of David" is a title typically used in healings and polemical situations to affirm that Jesus is the true Messiah (21:9, 15), who was sent to Israel and yet heals "outsiders": lepers (11:1-6), blind people (9:27; 12:22-23; 15:30-31), and Gentiles (15:22). Jesus' role as Son of David /Messiah is geared toward those who are not considered important.

The title "Son of Man" draws the attention of outsiders to the power that God gave Jesus (9:6; 12:8). This title seems to be secondary in Matthew (in contrast to Mark) since in the final scene it disappears. Instead of speaking of the Son of Man to whom power is given (Matt 26:64, see Mark 14:62), in Matt 28:16-20, the resurrected one who has received all authority and power is "Emmanuel" (28:20; cf. 1:23) who is continually present with us, is the Lord before whom the disciples kneel down, and the Son in the trinitarian formula (Matt 28:19).

There are other titles associated with others of Jesus' words and deeds: Jesus is Wisdom (Matt 11:16-19, 12:42, and 23:37). Jesus is like Moses (Exod 19–20; Deut 4–5; 9–10) because he teaches his people on a mountain (Matt 5:1-2 and 17:1-8), and because both the dying Moses (Deut 34) and the resurrected Jesus still provide guidance for the people on a mount (Matt 28:16-20).

What is noteworthy is that Matthew does not define any of these christological titles. The readers are supposed to define them on the basis of Jesus' deeds. Each title is associated with certain aspects of Jesus' ministry, and therefore none is sufficient by itself. One can say that the diverse narrative programs represented by the christological titles posit a revelation through praxis.

Integrating Teaching and Healings in Jesus' Ministry

Matthew brings together Jesus' roles as teacher and healer, as is clear in the summaries of Jesus' ministry in 4:23 and 9:35. Similarly, the fact that the Lord's Prayer forms the chiastic center of the Sermon on the Mount clearly indicates that this Sermon is centered on *prayer*, but prayer (including communal prayer) is assessed in ethical terms, that is, in terms of the deeds with which it is associated. Conversely, Matthew 8 and 9 are almost totally devoted to a description of Jesus' *deeds*, namely healings. But this praxis teaches about who Jesus is (8:1-17), about discipleship (8:18–9:17) and about the constitution of the group of disciples as a distinct group not separated from Israel.

Jesus' therapeutic ministry can serve as a model for the praxis/ministry of the community today. Matthew does not use the title Son of God to speak of Jesus when he heals. Rather he emphasizes that Jesus fulfills the prophetic texts about the Servant of YHWH (8:17; 12:17-21), presenting Jesus as a humble, obedient servant. This is the point where Christology and ecclesiology come together. Jesus is shown to be a model for the community, and the community through its praxis reveals the mysterious presence of Jesus today.

Discipleship and Church

In Jesus and in one's relation with him, one finds the new alliance and the faithfulness of God toward the people of God and toward the members of Jesus' family (12:46-50). The new assembly of God, the *ekklesia,* includes both the faithful remnant of Israel and those who accept Jesus and follow him as disciples.

For Matthew, this church is not an assembly of "saints." In the church, there are scandals (18:5-9), divisions (10:21), good and evil (13:24-30, 36-43). The disciples are those who (at last!) understand Jesus and his mystery (16:12) despite their "little faith" (14:33), and not people who are blameless or have "great faith."

Discipleship involves listening to him and following him (8:18-22; 9:9). This is what will insure that the church withstands the crisis, which according to Matthew, is part and parcel of the reality of the church's life (10:16-42). The church hopes for the kingdom; it is not the kingdom. It shows greatness when it is at the service of the weakest (18:6-14). This service is a testimony to others "so that they may see your good works and give glory to your Father in heaven" (5:16).

The church is a community that continuously seeks to understand the teaching of Jesus in new contexts, as Matthew's communities did by reinterpreting Jesus' teaching for new circumstances—exemplified in 5:38-42, applying Jesus' original teaching(5:39) to a court situation (5:40), forced labor (5:41), and someone asking for money from disciples in a financially secure position(5:42). As such, it is dynamic and not static. It must constantly pay attention to all justice issues and warn others about them (25:31-46). It is a community that should act with prudence and adapt itself to the problems of each historical time (17:24-27). For this, the church needs to look at the people from the perspective of Jesus' threefold ministry, teaching, preaching, and healing, which bring transformation and restoration.

Contextual Reflections on Matthew 2:1-23

"Your birth meant the death of the children in Bethlehem" (Acts of Pilate or Gospel of Nicodemus, 2:3, Elliott 1993, 172)

The "divine injustice" that Jesus was saved while the other children in Bethlehem were not (Erickson 1996, 5–27) is also present in our own situation. If we are saved through Jesus' grace, redeemed by God, then in an indirect way we benefit from an unjust act.

What concerns me did not seem to concern Matthew. Yet this issue fits the theological question that Matthew raises for us. Matthew's communities, as well as the early Christian communities and the patristic tradition, read Matthew 2 as a reference to a historical event. The Messiah is saved at the expense of others, according to the will of a Father who does not care for those little ones that his Son should take care. It is indeed his mission according to 1:21, because to "save his people from their sins" also means, in the theology of the Hebrew Bible, to save the people from the harm that awaits them in their daily lives.

Matthew's Midrashic Use of Scripture

"A voice was heard in Ramah, wailing and loud lamentation, Rachel weeping for her children; she refused to be consoled, because they are no more" (2:18). Can we not bypass this verse? Is it not the case that this quotation from Jer 31:15 has simply a literary function in Matthew 2? Is not its role to show that God, according to a prophecy, has saved God's chosen one? Is not Rachel's weeping for her children tempered by the promises of comfort for those who mourn (Matt 5:4)? The answers to these questions can be reassuringly affirmative for many. I refer to those interpreters for whom this text is disincarnated and ahistorical, even while they paradoxically defend the historical character of the text to better "freeze" it in the past and ignore its socio-political implications for today. The "historicity of the supernatural" limits their reading of the text to a certain aspect of reality which somehow excludes the sociopolitical (see Carter 2000).

In these contextual reflections, I first observe that Matthew uses the multiple meanings of the text of Jer 31:15 in a midrashic way. Midrash takes various literary genres, because midrash is first of all an interpretive attitude; a way to read the sacred text; a retelling of the sacred text as one relates it to a life-context. The distinction between midrash and history that modern scholars are tempted to make is not actually as clear cut as a distinction between pure literary creation and real fact. The biblical authors who practiced midrashic interpretation certainly thought that, in one sense or another, the Old Testament material they used was historical. In their midrash, they simply retold certain events, using the Old Testament as a reference tool. Such was certainly the case with Matthew. He probably thought that the events that he was retelling were historical, and he used midrash in either of two perspectives: as retelling historical traditions shared with Luke (for instance, those about Bethlehem, Nazareth, Herod) or as theological adaptation, starting with the person of Jesus.

The King as Benefactor of His People

Matthew 2 opens with a series of protagonists: the magi, Herod, Jerusalem, the chief priests and scribes, and the inhabitants of Jerusalem. The question "Where is the child who has been born king of the Jews?" (2:2) troubles some of these people, because it mentions another authority that challenges their claim to power. Matt 2:3 presents Herod as "*troubled*" (or "frightened" in the NRSV) "and all Jerusalem with him." Later in the gospel, all of Jerusalem responds to Jesus' coming: "When he entered Jerusalem, the whole city was in turmoil, asking, 'Who is this?'" (21:10). This response is deeply emotional and negative, because the religious authorities are present in the background, and Jesus' power and authority challenges theirs (see Neuviert, 1999, 139–142; Davies and Allison, Vol III, 1991–127).

This chapter is about "royalty": Herod's (2:1, 3, 9) and Jesus' (2:2, 6, 11). The relative values of these different types of royalty become explicit in the description of the intensification of violence (from 2:8 to 2:16) of Herod's efforts to hold on to his power over his subjects—efforts that ultimately lead to the destruction of Herod's royal power. As such, this chapter raises the question of what kingship is all about. A king should shepherd his people (2:6), watch over them, and therefore be a benefactor for his community, should he not?

Surprisingly, given Matthew's negative portrayal of Herod, there is historical evidence that King Herod did act as a benefactor of his people. He had large construction projects, as was typical of benefactors and patrons of cities or regions. Archeological evidence shows that Herod lived a life of luxury, a sign of greatness in that time. He built magnificent buildings in his own honor and he maintained order through military force. His government promoted the lifestyle of eastern Hellenism appreciated in cities such as Caesara, Jericho, and Herodium. Herod simultaneously acted as if he were a pious Jew by rebuilding the tomb of the patriarchs in Hebron, celebrating the memory of Abraham in Mamre, and rebuilding the Temple. All of these construction projects benefited the people when they resulted in full employment, a growing business, and commercial exchanges with Rome. This cultural integration seemed to give Judea prestige, peace and prosperity (see Josephus, AJ, 14:337-78).

Yet Herod was also a cruel man: he killed three of his children, one of his wives, and several potential rivals. Herod was a totalitarian. For him, power was the only reality, which in its logics requires the disappearance of the "other." Thus, his vision of power should be read in light of the temptation in Matt 4:8-10. It follows that for Herod, governing involved lying, as his interrogation of the magi shows (2:7-8). But Herod is outmaneuvered by God, who reveals Herod's plot to the magi (2:12). Power, which was the only reality, is now relativized.

Jesus is king, messiah, shepherd, and son of God. But as a character in the text he does not show kingly power like Herod's: he is simply "the child" or *paidon* (2:8, 9, 11, 13, 14, 20, 21). As such he is dependent and passive. Indeed, the child has power, as the magi acknowledge (2:11); yet he does not do anything. He is weak and vulnerable. He totally depends on God for his power.

The killing of the children at Bethlehem (2:16) deconstructs the mechanism of power that is not at the service of all (20:25-28). Two semantic fields are set in opposition. One is centered upon the power of brutal force used to kill and banish, forcing people to fearfully comply or to flee. The other semantic field is constructed by the actions of those who are pursued: avoiding the murderous rampage by "withdrawing" (*anachōereô*), a verb repeatedly used in 2:12, 13, 14, 22 and 4:12, 12:15, 14:13, 15:21 to speak about Jesus' withdrawing from a dangerous situation and about Moses' withdrawing from Egypt to avoid the fury of Pharaoh (Exod 2:15, LXX); returning to the "land" (2:20-21, return from exile is a sign of the presence of the living God, Ezek 20:36-40); returning to the people of "Israel" (2:20-21); resisting threats by going to Nazareth (2:22).

Matthew does not speak about the birth of

Jesus the Messiah but about his origin (*genesis,* 1:1). It is his origin that defines his identity. Matthew 2 continues this process by defining his messianic identity in terms of location. The magi's question is: *"Where is the . . . king of the Jews?"* (2:2). Matthew actually gives two answers to the magi's question. The first is: in Bethlehem (2:5). The second is: on the cross, on which the same phrase, "king of the Jews," is written (27:37). Jesus' messianic identity is defined by places of death: the cross where he dies and Bethlehem where his people (the children of his people) die (2:16).

The angel gave him the name Jesus, "he will save his people" (1:21). But the very people whom he should save, such as the children of Bethlehem, "disappear" (as people disappeared during the dictatorship in Argentina): the children are "no more" (2:16). In the beginning of the gospel, the identity of the Messiah and his function contradict each other; the hope of the poor is "fulfilled" in the death of the poor.

This is the problem that the story needs to address if it is to be good news for the people. "God with us" is portrayed against the backdrop of those who are no longer with us, those who have disappeared and "are no more" (2:18). What was presented in chap 1 as Jesus' task, namely that he will "save his people," is very much in doubt in chap 2, where Jesus does not seem to be able to carry out this program as the story of the gospel begins to unfold.

Set over against the portrayal of the benefactor king who also kills, Jesus seems to offer another model of kingship for the benefit of his people. He is presented as king-Messiah and as shepherd of his people (2:6). But this does not seem to be the case. Actually, the failure to implement the proposed and expected program leads to a crisis that ends in death.

The Uses of Scripture

In Matt 2:6, the quotation of Micah 5:2 is an integral part of the plot of the story: "And you, Bethlehem, in the land of Judah, are by no means least among the rulers of Judah;

for from you shall come a ruler." Herod receives the prophetic word that could be truly revelatory, but for him it becomes a tool for his attempt to maintain power and control and an impetus for murder. On the basis of *information* gathered from Micah 5:2, Herod charges the magi, "Go and search diligently . . . bring me word" (Matt 2:8). Herod appropriates the word of scripture in order to control a situation that is potentially threatening to his power. He uses it to deceive, claiming that he wants to "go and pay homage to" or "worship" the child; in reality, he wants to go and kill the child. In contrast, although the magi receive the prophetic word from a dubious source (Herod), nevertheless they act on this information and actually do "pay homage to" or "worship" the child (Matt 2:11).

A similar misuse of a revelatory word is found at the end of the gospel when the chief priests use the true information about the resurrection they received from the guards as a means to control a situation which is getting out of hand and threatens their authority (28:11-15).

Another kind of misuse of Scripture occurs when the chief priests and scribes cite the prophetic text (2:5-6) in response to Herod's question about where the child could be found: "In Bethlehem of Judea" (2:5). They use scripture as a shield to deal with the powerful Herod. Actually, they simply comply with Herod's order and hide behind the authority of scripture. They know the text of scripture. But because they use this text as a shield, they cannot recognize the fulfillment of the prophecy in Jesus, as Matthew invites his readers to do by repeatedly emphasizing such fulfillments (for instance, in 1:22-23, 2:15, and 2:17-18). In the hands of people who shield themselves behind it from dangerous powers and who carefully remain "neutral," the scriptural text becomes an instrument of death. Despite appearances and despite what they may think, the cry of Rachel is also against them.

One could object: Is it not Herod who is the main antagonist? Certainly, Herod is the one who seeks to ascertain the accuracy of the information with the hoped-for help of the magi. But the killings at Bethlehem (2:16) would not have taken place if these "neutral" readers had not provided Herod with the information they had found in scripture. Indeed, if we read carefully Mic 2:1-12 (as well as passages such as Mic 3:9-12 and Mic 5:3-5), it soon becomes clear that Bethlehem is mentioned as part of a general condemnation of Jerusalem and of its leaders. In Mic 3:9-12 Jerusalem is presented as a bloody city with corrupt rulers and priests who accept bribes as they render judgments. Their ideological/theological reason for this behavior is expressed in the affirmation, "Surely the Lord is with us!" (Mic 3:11a), held as a guarantee that nothing bad will happen to them (Mic 3:11b).

Throughout his gospel, Matthew presents a systematic critique of using scripture as to justify not intervening in a situation and denying any responsibility for the results of one's "neutrality." Knowing the scripture, and passing on the information to those in power has consequences for which one is responsible. In Matthew's presentation, this is the case with the chief priests and the scribes (2:4-6, 26:61-65 and 27:11-26). Those who are "in the know"—because they know scripture or other true information—seek to have Jesus condemned, even as they deny responsibility and wash their hands of what happens, as Pilate does.

From the beginning, Matthew demands that we analyze the characters' true intentions and their relationship to Jesus. In this perspective, Matthew invites us to find out how the king of the Jews succeeds in dismantling the oppressive and destructive power of those who deny him and try to hide the true meaning of his life story. The narrator empowers us to use resources from this twenty-eight chapter story about power: power that goes from Herod (and the chief priests and scribes) to Pilate, from Rome's vassal king (and his subordinates) to the Roman governor. Those in power, directly or indirectly through subordinates, take care of their people. But following the ideological logic of their view of power, they also kill, bribe, and deny or ignore what has been said to them, namely the possibility that the Messiah was born, that, after the crucifixion, he had been resurrected, and that there might be another way of exercising power/authority. This liberating praxis of power is actually signaled by the chief priests and scribes as they add to Micah 5:2 words from 2 Sam 5:2 and 1 Chr 11:2, "a ruler who is to shepherd my people Israel" (Matt 2:6).

There are of course other possible meanings to Matt 2:1-18, constructed by focusing the attention on the reference to Egypt (a favorite of patristic interpretations). Yet the echo of the confrontation with Jerusalem initiated by the quotation of Micah remains, and it is prolonged throughout the Gospel of Matthew. This becomes most explicit in Matt 21, the triumphant entrance of Jesus into Jerusalem with a multitude of outsiders (coming from Jericho with him, 20:29). As in 2:3, all the people in Jerusalem are "troubled." But in 21:10 the term used is even stronger; they are "shaken" (eseisthē—the verbal form of seismos, earthquake). Matthew also uses this term to refer to the storm that Jesus calms (8:24) and to describe the guards' experience of the resurrection (28:4). Matthew refers to earthquakes that will occur at the end-time in the apocalyptic discourse (24:7), as well as to describe what happened after Jesus death (27:54) and when the tomb was opened (28:2). In all these passages, the term "they were shaken" has an apocalyptic connotation, and therefore, Jesus' arrival with the crowd in Jerusalem has apocalyptic meaning.

Among those who come with Jesus there is a group of "children" (21:15; the same word used in 2:16 to describe the children of Bethlehem) who, after the triumphal entrance in Jerusalem and into the temple, proclaim who he truly is: "Hosanna to the Son of David." In the next verse, 21:16, Jesus defends these children and designates them as "infants and nursing babies." With these words Jesus quotes Ps 8:3, understood in Jewish tradition as referring to Exodus 15, when the "children of Israel" sang to the Lord after their victory (Davies and Allison, vol. 3, 1991, 140–141; see also Miler, 1999). In this way, the motif of the entrance into the temple is related to the exodus. Without going into the details (see Davies and Allison, vol. 3. 1991, 144), these observations are sufficient to recognize that Matthew expands the identification of Jesus as "son of David" by associating him also with Moses. It is as such that Jesus takes possession of the temple while he is surrounded by those who were normally excluded from the temple, "the blind and the lame," and children. These marginalized persons are those who reveal Jesus' full power/authority as he exercises it.

Herod unleashes the killing because he was "tricked" or "mocked" *(empaizô)* by the magi (2:16), as God mocked Pharaoh and the Egyptians "so that you may know that I am the LORD" (Exod 10:2; 1 Sam 6:6). In the Hebrew Bible (see Hab 1:10, Zech 12:3, Ezek 22:1-22) this mockery motif is directed against both God's people and their enemies. In Matthew, the mockery exposes the types of kings Herod and Jesus truly are. Herod (2:16) and Jesus (27:29) are both mocked: the true motives and the cruel character of Herod are revealed (2:16), while Jesus is revealed in his servanthood for all and in his dependence on God to be "the king of the Jews" (27:29).

In Matthew's narrative, Herod's deceitful manipulation of others is condemned along with the similar behavior of all the leaders and people in power throughout the gospel. When deceit and lies fail, the eruption of force and violence makes explicit the actual intention of the powerful. Herod's rage ("he was infuriated," 2:16) is contrasted to the great joy and happiness of the magi (2:10) when they find the child. This great joy, a breath of fresh air in this tense story, is shared by those who are persecuted in the Beatitudes (5:12) and by the shepherd who has found the lost sheep (18:13). This great joy is a sign of salvation and of discovery of "blessedness" (5:3-12) and the fact that God is with us. By contrast, rage ineluctably leads to desolation, to "they are no more" and to Rachel's lamentation (2:18).

The citation of Jeremiah 31:15 in Matt 2:17-18 is introduced as an indirect fulfillment ("then was fulfilled" rather than "this was to fulfill" in 2:15 and elsewhere) so as to mark that these killings did not happen according to God's plan, but according to Herod's plan and in the logic of his power-centered ideology—a logic which is once again controlling the penultimate phase of Jesus' story, the passion (Matthew 26–27). Yet this does not make this citation less important. Instead of being denied or ignored by those who do not assume responsibility for their use of scripture, this violence is assumed by scripture, assumed by God's word, assumed into God's plan.

Much could be said about the citation of Jer 31:15. Its Greek vocabulary links Matt 2:18 and 27:25 as the killing of the children is linked to the killing of Jesus. Also, Rachel weeping for her children (2:18) is associated with Jesus' lament over Jerusalem (23:37-38). Matthew's reference to Ramah broadens the "killing fields" ("in Bethlehem and in all that region," 2:16 RSV). In Jer 31:16-17 Rachel is consoled by the promise that her children will return from exile; so the killing of the children of Bethlehem is followed by the resurrection of Jesus. All these issues need to be clarified by comparing Matthew's use of Jer 31:15 with early rabbinic interpretations. In the limited space of this contextual commentary, it is enough to note that the voice of those who "are no more" resonates throughout the Gospel of Matthew. Rachel's weeping bears witness to violence that remains with us as we read the rest of the gospel. And her words demand a resolution of this violence.

This overcoming of violence starts with the flight to Egypt at night (2:13-15), which reflects the Passover night—an allusion reinforced by the citation of Hos 11:1—and continues with the return from Egypt (2:19-23). Here the central character, Joseph, follows a narrative pattern that is very different from Herod's: Joseph listens to and obeys the Lord. Repeatedly (see 2:13, 14, 20, 21) "he rises up" *(egeirō,* the same word that Matthew uses for Jesus' resurrection). Thus,

Joseph's actions anticipate the resurrection—an observation justified by all the parallelisms between Matt 2 and Matthew 26–28. But listening to what God says and obeying this word also means taking a risk (2:22-23), which settling in Nazareth only temporarily delays.

Jesus returns (from Egypt, 2:21-23). Contrary to the stories in which the hero comes back to defeat his enemies, the hero Jesus returns to share the fate of those whom he had left behind: the victims of oppressive power. As compared with traditional heroes, Jesus fails, because he dies in Jerusalem. And yet he is a manifestation of the presence of God ("God with us" 1:23; "I am with you always" 28.20).

Violence is "resolved" by being assumed rather than denied. The one who escaped came back to share the fate of those whom he had left behind. The text posits two options: the inclusion in life, which is an acknowledgment of God's central role and finds expression in Joseph's adoption of the child and the magi's homage to the child;

and the exclusion of life, represented by Herod. God the Father of Jesus does not *seem* to choose life, because he does not deliver his Son from the cross (27:43).

As we noted, the description of the killing of the children in 2:16-18 is first apprehended as the description of the hope of the poor shattered by the death of the poor. Thus, at first, the children's deaths cast doubt on the identity and mission of Jesus as the Messiah. But on the cross Jesus demonstrates his solidarity with the killed children. By renouncing the use of absolute power following a power-centered ideology (the use of "legions of angels," 26:53), Jesus deconstructs the mechanisms of power that engender the killing of the innocents or the disappearance of the "others" through their marginalization. It is in this solidarity with the children, the excluded, the crushed, the marginalized, that he is "Son of God" (27:54). He remains on the cross and dies, contrary to the power-centered ideology that thinks his Father should deliver him from the cross (27:43).

CONCLUSION

I have tried to show that Matthew provides us with tools to analyze the various kinds of confrontations we find in our societies. These are analytical tools that enable us to identify both in our societies and in the text the actors and their roles, and their different levels of responsibility for what is happening. From this identification, we can therefore develop an appropriate social critique.

1. The killing of the innocents in Matt 2 shows that one must assume responsibility for one's use of scripture and of its symbolic power. One cannot claim neutrality when using scripture.

2. The biblical text gives to the church—the people of God—the means to:

a) Analyze their particular contextual situation;

b) Analyze the contradictory representations of Jesus that one finds in one's

group and other groups; and more specifically,

c) Analyze the different representations of Jesus' resurrection and discuss those that are problematic;

d) Identify the modes of communication that either make visible or hide the presence of Jesus Christ in a situation;

e) Affirm that each community can and should formulate its own Christology and ecclesiology. The pluralism in the New Testament gives each community the right to do so;

f) Give us the hope that the righteous/just and the victims of injustice are those who will be resurrected. Matthew has brought together these righteous/just ones with all the little ones of his people who have been crushed by the power of the powerful. In Matt 2, having hope is a political act of resistance against death-wielding powers.

3. Matthew opens a door toward an ecclesiology characterized by Christian life-practices rather than theological views. It calls into question the intentions behind the quest for a uniform, monolithic Christianity that does not make room for diversity.

4. The exodus and its violent connotations, together with the violence of Matt 2 (and other passages of Matthew) are used to justify Christian violence against Jews.

A literalist theological reading of the exodus and of Matthew can accommodate violence by asking: Is it not appropriate that a message about our liberation begins with images of the death of innocent others? Yet one can also note that in Matthew the exodus is presented as a denunciation of oppressive powers and that the response to violence is not additional violence and killing. For example, Herod dies, but he is not killed. There is no death of the first-born of Herod and of the rest of Israel, as there was in Egypt.The theme of the killing of children is a description and denunciation of what one

sees in one's society. Is it not the case that our societies kill our children? Let us not forget how social disenfranchisement, unemployment, and marginalization in the so-called first world engender violence and death, indeed, the death of our children. Are we not killing our own children in wars, even as we deny these murders in name of power-ideologies? Do we not kill the future of our children by destroying the creation? This is not a hyperbolic statement, because the degradation of the planet will affect everyone and will help increase oppressive powers.

Our reading of Matthew and of our life context in terms of each other has just begun. We cannot pretend that our reading of Matthew is neutral. Either it contributes to the killing of the innocents, or it helps us to challenge the power-centered ideology that kills the innocents. Far from being inconsequential, pursuing our contextual reading of Matthew is a matter of life and death—the life and death of our children.

BIBLIOGRAPHY

Benoît, Pierre. *Les Récits Évangéliques de l'Enfance de Jésus. Exégèse et Théologie*. Tome IV. Cerf, Paris, 1984.

Carter, Warren. *Matthew and the Margins : A Sociopolitical and Religious Reading*. Maryknoll, NY: Orbis, 2000.

Davies, W.D.; D. C. Allison. *The Gospel According to Saint Matthew*. 3 vols. ICC. Edinburgh: T&T Clark, 1988-1991.

Elliott, J. K., ed. *The Apocryphal New Testament. A Collection of Apocryphal Christian Literature in an English Translation*. Oxford: Clarendon, 1993.

Erickson Richard "Divine Injustice? Matthew's Narrative Strategy and the Slaughter of the Innocents (Matthew 2,13-23)" *JSNT* 64 (1996) 5-27.

Luz, Ulrich. *Das Evangelium nach Matthäus*. 4 vols. EKK. Zürich Benziger; Neukirchen-Vluyn: Neukirchener Verlag, 1985-2002.

Miler, Jean. *Les Citations d'Accomplissement dans l'Évangile de Matthieu*. Rome: Pontificio Istituto Biblico, 1999.

Nieuviarts, Jacques. *L'entrée de Jésus à Jérusalem (Matt 21, 1–17): Messianisme et accomplissement des Écritures en Matthieu*. Lectio Divina 176. Paris: Cerf, 1999.

Patte, Daniel. *The Gospel according to Matthew: a Structural Commentary on Matthew's Gospel*. Philadelphia: Fortress, 1987. Valley Forge, Pa.: Trinity Press International, 1996.

Sim, David C. *The Gospel of Matthew and Christian Judaism: The History and Social Setting of the Matthew Community*. Studies of the New Testament & Its World. London & Edinburgh: Continuum & T & T Clark, 1998.

Strecker, Georg. *Der Weg der Gerechtigkeit; Untersuchung zur Theologie des Matthäus*. Göttingen: Vandenhoeck & Ruprecht, 1971.

MATTHEW 5–7: THE SERMON ON THE MOUNT AND INDIA

A Dialogue with Raja Rammohun Roy and Mohandas Karamchand Gandhi

R. S. Sugirtharajah

Selly Oaks Colleges, Birmingham, U.K.

LIFE CONTEXT OF THE INTERPRETATION

Among biblical texts, the Sermon on the Mount played a critical role in colonial India. It became an important narrative in the hands of the colonized in silencing any critique of "native" behavior. Two crucial figures, both Hindus, were engaged in an inventive and transgressive reading of the Sermon on the Mount: Raja Rammohun Roy (1774-1833) and Mohandas Karamchand Gandhi (1869-1948), better known as Mahatma Gandhi. Both played a crucial role in shaping modern India. Roy and Gandhi, in their respective times, dominated missionary and national discourses, appealing to different audiences: Roy addressed metropolitan society and Gandhi the masses. They appropriated the narrative that came with the Englishman's Bible and directed that same narrative against the colonialists and missionaries. Thus, Roy and Gandhi scuppered the missionaries' intention to convince the natives of their moral inferiority and depravity. In their hands, the Sermon on the Mount became a site for rigorous ethical scrutiny of both Christianity and colonialism. On this occasion, the persuasion flowed from the margin to the center and from the colonized to the colonizer.

One Sermon, Two Messengers

Roy and Gandhi came to the Sermon on the Mount by different routes. For Roy, any religion that was dogmatic, mysterious, irrational, and monotheistic, and that did not espouse the well-being of people, was not worth following. Roy had been engaged with his own Brahmanical tradition, trying to weed out elements that thwarted true worship, distorted the image of the Supreme Being, and hindered social welfare. The Sermon on the Mount, in Roy's view, contained the necessary ingredients that accorded with the expectations he had of religion. He wrote a booklet, *The Precepts of Jesus* (1820), which was a collection of the moral teachings of Jesus minus any of the historical or doctrinal components contained in the New Testament. Just as he had done with his own Brahmanical texts, he attempted in the *Precepts* to produce a purer form of Christianity that he felt the missionaries were incapable of achieving because of their obsession with doctrines and miracles. Naturally the *Precepts* starts straightaway with Matthew's account of Jesus preaching on the Mount: "And seeing the multitudes, he went up to a mountain." Except for some minor deletions,

---

R.S. Sugirtharajah was born in Sri Lanka and educated in Bangalore, India and Birmingham, U.K. His publications include *Postcolonial Reconfigurations: An Alternative Way of Reading the Bible and Doing Theology* (2003); *Postcolonial Criticism and Biblical Interpretation* (2002); *The Bible and the Third World: Precolonial, Colonial, and Postcolonial Encounters* (2001); *Asian Biblical Hermeneutics and Postcolonialism: Contesting Interpretations* (1998); as well as edited volumes such as *Voices from the Margin* (1991, 1995); *Postcolonial Bible* (1998); *Vernacular Hermeneutics* (1999); and *Dictionary of Third World Theologies* (2000, 2003).

Roy retains the Sermon on the Mount as it is presented in Matthew 5–7. In his view, the sayings contained in the 5th, 6th, and 7th chapters of Matthew are "the blessed and benign moral doctrines," and they include "every duty of man, and all that is necessary for salvation." More importantly for Roy, the Sermon expressly excludes "any of the mysterious or historical" accounts (Roy 1906, 555).

Gandhi was first attracted to the Sermon on the Mount by accidentally reading the Bible. Perturbed by meat-eating and alcohol-drinking among Christians, he was persuaded by "a good Christian from Manchester" to read the Bible in order to see for himself that these practices were not endorsed by the Bible. As he narrated in his *Autobiography*, Gandhi plodded through the Christian Old Testament without the "least interest or understanding." On the other hand, Gandhi wrote, "the New Testament produced a different impression, especially the Sermon on the Mount which went straight to my heart. I compared it with the *Gita*. The verses, 'But I say unto you, that ye resist not evil: but whosoever shall smite thee on thy right cheek, turn to him the other also. And if any man take away thy coat let him have thy cloak too'" in particular caught his attention (Gandhi 1927, 51). It was the Sermon on the Mount that changed Gandhi's perception of Christianity. In a talk that he gave on Christmas Day, 1931, on board the SS Pilsna, he told his audience that "for all I had then been given to understand was that to be a Christian was to have a brandy bottle in one hand and beef in the other. The Sermon on the Mount, however, falsified the impression" (Gandhi 1971, 438). On another occasion, he remarked: "Today supposing I was deprived of the *Gita* and forgot all its contents but had a copy of the Sermon, I should derive the same joy from it as I do from the *Gita*" (Gandhi 1941, 187). For Gandhi, the "Sermon on the Mount was the whole of Christianity" (Gandhi 1971, 438) and it was that Sermon that endeared Jesus to him. In his view, Jesus had given the "definition of the perfect *dharma* in those verses" (quoted in Chatterjee 1983, 51).

The strength of Roy and Gandhi was not in their detailed exegesis of the Sermon on the Mount but in their eclectic piecing together of the moral precepts scattered throughout it. They picked and discarded verses according to what suited their immediate hermeneutical concerns. A portion within the Sermon that attracted the attention of both Roy and Gandhi was the Lord's Prayer. The absence of idol worship and unnecessary ritual in the Lord's Prayer was alluring to Roy. He thought that there was nothing comparable to it and that it was "full of all good things, and spirit, and yet so short" (quoted in Shah 1977, 23). Gandhi likened the Lord's Prayer to the *Gayatri Mantra,* which has been recited by millions of Hindus for centuries and "yet their power has not diminished" (Gandhi 1972, 202). Jesus' teaching on wealth and anxiety in the Sermon did not elicit their enthusiasm. What attracted Roy was the Sermon's praxilogical intention and its insistence on orthopraxis rather than orthodoxy. At a time when Roy was seeking to reformulate some of the traditional ritual practices of Hinduism and channel them into service for community, he saw particular possibilities in the Sermon on the Mount. In his controversy with the Baptist missionary Joshua Marshman, Roy pointed out that "apparently to counteract by anticipation the erroneous idea that such conduct might be dispensed with, and reliance placed on a mere dogmatical knowledge of God, the following declaration seems to have been uttered: Not everyone that saith unto me Lord! Lord! shall enter into the kingdom of heaven, but he that doeth the will of my Father who is in heaven" (Roy 1906, 554). (On the controversy, see Sugirtharajah 1998, 29–53.) By prioritizing praxis over dogmatic allegiances, Roy dealt a severe blow to the undue emphasis the missionary seemed to be placing on traditional tenets such as the Trinity and the atonement. Roy taunted his missionary opponent to "show a commandment of Jesus directing refuge in the doctrine of the cross, in the same explicit way as he has enjoined love to God and to neighbors and obedience to his precepts as sufficient means for attaining eternal happiness" (Roy 1906, 693). What was crucial for Roy was Jesus' words: "Everyone then who hears these words of mine and acts on them will be like a wise man who built his house on rock" (Matt 7:24).

Gandhi used the Sermon on the Mount as a benchmark to test not only Christian behavior but also Christianity's belief system: "But negatively I can tell you that in my humble opinion, much of what passes as Christianity is a negation of the Sermon on the Mount. And please mark my words. I am not at the present moment speaking of Christian conduct. I am speaking of Christianity as it is understood in the West" (Gandhi 1969, 248). In a speech given at the Colombo YMCA, Gandhi recalled that when he had begun studying Christian literature earnestly, he had had to ask himself whether this was Christianity and had "always got the Vedic answer *neti neti* (not this not this)" (Gandhi 1969, 249).

There were two aspects of the Sermon on the Mount that attracted Gandhi. The first aspect was its message of "non-retaliation or non-resistance to evil" (Gandhi 1971, 438). He told J. J. Doke, a Baptist minister in Johannesburg:

> When I read in the Sermon on the Mount such passages as 'Resist not him that is evil; but whoever smiteth thee on thy right cheek, turn to him the other also,' and 'Love your enemies, pray for them that persecute you, that ye may be sons of your Father in heaven,' I was simply overjoyed, found my own opinion confirmed where I least expected it. The Bhagavadgita deepened the impression, and Tolstoy's *The Kingdom of God is Within You* gave it a permanent form. (Andrews 1929, 192)

The second aspect that appealed to Gandhi was its mundane practicality: "I think the Sermon the Mount has no meaning if it is not of vital use in everyday life to everyone" (Gandhi 1941, 278). If for Gandhi non-violence was central to Jesus' Sermon, for Roy, the grand and comprehensive moral principle which encapsulated the Sermon was the Matthean Golden Rule: "In every-

thing do to others as you would have them do to you" (Matt 7:12). Roy ended the preface to his translation of the Isa Upanishad with the words, "*Do unto others as ye would be done by*" (Roy 1906, 74, italics original).

Jesus: Not an Accidental Hero

Roy and Gandhi relied largely on the Sermon on the Mount to support their case for Jesus as a moral teacher. The fact that the Sermon did not contain any article of faith about Jesus was an added bonus to them. For Roy and Gandhi, Jesus was not irrelevant but they saw him as part of the eternal ethical lineage. They did not accept the traditional Christian claims for Christ. Neither saw Jesus as the Son of God or believed in his sacrificial and vicarious death. Interestingly, both believed in incarnation, but not in the traditional Christian sense, as the final revelation of God, but in the Indian sense of multiple appearances of God. For Gandhi, Jesus was "one among the most illustrious teachers and prophets the world has seen" (Gandhi 1967, 85). Neither Roy nor Gandhi was interested in the historical Jesus. Gandhi said that he would not care if someone were to prove that Jesus had never lived and what was narrated in the gospels was the "writer's imagination. For the Sermon the Mount would still be true for me" (Gandhi 1971, 438). What hermeneutically enthralled Gandhi was the "mystical Jesus of the Sermon on the Mount" (Gandhi 1970, 40). Roy, similarly, paid little attention to the historical Jesus, as indicated by the fact that he omitted any historical reference to Jesus' life in his *Precepts*. For Roy, Jesus completed the circle that started with Moses—a long line of faithful messengers through whom God had revealed his law: "It is true that Moses began to erect the everlasting edifice of true religion, consisting of a knowledge of the unity of God, and obedience to his will and commandments; but Jesus of Nazareth has completed the structure, and rendered his law perfect" (Roy 1906, 606). For Roy, Jesus was more than a teacher. He was a "Redeemer, Mediator and Intercessor with God in behalf of his followers" (Roy 1906,

608). Neither of them was interested in who Jesus was or where he was located, a question that was to plague Indian Christians later. Specifically, they were interested in what Jesus said.

Scriptures as One Continuum

For Roy and Gandhi, the value of sacred texts lay not in their literal meaning but in the ethical impetus they provided. If the ancient texts did not uphold the twin hermeneutical keys of truth and non-violence, Gandhi found them to be repugnant. He recalled: "My very first reading of the Bible showed me that I would be repelled by many things in it if I gave their literal meaning to many texts or even took every passage in it as the word of God" (Gandhi 1975, 333). Neither did he regard everything said in the Bible as exhaustive or even acceptable from the moral standpoint. One of the verses that Gandhi found morally objectionable was the saying of Jesus: "But I say to you that if you are angry with a brother or sister, you will be liable to judgment" (Matt 5:22). Such an inconsiderate saying in his view was inconsistent "with the *ahimsa* [non-violence] of Jesus." He treated many passages in the Bible as mystical: "For me 'the letter killeth, the spirit giveth life'" (Gandhi 1968, 46). For Gandhi, despite his admiration for the Sermon, it was the *Bhagavadgita* that provided the key to the Scriptures. As a Hindu, Gandhi found the Hindu Scriptures meeting the needs of his soul. His study of other religions did not decrease his reverence for or faith in Hinduism. In an address to missionaries in Calcutta, he said:

> I must tell you in all humility that Hinduism, as I know it, entirely satisfies my soul, fills my whole being, and I find a solace in the *Bhagavadgita* and *Upanishads* that I miss even in the Sermon on the Mount. Not that I do not prize the ideal presented therein, not that some of the precious teachings in the Sermon on the Mount have not left a deep impression upon me, but I must confess to you that when doubts haunt me, when disappointments stare me in the face, and when I see

not one ray of light on the horizon, I turn to the *Bhagavadgita* and find a verse to comfort me; and I immediately begin to smile in the midst of overwhelming sorrow. (Gandhi 1941, 51-52)

Likewise for Roy, it was the *Vedas* created by the Supreme Being that contain the law of God, "revealed and introduced for our rule and guidance" and "*Puranas* and *Agamas* without distinction, can impart divine knowledge to mankind at large" (Roy 1906, 130). The ultimate necessity was to recover "*the true meaning of our sacred books*" (Roy 1906, 90, italics original). To put it differently, for them the sources for moral renewal are to be found within one's own sacred narrative. For Roy and Gandhi no narrative was inherently better or purer than any other.

Some Reflections

Roy and Gandhi perceived the Sermon on the Mount as central not only to Jesus' teaching but also as a rallying point for all Christians. For them it was not about rules, obligations, and prohibitions. It was more about the quality of human behavior. When a Christian student asked Gandhi about his views on Christian organizations, worship, and ministry, Gandhi replied: "If Indian Christians will simply cling to the *Sermon on the Mount,* which was delivered not merely to the peaceful disciples but a groaning world, they would not go wrong, and they would find no religion is false, and that if they act according to their lights and in the fear of God, they would not [need] to worry about organizations, forms of worship and ministry" (Gandhi 1966, 169). For Roy and Gandhi, the Sermon represented an ethical ideal attainable by individuals and society. Gandhi stressed the potential of the individual to be transformed from within and believed that the transformed individual would in turn transform the community. For Gandhi the enemy was within oneself and one had to destroy the inner demons before society could be redeemed. This, he reckoned, was the message of the *Bhagavadgita,* the Sermon on the Mount, and the *Koran* (Gandhi 1969, 139). Roy, on the other hand, envisaged a transformed community creating transformed individuals. For both Roy and Gandhi truth was a matter of vigorous and conscientious performance and not a pious endorsement of a predetermined dogma. "Truth is the exclusive property of no single Scripture," wrote Gandhi (Gandhi 1941, 34).

The Raja and the Mahatma thought that Christianity could offer much to India but both felt that Christianity as it was professed, practiced, and promulgated in colonial India by colonialists, missionaries, and converted Indians did not offer much hope. This Christianity was interested in the salvation of souls and obsessed with doctrinal orthodoxy, and it denounced anyone who did not believe in the atoning power of Jesus' death. Roy and Gandhi were simply interested in Jesus as a moral teacher. What they did was to de-familiarize the Sermon on the Mount in its Christian context. A celebrated narrative of a Semitic tradition was made to lose its textual power and was placed in a totally radical textual and cultural milieu. This de-familiarization drained the text of its Christian meaning and exposed it as merely one among myriad contingent textual possibilities. For Gandhi and Roy no culture or textual tradition had a monopoly on good ethics. They conformed to the received notion of what the Sermon on the Mount should be but complicated it by rendering it as a concrete manifestation of eternal truth already embedded in their sacred texts. For Gandhi, non-violence was not something distinctive to the New Testament. It was common to all religions and had found the "highest expression and application in Hinduism" (Gandhi 1969, 167). Gandhi did not find anything new in the Sermon on the Mount. It vividly told what he had learned in his childhood: "There is nothing much in giving a cup of water to one who gave you a cup of water, or saluting one who salutes you, but there is some virtue in doing a good turn to one who has done you a bad turn. I have not been able to see any difference between the Sermon the Mount and the *Bhagavadgita*. What the sermon

describes in a graphic manner, the *Bhagavadgita* reduces to a scientific formula" (Gandhi 1941, 187). Roy found the sum total of the Sermon on the Mount the same as that set forth in the *Vedas:* faith in the Supreme Being, when translated into ethical practice, should lead the human race to social comfort and eternal happiness. Hence he incorporated the precepts of Jesus into his own canon as a basis for teaching morality, but he continued to champion the validity of *Vedic* texts while acknowledging errors that had accrued over the years, blurring their moral force. For Roy and Gandhi, truths could be constructed from a panorama of perspectives simply because truth is a matter of sound and scrupulous ethical practice.

In postcolonial India the Sermon on the Mount did not have the same hermeneutical purchase as it had during the colonial period. It fell out of favor for four reasons. First, in the wake of independence when nation-building was the prime concern, Indian interpreters turned to passages like Leviticus 19–25 where they found a roadmap for a well-ordered society, or elucidated the passages from Acts where the early church shared everything in common. Second, during the time of indigenization, the Gospel of John came to prominence, with its mystical teaching that resonated with Indian philosophy. The Fourth Gospel had the added advantage of invoking the Orientalist image of India as spiritual and mystical. Third, during the liberation theology phase, narratives like the Nazareth Manifesto (Luke 4:17-18) became the focus of hermeneutical attention. Fourth, with the emergence of identity hermeneutics, those most concerned—*dalits,* women, and *tribals*—seem not to have seen any potential in the Sermon. At a time when texts are being employed to advocate virulent fundamentalism, the likelihood is that the Sermon with its tolerance and reverence for life will recede still further. Gandhi's words, "become worthy of the message that is imbedded in the Sermon on the Mount, and join the spinning brigade," are unlikely to be heard (Gandhi 1941, 292) in the immediate future.

BIBLIOGRAPHY

Andrews, C. F. *Mahatma Gandhi's Ideas Including Selections from His Writings* [microform]. London: George Allen and Unwin, 1929.

Chatterjee, Margaret. *Gandhi's Religious Thought.* Foreword by John Hick. Notre Dame, Ind.: University of Notre Dame Press, 1983.

Gandhi, M. K. *The Story of My Experiments with Truth.* Trans. Mahadev Desai. Ahmedabad: Navajivan Publishing House, 1927-29.

Gandhi, M. K. *Christian Missions: Their Place in India* [microform]. Ahmedabad: Navajivan Press, 1941.

Gandhi, M. K. *The Collected Works of Mahatma Gandhi.* New Delhi: Publications Division, Ministry of Information and Broadcasting, Government of India, 1958-1975.

Roy, Rammohun. *The Precepts of Jesus: The Guide to Peace and Happiness, extracted from the Books of the New Testament, ascribed to the four evangelists with translations into Sungscrit and Bengalee.* Calcutta: The Baptist Mission Press, 1820.

Ghose, Jogendra Chunder, ed. *The English Works of Raja Ram Mohun Roy Vol. 1.* Vols 1-4. New Dehli: Cosmo Publications, 1906.

Shah, A. B., ed. *The Letters and Correspondence of Pandita Ramabai.* Compiled by Sister Geraldine. Bombay: Maharashtra State Board for Literature and Culture, 1977.

Sugirtharajah, R. S. *Asian Biblical Hermeneutics and Postcolonialism: Contesting the Interpretations.* Bible and Liberation Series. Maryknoll, N.Y.: Orbis, 1998.

MARK

Hisako Kinukawa

International Christian University, Lutheran Theological Seminary, and St. Paul Graduate School
Tokyo, Japan

LIFE CONTEXT OF THE INTERPRETATION

I live in Japan, a country that plays a significant role in globalizing the free market economy that undergirds capitalism. As is well known, Japan has colonized underdeveloped countries and benefited from hiring laborers at low wages in these countries. I cannot practice my hermeneutics of the Scriptures without critically analyzing both my own socio-cultural context and the political and economic context of my country in relation to other countries. I cannot forget the Asian countries that my country has invaded and colonized, in the past through war, and recently as one of the significant economic powers. I must painfully acknowledge the history of Japanese relations with other Asian countries. I must understand the victimization, pain, and suffering that other Asians endure and acknowledge my country's guilt.

At the same time, under the all-encompassing umbrella of its ally, the United States, Japan has recently been in danger of losing its autonomy. After 9/11, the government has been trying to replace the most important article of our constitution, Article 9, which declares that Japan will never fight another war, with a new law. I might say that Japan is invisibly colonized by the power of the United States, and thus Japan is both a colonizing and a colonized nation.

To be politically or culturally critical of my own country, especially its government, directly raises another serious question, namely the meaning of discipleship in the Christian churches in our country. If we want to dialogue with the Scriptures, we must expose ourselves to the political, social, economic, cultural, and religious situations of the ancient world where the writings were born and where the people did not necessarily enjoy peace and justice. Through this process, I would like to learn what the Gospel of Mark might have to say to Christians who seek peace and justice for the world and yet who live in an oppressive country like mine.

Because of my interests and concerns, my study focuses on the power relationships at work in certain texts Mark recorded in his gospel. What kinds of powers are covertly working as a hidden agenda underneath the easily grasped open, surface agenda? Under the oppression that people experienced in the time of Jesus and the early Christian communities, what did Jesus teach the disciples to be? What did Mark intend to convey to his community of faith, a community that was also assaulted by various oppressive powers that complicated the believers' lives? I would like to dig into the texts of Mark so that I may discern and embrace the urgent task that Christian churches in my country

Hisako Kinukawa is co-director of the Center for Feminist Theology and Ministry in Japan. She teaches feminist liberation theology, biblical interpretation, and gender issues in the Scriptures at International Christian University, Lutheran Theological Seminary, and St. Paul Graduate School in Tokyo. Recently she has taught feminist hermeneutics at San Francisco Theological Seminary (2002–2004). She is a coordinating committee member of the Asian Women's Resource Center [Malaysia] and on the Editorial Advisory Committee that oversees the Asian feminist journal, *In God's Image*. Her publications include *Women and Jesus in Mark: A Japanese Feminist Perspective* (1994) and many articles.

are called to undertake. My reading of Mark will also question the internalized and individualized faith commonly found among many believers in our churches to help them hear what Mark has to say about economic and political powers. Hearing this message, Christian believers in Japan's churches might adopt a post-colonial and post-imperial discipleship in line with Jesus' teaching.

CONTEXTUAL COMMENT

An Overview of Mark

For this, we must first recognize, with Ched Myers and others, that the Gospel of Mark constantly concerns itself with the establishment of a new order: the kingdom of God. In line with this concern, we can outline the Gospel as follows (adapted from Myers):

1:1-20 Prologue and Jesus' call to discipleship: a subversive call and mission;

1:21–3:35 Jesus' assault on the Jewish social order in Capernaum;

4:1-36 Jesus' sermon in parables on revolutionary patience;

4:37–8:21 Jesus' miracles as construction of a new social order and the execution of John;

8:22–9:30 Second call to discipleship, the courtroom, and the cross;

9:30–10:52 Teaching on the non-violent construction of a new social, economic, and political order;

11:1–13:3 Jesus' confrontation with the powers in Jerusalem;

13:4-37 Jesus' apocalyptic sermon on revolutionary patience;

14:1–16:8 Arrest, trials, execution by the powers, and resurrection;

I have chosen to focus my comments on three narratives, Mark 5:1-20, 7:24-30, and 9:14-29, which are usually categorized as miracle stories. Yet, none of them seems to be recorded simply for the sake of telling the miracles. The believers might have first transmitted these stories as oral traditions about the healing miracles they experienced. However, Mark may have used them with a subtextual or hidden agenda that I will attempt to disclose.

The Story of the Gerasene Demoniac: Mark 5:1-20

Issues We See in the Story

As we read this story, we are first astonished to encounter: 1) an ex-tended description of the demoniac's condition and behavior, and 2) the strange power that the demons have over this man. When the demons claim that their name is "Legion," we first suspect that the story may refer to the Roman Empire's colonial and military dominion. Thus, I propose to pursue the following questions: What kinds of power relationships are at work in this story? Why does the story tell us that the exorcism by Jesus took place in a foreign setting? Who is this Gerasene man with unclean spirits? Who are the people who ask Jesus to leave the region?

The Region of the Gerasenes

The story tells us that Jesus and his followers crossed the lake to the region of the Gerasenes. As many have pointed out, the city of Gerasa is located some fifty-five kilometers or thirty miles southeast of the Sea of Galilee. Gerasa is one of the ten cities of the Decapolis, and the story seems to identify it with the whole of Decapolis (5:20).

Decapolis was a loose confederation of territories created by the Roman Empire when Pompey integrated Syria into the Empire in 63 B.C.E. when the Hellenistic cities on the east side of the river Jordan were taken from Jewish control. The Roman legions stayed in the region to keep peace. Gerasa was one of the main Hellenistic cities that prospered through commerce. Jews continued to reside in the region. This historical background may be enough for us to suspect that the story reflects the tensions between the people of the Decapolis and the Roman legions, between the people of the Decapolis and their Jewish neighbors, and between Palestinian Jews and Rome as a colonial power.

The Demoniac:
a Man with Unclean Spirits

The story describes the situation of the sick man very vividly, repeating the gruesome words *chains* (three times), *shackles* (twice), and *tombs* (twice). The man is violently out of self-control; he behaves like a wild animal and even injures himself. The people's efforts to keep him chained and shackled are in vain. He continues to desecrate the graveyard, a sacred area, by living among the tombs, the space of the dead. The social and economic implications are clear: he has lost all relationship with his family; he has been cut off from all human contacts; he certainly feeds himself by begging from the people who visit the tombs to venerate their dead ancestors and relatives or taking the food brought for the dead (Deut 26:14; Job 4:17 Ps 106:28). Though living, he is treated as dead. Physically isolated from his kin, totally marginalized from the community and considered unclean, he is socially alienated as "other." In sum, he symbolizes society's outcasts.

The story also shows how utterly subject to the extraordinary force of the unclean spirits the man is. Who are these unclean spirits? The story states that the possessed man ran out to Jesus (5:6-7). Jesus, however, spoke not to the man, but to the unclean spirit, "Come out of the man, you unclean spirit" (5:8). After the detailed description of the man's wild behavior, the unclean spirits—the cause of the man's sickness—are the center of attention. For the readers in the Hellenistic world and Jewish society this was not surprising; exorcism was a common practice.

Some scholars point out possible social or cultural allusions: the possessed or mentally disturbed man might symbolize disabled people unable to maintain proper social relations in their community. The man's abnormal behavior might be his way of struggling with harsh circumstances. Or the man might represent someone with a mind colonized by demons, someone who has internalized the collective anxiety of a community under social, political, economic, or religious oppression. A subjugated community might repress its anguish and turn on itself, as symbolized by the possessed man. This latter interpretation is plausible and supported by the way in which the story describes the total control that the demons have upon the man. Thus, Jesus' exorcism can be read as a politically symbolic action against severe exploitation that prevents people from living decent human lives.

The Demon whose Name Is Legion

The reality of this exploitation becomes clearer when the demon replies, "My name is Legion; for we are many" (5:9). The name reveals the origin of the social, political, and economic oppression at the center of the story: the Roman Empire and its military might be stationed in the Decapolis. Usually a legion consists of two thousand to three thousand infantry, 120 cavalry, and associated auxiliaries organized into numerous cohorts and squadrons. When the story says that the spirits request "Send us into the swine; let us enter them" (5:12) and that, when they did so, "the herd, numbering about two thousand, rushed down the steep bank into the sea, and were drowned in the sea" (5:13), the story suggests that Mark chose the words *legion* and *swine* to mock the oppressing Romans. Some-times swine functions as a metaphor for foreigners, because most Jews avoid swine as unclean and inedible (Lev 11:7-8; Deut 14:8; Isa 65:4). Since a herd usually does not include more than three hundred swine, this herd functions symbolically. And since the number two thousand approximately corresponds to the size of a legion, it is another indication that this herd symbolizes a legion, possibly the Tenth Legion Fretensis, that was stationed in Syria since 6 C.E. and fought against Jerusalem in the 66-70 war (Theissen 1991, 110). This legion's standard included the image of a boar, and thus the boar/swine was quite possibly part of the legion's religious rituals.

The Aftermath of the Exorcism

The unclean spirits, "Legion," were exorcised from the man and driven into the swine that were drowned in the sea. The story states, "The swineherds ran off and told it in the city and in the country" (5:14). The swineherds are astonished and shocked. Considering the loss of their huge herd, for them this is an economic disaster. As hired hands of the owners of the herd, they will lose their livelihood and might be held responsible for the loss.

The owners, despite their higher economic and social status, will also be significantly affected by this economic loss. They were benefiting from Rome's colonial rule. For them, the presence of the legion to which they supplied food guaranteed a secure life. Despite Rome's oppressive control, these owners, and even the swineherds, were not eager to see a change of the status quo.

Yet the story implicitly insists that the removal of the Roman colonial control is imperative for the demoniac and thus for society's outcasts; they need to be liberated. But removing the legion threatens others; it would destabilize the whole structure of society and bring political dangers. Therefore the story continues: "They began to beg him to leave their neighborhood" (5:17). Those begging Jesus to leave are most certainly the swineherds' owners and keepers. Their pleading reveals their ambivalent feelings. They may desire the demise of the legion, the Roman control, yet they feel threatened by the resulting social changes.

In any situation of colonial and imperial oppression, whether during the time of the Roman Empire or today in Japan and Asia, the feelings of the colonized (whether politically or economically) toward the colonial powers that control their lives and their societies are always complex. This text contrasts the needs of the social outcast, the "other," the demoniac, with those who belong to the society and its class strata.

Who is the Gerasene Demoniac?

Who is the man with the unclean spirits? Is he a Jew or a foreigner? Since the Jews also lived in the region, he could be a Jew. Theissen (1991, 110) thinks he is a foreigner because the Jews regarded swine as unclean and disgusting. If he is a foreigner, we may say the story represents the beginning of Jesus' mission to Gentiles. In either case, I take the story as reflecting the torment, suffering, and pain caused by Roman oppression and the Jewish antipathy toward the empire, especially among those "others" marginalized by the rulers. There must be a reason for Mark and his community to express this antipathy in the guise of a healing story in a foreign setting. Galileans, mostly peasants known for being rebellious against Rome, might have been under stricter surveillance, especially if Galilee was the location of Mark's community.

Powers at Work

It is quite plausible to read the story as criticizing imperial/colonial hegemony. It is the hidden story, hidden from the Romans, of the alienated and the outcast's ardent desire for a drastic transformation of society. It is also the hidden story, hidden from the other colonized people, of the desire that the elite (the upper class of the hierarchical society) have to keep the status quo. These elite do not overlook the small, subtle signs of social transformation and diligently suppress them while they may easily control them.

Hierarchical imperial societies typically benefit a small elite group at the expense of the vast and impoverished majority. This was the case in the Decapolis and in Palestine under Roman colonial rule. This has also been the case in many Asian countries under past Japanese military rule and presently in the Western and Japanese free market economy.

Jesus stands with the victims of imperial oppression. His exorcism of the demon is a symbolic subversive political action against the oppressive occupation. In such situations, it is always dangerous to speak explicitly about resistance or subversion, so it might be prudent to speak about the troubles in a foreign land, here in Gerasa, but the message is clear.

As Jesus told several other persons he had healed, he told the man to go home to his friends, even though the man wanted to remain with Jesus (5:18-19). For the alienated, those labeled "others" by their communities and cut off from ordinary human relationships, it is most important to be reintegrated into their original communities. As Mark tells it, "He went away and began to proclaim in the Decapolis how much Jesus had done for him; and everyone was amazed" (5:20). The story keeps silent on what happened to his community after he went home or whether he became a follower of Jesus' movement. Thus for Mark the focus of the story is not on Jesus' foreign mission, but on the liberation of the "other," the person who is an outcast.

Conclusions

This story is heavily laden with power relationships. We recognize in it multiple levels of power struggles related to political, economic, social, religious, and ethnic conflicts:

1) Jesus' exorcism of the demoniac is a symbolic political action in the guise of healing. Through it he challenged Roman military control of the Decapolis and Palestine and symbolically destroyed Roman imperial domination.

2) The oppression was the severest for those at the bottom of the class ladder. The man with an unclean spirit calls our attention to the destitute situation of such people, who are easily victimized and receive very little benefit from the social system.

3) The destruction of the herd has brought serious economic damage to those benefiting from the imperial system. The swineherds and the swine owners exemplify those whose livelihood is tied to the social system and who are threatened by any change in the hierarchical society, even as they too suffer under its yoke.

4) Jesus sided with the expendables and

outcast, against the elite who benefit from this oppressive colonial situation, and thus he introduces tremendous social instability.

5) The destruction of the swine possibly affected religious rites and rituals (Mark 5:11–17). This suggests that the adherents and institutions of religions cannot stay neutral in political, economic, and social turbulence.

6) Jewish-Roman ethnic tension might also be present as a textual undercurrent. Such ethnic tensions are often hidden and exacerbated because colonized and subjugated people do not have effective means to address them.

Implications for our Churches

This story invites us to look at our present situation of economic imperialism and to recognize the power struggles behind its many political, economic, social, religious, and ethnic conflicts.

Historically, Japan colonized other Asian countries. Japan has now followed the U.S. request to send self-defense troops to the Middle East. The layers of colonizer/colonized continue as the economic power of Japan continues to oppress other Asian countries. Few Third World nations include Japan as part of the Third World.

Our churches have overtly and covertly raised their voices against violence of any form, especially war. Now, our churches are seriously challenged to exorcise the demons from our society that tempt us to change our constitution that prohibits our participation in war.

The Story of the Syrophoenician Woman (Mark 7:24-30)

Mark sets the story of the woman whom Jesus met when he "went away to the region of Tyre" (7:24) in the rural hinterlands surrounding the city of Tyre, a city located on an island just off the coast in the Mediterranean Sea. The woman is introduced as "a Gentile, of Syrophoenician origin" (7:26). The story begins with the woman's plea for the healing of her little daughter who has an unclean spirit.

Exegetical Concerns

Among the many questions that the story raises, we will focus on two that are inter-related:

1) Why did Mark put such harsh words in Jesus' mouth in response to the woman's plea? "Let the children be fed first, for it is not fair to take the children's food and throw it to the dogs" (7:27). The children represent the Jews and the dogs foreigners, including the woman and her daughter. Jesus overtly rejects her plea.

2) Why does Jesus speak about bread (*artos*), even though he knows her main concern is in the healing of her sick child? How does Mark relate healing to table fellowship?

By raising these two questions I already suggest that this story does more than report a miracle. Once again my concern is to uncover the power relationships between the dominant and subordinate by determining the story's social location.

Social Location of the Story

In the time of Jesus, both Galilee and Tyre were occupied by the Roman Empire. Despite imperial and colonial rule, the cities of Tyre and Sidon were two of the wealthiest and most important ports on the coast. In contrast, the residents of Galilee, mainly peasants, suffered under a threefold oppression: (1) Roman imperialism, (2) the Herodean monarchy subservient to Rome as client kings, and (3) temple politics in Judea. Jonathan L. Reed draws our attention to the fact that Tyre was closer to Capernaum than Capernaum was to Jerusalem (2000, 185). The region of Tyre might not have appeared foreign or distant to Galileans. Villages inhabited by Jews, Syrians, and Phoenicians were certainly intermingled in the area where the hinterland of Tyre bordered Galilee, with no clear border separating the two.

The Woman as a Greek

The woman is introduced as culturally Greek and ethnically Syrophoenician. The designation *Greek* might signal that she would have known the Greek language and probably was Hellenistic in culture. Yet the word Greek might simply indicate that she was a foreigner, and not a Jew—as in most New Testament texts. Mark might have wanted to suggest that Jesus opened up the possibility of foreign mission. The location of Jesus in the Tyrian hinterland suggests that the woman might have been from one of the peripheral villages, where people's lives were not as easy as in the wealthy urban centers.

The Devouring City of Tyre

The city of Tyre itself was well known for:

> its wealth based on metal work, the production of purple dye and an extensive trade with the whole Mediterranean region. Its money was one of the most stable currencies in circulation at this period. . . . This was certainly one reason why the temple treasury was kept in Tyrian coin, even though this meant accepting the fact that the coins of Tyre depicted the god Melkart. (Theissen 1991, 73)

Because the city of Tyre had very little space for farming on its island, "The Galilean hinterland and the rural territory belonging to the city (partly settled by Jews) were the 'breadbasket' of the metropolis of Tyre" (Theissen 1991, 74). Rich city dwellers purchased most of the produce, while the peasants in the hinterlands were always in want. Galilean peasants must have been resentful when they saw their agricultural produce sold to the highest bidders from urban Tyre, while they experienced a constant shortage of food and money, even though they labored from dawn to dusk. Tyre's economic drain on the region compounded its threefold oppression by the Romans, the Herodeans, and the temple. The Galilean peasants were deprived of a stable life.

The Impact of Jesus' Harsh Words

Taking into consideration the bitter economic relationship between the affluent city of Tyre and the exploited Galilee, Jesus' bitter words thrown to the woman would have had a powerful impact. These words, offensive as they were to the woman, also reflected the humiliating power relationship that Galileans suffered from urban Tyrians. Regardless of the woman's actual economic status, she seems to be identified with wealthy Tyre in some way. Jesus' words could mean: "First let the mouths of the poor people in Galilee be satisfied, for it is not good to take poor people's food and throw it to the rich Tyrians in the city." The words would overtly express the reality of the destitute Galilean peasants and show their resistance against the power exercised by the urban people of Tyre. By comparing the Tyrians, who devoured Galilee's agrarian produce, to dogs, Jesus may have expressed the popular feeling of the poor Galilean peasants toward the rich, Hellenistic, elitist Tyrians.

The Woman as a Syrophoenician

Yet if the Syrophoenician woman in this story is from one of the villages in the hinterland of Tyre, as is plausible, the woman with her sick child might not be rich or so privileged. Actually, the woman might be herself socially ostracized because of the unclean spirit in her child.

If this is the case, it is easier to understand why she is not offended by Jesus' words. From her attitude we learn she does not identify herself with the target of Jesus' harsh words. She is from a village in the vicinity of Galilee where her daily life may not be so different from that of Galilean peasants.

She enters the house where Jesus is and falls down at his feet, asking for a favor. Just like the demon possessed man (5:6) and Jairus, the synagogue leader (5:22-23), she assumes a subordinate position in relation to Jesus. However, in contrast to Jesus' quick response to these two men, Jesus shows great reluctance to grant her request.

Why this rebuff? The usual explanations are not convincing to me. Did Jesus rebuff her because she is a foreigner? But earlier in Mark Jesus healed a foreigner, the Gerasene demoniac in the Decapolis (5:1-20). Tolbert suggests that Jesus rebuffs her as "the opportunity for her faith to be fully revealed" (1989, 185). But her faith is not mentioned

in Mark, and the only concern she expresses is about her child. Some say she is rebuffed because she is a woman and that this passage reflects the sexism of the time. Yet the analyses above indicate that there are other concerns besides gender at work in this story.

If this metaphor reflects the power relationships between Galilee and Tyre, Jesus uses it to side with the destitute Galilean peasants and thus defends them against the Tyrians who benefit from exploiting the Galilean peasants. Her response is important because "The woman, though denigrated by Jesus, speaks in a supportive and affirmative way, for she is concerned with maintaining the relationship" (Kwok Pui-lan 1995, 74).

Toward a Dialogical Interdependence

Since she resides in a hinterland part of Tyre, the Syrophoenician woman identifies herself more closely with the Galilean peasants, and thus does not take Jesus' words personally, but as a rebuff of the populace of Tyre as a whole. In response, she says, "Yes, it is so, but, sir, even the dogs under the table eat the children's crumbs" (7:28; author's translation [a.t.]). She acknowledges that the Galilean peasants ought to have priority, since they are deprived of food because of Tyrian economic domination. At the same time, she reminds Jesus that other kinds of dogs also need to be fed, namely destitute Gentiles like her and her child. In this way, she raises a serious question to Jesus: Can he totally ignore a sick child while talking about feeding the children of Israel? It is appropriate that Jesus defends the needy children of Israel. But in this case, the woman insists, Jesus should also defend her and her sick child. She insists that Jesus' harsh words do not apply to her and her child. To the contrary, since she and her child suffer like the children of Israel, if Jesus does not feed them he will contribute to their oppression. Therefore she does not relent. She leads the dialogue toward an interdependent relationship among Jesus, the children of Israel, and herself and her child.

Listening to Jesus, she is made aware of the fact that she is from Tyre, a city noted for depriving the Galilean peasants of food by forcing them to sell their produce to Tyre. On the other hand, in hearing Jesus protect the "others" in Galilee, she is made aware of the fact that she is also one of these "others" in Tyre's society. Therefore she asks Jesus to expand his preferential option for the "others" to the "others" in Tyre, by asking how it is possible for Jesus to exclude her and her child from his table community. She asks Jesus to model equality in his treatment of the destitute. Had she not experienced being the "other" in her society, she would not be able to be as confident as she is in asking Jesus' help. Her tenacity can be read as evidence that she is neither rich nor privileged.

Change in the Balance of Power

Jesus fully accepts her request, "For saying that, you may go. . . . " (7:29). Jesus affirms her, as if he has learned a new lesson from her. In the first part of the encounter between Jesus and the woman, the balance of power is apparently in favor of Jesus. Toward the end it is reversed. The last verse, "So she went home, found the child lying on the bed, and the demon gone" (7:30) does not say anything about her faith, conversion, or religion. We must abstain from concluding she has become the first foreign female Christian regardless of how much Mark wants the audience to read the story in this way by placing it in the context of table fellowship. This story is not originally about table fellowship, but about the power relationships between Tyrian urbanites and Galilean peasants.

Conclusion

Two elements, the political and economic relationships between the regions of Tyre and Galilee, and Tyre's oppressive power over Galilean peasants, provide a context for understanding why Jesus throws such bitter words at the woman. His words reflect the urgent need of Galileans to secure food for their daily lives. They reveal the story to be about a most basic issue: the unfair distribution of food among rival colonies within the Roman Empire. The woman's words, however, demonstrate that she rejects being used as a foil in Jesus' conflict with the affluent urban Tyrians. Her words reveal that Tyrian society is also hierarchical and therefore Tyrians are not monochromatic. Instead she identifies herself with the destitute Galilean peasants, as also one of the destitute whose needs must be met. When Jesus heals her daughter, he acknowledges her claim. Only after we see her need fulfilled may we begin talking about the story as encouraging a table fellowship inclusive of all those in need, wherever they are.

Implications for our Churches

As Jesus heard the voice of the Syrophoenician woman, the churches in Japan might do well to hear the voice of the deprived and the poor in foreign lands, whatever their faith, who also struggle to defend the rights of the deprived in their own countries.

Through encountering this text, Japanese churches who claim to advocate for society's alienated may be made aware that they themselves are part of the affluent, dominant power over developing countries just as Tyre dominated Galilee. Our exposure to the influx of migrant workers from the suffering parts of the world also awakens us to our mission of advocacy, just as the Syrophoenician woman reminded Jesus of his mission. This particular story reminds us of the complicated situation in which our churches find themselves. Our commitment to discipleship is not easy to fulfill if our churches stick to the middle-class, individualistic faith that preserves their status quo in wealth and stability. This story is perceived as threatening to most such churches.

One question remains: what is faithful discipleship?

The Disciples, the Father and his Mute-deaf Son, and Jesus: Faith and Prayer (9:14-29)

The Context of the Story in Mark

The context of this miracle story in Mark seems quite significant. This story follows

Jesus' first passion prediction, Peter's negative reaction to it despite his earlier confession that Jesus is the Messiah (8:29, 32), and Jesus' teaching on discipleship (including the transfiguration) (8:27–9:13). The disciples have remained mute and deaf after Jesus' announcement of his suffering, death, and resurrection. Their crisis reveals an incredible lack of comprehension concerning Jesus' impending fate and the meaning of discipleship. We need to read the miracle story against this extraordinarily strained circumstance.

The Miracle Story (9:14-29)

Meyers observes that this story conforms to the model of the previous healing and exorcism stories (1990, 254). It has the same parts and character types: miracle-worker, sick person, demon, companion, crowd, opponents, and disciples. However, the dreadful description of the symptoms of the son's fits is surprising. They are almost as horrifying as those of the Gerasene demoniac. But here they are vividly described four times with diverse, striking terms. "He has a spirit that makes him unable to speak; and whenever it seizes him, it dashes him down; and he foams and grinds his teeth and becomes rigid" (9:17-18; see also 9:20, 9:22, and 9:26). Why does Mark repeatedly provide such detailed explanations about the patient's symptoms and the audience's fear and despair? Once again, Mark's primary intention does not seem to be simply to report another miraculous healing.

The son's life is literally threatened by death, and he is under the control of a power far beyond his will and consciousness. He is totally helpless, unable to manage himself or to have human relationships. The repeated description of the boy's fits also suggests his father's hopelessness, as both of them are certainly socially ostracized. After seeing the disciples' inability to cast out the spirit, the father may have reached the stage where he cannot but be skeptical about any possibility of healing, even when he asks for Jesus' help. He hesitates: "If you are able to do anything," and then continues, "have pity on us

and help us" (9:22). As the Greek word for *have pity, splanchnistheis* expresses, the father looks for someone who would share their pain, ordeal and agony—as, possibly, nobody has done before.

Disciples

Mark records that early in his ministry (3:15), Jesus gave the twelve disciples authority to cast out demons and they successfully cast out many demons and anointed with oil many who were sick and cured them (6:7). However, the father reports that they could not cast the spirit out (9:18). Literally, he says that they were not strong enough to cast the spirit out—using the same word, ischuos, used in 5:4 (no one was strong enough to subdue the demon) and in 3:27 (no one can enter a strong man's house and plunder his property without first tying up the strong man). Only Jesus has this strength. But what kind of strength is it? Why can Jesus cast out the demon? How can the disciples become like Jesus?

The story seems to suggest that the boy's incurable symptoms are the cause for the disciples' failure to heal him. But there is certainly more. In the previous chapter, Jesus told his disciples that he chose powerlessness, suffering, and dying on the cross—a statement that is absolute nonsense to the disciples. They cannot grasp the real meaning of Jesus' statements. Yet in the story Mark keeps reminding the reader that Jesus will soon be rejected and killed.

When Jesus sees their failure to exorcise the boy, he alludes to his impending death even as he expresses exasperation and anger (9:19). Mark seems to tell this story to highlight the tremendous gap in understanding between Jesus and the disciples. Consequently, our attention must shift from the healing to the issue of discipleship.

The boy's incurable symptoms may prefigure the life-threatening circumstances in which the disciples will be cast if they want to be Jesus' true disciples. It is a situation in which they feel useless and powerless and want to flee. What will enable them to break through the deadlock and overcome their fear? Jesus gives the answer in his brief teaching about faith (9:19, 23) and prayer (9:29).

The Father as a Model of Faith

Mark seems to present the boy's father as a model of faith. To the father who does not have complete confidence, Jesus replies: "If you are able!—All things can be done for the one who believes" (9:23). What matters is to believe. But what does faith entail? Let us consider how Mark describes the father.

The father had looked for someone who would share the pain, ordeal, and agony he and his son endure. This means that his real need was for a community of empathy; such a community would bring wholeness to his son's life. When this is recognized, we can see why he said, "I believe; help my unbelief!" (9:24). He vacillates between "unbelief" that reflects his miserable experiences and his son's ordeals, because they are deprived of a community of empathy, and "belief" that reflects his deeply held wish for empathy for the sake of re-gaining his son's wholeness. His brief cry expresses the true nature and ambivalence of faith—daring to believe when the situation appears desperate. By putting his trust in Jesus, he symbolically chooses the same difficult way of accepting suffering, death, and resurrection as Jesus does. We can interpret the description of the healing as verification of the father's faith. During the healing, the boy suffers terrible convulsions, appears to be a corpse, is thought to be dead (9:26), and then is "raised up" by Jesus (9:27). The father thus paradigmatically exemplifies the reality of faith as the struggle to keep belief despite unbelief, to keep faith in the resurrection even as one accepts suffering and death.

Disciples in Need of Prayer

Confronted by the unprecedented difficulty of healing the boy's serious sickness, the disciples are bewildered and can only argue (9:14). Afterward when they ask Jesus privately why they could not cast the spirit out, he teaches them the need for prayer: "This kind [of spirit] can come out only through prayer" (9:29). What kind of prayer do the disciples need? How do we relate faith and prayer in this context?

The narrative does not explain what kind of prayer Jesus is referring to. But its context clarifies this. The teaching about prayer (9:29) is quickly followed by the second passion prediction (9:31), which draws our attention to the earlier prediction of the suffering, death, and resurrection of Jesus. Jesus' life is the paradigmatic prayer. For the disciples prayer might be to "deny themselves and take up their cross and follow" Jesus (8:34). The type of prayer implied in this story is not something silent or static, but active. This is not to deny that meditative or solitary moments of prayer were important for Jesus. But by this story Mark advocates the type of prayer through which the disciples show that they are willing to "lose their life" for the Lord's sake and "for the sake of the gospel" (8:35).

Where do the disciples find the courage or confidence to take up such suffering and the cross and to identify with Jesus? Where do the disciples find the courage to pray for the boy and his father by taking upon themselves their own suffering? Jesus exemplifies through his life the way to stand with those who are outcast, ostracized, marginalized, and suppressed so much so that, like the deaf-mute boy, they lose their voice. Thus the story clarifies why it is not easy to be disciples of Jesus. Taking up, through prayer, the suffering of others who are reduced to silence by powers that oppress them is also taking up one's cross; it may cost the disciples their lives.

Through this story, Mark challenged the unconscientious disciples in his community of faith to transform themselves in their faith and prayer. The fact that there are only male characters in this particular story may suggest that Mark is more concerned to encourage male believers in his faith community to have faith, to pray, and to take up leadership.

Conclusion and Implications for our Churches

We can now see why Mark extensively records the son's symptoms. They symbolize the harsh circumstances Jesus' disciples must embrace to follow the paradigm of the suffering life of Jesus.

The story in 9:14-29 is no longer a miracle or exorcism story; it is a story showing the disciples how to surmount despair through faith and prayer. The vacillation of faith modeled by the father can result in resignation, abandoning any hope to change or transform an overwhelming situation. We often feel this hopelessness today because our lives are so dominated by the invisible powers manifested by the patriarchal and imperial society in which we live. No new vision of life is possible, or so it seems. Through this story Mark tries to teach disciples how to overcome this hopelessness, this resignation to the status quo, and this unbelief that leads to giving up the way of suffering.

One question remains: Should we say that faith is the strength to realize healing? And if so, what kind of faith is effective? What are the qualities that faith needs to have? The question arises when we hear Jesus deplore the little faith of the generation (9:19).

The cry of the father (9:22) may be valued as an expression of the reality of our faith when we cannot fully believe, even though we deeply wish to believe. At the same time, we must realize that the father's cry also reflects his refusal to accept his son's situation. His only wish is that his son be cured, a wish that Jesus fulfills in this story.

There are numerous disabled or mentally disturbed persons around us. The reality is that most of them are not cured, even though they may get some aid offered by medicine and other methods. Many are exposed to various kinds of inconvenience caused by the structure of life designed according to the standards of the able. They often suffer from discrimination that involves their families as well. What if the sick and their families are told by faith communities, following the example of this story, that their faith is not strong enough? Sometimes these differently-abled persons

are simply told how they are a blessing of God and are left alone. Often we fail to raise the question of what is expected from faith communities or disciples who surround the differently-abled or mentally disturbed persons. It is important to note on this point that the story in Mark asks the disciples, and not the father, to commit themselves to a new way of life through following Jesus.

In sum, the story challenges us to transform ourselves, our faith communities, and our societies so that the differently-abled and mentally disturbed can be accepted as they are and supported so that they may live their lives as comfortably as others. The story asks each of us to reflect critically upon our faith and prayer and to assess whether we really struggle against the despair and obstacles that may tempt us to give up on following Jesus. It can be a very personal struggle that requires us to fight against a spirit residing within us that makes us deaf and mute. The spirit that has been in us "from childhood" may have deteriorated our minds to the point that we submit to the powers that be. The story challenges us to believe that the life-giving power is stronger than the death-threatening demonic power and encourages us to choose the life-giving way that Jesus exemplifies through his whole life. Then a new vision of faith communities as inclusive communities becomes possible.

The story suggests that such an inclusive community cannot be engendered without a resolute willingness to act. The story describes the reality we face as full of obstacles that undermine our hope of bringing about the realization of our ideal. Mark knew from experience how much effort and dedication is required to break down the boundaries and to keep a community fully inclusive. Thus for Mark the ultimate model could only be Jesus' suffering life unto death for us disciples. From our own experience we can readily see that innumerable lives marked by suffering unto death is the cost required for bringing about a globally inclusive community.

CONCLUSION

What are the overall implications of these texts for today's Christian church in Japan?

First, in every sphere of life, political, economic, social, cultural, religious, and ethnic, the Roman Empire or the modern American and Japanese-led free market economy functions as the major power. We should not read the texts without acknowledging the effects, both the good and bad, of this power.

Second, we notice both in the ancient text and in today's world the differences in power among the colonized. Power struggles emerge among rival colonies, producing another type of hierarchy under the umbrella of the big power. Such internecine strife among the rival colonies prevents any significant challenge to the dominant power.

Third, each colonized nation establishes a similar hierarchical social structure within itself, with a small elite class that controls society and benefits itself at the expense of the others. This elite class strives to maintain the status quo and to keep the social structure secure, thus producing an oppressed majority. The most discriminated against, those at the bottom of society's ladder, are despised and subjugated as "others."

Fourth, in both the ancient and contemporary settings, discipleship is an invitation to to seek and struggle for the wholeness of every life in society. As disciples we are asked to cultivate a spiritual perception as to who are the most alienated and silenced. We are then asked to commit ourselves to empathize deeply with and share in the suffering of society's most destitute and invisible so that they may regain their life. This struggle will cause social turmoil as it touches the taboo, the despised outsider. Such discipleship follows the way of the cross as modeled by Jesus. His life exemplifies in the most condensed way how true faith and prayer may work.

Through this contextual analysis, these three stories reveal to us the life-giving gospel and the reality of a struggling faith, a teaching needed both by Mark's ancient faith community and by our contemporary churches.

BIBLIOGRAPHY

Carter, Warren. *Matthew and the Margins: A Sociopolitical and Religious Reading.* Bible and Liberation Series. Maryknoll, N.Y.: Orbis, 2000.

Fredriksen, Paula. *Jesus of Nazareth, King of the Jews: A Jewish Life and the Emergence of Christianity.* New York: Knopf, 1999.

Johnson, Earl S., Jr. "Mark 5:1-20: The Other Side." *IBS* 20 (April 1988): 50-74.

Kinukawa, Hisako. *Women and Jesus in Mark: A Japanese Feminist Perspective.* Bible and Liberation Series. Maryknoll, N.Y.: Orbis, 1994.

Kwok Pui-lan. *Discovering the Bible in the Non-Biblical World.* Bible and Liberation Series. Maryknoll, N.Y.: Orbis, 1995.

Myers, Ched. *Binding the Strong Man: A Political Reading of Mark's Story of Jesus.* Maryknoll, N.Y.: Orbis, 1990.

Perkins, Pheme. "Mark." Pp. 507-733 in *NIB* 8. Nashville: Abingdon, 1994.

Reed, Jonathan L. *Archaeology and the Galilean Jesus: A Re-examination of the Evidence.* Harrisburg, Penn.: Trinity, 2000.

Theissen, Gerd. *The Gospels in Context: Social and Political History in the Synoptic Tradition.* Trans. Linda M. Maloney. Minneapolis: Fortress, 1991.

———. *The Miracle Stories of the Early Christian Tradition.* Trans. Francis McDonagh. Ed. John Riches. Philadelphia: Fortress, 1983.

Tolbert, Mary Ann. *Sowing the Gospel: Mark's World in Literary-Historical Perspective.* Minneapolis: Fortress, 1989.

Wolmarans, J. L. P. "Who Asked Jesus to Leave the Territory of Gerasa (Mark 5:17)?" *Neot* 28 (1994): 87-92.

MARK'S HEALING STORIES IN AN AIDS CONTEXT

Musa W. Dube

University of Botswana, Gaborone, Botswana, and Scripps College, Claremont, Calif., USA

LIFE CONTEXT OF THE INTERPRETATION

Botswana: Healing Where There Is No Healing

As an activist and advocate for those living with HIV and AIDS in my home country of Botswana, and a professor of New Testament at the University of Botswana, I teach the gospels' healing narratives in a place where every student knows somebody—a relative, a friend, a neighbor, a colleague, a classmate—who is dying or has died of AIDS. The incurable nature of the disease, the prohibitive expense of treatment for it, and the devastation that it wreaks on even the most basic social interactions form the framework from which I read these stories. When one meets a friend after some time apart, and reads in the text of that friend's body the clear indications of AIDS, there seems to be no appropriate response. To speak of the disease is to force the friend to choose between facing the social stigma of AIDS or denying it, while not speaking of the disease makes all other interaction— even a greeting as innocuous as "good morning, how are you?"—cruelly absurd. The moment of meeting a person living with HIV and AIDS becomes a moment of reading a social text written in the invisible air, with a million conflicts. At the root of all of these tough encounters is the social stigma that initially associated HIV and AIDS with sexual immorality, the fear of infection, and the ugly face of death. This stigma has led many AIDS patients to be closed away and secretly kept by relatives, a fact that adds psychological strain to their physical state. The general public, shielded from seeing the truth about AIDS, becomes increasingly unprepared to deal with their own context. Consequently, those with HIV and AIDS who dare to walk outside tend to shock the average person, leading to lies, fears, and sometimes flight. One conclusion is clear about reading the social text of HIV and AIDS: we may not be all infected but we are all affected.

Analysis of the Context

For regions like Botswana that are highly infected by HIV and AIDS, the contemporary reader of the Synoptic Gospels cannot help but be stunned to find a Jesus who has extraordinary healing power over all diseases—for no money! Most Botswana have heard that some medical advancement allows HIV and AIDS patients to live longer and to clear the virus from the system, as long as they keep taking the cocktail drugs. Such medication, unfortunately, is too expensive for most individuals in the Two-Thirds World; hence AIDS is here virtually untreatable.

Musa W. Dube, formerly an associate professor at the University of Botswana, then a consultant on HIV/AIDS and theology for the World Council of Churches in Africa, now teaches at The Claremont Colleges, Scripps College. Her many publications include the following books: *Postcolonial Feminist Interpretations of the Bible* (2000); *HIV/AIDS and the Curriculum: Methods of Integrating HIV/AIDS in Theological Programs* (WCC 2003); *AfricaPraying: A Handbook of HIV/AIDS Sensitive Sermons and Liturgy* (WCC 2004); and the forthcoming *Grant Me Justice: HIV/AIDS and Gender Readings of the Bible*. The present article has been published in a different and longer form in the collection *Reading Communities, Reading Scripture: Essays in Honor of Daniel Patte* (Gary A. Phillips and Nicole Wilkinson Duran, eds., Harrisburg, Pa.: Trinity, 2002, 121–133) and is used with permission.

When I am teaching the Synoptic Gospels to my second-year students, the miracles of healing seem to be all over these texts. As we read them, we become conscious of reading two texts: the ancient biblical text and the text of our lives. The merging of these two texts is sharply ironic, for Jesus goes about healing all diseases and illness, while we believers in Christ know too well that there is no healing where we stand. Yet, Jesus, who heals all diseases instantly without demanding payment, represents our deepest prayers and wishes.

To read and teach the healing miracles of Jesus in an HIV and AIDS zone like Botswana is thus a challenge. It is to confront an ironic intertextual narrative that demands the reader's attention, for contradictions are too evident to be glossed over. It becomes a mind- and soul-searching practice. I find that I am forced to ask myself a number of questions, such as: How can I teach Jesus' miracles of healing to a class in which students are not only losing relatives, but also living with HIV and AIDS themselves? Should I go about "business as usual," teaching conventional methods of reading as if such stories do not strike too close to our hearts? Can I skip the healing miracles of Jesus and pretend they do not exist or are not important? How should I present these stories to my students: are they baseless myths (used in ancient biography to enhance the hero) or are they crucibles of divine power that surpass the scientific limitations of our world, offering us hope in hopelessness? Further, can I relate these stories to our HIV and AIDS context in the classroom without touching an emotional nerve amongst students who have to live with this hard reality?

While these numerous questions remain unanswered, the miracles of healing confront us, the readers in the HIV and AIDS context, with the yearning for healing, our deepest desire—the desire for that one touch that takes all the suffering away and makes our lives normal again. The healing miracles confront us with the impossible: namely, that healing is possible and that one does not need money for it, just faith. But is healing really possible? Is it really true that one does not need money for healing? Can we say it is true that faith heals HIV and AIDS? One fact is certain: these stories force us to recognize that we live in a context where there is no healing, where there is no money to pay for HIV and AIDS medical needs, and where we have learned that once ill one can only get worse by the day and die after long suffering. Faith seems to fail. Jesus seems to remain silent. How then should one read the healing miracles of Jesus in a context where there is no healing?

Teaching the Synoptic Gospels in an HIV and AIDS context forces me to rethink the purpose of the academy. I must ask myself what good my teaching does if it cannot address the most pressing needs of my students' society. I must ask myself what the point is of giving them knowledge and analysis that cannot improve their lives or speak to their situation. Indeed I must ask myself the question of "how"—how can I make my teaching of the Synoptic Gospels, which are full of the healing miracles of Jesus, become a social space for preparing students to live in their own context of HIV and AIDS (see bell hooks 1994, 15; Segovia and Tolbert 1998). The answers to the above questions are by no means readily available to me or to my students. Nonetheless, it has become increasingly clear to me that my approach to the healing miracles of Jesus would be highly inadequate or pretentious if I stuck to the "purely" academic analysis of the healing miracles of Jesus without relating them to our own context.

The Healing Narratives from a Contextual Perspective

What then would be an appropriate reading of the miracles of healing in an HIV and AIDS context? Such methods of reading and teaching are not clearly articulated in our textbooks or in the reference books in the library, for they were not written to directly address our HIV and AIDS context. To meet this challenge, my approach was that of "reading with" (see West and Dube 2000). Instead of just reading the library references and textbooks, I assigned stories of Jesus' healing miracles to students and asked them to design questionnaires from the passage in the light of HIV and AIDS and take them to the community outside the academic halls— that is, to read the miracles of healing with the general public, which is reading the Bible living in the frontlines of the battle with HIV and AIDS. Students brought their findings and we shared them in class. Although I would not say this approach provides "the answer" to teaching the healing miracles of Jesus in an HIV and AIDS context, it does provide a space of social gathering. The academic community meets in search of answers to scrutinize the basis of our attitudes toward the sick, and possibly to encounter new models of living. The classroom presentations become a social space of sharing and learning to talk openly about a problem that we can only regard as one too big to hide. In this conversational process, we participate in our own healing as we come to define ourselves as "all affected" by the HIV and AIDS in our country, region, and continent. The classroom becomes a social space for those tough encounters as we take a moment to talk about what is really happening and how best we can bring ourselves to live with each other with our situation.

What follows is one example of this process, the results of a questionnaire on Mark 1:40-44 (par. Matt 8:1–4, Luke 5:12–15), in which Jesus heals a leper through touch. This group of respondents, interviewed in Gaborone by my research assistant, Thato Ratsebe, were largely church leaders, partly to assess the view of the church toward people living with HIV and AIDS—to ascertain whether the church is on the condemnation or caring side. At the same time, the research earnestly sought the leaders' views on the significance of the healing miracles of Jesus in an HIV and AIDS context. Of the thirteen people interviewed, eight were men, ranging in age from twenty-eight to forty-five years, of whom five are church leaders. The remaining five were women, ages twenty-four to fifty-eight, of whom one is a church minister, while two others are theologically trained and working for church-related organizations. One woman did not identify herself as a church-goer. Their responses are presented here in their own words, not only to make their words available to those affected by HIV and AIDS and provide the healing that is desperately needed, but also to allow readers to carry out their own analysis.

CONTEXTUAL COMMENT

Mark 1:40-44: "I Desire it, Be Cleansed"

Our questionnaire asked four questions concerning the healing of the leper. They were as follows: (1) How is leprosy comparable to AIDS?; (2) If leprosy was an incurable disease, what is the significance of the leper's request; namely, "If you wish, cleanse me." Can Jesus make us clean in AIDS-ridden Botswana?; (3) If leprosy was a contagious disease, what is the significance of Jesus' act of touching him, when he could have cured the leper without touching him? and; (4) How is this story significant for Botswana AIDS patients?

The response of the two younger women was pessimistic. To the first question, they both said leprosy is similar to AIDS, for it is incurable. Responding to the second question, Ketso said, "Since Jesus does not exist, AIDS cannot be cured." Mpho acknowledged that "Jesus could heal leprosy while he was in the physical form," but she did not seem to have much hope, given that Jesus is not with us in a physical form today.

The middle-aged women respondents also asserted that AIDS and leprosy are similarly incurable. To the first question, Kgosiemang said, "AIDS and leprosy are the same." Mmangwedi held that "they are both incurable." Johnson gave a more explicit answer, saying, "People did not want [those with leprosy] near. So is AIDS. It attacks the body in such a way that people shun the patients" (cf. Myers 1988, 152-153; Lane 1974, 84-85). However, their responses contained more hope. Mmangwedi referred to John 5, holding that "we don't have power to heal, but Jesus has. So if we believe, Jesus can heal AIDS" (cf. Tolbert 1989, 137). For Johnson, "Jesus was a special person with special gifts. He had the power to heal [and] those who believed in him were healed."

In response to the third question, Kgosiemang held that, "Jesus was a measurer of people's faith." Mmangwedi said, "Jesus demonstrated love passion" and underlined that, "Botswana AIDS patients should have hope in God and keep praying." Johnson held that "Jesus was the son of God; he had power over everything. He was also demonstrating that sick people should not be shunned, they should be supported." In response to the fourth question, Kgosiemang said, "We will continue to show love to these people by visiting [and] helping them whenever possible. By so doing, we will be trying to show that Jesus loves them; they need to have enough faith that can sustain them for healing." Mmangwedi insisted that "Jesus has power to change" our situation, save that "it is not yet time for healing AIDS. We should keep on calling him patiently." Johnson, on the other hand, said, "The important thing with AIDS patients is that they should be healed in spirit. This means that if the attitude towards themselves is right, the suffering will be less. We are all going to die whether we have AIDS or not, but the question is, in what state of mind do we die: are we at peace with ourselves and the Lord?"

The men's responses were varied. Ezekiel Tafa did not really respond to this story, except to say, "Jesus is in heaven. He was on earth to cure people—it's all history." Several of the men—including church leaders—saw similarities between leprosy and AIDS, stressing the fact that both are terminal, incurable diseases that tend to marginalize the sick person. Molefe held that, "Apparently there was no known cure for leprosy at the time

[and] people were condemned to death by leprosy. These are the similarities between AIDS [and] leprosy." Moenga, on the other hand, differentiated between the two diseases, arguing that leprosy is not contacted through "sexual contact." Kgasa stressed that despite the apparent incurability of AIDS, "if Jesus wills to cure a person of AIDS, he can do it, for nothing is too hard for God."

That the leper's request for healing is positively met was seen by Kenneth to indicate that "we should keep praying . . . God may yield to our prayers one day." The leper's request also indicates that "We should also find some means of helping ourselves." Responding to the second and third questions, Molefe held that "miracles are needed in Botswana," that, "when Jesus touched the leper, this signified his caring nature." Just like lepers, "AIDS sufferers are equally isolated in our society. They need care and consideration." The leper's prayer is answered instantly, while in our context our prayers are not met. For Kenneth, this does not mean that AIDS cannot be healed; rather, "it is not yet time for God to heal us." For Molefe, "Jesus is represented by the church." While Molefe lamented that "the level of faith is not high enough for God's miracles to manifest themselves," he was optimistic that "if a group of individuals can commit itself to prayer [and] fasting for miracles to cure AIDS, it could happen." Moenga saw the story as indicating "trust in God." Basele said, "His faith works out for him."

Moenga interpreted Botswana's situation in light of this passage as calling us to have "faith in Jesus," and held that even if we are "not literally getting healed," it "does not mean that Jesus has no power," nor does it mean "that suffering victims cannot go to heaven." Basele insisted that it is the "knowledge of Christ which is important." For him, "the most important thing is for the infected to be healed or die in Christ." Like Basele, Chakane held that "there is healing in Jesus, not only the physical one, but spiritual, as it is more important than flesh." The Anglican priest held that "being healed does not necessarily mean getting well. Death is another way of being healed, because one is no longer suffering from the disease." Kgasa, on the other hand, said, "AIDS is a sign that Jesus is about to come. And if people die believing in him, He will raise them from death. When someone has AIDS he/she must be brought to Christ; he can heal if he wills."

Jesus touches a contagious leper to heal him, when he could have avoided it. Moenga reads Jesus' act as "compassionate love" and concludes that "as Botswana Christians we must love the infected." Basele, Chakane, and the Anglican priest made similar comments to the effect that "touching shows concern . . . We should love the infected" (see Lane 1974, 87; Malina 1981, 122; Myers 1988, 154). For Kgasa, "Jesus is the Way, the Truth, and the life. He knew the will of the Father was to touch and heal that leper. It is not God's will that everybody should be free from physical illness. But it is his will that all who are willing should be saved." As Kgasa said earlier, "If Jesus wills to cure a person of AIDS, he can do it, for nothing is too hard for God."

On the whole, the response of men and women indicates little or no gender differences. We find the same range of pessimistic and hopeful readings, with variations that are unrelated to gender. Perhaps this similarity exists because HIV/AIDS is a problem that affects men and women equally. Yet it might also be related to the choice of biblical text. If we had considered a passage about nursing the sick, differences might have become evident, since home-based care is a role that falls heavily on women. The question remains: what are the implications of these interpretations for the church and its response to HIV/AIDS?

Toward Healing Where There is No Healing

Is the attitude of the church on the side of condemnation or caring? In the early days of HIV and AIDS the church formed the majority of those who condemned the infected as sinners under God's punishment, suffering because of their supposed sexual moral laxity. Some of these comments came through in the above responses. To learn just how much condemnation continues would require additional research involving a wider analysis of the daily sermons of pastors or ministers. The general shift has gone toward caring as we increasingly come to regard the disease as a national crisis, affecting all of us, as we increasingly come to understand that one need not be promiscuous to be infected by HIV. The caring perspective of the church is captured by such comments as "we will continue to . . . show love to these people by visiting [and] helping them" (Kgosiemang). Johnson's view that Jesus' decision to touch the leper demonstrates that "sick people should not be shunned, they should be helped [and] supported," typifies the response to this aspect of the text that expresses concern for the ostracized victims. Moenga's statement that even if AIDS patients are not literally healed, "it does not mean . . . that suffering victims cannot go to heaven," is a strong indication of the shift from condemnation to caring. Their statements indicate that, together with the whole society, the church has come to regard HIV/AIDS as "our problem," a national disaster that calls for caring rather than condemnation. A number of respondents thus called for a focus on "following the instructions for reducing the spread of AIDS" (Johnson): we must "change our behavior" (Moenga), "take care of ourselves," and "find means of helping ourselves" (Kenneth). These responses indicate that the church is largely in agreement with the educational campaign that seeks to prevent further infections.

CONCLUSION

Save for three out of fifteen, who dismissed them, the respondents underline the relevance and importance of Jesus' miracles of healing. The fact that there is no cure at the moment makes the miracles even more important: "miracles are the only hope" (Kenneth). Miracles of healing signal that "God will ultimately heal our land" (Mmangwedi). Yet this healing is not only limited to the realm of hope. Respondents are seeing healing here and now, where there is no healing. They assert that spiritual healing (or peace with God), which is much more important than physical healing, can be experienced even when physical healing has not yet taken place. However, they have not completely given up on physical healing as a possibility. They express a firm trust that "Jesus can heal any disease, he is our hope [and] will provide us with medicine"

(Basele). Some call for more faith, more prayer, and more patient waiting for physical healing to be experienced. Instead of viewing the current situation as completely hopeless insofar as healing is concerned, some respondents insist that there is healing, even where there is no healing.

Editors' note: Since the time of the writing, one concern of the article has been addressed: Botswana has been able to make anti-retroviral medications available for free to those living with HIV or AIDS. In many other countries, however, the drugs remain unavailable and/or prohibitively expensive.

BIBLIOGRAPHY

hooks, bell. *Teaching to Transgress: Education as the Practice of Freedom.* New York: Routledge, 1994.

Lane, William L. *The Gospel according to Mark: The English Text with Introduction, Exposition, and Notes.* NICNT Vol. 2. Grand Rapids: Eerdmans, 1974.

Malina, Bruce. *The New Testament World: Insights from Cultural Anthropology.* Atlanta: Westminster John Knox, 1981.

Myers, Ched. *Binding the Strong Man: A Political Reading of Mark's Story of Jesus.* Maryknoll, N.Y.: Orbis, 1988.

Segovia, Fernando F., and Mary Ann Tolbert, eds. *Teaching the Bible: The Discourses and Politics of Biblical Pedagogy.* Maryknoll, N.Y.: Orbis, 1998.

Tolbert, Mary Ann. *Sowing the Gospel: Mark's World in Literary-Historical Perspective.* Minneapolis: Fortress, 1989.

West, Gerald O., and Musa W. Dube, eds. *The Bible in Africa: Transactions, Trajectories, and Trends.* Boston: Brill, 2000.

LUKE

Justin Ukpong

University of Uyo, Akwa Ibom State, Nigeria

LIFE CONTEXT OF THE INTERPRETATION

This reading focuses on Luke's approach to mission, and is done from the perspective of those being evangelized rather than that of the missionaries. Two well-known issues associated with the nineteenth- and twentieth-century Christian missionary work in sub-Saharan Africa—negative attitudes toward African culture and the missionaries' failure to directly confront colonial oppression—will be the contextual issues for the reading. Using the critical-analytical methodology of inculturation hermeneutics, I intend to show, with specific reference to Nigeria, how the Gospel According to Luke could be said to legitimate this approach to mission. Luke's interest in Gentiles and political figures is well known; this reading will focus on Luke's authorial motivation and ask why Luke was interested in these figures. I shall argue that, for Luke (and also the nineteenth- and twentieth-century Christian missionaries to Africa), mission was directed to Gentiles/non-Christians because they were perceived as dwelling in darkness without Christ. Christian mission meant bringing the light of Christ to them. For Luke, the Christ event culminating in the ascension marked the kairos for this mission, while, for the modern Christian missionaries, colonial exploration opened the way for mission. For neither did the process of evangelization involve direct confrontation of oppressive colonial power.

Christianity in Nigeria

Nigeria, a former West African British colony that became independent in 1960, is about four times the size of the United Kingdom and the fourteenth largest country in Africa. It stretches about 700 miles from east to west, and 650 miles from south to north. It is the eighth most populous country in the world (with 125 million people) and the most populous in black Africa (making up 20 percent of Africa's population). There are about 250 ethnic groups with different cultures. Though diverse, these cultures have many common traits. English, the official language, is spoken in the cities alongside pidgin English and the indigenous languages.

In the late nineteenth century, Nigeria, along with other countries in sub-Saharan Africa, was the site of intense Christian missionary activity. The missionaries, both Roman Catholic and Protestant, arrived by sea in the southern part of the country that borders on the Atlantic Ocean, and moved northwards spreading the gospel. By the middle of the twentieth century, Christianity had spread to the northern part of the country, which had been a Muslim stronghold since the eleventh century. Today, Christians make up about 50 percent of the population, and Muslims about 45 percent—a testimony to the great success of the Christian mission (practitioners of the traditional religion and other religious groups make up the rest of the population). In spite of this success, the early Christian missionary effort was marked by a negative attitude toward Nigerian culture and an absence of direct and open confrontation of the colonial oppression suffered by the people.

Justin Ukpong is a Catholic priest from Nigeria and professor of New Testament at the University of Uyo, Nigeria. His area of interest is inculturation, contextual hermeneutics and reading the Bible with ordinary readers. He is the author of *Essays in Contextual Theology* (1995) and *New Testament Essays* (1995) and is co-author of *The Gospel of Matthew: A Contextual Introduction* (2003), *The Bible in a World Context* (2002), and *Reading the Bible in a Global Village* (2002).

Contextual Issues

Negative Attitude Toward Nigerian Culture by Christian Missionaries

Christian missionary activity in Nigeria took place at a time when there was general ignorance of African culture in Europe. The information people received about Africa was generally distorted, unreliable, and exotic, and came from newspaper reports and travelers' accounts. In nineteenth-century Britain, in particular, a body of literature developed, exemplified by David Livingston's *Missionary Travels and Researches in South Africa* and Henry Morton Stanley's *In Darkest Africa,* in which Africans were depicted as savage, barbaric, pagan, primitive, lewd, and inferior to Europeans. Films depicted Africa as the dark continent—a fantasy at best, grossly racist at the worst. Europe's ethnocentric intellectual climate combined with Darwin's theory of evolution formed the basis for a theory of social evolution according to which human societies followed a linear development, with the so-called primitive societies at the bottom and European societies at the top. Africa was, therefore, portrayed in the poorest light.

Against this background, mission to Nigeria, for both Catholics and Protestants, meant bringing Christ to people outside the pale of God's salvation. Both groups possessed an exclusivist soteriology: "outside the church no salvation," for Roman Catholics, and "outside the word no salvation," for Protestants (Knitter 1984, 50–53). Nigerian culture was thought to be incompatible with Christianity and in need of being Europeanized before Christianity could take root in it. To this end, among other things, the missionaries introduced western education in Nigeria, which, rather than destroying Nigerian culture, led to the development of a Nigerian elite who started the struggle for Nigeria's political independence—an ironic situation the missionaries themselves did not intend or foresee.

The negative attitude toward African culture also manifested itself in the development of separate communities to shield the newly baptized from "contamination" by the local culture. In Nigeria, these were set up by the Roman Catholic missionaries in Topo Island near Lagos, and Aguleri near Onitsha, and were called "Christian villages." Modeled after similar institutions in Paraguay during the seventeenth- and eighteenth-century, Christian villages were physically remote and politically autonomous from the surrounding traditional villages. The Protestants had none in Nigeria but developed them in other African countries such as Zambia, and called them "mission villages." Unlike the Catholic villages, they were located within the traditional village around the church compound. The communities had only occasional contact with their non-Christian kith and kin, and tried to practice "Christian behavior"(i.e., European ways of doing things). The idea was to create "cells" of Christian civilization in Africa that would eventually cause the old social order to crumble. Because of conflicts and tensions between the Christian cells and the traditional villages, the project was later abandoned. It could not conform to the missionaries' ideal of Christian civilization.

In addition, Christian missionaries would not admit Nigerian cultural symbols and practices into Christian life and practice. The local language, musical tunes and accompaniments, and African liturgical expression in dance were considered unfit for Christian worship. Africans had to worship the European way, and to sing tunes from European hymnbooks. The use of indigenous African perspectives in theological reflection only began to surface in the 1960s, and was viewed with deep suspicion (Bujo 1992, 56–66).

Christian Missionaries' Failure to Confront Colonial Oppression

Christian missionaries from Ireland and England brought Christianity to Nigeria during the golden age of British imperialism in Nigeria. This came with the exploitation of the material and human resources of the country. Nigeria's palm produce, groundnuts, hide and skin, cocoa, tin ore, coal, and other products (with their prices fixed by the British merchants themselves) were exported cheaply to feed British industries. The people had no voice in the way they were governed; they paid taxes but had no say on how the money was spent. The country's infrastructure—roads, potable water, electricity, etc.—was not developed. Racial discrimination was rife. In the cities, the whites lived in special areas designated as "European Quarters" while Nigerians lived in the slums, separate centers of recreation existed for whites and blacks, and Nigerian workers received only a meager fraction of the wages of their white counterparts. Life for Nigerians was a bitter struggle. Poverty was everywhere. Above all, colonialism brought the dehumanizing commerce in human cargo. Nigerian villages were raided on a regular basis for able-bodied men and women who were carried away into slavery in America.

The Christian missionaries posed no direct challenge to colonial exploitation—particularly as colonialism was generally seen as bringing the light of European civilization to Africa. Besides, how could one expect them to criticize the very institution that provided them with protection and financial support in spreading the gospel? Even when they had opportunities to support the people against colonial oppression, they did nothing. For example, in 1949 the coal miners at Enugu, the seat of the Eastern regional administration, organized a demonstration to press their demand for a pay raise. The colonial police fired at them, killing nine people. When the miners' union organized a funeral service, neither the local Roman Catholic nor the Anglican Church—whose ministers were white—would permit the funeral to be held on their premises, even though some of the dead were Catholics and Anglicans. The union then moved to a small town, Aba, about forty miles west of Enugu, for the funeral. In protest against the attitude of the Christian churches, they had an open-air funeral, sang traditional religious songs, and used traditional religious rites invoking the ancestors. The occasion led to the founding of *Goddianism,* a modernized form of African traditional religion, a movement that could have been averted had the missionaries been sympathetic to the cause of the miners (Onunwa 1989, 116–125).

Luke's Gospel is open to multiple readings, depending on the reader's perspective and context. For example, it has been read in ways that inspire economic, social, and political liberation (see below, René Krüger's Luke's God and Mammon in a Latin American Perspective"). However, by focusing on Luke's authorial motivation (a choice made in view of the above interpretive context), this reading seeks to identify some of the inadequacies of Luke's missiology that seem to have influenced Christian mission practice in Nigeria, and that might be masked by the great success of Luke's Gentile mission. As already pointed out, Luke's motivation for the Gentile mission was the desire to bring Christ to people believed to be without him. However, the question is, did Christian missionaries bring Christ to the Gentiles? Was Christ not already present among these people even before the arrival of the missionaries? Luke's interest in political figures also stems from his desire to gain the goodwill of the empire's elite. While this may have well served Luke's cause, it is an inadequate paradigm for today.

CONTEXTUAL COMMENT

Following the general scholarly consensus, I date Luke's Gospel to about 80 c.e. (or shortly thereafter), and understand his intended audience as predominantly Gentile. Antioch in Syria is generally suggested as a possible location for the book's writing, but Rome or any major city in the Roman Empire could have been its base. Although some have proposed a female author, I share the majority opinion that the author is a male who may have been a Gentile or Diaspora Jewish convert to Christianity. Today, it is a matter of debate whether the author was a travel companion of Paul. He need not have been. For writing his story, he depended on Mark, Q, and other special sources that may have been either written or oral.

Like the rest of the New Testament, Luke's Gospel was written in the context of the first-century Christian mission movement. The Lukan community's experience of the mission issues of the time shaped the community's focus and goal, in the light of which Luke reinterpreted the tradition he had received. The Gospel begins with the birth stories of John the Baptist and Jesus (1:1–2:21); recounts the preparations for Jesus' ministry (3:1–4:13), Jesus' ministry in Galilee (4:14–9:50), and his ministry on the journey to Jerusalem (9:51–19:27); and concludes with his ministry, death, resurrection, and ascension in Jerusalem (19:28–24:43). Though he pays attention to history, Luke's approach is more theological and thematic than chronological. Luke has many concerns, including Gentiles, women, political figures, and the poor and their relationship with the rich.

As we shall see, for Luke, the Gentiles dwelt in darkness, and the Christ event marked the fulfillment of God's promise to bring the light of salvation to them. I shall explore this theme below by focusing on passages selected throughout the Gospel. With regard to his interest in political figures, Luke tries to present Christianity in a way that would attract the support of the middle-class elite of the Roman Empire but not appear to incite people against Rome's colonial authority. I find this accentuated in a second series of passages that I discuss in the second section below.

Interest in Gentiles

Luke's Gospel expresses a strong interest in Gentiles. He alone of the four evangelists gives a detailed account of the early church's mission to Gentile territory. By dedicating his two volume work to a Gentile, "Theophilus," (Luke 1:4) who may already have been a convert, was undergoing instruction to be converted, or was merely interested in Christianity. Luke indicates that his message has some relevance for Gentiles. Sym-

bolically, the Greek name (which means "lover of God") also points to Christians, particularly Gentile Christians, as addressees. Luke depicts Jesus as determined to include Gentiles in God's plan of salvation: Jesus is seen as the savior of all nations (2:32); Jesus' genealogy is traced to Adam, the father of all humanity (3:38); Jesus speaks positively of Gentiles (4:25-27); in the Sermon on the Plain, in contrast to Matthew's account, which presents a Jewish versus Gentile ethic (Matt 5:47), Luke presents a universal ethic for Jews and Gentiles (Luke 6:27-35); and a centurion acknowledges Jesus to be an upright man (23:47-48).

Luke's interest in Gentiles is shown in his understanding of the Gentiles as dwelling in darkness awaiting God's salvation. At the time Luke wrote, the frontiers of Christianity had extended beyond Palestine to Gentile lands, with Gentiles flocking to the church in large numbers. The large presence of Gentiles in the church raised questions, for Luke, of legitimizing Gentile mission and the near total Gentile "take-over" of an originally Jewish heritage. Luke saw, in the Christ event, the time of the fulfillment of God's Hebrew Bible promise of the redemption of Israel and salvation for the Gentiles who dwelt in ignorance of the true God (Acts 17:23).

In the Gospel's prologue, Luke states that his purpose for writing is to attest to the proper (scriptural) foundation of the Christian catechesis that Theophilus has received or knows about (Luke 1:4)—a catechesis whose genuineness is guaranteed by the tradition handed down by eyewitnesses of the life of Jesus, and his own careful research (Luke 1:1). As far as can be reconstructed from the Acts of the Apostles, the early Christian kerygma (which formed the substance of this catechesis) included a retelling of the story of Jesus' life as a fulfillment of ancient prophecies of God's salvation to all peoples as well as a call to repentance and acceptance of Jesus (Acts 2:14-36, 38-41; 3:13-26; 10:42-43; 13:17-41). Thus, one purpose of Luke's two-volume work was to testify to the arrival of God's time of universal salvation that included Gentiles. Luke announces this theme in the infancy narrative and, in his characteristic way, reviews and refers back to it in the rest of the Gospel (Tannehill 1986).

Luke 1–2: Gentiles Dwell in Darkness

In the infancy narrative, which introduces some of the major themes of the Gospel, Luke presents his theological viewpoint by commentating on the materials he received. He intersperses hymns (not all of his own composition) in his narratives of the visitation (1:39-56), the circumcision of John (1:59-79), the birth of Jesus (2:1-20), and Jesus' presentation at the temple (2:22-35) as his theological commentary on these incidents.

In the annunciation of John's birth, John's mission is set within Israel: he is to bring Israel back to God, effect a reconciliation, and prepare them for the approaching redemption (1:11-25). Israel is recognized as having defected but is not excluded from God's favor. In the Benedictus, Zechariah's hymn (Luke 1:67-79), the birth of John the Baptist inaugurates the dawn of Israel's freedom from its enemies, and the establishment of God's salvation and peace in Israel. Again, Israel is the focus of John's reconciling mission.

Unlike John, in the annunciation of Jesus' conception (Luke 1:26-38), his mission is ruling over Israel, which implies putting things in order and establishing peace. In Mary's Magnificat, the theme of God as the savior of Israel is prominent: what God does for her symbolizes what God will do for Israel. Thus, the time of Israel's redemption has come with the birth of the savior Jesus.

It is in Simeon's hymn, Nunc Dimitis (which is very likely Luke's own composition, Luke 2:29-32), that we find the core of the theme of Gentiles being without the light of salvation. Jesus is identified as the glory of Israel (2:32), an allusion to God's glory that dwelt with the chosen people in the desert on their way to freedom (Exod 40:34), and an indication of the arrival of Israel's time of redemption. Jesus is also identified as the bearer of "salvation" for all peoples (2:30-31), not just Israel. He is then specifically identified as a light for the Gentiles, a refer-

ence to Isaiah's "servant songs" (Isa 42, 49, 52) with the prominent theme of Israel as God's covenant people who will be a light to the Gentiles. Already in the Benedictus (Luke 1:67-79), we know that those for whom this light is to shine (2:32, Gentiles) dwell in darkness comparable to death (1:79). This does not, however, connote an inability to do good, as is clear from the rest of the Gospel (10:13-16; 23:47). Rather, it has to do with the absence of the knowledge of salvation (Isa 49:6b). Jesus is the "light" that makes salvation known to the Gentiles (2:31-32).

Thus, God sets divine salvation and glory within Israel (Isa 42:6-8). Though the salvation that Jesus brings is for all people, it is located in Israel, from where its light reaches out to the Gentiles (Isa 49:6, as read by Luke). Israel's glory and divine salvation are intertwined in Jesus. The resurrection is the point at which Scripture about God's salvation for the Gentiles is fulfilled and, thereafter, Christian missionaries are to bring the light of Christ to the Gentiles through their preaching (24:44-48). This preaching is important and must start from Jerusalem and reach out to the ends of the earth. Thus Luke locates the urgency of the Gentile mission and the explanation for the large Gentile influx into Christianity at the resurrection and ascension, whereby God's plan to bring salvation to the Gentiles is fulfilled. Up to that point, during Jesus' earthly ministry, such urgency is not apparent.

Gentiles on the Periphery: Luke 7:1-10, Cure of the Centurion's Servant

Having announced the theme of Gentiles dwelling in darkness at the beginning of his Gospel, Luke refers back to it in the rest of the book (Jervell 1979). He does this by negatively depicting the Gentiles as people peripheral to the Jews. In the Synoptic Gospels, the only two instances of Jesus healing at a distance involve Gentiles: the healing of a centurion's servant (Matt 8:5-13; Luke 7:1-10), a Q text, and the healing of the daughter of a Canaanite/Syro-Phoenician woman (Matt 15:21-28; Mark 7:24-30), a Markan text. Luke generally follows Mark, but omits the latter narrative. (This is a portion of Luke's so-called "great omission" of Mark; Luke makes no use of the materials in Mark 6:45–8:26.) Luke may have omitted this story because the saying that Jesus came for the Jews alone militates against his theology that Jesus also came for the Gentiles.

In a comparative analysis of Matthew and Luke's versions of the healing of the centurion's servant, Luke's redactional emphasis is on the centurion's peripheral position as a Gentile. In Matt 8:5-7, the centurion approaches Jesus directly with his request; in Luke, he approaches Jesus through Jewish elders. The ground for the Jewish elders acting on the centurion's behalf is that he is favorably disposed towards the Jews (Luke 7:3-5). His fate is therefore defined in relation to the Jews. In both Gospels, the centurion confesses his unworthiness to receive Jesus in his house (Matt 8:8; Luke 7:6-7), but in Luke the centurion is also too unworthy to approach Jesus in person.

Luke 8:26-39, Healing of a Demoniac

Three things invite our curiosity when we compare the story of the exorcism of the demoniac at Gerasa (8:26-39), a largely Gentile city with a non-Jewish population, with Luke's story of the exorcism of the demoniac in Capernaum (4:31-37), a Jewish city. First is the reaction of the crowds. In Capernaum, the Jewish residents were at first astonished, then came to appreciate and affirm the power of Jesus (4:36), an act consistent with a more "enlightened" point of view by a well-established and accepted people. However, in the case of Gerasa, the people who were probably Gentile were seized with fear and asked Jesus to leave their territory (8:37), an action consistent with marginal people. Second, at Gerasa Jesus expelled the demons into a herd of swine considered "unclean" by the Jews (Lev 11:7; Deut 14:8) but "clean" by the Gentiles. Destroying such a substantial means of livelihood underscores Jewish "enlightened" contempt for this Gentile "unenlightened" outlook. Lastly, Luke

states that, though the exorcized Gerasene sat at Jesus' feet (8:35) in an act of discipleship, Jesus does not accept him as a disciple (8:38-39). From the contextual perspective described above, it appears that, even though he acts as a disciple, he is not "worthy" to enter the mainstream of discipleship: a Gentile "disciple" is considered unfit to evangelize others except his own people (8:38-39).

Luke 23:1-25, Pilate's Vacillation at Jesus' Judgment

Luke's presentation of Pilate in the judgment of Jesus shows that while Pilate (a Gentile) wielded enormous political authority, he could not come to a decisive judgment on Jesus. He was convinced that Jesus was innocent, but hesitated many times, sent him to Herod, then condemned him to death on the basis of pressure from the Jews. From a contextual perspective, it appears that, in spite of his enormous political power, the Gentile Pilate acts from the periphery; it is the Jews that exercise the power in the situation.

Need to Bring Salvation to Gentiles (3:23-38; 4:16-30; 24:44-48)

Luke 3:23-38: Having presented Jesus as the glory of Israel and Gentiles as dwelling in darkness in the infancy narrative, Luke next records Jesus' ancestry, where he presents the ontological rationale for bringing the light of God's salvation to the Gentiles. Unlike Matthew, who traces Jesus' genealogy up to Abraham, the father of the Jewish people, Luke traces it to Adam, the father of all humanity, thus indicating Jesus' oneness with all humans. With his incarnation, the Gentiles with whom Jesus also identifies are no longer on the periphery; they may now see the light of God's salvation.

Luke 4:16-30: In this pericope of Jesus' preaching at Nazareth, Luke reinterprets the material he got from Mark by expanding it and moving it from its location in the middle of Jesus' ministry (Mark 6:1-6) to the beginning (Luke 4:16-30). The central text,

Luke 4:18-19, a programmatic statement of Jesus' ministry, is taken from Isa 61:1-2.

Within this strategic section we meet the first Jew/Gentile contrast on Jesus' lips (4:25-27). In this text, which is unique to Luke, the Jews (whom we know already to be the children of light) are unfavorably contrasted with the Gentiles (who dwell in darkness). This "preferential option" for Gentiles so infuriates the Jews that they want to throw Jesus over a cliff. But Jesus has made his point: though rooted in Israel (4:23-24), his ministry extends beyond Israel to the Gentiles. In this way, Luke claims a historical-theological justification for the mission to Gentiles. Here again, the background is Hebrew prophecy interpreted by Luke in a new light.

Luke 24:44-48: Luke closes his Gospel with Jesus pointing to the fulfillment of God's plan for universal salvation: the appointed time has come, hence the urgency and success of the Gentile mission.

Jew/Gentile Contrast

As in the other Gospels, we find harsh words for the Jews on the lips of Jesus in Jew/Gentile contrasts. In Luke 10:13-16 for example, the Gentile cities of Tyre and Sidon are favorably contrasted against the Jewish cities of Chorazin and Bethsaida. In the trial of Jesus (Luke 23), Luke contrasts the Jews who want Jesus killed and Pilate, a Gentile who sees Jesus as innocent. Another Gentile, a centurion, confesses Jesus' innocence (23:47) in contrast to the Jews who see him as guilty. For Luke, Gentiles are marginal people compared to the Jews. He argues this point with subtlety. The contrast is not between the Jews who rejected Jesus and the Gentiles who accepted him, for Luke gives instances (particularly in Acts) of acceptance and rejection on both sides. Rather, the contrast is between the Jews as the children of light, who should know better, and Gentiles who dwell in darkness, of whom not much is expected in the first place. Thus, their acceptance of Jesus becomes significant, while their rejection

does not command as much condemnation as that of the Jews.

Colonial Oppression Not Directly Confronted in Luke's Gospel

Luke wrote his Gospel against the backdrop of the first Jewish war (66–70 C.E.), the expulsion of Christians from the synagogue (80 C.E.), localized persecution of Jews/Christians, and the spread of fledgling Christianity into the wider arena of the Roman Empire. There are indications that, though he wrote for his community, he had an eye on the upper middle-class readership of the empire as well. The prologue (Luke 1:1-4) is written in elegant and technical Greek. This sets the work within the respected Greco-Roman literary tradition of the time, and makes it one destined to adorn the libraries of the elite. The book is dedicated to a certain Theophilus who bears the title "His Excellency" (1:3, author's translation [a.t.]) which was used for people of high social status like governors (Acts 24:2). This is an important indication that Luke expects the likes of Theophilus to read his story. Also, Luke constantly refers to the political authorities of the empire in his story: the annunciation of the births of John and Jesus took place when Herod was king of Judea (Luke 1:5); Jesus was born when Caesar Augustus was reigning in Rome (2:1); John and Jesus performed their ministries when Tiberius Caesar was reigning in Rome, Pontius Pilate was governor of Judea, and Herod was administrator in Galilee (3:1-2, 19-20); and the passion narrative is set in a similar political context (23:1-25, 47, 50-54). All this suggests that Luke wants to acknowledge the presence and authority of the Roman colonial power in Palestine during the period he writes about, and intends his story to be meaningful within that context.

Against this background, Luke wanted to present Christianity in a way that would not antagonize the colonial authority and would also appeal to the elite of the empire, as Christian communities needed the goodwill of such people to survive. This meant courting many ideological positions of that class without sacrificing Christian identity and principles. Thus, while not exonerating Pilate, he excuses him for the execution of Jesus by emphasizing that it was on the demand of the Jews that Pilate ordered Jesus' death (23:24-25). Compared to both Matthew (27:11-14) and Mark (15:2-5), who only record Pilate's confession of Jesus' innocence once, Luke records it three times (23:4, 14, 20-22), and has this corroborated by a Roman centurion (23:47). He presents a Jesus who did not directly confront the colonial authorities, but was critical of them within the circle of his followers, who was interested in the poor and marginalized in society, and was against the wrongful accumulation of wealth by the rich.

Contemporary historical research shows that the widespread existence of great poverty and deprivation in first-century Palestine was linked to the colonial occupation (Lapide 1986, 99). Luke is sensitive to this correlation for, in addition to reminding us of the presence of Roman colonial power in Palestine, his Gospel shows much concern for the poor. Jesus' programmatic statement of his mission is set within the context of the jubilee proclamation of liberation for the poor (Luke 4:18-19), with a pronouncement of blessing to the poor and woe to the rich (6:20-26), and there are more stories of God's favor towards the poor than in any other Gospel. Luke's own community may have been comprised of many who were poor (6:20). However, there is no indication that Jesus directly confronted the colonial power responsible for the grinding poverty in Palestine. The closest Jesus comes to directly confronting the colonial oppressors is his charge to his disciples to carry a sword in the passion story; even so, he restrained their use of it (22:36-38, 48-51). In contrast to the other Gospels, Luke presents a Jesus who represents peace. Unlike Mark, who uses the term *eirēnē* ("peace") once (Mark 9:50), and Matthew, who uses it four times (Matt 10:13, 34), Luke uses it fourteen times: angels pronounce peace on earth to herald Jesus' birth (2:13-14), Jesus' words to the sinful woman are "go in peace" (7:50), Jesus advocates making peace with the enemy in advance (14:32), and laments over Jerusalem for failing to know what would bring her peace (19:42). Thus, Luke presents Jesus as a peacemaker from birth, avoiding direct confrontation with the enemies of Israel who were responsible for the plight of the common people upon whom he focused his ministry.

However, to say that Luke's Jesus was a peacemaker and did not engage in direct confrontation with the Roman colonial authorities is not to say that he condoned the political status quo. Luke's Gospel contains indirect and covert revolutionary sentiments and actions against the political status quo. Luke records Jesus attacking the Jewish religious-political leaders, the scribes, Pharisees, and Sadducees, agents of the colonial authority (Luke 6:1-5; 11:37-44; 19:45-48; 20:45-47); Jesus did not defer to Herod, calling him a fox (Luke 13:31-33); he cautioned his disciples against the behavior of Gentile rulers who lorded it over their subjects (22:24-27); above all, the kingdom of God, the theme of Jesus' preaching, had characteristics antithetical to the "kingdom" of Caesar. In the material unique to Luke, the Magnificat celebrates God's overthrow of the mighty at the coming of Jesus (1:46-56); the Benedictus celebrates God's overthrow of Israel's enemies, the greatest being the Roman colonial power (1:67-79); *and* Jesus is accused of forbidding tribute to Caesar (23:2). These themes point to an indirect criticism of the colonial power.

Luke's handling of the tribute issue (Luke 20:20-26) sheds light on his strategy in presenting the political dimension of his story. Jesus' answer, "Pay Caesar what belongs to Caesar, and God what belongs to God" (Luke 20:25, a.t.), was an indirect, and covertly negative response to the question that was asked, "Should we pay tribute to Caesar or should we not?" For, since Israel was totally God's people, and God's right supersedes Caesar's, Caesar had no claim on Israel, and therefore no right to demand taxes from them (Ukpong 1999, 433-444). Luke alone records that, at his trial, Jesus was (falsely) accused of forbidding tribute to Caesar (23:2). Even though Jesus had raised doubts about paying tribute (in 20:25), Luke presents Jesus as indirectly refuting Pilate's question in the trial scene (23:3). In a similar way, in the entire Gospel, Luke presents a Jesus who did not confront the colonial authorities directly and openly though he did not condone the status quo. Therefore, Luke indicates that the movement Jesus founded to carry on his mission was not a political danger like the violent resistance of the zealots' movement.

CONCLUSION

The nineteenth- and twentieth-century Christian mission in Nigeria and Luke's interest in mission to the Gentiles share a common motivation—to bring the light of Christ where it was believed to be absent. Luke interpreted the prophecies in the Hebrew scriptures about the time of God's salvation as having arrived for the Gentiles, while the missionaries to Nigeria were influenced by the their cultural biases, misconceptions about Africans, and an exclusivist ecclesiology that denied the presence of Christ among non-Christians. The problematic idea is that Christian missionaries bring Christ to non-Christians. Was the risen Christ not already present and active among the Gentiles and in Africa before the missionaries arrived there? Though Jesus was confined to one locality and culture in his earthly life, by the resurrection he transcends time and space and is made present to all creation as the first fruits from all those who die (1 Cor 15:20-23). Besides, if Jesus is the logos through whom all creation came into being (John 1:1-8), and at the same time the way, the light, and the truth (John 14:6), then we must presume the light of Christ to have been already present among the Gentiles and Africans even before the arrival of the Christian missionaries (Shorter 1988, 83–85; Mbiti 1992, 21–30). This does not negate the need for missionaries but, rather, redefines their role in helping people discover Christ in their midst.

Because the political atmosphere in which he wrote was unfavorable to Christians, Luke's presentation of Christianity courted many ideological positions of the elite Romans so that it would not appear as a politically dangerous movement. Thus, despite his interest in the poor, he did not present Jesus as directly challenging the colonial authority responsible for the people's plight in the same way that Luke depicts Jesus challenging the Jewish religious leaders. Given Luke's influential position on mission to the Gentiles, this approach is potentially paradigmatic for contemporary mission practice, as it seems to have been for the early missionary efforts in Nigeria that did not openly challenge colonial exploitation of the people. Considering that, at the time of the Christian mission to Nigeria, the Bible was read in a spiritualized way, the missionaries did not draw inspiration for political action from Luke as we do today.

The mission to the Gentiles that Luke championed became a great success. Similarly, there has been an unprecedented phenomenal growth of Christianity in Nigeria because of the nineteenth- and twentieth-century missionary efforts. However, this success should not be allowed to mask Luke's missiological inadequacies for contemporary mission practice, nor should the success of the Christian mission in Nigeria be allowed to mask the inadequacies of its original bearers. Contemporary missionary efforts must take note of these inadequacies in Luke's missionary theology to avoid the mistakes of the past.

BIBLIOGRAPHY

Bujo, Benezet. *African Theology in Its Social Context*. Trans. John O'Donohue. Faith and Cultures Series. Maryknoll, N.Y.: Orbis, 1992.

Jervell, Jacob. *Luke and the People of God: A New Look at Luke-Acts*. Minneapolis: Augsburg, 1979.

Knitter, Paul F. "Roman Catholic Approaches to Other Religions: Developments and Tensions." *International Bulletin of Missionary Research* 8 (April 1984): 50–53.

Lapide, Pinchas. *The Sermon on the Mount: Utopia or Program for Action?* Trans. Arlene Swidler. Maryknoll, N.Y.: Orbis, 1986.

Mbiti, John S. "Is Jesus Christ in African Religion?" Pages 21–30 in *Exploring Afro-Christology*. Ed. John S. Pobee. Studien zur interkulturellen Geschichte des Christentums, Bd. 79. Frankfurt am Main: Peter Lang, 1992.

Onunwa, Udobata R. "Goddianism: A Resurgence of an Old Cult in Christian Garb." *Africa Theological Journal* 18, no. 2 (1989): 116-125.

Shorter, Aylward. *Toward A Theology of Inculturation*. Maryknoll, N.Y.: Orbis, 1988.

Tannehill, Robert C. *The Narrative Unity of Luke-Acts: A Literary Interpretation, Volume 1, The Gospel of Luke*. Philadelphia: Fortress, 1986.

Ukpong, Justin S. "Tribute to Caesar, Mark 12:13-17 (Matt 22:15–22; Luke 20–26)." *Neot* 33 (1999): 433-444.

LUKE'S GOD AND MAMMON, A LATIN AMERICAN PERSPECTIVE

Dr. René Krüger

Instituto Universitario ISEDET, Buenos Aires, Argentina

LIFE CONTEXT OF THE INTERPRETATION

More than half of the population of Latin America lives in conditions of poverty, exclusion, and misery. One of the main causes of this colossal crisis is the imposition of the neo-liberal economic model in all Latin America. Only the values of the market and the good merchant are promoted in the neo-liberal society. These values include: to know what to offer and in what moment; to take advantage of every available opportunity; to know when to sell and when to buy; to know how to deceive; to know how to lie; to know how to convince.

This serious situation challenges both our nations and our Churches. The Gospel demands that we clearly protest and denounce the neo-liberal project so profoundly destructive of Latin American life.

Contextual Comment and Hermeneutical issues

God calls the Church to raise her voice within the specific Latin American context and to act against the consequences of the European conquest, colonial and post-colonial exploitation of the people and the land, the impact of the military dictatorship, and the dramatic exclusion from access to basic resources caused by the globalized neo-liberal economy. How does the Church raise her voice and act? In part the Church does this through studying and reflecting on the Bible. The Bible contains numerous texts that deal with social and economic matters. These texts open up their message on these issues when read from the context of poverty, exclusion, violence, corruption, and destruction of life, because this specific context of reading provides hermeneutical codes that allow the reader to understand similar codes within the texts themselves.

Among the books of the New Testament, Luke and the Epistle of James are the outstanding examples of deeply rooted social message. Luke considers the antagonism between poor and rich, the cry for justice, God's option for the poor, the Church's organic commitment to the poor, the intentional development of fairness and justice within the community, the judgment on the rich, and the opposition between God and the Mammon. By telling the story (or stories) of Jesus, this author addresses some very serious problems in his communities: the increasing social and economic differences between the rich and the poor, the total disregard and contempt of certain social groups by others, the self-centeredness of some individuals. He shows how Jesus faced similar situations in his context, and through his narrative creates profound theological paradigms valid for all the Church throughout its history. He shows the link between Jesus and a group of people who were poor,

René Krüger, Professor of New Testament, is a Visiting Professor at the Presbyterian Theological Seminary in Mexico, and is an ordained minister of the Evangelical Church of the River Plate. He is author of several books, including *Dios o el Mamón. Análisis semiótico y hermenéutico del proyecto económico y relacional del evangelio de Lucas* (1987; German edition, 1997); *Interpretación Bíblica* (1994); *Arm und Reich im Jakobusbrief—von Lateinamerika aus gelesen. Die Herausforderung eines prophetischen Christentums* (2003); *Volver del abismo. Un modelo pastoral de abordaje del alcoholismo* (2003). He is co-author with Severino Croatto and Néstor Míguez of *Métodos Exegéticos* (1996); and co-editor of *Alternativas para un mundo justo. Globalización y probeza: Perspectivas bíblicas* (2004).

disregarded, and sinners. Simultaneously he shows Jesus' opposition to the selfish rich, who disregard others and imagine themselves to be self-sufficient people, and his call to them for sincere repentance and a changed life.

Latin American readers perceived these codes within the text of Luke as most significant because they, day after day, are confronted with these issues in their lives. From this contextual perspective, the Gospel is a persuasive instrument for God's global struggle for human survival, not only because the text is rooted in its socio-economic background, but also because—as the Word of God—it has a theological identity that gives coherence and transcendence to the commitment for human life.

CONTEXTUAL COMMENT

The following texts contain fundamental clues for the knowledge of Luke's socioeconomic project for his community. For each text, I will, if necessary, perform a brief exegesis and then concentrate on Luke's treatment of socioeconomic issues.

Luke 1:46–55: The Magnificat, the Announcement of an Alternative

The Magnificat begins with the individual and personal in the choice of the virgin Mary as mother of Jesus (Luke 1: 48) and expands to the community of the poor in (Luke 1:53). What God does to one humble person is projected onto all the humble. This line of thought continues in both Luke 6:20-26 (the Lukan Beatitudes), where Luke expands the same announcement to all the hearers, while the parable of Luke 16:19-31 focuses this message on a specific case.

The Magnificat presents God's option for the humble and God's inversion of the relationship between power and property as reflecting God's mercy and promises. God's action in favor of Mary and all the poor announces the authentic alternative based on Jesus as the only savior, instead of (and inverting) what is offered by the powerful and the rich who do not save and whose reigns will be destroyed.

Luke 6:20–26: The Total Inversion of Values and Relationships

In Luke's version, the Beatitudes are opposed to the Woes or announcements of disgrace. By setting the two groups in a parallel opposition, Luke declares that the poor are poor because the rich *have made them* poor; the hungry *are* hungry because those who are satisfied *have made them* hungry; those who cry do so because those who laugh make them cry; and the persecuted *suffer* because the prestigious, flattered, and famous *persecute* them.

By announcing the respective destinies of both groups, Luke inverts socio-economic values and relations. From the perspective of this literary inversion being rich is synonymous with living unjustly. This announcement also sharply judges the ethics and relationships maintained by the oppressive social and economic forces. In this way, the text highlights the gratuity (grace) of the Kingdom of God, which opposes those forces. The inversions brilliantly reject the ideology that justifies wealth as an indication of divine blessing and poverty as divine punishment.

Luke 12:13-21: The Social Function of the Riches

This story's message begins with the warning against *covetousness* (Luke 12:15), the actual site of the decisive conflict between the gospel and money. It is here where the struggle between two gods comes to light: the God of the poor and the god of the rich. Luke 12:15 is a fundamental warning against any kind of greed that would guarantee one's own life by increasing one's possessions. The parable of the silly rich man, who thinks only of his own well-being, connects such greed to the societal damage inflicted by stockpiling grain. The plans of the rich are not neutral; on the contrary, they are an identifiable sin: removing grain from circulation in order to maximize profits. Once grain was stockpiled, hunger and shortage followed, which allowed the monopolists to earn excess profits. This critical vision of the wealthy's criminal schemes is more than a sapiential warning about the foolishness of a life based on riches. This vision announces the deleterious societal effects of hoarding possessions.

Luke 16:1-31: The Decisive Option: God or Mammon

This chapter contains various examples of the Lukan Beatitudes (6:20-26). The parable of the steward (Luke 16:1–9) discusses the social significance of money. The parable of the rich and Lazarus (16:19-31) is not simply an inversion of personal destiny, but a radical critique of rich Christians. It makes them face up to the economic demands of their discipleship and shows them that the perpetuation of the socioeconomic inequalities is rooted in disobedience to God's will, as expressed in the Law and the Prophets.

Literarily, the text transforms Mammon into a divinity, an idol, that enslaves. There is no middle ground between Mammon and God, nor is it possible to agree with both by simultaneously being faithful to God and serving the Mammon. Instead the text proposes that one uses Mammon in accordance with God's will, which opens up life's full possibilities and promotes the survival of the excluded. As God's will is expressed in God's Law, the text opposes the Law of God to the law of capital, which wastes the opportunities that riches offer to commit oneself to one's neighbor.

Luke 18:18–30: The Mammon as an Impediment for Discipleship

The alternative presented in Luke 16:13, God or Mammon, is confirmed in Luke 18:18–22 when the rich magistrate is unable to sell everything, give the money to the poor, and follow Jesus. The immense difficulty that the rich have entering the Kingdom of God (Luke 18:24) also confirms 16:13. The hyperbole, comparing a large animal, the camel, to the smallest imaginable hole, expresses the desperate outcry of the poor who blame the selfish rich and also claim for themselves the possibility of God's intervention (Luke 18:27).

The Social and Economic Isotopic Theme

In semiotic analysis, an isotopy is a plane or a theme made up of the multiple narrative elements belonging to the same dimension, which makes possible a uniform and homogeneous reading of a text. Thanks to the isotopies, a discourse is not a simple succession of independent phrases, but precisely a discourse which makes sense.

Luke's social and economic isotopy has three thematic groups:

• The abyss between the poor and the rich;
• Jesus' solidarity with the poor; and judgment on the selfish rich;
• The ethics of sharing.

In Luke's text there is a dynamic relationship among these three groups, presented through stories, parables, beatitudes, sayings, which comfort the poor and confront the rich. On the one hand there is an ethics put into action, an applied economic ethics, a lived orthopraxis; on the other hand there is selfishness, an imminent downfall, and oppression in action.

The conflict between *rich and poor* is evident in the text's terminology. All the references to poor and rich are opposed to each other. Thus there are no isolated poor and no independent, "innocent" rich.

The term "poor" literally refers to the physically and economically impoverished. The situation of the poor is not a virtue, but a concrete reality; a state of hunger (without qualifications, cf. Matt 5:6), sorrow, persecution, lack of basic material goods for the maintenance and development of life. The only positive aspect of being poor is that they are guaranteed God's solidarity, received through Jesus. This affirmation excludes reading poverty as virtue, an ideal of the ascetic life, divine punishment, blind fate, test for future lives (from the perspective of reincarnation), consequence of irresponsibility or laziness, severe pedagogy, refuge of the satisfied or similar conceptual means of avoiding the evil of poverty and that we have to fight to abolish it. The Beatitude about the poor does not accept that the poor must remain poor, but instead advocates for the active overthrow of this deplorable state, since it states that those despised by the rich and prestigious are important and enjoy the love of God.

Jesus translates his solidarity with his poor contemporaries into a series of concrete liberating actions. Healing and resurrection are visible signs of God's presence in Jesus Christ. Liberating actions are social, economic, theological, cultural, and religious facts. They restore health, human dignity, social respect, and the access to God; they allow people to return to a dignified concept of work; and they destroy the ideology that ascribes respect and privileges to the healthy and the rich but contempt and punishments to the sick and the poor as sinners.

The Magnificat (Luke 1:46–55), the Beatitudes and the Woes (6:20–26), and the parable of the rich and Lazarus (16:19–31), each contain a significant image of inversion framed by the piety of Israel's poor, which states that God elevates the excluded and judges the rich and powerful.

With the promise of the Kingdom and his commitment to action, Jesus reveals that the God of the poor, the needy, the sick, the harmed, and the excluded is manifested in his person. Here we have an authentic alternative to a society that worships power and seeks success, affirmation, and salvation through political, military, economic, and religious systems; and because of that excludes the poor and the powerless.

The core of this isotopic theme is an economic inversion: the destruction of security based on wealth is transformed into the beatitude of the poor. Also this theme constructs a model for the rich to commit themselves to the cause of the poor. The rich are put to the severest test by being asked to actively commit themselves to the good of the poor.

The Challenge for the Rich

The term "rich" emphasizes the responsibility and personal guilt of every rich individual person and all the rich collectively. "The rich" as a collective concept derives from the prophetic criticism in the Hebrew Bible, which was not directed at any particular rich individual, but which launched a frontal assault on the entire rich class who were exploiters and oppressors.

The texts' criticism of the selfish rich takes several forms: inversions, open criticism, judgments, warnings, and reproaches. The judgment proclaimed against the rich is inversely related to the salvation, blessings, and share of the Kingdom proclaimed to the poor.

Luke contributes to the economic struggle on behalf of the poor by proposing that the rich are first criticized and then converted, and by highlighting the conjunction between God, Jesus, and the poor. The texts positively affirm the value of riches, appreciating their importance for human life, especially their ability to assist the poor. They call for the creation of a society in which all the people have the means to live with dignity; a goal achievable only if the rich become poor themselves through sharing their riches with the poor.

Luke uses the disciples (in the Gospel of Luke) and the first community in Jerusalem (in Acts) to confront the rich with the exemplary discipleship of the "first times", both by the disciples and by the first community in Jerusalem. The Gospel is a radical appeal to rich readers that demands a clear socioeconomic decision to place themselves on the side of the poor in this shameful conflict. The sterile controversy about the difference between a Luke who is "the evangelist of the poor" versus a Luke who is "the evangelist of the rich" is creatively resolved by noting that Luke is the voice of the poor and the judge of the rich. For that rich person who yields to this judgment and accepts the proposed conversion, Luke becomes the evangelist who shows him or her the way to salvation.

Luke uses the features of the topic "the poor and the rich" to formulate an alternative lifestyle for the Christian community, the common denominator of which is the praxis of sharing:

- *Renouncing* riches in favor of the poor.
- *Giving.* The receivers are the poor, the needy, the deprived. A concrete way of *giving* is *charity* (alms). Luke 12:33 explains the reach of charity: it covers all the facets of *giving* and *sharing*.
- *Lowering debts,* renouncing personal benefits, Luke 16:5-7.
- *Lending without expecting return,* Luke 6:34-35. Jesus destroys the theology of reciprocity in Luke 13:1-5; the commands of practicing goodness without expecting any recompense nullify the moral aspect (also, Luke 17:7-10). The gift of the Kingdom of God substitutes reciprocity of favors for fear of punishment.
- *Putting oneself at others' disposal both with service and riches.* Luke 8:1-3 exemplifies this praxis by commenting on the people who accompanied Jesus on his mission.
- *Inviting* the poor, the excluded and the chronically sick, Luke 14:13.21.
- *Doing good,* Luke 6:27.33.35; *Being compassionate,* Luke 10:33; Doing mercy, Luke 10:37; *Making friends with money,* Luke 16:9, are several of the explicit variants of sharing.
- *Offering* also takes place in this project,

and the rich who do not really offer are criticized, Luke 21:1-4.
- *"Wasting for love."* This wonderful figure of total selflessness appears twice in the text: Luke 7:36-50 and 15:22-32.
- *Making amends for damages,* as Zacchaeus promises, Luke 19:8.

Unmasking the fatal character of wealth publicly denounces the idolizing of wealth and negates the "theology of prosperity" that equates wealth with divine blessing. If the Mammon is not shared with the needy, it persists in being unjust and evil, it destroys the one who possesses it and leads this person to eternal damnation. If someone hears this judgment and responds in repentance, the possibility of an alternative praxis or way is opened. If God can miraculously convert a rich person, the latter can use his or her goods for the service of the poor and the exploited.

This economic project's originality consists of Jesus' identification with the poor, with the radical judgment of the selfish rich, and with the proposal for an economic conversion. The announcement (the good news of Jesus' identification with the poor) by itself would be a romance; by itself the pronouncement of a judgment against the rich is a legitimate, but inefficient protest; the third alone is a plan without foundation. Only the complete triad gives us the possibility of turning from the announcement and the judgment to the praxis of love that shares. With this, Luke offers a programmatic text, a project of life and for life. He aims to inform and reform the Christian community's orthopraxis, which has the possibility of practicing the early Jerusalem community's inversion paradigm (Acts 2 and 4).

CONCLUSION

In order to ethically evaluate a particular social, economic, and political system, from a theological perspective the key questions are: What are the consequences that

the given system has for human life and the realization of their full potential? Most importantly, what does life become for the weakest in the social body? Within his first century context, Luke removes the mask from the oppressive nature of the economy of his time by declaring that Mammon is an idol that opposes God and, consequently, true life and salvation.

At the same time, Luke shows that the poor are the most important members of the Christian and human community. The eschatological perspective of the Christian faith does not weaken in any way the application of the principles of justice and love to the needy in the concrete situation in which the Church lives. These principles of the Gospel, and the responsibility for the poor, prohibit rich Christians from avoiding that duty.

Luke calls the Church to the alternative praxis of forming a community without marginalization and without poverty. If we read his story in this light, it invites us into its grand vision of an alternative way of living.

BIBLIOGRAPHY

Duchrow, Ulrich, ed. *Colloquium 2000. Faith Communities and Social Movements Facing Globalization.* International and Interfaith Colloquium 2000 on Faith-Theology-Economy. Studies from the World Alliance of Reformed Churches. Geneva: WARC, 2002.

Fitzmeyer, Joseph A. *The Gospel According to Luke.* AB 28, 28 A. Garden City, NY: Doubleday & Co., 1983.

Klein, Hans. *Barmherzigkeit gegenüber den Elenden und Geächteten. Studien zur Botschaft des lukanischen Sonderguts.* Neukirchen-Vluyn: Neukirchener Verlag, 1987.

Krüger, René. *Gott oder Mammon: Das Lukasevangelium und die Ökonomie.* Luzern: Edition Exodus, 1997.

Moxnes, Halvor. *The Economy of the Kingdom. Social Conflict and Economic Relations in Luke's Gospel.* Philadelphia: Fortress, 1988.

Pilgrim, Walter E. *Good News to the Poor: Wealth and Poverty in Luke-Acts,* Minneapolis: Augsburg, 1981.

Schottroff, Luise and Wolfgang Stegemann. *Jesús de Nazaret, esperanza de los pobres.* Salamanca: Sígueme, 1981.

JOHN

Kyung-mi Park

Ewha Women's University, Seoul, Korea

LIFE CONTEXT OF THE INTERPRETATION

I read the Gospel According to John in Korea, a society currently marked by globalization, an economic and cultural phenomenon that deeply affects people's vision of life or "inner world" (as we like to say). Due to numerous technological developments, we perceive ourselves as members of humanity as a whole, and thus as much closer to people of other nationalities than ever before in history. Yet while these other people are very present to us, they remain invisible outsiders with whom we now must compete. As our shoulders sag with thoughts of competing with these outsiders, we forego living together in community with our next-door neighbors and our compatriots. It is ironic that today's individuals feel belittled and powerless in a world where people's freedom and prospects are greater than they have ever been. At first, globalization was welcomed, because it tore down the economic walls that separated nations. But as is clear in Korea, globalization has quickly become a formidable challenge for humanity as a whole, as well as for individuals and their "inner world."

Since the Gospel of John is the most spiritual of the Gospels, it is appropriate to approach it with questions raised by the disintegration of the vision of life—the inner world or symbolic world—that

people suffer in our time of globalization. Because we are constantly in the presence of all these invisible others who belong to various races and cultures, it becomes difficult for us to have a sense of belonging and security. The world, which earlier seemed more comprehensible and controllable, gradually becomes more terrifying, strange, and even hostile. Consequently, people aspire to otherworldly salvation in enthusiastic religious movements. Can John help us to reflect on this spiritual crisis and assess the present quests for a vision of life totally oriented toward a higher realm of human spirituality? Can it help us to make sense of spiritual quests that are prompted by the confrontation with unprecedented technical developments and with economic and cultural globalization? How can John help us to under-stand and address the distress of people whose inner world has been shattered?

As we bring these questions to the Gospel of John from this particular context of globalization, we will need to focus our attention on the spiritual character of this Gospel's theology. Furthermore, as we come to John with the present crisis of spirituality in a globalized Korea, we will focus on issues most directly related to the spirituality that one finds in our part of the world.

Kyung-mi Park received her theological training in Korea, where she earned her PhD from Ewha Women's University. Her publications include *New Heaven, New Earth, and New Woman: Feminist Interpretation of the Bible* (in Korean); many articles on the Gospel of John; and feminist interpretations of the New Testament. She is an active member of Korea Association of Women Theologians (KAWT).

CONTEXTUAL COMMENT

Major Themes of the Gospel of John from a Korean Perspective

From our Korean perspective, the most significant themes of the Gospel of John can be listed as follows:

a) *Jesus communicates mysteriously with those with whom he enters into dialogue.* Looking at John's use of language in comparison with mantras recited by Buddhist monks helps us to ponder its religious function for the community, and thus for present-day communities in our globalized world.

b) *A radical wall of separation exists between the divine world and the human world, and between the Johannine community and outsiders, especially "the Jews."* While this text communicates anti-Judaism to modern readers, a different message comes to the fore when it is read as reflecting the suffering of a group ostracized from a community. Looking at this twofold theme from the perspective of an ostracized community, when community life is as primary as it is for us (in contrast with the individualistic Western perspective), throws light on the theme of miscommunication. It also illuminates the symbolism, often colored with sorrow, through which John speaks about the mysteries of the division between the divine and the human world and of the miracle needed to bridge this division.

c) *The coming of the Paraclete is promised, who is identified as "the Holy Spirit, whom the Father will send in [Jesus'] name" (14:26).* The Paraclete, also designated as "the Spirit of truth, whom the world cannot receive" (14:17), but whom the ostracized community receives, can readily be understood in light of the Zen concept regarding the "spirit within, energy without." From this perspective, the Paraclete is the divine external energy that helps the community to love despite its ostracism and is correlated to the internal spirituality through which the community is in communion with Christ and/or God.

d) *Finally, the image of the vine and the branches is used to symbolize Jesus' relationship to his followers.* This symbolism conveys the vision of a community that, far from escaping into a mystical quietude of salvation and denying the world, is called to remain in the world and to embrace it in an unceasing mission.

The examination of these themes brings us to *a renewed understanding of John's theology of life.* No matter how hard and painful are the tests and trauma that we endure, John invites us to recognize that our life, however individualized, is directly in touch with nature, the universe, and the life of God, who orders us to be obedient and to remain faithful against all odds.

An Overview of the Gospel of John

I have outlined the Gospel of John following the work of Gail O'Day in the *New Interpreter's Study Bible.* I have expected discussion on passages of special interest in the contextual commentary below.

I. The Prelude to Jesus' Ministry, 1:1-51

II. The Beginning of Jesus' Ministry, 2:1–5:47

   Special attention to Jesus and Nicodemus, 2:23–3:21 and other instances of communication/miscommunication

III. Jesus' Ministry Continues: Conflict and Opposition Grows 6:1–10:42

   With special attention to the exclusion from the synagogue, 9:1–10:21

IV. The Prelude to Jesus' Hour, 11:1–12:50

V. The Farewell Meal and Discourse 13:1–17:26

   With special attention to the Farewell Discourse, the promise of the Paraclete, and the vine and the branches 14:1–16:33

VI. Jesus' Arrest, Trial, and Death, 18:1–19:42

John's Historical Context and Our Globalized Context

The earliest possible date for the Gospel of John is 75-80 C.E., that is, after the destruction of Jerusalem and the temple. At this time Jews were seeking to redefine their identity without the temple, a process that led them to reject those who did not conform to this identity, including the Jewish Christians. This exclusion from the synagogue is mentioned in 9:22; 12:42; 16:2 (see comments below). Although no consensus exists on the precise circumstances, with a number of scholars we can say that the Gospel of John reflects a situation in which an ostracized Christian community was in the process of defining its identity (a) independently from the Jewish community, and (b) in a Hellenistic world dominated by the Roman Empire that had recently destroyed Jerusalem and a rebellious Palestine.

Our present situation, characterized by globalization, is very similar to that of the late Hellenistic period when Christianity was in its early stages. People suffered and were haunted by similar crises of their inner world. The globalization of that period, much like that of today, was spurred by economic factors in the context of political empires. In Alexander the Great's Hellenistic Empire, as well as in the Roman Empire, East and West met. The great cities in the East, such as Antioch of Syria, Ephesus of Asia Minor, and Alexandria of Egypt, became economic and cultural pillars and, as such, places where East and West were open to each other. Out of trade a single economic community grew. Through the unlimited exchange of ideas, which helped people shed their "provincialism" and become more cosmopolitan, a single civilization was born.

However, Hellenistic globalization was not without problems. Conflicts existed between the rulers and the ruled, between cities and rural areas, and between the Hellenized elite and the mass of people clinging to their traditional way of life, that is, their religious, socio-economic, and cultural legacies. In this confrontation of East and West, revolution or resistance against the ruling class was understandable. The Jewish War of 66-70 C.E. exemplified how much this anti-Roman and anti-Hellenistic resistance mixed together political, religious, and cultural factors.

The subjects of the Roman Empire, people of various races and cultures, must have found it difficult to gain a sense of belonging or security. The cosmos that had seemed comprehensible, as well as controllable in the traditional cultures, gradually became more terrifying, strange, and even hostile. People aspired to another world for their salvation, a religious world where they could forget about this world's changes and worries. In this atmosphere of late Hellenism, ancient oriental religions were reborn as popular religions in which oppressed people's fervor for salvation often developed into eschatological visions. For individuals who had lost their identity in the vast Hellenistic Empire, these religions provided not only a sense of belonging and security but also new means for understanding this changeable world.

The Gospel of John rather introspectively speaks about the crisis that the people of the Hellenistic period were going through. Although it does not provide a concrete description of this crisis, the Gospel depicts in vivid detail the suffering caused by the shattering of people's inner world. With great literary and theological creativity, John's Gospel depicts the world's hostility toward Christ and the believers' fervent desire to break away from oppression and to fly high up into the sky like an eagle.

The Gospel of John has been called "the spiritual Gospel" or "the theological Gospel," in contrast with the synoptic Gospels whose descriptions of Jesus' life are, so to speak, about the "flesh." This contrast is not quite appropriate, as is shown by the remarkable progress made in understanding John's Gospel by studying John's community. Scholars have clarified how the community's conflicts with Judaism and its painful experience of expulsion from the Jewish community are reflected in the particular way in which the Gospel retells the stories about Jesus. This socio-historical study opens new possibilities for understanding this Gospel. Without denying its spirituality, this study fleshes out the spiritual gospel by bringing us ever closer to those fierce spiritual struggles in which John's community was caught. This study brings us closer to the gospel's spirituality by relating it to the concrete and physical reality of life, and thereby leads us to a more holistic understanding of the text.

The legendary symbol for John's Gospel is an eagle. Raymond Brown said, "If the Johannine eagle soared above the earth, it did so with talons bared for the fight" (1979, 24). This sentence expresses well the nature of the gospel's spirituality. What does it mean that John's gospel and his community are spiritual? Does it mean that the community enjoyed quiet introspection or blissful states of enthusiasm? Indeed, the gospel leads its readers into a deep relationship with Jesus. However, this empowering spirituality originates in the life and struggles of a community that was intrinsically and actively interacting with the surrounding world. The spiritual experience of the community was incarnated in a most concrete way as its members testified to Jesus amid the hostile world. The eagle symbolizing the gospel flies ever higher and ever deeper into the spiritual heaven toward its invisible end, but it has been injured from battles on earth. Although it is hurt, with undying love and persistent expectations for the earth, it will continue to soar up into the sky dreaming of the day of its beautiful landing.

The Language of John

At the bottom of the unfathomable world of religion there are always mysterious experiences. John invites readers to meet face to face with this world of mystery by eavesdropping on dialogues between Jesus and people such as Nicodemus (3:1-21) and a Samaritan woman (4:1-42). These dialogues

remind us of Buddhist monks reciting mantras each in his own "language." As outsiders, we cannot perceive a common system of communication. This is what happens when God's words enter human speech. Disruptions and contradictions become pervasive, as is the case in the language and the theological vision of John's Gospel. The readers' first impression is that these dialogues represent a confusing breakdown in communication, because the expected gradual progression of perception is missing. Nicodemus and the Samaritan woman eventually gain a partial insight into the mystery of Jesus, but never a complete one. Furthermore, despite their eagerness, they do not gain this insight as a result of a growing perception following step-by-step the unfolding of the conversation. Their incomplete enlightenment is very slow in coming. For instance, Nicodemus is unable to understand what Jesus said about spiritual rebirth (3:3); for him, it simply means re-entering into his mother's womb (3:4). The Samaritan woman, upon hearing Jesus' unmistakable self-revelation, "I am he" (*ego eimi*) (4:26), responds hesitantly, "[He] told me everything I have ever done! He cannot be the Messiah, can he?" (4:29, NRSV; other translations tone down this hesitation).

In contrast, Jesus, as depicted by John, knew human beings only too well. According to John, many people believed in Jesus' name upon seeing his signs, but he did not like to rely on the use of signs, because "he knew all people" (2:24-25). Jesus' knowledge of their minds hindered, rather than helped, the development of intimate relationship between them. As described by John, Jesus intentionally made his teachings obscure, so that outsiders would readily misunderstand them, and so that his community alone would grasp the revelations. Because of the difficulty of communicating divine knowledge, the Jews and "the world" are left out of this communication, even though Jesus ostensibly addresses them again and again. John presents the world of faith as characterized by knowing; however, this know-ledge is never fully explained so as to prevent the common people from understanding.

Between Jesus and the world stands a high wall of silence, through which no communication is possible—a feature of the Gospel particularly apparent in a cultural setting that is not framed by Christian perspectives.

Unless you step into the world to which John guides you, his unique, introspective language will never open to you. By following John as he leads you by the hand, you eventually end up in that symbolic world depicted in the Gospel by simple yet mystical words. Then, when you look from inside, you discover that the door to it was open all along. "The wind blows where it chooses, and you hear the sound of it, but you do not know where it comes from or where it goes" (3:8). These words may be applied to John's own language. We can see that the meaning of his language changes freely just as the wind blows randomly in every direction. Though we cannot possibly know from where the wind blows, we can feel it rushing past us; so it is with John's language. Just as we are unable to catch the wind with our hands, so his language is out of reach. Just as we feel the wind with our body, so must we feel the language of John with our hearts and with our lives. When the language is felt in this way, it empowers us and our communities to resist being disoriented by globalization.

In spite of its closed nature, the Gospel of John keeps inviting its readers with its alluring voice to enter its own world—calling them to surrender to its unique flow of thought. Many scholars have observed that John's way of thinking is circular. His way of thinking, which helped him conceive and communicate a particular revelation, is based upon his unique convictions about revelation. Ideas are often so interconnected that the basis of one conclusion becomes the premise of another, which in turn becomes the basis of the first. Thus, John's closed and circular way of thinking puzzles those outside, even though it is readily understood by those inside. From John's perspective, knowledge about the revelation cannot be explained; it can only be vindicated within its hermeneutical circle. Where faith is already established, this circular thinking possesses a remarkably persuasive power, which draws people with an irresistible force, holding their "inner world" together. The power of this circular thinking of faith is the exact opposite of the power of globalization that shatters people's inner world.

The closed nature of John's circular thinking is a way of expressing the closed nature both of the symbolic universe of his gospel and of the Johannine community. Therefore we need to understand the context circumscrib-ing the concrete life of John's community.

The Reality of Suffering

In John 3:3, Jesus says, "No one can see the kingdom of God without being born from above or again (anōthen)." John strongly believed that there was no way for the world to truly go near God. To express this conviction, John used the phrase "to be born from above, or again" in Christ's dialogue with Nicodemus. His use of this phrase betrays his radical theological conception about the division between the two worlds, divine and human. In fact, this conception is rooted in the experiences of painful persecution suffered by John's community.

The Jews are depicted more negatively in John's Gospel than in any other part of the New Testament. While *Jews* mostly refers to Jewish leaders and can be viewed as reflecting a family dispute, for readers this term symbolizes non-believers refusing to accept Jesus' words, whoever they might be. One has to acknowledge and deplore that the gospel conveys anti-Judaism in this way, as is clear from a post-Holocaust perspective. But rather than ignoring this painful aspect of the Gospel, we have to ask: Why did John use the word *Jews* in describing those who were against Jesus? The tense relations between John's community and contemporary Judaism certainly played a role. His description of confrontations between Jesus and the Jews reflect the situation in his time. The passages where John describes those conflicts are two-dimensional dramas (Martyn 1979). When John talks about Jesus, he also speaks of his community.

The story about the healing of a blind man in John 9 is such a two-dimensional drama (following Martyn's interpretation). The reference to excommunication from the synagogue (9:22) clearly refers to the real situation of John's community. This ostracism did not take place during Jesus' ministry, but in the time following the Jewish War of 66-70 C.E.

The Pharisees were the only Jewish group that survived after the destruction of Jerusalem, because they did not associate themselves directly with the resistance movements against Rome during the war. Having launched a movement to rebuild Judaism in Jamnia, they viewed Johannine Christians as heretics who must be expelled from the synagogue. According to John 9 and 15:18–16:4a, John's community suffered greatly under this measure. Expulsion from the synagogue meant ostracism from the Jewish community and thus both religious and economic isolation; they fell into legal uncertainties and economic hardship. Their expulsion had an adverse effect upon their relations with the occupying Roman forces; Christians were in no position to receive any protection from the Roman authorities, because they were no longer part of an authorized religion.

Coming back to John 3:3, considering these painful experiences, the phrase *being born again* shows the closed nature of John's symbolic world, as well as the unique self-understanding of his community. As was the case with Nicodemus, it is almost impossible for outsiders to approach the gospel and understand its logic because it is fully conviction-driven. Understanding has become a miracle of new birth, entering into a new system of symbols. More than anybody else, John was acutely aware of the conflicts and discontinuity lying between the two worlds—theologically speaking, the divine world and the human one, and sociologically speaking, John's community and its outside world. Perhaps all of the mysteries and symbols he depicted bear the subdued color of sorrow for this reason. Between the two worlds stood a long wall of silence, through which no communication was possible. John is aware that this wall returns only echoes of bitter accusations in response to his words, no matter how sweet they are. John's simple yet enchanted words are precious stones that have been polished in the process of this incisive perception.

The Paraclete

According to the New Testament, believers are born again and come into being through their spiritual experiences. The book of Acts shows that spiritual experiences and church mission are closely related; after Jesus' death, the Holy Spirit turns the trembling disciples into courageous missionaries (Acts 1:8). Furthermore, in the Synoptic Gospels, whenever Jesus talks to his followers about their destiny, he speaks of their coming persecution and trials, in the midst of which the Spirit would help them to give testimony (Matt 10:20; Mark 13:11; Luke 21:12-13).

Similarly, in John the Paraclete is the power that helps the disciples' testimony to succeed against all odds (15:26-27). As if to reflect these forensic circumstances of trials in persecution settings, John uses the term *Paraclete,* which commonly designated a trial advocate for the accused. But now John uses this term as a title for the Spirit, depicting it as a person, and thus making it possible to identify the Spirit with Christ. When other New Testament writers used the term *pneuma*—the neutral noun most commonly used in the New Testament as a designation for the Spirit—they did not relate the Spirit to the person of Christ, despite its power to inspire and change human beings. The term Paraclete allows John to present the Spirit as a person who is closely related to Christ. In the eyes of John, the Paraclete is Christ, present in the form of the Spirit after Christ's glorification on the cross. This term further denotes the roles of the Spirit / Christ for Jesus' followers as advocate for the accused, and far beyond, as prosecutor, comforter, and exhorter. By calling the Spirit Paraclete, John introduces spiritual experiences into the literary framework of the trial scenes of his Gospel. In effect, John identifies the manifestations of the Spirit in the midst of persecutions and trials in the disciples' mission (as in the Synoptic Gospels) with Jesus' ministry. Throughout the Gospel, Jesus is described as under trial; John seems to say that the persecution his community presently suffers is comparable to Jesus' own trial. Through this identification, Jesus is standing for the community. Through these shared circumstances of persecution and harassment, the community and Christ become one through the Paraclete.

Thus the Paraclete is the Spirit that leads the community to concentrate on life here and now. God's history and future plans are manifested in their life, burdened with persecution and missionary work. Here and now, in the life of the community, the past and the future are integrated. The Paraclete transformed the present time (in which the community experienced the presence of Christ amid its persecutions) into God's time (an eschatological time). This transformation was possible because John's community understood its life as being strictly Christ-centered. The church went on with its missions for Christ (17:18; 20:21), while "living him." Through the Paraclete, John's community manifested the presence of Christ in the world, and so to speak, kept him alive.

The Paraclete played an essential role in the ongoing life of a community that struggled to hold onto Christ's revelations despite persecution. Through its spiritual experiences the community could realize perfect oneness as well as perfect love. In the farewell discourse (John 14–16) Jesus eloquently speaks about such oneness and perfect love. The Paraclete is the spirit of accord and consolation that heals the grieving community after Jesus' departure, and changes its sorrows into convictions about the future. The Spirit weaves everything within Jesus Christ, seeping quietly like water and blowing in silence like the wind. Like the vine and its branches, Christ and the community are one (15:1-6); John's shepherd and his sheep know each other perfectly (10:11-16). This communion is the basis of the Johannine community's love. Its members are able to love because the Paraclete enables them

to live with Jesus though he is physically absent. Furthermore, because the Paraclete is the presence among them of both the Spirit and Christ, it brings back the memory of Christ's love for them (14:26; 15:26-27).

The community lives forever in this memory of the love it had experienced. John's shepherd dies for his sheep (10:11), unlike ordinary shepherds, who would consider their own life more precious than one of their possessions. Here, we can glimpse John's specific way of thinking—the tendency to envision reality in most radical ways, in terms of life and death. Presumably John drapes all his symbols in sadness because of his community's terrifying situation. These emergencies might have led John to picture Jesus as a good shepherd, so that his community might live in the memory of that love. The memory of such sacrificial love (15:13) might have empowered the community to survive without betraying each other in the face of persecution and threats of death. As Jesus, the good shepherd, sacrificed his life for the community, the sheep, so that they might find eternal life, so John's community had to prepare its members to give their lives for each other in times of imminent danger. Sacrificial love enables communion and perfect knowledge between the one who gives up his or her life and the one for whom the sacrifice was made.

The foundation of all love relationships in the community is the love between the father and the son. At the bottom of the love among the community lies the shepherd's love, and at the bottom of his love lies that of his father who sent him to watch for the sheep. In Christ we partake of the relationship of love between Christ and the father: "As the Father has loved me, so I have loved you; abide in my love" (15:9). Thus, perfect oneness or the relationship of perfect love becomes possible in the community. The Spirit present among them is the foundation of their accord and communality.

What is the dominant symbol for the Spirit in John? In the Bible, Spirit is most conspicuously associated with fire and water. The Spirit, as fire, appears in the form of glossolalia or violent mystical experiences, while, as water, it seeps through to bring enlightenment. We find this latter symbolism in the dialogue with the Samaritan woman, 4:10-26, more cryptically in other parts of the Gospel (e.g., 19:34), but most directly in 7:37-39 where water and spirit are explicitly brought together:

> "Let anyone who is thirsty come to me, and let the one who believes in me drink. As the scripture has said, 'Out of the believer's heart shall flow rivers of living water.'" Now he said this about the Spirit, which believers in him were to receive; for as yet there was no Spirit, because Jesus was not yet glorified.

Thus water is associated with the Spirit and more broadly with the spirituality of John's community, as that community was banned from the synagogue and stripped of its right to exist. John's community strove to become one with Christ by adopting a communal life in the midst of the world, rather than indulging itself in collective enthusiastic experiences beyond human understanding. The Spirit / Paraclete is the spirit of accord and oneness that enabled them to become one with Christ, to live in Christ, and thus to keep Christ alive.

What is the spirit for us today? In my cultural context I envision it both in a biblical and a Korean way. The spirit in me is that which is in touch with God, with myself, with my neighbors, and with nature. Spirituality is our attitude toward the experience and practice of transcendence. In Hebrew *(ruah)*, Greek *(pneuma),* and Latin *(spiritus),* spirit means wind or breath. The wind is an invisible, unpredictable, and uncontrollable force. Breath is a feeble wind blowing within life—the substance of life. All lives exist through breathing and are connected with each other through breath. Therefore, the spirit is necessarily integrated with the body, and the spirit refers to that which is within you and beyond you. According to Asian Zen philosophy, only when the three elements of *Chong* (body), *Ki* (energy), and *Shin* (spirit or mind) are united as one can

we reach *Tao* (the Way). The spirit or deity is a transcendent, divine life corresponding to the intimate life force. Thus, they say spirit within, energy without.

The Paraclete is appropriately understood as the breath or the life energy for John's community, its "spirit within, energy without." The Spirit internally enabled the community to get in touch with Christ or God (spirituality within) and to help them to love others (energy without) and live with them without falling into the abyss of despair and hatred that could have been their response to a world that hated them without any reason.

The Vine and Its Branches: John's Community

Be it in the time of John or today, community life supports Christian mission and Christian life for individual believers. All the more so for John's community, whose members kept their convictions despite persecution. Consequently, the members regarded their community identity and the power that unified them as most important. This may be illustrated by stories found in John 10 and 15. John 15:1–16:4a helps us to understand relations within the community (15:1-17) and with the world outside it (15:18–16:4a). In 15:1-17, the branches belonging to the vine must bear much fruit (15:2, 5, 8). Since the community has received its eschatological salvation from Christ the vine, the community was required to display and perpetuate its status of salvation in its praxis, through deeds of love within its life (15:12-17). Through this love, the community proves that its members are disciples of Jesus and thus glorify the Father (15:8). After Easter, the community becomes the messenger of the revelation, but not through doctrinal statements about salvation or faith or through fiery slogans. The life of love exemplified by the community functions to share the revelation and fulfill its missions toward the world (10:37-38; 14:10-11; 15:8).

What should be specifically noted about the community in John's gospel is its intimate relationship with Jesus. The believers are led to Christ, "reside" and "live" in Christ, and are invited to form with him a community "in him." The world in which Christ resides could be characterized by love. Moreover, it is important to remain in this love and practice love with each other (13:34-35; 15:9-10, 12, 17; 17:26). That is, according to 15:1-17, the integral part of communality is to draw its members inside Christ and lead them to the revelation of love. Here the church is not an institution that gathers a few people for some agreed-upon purposes. Rather the church is the community in which Christ and the members, like the vine and its branches, are joined together as one in a mystical way.

In 15:18–16:4a, John's community stood as a witness to Jesus before the Jews who were its contemporaries. After their expulsion from the synagogue, the Johannine Christians had to explain the reason for the Jews' hatred and persecution. John does so in 15:18–16:4a by positing a dualism between the community and the world. John's community, as chosen by Jesus, is separate from the world; it stands in sharp contrast to a hostile world. The world hates the community, because it is not of the world (15:19). Yet, by showing that the fate of Christians who are hated and persecuted by the world is the same as that of Jesus himself, John empowers the community to continue its testimony with the help of the Paraclete (15:26-27).

While 15:18–16:4a presents a dualism between the community and the world, as Onuki points out, this dualistic teaching does not suggest that the community should stand aloof and isolated from the world; on the contrary, it encourages the community to be involved in the world again (1984). Thus, surprisingly, John's dualistic conception leads the community to a monistic conduct of integration. By reaffirming that his community has rid itself of worldliness and is different in essence, John paradoxically leads his community to proclaim and exemplify the gospel for the world, rather than extricating themselves from it.

John's Gospel, contrary to common perceptions, is not a static, mystical document that calls people to settle down in the intimate quietude of salvation. Rather it demands that people rush into the world that refuses them and hates them, and wrestle with this world to reform it. John's Gospel demands that the community be both courageous and proactive in its interaction with the world. John's community is not a closed-in group, but a society again and again opened up by a centrifugal force centered around Christ. The internal cohesion of its members with Jesus as the center was not designed to deny the world or set the community apart from it, but to rush toward it, and to embrace it. Perhaps, this kind of activism and vitality might explain the dynamism of the early Christians, including Johannine Christians, despite their suffering and persecution in the Hellenistic age.

CONCLUSION

While the Synoptic Gospels used the phrase "kingdom of God" to express the reality of salvation, John prefers the word "life," including expressions related to "eternal life." In this way he expresses the anthropological and psychological dimensions of the salvation event.

As far as John's Gospel is concerned, salvation and the eschatological realization of expectations related to the conferring of life or of the Spirit are related to the time of Jesus' being *glorified*. It is well known that in John's Gospel, Jesus' glorification is connected with the event of the cross. The word *glorified* has a variety of meanings. In depicting those multiple events that involved Jesus—his death, resurrection, ascension, and the spiritual anointment—John uses the Greek verb *"doxazō"* (to glorify), which denotes God's decisive act of salvation (12:23, 28; 17:1). Strictly speaking, the events of Jesus' death, resurrection, and ascension each happened at different times, as John's successive narratives express. Yet, he manages to describe, by means of his own unique language, Jesus' death, resurrection, and ascension as if they happened in one single eschatological glorification.

Likewise, the verb *hypsoō,* meaning to *lift up* as used by John, also carries a compound meaning. In his gospel, this verb is used to mean "to be lifted onto the cross" as well as "to be raised to heaven." (In Acts 2:33, Luke uses the same word to speak exclusively of the ascension.) By using two meanings of one word to describe the two very different events, John manages to bring these events together as inseparable—as the horrific cross was the way to heavenly glorification. Without the crucifixion, there could be neither the ascension nor the conferring of the spirit. Here, we witness John's theological and literary genius.

The glorified ascension is related to the painful crucifixion, but unlike Luke 24 and Acts 1, John does not describe the ascension as a dramatic scene of Jesus rising high into the air. This leaves open the possibility that Jesus might still be with his community of followers here on earth. Despite the fact that John knew these events belonged to the eschatological time, he dared to describe them as one whole. Thus, the cross holds the potential fulfillment of the eschatological expectations of the ascension and the conferring of the Spirit.

If we were to accept John's overall theological framework, our attitudes toward life and pain might change. John does not make any empty promises that a blessed future will follow after suffering. Nor does he make any drab hackneyed promises that the present life, though painful, will be rewarded with eternal happiness in our next life in heaven. He tells those who are suffering hardships not to run away, but does not beautify life with hollow words. By encouraging the sufferers to find the eternal life of God amidst the changing time that swallows everything, he just tries to show that they might psychologically overcome their hardships. Just as the disgraceful cross is glorification and is being lifted up to God, so our present life of suffering itself is a blessing. In this sense, John presents a rather heroic attitude toward life.

John's overall theological framework provides a way to overcome the disintegration of the vision of life—of the inner world—that people suffer in our time of globalization. To those who are groaning under the crushing weight of global history, God, who is the master of time, might seem coldhearted and merciless. The rolling wheels of time, which mercilessly destroy everything in their path, do so without regard for personal feelings or for underlying concepts about good and evil. None of the great theological insights deny human agony or travails. Nevertheless, religion in general, and Buddhism in our context, often tells people that suffering and hardship are in essence a path to peace and to the ultimate life, and further recommends that people recognize that peace and life are hidden in such suffering. As we saw reading the Gospel of John from a context where Christians cannot ignore the presence of Buddhists around them, the oneness between God and human beings is possible only when we free ourselves from all the existing dualistic conflicts—such as good and evil, man and woman, and you and I—and transcend our self-centeredness. By giving up this sense of dualistic conflict, one can enter the realm of faith; then the fearful and cruel aspects of God dissolve.

The crucifixion of Christ may be said to represent the fear and cruelty of time, and to symbolize the reality of life in which suffering is ever present. John's Jesus, it seems, overcomes fear through the crucifixion and maintains his dignity by offering and absolving all those horrendous, untamable tragedies rendered by the vast, merciless universe.

The wonderful mystery of religious insight lies in the way it transforms the tragedies and degeneration of life into praise for life. Irony and paradox are found in all great religious teachings. Here, in John's Gospel, the mystery about God—always self-contradictory—parallels that of the incarnation in which God's Word becomes flesh and resides in a humble manner among us. By nature life is subjected to time; God's love is God's affection for the existence in time. For this reason, in the story of the incarnation, God enters into the flow of time that incessantly moves from birth to death, by lowering God's self.

Through his discourse about a suffering God who offered Self as a sacrifice, John could have eloquently explained away the paradoxical truth of life. The flesh of Christ, who is God, is nailed to the cross, a wooden frame of death. To abandon oneself to God is to accept abandoning life. There would be no longer any paradox about life. However, for John the cross is none other than the tree of life. John readily sees the flower of the resurrected life blooming on the cross, the frame of death. This perspective enables us to be truly loyal to life, to obey its order to go on living. When one accepts this order, all individual fears, dreads, and pains become secondary. Like a nameless wildflower that blooms in a field, it is possible to live to one's fullest as long as one has breath, without care from anyone, however feeble, vain, and fragile life may seem. Perhaps John came to grasp this nature of life in the midst of the painful persecution and trauma he endured as part of an ostracized group. Maybe he is declaring that no matter how hard and painful the tests, one must recognize that one's life, however individualized, is directly in touch with nature, with the universe, and with the life of God. Being in touch with the life of God in this way requires that we live on against all odds.

BIBLIOGRAPHY

Barrett, C. K. The Gospel According to St. John: An Introduction with Commentary and Notes on the Greek Text. 2d ed. Philadelphia: Westminster Press, 1978.

Brown, Raymond E. The Gospel According to John. AB 29-29A. Garden City, N.Y.: Doubleday, 1966/1970.

———. The Community of the Beloved Disciple. New York: Paulist, 1979.

Burge, Gary M. The Anointed Community: The Holy Spirit in the Johannine Tradition. Grand Rapids: Eerdmans, 1987.

Culpepper, R. Alan. Anatomy of the Fourth Gospel: A Study in Literary Design. Foreword by Frank Kermode. Foundations and Facets. Philadelphia: Fortress, 1983.

Martyn J. Louis. History and Theology in the Fourth Gospel. 2d ed. Nashville: Abingdon, 1979.

Meeks, Wayne A. "The Man from Heaven in Johannine Sectarianism." JBL 91 (1972), 44-72.

O'Day, Gail R. "The Gospel According to John." Pages 1905-51 in The New Interpreter's Study Bible. Edited by Walter J. Harrelson. Nashville: Abingdon, 2003.

Onuki, Takashi. Gemeinde und Welt im Johannesevangelium: ein Beitrag zur Frage nach der theologischen un pragmatischen Funktion des johanneischen Dualismus. WUANT 56. Neukirchen-Vluyn: Neukirchener Verlag, 1984.

JOHN IN AN ORTHODOX PERSPECTIVE

Petros Vassiliadis

Aristotle University of Thessaloniki, Thessaloniki, Greece

LIFE CONTEXT OF THE INTERPRETATION

The Fourth Gospel, or the "Gospel of John" as it is traditionally called, is unique in world religious literature because it challenges the conventional approach to many religious issues. Ironically, it is also the theological treatise that has shaped the identity and self-understanding of the Christian church, especially of the Eastern Orthodox Church, thus becoming *the* Gospel of Christianity. Its transcendent theology concerning Jesus (observed by Pseudo-Dionysios the Areopagite) determined Christian doctrine. Yet in my view, it is its profound reflection on eucharistic theology that makes it most important for today.

This short commentary will attempt to analyze and elaborate on this particular aspect of the text. I will interpret John's Gospel from the life-context of both post-modernity and Eastern Christianity. This latter traditional or denominational context, however, can also have wider ecumenical implications.

The Fourth Gospel's originality provoked strong controversy in early Christianity. This controversy continued in the modern era, though for quite different reasons. John gained recognition, respect, and renewed consideration only in post-modernity. Post-modernity has challenged the priority of the *texts* over *experience,* a priority that dominated, and perhaps still dominates, modern scholarship. As appears most clearly in the context of Eastern Christianity, post-moder-

nity has even challenged the priority of *faith* over the eucharistic *communion* experience of the kingdom of God. After the Reformation and the Enlightenment all scholarly theological perspectives were framed by the dogma that the basis of the Christian faith must be extracted exclusively from a certain historical and critically defined *depositum fidei.* In post-modern time, scholarship no longer holds this dogma to be self-evident. Scholars now realize that equal, if not major, attention must be paid to the eschatological/eucharistic communion experience that produced this *depositum fidei.* And whereas in modernity biblical theology focused mainly on the Jesus tradition in the synoptic gospels, in post-modernity it places greater emphasis on the Johannine tradition.

Postmodern biblical scholarship is moving away from the old affirmation that the Christian community was originally initiated as a faith community by the story (the proclaimed gospel, the written Gospels, and other "historical" accounts). Rather, more scholars are now inclined to think that the story. It is now thought that Christianity started around a table, a normal messianic Jewish banquet, meant as a foretaste of the coming kingdom of God, a proleptic manifestation within the tragic realities of history of an authentic life of communion, unity, justice, and equality. Such an authentic life is, after all, the meaning of the Johannine term *aiōnios zoē* (eternal life).

Petros Vassiliadis is the author of *Eucharist and Witness: Orthodox Perspectives on the Unity and Mission of the Church* (1998) and *Logoi Ihsou* (1999). He is the editor for eastern and southeastern Europe of the monograph series "International Studies in Formative Christianity and Judaism" of the University of South Florida, as well as editor of the monograph series "Commentaries of the N.T.," "Bibliotheca Biblica," and "Ecclesia-Koinonia-Oikoumene." He is a commissioner at the Conference of the World Mission and Evangelism of the World Church Council, president of the World Conference of Associations of Theological Institutions, and vice-president of the Society for Ecumenical Studies and Inter-Orthodox Relations.

In this respect, John offers a dynamic reinterpretation of the traditional (Pauline and synoptic) understanding of the Eucharist as a unique rite regarding the relationship between God, the church/People of God, and the world. In this way, John provides an excellent basis for reflection on unity, reconciliation, communion, sharing, and diaconal service.

CONTEXTUAL COMMENT

The Theological Background of the Gospel of John

John presupposes the synoptic tradition but moves beyond its logic, as well as beyond some of the earlier (Pauline) theological views. Theologically the Fourth Gospel approaches the enduring problems of history, human destiny, death, and the salvation of humankind starting from *Christology,* rather than from anthropology. Christology in John, however, cannot be understood apart from its pneumatology, since "the Advocate, the Holy Spirit" (14:26), according to John's terminology, can be easily defined as the "alter ego" of Christ ("and I will ask my father and he will give you another Advocate to be with you forever," 14:16). This other Paraclete who "will teach you all everything" (14:26) is "the Spirit of truth" (14:17; 15:26; 16:13), and ultimately the one that will "guide you into all the truth" (16:12). Consequently human beings are in communion with "the way, the truth and the life," who is Christ, only through the Holy Spirit, whom he bestows upon the world as a gift of God the Father.

The crucial question is how and on what condition one can become a bearer of the Spirit. In answering this question, modern exegetes are dramatically divided. In the context of eastern Christianity, conservative scholars insist that according to John this can only happen within the church through the sacraments, whereas liberal critics argue that salvation comes through keeping the word of God and being in communion with Christ.

In John, as in the early Christian tradition, the Christian community is not perceived as a mere institution, as an organization with a logically-defined set of doctrines and/or a specific rule (as religious orders have). Instead the Evangelist envisions them as being in communion with Christ when they keep his word and believe in the one who had sent him, just as Christ is in communion with the Father (10:30; 17:21-23). They are "of the truth" when they hear his voice, just as the sheep hear the voice of the good shepherd (10:1-16). This happens when they change their lives, i.e., when they are born from above (3:3), by the Spirit (3:5-8). But this birth by the Spirit is the work of God that no one can control, just as no one can control the wind. "The Spirit blows where He or She wills [here the evangelist moves from the meaning of the Spirit to that of the wind, since the Greek *pneuma* can have both meanings] and you hear its sound, but you do not know from where it comes or where it goes. Thus it is with everyone who is born of the Spirit" (3:8, author's translation [a.t.]). For this reason the proper worship of the community has to be "in spirit and in truth" (4:24).

This extremely charismatic ecclesiological view, however, alternates with a number of sacramental references, which so far have been either rejected in modern scholarship as later additions or interpolations, or explained in a conventional "sacramentalistic" (i.e., quasi-magical, and therefore premodern) way. No other issue has so divided modern Johannine scholarship as the sacramental or non-sacramental character of John. Those who view John sacramentally support their argument by citing and discussing those passages that seem to speak of baptism and Eucharist in a veiled or symbolic manner. Those on the opposite side support their argument by pointing out the Gospel's apparent silence regarding baptism and Eucharist. Today, according to the postmodern approach the issue at stake is whether the various "sacramental" references are at all related to the "sacramental-istic" views of the ancient, Hellenistic mystery cults contemporary with the early church, or whether they have much more dynamic connotations.

Eucharist as a "Mystery" and its Meaning for the Unity of Humankind

John, although it omits the words of institution of the Eucharist, is rightly considered the sacramental book par excellence. The miraculous change of the water into wine at the Wedding in Cana (2:1-11) at the outset of Jesus' earthly ministry, the symbolism of the vine and the branches in the Farewell Discourses (John 15), the flow of blood and water from the pierced side of the crucified Jesus (19:34) and the verses and expressions discussed below make John's sacramental and eucharistic character inescapable. The most discussed texts in this discussion are John 6 (especially 6:51b-58) with its Eucharistic Discourse; the washing of the disciples feet, which actually replaces the synoptic account of the institution of the Eucharist, and all of John 13; the anointing of Jesus in 12:1-8; and the so-called High-Priestly Prayer in John 17, as a model of eucharistic prayer and a plea for the unity of humankind. We will briefly analyse these pericopes, starting with the indispensable theological framework of 11:51-52.

The Eschatological Framework of John's Eucharistic Theology (11: 51-52)

It has long been recognized that in the Gospel of John, the ultimate gifts of God, usually associated with the end times of history, are already accessible to the believer "in Christ." This claim is made, however, without compromising the future dimension of those gifts. The Fourth Gospel insists that these eschatological realities are present in the life of the believer, although there is still a future and unfulfilled quality to them. In doing this, it invites readers to turn their attention from the future to appreciate the quality of Christ-

ian existence in the present. Nevertheless, it perfectly keeps the balance between the present and the future, giving the impression that it attempts to correct an excessive orientation toward the future without dispensing with the value of the future for the believer.

This ambivalence is evident in the teaching, and especially the life and work, of the Jesus of history. This cannot be properly understood without referring to the messianic expectations of Judaism; i.e., the coming of a Messiah, who in the "last days" of history *(eschaton)* would establish his kingdom by calling all the dispersed and afflicted people of God into one place to become one body united around him. The idea of "gathering into one place the scattered people of God and of all the nations," coupled with the descent of God's Spirit upon the sons and daughters of God, is found in the prophetic tradition (e.g., Isa 2:2, 59:21; 66:18, Ezek 36:24; Joel 3:1), but is also evident in the early Christian literature (e.g., Matt 25:32; Rom 12:16; *Did.* 9:4b; *Mart. Poly.* 22:3b; Clement of Rome, 1 Cor 12:6). Most importantly, John interprets the words of the Jewish High Priest by affirming, in a statement generally overlooked in modern biblical scholarship, that "he prophesied that Jesus was about to die...not for the nation only, but to gather into one the dispersed children of God" (11:51-52).

According to John, Jesus of Nazareth identified himself with the Messiah of the end time, who would be the center of the gathering of the dispersed people of God. This radical eschatological teaching about the kingdom of God was the basis for early Christian community's developments in its theology, ecclesiology, spirituality, and its mission. It is exactly this gathering that has ever since been reenacted in the liturgical practice of the Eucharist. Already Paul had stated that all who believe in Christ are incorporated into the one people of God and mystically united into his body through baptism. John further develops this teaching about the unity of the people of God by pointing out that this incorporation into Christ's body takes place in the Eucharist, a significant act of personal and corporate identity that was seen not as a mystery cult but as a foretaste of the expected eschatological kingdom.

The Eucharistic Theology of John 6

To decipher John's overall eucharistic theology one must undoubtedly start from chapter six. The chapter begins with three wondrous deeds: the feeding of the multitude, Jesus walking on the sea, and the miraculous landing of the boat (6:1-21). A lengthy discourse on the "bread of life" follows, where Jesus makes high claims for himself consistent with the Gospel's prologue (1:1-18). This results in a schism among his hearers, with many who had believed now leaving him (6:22-71).

The author no doubt wanted to set the Christ event within the framework of the Exodus-Passover theme. In the Johannine passion story, Jesus is made to die at the very time the lambs are being slaughtered in preparation for that same evening's Passover meal (19:14). The symbolism suggests that Christ is the new Passover lamb by which God liberates humanity from oppression, just as Israel was freed from slavery in Egypt.

This Passover framework, however, is interpreted through clear sacramental references. Only the passage about Jesus walking on the sea (6:16-21) seems to be outside this scheme. But this is probably due to the fact that this very unit was preserved in the earlier synoptic tradition (Matt 14:13-27; Mark 6:30-52) coupled with the account of the multiplication of loaves. At any rate, the entire "bread of life" discourse (6:22-59) is a continuation of, and a commentary on, the miraculous feeding of the five thousand, which already had an accented eucharistic dimension in the synoptic tradition (Mark 6:41).

In general, if Paul and the Synoptic Gospels underline the significance of the soteriological/sacramental understanding of the Eucharist, it is John that gives a life-orientation to it. Without losing its connection with Jesus' death (19:34), the eschatological meal of the community is essentially distanced from death and instead associated with life ("the bread that I will give for the *life* of the world is my flesh," 6:51; see also 6:33, 58). The antithesis between bread and manna perfectly illustrates this truth, for whereas the Jews who had eaten the manna in the desert died, those who partake of the true bread will have life eternal (6:33, 58).

Reading carefully through the entire Johannine eucharistic discourse (6:22-71) one notes a clear change of vocabulary and content in 6:51b-58. In these verses, faith in Christ is no longer the basic presupposition for eternal life ("whoever believes has eternal life. I am the bread of life," 6:47-48; also 6:35). Eternal life now is linked with eating the flesh and drinking the blood of Christ: "Very truly, I tell you, unless you eat the flesh of the Son of Man and *drink his blood,* you have no life in you. Those who eat my flesh and drink my blood have eternal life . . . so whoever eats me will live because of me" (6:53-54, 57). The profound meaning of these sayings, however, is given by the concluding remark of 6:56: "Those who eat my flesh and drink my blood *abide in me, and I in them.*" With these words John denotes an unbroken relationship, communion, and abiding presence of God surpassing both the Hellenistic concept of ecstasy and the classical conception of Jewish prophecy, for it transforms the eschatological expectation from a future event to a present reality. But at the same time it avoids any trace of pantheism, since there is no hint that the initiate identifies with the deity, which was an important teaching of most contemporary mystery cults.

Here we have the beginnings of what has become axiomatic in later Christian tradition: to have "eternal life" (in other words to live an authentic and not just a conventional life) one must be in communion with Christ. This communion means participation in the perfect communion that exists between the Father and the Son: "Just as the living Father sent me, and I live because of the Father, so whoever eats me will live because of me" (6:57). What we have here in the Gospel of John is a parallel expression to the doctrine of *theosis* (divinization; cf. the classic statement of 2 Pet 1:4, "participants of the divine nature") in later patristic literature. John, however, expresses this idea in a more dynamic and less abstract way.

Taking this argument a little further, one can say that John further developed an understanding of the Eucharist as the unceasingly repeated act of sealing the "new covenant" of God with a new people. This interpretation is of course evinced also in the earlier synoptic and Pauline traditions, although there the covenantal interpretation of Jesus' death in the phrase "this is my blood of the *covenant* " is somewhat hidden by the soteriological formula "which is shed *for* you" (Mark 14:24; 1 Cor 11:25).

This eucharistic theology of the Gospel of John, which directly emphasizes the ideas of the covenant and communion, accords with Jeremiah's vision, which was at the same time also a promise. As the prophet said: "and I will make a *covenant . . . a new covenant*" (Jer 31:31), and "I will give them a heart to know that I am the Lord; and they shall be my *people*" (Jer 24:7). In John, as in Jeremiah, the ideas of *a new covenant,* of *communion,* and of the church as a *people* are most strongly emphasized.

The Diaconal Dimension of the Eucharist in John 13

The covenantal dimension of Eucharist, however, is not the only feature emphasized in John's Gospel. The pericope "Jesus Washes the Disciples' Feet" (13:1-20) reveals a further aspect in the John's understanding of the Eucharist. This incident, preserved only in the Fourth Gospel, is placed in the context of the Last Supper, and directly connected to Judas' betrayal. This is the exact place in the Synoptic Gospels where the so-called dominical sayings of the institution of the Eucharist are recorded (Mark 14:22-25 par.). Given the author's almost certain knowledge of the synoptic tradition, one can fairly argue that John has actually replaced the account of the institution of the Eucharist by the symbolic act of Jesus' washing of his disciples' feet. A careful reading of the new love commandment (13:34-15), in the same context, brings immediately to mind the institution narratives of the synoptic tradition. The "*new* commandment" sounds very similar to the "*new* covenant" of these institution narratives.

In sum, John understands the Eucharist not as a mere "cultic" and "sacramental" act, but primarily as a diaconal act and an alternative way of life with clear social implications. In the first century, washing a disciple's feet was more than an ultimate act of humble service (technically known as *kenotic diakonia*). It was also an act of radical social behavior, a rite of social role inversion. This radical behavior and Jesus' admonition to his disciples, and through them to his church: "For I have set you an example, that *you should do as I have done to you*" (John 13:15), make the diaconal implications of the Eucharist an imperative.

The Pericope of the Anointing of Jesus and its Wider Connotations: John 12:1-9

It is almost an assured result of modern biblical and liturgical scholarship that the Eucharist was "lived" in the early Christian community as a foretaste of the coming kingdom of God, a proleptic manifestation within the tragic realities of history of an authentic life of communion, unity, justice, and equality, in which there was no practical differentiation (soteriological, sociological, communal, and in leadership roles) between men and women.

If this was the authentic original meaning of the Eucharist, then John's redaction of another pericope, "Mary Anoints Jesus" (12:1-8), full of ritual connotations and closely related to the eucharistic incident of the washing of the disciples' feet, may not be accidental. John not only placed this famous pericope in the same Passover setting as the pericope of the washing of the disciples' feet (John 13:1-20), he also replaced the unknown woman with Mary, a figure from the family of Lazarus, a family beloved by Jesus. More importantly, by replacing the original and more authentic anointing of Jesus' hair (Mark 14:3 par. Matt 26:7, originally understood as a prophetic act of messianic character, parallel to St. Peter's confession at Caesarea of Philip, Mark 8:27-29) with an anointing of Jesus' feet (John 12:3), John made a woman anticipate the incident of Jesus washing his disciples' feet. By so doing, the "disciple of love" (John, according to the Christian tradition) changed an act of witness into an act of diakonia.

The High-Priestly (Eucharistic) Prayer and the Unity of Humankind (John 17)

It is commonly accepted that John is structured in two major parts: the "Book of Signs" (John 1–12) and the "Book of Glory" (John 13–20). Both are woven around the notion of Jesus' "glorification," his "hour." In the first part Jesus' "hour has not come" (2:4; 7:30; 8:20), but throughout the second, the presence of the "hour" of Jesus—his death and resurrection—is clearly affirmed (13:1; 17:1). In the second part, the Gospel presents Jesus addressing his disciples alone (John 13–17) and reflects on the passion and resurrection experience (John 18–21).

John 14–16, the so-called Farewell Discourses, contains Jesus' final instructions to his disciples. These chapters consist of a mosaic of themes introduced, explored, dropped, and reintroduced. The central point of this discourse is the promise of the sending of the "Paraclete," "the Spirit of the Truth"—the first serious pneumatological reflection in Christian literature, the second and more decisive being that of St. Basil the Great in his treatise, *On the Holy Spirit*.

Nevertheless, the most important material is undoubtedly John 17, sometimes known as Jesus' High-Priestly Prayer. However, Jesus' prayer in John 17 is not only a prayer on behalf of his disciples and their glorification in his glorification, but also "on behalf of those who will believe in [Christ] through their word" (17:20). All the motifs and symbols used in this chapter remind us of the "eucharistic prayer," the "anaphora" of the later Christian liturgy, which as a "reasonable worship" and "bloodless sacrifice" is being offered not only for the Christian community itself, but also for the "*oikoumen*," "for the life of the whole world." In addition, the basic aim of Jesus' prayer is "that they may all be one" (17:21), and by extension for the unity of humankind. Characteristically, this gospel develops its whole argument on the model of the perfect unity that exists between Christ and His Father, i.e., the unity that exists within the Holy Trinity ("as you, Father, are in me and I am in you," 17:21; "that they may be one, as we are one," 17:22). It is not accidental that the Eucharist, the Church's Mystery par excellence, is also an expression of unity, indeed, the ultimate act of unity. Nor is it accidental that it is a rite of glory, experienced as such in almost all Christian traditions, perhaps most evidently in the Eastern Orthodox Church.

CONCLUSION

If any conclusion is to be drawn from the above short commentary of the Johannine eucharistic passages, it is that they constitute an affirmation of the ecclesial and diaconal dimension of the Eucharist as a communion event (an act of unity) and not as an act of personal devotion. The Eucharist is an act of diakonia and sharing, and not a sacramentalistic, i.e., quasi-magical rite; it is an expression of the church as the people *(laos)* and household *(oikos)* of God and as the Body of Christ mystically united with its head, and not as a mere cultic and/or witnessing institution. In other words, the Eucharist as the unique and primal Mystery of the church is a reflection of the communion that exists between the persons of the Holy Trinity, and above all, a "thanksgiving" prayer to God *(eucharistia)* for the unity of humankind and a proleptic manifestation of the kingdom to come. If one pushes these conclusions a little further, one can easily argue that the relationship of God's people and the world is a liturgical relationship; one can even say that daily life in society and the world is a eucharistic liturgy through which this unity of humankind in God and the preliminary manifestation of the future kingdom are made present. In a post-modern world these Johannine insights are a challenge not only for all the churches, but also for the secular communities.

BIBLIOGRAPHY

Adam, A. K. M. *What is Postmodern Biblical Criticism?* Guides to Biblical Scholarship: New Testament Series. Minneapolis: Fortress, 1995.

Brown, Raymond E. *The Community of the Beloved Disciple*. New York: Paulist, 1979.

Barrett C. K. *Essays on John*. Philadelphia: Westminster, 1982.

Cullmann, Oscar. *Les Sacraments dans l'Évangile Johannique : la vie de Jésus et le culte de l'église primitive*. Études d'histoire et de philosophie religieuses 42. Paris: Presses universitaires de France, 1951. Reprint pages 37-119 in *Early Christian Worship*. Translated by A Stewart Todd and James B. Torrance. SBT 10. London: SCM, 1953.

Vassiliadis, Petros. *Eucharist and Witness: Orthodox Perspectives on the Unity and Mission of the Church*. Geneva: WCC Publications, 1998.

Witherington, Ben III. *John's Wisdom: A Commentary on the Fourth Gospel*. Louisville: Westminster John Knox, 1995.

ACTS

Benny Tat-siong Liew

Chicago Theological Seminary, Chicago, Ill., USA

LIFE CONTEXT OF THE INTERPRETATION

Chinese have been a part of U.S. society since the beginning of the California Gold Rush (1849), although our presence has always been fraught with social and/or legal illegitimacy. The only law in U.S. history that explicitly prohibited immigrants from a specific racial/ethnic group is the Exclusion Act against the Chinese (1882). In addition, there were various anti-miscegenation laws, as well as the 1924 National Origins Law (which effectually barred Chinese students and Chinese wives of U.S. citizens from entry). With courage and cunning (like the "conception" of "paper sons"), the Chinese in America were able to challenge and circumvent these discriminations despite their primary makeup as a bachelor society. With the repeal of these laws by 1943 as well as the Immigration Act of 1965, the Chinese population in the United States continues to grow through international immigration and native birth. Depending on many factors (especially the diplomatic relations between the United States and China at a given time), the Chinese in the United States continue to experience oscillations between welcome and socio-political disfranchisement. Anti-Chinese sentiments previously expressed in discriminatory laws may,

for example, (re)emerge in the execution of "color-blind" legislation. The more recent and most publicized anti-Chinese hate crime is arguably the murder of Vincent Chin in Detroit (1982). Two men, after beating Chin to death with a baseball bat, were sentenced to only three years of probation and a fine of $3,000.00. Neither served a day in jail for taking a (Chinese) life.

As mainstream U.S. society pushes to accelerate globalization in the twenty-first century, it is simultaneously haunted by this process of global (inter)relation and (inter)penetration. Anxious about its own national identity, integrity and invulnerability, this nation's imagination once again makes the Chinese one of its threatening and undesirable "others" (Chuh and Shimakawa 2001, 1-3). It is not mere coincidence that Chinese Americans were accused in the "campaign finance scandal" in 1996 (John Huang) and the "technological espionage scandal" in 1999 (Wen Ho Lee). Finance and technology, being key to globalization, also become suspect areas through which Chinese—who are by (racialized) definition "foreign" and "alien"—would attempt to infiltrate, pollute, and/or betray the U.S. national body.

CONTEXTUAL COMMENT

Contextual and Hermeneutical Issues

Most New Testament scholars agree that the same person authored Luke's Gospel and Acts. Beyond that, scholars disagree on the specific nature of their relation-

ship: Is Luke-Acts a two-volume work? Is Acts a later sequel to Luke's Gospel? Do the books share a coherent outlook?

Acts is a narrative with two interconnected foci. It sketches the formation of the Christ(ian) community, and it depicts the

Benny Tat-siong Liew was born in Hong Kong and has studied in Canada and the USA, he is Associate Professor of New Testament at Chicago Theological Seminary in Chicago, Ill. USA. He is the author of numerous articles and *Politics of Parousia: Reading Mark Inter(con)textually* (Leiden: Brill, 1999), and editor of *The Bible in Asian America* 90/91 (Atlanta: SBL, 2002).

community's evangelization of various peoples in different places (which leads to further [re]formation of the community). Even a cursory reading of Acts will bring out many interests that intersect with Chinese-American communities. Acts has many episodes that demonstrate an awareness of linguistic and ethnic differences. In addition to the linguistic miracle among ethnic Jews in the Jerusalem Pentecost (2:6-11), one finds the people of Lystra speaking in Lycaonian (14:11), and Paul being fluent in both Greek and Hebrew as an ethnic Jew from Tarsus (21:37, 39-40; 22:2; 26:14). There is also a mixed marriage between the Roman procurator (or governor) Felix and his Jewish wife, Drusilla (24:24). While Lysias' mistake regarding Paul's ethnicity (21:38) confirms (post)modern scholarly argument that race (being visibly identifiable) and ethnicity are not the same, the continuing exchange between Lysias and Paul about their respective Roman citizenship (22:25-29) illustrates the significance of nativity. As is well-known within Chinese America, native-born and immigrant Chinese may share a U.S. passport, but barriers and conflicts between them are all too real and prevalent.

I would like to follow the trails of three Chinese-American scholars (Yeo Khiok-khng; David W. Pao; and Timothy Tseng) to explore what Acts and Chinese Amer-icans may have to say about three issues that are of significance to the contextual situations of both the biblical text and Chinese Americans: community integration, religious diversity, and colonialism.

Community Integration

The historic and continual portrayals of Chinese as "foreign" or "heathen" make it difficult for Chinese to be fully integrated into mainstream U.S. society, even if one was born in the United States or has faithfully gone through the naturalization process. We have already seen from the exchange between Lysias and Paul (22:25-29), the Lukan sensibility about Roman citizenship (also 16:35-40). Acts also hints at integration problems within the Jewish community. In addition to linguistic and cultural issues (2:5-13; 6:1-7), it points to the issue of the Sadducees and the Pharisees (23:6-10), or perhaps even to people of different social status (the "synagogue of the Freedmen," 6:9). Integration within Acts' early Christ(ian) community is significant for two reasons. First, Acts seems to link, as sociologists of religion do, conversion with integration into a new community. Second, one of Acts' emphases has to do with the integration of Jews and Gentiles into one people of God through Jesus Christ.

The integration of Jews and Gentiles certainly receives major coverage in Acts, with the length of the narrative (8:26–15:35) signifying perhaps a long and drawn-out struggle. That is, however, by no means the only source of conflict within the early Christ(ian) community. Tseng's article concentrates on the conflict between Hellenistic and Palestinian Jews (6:1-7). In addition, we find Ananias and other Jerusalem disciples being suspicious of a new Christ-follower like Paul (9:10-16, 26). Barnabas, after mediating for Paul (9:27-28), ends up falling out with Paul over John Mark (15:36-41). Acts' Christ(ian) community does not integrate (new) people into its midst as "peacefully" and seamlessly as 9:31 seems to indicate.

Paul, responding to the Philippian jailer's question, states that faith in Christ is the means to or the requirement for salvation (16:31). However, we have learned previously from Peter that concerning community integration, the giving/receiving of the Holy Spirit is the eraser of (ethnic) difference (15:8-9). Faith in Christ without having the Holy Spirit is incomplete or inferior, according to the cases of the Samaritans (8:14-17) and the Ephesians (18:24–19:7). The Holy Spirit in Acts comes and goes, however, as it pleases (González 2001, 108-109). While the Samaritans experience a time lag between their baptism in Jesus' name and their receiving of the Holy Spirit (8:16), the Ephesians receive the Holy Spirit upon (or at least closely following) their baptism (19:5-6). In the case of Cornelius at Caesarea, the Holy Spirit comes on him and his household even before they are baptized (10:44-48). If faith in Christ is like obtaining a "green card" that grants entry and residency, the coming of the Holy Spirit is comparable to the "naturalization" process that (theoretically) turns a "green-card" holder into a citizen eligible for equal rights and benefits. Yet in Acts, the newcomer cannot decide if and when he or she would satisfy this requirement of integration or "naturalization" by receiving the Holy Spirit. The matter is simply beyond human control.

Acts reveals additional hurdles to full integration into the Christ(ian) community. Shortly after the Jerusalem Pentecost (2:1-13), we read about the early church as a community with "all things in common" (2:44-45). After a similar description and a positive example of "selling and sharing all" in Barnabas (4:32-37), Acts presents us with a negative example in Ananias and Sapphira (5:1-11). This couple, guilty of withholding for themselves part of the money they receive from selling their property, is struck dead (presumably by the Holy Spirit). Their death, which brings "great fear" upon "the whole church" (5:11), implies that, in addition to receiving the Holy Spirit, members of the Christ(ian) community must further share a specific attitude and action toward material possessions. Otherwise, not only is their integration into the community open to question, their very presence in the community may literally be removed.

The importance of money matters in Luke's community construction is well-known. Scattered throughout Acts are Christ believers characterized by works of charity or almsgiving, like Tabitha or Dorcas (9:36), Cornelius (10:24), and the Christians at Antioch (11:25-30). On the issue of integration, Simon in Samaria (8:9-24) is another telling episode. Acts is clear that Simon has believed and received baptism in the name of Christ (8:13, 16). Simon's desire to purchase the role as an authoritative agent or conduit of the Holy Spirit after the Holy Spirit has come upon the Samaritans results, however, in Peter's warning that Simon will "have no part or share in this" (8:21). While "this" may

refer to Simon's specific verbal request (8:19), Peter's specific reference to death or destruction (8:20) implies that Simon will be deprived of his very participation in the "word," and thus the people/community, of God (8:14). While Peter's threat to remove Simon may have to do with Simon's magical worldview, Peter's response in 8:20 locates the problem clearly with a double reference to Simon's (high) view of money (8:20).

Acts has yet another quality or qualification for integration into the Christ(ian) community. Willingness to suffer for one's faith in Christ becomes an issue with the beginning of persecution in Acts 4. Ignoring the verbal warning from the Jewish leaders that they should not "speak or teach at all in the name of Jesus" (4:18), the apostles are arrested and flogged (5:17-23, 34-40), but only to "rejoice" for being "considered worthy to suffer" in and for Jesus' name (5:41). Other "worthy sufferers" in Acts would include Stephen (6:8–7:60) and Paul (9:16; 14:19; 16:19-24; 20:23-24, 26-30; 21:13). As Paul and Barnabas return to Lystra, Iconium, and Antioch at the end of their first missionary journey, their encouragement and reinforcement of their converts also include the "must" of sufferings (14:22).

These two additional qualities or qualifications are actually two sides of the same coin. Negatively, the quality or qualification of being free from monetary concerns contrasts those who belong to Christ with those who live and act for material gain. In contrast to Christ-followers who sell and share all, we find in Acts some unnamed Philippian slave-owners and one silversmith called Demetrius who, because of falling income, accuse Paul with civic and religious pretenses (16:16-21; 19:23-29). By the time of the Jerusalem council, suffering persecution has become a distinguishing mark of certain membership in the community (15:26, "certain" in the doubled sense of "some" and "sure"). Unlike the examples of Theudas and Judas the Galilean given by Gamaliel (5:36-37), death and dispersion do not spell an end to the Christ(ian) movement, because the latter keeps evangelizing despite such sufferings

(8:1-4; 11:19; 13:44-52; 14:5-6, 19-21; 17:13-17; 20:17-25; 21:10-14; 28:30). This positive response to suffering and persecution itself may be(come) a means of evangelism. More important, in the case of Stephen, suffering persecution (in fact, martyrdom) is specifically and directly linked to a welcome entry into God's community (7:54-60). The quality or qualification of being worthy of suffering thus functions positively to legitimate not just the Christ(ian) community, but also the sufferer's own place in the community. These negative and positive legitimations of one's membership or belonging are clearly seen in Paul's farewell speech to the Ephesian elders at Miletus (20:17-38), where Paul establishes his ethos as a credible leader/teacher in the beginning and at the end of his speech. In the beginning, Paul highlights his endurance of persecution in the past, and his present decision to head toward Jerusalem despite certain dangers (20:18-25); in the end, he emphasizes his disinterest in personal material gains (20:32-35).

Acts shows that despite fulfilling earlier qualifications (faith, baptism, and the ever-elusive coming of the Holy Spirit, 2:38), one's legitimacy in the larger Christ(ian) community may still be questioned on the basis of economics and demonstrated loyalty. Such dynamics are too painfully familiar to many Chinese Americans. A Chinese born or "naturalized" in the United States is still illegitimate without demonstrating loyalty to certain economic or patriotic principles such as capitalism, model minority upward mobility, or military "defense" of national "safety" at the risk of injury or death. As the disputes over "daily distribution" (6:1-6) and circumcision (10:1–11:30, 13:1–15:35) show, the problem of community integration in Acts is entangled with matters of language and ethnicity.

Feminist scholars have already sensitized us to the gender problem in Acts. Only "men" are eligible to be apostles (1:21) or one of the seven "servers" (6:3), while women are generally involved in "the ministry of benefaction and hospitality" rather than that of preaching and teaching (D'An-

gelo 2000, 68). In addition, Acts has an ethnicity problem. Acts contains many references to the community's successful mission to Gentiles, but the work of mission and evangelism is restricted to Jews (Palestinian or Hellenistic). This is true not only of the "major" missionaries like Peter, Philip, Barnabas, or Paul, but also of "minor" ones like Apollos (18:24) or Apollos' "instructors," Priscilla and Aquila (18:1-2, 26). Luke never presents the activity of any non-Jewish missionary. This ethnic monopoly (a kind of "glass ceiling" for Gentile Christ-followers?) may explain why Paul circumcises Timothy, who has a Greek father and a Jewish mother (16:1-3). Paul's act is puzzling since this episode is sandwiched by references to the Jerusalem decision that Gentile disciples need not be circumcised (15:12-31; 16:4-5). What distinguishes Timothy is Paul's desire to make him a missionary partner (16:3). Although the preaching of Stephen, Philip, and Paul in Acts demonstrates that the Holy Spirit's thwarting of the Jerusalem apostles' attempt to reserve the preaching ministry to themselves (6:2-4; González 2001, 88-94), the Holy Spirit does *not* thwart such attempts in the missionary activities of only ethnic or proselyte Jews! Even if the leaders or elders whom Paul appoints "in each church" during his missionary journeys are indeed new Gentile converts (14:23; see also 20:17), there is *no* reference to their preaching or missionary activities. Paul's message to the Ephesian elders refers only to Paul's own preaching (20:25-27), while the elders are specifically charged with the ministry of supervision and care (20:28-30). Note also Acts' thrice-repeated statement that Spirit-filled Gentile disciples are nevertheless required to fulfill certain Mosaic commandments short of circumcision (15:19-21, 28-29; 21:25). The legitimating role that the Jerusalem apostles repeatedly perform upon missions and conversions that they did not begin or mediate (8:14–16; 9:26-29; 11:22-23; 12:24-25; 15:12-35) may imply other bases of discriminatory integration, such as language and/or geography.

The legitimating role of the Jerusalem apostles is related to the interweaving parallels among the major missionary/ preacher figures in Acts as well as between these figures and the Lukan Jesus. Paul's raising of Eutychus (20:7-12) parallels Peter's raising of Tabitha/Dorcas (9:36-43), and both parallel Jesus' raising of a widow's son in Nain (Luke 7:11-17). In Luke's Gospel, Jesus' ministry begins with his inaugural sermon, which is followed closely by his healing of a lame or paralyzed person (4:16-21; 5:17-26). In Acts, this same sequence of and proximity between an inaugural sermon and a healing of a lame person appears in the ministry of Peter (2:14-36; 3:1-10) and Paul (13:13-42; 14:8-11). A key to interpret these parallels may be the different interactions within these three healing stories (Tannehill 1994, 51-53). In Luke, the scribes and Pharisees accuse Jesus of blasphemies, but Jesus affirms his authority to forgive sins *as* God does by healing the bed-ridden person (5:21-24). In Acts, people respond so positively to the healing of a lame person that Peter and Paul have to correct, clarify, and confirm their own human status (3:11-12; 14:11-18). Luke thus wants to emphasize, but simultaneously distinguish Jesus as the original, and Peter and Paul as the (faithful) copies. What gives the Jerusalem apostles the privilege of legitimation is this concern to be "faithful to the origin(al)," since Acts tells us early that having accompanied Jesus from the *beginning* is a prerequisite for apostleship (2:21-26). In fact, Acts repeatedly legitimates both the ministry of Jesus and the mission to the Gentiles not as "new" developments, but fulfillments of Hebrew Scripture (3:17-18; 13:22-27, 32-41, 46-48; 15:15-21; 17:2-3; 28:25-28). The question of who and what defines the "origin(al)" is of course important and debatable, but its (howsoever defined) tyranny has been a long struggle for many Chinese Americans. Tseng shows how both mainstream U.S. society and Chinese-American (church) communities have used the "origin(al)" to premise inclusion or integration on acquiescence to tradition, assimilation, and acculturation. It is precisely these opposing but similar tyrannies

that Maxine Hong Kingston struggles against when she writes in succession: "Those of us in the first American generation have had to figure out how the invisible world the emigrants built around our childhoods fits in solid America. . . . Chinese-Americans, when you try to understand what things in you are Chinese, how do you separate what is peculiar to childhood, to poverty, insanities, one family, your mother who marked your growing with stories, from what is Chinese? What is Chinese tradition and what is the movies?" (1989, 5-6). Like Acts' (re)presentation of community and mission, both "solid America" and Chinese "tradition" are claiming the privileged status of original blueprints that others have to fit in. Such a process of fitting-in is, as I have shown above, seldom a finished business. Instead, it is a matter of continuous, if not eternal, insecurity, whether the rhetoric is the "melting pot" of the United States or the "universalism" of Luke.

Religious Diversity

Yeo argues that Paul's Areopagus speech (17:16-31) is a model for interreligious dialogue (1998, 165-197; see also Dibelius 1956). The significance of this issue lies not only in the long history of religious diversity within Chinese America, but also in the equally long history of marginalization that Chinese Americans face in this society because many of them were/are not Christians.

In contrast to Yeo, I would suggest, first of all, that Acts (including 17:16-31) is not interested in religious diversity or interreligious dialogue. Acts is, after all, a book of mission, and is thus more interested in conversion than conversation (the latter is at most a means to achieve the former).

This focus on mission is particularly visible in Peter's statement that "there is salvation in no one else [besides Jesus]" (4:12). Paul does demonstrate knowledge and even sensitivity to the religious traditions of both Lystra and Athens, and emphasizes to a degree the unity of all humanity (14:16-17; 17:22-28). He nevertheless sees these other religions as "worthless" and "ignorant," and thus argues that their adherents must "turn" and "repent" to faith in the "appointed" and risen Christ (14:15; 17:29-31). Since Jesus Christ is necessary for Jews as well as Gentiles (2:38; 13:36-41; 15:10-11), Acts' goal is religious monopoly rather than diversity. I therefore do not see Acts' Paul, despite his being persecuted by both Jews and Gentiles for his proclamation of Christ (14:5; 16:19-23; 17:1-7; 18:12-13; 19:23-31; 21:19-22, 27-36), as occupying an interstitial location comparable to Kingston's description above. What Paul promotes in Acts is not an alternative identity to stand between Jews and Gentiles, but the elimination of all other ethnic/religious identities for all people. The riot caused by Demetrius' appeal to Artemis (19:23-34), along with the many accounts of persecutions by "Jewish plots" (20:3, 19; 21:27-31; 23:30), show that Acts is well aware of the conflicts and violence that result from religious and ethnic intolerance. Such awareness does not, however, keep Acts from pushing for mission and conversion. Instead, Acts presents suffering and martyrdom as legitimizing the Christ(ian) movement as well as verifying one's membership in the community.

One can find, however, within Acts a slender, different thread when Paul makes the trip as a prisoner to Rome to appeal to Caesar (27:1–28:16; Tannehill 1994, 330-38). Although there are Roman soldiers, sailors, and other prisoners on board, there is no reference to Paul preaching or sharing the gospel. The narrative of this treacherous trip contains but two references to religion or divinity. The first is Paul's reference to a divine vision that points, first of all, to Paul's awareness that others on board do not share his religion, for he specifically refers to God as "the God to whom *I* belong and whom *I* worship" (27:23; emphasis mine). Nevertheless, Paul promises on the basis of this divine vision that everyone on board will be "saved" without (religious) discrimination (27:24-26, 31). The second reference is found when the natives of Malta, upon seeing Paul surviving a snake's bite without any harm, mistake Paul as "a god"

(28:3-6). When comparable mistakes have appeared previously in Acts, Peter, Barnabas, and Paul have resisted and attempted to correct such misidentifications (3:11-12; 10:25-26; 14:11-15). In contrast, Herod, who fails to refute a similar misconception others have of him, becomes infested with worms and dies (12:20-23). It is therefore surprising that Acts makes no remark on Paul's response to the islanders' misunderstanding, other than Paul's performance of more miraculous healings on and for the island natives (28:7-9). Even if Paul is in effect dis-identifying himself from divinity when he prays (presumably to God) for the healing of the island chief's father (28:8; Talbert 2003, 184), Paul does not ask the natives of Malta to repent, turn away from other gods, and turn to Jesus alone. Even if one extends Talbert's argument and reads Paul's prayerful healing of the natives as "friendship evangelism," what we have here is at most an adhesion (adding of new religious traditions *without* leaving or turning away from existing ones) rather than a conversion (Finn 1997, 32-33).

What is essential to this more tolerant thread in Acts is Paul's acknowledgment through the divine vision that (to use the well known first person plural in this part of Acts) "we" are literally in the "same boat," and thus "we" will live or die together. This recognition helps Paul put religious differences and his great missionary zeal aside (if only temporarily, since Paul will quickly resume his missionary acts upon arrival at Rome, 28:23-31), and concentrate his efforts for the common good. He informs the Roman soldiers of the sailors' plan to "jump ship" (27:27-32), and encourages others on board to eat and keep their strength (and spirits) up (27:33-38). This expression of (unconditional) goodwill causes others to reciprocate: the centurion protects Paul, prevents his soldiers from killing the prisoners, and orchestrates a procedure for all to escape safely to land (27:39-44). Similar reciprocity operates again on the island of Malta, although Acts is clear this time that the natives are the initiators and Paul a recipient (28:1-2). When Paul reciprocates by healing many on the island, his reciprocation leads to more reciprocation of goodwill and generous sharing on the part of the natives (28:7-10).

Is this (passing) picture of (religious and ethnic) tolerance and harmony in Acts an affirmative answer to Rodney King's plea after the multi-racial/ethnic uprising in Los Angeles, 1992: "Can we all get along?" (*Time*, May 1, 1992). There is no denying that racial/ethnic and religious crises are mounting in the (inter)national politics of the United States. What Acts 27:1–28:16 reminds us of is the importance of King's often-forgotten, but arguably more insightful statement that follows his over-quoted question: "We're all stuck here for a while." Diversity and tolerance depend on a deep and durable re-cognition of everyone's co-existence and interdependence despite, or perhaps even because of racial/ethnic and religious differences. Without that re-cognition, "all getting along" is just a romantic slogan.

(Anti-)Colonial Dynamics

According to Pao, Acts is a rewriting of the "Isaianic new exodus" (2002). Like the post-exilic Isaiah (chs. 40–66), Luke struggles to affirm, as he faces the need to redefine and rebuild, the people of God after the trauma of the first Jewish-Roman war. It is well known that Acts often quotes from the Septuagint, especially Isaiah (Acts 7:49-50; 8:32-33; 13:34, 47; 28:26-27). There are, however, other more implicit allusions. As Isaiah uses "the way of the Lord" (40:3) to refer to God's "new exodus" for God's people after the Babylonian exile (see also Isa 43:16-19), Luke uses "the way" as the self-designation of the early Christ(ian) movement (9:2; 19:9, 23; 22:4; 24:14, 22). There are also many parallel emphases between Isaiah and Acts, like the ingathering of exiles (Isa 40:11, 43:5-7; Acts 2:9-11), the universal revelation of God's glory or salvation (Isa 40:3-5; Acts 26:23, 28:28), the power of God's word (Isa 40:6-8; Acts 6:7, 12:24, 19:20), the centrality of Jerusalem (Isa 40:9-11; Acts 1:4-5), the work and power of the Holy Spirit (Isa 42:1, 44:1-4, 61:1-2; Acts 2:1-4; 10:38; 13:1-4), the

(re)creation of God's people that includes both Jews and Gentiles (Isa 43:15-21, 49:6; Acts 10:44-48, 14:1, 15:12-31), as well as other previous outcasts like eunuchs (Isa 56:4-5, 8; Acts 8:26-40). The verse that many have taken as the summary outline of Acts, 1:8, captures several main ingredients of Isa 40-55. The geographical sequence of the verse signifies the centrality of Jerusalem ("in Jerusalem [first]"), the reunification of Israel ("in all Judea and Samaria"), and the inclusion of Gentiles ("and to the ends of the earth"). This verse is further sandwiched by two references to the focus of the Isaianic new exodus: Israel's restoration or reconstitution. The first is the disciples' question (1:6), which prompts the "programmatic" promise from the resurrected Jesus. The second is the election of Matthias to replace Judas, which completes the "twelve," the number of the original apostles as well as the tribes of Israel (1:12-26). Pao, however, ends up using this intertextual connection to argue for a narrower contextual conflict: Luke's concern to establish the church as the true heirs of Israel (2000, 123-129). In effect, Pao (dis)misses the very imperial or colonial dynamics that are present in the exodus from Egypt, in (deutero-) Isaiah's (post)exilic struggles, as well as in Luke's context of the Jewish-Roman war.

Focusing on another set of intertextual relations, Marianne Palmer Bonz manages to highlight at the same time inter-contextually (Luke-)Acts' imperial or colonial dynamics. As Virgil's *Aeneid* presents the Romans as being ordained by the gods to take the best out of the ruins of Troy to become the rulers of the world, Luke is, according to Bonz, not only imitating Virgil, but also presenting the Christians as the new ordained conquerors of the universe. Christians emerge in Acts as heirs of the very best of the Jewish tradition, despite the destruction suffered by the latter in the first Jewish-Roman war (2000, 182).

My interest here is not to limit or adjudicate Acts' intertextual relations, since I do not think that Isaiah and Virgil are mutually exclusive. I want to use both Pao and Bonz together to argue for the anti-colonial implications of Acts. Acts is certainly not shy about Israel's political subjugation. Stephen refers back to the slavery in Egypt and the exodus at length and in detail (7:6-38). There are also in Acts at least a couple of direct references to diasporic existence, Jewish or otherwise (2:5, 9-11; 17:21). As Acts progresses, one finds more and more references to both the presence and the power of Rome (16:12; 18:1-2; 19:35-41). More specifically, both Paul and Paul's opponents have to work through Roman power to achieve their respective ends (16:16-22, 35-40; 17:5-8; 18:12-17; 21:31-32; 23:10; 24:2-3, 10; 25:10-12). At the same time, Acts contains several incisive if indirect jabs at the Romans. Many readers are familiar with Luke's unflattering representations of the Roman officials surrounding Paul's arrest (Tannehill 1994, 295-313). While Lysias writes a report to make himself look better than he actually is to impress his superior (23:25-30), Felix keeps someone in jail to get a bribe from the prisoner (24:26), and Festus (like Felix) is always concerned with accumulating his own political capital (24:27; 25:3, 9, 11). All three of them know Paul to be innocent, but none of them is willing to set Paul free (23:29; 24:22-27; 25:24-27; 26:31-32).

I will simply point to one episode that Bonz overlooks, but I think will further support her thesis about Acts as a competing version of Virgil's *Aeneid*. The major character in the *Aeneid* who represents the Trojans, who migrates to Italy under divine providence and founds a city that ultimately leads to the triumph of Rome is, of course, Aeneas. Interestingly, there is also a character in Acts by the same name. This Aeneas is,

however, a bedridden invalid at Lydda, who is healed by Peter in the name of Jesus Christ (9:32-35). While symbolically Peter's healing of Aeneas may seem pro-Roman, one must remember that this episode involves a clear difference in health and strength. Peter, not Aeneas, is the one who is healthy and strong. Later in Acts, we will find Paul making a Roman governor his first convert of his first missionary journey (13:1-12). Even when Paul comes under Roman custody, he will debate with another Roman governor about "justice, self-control, and the coming judgment," and the governor (Felix) will retreat in fear (24:25). This resistant and subversive move within Acts may also account for its emphasis on God's rejection of (only) unbelieving Jews (13:46-47; 18:6; 28:25-28) as an(other) illustration of status reversal (Talbert 2003, 161-73).

I have already intimated that imperial/colonial dynamics are important to Chinese Americans on two fronts. Externally, China continues to be one of the most desired and feared "partners" of the global world (read: U.S. imperialist) order. Chinese America, like other racial/ethnic minority Americas, is an internal colony. My reading of Acts becomes uneasily complex since "manifest destiny" is not only a theme of both Virgil's *Aeneid* and Luke's Acts, but also a claim of the United States in its imperialist project. In fact, one of the ways that dominant U.S. society colonizes and racializes its Chinese members is through religion. If Acts was once a tool of resistance against Roman colonialism, its rewriting of Isaiah's new exodus and Virgil's *Aeneid* has—despite its intention—duplicated in effect the lamentable link between (the first) exodus and conquest.

CONCLUSION

Within Acts one can find both liberating and oppressive elements regarding community integration, religious diversity, and colonialism. Acts thus indicates that the Bible and the church are capable at times of inspiring us to be, or to go beyond, our very best. At other times, the Bible and the church

can also sadly resemble the worst that the world has to offer.

If Acts is a complex book, reading Acts is an even more complex business. Changes in a reader's identification of or with different characters in a narrative will dramatically change the implications of a story, as Tseng's reading of Acts 6:1-7 shows. My discussion of (anti-)colonial dynamics has shown that the same is true for readers who come to Acts with varying and shifting (con)texts. Readers come, however, not only with a context of themselves as readers, but also that of Luke as author. According to Tannehill, Paul's brief cessation of missionary activities on his trip to Rome (27:1–28:16) reflects Luke's realization of the Christ(ian) movement's minority status within a largely non-Christian Roman society (338-39). Of course, the minority status of the Christ(ian) movement may also account for Luke's overwhelming emphasis on mission and conversion. That is to say, Luke's missionary zeal comes from his concern for survival; when survival is not in question, then his missionary zeal may also wane. This is not, however, how Tannehill sees it. Wittingly or unwittingly, Tannehill gives the impression that the picture of religious and ethnic tolerance and cooperation is Luke's compromise with a dominantly non-Christian environment. For Tannehill, the singularity and the brevity of Paul's voyage to Rome in Acts show that mission and conversion are Luke's norm, whereas diversity and tolerance are his exceptions.

Some Chinese-American readers, being sensitive to the frustration of many Chinese-American writers over the publishing industry's politics, may relate the same episode to a different Lukan context and come up with a rather different interpretation. Instead of the minority status of the Christ(ian) movement, one may relate the differing theology or ideology regarding religious diversity in Acts to Luke's writing under someone's patronage (a likely scenario in Roman patronage society despite however fictive the name or figure "Theophilus" [1:1] may be). While it is impossible to ascertain which theological or ideological thread is Luke's nod to his patron, the power of the patron or publishing institution will steer one to make exactly the opposite conclusion from Tannehill's. It is precisely the singularity and the brevity of Paul's sea voyage to Rome within Acts that evidence diversity and tolerance to be Luke's more treasured, if—or thus—more hidden perspectives.

Explicitly inter-contextual interpretations are therefore admittedly inconclusive interpretations that (ideally) should lead to humble but active engagement with other interpretations. One's (dis)com-fort with such interpretations may also be contextual. My bicultural or transcultural experience has led me to share Kingston's sentiment: "I learned to make my mind large, as the universe is large, so that there is room for paradoxes" (1989, 29). This contextual sentiment also explains my intention to highlight both the liberating and oppressive elements in Acts. Knowing the importance of religious diversity in general, and the role that the Bible has played in the history of racializing Chinese Americans as "foreign heathens" in particular, as well as being sympathetic to the colonial context from which Acts emerged, I have chosen not to be too politically (in)correct about anything, including my act(s) of reading Acts.

BIBLIOGRAPHY

Bonz, Marianne Palmer. *The Past as Legacy: Luke-Acts and Ancient Epic*. Minneapolis: Fortress, 2000.

Chuh, Kandice, and Karen Shimakawa. "Introduction: Mapping Studies in the Asian Diaspora." Pages 1-21 in *Orientations: Mapping Studies in the Asian Diaspora*. Edited by Kandice Chuh and Karen Shimakawa. Durham, N.C.: Duke University Press, 2001.

D'Angelo, Mary Rose. "The *ANHP* Question in Luke-Acts: Imperial Masculinity and the Deployment of Women in the Early Second Century."

Pages 44-69 in *A Feminist Companion to Luke*. Edited by Amy-Jill Levine (with Marianne Blickenstaff). Feminist Companion to the New Testament and Early Christian Writings 3. New York: Continuum, 2002.

Dibelius, Martin. "Paul on the Areopagus." Pages 26-83 in *Studies in Acts of the Apostles*. Edited by Heinrich Greeven. Translated by Mary Ling and Paul Schubert. London: SCM, 1956.

Finn, Thomas M. *From Death to Rebirth: Ritual and Conversion in Antiquity*. New York: Paulist, 1997.

González, Justo L. *Acts: The Gospel of the Spirit.* Maryknoll, N.Y.: Orbis, 2001.

Kingston, Maxine Hong. *The Woman Warrior: Memoirs of a Girlhood among Ghosts.* New York: Vintage, 1976; Repr. 1989.

Pao, David C. *Acts and the Isaianic New Exodus.* WUANT 2. Tubingen: Mohr Siebeck, 2000.

Talbert, Charles H. *Reading Luke-Acts in its Mediterranean Milieu.* NovTSup, v. 107. Leiden: Brill, 2003.

Tannehill, Robert C. *The Narrative Unity of Luke-Acts: A Literary Interpretation. Volume 2: The Acts of the Apostles.* Minneapolis: Fortress, 1994.

Tseng, Timothy. "Second-Generation Chinese Evangelical Use of the Bible in Identity Discourse in North America." *Semeia* 90/91 (2002): 251-67.

Yeo Khiok-khng. *What Has Jerusalem to Do with Beijing? Biblical Interpretation from a Chinese Perspective.* Harrisburg, Penn.: Trinity, 1998.

ROMANS

Daniel Patte
Vanderbilt University, Nashville, Tennessee, USA

LIFE CONTEXT OF THE INTERPRETATION

I write this commentary as a French Huguenot and a white male who lives and teaches in the southern region of the United States, and I write after September 11, 2001. These contexts, separately and combined, frame my interpretation of Romans, even as my reading of Romans helps me to see them in a new light. By looking at these life contexts in light of Romans, I see that the gospel proclaimed by Paul (Rom 1:16-17) reveals that anti-Semitism, racism, sexism, colonialism, imperialism, and similar victimizations of others are rampant manifestations of the evil God condemns (1:18-32; see also 2:1–3:9). The gospel also reveals the quandary in which we Christians find ourselves. To our shame, we often condone and participate in these evils, even as we self-righteously reject and "condemn" them (2:1-3). However, by reading Romans with these contextual issues in mind, I can envision how the gospel as "power of God for salvation" (1:16) opens a way out of this impasse.

French Huguenots and Anti-Semitism during World War II: Our Dilemma in Light of Romans

I have vivid memories of my childhood during World War II, when I was learning from my parents to read the Bible as the Word to live by. I remember my fear of the German soldiers who occupied our village at the foot of the Alps in the south of France and who, for a while, camped on our farm. I also remember that, despite the soldiers' proximity, worn-out visitors often came, stayed for a few days in our home, and disappeared in the night. Later I learned that these were Jewish refugees desperately trying to escape the Holocaust, the Shoah, the systematic slaughter tha engulfed six million European Jewish men, women, and children during World War II. The weary eyes of those refugees in our home remain with me of the mysterious presence of God's chosen people among us and of the terrible offense that anti-Semitism is.

Heirs of Huguenots who endured centuries of persecution, my parents and our small congregations of the Reformed Church of France taught me that anti-Semitism is totally incompatible with the gospel of Jesus Christ. In our reading, the Bible, including the New Testament, teaches that Israel is in an irrevocable relationship with God as the chosen people—a mystery we should contemplate in awe (11:25-36).

Yet, as I pursued my studies, I soon discovered that many readings of the Christian Scriptures propose anti-Jewish teachings that throughout history readily became the basis of anti-Semitic attitudes and deeds. I shivered when I recognized that it was this

Daniel Patte is the general editor of the *GBC* and professor of New Testament and Early Christianity. A French Huguenot (Église Réformée de France), he taught two years in Congo-Brazzaville and "read the Bible with" people in France, Switzerland, South Africa, Botswana, and the Philippines, as well as in the United States. His publications include books on hermeneutics and semiotics (*Early Jewish Hermenutics,* 1975; and *The Religious Dimensions of Biblical Texts,* 1990) and on Paul and Matthew *(Paul's Faith and the Power of the Gospel,* 1983 and *The Gospel According to Matthew: A Structural Commentary on Matthew's Faith,* (1987). Publications that relate to the *GBC* include *Ethics of Biblical Interpretation* (1995), *The Challenge of Discipleship* (1999), *Reading Israel in Romans: Legitimacy and Plausibility of Divergent Interpretations* (edited with Cristina Grenholm, 2000), and *The Gospel of Matthew: A Contextual Introduction* (with Monya A. Stubbs, Justin Ukpong, and Revelation E. Velunta, 2003).

kind of "biblical" teaching that fueled the fire of the Holocaust. This massive, monstrous evil could not have taken place if, throughout Europe, a mass of Christians had not felt justified by such anti-Jewish teachings either to participate directly in its perpetration or to give their tacit consent to it. Of course, for these Christians, the murder of innocent victims was an evil they condemned. But, for one or another well-intentioned reason (e.g., the security of their families), they ended up condoning and doing the evil they did not want to do and that they hated (7:15-19).

Unfortunately, we French Huguenots cannot claim to be exempt from complicity with this evil (cf. 3:23). Even as we helped a few of its victims, we ignored most of them. Against our best intentions we participated in this evil. The wartime sense of emergency twisted all our relations to others. Its logic unfolded quite innocently. First it required vigilance. In a state of emergency, was not vigilance against all possible threats to us and our families appropriate? Then our relation to those victimized by the worst of the persecutions was warped. Their anxious eyes calling for compassion became the frightening reflection of a threat that we should urgently flee. Consequently, too often, instead of welcoming them as sisters and brothers in need, we turned away from them. By prudently and "innocently" making ours this wartime sense of emergency—a "natural" attitude, isn't it?—we became active participants in the warped universe where the murder of millions of people was institutionalized simply because they were different—Jews, but also Gypsies, homosexuals, communists, and mentally handicapped people (another six million victims of the Holocaust).

Confronting Racism, Sexism, and Other Oppressions in the United States: Our Dilemma in Light of Romans

Teaching at Vanderbilt University both in the Department of Religious Studies and in the Divinity School I find the same ambivalence. I readily identified myself with the history of the Divinity School's prophetic role during the civil rights struggle and its clear "commitment to do all in its power to combat the idolatry of racism and ethnocentrism" (Vanderbilt Divinity School 2000–2001, 9). This part of the divinity school's mission statement is carefully and realistically ambivalent. It is a definite commitment that faculty and students strive to implement. But it is also an acknowledgment of the limitations of this commitment.

The school does not claim to be free from racism but "to do all in its power to combat" it. Why? Because the very claim to be free from racism would demonstrate that we fail to recognize that racism is a systemic evil in which one participates simply because it seems to be the normal or natural way of life, and that, as an individual, one cannot free oneself from racism. As the African-American novelist Alice Walker says, the best that people can do is to be "enemies of their own racism" (1989, 287). We who ostracize and marginalize others, or who simply condone such victimization of others, must assume responsibility for racism and strive to overcome this evil. But how? Committing oneself to do so is important, yet it is not enough because, as Martin Luther King Jr. emphasized, the victimizers are themselves entrapped by racism. As Paul would say, racism is intertwined with all that is "holy and just and good" (7:12) in our way of life, including our good commitment to combat racism. Such is the predicament we face.

Paul helps us to clarify our confusing and confused situation. All of us are appropriately convinced that our usual way of interacting with others in family, in community, and in society is for the good of all those involved, provided that this order be respected. Our "conscience" confirms it (2:15). It gives us a pang whenever we stray from this way of life by hurting others rather than expressing love, by disrupting community life, or by transgressing the economic, social, political, and cultural order. For us, this is a good and necessary way of life that "promise[s] life" (7:10), including prosperity, security, and justice for all. For us, it is "holy," a manifestation of God's will, or, in secular terms, the most reasonable and humane way of life. And so it is.

The problem is that this holy, just, and good American way of life is impregnated with racism. It gives birth to elitist attitudes that denigrate other cultures, to authoritarian laws that subjugate entire sections of the population,* to discriminatory social practices that marginalize those who are different, to an out-of-kilter workplace and a global economy in which the gap between the rich and the ever-growing mass of the poor becomes wider and wider. The problematic character of our way of life usually remains invisible to us. Yet, we readily recognize the injustice in other people's ways of life. How could it have been normal and appropriate ("holy and just and good") for Christians in the southern region of the United States to have an economic and social way of life that demanded the enslavement of people of African ancestry? Or more recently, the Jim Crow segregated way of life? Of course, because of their conscience, some good Christians refused to participate in the abuses of this system. Yet, racism and oppression remained embedded in their way of life.

For me, a European-American male living in the United States at the beginning of the third millennium, the question is, are we not in the same situation? Are we not blind to the oppressive power that is intertwined with all that we hold to be good in our own way of life? Are we not contributing to these oppressions? Not only the voices of the victims of racism but also those of the victims of sexism, of homophobia, of religious exclusivism, of anti-Semitism, of colonialism, of neo-colonialism, and of imperialism (all of which the Vanderbilt Divinity School also denounces) should remove any doubts that these people are victimized by the very way of life we take for granted.

Nevertheless, we give thanks to God for all the blessings this way of life brings to us. Is it not appropriate to give thanks to God for food, family life, healthcare, education, a job, intellectual and cultural opportunities, travel and communication, and freedom to worship? Yes, it is. Is this thanksgiving self-centered and hypocritical? Of course it can be, but in many instances it is not. We also give thanks for a way of life that brings all of these benefits to many people who were deprived of them. Thus, through the filter of our conviction that our way of life is good, just, and a gift of God, we hear the cries of the victims of oppressions as if they are calling us to help them to share in this way of life and its benefits. Thus, we commit ourselves "to do all in [our] power" (Vanderbilt Divinity School, 2000–2001, 9) to combat oppressions. But from the perspective of Romans we have to ask, what resources will we use to combat oppression? Where do they come from? Is not this well-intentioned attitude similar to that of slave masters who, in response to the cries of their slaves, "generously" treated them more humanely with the resources generated by the slavery system, which in the process was further reinforced and justified?

Again and again we find ourselves in the same quandary. Even as we strive to do good, we end up doing the evil we denounce and want to avoid (7:15-19). To his own cry of despair, "Who will rescue me from this body of death?" Paul responds, "Thanks be to God through Jesus Christ our Lord!" (7:24-25). How does the gospel "rescue" us from our own racism, anti-Semitism, exclusivism, sexism, homophobia, colonialism, and imperialism? I bring this question with me as I read Romans for this commentary.

CONTEXTUAL COMMENT

Overview: Romans
and Its Interpretations

Through the centuries Christian believers and preachers have read Romans in many different ways. Rather than resolving these divergences, biblical scholars seem to have exacerbated them. Scholars are sharply divided into three broad camps. Yet one can note that these groups use different critical methodologies in different life contexts.

1. Forensic Interpretations (often supported by Lutheran scholars) use philological historical-critical approaches to elucidate the theological argument of the letter. This argument provides forensic evidence for the justification of the guilty (sinners) by the grace of God, the righteous judge, and through faith in Christ.

2. New Covenant interpretations, also known as those of the *new perspective,* were developed after World War II. They depart from forensic interpretations by using a combination of rhetorical and socio-historical analyses to read the letter as a discourse through which Paul seeks to persuade his readers to change their behavior, especially in Jewish-Gentile relationships (see Stendahl). Through Christ's faithfulness, the Gentiles are now in a covenantal relationship with God, similar to that of the Jews.

3. Apocalyptic Gospel interpretations start with a more pessimistic post-World War II outlook. These interpretations use the methods of history of religions and structural studies to clarify the religious experience and symbolic world presupposed by the letter and characterized by convictions about the gospel as the power of God for salvation from apocalyptic powers. In Christ and Christ-like people (from Abraham to "the body of Christ," 12:5) and through resurrection-like interventions, God defeats the powers of sin, death, and other evils.

These three kinds of interpretations, or readings, despite their radically different conclusions, are not in conflict. Each is legitimately grounded in the text. Each focuses on one of the three main textual features through which the letter affects its readers/hearers.

1. Forensic interpretations focus on the letter's *theological argument,* through which Paul conveyed to the Romans certain kinds of information—*a theological knowledge*—about the gospel he proclaimed. In a context in which the guilt of individuals is prevalent, this theological argument can become the basis of a forensic teaching.

2. Covenantal interpretations focus on the letter's *rhetorical discourse,* through which Paul attempted to persuade his readers—tried to establish their *will*—to change their behavior toward each other in their community and to support his mission to Spain (12–15). In a context in which the prevalent problem concerns communities and their respective relationship, this rhetorical discourse can become the basis of a covenantal teaching.

3. Apocalyptic interpretations focus on the letter's *religious discourse,* through which Paul *empowered* his readers by sharing with them his deepest *convictions* concerning God's power manifested in Christ, in the gospel, and in the believers' lives. In a context in which people are overwhelmed by the immensity of evil and feel totally powerless, religious discourse helps them to recognize the Christ-like divine interventions in their present and empowers them by the good news of the defeat of these apocalyptic powers.

Preachers should not be surprised that this letter conveys several messages, for their sermons do the same. Through their sermons, preachers simultaneously convey knowledge (e.g., about a biblical text), exhort their hearers (influence their hearers' will), and share their faith (or convictions). Even though each sermon gives priority to one of these three types of messages, all are necessarily present. Consequently, preachers often find that their parishioners are most directly touched by an aspect of their sermon they did not intend to emphasize but that nevertheless challenged these persons or addressed their particular needs at the time. So it was for Paul. He could not communicate one of these messages without also communicating the two others.

One could ask which of these three interpretations, or readings, was the primary intention of Paul. Scholars disagree and argue at length in favor of one or another. This debate is most helpful because it clarifies the different messages of Romans. However, we do not need to reach a firm conclusion. It is enough to recognize that Romans carries these three kinds of messages and that each of them challenges and/or addresses the needs of different people at different times. The question is not, which one of these three types of interpretation is truly grounded in the text? All are. The question is, which of these messages is the most helpful in order to address the contextual issues raised at the beginning of this chapter?

The Theological Argument of Romans: Are Oppressive Attitudes Due to a Lack of Knowledge of the Gospel?

Paul's clarification of his particular understanding of the gospel is necessary because he did not have a personal relationship with the Roman church (1:13; 15:22). In Galatia and Corinth there had been many controversies due to misunderstandings regarding the teaching of the "apostle to the Gentiles" (11:3), especially on the part of Jewish Christians. Thus, Paul needed to clarify his teaching before asking for support from the Romans for his forthcoming missionary activity in Spain (15:23-24). From this perspective, the primary message of the letter is its theological argument that clarifies the logic of the gospel for both Gentile and Jewish Christians in Rome.

The "Jews" (Jewish Christians) —whom Paul addresses directly in 2:17, 7:1, and, according to this interpretation, also in 2:1— are composite figures he constructed from the actual Jewish Christians who misunderstood his teaching in other churches, including "the saints" in Jerusalem whom he plans to visit (15:25-27). Similarly, the Gentiles— whom Paul addresses directly in 1:5-6, 1:14, and 11:13—are a construct of Gentile Christians who misunderstood his teaching in other churches. Paul's other letters, especially Galatians, are therefore most helpful for understanding Romans.

There is a broad consensus regarding the overall interpretation of Romans from this perspective. I present here a reading of Paul's teaching in Romans already found in Rudolf Bultmann's commentary and still in commentaries by Joseph Fitzmyer and Peter Stuhlmacher. Francis Beare's outline in *The Interpreter's Dictionary of the Bible* (1962, 115) summarizes it well, and portions of it appear here. Note Beare's vocabulary; the words between square brackets are mine.

I. Introduction, 1:1-15

II. The main theme: the gospel of salvation [the justification of sinners], 1:16–8:39. The universal need of salvation, 1:18–3:20 (guilt of the Gentile world, 1:18-32; equal guilt of the Jews, despite their complacent assumptions of superiority, 2:1-24; knowledge of the law does not mitigate Jewish guilt, 2:25–3:8; sin and guilt are universal, and law does not remove them, 3:9-20); the grace of God brings deliverance through Christ to all who believe, 3:21-26; no place is left for human pride in moral achievement, 3:27-31; testimony of the ancient scriptures: Abraham, counted righteous through his faith, ch. 4; the new relationship with God, entered through faith, 5:1-11; life under grace: deliverance from sin and law, chs. 6–7; and [life in the Spirit, with] the assurance of the love of God in Christ, 8:1-39.

III. Subsidiary theme: the faithfulness [or righteousness] of God and the failure of Israel. Problem: Has God failed to fulfill his promises to Israel, since the blessings of the gospel are being received chiefly by Gentiles? Chs. 9–11. [No,] God's promise [was] not made to all the Israel of natural descent (9:6-13); God's will, however arbitrary, is not subject to human challenge, 9:14-24; God's promise has always included Gentiles as well as Jews (9:25-29); [the] cause of Israel's failure [is] the effort to establish their own righteousness through the law, in place of righteousness of faith (9:30–10:4); testimony of the ancient scriptures to the righteousness of faith (10:5-21); the failure of Israel has brought salvation to the Gentiles [but it is not final] (11:11-16).

IV. Ethical instruction and exhortation: the law of love, 12:1–15:13. Appeal for dedication to God (12:1-2); the corporate life: responsibilities of each for the service of all [life in the body of Christ for the service of all] (12:3-13); love of enemies (12:14-21); obedience due to civil authority (13:1-7); love the sum of all commandments (13:8-10), [acknowledge] the right to differ (14:1–15:13); [and call for] self-denial [following] the example of Christ (14:1–15:13).

V. Concluding remarks [and travel plans], 15:14-33. This interpretation is called *forensic* because it emphasizes the metaphor of a court of justice in the passages about God's judgment (2:2-16; 3:6-7; 5:16; 14:10) of sinners who deserve God's wrath (1:18, 2:5, 2:8, 3:5, 9:22, 12:19, 13:4) but who are acquitted or justified through faith in God's grace manifested in Christ (3:21–5:21). The gospel is both the revelation of the sinfulness of all—prompting guilt and hopefully repentance—and the good news that through Christ sinners are justified, freed from guilt, if they believe. Justification through faith is understood as the deliverance from the guilt individual sinners have; it frees them for a life under grace and in the spirit (6:1–8:39) in which they can have a proper moral life governed by love, rather than a life determined either by sinful human nature or by their (cultural, social, and political) environment (12:1–15:13; Beare 1962, 121). Thus understood, the gospel also explains God's righteousness (or justice). Those who, like the Jews, deceive themselves by thinking that they can rely on works of the law to escape God's condemnation are sinners like any other sinner. God would be just in condemning them. But God's justice has been satisfied through Jesus' death, and this good news is also for the Jews. By believing this good news, they will also be freed from their guilt and from their fear of the wrath of God.

Contextual Implications

In many life contexts, especially when individuals are heavily burdened and paralyzed by guilt, the teaching based on this reading of Romans is most helpful. The gospel is the good news that all people— Jews and Gentiles, the church-going and the nonreligious—have been forgiven by God.

This forgiveness has been achieved through Christ's death on the cross for all sinners, even when both Jews and Gentiles were still "sinners" and "enemies" of God (5:8-10,19). Although all deserve God's condemnation, God lovingly welcomes us despite our sins. Through our faith, we have the assurance of salvation and are freed from guilt and fear of divine judgment and death. This is good news indeed.

When we feel guilty and ashamed by our racist, anti-Semitic, sexist, or oppressive deeds, this teaching addresses some of our needs. But it does not show how the gospel rescues us from our racism or other oppressive inclinations. Actually, this teaching could even mislead us into thinking that everything is resolved when we discover we are forgiven. In fact, nothing is resolved (see Tamez). People around us continue to be hurt and to die as a result of our racist, anti-Semitic, and/or oppressive ways of life. The unending cycle of violence remains and we are caught in it, still contributing to it, much like an abusive husband begs for forgiveness from his wife for hurting her is forgiven but again and again mistreats her and needs to beg her for forgiveness. Hopefully, another dimension of Romans offers a teaching that can better address our predicament.

The Rhetorical Discourse of Romans: Are Oppressive Attitudes Due to Arrogance?

The Letter to the Romans is also a rhetorical discourse through which Paul hopes to convince the Romans to change their behavior toward each other in an integrated church that includes Gentile and Jewish members, and toward outsiders, including Roman authorities. This is what Stanley Stowers and John Gager underscore, each in his own way, as they prolong Krister Stendahl's insightful criticism of the forensic interpretation. I affirm the legitimacy of their interpretation, but against their suggestion I want to emphasize that this does not exclude the two other interpretations; yet we should not collapse them into a single interpretation (as

James Dunn appears to do). I primarily present Stowers's interpretation, although I allude to other scholars in this group.

The rhetorical goal of Romans is easier to see by first considering its conclusions: four chapters of exhortations and ethical teachings (12–15). In chapter 15, it is clear that Paul hopes to persuade the Romans to support his mission to Spain (15:23-24) and heed his exhortations, at times expressed in very strong terms (15:15). He has "admonished them" as he expects them to "admonish each other" in a good and responsible way (15:14, author's translation [a.t.]; the NRSV translation, "instruct one another," is too mild). Similarly, the goal of 14:1–15:13 is to transform the way "the strong" and "the weak" interact.

It is right for the Romans to admonish each other for mutual correction and for "building up" the character of the weak (15:2), yet they should do so appropriately. Instead of despising as superstitious those who are weaker and condemning them (14:1-4, 10-12), the strong should welcome the weak as God did by adapting their behavior to meet the need of the weak (14:13–15:2). As Christ "did not please himself" but "has become a servant" to the Jews in order to confirm the promises given to the patriarchs about the Gentiles (15:1-12), so the strong should adapt themselves to the varied needs of the weak. In sum, Paul's goal is to bring the Romans to abandon the Greco-Roman practice of mutual correction that includes shaming the weak for their weaknesses. Instead, they should adopt a practice of mutual exhortation that follows "the model of Christ's adaptability to the needs of others" (Stowers 1994, 41, 320–23). This is the way to empower the weak (15:2). By the end of his discourse, Paul is confident his readers will change their behavior because they are now enabled to follow the model of Christ (15:14).

What is the root of the problem that Paul's rhetorical discourse helps his readers overcome? Most generally, arrogance: the arrogance of "the strong" toward "the weak" (14:1–15:13); the arrogance of the Gentile Christians toward the Jews who do not believe in Jesus as the Christ (11:13-25); the arrogance of the imaginary Jewish teacher with "his condescending pride in teaching gentiles to observe works of the law (3:7, cf. 2:17-20, 23)" (Stowers 1994, 38; see also 2:17–4:22); the arrogance of the imaginary person (in this reading, a Gentile) who condemns others (2:1-4; cf. 2:1-16); and, I add, the arrogance of the (Gentile) sinners who claim to be wise (1:22) even as they commit all kinds of sin (1:18-32). Arrogance is a belief that one has self-mastery and that others do not have it, and thus a belief that one needs to help others to gain the same self-mastery that one has. Paul's teaching is that those who are arrogant and judge others actually lack character, self- control, and self-mastery because, like the others (2:1-2), they are dominated by passions (1:18-32) or sin as desire (7:7-25).

How does the gospel overcome this arrogance? In its entirety, this letter as rhetorical discourse is addressed to the Romans as Gentiles. This is explicit in 1:5-6 and 13–15, and it is clarified by the recognition that, following common practices of the diatribe, Paul enlivens his discourse by addressing imaginary people, including Gentiles in 2:1-16 and a Jewish teacher from 2:17 to 4:22. "Romans tries to clarify for gentile followers of Christ their relation to the law, Jews, and Judaism" (Stowers 1994, 36), a relation that has been vitiated by arrogance on all parts. If one wants to escape condemnation by God, self-mastery is the goal to be achieved, as Greco-Roman Gentiles think. Indeed, Gentiles can be expected to condemn the sinners enslaved to passions and desire (1:18-32), as they do according to 2:1-2; but they should not condemn others because they are in the same situation (2:1-16).

Gentile followers of Jesus might think that becoming a Jew by fulfilling the law, as the imaginary teacher teaches, will provide them with all they need to overcome sin (passion and desire) and thus to be in right relationship with God and have self-mastery. But this is an inappropriate understanding of the relationship between Jews and Gentiles—all are sinners (2:17–3:9). Thus, still in the diatribe style, Paul conveys that "the [imaginary Jewish] teacher needs to understand that in the present moment God is effecting his just solution not through the Jewish law (3:19-21) but in the gentile mission based on Christ's faithfulness (3:22-26)" (Stowers 1994, 37). Stowers (as well as Neil Elliott and other scholars) translates 3:22 as "God's righteousness has been manifested *through the faithfulness of Jesus Christ* for all who are faithful." The faithfulness of Jesus Christ is comparable to that of Abraham, who is the ancestor of both Jews and Gentiles (4:1-25).

Gentile followers of Jesus must imitate Christ's faithfulness; this is what having faith is all about. As "Christ adapted himself to their need, dying for them as they were ungodly (5:1-11)" (Stowers 1994, 38), so Gentile believers must reenact his death and resurrection in baptism (6:2-11). In the process of dying to self they are freed from the dominion of sin and passions (6:12-14); they receive self-mastery. This freedom applies beyond baptism as well. The enslavement to desire and passion described in 7:7-23 is overcome through Christ, who adapted himself to the believers' needs, and through the Spirit that empowers them to be faithful as Christ was (ch. 8). Consequently, Gentiles share in Christ's privilege and relationship with God as son (8:15-23, 29), a kinship with God that Israel always had (9:4).

Gentile believers are then in a position to understand the mysterious way in which God deals with Israel and Gentiles (9–11). This is the mystery of God's adaptation to the needs of Gentiles—and this is without denying the covenant and promises to Israel (11:13-36). Acknowledging this mystery of God's faithfulness (11:25, 33-36) is the condition for Gentiles to be free from their arrogance toward the Jews (11:17-18) and then to be free to imitate Christ's faithfulness.

What is this faithfulness by which the Romans as Gentile believers should live? It involves giving one's body in "living sacrifice" as Christ did (12:1-2). Paul admonishes the Romans to make Christ's faithful adaptability to the needs of others (i.e., love) the

basic principle for their life in a diversified community (12:3-13; 14:1–15:13) and in relationship with outsiders (12:14–13:7). This love fulfills the law and frees Christ's followers from the flesh and its desires (13:8-14). Thus, the Romans should admonish one another and build up the character of the weak (still enslaved by their weakness) by adapting themselves to the needs of the weak, as Christ did.

Contextual Implications

When the rhetoric is viewed as the most significant dimension of the letter, the issue is no longer guilt but rather arrogance. Arrogance consists in "generously" wanting to help others to become like oneself, because one views oneself as better than others—an attitude related to the honor-shame code of Greco-Roman culture (see Jewett). Through its forceful rhetorical presentation of the gospel, the letter seeks to overcome the believers' arrogance vis-à-vis less mature Christians and outsiders.

In Paul's time, the letter strove to overcome the arrogance that believers in Christ from Jewish and Gentile origins had toward each other and toward Jews through admonishments and exhortations—parts of character formation and of sanctification. It is a matter of changing the will of people who have an inappropriate, deficient, or weak will. Paul emphasizes, from beginning to end, that this character formation is mutual (1:12 and 15:14): members of the church need to exhort, encourage, comfort, and instruct each other, as Paul himself expected to be exhorted and supported by the Romans (1:12 and 15:30). Arrogance is not a proper way to exhort others; rather, believers must imitate Christ and "adapt themselves to the needs of the weak." This is what Paul did with the Romans, adapting himself and his discourse to their needs by, as Stowers argues, entering their way of thinking regarding the importance of character formation (1994, 41, 320–23). This kind of teaching about mutual support is much needed today by individualistic Christians in the Western world who forget that they need the support of a community to progress in their faith journey. It is also needed by those Christian communities for whom exhortation and encouragement have lost their mutual character and who have become arrogant.

At first, this teaching also seems to address the problem of racism and the similar problems of sexism, colonialism, and imperialism. Is not arrogance (because of one's race, gender, or social, economic, or cultural status) the root of each of these problems? Yet, for the victims of racism, sexism, colonialism, or imperialism, the second part of this teaching—the exhortation to adapt themselves to the need of others—is suspicious. They have too often offered their bodies in "living sacrifice" (12:1-2) and been abused in the process. Furthermore, the exhortation to the strong to adapt themselves to the needs of the weak is fine when true reciprocity is possible, such as among members of a community of equals. But this attitude reinforces racism, sexism, colonialism, and imperialism when it is practiced in a relationship in which mutuality cannot be truly envisioned because the relationship is primarily characterized by inequality. In such cases, the weak—people from other races, religions, genders, or cultures—are like children who need to be kindly instructed and taken care of by condescending, strong people like, for instance, well-intentioned, white, male, European Christians. This has unfortunately been illustrated after 9/11 by the United States seeking to bring the gift of freedom and democracy to Afghanistan and Iraq. When this teaching is applied outside of a community of equals, it is part of the problem rather than the hoped-for solution.

Ultimately, this teaching cannot truly address our predicament because racism and other oppressive attitudes *are not a matter of will*. The weakness of the victims of racism and oppression is not due to a lack of will; it is not due to, for example, their so-called laziness or slothfulness! It results from oppression. Conversely, oppressors remain oppressors even when they are well intentioned and have the right kind of will.

The evil of racism and oppression is due neither to a lack of knowledge (e.g., of God's love) nor to a wrong will (e.g., arrogance). It is a matter of power that entraps both the perpetrators and the victims of racism and other oppressions. Hopefully, another dimension of Romans involves a teaching about the way the gospel can rescue us from our own racism, anti-Semitism, or other oppressive drives.

The Religious Discourse of Romans and Paul's Convictions: Oppressive Attitudes as Signs of Bondage to Evil Powers Overcome by the Gospel as Power of God for Salvation

A condition for the effective communication of a religious message—concerning the *knowledge* about the gospel of justification through faith (the first reading, forensic interpretations) or the *will* to abandon their arrogance and be faithful followers of Christ (the second reading, covenantal interpretations)—is that this message also convey a clear sense of the preacher's convictions. In his letter to the Romans, Paul also shares his deepest convictions regarding God's role in the world and in the believers' experience.

This most religious dimension of Romans is often overlooked because it is diffuse and difficult to apprehend. We miss Paul's convictions if we ask either, What is the central theological point of this letter? or What rhetorical effect does it seek to achieve? Paul's convictions are found neither at the center of his argument nor in the trajectory of his discourse because they provide the symbolic universe in which this argument and discourse take place and make sense. The appropriate questions are, how is Paul's symbolic universe constructed or structured? What religious symbolism is he using? How is it related to Hellenistic religions (see Schweitzer and other historians of religions)? To Pharisaic and early Rabbinic Judaism (see Davies and Sanders)? To Apocalyptic Judaism (see Käsemann and Beker)? To the symbolism of the Roman Empire (see Elliot)? What are the theological oppositions emphasized in the letter (see Patte)?

The latter question is helpful for locating Paul's convictions because the believers' convictions are self-evident truths that are like the air they breathe. As we desperately gasp for breath when our air supply is threatened, so, when our convictions are threatened, we emotionally affirm them by denying that we believe something else, setting up theological oppositions. When we consider these oppositions in Romans, it soon appears that Paul's symbolic universe should *not* be envisioned as a building with walls that separate an outside, the world, from an inside, the church. Paul's symbolic universe is better envisioned as a powerful movement that sweeps through the entire world and creation, transforming them as it conquers them. In this brief commentary, it is enough to examine two kinds of "figures," which, as implicit metaphors, express both what the gospel is *like* and *unlike*: political Roman figures and Jewish eschatological and apocalyptic figures.

Political Roman Figures: The Gospel as Inverted Imperial Conquest

A part of Romans appropriately represents the gospel as an inverted imperial conquest. The proclamation and spreading of the gospel of the lordship or dominion of Jesus Christ is like—and unlike—the proclamation and spreading of the good news of the lordship or dominion of the Roman emperor. Like the Roman emperor, Jesus Christ is Son of God and Lord (1:4). The task of the servants of this Lord—Paul (1:1) and the entire body of Christ (12:5)— is to bring to the "obedience of faith" (1:5) the Gentiles and the barbarians (1:14) and to "overcome evil" (12:21) by putting on "the armor of light" (13:12); that is, they are to "put on the Lord Jesus Christ" (13:14). This is just as the Roman legionnaires put on their armor and overcome evil in the name of the lord Caesar by bringing order, security, and peace (the *Pax Romana*) for the good of all people (13:3-4), by forcing people into subjection by the power of the sword (13:4-5), and also and primarily by bringing people to the "obedience of voluntary submission" (the meaning of the phrase "obedience of faith," 1:5) to Roman authority.

Contextual Implications

The gospel is the good news concerning the establishment of the empire of God through the voluntary submission (faith) of people to the Lord Jesus Christ and to God. In this sweeping imperial conquest of the Lord Jesus Christ, the Roman authorities are themselves subjected to the authority of God's empire; indeed, they are servants of God (13:4). God's empire is also established with "power," but unlike Roman imperial power, the power of the gospel is manifested in offering oneself in living sacrifice for others (5:8-10; 12:1-2).

Jewish Eschatalogical and Apocalyptic Figures: The Urgency of the Gospel's Imperial Conquest

The gospel's imperial conquest encompasses the entire inhabited world, from Jerusalem to the Adriatic Sea ("Illyricum," 15:19), and in between—Asia Minor and Greece ("Macedonia" and "Achaia," 15:25-26)—to Rome and to Spain (15:23-24), the end of the (known) world. For Paul, this conquest of the entire world is all the more urgent because this is the time of the end (the *eschaton*), when God sends the Messiah, the Christ Jesus (1:1, 3; 8:3), and fulfills the prophecies of Scriptures (1:2); when the resurrection from the dead has already begun with the resurrection of Jesus (1:4); when the Spirit of God, through the resurrection, establishes Jesus as "Son of God with power" (1:4), transforms believers into "children of God" (8:14; see 8:9-17), and will soon transform the rest of creation (8:18-23), since the time of salvation is near (13:11). In sum, for Paul it is self-evident that with the coming of Christ and his resurrection the end time (the eschatological time) has begun. This basic conviction is confirmed by the transformative work of the Holy Spirit and of the resurrected Christ in the believers' experience, who repeatedly rescues them from their sin (or "take[s] away their sins," 11:27).

Paul's symbolic universe is also apocalyptic in the sense that the envisioned end time is marked by the struggle between the power of God and Christ and the powers of evil, including "powers," "rulers" (on high, under the earth, or in life), and "death" (8:38-39). This is the time of God's judgment, when God's "wrath" is manifested against all "ungodliness and wickedness" (1:18). The gospel is "the power of God for salvation" (1:16). Even though the final victory over evil is still to come, some of the powers of evil are already being defeated, including "sin" as a power that enslaves people (3:9). Sinners are overwhelmed by desires to which God has abandoned them (1:24; see 1:26, 28); they are possessed by all kinds of evil (1:29). Thus, even if they "know" what is good to do and "want" to do it, they end up doing evil because they are possessed by sin and under its power (7:18-20).

Contextual Implications

This apocalyptic view, with its emphasis on sin and evil as powers that enslave us, makes sense when speaking about anti-Semitism, racism, sexism, and other oppressive attitudes. Despite our best intentions (against our will) and despite our efforts to avoid those attitudes we know to be wrong and evil, they dwell in us (7:18), possess us, and enslave us (7:14). Sin brings about not only our own destruction (death, 1:32; 7:10-11) but also the destruction of others and of all aspects of life in relation to others (1:24-31). Thus, it is indeed good news to hear that the gospel "is the power of God for salvation" (1:16); that is, the gospel is the power through which we can be freed from slavery to sin, or from all its destructive effects on individuals and communities.

While sin as guilt and "condemnation" (the focus of the first reading), instead of sinners, has been overcome once and for all by Jesus' death (e.g., 3:25; 8:1), sin and other evil powers are still at work in Paul's present and in our present. People, including Christian believers, are still in bondage to these powers. The dictum "all have sinned and fall short of the glory of God" (3:23) still applies to them. Every day there are new victims of anti-Semitism, racism, sexism, imperialism, and other oppressive attitudes, and Christian

believers are among the oppressors. Therefore, Paul's cry in 7:24 is also that of any Christian believer—"Who will rescue me from this body of death?" Who will rescue me from bondage to these evil powers?

The Gospel as Power of Salvation: What Is the Power of Sin?

The power of sin remains a reality for Paul the apostle. Day after day, like everyone else, Paul needs to be rescued from manifestations of the power of sin. But Paul also expresses his conviction that his cry for help (7:24) is answered: "Thanks be to God through Jesus Christ our Lord" (7:25). God—through the resurrected Christ, his power (1:4), and the Spirit (8:1-39) —saves people from the powers of evil. This is "the power of God for salvation" (1:16), the gospel as a process that will be ongoing until all God's enemies, including death, are defeated (1 Cor 15:24-26).

How does the gospel rescue believers from the powers of evil? Paul's convictions on this central point become apparent in the numerous theological oppositions of chapters 1, 7–8, and 12. In 1:18-32, the powers of evil to which people are abandoned by God are those of "coveting desires" (1:24, a.t.),** "passions" (1:26), and "debased mind" (1:28). Paul's reference to idolatry is most helpful, provided we note the unexpected way in which he presents it. Three points are essential.

1) For Paul, idolaters are people who have received a true revelation from God in creation: a revelation of God's "eternal power and divine nature" that is recognizable in the creation (1:19-20). This true revelation (1:21) is partial; it is not complete since it does not include, for instance, the revelations to Israel and in Jesus Christ.

2) Far from ignoring or denying this revelation, idolaters are obsessed by it and absolutize it. They view this partial revelation as the complete and final revelation; they worship the creatures instead of the creator (1:23), the mani-

festations of this revelation rather than the mysterious God toward whom they point. This delusive absolutization comes from a warped, "darkened" mind (1:21-22, 28) made foolish by deeply rooted desires to own, possess, and control this divine revelation—"coveting desires" (1:24, 7:7-8, a.t.) to possess what does not belong to them.

3) Idolaters are then trapped into their idolatry as a manifestation of God's "wrath" (1:18, 24, 26, 28). The more they strive to worship God, revealed to them in creation, the more, in their obsession for this revelation, they end up worshiping the creation and thus an idol (1:23). The more they welcome God's good gifts of human relations—sexuality (1:24-27) and community relations (1:28-32)—the more their obsession and passion transform these good gifts into self-destructive and oppressive behavior.

Paul underscores in Romans (and Galatians) that his own experience as a Jew is similar to that of Gentile idolaters.

1) The true revelation and gifts the Jews have received from God include the covenant, the irrevocable election as children of God, Torah (the commandment, which is "holy and just and good," 7:12), the promises and oracles of God (3:1-2; 9:4-5; 11:28-29), and worship (9:4).

2) Far from hypocritically ignoring and denying this revelation, Jewish believers have a great "zeal" for God (10:2); they follow the Law/Torah with the conviction that, as promised, it will bring them life (7:10). But because their zeal is obsessive ("not enlightened," 10:2), they have absolutized the Law/Torah, viewing it as the way to righteousness (instead of being open to the righteousness that comes from God, 10:2-5).

3) Like any idolater, they are then trapped, destroyed, and killed by their obsession for this revelation. Sin

"deceived" Paul the Jew through the law (7:12). The more he wanted to do God's will, the more he did the evil he hated, including idolatry (i.e., viewing as an absolute what is not, 7:15-23).

Such is the story of all religious persons who view what they have received from God as the complete and final revelation. This applies to arrogant Christians (Rom 11 and 13–15; see the second reading), who obsessively view their particular understanding and practice of the gospel as the complete and final revelation that everyone should adopt.

The Gospel as Power of Salvation: Being Freed from the Power of Sin

The way out of all these obsessions passes through the recognition that the revelation or gift one has received from God is not the complete and final revelation. ("For we know only in part . . . For now we see in a mirror, dimly," 1 Cor 13:9-12). But how can we be freed from our obsessions about the revelation or gift we received from God? Paul's answer: through the gospel as "the power of God for salvation" (Rom 1:16). Is this a divine lightening bolt through which idolaters and arrogant believers are shocked out of their obsessions? Paul surprises us: this powerful salvation is through a revelation of God's righteousness "from faith to faith" (1:17, a.t.); that is, it is transmitted from believers to believers. This seems strange (so the NRSV translates it as "through faith and for faith") until one recognizes two things: 1) receiving a revelation from someone else involves acknowledging that the revelation one has is *not* complete or sufficient and 2) encountering unexpected manifestations of God in other persons or groups (such as Jews or Gentiles) transforms us (12:2). The liberating power of the gospel is at work for someone when that person acknowledges the truth of the *different* revelations and divine gifts that others have received and manifested; that is, when one encounters the presence of God as manifested in the different experience of those others—in their otherness.

For Paul, this power of the gospel is at work in the "body of Christ" (12:5). Each Christian believer has received a "measure of faith" (not the whole of faith, 12:3). Consequently, each should acknowledge the different "gifts" (*charismata*) that others have received from God (12:6) and be open to benefit from them. Being part of the body of Christ involves acknowledging that the gift one has received is never self-sufficient; it needs to be complemented by the gifts others have (12:3-8). Therefore, the only possible attitude is to honor others ("putting others before yourselves in honor," 12:10, see NIV). Christians cannot but "regard others as better than [themselves]" (Phil 2:3) when they contemplate others and view them as bearers of divine gifts or revelations they lack. Encountering God's manifestation in others frees believers from the destructive obsession that kept them in bondage.

The same applies to Paul himself. Paul, with his superb credentials (see Rom 1:1-6), is tempted like everyone else to obsessively believe that the exceptional revelations and gifts he has received puts him above others and that he is to share these revelations and gifts with others without needing to receive anything from them. He actually falls into this trap when he writes, "For I am longing to see you so that I may share with you some spiritual gift to strengthen you" (1:11). However, he realizes immediately what he has done and corrects himself, "or rather so that we may be mutually encouraged by each other's faith, both yours and mine" (1:12). Of course! He has to receive something from the Romans. Indeed, he should regard them as better than himself because they have gifts (*charismata*) he lacks. He needs to honor them; that is, he needs to discern the gifts they are bringing to him.

Paul (barely) escapes an obsessive idolatrous attitude by acknowledging that he has much to receive from other Christians. What about his attitude toward Gentile idolaters? We have noted that Paul acknowledges that they have a true revelation (1:18-19). Is this a revelation that he believes he needs to receive from them? In 1:14 Paul signals that

he does, writing, "I am a debtor both to Greeks and to barbarians, both to the wise and to the foolish." This statement refers to a debt that he has incurred by receiving something from these other people (rather than to a general sense of obligation toward them). For Paul, bringing the gospel to the Greeks and to the barbarians involves acknowledging that they have revelations and gifts he needs to receive from them, even though they might have transformed them into destructive, idolatrous obsessions. This is what Paul does in 13:4 by recognizing "God's servant" in the Roman emperor cloaked in his destructive imperialistic idolatry. Far from viewing the gospel as the complete and final revelation, for Paul the gospel calls Christians to discern the many revelations and divine gifts that other people have and to be ready to receive these from them.

Paul exhorts the Romans to adopt the same attitude: "Do not be conformed to this world, but be transformed by the renewing of your minds, so that you may discern what is the will of God—what is good and acceptable and perfect" (12:2). Far from stepping out of the evil "world" and rejecting it, Christians should contemplate it, discern in it what is from God, affirm what is good and acceptable and perfect in it (or "holy and just and good," as Paul says about the Law/Torah in 7:12), and be ready to receive it as a gift from God, who is actively present in "this world."

However, Christians should not "conform" (12:2) themselves to this world; they should not participate in the idolatrous, destructive obsessions of this world. They should follow the example of Christ, who did not conform to the world into which he was sent and thus appeared to be sinful from the warped (sinful) perspective of that world (he was "in the likeness of sinful flesh according to sin [*peri hamartias*]," 8:3, a.t.). By not conforming to and sinning against this world (transgressing the rules of this world), Christian believers "present [their] bodies as a living sacrifice" (12:1) as Christ did (3:25). They will be rejected and persecuted for threatening what this world obsessively views as most sacred. But, when through some manifestations of God they are shown to be truly sent by God (as Christ was shown to be Son of God through his resurrection, 1:4), then (some) people from this world are freed from bondage to their destructive obsessions.

CONCLUSION

For present-day Christians who struggle with their exclusivist attitudes, the implications of Paul's view of religious obsession are striking. Our knee-jerk reaction is to reject or despise those who have religious views and practices that we perceive as nonsensical, childish, and dangerous because they contradict our convictions. We despise believers of other religions, followers of anti-religious ideologies (e.g., atheists or communists), and also Christians of traditions other than ours. As Paul warns us, this knee-jerk reaction is doubly problematic: we "condemn" ourselves (2:1) because it is a sign that we ourselves have absolutized a partial revelation or gift from God, and we deprive ourselves of the good gifts and revelations that, surprisingly, God offers us through them.

How can we escape this vicious circle? It is neither a matter of theological knowledge (see the first reading) nor a matter of will (see the second reading). It is a matter of convictions. As self-evident truths, convictions have power upon believers either to drive them into an obsessive behavior (idolatrous convictions) or to empower them and free them from such behavior (iconoclastic convictions).

For Paul, the gospel has this iconoclastic power that transforms people through a "renewing of [their] minds," which empowers them to discern what is (and what is not) from God in the world around them (12:2). Contemplating all those around us through the corrective lenses of the gospel, we can recognize that, behind the grime and destructiveness of their obsessive behavior, all of these persons have received good, acceptable, and perfect gifts from God *(charismata)*, which they offer to us. We can see that God is truly at work in their experience and that they are sent by God. Then, we can honor others (12:10), considering them as better than ourselves (Phil 2:3); that is, as

people to whom we are indebted (Rom 1:14) because of the gifts they share with us. These other people we honor include Jews and people from other races, from the other sex and of other sexual tendencies, from other cultures, from other economic status—indeed, all people who are somehow different from us. By the very fact of honoring them we are freed *for a moment* from anti-Semitism, racism, sexism, elitism, colonialism, imperialism, and other oppressions. But it is only for a moment because the root of sin (coveting desires) remains within us. As soon as we stop contemplating others around us through the corrective lenses of the gospel, we are back in bondage to our sins. Constant empowerment by ongoing contemplation of the world through the corrective lenses of the gospel is a condition for being rescued from our multifold obsessive and destructive bondage by those others who, in their mysterious difference, bring divine gifts to us.

The gospel is also the power of God for salvation because, when we look at this world as though through corrective lenses, it also reveals to us what God condemns (1:18), what in this world is not from God, and thus to what we should not conform ourselves (12:2). Contemplating the world around us through the gospel, we are empowered to discern not only obsessive, idolatrous, destructive, abusive, hurtful, and deadly types of behavior but also their systemic, cultural, economic, social, and political causes. This recognition is a call to not conform to this world and thus to offer ourselves in "living sacrifice" (12:1) as Christ did. Refusing complicity with the powers of this world—for instance, refusing to live in the warped world of a constant state of emergency—involves putting oneself and those we love at risk. But this sacrifice is not in vain because, as the gospel promises, it is never the end of story. By his resurrection the crucified was shown to be the Son of God through whom the power of God for salvation was manifested among the Jews (1:4, 16). In the same way, when Christian believers offer themselves in sacrifice by not conforming to the evil of this world, they can count on resurrection-like interventions of God that will transform their apparently futile gesture into a manifestation of the power of God through which at least some of the victims of evil will be freed from their bondage.

BIBLIOGRAPHY

Beare, Francis W. "Romans, The Letter to the." Pages 112–22 in *The Interpreter's Dictionary of the Bible*. Edited by George Arthur Buttrick et al. Vol. R–Z. Nashville: Abingdon, 1962.

Beker, J. Christiaan. *The Triumph of God: The Essence of Paul's Thought*. Translated by Loren T. Stuckenbruck. Minneapolis: Fortress, 1990.

Bultmann, Rudolf. *Theology of the New Testament*. Translated by Kendrick Grobel. 2 vols. New York: Scribner, 1951–1955.

Davies, W. D. *Paul and Rabbinic Judaism: Some Rabbinic Elements in Pauline Theology*. Philadelphia: Fortress, 1965.

Dunn, James D. G. *Romans*. WBC 38A-B. Dallas: Word Books, 1988.

Elliott, Neil. *Liberating Paul: The Justice of God and the Politics of the Apostle*. Bible and Liberation series. Maryknoll, N.Y.: Orbis, 1994.

Fitzmyer, Joseph A. *Romans: A New Translation with Introduction and Commentary*. AB 33. New York: Doubleday, 1993.

Gager, John G. *Reinventing Paul*. Oxford: Oxford University Press, 2000.

Grenholm, Cristina, and Daniel Patte, eds. *Reading Israel in Romans: Legitimacy and Plausibility of Divergent Interpretations*. Romans through History and Culture series. Harrisburg, Penn.: Trinity Press, 2000.

Jewett, Robert. *Saint Paul Returns to the Movies: Triumph over Shame*. Grand Rapids, Mich.: Eerdmans, 1998.

Käsemann, Ernst. *Commentary on Romans*. Translated and edited by Geoffrey W. Bromiley. Grand Rapids, Mich.: Eerdmans, 1980.

Patte, Daniel. P*aul's Faith and the Power of the Gospel: A Structural Introduction to the Pauline Letters*. Philadelphia: Fortress, 1983.

Sanders, E. P. *Paul and Palestinian Judaism: A Comparison of Patterns of Religion*. Philadelphia: Fortress, 1977.

Schweitzer, Albert. *The Mysticism of Paul the Apostle*. Translated by William Montgomery. New York: Macmillan, 1931.

Stendahl, Krister. *Paul among Jews and Gentiles, and Other Essays*. Philadelphia: Fortress, 1976.

Stowers, Stanley K. *A Rereading of Romans: Justice, Jews, and Gentiles*. New Haven: Yale University Press, 1994.

Stuhlmacher, Peter. *Paul's Letter to the Romans: A Commentary*. Translated by Scott J. Hafemann. Louisville: Westminster John Knox Press, 1994.

Tamez, Elsa. *The Amnesty of Grace: Justification by Faith from a Latin American Perspective*. Translated by Sharon H. Ringe. Nashville: Abingdon, 1993.

Vanderbilt *Divinity School. Divinity Catalog: Vanderbilt University, 2000–2001*. N.p.: 2001. Cited April 14, 2004, online: http://www.vanderbilt.edu/catalogs/divinity/index.html.

Walker, Alice. *The Temple of My Familiar*. New York: Pocket Books/Washington Square Press, 1989.

Yeo, K. K., ed. *Navigating Romans Through Cultures: Challenging Readings by Charting a New Course*. Romans Through History and Cultures Series. New York: T & T Clark International, 2004.

---

* According to the Bureau of Justice Statistics, at the end of 2002, U.S. prisons and jails held 2,033,331 prisoners. There were "3,437 sentenced black male prisoners per 100,000 black males in the United States, compared to . . . 450 white male inmates per 100,000 white males." U.S. Department of Justice. Office of Justice Programs. Bureau of Justice Statistics. "Prison Statistics." No pages. Cited April 12, 2004. Online: http://www.ojp.usdoj.gov/bjs/prisons.htm.

** The NRSV translates epithymia as "lusts" in 1:24 and as "covetousness" in 7:8.

1 CORINTHIANS

Joseph Pathrapankal, CMI

Faculty of Theology, Dharmaram Vidya Kshetram, Bangalore, India

LIFE CONTEXT OF THE INTERPRETATION

India is the most populous country in the world after China. It has a polygenetic population, subdivided into twenty-eight states, with eighteen official languages and hundreds of dialects. As such, India is a land of ethnic, social, religious, and cultural pluralism. It is the birthplace of some of the major religions of the world, like Hinduism, the religion of the Aryans. Two other religions, Buddhism and Jainism, arose during the sixth and fifth centuries B.C.E., while Sikhism developed during the sixteenth century. India has also accommodated many other religions from outside, such as Islam (since the eighth century C.E.), Christianity, Judaism, and Zoroastrianism. Hinduism is the religion of more than 75 percent of the Indian population, while only a small minority, 6 percent, profess Christianity. Since India's independence (1947) and the establishment of a democratic republic (1950), the Indian Consti-tutions provides complete freedom and equality for all religions.

According to a living tradition, Thomas, one of Jesus' twelve disciples, came to India in 52 C.E. and spread the message of Christ in South India. From the sixteenth century C.E. onwards, the Portuguese, Dutch, and British brought Western Christianity to India, which succeeded in destroying many meaningful traditions prevalent among its early Christians. These encounters resulted in many tensions and divisions among the Christians through the centuries. As a result of this complex history of Christianity in India, the Churches in India constitute a multifaceted reality, a reality that becomes even more complex when viewed against the background of India's religious pluralism. Moreover, Christianity's presence is not uniform throughout India.

How 1 Corinthians Addresses the Relationship of God's People to the People of other Faiths in India

In a land of religious pluralism, Christianity has its own strengths and weaknesses. Though it constitutes only a small percentage of the Indian popula-tion, the impact this religion has on the Indian cultural scene and the outside world is unique and unparalleled. Through its many educational institutions, vast health programs, and many socio-economic development projects, Christianity in India projects a very impressive image of a committed and involved religion. At the same time, because it exists and operates in the context of a religious pluralism that is unique in the world, Christianity needs to sincerely and seriously reflect on the image that it projects among the followers of other religions (see Paul's similar concerns in 1 Cor 14:23). What image of itself does Christian divisiveness—including the divisions between the Roman Catholic, Protestant, and Orthodox Churches—give to the followers of other religions? The impact of the great Eastern Schism in 1054 c.e., the sixteenth-century Protestant Reformation, and the Anglican Schism is clearly visible in India where there

Joseph Pathrapankal, CMI, is a Professor Emeritus of New Testament and Theology. He holds a doctorate in Biblical Theology from the Gregorian University, Rome, and an honorary doctorate in Theology from the University of Uppsala. He is the author of several books including, *Critical and Creative* (1986), *Text and Context* (1993), *The Christan Programme* (1999), *Dimensions of the Word* (2000) and *Time and History* (2002). He was honored by a Festschrift: *Indian Interpretation of the Bible* (Augustine Thottakara, ed. 2000).

is an ever-increasing number of churches and denominations, many of which are so-called "Independent" churches. These trends toward division and tensions between the various groups are visible within the same church, whether Roman Catholic, Protestant, or Orthodox. The result is that Christianity cannot claim to bear witness to the message of the gospel preached by Jesus Christ. There is a credibility gap. Thus, our first question will be: How does 1 Corinthians help us address the problem of internal divisiveness and the negative image of Christianity this conveys to followers of other religions?

From the colonial times to the present, Christianity has projected the image of being a foreign religion in India. Though the indigenous church of the early centuries was very much an Indian reality, "inculturated" or indigenously nurtured in the Indian soil and committed to the cultural and social characteristics of the people, the colonial powers destroyed these cultural and social traits, claiming that they were opposed to the Christian faith. Closely related to this rejection of indigenous Indian Christianity was the missionaries' negative attitude toward the followers of other religions. Basing their arguments on the great commission of the risen Christ—making disciples of all nations and baptizing them (Matt 28:18-19)—the missionaries competed with each other to convert the followers of other religions to their respective churches and denominations. Thus, our second question will be: How does 1 Corinthians help us overcome the rejection of inculturated Indian Christianity and indigenous culture that we inherited from the colonial period?

The cumulative effect of these historical developments is that Christianity in India manifests the symptoms and characteristics of a church that is not fully aware of its true nature and heritage. In this respect, the churches in India can be compared to the Corinthian church. In a certain sense, Paul's writings are mirrors in which churches of every age, as well as Christians of every generation and culture, can find their own image reflected, causing alarm and anxiety but also offering courage and consolation. Even if Paul did not directly emphasize all the ideas that we discern in his letters today, we have to acknowledge the power that his writings carry within themselves. Indeed, we need to rediscover the power of these texts to bring new vision within our communities, and help us see our communities in a new light. This is not eisegesis, but rather a critical analysis of these texts in which exegetes bring together historical (diachronic) observations, literary (synchronic) analyses, and contextualized theological reflections. Paul himself legitimates such an approach because, though 1 Corinthians is addressed to the Corinthians as the "church of God," it is also addressed to "all those who in every place call on the name of our Lord Jesus Christ, both their Lord and ours" (1:2). Beginning with the church of Antioch (Acts 15:22-35), local churches were encouraged to understand their faith in terms of their cultural settings.

We will use two approaches to understand how 1 Corinthians applies to India's current state of affairs. First, we will use the insights of critical New Testament scholarship to understand the situation in first-century Corinth. Second, we will rely on the idea of "inculturation," which is "the creative and dynamic relationship between the Christian message and a culture or cultures" (Shorter 1988, 11). How does the syncretistic and religiously plural setting of ancient Corinth inform our understanding of and ministry to the religiously pluralistic setting of contemporary India?

CONTEXTUAL COMMENT

An Overview of First Corinthians

The origin of the Corinthian church is associated with challenges. Accor-ding to the Acts of the Apostles, Paul took a risk in preaching the gospel to the Corinthians (Acts 18:1-18) immediately after preaching in Athens (Acts 17:16-33). Though the narratives about Paul's preaching in Athens and

Corinth are not to be understood literally, Paul's own words about his first visit to Corinth (1 Cor 2:1-5) indicate that there is a historical nucleus behind the Acts narrative. After his encounter with the inner contradictions of the Greek culture in Athens, Paul had to deepen his commitment to being the apostle to the Gentiles.

The major issue Paul had to deal with in Corinth was related to the question of Greek knowledge (*gnōsis*) and the Corinthians' confusion of it with the wisdom (*sophia*) of the gospel. The results of this cult of knowledge were the ever-growing divisions among the members of the community (1:10–3:4), as well as a false understanding of the role of its leaders in the community (3:5–4:21).

The divisions in Corinth did not stop there. They evolved into controversies among the members, resulting in conflicting ideologies (1 Cor 5–14). The central issue is that, when people allow themselves to be guided by conflicting ideologies, divisions multiply limitlessly. This is precisely what we see, not only in the Corinthian community, but also in the long history of the church in India, the Untied States, and Europe.

In Corinth there were both proto-gnostic Christians as well as libertines. Whereas the former tended towards austerity, the latter practiced extreme licentiousness, including incest (1 Cor 5:1-13) and prostitution (6:12-20). The ascetic proto-gnostic Christians (who were, perhaps, "over-converted") advocated sexual abstinence even as the ideal for married couples (7:1) and encouraged abstinence of other kinds. Paul had to deal with questions about marriage and virginity (7:1-40), about eating or not eating meat offered in the shrines of other religions (8:1-11:1), about church discipline (11:2-34), and about gifts of the Spirit (*charismata*) (12:1-14:40). These preliminary remarks about 1 Corinthians already suggest some of the issues the churches in India (and elsewhere) might need to consider regarding their own internal divisions, especially by considering 1 Cor 1:1-4:5 and 11:17-34.

Besides these divisions, other issues also added to the disharmony among the members of the church in Corinth—tensions among the rich and the poor, among Jewish and Gentile Christians, among those practicing asceticism and others indulging in permissiveness (1 Cor 5:1-6:20), and enthusiasts with exaggerated understanding of spiritual gifts (12:1–14:40)—all led to a serious lack of unity among the members of the community.

For Paul, the most serious issue was the role of Christ in the makeup of the community. Hence Paul raises the challenging question: "Has Christ been divided?" (1:13). It was not Paul who was crucified for the Corinthians, and it was not in the name of Paul that the Corinthians were baptized. Christ is the uniting agent of the community, a unity that transcends all diversities. Before the person of Christ, all discriminatory behaviors must disappear; Christ should unite the whole community. The major issues analyzed in this section relate to Paul's experiences during his stay in Corinth and also what he came to know from Chloe's people (1:11). The fundamental question was about the insidious divisions in the community. Writing to them from Ephesus during his third missionary journey (ca. 56-57 C.E.), Paul alternated between teaching, pleading, and expressing indignation as he tried to introduce some good sense into the new version of Christianity that had evolved on the Greek soil. The churches in India and elsewhere in the world may learn something about inculturation and interreligious relationships from 1 Corinthians, especially from 8:1–11:16.

Church Divisions, a Cult of Knowledge (Gnosis) Divorced from Christian Wisdom, and a Lack of Understanding of Church Leadership (1 Cor 1:18-4:5; 11:17-34)

The divisions in Corinth seem to have arrested Paul's attention so much that all other issues fade into the background. For Paul, this was the root of all the problems of orthodoxy and orthopraxis in the community. Paul was fully convinced of the devastating effect of divisions for this young church with its cosmopolitan character. His lengthy stay with the Corinthians did not seem to have produced the desired unity. In fact, toward the end of 1 Corinthians Paul hints at the major estrangements between leaders and the community. Paul asks the community not to oppose Timothy (16:10-11) and he also mentions Apollos, a patron of a strong group in the community, explaining that he was not willing to visit the community in spite of Paul's sincere request.

As a theologian committed to radical thinking, Paul analyzed the problem of Corinthian factionalism from two main perspectives, claiming the divisions arose, first, from a false understanding of Christian wisdom and, second, from a wrong understanding of the role of the apostles in the community. At the heart of these divisions is the polarization within humans between the spirit and flesh (1 Cor 3:1, 3; 5:5; 6:16; 15:39, 50). Yet, since humans are rational creatures, the problem lies still deeper, as Paul analyzed in his reflections on divine and human wisdom. Christian wisdom is identified with the divine, not with the human. As the Greeks were committed to the pursuit of wisdom as their privilege and right, it was only natural that they had their own cultural understanding of wisdom, despite the fact that it did not assist them in clearly understanding the gospel.

Contrast Between Divine and Human Wisdom: 1 Cor 1:18-25

Paul explains that the true nature of Christian wisdom is derived from the wisdom of God as revealed in the wisdom of the cross. The topic is so incomprehensible for rational thinkers that Paul has to describe it from multiple perspectives: the "wisdom of God," the "wisdom of this world," the "folly of preaching Christ crucified," the "folly to the Gentiles," the "power of God," the "foolishness of God" and the "weakness of God." The basic idea is clear enough. The human view of wisdom is not God's view. The way of faith alone leads to understanding the wisdom of God revealed in the cross, and to salvation. This is a reversal, an inversion of the human way of thinking of and understanding Christianity (which, from this human perspective, is merely a grouping of parties, a clustering of factions). Moreover, in human eyes, the gospel itself is both offensive and absurd. To the Jews, the concept of a crucified messiah was contradictory. Similarly, Jesus' crucifixion had led the Greeks to conclude that it was folly to make him a hero. But Paul maintains that the crucified Christ has done something for humankind that the wisdom and power of humans could never accomplish. Paul's apparently negative attitude toward rational wisdom in this passage must be understood from the specific Greek context in which he was trying to make the Corinthians see the absurdity of their divisions in the Church. What would make us see the absurdity of our own divisions today?

The Wisdom of God Revealed in the Call of the Corinthians: 1 Cor 1:26-31

In light of this contrast of divine and human wisdom, Paul spoke to those Corinthians, from the lower strata of the community, the "have-nots" who formed the majority of the cosmopolitan city. Paul refers to the wisdom of God revealed in God's call to the have-nots. They were just ordinary people. The same principle is applied also to those who were of a nobler origin. Boasting *(hybris)* is excluded from Christian life. The least and the last are those who are preferred by God. This may be our first lesson. Following the egregiously bad example of the colonial era, are we not looking at the wrong people to find those who have authority in the church?

The Wisdom of God Shown in the Apostolate of Paul in Corinth: 1 Cor 2:1-5

Here Paul refers to his initial visit to Corinth after his attempt to communicate the gospel in Athens failed because of the arrogance of human wisdom, which rejected the message of the resurrection. Hence, his visit to Corinth was associated with much "weakness, fear, and trembling" because he did not know how to proceed in his mission of preaching the gospel. To survive in a city like Corinth, faith needed a supernatural basis ("so that your faith might rest not on human wisdom but on the power of God," 1 Cor 2:5). Paul may be referring to the lack of sophistication and rhetorical skill in his speeches (2 Cor 10:10) compared to the eloquence of Apollos, which became yet another issue in the Corinthian church that caused division and preferences among its members.

The True Wisdom of God:
1 Cor 2:6–3:4

The main theme here is that human comprehension of the plan of God revealed in Christ depends on the enlightenment given by the Spirit *(pneuma)*. In fact, Paul maintains that all humans possess the spirit, a principle or basic source of discernment. But those who rely solely on their natural reason cannot understand the truths taught by the spirit; only those who allow their spirit to operate can understand these truths. This joint operation of the human spirit and the divine Spirit requires close analysis. When people allow themselves to be guided by their spirit, their spirit opens itself to the divine Spirit and they begin to think and live in maturity (2:9-16). There is an implied rebuke to the Corinthians for their criticism that Paul had not taught them "wisdom" as Apollos had done. In fact, he refrained from teaching them the higher wisdom, not because he did not know it, but because the Corinthians were not capable of receiving it. They were still in their state of infancy, for the divisions in Corinth were proof that they were living by human standards (3:1-4).

The Role of the Apostles:
1 Cor 3:5-4:5

In the context of the personality cult in Corinth, Paul analyzes the nature of an apostle's work and its value in God's eyes. The apostles are only servants, instruments God has used to bring faith to the Corinthians, each of them according to the gift received

from God. Paul uses two metaphors of planting and building to describe the work the apostles are engaged in. It was Paul's task to sow the seed, and Apollos' task to water it, but only God could make the plant grow. Both are instruments cooperating with God, not rivals. The second metaphor is one of building: the Corinthians are the building, Paul laid the foundation for the building, and others, including Apollos, have built on it. All workers must be careful about how they build. Most importantly, they should not disturb the foundation, which is Christ himself. Paul then refers to the evaluation of each one's work made at the final judgment. After another attack on human wisdom (3:18-23) Paul concludes his formal arguments against those who were engaged in creating divisions at Corinth (4:1-5). Is this not a teaching that we should take to heart concerning our understanding (or misunderstanding) of leadership in contemporary church divisions?

Divisions in the Celebration
of the Lord's Supper:
1 Cor 11:17-34

These divisive tendencies led to serious ethical consequences in the Corinthians' celebration of the Lord's Supper (11:17-34). Therefore, Paul had to dwell on the challenging message of the Lord's Supper as the proclamation of the death of the Lord (11:26). First Corinthians 11:23-26 is uniquely important insofar as this is a tradition that Paul considers as having great significance for Christian life. But for many Corinthians, the celebration of the Lord's Supper was nothing more than a meal, a mere social gathering, and they could not discern the relationship of this ritual to Christ. The problem seems to have been the division between the rich and poor in the Corinthian Christian community. Whatever the real issue, Paul found the Corinthian situation alarming and had to exhort and warn the community about the serious consequences of their divisiveness in the celebration of the Lord's Supper.

Looking at the situation in both India and the rest of the world, it seems that what Paul condemns in Corinth is precisely what has taken place in the Christian world throughout history. Despite the theological and ecclesiological arguments used to legitimize these divided celebrations, the fact remains that the celebration of the Lord's Supper in these divided houses of God is the Christian movement's most extreme scandal, especially when it occurs in a pluralistic setting such as India. Christianity's characteristic emphasis on unity is evidenced not through its doctrine, but through its celebration of the Lord's Supper.

Advice about Interreligious Relationships and Inculturation from Paul, a Prudent and Mature Pastoral Theologian (1 Cor 8:1-11:16)

Living as a Christian in ancient Corinth, in the shadow of Greco-Roman religions, was demanding and challenging. There were conflicting Christian attitudes toward the larger culture: some scrupulously avoided all contact with their Gentile neighbors, while others claimed to have an advanced knowledge of spiritual reality and ignored their weak brothers and sisters. Therefore, Paul, a gifted pastoral theologian, had to discuss interreligious relationships and Christian adaptation to the surrounding culture with prudence and maturity (1 Cor 8:1-11:16).

It is worth meditating upon these chapters and the way in which Paul carefully tried to preserve the cultural character of the Corinthians without in any way introducing his own personal preferences, except to demand the values of the gospel (see 10:20-21). He made a clear distinction between issues that are specifically related to the demands of the Christian faith and matters that had only social and cultural aspects. Regarding the former, Paul insisted that there can be no compromise with the basic truth of the gospel. With respect to the latter, there was freedom. Christians attended the social gatherings of Gentile neighbors (10:27). Here is an excellent example of how Paul could maturely instruct a relatively young Christian community about interreligious relationships. There is no evidence here of the negative attitude toward other religions that colo-nial missionaries taught and practiced with devastating consequences throughout the world.

Paul maintains that, in such gatherings with Gentiles, the Christians should be extremely careful about edification, deference, and respect for the followers of other religions, even if it meant sacrificing their freedom of conscience. For Paul, as a rule, "the other" should be the criterion and controlling factor of Christian behavior: "Give no offense to Jews or to Greeks or to the Church of God" (1 Cor 10:32). Again and again he points to the importance of love (agapƒ?) (8:1, 3), care and concern for others (8:9-13), and seeking the best for others (10:24) as the controlling principles in choosing how to incorporate certain practices or views associated with the larger culture into one's Christian life (see 10:25–11:1). Whereas egoistic knowledge puffs one up and destroys others, altruistic love builds up both oneself and the community (8:1). Consequently, those who are committed to the service of the gospel must have an attitude of appropriately adapting and appreciating their cultural milieu. This is precisely what Paul could claim: "To the Jews I became as a Jew, in order to win Jews. To those under the law I became as one under the law (though I myself am not under the law) so that I might win those under the law. To those outside the law I became as one outside the law (though I am not free from God's law but am under Christ's law) so that I might win those outside the law. To the weak I became weak, so that I might win the weak. I have become all things to all people, that I might by all means save some" (9:20-22). Paul's bold statement is challenging: "If food is a cause of [my brother's] falling, I will never eat meat, so that I may not cause [my brother] to fall" (8:13). Taken as a whole, this letter is a model of inculturation and interreligious relationship for all in our times. Rather than rejecting different cultures and religions, Christians should remain open to them, even as they proceed in their daily lives with all the prudence exemplified by Paul.

CONCLUSION

First Corinthians is a letter whose message has profound implications, not only for the first-century Christians, but also for today's Christians of India and for Christians throughout world. "Become what you are" (see 1 Cor 7:17) is the controlling thought of the entire letter; the Corinthians had to put into practice what they already were. Christ is the uniting power for all. This Christ is not and cannot be divided (1:13). In union with Christ they have been washed and sanctified, and have become acceptable in the name of Christ and in the Spirit of God (6: 11). Since Paul had been brought to a new life through the overarching message of the gospel, he wanted all the members of his communities to pattern their lives in light of the resurrection of Christ. Divisions, sexual permissiveness, and lawsuits are alien to the spirit of the resurrection. Individual freedom must always be accommodated to one's social responsibility toward fellow humans.

Even as the world becomes a global village through the abolition of ethnic and social discrimination, new divisions develop among people, as seen in the various conflicts and forms of aggressions throughout the world. The September 11, 2001 attack on the World Trade Center was a horrific, visible proof of the power of evil still lurking and active in the world. The divisive and diabolic power loosed at the beginning of human history through fratricide still operates among humanity in a various forms. Division within the church and its consequences, which Paul encountered in Corinth, serve as a reminder to the churches of all times how their members need to become instruments of peace and harmony in the world. The great responsibility of the Christian movement in a postmodern world is precisely the same. We need to guide Christian communities to work toward both unity in the human society and harmonious interaction and dialog with followers of other religions.

BIBLIOGRAPHY

Blenkinsopp, Joseph. *The Corinthian Mirror: A Study of Contemporary Themes in a Pauline Epistle*. London and New York: Sheed & Ward, 1964.

Conzelmann, Hans. *1 Corinthians*. Hermeneia. Minneapolis: Fortress, 1975.

Fee, Gordon D. *The First Epistle to the Corinthians*. NICNT. Grand Rapids: Eerdmans ,1987.

Green, Michael. *To Corinth with Love: The Vital Relevance Today of Paul's Advice to the Corinthian Church*. London: Hodder and Stoughton, 1982.

Martin, Ralph P. *The Spirit and Congregation: Studies in 1 Corinthians 12-15*. Grand Rapids: Eerdmans, 1984.

Orr, William F., and James Arthur Walther. *1 Corinthians*. AB 32. Garden City: Doubleday, 1976.

Pathrapankal, Joseph, CMI. *Text and Context in Biblical Interpretation*. Bangalore: Dharmaram, 1999.

Robertson, A., and Alfred Plummer. *A Critical and Exegetical Commentary on the First Letter of St. Paul to the Corinthians*. ICC 33. Edinburgh: T & T Clark, 1963.

Shorter, Aylward. *Toward a Theology of Inculturation*. Maryknoll, N.Y.: Orbis, 1988.

Schmithals, W. *Gnosticism in Corinth: An Investigation of the Letters to the Corinthians*. Trans. John E. Steely. Nashville: Abingdon, 1971.

Thottakara, Augustine, ed. *Indian Interpretation of the Bible: Festschrift in Honour of Joseph Pathrapankal*. Bangalore: Dharmaram, 2000.

Witherington III, Ben. *Conflict and Community in Corinth: A Socio-Rhetorical Commentary on 1 and 2 Corinthians*. Grand Rapids: Eerdmans, 1995.

1 CORINTHIANS 11 IN CHRISTIAN AND MUSLIM DIALOGUE

Derya Keskin Demirer,
Ohio State University, Ohio, USA and

Nicole Wilkinson Duran,
Rosemont College and Villanova University, Philadelphia, Pa.

LIFE CONTEXT OF THE INTERPRETATION

In this excursus, we will use some of the history of women's headcovering in Christianity and Islam to illumine Paul's notoriously obscure comments on headcovering in 1 Corinthians 11:2-16. This passage begins with a dishearteningly flat statement of the cosmic hierarchy—from woman at the lower end through man and then Christ, to God (v. 3)—followed by a similar statement about the relative shame of men and women covering their heads (vv. 4-5). He then offers an argument from culture equating a woman's uncovered head with a shaven head (vv. 5-6), and an argument from Scripture that woman was created for man and from man and so reflects his, rather than God's, glory (v. 7). The argument then stalls as Paul concedes that neither gender is independent of the other (v. 11), and he asserts their mutual origin in God (v. 12). In the end, he appeals to the Corinthians' (cultural) common sense, asking whether it is not obvious that long hair, and thus head covering, is appropriate for a woman and not for a man (vv. 13-15). Finally, he answers possible contention with the statement that the church has "no such custom" (v.16).

Text and Context in Dialogue

We write from the context of the United States, within two years of 9/11, when the relationship between Islam and Christianity, Middle East and West, has become a matter of life and death. As feminists and scholars we have both noted with interest and alarm the recurrent image of the covered woman as a metonym for Islam. This western equation of women's headcovering with Islam prompted us to explore the function of headcovering in early Christianity, in hopes that the current Muslim practice and the ancient Christian text might illumine one another. We end the article with some lingering questions that this preliminary discussion has raised for us.

Nicole: As a woman who has married into Turkish culture, I read this passage in Paul partly in a continuing struggle to understand the meaning of women's headcovering in Turkey and in other Muslim societies. At the same time, I read 1 Corinthians 11:2-16 as a Protestant Testament at a Protestant seminary, clergywoman, teaching an introduction to where most of my students are African-American and evangelical, and where many

Nicole Wilkinson Duran, after teaching New Testament in the USA, South Africa (Zululand), and Turkey, is currently teaching part-time and, with her husband, raising twin sons in the suburbs of Philadelphia, Pa. She has published articles on gender and race in Esther, the unread Bible in Toni Morrison's novels, and body symbolism in the story of John the Baptist's execution. She has edited (with G. Phillips) *Reading Communities, Reading Scripture* (2002). She is an ordained Presbyterian minister and does occasional preaching and adult Christian education.

Derya Keskin Demirer received a master's degree in Near Eastern languages and cultures at Ohio State University in Columbus, Ohio. She wrote her thesis on the cultural and political implications of modernity, Islam, and orientalism, both in the East and in the West, in terms of gender and specifically examined the headscarf issue in contemporary Turkey.

struggle with the Pauline letters' implications for the ordination of women. The center of this crucial interpretive issue, it seems to me, lies in our selected passage.

Derya: I come to this text as an outsider to the Christian religion, a woman from a Muslim culture, and a student of women's issues in a western school. Studying women's position in general and veiling in particular in the Islamic context has directed me to the study of early Islam, and thus to early Christianity—for I learned that veiling did not begin with Islam. At that point, many questions arose: Is veiling then not really a Muslim tradition? Whatever happened to veiling within Christianity? How did this piece of cloth become an enormous symbol of not only Muslim women but also the whole religion of Islam for western Christian cultures? Coming from a Muslim culture, I grew up with women who covered their heads, including my own mother. For me, it was part of our culture and not part of the Christian culture. When I came to study this issue, I had two tasks in front of me: (1) to understand how this practice became a Muslim practice, and (2) to understand the place of this practice in Christianity.

Nicole: It interests me that neither Derya nor I initially saw headcovering as a Christian practice. In fact, headcovering for women in worship is alive and well in many forms of Protestantism around the world, and was only abandoned by the Roman Catholic Church with Vatican II. Within my own white mainline Protestant world, however, even supposed literalists often blithely read over this passage as either not truly recommending veiling or as culturally conditioned and consequently irrelevant to the practice of contemporary Christian women.

Derya: Similarly, whether the veil (either a headcovering or *hejab* that covers the whole body except the face) is truly an Islamic practice in its historical context has been the subject of a wide range of literature. Perceptions differ tremendously even among Middle Eastern women scholars. For instance, while some scholars mainly draw attention to fundamentalist Islam and the

oppressive features of the veil (e.g., Haideh Moghissi 1999, Nawal El Saadawi 1997), others pay more attention to the indigenous, religious, and positive aspects of the veil (e.g., Leila Ahmed 1982), and some even reinterpret the Koran and the other Islamic sources and criticize those who have misinterpreted them (e.g., Fatima Mernissi 1993). This variety of perspectives sheds light on both the varied perceptions and the multifaceted character of the veil.

Nicole: Within Christianity, interpretations also vary drastically. Paul's argument is so tangled that one cannot even be sure that he concludes that women should cover their heads. The entire discussion, after all, concerns the dress of women when "pray[ing] or prophesy[ing]" (vv. 4-5), that is, while they lead communal worship. Paul also stresses the interdependence of the genders (v. 11) and points out a fact that patriarchy often seems built to erase—that man is born from woman (v. 12). His wording in the phrase "authority on her head" (v. 10) leaves open the possibility that he refers not to someone else's authority over her, but her own authority—so perhaps the authority is not synonymous with the veil at all.

Derya: Even though Paul's text is not completely clear, we can still extract some clear ideas from it. First, in 1 Corinthians 11:3, he implies that the woman's head belongs to the man in some way, and the headcovering symbolizes this belonging. I read verses 8-9 as statements of women's inferiority. Distinguishing a woman's social position from a man's in such a way clearly indicates that women are of lesser value. He concludes, "Judge for yourselves: is it proper for a woman to pray to God with her head unveiled?" (v. 13), implying that women should cover their heads.

First Corinthians 11:15 is puzzling: "but if a woman has long hair, it is her glory." First it seems to indicate that hair itself is the cover, in which case, women apparently do not need a headcovering. Here I find it helpful to compare the meanings of long and short hair in the Islamic cultural context. Whether it is part of Islam itself or of the surrounding culture, some religiously observant people in Turkey consider a woman's cutting her hair short to be a sin. Similarly, a woman with a shaved head would be considered more disgraceful than a woman with an uncovered head. At the same time, in another cultural context, the practice of wearing the headscarf itself can be more important than simply covering the hair, since some women leave their hair partly out, neither covering the whole head nor the hair. In other words, what the headscarf (culturally) symbolizes can be more important than its ostensible (religious) function.

Nicole: Mary Rose D'Angelo (1995, 134) has suggested that in this passage Paul conceives of woman's hair as analogous to pubic hair. That is, nature covers both the genitals and the woman's head with abundant hair as an indication of how much both need to be covered, how shameful the exposure of either one would be, so that the hair is not a sufficient social covering, but simply a sign from nature of what must be covered. In this case, as Derya implies, the woman's longer hair signifies nature's greater desire to cover the woman's head.

I agree that despite the few open spaces in the text, the overall logic drives toward the conclusion that women's heads must be covered because women are lower in the universal hierarchy than men. Paul states famously in Galatians 3:28 that there is in Christ "neither male nor female." In 1 Corinthians, however, this conviction seems to trouble him. My sense is that this tension between the conviction and the practice accounts for the twists and turns in Paul's argument. He believes that in Christ, distinctions, including gender, are defunct, and yet he seems to be urgently searching for a reason why women ought to cover their heads. Finally he reverts to the argument from nature, an argument that fails with contemporary readers for the good reason that he is discussing culture and not nature at all.

Unfortunately for later Christians, Paul's inability to follow through in practice on his egalitarian convictions has been understood as authorization for the systematic oppression of women within Christianity. This reading of Paul begins within the canon itself, in 1 Timothy and elsewhere. Paul's statements on why women must cover their heads came quickly to be read not just as dictating the attire of women leading worship, but as affirming and legitimating the subordinate place of all women in Christian culture.

Derya: Within contemporary Islam, the question of what the veil means about women's place in society, and whether or not it means subservience, is widely debated. As in the interpretation of the Koran and the hadith, there are varying perceptions of the veil throughout Middle Eastern societies. One can find contradic-tory perceptions and practices regarding the veil even within one society. Some women wear the veil simply because it is part of their traditional attire, not because they are particularly religious. Others wear it only for religious reasons. Still others wear it for both religious and political reasons, as the newly veiled women within the Islamic revivalist movements do. Not only the reasons but also the styles of the practice change from one place to another and from one woman to another within the same place, which makes generalizing impossible. In short, one has to pay attention to the different cultural and historical contextual meanings attributed to the practice of veiling.

As the practice and the meaning of the veil change from one place and one woman to another, the metaphorical empowerment or oppression of the veil also changes depending on the context in which it is viewed. Certainly, the veil would mean oppression for a woman who is forced to wear it, while it could mean modesty, privacy, or simply the fulfillment of a religious requirement for pious observant Muslim. On the other hand, it could be a powerful tool for a woman who is newly veiled for political reasons. In Iran, for example, previously unveiled women veiled and marched in the streets, in solidarity with women who refused to unveil when the Shah ordered them to do so. In this context, forcing a woman to unveil would be as oppressive as forcing her to veil. Thus, the agency behind the veil gains a great importance, and the understanding of the veil depends on that agency.

Nicole: One of the most troubling aspects of this passage in 1 Corinthians is exactly the issue of agency. Paul appears to be prescribing something for the women that the women themselves have not been doing—something they apparently have no wish to do. If the women cover their heads on account of Paul's letter, they do so less for the reasons Paul gives than simply because Paul—and "the churches of God" (v. 16)—say they must.

CONCLUSION

Lingering Questions of Text in Context

How can the Christian practice of head-covering be traced through the diverse Christian cultures from Paul's time to our own? When and how did some churches abandon the practice? When and how did other denominations cling to or reinvent it? What kinds of cultural forces and rationales are at work in this complex history?

We need to know more about Muslim women's self-understanding on the issue of headcovering. For example, do the women who normally are not veiled but cover their heads at a funeral see themselves as doing this for religious or cultural/traditional reasons—out of respect for God or for the community?

We need to explore further the issue of agency raised by headcovering in both Islam and Christianity. What we read as a silencing and subordinating of women can become in practice a celebration of gender, ethnicity, and membership in the religious community, as it has sometimes been for those African-American denominations wherein Corinthians 11:2-16 remains a key text. How does the painful logic of the text itself jibe with the occasional joy of the practice? At the same time, women in Muslim or Christian contexts who choose to cover their heads will surely by this use of their agency affect the agencies of other women. How does the practice alter the meaning of the text/traditions that recommend it—to what extent can the practice subvert and reconstitute the tradition?

BIBLIOGRAPHY

Ahmed, Leila. "Western Ethnocentrism and Perceptions of the Harem." *Feminist Studies* 8/3 (Fall 1982).

D'Angelo, Mary Rose. "Veils, Virgins, and the Tongues of Men: Women's Heads in Early Christianity." Pages 131–164 in *Off With Her Head: The Denial of Women's Identity in Myth, Religion, and Culture."* Edited by Howard Eilberg-Schwartz and Wendy Doniger. Berkeley: University of California Press, 1995.

Derrida, Jacques. "A Silkworm of One's Own." In *Acts of Religion.* Ed. Gil Anidjar. New York: Routledge, 2002.

El Guindi, Fadwa. *Veil: Modesty, Privacy and Resistance.* Dress, Body, Culture 1360-466. Oxford and New York: Berg, 1999.

El Saadawi, Nawal. *The Nawal El Saadawi Reader.* New York: Zed, 1997.

Mernissi, Fatima. *Women and Islam: An Historical and Theological Enquiry.* Trans. Mary Jo Lakeland. New Delhi: Kali for Women, 1993.

Moghissi, Haideh. *Feminism and Islamic Fundamentalism: The Limits of Postmodern Analysis.* New York: Zed, 1999.

2 CORINTHIANS

Ukachukwu Chris Manus

Obafemi Awolowo University, Ile-Ife, Nigeria

LIFE CONTEXT OF THE INTERPRETATION

Paul and Timothy, writing about 55-56 C.E., addressed 2 Corinthians to a church divided by internal squabbles and destabilized by the presence of competing Christian missionaries. Their letter seeks to address the resulting breakdown of discipline and disparagement of Paul's apostleship (2 Cor 1:15–3:3; 4:1–6:13; 7:2-16; 11:1-33).

I read 2 Corinthians in Nigeria, a nation marked by interdenominational rivalries and competition that first arose during nineteenth-century Christian missions, a situation resembling first-century Corinth. Christian evangelism and church planting in Nigeria dates back to 1841 and Sir Thomas Fowell Buxton's expedition up the River Niger sponsored by the Society for the Extinction of the Slave Trade and for Civilization of Africans. The expedition had an evangelistic slogan, *"Bible and Plough"* (Crowder 1966, 140–149). In the spirit of the partition of Africa in 1884–1885, this British society partitioned Nigeria into discrete mission fields among English Protestants: Calabar in today's south Nigeria was given to the Church of Scotland Mission; the Niger Delta and up the Niger river to the Anglican Church Missionary Society (CMS); different parts of Yorubaland to the Methodists, the CMS, and the Baptists. For thirty years, these unquestioned spheres of English Protestantism remained unchallenged. Not until 1885 did the French Roman Catholic Spiritan Missionaries arrive on the bank of the Niger from Gabon. The team led by Father Joseph Lutz was welcomed in Onitsha with the slogan: "Catholic Missionaries have come to plant the flag of truth" in Nigeria (Ekechi 1972,71–73). The conflict resulting from what the CMS saw as a Catholic "invasion" (Ekechi 71) was not only due to "traditional Protestant and Catholic antagonism," but also to the British and French political rivalry of the period.

In the present-day Nigerian socio-religious context, these rivalries take new forms. The churches boast of teeming numbers of ardent Bible-believers and committed churchgoers who see themselves as the addressees of Paul's Second Epistle to the Corinthians. Many Nigerian Christians are attracted by Paul's gospel of peace, reconciliation, and solidarity, themes that resonate with their own desires. They value the egalitarian principle that 2 Corinthians proclaims in a country where overt ethnic animosities are prevalent. Yet, Paul's teaching also makes apparent the rivalries that mark the many jam-packed crusade grounds, revival gatherings, and miracle and healing centers. Huge crowds attend the open-air rallies and Holy Ghost Fire Nights of the more ebullient and charismatic pastors and priest-healers. Evange-

Ukachukwu Chris Manus (PhD Leuven) is a professor of New Testament studies and African Christian theology. He is a member of the editorial board of *Bulletin of Ecumenical Theology,* Journal of the Ecumenical Association of Nigerian Theologians. His publications include *Christ, the African King: New Testament Christology* (1993); *Intercultural Hermeneutics in Africa: Methods and Approaches* (2003); and numerous articles, including "African Christologies: The Centrepiece of African Christian Theology" (*ZMR,* 1998); "Towards the Promotion of African Women's Rights: A Re-reading of the Priestly-Jahwist Creation Myths in Genesis," (*NZM,* 1999); "Methodological Approaches in Contemporary African Biblical Scholarship: The Case of West Africa," in *African Theology Today* (ed. E. Katongole, 2002); "Towards a Theology of Concerned Leadership in the African Churches: A Rereading of Matthew 18,12-14; Luke 15,1-7; Gospel of Thomas 107" (*AJBS,* 2002).

lists, including Nigerian women, preach the Bible and claim miraculous cures of incurable sicknesses and deliverance from demonic possession. They declare war against poverty, and found churches by promising eternal salvation (Shorter and Njiru 2001, 7-9).

The various Christian groups interpret the gospel along confessional lines. More often than not, they use the Bible to fan the embers of hatred and religious intolerance among Christian communities and to tear apart family and kinship relations. They pit white-controlled churches and African-led churches against each other (Kalu 1978),

causing division between those who accept Western culturally-derived dogmas and those nationalist and splinter groups that denounce these dogmas as forced upon Nigerian converts (Hackett 1987).

In this context, one readily recognizes in 2 Corinthians a sense of injury and division occasioned by mission rivalry. Soon other hermeneutical and theological issues are raised when the Nigerian situation and the tension under which Paul struggled are put in dialogue. Does not the final part of 2 Corinthians, where Paul brutally and sarcastically defends his ministry, directly challenge contemporary Nigerian church leaders?

CONTEXTUAL COMMENT

An Overview of 2 Corinthians

In 2 Corinthians 1:1-11, Paul opens with a greeting in which he identifies himself as an apostle of Jesus Christ called by God's will. Instead of his usual thanksgiving, he enumerates his hardships and closes with a benediction. In 1:12–2:13, he tries to mend fences with the Corinthians. He maintains that he is sincere and speaks the truth about the delay in his plans to revisit the community. He seeks reconciliation between himself and the community, which has punished the member who had insulted him and challenged his apostleship. Three major sections address this theme from three different standpoints, each with implications for the contemporary Nigerian situation:

2 Cor 2:14–7:4 Paul's apostleship as a ministry of the new covenant;

2 Cor 8–9 Paul's apostleship as symbolized in the collection, a *community self-help project, a harambee* that he launched for the distressed Jerusalem community;

2 Cor 10–12 Paul's apostleship negatively and graphically portrayed in his self-defense.

These three sections will be read in the context of Nigeria where mission rivalries and factions prevail among the Christian communities.

2 Corinthians 2:14–7:4

In this section, Paul forcefully defines the true apostolic ministry by contrasting it with incompetent missionary work. Apostolic ministry is a special vocation from God, which has a decisive effect on hearers. It is God in Christ who makes missionaries successful and crowns their ministry with manifestations of his glory and power. God commissions real apostles, and God's work in the heart of people is their letter of authorization. Their commission and letter of authorization *is not* from some human institution, whether it be the Jerusalem Church, the Church Missionary Society (1842) or the *Propaganda Fide* (1622). False missionaries boast of permits written on "tablets of stone," but genuine messengers of God have their identity cards embossed "with the spirit of the living God" which imprints itself indelibly on "tablets of human hearts" where the message effects change.

Paul contrasts the old and the new covenant. This midrash on Exodus 34:29-35 affirms that in the Lord Jesus the veil of ignorance is removed. The glory of God is made manifest in the gospel through the presence of God's power. The Spirit of God reveals the glory of Christ who is God's image. In sum, he cautions that the success of the gospel does not depend on the missionary's power or dignity. The success of a ministry does not depend on the missionary's human skill, but on God's work. Missionaries are merely torches through which divine light is shed on the converts, yet they are disposable, often rejected and afflicted. Often, death is their lot.

Apostles have hope for a future glory. They should hope with their converts for their share in Jesus' resurrection (4:14). Their suffering has an eschatological dimension. For the sake of their converts, they re-live Jesus' life and death, giving themselves for others as Christ did (5:14-15).

This is new life given by the Spirit. It is a new covenant, a new creation (5:17). It calls for a new lifestyle and new relationships with others. The Spirit shapes the life of believers in the likeness of Jesus. What counts in life is no longer individual happiness and self-fulfillment but service to fellow humans, no longer personal rights that lead to alienation but self-sacrifice that leads to reconciliation. For in Christ "God was reconciling the world to himself" despite human transgressions. He has chosen the apostles and indeed all believers to preach this message of reconciliation (5:19), and to become agents of God in the ministry of reconciliation (5:20). The crucifixion and the resurrection of Jesus remain the basis for this reconciling ministry. It is through the cross of Christ that God's power is recognized in the world.

The Contextual Lessons

The qualifications of the missionaries and the consequences of their preaching are most appropriate lessons for Nigeria. Against the missionary rivalries described above, Paul teaches that God is the author of any successful planting of the gospel. The competency of evangelists and pastors is measured not by overflowing numbers of devotees at crusade grounds and redemption camps but by whether the spirituality of these believers truly resonates with the manifestations of divine glory and with the power of Christ. The evangelists' and pastors' claim that this spiritual focus is the case can be verified by asking: Does the gospel they preach call their hearers to a decision to live for God and neighbor? How much of today's social evils do they confront?

Many contestants occupy the African mission field, all making different "holy" noises and claiming to have been sent by Christ. There are, no doubt, charlatans and crooks in mission and evangelization work in Nigeria and in all of Africa. How many of our contemporary preachers and pastors can show themselves to be genuine apostles who can boast that their identities are engraved in "tablets of human hearts" where real conversion is effected by the Spirit? Paul warns against excessive legalism. And for those who idealize the Spirit and claim its power at jam-packed Holy Ghost Fire Nights, Paul offers some alternative advice: the life-giving Spirit that raised Jesus must be fully proclaimed to counter the forces of evil and death that menace the people of God.

The Financial Collection: 2 Corinthians 8:1–9:15

The church in Jerusalem had a large number of indigent members "who lived a precarious existence on the level of bare subsistence" (Murphy-O'Connor 1991, 75). Many ordinary people in the city lived on rations and food aid, as is the case today in many war-torn African nations. In view of this situation, Paul launched a *harambee* (a Kiswahili word for a community self-help project) in the richer communities, those of the Gentile missions. He enjoined them to share with the less fortunate in Jerusalem, remembering the request of the authorities at the Jerusalem Council in 49 C.E.(Gal 2:10). This voluntary gift (2 Cor 8:12; 9:5) was a symbol that the Gentile churches acknowledged Jerusalem's status as the mother church.

Between the years 56–57, this "service to the saints" had preoccupied Paul's missionary work (Brown 1997, 553). Members of the Corinthian church had agreed to participate in the project. But the intrusion of the opponents put their commitment into question. In 2 Corinthians Paul once again seeks to motivate them to contribute generously as a sign of their concern for people in distress. He cites the example of Jesus' poverty (8:9) and entreats them to resume what they had started. He also cites as an example the Macedonians, who had contributed liberally in spite of their poverty. Their self-sacrificing love in imitation of Christ's love enabled them to give more than they had. He sends Titus and an unnamed brother "who is famous among all the churches for his proclaiming the good news" (8:18) to manage the collection among the Corinthians—rather than doing so himself—and also as delegate to bring the funds to Jerusalem (8:19), so as to avoid any doubt about his motives (8:20).

Paul underscores that the Corinthians' gift would not only reflect their appreciation and thanksgiving to God for all that they had received (9:12), but also show their obedience to the spirit of the gospel (9:13). When Christians give out of their poverty (8:2), they demonstrate their faith in life for others (7:2). Material blessings are neither for safekeeping nor for displays of pride. They are given to us to be freely shared in order to build up others in compliance with the mind of Christ (8:9). Paul seemed to have achieved a measure of reconciliation with the Corinthians and they apparently became involved in the collection.

Contextual Lessons

Paul's *harambee* has much to commend itself to the Nigerian context as well as elsewhere in Africa. Christianity is still young on the continent with some churches just celebrating their 150th. Human and financial resources are required to build up and consolidate the faith of God's people. New mission houses are to be opened; old churches need expansion and renovation. Church schools and hospitals need financial assistance in order to be able to provide traditional services to Christian families and health care for the sick. Some Nigerian congregations are unable to feed their pastors, pay their workers, or build a decent sanctuary. God's church in Africa is afflicted with the HIV/AIDS pandemic, which affects many of its members. Many youths are uneducated, jobless, famished, and poor. In these situations, the example of Paul's *harambee* from the more well-to-do Gentile churches to contribute to the needs of Jerusalem's distressed community is a worthy ecclesial practice that needs to be emulated in the African churches. Furthermore, Paul provides a good model for handling funds raised from the *harambee*. To avoid the difficulties associated with fund-raising and misappropriation that plague many contemporary Christian establishments, pastors should not hold church money by themselves. Let us learn from Paul, who took with him delegates to bring the collection to Jerusalem.

Today, many churches in Nigeria's urban areas are financially rich. Many pastors of big Pentecostal and charismatic churches live ostentatiously, owning several chauffeur driven cars and living in expensive mansions with many servants. Paul's example calls these people to discard the belief that their heaven is here on earth. He enjoins them to recognize that they need to redistribute church wealth by using their surplus to assist poor churches and members.

Paul's effort to unify Gentile communities with Jerusalem symbolizes the unity, cooperation, and solidarity that should mark intrachurch relations in Nigeria (Kalu 1978). Annual end-of-year harvests and collections at Thanksgiving services must be encouraged in modern dioceses and parishes as occasions for raising funds to alleviate the poverty of younger parishes and small outstations in rural areas. Paul's *harambee* makes clear that generosity toward sister churches is one of the obligations of Christian solidarity and love. The spirit of giving and sharing the little we have is the hallmark of Christian unity and community up-building. Beyond denominational loyalties, such donations should promote inter-church fellowship and reconciliation that can heal the wounds of discord inherited from the rivalries and divisions associated with the earliest missionaries.

2 Corinthians 10–12

The situation that Paul faces in Corinth necessitates his apology for his apostleship. He is confronting foreign missionaries who have gained influence in his mission field: "super-apostles" who in their boastful style have severely criticized his ministry (Manus 1981, 195).

10:12-18: The Futility of Self-Commendation: 2 Corinthians 10:12-18

Paul refutes the accusation of vain boasting leveled against him by his rivals, and taunts them for glorying in other people's work, and for their self-commendation (Manus 1981, 206-207). They misunderstand what apostleship and Christian life mean. He accuses them of being opportunistic apostles. By contrast, God conferred authority on Paul to serve a mission field; he conceives his mission in geographical terms (Barrett 1964, 292–293; Manus 1993, 266).

Paul's Foolish Speech: 2 Corinthians 11:1–23a

Paul opens this long discourse by asking the Corinthians to join him in the folly of boasting (Manus 1993, 377). Jealous of the success of his ministry, the rival missionaries have leveled accusations against him and his credibility, and have mocked his amateurish eloquence (Manus 335). They have asserted their legitimacy and superiority by their power of speech and knowledge (11:6) and boasted of their qualifications and origins (11:22-23). Further, they have pushed the community to despise Paul for rejecting material and financial support (11:7-9). Paul denies all the charges and emphasizes that, while not a trained rhetorician, he has knowledge to impart. These arguments constitute, for him, foolish boasting, made necessary by the Corinthians who love fools (11:6; 19) (Murphy-O'Connor 1991, 108), and who are easily led astray by a false gospel (Manus 328). In an outburst, Paul calls his rivals "false apostles," "deceitful workers" (11:13), and disguised agents of Satan (11:14-15). For Paul, missionary praxis must be Christ-like. A true apostle replicates the life of Jesus by continually risking health, personal security, and comfort in order to bring God's message to others.

Paul's Foolish Boasting: 2 Corinthians 11:23b–12:13

Paul further underscores the differences between his opponents' ministry and his own, which involved near-death experiences, imprisonments, Jewish floggings, Roman rod-beatings, and stonings. He has suffered for Jesus and undertaken very perilous journeys. Marauding gangsters have freely ransacked and pillaged his goods, as happens today in most African urban areas, rural regions, and on the highways. He had to bribe his way through and at the same time support himself, yet he was concerned for the churches he had founded. He even had to escape shamefully from Damascus (11:32-33).

In 12:1, Paul criticizes the value that his opponents place on visions and revelations. Visions and revelations neither authenticate an apostle's ministry nor promote the community's spirituality. He cites a revelatory experience he had had long ago that included an ascent to paradise (12:2–5), but that he had not talked about before. Such ecstatic mystical experiences do not deserve to be mentioned publicly. Rather Paul wishes to be judged by his personal conduct and preaching (12:6). The God-given signs, wonders, and mighty works in his ministry are for the strengthening of the community (12:12) and not for his own fame and prestige. Hence, miracles should not be given too much prominence in the apostolate. Indeed, God does not tolerate egotism in a minister. Paul recalls how God afflicted him with "a thorn given him in the flesh," a weapon readily used by Satan, his inveterate enemy. This problem, whatever it might be, was one of his major signs of weakness in the catalog of hardships he endured as a minister of Christ. But his crown is that churches had been founded, and converts had been won to Christ and had committed themselves to a new way of life. The power of Christ has brought about transformation.

Contextual Lessons

African churches need to make Paul's view of mission, focused on a cross-centered Christology, their own. This view is far from the prosperity gospel proclaimed by many African Christian preachers and pastors. The task of the true African apostles is to proclaim and represent Jesus Christ, emphasizing his death on the cross, so that the people of God might recognize the christological and soteriological significance of suffering in Africa. By the hostility and suffering they face daily, such African apostles would be representing the crucified Christ, as Paul did. While many emphasize a triumphalistic Christology and engage in an aggressive supposed "Spirit-led" evangelism, Paul-like preachers should de-emphasize such a theology by balancing it with a theology of the cross. Christ in his crucified "weakness" empowers missionaries to conform to the sufferer and to embody him. We see here the tension between two christologies and missiologies that must be kept in balance: one rooted in the power displayed in the risen and living Lord, and the other in the power hidden in the weakness of the crucified Lord. In contemporary African Christianity, most of the African Initiated Churches, the Pentecostals, and the charismatics promote a Christology of the glorified Jesus and boast of Spirit-filled ministers blessed with affluence, while the theology of the cross is gradually relegated to the background despite the teeming number of suffering Africans whom they shepherd. The two theologies and missiologies must be correlated so as to address together the situations of suffering among the people of God in Nigeria and Africa.

Paul promotes the interface between Jesus' crucifixion and resurrection in mission. In his missiology, suffering and weakness are juxtaposed to new life and glorifi-cation in order to teach the contradictions the missionary will always encounter. Modern missionaries must be prepared to undergo suffering and pain. They must take on the challenge to minister toward *change* in an African world marked by corruption, graft, selfishness, conflicts and wars, civil unrest and opposition, tribulation and persecution in spite of the abiding presence of the glorified Jesus. Our age still thrives on ungodliness. The murder of missionaries is still commonplace, political killings the order of the day.

Paul's central teaching on the suffering, cross, and death of Christ reminds us that God in Christ is living with all Nigerians and Africans who suffer and are afflicted by disease, hunger, poverty, and the consequences of bad government. In Christ, God dwells with the people. He is alert to their plight, pain, and cries. God in the crucified Christ encounters pain in their world. In Christ's glorification, he struggles with well-intentioned humanity to overcome human afflictions.

Second Corinthians reminds us Africans to take seriously the challenge to be missionaries to ourselves and to our continent. African missionaries must be willing to find themselves where the people of God are suffering from oppression; where children are abandoned on the streets; where a caste-system is used to depersonalize people, as in Igboland, Nigeria; and where under-aged children are forced to work for the wealthy and to carry arms for warlords. It is within these contexts that the love of Christ invites us as missionaries to come, share, and alleviate the agony and desperation of the people of God. Here, African apostles must replicate Christ, his resurrection empowering them to transform their communities. Paul calls for this healing and reconciling ministry as he puts before us Christ's ministry of reconciliation (5:18–21). In sum, the Nigerian church, and the church throughout Africa, must identify with the "divided people of God" to quickly bring about the healing and transformative power of the risen Lord.

CONCLUSION

Of course, modern ecumenical missiologists may want to set aside some views conveyed in this letter, such as Paul's intolerance toward the activities of other "servants of Christ" and his insistence on territorial integrity in mission. But local African church leaders have much to learn from this letter to help reorient their vision of mission and Christian ministry.

Suffering and Christian Life

Extensive suffering takes many forms in Nigeria and in Africa, giving the people of God the feeling that they are abandoned by God, the Father. It rouses the feeling that their suffering is a retribution for sin. Jesus' suffering, on which Paul has patterned his life, should transform the Nigerian believers' sense of suffering and their sense of the transition from powerlessness to eventual glorification. Second Corinthians shows that the transformative power of God's grace gives meaning to the lives of the suffering people of God.

The African Churches and the Alleviation of Poverty

Today, Nigeria, Kenya, South Africa, and other African states are instituting poverty alleviation, reduction, or elimination programs targeted at the grassroots (the *Ogbenye* or the *wananchi*). Paul's initiation of a *harambee* for poverty alleviation in one Christian community of his time makes clear that misery and wretchedness are not God-ordained. Poverty, whether systemic or localized, should be treated with relief. Fund-raising should be conducted for needy communities irrespective of denominational affiliations. We know these days that the Jerusalem and Gentile churches had their own disagreements (Gal 2:1-14)!

Teaching on Wealth

Together with many African pastors and evangelists who preach the "prosperity gospel," Paul insisted in chapters 8–9 that material prosperity is the fruit of divine grace. But he also insisted that what belongs to God belongs to all (as Cyprian, one of the illustrious African church fathers, phrased it) and that God's blessings are never given without a purpose. Wealth is given to expend in generosity (9:11), so that the poverty and suffering of less fortunate persons and churches should be relieved.

Generosity

Nigerian peoples and Africans in general are notoriously generous. A visitor to an African home or village walks away, in spite of pervasive poverty, with plenty of gifts. The tradition of sharing the little that one has with others is quite at home in all of Africa. Therefore, Paul's understanding of Christianity should be fully at home in Africa. Giving and receiving promote the emergence of new life; they have nothing to do with avoiding loss of face or impressing the public. Africans can therefore readily understand that the special grace to "exchange ourselves" in our acts of giving transforms Christians into the image of God. Jesus' giving of himself has set the benchmark for the virtue of generosity (8:9). As in the case of African peoples, the attitude of the givers, who might be in abject poverty, is more important than the actual value of what is given (8:12). True generosity is a gracious act (8:7). When a generous gift is made it is a self-giving act, which wins grace for the cheerful giver.

BIBLIOGRAPHY

Barret, Charles K. "Christianity at Corinth." *BJRL* 46 (1964): 269–297.

Brown, Raymond E. *An Introduction to the New Testament*. ABRL. New York: Doubleday, 1997.

Crowder, Michael. *A Short History of Nigeria*. Rev. ed. New York: Praeger, 1966.

Ekechi, Francis K. *Missionary Enterprise and Rivalry in Igboland 1857–1914*. London, Frank Cass: 1972.

Hackett, Rosalind I. J., ed. *New Religious Movements in Nigeria*. African Studies 5. Lewiston, N.Y.: E. Mellen Press, 1987.

Kalu, Ogbu U. *Divided People of God: Church Union Movement in Nigeria, 1875–1966*. Foreword by James I. McCord. New York: NOK, 1978.

Manus, Chris U. "The Opponents of Paul in 2 Corinthians 10–13: An Exegetical and Historical Study." Ph.D. diss., Katholieke Universiteit te Leuven, 1981.

———. *Christ, the African King: New Testament Christology*. Studien zur interkulturellen Geschichte des Christentums 82. Frankfurt/Main: Peter Lang, 1993.

Metuh, Emefie I., and Chris I. Ejizu. *Hundred Years of Catholicism in Eastern Nigeria 1885–1985. The Nnewi Story: A Historico-Missiological Analysis*. Nimo: Asele Institute, Nigeria, 1985.

Murphy-O'Connor, Jerome M. *The Theology of the Second Letter to the Corinthians*. New Testament Theology. Cambridge: Cambridge University Press, 1991.

Odozor, Paulinus I. "How Can the Gospel be Heard in the Secular Cultures of Africa's Cities." Pages 63–84 in *The Gospel as Good News for African Cultures: A Symposium on the Dialogue Between Faith and Culture*. Ed. G. M. Tonucci, et. al. Nairobi: Catholic University of Eastern Africa, 1999.

Shorter, Aylward Joseph N. Njiru. *New Religious Movements in Africa*. Nairobi: Paulines Publications Africa, 2001.

Ukpong, Justin S. "Rereading the Bible with African Eyes: Inculturation and Hermeneutics." *JTSA* 91 (1995): 3–14.

GALATIANS

Néstor Oscar Míguez

Instituto Superior Evangélico de Estudios Teológicos, Buenos Aires, Argentina

LIFE CONTEXT OF THE INTERPRETATION

Liberty and (Neo)liberalism

Latin America is experiencing the effects of the new economic globalization, advances in technology, new means of communication, and improved production and management, thanks to the impositions of the neo-liberal economy. After enduring years of military dictatorships in the 1970s, the weak recovering democracies were left at the mercy of the international economic powers. The consequences have been devastating. My country, Argentina, is experiencing the worst economic and political crisis in its history. Five consecutive years of recession have undermined the financial and economic reserves and have affected the social and moral condition of the population. The political leadership has shown itself to be corrupt and inefficient, and is now repudiated by the citizenry. The crisis has ended several governments, but even worse, it has eliminated small and medium-size industries (and some of the bigger ones too), millions of jobs, and the savings of the middle class. It has also imposed regulations on public programs of education, health, retirement, and any other social safety nets. This situation is threatening to become permanent.

In less than six months (December 2001 through June 2002), more than half of the population had fallen below the poverty line. Many workers who had steady jobs in factories and offices are now roaming the streets, rummaging through the garbage in search of recyclable materials or food. Individuals and families are experiencing psychological problems caused by displacement and insecurity. These problems lead to an increase in neglect, domestic violence, and street violence. Social and economic exclusion are played out in all their human drama. Some, out of desperation, return to their conservative views and rabid nationalisms, and establish new prejudices. The poor fight among themselves over the system's leftover morsels.

A new government, with a socio-economic program that differs from the previous neo-liberal trend, has come to power recently, and has partially reversed the situation. If new forms of solidarity are made possible, if there is a chance to resist the social, political, and economic dominance of the financial elite, and the search for viable alternatives is restored, there might be hope for the future. But the truth is that the human and social cost of this system is tremendous, and any way out will require a considerable amount of time and effort.

The temptation is to place the blame on the "outside," on globalization and imperialistic policies of the dominant powers. However, we have our own local share of blame: omnipresent corruption, preferential treatment, the insatiable ambition of the financial sector, the "immediacy" of the business sector, the superiority of the wealthy regions over the poorest sectors and regions of the country, among others. But an even more corrupt, ambitious, and domineering global financial system tolerates, and even stimulates these local problems.

Néstor Oscar Míguez was born in Rosario, Argentina. His recent publications include articles on Philippians, Paul, and Revelation from a socio-economic hermeneutic perspective. He is the author (with Pablo Andiñach) of *Manual de Introducción al Texto Biblico* (1998). A pastor of the Iglesia Evangélica Metodista Argentina, he lectures in universities, churches and ecumenical centers throughout the world.

The new rules of the game imposed by globalization are the laws of the market. They direct human life through the "deregulation" of the market as a whole. While capital circulates freely and goods are distributed at the convenience of the powerful, many people are confined to poor areas with tougher migration laws and virtual, as well as physical barriers, impeding their mobility. Capital moves freely, but human beings, especially the poor, are kept chained.

Galatians: Resonances with the Argentine Context

The ideology of a free market portrays itself as a "natural law," a normal way of behaving, although in reality it is a distinct cultural construction. Many people have naively accepted its claims, including many Christian groups and churches. Competition is thought to be the great panacea for all social ills. But this kind of competition is unfair, because it forces non-equals to compete, suppresses the weak, and enslaves the losers of that competition. It becomes a *law of death,* as we see its effects in the poorest communities.

The market is a mechanism created by human beings as a place where both material and nonmaterial goods are exchanged, and where products and work contracts circulate. As with every human activity, it has its own virtues and problems. The problem with the ideology of the *total* market is that it pretends to be the only viable economic mechanism, i.e., a "free" market, a market auto-nomous of the human condition, free of social consequences or ethical dimensions. And because it is *total,* it seeks to establish itself as the arbiter of all human activity, to occupy every space of creation and exclude anything or anyone who does not submit to its rules. The players in the global free market take hold of what has been created (privatization) and do not allow the participation of those who are not of any benefit to them, denying them access to the goods and relationships that are necessary for life. This market becomes a tyrannical and absolute *idol* that tries to impose its practices and cultural develop-

ments as the only valid ones. It does not know the realities of life beyond its game of power. The private ownership of every living thing is its law, as if it were possible to take private possession of all the resources created by God. Real human beings are kept hidden behind the fiction generated by the speculations of financial capital.

To study Galatians in the modern Argentine economic context is to be willing to recognize how cultural conflicts, the dynamics of power, and the tension between law and liberty affect the lives of believer and non-believer alike. In this particular situation we need to consider how reading the Bible can guide Christians to understand the tensions and consequences of giving in to "the *elements* of this world," of yielding to the dominant powers the prerogative to determine what is right and wrong, what is good and bad, and what is life and death. The imposition of a "standard universal culture" and the ideology of globalization should be seen in the true light of their destructive powers. This does not mean we ought to deny the achievements and efforts of people in their use of liberty and their advancements in science and communication. Nor does it mean we should undermine the value of cul-tural exchanges, but rather discover how these can be redeemed and become instruments of solidarity and expressions of creativity.

Pauline literature lends itself to an interpretation that allows us to draw parallels with present globalization. On the one hand, we have to recognize the drastic differences in time periods and social organization to keep from making naïve comparisons. But on the other hand, the Roman Empire was the greatest example of "globalization" in the ancient Mediterranean basin. Paul was a resident of that globalization. He traveled across a large part of the Empire and traversed the diverse cultures and subcultures that inhabited it; he suffered in jail at the hands of arbitrary authorities and was confronted by their ideology in several ways. However, he was also nourished by this world (Stegemann 1987, 200-229). Paul wrote his letters against the backdrop of the *Pax Romana* as an ideology, an enslaving economy, and imperialistic politics. It is with the backdrop of the *Pax Americana,* the neoliberal economy, and imperialistic power that we read Pauline literature today.

In Galatians, Paul shows the problems that arise when a group—the churches in Galatia—tries to preserve its identity through rigid legalism and crushes the life of a community, destroying its solidarity (Gal 2). Paul addresses the issue of law as a way to clarify the situation. He also addresses the absurdity of forgoing Christian liberty by favoring exclusionary laws that reduce real life to ideologies that subject us to the things of this world (Gal 3–4). Building loving relationships is the way of Christian liberty (Gal 2:10; 5–6).

It is important to clarify that Galatians—or any other biblical text, for that matter—does not directly refer to our present-day situation. Its language, questions, and metaphors occurred in a specific historical situation. The validity of the exegetical and hermeneutical task is in trying to find guiding principles from the text that, in light of faith, will allow us to analyze the new issues of our contemporary context and to assess how the text addresses these issues. This involves recasting the issues that Paul faced in new terms, those of the contextual reality in which we live. The question should not be, "What did Paul say?"; rather, we should explore how his ancient words point to answering the questions of our times, thus increasing our own faith.

CONTEXTUAL COMMENT

An Overview of Galatians: Pertinent Points for our Interpretation

F ew people today doubt that Paul wrote the Epistle to the Galatians. But scholars disagree about the identity of the original readers and the place and time of the writing. Some believe that the letter was addressed to the churches of the southern region of the province of Galatia, which were established during Paul's first missionary journey to Asia Minor (Acts 14). Others argue that it was addressed to the communities in the northern region called Galatia, which were likely established in the journeys mentioned in Acts 16:6 and 18:23. There are those who believe that the letter was written at an earlier date, circa 53 C.E.., and others who favor the view that it was written later, circa 57 C.E. These issues do not affect our interpretation. (Personally I tend to favor the theory that the letter was addressed to the communities of the northern region, and was written at a later date.)

There is another and more significant controversial point: Who are the "adversaries" that Paul confronts in his writing? Commentators have not agreed on the identity of these people whose teachings have to

be read in light of what Paul combats in them. The traditional view is that Paul confronts "Judaizers," or Jewish Christians who were followers of James, as illustrated in the discussion between Peter and Paul in Antioch (ch. 2). Others perceive an anti-Gnostic controversy. Some argue that the issue is not so much about whom Paul's opponents were, but rather about the conflicts within Christian communities. From this perspective, it is important to note that these conflicts between factions emerge from the doubts, questions, and issues that develop when people of different ethnic and religious origins coexist. These different groups have yet to resolve their differences, and they carry with them old habits and behaviors from their former socialization. For the purpose of our discussion, we will keep in mind the dominating ideology of the Roman Empire. Our interpretation will follow this line of thinking, while recognizing that other issues are present in the text.

Galatians raises a number of significant issues for our present reading context. Several cultures shared the region of Galatia: its original inhabitants, Celtic tribes that came into the region in the third century B.C.E., people associated with the Hellenization of the region and later with the Roman occupation, as well as certain groups of Jewish origin. It is most likely that this mixed religious backdrop confused the new Galatian believers and caused their indecision. Consequently, as long as scholars are primarily concerned with identifying a single source of opposition or conflict they cannot but vacillate. The Galatian communities were probably subjected to a wide variety of cultural and religious influences. Paul himself, because of his own tradition and cultural conditioning, perceives some influences and not others. Perhaps we find a conflicting experience among groups, each of which is trying to preserve its particular identity without recognizing the solidarity that unites them.

To preserve their cultural, religious, and ethnic identities, the Galatians needed to rely upon stable rituals, the security of religious laws or normative conventions, and material markers for their place in the world (food, days). We also see this in our reality, where anonymity and standardization produced by the "globalized culture" has often resulted in the exacerbation of ethnic conflicts and the search for an identity based on tradition or artificially reconstructed historical roots.

However, the Christian freedom of the Galatians and of the Argentineans is at stake in this attitude. Whichever of the above options they choose, they will carry its mark; a ritualistic or rigid letter-of-the-law attitude owns them; they end up in submission, a new slavery. This is how Paul understood the Galatians' situation, so he underscores the tension between being freed and submitting to slavery, a very apt metaphor in a slave-based Roman economy. There is always the temptation to adhere to new laws, to hang on to earthly and carnal rituals instead of being guided by the Spirit. Today, we call these laws and rituals dominant ideologies, which appear so natural and are so invisible that they completely control people. Through this ability to control, these ideologies engender habits and behaviors that destroy the bonds of community. The artificial identity they

establish for people denies the fairness and solidarity created by the new relationships "in Christ."

Paul introduces the concept of "grace," that which is freely given (which he develops more extensively in Romans). Life does not depend on security and laws, or on profit/loss statements and rituals, but on what is priceless, what God offers through Christ. The neo-liberal "free" market economy has no place for grace, for what *is* free. For market economy, it is inconceivable that life and justice have no price. In fact, the gospel defies the essential law of the market, the game of prices and competition. The "invisible hand of the market," as classic economists call it, becomes very visible in times of hunger, repression, and social exclusion.

Between Identity and Solidarity: Galatians 2:11-21

In this passage Paul talks about an apparent theological conflict, which is also a personality conflict (between Peter and Paul). Yet this conflict can be understood as fundamentally ethnic and cultural. The tension he alludes to in 2:15-21 probably originated in one or more Galatian communities and threatened to destroy the existing solidarity.

Paul indirectly refers to this conflict when he describes what happened in the Christian community of Antioch (2:11-14), where the first Gentile community originated (Acts 11:19-26). Here, apparently, we also see the first controversy regarding "ethnicity" (Acts 15:1-5). At first, the coexistence of Jewish and Gentile Christians was possible. But, as their community grew, the Jewish Christians—whom Luke identifies as "Pharisees" (Acts 15:5)—insisted that salvation was obtained by adhering strictly to the Mosaic Law, with special emphasis on circumcision, a sign of true Judaism. Paul, however, ascribes this disunity to followers of James from Jerusalem.

In some fashion, the identity of a (Jewish) subgroup was imposed on the whole group's identity, thus disrupting group unity. Identity is viewed as being separate, as being in a reserved space. This breach in community solidarity is symbolically expressed at the shared table (Gal 2:12) and leads to other kinds of segregation, such as distinctions in legal status (free or slave) or gender (Gal 3:28). If this ethnic division is permitted, then others can be allowed, and the entire community collapses.

Paul does not suggest that all former identities should dissolve into one new all-encompassing identity (for example, that everyone should be Jewish, or everyone should be Gentile). This is precisely what he fights against. He points out that group identity trumps subgroup, and that this relationship is expressed in community solidarity. The problem with Peter is not that he is Jewish; Paul is also legitimately Jewish (2:15). But this identity is not to be considered as exclusive or as a requirement; rather it is part of a tradition (1:14) that should be renewed. The problem arises when that identity turns into a law so narrow and restrictive that it hinders the creation of alternative identities and impedes freedom.

Appropriately, Paul states that "false believers . . . slipped in to spy on the freedom we have in Christ Jesus, so that they might enslave us" (2:4). To force someone to adopt certain practices or laws for the sake of identity reduces life to slavery. Paul himself uses Jewish tradition to refer to his calling and ministry, placing himself in the line of the prophets (1:15). However, he uses this tradition freely and creatively in order to affirm the new kinship with Gentiles. If identity turns into or depends on a law, it loses the possibility of becoming a source of justice, since this law and its commands cannot bring about justice (2:16). Justice requires that a person be acknowledged as kin, an acknowledgement truly possible only through faith in Christ.

The cross of Christ allows Paul to understand his culture, the law in which he was educated, anew (2:20). It is the determining factor that allows him to discover that a law without grace cannot bring about justice. Rituals and preoccupations with cost and price, profit and loss, shut out life. Christ dies because his mercy cannot be received within the framework of the law. But by the grace of God he lives, in his resurrection, in Paul, and in believers. Because of his experience in Christ, the one who persecuted others in the name of the law (1:23) now announces God's new justice, a justice based not on the law but on mercy. If there are elements of the Jewish identity that become barriers to a merciful life, these elements should be reconsidered. Partial identities need not be denied, provided they clearly contribute to a new identity that participates in constructing a community of solidarity now based on justice, on the fact that we are now made right with God through Christ. A person dies to the law in order to live in love.

Beyond the issues related to law and grace that have dominated scholarly discussion about this epistle and all of Pauline theology, this passage raises another issue. As Paul reexamines his own theology and culture, the cross becomes the basis by which he determines what he should uphold and what he should modify in his theology and culture. The temptation to uphold one's culture as a whole, for instance, to maintain a separate space in the face of globalization, is tremendous. We try to recreate our identity by asserting the past or a tradition. But because this asserted past is actually emblematic and intangible, its reconstruction is too often artificial. Instead one must recreate an identity and uphold it solely for the sake of community with others who have different identities. The goal should be to be Jewish, or Gentile, *at the shared table*. An identity that promotes liberty and rests on our merciful God's justice is an identity with purpose and one that promotes neither fragmentation nor isolation, but mutual recognition.

The cross of Christ shows us the new face of God's justice, and on this basis all traditions and cultures can be renovated. Every tradition and culture bears ambiguities and internal oppressions. (Paul makes this point at length in the first chapters in his letter to the Romans, where he explains the tensions between the Gentile and Jewish cultures.) Yet, every tradition and culture can be renewed thanks to God's liberating grace. This differs from Christian imperialism, which imposes the cross and becomes oppressive—or from a globalization that erases and overshadows rich and diverse traditions and histories. Oppression that was once destroyed by God's liberating grace is rebuilt, as the history of Christianity has so often, and unfortunately, demonstrated: "But if I build up again the very things that I once tore down, then I demonstrate that I am a transgressor" (2:18). If justice is achieved solely by imposing a universal identity—or contrarily, by building walls of separation, division, or isolation—then the grace of God is nullified and Christ died needlessly (see 2:21).

Ideologies and Real Life, Slavery or Freedom: Galatians 3:23–4:16

These verses are so important that many consider them to be the letter's focal point. In fact, several authors consider 4:1-10 to be the center of a concentric structure that encompasses the entire text (Bligh 1969, 39; Michelin-Salomon 1997). The surrounding passages help give the center meaning and significance. For this reason I have included the preceding verses, which clearly refer to slavery and freedom, one of the main themes of this passage; I also refer to the first verses in the succeeding passage, because Paul there again becomes autobiographical, giving us a key to personalizing this teaching.

This section's theme centers on the slave/free distinctions, as is the case in 3:28: "There is no longer Jew or Greek, there is no longer slave or free, there is no longer male and female; for all of you are one in Christ Jesus." Here, the privileged status (Jewish, male) appears first, and the underprivileged, second (Gentile, female). This order is not unintentional, as becomes clear with "slave/free" where this order is reversed. Actually, Paul's entire argument is based on the possibility of moving from a state of slavery to freedom; those who were once slaves can be set free: "For freedom Christ has set us free" (Gal 5:1). Each of the three distinctions is addressed differently in the

letter (Bligh 1969, 320-329; Betz 1979, 181-201). While we can draw parallels between these distinctions, careful study shows that these similarities also point to important differences. Paul has discussed Jews and Gentiles; it is not necessary for a Jewish person to become a Gentile, or for a Gentile to adopt Jewish rituals in order to overcome their differences in Christ, or participate in one baptism to encourage solidarity around the shared table. Despite its mention, the male/female distinction (curiously, Paul carefully avoids using the word *woman* here), does not receive special attention in this letter. One might think that Paul does not dare delve into the consequences of his own statement. By contrast, in the case of the slave/free distinction, "in Christ" the difference is abolished, because the slave knows freedom in Christ. The difference between slave and free is cancelled out, at least ideally, since in Christ we are all free. Slavery imposed by the law is surmounted by a new form of relationship. While it is true that Paul emphasizes his metaphorical usage here, one cannot ignore that, against the backdrop of a Roman society and economy based on slavery, the social and legal implications of this language would resonate loudly (Betz 1979, 181-201).

Significantly, Paul's distinction is not "slave/master," but "slave/free." Paul does not ignore the social and economic conditions of exploitation (Míguez 2000, 413-437), but rather refers to the legal issue. From Paul's perspective there is a law that enslaves, and this is the law from which Christ frees us. Christ's action transforms us, so that instead of being slaves we are now heirs. Ancient inheritance laws restricted inheritances to those who had the appropriate status (a) by belonging to the lineage (only Jewish people were heirs to the promise); (b) by being free (slaves could not receive an inheritance, although in some cases they were granted freedom by way of their masters' will and testament); and (c) by being males (women did not receive an inheritance). All of these restrictions regarding inheritance are surmounted in Christ; the inheritance established by Christ is for everyone, thus all distinctions among those who receive the Promise (3:29) are erased. Therefore, in Christ, all hierarchical distinctions are eliminated, and complete human equality is achieved—a basic condition of freedom.

Human maturity is reached when there is no longer a need for a guardian who limits our actions, such as the law, a tutor or teacher (3:24), or a trustee (4:2). In this case, Paul totally favors freedom. He knows, by experience, that freedom is restricted by worldly powers that do not understand it and look to overpower it, and that unjust people set themselves up as judges of the saints (see, for example, 1 Cor 6:1-11). However, Christians can and should look for ways to avoid these oppressive forces that drown out Christ's call to freedom.

The status of slave is changed to that of heir. An inheritance is a gift that is received from the Father. An inheritance cannot be bought; it does not belong to business people, but to sons and daughters. It is not an object in a transaction; it is a free gift. Inheritance is not the individual experience of sons and daughters; rather it is a community-building experience. By being made sons and daughters we become brothers and sisters. In 4:7 Paul states the personal dimension of this experience, but in 4:8 he reverts to the plural form. It is the person in the community—and the good of the individual as well as the community—that constitutes the center of this inheritance created by Christ's action.

Since the Creator is the one who gives this inheritance, the whole world is part of this gift. Therefore, the world cannot have private owners who expropriate the inheritance of other brothers and sisters: "You are all children of God" (3:26; see 4:7). After receiving this divine inheritance it is foolish to submit oneself once again to the "powers of this world" in a new slavery (4:8-9).

These verses show that Paul confronts certain religious and ideological notions that need to be modified. Human immaturity has subjected human beings to what Paul calls "the powers [Gr. stocheia] of this world."

Stocheia has several meanings; Paul's usage in this text (4:3, 9) is much debated. In Greek philosophy and later in Hellenism, it could refer to the basic elements that make up the world (fire, air, water, and earth), as well as to plants and other components of the physical world. It could also refer to the natural and supernatural forces that have power upon humans—such as astrological powers and other kinds of supernatural powers associated with mystery religions and beliefs. Paul states that the Galatians have been set free from these powers and elemental spirits through Christ, but they soon yield again to them, not knowing how they can be rescued from these powers and not understanding how they can remain free from them.

Jesus, a man born of a woman, born under the law, is the one who *takes off* the yoke and gives his life in order to be set free and to set free those who are slave to the law. He is the slave who *takes on* humanity in obedience to God. Our faith experience is what allows us to acknowledge the story that changes our story. Nevertheless, Paul points out how, even after acknowledging that story (3:1), people go back to being enslaved by the "weak and beggarly elemental spirits" of the world, which Paul calls "the present evil age" (1:4). He points out how, as result of serving those who "by nature are not gods" (pagan gods, and perhaps even the Emperor), believers who have been set free from this dictatorial domination, now give up their freedom to place themselves under a new dictatorship, that of the powers of this world (4:8-9). Knowing the only God of truth, or better yet, says Paul, being known by God as a son or daughter is what sets us free. Why, then, should we return to "the weak and beggarly elemental spirits" of this world? Why, in our search for false securities, do we give up our freedom?

Although the Galatians could not know this yet, it is the principle of every empire, of all policies fashioned according to the Nazi, or any tyrannical, plan: people relinquish freedom out of fear and seek security-giving rituals and enslaving mystical identities and images of power (Fromm 1960). Because of their fear of freedom, people exchange their freedom for submission to created things (days and months, times and rituals). In so doing, their experience of freedom becomes a dead-end street.

It is in real, concrete life that Paul finds a counter-example to such behaviors: the experience of liberating love. Thus, he refers to his own experience of illness and weakness when he proclaimed the gospel in Galatia (4:13). The Galatians' faith was built up when they accepted a person who seemed despicable. It was their willingness to "pluck out [their] eyes" that demonstrates how the gospel works in us (4:15). It is from this attitude—which has nothing to do with laws, profit, or competition—that this gift is reinstated as a gift. The spirit of the market is not the Spirit of love that enables us to say "Abba! Father" (4:6), but rather the spirit of competition and profit. Christ's freedom is something else; it points directly to humanity, to our neighbor, and it invites us to a common faith. God's gift is demonstrated in such human interaction.

Freedom that Triumphs over All Oppression: Galatians 5:13-26

In order to verify that our interpretation properly accounts for Paul's argument, we will delve into the letter's exhortations, the place where Paul applies his teachings to the believers' conduct. This section, 5:13-26, is a counterpart to the first section we have already analyzed (2:11-21; Michelin-Salomon, 1997; cf. Bligh 1969, 39, who has a different analysis).

Galatians 5:13-15 begins a new section, which complements what has been previously discussed (with Betz 272; against Bligh 39). Verse 13 could not be any clearer. Human freedom is not acquired by returning to old, destructive patterns and regulations, but rather by refocusing on the communitarian meaning of freedom, the sense of mutual belonging. The expression "one another" (Gr. *allēlōn*) appears three times in these verses. We can either build one another up or destroy one another. The command to love your neighbor as yourself also appears here. It is precisely this sense of mutuality that leads us to the freedom to which Christ calls us. Paradoxically, after advocating freedom from slavery (*douleia*), we now read about a freedom that is obtained "through a slavery of mutual love" (*douleuete allēlois*). Conduct "in the flesh" denies our neighbor or sees the neighbor as a boundary, as a rival or competitor, or a means for our own pleasure. The behaviors classified as being "of the flesh" in 5:19-21 are behaviors that disregard God or dishonor our neighbor, break down community relationships, and destroy our lives and the lives of others. Paul does not list these as prohibitions, but as the consequences of living a life without the Spirit.

On the other hand, the behaviors that are "of the Spirit" are those that build community and affirm our relationships with our neighbor. This list does not include ritualistic conduct, the essence of religiosity in the ancient world. Rather these behaviors are, in a sense, earthly virtues that can be lived out in the real world as alternatives to all forms of domination, be they those of the Roman Empire's hierarchical and enslaving system or those of ritualism and legalism, such as those of the Essenes of Qumran.

The law of loving your neighbor is the only law that endures because it builds relationships. It places others in the middle of our lives; it forces us to build a community. Our neighbor is neither a competitor nor a threat, but an occasion to define freedom as service. Centuries ago, Paul criticized the laws of the market and the idea that competition is the only regulator of human activity, and warned: "If . . . you bite and devour one another, take care that you are not consumed by one another" (5:15). Similarly, freedom is not a license to "do what you want" (5:17c); it is, however, an opportunity to discover the presence of the Spirit that sets us free. The Spirit is not a new form of evasion, but rather a new means of living one's life in relation to neighbors who by their presence unmask whenever freedom is threatened or denied.

CONCLUSION

When Liberty Is Not (Neo)liberalism

We have all memorized this liberal slogan back in our school days: "My freedom ends where the freedom of others begins." One possible outcome of this understanding is that my neighbor becomes a boundary, an obstacle to my freedom, and consequently, if I want to increase my freedom, I should limit the freedom of others. So, for some, market deregulation results in the exclusion of others. For the market, neighbors in need no longer exist. And since the market encompasses the whole of our lives, if these neighbors do not exist for the market, they do not exist at all. The liberal logic has been taken to the extremes of the neo-liberal logic. In the name of freedom (capital freedom, freedom of the market, freedom of deregulated labor contracts) all others are being excluded. Freedom granted to corporations actually results in the oppression of real people. Our neighbors, hidden behind these legal fictions, end up being excluded.

After suffering at the hands of dictators, we Argentineans are now subjected to a new kind of slavery by the false proclamation of neo-liberal freedom. We are in subjection to the dictatorship of the market whose "deregulated" laws make its oppressive power even more anonymous. Once we could name the dictators, but now they hide behind the impersonal empire of the market. The market is a structure without spirit. The market has laws, but has no spirit and no life. The hopes and even the rights of real human beings are subject to the norms and power of fictitious beings (corporations, public limited companies, virtual currency, and artificial legal entities) created by the market. We are dominated by those who "by nature are not gods"; indeed, they are not even human. They are fictitious entities, beggarly elemental spirits of this world, and they wield the power of death. These new hidden powers present themselves as an expression of the divine will, but are merely human creations that enslave us. The market economy and its powers offer themselves as "free," but they demand from people total surrender to the injustices of unlimited accumulation. Freedom for the market results in the exclusion of the majority, a natural world violated by the appetites of unlimited consumption, and enslaved real human beings.

When faced with this reality, some look for a way to bring back the past. They enforce laws that will, they hope, reestablish the role of the nation-state as a self-sufficient authoritative framework. They return to nationalistic essentialisms in religious or patriotic rituals, which only increase the number of enslaving masters. But, as Paul shows, the solution to facing oppression and slavery is not relinquishing freedom to yet another enslaving master. We in Argentina have already experienced what happens when authoritarianism and nationalism increase. Following Paul's thought in Galatians, we should confront the logic of profit with the logic of freedom, with the grace that liberates. We are invited to replace the "naturalized" logic of slavery with the logic of community affiliation, and with the Spirit of mutual recognition through which we acknowledge each other as sons and daughters of God. It is also a matter of discovering freedom as an opportunity to serve. Our neighbor, according to Paul's logic, is not the boundary of my freedom, but rather the opportunity of my freedom. My freedom begins when my real neighbor—especially the poor, the weak, the needy—becomes the motive of my actions, when individualism is overcome by community. The cross of Christ places our neighbor—especially our afflicted neighbor—in the center of all moral actions. "So then, whenever we have an opportunity, let us work for the good of all . . ." (6:10).

We should not expect the world to function in this way, for it does not know or recognize the full humanity of all of God's children. The world continues in the ways of sin. Empires behaved like empires then, and they still do now. But those who have learned to live by the Spirit that cries "Abba" know that an alternative path lies ahead of them. They must proclaim that human rights belong to human beings—not corporations. They must assert that creation cannot be expropriated from everyone and appropriated for some; rather its fruits should be cared for and distributed, because the truth is that "the earth is the LORD's, and all that is in it" (Ps 24:1). When we build up unified communities and remember the poor, we will gain victory over the mechanisms of exclusion.

Galatians does not invite us to deny the achievements and advances in science in the area of communications or to preserve cultures intact like museum objects; it does not require us to return to a simplistic natural-ism. This would be impossible. Rather this teaching asks us to continue searching for the human maturity to which Christ calls us, by offering our human achievements (including the market as an economic mechanism), but without declaring any of these as absolute or as the only possible ones. This road to human maturity involves acknowledging that we are called to freedom by placing our neighbor, as Paul suggested, in the center of that freedom. Then, as mature humans we can recognize that our ethnic, cultural, or social identity has no value in and of itself, unless it becomes a new creation in Christ: "For neither circumcision nor uncircumcision is anything; but a new creation is everything!" (6:15).

BIBLIOGRAPHY

Betz, Hans Dieter. *Galatians: A Commentary on Paul's Letter to the Churches in Galatia.* Hermeneia. Philadelphia: Fortress, 1979.

Bligh, John. *Galatians: A Discussion of St. Paul's Epistle.* Householder Commentaries 1. London: St. Paul, 1969.

Borón, Atilia. *Imperio & Imperialismo: Una lectura crítica de Michael Hardt y Antonio Negri.* Colleción de ciencias de la Secretaría Ejecutiva de CLASCO. Buenos Aires: CLACSO, 2002.

Chomsky, N. *Latin America: From Colonization to Globalization.* Melbourne; New York: Ocean Press, 1999.

Fromm, Erich. *The Fear of Freedom.* London: Routledge & Kegan Paul, 1960.

Garcia Canclini, Néstor. *Culturas Híbridas: estrategias para entrar y salir de la modernidad.* Los Noventa 50. Grijalbo, México: Consejo Nacional para la Cultura y las Artes, 1990.

———. *Consumidores y Ciudadanos: conflictos multiculturales de la globalización.* México: Grijalbo, 1995.

———. *La globalización imaginada.* Paidós estado y sociedad 76. Buenos Aires: Paidós, 1999.

———. *Latinoamericanos buscando lugar en este siglo.* Paidós estado y sociedad 105. Buenos Aires: Paidós, 2002.

Gray, John. *False Dawn: The Delusions of Global Capitalism.* New York: New Press, 1998.

Hardt, Michael, and Antonio Negri. *Imperio.* Buenos Aires: Paidós, 2002.

Potter, Philip, and Bärbel Wartenberg. *Libertad para liberar: estudio de la Epístola a los Gálatas.* New York: Board of Global Ministries, United Methodist Church, Oficina de Recursos en Español, Editora de Recursos en Español, 1990.

Míguez, Néstor Oscar. "La libertad de ser humano: Lectura de Filipenses 2:6-11 como canto libertador." Pages 413-437 in *A Los caminos inexhauribles de la Palabra: Homenaje a J. S. Croatto en su 70 aniversario.* Buenos Aires: Lumen-ISEDET, 2000.

Michelin-Salomon, Alvaro. *Estructura literaria y hermenéutica de la Epístola a los Gálatas.* PhD diss., ISEDET, Buenos Aires, 1997.

Ramos, Federico. *La libertad en la carta a los Gálatas: estudio exegético-teológico.* Teología I, 6. Madrid: Eapsa, 1977.

Stegemann, Wolfgang. "War der Apostel Paulus ien römischer Burger?" *ZNW* 78 (1987): 200-229.

Tamez, Elsa. *Contra toda condena.* San José, Costa Rica: DEI, 1991.

EPHESIANS

John Riches

Department of Theology and Religious Studies, University of Glasgow, Scotland, U.K.

LIFE CONTEXT OF THE INTERPRETATION

Scotland

The two kingdoms of Scotland and England were joined by personal union as a result of James VI's accession to the English throne in 1603 and then formally by Act of Union in 1707. Throughout its history, Scotland has developed a strong sense of national pride and strong national institutions: churches, universities, schools, and its own legal system. In 1999, a Scottish Parliament was reestablished after nearly three hundred years. It is seeking to develop new forms of participatory democracy and to develop an appropriate sense of Scottish identity.

Post-Colonial Scotland

Many Scots emigrated in the eighteenth and nineteenth centuries, not least as a result of political oppression and economic hardship at home. Many contributed to the development of North American forms of democracy and enterprise. Others were active as soldiers, engineers, entrepreneurs, or civil servants in the spread of the British Empire. Scotland was also deeply involved in the missionary movement; it retains strong links with countries overseas. It was one of the centers for the Anti-Apartheid movement and for the campaign on international debt. But some Scots have strong financial and personal interest in forms of neo-colonialism. In the recent war against Iraq, the churches and many of their leaders were actively involved in opposition to the war; at the same time, Scottish troops were prominently involved in the fighting and enjoyed considerable support.

Post-Industrial Scotland

Scotland contributed greatly to and benefited hugely from the industrial revolution. However, the resultant wealth was by no means equally shared. Glasgow was also home to "Red Clydeside," so-called after the strong communist presence in the shipyards around Glasgow. Over the last fifty years Scotland has transitioned from an economy based on heavy industry to one based partly on oil, partly on service industries, culture, tourism, and education. This transition has left areas of urban deprivation that prove difficult to revive. There has been large-scale migration from the rural areas to the cities, though recent years have seen some renewal of the rural economy. The gap between rich and poor, unemployed and employed has grown over the last twenty years.

Ethnic and Gender Issues

The industrial revolution created a demand for labor, which was met by large-scale immigration from Ireland, both Protestant and Catholic. The last hundred years have seen many new immigrants: Jews, Italians, Poles, Indians, Pakistanis, and Chinese, most recently asylum seekers from a wide range of countries. Scotland is reasonably comfortable with its multicultural character,

John Riches, Professor Emeritus of Divinity and Biblical Criticism, is the author of numerous articles and books including, *Jesus and the Transformation of Judaism* (1982); *The World of Jesus* (1991); *A Century of New Testament Study* (1993); *Matthew* (NT Study Guide, 1996); *The Bible: A Very Short Introduction* (2000); and *Conflicting Mythologies: Identity Formation in the Gospels of Mark and Matthew* (2000). *Galatians,* a reception historical commentary in Blackwells Biblical Commentary, is forthcoming. With David C. Sim, he edited, *Matthew* in *Colonial Perspective*. He is co-founder of the Scottish Contextual Bible Study Group and convener of the Mission Board, Scottish Episcopal Church.

though there are still concerns about sectarianism (Catholic/rotestant antipathies) and there have been some disturbing attacks on asylum seekers. There is a small but creative interfaith council. Traditionally, women were effectively debarred from many positions within society and were discriminated against in marriage legislation. There has been significant improvement in many areas but there is still a disturbing level of violence against women; the women's shelters are very busy.

The Churches in a Post-Christian Age

The churches have played a complex role in Scottish society. The Reformation saw a prolonged struggle between Presbyterians and Episcopalians. From that struggle the Presbyterian Church emerged as the national church; for nearly three hundred years its General Assembly was in many ways the voice of the nation before the Scottish Parliament was reestablished. Its voice has often been prophetic, particularly on issues of peace and disarmament, world poverty, and women's rights. Yet it has also represented the Lowlands rather than the Highlands (which have their own, Sabbatarian, form of Presbyterianism) and among the working classes has often been confronted with strongly Catholic communities. The Episcopal Church is often identified popularly with the wealthier classes and with English immigrants. However, it also has deep roots in Scottish history; recently it has been more willing than most churches to be identified with an open, liberal agenda. The Catholic Church too has deep roots in Scottish history and also has strong links with the Irish immigrants of the nineteenth century. It has suffered much discrimination. Sectarianism has dogged the peripheral housing estates of Glasgow and the mining villages of Lanarkshire. Ecumenism has overcome a good deal of this, but a strong legacy of bigotry remains in the unchurched population.

Culturally the churches have contributed a great deal to education; until recently, there was a great tradition of Bible reading and theological debate. However, the legacy of Calvinism in all churches has engendered a deep sense of human weakness and a deep mistrust of attempts at political liberation: one professor described the church's task as "washing the faces of the faithful for judgment day." Recently there has been a dramatic loss of Christian influence in society at large, and all churches find themselves culturally marginalized, even though they continue to exercise considerable influence on political life. (Church members were very active in a campaign against the repeal of a law that forbade the "promotion" of homosexuality in schools.)

Scottish culture has become both more diverse, which allows for members of small churches to live reasonably comfortably, and also much more influenced by popular mass culture, which has little or no place for traditional forms of institutional religion and which leaves Christians feeling marginalized and subject to ridicule. The churches urgently need to find a new role for themselves in relation to society, but this role may now be exercised more from the margins (as with Jubilee 2000, the campaign on international debt) than from positions in the center that make confusing claims about their authority.

Ephesians and the Relationship of God's People to the World in Scotland

Read in this context, Ephesians raises a number of crucial issues, which can conveniently be linked to certain passages.

a) **1:15-23.** This passage raises issues relating to the churches' sense of diminished power and position within society, and also about the possibilities of recovering a new sense of their place within society. What can be learnt from this letter to a marginalized community, which proclaims such a high view of the church's place in God's world? Is its vision encouraging or daunting?

b) **2:1-10; 3:14-21.** As noted above, many people suffer from a deep lack of confidence, which is probably related to certain theological traditions, both Catholic and Protestant, with deep roots in various forms of Puritanism, Calvinism, and Jansenism. To what extent do readers in Scotland evince such attitudes? How far are they able to share Ephesians' view of the Christian life and to overcome their low self-esteem?

c) **2:11-22.** This passage will be used to raise questions about identity in a multicultural society. How far can the vision of the unity of Jews and Gentiles in the church provide encouragement for Christians to engage in open encounter and dialogue with people from other countries and faiths?

d) **4:1-16.** The potential for division among the churches is great. There are deep-seated historical divisions over episcopacy and considerable suspicion of newer movements within the church: evangelicalism, pentecostalism, and postmodern forms of Christianity. What forms of unity are suggested by this text?

e) **5:21-33.** Domestic violence is widespread in Scotland. Patterns of marital relationships are changing rapidly, though patriarchal traditions die hard. How is this text, with its requirement of wifely submission, seen in the light of a very different text like Gal 3:28?

CONTEXTUAL COMMENT

An Overview of Ephesians

The letter divides neatly into two halves, chapters 1–3 and 4–6. The first section, lyrical in style and taking the form of blessings and prayers, sets out certain truths about God, Christ and salvation, the church, and Christians, the latter especially in regard to the Gentiles. The second section is ethical, containing some fairly general instruction: to preserve unity, to put on Christ and keep separate from darkness, and to avoid obvious sins. It continues with some specific instructions, sometimes known as household codes, addressed specifically to husbands and wives, children and their parents, to slaves and their masters. It finishes with general instruction, comparing Christian virtues to a soldier's armor.

Ephesians 1:15-23 immediately follows the blessing with which the letter, rather unusually within the Pauline corpus, opens. It takes the form of a thanksgiving for the faith of the Ephesians and a prayer for their understanding of the mystery of God's work in Christ. This is actually more than one would expect at the start of a letter from Paul.

Ephesians 2:1-10 and 3:14-19 continue this theme by giving instruction about the Ephesians' salvation from their old way of life, followed by a prayer for the Father's continuing power in the Ephesians' lives.

Ephesians 2:11-22 continues the exposition of God's work of salvation by discussing the incorporation of the Gentile believers into God's people, as the barrier between Jews and Gentiles is broken down and a new people is created.

The remaining two passages are selected from the ethical material in the second half: the first dealing with unity among Christians, the second with the relations between Christian husbands and wives. The latter injunctions compare the relation between husband and wife with the relation between Christ and the church.

How This Contextual Commentary Was Developed

A key role in the development of this commentary was played by the contextual Bible study group in Scotland. This body encourages Christians across Scotland to read the Bible closely in communal, critical, and contextual ways. Groups work through a series of questions that help them first to read the text closely and then to make links between it and their own experience. This commentary is based on reports from five groups who read the passages described above. The groups represented different denominations: Catholic, Church of Scotland (Reformed), and Episcopalian (Anglican). One group was composed of women only. The groups came from different geographical and social locations.

Ephesians 1:15-23

This intimate prayer of thanksgiving for the faith and mutual love of the Ephesians, with its request that they should grow in understanding of the mystery revealed to them, clearly arouses mixed feelings in many readers in Scotland today. On the one hand the language is too exalted, the vision of God's power poured out in the church too incompatible with the experience of the church as a marginalized community, largely deserted by the young and seen as irrelevant by many of all ages. For some, indeed, talk of the church as "the fullness of him who fills all in all" (1:23) seemed like a "foreign language." On the other hand, people in the study group recognized points of considerable similarity between their situation and that of the Ephesians. While it is difficult to be precise about its social standing, the Ephesian church was likely a small and marginal community within the flourishing commercial city of Ephesus.

The exultant language of power in expressions like "the immeasurable greatness of his power" (v. 19) was felt to be ambiguous: did it echo the pretensions to secular power of some richer members of the Ephesian community (the educated ones who could read) or did it express a subversive, almost revolutionary vision of the church's place in society? Similar tensions exist today. Some still see the church as part of the Scottish establishment. Others take a more critical, subversive stance and respect the churches for their protest against nuclear weapons bases and their role in the campaign against international debt.

Some people in the group took encouragement from this passage, while realizing that significant change would be necessary for its more radical reading to take root in the present church. But that too was the case with the Ephesians. They, too, needed "the eyes of [their] heart" to be enlightened (v. 18, not just an intellectual understanding but a transformation of the whole person). Everyone was promised that they could participate in the "spirit of wisdom and revelation" (v. 17), but this promise required an active response. For women who feel excluded from the church's ministry in Scotland, this is an inclusive promise that encourages them to continue working for greater recognition. Others saw here a call for the church to face up to its failings, to allow the "bad things" to come out (e.g., cases of sexual abuse in church-run institutions), so that the church can go forward. The church is deeply needed in today's materialistic society, but it will only be heard when it has itself been filled with the spirit of enlightenment. Others felt that the force of the writer's convictions drew them into the text in such a way that they heard it as a personal message of what the Spirit would do for them. For some the passage was inspiring but they recognized that it would make costly demands on those who were drawn into its vision. It would require discipline in prayer to discern what to do and to do it without worry, trusting in the Spirit. It would lead to a communal sense of empowerment, a "living out of a relation to something much bigger than we are ourselves, giving confidence in the midst of the cost, bringing difficulty but also joy." They spoke of a Gethsemane experience—"of fear, but a fear that is cast out by love." This vision was felt to be "both enticing and at the same time too good to be true." The church was too complacent and needed to be challenged, to become less comfortable, to be disturbed by the Holy Spirit.

Ephesians 2:1-10; 3:14-19

These passages describe in sharp contrasts the Ephesian converts' former way of life and their present life as Christians. The language is again powerful and contrasts the restlessness of their former life, "following the course of this world" (2:2) "following the ruler of the power of the air" (v. 2), "following the desires of the flesh and senses" (v. 3) with their present, stable life, "seated . . . in the heavenly places in Christ Jesus" (v. 6), being rooted and grounded in love. (This emphasis on Christ's ascension into the heavens and the Christian's participation in his exalted state is one of the most striking features of the letter.) The text also contrasts the deadness of their former state with their present life: they have been made alive, they are to be strengthened internally by the Spirit, Christ is to dwell in their hearts, and they are to be filled with all the fullness of God.

As in the first three chapters, the language here is extremely rich, and different people in the study group focused on different phrases and ideas, which brought out their amazement at the exaltedness of the vision. Some seemed almost overwhelmed by the vision: "the more we look to God, the more insignificant we make ourselves feel, the more we see our sinfulness." They found comfort in the letter's emphasis on God's mercy and grace: that they were saved not by their own doing. Others were encouraged to see that their lives might be illuminated and transformed by this vision.

Some in the Bible study group felt that the contrasts between converts and non-Christians were too sharply drawn. They could not think of their non-Christian neighbors as "following the ruler of the power of the air" (2:2) and felt that the presentation was probably influenced by Paul's own dramatic conversion. Nonetheless, they recognized that such stark contrasts do occur in society, that those who have been brought up in a violent environment, without security and love, are often unable to control their emotions or behavior, and need love and a safe, stable environment in order to come to terms with their conflicting emotions and desires. The church can provide a place of sanctuary where people can find restoration. Christians also need to recognize the changes that have occurred in their own lives and celebrate these as enriching and empowering gifts from God.

People were asked what the text might affirm and what it might critique in present Christian practice and worship. Much might be critiqued: the lack of vision, the resignation and acceptance of a low view of Christians and the church ("it has always been like that"), the lack of personal commitment and courage to stand up for one's convictions, and the lack of "teaching of God's invitation to relationship with him." On the positive side, a number saw this text as affirming of Christians' participation in the divine life and linked this text to a strong desire for a shared Eucharist between all denominations. If Christ dwells in Christians and they participate in his fullness, how can they deny one another this central act of communion with God in Christ? We should encourage liturgies that reflect a greater sense of joy and confidence in Christ's presence in the church, so that troubled people can turn to the churches for comfort and support. We should encourage the church's movement toward a greater inclusiveness, not least of women, in all aspects of the church's life.

Ephesians 2:11-22

All groups read this as a text that, while it specifically speaks to divisions in the first-century church at Ephesus, also speaks more widely to issues of ethnic, cultural, and economic division today. The text speaks foremost of Christ's action in overcoming the age-old divisions between Jews and Gentiles, and does so through a rich variety of metaphors (which however did not particularly resonate with our Scottish readers). Groups focused on Christ's action in abolishing the law and building up the church out of opposing ethnic groups. But here interpretations differed. Some saw the abolition of the law as referring to the abolition of "human rules," which were replaced by Christ himself as the foundation of the church. Others saw it as referring to the abolition of "pernickety practices, where observation is more important than intention." Yet others saw Christ's action as replacing God's old law with a better one, created for a new humanity. Significantly, this latter reading came from the women's group, who saw the new humanity as leaving behind a patriarchal society whose laws reflect and reinforce the subordination of women to men. An interesting distinction emerged between those who interpreted this passage as promoting a deep critique of religious structures and those who read it as marking a division between the world with its "man-made [sic!] rules" and the church with its foundation in God's (new) law.

But how is this text to be read in the light of our present divisions, not least the continuing divisions between Jews and Gentiles in Israel? What is described here as already existing in reality for the church in Ephesus has not been realized in the world in two thousand years. Peace between Israel and Palestine still seems far off. Indeed, to what extent was the hostility between different ethnic groups in ancient Greco-Roman cities fully overcome in the early church at Ephesus? How might this answer affect our way of applying these texts to problems of intergroup rivalry today?

Various divisions were identified: some groups focused on divisions within the church, between "culture Christians'" and "believing" Christians, between "born-again" Christians and "just churchgoers"; others focused on differences between Christians and other faith communities. A more disciplined, prayerful life, sharing in dialogue in small groups, could help to break down barriers and to identify common denominators between different parties in the churches. A similarly prayerful and dialogical approach is needed to bring greater unity among people of different faiths. Others saw an urgent need for Christians to seek to heal divisions and inequalities in present-day society. For example, Christians should promote understanding of the causes of conflict between asylum-seekers and people on run-down housing estates where the asylum-seekers are temporarily housed. Others considered questions of the divisions between the Northern and the Southern hemispheres. Just as the Jews had to give up more than the Gentiles to bring the Gentiles into equal status with themselves, so too the rich nations, corporations, and individuals in the Northern Hemisphere need to abandon power, wealth, and privilege in order to allow the inhabitants of the Southern Hemisphere to enjoy equal status and access to opportunity. The less powerful (those in the Southern Hemisphere) must forgive present injustices. In the same way, in the church, men must give up power and women must forgive the injustices and discrimination of the past. Both need to draw inspiration from Christ's costly, sacrificial death.

Ephesians 4:1-16

This passage impressed the reading groups with its elaborate metaphor of the parts of the body being joined together and its vision of the church's growth in unity and into maturity. The vision is of Christ filling the whole universe with his presence and all the individual parts of his body receiving the power, through a diversity of gifts, to discharge their role in his mission to the world. Again most found this inspiring and challenging; some found it akin to a foreign language. Some also saw a note of anxiety in the passage. Paul, in prison (others read "prisoner of the Lord" [v. 1] as a metaphor, like a "slave of Christ"), is concerned about deceivers subverting his teaching and destroying church's unity.

The passage is concerned with unity and diversity, but there is no mistaking the emphasis on unity: one body, Spirit, hope, Lord, faith, and baptism. But baptismal unity, recognizing baptism as conferring equal status on all members of the church, brings diversity, as do the gifts conferred by Christ through the Spirit. This diversity needs to be brought together into an articulate, coordinated whole (into an interactive form of unity). Not all gifts are the same; they complement and support each other, if they are allowed to. Nor indeed are the same gifts always present in the church at any time. This text marks the emergence of church order in Ephesus. There may be a form of hierarchy in "apostles, prophets, evangelists, pastors and teachers" but it does not coincide precisely with present forms of church order in most mainstream denominations. The writer emphasizes that the whole church needs to grow into the fullness of Christ's love and truth. Truth is neither to be found in constantly changing fads and fashions, "wind[s] of doctrine" (4:14), nor in the simple formulations of penny catechisms. Truth has to enlighten the eyes of our heart.

Interestingly, the reading groups had different perceptions of what the main obstacles to unity among today's churches are. For some, the major problem is the Catholic-Protestant divide, which feeds on exclusive attitudes, an uncritical sense of one's own rightness and another's wrongness, on thoughtless opinions, prejudice, and banter. All this needs to be countered with a willingness to learn about and *from* the other. Such dialogue is also important for those concerned about lack of unity *within* churches and individual congregations. A patriarchal, authoritarian, clerical church can easily fail to listen to the voices and to acknowledge the gifts of the laity, especially women, and so fail to grow into mature unity.

Others felt that the main problem lies with the traditionalist church's refusal to acknowledge the value of newer groups among the Christian churches: evangelicals, Pentecostals, and charismatics. They saw such groups as bringing different gifts to the body and believed they can and should work together. Interes-tingly, they hoped for strong "spirit-filled leaders" while also believing that they should look for God's presence in unusual places: among the marginalized, e.g., among people with learning difficulties.

Others saw the need for churches in different parts of the world to share their gifts, to develop partnerships and friendships, and to act in solidarity where there is suffering and oppression. The churches can draw great strength from each other. Moreover, the powerful churches in the Northern Hemisphere need to hear what churches in the rest of the world are saying about the north's role in their predicament and to respond to the south's call for help.

Ephesians 5:21-33

This was read alongside Gal 3:23-29. This passage, which comes toward the end of the letter, begins the series of instructions to members of Christian households. The subject is specifically the behavior of Christian husbands and wives, whose relationship is compared to that of Christ and the church. The section opens with Christians being enjoined to be subject to one another, a phrase that seems to undermine the notion of subjection altogether. But the subsequent sections speak clearly enough in terms of the subjection of one group (wives, children, slaves) to another (husbands, parents, masters). The language of subjection—"in everything" (5:24) —is emphasized in this passage, but it is also qualified: "as you are to the Lord" (v. 22) and husbands are enjoined to love their wives as Christ loved the church (v. 23).

Some felt this to be an impossible ideal, reinforced by the image of Christ's cleansing the church and presenting her (to himself) holy and without blemish. Such exalted idealism can put huge pressure on all concerned.

In contrast with the strongly hierarchical language of Ephesians, Galatians speaks of the relation between believers and Christ in more intimate terms: Christians are children of God by virtue of their union with Christ, they are clothed with Christ, and this union means that they are equal to one another and that all other differences become unimportant.

Generally speaking, groups were critical of marriages characterized by a strong relationship of headship/subordination between husband and wife. Such relationships give men *carte blanche* for their actions, deny women their identity, and lead to women's resentment and depression. Women become inhibited and subdued; subjection causes pain and anger. At worst the text's demands of subjection, obedience, and perfection, with its underlying image of the husband presenting his wife as perfect, could put pressure on both partners, raise impossibly high expectations, and lead to deep frustration spilling over into violence.

Yet, while Galatians was recognized to be a more inclusive text, which creates greater opportunities for justice and equality in male/female relationships, there was also an awareness that a simple recognition of the equality of husbands and wives was not sufficient to deal with the need for them to take different roles, to acknowledge and complement each others' strengths and weaknesses. Simply sharing the tasks of housekeeping and parenting could lead to severe problems and fail to meet the particular needs of either partner. There was great concern over the privatization of marriage, and of how couples are left on their own to work out their relationships without adequate support systems or traditional roles to follow. Thus, while people took some encouragement from Galatians, and were generally critical of traditional marriage relations, they did not see either text as simply providing a model of marital relationships. They did, however, value the emphasis in Ephesians on the quality of relationships between husband and wife: the emphasis on love, respect, and reciprocity. Other questions were left undecided: do we want clearly defined roles in marriage, or simply an emphasis on the quality of relationships with any given structure of marriage relationship?

CONCLUSION

It is hard not to be struck, when reading Ephesians, with the breadth of its vision, its universality, its sense of the all-pervading presence and activity of God, filling all in all. This vision both excites and repels. To the same reader, it can speak deeply at one moment and the next appear like a foreign language. This is, I suspect, not least because of the stark contrast between the present, marginal, liminal state of the church in Scotland and the vision of Christ's body as filling everything. Yet these contrasts also existed for the original readers/hearers and the letter clearly addresses this disjunction between ideal and experience with its emphasis on growth: in knowledge, in the development of individual gifts, in the overcoming of divisions and threats to church unity. As so often in the Pauline/deuteropauline literature, tension appears between the claims that are made about Christians and the church (here: that it fills the world) and the injunctions to become more like what they are supposed to be (here: to grow in knowledge and mutual love so as to fill the world).

This tension in turn leads to the possibility of rather different emphases in the reading of the text: either on the internal question of growth and development within the church itself (matters of urgent importance for its survival) or on the interaction between church and world, as it fills and interacts with the world, overcoming the old ways ("following the prince of the power of the air," "following the desires of body and mind") and living out of God's love, empowered by God's Spirit. Perhaps understandably, these readings focused considerably on possibilities for inner church renewal, but still evoked some important views about the church's interaction with society in Scotland and beyond.

The vision of a dialogical church begins to emerge from these discussions. It is a church where the "eyes of the heart" can be enlightened through dialogue with other Christians based on their reading of Scripture. Listening to each other with respect and trust is necessary if the gifts of all are to be recognized and given room to develop within the church, as it is for their coordination and cooperation. This need for dialogue applies especially to the relations between men and women in the church. Through such respectful conversation, God's love can operate in and through the church, allowing it to fulfill its mission. This fulfillment requires discipline, courage, and persistence. The effort will come with a cost. If the church is to be genuinely open to the Spirit of God—being poured out into the world—it will have to endure its Gethsemane experiences, but it will also be filled with that love that casts out fear.

How is the church to exercise its power in the world? No longer as a powerful institution alongside other secular institutions. The church can serve as a place where people can find security and consolation, and as a community where they can begin to refashion their lives. It can serve as a mediator in conflicts between different factions within society, seeking to draw warring parties into dialogue, speaking the truth prophetically yet in such a way as to leave room for rapprochement and reconciliation. It has done this remarkably in some of the conflicts in Africa; however, its role in Northern Ireland has not been made easier by the churches' involvement in the conflict itself. It can influence newly emerging, more participatory forms of governance in Scottish society. It can continue to promote greater equality between people of different gender and ethnicity. It must continue to search for ways of empowering people in areas of rural and urban deprivation. It can also take a more active part in pursuing justice in international relations between rich and poor nations, as it has done to some effect in the Jubilee campaign on international debt and through campaigns to persuade pharmaceutical companies to provide or permit the sale of cheaper drugs to combat HIV/AIDS. Here it faces the greatest challenge: to encourage the rich to renounce power, privilege, and wealth; to give power, dignity, and respect to the poor; and encourage the poor to offer reconciliation and forgiveness.

Underlying this challenge is the emergence of a renewed vision of God's power, not the power of domination (though such notions are to be found in Ephesians: "put[ting] all things under his feet," 1:22), but rather one of interaction with God's people and God's world, cultivating growth, giving gifts, and encouraging their development and coordination. God is not simply set over and above God's world, subjecting all things to an inflexible will, constantly reminding believers of their failings and inadequacy. Rather, God is present through Christ and the Spirit, bringing all things into a creative and living relationship of interdependence, mutual support, and inter-animation. Such an understanding of power also needs to inform and critique our secular understandings and exercise of power.

BIBLIOGRAPHY

Best, Ernest. *Ephesians*. NTG. Sheffield: JSOT Press, 1993.

Forrester, Duncan B. *On Human Worth: A Christian Vindication of Equality*. London: SCM, 2001.

Holloway, Richard. *Doubts and Loves: What is Left of Christianity?* Edinburgh: Canongate, 2001.

Holman, Bob. *Towards Equality: A Christian Manifesto*. London: SPCK, 1997.

Muddiman, John. *A Commentary on the Epistle to the Ephesians*. BNTC. London: Continuum, 2001.

Newlands, George. *Generosity and the Christian Future*. London: SPCK, 1997.

West, Gerald O. *The Academy of the Poor: Towards a Dialogical Reading of the Bible*. Interventions 2. Sheffield: Sheffield Academic Press, 1999.

PHILIPPIANS

Demetrius K. Williams

Tulane University, New Orleans, Louisiana, USA

LIFE CONTEXT OF THE INTERPRETATION

I write this commentary as an African American male, born and raised in the northern Midwest of the United States during the height of the civil rights movement. Nurtured religiously and ordained as a minister in the black Baptist tradition, and trained academically in religious studies and New Testament and Christian origins, I currently teach at a private university in the South. These elements inform my approach to Philippians and the life context of African American Christians. As I view these life contexts from the perspective of Philippians, it becomes apparent that after much religious, social, and political struggle to overcome the obstacles of economic injustice, racism, and Jim Crow policies (separate but "unequal"), American Christians in general and African American Christians in particular are in danger of compromising the integrity of the gospel (1:27-30). Instead of remaining in partnership *(koinonia)* with others (1:5, 7, 25; 4:14-16) who continue to suffer (1:12-26, 29) from racial and economic injustice, many African American Christians who have benefited from the former struggles are seeking rather to profit selfishly from social and economic gains (3:5-8), which are presented in the guise of a gospel of prosperity. The gospel of liberation and equality that guided the churches' protest and agitation for social change is being co-opted by a gospel of prosperity.

African American churches, whether historically activist, moderate, or accommoda-tionist, realized during the civil rights movement their true potential to bring about the structural social changes for which they had long preached, sung, and prayed. The social and political gains of the civil rights movement were viewed in biblical imagery—the long-sought promised land of social and economic freedom and opportunity was coming to pass. Such a perspective on historical events was not uncommon in African American religious history. African Americans have historically viewed the Bible as a document that supported their quests for freedom and equality, and have ex-pressed their longings in biblical language and imagery (Wimbush 2003). Just as the ancient children of Israel entering the promised land were instructed that freedom entailed responsibility to God and community, many African Americans were likewise taught in church and at home that new responsibilities came with these new opportunities. No matter how successful we might become in the land of opportunity, we were to remain faithful to our heritage of struggle for justice and equality for all and to remember those who struggled for our liberation.

As a result of this movement, African Americans made several social and economic gains in line with the Declaration of Independence; it was increasingly recognized that "they are endowed by their Creator with certain unalienable Rights, that among these are Life, Liberty, and the pursuit of Happiness." In varying degrees African

Demetrius K. Williams (PhD, Harvard Divinity School in New Testament and Christian Origins) teaches New Testament, directs Religious Studies, and participates in the African and African Diaspora Studies Program at Tulane University. He has published works on Paul, including the book *Enemies of the Cross of Christ: The Terminology of the Cross and Conflict in Philippians* (2002), and works on the meaning of scripture within the African American religious context, including the book *An End to This Strife: The Politics of Gender in African American Churches* (2004). Dr. Williams is an ordained Baptist minister.

American representation can now be found in almost all civil, economic, social, educational, cultural (including mass media and music), and political aspects of American life. To be sure, some believe that as a people African Americans have entered into the promised land of equal opportunity. Nevertheless, many African Americans remain at the bottom of the social and economic heap. These individuals often are the ones who struggle to carve out an existence and who fill black churches of all denominations on Sunday mornings.

These church people continue to endure subtle forms of racism, urban blight, and economic injustice as they attempt to live out the gospel. They come to church to hear a gospel relevant to their quest for human liberation and wholeness, but a growing number of them hear a gospel that implies that the hope for their deliverance is to get on the prosperity train. An increasing number of highly visible African American Christian leaders and pastors teach that those who continue to suffer are themselves at fault because of their inadequate faith. In many cases, the gospel and indeed the Bible

are exploited as mere roadmaps or paradigms for crass material gain, which can be accessed with the proper faith-practice. Some African American Christian leaders in this category boast of their private jet planes, luxury automobiles, and grand mansions all in the name of the Christ who "emptied himself" of privilege (2:7) so that he might participate in the human situation and liberate those who were oppressed and exploited. Prosperity preaching presumes that if one person can achieve his or her goals by faith, then so can others?

It appears to me that some of God's people in this context have lost sight of the tradition of joining in partnership with those who struggle for freedom, justice, and equal opportunity. Identification with free market gain and the cult of personal success have replaced social-political concern for those who "suffered the loss of all things" (3:8) in the capitalistic game—a game in which poverty, racism, and victim-blaming play in favor of the system. Used with caution, Paul's presentation of the examples in Philippians provides new lenses with which to view this growing trend.

CONTEXTUAL COMMENT

An Overview of Philippians

After traditional historical-critical and literary-critical analyses, scholars in the mid-seventies rediscovered classical rhetorical analysis to interpret biblical texts. This approach is best suited to expose the rhetorical function and motivation behind Paul's use of hortatory examples. His goal is to show the Philippians the attitudes and behaviors that are advantageous or harmful, expedient or inexpedient, through a comparison of positive and negative examples.

In his greetings to the Philippians, "Paul and Timothy, slaves of Christ Jesus" (1:1, a.t.), Paul identifies himself (and Timothy) as a slave. This identification is unusual; it appears in the uncontested letters only in Romans 1:1. But Paul introduces himself in this way to underscore a key theme of the primary example he proposes, namely that of

Jesus who "emptied himself, taking the form of a slave" (2:7). By this self-designation in 1:1, Paul begins to persuade his audience that he exemplifies a Christlike existence.

Paul's relationship with the Philippian community is generally assumed to be strong and positive. Yet there are hints of tension that may have been generated by Paul's imprisonment (Peterlin 1995). Why would his imprisonment be a problem? Some interpreters suspect that a segment of the Philippian congregation may have felt that the partnership (*koinonia*) that they had established with Paul was now compromised. This partnership was a formal agreement wherein the Philippians agreed to support Paul financially and to participate with him in the spread of the gospel, a cooperative enterprise that Paul mentions in several places: he writes that he is thankful "for your *partner-*

ship in the gospel from the first day until now" (1:5, a.t.), adding, "you are all *partakers with me* in this grace" (1:7, a.t.). Because of this partnership, Paul assures the Philippians that "the one [God] who began a good work in you will bring it to completion at the day of Jesus Christ" (1:6, a.t.). Paul wants to assure them that his imprisonment and possible martyrdom will neither hinder the gospel's progress nor cause a breach in their partnership. Far from hindering the gospel, his imprisonment has served to advance it (1:12-18). Hence, whether he lives or dies, Christ will be glorified (1:19-26). Paul's concern, which governs the entire letter, is that the Philippian church live as a community in a manner "worthy of the gospel of Christ," especially in the face of their adversaries (1:27-30). He reinforces this call to live in a manner worthy of the gospel by offering them the example of Christ.

The Example of Christ: The Paradigm of Partnership

In chapter 2 Paul attempts to redirect the attitude of the Philippian church toward modes of thinking and behaving that can assist them through their present internal crisis (2:1-4). They should share common goals and concerns. The appeal in 2:3 drives home Paul's concern: "Do nothing from selfishness or conceit, but in humility count others better than yourselves"(a.t.). Earlier, in 1:15, Paul used a similar phrase to describe those at his present locale (Ephesus?) who, hoping to increase Paul's suffering, were preaching Christ "out of envy and rivalry" (1:15, a.t.), rather than out of love (1:16). People with such a mind-set not only stand over against Paul but also against the gospel of Christ Jesus, who joined in partnership with humanity and suffered death on a cross (2:7-8). In this way Paul contrasts positive and negative examples to instruct the Philippian community, and shows that having the *right attitude* leads to proper community harmony and goals.

The example of Christ is the key to the Philippians' unity, because it instructs them to "look out for the interests of others" (2:4, a.t.).

This teaching is neither mere ethical exhortation nor nice moralism, but what Paul believes to be the foundation for successful communal living and true partnership. The Philippians had seeds of dissension, a mindset that could cause them to miss their eschatological goal (1:10; 3:20-21). So to put them back on track Paul provides them with a paradigmatic example of the proper attitude or mind-set, that of Jesus Christ (2:6-11).

The interpretation of the "Christ hymn" hinges on the translation of 2:5, for which we may choose among three alternative interpretations: ethical, kerygmatic, or rhetorical.

According to the ethical interpretation (dominant from the Reformers until the middle of the twentieth century), Philippians 2:5 presents the experience of Christ in 2:6-11 as a moral example for the congregation, a model to imitate. Then one translates 2:5, "Let the same mind be in you that was in Christ Jesus" (NRSV, supplying the verb "be" because there is no direct object for the verb). In such a case, Paul presents the example of Christ as a way of life characterized by humility and self-sacrifice. With this interpretation, 2:5 can be rendered as, "adopt towards one another, in your mutual relation, the same attitude [or mind-set] that was found in Christ Jesus" (a.t.). This traditional interpretation is problematic in the African American context because it can be used to encourage believers to submit to suffering and humiliation, following the example of Jesus.

The kerygmatic interpretation emerged among scholars in the 1950s. This line of interpretation argues that, since Paul quotes a hymn composed earlier than the letter, he wants to remind the Philippians of how they came to be "in Christ Jesus." The phrase "in Christ Jesus" is part of Paul's familiar theological language and refers to the union of believers with Christ as members of his body. Here one translates 2:5 as: "Have this mind among yourselves, which you have in [towards] Christ," that is, "adopt towards one another, in your mutual relations, the same attitude you adopt towards Christ Jesus, in your union with him" (a.t.). Therefore, the expression points to the salvation event; Christ's example is held up to explain to the Philippians how they came to be "in Christ." This interpretation avoids promoting a theology of suffering, which I try to avoid for the sake of the African American churches, but it still misses the rhetorical force of the gospel that Paul sought to convey and that we also need today.

A rhetorical interpretation offers another alternative needed to capture the rhetorical function of the hymn and its connection with Paul's use of other examples in the letter. Although problems exist with the ethical interpretation, it appropriately recognizes that Paul's object in using the hymn is to encourage an attitude in the Philippians that was described in 2:1-4 and was also exemplified in Jesus Christ. In my interpretation, this attitude is not one of suffering and self-sacrifice, but one of willingness to participate with others in creating a community of wholeness. Partnership implies mutual cooperation for a common goal without entailing structures of dominance—two equal parties agree to cooperate. It is along these lines that I examine the Christ hymn.

Three important narrative movements appear in the hymn: privilege (2:6), voluntary loss of privilege culminating in death on a cross (2:7-8), and exaltation (2:9-11). This pattern can be described as the privilege-loss-exaltation scheme.

The redeemer's privileged status is stated in 2:6: "though he was in the form of God [divine], [he] did not regard equality with God as something to be exploited." The one who has equality with God has the selfless attitude or mind-set that Paul wants to promote among the Philippians, instead of "selfish ambition" (2:3). This selfless mind-set expresses itself in "humility," as they "consider" one another better than themselves (2:3b, a.t.). Then, with the phrase "not consider[ing] equality with God as something to be exploited," he reiterates the appeal to "not look out for one's own interests" (2:4, a.t.) because Christ freely gave up his privileged status to join in partnership with others who were struggling to realize liberation.

The second movement, 2:7-8, describes how Jesus Christ "emptied" himself and became a slave, taking on the lowest status in human society. The verb, "to empty," regularly means "to become powerless," or "to be emptied of significance." Here it contrasts with the empty glory of those whom Paul mentions in 2:3 (like the phrase, "he became poor," in 2 Cor 8:9). Instead of pursuing his own will and privilege, Christ "emptied himself" of these, and exhibited a willingness to join those at the bottom of society who had been excluded from privilege. The following phrases, he was "born [came to be] in human likeness" and "being found in human form" (2:7), reflect the quality of his partnership with humankind. The next phrase, "he humbled himself and became obedient" (2:8), is linked with the exhortation to humility of 2:3 through the word "humble"—a term that can carry meanings such as "base-minded," "shabby," and "of no account." Humility was not seen as a positive virtue in Greco-Roman antiquity; it could be viewed as having the mentality of a slave, the connection Paul makes regarding Christ in 2:7 and regarding himself and Timothy in 1:1. The concept of humility is directly linked with partnership. Jesus "humbled" himself, sparing nothing, to participate in the human condition for the cause of human liberation. In such partnership, no room remains for pride or selfishness, attitudes that breed competition, rivalry, and division in community. Having a mind-set (phronein) of selfishness contradicts that exhibited in Christ's humility.

Christ was also "obedient to the point of death, even death on a cross" (2:8). The final phrase, "death on a cross," is more than a mere addition. The repetition of the word death and the mention of the cross form the rhetorical climax to which the preceding verses pointed. Paul added these words to the original hymn (D. K. Williams 2002) to emphasize Christ's willingness to participate in the cause of liberation with suffering humanity, in contrast with those who are unwilling to do so, the "enemies of the cross of Christ" (3:18)—whether these be Paul's opponents (1:15-16) or those who threaten the Philippians' community (3:1-21). Accordingly, as we shall see below, when Paul presents himself, Timothy, or Epaphroditus as examples for the Philippians, Paul makes sure that these examples follow the cruciform pattern of the Christ hymn.

The final narrative movement of the hymn (2:9-11), the exaltation, should not be simply viewed as a reward for Christ's previous obedience and the cross. Rather, the exaltation puts Christ in a position to bring about liberation. It is the next stage in bringing about liberation, initiated by Christ's willingness to empty himself of privilege and to participate in the cause of liberation with suffering humanity. The exalted Lord brings about this liberation. This final movement gives the Philippian community the necessary hope for exaltation. They are in Christ, to be sure, yet they are struggling in their present reality. If they cease dissention and join together in unity and partnership, they too can be victorious over the obstacles that hinder their progress and share in Christ's ultimate victory and exaltation.

The Example of Timothy: Exhibiting the Christlike Attitude about Partnership

Paul looks forward to sending Timothy to the Philippians so that he may obtain news of the Philippians' well-being (2:19), and so that Timothy might help to resolve the tensions in the community. Here Paul uses Timothy as an example of partnership: "I have no one like him [like-minded] who will be genuinely concerned for your welfare" (2:20). The word *isopsykos* that Paul uses for "like-minded" is rare in Greek and literally means "having one soul." Paul and Timothy share the same life principle, indeed the same life, a sharing that is a basis for partnership. Timothy's partnership stands in sharp contrast to the attitudes of those who "out of rivalry" intend to increase his affliction (1:17, a.t.). Timothy's coming reflects that he is genuinely concerned about them, rather than seeking his own interests as in 2:3-4. In sum, Timothy is a living example of humility and concern for others, as repre-

sented in the Christ hymn; he is an example of right attitude in partnership.

The Example of Epaphroditus: Exhibiting the Christlike Behavior of Partnership

Epaphroditus was apparently sent back to Philippi (2:25-30) early, possibly before the outcome of Paul's trial. In Paul's lengthy explanations, some interpreters recognize a hint of tension. Yet one can also see the recommendation of Epaphroditus as Paul's presentation of another example of an individual who exhibits the selfless behavior of Christ in the hymn. In 2:25 Paul combines a number of favorable labels regarding Ephaphroditus: "brother and co-worker and fellow soldier, your messenger and minister to my need." Paul lists the qualities that make Epaphroditus useful to himself and to the Philippians. In his service on behalf of the Philippian church to Paul, Epaphroditus fell ill, indeed almost to the point of death (2:27, 30). This example of service certainly recalls the Christ hymn (especially 2:8) and for this reason, Epaphroditus is to be honored and received with joy because "he came close to death for the work of Christ, risking his life to make up for those services" that the Philippians could not perform (2:30). Epaphroditus' Christlike behavior is lifted up to further drive home Paul's message about Christ's willingness to share in the human situation even to the point of death.

The Example of Paul: Partnership with and in Christ

Paul opens chapter 3 with invectives against a group that promotes circumcision (3:2-3). In this case Paul presents his own example (3:17) to counter that of his rivals. His former status and achievements in Judaism are an example of his former code of values, which he now views as "confidence in the flesh" (3:4). He then presents himself as an example following the narrative pattern of the Christ hymn: privilege (3:4-6), loss (3:7-8), and the *hope* of exaltation (3:11-16). Paul relates the complete reversal of his values on the basis of "the surpassing knowledge of Christ Jesus my Lord" (3:8, a.t.). What he once persecuted and tried to destroy, he now recognizes to be the only goal worth pursuing. His experience of Christ caused him to reconsider the significance of his religious heritage (3:5-8) in favor of the "the righteousness from God based on faith" (3:9). As a result of his reconsideration, he now strives to know Christ and to participate with Christ: "the sharing *[koinonia]* of his sufferings by becoming like him in his death" (3:10).

Paul describes his opponents as self-serving, shameful, and divisive (3:18-19). One should avoid their example at all costs, despite its surface appeal. Their offer of circumcision and status in Judaism provided a means of avoiding persecution from the civil authorities (because Judaism was a recognized religion with certain privileges). But it could never help them to attain eschatological union with Christ (3:20-21). Paul encourages the Philippians not to sell out their new "heritage" in Christ for mere earthly, transient gain. Their status "in Christ," and thus in the church, provides an identity that sur-

passes ethnic loyalties as well as the power dynamics of Greco-Roman society. It offers an alternative "identity" and "society" to that of Rome. Paul de-emphasizes ethnicity, even his own (3:5-10), with respect to the new identity that really matters for him, namely, being a Christian or being in the church (Braxton 2003).

The Example of the Philippians: Partnership in the Gospel

The Philippians community itself provides the final noteworthy example of partnership *(koinonia)* in the gospel. Their financial gift, and other kinds of support for Paul, provides an example of committed partnership for the sake of the gospel. They had supported Paul in the past (Phil 1:5-7; 4:10, 15-16; 2 Cor 8:1-6; 9:2-4) and despite the tension about his imprisonment, they continued faithfully in their partnership with him. Their envoy Epaphroditus (4:18) brought this gift to Paul. Paul gives thanks to the Philippians for their financial support and formally acknowledges its receipt (4:10-20), and ends this segment with a benediction and a doxology (4:20).

CONCLUSION

Contemporary African American Christians can certainly benefit from the examples of committed partnership in the cause of the gospel of liberty that Paul presents in his letter to the Philippians. Such examples of proper attitudes and actions for the greater good and betterment of the community in the face of hostility and conflict can remind African American Christians of their heritage of struggle against injustice. However, there are also reasons for caution. The interpreter and preacher of Philippians must neither reinscribe a slave mentality among the oppressed, nor valorize the language of servanthood/service (Grant 1993), nor sacralize suffering (D. Williams 1991).

The American antebellum slave regime used the Bible as a tool to support an ideology of God-ordained slavery. A skewed portrayal of Jesus was a significant component of this regime. Philippians' portrayal of

Christ in the hymn as the ultimate obedient slave who suffers willingly can fall into this ideological trap.

Following Briggs (1989, throughout this paragraph) we first must recognize that Philippians draws its imagery and makes its christological statement from the social-cultural background of the Greco-Roman ideology of slavery. On can grant that Philippians is neither about slavery as a social institution nor a critique or apology for slavery. Metaphorically, Christ is the slave *(doulos)* that has become lord *(kyrios)*. But he did not begin as a slave, but with "equality with God" (2:6). As such, according to Greco-Roman ideology, Christ was much too worthy to become enslaved. Nevertheless, Christ is presented as the ideal slave and his obedience makes him worthy of exaltation. The end of Christ's enslavement, however, is not manumission but a return to his original status of glory and honor. Such a scenario has parallels in Hellenistic novels in which highborn persons are enslaved and suffer humiliation until the subsequent recognition of their identity. Yet, the problem remains. What action did God deem favorable? It is not the death on the cross as such but what precedes it—Christ's obedience. God is therefore described as having the same expectation of Christ (as a slave) as a human master had of his slave in Greco-Roman and antebellum American society: obedience, a chief virtue for a slave in such contexts. Christ is the ideal slave and his obedience makes him worthy of exaltation. Thus Philippians 2:6-11 for the people of God in my context is quite problematic because it idealizes the slave's role.

Also problematic is the idea that God has given the oppressed the privilege to suffer (1:29), while others have the liberty and freedom to pursue happiness. This idea has been influenced by the traditional view of the theology of the cross; we have been taught that the cross entails suffering. But such language has also been used by ruling regimes to perpetuate the suffering of the oppressed. In our interpretation, the cross does not function as a symbol of suffering, but as a representation of the lengths to which Christ would go to participate with the oppressed in their cause for wholeness and freedom.

Finally, the question of rejecting one's ethnicity for the sake of the gospel must be addressed (Phil 3:4-11). African American people were taught and forced to "count their ethnic African background as loss" in order to adopt a new identity as "Negro slaves" without a history. They did, however, create a new identity as they merged their African heritage with their Christian heritage. Many African Americans today are proud members of the African American Christian tradition—a tradition that has so indistinguishably mingled the ethnic and the religious that to single out or prioritize the parts may substantially and negatively alter the whole (Braxton 2003). Therefore, many African Americans might reply to Paul that they have *not* counted their heritage and background as loss because it is through the unity of the religious and ethnic that they have realized the surpassing value of knowing Jesus Christ as the one who willingly participates in their freedom struggles.

For these reasons, I see the growing wave of prosperity preaching among African Americans as contrary to the heritage of struggle and as a de-radicalization of the African American religious heritage. We give thanks to God, how-ever, that Paul's letter to the Philippians offers us a number of examples of those who radically and unselfishly participated in the gospel. They beckon us to join them.

BIBLIOGRAPHY

Braxton, Brad R. "The Role of Ethnicity in the Social Location of 1 Corinthians 7:17-24." Pages 19-32 in *Yet With a Steady Beat: Contemporary U.S. Afrocentric Biblical Interpretation*. Edited by Randall C. Bailey. SemeiaSt 42. Atlanta: Society of Biblical Literature, 2003.

Briggs, Sheila. "Can an Enslaved God Liberate? Hermeneutical Reflections on Philippians 2:6-11." *Semeia* 47 (1989): 138-153.

Gould, N. D. "'Servants of the Cross': Cross Theology in Philippians." *ResQ* 18 (1975): 93-101.

Grant, J. "The Sin of Servanthood and the Deliverance of Discipleship." Pages 199-218 in *A Troubling in My Soul: Womanist Perspectives on Evil and Suffering*. Edited by Emilie M. Townes.

Bishop Henry McNeal Turner/Sojourner Truth Series in Black Religion 8. Maryknoll, N.Y.: Orbis, 1993.

Martin, Ralph P. *Carmen Christi: Philippians 2:5-11 in Recent Interpretation in the Setting of Early Worship*. SNTSMS 4. Grand Rapids: Eerdmans, 1983.

Peterlin, Davorin. *Paul's Letter to the Philippians in the Light of Disunity in the Church*. NovTSup 79. New York: E. J. Brill, 1995.

Terrell, JoAnne Marie. *Power in the Blood?: The Cross in the African American Experience*. Bishop Henry McNeal Turner/Sojourner Truth Series in Black Religion 15. Maryknoll, N.Y.: Orbis, 1998.

Williams, Delores S. "Black Women's Surrogacy Experience and the Christian Notion of Redemption." Pages 1-14 in *After Patriarchy: Feminist Transformations of the World Religions*. Edited by Paula M. Cooey, William R. Eakin, and Jay B. McDaniel. Maryknoll, N.Y.: Orbis, 1991.

Williams, Demetrius K. *Enemies of the Cross of Christ: The Terminology of the Cross and Conflict in Philippians*. JSNTSup 223. London: Sheffield Academic Press, 2002.

_____. "Paul's Anti-Imperial Discourse of the Cross: The Cross and Power in 1 Corinthians 1–4." Pages 796-823 in *Society of Biblical Literature Seminar Papers 2000*. Atlanta: SBL Press, 2000.

Wimbush, Vincent L. *The Bible and African Americans: A Brief History*. Facets. Minneapolis: Fortress, 2003.

COLOSSIANS

Teresa Okure, SHCJ

Catholic Institute of West Africa, Port Harcourt, Nigeria

LIFE CONTEXT OF THE INTERPRETATION

I read this letter as a Nigerian and a Roman Catholic who is a member of an international religious congregation, the Society of the Holy Child Jesus. In the Nigerian and Roman Catholic contexts, a major issue raised by Paul's Letter to the Colossians is Jesus' uniqueness as the only savior of the world. A favorite chorus among Nigerian Christians of all denominations is the hymn based on Phil 2:6-11:

He is Lord, he is Lord. Amen.
He has risen from the dead, he is Lord.
Every knee shall bow
Every tongue confess that
Jesus Christ is Lord.

In the name of Jesus
There is power.
In the name of Jesus
Every knee shall bow.

In 2001, the Declaration of the Congregation for the Doctrine of the Faith, *"Dominus Iesus:* On the Unicity and Salvific Universality of Jesus Christ and the Church," entered into the discussion in a manner that created a furor among Catholics, Protestants, and people of other faith communities. Many saw the declaration as reversing the significant progress that had been made, especially during the pontificate of John Paul II, on ecumenical and interfaith dialogue. Others—Catholics and, especially,

Pentecostal and Charismatic Christians, who have an uncompromising faith in the unique lordship of Jesus—welcomed it as timely, if not long overdue. Yet both Nigeria and my church have ratified the Universal Declaration of Human Rights, which declares that no one shall be discriminated against on the basis of religion, and that each person has the freedom of worship. Does this affirmation not imply that all religions are equal, and hence that the preoccupation of Catholics (since the Second Vatican Council) and other Christians with Jesus' universal lordship is at best outdated and misleading and at worst a downright insult to other Christians and peoples of other faiths? How does a believing Catholic and staunch Christian cope with this apparent contradiction?

The affirmation of the lordship of Jesus was not invented by the Catholic Church but is a solid core of our New Testament faith, of which the Letter to the Colossians is but one example (e.g., Acts 4:12; Phil 2:6-11). As Christians, our faith is first and foremost biblical before it becomes theological or denominational. What light does the Letter to the Colossians shed on this matter, and how can reading the letter from the perspective of the contemporary situation help to shed light on the christological affirmations in the letter itself?

Teresa Okure, SHCJ, a graduate of the University of Ibadan, the Sorbonne, École Biblique of Jerusalem, and Fordham University (PhD), is a professor of New Testament and gender hermeneutics. She has served on executive committees of several associations, including EATWOT (Ecumenical Association of Third World Theologians, as Executive Secretary), the International Association for Mission Studies (IAMS), and the Society for New Testament Studies (SNTS). She has published more than one hundred articles and six books, including *The Johannine Approach to Mission: A Contextual Study of John 4:1-42* (1988). She edited *Evaluating the Inculturation of Christianity in Africa* (1990) and *To Cast Fire upon the Earth: Bible and Mission Collaborating in Today's Multicultural Global Context* (2000).

The Lordship and Uniqueness of Jesus the Nigerian Context

Nigeria is the most populous country inAfrica, with about 120 million inhabitants and more than four hundred ethnic groups. It is located in West Africa, one of the most turbulent areas of the continent, which has witnessed civil wars in Liberia, Sierra Leone, and currently Côte d'Ivoire (Ivory Coast). The recurrent religious conflicts between radical Muslim fundamentalists in northern parts of the country and the ethnic clashes which occur indiscriminately everywhere are but examples of this turbulence fomented, many believe, by ex-generals who do not want democracy to succeed after some thirty-five years of military rule. Radical Muslim fundamentalism, mostly in the service of politics and power, is sustained through the unconstitutional application of the *sharia* law in many northern states. Some Pentecostal and Charismatic Christians also help to trigger these religious conflicts by recklessly claiming their right to freedom of worship, proclaiming the lordship of Jesus through huge public rallies organized in predominantly Muslim areas.

From the perspective of the Roman Catholic Church, not only *Dominus Iesus* but the reiterated calls of John Paul II for ecumenism and interfaith dialogue stand side by side with an emphasis on the indispensable duty of Christians to proclaim the gospel to every creature. Here proclamation is meant as actually preaching the gospel to those who have not yet heard it, not merely being present to them so that by seeing our actions they may come to believe in Jesus. This call, too, is done in fidelity to Jesus' mandate to his disciples to go out to the whole world to proclaim the good news and be his "witnesses till the end [not ends] of the earth" (Acts 1:8, a.t.; Matt 28:19-20). The church must accept this mandate as a duty even as Paul did ("Woe to me if I do not proclaim the gospel," 1 Cor 9:16) or risk being unfaithful to her identity and mission. Many

Protestants would agree with John Paul II on this imperative to proclaim the gospel, in contrast with some liberal Catholics who see little or no need for such a direct proclamation or who are inclined to equate Jesus with the savior figures of other religions. Though few, if any, Nigerian Christians hold this liberal view, its presence among Christians in other contexts makes some Nigerian preachers more adamant in proclaiming the lordship of Jesus polemically, for fear the ordinary Christian's faith will be eroded by this liberal view as spread through literature and the media in our globalized world. Hence, though the debate on the uniqueness of Jesus is not directly a Nigerian problem, Nigerian Christians are not ignorant of or indifferent to it.

These conflicting affirmations of the church (upholding each person's right to freedom of worship, commitment to ecumenism and interfaith dialogue, yet at the same time encouraging Christians to proclaim the absolute necessity of Jesus for salvation) raise the fundamental questions: How can a Christian simultaneously hold these (possibly) conflicting truths? Can the affirmations themselves hold together at all, or do they amount to one enormous theological deception? What did Jesus mean when he commissioned his disciples to be his witnesses, to proclaim the good news to the end of the earth, and to make disciples of all nations, promising to be with them himself in the undertaking? Is Jesus present outside the Catholic Church or Christianity or must a faithful Christian believe absolutely that outside Christ there is no salvation? Though posed in the Nigerian context, this problem is a most vexing one for Christians worldwide because of the globally accepted universal human right to freedom of worship.

The history of Christianity in Nigeria further compounds this problem. Nigerians, like most Africans, received a divided Christianity. The political, national, and economic quarrels of Europe were transmitted to Africa as part and parcel of the "good news."

African Christians received a Christianity deeply divided over politics, economics, and ethnicity and over time have added and multiplied their own divisions, especially after the Biafran civil war. Previously, missionaries taught Christians to hate and vie with one another over the number of converts won for their different denominations (not for Christ). Now the fashion is for some "mushroom churches" to go "soul harvesting" in the established churches, to enrich their own churches while trying to undermine these established churches. This practice inspired by the same ideology of power, control, and Mammon that largely motivated the division of Christianity in Europe.

Ironically, those who brought and spread a deeply divided Christianity in Africa saw Africans as "pagans," people who allegedly had no knowledge of God. They said Africans were under the power of Satan, what Colossians would call "the power of darkness" (1:13). These divided Christians, who had already subjected the gospel to the service of the empire, and who to all intents and purposes had betrayed the very essence of the gospel by dividing up Christ instead of building him up (cf. 1 Cor 1:13) traveled far and wide to bring more members into the divided body of Christ as they undertook the mission to save "pagan" Africans. And they saw nothing wrong with the scandal of dividing up the body of Christ.

Yet, by both nature and nurture, Africans were traditionally very much a gospel people, a community people who practiced and still practice that native hospitality of giving "the other" the room and the freedom to be. Inclusiveness remains their cultural instinct.

Even today, despite the received heritage of deeply divided Christianity and the onslaught of fundamentalist Muslims, one can find within the same family, a Catholic, a Protestant, a Muslim, and a follower of the African Traditional Religion (ATR). This inclusiveness and tolerance are based on the belief that "blood is thicker than water." The blood of the common ancestor that unites the members of a family transcends all other personal affiliations within the family, because such affiliations among the descendants could not exist without the primary gift of life transmitted through the ancestral blood.

Some Nigerian Christians today adamantly proclaim Jesus as Lord and are inclined, as were the missionaries of old, to view non-Christians, especially followers of the ATR, as pagans. The question remains whether or not they have actually understood what this proclamation entails for them personally, and what it demands of their lives in the Lord Jesus.

Ultimately, what does it mean concretely for a Christian to confess and proclaim Jesus as Lord with undaunted conviction in such a religiously diverse context? What, if anything, can the Nigerian and African cultural heritage and the history of the transmission of the Christian faith contribute toward a clearer understanding of the universal lordship of Jesus, if not toward its solution? What corrective lens can the Letter to the Colossians offer to help us address these issues and how can these issues in turn shed light on our understanding of the letter? These are the questions that guide this reading of Paul's Letter to the Colossians.

CONTEXTUAL COMMENT

An Overview of Colossians

The Letter to the Colossians conveys the impression that the Colossians addressed problems similar to those experienced in our Nigerian Church context. In the letter, Paul (an apostle) with Timothy (a brother in the faith) address other brothers and sisters (saints, consecrated persons) in the Lord Jesus. The letter and its contents are primarily for their use as believers, not for use by non-Christians. It is intended to help them gain a better understanding of themselves as Christians and live out the consequences of their faith in Jesus.

This point is important. The letter is intended to equip the Colossians with the theological or christological resources necessary for dealing practically with the faith challenges in the context of their daily lives. It is not for dialogue with peoples of other faiths whom Paul refers to only briefly at the end of the letter (4:5). The question of Jesus' lordship is purely a functional response to this need, since the members of the church are under pressure to serve other gods in their lives, whether these be the principalities and powers described in the text, their previous religious observances, or new religious practices proposed to them by the Judaizers.

In the letter, Paul discusses Jesus' uniqueness in creation, and in the church, over all other possible messiah figures that can claim their allegiance. His proclamation aims to persuade them that, in the Lord Jesus, they will find their true identity and the principle of unity for their checkered/unstable lives. Consequently, they will not allow themselves to be tossed about by every new teaching that sundry preachers feed to them. In brief, Paul's proclamation of Jesus as Lord has implications primarily for the Colossian Christians themselves. For instance, John the Baptist's confession, "I am not the Christ," precluded any effort on his part to proceed to act as if he were the Christ; his confession carried the personal acceptance that he must *(dei)* decrease while Christ must *(dei)* increase (John 3:30). So too must the Colossians' confession result in a practical way of living within their own context.

Though little is known about Colossae, this much can be affirmed: it was a Phrygian city inhabited by a mixture of Jews and Gentiles. The Christian community would also have been mixed, with Gentiles in the majority. The letter mentions Greeks, Jews, barbarians, Scythians, free born people, and slaves, who by virtue of their Christian faith have now all become one person in Christ (3:11). The origin of their problems cannot be categorically identified. Was it from the Judaizers, the Gnostics, or a remainder from their traditional (pagan) religions? It would seem from the letter's contents that the problem was primarily the influence of the Judaizers, perhaps already tinged with Gnosticism (the reference to knowledge of God's mystery, the treasury of which is hid in Jesus, 2:2-3). The Gnostics believed that access to secret knowledge resulted in a certain way of life and qualified one for salvation. In the early church, the confession of Jesus often ran into conflict with the converts' previous or traditional religious practices or with the Jewish Christians' insistence that Gentile converts must be circumcised and live according to the law of Moses as a condition for being saved.

Against this teaching, Paul posits that baptism in Christ is the true circumcision (2:11-15). This circumcision is God's own work, not something effected in the flesh by human beings. Unlike the circumcision of the flesh which obliges one to obey laws promulgated by angels and supernatural powers (2:16-23), this circumcision gives one supremacy over all these other powers since it makes the believer one with the risen, exalted, and glorified Christ. Thus, against Gnostics and Judaizers, Paul affirms that to accept other religious practices and observances as a condition for being saved is to betray one's own Christian identity or to debase oneself after one has been raised by God to glory in Christ (2:18-19). The rest of the letter works out the implications of the exaltation of the Christian through his or her baptism in Christ. It shows the Colossians why, on the one hand, they should not allow themselves to be preyed upon by these false preachers, and, on the other, what this exalted status in Christ requires of them. In this respect, Paul makes a key affirmation, often missing in contemporary debates about Jesus' lordship: The issue is not so much Jesus' lordship per se (since its truthfulness does not depend on human beings' belief or lack of it), but its implications for the Colossians themselves in their self-perception and in their relationships with God, other Christians (including all the preachers), and their participation in Christ's work.

Against this general historical background and our contextual concerns, we may study the letter in three parts: Paul's introduction, gratitude and prayer for the Colossians (1:1-12); his presentation of the person and work of Jesus (1:15-23, with vv. 13-14 as transition), and its implications for him as an apostle, the christological section (1:24–2:5); and last, but not least, its implications for the Colossians themselves (2:6–4:17), who form part of creation. The key areas of interest are the christological and consequential parenetic sections addressed to the Colossians themselves.

Paul's Gratitude and Prayer for the Colossians

As an apostle to the Gentiles, Paul joyfully and gratefully received from God the news of the conversion of the Colossians through Epaphras (1:7; 4:12). Unlike the missionaries to Africa, Paul did not personally convert the Colossians. Still news of their conversion filled him with joy and moved him to recognize, celebrate, and express thanks to God for their conversion through Epaphras. Paul's recognition that the conversion is God's work (though he in turn has to labor and toil to make this divine work manifest, 1:24–2:5) contrasts sharply with the attitude of the missionaries to Africa. An important aspect missing in missionary activity then and today is this profound recognition that God alone is the author of our or any other person's conversion. Accordingly, every missionary has a duty to thank God ceaselessly and to encourage the converts themselves to do likewise (3:16-17).

This spirit of gratitude rules out judgmental and triumphalist attitudes that pride the self in missionary achievements (as if one earned the grace of conversion of others) and judge others as "pagan," or not of the "true" denomination. The spirit of gratitude is a recognition and a celebration of the God who alone transfers both the believer and the missionary from

the dominion of darkness (un-conversion) to the influence of God's own reign effected through Jesus' beloved divine and perfect representative (this is the fundamental meaning of Son). Epaphras, Paul's fellow servant, probably reported to Paul the problems the new converts experienced in living out their faith. Paul's acknowledgment of the role of other co-workers (1:1; 4:7-17) is itself an essential aspect of one's confession of faith in Jesus as Lord. The prayerful attitude ensures that one never loses sight of God who continually sustains the missionary and the convert in their faith; otherwise both would fail. It is all God's work, an act of pure grace (1:12-14).

Christ's Mission and Work (1:9-23) and Paul's Participation in It (1:24–2:8)

After expressing his prayerful gratitude, Paul presents the person and work of Jesus, who is both the content and ground/source of the believer's faith. In early Christian kerygma, "the Lord Jesus" was the content of the proclamation (Rom 1:1,16; Acts 11:20), not philosophical, dogmatic, or creedal definitions of him, still less the different denominational tenets elaborated over the centuries by theologians and church leaders. The core of this proclamation is 1:15-23. What briefly is the message here?

Here Paul uses a hymn already known and used by the Colossians (see his similar use of a pre-existing hymn in Phil 2:6-11). The hymn celebrates the lordship of Jesus on two grounds: because he is the image of God (the perfect and visible representative of God who participates in God's act of creation) and because he is the source and principle of God's redemptive work, the church. Because he is the image of God, all things were created through him and for him (1:16-17a). Therefore, in him all things visible and invisible, in heaven and on earth hold together, whether thrones, dominions, principalities, or powers (categories already familiar to the

Colossians and presented by Paul as possible rivals to Christ's supremacy). Far from competing with Christ for lordship, the entire creation is his work and belongs to him. He maintains them in being and unites them to himself. As his property, the entire created reality, visible and invisible, owes its identity and continued existence and has its ultimate goal in him.

The hymn portrays Jesus in terms similar to that of the Lady Wisdom in Prov 8:22-31. Here personified wisdom (*sophia*) presents herself as the first of God's works who then becomes the principle of creation. This was as far as the Hebrew Bible could go, given the belief in monotheism that allowed of no trinitarian concept of God. Yet the conception of the work of Wisdom is identical with that which the New Testament ascribes to the Word made flesh, the divine *logos*, who is clearly not a creature, but God in person (John 1:1-5, 14, 18). The hymn, influenced perhaps by this wisdom figure, describes Jesus as "the firstborn of all creation" (Col 1:15). As Wisdom/Word, Jesus sustains creation in being, and guides, directs, and reconciles all things to the divine self. He establishes this unity in his person: "in him all things hold together" (*synestēken*, literally "stand bonded together," v. 17). The irony is that anybody could cite him, the agent of unity, as the principle of division and marginalization of others for whatever reason. Jesus himself would say to such persons, "Therefore what God has joined together, let no one separate" (Mark 10:9).

From Christ's identity and role in creation, the hymn moves to his identity as Word incarnate and his place and role in the mystery of redemption. It sees Jesus as the incarnate *logos, sophia*. As he was the principle and agent of creation, so is he the principle and agent of redemption. As he was the firstborn of creation, so is he "the firstborn of the dead." As he holds the universe together in his person as its creative source, so does he hold together his body the church, where all are inseparably joined and knit together as through joints and ligaments (2:19). The affirmation that he is the image of the invisible God is repeated now with nuanced emphasis that in his incarnate person, the fullness of God was pleased to dwell (1:19) "bodily" (*sōmatikōs*, 2:9). Through him God reconciles all things, in heaven and on earth, to the divine self. All things visible and invisible stand bonded together in his body, the church. Thus he becomes preeminent in all things.

This divine reconciliation, the establishment of perfect harmony (peace, *eirēnē, shalom*) is said to be through "the blood of his cross" (1:20b). This is a strange expression, especially as there is no textual variant. Seemingly, it is the cross, not Jesus, that sheds blood. The purpose of this New Testament *hapax legomenon* may be to firmly emphasize that Jesus' death was real. His death entailed a real shedding of blood that stained the cross, not a mere appearance as the Docetists held. For them Jesus did not really suffer and die on the cross, he only appeared to die. But the bloodstained cross rules out such theological subterfuge.

The section on Paul's suffering may shed light on this issue. Writing from prison (4:10) where he was imprisoned for preaching the Lord Jesus, God's gospel (Rom 1:1, 16), Paul knows that his participation in Christ's redemptive work is costly to him personally. It is not merely a matter of delivering beautiful sermons to others on the importance of the cross. One needs to know and to experience that one's belief in the crucified Jesus invites one to a death to self, or put to death all anti-Christ-like attitudes and practices in one's life, i.e., whatever stands in the way of building up his body the church.

This reading of Paul's discussion about completing the things that are lacking in Christ's sufferings, for the sake of his body the church, makes sense. In itself, Christ's death leaves nothing wanting, but we who claim to be in him need to participate in his death—a death to self, to sin, to our divisive attitudes—so that we can in turn become effective members of the body for which Christ died. Only then we will be able to help or free others to become members of that same body. For this reason, Paul later exhorts the Colossians to put to death in themselves—or "put off"—all the anti-Christlike attitudes and practices of their former lives (anger, quarreling, etc., 3:5-11) and instead to "put on" actions that reveal they are now in Christ (compassion, kindness, meekness, forgiveness, etc., 3:12-17).

As incarnate *logos,* Jesus transferred his divinity to his humanity and allowed this humanity to die or be further transformed. This death enabled his humanity to become fully one with the divinity, no longer subject to death. This death in turn became the creative source and principle of unity for his body the church. By undergoing death, Jesus defeated—for all persons—death, the ultimate enemy of life, and the cause of radical separation from the self, from other persons, and from God. Henceforth divinity in its fullness not only dwells bodily in him, but also in all others incorporated in this body. Because the divinity in its fullness dwells and acts in and through this body, this embodied divinity becomes as supreme in all things as God is supreme in all things. Viewed thus, Christ's body here is not merely the Christian church, but God's gathering *(ekklēsia tou theou).* The believing church is the first fruits of his risen body, but does not exhaust its scope. To then use this visible body, the church, as the criterion for excluding and marginalizing others is equally to miss the whole point of this mystery and to betray one's identity as a member of this body.

No Christian who believes in the mystery of the incarnation would question the hymn's affirmation about Jesus (though some Christians doubt whether Jesus was really God). The problem for the Colossians is not one of belief (intellectual assent), but of a belief that manifests

itself in actions full of love. From here Paul moves to explore how this faith should affect their self-perception (their status and identity) and the challenges it poses for them. But first, how do Christians enter into this mystery of Christ so that they share in his fullness of life (2:10) and in turn become God's visible image and principle of unity in the world (3:1-4, 10)?

The New Life in Christ

Paul answers briefly that this entrance is through baptism (2:12-15). Through this ritual, God graciously cancels the believer's sins, destroys all possible debts to any powers, and transfers him or her from the sphere of darkness and sin (3:5-9) to Jesus' sphere of influence (3:2-4). By this transfer (1:12-14), God empowers the Christian to put off the old way of life and put on the new one, created and renewed *daily* in the image of the creator. This transfer is also an ongoing activity which requires the active participation of the one transferred. This new manner of living and relating gives flesh to, and makes concretely visible, the divinity that dwells in the believer. Because such a person is a member of Christ's own body in whom the fullness of the divinity dwells (3:10), this person shares in this indwelling of the divinity. This new way of life also gives flesh to our faith in the risen and glorified Christ and testifies to our sharing in that glory. It testifies that we are rooted in Christ, holding fast to the head instead of being carried away by empty human reasoning and philosophies (2:18-19). Paul calls such philosophies "empty reasoning" (*kenē apatē*); they lack substance and are rooted in the elemental spirits of this world (2:8). By their very human origin they are powerless or incapable of empowering one to live the divine life. But in Jesus the believer actively participates in building up his cosmic body joined together by joints and ligaments. This is not pantheism but rather the real unity and values we should attach to all peoples and creation, if we see ourselves as being in Christ.

This new nature is progressively renewed in the knowledge of the creator (3:10). Like Jesus, the believer becomes in him the image of the invisible God. That imaging rules out and destroys all divisive and exclusive attitudes. Since one has deep awareness that all things in heaven and on earth belong to God who keeps, loves, and sustains them in being (Wis 11:21–12:1) in and through Christ, then one should see the self as also belonging to Christ. Then the believer should learn to cherish and relate to all things with the very love of God in Christ.

The final section of the letter spells out what this new relationship should be within the family, the domestic church (Col 3:18–4:5), and among the preachers themselves (4:7-18). The call on wives to be subject to husbands needs to be read in the patriarchal context in which the letter was written, and in a context where Christians were probably in a minority and where mixed marriages existed. Paul in that context may have been careful not to disrupt the social order. Nonetheless, John Paul II has recognized, in his *Mulieris dignitatem*, with women theologians, that these and similar New Testament passages were culturally conditioned and need to be reinterpreted christologically. The same argument applies to the exhortation to slaves to be subject to their masters, since such arguments go against the basic equality in Christ unmistakably proclaimed in the letter (Col 3:11; also Gal 3:25-29). These passages notwithstanding, Paul went beyond his time by addressing the wives and slaves as persons, a dramatic departure from ancient household codes.

CONCLUSION

In the letter, Paul affirms that the faith in Christ as Lord and principle of creation and redemption, celebrated liturgically by the Colossians, has implications and challenges for them as individuals and as a church. His treatment of Jesus' lordship originates from his concern to build up the Colossians and help them understand better their own dignity and status in the risen and exalted Christ. The issue is not the lordship of Jesus in itself, but the meaning of this lordship for them. These implications and challenges within the faith context of Paul and the Colossians are described in terms of the temptations of idolatry, externalism in religion (observances of empty practices instead of concentrating on substance, possibly alluding to Platonic philosophy in which perfect forms existed in heaven and earthly ones were only their shadows or at best imperfect forms), and fear of supernatural powers (known as evil spirits in modern Nigeria). He exhorts them not to debase themselves with such practices, since God has graciously raised and exalted them to a new status and life in Christ.

Though the question of Jesus' lordship in the Nigerian Church context is not exactly the same as in Paul's context, Paul's approach can enable us to address our own contexts with the same christological faith with which he addressed his. In the Nigerian context, we share Paul's firm belief in the supremacy of Jesus, rooted in the further belief in his uncreated divinity. Though "Word" is not used in the letter (cf. Col 1:15, 17; 2:9; John 1:1-5, 14, 18), Jesus in his humanity remains the preexistent Word through whom God created and sustains the universe and who alone reveals God's uniqueness. He remains the principle of unity for both creation and redeemed humanity. By making peace and restoring harmony through his sacrificial death, he broke down all divisive barriers that humans erect between themselves and God, especially the anthropological ones—racism, sexism, classism, ethnicism—and all the prejudices that lead us to judge, condemn, and dismiss others who differ from us or are not privileged to receive Christ as we are.

Today we would need to include those barriers between the whites and the blacks, the north and south, the two-thirds and one-third world, and where the minority exploit and feed on the fat of the land given freely by God to all, look down on those they exploit as being lazy and humanly inferior, yet still call themselves Christians. If our belief in Jesus' lordship means anything to us, then we will have to study concrete ways of being God's agents of reconciliation to ourselves as Jesus reconciled us to his own body and paid the visible price for it on the cross, that of a love unto death and resurrection. In Nigeria we accept the responsibility to promote the same ministry of reconciliation in our contexts of tribalism, religious fanaticism, and deeply divided Christianity, while we draw from the Gospels and our traditional resources of hospitality. Confession of Jesus as Lord challenges us also to that prophetic mission as a way of sharing in Christ's life-giving sufferings as Paul did, so that we in turn may complete what is still lacking in the actualization of God's gift of reconciliation in Christ. We do this for our sake and for that of others who, with the entire creation, form his body the church.

Our belief that Jesus is God makes it equally pointless to debate his uniqueness or to compare him to others as equal means of salvation. In the christological faith of Colossians, which we share, we believe that these other messiahs and religious leaders were created through Christ and for Christ. If God chose to act in person in Jesus, we human beings have no power to alter that decision or reality, however much we may dislike or dispute it. Instead we recall that this faith challenges us to "do justice, and to love kindness, and to walk humbly" with our God (Micah 6:8). Paul counsels the same when he urges the Colossians to conduct themselves "wisely toward outsiders, making the most of the time. Let your speech always be gracious, seasoned with salt [salt is a preservative], so that you may know how you ought to answer everyone" (4:5-6). Peter counsels the same to Christians of the Diaspora (1 Pet 3:15-18).

Finally, we recall that the heretical groups among the Christians themselves caused some of the problems in the Colossian church. Today our heresy may not be Gnosticism, but that divisive spirit which gives Christians a triumphalist air over others or makes us want to convert them by force. Such an approach is not from Christ but from the elemental spirits of the universe. We must not stop searching for appropriate ways to proclaim Christ and to help others to discover for themselves what God has done for them in Christ. To not do so would be to fail in our Christian responsibility and mandate from Jesus. Paul went from fanaticism through a personal encounter with Jesus to become a committed but discerning preacher (1 Cor 9:19-23). Paul invites and challenges us to put on Christ's mind. God's offer in Christ is for all, exclusive of none. Consequently, Paul invites us to share in the celebration of the God who transfers both the believer and the missionary from the dominion of darkness to the influence of God's own reign. This prayerful attitude ensures that one never loses sight of God's work in others through the lordship of Christ (Col 1:12-14). In sum, the proclamation of our faith in the unique and universal lordship of Jesus challenges us as confessors to become Christ in the world, both in deed and in truth. Then Jesus will be truly seen in our lives to be uniquely the living, loving, and caring savior of all, who loves us all to the point of laying down his life and inviting us to share in his resurrection and exaltation.

BIBLIOGRAPHY

Congregation for the Doctrine of the Faith. *"Dominus Iesus:* On the Unicity and Universality of Jesus Christ and the Church." *L'Osservatore Romano,* Weekly Edition in English, Special Insert N. 36 [1658], 6 September 2000.

John Paul II. *Novo millennio ineunte: Apostolic Letter to the Bishops, Clergy and Lay Faithful at the Close of the Great Jubilee of the Year 2000.* Vatican City: Editrice Vaticana, 2001.

Lohse, Eduard. *Colossians and Philemon: A Commentary on the Epistles to Colossians and to Philemon.* Translated by William R. Poehlmann and Robert J. Karris. Edited by Helmut Koester. Hermeneia. Philadelphia: Fortress, 1971.

MacDonald, Margaret Y. *Colossians and Ephesians.* Edited by Daniel J. Harrington. SP 17. Collegeville, Minn.: Liturgical, 2000.

Miller, J. Michael, ed. *The Encyclicals of John Paul II.* Huntington, Ind.: Our Sunday Visitor, 1996.

Okure, Teresa. "The Global Jesus." Pages 237–249 in The Cambridge Companion to Jesus. Edited by Markus Bockmuehl. Cambridge: Cambridge University Press, 2001.

———. "'In him all things hold together': A Missiological Reading of Colossians 1:15-20." *International Review of Mission* 91, no. 360 (January 2002): 62-72.

Osiek, Carolyn. "The New Testament Household Codes." Page 1707 in *International Bible Commentary: A Catholic and Ecumenical Resource for the Twenty-First Century.* Edited by William R. Farmer, et al. Collegeville, Minn.: Liturgical, 1998.

Paz, A. M. Cesar. "Colossians." Pages 1697–1709 in *International Bible Commentary [IBC]: A Catholic and Ecumenical Commentary for the Twenty-First Century.* Edited by William R. Farmer, et al. Collegeville, Minn.: Liturgical, 1998.

1 THESSALONIANS

Yeo Khiok-khng (K.K.)

Garrett-Evangelical Theological Seminary, Chicago, Illinois, USA

LIFE CONTEXT OF THE INTERPRETATION

Chinese Christians in China, Hong Kong, and Taiwan live in countries that used to hope for freedom from the oppression of western imperialism and economic depression. Now these countries look for modernization embodied in the cultural ethos of individualism, the political system of liberal democracy, the capitalist market economy, and the western consumer lifestyle. Today the East looks very much like the West. The problems of regional conflict (e.g., the tensions between India and Pakistan or China and Taiwan), religious chaos (e.g., Falung Gong), neocolonialism, military occupation, terrorism, sex slavery, urban chaos, and ecological devastation seem to point to the end of the world. Are we the "last generation"? Is "millenium anxiety" our lot? Is Chinese national history heading toward Armageddon? How should Chinese Christians respond to the peaceful coexistence of China, Taiwan, and Hong Kong? How can the church provide a model of hope for the meaning of history?

1 Thessalonians and the Relationship of God's People to the World in this Life Context

To overcome either despair or overconfidence in military or economic power, 1 Thessalonians points to the necessity for Chinese Christians to adopt a peaceful ethic grounded in love and hope. This peaceful ethic for one's life and for life with others is anchored in Christ, who is the *telos* (goal or purpose, Rom 10:4) of human history and of meaningful life. This is a key teaching of 1 Thessalonians, which resists setting a date for the end-time, because Christ as the goal of history is always about salvation rather than judgment (1 Thess 5:9).

Christians in China and Taiwan are called to present the good news of peace. The church should serve as a model of reconciliation and hope for Chinese in the "three regions across the straits." In 1 Thessalonians 1:4 Paul affirms to the congregation that, as "brothers and sisters beloved by God" (repeated in 2 Thess 2:13), they are accepted by God's unconditional love. Not knowing God's unconditional love means living in fear that will ultimately breed hatred and military violence.

First Thessalonians is a theological document responding to the Roman ideology of conquest and domination that lies behind the *Pax Romana*. In this ideology, peace and prosperity are achieved through bloodshed. Paul argues that hope lies in the spirit of Christ and in the courage to conquer death, sin, and evil in the life of individuals, institutions, and governments.

The spirit of the anti-Christ is one that is deceitful, boastful, and unwilling to accept its own vulnerability and limitations, and therefore strives to be God. Such a spirit can be discerned in Marxism and capital-

Yeo Khiok-khng (K.K.), a Malaysian Chinese, is Harry R. Kendall Associate Professor of New Testament at Garrett-Evangelical Theological Seminary and Advisory Member of the Graduate Faculty at Northwestern University. He is an ordained elder of the Chicago Chinese Churches Association. He is a visiting professor at major universities in China and has published eighteen books and numerous articles in both English and Chinese, including *What Has Jerusalem to Do with Beijing?* (1998), and *Chairman Mao Meets the Apostle Paul* (2002) and *Navigating Romans Through Cultures* (ed. 2004).

ism, communism and democ-racy, the cults and the occult, religion and atheism alike. The hope of the Pauline proclamation in 1 Thessalonians assures us that, even though

death, evil, and sin might now dominate human history, life and resurrection will prevail at the Parousia when the salvation of Christ will define human destiny.

CONTEXTUAL COMMENT

An Overview of 1 Thessalonians

The Thessalonian congregation faces affliction and suffering (1 Thess 1:6-8, 2:14-16, 3:3-4). Their conversion, which involved breaking with their past and social environment, has brought hostility upon them. They are persecuted because of the politically inflammatory connotations of their Christian proclamation, especially their apocalyptic and millennial faith, and because of their alleged polemical attitude toward the civic cult. The Thessalonian community is shaken and disturbed (3:3). Some members grieve over members who have died (4:13-18); some are without hope with regard to the Parousia (5:1-11); some reject Paul's traditional ethic (4:1-12). The problem of hopelessness for the Thessalonian Christians is doubly compounded by the absence of Christ (their Benefactor) and Paul (the agent of their Benefactor).

Paul's theology of hope in 1 Thessalonians points to the presence of the living God (3:9; 4:8, 17). God is the One who chooses (1:4), calls (2:12), gives the Spirit (4:8), wills the believer's sanctification (4:3), and makes each believer perfectly holy (5:23). Being the divine agent of this loving parent, Christ has died and been raised for the sake of the Thessalonian congregation (1:10; 4:14; 5:10). He is destined to be the saving and sanctifying instrument (5:9, 18, 23), the one who distributes divine wrath to oppressors and peace to believers (1:10; 5:28). He is the source of their hope as they wait for his return (1:3, 10; 4:15; 5:23).

1 Thessalonians 2:12, 4:9-12, and 5:2, 15 and Their Teaching

Paul tells the congregation in 1 Thessalonians 2:12 that he is "urging and encouraging you and pleading that you lead a life

worthy of God, who calls you into his own kingdom and glory." The kingdom and glory language is best understood in the context of the political messianism of the time: the Augustan Roman expectation of the new age with a divine ruler. This form of messianism and its realized eschatology must have appealed to some in the audience more than Paul's message about Christ whose kingdom is yet to come. The realized eschatology of the *ataktoi* (disorderly ones) was a case in point. But Paul suggests the dynamic, progressive, and yet-to-be-consummated reality of the kingdom and glory of God by using the present tense of "calling" (*kalountos*) in 1 Thessalonians 2:12.

Paul charges the Thessalonians to live a life of quietness (not disruption), order (not chaos) and familial love (not enmity). Paul says, regarding this tradition, that the Thessalonians are "God-taught" (4:9, *theodidaktoi*)—a word used by the author of Isaiah 54:13; see also John 6:45) in which the children of Zion were looking forward to the age of salvation. If the Thessalonians are "God-taught," they now participate in the new age of salvation, energized by the Spirit. The community is to love one another (4:9), to sharpen their identity and mutual tie with love, as well as to gain the respect of outsiders by their fruit of love (4:12).

In line with what God has taught them, Paul exhorts and charges the Thessalonians by means of four infinitive clauses. They are to love more and more, to aspire to live quietly, to be responsible for their own affairs, and to work with their hands (4:10-11). The aim of the exhortation is to lead the Thessalonians to share the community resources among themselves and to build the community of God. The exhortations make clear that the Pauline community in the pagan world of Thessalonica has to be internally harmonious and self-sufficient as well as externally reputable.

This love toward one another is vital in the Christian community; it serves to reinforce the spiritual ties of its members. Brotherhood (and implicitly, sisterhood) is not only a metaphor; it is a reality for Christians whose conversion often means the breaking up of familial ties. No wonder the word "brother and sister" (NRSV) is used repeatedly in 1 Thessalonians (1:4, 2:1, 9, 14, 17; 3:2, 7; 4:1, 9, 10, 13; 5:1, 4, 12, 25, 26, 27). The word "brothers" (Gr., *adelphoi,* to be read inclusively as "brothers and sisters") is used explicitly thrice in contrast to outsiders (4:8-12), to the rest (of people, 4:13) and to those who will be destroyed (5:3) as a way to emphasize the unique identity and bonding of the Thessalonian Christians. In the same vein, God is addressed as "Father" not just of Jesus, but also of believers. Therefore, the spiritual brotherhood/sisterhood of all believers in Christ is underscored as a divine election to redemption, rather than to destruction (1 Thess 5:9). Spiritual brotherhood/sisterhood, if realized in a new community in Christ, would mean true brotherly/sisterly love that is as precious, if not more so, than familial brotherly/sisterly love.

Brotherly/sisterly love is the hallmark of a Christian community that reflects its vitality, but also is a microcosmic representation of this Christian community as an ideal model for the wider culture. To the non-Christian community or "the outsider"—a term often used to refer to those outside the church (Mark 4:11; 1 Cor 5:12; Col 4:5)—the disruptive behavior of the Christians who refuse to work would be perceived as a scandal or even as a burden (1 Thess 4:11). Paul and the members of the early Christian community depended not on themselves as individuals, but on God and on one another (see Gal 6:2-5 and Phil 4:10-14) in a mutuality that did not burden each other.

In 1 Thessalonians 5:2, Christ is the eschatological Lord-Judge. The wrath of the Lord-Judge is yet to arrive, and all persons will be subjected to it. Christians can take courage, but not because of their virtue. The source of their courage is rather that God has destined them not for wrath, but for salvation. In other words, fatalistic doctrines and escapist ethics are not the core of Paul's teaching; rather, realistic hope and responsible ethics are! Paul writes, "See that none of you repays evil for evil, but always seek to do good to one another and to all" (1 Thess 5:15). This verse addresses how the congregation should treat not only the in-group but also the outsiders—"to one another and to all." Paul does not accept the traditional wisdom of *lex talionis.* Instead, he ignores retaliation and encourages respectful coexistence and mutual transformation through love and hope. His mandate is "seek to do good to one another and to all." It would be a disgrace if Mainland China and Taiwan, nations of the same ethnic family, could not coexist and in the end mutually destroyed each other.

The Thessalonians are asked to live honorably as children of the Great Benefactor who benefit from God's favor (grace). Chinese Christians are asked to be benefactors to all. In other words, in the "todayness" of God's future (an eschatology of the "already and not-yet"), they are God's channels of blessing (1 Thess 1:7-8). Using honor language to speak of these Christians in 1 Thessalonians 1:7-8, Paul leads them to see honor with an eschatological eye focused on the ultimate, viz., the imminent day of the Lord, rather than with a temporal eye focused on the present. It is honorable to turn from idols to serve a living and true God and to wait for God's Son from heaven, whom God raised from the dead, Jesus who delivers us from the wrath to come (1:9–10). It is honorable to lead a life worthy of God, who calls us into God's own kingdom and glory (2:11–12). It is honorable to belong to our God and Father, who makes our hearts holy to prepare us for the coming of our Lord Jesus with all his holy ones (3:12–13). It is honorable to have the destiny of obtaining salvation rather than wrath (5:9). And it is honorable to trust in hope that the God of shalom will make us whole and blameless at the coming of our Lord Jesus Christ (5:23).

The interactive relationship of faith, love, and hope is a central motif in 1 Thessalonians. By trusting in God (rather than in the political propaganda of the *Pax Romana* described in 1 Thess 5:3) through the gospel of salvation (5:9) brought about by the death and resurrection of Jesus Christ (4:14), Christians (1:7) are called (1:4) and taught (4:9) a dynamic faith (5:23) that is manifested in love (1:3; 3:6; 4:9, 10; 5:8) and hope (1:3; 2:19; 4:13; 5:8). Love is a harmonious, joyful, interactive relationship among the Thessalonians (and Chinese) as well as between the called community and the calling God. As a community, they are the corporate "in Christ" (2:14; 3:8; 4:1, 16; 5:12,

18). As they are God-taught to love one another (4:9), so, according to Paul's exhortation, they should more and more actualize the gift of love in their lives (4:10, 12).

Faith without hope results in fear and uneasiness of mind. Faith without hope is like an exhausted engine, a car out of gas. In times of affliction, hope energizes believers by giving them the joy and assurance of God's love, a purpose in life, and a calling they can follow. The Pauline theology of Parousia-hope offers humanity a way to reach holistic faith, love, and hope. The whole reality of salvation in Christ is promised in the death and resurrection of Christ, but fulfilled and consummated in the Parousia anticipated by believers in the here and now (5:23).

CONCLUSION

Chinese Christians, who understand eschatological hope and practice love, embody the message of community (national and global) reconciliation. This message refuses the government's "will to power" that could end in national lawlessness and self-destruction (5:3). First Thessalonians encourages believers to have the hope that leads them to live a life worthy of the gospel (2:12; 4:1)—that is, a life of sanctification (4:3, 4, 7; 5:23) and blamelessness (3:13; 5:23), rather than a life of porneia (immorality, 4:3), transgression (4:6), and destined for wrath (5:8-9). In waiting for the Parousia, believers "serve a living and true God" (1:9). A Christian ethic is informed and motivated by eschatology, in contrast to the non-eschatological theologies and modern ideologies that have no sense of an ethical lifestyle. Hope assures the validity of traditional ethics and the proper mission of the church within the world.

Pauline eschatology is not exclusively preoccupied with the future; it is very much concerned with the present as offering us a decisive opportunity to transform the world. Paul's concern in this letter was with the survival, meaningfulness, and holiness of a Thessalonian congregation in the midst of suffering, ambiguity, and impurity. All this teaching directly applies to the present Chinese Christian communities, for which Pauline eschatology constantly nurtures imaginative hope.

BIBLIOGRAPHY

(See 2 Thessalonians)

2 THESSALONIANS

Yeo Khiok-khng (K.K.)

Garrett-Evangelical Theological Seminary, Illinois, Chicago, USA

LIFE CONTEXT OF THE INTERPRETATION

In the midst of the political struggles between the right and the ultra-left campaigns during the Cultural Revolution, Chinese Christians, and the rest of the Chinese people, suffered greatly. During the ten catastrophic years (1966-1976) of the "Cultural Destruction," all churches were closed and many congregations met in homes or went underground. There were 700,000 Protestant Christians in a population of about 500 million in 1949, but by September 1976, there were an estimated 10 million Christians, and by 2000 the estimated numbers were between 40 and 80 million. The eschatological hope of 2 Thessalonians had sustained the vitality of Chinese Christianity.

2 Thessalonians and the Relationship of God's People to the World in China

Chinese Christians accepted the eschatological hope in 2 Thessalonians that God called them for the purpose of enduring affliction and persecution. They were able to see the final destiny of this despairing world in light of the divine purpose, so their faith abounded and their love increased (2 Thess 1:3).

The idea that the justice of God ruled over the world encouraged Chinese Christians to counter the communist worldview. The righteous seemed to suffer while the wicked flourished; the world seemed to be ruled by evil, not by God. But that was only part of the picture. With its ultimate hope for Christ's coming, 2 Thessalonians 2:1-11 gave them a larger view (2 Thess 1:7; cf. 1 Thess 5:1-11). This eschatological worldview assured Chinese Christians that God's kingdom would surely come, and that they could maintain their faith in the one, all-powerful and righteous God in the face of the harsh realities of evil in the world.

CONTEXTUAL COMMENT

An Overview of 2 Thessalonians

Second Thessalonians corrects the wrong assumption regarding the realized Parousia ("the day of the Lord is already here," 2:2) by contrasting the false and real Messiah, the false and real Parousia and hope, and the false and real ethic. Paul corrects the problem of suffering by affirming the sovereignty of the Lord (of the eschatological day). The major exhortations of the epistle concern moral integrity (1:11; 2:16-17; 3:1-3, 5, 16) and love of truth.

The justice of God in 2 Thessalonians is a prominent motif helpful to Christians enduring persecution. God has called believers,

Yeo Khiok-khng (K.K.), a Malaysian Chinese, is a Harry R. Kendall Associate Professor of New Testament at Garrett-Evangelical Theological Seminary and Advisory Member of the Graduate Faculty at Northwestern University. He is an ordained elder of the Chicago Chinese Churches Association. He is a visiting professor at major universities in China and has published eighteen books and numerous articles in both English and Chinese, including What Has Jerusalem to Do with Beijing? (1998), *Chairman Mao Meets the Apostle Paul* (2002), and *Navigating Romans Through Cultures* (ed. 2004).

and they suffer to demonstrate the just judgment of God (1:5). The justice of God is shown when those who suffer are vindicated and rewarded and the persecutors punished. God is the executor of justice, the apocalyptic judge, and Christ is God's agent. Jesus the Lord, the final judge of the coming Parousia, is able to take away the power of the lawless one by the breath of his mouth (2:8). He will punish the persecutors (1:9). The persecutors who do not obey the gospel of Christ (1:8) and who refuse to love the truth (2:10) will experience God's eschatological wrath. Christians, however, are called "through belief in the truth" (2:13), and they will obtain the glory of Jesus Christ (2:14). The hope and salvation of Christians is not only in their present baptism but in the future arrival of the Lord, when they will gather before him (2:1). The Lord "will strengthen you and guard you from the evil one" (3:3).

2 Thessalonians 2:3-15: Truth against Lawlessness and Deception

Mao's revolutionary ideology was also eschatological in the sense that it proclaimed an imminent paradise on earth. Mao boldly gave new names to China, such as "new humanity," "new society," and "new China" during the Cultural Revolution. By these names he implied that the unprecedented new reality of hope had already arrived.

In demonstrating his conviction that the Day has not yet arrived, Paul provides his readers with a fourfold apocalyptic schema, a series of signs-events, which will precede the arrival of that Day. These end-time signs-events were partially fulfilled then, but the Parousia had not yet arrived.

The first sign is apostasy (2:3). In light of the religious context of the pericope and the reference to the temple in 2:4, the apostasy here is best understood as a religious apostasy, but with a political connotation. It could be a departure from the divine order, immorality, or a rejection of the gospel message. In the context of this passage, it probably means turning away from the "love of truth" (2:10) and the immorality that results from it, leading to destruction.

The second sign is the manifestation of the "lawless one," also called, literally, "the son of destruction" (2 Thess 2:3). The genitive "of destruction" refers to the quality of the person, that is, he is the destructive one, although he is also the one who is "destined for destruction" (as NRSV translates). Verses 3-7 speak of the destruction done by the lawless one, while alone 2:8 predicts his destiny—Jesus will destroy him. The noun "destruction" in v. 3 becomes a participle in v. 10, indicating the irony of the result of the lawless one's activity: he ends up being destroyed!

The identity of the lawless one is expressed in the two participles of 2:4: "opposing and exalting" himself over "every so-called god" (author's translation [a.t.]). He is imitating the divine in order to become the anti-benefactor. The man of destruction's thirst for veneration is evident in the way he seeks to occupy the shrine alone. He is not satisfied to sit alongside others in a pantheon. He wants to be God! The activities of the lawless one are satanic in nature, for he is the agent of Satan who opposes the divine and moral realms. Paul acknowledges that the mystery of lawlessness is already at work now, but the lawless one has not yet been revealed because he is under restraint.

The third sign is the fact that the lawless one is "restrained," the reason for his delayed arrival. The congregations already knew about the "restrained" one and the "mystery of lawlessness" (2:6-7) from Paul's traditional eschatological doctrine ("do you not remember that while I was still with you, I often told you these things," 2:5, a.t.). Unfortunately, this information is not available to later readers.

The fourth sign is Jesus' destruction of the lawless one: "The Lord Jesus will slay [the lawless one to be revealed] with the breath of his mouth and will bring [the lawless one] to an end at the sudden appearance of his manifestation" (2:8, a.t.). Borrowing the imagery from Isaiah 11:4 (LXX; "he will smite the earth with the word of his mouth and with the breath of his lips he will slay the wicked"), Paul combines the two clauses and then adds a parallel to it. The two means by which the lawless one will be destroyed are the breath of Jesus' mouth and Christ's manifestation.

After the four signs, Paul shows the sovereignty of God (2:11-12): "God sends them a deluding influence" (2:11, a.t.). Righteousness is the virtue of the apocalyptic benefactor, and deception is the hallmark of the false benefactor. Delusion is sent to those who previously rejected the gospel when they heard it. At this climactic anti-Parousia, God intervenes by sending this deluding influence as a judgment "so that they may believe the lie." The lie/deception here is contrasted with truth in the next verse (2:12). The belief that "the Day of the Lord is already here" is the lie that this passage is trying to correct.

The primary intention of 2:1-15 is to contrast the pseudo-Christ and the real Christ in order to prove that the Parousia has not yet arrived. The lawless one is an anti-Christ in his anti-Parousia, anti-reign-of-God, and anti-divine-judgment activities. Demonic force is operative on those who oppose the law, such as the lawless one who has "refused to love the truth and so be saved" (2:10).

The Day of the Lord, as described in this passage, does not just portray God's sovereignty in judging the evil ones; it also portrays God's sovereignty in delivering the suffering righteous. The sovereignty of God is stressed by the effect of the "delusion" sent by God; it confirms the belief in the falsehood spread by the lawless one. Christ, the apocalyptic Benefactor, protects the Thessalonians from this evil one. In contrast to those who reject the gospel and end up being punished, those who "have faith in the truth" (2:13) and "love the truth" (2:10) will be delivered in the end.

Retaliation against the Red Guards was not the revenge of the Chinese Christians.

Chinese Christians have learned that the Crucified God in his death does not accept the "will to power" of the "permanent revolution." The cross is a violent event, but it does not condone violence. Christ's violent death on the cross publicly demonstrates God's wound of love rather than the human power to kill. The church, as the body of Christ, is to live out the faithful life of the incarnated and crucified and coming Christ. The church is born, called, and sanctified by God to be the agent of God's benefaction and salvation in the world. The church is a political-theological reality in that, though it does not seek to form a government for a nation-state, it is the radical realization of God's grace and of God's justice upon the world that creates God's community of trust, faithfulness, equality, and accountability.

As bearers of the holy in China, the Chinese churches are the *ekklēsia* of God in New China. Ekklēsia is a common term referring to the citizens' assembly or a trade guild or burial society in Paul's day. Early Christianity then adopted the term as a sacralization of the secular *polis* into a heavenly *politeuma* or state. The church as the body of Christ practices the love-feast and proclaims the divine future of hope, wholeness, and salvation in midst of the suffering world. The church's task is to proclaim the radical future of God that offers hope and possibilities in a world where violence and possible destruction are the old scripts of life. Its task is to encourage people to place their faith in God and give them new courage to live against the odds of life.

The Pauline interpretation of the "anti-Christ" who claims to be God remains the most illustrative example of how a political or religious leader claims to be God and assumes hegemonic power and thus brings about lawlessness by eliminating *religious* virtue among people. The "anti-Christ" in 2 Thessalonians and Mao Zedong in China used realized eschatology and de-eschatology (no eternal hope) to breed violence and destruction.

CONCLUSION

Hope has produced miracles among Chinese Christians for the past forty years. The blood of the martyrs is the seed of faith, and Christian hope nurtures that faith. Most Chinese congregations have loved to study the New Testament's eschatological theology, from which they have derived strength, faith, and hope. Christians "remembered" (1 Thess 2:9) and "knew" (1 Thess 1:5; 2:1, 2, 5, 11; 3:3, 4; 4:2, 4, 5) what they had been "told" (1 Thess 3:4, 4:6; 2 Thess 2:5, 15) and "received" (1 Thess 2:13; 4:1; 2 Thess 2:15), and instructed (1 Thess 4:2, 11). In contrast to Mao's followers, Chinese Christians have seen the whole picture of God's revelation working itself out in history. They have seen the end (*telos* as goal) of history, which grants them the assurance of victory, comfort in suffering, and hope in the midst of dismay. They have learned to be open to God and to the future in an attitude of obedience and surrender.

BIBLIOGRAPHY

Bultmann, Rudolf. *The Presence of Eternity: History and Eschatology.* New York: Harper, 1957.

Collins, Raymond F., ed. *The Thessalonian Correspondence.* BETL 87. Leuven, Belgium: Leuven University Press, 1990.

Donfried, Karl Paul, and Johannes Beutler, eds. *The Thessalonians Debate: Methodological Discord or Methodological Synthesis?* Grand Rapids: Eerdmans, 2000.

Evans, Robert. "Eschatology and Ethics: A Study of Thessalonica and Paul's Letters to the Thessalonians." PhD diss., University of Basel, 1967.

Malherbe, Abraham J. *The Letters to the Thessalonians.* AB 37B. New York: Doubleday, 2000.

_____. *Paul and the Thessalonians: The Philosophic Tradition of Pastoral Care.* Philadelphia: Fortress, 1987.

Jewett, Robert. *The Thessalonian Correspondence: Pauline Rhetoric and Millenarian Piety.* Foundations and Facets. Philadelphia: Fortress, 1986.

Richard, Earl J. *First and Second Thessalonians.* Ed. Daniel J. Harrington. SP 11. Collegeville, Minn.: Liturgical, 1995.

Wanamaker, Charles A. *The Epistles to the Thessalonians: A Commentary on the Greek Text.* NIGTC. Grand Rapids: Eerdmans, 1990.

Yeo Khiok-khng. *Chairman Mao Meets the Apostle Paul: Christianity, Communism, and the Hope of China.* Grand Rapids: Brazos, 2002.

1 TIMOTHY

Elsa Tamez

Universidad Bíblica Latinoamericana, Costa Rica

Translated from the Spanish by Rubén A. Muñoz

LIFE CONTEXT OF THE INTERPRETATION

The southern *barrios* (neighborhoods) of San José, Costa Rica are very different from the exuberant forest and beaches that tourists see. These barrios, where jam-packed living conditions are the order of the day, are overpopulated, unhealthy, and poor. This is true for the majority of San Jose's neighborhoods, but here in the southern barrios the problems are more visible: cheap drugs, alcoholism, robbery, domestic violence, lack of clean drinking water, and unemployment prevail. Many women are involuntary heads of households because their husbands have abandoned them for another woman, migrated to the mainland United States with the promise to send money to their families, or are alcoholics unable to support their families. Thus, everyone struggles to survive one day at a time, working hard in any possible job. These barrios attract politicians at election times; because of their high population-density, they are important if one wants to win the popular vote. These barrios are also the home of highly religious women who have emerged as leaders of the community. It is from this context that I am reading 1 Timothy.

1 Timothy and the Church's Relationship with the World

In these barrios, church attendance is very high, no matter what the denomination, because people need to feel closer to God. They want to have God as a friend who listens to their problems. The more they lose confidence in politicians who make promises but never fulfill them, the more they hope that God will meet their needs. Women regularly attend these churches, even though men are most often the church leaders. In some congregations women hold positions of authority as senior ministers.

The Rejection

Studying 1 Timothy is a challenge for us women because, in this epistle, it is not easy to find God as a liberator who hears the cry of the people, of the poor, of those who struggle for daily life. For this reason, 1 Timothy is almost never studied in the *barrios*. Sometimes texts such as 1 Timothy 4:12 are read to motivate the youth in their fight for purity, but such readings do not take into account the ancient contextual problems that these passages addressed.

Women play a crucial role in the base Christian communities and the neighborhood-associations of the barrios by leading, sustaining, and motivating these communities. To read a text such as 1 Timothy 2:12, "I permit no woman to teach or to have authority over a man; she is to keep silent," without discernment and proper understanding would be to undermine the

Elsa Tamez, Professor of New Testament, the Latin American Biblical University in Costa Rica, leads workshops through all Latin America on contextual reading of the Bible. The recipient of the Award of Excellence on Biblical Interpretation (Associates Church Press, 1979) and of the Hans-Sigrist Award (University of Bern, 2000) for Contextual Biblical Hermeneutic, she is the author of numerous publications including *The Bible of the Oppressed* (1982); *The Scandalous Message of James* (1989); *The Amnesty of Grace: Justification by Faith from a Latin American Perspective* (1993); and *When the Horizons Close: Rereading Ecclesiastes* (2000).

accomplishments of these women. For them, being silent would involve submitting to a family model that does not exist in their daily life.

In addition, texts such as 1 Timothy 6:1-2, which instructs slaves to obey their masters, are very problematic. Similarly repulsive are those texts that display intolerance for a dialogue between traditional customs and new theological arguments (1:3-4; 4:1-3) and those that treat any defiance of the ironclad tradition as if any innovation were evil (1:10, 20; 6:20). Furthermore, texts that defend doctrine against their enemies with apologetic statements using military metaphors are horrifying (1:18; 6:12). It is much easier to understand how threatening these teachings are when one hears people speaking of their lives and persecutions under the military dictatorships of Nicaragua, El Salvador, and Guatemala. In such situations, the simple fact of being singled out as someone who thinks differently or as a friend of "the other group" has fatal consequences.

These are some of the reasons why there are no popular studies and commentaries about 1 Timothy in Latin America. People want a God who sides with them when society is against them. As a woman who works among these groups, I cannot view 1 Timothy as a normative text. Galatians 3:28 and the texts about Jesus' interactions with women are more important. Many sincere believers who read the Bible as literally inspired by the Holy Spirit and who approach the Bible as normative struggle with this issue. Why does God's point of view change in these texts? Others encounter these texts with anger for the centuries of painful history during which 1 Timothy has set the norm for the life of the church.

The Search for Understanding

Women from the *barrio* congregations love the Bible, and they want to understand it and to struggle with it. Their religious experience does not allow them to toss a biblical book in the trash just because it does not speak about liberation. We biblical scholars in these groups know that it is impossible to apply the hermeneutic of liberation that we are accustomed to practicing. We must envision a process of reconstruction and be ready to reject some of the teachings of this text. We must understand why particular teachings are affirmed in the particular historical and cultural context of 1 Timothy, and have the freedom not to accept those teachings that paradoxically contradict the will of a God who is in solidarity with the poor and the oppressed. In our context, this new step in popular hermeneutic must be truly liberating.

When we distance ourselves from 1 Timothy and reject it, it becomes impossible to consider important and interesting aspects of this letter: its proclamation of universal salvation (4:10); its critique of riches and wealth (6:17-19); its reference to wealthy women (2:9); and especially its identification of the desire for money as a root of all evils (6:9). These topics are worthy of reflection. However, one must also take into account those passages that legitimize marginalization and oppression. A uniform reading is necessary; the themes and textual features of the epistle must be read in terms of the entire epistle. In order to understand the misogynistic features of the epistle, I highlight gender and social class.

CONTEXTUAL COMMENT

An Overview of 1 Timothy

The letter, written at the end of the first century or beginning of the second under the pseudonym of Paul the apostle, is best understood when one seeks to understand its historical context. The letter does not describe the community. Its instructions and exhortations should not be confused with descriptions of the community (Schüssler Fiorenza 1983, 310). It presents instructions to Timothy that reflect the author's convictions, but that are also certainly motivated by particular circumstances.

The author had four primary concerns regarding the behavior of the Ephesian community (1:3; 3:14-15): (a) the powerful presence of some wealthy people, especially female benefactors (2:9-10; 6:7-10, 17-19); (b) the disturbing participation of women (2:9-15; 5:3-16); (c) teachings that differ from the regular or accepted tradition (1:3-4; 4:1-10; 6:3-5; 6:20-21) and; (d) the opinions that the Greco-Roman society might have about this Christian group (2:2; 3:4, 7, 12; 5:14; 6:1). These four concerns are related to the power struggle between the female benefactors and the officially elected leaders— a struggle with implications for the relation of the Christian community with the Greco-Roman society.

This church seems to be astray: more and more the wealthy impose their views on others. However strange in light of tradition, new theological doctrines and practices are proving very attractive, especially to women. Also, the Pauline heritage of an equalitarian community (Gal 3:28), highly regarded among women and slaves, is problematic for the Greco-Roman patriarchal society. The author responds with a strongly patriarchal discourse intended both to resolve the conflicts *and* to regain power over the community. For him, these power struggles endanger the proclamation of the gospel to others, as well as endangering the tradition and the community itself. The author exhorts his readers to apply the patriarchal, socio-cultural code of conduct within the community in the same way a father runs his family (3:4-5, 12, 14-15).

Timothy is caught between a church where the rich and powerful rule and a set of authoritarian instructions that he must enforce in the congregation and that will exclude all women, rich and poor, from leadership positions—a most serious dilemma. Today, it is important to have this particular ancient context clearly in mind when this letter is read in the church. Knowing Timothy's situation allows us to read the letter without fear of its being a universal, immutable teaching. We can then better understand the author and the text, and be free to distance ourselves from these exhortations when they do not reflect the teachings and practices of the Jesus movement.

The Rich Women and the Power Struggle (2:9-12)

First Timothy is commonly viewed as a book against all women, whatever their social status. From the perspective of the women of the southern *barrios* in San José, it is immediately apparent that the restrictions upon personal dress concern rich women. If these exhortations ended in the middle of 2:9, the women's social status could pass unnoticed. It could be normal in this pious tradition for women to dress modestly (*aidōs*), simply, and decently (*sōphrosynē*). However, the author does not stop here; he emphasizes that it is not proper in the Christian community to see women with braided hair (*plegma*) and adorned with gold, pearls, and expensive clothes. Some ancient artifacts show rich women with elaborate hairstyles braided with golden and precious stones and brooches. Pearls could be worn on rings, necklaces, and earrings. The author contrasts simplicity and modesty (2:9a) with wealthy women's ostentation (2:9b).

Why does the author attack these rich women? Is it because they are women? Because they are rich? Or for both reasons? It is also plausible that this authoritarian and patriarchal text reflects a power struggle between rich women and elected church leaders. Perhaps these women benefactors thought they had the right to impose their views and to rule over the rest of the congregation as patronesses. The phrase, "Let no one despise your youth" (4:12) and the author's suggestion that the elders should receive double pay (5:17) could be signs of such a conflict. Similarly, the exhortation that rich people should expect rewards from God for sharing their goods with the poor (6:17-20) might be understood as duplicating the patron-client relationship in the Roman Empire. In this relationship rich people expected reciprocity for a favor to a client, although the rewards are now given by God and not by the client. However, this exhortation can also be understood as a criticism of the patron-client system, calling the rich in the congregation not to be haughty, and underscoring that their role is to give generously without expecting rewards or reciprocity in this world (Kidd 1990, 155-6).

When one reads 1 Timothy 2:12, one should note that this prohibition against women teaching or having authority over men is found in the passage about the rich women benefactors. Although the Greek word *andros* could be translated "husband," in the context of the congregation it probably referred to a male leader. Even though the text is directed to all women in the community, its emphasis is on the leadership role of rich women (2:9b). This prohibition shows that women were in fact teaching in the church, a common occurrence among early Christian communities. For some reason, the author insists that this practice should stop. Perhaps the author views their teaching as foreign to the gospel, or he thinks that these teachers have created tensions within the community by sharing their great power and influence with other women. Another alternative is that only one or a few rich women, through the Greco-Roman patron-client system, exercised too much power over the male leadership.

Therefore 1 Timothy reflects a power struggle between male leaders and rich women who taught without official authorization and perhaps aspired to the position of bishop (3:1). In response, the author sends instructions to take power and authority away from these women. First Timothy 2:13-15 tries to offer scriptural and theological reasons for the view that a woman should not teach and exercise authority over a man, and to explain the differences between gender roles. The

text justifies the traditional theological understanding of domestic roles. Because of childbearing, women's place is in the house and they should submit to their husbands; hence they should not have leadership positions in the Christian community.

Today, this teaching is readily grasped in the poor churches. Commonly such churches have one rich family, or a rich woman or a rich man, who has authority over the community's leadership simply because of her or his social position. Today, we women in such churches understand and reject this situation. Yet, we also reject the author's proposal to neutralize women, because such a proposal penalizes women of every social status.

It is somewhat unusual that the author relates maternity to salvation (2:15), because this connection is neither a part of Pauline theology nor the theology of the other Pastoral Epistles. Thus one might argue that the author uses the phrase "she will be saved (*sōthēsetai*) by bearing children" in a spiritual or theological sense. This sense is based upon an orthodox interpretation of "having children" as referring to Eve and her promised descendant, the Messiah, who as the savior will rescue her together with Adam. If one accepts this interpretation, then one must understand the woman's task of performing household chores in the same spiritual sense. The problem is that in early Christianity, there was neither a single orthodox theology nor an established canon, but a diversity of theological trends and interpretations of Genesis.

The phrase "she will be saved through childbearing" (2:15) is thus best understood as an argument used to convince women to continue in their assigned traditional roles. Of course, it is one thing to affirm that the text must be read in this way and another to accept its perspective. This teaching is most difficult to accept in our modern context and with our modern beliefs. Raising children (*teknogonias*) is related to getting married and establishing a family, a main topic in this letter. The salvation of women through childbearing (2:15) cannot be read independently of 4:1-3, where the author explicitly rejects the teaching of those who "forbid marriage."

For the author, those who forbid marriage (and promote other ascetic practices) "renounce the faith by paying attention to deceitful spirits and teachings of demons" (4:1). Likewise, 2:15 cannot be read independently from the teaching regarding younger widows who are in a dilemma after having made a vow of chastity; thus the author states, "I would have younger widows marry, bear children, and manage their households, so as to give the adversary no occasion to revile us" (5:14).

In sum, the problem in the ancient community was much broader than conflicts with rich women benefactors. The problem's starting point might have been a conflict with two or three rich women. However, some (rich and poor) male members of the congregation found problems with the behavior of certain (rich and poor) women in the community, including the younger widows who did not follow the usual prescribed domestic roles. The patriarchal ideology of the early church extended through all social strata, as is also the case in present-day Latin America.

The Option for the Widows, Poor but Obedient (5:3-16)

A concern for the widows is an important theme in the letter. The text is complex because it mixes together the issues of the widows' economic situation, their age, and their role in the church. There are poor widows who need financial aid, younger widows who are "too active" (from the author's perspective) and families who do not provide for the widows who are their relatives. In addition, there was a special registry of widows in the Christian community, divided according to age, economic situation, and whether or not their behavior was consistent with the traditional Greco-Roman role of widows.

Apparently, there were not enough funds to help all the widows (5:3-4, 16). Thus it appears that only the really impoverished ones were eligible for support. However, other factors, apart from economic necessity, played a role in enrolling women on the official registry of widows, namely age and behavior. Certain widows, especially the younger ones, were to be denied enrollment because their behavior did not conform to the patriarchal ideal that the author wanted to enforce.

The author wanted both to regulate the assistance to the widows and to update the official registry of widows. In both cases, economic needs played a significant role. But so did patriarchal ideology and the struggle for power between the male leadership and some rich women. In 5:5-6 social status is clearly marked; real widows are poor and abandoned, and put all their confidence and hope in God. According to the author, the false widows, the ones who are not poor, have an easy life abandoning themselves to pleasures.

For the author, wealth and a libertine lifestyle go together, whether or not this happens in actual practice. The author wants to lower the rich women from the positions they assumed due to their power and influence (rather than from being elected.) For this purpose, he calls into question their morality. Latin American women easily understand this moral argument because it is still used today when one wants to discredit women.

Therefore we may infer that the author wanted both to stop financial assistance to some widows and to eliminate them from the registry. He targets especially those widows, poor or not, who do not fulfill their traditional roles in a patriarchal household, and who prefer to work for the church and the community. The author is also much concerned about the way in which the congregation is perceived by the wider patriarchal Greco-Roman society, which also looked down on women who did not fulfill their traditional family role and did not submit to the head of the household. In addition, it is important to note that the male leaders of the church, confronted by these widows, also have a public role in the larger community; as men they have the privileges of patriarchy. On this basis the author emphasizes that the widows on the official registry must maintain moral behavior, especially in the case of the young widows (5:9-15). Furthermore, there must be a clear distinction between the devout and pious widows and those who are not, especially those who, the author states, live for pleasure (5:6). In summary, the author of 1 Timothy maintains an "option for the poor" widows. He is committed to supporting them, but his commitment is predicated upon their obedience to the traditional Greco-Roman domestic code.

Excluding certain widows from the registry is understandable: those supported by their relatives (5:4-8); those appropriately assisted by rich women (5:16); and those widows who are themselves rich. The young widows were not necessarily rich and thus could be supported by the church. But then, if they did not need to work in order to survive and had free time to visit, teach, and comfort one another in their homes, they would not fulfill their domestic role as defined by the patriarchal society. Thus the author suggests that it is better for them to get married, to have a family (a traditional patriarchal family, of course), and to be busy with children at home.

The language used about the young widows does not have much weight in itself as a rhetorical discourse; it works only because of the patriarchal ideology and its artificial definition of women. It is only a myth that young widows "want to marry" (5:11) and "live for pleasure" (5:6), and that they are being "idle," "gossiping," and "gadding about from house to house" (5:13). Today, in patriarchal Costa Rica and Latin America it is also believed that young widows

> "madly want to get married, have all the time in the world, are lazy, visiting girlfriends and boyfriends all the time, filling their minds with dumb things, intruding in other peoples' lives and talking unceasingly about stupid things."

A widow who does not stay at home as a recluse is called *viuda alegre,* a joyful widow. But we know that that image does not correspond to reality. The great majority of single women, widows or not, never

have any time for themselves because they work day and night to sustain their children. Some women have a better life, and are therefore "free" to participate in activities outside the house, but this does not make them idlers or gossipers. (Of course, some women are gossipy and nosy, but so are some men.) In all societies, it is a great challenge for single women to find self-fulfillment as human beings, especially because of such patriarchal caricatures of single women and young widows.

Throughout the rhetorical discourse of 1 Timothy, we observe that there were young widows who were possibly on the official registry of the Christian community, and that these widows were doing pastoral visits. They apparently took vows of celibacy, similar to those of modern religious orders (5:12). If the author wanted to restrict these visits, perhaps it was because they threatened the patriarchal family order, and because the topics discussed during these visits diverged from sound doctrine. Therefore the author wanted to limit the official registry of widows on the basis of age (5:9). Older widows of more than sixty years did not have energy for visitation and were not a threat to the order of the households or of the congregation. Moreover, with all other women faithfully fulfilling their domestic roles as married women, mothers, and wives and with fewer widows on the official church registry, there would be fewer economic and ideological problems in the congregation and in its relation to the Greco-Roman imperial patriarchal society.

The clearly patriarchal teaching found in this text does not prevent the possibility of another reading that would underscore that this teaching was first of all a response to the Roman Empire, which viewed the subversion of traditional family roles as a threat. The fragile Christian community needed to have a consistent teaching in order to enhance the mission of the church, so much so that this teaching was accepted and promoted in Ephesus by the women themselves. However, the restriction of women to domestic values that confine them to the home, exclude them from leadership, and prevent their self-realization as human beings contradicts the proclamation of the gospel and the vision of a kingdom of God characterized by equality and justice.

Questions concerning the struggle for power, women, and social class can now be raised: Are the poor, as well as women, excluded from the possibility of assuming leadership positions such as that of bishop in 3:1-7? Regarding women, one is not surprised to see that in 2:12 the author prohibits them from teaching and exerting any kind of authority over men. First Timothy 3:4-5 envisions a *"paterfamilias"*—a father who is the head of a family. If only rich males could fulfill the requirements for becoming bishop, the letter is self-contradictory, since it criticizes the wealthy. However, the interpretation depends on the way "house" (*oikos*) is translated. Is this term used to refer to a mansion (*domos* in Latin), or to a small house in an apartment complex (*insula*)? I think it refers to something more than a building, namely to a household—the ideological construct of a patriarchal household that was found in all social strata. It might represent a well-to-do family with a small workshop where the wife, children, and perhaps even slaves

work. It might also represent a poor family, without slaves, of course, but where the father is seen as the head of the household and the wife and children as submissive and obedient dependents. According to the patriarchal ideology, the father was in charge of rearing and guiding his house and family.

We women in modern Latin American society are surprised by the similarities between the patriarchal ideology of the first centuries and the reality of our twenty-first century society. Today, despite all the scientific and technological developments and the growing recognition of women in the West, the ideology of the patriarchal household remains almost the same. In the southern barrios of Costa Rica and throughout the country, the killings, beatings, and abuses of women of all social classes, simply because they are women, show that this ideology is still very present. It is very sad that in the Christian churches one finds a prevalence of ahistorical readings of 1 Timothy and other texts that reinforce contemporary patriarchal ideology and legitimate violence against women. To be faithful to the gospel of Jesus Christ, Christian communities must challenge this use of the text.

CONCLUSION

To the women of poor Christian communities, it is important that 1 Timothy be understood as a text that arose in response to a well-known problem: the authority of rich people who believe that their power and wealth gives them the right to rule over the community and its leaders. First Timothy rejects the patronage system that enslaves those who receive favors from benefactors; this is a good stance. However, since the benefactors of the community were rich women, and since their role was related to the presentation of problematic "other doctrines" and to a pattern of behavior that could engender tensions with the empire's patriarchal system, the author addressed

its message against all women without measuring the consequences of this emphasis. The women from the *barrios* may recognize in 1 Timothy an option for the poor, that is, a message that addresses the plight of the poor. But it fails to address the plight of women. For this reason, it is important when reading a biblical text to discern the face of the poor, including gender, race, and class.

We women must understand the struggle for power and affirm the author's rejection of any authority that derives from social status. Yet, on the basis of this teaching, we must also reject the other part of the author's teaching according to which women should be excluded from positions of authority because of their gender. When we have understood the letter's internal contradiction, our task is to re-write it so that the letter more closely reflects the practice of Jesus. In order to do this, we may draw upon other biblical texts from the same period, such as the Gospel of John, wherein women are portrayed as leaders. These positive images of women with authority inspire us to rewrite the letter for their time and ours.

BIBLIOGRAPHY

Countryman, L. William. *The Rich Christian in the Church of the Early Empire: Contradictions and Accommodations.* Text and Studies in Religion 7. New York: Edwin Mellen, 1980.

Kidd, Reggie M. *Wealth and Beneficence in the Pastoral Epistles: A "Bourgeois" Form of Early Christianity?* SBLDS 122. Atlanta: Scholars Press, 1990.

Knight, George W., III. *The Pastoral Epistles: A Commentary on the Greek Text.* NIGTC. Grand Rapids: Eerdmans, 1992.

Marshall, I. Howard, and Philip Towner. *A Critical and Exegetical Commentary on The Pastoral Epistles.* ICC. Edinburgh: T. & T. Clark, 1999.

Oberlinner, Lorenz. *Die Pastoralbriefe: Erster Timotheusbrief.* HTKNT, Bd. 11, 2. Freiburg: Herder, 1994.

Osiek, Carolyn, and David L. Balch. *Families in the New Testament World: Households and House Churches.* The Family, Religion, and Culture Series. Louisville: Westminster John Knox, 1997.

Quinn, Jerome D., and William C. Wacker. *The First and Second Letter to Timothy: A New Translation with Notes and Commentary.* Eerdmans Critical Commentary. Grand Rapids: Eerdmans, 2000.

Schüssler Fiorenza, Elisabeth. *In Memory of Her: A Feminist Theological Reconstruction of Christian Origins.* New York: Crossroad, 1983.

Tamez, Elsa. "1 Timothy: What a Problem!" Pp. 141-156 in *Toward a New Heaven and a New Earth: Essays in Honor of Elisabeth Schüssler Fiorenza.* Ed. Fernando F. Segovia. Maryknoll, N.Y.: Orbis, 2003.

Thurston, Bonnie Bowman. *The Widows: A Women's Ministry in the Early Church.* Minneapolis: Fortress, 1989.

2 TIMOTHY AND TITUS

Daniel C. Arichea, Jr.

Union Theological Seminary, Dasmariñas, Cavite, Philippines, and
Duke Divinity School, Durham, North Carolina, USA

LIFE CONTEXT OF THE INTERPRETATION

My Filipino Life Context

I am a Filipino. I come to these two biblical books with Filipino eyes, with the aim of discovering what 2 Timothy and Titus can say to Filipinos, and what Filipinos can appropriate from these books. At the same time, I also want to find out whether Filipinos can contribute to a better understanding of these books in other contexts beyond that of the Philippines.

The Philippines is part of Asia and the Pacific. Culturally and politically it is linked to Southeast Asian countries, such as Malaysia, Singapore, Brunei, Indonesia, Laos, Cambodia, Vietnam, Thailand, and Myanmar. In the area of religion, however, the Philippines is distinct from its neighbors. While Christians comprise only a small segment of the population in these countries, they constitute over 90 percent of the population in the Philippines. Yet there is presently a crisis of church leadership in the Philippines related to the lack of a clear vision of its mission. The questions are therefore: What can these letters say to communities of faith that are scattered far and wide in the Philippine archipelago? How can these letters help the Philippine church to become more aware of its mission to the Philippines, and Southeast Asia, and to the rest of the Asian continent?

These two letters, together with 1 Timothy, are commonly designated as the Pastoral Letters and can be viewed in two ways. First, they can be regarded as leadership manuals for the Christian community, with the older leader providing instructions to younger leaders both by word and example. The older leader, represented by Paul, often points to himself as an example to be followed by the younger leaders of the church, represented in these letters by Timothy and Titus. The young leaders are invited to imitate Paul's way of life (2 Tim 3:10), to follow Paul's teachings (2 Tim 1:13; 2:2), to share with Paul in his ministry and in his suffering (2 Tim 1:8b; 2:3), and to develop the spiritual gifts that they received when they were set aside for their special task within the church (1 Tim 4:14, 2 Tim 1:6). Furthermore, the young leaders are assured of the support of the older leader through prayer (2 Tim 1:3).

Second, the letters are written to give pastoral guidance for the whole Christian community. While they are addressed to individuals, these individuals were apparently expected to read the letters to the whole congregation, as is shown by the fact that, while the younger church leader is addressed in the second person singular, the concluding blessings are in the second person plural. Through these letters, then, the community is made aware of the true message of the gospel and simultaneously reminded of the lifestyle it should have in order to witness effectively to the larger society.

Daniel C. Arichea, Jr. (PhD, Duke University) is currently bishop in residence at Union Theological Seminary, Dasmariñas, Cavite, Philippines and at Duke Divinity School (half the year in each location). He spent 26 years with the United Bible Societies as a translation consultant for Southeast Asia and as regional translation coordinator for the Asia-Pacific region. He was elected to the Episcopacy of the United Methodist Church in 1995. He co-authored four volumes in the UBS Handbook Series: *Galatians* (1976), *1 Peter* (1980), *Jude and 2 Peter* (1993), and *Paul's Letters to Timothy and to Titus* (1995).

CONTEXTUAL COMMENT

An Overview of 2 Timothy and Titus as Related to 1 Timothy

The Pastoral Letters were written at a time when some people within the church advocated various teachings and ethical positions that contradicted the accepted teachings of the Christian faith. While these false teachers are not clearly identified, clues in the letters indicate that they were in fact members of the Christian community (1 Tim 1:3, 19-20; 2 Tim 1:15; 3:8; Titus 1:10). These heretical teachers were interested in myths and genealogies (1 Tim 1:4; 4:7; 2 Tim 4:4; Titus 1:14; 3:9), as well as in arguments and speculations (1Tim 1:4, 6; 6:4, 20; 2 Tim 2:14, 16, 23; Titus 1:10; 3:9). This has led them to advocate abstinence from marriage and from various kinds of food (1 Tim 4:1-5). There was immorality among them (1 Tim 1:19, 20; 2 Tim 2:16, 19, Titus 1:15-16), and religion was used as a way of taking advantage of weak women and obtaining material gain (1 Tim 6:5, 2 Tim 3:2, 4; Titus 1:11).

What is the appropriate response to these false teachers and their heretical teachings? The true message of the gospel needs to be reemphasized. This is done in many parts of these letters. But this message cannot be limited to isolated individuals; it should be related to the whole faith community. The lifestyle of the community should be such that the community becomes a faithful and effective witness to society as a whole. But for this to happen, the leaders should be faithful to the truth of the gospel. These letters make the community aware of the importance of professional leadership, as well as of the qualifications and responsibilities of church leaders. Finally, the letters also address the need for an organizational structure in the church to protect the gospel's true message from corruption. The Pastoral Letters replace the offices of apostle, prophet, and teacher, which are mentioned by Paul in 1 Cor 12:28, with those of bishops, elders, deacons, and widows. Furthermore, they explain the qualifications of these church leaders in specific passages (e.g., 1 Tim 3 and Titus 1). Finally the Letters refer to a ceremony of setting these leaders apart from the rest of the community: this is done by the laying on of hands (1 Tim 4:14; 2 Tim 1:6).

Both Second Timothy and Titus contain much teaching that promises to help address our concerns for leadership in the church in the Philippines and the lack of clear vision of its mission. The following passages are particularly helpful: 2 Tim 2:1-14, regarding Timothy's responsibilities; 3:14-17, about the role of Scriptures; 4:1-5, regarding the importance of proclamation as part of the mission of the church; 4:6-8, Paul's final testament; and Titus 3:1-8, about the proper conduct of the faith community.

2 Timothy 2:1-14: Timothy's Responsibilities

Since Timothy is the guardian of the truth (2 Tim 1:13-14), he should have qualities and virtues that would ensure his effectiveness in this task. What are some of these qualities?

In 2:1, Timothy is urged to continue to be "strong" (the verb is in the present tense) "in the grace that is in Christ Jesus," that is, in the undeserved love and favor that God freely gives to those who are united with Christ. Timothy should also recruit and develop leaders who are "faithful," that is, trustworthy, dependable and reliable, and who are "able to teach others as well" (v. 2).

In 2 Tim 2:3, Timothy is told to "share in suffering," that is, to have a part in the sufferings being experienced by Christians because of their faith in and faithfulness to Jesus Christ himself. In 2:4-6, Timothy is told to have the single-mindedness of a soldier, to follow the rules as athletes do, and to work as hard as a farmer does.

Second Timothy 2:8-13 contains a theological basis for the instruction to Timothy. The center of this statement is Jesus Christ (2:8). This verse affirms Jesus' divine nature (for reference to his resurrection, see Rom 1:4) as well as his humanity (for reference to his Davidic ancestry, see Rom 1:3). This is what Paul refers to as "my gospel," for which he has suffered and continues to suffer through imprisonment. Suffering, however, does not hinder the gospel: "the word of God is not chained" (2 Tim 2:9). All this suffering has a purpose, which is to enable "the elect," God's chosen people, to experience salvation in Christ, so they may live forever with God, who will give them "eternal glory" (2:10). A hymn follows, which challenges Christ's followers to remain faithful to him, and affirms Christ's faithfulness to them even when they become unfaithful (2:11-13).

Second Timothy 2:15-16 contains a summary of Timothy's role as a church leader. Positively, he should do his best to present himself "to God as one approved by him," and as one who boldly and confidently interprets and expounds the true meaning of "the word of truth." Negatively, he is to keep away from "profane chatter," or silly discussions that show no reverence for God and in fact lead people to "impiety," that is, away from God.

2 Tim 3:14-17: The Scriptures

For the true message to prevail there has to be a visible basis for it. And in fact, there is! The truths of the gospel are contained in and based on the Scriptures. In this context, Scripture refers to the Hebrew Scriptures, commonly known among Christians as the Old Testament.

Scripture is characterized as "inspired by God" (*theopneustos* 3:16). This single term has generated a great deal of controversy among Christians. The literal rendering is "God-breathed," which seems to refer to the first man, Adam, who became alive when God breathed into him. These writings therefore are "alive" and are able to confront people in order to fulfill specific functions for which these writings were produced. That is why it is noteworthy that the text reads, "All scripture is inspired by God and is useful . . . " The passage mentions some specific functions such as giving people wisdom that leads to salvation through faith in Jesus Christ (3:15), nurturing believers in their faith, defending the faith from error, correcting wrong behavior, "and training in righteousness," that is, providing instruction in right living. The overall purpose is summarized in 3:17: to equip and enable God's people (either generally or specifically church leaders) to do what they are supposed to do in their various ministries.

2 Tim 4:1-5: The Importance of Proclamation

The instructions to Timothy are coming to an end. In view of the serious situation that is faced by the faith community, and in view of a future characterized by unfaithfulness to the truth of the gospel, Timothy is urged to continue to proclaim the gospel message regardless of the circumstances. His faithfulness in this task is even more compelling considering the fact that he will soon be left alone, because his teacher will soon pass away, as 2 Tim 4:6-8 clearly indicates.

The charge to Timothy regarding his preaching and teaching ministry is summarized in nine imperatives (five in 4:2, and four in 4:5) as follows: preach the word; "be persistent," that is, insist upon preaching it whether it is convenient or not, and whether people want to hear it or not; "convince, rebuke, and encourage"; always "be sober," that is, be alert and controlled; "endure suffering, do the work of an evangelist," proclaiming the good news also to those outside the church; and finally, "carry out your ministry fully," or in other words, do everything necessary in the performance of your duties as a servant of God.

2 Timothy 4:6-8: Paul's Final Testament

This passage is often known as Paul's final testament. One cannot read these words without sensing that they belong to someone who has lived and toiled for the gospel, but who recognizes that he has reached the end of his earthly journey. Since the letter appears to be written from prison, one gets the impression that Paul did not expect to survive his imprisonment.

This passage is connected with what immediately precedes it, namely the urgent advice to Timothy to be faithful in his ministry, particularly in the proclamation of the gospel. It is as if the older leader is saying to the younger one, "I will not be there to help you, so do your best." The older leader is leaving, and the younger leader must now take over and fill the space created by the older leader's departure. The hour has come for him to move on: "the time of my departure has come." His life is "poured out as a libation," like wine being poured at the altar as a sacrifice to the Lord (Num 28:7). He is like a Roman or Greek athlete who fights to the very end or a runner who runs until the finish line. He does not focus on winning, but on finishing. Finally, he exclaims victoriously, "I have kept the faith." I have been faithful to the very end. What a glorious way to die!

Titus 3:1-8:
Conduct of the Faith Community

How should the members of the faith community conduct their lives? What should be their attitude toward those who deliberately teach false doctrines and threaten the unity and harmony of the community? This passage from Titus offers some guidelines.

First, the community members are reminded that their attitude toward political rulers and government officials should be characterized by submissiveness and obedience (Titus 3:1a). Elsewhere, Christians are urged to pray for those in authority (1 Tim 2:1).

Second, the members of the community are reminded of the kind of behavior they should demonstrate as they relate to others, both within and outside the community (Titus 3:1-2). Five elements are mentioned. First, they "are to be ready for every good work," that is, to do good deeds for the benefit of others. Second, they "are to speak evil of no one" (literally "to blaspheme"), that is, to refrain from insulting and slandering other people. Third, they are to "avoid quarreling," or stated positively, they should strive to be at peace with others. Fourth, they are to be "gentle," that is, courteous, reasonable, and considerate in dealing with others. Finally, they are "to show every courtesy to everyone," that is, polite in every way to everybody.

The next part of the passage gives a theological basis for the kind of behavior that is being advocated for members of the faith community. They are reminded in Titus 3:3 that at one time, they were "foolish, disobedient, led astray, slaves to various passions and pleasures," passing their days in "malice and envy, despicable, hating one another." This language describes people who have not yet heard or responded to the gospel message.

The answer to this depraved human condition is contained in Titus 3:4-8. The passage describes God's nature as good, loving, kind, and as willing to bestow salvation solely on the basis of such loving-kindness, and not because of the good deeds that people (even good people!) do. This salvation is effected "through the water of rebirth and renewal by the Holy Spirit" (3:5b). This latter expression is ambiguous, but its appropriate meaning can be expressed as follows: Water stands for spiritual cleansing, and it is the means by which the Holy Spirit works out rebirth and renewal in the lives of people. This Spirit is "poured out on us richly" (that is, abundantly, generously) by God "through Jesus Christ our Savior." In these letters, Savior occurs many times and is used of both God and Christ. People are "justified by his grace" and become "heirs according to the hope of eternal life" (3:7). "Justified" refers to God's activity of righting a wrong. In this present context (and elsewhere, e.g., Gal, Rom), people are the target of such "righting." To be justified means to be put in a right relationship with God. This justification is through God's "grace," that is, God's unconditional and undeserved kindness and favor. Those who are justified have the hope of receiving eternal life, as God has promised.

The end of the passage, Titus 3:8, reminds the community once again of the importance of doing good: believers should "devote themselves to good works." Their actions should not be self-serving and motivated by self-gain; instead they should be "excellent," that is, good, and "profitable," that is, useful to everyone.

CONCLUSION

The Letters and the Philippine Churches

Discerning the teaching of these letters for the churches in Asia involves considering how the content of the letters applies or does not apply to our particular life context. These letters, written in and for another life context, are not recipes that the church could simply follow today in order to meet present-day challenges. The challenges facing the churches in Asia are quite different from those that the early church had to confront.

Leadership

There is a crisis of leadership in Philippine churches. It is not only in the matter of recruiting people and training them for leadership positions, but it is also in the quality of leadership. Very few leaders today would measure up to the standards set for us in the Pastoral Letters, both in terms of qualifications and qualities. And, as is often the case, leaders are evaluated not by the best but by the worst among them. The Philippine churches have a continuing need for the development of effective, efficient, educated, and dedicated leaders who are ready and willing to propelling the church into the future.

Leadership succession is another matter. One of the greatest problems in Asian society is the transfer of leadership from the old to the new. This problem exists in the church as well as in other segments of society. The high regard for age has been exploited by many older leaders as a reason for remaining in their positions. In some cases, even when new leaders are already in place, the old leadership still continues to insist on its own way, leaving no space for the development and growth of the new leadership. We need to learn a lesson from the passage in 2 Tim 4:1-6, where the old leader passes on leadership responsibility to the younger leader.

Church Structures

Philippine churches need to recover the functional aspects of leadership positions that were advocated within the early church. The church structure depicted in the Pastoral Letters was intended to meet the challenges of the Christian community at that time, and was not meant to be a permanent fixture of future Christian communities. Church structures, including leadership positions, should always be mission driven. In other words, the mission of the church should determine the structure of the church. It is therefore imperative for Christians in Asia to ask what our mission is and then adjust our ecclesiastical structures accordingly, even if this adjustment deviates from traditional Western models.

Attitude towards Political Authority

There is a place for the posture toward government that is reflected in the Pastoral Letters, particularly if the government is fulfilling its role of promoting the common good (cf. Rom 13:1-7). In situations where a government no longer exists for good but for ill, Christians are justified when their attitude toward such government changes from obedience to disobedience and prophetic denunciation, as is evident in the book of Revelation (see especially Rev. 13). Unfortunately, many governments in Asia can be characterized as belonging to the second of these categories. In such cases, Christians should not simply submit and obey the political authorities, but should exercise their prophetic function in order to remind government of its primary obligations.

The Community's Relation to Society

The exhortations found in Titus 3 can be viewed in two ways. On one hand, Christians are often expected to be so nice that they are not encouraged to exercise their prophetic role in society. They do not speak and act against injustice and unfairness, for to do so would violate their "Christian" character as nice, good people. This expectation leads some Christians to tolerate and ignore conditions in society that lead to suffering and dehumanization. This attitude also makes faith relevant only for the "religious" side of life and irrelevant for the secular side. It creates a dichotomy between religious and secular, heaven and earth, soul and body, church and world, with faith relevant only on one side of the equation.

On the other hand, Christians may give the impression that they are conscious of their own goodness, and as a result others perceive them as proud, arrogant, self-righteous, and self-important. It is unfortunate but often true that the more faith people have, the more arrogant they seem to become. Both of these elements need to be inculcated in the consciousness of Christians, especially in situations where they are a very small segment of the total population, as is the case in most of Asia.

The focus on good deeds is quite significant. In the end, it is not words but actions that count. It is what Christians do that defines who and what they are.

BIBLIOGRAPHY

Arichea, Daniel C., and Howard A. Hatton. *Paul's Letters to Timothy and to Titus*. United Bible Societies Handbook Series. New York: United Bible Societies, 1995.

Bassler, Jouette M. *1 Timothy, 2 Timothy. Titus*. ANTC. Nashville: Abingdon Press, 1996.

Hanson, Anthony Tyrrell. *The Pastoral Epistles*. NCB Commentary. Grand Rapids: Eerdmans, 1982.

Houlden, James Leslie. *The Pastoral Epistles*. London: SCM Press, 1989.

Johnson, Luke Timothy. *1 Timothy, 2 Timothy and Titus*. Atlanta: John Knox Press, 1987.

Mounce, William D. *Pastoral Epistles*. WBC 46. Nashville: Thomas Nelson, 2000.

Oden, Thomas C. *First and Second Timothy and Titus*. Louisville: Westminster John Knox, 1989.

Towner, Philip H. *1–2 Timothy and Titus*. Downers Grove, Ill.: InterVarsity, 1994.

PHILEMON

Jean K. Kim

Moravian Theological Seminary, Bethlehem, Pennsylvania USA

LIFE CONTEXT OF THE INTERPRETATION

Korean Christianity has been offered as a successful instance of conducting Christian mission; like the student who goes on to become a teacher, it now plays a major role in world Christianity, leading active ministries on virtually every continent and spreading Christianity around the world. Domestically, however, mainstream evangelical Christianity has been criticized for measuring the success of its ministries according to a materialistic standard. During successive Korean military governments, the mainstream evangelical churches also supported a Cold War ideology that was used to justify the legitimacy of the military government as well as the priority of economic development at the expense of the workers' well-being, rather than raising a prophetic voice against government abuses. By exclusively emphasizing justification by faith and the transcendental dimension of the Bible, the churches have justified themselves and continuously ignored issues of social justice and human rights. These mainstream churches have been challenged by *Minjung* theologians who have begun to see the Bible through the lens of *Minjung,* that is, of the marginalized people, and to seek the Bible's liberating message from a socio-political perspective, with awareness that the Bible itself is a socio-political product.

After Korea overcame its economic difficulties, it faced a different situation in the exploitation of cheap labor connected with globalization. Recently, more than eight hundred cases of human rights abuses against foreign workers were uncovered in Korea: workers have been discriminated against, exploited, poorly paid or cheated of their wages, and threatened with deportation. Since these victims are illegal immigrants, it is risky to help them. Only a few Minjung churches and organizations (e.g., Korean National Council of Churches, *Ansan* Migrant Shelter, Jubilee Mission) have begun special ministries aimed at protecting foreign workers and their labor rights from unjust employers and governmental laws directed against them.

Although both evangelical and Minjung Christians appeal to the Bible to support their agendas, their respective uses of the Bible presuppose very different values. The application of the Bible is a matter of decision and action. These actions and decisions are determined by the tension between the salvation a Christian already has and the Christian's hope in Christ. In Korea, Minjung theologians are fond of saying that "Minjung is rice" (the staple food in Korea, corresponding to bread in the West), and that "the heart of the heavenly being is that of Minjung." The first saying describes the situation: Minjung (as those who grow rice) are vulnerable because they can be exploited (that is, eaten) by the powerful, especially when

Jean K. Kim, born and raised in Korea, graduated from Ewha Women's University and earned an MA and a PhD in the United States. An assistant professor of New Testament, she is interested in a seamless interweaving of biblical interpretation with the realities of church life and society in a postmodern, postcolonial world. Her publications include a forthcoming *Woman and Nation: An Intercontextual Reading of the Gospel of John* (Brill, 2005), and many articles, including "Adultery or Hybridity? Reading John 7:53–8:11 from a Postcolonial Context" in *John and Postcolonialism* (2002).

they are denied the benefits of the harvest. The second saying seeks to protect Minjung from their vulnerability by equating Minjung with the heavenly being. These sayings also emphasize that the interconnection of human beings' lives is vitally important by stressing that rice is life and life is also rice (cf. John 6:33-51).

CONTEXTUAL COMMENT

In this life-context, the message of Paul's letter to Philemon can speak not only to pastors of Korean churches serving the rich (who might be the employers of many foreign workers) but also to those whose churches serve the poor. It can be a living witness for the church and all the people of God as it depicts Paul's attempt to mediate between a powerful slave-owner and a powerless slave despite the danger of losing Philemon's support for his ministry. The message it offers is then: we, as people of God, envision a Christian society where social distinctions are erased and where the church risks its own comfort to help the powerless. This vision of new social relations is actualized when we change the metaphors through which we envision our relationship with the powerful and the powerless.

Paul's letter to Philemon appears to be a private letter regarding a personal matter. Yet the observations that both senders and addressees are plural (vv. 1-3), that numerous persons are mentioned in the closing (vv. 23-24), and that private matters are connected with communal concerns show that the letter to Philemon is more than a private letter. Paul was imprisoned and somehow Onesimus encountered him there. Although it is not clear what brought Onesimus to Paul or what exactly Paul was asking of Philemon, we can say that Paul wrote the letter on behalf of Onesimus (v. 10).

The Roman Empire in the first century was a strongly authoritarian society where severe laws punished those who interfered with the rights of slave owners, because slavery was a part of the legitimate social order. In that society, it was far from obvious what impact, if any, Onesimus' conversion to Christianity might have on his legal status. Possibly because Paul recognized Philemon's legal rights and anticipated that Philemon might reject his request, Paul proceeds diplomatically: he mentions fellow-patrons (Apphia, Archippus, v. 2) with whom Philemon might be familiar (cf. Col 4:17) in order to set up a larger audience that might influence Philemon's decision.

Paul's appeal to Philemon is developed in a deliberative manner. In the thanksgiving section (vv. 4-7), Paul first builds up goodwill between himself and Philemon by complimenting Philemon's past behavior, including his "love for all the saints" (v. 5). In this way he furthers his case by softening Philemon's disposition and subtly encouraging him to act with the same love in the future. Furthermore, by establishing a brotherly relationship between himself and Philemon (v. 7), Paul posits an egalitarian relationship between them. Yet Paul gradually changes tone as he ensnares Philemon into a net of power relations based on love-patriarchalism: he is not commanding him, but rather appealing to him "on the basis of love" due to "an old man" who is "a prisoner of Christ Jesus" (vv. 8-9). After explaining, through his wordplay on the name "Onesimus" (useful), how useful the formerly useless Onesimus is (v. 11), Paul expresses the wish that Philemon accept Onesimus not as a slave but as a brother (v. 16).

It is not clear what kind of a favor Paul was asking of Philemon on behalf of Onesimus. If Paul were requesting Philemon's manumission of Onesimus, this might have put Philemon in a dilemma arising from the inequality in the relationship between a Christian slave-owner and a Christian slave. Paul depended mainly on patrons wealthy enough to provide house-churches for his congregations (Rom 16:23; 1 Cor 1:11-16; cf. Acts 16:15, 34; 18:8). In the Roman society, these patrons were slave-owners. Therefore, the manumission of Onesimus by Philemon would be a precedent that might engender a whole range of problems for Paul and for the house-churches. For example, the churches might face financial liability in compensating slave-owners for the loss of their slaves, or the churches might be inconvenienced by having a worship service in a house without the slaves' assistance. In sum, neither Onesimus's manumission nor his continued status as a slave was a satisfactory resolution for Paul (for similar ambivalent attitudes regarding slavery see Herm. *Mand.* 8.10; Herm. Sim. 1.8; Ign. Pol. 4.8).

Recognizing the tension between the social reality and the relationship in the Christian community, Paul uses the relationship within a patriarchal family as a metaphor that posits a relationship between Onesimus and Paul and Philemon that is closer than the one that manumission could provide: Paul introduces Onesimus as another household member, as his child, and himself as the father of Onesimus; he establishes a familial bond between himself and Onesimus (v. 10). In a patriarchal society where only the senior male could hold domestic as well as public authority over all members of the house, Paul's claim based on his parent-child relationship with Onesimus superseded Philemon's authority over Onesimus: Paul speaks to Philemon as an elderly man (presbutes, v. 9). He then not only asks Philemon to receive his runaway as a beloved brother (v. 16a), but also puts pressure on Philemon by emphasizing that Onesimus is in this familial relationship "especially to me [Paul] but how much more to you, both in the flesh and in the Lord" (v. 16b). By being Paul's child and a part of Paul's self (v. 12), Onesimus also becomes Philemon's beloved brother. In a patriarchal family based on love-patriarchalism, Philemon and Onesimus as brothers are also Paul's children (cf. Gal 4:1-7; 1 Cor 4:14-21; 1 Thess 2:11-12). If Philemon accedes to Paul's request, Onesimus will be forgiven his former wrongdoing and also will no longer be treated as a slave but as a brother. Paul constructs the family metaphor as a strategy for challenging and subverting Philemon's authority and achieving his goal of giving Onesimus a better status.

Paul's authority over Philemon continues through the theme of indebtedness. Paul had complimented Philemon for his past behavior (vv. 4-7) and referred to Onesimus's conversion and return (vv. 10-16). It is thus only after highlighting the positive that Paul alludes to Onesimus's wrongdoing and his debt toward Philemon, expressing in the same breath his willingness to pay off Onesimus's debt (vv. 17-19a). Using a rhetorical trope (*Occultatio / Parasiopesis*), Paul skillfully emphasizes the fact that Philemon is also indebted to him by pointedly seeming to pass over it (v. 19b). Paul then demands that Philemon receive Onesimus, begs for compliance in the name of the Lord, and finally expresses his confidence in Philemon's obedience to his bold apostolic authority (vv. 20-22).

CONCLUSION

Paul's life-context may not be the same as my life-context: the ideology of capitalism and globalization emanating from the One-Third World countries has created different kinds of slavery in the Two-Thirds World as the West expands its economic and political power. In Paul's context, it was not the powerful Philemon but the powerless Onesimus who broke a social rule, whereas in my life-context it is both powerful Korean employers and powerless foreign employees who transgress such rules. Yet being true to the liberating message of the biblical tradition does not mean proceeding to a meta-historical photocopying of what happened in Paul's context, but rather pushing forward in the liberating direction to which Paul points.

Despite its success abroad, Korean mainstream evangelical Christianity has been criticized for measuring the success of its ministries according to the size of the church; for emphasizing salvation of individuals as an end in itself; for allowing quasi-hereditary senior pastor positions to become established within the so-called mega-churches; and for supporting the status quo while remaining silent on issues of social justice. In effect, Korean mainstream evangelical Chris-tianity duplicates the love-patriarchalism found in Paul's letter without considering Paul's socio-historical context; it is a meta-historical photocopying of what happened in Paul's context.

In contrast, marginalized Minjung Christian leaders have struggled to fight against unjust social systems on behalf of the powerless. In this life-context, we need to prolong the liberating line of Paul's teaching. Indeed, Paul gives us a very important lesson. In spite of the risk of losing the support of Christian slave-owners for his mission, Paul demands that Philemon accept a fundamental change in his relationship with Onesimus by emphasizing kinship ties in the Lord. As a model of church leadership, Paul's courage and love based on his faith in Christ not only challenges pastors of the mainstream Christian churches to move in a liberating direction but also encourages those of Minjung churches to continue their mission for the powerless. In so doing, as Paul sought the unity of the church, the Korean churches from both sides can move together toward an overall Christian community. Paul's message can be a living witness only when the people of God take the risk to enter into dynamic, inspiring relationships with all their neighbors envisioned as brothers and sisters with the help of new metaphors arising from their particular contexts. "Minjung is rice." Who are the people who are like Onesimus? Who are eaten up like rice by others? Such people are beloved brothers and sisters "both in the flesh and in the Lord" (v. 16); thus one needs to recognize that "the heart of the heavenly being is that of Minjung."

BIBLIOGRAPHY

Barclay, John M. G. "Paul, Philemon and the Dilemma of Christian Slave-Ownership." *NTS* 37 (1991): 161-86.

Church, F. Forrester. "Rhetorical Structure and Design in Paul's Letter to Philemon." *HTR* 71 (1978): 17-33.

De Vos, Craig S. "Once a Slave, Always a Slave? Slavery, Manumission and Relational Patterns in Paul's Letter to Philemon." *JSNT* 82 (2000): 89-105.

Elliot, John H. "Philemon and House Churches." *BTB* 22 (1984): 145-50.

Frilingos, Chris. "'For My Child, Onesimus': Paul and Domestic Power in Philemon." *JBL* 119 (2000): 91-104.

Kim, Ji-ha. *Bab* (Rice). Waigwan: Bundo, 1984.

Lohse, Eduard. Colossians and Philemon: *A Commentary on the Epistles to the Colossians and to Philemon.* Translated by William R. Poelmann and Robert J. Karris. Edited by Helmut Koester. Hermeneia. Philadelphia: Fortress, 1971.

Nordling, John G. "Onesimus Fugitivus: A Defense of the Runaway Slave Hypothesis in Philemon." *JSNT* 41 (1991): 97-119.

Petersen, Norman R. *Rediscovering Paul: Philemon and the Sociology of Paul's Narrative World*. Philadelphia: Fortress, 1985.

Polaski, Sandra Hack. *Paul and the Discourse of Power*. Gender, Culture, Theory 8. Biblical Seminar 62. Sheffield: Sheffield Academic Press, 1999.

HEBREWS

Stelian Tofanâ

School of Orthodox Theology, Babes-Bolyai University, Cluj-Napoca, Romania

LIFE CONTEXT OF THE INTERPRETATION

I write this commentary from a *didactic* and *sacerdotal* context. As a professor of New Testament at an Orthodox theological seminary, I have always considered the Epistle to the Hebrews most important in teaching New Testament Christology. As an orthodox priest, the book of Hebrews is part of the mystical reality I experience in every holy liturgy, at the altar on which Christ sacrifices himself continuously for each person, being there in a sacrificial state forever. So I read Hebrews from the liturgical context of a permanent sacerdotal relation with the eternal high priest—Jesus Christ—in his continuous sacrifice for God's people. This liturgical context encompasses heaven and earth, and thus daily life in society and in the natural world, where Jesus Christ, the high priest, offers his continuous sacrifice.

Hebrews and the Church's Relationship with the World

By its unique theme—the eternal high priesthood of Christ—Hebrews raises, first of all, the contextual issue of the relationship between Christ's priesthood and the sacramental priesthood of the church, which prolongs Christ's priesthood and sacrifice, and eternalizes them in history. This eternalized historical reality is expressed in 13:8: "Jesus Christ is the same yesterday and today and forever." Christ is present not only in his abstract transcendence, but also in the concreteness of the visible world in his church. The Christian meets him and becomes one with him in the sacrament of holy Eucharist, taking upon oneself the effect of his unique sacrifice. Thus each Christian becomes a "priest by participation" at his sacrifice, eternalized today through the church is liturgy.

From this standpoint, the priesthood of all Christians, the sacramental priesthood of the church, and Christ's high priesthood do not exclude one another. They are rather in perpetual communion and mutual interdependence. The church becomes entirely sacrifice and entirely priesthood by the power of Christ's sacrifice and high priesthood, the source of all sacrifices and priesthood.

Viewed in this way, Hebrews raises the contextual issue of ecumenical relations. It is actually an excellent ecumenical guide that includes all necessary rules, prescriptions, and motivations for striving to unite Christian churches all over the world. All Christians are united by the fact that "[Christ] always lives to make intercession for them" (7:25), regardless of their faith, of their ways of expressing it, and regardless of nationality, sex, and social or moral status.

Stelian Tofanâ, an Orthodox priest, is also a professor of New Testament and executive director of the Center for Biblical Studies. His publications include, in addition to many articles, five books (in Romanian): *Jesus Christ, Forever High Priest According to the Epistle to Hebrews* (1996); *Introduction to the Study of the New Testament* (3 vols.); Vol. 1: *Text and Canon: The New Testament Epoch* (1997); Vol. 2: *The Gospels of Matthew and Mark: The Document Q* (1998); Vol. 3: *The Gospels of Luke and John: The Synoptic Problem* (2002); and *The Symbolism and the Sacramental Theology of the Fourth Gospel* (2003).

A third contextual issue raised by Hebrews is related to the past and present situation in Romania and the role of faith in it. Hebrews 11:1 offers the most explicit definition of faith in the New Testament: "Now faith is the assurance of things hoped for, the conviction of things not seen." According to this definition, Christians can always find comfort even in the most difficult situations as they hope for the fulfillment of God's promises. This faith has always been preached in Romanian churches, keeping alive the hope of redemption from communist terror. Through this teaching about faith, Hebrews was the beacon of our hopes in those difficult times, as it still is today.

A fourth contextual issue is related to the moral teaching of Hebrews, a much needed teaching in a world where injus-tice, hate, cynicism, exploitation, deceit, and indifference are often elevated to the rank of legitimate doctrines. In 13:1-21, an appendix about moral and practical teachings, the author encourages the prac-tice of Christian love, hospitality, gen-erosity toward prisoners and toward the oppressed, and renunciation of the love of money and false teachings. Such virtues are still unknown to many Christians who are caught in the contemporary world where injustice, exploitation, and cyni-cism are the rule. For such Christians and for the world, Hebrews offers an alterna-tive paradigm, a real moral paradigm. The words, "Pursue peace with everyone, and the holiness without which no one will see the Lord" (12:14), are both an exhor-tation for Christians and a warning for a secularized godless world.

CONTEXTUAL COMMENT

An Overview of Hebrews

Hebrews is one of the most controver-sial epistles of the New Testament regarding authorship, authenticity, liter-ary style, and also regarding its central theological theme, the eternal high priest-hood of Christ.

The Author of the Epistle

In the Eastern Church, Paul's author-ship of the Epistle to the Hebrews was recognized from the very beginning. Clement of Alexandria affirmed it and referred to an older tradition (from "the happy priest," Panthenus). In the nine-teenth and twentieth centuries a great majority of exegetes rejected Paul's authorship. However, a careful compari-son of Hebrews with the Pauline Epistles shows that their respective christologies have several particularities in common and have a greater affinity than Hebrews has with any other writings of the New Testament. Compare Heb 1:3 with Col 1:15-17; Heb 1:4-5 with Col 2:10; Heb 1:2 with Rom 11:6 and 1 Cor 8:6b; Heb 9:24 with Rom 8:34; and Heb 5:7-9 with Phil 2:7-8. If Paul were the author, its date would be about the same as the epistles of captivity (Colossians and Philippians), close to his martyrdom, in the years before the destruction of the temple in Jerusalem in 70 C.E.

My primary point is that the content of Hebrews is not at odds with the major ideas of Paul's theology, although the arguments against Paul's authorship should not be disregarded. Who is the real author? We cannot know for sure. Hebrews has probably been conceived, adapted, and edited by one of Paul's dis-ciples (13:23). Yet, we can say that the author, his style, and his choice of the eternal priesthood of Christ as a major theme were strongly marked by his cul-ture and theological formation in a Jew-ish-Hellenistic setting. Reading Hebrews together with the (other) Pauline Epistles amplifies important themes in Hebrews; conversely, reading the (other) Pauline

Epistles together with Hebrews brings out the liturgical and sacrificial dimensions of Paul's theology, as is important from an Orthodox perspective.

The Addressees of Hebrews

The hypothesis held by the majority of interpreters is that Hebrews was addressed to Jewish Christians living in Palestine, maybe even in Jerusalem. For the author these addressees are in a spiritual crisis because of:

a. Doubt regarding the reality of "the new time" inaugurated by Jesus Christ's arrival;

b. Doubt regarding the possibility of redemption;

c. Tension resulting from living in the intermediate time between the arrival of Jesus Christ, an eschatological time (9:28; 10:10, 14), and its future fulfillment in "the promised eternal inheritance" (9:15).

The author tries to overcome his readers' doubts by showing that:

— A "new time" of complete redemption and full eschatological renewal has been inaugurated through Jesus Christ;

— Christians can be certain about their own salvation, because they have a high priest, holy and flawless (7:26), who "sympathize[s] with [their] weaknesses" (4:15);

— The high priest "always lives to make intercession for them" (7:25; 9:24) so that they might "receive the promised eternal inheritance" (9:15).

The Thematic Frame

The doctrinal contents of Hebrews reflect theological and moral problems regarding the relationship between Christians as the people of God with their Creator and regarding the relationship between Christians and the world they live in. We will focus our attention on four sections concerning:

I. The incarnated Son of God as fulfillment of the revelation and beginning of our salvation (1:1–2:18);

II. The heavenly calling of Jesus Christ as high priest (3:1–5:10);

III. Jesus Christ as heavenly high priest (7:1–9:28), the climax of the Epistle;

IV. The present and future effectiveness of Christ's sacrifice for the whole of humankind (10:1-25; 13:7-17).

The Incarnated Son of God (1:1–2:18)

Sending God's Message through the Son

From the start Hebrews presents the Son not only as the one who brings salvation, but also as the one "through whom [God] also created the worlds" (1:2b). He brings the supernatural revelation through which God spoke to the people "in these last days": "God who, at various times and in various ways spoke in time past to the fathers by the prophets, has in these last days *(ep eschatou tōn hēmerōn)* spoken to us *(hēmin)* by His Son *(en huiō)*" (1:1-2a, [a.t.].

These last few words are of special interest. By emphasizing "the last days," the personal pronoun "us," and the noun "the Son," the author conveys that God also speaks to us today through the Son in the gospel, always expanding the depths of our knowledge of the person of Christ. "The last days" refers to the present in its historical stretch throughout time, a present that also includes us. The coming of the Son marks the difference between the time when the revelation was given (in the past) and the time when it is *fulfilled*. Our present context is the time when the revelation is fulfilled.

Jesus Christ,
the Initiator of Salvation

"It was fitting that God. . . . should make the initiator (*archēgon*) of their salvation perfect through sufferings" (2:10). The presentation of the Son as the initiator of salvation through Calvary, suffering, and sacrifice (2:5-18) is a second feature of Hebrew's Christology. The key word "suffering" links Jesus to the Christians and thus defines the relationship between the "Son" and the "sons."

The beginning of the salvation process is accomplished by Jesus Christ the High Priest through his lowering or *kenosis* (2:4-18): "But we see Jesus, who was made a little lower than the angels, for the suffering of death, crowned with glory and honor, that He, by the grace of God, might taste death for everyone (*hyper pantos geusētai thanatou*)" (2:9, a.t.). From this perspective, Christ's incarnation, suffering, humiliation, and death are examined by the author from both a christological and a soteriological perspective:

a. Christologically his death represents the condition for his being "crowned with glory and honor";

b. Soteriologically, his death was necessary for all of us: "that so by the grace of God he might taste death for everyone" (2:9).

Viewed from this perspective, 2:14-18 explains this "necessity" (*eprepen*, "it was fitting, proper, necessary" 2:10) for the Son's suffering and lowering. "Since, therefore, the children share flesh and blood, he himself likewise shared the same things, so that through death he might destroy the one who has the power of death, that is, the devil" (2:14). This verse explains the way in which the solidarity principle between the "Son" and the "sons" (children) became effective in the mystery of the incarnation. (We need to reproduce the androcentric language of the text in order to appreciate how the text conceives of the solidarity of the Christians with Christ.)

The total solidarity between the Son (as mediator of salvation) and human beings, between the Son and Christians, and also among Christians, is demonstrated through the fact that the latter are appointed as "sons" (*huioi*, 2:10). This shows again that he who saves and those who need to be saved, he who sanctifies and those who are being sanctified, "are all of one" (*ex henos pantes*): "For both he who sanctifies and those who are being sanctified are all of one, for which reason he is not ashamed to call them brethren" (2:11, a.t.).

This solidarity between Jesus and his brethren is substantiated by their common origin (*ex henos*—"from one," i.e., from God), by the incarnation and by the sanctifying and saving action of the Son, brought about through his suffering and death. "Therefore he had to become like his brothers and sisters in every respect, so that he might be a merciful and faithful high priest in the service of God, to make a sacrifice of atonement for the sins of the people" (2:17).

The Heavenly Calling
of Jesus Christ as High Priest
(3:1– 5:10)

The Attributes of Christ as High Priest

While the first two chapters clarify the place and role of Jesus in the universe and in the divine plan for the world's salvation, 3:1–5:10 places Jesus Christ in relation with Israel's religious history and its most significant representative, Moses, and presents his heavenly calling as high priest. In this context, Christians are advised to focus entirely on Jesus, not so much on the Ascended One but first of all on the One made "in all things . . . like his brethren" (2:17, a.t.), revealing himself a merciful and faithful high priest.

Jesus Christ's "faithfulness" as high priest is revealed first of all in his temptations, suffering, and martyrdom through which he remained faithful to the One who sent him and also to the soteriological mission entrusted to him (2:9, 14, 18; 5:7). His faithfulness to God is the basis for our trust in his present intercession for his people as an eternal high priest before God.

His faithfulness is also the basis for the certainty of Christians that he is "the source of eternal salvation for all who obey him" (5:9). Jesus is the compassionate (*eleēmōn*) high priest (2:17), willing to suffer with us (*sympatheō*, 4:15)in our weaknesses, because he is in complete solidarity with human beings through his perfect resemblance to them ("in all things he had to be made like his brethren," 2:17, a.t.). The verb *sympatheō* (to suffer with us) in 4:15 must not be understood metaphorically (as suggested by the NRSV translation, "to sympathize with our weaknesses"), but literally: he is a high priest "who in every respect has been tempted as we are, yet without sin" (4:15, RSV). But his "suffering with us" should not be limited to Jesus' earthly life, considered as a past historical reality. As an eternal high priest, he suffers with us and will continue to do so. Thus his "suffering with us" has a profound effect upon the present world.

Jesus Christ as high priest is never far from "his brothers and sisters" because he eternally remains human. He does not allow his superiority to estrange him from Christians' weaknesses and temptations. Therefore they can approach him "with confidence" (*meta parrēsias*) and "find grace and help in time of need" (4:16, a.t.), even in our present day. Jesus, our high priest, is thus present in our life-context today.

The Calling of Christ as High Priest

This calling as high priest has two facets. It is as the Son of God that Christ received his calling as high priest from God: "And one does not presume to take this honor, but takes it only when called by God, just as Aaron was. So also Christ did not glorify himself in becoming a high priest, but was appointed by the one who said to him, 'You are my Son, today I have begotten you'" (5:4-5). Yet he accomplished his calling through the human side of his person and his suffering "in the flesh":

> In the days of his flesh, Jesus offered up prayers and supplications, with loud cries and tears, to the one who was able to save him from death, and he was heard because of his reverent submission. Although he was a Son, he learned obedience through what he suffered. (5:7-8, RSV)

Jesus' saving mission first applies to his own human nature, which he assumed in his divine nature. Through his sacrifice he fills his humanity with his Lordship and sets it free from any faults and passions, and from death, the consequence of sin. In this way "he became the author (or source) of eternal salvation for all who obey him" (5:9, a.t.), by his incarnation through which he assumed our human nature into his human nature and by the sacrifice through which he brought his humanity to perfection (*teleioō*). Through his ongoing incarnation, he sanctifies and brings to perfection "his brothers and sisters," that is, the entire people of God. It is this "bringing to perfection" of our humanity that is taking place in our world today as Christ fulfills his calling as high priest for us.

Jesus Christ, Heavenly High Priest (7:1–9:28)

Christ the High Priest according to the Order of Melchizedek

The high priest according to the order of Melchizedek is an "eternal high priest" (6:20, a.t.) since, according to 7:1-3, Melchizedek is presented in Genesis as an eternal priest (7:1-3). The comparison of Christ to Melchizedek emphasizes the superiority of this kind of priesthood as compared to the old Levitical priestly order of a "weak and ineffectual" law (7:5-25) by stressing that:

1. The old priesthood cannot lead to perfection (*teleiōsis*, 7:11).
2. The priest according "to the order of Melchizedek" is not supposed to be a descendent from a sacerdotal tribe, Levi, but from Judah, "another tribe, from which no one has ever served at the altar. For it is evident that our Lord was descended from Judah . . ." (7:13-14).
3. The service of the old priesthood is transitory, while the intercessory ministry of Jesus the great high priest continues eternally in the heavens: "he always lives to make intercession for them" (7:25).

The Liturgical Service of Jesus Christ as High Priest in "the Most Holy Place" in the Heaven

If the existence of a heavenly high priest is accepted, then logically there must also be a heavenly service and a heavenly altar (8:1-2). This means, as Saint Ambrosius underscored, that Jesus' priesthood and ministry as high priest are not limited to his sacrifice on Golgotha but are continuing in "the most holy place" in the heavens, at the true and eternal altar (Ambrosius, *De fide*, XI, 87, PL 16, G 32). The holy fathers of the church deepen and spiritualize the meaning of the notions "tent" and "temple" as places of service for Christ the eternal high priest. They consider them from a Christological-soteriological angle, under-standing "the tent" and "the temple" as the temple of his resurrected and glorified body.

According to 8:2-6, "today," between his first and second coming, Christ the Savior is *leitourgos* (a minister of the sanctuary) in heaven. This means that he is willing to sacrifice himself, thereby entering the realm of eternal life. He became eternal with his pure blood, due to the sacrifice that purified him. Therefore,

his state of eternal sacrifice in heaven means the perpetual manifestation of his humanity sacrificed to the Father. This gesture constitutes the altar dimension of his heavenly liturgy.

Jesus Christ's eternal service as high priest has three soteriological effects:

a. *Intercession for us:* "appear[ing] in the presence of God on our behalf" (9:24).
b. *Destruction of sins:* "But now, at the end of the ages he has appeared once (hapax) to put away sin by the sacrifice of himself" (9:26, a.t.), mentioning then its unique effect: "by that will we have been sanctified through the offering of the body of Jesus Christ once for all" (*ephapax*, 10:10, a.t.).
c. *Bringing salvation at the end of time:* Christ "will appear a second time, not to deal with sin, but to save those who are eagerly waiting for him" (9:28, a.t.).

The Effectiveness of Christ's Unique and Ultimate Sacrifice (10:1-25; 13:7-17)

By comparing Jesus Christ's unique sacrifice with other sacrifices (10:1-10), Hebrews clarifies three kinds of relationships:

a. *Resemblance:* the sacrifice material ("gifts and sacrifices," 8:3), the necessity of the victim's death ("a death . . . that redeems them from the transgressions," 9:15-16), the redeeming role of the blood (9:7, 14, 18, 24).
b. *Differentiation:* instead of the "gifts and sacrifices" brought by the high priest of the old covenant (9:6-9), Christ "through the eternal Spirit offered himself without blemish to God" (9:14).
c. *Superiority:* the effectiveness of Christ's sacrifice does not limit itself

to ritual purification; it secures an *"eternal redemption"* (9:12).

In sum, Christ's sacrifice has an eternal effectiveness for Christians' salvation: "by God's will . . . we have been sanctified through the offering of the body of Jesus Christ once for all. . . . For by a single offering he has perfected for all time those who are sanctified" (10:10, 14).

CONCLUSION

In my didactic context as a professor in an Orthodox seminary, the novelty of the Epistle to the Hebrews is not only the theme of Christ's service as a high priest that it introduces into New Testament Christology, but also and mainly its emphasis on the eternal duration and effectiveness of Christ's sacrifice: "By a single offering he has perfected for all time those who are sanctified" (10:14). This message renews every Christian generation in its particular context in society and the world. It also completes the whole message of the New Testament about Jesus Christ's human-divine person and about his saving work. From my perspective as an Orthodox theologian, the New Testament's Christology would remain incomplete without the Epistle to the Hebrews.

In my sacerdotal context as an Orthodox priest, the Epistle's essential message to the world, to God's people, is that Christ sacrifices himself continuously for each person, remaining in a sacrificial state forever because of his unchangeable priesthood. He can save those who come to God through him, since he always lives to make intercession for them (7:24-25). This effect of Christ's sacrifice is part of the mystical reality I experience in every holy liturgy.

Yet this effect of Christ's sacrifice is also eternalized in the concreteness of the visible world in his church as each Christian becomes a "priest by participation" at his sacrifice. Ecumenical interactions with all Christians is called for by the simple fact that Christ continuously makes intercession for all of us, regardless of our faith, of our ways of expressing it, and regardless of nationality, sex, and social or moral status. Further, the priesthood of all Christians makes of our daily lives in today's world a liturgical space where the church can be both a sign of hope (as the Romanian Church was even during the communist terror) and a sign of the ongoing redemption of the world. Indeed, as Christ fills his humanity with his Lordship and sets it free from faults, passions, and death—bringing his humanity to perfection—so today he sanctifies and brings to perfection "his brothers and sisters," that is, the entire people of God. It is this "bringing to perfection" of our humanity that is taking place in our world today as Christ fulfills his calling as high priest for us.

BIBLIOGRAPHY

Ambrose (Ambrosius Medidanensis). *De fide ad Gratianum Augustum,* XI, 87. In vol. 16 of Patrologia Latina. Edited by J. P. Migne. 217 vols. Paris, 1844–1864.

Andriessen. "Paul. L' Eucharistie dans l'Epître aux Hébreux." NRTh 94:3 (1972): 269–277.

Grässer, Erich. *An die Hebräer.* Evanelisch-Katholischer Kommentar zum Neuen Testament 17. Zurich: Neukirchener Verlag, 1990.

Guthrie, Donald. *The Letter to the Hebrews: An Introduction and Commentary.* TNTC 15. Grand Rapids, Eerdmans, 1983.

Hugedé, Norbert. *Le sacerdoce du Fils: Commentaire de l'Epître aux Hébreux.* Paris: Editions Fischbacher, 1983.

Roloff, Jürgen. Der mitleindende Hohepriester. Zur Frage nach der Bedeutung des irdischen Jesus für die Christologie des Hebräerbriefes. Pages 143–166 in *Jesus Christus in Historie and Theologie, festschriften fur H. Conzelmann.* Edited by Georg Strecker. Tübingen: Mohr, 1975.

Vanhoye, Albert. *Le Christ récreation de l'homme et réstaurateur de ses droits selon l'Epître aux Hébreux.* Roma: Editrice Pontificio Instituto Biblico, 1984.

Weiss, Hans-Friedrich. *Der Brief an die Hebräer: Übersetzt und erklärt.* KEK Bd. 13. Göttingen: Vandenhoeck & Ruprecht, 1991.

HEBREWS: SACRIFICE IN AN AFRICAN PERSPECTIVE

Teresa Okure, SHCJ
Catholic Institute of West Africa, Port Harcourt, Nigeria

LIFE CONTEXT OF THE INTERPRETATION

At a 1995 meeting in Leuven, Belgium, contributors to the *International Bible Commentary: A Catholic and Ecumenical Commentary for the Twenty-First Century,* launched a heated discussion about how the writer who was assigned to comment on the book of Hebrews would tackle the topics of sacrifice and blood. Many felt that this issue was no longer relevant for the modern reader. The two African scholars present maintained that the value of sacrifice and blood is still very relevant for Africans and people in other parts of the world. They cited as evidence the resurgent cultic practices worldwide with their accompanying sacrificial acts. About a year later, an Irish missionary nun in Nigeria, expressed that given the importance that Africans attach to sacrifice, it was a pity that preachers give little or no attention to explaining the importance of the Eucharist as a sacrifice, not simply as a communion meal. Effectively, this nun noticed that preachers in Africa fail to do for the people what the author of Hebrews did for his readers.

Issues Raised by Hebrews about Sacrifice in Africa and Elsewhere

The impression created by these two incidents is that sacrifice is primarily, if not exclusively meaningful to Africans. This impression is not without justification. Available historical, documentary evidence shows clearly that sacrifice with its accompanying requirements of priest, priestess, temple and sacrificial offerings originated in Africa, as far back as the fourth millennium B.C.E., in the Egypt of the Pharaohs, where the Israelites spent over 430 years and became for the first time "a great nation" (Deut 26:5). Moses their lawgiver and cult initiator grew up in this court, a Pharaoh's daughter's son (Exod 2:5-10). Sacrificial practices form the heart of African Traditional Religions. Throughout modern Africa many Christians still believe, especially in times of crisis, in the effectiveness of traditional religious sacrifices, designed to meet their diverse needs. It would be grossly misleading, however, to conclude from this evidence that sacrifice is of value mainly or only for Africans.

Sacrifice, as noted by many African and other scholars, is of the very essence of all known religions worldwide from the earliest times. Its purpose is to establish, regulate or rectify the relationship between humans and God or to appease the ancestors and the land. Through sacrifice, humans seek to encounter the divine, project themselves into the invisible world, penetrate into the divine presence and commune with the deity. Sacrifice creates a bridge between humans and God and serves to sustain the established relationship. Its different forms

Teresa Okure, SHCJ, a graduate of the University of Ibadan, La Sorbonne, École Biblique of Jerusalem, and Fordham University (PhD), is Professor of New Testament and Gender Hermeneutics. She is or has been a member of the executive committees of EATWOT (Ecumenical Association of Third World Theologians), the International Association for Mission Studies (IAMS), and the Society for New Testament Studies (SNTS). She has published more than one hundred articles and six books including *The Johannine Approach to Mission: a Contextual Study of John 4:1-42* (1988), ed. *Evaluating the Inculturation of Christianity in Africa* (1990) and ed. *To Cast Fire upon the Earth: Bible and Mission. Collaborating in Today's Multicultural Global Context* (2000).

depend on the nature of the relationship or favor sought from the deity. Ultimately, sacrifice is a human activity. Its primary beneficiaries are the humans who offer them, not God or the deities to whom the offerings are made.

Underlying the practice of sacrifice is the awareness that sin in its diverse forms (the destruction of right relationship with God, the ancestors, the land) creates a barrier between God, the invisible world and humans. Genesis 3 gives a primordial expla-

nation of this idea. Adam and Eve, who previously communed with God "walking in the garden in the cool of the day," later saw their sin to be a barrier between them and God; so they hid from God (3:8, a.t.). Only after that sin does the notion of sacrifice, of Abel and Cain, arise in the Bible (Gen 4:3-5). From then on humans seek to remove this barrier of sin or to celebrate the restoration of the relationship through various forms of sacrifice. Sacrifice in Leviticus systematizes this practice.

CONTEXTUAL COMMENT

The Letter to the Hebrews, Ineffective Human Sacrifices, and Christ's Sacrifice

This brief background helps one to understand the main thesis of the Hebrews' author on the nature and permanent effectiveness of Christ's sacrifice vis-à-vis the many sacrifices of the Old Testament. The thesis, given succinctly in Hebrews 10:1-17 (see also 7:23-9:28), is that compared to Christ's sacrifice, the many repeated sacrifices of the OT did not remove the barrier of sin between God and the people, or establish a permanent relationship or communion between God and the people because the priests who offered these sacrifices for sin, and the people on whose behalf the sacrifices were offered, were in the grip of sin. Secondly, the blood of victims offered in sacrifice (of bulls, goats, etc) did not initiate the desired communion between God and humans.

Because the sacrifices that humans offered to God in the OT did not give them the lasting communion with God that they wanted, God in the person of Jesus decided to make the sacrifice which would establish the communion with God that humans sought in vain to establish. This sacrifice has two dimensions. First, Jesus, God's Word/Son (Heb 1:2), became one with us ("like us in all things but sin," the basic obstacle between us and God; 4:15; cf. 2:14-17). Second, since the desired com-

munion was between bodied human beings and God—Jesus, having assumed our humanity, made that same body as the sacrificial offering, thereby establishing a permanent and indestructible relationship between humans and God. The permanent union between humans and God happened first in his person. Then through that same body, offered in sacrificial death (his passion, death, resurrection and ascension), Jesus unites all who are incorporated into him permanently to God and transforms them from within through the shedding of his own blood—blood signifying life. He thereby succeeds in effecting once and for all that union which repeated sacrifices (OT and otherwise), sought in vain to effect. He breaks the barrier of sin of separation between God and human beings, establishes a permanent relationship between them and God, penetrates into the divine, invisible presence and lives there permanently at God's right hand making intercession for us (8:1-2; 9:12, 14, 24). In Christ, in his person, all human beings, whom he was not ashamed to call his brothers and sisters, especially believers, share in this permanent relationship and access to God in their new capacity and status of the first-born (12:23). Legally, all first born belonged to God as his unique portion.

An amazing twist in the notion of sacrifice presented in Hebrews (and the NT generally) must not be overlooked. Sacrifice, as earlier noted, is the means by which humans seek to make themselves sacred, to penetrate into the divine realm and community with God. It is essentially a human activity undertaken to appease God or create a bridge between humans and God. The higher the relationship or favor sought, the greater the victim offered in sacrifice. But sacrifice in Hebrews essentially reverses this process. In the sacrifice of Jesus, it is not human beings who seek to establish a communion relationship with God, but God, who in the person of "his Son" valuates us very highly and seeks to establish this relationship with us. God works to make us sacred by offering the divine self and life for us. Jesus himself was valuated at thirty pieces of silver, which was the price of a slave. But to reveal how much God loves/values us, Jesus himself valued us at the price of his own life. "No greater love has one than this, to lay down one's life for one's friends" (John 15:13, a.t.). "God loved the world so much that he gave his uniquely begotten Son so that all who believe in him may not perish but have eternal life" (John 3:16, a.t.). This incredible value which God places on us, the divine commitment to establish and sustain an unbreakable relationship with us, is the comprehensive or all embracing framework within which the author of Hebrews understands the meaning of Christ's sacrifice and shares it with his readers. His central message is that the desire of humans to remove the obstacle of sin between them and God or to establish a permanent communion with God through sacrifice has already been fulfilled for us once and for all by God in the person of Jesus. It is, therefore, futile to indulge in or go back to all other types of ineffective sacrifices in the hope of achieving the same end when God has already done it for us, free of charge and at great cost to the divine self in the person of Jesus.

CONCLUSION

Ineffective Modern Sacrifices and Christ's Sacrifice

If such is the message of Hebrews concerning Christ's sacrifice, does sacrifice have any relevance for the modern reader? Can the modern Christian, whatever his or her location, treat the sacrifice in Hebrews as an outdated concept? Its religious dimension apart, sacrifice is an essential component of human life or of the reality of being human. Today people may not sacrifice goats, bulls or shed human blood to appease the gods and get what they need from them. But do people not engage in all types of sacrifice daily? In this general context, sacrifice may be understood as spending something of value to acquire another and higher value that lies outside what is spent. We spend time, for instance, for study, money for purchasing items, and so forth. The time and money thus spent for the values sought cannot be regained and re-spent for other values, except, perhaps, in the case of a refund from an unsatisfactory item purchased. Furthermore, human beings sacrifice people for money (e.g., laying off of workers to replace them by machines). In occult practices people sacrifice their parents, wife, children, even their entire families to gain wealth, fame and power. In exploitative capitalism, engineered today by globalization, multinational corporations sacrifice small local businesses to make a large, fast, and easy profit. In Africa and elsewhere, political leaders sacrifice their people's welfare to stay in power. Powerful countries use all kinds of excuses to invade and exploit poor nations. Even in the churches, many modern preachers sacrifice the God-given dignity and status of their people for their own selfish and money making ends. Like false OT prophets, they "ply their trade through the land and lack knowledge" of God and God's high value of his people.

Ironically, these modern sacrifices are essentially anti-sacrifice. They benefit neither the ones who offer them (for it dehumanizes them) nor the ones sacrificed on these modern altars of fame, power, sex, money and materialism. How can the believer re-appropriate the unique value of sacrifice in Hebrews in such a way that it will serve to correct false modern sacrifices as the author of Hebrews did for himself and his audience? Does not the daily participation in Christ's self-sacrifice in the Eucharist challenge the contemporary Christian to do this? "Sacrifice and offerings you have not desired, but a body you have prepared for me. . . Then I said, 'See God, I have come to do your will . . .' " (Heb 10:5-7). "A new commandment I give you that you love one another as I have loved you" (John 13:34). Why do we sacrifice money, time, and energy on what cannot give and sustain life, let alone divinize us? "In the fight against sin you have not yet resisted to the point of shedding your blood" (Heb 12:4). I consider the fight against sin to be the struggle to eliminate all barriers between human beings and God and among human beings themselves. Have we carried on this fight to the point of shedding our blood? Is the notion of sacrifice in Hebrews really as irrelevant for the modern Christian as was intimated at the beginning of this very short study?

BIBLIOGRAPHY

Awolalu, J. O. *Yoruba Beliefs and Sacrificial Rites*. London: Longman, 1979.

Babalola, E. O. Pages 78-91 in "The Continuity of the Phenomenon of Sacrifice in the Yoruba Society of Nigeria." *Africa Theological Journal* 21/1 Arusha, 1992.

Barclay, William. *The Letter to the Hebrews*. The Daily Study Bible. Louisville: Westminster John Knox, 1976.

Casey, J. *Hebrews*. New Testament Message 18. Dublin: Veritas, 1980.

Diop, Cheik Anton and Cook, Mercer, eds. *African Origin of Civilisatio: Myth or Reality*. Translated by Mercer Cook. Chicago: Chicago Review Press, 1989.

Dunnill, John. *Covenant and Sacrifice in the Letter to the Hebrews*. MSSNTS 75. Cambridge: Cambridge University Press, 1992.

Olowola, C. *African Traditional Religion and the Christian Faith*. Achimota, Ghana: African Christian Press, 1993.

Sawyerr, Harry. "Sacrifice." Pages 57-82 in *Biblical Revelation and African Beliefs*. Edited by Kwesi Dickson and Paul Ellingworth. Maryknoll: Orbis Books, 1969.

Ukpong, J. S. *Sacrifice: African and Biblical*. Rome: Urbaniana University, 1987.

Vanhoye, Albert. "Hebrews." Pages 1765-1785 in *International Bible Commentary: A Catholic and Ecumenical Commentary for the Twenty-First Century*. Edited by W. R. Farmer et al. Collegeville: The Liturgical Press, 1998.

JAMES

Cristina Conti
Seminary of the Salvation Army, Buenos Aires, Argentina

LIFE CONTEXT OF THE INTERPRETATION

I come from Uruguay, a small country on the coast of the Atlantic Ocean and the River Plate. On the map it looks like a little wedge inserted between Argentina and Brazil.

Unlike our big neighboring countries, we have had a long history of democracy, only interrupted by eleven years of a military regime in the 1970s and early 1980s. This democratic background, the "sanctity" of the banking system, and the thorough reform of the state in 1917, which, among other things, implemented the separation of church and state and also a wide-ranging welfare state, caused Uruguay to be called "the Switzerland of America."

We used to have the highest rate of human development in Latin America and illiteracy was practically erased from the country in the first decades of the twentieth century. In more recent times, though, little remains of our past glories. Neoliberalism, globalization, and other peculiarities of the present world have left their mark on our small country, which has few natural resources. Furthermore, corruption is rampant in most decision-making spheres. Those in power use their influence to give preferential treatment to friends, relatives, and colleagues. Favoritism and nepotism may seem relatively harmless, but they have done much harm to the economy of our country. These practices progressively lead to wide-ranging social injustice, until it appears normal for the political class to rule mostly for the benefit of the powerful.

Uruguay is quickly becoming, like most Latin American countries, a land of strong socioeconomic contrasts. The gap between rich and poor is widening. In the last few years the middle class, which included the vast majority of the population, has dramatically shrunk because many have been forced back into the lower classes. The unemployment rate is constantly rising. Approximately 30 percent of the population is now below the poverty line.

James and the Relationship of God's People to the World

James writes to churches with clear socioeconomic inequalities and with leaders who discriminate against the poor and show favoritism toward the rich. The economic struggle of Christians who are in need is a recurrent theme in the book, and indeed at its center.

The first textual feature I propose to highlight is the semiotic structure of the whole book. It has a concentric structure, with 2:1-13 as its center. This passage deals with a church that gives preferential treatment to the rich. The central section

Cristina Conti is a professor of New Testament and Greek and pursues research in gender hermeneutics. She has taught as a visiting professor at Garrett-Evangelical Theological Seminary (2000). Her publications include "Propuesta de estructuración de la Carta de Santiago" (*RIBLA*, 1998); "Hermenéutica feminista" *(Alternativas,* 1998); "Infiel es esta Palabra. 1 Timoteo 2, 9-15" (*RIBLA*, 2000); and "Ecritos y conferencias de J. Severino Croatto" (a copiously annotated bibliography), in *Los caminos inexhauribles de la Palabra: Homenaje de colegas y discípulos a J. Severino Croatto* (2000). Cristina Conti is responsible for preparing a Spanish edition of this *Global Bible Commentary*.

will be analyzed in full, both because of its central position in the structure of the book and also because of its significance for the life context in Uruguay. In order to clarify what the text says about this issue, I will also analyze related passages that treat similar issues. The most important of these are 1:9-11 and 4:13–5:6, as well as 1:27 and 2:14-26, which are paired in the structure of the book. Both sets of passages have to do with the living faith that becomes evident in the concern for those in need. As will become clear, the five passages are relevant for the Uruguayan life context.

CONTEXTUAL COMMENT

An Overview of James

The book of James is one of the so-called Catholic (i.e., universal) Epistles, since it is not addressed to a particular church. Rather than being known by the names of their addresses (Romans, etc.), the Catholic Epistles are known by the names of those who, according to the early church tradition, were supposed to be their authors: James, Peter, John, Jude.

Tradition has attributed this book to James, the brother of the Lord. However, there is no firm ground for such an assumption. The author shows a mastery of the Greek language that can only be explained if it was actually his mother tongue. He uses Hellenistic literary devices such as diatribe (Jas 1:13; 2:14-17; 3:2-5), imaginary opponent (2:18-26); Stoic paradox (2:10), Stoic expressions (1:25; 2:12), phrases from secular Greek (2:15-16), Greek metaphors (3:3-4, 7; 4:14), and Greek sayings (4:15). Besides, there are no traces of Aramaic influence, and the biblical quotations are taken from the Septuagint. So, unlike Jesus' brother, the writer was not a Palestinian Jew. We can say that he probably was a Hellenistic Jew, in view of his proficiency in Jewish Wisdom literature, his arguments based in the Hebrew Scriptures, and his use of Semitic concentric structures. He was also a teacher (3:1).

The addressees, according to the salutation, are "the twelve tribes in the Dispersion," meaning the new Israel, the Christian church as heir of the patriarchs. By the time James wrote his book toward the end of the first century, the church had spread from Palestine to other regions of the empire; it was therefore "in the Dispersion."

The book of James is the only work of Wisdom literature in the New Testament. The author is especially concerned for social justice, and also for the ethical and practical issues of Christian life. He is clearly on the side of the poor, the marginalized, and the powerless, as Jesus was—a point James emphasized with the structure of his book.

Overall Structure of James

At first sight, the book of James appears a somewhat disorderly text, but it actually follows a precise scheme. In the first part the author presents the topics that he will develop in the rest of the text. As the topics are expounded in the opposite order, a concentric structure emerges. Even though this structure does not touch each and every detail, at least it shows the general design of the writing. In this kind of structure, the center is the main message of the whole text. Concentric structure was a characteristic form of expression by Near Eastern peoples.

A (1:2-8) **(a)** joy in the midst of trial **(b)** endurance **(c)** asking in faith **(d)** one who doubts **(e)** will not receive anything **(f)** a two-souled man **(a)** unstable **(b)** in all his ways

  B (1:9-11) (the paths of the rich) **(a)** boasting **(y)** exaltation **(z)** humiliation **(b)** (comparison) flower of the grass // grass (withers) flower (falls) **(c)** journeys of the rich

    C (1:12-15) **(a)** problems because of lustfulness **(b)** sin

      D (1:16-25) **(a)** perfect gift **(b)** from above **(c)** all filth and abundance of evil **(d)** with sweetness **(e)** doing

        E (1:26) **(a)** restraining **(b)** the tongue

          F (1:27) **(a)** religion in deeds **(b)** helping those in need **(c)** "orphans and widows"

            XX (2:1-13) making distinctions between the rich and the poor (= transgression of the law)

          F' (2:14-26) **(a')** faith in deeds **(b')** helping those in need **(c')** "brother or sister"

        E' (3:1-12) **(a')** restraining **(b')** the tongue

      D' (3:13-18) **(e')** deeds **(d')** with sweetness **(c')** every evil action **(b')** from above **(a')** wisdom as a perfect gift

    C' (4:1-12) **(a')** problems because of lustfulness **(b')** consequences of sin

  B' (4:13-5,6) (the paths of the rich) **(c')** we shall journey **(b')** (comparison) vapor **(a')** boasting **(y')** showing off **(z')** humiliation

A' (5:7-20) **(a')** patience in suffering **(b')** Job's endurance **(c')** prayer of faith **(d')** Elijah did not doubt **(e')** Elijah received **(f')** one who converts the sinner from the deviation **(b')** of his/her way **(a')** will save his/her soul

As we can see, far from being a disorderly text, the book of James has order and coherence. Note for example, the correspondence between frames **F** and **F'** particularly in regard to the corresponding development of topics (**a** and **a'**, **b** and **b'**, **c** and **c'**).

The Frame of the Center (1:27 and 2:14-17)

The center (2:1-13) is directly framed by 1:27 and 2:14-17. The latter is part of the well-known passage that deals with faith and works (2:14-26). Both framing texts have to do with social justice. Both explain the meaning of true religion or faith. In 1:27 we see that pure and undefiled faith is verified by good deeds assisting the needy, described as the paradigmatic orphans and widows. They were the most destitute groups in ancient society, because the death of the head of the patriarchal family—the husband and father—deprived orphans and widows of protection and legal status. They could only count on the protection of God. The Law, the Prophets, and the New Testament abound in references about God's concern for orphans and widows.

Their counterparts in the parallel text (2:14-17) are "the brother or sister" in need. Thus we find a parallelism—masculine / feminine (orphans and widows // brother or sister)—that cannot but be intentional. The first-century author is using inclusive language!

The response given to those in need (2:16) is suggestive: "Go in peace!" is a Semitic idiom of farewell; the imperatives can be understood in the passive voice as, "May you be warmed and filled!" The implication is that those who could help simply consign the needy to the providence of God.

The Central Message of the Book (2:1-13)

Faith in Jesus and the practice of partiality are incompatible according to 2:1. The word prosōpolēmpsía (literally: receiving the face) means judging by appearances, by a person's exterior.

In 2:2-3, the author gives a hypothetical example of the usual partiality and favoritism of the addressees in their "synagogue." This term is commonly and appropriately translated "assembly," because it certainly refers to the church, or a church-court in the manner of the courts of the Jewish synagogue. In either case, the addressees function as leaders. The man with gold rings and the poor person represent all those who have been judged by their appearance and treated with partiality.

In 2:3 there is a suggestive repetition of two opposite prepositions: epi (over) and hypo (under). The author repeats epi when he is referring to the behavior of the leaders toward the rich man (looking with respect to this man), and hypo regarding their conduct with the poor person ("sit under my footstool"). The play with the prepositions underlines the place assigned to both characters.

The author refers to the rich in an indirect way—as the "man with gold rings" and "the one who wears the resplendent dress"—to highlight the visual aspect of brilliance, which seems to be so blinding for the addressees. They prove to be unable to see beyond the external. The fact that the descriptions of both the rich and the poor remain in the visual sphere is highly suggestive. Nothing is said about the inner self of either, for the simple reason that discrimination and partiality are precisely based on external aspects.

The rich man is depicted as the stereotype of a patron, so the leaders seem to be looking for his favor. They invite the rich to sit "here," close to them. On the contrary, they tell the poor person to "stand there," at a distance. What follows is remarkable, not only because of the place where the poor is told to sit and what it implies, but also because of the wordplay involving the preposition hypo (under). The leaders tell the poor to sit literally "under my under-foot," that is under a footstool. There cannot be a lower position. The expression implies degradation—a loss of dignity as a human being.

In 2:4, a rhetorical question concludes the preceding example. It is an accusation to the addressees. Partiality is a transgression of "the royal law," the law of the kingdom of heaven, which is quoted in 2:8: "You shall love your neighbor as yourself." Together with the commandment to love God, it is a summary of the whole law (Matt 22:36-40).

There is a blatant opposition between what we could call the option of God—who chooses those who are poor according to the world (Jas 2:5)—and the option of the addressees, who, together with the world, despise the poor (2:3b and 6a). This opposition brings us back to 1:27 and its statement that the pure and immaculate religion consists in helping the needy and "keep[ing] oneself unstained by the world."

The bitter accusation that follows ("But you have dishonored the poor" [2:6] emphasizes the pronoun "you," which instead of being implicit as is usual, appears explicitly at the beginning of the sentence. In that society, honor was the highest value. To deprive a man (especially a man) of his honor was to ostracize or marginalize him from society. The author wants to mark the contrast between God's attitude toward the poor and that of the addressees. While their option is for the rich, the option of God is for the poor. This point is in keeping with the tradition that saw the poor as the objects of God's care and blessing. On the contrary, the rich are depicted as oppressors who are unjust and even blasphemous (2:6b-7).

The Greek language has two different words for "the poor": *penētes* and *ptō-choi*. The former are people who have to work for living, but are above the level of subsistence. The ptōchoi, on the contrary, have neither work nor the means to obtain what is needed for life; they are forced to beg. Jesus was always talking about this kind of poor, and he said they were blessed because the kingdom of God belonged to them (Luke 6:20). It is worth noting that this Lukan blessing corresponds to James 2:5, where these people—who are *ptōchoi* in the eyes of the world—are proclaimed to be "rich in faith and heirs of the kingdom."

The *ptōchoi* in our Uruguayan context are the unemployed, the homeless, the families who live in shantytowns, the children who live in the streets, and all those who are below the poverty line. Their lives depend on the charity of other people and on the mercy of God.

In the accusation of James 2:4 the author used the verb *diakrinō* (discriminate, make distinctions), which has the same root as *krinō* (judge), *kritai* (judges), and *krisis* (judgment). This verb establishes a connection with the end of the passage (2:12-13) and its threefold repetition of words of the same root. Such connection cannot but be intentional, especially if the context is a church-court. The addressees establish themselves as judges by making distinctions, and so they arrive at evil decisions (2:4). Nevertheless, they will be judged according to the "law of liberty" (2:12), that is, the law of love. This explains the enigmatic phrase at the end: "Mercy triumphs over judgment" (2:13). If, in spite of their partiality, they are going to be judged by the law of love, mercy will be the determining factor. God's mercy demands from them to be merciful, thus performing the law of love. From the point of view of classical rhetoric, 2:12-13 is a fitting conclusion to the argument.

Critique of the Rich in the Church (1:9-11 and 4:13-17)

The passages B and B' in the overall structure also have to do with the rich people, those in the church (1:9-11; 4:13-17) and those outside the church (5:1-6).

In 1:9-11 the author addresses the humble brother and then the rich person, who is implicitly also a brother, as seems confirmed by the antithetic parallelism:

a Let the humble brother boast
  b in his exaltation,
a' but the rich
  b' in his humiliation . . .

The humble brother can boast in being exalted by God. On the other hand, the rich brother, who is asked to become humble, may boast in his future reward. His present humiliation might imply social and economic loss. The rich were involved in a complex web of relations with their equals, a web on which their social status as males and even their sources of wealth depended.

In James 4:13-17 the addressees are self-sufficient rich merchants who are believers; otherwise the author's exhortation to say, "If the Lord wants . . . " (4:15, a.t.), would be irrelevant. The only non-Christian rich people in the book seem to be those mentioned in 2:6-7—who oppress the addressees and blaspheme the name of Christ—and the rich landlords of 5:1-6.

Condemnation of the Rich Oppressors (5:1-6)

This passage also deals with the rich, but this time they are not members of the church. These rich people are guilty of oppression, exploitation, and greed. They may even be murderers (5:6). The author predicts for them a punishment that will come directly from God, who has heard the clamor of their oppressed laborers.

The withheld salary of the laborers is personified as crying out to heaven (5:4) like Abel's blood (Gen 4:10). Laborers had to receive their pay at the end of the day (Lev 19:13; Deut 24:14-15), because they and their families depended on it for their subsistence. To withhold wages amounted to murdering them (Jas 5:6).

The language of the passage resembles that of the prophets or the Jewish apocalyptic writers, but it also resembles Jesus' warnings to the rich in Luke 6:24-25. This is not a call to repentance, but a warning of impending condemnation. However, the rich landlords are not the real addressees. As in apocalyptic literature, the injunctions are actually a consolation for the oppressed, a call to trust in the justice that God will bring.

CONCLUSION

The church and the people of God should have a message of hope to proclaim in the seemingly hopeless situation of a lot of impoverished people in Uruguay. Such a message—unlike the position of some charismatic churches—must not be perceived as escapism that drives deprived people into a magic present realm and a purely eschatological expectation. Instead, as the book of James does, this message should keep them with their feet on the ground and their heads in search of practical solutions.

Furthermore, the increasing rate of unemployment will not be solved by simply assisting people in need. They need to be taught how to help themselves and, above all, their self-respect must be rebuilt.

To this end, the book of James is an invaluable source of encouragement and empowerment. It teaches that God disapproves of inequality and favoritism, oppression and injustice, and any practice that might hinder the freedom and the dignity of any person. Every human being is valuable, respectable, and a full person before God, regardless of class or wealth, and, consequently, regardless of race, age, gender, sexual orientation, or anything else. The above teaching, though it is expressed in androcentric terms and reaffirms patriarchal structures, needs to be turned against itself on this point.

James is clearly on the side of the poor and the powerless. He shows that God and Jesus are also on their side. As Christians, we should also be this way.

BIBLIOGRAPHY

Cargal, Timothy B. *Restoring the Diaspora: Discursive Structure and Purpose in the Epistle of James.* SBLDS 144. Atlanta: Scholars Press, 1993. This work contains excellent structural analyses of James.

Davids, Peter H. *The Epistle of James: A Commentary on the Greek Text.* NIGTC. Grand Rapids: Eerdmans, 1982. This work contains excellent structural analyses of James.

Laws, Sophie. *A Commentary on the Epistle of James.* London: Adam & Charles Black, 1980.

Maynard-Reid, Pedrito U. *Poverty and Wealth in James.* Maryknoll, N.Y.: Orbis, 1987.

Tamez, Elsa. *The Scandalous Message of James: Faith without Works is Dead.* Translated by John Eagleson. New York: Crossroad, 2002.

1 AND 2 PETER, JUDE

Sharon H. Ringe

Wesley Theological Seminary, Washington, D.C., USA

LIFE CONTEXT OF THE INTERPRETATION

I write this commentary as a woman from the dominant culture of the United States and as a feminist who is a tenured professor in a theological seminary and an ordained minister in a liberal Protestant denomination. I write also as a person in solidarity with Latino/Latina communities in the United States and with communities in Central America and the Caribbean that have been left desolate and impoverished by decades of military intervention and economic exploitation that originated in my country. This multifaceted context intersects with the Petrine letters at several points.

1 and 2 Peter and Jude about the Church's Relationship with the World

These letters that claim to stem from Peter and from "brother of James" (Jude 1:1) are actually the product of theologians of a subsequent generation who attempt to interpret the gospel for a context far from its origin. They wrestle with issues of exile and homelessness (literally and metaphorically), with life in the context of the Roman Empire, and with the intersections of the gospel and the diverse cultures that surround them. From my context I also wrestle with the gospel as a privileged citizen of the leading imperial power, in the midst of a global crisis of uprooted peoples (a term that encompasses both those displaced within their own countries by eco-

logical and economic disasters or war, as well as those who meet the legal definitions of refugees and asylum seekers). Given my context of origin and my context of commitment, I find myself joining the author of 1 Peter in straddling the gulf between the imperial center and the life of exiles. From the center, I cannot speak for those on the margins. Unlike the authors of these letters, I would not speak to them about the shape their faith should take, for I am committed to the epistemological privilege of persons on the margins in matters of the gospel.

The homelessness of the Latino/Latina communities in the United States with whom I read is both physical and metaphorical. Many members of these communities are literally homeless in the sense that they are refugees from political and economic turmoil in their home countries, or they are undocumented fugitives from the legacies of decades of war. Many also live in crowded and substandard conditions verging on literal homelessness while they try to support family members "back home" with incomes from the lowest-paid jobs available in a country that disdains their very presence. Others may not know the pain of physical homelessness, but they do know the experience of cultural exile in which they must always translate between the values and assumptions of the dominant groups and institutions while defending the legitimacy of the culture that has nurtured and shaped them.

Sharon H. Ringe is Professor of New Testament at Wesley Theological Seminary in Washington, D.C., and a visiting professor at the Universidad Biblica Latinoamericana in San Jose, Costa Rica. She is the co-editor of *Women's Bible Commentary* (1992, 1998), the author of *Wisdom's Friends: Community and Christoloty in the Fourth Gospel* (1999) and *Luke* 1995), and co-author with Frederick C. Tiffany of *Biblical Interpretation: A Roadmap* (1996).

Within the church, such external consequences of homelessness and exile are often addressed by various mission efforts to meet immediate needs (and even to change the root causes and conditions). At the same time, these consequences are compounded by the coalition of Christian theology and practice with the dominant culture of the West, and especially of the United States. Instead of being havens of safety and hospitality, congregations often exacerbate the loneliness of persons from other cultures by the way they formulate belief and practice. This happens when they equate the values of middle-class white society, a capitalist economic order, and a priority on individual rights with the heart of the gospel. Being part of the church requires formulation of one's faith in categories that ignore the symbols, narratives, and values of one's own culture.

In both the context of the challenges of cultural diversity and my identity as a feminist, I find myself wrestling also with the issue of "right teaching" that underlies 2 Peter and Jude, and with questions of the relationship between the gospel and the cultural norms and values that are woven through both letters. Who decides what is an acceptable formulation of the faith or what values conform to the gospel when interpreting it for new times and places? According to what criteria are those decisions reached? Who benefits by those decisions, and who is harmed or rejected?

CONTEXTUAL COMMENT: 1 PETER

An Overview of 1 Peter

1 and 2 Peter are called *general* or *catholic* letters because they are addressed to a wide range of Christian communities. The "exiles of the Dispersion" (1:1) to whom 1 Peter is addressed have been understood literally as Jewish Christians living outside of Palestine, or even as all Christians in exile from their true heavenly home. The letter itself points in another direction. Baptismal references, language of "being chosen," and an emphasis on a recent change in one's status before God suggest the letter is addressed not to Jews but to Gentiles who have become heirs to God's promises through Jesus Christ (a similar argument is found in Romans 9–11). These Gentiles now live as resident aliens (1:17 and 2:11), perhaps literally, but certainly as a minority community surrounded by a pagan culture. The crescent sketched by the list of place names in 1:1—Pontus, Galatia, Cappadocia, Asia, and Bithynia—further situates these addressees in northern Asia Minor (modern Turkey).

The traditional connection of Peter with Rome, coupled with the letter's own claim of authorship by Peter, suggests that Rome is the letter's place of origin, a city from which Asia Minor would seem like a distant exile indeed. However, there are similarities between this letter and other letters from the final third of the first century, and there is no discussion of the need to observe torah or of other points of contention in relations between Jews and Gentiles in the church of the time of Peter. These points suggest the letter was likely written by a follower of Peter, probably in 70 to 90 C.E. I use masculine pronouns to refer to the author, whose perspective (for example, see the household code of 2:18–3:7) is clearly that of a dominant male.

References to suffering pervade the letter and raise questions about the specific circumstances that caused it. Nothing points to political persecution of a formal sort being threatened against Christians. We are told nothing about conditions of extreme poverty or other physical suffering, though the lives of people with the tenuous status of resident aliens might well have included economic difficulties. What is clear is that the addressees are exiles in the sense of being surrounded by a world that does not recognize their religious commitments and scruples. In a culture where relative honor is a crucial factor, these are people without honor and respect because of their differences; they are outsiders in their place of residence. They may have been harassed, slandered, or otherwise pressured by the surrounding communities to abandon their faith and conform to society's norms. The author of this letter offers encouragement and guidance that confirms members of the Christian community in their identity as God's chosen people (2:9-10), helps them withstand pressures from their surroundings (3:8-22), and understands their sufferings in the context of their faith and of the gospel (4:12-19).

Between the address and greeting (1:1-2) and the closing (5:12-14), the body of the letter has three sections. The first (1:3–2:10) directs the readers' attention back to God's election of them through the sacrifice offered by Christ and through the revelation of the Holy Spirit. This section accents the wonder of God's act and the foundation of joy that is stronger than any temporal sufferings. Christ's own rejection by humans and being chosen by God (2:4-8) is mirrored by the readers' own status before God, regardless of their circumstances (2:9-10). The third section (4:12–5:11) resumes the message of encouragement, exhorting the addressees to see their present suffering in the context of Christ's and to look forward to the glory that will be theirs at the final judgment. Between the past model and the future promise are the author's ethical guidelines for living in the present (2:11–4:11).

The second section is the focal point of the letter. It opens by summarizing the ethic of submission that the author advocates (2:11-17) and climaxes with injunctions to "Honor everyone. Love the family of believers. Fear God. Honor the emperor" (v. 17). That summary is elaborated in a set of rules for members of a household (2:18–3:7); in injunctions to live, as an expression of the changes wrought in them by their baptism, a blameless life without vindictiveness in the face of suffering (3:8–4:6); and in counsel for behavior toward others in the community (4:7-11). Both the household code (2:18–3:7) and the teachings about suffering and righteous conduct (3:8–4:6) merit a closer look.

The Household Code (2:18–3:7)

Lists of obligations (household codes) of various members of the household to the paterfamilias (the male head of the family) are common in the writings of the Stoic philosophers. It is unclear whether they reflected norms of society (accepted, at least, by the powerful) that were followed as self-evidently appropriate or whether they were ideals that were never achieved. A similar uncertainty surrounds their status in the early church and thus their role in the literature. While the three letters in which these codes are found (Col 3:18–4:1 and Eph 5:21–6:9, in addition to 1 Pet) provide different theological rationales for their rules and regulations, they share some commonalities.

Even though modern egalitarian sensibilities find both the institution of slavery and the notion of women's submission to men abhorrent and unacceptable, both may have been an accepted part of life in the ancient world. One possibility, then, is that these social norms seemed threatened by the proclamation of the freedom of the gospel and by the significant roles played by women in early Christian communities. Both of these factors may have figured in the suspicion and slander heaped on these communities by their neighbors and in a perception that Christians were a threat to the good order of society, even to the well-being of the empire itself.

Interpreters who follow this line of argument suggest that such rules may have found their way into Christian teaching as a way to reduce social and political tensions. Even subordinate members of the household might have been willing to go along with the rules for the sake of peace and survival, though their adoption would have clearly been more advantageous for the husbands, fathers, and slave owners than for the wives, children, and slaves. Other interpreters posit a more positive role for these teachings, as leaders of the early church sought to negotiate the relationships between their beliefs and the surrounding culture. These scholars suggest that the incorporation of the household codes into Christian writings and their interpretation in categories from Christian theology would have helped the members integrate their faith with social norms and feel at home in an otherwise alien environment. Both of these rationales resonate with the context to which 1 Peter was written.

The code in 1 Peter is unique in several respects. While most codes address three pairs of relationships—wives and husbands, children and parents, and slaves and slave owners—this code does not mention children and parents. Furthermore, instead of beginning with husbands and wives as most do, this code begins by addressing slaves and includes no word of advice to slave owners. Both slaves and wives are counseled to accept the authority of masters and husbands, in specific elaborations on the general counsel in 2:13, "For the Lord's sake accept the authority of every human institution." Husbands, in turn, are urged to "show consideration" for their wives for the sake of their own spiritual well-being (3:7).

Instructions to both slaves and wives are given specific theological rationales under the general rubric of accepting the authority of their duly established social superiors. For slaves, the theme is the value of suffering unjustly under harsh masters. Thus, not only do they have "God's approval" (2:20), but they follow the example of Christ, who is interpreted through the image of the Suffering Servant of Isaiah 53 (2:21-25). Wives are advised that their exemplary conduct might win over their non-Christian husbands (3:1-2), suggesting that a subtext of this letter might be life in religiously disparate households. Wifely submission to husbands is also said to be expressed in simple and even austere dress (3:3-6), perhaps in contrast to the behavior of adherents of some other religions, whose devotees attired themselves in extravagant finery, especially for worship, as a way of honoring their deities.

When I read this section of the letter in my own context, I see only its negative potential. This text and its parallels in Colossians and Ephesians are held over the heads of women to exhort submission to their husbands and even to justify spousal abuse when women do not behave according to these norms. Whatever the cultural origins in the ancient world, the inclusion of these texts in the Christian Scriptures appears to give such norms religious approval, even in cultures whose egalitarian secular values seem more in keeping with the practice and teachings attributed to Jesus elsewhere in the New Testament. What then should we do with texts such as these? Some would say to ignore them, but I think it would be better to attempt to understand the struggles and questions of early Christian women and men over the intersections of faith and culture, and to continue that same wrestling in our own context. The questions continue to engage us, even when we cannot follow them in their answers.

Suffering and Righteous Conduct (3:8–4:6)

The advice to slaves is applied to the entire community in this section. All are to answer evil or abuse with blessing and doing good, even if one suffers more for doing so. Once again, the sufferings of Christ are the model for the believers, who are to prepare for the final judgment that is at hand by living exemplary lives in the face of hostility.

The instructions are hard to bear in any circumstance, even in the private slights of everyday social relationships. But in a context of social oppression or abuse by people who are more powerful, the equation of faithfulness with accepting unjust suffering becomes a distortion of Jesus' message of life and hope. When these words are spoken by someone standing in solidarity with those who suffer, the words are difficult enough. Spoken by those with power to those without it, and spoken at a safe distance from all risk, they become cruel.

This passage resonates in my context as a dangerous text, because it can so easily become a text to reinforce the powerful as they prescribe obedience and submission—whether legal, economic, or famil-ial—to those under their power. It is used by persons in power and by their unwitting supporters to endorse as legitimate, and even praiseworthy, the suffering of such vulnerable communities as new immi-grants and refugees, people who are poor or disabled, children, or the elderly. When it becomes a generalized counsel for those who suffer, the model of the powerful and godlike Christ who accepted suffering for the sake of the life of the world (in the powerful imagery of the hymn of Phil 2:5-11) risks excusing the very death-dealing circumstances Christ came to end.

CONTEXTUAL COMMENT: 2 PETER

Overview and Comment

The author identifies this as his "sec-ond letter" (3:1), thus connecting this later work to the one we know as 1 Peter. He looks back on Paul's letters as writings that, while equivalent to other Scriptures, are sometimes unclear and in need of interpretation (3:15-16). He makes use of the letter of Jude as a source for most of chapter 2. The author wrestles with two issues: the implications that the delay of the anticipated second coming of Christ had on the beliefs and conduct of the church (ch. 3) and the treatment of "faith" as a deposit of beliefs (1:16) rather than with the relationship with God "by faith" meant in the Pauline letters. These are factors that mark this as a late writing, perhaps even the latest in all the New Tes-tament. It has a number of similarities to 1 Clement, which confirms it as a docu-ment of the early second century, perhaps written around 130 C.E.

Aside from the author's identification of it as the second letter, there is nothing that explicitly identifies this letter as com-ing from the same hand as 1 Peter. The fact that there is little overlapping vocab-ulary and a difference of topic suggests a different author, who may come from the same general community that traced its authoritative links to Peter and to the "brothers of the Lord." Again, I use mas-culine pronouns to refer to the unknown author, who is in a position of authority at a time when women were increasingly excluded from such leadership roles in the church.

The three chapters of the letter develop the author's three principal concerns. Chapter 1 is an unequivocal exhortation to virtue, with only the slightest attempt toward casting that exhortation as a letter (1:1-2). The second chapter, which deals with the danger of false teachers, repli-cates the letter of Jude, with only minor editorial changes of images and Scriptural references. The author's deliberations concerning the delay of Christ's second coming fill the third chapter.

Instead of looking at the impact of cul-ture on the everyday life of the commu-nity, as the author of 1 Peter does, 2 Peter's author is principally concerned that factors in the shifting culture will affect core beliefs. "False prophets" are perceived as the greatest threat (2:1), and their intellectual mischief is linked also to immorality and "lust" (1:4-7). The author assumes the role of arbiter of such mat-ters, but he does not identify the basis of his authority to do so. His reminder of the impending judgment is connected to his call for moral righteousness in a style reminiscent of the old threat to disobedient children, "You just wait till your father gets home!"

This letter resonates with challenges that have been leveled against indigenous communities in the Americas (and elsewhere) and against feminists who have sought to bring new language and new world views to the articulation of their faith (of which continuing battles over inclusive language are just one expres-sion). Efforts to incorporate the affirmation of nature or the human body into their spirituality are often rejected by official leaders of the churches as contrary and even dangerous to the faith and the faithful. Now, as in the first century, concerns of personal morality (especially sexual morality) dominate much of the church's ethical discourse and are identified as determinative of theological orthodoxy.

CONTEXTUAL COMMENT: JUDE

Overview and Comment

The author of the letter of Jude identifies himself as "a servant of Jesus Christ" and "brother of James" (1:1). If that were literally true, the letter would represent the voice of a first-generation follower of Jesus aligned with the conservative (compared with Paul, at least) leadership of the Jerusalem church. While that is not impossible, it is more likely that the letter was written by someone who identified with such authorities but wrote at a later time—perhaps between 90 and 100 C.E. That later date fits with the reference in verses 17 to 18 to the apostles as people who lived in the past. Although nothing in the letter suggests a geographical or social setting for the recipients or the author, a connection to Rome (which seems to have enjoyed a close relationship to the Jerusalem church) is possible, especially given the duplication of much of this letter in 2 Peter, which appears to have come from the same city.

The situation that provoked the letter is unclear. Instead of being a communication to a particular community in response to specific events, it is generally directed to any and all communities plagued by the arrival of disruptive "intruders" whose theological apostasy is matched by their moral licentiousness (v. 4). Exactly what the charges are, either ethically or theologically, is not specified. Only the one claiming the authority to write this letter is opposed to what he perceives is going on.

While this communication is cast in the form of a letter, with a greeting (vv. 1-2) and benediction (vv. 24-25) reminiscent of Paul's letters, the body of the letter appears to be an essay exhorting the recipients to moral integrity and to fidelity to "the faith" (v. 3). For this author, *faith* is a body of doctrine to be maintained and transferred to new believers (vv. 3, 20), rather than Paul's understanding of it as the dynamic response to God's grace. The fact that those to whom this letter is addressed and the intruders about whom the author writes are warned about their immoral behavior suggests that, while the author can appeal to traditions from the Hebrew Bible and other Jewish literature, these people have divorced their understanding of faith from ethical responsibilities. They are not unlike those whom the author of the letter of James feels called upon to warn that "faith by itself, if it has no works, is dead" (James 2:17).

Several points in this letter are of interest to the contexts from which I read. First, while the author concludes that these intruders "deny our only Master and Lord, Jesus Christ" (Jude 4), the discussion focuses less on traditions about Jesus than on scriptural witnesses to God's saving acts as models of the coming judgment and salvation God will carry out. That God-centered proclamation stands as a challenge to the more exclusive Christ-centered or even Jesus-centered emphasis of much of Protestant Christianity.

A second point of interest is the breadth of scriptural witnesses to which the author appeals without differentiation. In addition to texts from the Hebrew Bible, he appeals to *1 Enoch* (in vv. 14-15) and to the *Assumption of Moses* (in v. 9). Although these texts are still from the religious literature of Judaism, they reflect an openness on the author's part to faithful witnesses wherever they are found. Clearly a criterion other than formal status in the canon governs his selection of authoritative sources. That openness to witnesses from outside his own community offers a helpful model to those of us who work in a world marked by religious pluralism. On a less helpful note, the author's ready use of pejorative language for those whom he opposes and his "behave or else" strategy of persuasion are not approaches to pastoral or theological argument that acknowledge the integrity and human dignity of those with whom one differs.

CONCLUSION

The questions underlying these three letters intersect the context out of which I write at a number of points, but the authors' answers pose serious difficulties for me. The concerns of the author of 2 Peter for personal morality (especially sexual morality) eclipse any effort by indigenous communities and feminists to articulate their faith in and for their present contexts. From this perspective, as I just noted, the author of Jude is more helpful through his openness to witnesses from outside his own community. The author of 1 Peter seeks, as I do, to interpret the gospel among people who suffer. For one who writes from the seat of power and a position of authority, how-ever, attributing merit to suffering that has been inflicted unjustly is gratuitous, even cruel. Similarly, while all members of a minority community struggle to survive surrounded by a dominant culture and social order, for one of the dominant group to advocate harmony at the price of the community's most vulnerable members hardly conforms to the gospel attributed to Jesus. While at every point the Christian message must take on flesh in specific cultures and circumstances, the struggle is always over the extent to which that message stands against cultural and social norms and the extent to which those values can be seen as appropriate challenges to our understanding of the gospel. The questions posed at the outset still trouble me: Who answers these questions, and by what criteria?

BIBLIOGRAPHY

Balch, David L. *Let Wives Be Submissive: The Domestic Code in 1 Peter.* SBLMS. Chico, Calif.: Scholars Press, 1981.

Bartlett, David L. "The First Letter of Peter: Introduction, Commentary, and Reflections." Pages 229–319 in *The New Interpreter's Bible: General Articles and Introduction, Commentary, and Reflections for Each Book of the Bible Including the Apocryphal Deuterocanonical Books in Twelve Volumes.* Edited by Leander E. Keck et al. Vol. 12. Nashville: Abingdon, 1998.

Brown, Raymond E. *An Introduction to the New Testament.* ABRL. New York: Doubleday, 1997.

Craddock, Fred B. *First and Second Peter, and Jude.* Westminster Bible Companion. Louisville: Westminster John Knox, 1995.

Dowd, Sharyn. "Jude." Page 468 in *Women's Bible Commentary.* Exp. ed. Edited by Carol A. Newsom and Sharon H. Ringe. Louisville: Westminster John Knox, 1998.

_____ . "1 Peter." Pages 462–64 in *Women's Bible Commentary.* Edited by Carol A. Newsom and Sharon H. Ringe. Louisville: Westminster John Knox, 1998.

_____ . "2 Peter." Pages 465 in *Women's Bible Commentary.* Exp. ed. Edited by Carol A. Newsom and Sharon H. Ringe. Louisville: Westminster John Knox, 1998.

Elliott, John H. *A Home for the Homeless: A Sociological Exegesis of 1 Peter, Its Situation and Strategy.* Philadelphia: Fortress, 1981.

Neyrey, Jerome H. *2 Peter, Jude: A New Translation with Introduction and Commentary.* AB 37C. New York: Doubleday, 1993.

Perkins, Pheme. *First and Second Peter, James, and Jude.* IBC. Louisville: Westminster John Knox, 1995.

Watson, Duane F. "The Letter of Jude: Introduction, Commentary, and Reflections." Pages 473–500 in *The New Interpreter's Bible: General Articles and Introduction, Commentary, and Reflections for Each Book of the Bible Including the Apocrypha/Deuterocanonical Books in Twelve Volumes.* Edited by Leander E. Keck et al. Vol. 12. Nashville: Abingdon, 1998.

_____ . "The Second Letter of Peter: Introduction, Commentary, and Reflections." Pages 323–61 in *The New Interpreter's Bible: General Articles and Introduction, Commentary, and Reflections for Each Book of the Bible Including the Apocrypha/Deuterocanonical Books* in Twelve Volumes. Edited by Leander E. Keck et al. Vol. 12. Nashville: Abingdon, 1998.

1, 2, AND 3 JOHN

Johannes Beutler, SJ

Pontifical Biblical Institute, Rome, Italy

LIFE CONTEXT OF THE INTERPRETATION

I interpret the Johannine Letters from the perspective of a European who grew up in a metropolis of Germany (Hamburg), spent most of his life in Frankfurt (the financial center of the European Community), and now lives in Rome, Italy. The personal approach taken here is that of a Roman Catholic priest and a member of the Society of Jesus, with its international connections. Teaching students in different parts of the world (Africa, Latin America) and in Rome, from all parts of the world, has sharpened my eye for the social, economic, religious, and cultural problems of the world in which we live.

Living in Western Europe means living in a world of affluence. Germany belongs to the leading industrial nations. Despite increasing unemployment, the majority of the population is still wealthy. Registered and unregistered immigrants from the nations of the southern hemisphere come to share the economic and social benefits of the north. They are a constant challenge to everybody who believes in a "One World" with brothers and sisters enjoying equal rights.

In Western Europe material wealth is accompanied by spiritual poverty. The established churches have increasingly lost their influence on people, especially on the young generation. The great social utopias of the 1960s have succumbed to a new individualism, which seeks happiness in personal experiences and private relations. However, the generation of the late 1960's "cultural revolution," which believed that religion was relegated to the past, was proved mistaken. New forms of religiosity spread in Europe, inspired partly by the influence of North America and partly by the influence of Eastern religions. Inside the churches, the charismatic movement increasingly found adherents from all generations. A common denominator of the development seems to be the idea that religion is a form of personal experience. While modern secular movements seek this experience in meditation, Christian movements seek it in a charismatic experience, shared in small groups, community gatherings, or large outdoor meetings.

In general, religion and ethics have become disassociated. Modern secular movements concentrate on the believer's personal spiritual growth, while charismatic groups primarily emphasize the sharing of spiritual experiences and group solidarity. Often, both groups disregard the social and political aspects of life. For Christian fundamentalists, the "world" is evil, and Christians must wait for the return of their Lord who will establish his kingdom at the end of time.

The Letters of John, especially 1 John, seem to presuppose a similar situation. We may suppose that the communities where the letters originated were charac-

Johannes Beutler, SJ, born in Hamburg (Germany), teaches exegesis of the New Testament. Several of his numerous books (in German and French) treat topics concerning Johannine studies: the idea of witness in John (Martyria: traditionsgeschichtliche Untersuchungen zum Zeugnisthema bei Johannes, 1972), the Farewell Discourses (Habt keine Angst: die erste johanneische Abschiedsrede (John 14), (1984), miscellaneous biblical themes of importance for today (Heute von Gott redden, 1998) and a recent commentary on the Letters of John (Die Johannesbriefe, Regensburger Neues Testament, 2000). From 1993 until 2001 he was a member of the Pontifical Biblical Commission.

terized by great inequality in wealth and social status. With tradition, we may think of the metropolis of Ephesus, one of the major centers of the Roman Empire in the East with its Jewish and Christian communities, as the setting of the redaction of these letters. The author's repeated invitations to love one's brother or sister become very concrete in 1 John 3; not sharing one's bread with one's hungry brother or sister is equivalent to murder.

On the other hand, the author of 1 John is concerned with helping his addressees to develop a right understanding of faith. Commentaries have often distinguished between two aspects of possible doctrinal aberration among the addressees: a Christology that neglects the human nature of Christ, and a form of ethics that neglects the responsibility for one's brother or sis-

ter. The adversaries criticized by our author in 1 and 2 John may share a similar self-understanding and anthropology (see Beutler 2000, 20-24; Grayston 1984, 14-22). These adversaries seem to have come from the Johannine community but to have left it at a certain moment (1 John 2:18-19). There may be reason to assume that they were "ultra-Johannine" Christians who were deeply convinced that they possessed the Spirit beyond measure. As the "anointed ones" they no longer saw the need for redemption by the blood of Christ or for any salvific role of a "Christ" (the "Anointed One"). As spiritual persons they perhaps also felt they were no longer bound by any moral commandment, in particular the commandment to love one's brother or sister. We shall see how our author responds to these views.

CONTEXTUAL COMMENT: 1 JOHN

How to have communion with God and with each other: this seems to be the central topic of 1 John. Communion with God is seen in 1 John in terms of the new covenant relationship (Malatesta 1978, 3). The community sees itself as the people of God who have been promised a new, unending covenant with God, knowledge of God, God's love and inhabitance, and the gift of God's Spirit (cf. Jer 31:31-34; Ezek 36:26-27; 37:26-28.). According to Malatesta (1978, 40-41), even the structure of 1 John is determined by three different explanations of how to obtain the new covenant relationship with God. After a prologue (1:1-4) we can distinguish the new covenant relationship with God: 1) in terms of light (1:5–2:27); 2) in terms of justice and of being children of God (2:28–4:6); and 3) in terms of love (4:7–5:13). Basically, all the three parts of the letter have the same structure: Part 1) Breaking with sin, walking in the light (1:5–2:2); keeping the commandments, loving one's brother/sister (2:3-11); breaking with the world, authentic faith (2:12-27); Part 2) Breaking with sin,

doing justice (2:28–3:10); keeping the commandments, loving one's brother/ sister (3:11-24); breaking with the world, authentic faith (4:1-6); Part 3) Keeping the commandments, loving one's brother/ sister (4:7-21); gaining victory over the world through faith and love and possessing life (5:1-13); and epilogue (5:14-21).

The Prologue
(1:1-4)

The central concept of this literary unit is "the word of life" (1:1). This word has become incarnate in such a way that it can be seen, heard, and even touched with the hands. It inspires life and creates fellowship with God and among the members of the community as the source of joy. Authors agree that this "prologue" echoes that of the Gospel of John (John 1:1-18), even as the gospel echoes the beginning of the book of Genesis: "In the beginning . . . God created the heavens and the earth" through his life-giving word (Gen 1:1-5). In the prologue of John's gospel, the Word Incarnate stands at the center, while in the prologue of 1 John "the word of life," the same Word Incarnate, becomes the content of Christian preaching and witness. The incarnation itself is underlined by a series of expressions that manifest the real human existence of Christ as the Word Incarnate. With this rereading of the prologue of John's gospel, our author interprets the message of the Fourth Gospel in a new way for readers who need clarification and encouragement in their faith in Christ as God's living word, who had become incarnate for the life and salvation of the believers. For this reason, Brown (1982) sees 1 John in its entirety as a commentary on the Gospel of John.

New Covenant with God: Light (1:5–2:27)

For the first time, the author exhorts his readers to break with sin. This rejection of sin is equivalent to walking in the light. The most important point is not to be free from darkness, but to be sincere and to confess one's own sins in order to receive forgiveness through the blood of Christ. Here two different ways of understanding oneself appear as possibilities: either one can deceive oneself about one's status before God, thereby making God a liar (1:5–2:2), or alternatively one can have sincere faith and authentic love (2:3-11). Only those who love their brothers or sisters are entitled to say that they know God and live in the light. This point is revisited and further developed in 3:11-24 (see below). The author's message is applied to the different generations in the community. Young and old are exhorted not to conform to this world and its desires but to do the will of God (2:12-17). They all are "anointed ones," but they are still in need of Christ as the "Anointed One" and must confess him as the One who became incarnate (2:18-27).

New Covenant with God: Justice and Children of God (2:28–4:6)

At the beginning of the second part of the Letter stands an invitation to abide in Christ, the Just One. This is equivalent to breaking with sin, a subject that is treated in more depth in this section (2:28–3:10).

While 1 John 1:5–2:2 affirmed that Christians must admit that they are sinners, the present section suggests that they cannot sin at all. The apparent contradiction is resolved if one sees the difference of perspective in each paragraph: in the first text, Christians are taken as they are, independent of their life in faith; in the second, they are considered as Christians, as rooted in Christ, "abiding" in him. As long as they are one with Christ as God's children, they are unable to sin.

As in the first part of the letter (1:5–2:27), so also in the second part of the section about breaking with sin is followed by a section about keeping the commandments, in particular the commandment to "love one another" (3:11-24). This commandment frames the whole section (3:11-23). If we consider these verses as the introduction and the conclusion of the paragraph, the remaining verses form its body. It consists of three antitheses. First, loving one's brothers and sisters is the criterion for considering oneself a child of God. Not loving is equivalent to murder. Those who do not love their brothers or sisters are full of hate and cannot have the life of God abiding in them (3:13-15). Authentic love can be recognized according to one's readiness to give one's life for one's brothers and sisters, following the example of Christ. The alternative would be to close one's heart against the needs of one's brother or sister. Here, the author becomes very concrete: "How does God's love abide in anyone who has the world's goods and sees a brother or sister in need and yet refuses help?" (3:17). In other words, readers should love their fellow Christians "not in word or speech, but in deed and action" (3:18). The final verses (3:19-22) treat the sincerity of one's readiness to love one's brother or sister. In 3:19-20 the author does not want to "reassure" his readers when their heart condemns them, but rather to convince them to act according their conscience, since God looks into the heart and "knows everything." When, however, their heart does not condemn them, they may have confidence before God and can hope for the fulfillment of their prayers (3:21-22).

Contextual Observations

This section is perhaps the most concrete and relevant of the whole of 1 John. Love consists in the readiness to share one's wealth and ultimately to give one's life for brothers and sisters. The author thinks concretely of persons who "have the world's goods," probably members of the community (his own or that of the addressees) who live in affluence while other members of such communities suffer from hunger and starvation. One may regret that our author seems to think exclusively in terms of solidarity among Christians, and that he does not in any way question his society's unjust structures. In this latter aspect he is a child of his time. But notice the concept of "justice" and "being just" as leading ideas of this section. As to the aspect of exclusive solidarity among the members of the Christian community, we should notice that at the beginning of the paragraph the author introduces Cain, the son of Adam and Eve who murdered his brother. By introducing this figure, our author widens the perspective beyond the people of God: all humankind is concerned. This impression is confirmed by the wording used to describe a person who hates a brother or sister: this person is guilty of "murder" or "homicide" (Gr. *anthrōpoktonos*), not just "fratricide" (3:15). This wording gives the author's exhortation a universalistic ring that is relevant for modern readers. Christians living in affluence must share their material goods with their brothers and sisters beyond the boundaries of their Christian communities on a worldwide scale and challenge unjust social structures. Not doing so would be equivalent to murder.

Toward the end of the section (3:24), the author prepares and announces the succeeding one (4:1-6) about the discernment of the Spirit. The decisive criterion for the possession of the Spirit is the confession of Christ as Son of God Incarnate. One may see a connection between the love commandment and the commandment to confess Christ as Son of God Incarnate. Both commandments contain an element of concreteness: as brothers or the sisters in need must be seen in their concrete life-situations, so also Christ must be seen as a historic member of the human family, as one who suffered from hunger, thirst, and even death. The author mentions this suffering explicitly in 5:6, where he states that Jesus came "not with the water only but with the water and the blood."

New Covenant with God: Love (4:7–5:14)

The final part of 1 John does not begin with an exhortation to break with sin since this message seems to be taken for granted at this point of the letter. Thus, the author moves immediately to the subject of love (4:7-21). Two remarkable features appear in this section: the unique statement that "God is love" (4:8, 16), and the constant exhortation to respond to God's love by loving one's brother or sister. The final section (5:1-13) sums up the previous chapters: love and faith are shown in their unity as the basis for the victory over the world (5:1-4), and the relevance and particular character of faith is once more explained (5:5-13): faith in God's Son, based on true divine witness, leading to eternal life.

The Final Verses (5:14-21)

The final verses revisit previously treated subjects and add new ones: confidence in the power of prayer for believers and also for their sinning brothers or sisters, and trust in God despite the attacks of the Evil One. The letter's last word has been subject to debate: "Little children, keep yourselves from idols" (5:21). We may legitimately see these "idols" as all created things, including wealth, given to humans for their use, in which humans have mistakenly placed their ultimate value (cf. Martin Luther's interpretation of the first commandment).

CONTEXTUAL COMMENT: 2 AND 3 JOHN

The two shorter Letters of John, 2 John and 3 John, took some time to gain general acceptance in the early church, perhaps because the apostolic identity of the author was not generally recognized and because these letters are of limited theological interest. The author calls himself "the Elder" and may be one of the persons of the early post-apostolic era who were recognized as tradition-bearers of the apostolic tradition—in this case, of the Johannine tradition. The Elder appears concerned about the unity of his communities and their faithfulness to the instruction once received. He tries to ensure that these goals are met by reminding them of his authority and of tradition. It seems reasonable to date these letters later than 1 John, and 3 John probably after 2 John, since the author writes 2 John from a position of strength and 3 John from a position of weakness. The social background of these letters seems to be a group of house-churches connected with each other in a network in which the Elder still had a dominant role, which was however increasingly contested by rivals like Diotrephes of 3 John.

Second John: Overview and Contextual Observations

Second John follows the structure of Hellenistic private letters. After the initial greeting (vv. 1-3) comes the body of the letter, consisting of two halves: a thanksgiving together with an exhortation to remain faithful to the commandment of loving one another (vv. 4-6), and instructions to be on guard against false teachers (vv. 7-11). The final greeting forms (with the concept of "joy" and a reference to the community as "beloved sister") an inclusion with the opening (vv. 1-3).

Contemporary readers may appreciate two aspects of this short letter. The first one is the correspondence of "truth" and "love" as key concepts. Verses 4-6 are dominated by the subject of "love." This love is characterized, however, as "truth," divine revelation, which illuminates the path of the faithful. Verses 7-11 are dominated by the subject of sound doctrine, but stand parallel to the previous section and show the internal coherence of both aspects of Christian teaching. The other important feature of the letter is the author's attempt to handle an internal conflict within his communities. He appeals to tradition (v. 9) and to his authority to excommunicate messengers from other communities that he regards as heterodox (to the point of classifying them as "antichrist," v. 7). Such messengers should not be received in the houses of his readers (vv. 10-11). It is doubtful whether this strategy was successful; soon the author would find himself in the situation of someone excommunicated by a different community and its leader.

Third John: Overview and Contextual Observations

The Third Letter of John belongs, with 2 John, to the shortest documents of the New Testament. Still more than 2 John, this letter represents the literary form of a Hellenistic private letter. After the prescript, naming sender and addressee (v. 1), comes the traditional wish for the health of Gaius, here in the form of spiritual health (v. 2), and the expression of joy about the good news about him (vv. 3-4). The body of the letter (vv. 5-11) is followed by a recommendation of a certain Demetrius (v. 12). Conventional expressions about the shortness of the letter and the wish to see the addressee (vv. 13-14) are found at the end of the document, together with greetings and a wish of peace (v. 15).

In the body of the letter, praise for Gaius and his hospitality (vv. 5-8, 11) frames the condemnation of Diotrephes, who asserts his own authority and denies acceptance to the emissaries of the Elder (vv. 9-10). The author announces his imminent arrival when Diotrephes will have to give account for his conduct.

From a theological point of view, the emphasis on the concept of truth is a striking feature of this text. Even if the controversy with Diotrephes and his group was not on doctrine, it points clearly to the importance of truth for settling conflicts inside the community. From a sociological point of view, 3 John bears witness to a form of church organized by a network of house churches. In such a church structure, readiness for dialogue is essential, and apparently this readiness was lacking. As the Elder denies acceptance to the emissaries of the heretics (2 John v. 10-11), his messengers are denied hospitality by Diotrephes (3 John 9-10.).

CONCLUSION

In sum, we can say that 1, 2, and 3 John have a message for the readers of today: faith and love belong together. In 2 and 3 John this message is more focused on the correspondence of "truth" and "love," which leads to a way of resolving conflicts through the rejection of those with whom one disagrees by declaring them heterodox. We noted that, in our view, this way of dealing with conflicts among brothers and sisters is problematic. But in 1 John the message regarding faith and love as belonging together is quite different.

First, for 1 John, believers take seriously their own situation as sinners and their need for Christ as Redeemer. And they do need redemption! Indeed, the gift of the Spirit does not exonerate them from assuming responsibility in their concrete life context. This responsibility requires individual Christians to share their material goods in order to live according to the commandments of Christ. For the nations of the northern hemisphere, this responsibility means sharing their wealth with the nations of the south. But this commandment also applies to the developing nations that are characterized by vast inequality in material wealth. A rich ruling class often exploits the masses of the poor. According to 1 John, those who do not share with their brothers or sisters commit murder. By living in the Spirit of Christ, Christians will overcome their sinful attitudes and live as children of their common Father in heaven.

BIBLIOGRAPHY

Beutler, Johannes. *Die Johannesbriefe: übersezt und erklärt von Johannes Beutler.* Regensburger Neues Testament. Regensburg: Pustet, 2000.

Brown, Raymond E. *The Community of the Beloved Disciple.* New York: Paulist, 1979.

———. *The Epistles of John.* Translated with introduction, notes, and commentary. AB 30. Garden City, N.Y.: Doubleday, 1982.

Grayston, Kenneth. *The Johannine Epistles: Based on the Revised Standard Version.* NCBC. Grand Rapids: Eerdmans, 1984.

Lieu, Judith. *The Second and Third Epistles of John: History and Background.* Edited by John Riches. Studies of the New Testament and Its World. Edinburgh: T & T Clark, 1986.

Malatesta, Edward. *Interiority and Covenant: A Study of einai en and menein en in the First Letter of Saint John.* AnBib 69. Rome: Biblical Institute Press, 1978.

Painter, John. *1, 2, and 3 John.* Ed. Daniel J. Harrington. SP 18. A Michael Glazier Book. Collegeville, Minn.: Liturgical Press, 2002.

REVELATION

Christopher Rowland

Queen's College, Oxford, England, United Kingdom

LIFE CONTEXT OF THE INTERPRETATION

The book of Revelation (or Apocalypse) has always been linked with martyrdom and persecution, with the outlook of an embattled minority whose perspective on God and history needed to be expanded. This is a voice from the margins of the scriptural canon and yet its universal challenge is apparent. Of all the New Testament books, it especially challenges the rich and powerful while encouraging the weak and vulnerable.

I write from the heart of an ancient academic establishment, with a secure position in the world of scholarship. But, in addition to being shaped by the First-World academy, my theological formation has also been influenced by the theology of the grassroots in Brazil and by working with urban theology groups in Britain. My perspective on Revelation is that of one who, like John, has found himself taken out into the wilderness to see afresh the world as it is and privileged to see the pervasive and subtle ways in which the culture of Babylon is at work undermining the human flourishing of the majority of the world's population.

Issues Raised by Revelation for the People of God in this Life Context

Since the Enlightenment there has been a widespread belief that the affairs of religion are an individual matter, not signifi-cantly affected by their social and political context. The experience of Brazil showed that this privatization of religion and its domestication within the confines of ecclesial sanctuaries made no sense to people who believed that they were meeting God day by day in the struggle for justice in their world. The book of Revelation, which bears witness to the way of the Lamb (against the power of the beast and Babylon) and the hope for a better world, has both inspired and challenged many Third-World Christians.

So, whereas Revelation has either been ignored or become part of a frightening scenario about the end of the world and the opting out of history, particularly in some conservative Christian circles in North America and Europe, for many committed people influenced by liberation theology Revelation has been a bedrock of the struggle for justice, peace, and the hope that God's ways will be demonstrated in the world of flesh and blood. Revelation is the foundation text for a strand of Christianity as ancient as it has been persistent. Its very existence bears witness to the fault line in Christian theology. On one side are those who believe that the coming of God's kingdom *on earth* involves a hope for the transformation of the world. On the other hand are those who reject this belief and see the

Christopher Rowland, a professor of scriptural exegesis, has been a member of the Board of Christian Aid and chair of its Latin American and Caribbean Committee. He is much involved with the practice of grassroots theology in Britain, and with John Vincent Rowland has edited the periodical *Liberation Theology United Kingdom*. His publications include *The Open Heaven: A Study of Apocalyptic in Judaism and Early Christianity* (2002); *The Cambridge Companion to Liberation Theology* (editor, 1999); *Liberating Exegesis: The Challenge of Liberation Theology to Biblical Studies* (1990); *Radical Christianity* (1988); *Radical Christian Writings: A Reader* (with Bradstock, 2002); *Revelation: The Apocalypse of Jesus Christ* (with Judith Kovacs, 2002); and *Christian Origins: From Messianic Movement to Christian Religion* (1986; revised ed. 2002).

divine purposes being fulfilled in heaven and in escape from a wicked, fallen world.

The Revelation is unique in the New Testament. It is the only visionary report in which a message from "beyond" confronts humanity. It is the product of a visionary's imagination rather than the careful passing on of tradition or articulation of an argument. It demands of its readers particular interpretative skills and a readiness to engage it at an imaginative level. It offers no blueprint for a better world. Rather, its images inspire reflection in situations where oppression and injustice dominate—as is the case in a globalized economy that involves all those who benefit from the cheap labor and goods from Third-World countries. None of the New Testament books more explicitly enunciates the economic critique of the benefits to the minority and the consequent impoverishment of the majority (chs. 18–19).

In their emphasis on revelation, apocalyptic works can seem to offer a solution to complex theological problems. But Revelation does not provide answers. To explain every detail of Revelation, as if it were a kind of scriptural puzzle whose only function was to conceal, fails to take seriously the apocalyptic medium whose aim is to question and to disorientate before offering a fresh perspective on reality through its extraordinary imagery. Revelation can make visible a horizon of hope. Apocalyptic symbolism can enable the oppressed to find and maintain a critical distance from an unjust world from the prospect of the hope of a reign of justice.

How Revelation engages us and transforms us will be as much a story of apocalypse/revelation taking place in us with every reading, every digesting of this text, as a new

moment of unveiling occurs through the impact of its images—these images that John has bequeathed to us as a precious work of art. The book is a classic example of art that stimulates rather than prescribes. By demanding this suspension of what counts for normality we may perceive where the beast and Babylon are to be found.

Revelation is the most "unchurchy" book in the New Testament. Revelation, like the Gospel of Matthew (e.g., Matt 7:21-23; 25:31-45), suggests that membership in a specific religious group is less important than nonconformity with the culture of the beast and Babylon. In Revelation we have a book that rejects the sense of the church as a haven against the world in favor of prophetic witness and the life of exile, resistance, and endurance (Rev 14:12). The corporate identity of the church as the body of Christ has to be subverted because of the positive response of many of its members to the culture of Babylon. Revelation is if anything just as much a challenge to the lukewarm, comfortable Christians of Ephesus as an encouragement to the weak and vulnerable of Smyrna and Philadelphia.

Consequently, this commentary is contextual precisely by presenting ways in which the book of Revelation challenges us to enter its vision, invites us to digest it, with the hope that a new moment of unveiling will occur in our context in the Western world. Like the parables of Jesus, Revelation offers a mode of moral reasoning that prompts, tantalizes, and challenges its persevering readers to understand reality in ways that will lead to amendment of their lives. This is all the more urgent when the present reality is that of an unjust world that longs for a reign of justice.

CONTEXTUAL COMMENT

An Overview of Revelation

No visionary text is easily summarized. Revelation is no exception. However, despite the fact that the book contains sudden transitions (as between chs. 11 and 12), we might discern three major themes.

First of all, in the various sequences of

sevens, two of these are interrupted before their completion (6:12-17; 9:13-21). As a result this text creates a pervasive sense of being on the brink, of not having arrived, and, in those circumstances, of needing to resist, endure, and bear witness to something different and better.

The second theme concerns *the location of God's throne*. In chapter 4 it is located in heaven whereas in chapter 21, at the book's climax, the throne of God is on earth in the New Jerusalem where God dwells and people will see God face to face (22:4). That movement from heaven to earth and the merging of the two is *the* story line of Revelation.

Finally, in the midst of the chaos of a disordered world John is called to prophesy (Rev 10) and is shown in a vision the kind of prophetic witness that is expected in the midst of ordinary life (11:3-6). Churches that are tempted to compromise with the life of Babylon are recalled to their vocation. This witness is directed against the all-encompassing demands of empire and its political exemplification in Babylon.

The God Revealed in John's Vision: A God of the Lowly Who Receives Priesthood and Kingship (1:1-9)

John's revelation is a vision, an apocalypse. Its images bypass the usual canons of rational discourse and appeal directly to the imagination. Despite its awesome apocalyptic message, John is not commissioned to write some abstract collection of eschatological predictions. John's vision occurs not in some holy place but in a place of exile, albeit when John would recall the risen Christ, the prototypical witness and victim of injustice, on the day of resurrection ("Lord's day," 1:10). Just as the prophet Ezekiel before him had seen God in exile in Babylon—in a place far removed from the ark of the covenant in the holy place of Israel, the temple in Jerusalem—and as Jesus had seen the heavens open and the Spirit of God descending upon him in the wilderness (Mark 1:10), so here too God appears to a member of a suffering and oppressed people. It is that kind of God that Revelation tells us about: a God who identifies with Hebrew slaves, with a beaten people in exile in Babylon, with a crucified Messiah, with an exiled Christian.

The message reveals the character of God as one who is eternally present (Rev 1:4). The claim in 1:7 that all peoples of the world shall lament seems incredible when viewed from the perspective of isolated and, in some cases, weak communities. These words remind them of the significance of their position. They are the ones who, despite their lowliness, may be destined to share in the messianic governance. Similarly, the crucified messiah, whose death seemed to be another sad episode in the story of the exercise of colonial power, is the one whose way will ultimately be vindicated (1:7). Then God will be recognized as Creator and Lord of the universe (1:8). Those addressed are themselves given privileged positions. The view of priesthood and kingship is inclusive. All who are part of God's people share this role; it is not confined to a priestly elite or royal dynasty. Traditional notions of hierarchy are challenged.

Letters to the Angels of the Churches: Supporting the Weak and Challenging the Complacent (2–3:22)

The tremendous drama of human history told in much of the book of Revelation is sandwiched between letters to the angels of the seven churches (chs. 2–3 and 22). The message is a telling reminder that the activity of individuals and communities is no ordinary matter, for religion extends to all parts of life. The account of God's purposes for the universe starts with a direct challenge to the churches. It is a contemporary message directed to their situation. The letters indicate that present behavior determines eschatological standing. What goes on *here and now* is therefore intimately related to the eschatological drama. What is more, the letters stress the importance of good works (2:2, 19, 26; 3:1, 8, 15), for works will be the criterion of judgment (18:6; 20:12).

Such a mixture of encouraging comment, searching criticism, and exhortation is a prerequisite of pastoral practice that is grounded in Christ. Most of the time, however, all of us are that mixture of faithfulness and folly that is accurately represented in most of the letters. What is offered in the letters, therefore, represents a pattern of affirmation and correction, challenge and comfort, supporting the weak and challenging the complacent, which is the foundation of our pastoral and preaching ministry.

The conclusion of the letter to Laodicea offers a graphic portrait of Christ standing *outside* the community of faith seeking to enter. The Laodicean community in its comfortable fellowship and complacency failed to recognize that it had excluded the principal guest from the feast (3:20). The living Christ refuses to be tied down by ecclesiastical formulae and prejudices. It is not those who are most certain and powerful in the faith that necessarily have the right to claim the presence of the humble Son of Man, who had nowhere to lay his head, with them (cf. Matt 7:21-3; 8:20).

Escape from Life and from Witness as Contrary to True Worship (Ch. 4)

John is given access to another perspective on reality as he enters the divine presence (4:1) and as a result can see the world below differently. He is shown that the empires of the world are not in fact the ultimate source of authority and power in the universe and that however powerful the Roman Empire might be it does not have the last word. John's visionary perspective enables him to see the contrast between how the world actually is and what it will be under God.

Those who worship God the Creator must exhibit a pattern of everyday behavior in the midst of the temporary dominance of empire (4:8-11), a pattern that manifests in particular deeds the fact that creation is God's, and that humans have a due responsibility in it (cf.11:18, where the destruction of creation is laid firmly at the door of humanity). Those who worship God truly will not worship the beast (14:9). To have the character of God means, above all, commitment to a particular style of life. One cannot have true worship without doing the works of God (cf. 1 John 3:17). Therefore, when worship becomes an escape from life and from witness, it has lost touch with the true worship that God expects. Thus, worship does not allow us to escape from the hurly-burly of existence into another world but brings us face to face with the justice of God and with the divine purposes.

The Key to History: A Powerless Victim of Injustice and of the Culture of Violence (Ch. 5)

The scene in heaven in chapter 4 is transformed by the coming of a Lamb "with the marks of sacrifice *(sphragizo),* standing with the four living creatures, between the throne and the elders" (5:6, a.t.). The arrival of the Lamb both vindicates this creature and effects God's liberating work, described in the rest of the vision. A weak creature with no mark of triumph but the marks of its own slaughter should turn out to be the agent of God's purposes. The moment of utter defeat when a would-be messiah died in apparent failure turned out to be the decisive moment in history (Mark 15:35-38). An event of little concern to the writers of the age, when a troublemaker received the just reward for his actions, cried out to heaven for vindication (Acts 2:24). God's relationship to creation could never be the same again; humanity is taken into the godhead, thus enabling those who identify with this improbable messiah to become God's priests and to exercise the messianic reign in the future (5:10; cf. Matt 19:28; 1 Cor 6:3). An apparently powerless victim of injustice and of the culture of violence, which typifies the power politics of this age, turns out to be the key to history, not the military might of empire. Thereby the world of violence and the structures of oppression that it upholds are seen for what they are and are subject to judgment.

Putting Right the Wrong of a Disordered World Where Death and Destruction are the Lot of Millions (Chs. 5–7)

The opening of the seals (chs. 5–7) sets in train the demonstration of the extent of evil and injustice and the proclamation that they will not always prevail. The maintenance of a structural injustice—which is unresponsive to the need for change in line with God's will—results in destruction. God is not one who will allow the cry of the weak and the oppressed to go unheard (Exod 3:7). Revelation shows that in a disordered world death and destruction are the lot of millions and the putting right of wrongs demands a seismic shift of cosmic proportions, which will happen even if humankind does not repent (Rev 9:20-21).

The book draws a contrast between those who follow the way of God and those who follow the way of unjust world order. Those marked by "the seal of the living God" (7:1-3) are from every nation (7:9), and here is stated more clearly than anywhere in the New Testament the place of the Jewish people in God's purposes (7:4-8). As will be stressed in chapters 13–20, the true servants of God are those who refuse to succumb to the worship of the beast. God's graciousness to those who follow the Lamb is tenderly brought out in 7:16-17. In the midst of death and destruction a glimpse is offered of those who have with integrity refused to conform and have accepted that they must be willing to pay a price for it, as will be stressed in 13:16 and 17:14. Washing robes and making them white in the blood of the Lamb is therefore no specifically "churchy" affair. It is not a matter of being strict in belief or devoted in ecclesiastical practice, but identifying with the Lamb who was a victim of injustice also (John 18:38–19:2). What is fundamental is the task of not conforming to the negative aspects of the prevailing culture and holding on to a way of life that is different. Doing this is nothing less than identification with the way of Jesus, the Lamb, which for him ended up in the brutal death on the cross (Mark 8:38).

The Importance of Silence and Prayer (Ch. 8)

Although there seems to be a hope that some will escape the torment of judgment (9:4; cf. 7:3), references elsewhere in Revelation indicate that God's servants will not escape (2:13; 11:7). There is no miraculous escape from the horrors of suffering and tribulation, for the tasks of prophetic witness and service must be carried out. The gruesome catalogue that issues forth from the trumpet blasts (8:6–9:19) are threatening to the earth and its inhabitants. Creatures take on a fearsome aspect in John's vision. The full destructive power of nature is set loose. In nature and in society the destructive power results from rebellion against God's justice.

The opening of the seventh seal brings about silence in heaven (8:1). The seemingly inevitable process is interrupted and the pause enables reflection on what is happening, even in heaven. Silence and reflection are appropriate in the midst of the tumult of life (Ps 46; Zech 2:13). Before the trumpets begin to sound there is the offering of prayers of the saints at the heavenly altar (Rev 8:3-5). There is a potent reminder of the effectiveness of the human activity of prayer and witness. Here is a theme that runs through the book. For people who thought it did not matter whether they prayed, how they behaved, or whether they stood up to be counted, the thunder and lightning (8:5; cf. 4:5; Exod 19:16; and Isa 29:6) emphasize the significance of the prayers in the divine economy. The smoke of the incense and the prayers of the saints are an acceptable offering, not a threat to the world, though the prayers stand as a reproach to the injustice and lack of repentance (9:20-1).

True Prophetic Witness in Society Opposed to God's Justice (Chs. 9–11)

Humanity longs for release (9:6) but does not find it. It is brought face to face with the full horror of the world it has created. The ultimate idolatry is to make the creature the end and measure of creation, which leads to darkness (9:2), disfigurement, and the unbalancing of the natural world. Despite the upheavals there is no understanding of the reason for the disorder in the world (9:20-21). Humanity does not comprehend that the vindication of the innocent victim of injustice is the key to the meaning of history and that only the recognition of this and a radical change in behavior and in the structures of the world order can stave off disaster.

Throughout these chapters there is a repeated interruption of the sequence of seven after the sixth. This emphasis on the "penultimate" is typical of John's message. Revelation encourages readiness, waiting, and vigilance but not the assurance of having arrived.

The seer is involved in the unfolding eschatological drama of the apocalypse when he is instructed to eat the scroll and commanded to prophesy (10:8-9). Here there is a direct call to participate actively as a prophet rather than merely be a passive spectator (10:11). Like the Lamb in chapter 5 the prophet of the Lamb takes the scroll. The universal sovereignty of the Lamb (5:9) is reflected in the universal scope of the message of the prophet (10:11). The message is internalized (10:9) and forms part of the very being of the prophet. All of the true prophets of God experienced prophecy not merely as an uttering of oracles but as an activity involving the whole of life (Luke 11:49). Prophets could expect a life of witness, suffering, and death, so that their lives would be an imitation of their Lord's suffering (11:8). Ironically, in the story of Jesus, the holy city is the site of profanity, which continues the rejection of the prophets (Matt 23:34-36).

The prophetic commission is followed in Rev 11 by a vision that offers a paradigm of the true prophetic witness as it sets out to fulfill its vocation to prophesy before the world. Utilizing the ideas connected in the Bible with the figures of Moses and Elijah (11:6; cf. Exod 7–11 and 1 Kgs 17), the prophetic witness takes place in a society opposed to God's justice—where that witness must take place even though it ends in martyrdom.

Individual, Political, Economic Struggles against the Powers of this Age (Chs. 12–14)

The bringing to birth of the messianic age and its different values is a threat to those who would support the powers of this age. A cosmic struggle is involved. The heavenly struggle (12:7-8) is closely linked with the earthly struggle of those who seek to be disciples of Jesus to maintain their testimony (12:10). The maintenance of that testimony in the face of temptations to compromise is a conquest equivalent in the realm of flesh and blood to the overcoming of the forces of darkness in heaven by Michael and the angels of light (12:11; 13:14). The defeated Satan, thrown out of heaven (12:9), conducts a campaign with threats, bribes, deception, and social and economic ostracism (13:16). It is a war waged against the woman's seed, the goal being the prevention of obedience to God's commands and the witness to Jesus (12:17). This is not to be seen solely as an individual struggle, for, as Revelation 13 makes clear, it is just as much a struggle in the political and economic sphere.

In chapter 13 the reasons for the shortcomings of the state are laid bare. The beast incarnates the powers of the devil (13:2) and attracts universal admiration for acts that appear to be beneficial (13:3). The imagery here is well known in Jewish apocalyptic literature (it is based on Dan 7) as a way of referring to world governments, and in John's day would have applied particularly to Rome (cf. 4 Ezra 11–12). The wonder of the world is rooted in its military power (13:4). Public opinion goes along with the propaganda of the beast and its supporters. The pressure is to conform and be marked with the mark of the beast (Rev 13:14). Those who refuse to do so are offered reassurance that being marked with the Lamb is a sign of righteousness even if it means social ostracism (13:16). In the present age those marked with the beast apparently have freedom to go about their activities, whereas those who refuse to be so marked and side with God and the Lamb are persecuted and their deaths are greeted with glee by the inhabitants of the earth (11:10). Those who persevere (an important theme of Rev, see 14:12) will be shown that the might of state power is itself extraordinarily fragile, and its affluence, so attractive and alluring, is destined for destruction by precisely that power which has maintained it (17:16).

In 13:11-17 we have a graphic portrait of the creation of an ideology that sets out the effect of a prevailing set of ideas to form our minds. It makes one think that the ideas that are widely held are "obvious," "commonsense," and "normal," when in fact they often cover up the powerful vested interests of a small group that has and wants to retain power. In John's vision the task of the second beast from the land is to persuade ordinary people that what they see in the first beast is normal and admirable so that any deviation or counter-attraction is regarded as strange, antisocial, and to be repudiated. John's vision helps to unmask these processes. What everybody does is not necessarily right and worthy of emulation, even though it might have marks of credibility— a parody of the reality of the way of Christ— just like the beast (13:3, 8).

One of the most fascinating texts found in the vicinity of the Dead Sea, the War Scroll (1QM), offers in minute detail the inventory of preparations necessary for the fight between the sons of light and sons of darkness. This is a conventional battle in that it uses weapons of war. But it is apparent that this battle is not only between humans but also between angelic forces who fight alongside humans (cf. Josh 5:14). The contrast between Revelation and the War Scroll is in this respect quite remarkable. Certainly a war takes place in heaven in Revelation (12:7), but here the elect do not fight (13:10; cf. John 18:36). They struggle by rejecting the deceitfulness of the beast and taking a stand against injustice.

Revelation 14:4 stands in a long tradition of ascetic practice whose social as well as religious importance should be noted. In a world of affluence on the one hand, and of enormous suffering and deprivation on the other, there are limited choices available for taking a stand against the status quo. Renunciation offers an important avenue for resistance. Thus, the vocation of renunciation is one that Christian women, who have particular experience of exclusion and oppression, have taken both as a way of discipleship and a means of self-affirmation in a male-dominated world. Virginity is honored because distance from family meant distance from the normal pattern of society and commitment to a different way of being community (Mark 3:34-5).

The Male-Centered Description of Babylon (Ch. 17)

John is taken to a desert place (17:3; 21:10) where he can clearly see Babylon for what it is, a place of exile and alienation (Ps 137; 1 Pet 5:13) where the people of God will never feel at home. The wilderness is a place for seeing the world in proper perspective (Hos 2:14) without the lures of surrounding culture. The iniquity of Babylon and its relationship with the beast can be seen with stark clarity.

Babylon is supported (17:3) by a whole regime whose outlook is idolatrous (ch. 13). The Lamb and its followers are targets for hostility (17:14). The vision of Babylon seated on many waters (17:1, 15) supported by the beast (17:3) is inherently unstable, however. Resting on water and a beast, Babylon is destined for collapse and destruction (17:16). That which has caused intoxication and power will itself be turned on and destroyed. God will allow Babylon's poverty to be seen for what it really is. Her wealth and "false" clothes mask her need and destitution.

Rightly, reservations have been expressed about the negative image of woman here (17:3). Babylon as a woman has led the nations astray by virtue of her sexuality. We have to face squarely the male-centeredness of this text, which is also expressed by the figures of Jezebel and of the New Jerusalem, who is portrayed merely as an adjunct of the bridegroom. The ultimate inspiration for the immoral behavior lies with the beast supporting the woman, however. Babylon is also in part a victim and is deceived by the beast. Similarly, a passive role is accorded to the acceptable feminine images. Never-theless "endurance" is a dominant characteristic. Neither men nor women are mere spectators. Their activity is focused in faith (12:9) and perseverance through thick and thin.

The Unjust Wealth of Babylon that Makes People Mere Commodities (Ch. 18)

Revelation 18 enables readers to understand how the wealth of Babylon comes by ways other than those required by God's justice. It comes at the expense of millions (particularly 18:13). It is a telling reminder that the world power is an oppressor and that the world is a place of exile, not of comfort and prosperity, for those with integrity. The nations of the world might think that they have achieved great prosperity as a result of Babylon's power (18:2), but God's view is very different.

The description of Babylon (together with the account of its wealth) owes much to Ezek 27–28 and Jer 51. The passage from Ezekiel is important because of its emphasis on the economic activity and success of Tyre. This element comes to the fore in both chapters 17 and 18, with the long lists of goods that are part of the commerce promoted by Babylon's power. The goods are in large part luxuries, hardly the basic necessities that formed the subsistence of most people in John's (or in our) day (Rev 18:11–13; cf. Ezek 27:12–24). The description of Babylon in 17:4 suggests conspicuous consumption. Luxury goods gravitate to the all-powerful center to supply the insatiable needs of its well-to-do inhabitants. This flow of goods has the effect of marginalizing the rest of the world, so that those on the periphery become merely means of supplying the needs of others. The list of goods in 18:12-13 consists almost entirely of items whose production depends on human labor. Slave labor, along with military conquest, enabled Babylon to become great. Rome increased its might through conquest and the exploitation of slave labor, in a way reminiscent of Europe's exploitation of the Americas from the sixteenth to the nineteenth centuries. As in 13:16, buying and selling are not innocent enterprises at all, for their conditions are bound up with the whole demonic edifice of that social and economic system. The long list of commodities that were part of the trade of Babylon in 18:12-13 ends with "slaves—and human lives." A society that treats people as mere commodities has departed from the religion of God and follows the beast.

In 18:9, 11, 15, and 17, we have the perspective of the beneficiaries of Babylon's wealth. Some real sadness is expressed at the passing of the splendor of Babylon (18:22-23). There is a hint of the appreciation of human endeavor, however misguided, that has contributed to Babylon's greatness. We know from the vision of the New Jerusalem that the kings of the earth are described as bringing their glory into it (21:24). It is not true, that the nations must be rejected simply because of their glory. In this case the acquisition of wealth and glory is the result of deceit (18:23), and at enormous human cost (18:13, 24). Babylon is entirely a human creation, which, like idols, involves distorted perceptions and unjust acts and which in its splendor seems invincible (18:10, 19). It is in reality less than human in its savagery and in the defacement of its own dignity and worth in pursuit of glory (18:23).

Those who have profited from Babylon's greatness include all of us who have become prosperous. We are reminded of the ephemeral nature of that prosperity when viewed from God's perspective (3:17). If we find ourselves identifying with the lament of the kings, we shall be reminded that a price has had to be paid for the creation of that grand edifice in human labor and life. John's lament, which looks at the event from the perspective of the merchants, reminds us readers in the rich world that another world's impoverishment is the price to be paid for our ease and wealth.

Looking Forward to the Messianic Reign on Earth (Ch. 20)

Revelation 20 has not received the attention it deserves. It looks forward to a period when the messianic reign would take place *on earth*. It is a fulfillment of the prayer of Jesus: "thy kingdom come, thy will be done on earth as it is in heaven" (Matt 6:10, RSV). However, it has become a commonplace in Christian belief to suppose that the blessed are destined to be with God in heaven. Thus, it comes as something of a surprise to note that for much of the first two hundred years of the church's life, together with contemporary Jewish writers, virtually all Christians looked forward to the coming of the reign of the Messiah on earth.

Belief in the millennium (20:2-3) deserves much greater prominence than it has had. At the center of Christian faith is the confession that Jesus is raised from the dead. Resurrection from the dead is after all the transformation of those destined to death to share the life of a renewed world. Therefore, salvation does not involve an escape into a world beyond. We do not in our creeds confess our belief in the immortality of the soul but in resurrection from the dead. The hope for a thousand-year reign of the Messiah on earth (20:2-3) is entirely consistent with that hope. The inspiration for the pattern of human existence that led to the death, destruction, oppression, and other acts described in the previous chapters will be absent. Satan will be bound, and deceit and confusion will no longer lead the nations astray. Those who reign have shown themselves fit to do so because they are the ones who have identified themselves with the Lamb even at the cost of their lives (21:4) and have opted for a different vision of human existence. Those whose lives follow in the footsteps of the Messiah by refusing to accept the injustice of the old order and holding out for a reign of justice can truly represent humanity to God and God to humanity.

Christ's coming as judge (19:11-21) manifests some of those basic characteristics of the gospel presentation. He comes with garments dipped in blood (19:13). Christians cannot be fatalistic about the present state of affairs and imagine that the God they worship can allow the injustices of human history to remain forever. The judgment itself (20:11-15) is an interlocking process of consultation of two books (Daniel 7:10). The Lamb's book of life is intimately linked with refusal to compromise with the beast and Babylon (Rev 13:8). The twofold emphasis on judgment according to works (20:12, 13) is consistent with the rest of the book, which encourages believers (chs. 2–3) and nonbelievers alike (9:20) to repent.

New Creation: When the Barrier between God and the World Has Been Destroyed (Chs. 21–22)

The contrast between heaven and earth disappears in the new creation. Now the tabernacle of God is with men and women, and they shall be God's people (21:3). God's dwelling is not to be found above the cherubim in heaven, for the throne is set right in the midst of the New Jerusalem, where the living waters stream from the throne of God (22:1) and God's servants marked with the divine name will see God face to face (22:4). Only in the new creation will the conditions be present for God and humanity to dwell in that harmony that was impossible while divine justice was rejected in human affairs. Heaven on earth is the fulfillment of God's purposes. God is no longer apparently far off but immediate and manifest—very much part of that world of perfection and evident in it as God was in paradise (Gen 3:8). The inhabitants will be God's children and carry God's name on their heads:

they will be identified with the character of God and enjoy the divine presence unmediated. But, as Paul reminds us in 2 Corinthians 5:17, Christians are not merely to look forward to that new creation. In Christ, in the power of God's spirit, there is already the possibility of bringing about that new creation in individual lives and corporate action, albeit of witness against injustice and on behalf of a better world (Rev 11:3-10).

Once the barrier between God and the world has been destroyed, God's will can be manifested directly. At the moment of triumph of divine righteousness the needy are remembered: "To the thirsty I will give water as a gift from the spring of the water of life" (21:6; cf. Matt 5:6). Just as the divine spirit enabled those who accepted the Messiah, the son of God, in the midst of the old order to be sons and daughters of God (Gal 4:6), so now that promise is fulfilled. The promise to David is extended to the whole people (2 Sam 7:14). Two lists enumerate those who will be excluded from the New Jerusalem (Rev 21:8, 27; 22:15). They are those who behave in the manner of Babylon, believing they can take shortcuts to satisfy their desires or to practice righteousness, or hoping to manipulate God through sorcery.

No temple exists because the whole city is a holy place, and God does not need to be confined to a holy space in the New Jerusalem. This point is echoed elsewhere in the New Testament (e.g., 1 Cor 3:16; 6:19; 2 Cor 6:16). The writings of the early Christians reflect ambivalence, even hostility, toward the temple (Acts 6:7; cf. Mark 14:58 and John 4:25). The first Christians viewed holiness as rooted in practical living in the midst of the variety of human community. The centralization of religious life in a building has enormous attractions as a way of dealing with the human need for reassurance. It is likely that in postexilic Judaism some Christians resisted the restoration of the temple (Isa 58 and 66) and the narrowness of vision that it involved, especially when

it meant denial of God's justice and the true mission of Israel to bring that justice to the nations (Isa 49). It is possible that Jesus, Stephen, and some of the New Testament writers the author of the Gospel of John, the author of Hebrews, and John of Patmos) may have stood in this Judaic tradition that was suspicious of the temple, particularly when support for its upkeep was at the expense of justice (Isa 58).

This tradition raises an important question about the church's enormous investment through the centuries in its buildings. Revelation evokes a most physical structure for the eschatological space; yet it is clear that the face-to-face relationship between God and humanity at the center of its life (Rev 22:4-5). The temple is superfluous in Revelation's vision of the new age. Yet a special space or place has become central to our understanding of religion. What is most apparent in Revelation is that the presence of divine holiness and the testimony to the divine purposes are in no way dependent on buildings but on the maintenance of human community where God in Christ is acknowledged and the alternative vision of reality maintained and celebrated. The hope and commitment to the crucified Messiah, which is folly to humanity, do not depend at all on a building but on the creation of a holy people where God's spirit can dwell. It is in that sharing and engagement that life in the New Jerusalem can be glimpsed.

This is not an exclusive vision. The light of God's glory is a light for the nations (Rev 21:24-26; Isa 60). Only those who ignore God by raising the material to the level of God and their own self-interest above God's justice are excluded (Rev 21:27). Those whose names are not written in the book of life are explicitly linked with those who have compromised and collaborated with the old order (13:8). At the head of the list of those excluded from the New Jerusalem are the cowards (21:8), those who refused to stand up and be counted when protest against injustice was needed. In 21:8 (cf. 22:15) those who were infected with the sorcery of Babylon, the deceit of wealth, and the temptations produced by trade are also excluded.

John's vision of a city is communal rather than individual, a reminder that biblical hope is centered from first to last on relationships between humanity and God and with one another. Christianity has in its history focused so often on hope for the individual that it has lost sight of the central place community plays in past, present, and future expressions of human destiny. The fulfillment of God's purposes is centered on a city, in a community that reflects the situation of paradise (Rev 22:1; Gen 2:10). This is God's paradise. It contradicts the presumption of the earthly city, which believed that wealth could make paradise (Ezek 28:12). That travesty, which led to the exploitation of human lives as a pseudo-paradise, was created for a few at the expense of the many.

CONCLUSION

Revelation suggests a rather different approach to the practical engagement of political theology. It is so different, in fact, that it raises the question of whether theology (at least as it is understood in Western academies) is the most appropriate way of describing the quality of the engagement. It will be more oblique, less logical, embracing of different kinds of routes. The poetry of image and oxymoron often leads to lateral thinking, in which anecdote and analogy, rudely juxtaposed, all contribute to the pursuit of truth. Poetic language opens up the possibility of a critical reexamination of the premises of one's own life and of one's society.

The book of Revelation (or Apocalypse) summons us to be confronted by and infused with its images, rather than to be primarily interpreters or calculators of a precise eschatological program, or even providers of careful explanation. In fact, we are summoned to become participants in a spiritual and moral agony, which wrenches us from the easy compromises we make every day with the beast and Babylon. Revelation summons its reader (or hearer) to participate in another way of speaking about God and the world, which refuses to be tied down to the niceties of carefully defined formularies.

John has bequeathed to us an apocalypse, a revelation, a prophecy. It is a text requiring of its readers different interpretative skills, such as imagination and emotion. The theological function of Revelation as apocalypse depends on the reader's ability to allow its images to inform by means of a subtle interplay of text, context (biblical and social), and imagination. It summons us to see the world from an unusual point of view and to entertain the possibility that a different perspective will lead to a different insight and practice. An imaginative approach to this visionary text, in the course of the actual practice of witness to Jesus, is a more appropriate context for understanding than a detached study of the text in an academic context. An engagement with the text, in which imagination is allied to practical discipleship, suggests a different kind of Christian pedagogy. Revelation bids us put at the center a politically committed engaged discipleship of Jesus as a necessary component of understanding the divine will.

BIBLIOGRAPHY

Aune, David E. *Revelation*. WBC 52A-52B. Waco, Tex.: Word, 1997. The most recent and comprehensive commentary in the historical critical tradition.

Bauckham, Richard. *The Theology of the Book of Revelation*. New Testament Theology. Cambridge: Cambridge University Press, 1993.

Bradstock, Andrew, and Christopher Rowland, eds. *Radical Christian Writings: A Reader*. Oxford: Blackwell, 2002.

Collins, John Joseph. *The Apocalyptic Imagination: An Introduction to the Jewish Matrix of Christianity*. New York: Crossroad, 1984. A guide to the varying characteristics of the apocalyptic genre in ancient Judaism.

Kovacs, Judith L., and Christopher Rowland. *Revelation: The Apocalypse of Jesus Christ.* Blackwell Bible Commentaries. Oxford: Blackwell, 2004. A commentary whose focus is on the history of interpretation.

Richard, Pablo. *Apocalypse: A People's Commentary on the Book of Revelation.* Bible and Liberation Series. Maryknoll, N. Y.: Orbis, 1995.

Rowland, Christopher. *The Open Heaven: A Study of Apocalyptic in Judaism and Early Christianity.* New York: Crossroad, 1982.

———. "The Book of Revelation." *NIB* 13. Nashville: Abingdon, 1998.

Schussler Fiorenza, Elisabeth. *Revelation: Vision of a Just World.* Proclamation Commentaries. Minneapolis: Fortress, 1991.

Wengst, Klaus. *Pax Romana: and the Peace of Jesus Christ.* Translated by John Bowden. London: SCM, 1988; Philadelphia: Fortress, 1987.